Visit classzone.com and get connected

Online resources provide instruction, practice, and learning support correlated to your text.

- **Online examples** offer extra at-home support.
- **State test practice** prepares students for assessments.
- **Self-scoring quizzes** provide comprehension checks.
- **Flashcards and crosswords** help students review vocabulary.
- **Teaching resources** offer answer keys and other support.

You have immediate access to *ClassZone's* teacher resources.

MCDTKASTMSMZ

Use this code to create your own username and password.

Also visit *ClassZone* to learn more about these innovative online resources.

- eEdition Plus Online
- eTutorial Plus Online
- eWorkbook Plus Online
- EasyPlanner Plus Online

Try our *Test and Practice Generator* CD-ROM

Now it all clicks!™

CLASSZONE.COM

COURSE 1

McDougal Littell Middle School
Math

Teacher's Edition

$$\frac{1}{4} = \frac{25}{100} = 25\%$$

$$3x = 18$$

Larson   Boswell   Kanold   Stiff

McDougal Littell
A HOUGHTON MIFFLIN COMPANY
Evanston, Illinois • Boston • Dallas

Contents

About Middle School Math Course 1

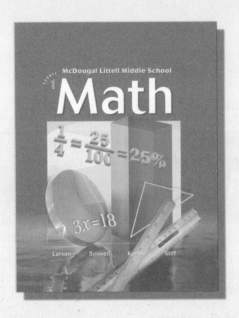

McDougal Littell Middle School Math will help your students be successful in this course. The clearly written lessons with frequent step-by-step examples make even difficult math concepts and methods easier to understand. The number and variety of problems, ranging from basic to challenging, give your students the practice they need to develop their math skills. This book will also help them develop their notetaking and problem-solving skills. Look for notetaking strategies and Help Notes that support problem solving, vocabulary, reading, homework, technology, and review. To help your students get ready for tests, there are test-taking strategies and test-taking practice exercises throughout the book. Your students will also enjoy the Brain Games — they will challenge their thinking skills!

Contributing Authors and Reviewers

The authors wish to thank the following individuals for their contributions.

Reading, Writing, Notetaking; CRISS *(pp. T45–T47)*—Joan Smathers, National CRISS Trainer, Former Language Arts Supervisor, Brevard County, FL; Marie Pettet, Reading and Language Arts Curriculum Specialist, Former K–12 Language Arts Coordinator, Fulton County, GA

Differentiating Instruction *(pp. T35, 1E–1F)*—Donna Foley, Curriculum Specialist for Math, Chelmsford Middle School, Chelmsford, MA; Mark Johnson, Mathematics Education Consultant, Teacher of Mathematics, Gardner High School, Gardner, MA

Universal Access *(pp. T50–T53)*—Catherine Barkett, Vice President, Director of Training, Calabash Professional Learning Systems, Sacramento, CA

English Learners *(pp. T54–T55, 1E–1F)*—Olga Bautista, Vice Principal, Will C. Wood Middle School, Sacramento, CA; Judy Lewis, Director, State and Federal Programs, Folsom Cordova Unified School District, CA

ISBN: 0-618-24973-7   123456789–DWO–07 06 05 04 03

Internet Web Site: http://www.mcdougallittell.com

RON LARSON

Ron Larson is a professor of mathematics at Penn State University at Erie, where he has taught since receiving his Ph.D. in mathematics from the University of Colorado. Dr. Larson is well known as the author of a comprehensive program for mathematics that spans middle school, high school, and college courses. Dr. Larson's numerous professional activities keep him in constant touch with the needs of teachers and supervisors. He closely follows developments in mathematics standards and assessment.

LAURIE BOSWELL

Laurie Boswell is the mathematics department chair at Profile Junior-Senior High School in Bethlehem, New Hampshire. A recipient of the Presidential Award for Excellence in Mathematics Teaching, she has also been a Tandy Technology Scholar. She serves on the National Council of Teachers of Mathematics Board of Directors. She speaks frequently on topics related to instructional strategies and course content.

TIMOTHY KANOLD

Timothy Kanold is the superintendent of Adlai E. Stevenson High School District 125, where he served as a teacher and the Director of Mathematics for 16 years. He recently received his Ph.D. from Loyola University Chicago. Dr. Kanold is a recipient of the Presidential Award for Excellence in Mathematics and Science Teaching and served on The Academy Services Committee for NCTM. He is a frequent speaker at mathematics meetings where he shares his in-depth knowledge of mathematics teaching and curriculum.

LEE STIFF

Lee Stiff is a professor of mathematics education in the College of Education of North Carolina State University at Raleigh. His extensive experience in mathematics education includes teaching at the middle school and high school levels. He has received the W. W. Rankin Award for Excellence in Mathematics Education, and was Fulbright Scholar to the Department of Mathematics of the University of Ghana. He served as President of the National Council of Teachers of Mathematics (2000–2002).

T3

CURRICULUM ADVISERS AND REVIEWERS

Donna Foley
Curriculum Specialist for Math
Chelmsford Middle School
Chelmsford, MA

Barbara Nunn
Secondary Mathematics Specialist
Broward County Schools
Fort Lauderdale, FL

Wendy Loeb
Mathematics Teacher
Twin Groves Junior High School
Buffalo Grove, IL

Tom Scott
Resource Teacher
Duval County Public Schools
Jacksonville, FL

TEACHER PANELS

Florida Panel

Kathy Adams
Mathematics Teacher
Allapattah Middle School
Miami, FL

Micki Hawn
Mathematics Teacher
Pompano Beach Middle School
Pompano Beach, FL

Barbara Schober
Mathematics Department Chair
Okeeheelee Middle School
West Palm Beach, FL

Sue Carrico-Beddow
Mathematics Teacher
Bayonet Point Middle School
New Port Richey, FL

Pat Powell
Mathematics Department Chair
Stewart Middle School
Tampa, FL

Laurie St. Julien
Mathematics Teacher
Oak Grove Middle School
Clearwater, FL

Melissa Grabowski
Mathematics Teacher
Stone Middle School
Melbourne, FL

Kansas and Missouri Panel

Linda Cordes
Department Chair
Paul Robeson Middle School
Kansas City, MO

Rhonda Foote
Mathematics Department Chair
Maple Park Middle School
North Kansas City, MO

Jan Rase
Mathematics Teacher
Moreland Ridge Middle School
Blue Springs, MO

Linda Dodd
Mathematics Department Chair
Argentine Middle School
Kansas City, KS

Cas Kyle
District Math Curriculum Coordinator
Richard A. Warren Middle School
Leavenworth, KS

Dan Schoenemann
Mathematics Teacher
Raytown Middle School
Kansas City, MO

Melanie Dowell
Mathematics Teacher
Raytown South Middle School
Raytown, MO

Texas Panel

Judy Carlin
Mathematics Teacher
Brown Middle School
McAllen, TX

Judith Cody
Mathematics Teacher
Deady Middle School
Houston, TX

Lisa Hiracheta
Mathematics Teacher
Irons Junior High School
Lubbock, TX

Kay Neuse
Mathematics Teacher
Wilson Middle School
Plano, TX

Louise Nutzman
Mathematics Teacher
Sugar Land Middle School
Sugar Land, TX

Clarise Orise
Mathematics Teacher
Tafolla Middle School
San Antonio, TX

Wonda Webb
Mathematics Teacher
William H. Atwell Middle School
and Law Academy
Dallas, TX

Karen West-Young
Mathematics Teacher
Workman Junior High School
Arlington, TX

FIELD TEST TEACHERS

Kathryn Chamberlain
Mathematics Teacher
McCarthy Middle School
Chelmsford, MA

Sheree Daily
Mathematics Teacher
Canal Winchester Middle School
Canal Winchester, OH

Deborah Kebe
Mathematics Teacher
Canal Winchester Middle School
Winchester, OH

Jill Leone
Mathematics Teacher
Twin Groves Junior High School
Buffalo Grove, IL

Wendy Loeb
Mathematics Teacher
Twin Groves Junior High School
Buffalo Grove, IL

Melissa McCarty
Mathematics Teacher
Canal Winchester Middle School
Canal Winchester, OH

Deb Mueth
Mathematics Teacher
St. Aloysius School
Springfield, IL

Jan Rase
Mathematics Teacher
Moreland Ridge Middle School
Blue Springs, MO

Gail Sigmund
Mathematics Teacher
Charles A. Mooney Middle School
Cleveland, OH

REVIEWERS

Chris Acosta
Grand Bay Middle School
Grand Bay, AL

Jennifer Clark
Mayfield Middle School
 (Putnam City Schools)
Oklahoma City, OK

James Cussen
Candlewood Middle School
Dix Hills, NY

Kristen Dailey
Boardman Center Middle School
Boardman, OH

Dorene Ellis
Kimpton Middle School
Munroe Falls, OH

Shannon Galamore
Clay-Chalkville Middle School
Pinson, AL

Tricia Highland
Moon Area Middle School
Moon Tap, PA

Jessica Kent
Westside Middle School
Omaha, NE

Myrna McNaboe
Immaculate Conception High School
East Aurora, NY

James Richardson
Booker T. Washington Middle School
Mobile, AL

Ray Scacalossi
Hauppauge High School
Hauppauge, NY

Wendee Siegel
Orchard Park Middle School
Orchard Park, NY

CHAPTER

1

Number Sense and Algebraic Thinking

 **Notetaking and Student Help**

 BrAiN GAME

Internet Resources

- eEdition Plus Online
- eWorkbook Plus Online
- eTutorial Plus Online
- State Test Practice
- More Examples

Pre-Course Assessment

Exercise 49, p. 9

Notetaking and Student Help

Notetaking, 54, 57, 61, 62, 76, 93, 94, 98
Reading, 69, 89
Vocabulary, 56
Solving, 57
Review, 63, 73, 79
Watch Out, 62

BrAIN GAME

Desert Math, 52
Optical Illusions, 60
Lucky Sevens, 97

Internet Resources

· eEdition Plus Online
· eWorkbook Plus Online
· eTutorial Plus Online
· State Test Practice
· More Examples

Measurement and Statistics

Example 1, p. 88

Contents **vii**

Decimal Addition and Subtraction

Example 4, p. 119

CHAPTER 4

Decimal Multiplication and Division

Notetaking and Student Help

Notetaking, 152, 155, 159, 164, 169, 174, 176, 177, 180, 187, 196
Solving, 153, 165, 170, 176, 180, 192
Review, 159
Watch Out, 165

BrAIN GAME

Operation Cover-Up, 150
Matching Cards, 173
Fruit Punch, 195

Internet Resources

· eEdition Plus Online
· eWorkbook Plus Online
· eTutorial Plus Online
· State Test Practice
· More Examples

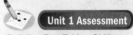

Unit 1 Assessment

Building Test-Taking Skills: Multiple Choice, 202
Practicing Test-Taking Skills, 204
Cumulative Practice, 206

Exercise 8, p. 171

Contents **ix**

Number Patterns and Fractions

Notetaking and Student Help

BrAIN GAME

Exercises 23–24, p. 225

Addition and Subtraction of Fractions

Exercise 10, p. 300

Contents   xi

CHAPTER 7

Multiplication and Division of Fractions

Notetaking and Student Help

Notetaking, 312, 313, 321, 331, 334, 356
Vocabulary, 345
Solving, 314, 321, 322, 326, 351
Technology, 355
Watch Out, 322, 335, 340, 350

BRAIN GAME

Mixed Number Race, 310
Triple Jump, 311
Making Up Your Own Unit of Measure, 330
Fill in the Fractions, 332
A Pattern of Measures, 357

Internet Resources

· eEdition Plus Online
· eWorkbook Plus Online
· eTutorial Plus Online
· State Test Practice
· More Examples

Unit 2 Assessment

Building Test-Taking Skills: Short Response, 362
Practicing Test-Taking Skills, 364
Cumulative Practice, 366

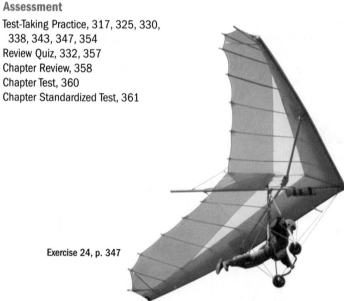

Exercise 24, p. 347

C H A P T E R

8

Ratio, Proportion, and Percent

Notetaking and Student Help

Notetaking, 372, 383, 392, 395, 396, 401, 406, 408, 412
Reading, 379, 383
Solving, 400
Review, 375, 385, 389
Technology, 411

Number Challenge, 370
Ratio Puzzlers, 378
Target 203, 413

(i) **Internet Resources**

· eEdition Plus Online
· eWorkbook Plus Online
· eTutorial Plus Online
· State Test Practice
· More Examples

Example 3, p. 400

CHAPTER 9

Geometric Figures

Notetaking and Student Help

Notetaking, 420, 431, 437, 442, 445, 461, 464
Reading, 422, 426, 450
Vocabulary, 431, 449
Solving, 461
Review, 452
Watch Out, 427

BrAiN GAME

Mix and Match, 418
Computer Graphics, 419
Flag Team Challenge, 429
Triangle Teaser, 453

Internet Resources

· eEdition Plus Online
· eWorkbook Plus Online
· eTutorial Plus Online
· State Test Practice
· More Examples

EXPLORING MATH IN SCIENCE

The Geometry of Crystals, 470

Exercise 14, p. 463

Geometry and Measurement

Example 3, p. 511

C H A P T E R

11

Notetaking and Student Help
Notetaking, 532, 539, 544, 545, 548, 550, 555, 574
Reading, 534
Solving, 539, 567, 568
Review, 562

BRAIN GAME

Constellation Mapping, 530
Unidentified Symmetrical Object, 531
Magic Square, 549
Mystery Dog, 558

Internet Resources

· eEdition Plus Online
· eWorkbook Plus Online
· eTutorial Plus Online
· State Test Practice
· More Examples

Integers

Example 3, p. 555

Notetaking and Student Help

Notetaking, 582, 589, 593, 596, 599, 613, 618
Reading, 603, 606
Solving, 589, 606, 614, 616
Review, 598, 602
Watch Out, 584, 593

BrAIN GAME

Expression Race, 580
Symbologic, 597
Function Assembly Line, 609

Internet Resources

· eEdition Plus Online
· eWorkbook Plus Online
· eTutorial Plus Online
· State Test Practice
· More Examples

EXPLORING
MATH in SCIENCE

Investigating Elephant Tracks, 624

Equations and Functions

Exercise 39, p. 586

Contents   **xvii**

Probability and Statistics

Notetaking and Student Help

Notetaking, 628, 630, 646, 663, 666
Solving, 631, 649, 657
Review, 649
Technology, 635
Watch Out, 653

BrAIN GAME

Spider Web Maze, 626
Butterfly Challenge, 627
Create a Spinner, 647
Solve the Riddle, 661

 Internet Resources

· eEdition Plus Online
· eWorkbook Plus Online
· eTutorial Plus Online
· State Test Practice
· More Examples

 **Unit 4 Assessment**

Building Test-Taking Skills:
Extended Response, 672
Practicing Test-Taking Skills, 674
Cumulative Practice, 676

End-of-Course Assessment

End-of-Course Test, 679

Exercise 14, p. 639

Contents of Student Resources

McDougal Littell Middle School

COURSE 1

Math

The right math,
the right way,
the right results

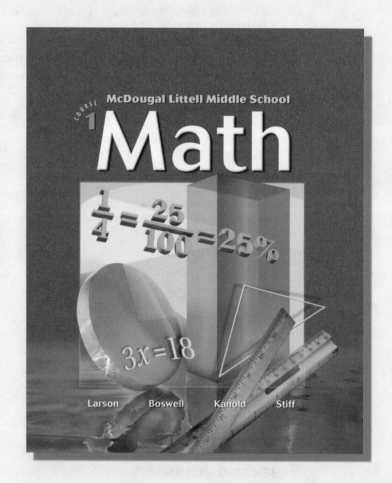

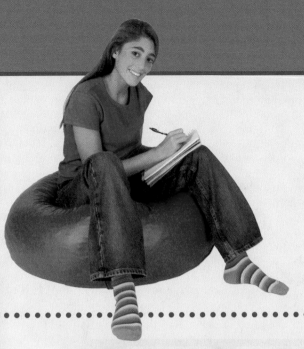

Our middle school program provides the math your students need to know in a way that they can understand. Fully integrated problem solving, notetaking, and assessment strategies help your students succeed.

Understand

Give your students math they can read, understand, and practice with built-in learning support, clear examples, and engaging review games that emphasize critical thinking.

Organize

Help your students organize their approach to new concepts with fully integrated notetaking and study strategies, as well as stepped-out examples.

Achieve

Prepare your students for success on local and state tests with frequent assessment strategies and practice opportunities.

Accessible Content

Our middle school program provides clear, concise math in a student-friendly voice.

EXPLORE IT!

Quick, hands-on activities help build conceptual understanding before the lesson begins.

THINK ABOUT IT!

Critical-thinking questions ask students to reflect on the exploration.

4.3 Hands-on **Activity**

GOAL
Use an area model to find the product of two decimals.

MATERIALS
• graph paper
• colored pencils

Multiplying Decimals Using Models

In this activity, you will use area models to multiply two decimals. The decimals will represent the length and width of a rectangle. The area of the rectangle will represent the product of the decimals.

Explore Model 0.8×0.7 using an area model.

① Start with a 10-by-10 square drawn on graph paper.

The whole square represents 1.

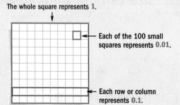

Each of the 100 small squares represents 0.01.

Each row or column represents 0.1.

② Use a colored pencil to shade a rectangle that is 8 rows long by 7 columns wide.

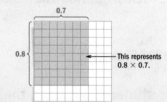

0.7

0.8

This represents 0.8×0.7.

③ The area of the rectangle represents the product 0.8×0.7. Count the number of squares in the shaded rectangle. Because each small square represents 0.01, 56 of the small squares represent 0.56, or fifty-six hundredths. So, $0.8 \times 0.7 = 0.56$.

Your turn now Use a model to find the product.

1. 0.3×0.9 **2.** 0.4×0.4 **3.** 0.5×0.6 **4.** 0.7×0.3

5. In Step 3 above, is the product *greater than* or *less than* each of the numbers being multiplied?

Stop *and* **Think**

6. Critical Thinking Use a model to find the product 0.7×0.8. Is the result any different than the result in Step 3 above? Why or why not?

Lesson 4.3 Multiplying Decimals **163**

LESSON 4.3
Multiplying Decimals

BEFORE	▶ Now	WHY?
You multiplied decimals by whole numbers.	You'll multiply decimals by decimals.	So you can find the distance traveled by a turtle, as in Ex. 30.

📖 **Word Watch**

Review Words
factor, p. 16

In the Real World

Sloths The sloth is commonly referred to as the "slowest mammal on Earth." Its top speed on the ground is about 0.2 mile per hour. What is the farthest a sloth might go in 0.6 hour?

EXAMPLE 1 Using a Model to Multiply Decimals

To find how far a sloth might go in the question above, use a model to find the product 0.2×0.6.

① Draw a 10-by-10 square. The whole square represents 1. Each small square represents 1 hundredth, or 0.01. Each row or column represents 1 tenth, or 0.1.

② Shade a rectangle that is 0.2 by 0.6. The area is 12 hundredths, because 12 small squares are shaded. So, $0.2 \times 0.6 = 0.12$.

ANSWER The farthest a sloth might go in 0.6 hour is 0.12 mile.

Your turn now Draw a model to find the product.

1. 0.1×0.7 **2.** 0.3×0.8 **3.** 0.9×0.7

📓 **Multiplying Decimals**

Words Multiply decimals as you do whole numbers. Then place the decimal point. The number of decimal places is the total number of decimal places in the factors.

Numbers $\underset{\text{2 places}}{3.14} \times \underset{\text{1 place}}{15.6} = \underset{\text{3 places}}{48.984}$

164 Chapter 4 Decimal Multiplication and Division

EXAMPLE 2 Placing a Decimal Point in a Product

Place the decimal point in the correct location.

$\underset{\text{2 places}}{252.64} \times \underset{\text{3 places}}{0.842} = \underset{\text{5 places}}{212.72288}$

The first factor has 2 decimal places. The second factor has 3 decimal places. Because $2 + 3 = 5$, the answer has 5 decimal places.

ANSWER $252.64 \times 0.842 = 212.72288$

✓ **Check** Estimate: $252.64 \times 0.842 \approx 250 \times 1 = 250$. So, the product 212.72288 is reasonable.

EXAMPLE 3 Multiplying Decimals

Find the product.

a. 5.08×2.1 **b.** 1.159×0.03 **c.** 7.215×4.8

Solution

a.
$$\begin{array}{r} 5.08 \\ \times\ 2.1 \\ \hline 508 \\ 1016 \\ \hline 10.668 \end{array}$$
2 decimal places
+ 1 decimal place

3 decimal places

b.
$$\begin{array}{r} 1.159 \\ \times\ 0.03 \\ \hline 0.03477 \end{array}$$
3 decimal places
+ 2 decimal places

5 decimal places

c.
$$\begin{array}{r} 7.215 \\ \times\ 4.8 \\ \hline 57720 \\ 28860 \\ \hline 34.6320 \end{array}$$
3 decimal places
+ 1 decimal place

4 decimal places

Watch Out!

You may need to write zeros in the product as placeholders in order to place the decimal point correctly.

Once you place the decimal point, drop the zero at the end of the final answer. You write the product as 34.632.

Your turn now Multiply. Use estimation to check your answer.

4. 2.15×5.4 **5.** 12.7×2.9 **6.** 6.289×0.2 **7.** 0.86×0.04

Lesson 4.3 Multiplying Decimals 165

T23

Organize it!

Study Strategies

Integrated notetaking and study strategies support the development of learning skills.

PREPARE FOR IT!

Prerequisite-skills review opens each chapter and prepares students for the chapter.

CHAPTER 2 Getting Ready to Learn

Review What You Need to Know

Using Vocabulary Copy and complete using a review word.

Word Watch

Review Words
perimeter, p. 702
area, p. 702
data, p. 704
bar graph, p. 704
line graph, p. 705

1. The _?_ of a figure is measured in square units.

2. In a _?_, you connect the data points with line segments.

Find the perimeter of a triangle with the given side lengths. *(p. 702)*

3. 5 feet, 2 feet, 6 feet

4. 10 inches, 10 inches, 10 inches

The medal count for the United States in the 2000 Summer Olympics is shown in the bar graph. *(p. 704)*

5. About how many gold medals did the United States receive?

6. About how many silver medals did the United States receive?

7. About how many medals did the United States receive in all?

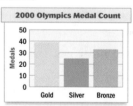

2000 Olympics Medal Count

Evaluate the expression when $x = 8$ and $y = 2$. *(p. 29)*

8. $2x$

9. $4y$

10. $x + y$

11. $2x - y$

Note book

NOTE IT!

Notebook strategies provide examples of how to take good notes.

Note book

You should include material that appears on a notebook like this in your own notes.

Know How to Take Notes

Taking Notes While Reading Leave extra space while you take notes in class. Then review the lesson in your textbook to correct or add to your class notes. You may also want to copy the "Help" notes from the textbook in your own words, as shown below.

$m = 3, n = 4$

$m + 2n = 3 + 2 \cdot 4$ ← Follow the order of operations after substituting.
$= 3 + 8$
$= 11$

The reminder above will be helpful in Lesson 2.8 when you learn about finding averages.

Perimeter and Area

BEFORE	▶ Now	WHY?
You found the square of a number.	You'll use formulas to find perimeter and area.	So you can find measurements, such as poster areas in Ex. 28.

In the Real World

Word Watch

perimeter, p. 61
area, p. 62

Carnival A carnival is going to be held in your school's parking lot. How much rope is needed to enclose the carnival? To answer this question, you can find the carnival's *perimeter*.

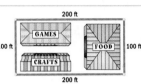

200 ft
100 ft   100 ft
200 ft

The **perimeter** of a figure is the distance around the figure. Perimeter is measured in linear units such as feet, inches, or meters.

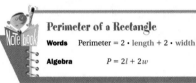

Perimeter of a Rectangle

Words   Perimeter = 2 · length + 2 · width

Algebra $P = 2l + 2w$

EXAMPLE 1   **Finding the Perimeter of a Rectangle**

To answer the real-world question above, find the perimeter.

$P = 2l + 2w$ Write the formula for perimeter of a rectangle.

$= 2 \cdot 200 + 2 \cdot 100$ Substitute 200

$= 400 + 200$ Multiply.

$= 600$ Add.

ANSWER The amount of rope needed to encl

Your turn now   Find the perimeter of the r

1. length = 9 m, width = 5 m   **2.** le

Lesson 2.

WRITE IT!

Integrated notetaking features remind students to write new concepts in their notebooks.

REVIEW IT!

Mid- and end-of-chapter reviews help students review notes and prepare for tests.

USE IT!

Vocabulary exercises give students an opportunity to use key terms.

Notebook Review

Review the vocabulary definitions in your notebook. Copy the review examples in your notebook. Then complete the exercises.

Check Your Definitions

inch, p. 55	centimeter, p. 56	scale drawing, p. 68
foot, p. 55	meter, p. 56	scale, p. 68
yard, p. 55	kilometer, p. 56	data, p. 72
mile, p. 55	perimeter, p. 61	frequency table, p. 72
millimeter, p. 56	area, p. 62	line plot, p. 73

Use Your Vocabulary

1. Writing Define area and perimeter.

2.1–2.2 Can you find perimeter and area?

EXAMPLE Use a ruler to find the length of the rectangle in centimeters. Then find the perimeter and the area.

2 cm

$P = 2l + 2w$ $A = lw$

$= 2 \cdot 3 + 2 \cdot 2$ $= 3 \cdot 2$

$= 10$ cm $= 6$ cm^2

cm   1   2   3

 2. Find the perimeter and the area of a 7 inch by 7 inch square.

3. Estimate then measure the length of this sentence in inches.

2.3 Can you use a scale?

EXAMPLE The length of a wall on a scale drawing is 192 millimeters. Find the actual length if the scale on the drawing is 8 mm : 2 m.

$\times 24 \begin{cases} 8 \text{ mm} : 2 \text{ m} \\ 192 \text{ mm} : \underline{?} \text{ m} \end{cases}$ You multiply by 24, so the actual length is 48 m.

 Find the actual length of the wall in the Example above using the given scale.

4. 3 mm : 1 m **5.** 4 mm : 2 m **6.** 12 mm : 4 m **7.** 6 mm : 6 m

T25

Achieve it! Assessment Preparation

Assessment tips and practice opportunities help students achieve their goals.

UNIT 2 Chapters 5–7

BUILDING **Test-Taking Skills**

Scoring Rubric

Full credit
- answer is correct, *and*
- work or reasoning is included

Partial credit
- answer is correct, but reasoning is incorrect, *or*
- answer is incorrect, but reasoning is correct

No credit
- no answer is given, *or*
- answer makes no sense

Strategies for Answering
Short Response Questions

Problem

There are $3\frac{1}{2}$ cups of flour in one pound of flour. Your recipe for Key Lime cake calls for $1\frac{1}{2}$ cups of flour. How many cakes can you make using a 5 pound bag of flour?

Full credit solution

The number of cakes you can make is the number of cups of flour in a 5 pound bag divided by the number of cups of flour in each cake. — This reasoning is the key to choosing the operations you need.

The steps of the solution are clearly written. — Cups in 5 lb bag = Pounds per bag × Cups per pound

$= 5 \times 3\frac{1}{2} = \frac{5}{1} \times \frac{7}{2} = \frac{35}{2} = 17\frac{1}{2}$

Number of cakes = Cups in 5 lb bag ÷ Cups per cake

$= 17\frac{1}{2} \div 1\frac{1}{2} = \frac{35}{2} \times \frac{2}{3} = \frac{35}{3} = 11\frac{2}{3}$

The question asked is answered correctly. — You can make 11 cakes.

Partial credit solution

There are $17\frac{1}{2}$ cups of flour in a 5 pound bag. — The reasoning and calculations are correct.

$17\frac{1}{2} \div 1\frac{1}{2} = \frac{35}{2} \times \frac{2}{3} = \frac{35}{3} = 11\frac{2}{3}$

The answer makes no sense. You cannot make a fractional number of cakes. — You can make $11\frac{2}{3}$ cakes.

Partial credit solution

Without explanation, the reasoning behind this calculation is unclear. — $\frac{35}{2} \times \frac{2}{3} = \frac{35}{3} = 11\frac{2}{3}$

You can make 11 cakes. — The answer is correct.

362 Unit 2 Fraction Concepts and Operations

PLAN IT!

Test-taking strategies help students perform well on assessments.

EXPRESS IT!

Sample solutions help students analyze problems and write full-credit solutions.

Chapter Standardized Test

Test-Taking Strategy Look for choices that are obviously not the right answer and eliminate them first.

Multiple Choice

1. Which number is a prime number?

   A. 62   **B.** 87   **C.** 109   **D.** 129

2. Which number is divisible by 2, 3, 5, 6, 9, and 10?

   F. 120   **G.** 150   **H.** 180   **I.** 600

3. Which number is *not* a multiple of 7?

   A. 98   **B.** 112   **C.** 147   **D.** 163

4. What is the GCF of 20 and 35?

   F. 5   **G.** 7   **H.** 10   **I.** 15

5. What is the LCM of 15 and 45?

   A. 15   **B.** 45   **C.** 90   **D.** 139

6. **Tile Designs** A square tile has a side length of 14 centimeters. A rectangular tile has a length of 20 centimeters. If the tiles are laid out in a line in two separate rows of the same tiles, at what point will the rows be the same length?

   F. at 120 cm   **G.** at 140 cm

   H. at 210 cm   **I.** at 320 cm

7. Which fraction is equivalent to $\frac{7}{15}$?

   A. $\frac{70}{150}$ **B.** $\frac{14}{45}$ **C.** $\frac{28}{80}$ **D.** $\frac{56}{140}$

8. Which fractions are in order from least to greatest?

   F. $\frac{5}{16}, \frac{3}{8}, \frac{1}{4}, \frac{9}{16}$ **G.** $\frac{1}{4}, \frac{5}{16}, \frac{3}{8}, \frac{9}{16}$

   H. $\frac{3}{8}, \frac{9}{16}, \frac{1}{4}, \frac{5}{16}$ **I.** $\frac{9}{16}, \frac{1}{4}, \frac{3}{8}, \frac{5}{16}$

9. Which number is equal to $3\frac{3}{4}$?

   A. $\frac{9}{4}$ **B.** $\frac{10}{4}$ **C.** $\frac{13}{4}$ **D.** $\frac{15}{4}$

10. Which number is equal to 2.08?

    F. $2\frac{2}{25}$ **G.** $2\frac{1}{8}$ **H.** $2\frac{1}{4}$ **I.** $2\frac{8}{25}$

11. Which statement is *false*?

    A. $1\frac{11}{12} > 1.9$ **B.** $\frac{27}{10} < 2\frac{7}{9}$

    C. $\frac{23}{8} > 2.88$ **D.** $3\frac{5}{6} > 3\frac{4}{5}$

Short Response

12. Use the digits 2, 5, and 9 to write a fraction of the greatest possible value. Write this fraction as a mixed number. Is the fraction part in simplest form? Explain.

Extended Response

13. List all the pairs of factors of 60 and write the prime factorization. Describe a relationship between the prime factors and any pair of factors.

f fruit juice. How much does the juice cost

ct. Then find the value. *(Lesson 1.3)*

58. 7^3 **59.** 1^5

umbers from least to greatest.

414, 41, 4, 404   **62.** 555, 50, 510, 505

PRACTICE IT!

Multiple-choice, short-response, and extended-response questions prepare students for a variety of test-taking experiences.

Test-Taking Practice

63. **Multiple Choice** What is the first step in evaluating $3 + 5 \times 8 - 7$?

    A. $3 + 5$ **B.** 5×8 **C.** $8 - 7$ **D.** $3 + 7$

64. **Multiple Choice** Evaluate the expression $6 + 18 \div 3^2$.

    F. 8   **G.** 31   **H.** 42   **I.** 64

BRAIN GAME

Solve the Riddle

Match each numbered expression in the first column with the letter of the expression in the second column that has the same value. Then replace the number in each box with its matching letter to find the answer to the riddle.

What goes around the world and stays in the corner?

| 3 | 4 | 1 | 3 | 5 | 2 |

1. $3 + 2 \div 1 - 4$
2. $4 - 2 + 9 \div 3$
3. $8 \div (1 \times 2) - 2$
4. $7 + (8 - 4 \times 2)$
5. $1 + 3 \times 4 - 3$

R. $(8 - 4 + 2) \div 2$
S. $0 + (15 - 1) \div 2$
T. $10 - (4 + 3) - 2$
E. $2 \times (12 - 8) + 5$
P. $(10 \div 5) \times 4 - 3$
M. $(7 - 4) \times 3 + 1$
A. $11 - 6 - (12 \div 4)$

SOLVE IT!

Test-Taking Practice with every lesson and frequent Brain Games provide ongoing assessment.

 Connect to it!

CLASSZONE.COM

eEdition Plus Online
provides an interactive, online version of the text that engages students and facilitates teaching.

eWorkbook Plus Online
includes interactive practice opportunities that correspond to the text.

eTutorial Plus Online
offers an Internet tutorial that makes it easier than ever to help students master skills and concepts.

State Test practice
helps support students as they prepare to achieve their goals on state tests.

More Examples
include additional, online support that helps students master new concepts.

Online Quizzes
help students assess their own progress.

Vocabulary Support
provides interactive practice with vocabulary.

Activities
help students become engaged with the mathematics.

T27

Teacher's Resource Package

This package is conveniently organized and includes a variety of materials to help you adapt the program to your teaching style and to the specific needs of your middle school students!

Teacher's Resource Package includes:

Chapter Resource Books
(one for each chapter, organized by lesson)

Assessment Book

Notetaking Guide Teacher's Edition

Practice Workbook Teacher's Edition

Teacher Survival Kit
(includes the Professional Development Book, the Special Activities Book, and the Poster Package)

Warm-Up Transparencies with Daily Homework Quiz

Worked-Out Solution Key

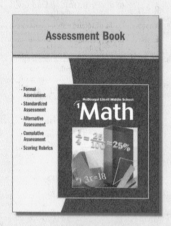

Chapter Resource Books

Chapter Resource Books allow you to carry the resources you have for a chapter in one manageable book. The materials in each Chapter Resource Book are organized by lesson so that you can easily see everything you have available.

Chapter Resource Books include:

- Tips for New Teachers
- Parents as Partners
- Games Support Master
- Lesson Plans
- Lesson Plans for
- Block Scheduling
- Activity Masters
- Technology Activities and Keystrokes
- Practice (Levels A, B, and C)
- Study Guide
- Real-World Problem Solving
- Challenge Practice
- Chapter Review Games and Activities
- Real Life Project with Teacher's Notes
- Cooperative Project with Teacher's Notes
- Independent Extra Credit Project with Teacher's Notes
- Cumulative Practice
- Resource Book Answers

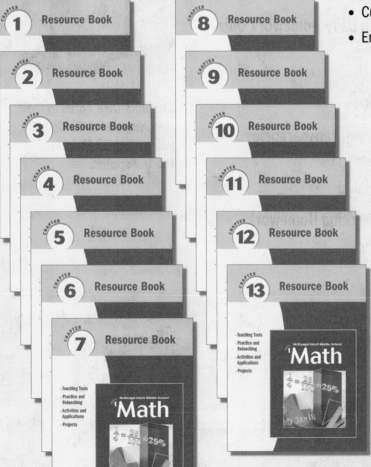

Assessment Book

- Diagnostic Pre-Course Test
- Quizzes
- Chapter Tests (Levels A, B, and C)
- Standardized Tests
- Alternative Assessment with Math Journal and Rubric
- Unit Tests
- Cumulative Tests
- End-of-Course Test

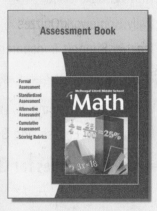

Transparency Packages

The transparency packages give you many easy-to-use options for reviewing homework, starting class, and teaching notetaking and problem solving strategies.

Notetaking Guide Transparencies

- Promote notetaking skills
- Reinforce key concepts

Warm-Up Transparencies with Daily Homework Quiz

- Warm-Up Exercises
- Daily Homework Quizzes
- Teacher Support Transparencies

English-Spanish Problem Solving Transparencies

- Worked-Out Problems
- Presented in English and Spanish

Answer Transparencies for Checking Homework

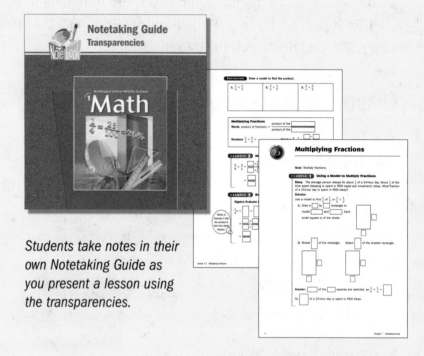

Students take notes in their own Notetaking Guide as you present a lesson using the transparencies.

Teacher Survival Kit

This kit provides professional development ideas, helpful activities, and materials to enhance your classroom environment.

Teacher Survival Kit includes:

- Professional Development Book
- Special Activities Book
- Poster Package

Math Tutor Place

Math Tutor Place helps students practice and master essential math topics. The instruction and practice are provided by 104 cards divided into five main categories:

- Whole Numbers and Decimals
- Fractions
- Ratio, Proportion, and Percent
- Geometry and Measurement
- Algebra

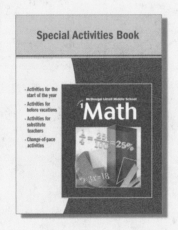

Notetaking Guide

This workbook promotes notetaking skills and helps build understanding by providing students with a framework for recording the key concepts of every lesson. This workbook is also useful in helping students review and prepare for tests.

Practice Workbook

The Practice Workbook includes practice exercises for every lesson.

World Languages Resources

A variety of resources are available to help you address the needs of English learners.

English-Spanish Chapter Reviews and Tests
The Chapter Reviews and Chapter Tests from the text are reproduced with English and Spanish side-by-side.

English-Spanish Problem Solving Transparencies
The transparencies provide worked-out problems, correlated to the textbook, with English and Spanish side-by-side.

Spanish Study Guide
The Study Guide pages from the Chapter Resource Books are reproduced in Spanish.

Multi-Language Glossary
The textbook's visual glossary is translated into 9 languages.

Chapter Audio Summaries CDs
Available in English, Spanish, and Haitian Creole.

Technology Resources

McDougal Littell offers resources online and on CD-ROM to enhance lessons and help students build understanding.

Online Resources:

Online resources at www.classzone.com are linked together and provide instruction, practice, and learning support.

- **eEdition Plus Online** This electronic version of the book is enhanced by interactive extensions that allow students to explore concepts and self-assessment questions that check understanding. Reports on individual student performance help you track student progress.

- **eWorkbook Plus Online** This interactive software presents students with algorithmically generated problems correlated directly to the lessons and tracks their performance for your review. The problems can be accessed straight from the eEdition or directly from the Web site.

- **eTutorial Plus Online** An interactive program provides students additional material and reinforces key skills. The tutorial can be accessed straight from the eEdition or directly from the Web site.

- **Chapter-Based Support** State test practice, vocabulary support, self-quizzes, and other engaging student activities are provided online.

- **EasyPlanner Plus Online** This planner provides you access to all materials that come along with the program. It allows you to organize them into lesson plans and provides correlations to your state standards.

Other CD-Rom Resources include:

- **Chapter Audio Summaries CDs** These CDs summarize the key concepts of each chapter in English, Spanish, and Haitian Creole.

- **eEdition CD-ROM**

- **eTutorial CD-ROM**

- **EasyPlanner CD-ROM**

- **Electronic Lesson Presentations** PowerPoint™ slides help you walk through key concepts in a stepped out presentation.

- **Test and Practice Generator** The power of the Internet and the computer lab are available to you with this new generation of software.

eEdition Plus Online

eTutorial Plus Online

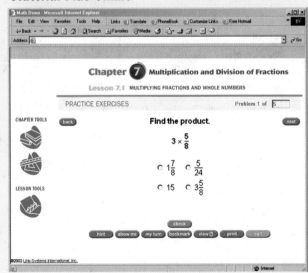

Planning the Chapter

- Regular and Block schedules for pacing the course

- A handy guide for integrating resource materials into your lessons

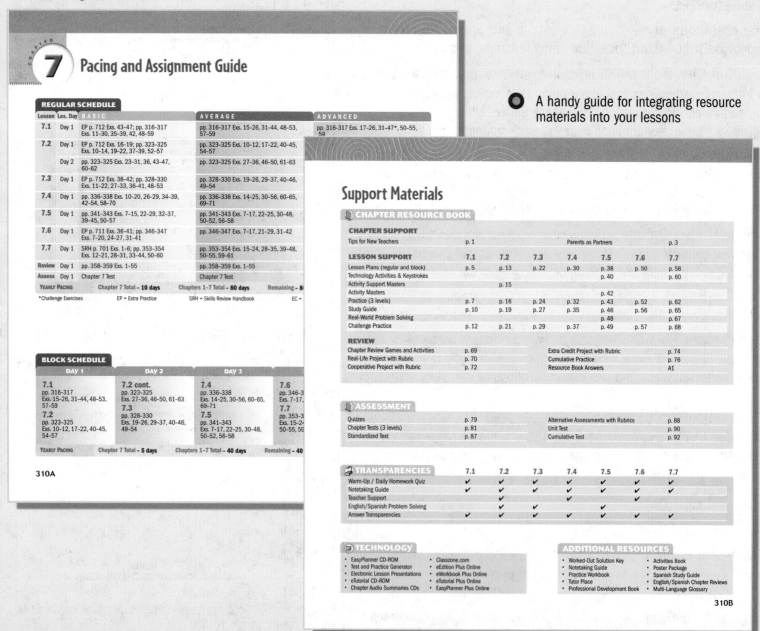

CHAPTER 7 — Pacing and Assignment Guide

REGULAR SCHEDULE

Lesson	Les. Day	BASIC	AVERAGE	ADVANCED
7.1	Day 1	EP p. 712 Exs. 43–47; pp. 316–317 Exs. 11–30, 35–39, 42, 48–59	pp. 316–317 Exs. 15–26, 31–44, 48–53, 57–59	pp. 316–317 Exs. 17–26, 31–47*, 50–55, 59
7.2	Day 1	EP p. 712 Exs. 16–19; pp. 323–325 Exs. 10–14, 19–22, 37–39, 52–57	pp. 323–325 Exs. 10–12, 17–22, 40–45, 54–57	
	Day 2	323–325 Exs. 23–31, 36, 43–47, 60–62	pp. 323–325 Exs. 27–36, 46–50, 61–63	
7.3	Day 1	EP p. 712 Exs. 38–42; pp. 328–330 Exs. 11–22, 27–33, 36–41, 48–53	pp. 328–330 Exs. 19–26, 29–37, 40–46, 49–54	
7.4	Day 1	pp. 336–338 Exs. 10–20, 26–29, 34–39, 42–54, 58–70	pp. 336–338 Exs. 14–25, 30–56, 60–65, 69–71	
7.5	Day 1	pp. 341–343 Exs. 7–15, 22–29, 32–37, 39–45, 50–57	pp. 341–343 Exs. 7–17, 22–25, 30–48, 50–52, 56–58	
7.6	Day 1	EP p. 711 Exs. 36–41; pp. 346–347 Exs. 7–20, 24–27, 31–41	pp. 346–347 Exs. 7–17, 21–29, 31–42	
7.7	Day 1	SRH p. 701 Exs. 1–6; pp. 353–354 Exs. 12–21, 28–31, 33–44, 50–60	pp. 353–354 Exs. 15–24, 28–35, 39–48, 50–55, 59–61	
Review	Day 1	pp. 358–359 Exs. 1–55	pp. 358–359 Exs. 1–55	
Assess	Day 1	Chapter 7 Test	Chapter 7 Test	
YEARLY PACING		Chapter 7 Total – **10 days**	Chapters 1–7 Total – **80 days**	Remaining – 8

*Challenge Exercises   EP = Extra Practice   SRH = Skills Review Handbook   EC =

BLOCK SCHEDULE

DAY 1	DAY 2	DAY 3	
7.1 pp. 316–317 Exs. 15–26, 31–44, 48–53, 57–59	**7.2 cont.** pp. 323–325 Exs. 27–36, 46–50, 61–63	**7.4** pp. 336–338 Exs. 14–25, 30–56, 60–65, 69–71	**7.6** pp. 346–3 Exs. 7–17,
7.2 pp. 323–325 Exs. 10–12, 17–22, 40–45, 54–57	**7.3** pp. 328–330 Exs. 19–26, 29–37, 40–46, 49–54	**7.5** pp. 341–343 Exs. 7–17, 22–25, 30–48, 50–52, 56–58	**7.7** pp. 353–3 Exs. 15–2 50–55, 59
YEARLY PACING	Chapter 7 Total – **5 days**	Chapters 1–7 Total – **40 days**	Remaining – 40

310A

Support Materials

📖 CHAPTER RESOURCE BOOK

CHAPTER SUPPORT

Tips for New Teachers	p. 1			Parents as Partners		p. 3

LESSON SUPPORT

	7.1	7.2	7.3	7.4	7.5	7.6	7.7
Lesson Plans (regular and block)	p. 5	p. 13	p. 22	p. 30	p. 38	p. 50	p. 58
Technology Activities & Keystrokes					p. 40		p. 60
Activity Support Masters		p. 15					
Activity Masters					p. 42		
Practice (3 levels)	p. 7	p. 16	p. 24	p. 32	p. 43	p. 52	p. 62
Study Guide	p. 10	p. 19	p. 27	p. 35	p. 46	p. 56	p. 65
Real-World Problem Solving					p. 48		p. 67
Challenge Practice	p. 12	p. 21	p. 29	p. 37	p. 49	p. 57	p. 68

REVIEW

Chapter Review Games and Activities	p. 69	Extra Credit Project with Rubric	p. 74
Real-Life Project with Rubric	p. 70	Cumulative Practice	p. 76
Cooperative Project with Rubric	p. 72	Resource Book Answers	A1

📋 ASSESSMENT

Quizzes	p. 79	Alternative Assessments with Rubrics	p. 88
Chapter Tests (3 levels)	p. 81	Unit Test	p. 90
Standardized Test	p. 87	Cumulative Test	p. 92

🖥 TRANSPARENCIES

	7.1	7.2	7.3	7.4	7.5	7.6	7.7
Warm-Up / Daily Homework Quiz	✔	✔	✔	✔	✔	✔	✔
Notetaking Guide	✔	✔	✔	✔	✔	✔	✔
Teacher Support		✔		✔	✔		
English/Spanish Problem Solving		✔	✔		✔		✔
Answer Transparencies	✔	✔	✔	✔	✔	✔	✔

💻 TECHNOLOGY

- EasyPlanner CD-ROM
- Test and Practice Generator
- Electronic Lesson Presentations
- eTutorial CD-ROM
- Chapter Audio Summaries CDs
- Classzone.com
- eEdition Plus Online
- eWorkbook Plus Online
- eTutorial Plus Online
- EasyPlanner Plus Online

ADDITIONAL RESOURCES

- Worked-Out Solution Key
- Notetaking Guide
- Practice Workbook
- Tutor Place
- Professional Development Book
- Activities Book
- Poster Package
- Spanish Study Guide
- English/Spanish Chapter Reviews
- Multi-Language Glossary

310B

● Math background and teaching strategies provide suggestions to help you present each lesson and to increase student understanding

7 Math Background and Teaching Strategies

Lessons 7.1 through 7.3

MATH BACKGROUND

When you multiply any number (whole number, fraction, mixed number) by a fraction less than 1, the product is less than that number because you are only looking for a part of it.

TEACHING STRATEGIES

Suppose there are 18 students in your class, and that in a survey two-thirds of them say they like using a word processor better than writing by hand. How many students prefer using a word processor? Since not all of the students prefer using a word processor, you know that the number who do is less than 18. To solve this problem you would multiply $\frac{2}{3} \times 18$.

USING A MODEL You can find $\frac{2}{3} \times 18$ by drawing a picture.

So, $\frac{2}{3} \times 18 = 12$. (Point out that 12 < 18.)

TEACHING STRATEGIES

On the board, draw a circle divided into sections that are $\frac{1}{2}$, $\frac{1}{4}$, $\frac{1}{8}$, and $\frac{1}{16}$ of the circle as shown at the right. Shade each section with a different color of chalk but do not label the sections. Ask students what fraction of the circle each colored section models. Then ask questions such as "What is $\frac{1}{4}$ of the orange section?" Students then draw pictures and work together to answer the questions.

In a bike race, suppose $\frac{1}{3}$ of the course is paved road. If the course is $1\frac{1}{4}$ miles long, what length is paved road? To

solve the problem, you need to multiply $\frac{1}{3} \times 1\frac{1}{4}$. Draw this diagram.

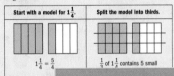

Start with a model for $1\frac{1}{4}$.	Split the model into thirds.
$1\frac{1}{4} = \frac{5}{4}$	$\frac{1}{3}$ of $1\frac{1}{4}$ contains 5 small

Each small shade...

So, $\frac{1}{3} \times 1\frac{1}{4} = \frac{5}{12}$...

Lesson 7.4

MATH BACKGROUN...

Reciprocals are n... find the reciproca... you have a whole... fraction first and t...

TEACHING STRATEG...

USING AN ALGO...

fabric. Into how m...

fabric? To solve th... involves using the...

Multiply the divi... **the divisor's recip...**

Write the produc... **simplest form.**

So, two $\frac{3}{8}$-yard pie...

Lesson 7.5

MATH BACKGROUN...
To find the numb...

310C

● Strategies for enabling all students to learn mathematics

7 Differentiating Instruction

Strategies for Underachievers

PROVIDE AND CREATE MANIPULATIVES AND TOOLS FOR CONCRETE LEARNING

Many students, especially concrete learners, learn better if they are able to see, touch, and manipulate objects that represent the concept being taught. Chapter 7 provides many opportunities for you to reach these learners.

MANIPULATIVES In Lesson 7.1, Hands-on Activity 7.2, and Lesson 7.2, you may want to provide students with fraction tiles for them to manipulate when showing multiplication of fractions and whole numbers. The use of tiles allows students to quickly build several examples of these operations. This helps students gain a concrete grasp of how to find these products before they move on to using an algorithm.

Hands-on Activity 7.4 can be adapted for underachieving students by starting with a ruler marked with increments of only $\frac{1}{4}$ inch. You may wish to draw the following table for students to complete.

Dividend	Divisor	Quotient	Dividend	Multiplier	Product
2	÷ $\frac{1}{4}$	= 8	2	× $\frac{4}{1}$	= 8
$\frac{3}{4}$	÷ $\frac{1}{4}$	= ?	$\frac{3}{4}$	× $\frac{4}{1}$	= ?
$1\frac{1}{2}$	÷ $\frac{1}{4}$	= ?	$1\frac{1}{2}$	× $\frac{4}{1}$	= ?

Depending upon the level of understanding of your students, you may also wish to complete a similar table using $\frac{3}{4}$ as the divisor.

In Lesson 7.7, to reach all students, you may wish to provide them with numerous items whose weight can be estimated. It is a good idea to pass the items around the room, having students record their estimates in a table that lists the names of the items. Make sure students have labeled their weights; stress that giving an answer without a unit label is unacceptable. Now choose individual students to come to the front of the classroom and weigh the items on a balance or a scale. Students should compare their estimates to the actual weights of the items. This

activity will help you determine whether your students have a grasp of the relative weights of objects. After several of the objects have been weighed, you might wish to pass the remaining ones around the room again, allowing students to change their estimates if they wish to do so.

USE SCAFFOLDING

Because many of the concepts in this chapter require students to execute multiple steps, you may first wish to provide review, practice, and reinforcement of previously-learned concepts that students will need.

ESTIMATION In Example 4 of Lesson 7.1 on page 315, students are shown the use of compatible numbers to make an estimate. You may wish to take some time to review *compatible numbers* and *multiples* before beginning the estimation problems in Exercises 6–8 and 27–34. Students who have not mastered their multiplication facts will need a table to assist them.

UNIT CONVERSIONS In Lesson 7.7, many students will need a table of conversions. For some students, you may wish to provide a table that instructs them when to multiply and when to divide to make a conversion.

USE A GRAPHIC ORGANIZER

VISUAL AID When multiplying or dividing with mixed numbers, students may benefit from creating a graphic organizer to detail the many steps they must follow. For multiplying two mixed numbers, you might wish to provide students with a graphic "hamburger" organizer like the one shown below, which instructs them on how to fill in each portion.

Given Problem
Change to Improper Fractions
Multiply Fractions
Simplify if Necessary
Solution

310E

Planning the Lesson

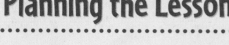

① PLAN

SKILL CHECK

1. Simplify $\frac{6}{10}$. $\frac{3}{5}$
2. Simplify $\frac{7}{4}$. $1\frac{3}{4}$
3. Multiply $\frac{2}{3}$ by 5. $3\frac{1}{3}$
4. Multiply 4 by $\frac{1}{8}$. $\frac{1}{2}$

LESSON OBJECTIVE

Multiply fractions.

PACING

Suggested Number of Days
Basic Course: 2 days
Average Course: 2 days
Advanced Course: 2 days
Block: 0.5 block with 7.1
0.5 block with 7.3

TEACHING RESOURCES

For a complete list of Teaching Resources, see page 310B.

 TRANSPARENCY

Warm-Up Exercises for this lesson are available on a transparency. A support transparency is available for Example 1.

② TEACH

MOTIVATING THE LESSON

Show students that the rule for multiplying a fraction by a whole number could be written as $\frac{a}{1} \cdot \frac{b}{c} = \frac{a \cdot b}{1 \cdot c}$. Then ask what the rule for multiplying $\frac{a}{b}$ by $\frac{c}{d}$ might be. $\frac{a \cdot c}{b \cdot d}$

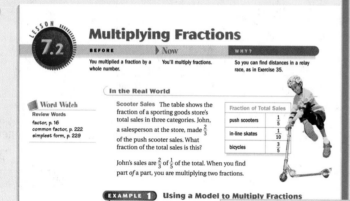

LESSON 7.2 Multiplying Fractions

BEFORE You multiplied a fraction by a whole number.

Now You'll multiply fractions.

WHY? So you can find distances in a relay race, as in Exercise 35.

Word Watch

Review Words
factor, p. 16
common factor, p. 222
simplest form, p. 229

In the Real World

Scooter Sales The table shows the fraction of a sporting goods store's total sales in three categories. John, a salesperson at the store, made $\frac{2}{3}$ of the push scooter sales. What fraction of the total sales is this?

Fraction of Total Sales	
push scooters	$\frac{1}{5}$
in-line skates	$\frac{1}{10}$
bicycles	$\frac{3}{5}$

John's sales are $\frac{2}{3}$ of $\frac{1}{5}$ of the total. When you find part *of* a part, you are multiplying two fractions.

EXAMPLE 1 Using a Model to Multiply Fractions

To answer the question above about John, find $\frac{2}{3}$ *of* $\frac{1}{5}$, or $\frac{2}{3} \times \frac{1}{5}$.

① Draw a 3 by 5 rectangle to model thirds and fifths. Each small square is $\frac{1}{15}$ of the whole.

② Shade $\frac{1}{5}$ of the rectangle.

③ Select $\frac{2}{3}$ of the shaded rectangle.

ANSWER Two of the 15 squares are selected. John's push scooter sales are $\frac{2}{15}$ of the s...

Your turn now Draw a model to find ...

1. $\frac{1}{2} \times \frac{1}{5}$ $\frac{1}{10}$
2. $\frac{2}{3} \times \frac{2}{5}$ $\frac{4}{15}$

320 Chapter 7 Multiplication and Division of Fractions

320

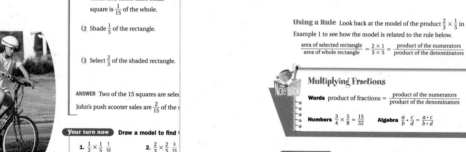

Using a Rule Look back at the model of the product $\frac{2}{3} \times \frac{1}{5}$ in Example 1 to see how the model is related to the rule below.

$$\frac{\text{area of selected rectangle}}{\text{area of whole rectangle}} = \frac{2 \times 1}{3 \times 5} = \frac{\text{product of the numerators}}{\text{product of the denominators}}$$

Note book

Multiplying Fractions

Words product of fractions = $\frac{\text{product of the numerators}}{\text{product of the denominators}}$

Numbers $\frac{3}{4} \times \frac{5}{8} = \frac{15}{32}$ **Algebra** $\frac{a}{b} \cdot \frac{c}{d} = \frac{a \cdot c}{b \cdot d}$

EXAMPLE 2 Multiplying Two Fractions

$\frac{2}{5} \times \frac{4}{3} = \frac{2 \times 4}{5 \times 3}$ Use the rule for multiplying fractions.

$= \frac{8}{15}$ Multiply. The product is in simplest form.

HELP with Solving

Notice in Example 3 that the product of $\frac{1}{3}$ and $\frac{2}{7}$ is less than either fraction.

EXAMPLE 3 Evaluating an Algebraic Expression

Algebra Evaluate the expression $\frac{1}{3}n$ when $n = \frac{2}{7}$.

$\frac{1}{3}n = \frac{1}{3} \times \frac{2}{7}$ Substitute $\frac{2}{7}$ for n.

$= \frac{1 \times 2}{3 \times 7}$ Use the rule for multiplying fractions.

$= \frac{2}{21}$ Multiply. The product is in simplest form.

Your turn now In Exercises 4–7, find the value.

4. Find the product $\frac{1}{3} \times \frac{1}{6}$. $\frac{1}{18}$
5. Find the product $\frac{3}{7} \times \frac{1}{4}$. $\frac{3}{28}$
6. Evaluate $\frac{3}{4}n$ when $n = \frac{3}{5}$. $\frac{9}{20}$
7. Evaluate $\frac{2}{3}x$ when $x = \frac{4}{9}$. $\frac{8}{27}$
8. Is the product in Example 2 less than both fractions? no

Lesson 7.2 Multiplying Fractions **321**

TIPS FOR NEW TEACHERS

Check students as they complete the exercises to make sure that they multiply numerators by numerators and denominators by denominators when they find the product of two fractions. See Tips for New Teachers in the *Chapter 7 Resource Book.*

EXTRA EXAMPLES

Example 1 Draw an area model and use it to find $\frac{3}{5} \times \frac{1}{4}$.

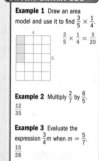

$\frac{3}{5} \times \frac{1}{4} = \frac{3}{20}$

Example 2 Multiply $\frac{2}{7}$ by $\frac{6}{5}$. $\frac{12}{35}$

Example 3 Evaluate the expression $\frac{3}{4}m$ when $m = \frac{5}{7}$. $\frac{15}{28}$

VISUALIZE

When students visualize or draw area models such as the one for Example 1, be sure they understand that the dimensions of the rectangle correspond to the denominators of the fractions being multiplied.

MULTIPLE REPRESENTATIONS

Students should understand that $\frac{a}{b} \times \frac{c}{d}$ and $\frac{a \times c}{b \times d}$ are two different representations of the same value.

321

TEACH

○ A Motivating the Lesson note at the beginning of each lesson

○ Extra Example for each example in the book

○ Concept Check question at the end of each lesson

○ Teaching Tips, Common Error notes ... AND MORE

PLAN

○ Skill Check
○ Lesson Objective
○ Pacing Summary
○ Teaching Resources

7.2 Exercises
More Practice, p. 714

Getting Ready to Practice

1. **Vocabulary** How can you tell whether a fraction is in simplest form? *if the GCF of the numerator and denominator is 1*

2. Draw a model to find the product $\frac{2}{3} \times \frac{4}{5}$. $\frac{8}{15}$

3. Find $\frac{3}{5}$ of $\frac{1}{2}$. $\frac{3}{10}$ 4. Find $\frac{1}{6}$ of $\frac{6}{11}$. $\frac{1}{11}$ 5. Find $\frac{7}{8}$ of $\frac{4}{5}$. $\frac{7}{10}$

Algebra Evaluate the expression when $x = \frac{3}{4}$.

6. $\frac{1}{5}x$ $\frac{3}{20}$ 7. $\frac{8}{9}x$ $\frac{2}{3}$ 8. $\frac{3}{4}x$ $\frac{9}{16}$

9. **Find the Error** Describe and correct the error in the solution. *The GCF of 3 and 9 is 3, and 9 divided by 3 is 3, not 2. The solution is $\frac{5}{12}$.*

$$\times \quad \frac{3}{4} \times \frac{5}{9} = \frac{\cancel{3} \times 5}{4 \times \cancel{9}_2} = \frac{5}{8}$$

Practice and Problem Solving

with Homework

Example	Exercises
1	10
2	11–18, 22, 35
3	19–21
4	23–30, 36
5	31–34

Online Resources
CLASSZONE.COM
· More Examples
· eTutorial Plus

A 10. Draw a model to find the product $\frac{3}{5} \times \frac{1}{4}$. Use the model to explain why the product is less than 1. $\frac{3}{20}$ *Sample answer: A part of a part is less than either part.*

Find the product.

11. $\frac{1}{3} \times \frac{4}{7}$ $\frac{4}{21}$ 12. $\frac{1}{3} \times \frac{1}{3}$ $\frac{1}{9}$ 13. $\frac{3}{4} \times \frac{1}{4}$ $\frac{3}{16}$ 14. $\frac{7}{8} \times \frac{1}{2}$ $\frac{7}{16}$

15. $\frac{1}{2} \times \frac{3}{10}$ $\frac{3}{20}$ 16. $\frac{4}{5} \times \frac{6}{7}$ $\frac{24}{35}$ 17. $\frac{2}{5} \times \frac{9}{9}$ $\frac{2}{45}$ 18. $\frac{6}{5} \times \frac{3}{7}$ $\frac{18}{35}$

Algebra Evaluate the expression when $x = \frac{1}{5}$.

19. $\frac{1}{7}x$ $\frac{1}{35}$ 20. $\frac{7}{10}x$ $\frac{7}{50}$ 21. $\frac{6}{11}x$ $\frac{6}{55}$

22. **Soap Bubbles** You and a friend want to make one half of a batch of soap bubble solution. How much dishwashing liquid do you need? $\frac{1}{8}$ c

SOAP BUBBLE SOLUTION
1 cup warm water
$\frac{1}{4}$ cup dishwashing liquid
1 teaspoon salt
Combine all ingredients.
Mix well until salt dissolves.

Lesson 7.2 Multiplying Fractions **323**

---

3 APPLY

ASSIGNMENT GUIDE

Basic Course
Day 1: EP p. 712 Exs. 16–19; pp. 323–325 Exs. 10–14, 19–22, 37–39, 52–57
Day 2: pp. 323–325 Exs. 23–31, 36, 43–47, 60–62

Average Course
Day 1: pp. 323–325 Exs. 10–12, 17–22, 40–45, 54–57
Day 2: pp. 323–325 Exs. 27–36, 46–50, 61–63

Advanced Course
Day 1: pp. 323–325 Exs. 10, 15–22, 40–46, 52–55
Day 2: pp. 323–325 Exs. 29–36, 47–51*, 58–63

Block
pp. 323–325 Exs. 10–12, 17–22, 40–45, 54–57 (with 7.1)
Exs. 27–36, 46–50, 61–63 (with 7.3)

EXTRA PRACTICE
• Student Edition, p. 714
• Chapter 7 Resource Book, pp. 16–18
• Test and Practice Generator

TRANSPARENCY
Even-numbered answers are available on transparencies. A support transparency is available for Exercises 2 and 10.

HOMEWORK CHECK
When you review students' homework for this lesson, go over the following exercises to check understanding of key concepts.
Basic: 10, 11, 19, 23, 31
Average: 10, 12, 20, 27, 32
Advanced: 10, 15, 21, 29, 33

ASSESS AND
FOLLOW-UP

⬤ Assessment Resources
⬤ Mini-Quiz for each lesson
⬤ Reteaching/Remediation
⬤ Challenge/Enrichment
⬤ English Learner Support

APPLY

⬤ Assignment Guide
⬤ Extra Practice references
⬤ Homework Check exercises

...duct.

... $\times \frac{16}{21}$ $\frac{4}{13}$ 48. $\frac{48}{77} \times \frac{33}{52} \times \frac{7}{18}$ $\frac{2}{13}$ 49. $\frac{36}{49} \times \frac{25}{54} \times \frac{21}{40}$ $\frac{5}{28}$

...ll This season the school ...ll team played $\frac{3}{7}$ of their games ...and $\frac{4}{7}$ of their games during the day. ...$\frac{3}{4}$ of their night games and $\frac{1}{2}$ of their ...es. What fraction of their games did ...during the season? Explain how you ...ur answer.

...ge Use number sense to order the expressions from least to ...without finding the products. Explain how you decided.

$$\frac{7}{12} \times \frac{13}{27} \qquad \frac{18}{19} \times \frac{7}{12} \qquad \frac{7}{12} \times \frac{1}{2} \qquad \frac{7}{12} \times \frac{2}{21}$$

...view

...mplete the statement. *(Lesson 5.6)*

52. $4\frac{2}{5} = \frac{1}{5}$ $\frac{2}{5}$ 53. $5\frac{1}{3} = \frac{16}{?}$ 3   54. $\frac{17}{6} = ?\frac{5}{6}$ 2   55. $\frac{25}{7} = 3\frac{?}{7}$ 4

Use compatible numbers to estimate the product. *(Lesson 7.1)*

56. $\frac{2}{5} \times 31$ 12   57. $\frac{5}{8} \times 18$ 10   58. $40 \times \frac{5}{6}$ 35   59. $28 \times \frac{2}{3}$ 18

Basic Skills Use clustering to estimate the sum. *may vary.*

60. $28 + 33 + 31 + 27 + 30 + 32$ $\frac{180}{}$ 61. $209 + 195 + 211 + 193 + 198$ $\frac{1000}{}$

60–61. Estimates may vary.

...of $\frac{7}{12}$, so compare the other factors to find the order.

Test-Taking Practice

62. **Multiple Choice** Which product is equal to $\frac{3}{5}$? D

A. $\frac{1}{5} \times \frac{2}{5}$ B. $\frac{3}{7} \times \frac{7}{10}$ C. $\frac{5}{6} \times \frac{9}{25}$ D. $\frac{5}{8} \times \frac{18}{25}$

63. **Short Response** A town is building a new school that will be about $\frac{1}{2}$ of a block wide and about $\frac{2}{3}$ of a block long. Draw a rectangle to represent one block and model the area of the school on the rectangle. Then give the area of the school in square blocks.

Check drawings; $\frac{1}{3}$ square blocks.

Lesson 7.2 Multiplying Fractions **325**

---

4 ASSESS

ASSESSMENT RESOURCES
For more assessment resources, see:
• Assessment Book
• Test and Practice Generator

MINI-QUIZ
Find each product.
1. $\frac{2}{3} \times \frac{4}{5}$ $\frac{8}{15}$
2. $\frac{3}{7} \times \frac{2}{11}$ $\frac{6}{77}$
3. $\frac{5}{12} \times \frac{6}{7}$ $\frac{5}{14}$
4. $\frac{4}{15} \times \frac{3}{8} \times \frac{1}{5}$ $\frac{1}{50}$
5. A rectangle has length $\frac{3}{5}$ inch and width w inches. Find the area of the rectangle if $w = \frac{7}{8}$ inch. $\frac{21}{40}$ in.^{2}

5 FOLLOW-UP

RETEACHING/REMEDIATION
• Study Guide in Chapter 7 Resource Book, pp. 19–20
• Tutor Place, Fractions Card 15
• eTutorial Plus Online
• Extra Practice, p. 714
• Lesson Practice in Chapter 7 Resource Book, pp. 16–18

CHALLENGE/ENRICHMENT
• Challenge Practice in Chapter 7 Resource Book, p. 21
• Teacher's Edition, p. 310F

ENGLISH LEARNER SUPPORT
• Spanish Study Guide
• Multi-Language Glossary
• Chapter Audio Summaries CDs

Pacing the Course

The Pacing Chart below shows the number of days allotted for each chapter. The Regular Schedule requires 160 days. The Block Schedule requires 80 days. These time frames include days for review and assessment: 2 days per chapter for the Regular Schedule and 1 day per chapter for the Block Schedule. Semester and trimester divisions are indicated by green and blue rules, respectively.

	SEMESTER 1							SEMESTER 2					
Chapter	1	2	3	4	5	6	7	8	9	10	11	12	13
Regular Schedule	12	12	8	14	12	12	10	14	14	12	14	14	12
Block Schedule	6	6	4	7	6	6	5	7	7	6	7	7	6

TRIMESTER 1	TRIMESTER 2	TRIMESTER 3

Assignments are provided with each lesson for a basic course, an average course, an advanced course, and a block-schedule course. Each of the four courses covers all thirteen chapters.

Basic Course

The basic course is intended for students who enter with below-average mathematical and problem-solving skills. Assignments include:

- spiral review of pre-course and on-level topics through Skills Review Handbook and Extra Practice references

- substantial work with the skills and concepts presented in the lesson

- straightforward applications of these skills and concepts

- test preparation and mixed review exercises

Average Course

The average course is intended for students who enter with typical mathematical and problem-solving skills. Assignments include:

- substantial work with the skills and concepts presented in the lesson

- applications of these skills and concepts

- test preparation and mixed review exercises

Advanced Course

The advanced course is intended for students who enter with above-average mathematical and problem-solving skills. Assignments include:

- substantial work with the skills and concepts presented in the lesson

- more complex applications and challenge exercises

- test preparation and mixed review exercises

- optional extra challenge exercises provided in the Teacher's Edition and in the Chapter Resource Books

Block-Schedule Course

The block-schedule course is intended for schools that use a block schedule. It covers the same content as the regular-schedule course. The exercises assigned are comparable to the exercises for the average course.

The Pacing and Assignment Guide for each chapter is located on the interleaved pages preceding the chapter. Part of the Pacing Chart for Chapter 7 is shown here.

Regular-Schedule Chart This chart provides pacing for the basic, average, and advanced courses.

Lesson	Les. Day	BASIC	AVERAGE	ADVANCED
7.1	Day 1	EP p. 712 Exs. 43–47; pp. 316–317 Exs. 11–30, 35–39, 42, 48–59	pp. 316–317 Exs. 15–26, 31–44, 48–53, 57–59	pp. 316–317 Exs. 17–26, 31–47*, 50–55, 59
7.2	Day 1	EP p. 712 Exs. 16–19; pp. 323–325 Exs. 10–14, 19–22, 37–39, 52–57	pp. 323–325 Exs. 10–12, 17–22, 40–45, 54–57	pp. 323–325 Exs. 10, 15–22, 40–46, 52–55
	Day 2	pp. 323–325 Exs. 23–31, 36, 43–47, 60–62	pp. 323–325 Exs. 27–36, 46–50, 61–63	pp. 323–325 Exs. 29–36, 47–51*, 58–63

*Challenge Exercises   EP = Extra Practice   SRH = Skills Review Handbook   EC = Extra Challenge

Block-Schedule Chart This chart provides pacing for the block-schedule course.

DAY 1	DAY 2	DAY 3	DAY 4	DAY 5
7.1 pp. 316–317 Exs. 15–26, 31–44, 48–53, 57–59 **7.2** pp. 323–325 Exs. 10–12, 17–22, 40–45, 54–57	**7.2 cont.** pp. 323–325 Exs. 27–36, 46–50, 61–63 **7.3** pp. 328–330 Exs. 19–26, 29–37, 40–46, 49–54	**7.4** pp. 336–338 Exs. 14–25, 30–56, 60–65, 69–71 **7.5** pp. 341–343 Exs. 7–17, 22–25, 30–48, 50–52, 56–58	**7.6** pp. 346–347 Exs. 7–17, 21–29, 31–42 **7.7** pp. 353–354 Exs. 15–24, 28–35, 39–48, 50–55, 59–61	**Review** pp. 358–359 Exs. 1–55 **Assess** Chapter 7 Test

YEARLY PACING   **Chapter 7 Total** – 5 days   **Chapters 1–7 Total** – 40 days   **Remaining** – 40 days

Assignment Guide An assignment guide for each lesson is provided at the beginning of the exercise set. Assignments are given for basic, average, advanced, and block-schedule courses.

Basic Course
Day 1: EP p. 712 Exs. 16–19; pp. 323–325 Exs. 10–14, 19–22, 37–39, 52–57
Day 2: pp. 323–325 Exs. 23–31, 36, 43–47, 60–62

Average Course
Day 1: pp. 323–325 Exs. 10–12, 17–22, 40–45, 54–57
Day 2: pp. 323–325 Exs. 27–36, 46–50, 61–63

Advanced Course
Day 1: pp. 323–325 Exs. 10, 15–22, 40–46, 52–55
Day 2: pp. 323–325 Exs. 29–36, 47–51*, 58–63

Block
pp. 323–325 Exs. 10–12, 17–22, 40–45, 54–57 (with 7.1)
Exs. 27–36, 46–50, 61–63 (with 7.3)

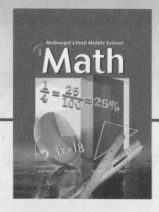

A Program *you can* trust

The right math, presented in the right way.

McDougal Littell Middle School Math, Course 1, is a program you can count on to teach the mathematical concepts and methods that your students need to know in order to meet high curriculum standards and succeed on high-stakes tests. Including the appropriate content, however, is not enough. The math must be presented in a way that students can understand and that will motivate them to learn. The distinguished author team of *McDougal Littell Middle School Math* and the thorough, research-based planning and development process ensure that this program both includes the right math and teaches the math in the right way, so that students gain conceptual understanding and achieve success on important assessments.

DISTINGUISHED AUTHOR TEAM

The experienced, expert author team of Ron Larson, Laurie Boswell, Timothy Kanold, and Lee Stiff brings a wealth of mathematical expertise, writing talent, and classroom teaching and curriculum planning experience from middle school through college to the creation of this new program. Lead author Ron Larson has been writing highly-respected and widely-used textbooks for more than 20 years, and each new book benefits from the comments of the many teachers and students who used earlier editions.

STANDARDS-BASED INSTRUCTION AND ASSESSMENT

State and National Standards In planning the outlines and writing the textbook, the authors paid careful attention to state curriculum standards and state assessment objectives from all states to make sure that the important mathematical concepts and skills were included and given appropriate emphasis. The authors also made sure that the outline and course content fully addressed the standards of national organizations such as the National Council of Teachers of Mathematics (NCTM) and the National Assessment of Educational Progress (NAEP). A correlation to the NAEP objectives appears on page T56 and a correlation to the NCTM Standards can be found on page T57.

SUPPORTING BEST PRACTICES FROM RESEARCH

Educational and Cognitive Research Recent research studies have confirmed strategies for increasing student achievement. These strategies, which reflect the best practices of successful teachers, can help all students learn more effectively. The authors kept this research in mind as they planned and wrote *Middle School Math*, so that the content, organization, and instructional strategies in the program would make it easy for you to implement best-practice instruction in your classroom.

...validated by research

COMPREHENSIVE RESEARCH, REVIEW, AND FIELD-TESTING

About three years prior to the publication of this book, the authors and teams of editors, consultants, graphic designers, professional researchers, and experts in content, instruction, and technology began gathering and analyzing the extensive data on which the plans for this program are based. Data were gathered in a variety of ways, starting with school visits and concluding with field testing.

- **Classroom Visits** Discussions and classroom observations took place in schools throughout the country to determine the key needs of teachers and students, the obstacles that they face in achieving their goals, and the types of materials that can help them achieve success.

- **Nationwide Research Surveys** Comprehensive mail surveys on middle school math curriculum needs, instructional practices, student achievement levels, and teacher preferences regarding instructional materials were conducted early in the development process to guide the planning of the program.

- **Teacher Panels** Panels of expert teachers from different areas of the country participated in the development of the program by identifying instructional and curriculum needs, reviewing prototype outlines and sample materials for both print and electronic materials, and providing suggestions for teaching-support publications.

- **Student Discussion Groups** Discussion groups were held with middle school students to determine the textbook characteristics that make it easy or hard for them to learn and the extent to which they have access to and feel comfortable using electronic products.

- **Focus Tests** Focus tests in which teachers discussed their instructional goals and evaluated sample student and teacher materials were held in different areas of the country. The teachers participating in the focus groups were chosen to represent the wide range of types of schools, philosophies of instruction, and teacher characteristics (like number of years of teaching) in the teaching population. The feedback from these diverse groups of teachers was used to revise and refine the project plans prior to writing.

- **Curriculum Advisers and Reviewers** The Curriculum Advisers and Reviewers listed on page T4 participated in planning the program and read all the proof for the student edition in detail with regard to clarity, accuracy, and appropriateness for classroom use. Other teacher reviewers read selected chapters for these characteristics.

- **Field-Testing** Selected chapters from each grade level were taught in the classroom to test how successful students were in learning from the textbook. Some of the aspects tested were student achievement as measured by pre- and post-test scores, students' ease of learning from the material, and students' interest in the material.

Reaching *All* students

No Child Left Behind

The new federal law known as *No Child Left Behind* (NCLB) highlights the need to ensure that all students, whether they are struggling, average, or advanced learners, have opportunities to make continuing progress in developing the skills they need to become successful adults. This law charges the states with the responsibility of establishing statewide accountability systems based on challenging standards, annual assessment in Grades 3–8, and annual statewide progress objectives.

Intervention begins with diagnosis.

McDougal Littell Middle School Math supports the goals of NCLB. The program is based on challenging state curriculum standards and assessment objectives *(see page T40)*. It provides you with helpful materials for diagnosing how well students understand the material, for differentiating instruction to reach all students, for assessing student progress, and for providing remediation. It also emphasizes important test-taking skills and problem-solving strategies.

ONGOING DIAGNOSIS

Materials to diagnose student understanding are provided before, during, and following each chapter and lesson.

- **Pre-Course Tests** in the Student Edition and the Assessment Book help you diagnose how well students have mastered key prerequisite skills for the course.

- **Chapter Warm-Up Games** and **Getting Ready to Learn** exercises at the beginning of each chapter provide two different mechanisms for reviewing pre-chapter skills and vocabulary.

- **Skill Check** exercises in the Teacher's Edition and **Warm-Up** exercises on transparencies provide practice with prerequisite skills for the upcoming lesson.

- **Your Turn Now** and **Getting Ready to Practice** exercises in the Student Edition, along with **Concept Check** items in the Teacher's Edition, help you monitor how well students are grasping the vocabulary, skills, and concepts as you present each lesson.

- **Homework Check** boxes in the Teacher's Edition identify exercises from the homework assignment that you can use to determine whether or not students have mastered the key skills and concepts.

- You can also use the **Test and Practice Generator** to create online practice sheets and see a report of the results to monitor individual progress.

...in your diverse classroom

DIFFERENTIATED INSTRUCTION AND PRACTICE

Being able to differentiate instruction and practice can help you reach all students. The list below highlights a few components of *Middle School Math* that are designed to help you in this effort. You can use **EasyPlanner Plus Online** to preview and select the resources as you develop your lesson plans. *(See also pages T50–T55 and the E and F pages preceding each chapter.)*

INSTRUCTION

- Hands-On Activities in the Student Edition and a Special Activities Book
- Visualize and Multiple Representation notes in the Teacher's Edition
- Notetaking Guide workbook and transparencies
- English-Spanish Problem Solving Transparencies
- Chapter Audio Summaries CDs (in English, Spanish, and Haitian Creole)
- Electronic Lesson Presentations
- Online Activities and Vocabulary Support

PRACTICE

- Leveled exercises labeled in the Teacher's Edition; leveled homework assignments; leveled practice worksheets
- Challenge exercises in the Student Edition; Daily Puzzlers in the Teacher's Edition; and Challenge Practice masters in the Chapter Resource Books
- Math Tutor Place cards with practice on essential math topics
- Cooperative Learning Projects in the Chapter Resource Books
- Spanish Study Guide

ASSESSMENT

Middle School Math provides diagnostic, formative, and summative assessment resources for measuring student progress on an ongoing basis.

- The **Student Edition** has test-practice questions at the end of every exercise set, including multiple choice, short response, and extended response items. Also included are quizzes, reviews, traditional and standardized chapter tests, and an end-of-course test.
- The **Teacher's Edition** has a quiz for every lesson. An alternate quiz is available on a transparency.
- The **Assessment Book** has alternate forms of all the quizzes and tests in the textbook, PLUS leveled chapter tests, alternative assessments, unit tests, and cumulative tests.
- You can use the **Test and Practice Generator** to create your own customized quizzes and tests. **Online quizzes** and **State Test Practice** are available at www.classzone.com.

Students need practice with the various types of questions on standardized tests.

BUILDING TEST-TAKING SKILLS

It is more important than ever for students to build strong test-taking skills in order to be successful on annual assessments required by the NCLB Act. *Middle School Math* provides instruction and practice with test-taking skills at the end of every unit in the textbook.

- **Multiple Choice Questions** Students are encouraged to use number sense and estimation skills to decide whether answer choices are reasonable.
- **Short Response Questions** Students are given guidance about how to write complete answers and show their work.
- **Context-Based Multiple Choice Questions** Students practice answering multiple-choice questions that involve interpreting diagrams and graphs.
- **Extended Response Questions** Students learn how to write complete answers to multi-step problems.

Continued

Reaching *All* students Continued

RETEACHING AND REMEDIATION

Students sometimes need reteaching in order to understand concepts better or additional practice in order to master key skills. *Middle School Math* provides a variety of resources to help students achieve success. Some of these same resources can also be used by absent students to help them catch up.

Strong problem solving skills help students become successful adults.

- **Student Edition** Includes **Help with Review** notes that direct students to appropriate review materials, **Notebook Reviews** after every three or four lessons that summarize and practice key vocabulary and skills, **Chapter Reviews** with more vocabulary and skill practice, **Cumulative Practice** at the end of every unit, a **Skills Review Handbook** with reteaching and practice for pre-book skills, and **Extra Practice** for every lesson.

- **Teacher's Edition** Includes **Extra Examples** and **Common Error** notes that can be used to help clarify understanding.

- **Chapter Resource Books** Include **Practice** masters (Levels A, B, C), **Challenge Practice** masters, **Cumulative Practice** masters, **Study Guide** masters with worked-out examples, and **Chapter Review Games and Activities**.

- **Math Tutor Place** Includes 104 cards organized by mathematical strand to give students reteaching and practice on important concepts.

- **Technology Resources** Include a variety of interactive and engaging materials for reteaching and practice. *(See page T33 for descriptions.)*

PROBLEM SOLVING STRATEGIES

Questions on state and national tests are often posed as word problems. In order for students to demonstrate mastery of computational skills, they must be able to read and interpret word problems and apply appropriate strategies to solve them. *Middle School Math* incorporates problem solving throughout the textbook to help students learn to apply computational skills in context. *(See also the Professional Development Book, the Chapter Resource Books, and the English-Spanish Problem Solving Transparencies.)*

- **Problem Solving Plan** A four-step problem solving plan, where students read, plan, solve, and look back, is introduced in Chapter 1.

- **Problem Solving Strategies** A familiar or new problem solving strategy is featured in every chapter. Each feature includes practice on that strategy as well as mixed practice. The strategy is then applied in the lesson that follows. Choose a Strategy exercises provide ongoing review.

- **Word Problems at All Levels** Word problems appear at all three exercise levels and in the Getting Ready to Practice section.

- **Multi-Step Problems** Guided Problem Solving and Extended Problem Solving exercises help students prepare for multi-step problems on state and national tests.

- **Test Practice** Test-practice exercises at the end of each lesson, chapter, and unit are stated in words.

Reading, *Writing, Notetaking*

Vital Skills for Today and the Future

Vital Skills Today more than ever, students need strong skills in reading, writing, and notetaking in mathematics in order to understand course content, be successful on important state and national assessments, and develop the ability to become independent learners. Acquiring these skills in middle school will build an important foundation for more advanced courses and for adult life. *McDougal Littell Middle School Math* provides many opportunities in the textbook and in the teacher's materials to help students develop their reading, writing, and notetaking skills.

Recent Research Recent brain research and classroom research in reading and writing have provided new insights into learning and also confirmed the value of well-known practices of successful teachers. Although the focus of this research is often on reading in language arts and social studies, many of the strategies also help those reading mathematical material. Two important aspects of reading addressed by research are vocabulary development and reading comprehension. *McDougal Littell Middle School Math* offers substantial learning support in these core areas.

VOCABULARY DEVELOPMENT

The textbook provides strong support to students in learning, practicing, and reviewing vocabulary. On the Getting Ready to Learn page at the start of each chapter, the important review words are listed and practiced in the Using Vocabulary exercises. Then, at the beginning of each lesson, the key vocabulary for the lesson appears under the Word Watch list, and new vocabulary in the lesson is emphasized by boldface type with yellow highlighting. The Help Notes in the margin serve as a built-in vocabulary, reading, and problem solving tutor. *See pp. 93, 106, 345, 431.*

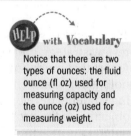

HELP with **Vocabulary**

Notice that there are two types of ounces: the fluid ounce (fl oz) used for measuring capacity and the ounce (oz) used for measuring weight.

In the Exercises, the Getting Ready to Practice exercises (which provide guided practice prior to homework) include vocabulary as well as computational and problem solving practice. The Notebook Review pages (two per chapter) and the Chapter Reviews also list key vocabulary and include vocabulary exercises. In addition, there is a complete Glossary that includes examples and diagrams at the back of the book. *See pp. 193, 392-393, 518-519, 739.*

The teacher's materials give specific suggestions for helping students understand and remember vocabulary. *See, in particular, the Professional Development Book, pp. 15-22.*

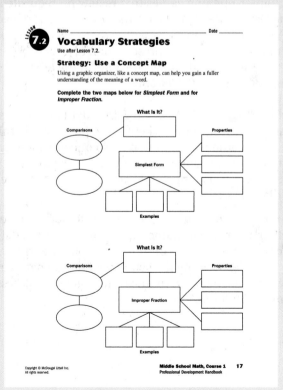

Continued

READING COMPREHENSION

The Student Handbook on pp. xx–xxv gets students off to a good start with reading the textbook by giving tips for identifying the main idea, understanding the vocabulary, knowing what's important in a lesson, being an active reader, and reading word problems.

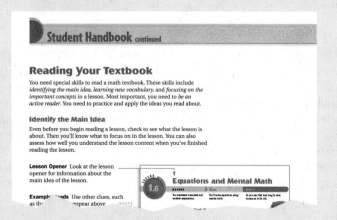

Establishing a Context A useful comprehension strategy supported by both brain and classroom research is connecting new learning to prior knowledge. This strategy is incorporated throughout *Middle School Math* in the Before/Now/Why lists at the beginning of chapters and the beginnings of lessons; in the chapter-opening games that review prerequisite skills; and in the Getting Ready to Learn pages at the start of each chapter. Also, each lesson starts with either a real world example, a short activity, or a visual presentation of a math idea in order to set the stage for the new concepts in the lesson. *See pp. 228, 267, 310, 383, 532.*

Facilitating Understanding In order to create a student-friendly book, the authors kept these principles in mind as they wrote: Students can learn new concepts more easily when they are presented in short sentences that use simple syntax and are accompanied by appropriate tables, charts, and diagrams.

Clear definitions that enable students to determine easily whether a particular mathematical object fits the definition or not are essential for comprehension. Students need special help in understanding the symbols of mathematics and knowing how to use them in writing algebraic expressions. *See pp. 449, 533, 583.*

Reflecting on Learning An effective strategy for increasing both reading comprehension and thinking skills is reflection on what has been read or learned (metacognition). The Stop and Think questions throughout the book, the worked-out examples that encourage students to consider whether an answer is reasonable, and the exercises that ask students to explain their reasoning all help students develop metacognitive skills. *See pp. 143, 154, 211, 280.*

Using Graphic Organizers Graphic organizers such as charts, Venn diagrams, or concept maps can be especially helpful for classifying mathematical objects such as types of numbers or types of geometric figures. These organizers are used throughout the textbook, and suggestions on how to use them are given to students in the Know How to Take Notes sections. *See pp. 420, 445.*

WRITING OPPORTUNITIES

In order to become good writers, students need frequent opportunities to practice their writing skills. These opportunities occur throughout the textbook in the Exercises; in the Stop and Think questions in the chapter-opening games, the activities, and the Notebook Reviews; and in the Exploring Math in Science sections. *See pp. 75, 105, 148–149, 234, 473.*

EFFECTIVE NOTETAKING

Taking effective notes is an important reading, learning, and review strategy, and yet math teachers throughout the country report that many students enter middle school with few if any notetaking skills. Thus, the authors identified the goal of helping students develop their notetaking skills as an important objective of the program, and they have incorporated many notetaking aids into the program. See, especially, the Getting Ready to Learn pages and the Notebook Reviews in the textbook, and the Notetaking Guide workbooks and overhead visuals in the teacher's materials. *See pp. 474, 548–549.*

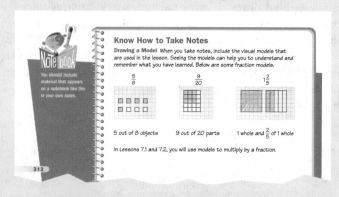

CRISS: CReating Independence through Student-owned Strategies

Project CRISS was founded to help develop thoughtful, independent readers and learners through instruction based on strategies arising from scientifically-based cognitive and social learning research of the past 25 years. The chart below lists the key CRISS principles, together with examples from *McDougal Littell Middle School Math, Course 1* that support them.

Background Knowledge Background knowledge is a powerful determinant of reading comprehension. Look for introductory material that both builds upon and provides background knowledge.	Chapter Warm-Up Games, 52–53, 210–211, 310–311, 370–371, 530–531; Getting Ready to Learn, 54, 212, 266, 312, 372, 532; Stop and Think, 53, 211, 311, 372, 531; Help with Review, 159, 271, 385, 493, 562
Active Involvement Good readers are actively involved with the text and in their learning. Look for methods and activities that show students how to be active and that provide ways for them to be active.	Know How to Take Notes, 106, 212, 372, 474, 532; Notebook, 21, 108, 214, 313, 476, 539; Notebook Review, 196, 282, 498; Chapter Review, 100, 260, 358; Worked-out Examples, 21, 107, 228, 278, 313, 476
Discussion Students need many opportunities to talk with one another about their reading and about what they are learning. Look for activities that open doors for discussion, in pairs, in groups, and with the whole class.	Chapter Warm-Up Games, 52–53, 210–211, 310–311, 370–371, 530–531; Brain Games, 97, 173, 330, 453; Activity, 187, 460; Hands-On Activity, 92, 112, 444, 537; What Do You Think?, 154, 280, 353
Metacognition Good readers are metacognitive. They are goal-directed, and they know how to interact with print to construct meaning. Look for opportunities to help students become more aware of and to discuss the *how* and *why* of their learning.	Help with Review, 159, 271, 385, 493, 562; Help with Solving, 57, 153, 215, 236, 351, 589; Help with Homework, 70, 167, 273, 381, 451, 569; Help with Notetaking, 107, 313, 445; Help with Reading, 138, 379, 450; Help with Technology, 257, 355, 411; Help with Vocabulary, 56, 345, 431; Watch Out, 125, 299, 492, 584; Building Test-Taking Skills, 202
Writing Students need multiple opportunities to write about what they are learning. Look for activities that occur naturally throughout the textbook and activities in teacher's materials that are correlated to the textbook.	Know How to Take Notes, 106, 212, 372, 474, 532; Notebook, 108, 214, 383, 480, 539; Notebook Review, 98, 196, 282, 356, 412, 498; Help with Notetaking, 107, 313, 445; Short Response, 103, 205, 281, 343, 410; Extended Response, 133, 205, 208, 365; Stop and Think, 53, 129, 259, 465; Writing, 116, 274, 387, 448, 513; Exploring Math in Science, 148
Organizing for Learning Good readers know a variety of ways to organize information for learning. Look for suggestions for use of tables, charts, graphic organizers, and other devices that help students organize and interpret their learning.	Know How To Take Notes, 106, 212, 372, 474, 532; Problem Solving Strategies, 134, 185, 296, 348, 458; Help with Notetaking, 107, 187, 228, 278, 313, 445, 476
Explanation and Modeling Students become strategic when teachers model processes. Look for modeling that explains the *why* of a method or strategy.	Worked-out Examples, 21, 107, 228, 278, 313, 476; Problem Solving Strategies, 134, 185, 296, 348, 404; Technology Activities, 87, 141, 158, 295, 441; Special Topic, 496
Teaching for Understanding Students come to understand by doing a variety of activities. Look for a rich variety and choice of activities, exercises, and projects.	Extended Problem Solving, 133, 218, 452, 513; Stop and Think, 99, 197, 283, 499; Critical Thinking, 121, 225, 342, 488; Challenge, 65, 140, 232, 434, 536; Brain Games, 123, 219, 357, 429; Activity, 107, 187, 313, 506; Hands-On Activity, 163, 289, 394, 537; Writing, 116, 274, 448, 513; Short Response, 205, 343, 512; Extended Response, 205, 206, 367, 521

Further reading: A helpful reference is *Teaching Reading in Mathematics*, by Mary Less Barton and Clare Heidema, published by Mid-continent Research for Education and Learning (MCREL), Aurora, Colorado.

Research-Based *Solutions*

The *McDougal Littell Middle School Math* program reflects current research in education. The student editions (**SE**), teacher's editions (**TE**), Chapter Resource Books (**CRB**), and other ancillary materials provide opportunities for teachers and students to experience a number of different learning strategies both in school and at home.

Research supports a variety of learning strategies.

One group of instructional strategies used in this program are the instructional strategies presented in *Classroom Instruction that Works**, a publication from the Association for Supervision and Curriculum Development. The nine strategies discussed in that publication are summarized below, along with some specific instances of the strategy's use in the *McDougal Littell Middle School Math, Course 1* program.

1. Identifying Similarities and Differences

This strategy includes comparing and classifying, and suggests representing comparisons in graphic or symbolic form.

Course 1 examples include *compare* exercises throughout the chapters, contrasting units of measure and types of geometric figures, and making concept maps and Venn diagrams.

See, for example, SE194, SE350, SE703, TE137, TE420, CRB3 p. 25

2. Summarizing and Notetaking

This strategy includes deciding when to delete, substitute, or keep information when writing a summary and using a variety of notetaking formats — e.g., outlines, webbing, or a combination technique — and suggests encouraging students to use notes as a study guide for tests.

Course 1 examples include the entire Notetaking Guide; Know How to Take Notes, Help with Notetaking, Notebooks (SE); Notetaking Strategies, Notetaking (TE)

See, for example, SE54, SE169, SE278, SE628, TE30, TE312, TE501, CRB2 p. 3

3. Reinforcing Effort and Providing Recognition

This strategy includes making the connection between effort and achievement clear to students and providing recognition for attainment of specific goals to stimulate motivation.

Course 1 examples include Your Turn Now, Getting Ready to Practice, Guided Problem Solving (SE); Motivating the Lesson, Concept Check, Mini Quiz (TE)

See, for example, SE138, TE59, TE272, TE275, CRB2 p. 4

4. Homework and Practice

This strategy includes making the purpose of homework assignments clear to students and focusing practice assignments on specific elements of a complex skill.

Course 1 examples include Math Tutor Place; Homework Help, Practice and Problem Solving, Notebook Review, Extra Practice (SE); Diagnosis/Remediation, Homework Check, Skill Check (TE); Practice A, B, C (CRB)

See, for example, SE106, SE224, SE258, TE312, TE316, TE320, CRB2 pp. 33, 83, CRB3 p. 20

5. Nonlinguistic Representations

<u>This strategy includes</u> creating nonlinguistic representations — including creating graphic organizers, making physical models, generating mental pictures, drawing pictures and pictographs, and engaging in kinesthetic activity — to help students understand content in a whole new way.

<u>*Course 1* examples include</u> Know How to Take Notes, Problem Solving Strategies, Brain Games (SE); Differentiating Instruction, Visualize, Multiple Representations, Alt. Strategy (TE)

See, for example, SE372, SE458, SE582, TE17, TE126, TE383

6. Cooperative Learning

<u>This strategy includes</u> a description of the five defining elements of cooperative learning — positive interdependence, face-to-face interaction, individual and group accountability, interpersonal and group skills, and group processing — and gives suggestions for grouping techniques.

<u>*Course 1* examples include</u> Chapter Warm-Up Games, Hands-On Activities, In-lesson Activities, Brain Games (SE); Grouping (TE); Cooperative Projects (CRB); see also the Special Activities Book

See, for example, SE150, SE187, SE248, TE158, TE186, CRB2 p. 79

7. Setting Objectives and Providing Feedback

<u>This strategy includes</u> using instructional goals to narrow what students focus on and suggests providing feedback that is specific to a criterion and encouraging students to personalize their teacher's goals and to provide some of their own feedback.

<u>*Course 1* examples include</u> Before/Why/Now lists in student lessons and scoring rubrics on Building Test-Taking Skills pages (SE); Lesson Objectives, Activity Goals, Assess rubrics (TE); goals and objectives given on Activity Master and Technology Activity pages and rubrics provided with projects (CRB); discussion of rubrics in the Professional Development Book; Online self-assessment quizzes

See, for example, SE61, SE362, TE149, TE289, CRB3 p. 67

8. Generating and Testing Hypotheses

<u>This strategy includes</u> using a variety of structured tasks to guide students through generating and testing hypotheses, using induction or deduction, and suggests asking students to clearly explain their hypotheses and conclusions to help deepen their understanding.

<u>*Course 1* examples include</u> Hands-On Act., Predict exercises throughout book (SE); Activity/Key Discovery, Math Reasoning (TE)

See, for example, SE316, SE435, TE35, TE68, TE90

9. Cues, Questions, and Advance Organizers

<u>This strategy includes</u> asking questions or giving explicit cues before a learning experience to provide students with a preview of what they are about to experience; using verbal and graphic advance organizers, or having students skim information before reading as an advance organizer.

<u>*Course 1* examples include</u> Before/Why/Now lists at beginning of lessons, pre-reading lesson elements such as Word Watch lists and Example heads throughout book, problem solving plan (SE); Motivating the Lesson (TE); discussion of problem solving in the Professional Development Book

See, for example, SE113–114, TE16, TE21, TE130, TE421

*Marzano, Robert J., Debra J. Pickering, and Jane E. Pollock, *Classroom Instruction that Works: Research-Based Strategies for Increasing Student Achievement* and its accompanying handbook. Alexandria, Virginia: Association for Supervision and Curriculum Development, 2001

Providing *Universal Access*

With careful planning, teachers can help <u>all</u> students reach a level of mathematical competence needed to continue their education in mathematics.

DIVERSE STUDENTS

In most classrooms, students present a variety of achievement levels, skills, and needs. The goal for all students is the same: We want them to develop sufficient computational, procedural, and problem solving skills to provide a solid foundation for further study in mathematics. However, all students do not arrive at these competencies at the same time or in the same way. In this article we suggest research-based strategies teachers can use to modify curriculum and instruction for special needs students. The basic instructional plan in *Middle School Math* is designed for students who are achieving at near grade level; but just prior to each chapter we include specific suggestions for students who are achieving above and below grade level, and for students who are not fluent in English (see also the article titled "Adapting Curriculum and Instruction for English Learners").

Student Groups Teachers may find it helpful to view students as members of four basic groups, as shown on the facing page. (English learners can be found in all four groups.) Teachers do not need to place students in these groups; the categories are suggested so teachers can plan ahead to meet different needs of students. Note the use of the term *underachievers*. This term is not synonymous with special education. It may include some special education pupils but includes many more students whose low achievement levels are the result of inadequate prior schooling or attendance, high mobility rates, or a host of other reasons that have nothing to do with their abilities or disabilities. The term *underachievers* is not meant to be a negative term. On the contrary, we believe that students achieving below grade level can be successful in mathematics given carefully designed instruction.

SETTING THE RIGHT TONE

There are three key strategies recommended for teachers as they adapt any program to students' needs:

- Use frequent assessment as a way to determine what each student does or does not know, and use that assessment as the basis for planning.

- Plan modifications of curriculum and instruction ahead of time so that you are ready to differentiate as the need arises.

- Use a variety of grouping strategies to facilitate learning. A combination of whole class instruction and temporary groupings of students, with groups organized around students' needs, will facilitate management of the variety of achievement levels and learning needs in the classroom.

Assessment, planning, and flexible grouping are essential to ensuring that your students have the optimal chance for success. In addition to these three key strategies, general guidelines for establishing a classroom designed to meet students' needs are:

1. Establish an atmosphere where students feel comfortable asking questions and are rewarded for asking about things they don't understand.

2. Maintain the same goals for all students. Allow additional time and practice for students who need it, and provide challenging alternatives for those who are ready to move more quickly.

3. Clearly identify the skill, concept, or standards you are working on and measure progress toward those ends.

4. Have students show their work. It is much easier for teachers to understand where a student gets confused if they have evidence of the student's thought process.

5. Try small modifications in curriculum and instruction before more drastic ones.

6. Don't persist with a strategy that is not working. Try something else.

7. Encourage effort and persistence, and celebrate successes with your students.

VARYING CURRICULUM AND INSTRUCTION

1. **Time** Most students whose achievement is below grade level will need more time. Students who are not fluent in English will need more time. The contents of this book might be offered over a two-year period, or two periods a day. Perhaps the day can be extended through study hall, regular homework assignments, tutoring, or Saturday, summer, or "off track" catch-up sessions. Advanced students might "test out" of portions of the book and complete the material in half a year, or they may compact two courses into one.

2. **Presentation** Instructing in a variety of ways and taking a single concept and explaining it verbally and visually with concrete and abstract examples provide students multiple opportunities for understanding. Area, for example, is a key concept in geometry. In earlier grades students have found areas of simple objects, both by using tiles to cover an area, and by applying algorithms. Later, students practice with unusual shapes, dividing them into simpler ones. Finally, students tackle sophisticated examples like finding the shape with the maximum area given a fixed perimeter, using both trial and error and more abstract methods.

3. **Task parameters** Multi-step problems can be especially difficult for students. These types of problems are just combinations of simpler problems and can be broken down into those simpler steps, with additional help and practice at each step. Confusing elements can be minimized and extraneous material can be eliminated. For advanced students, simpler problems can be eliminated and more challenging ones (as suggested in each chapter) may be substituted.

4. **Methods of assessment** Students learning English may be able to demonstrate on paper what they cannot yet verbalize. Students with physical challenges may be unable to draw a graph but may be able to select the right graph from a series of options or verbally describe the graph so that someone else can draw it. Allow students to demonstrate their knowledge in a variety of ways while helping all students to master the skills and knowledge necessary to exhibit their understanding in standard ways.

Middle School Math is organized so that much of the differentiation for special needs students is built into the design of the program. Note that simpler concepts are introduced before

FOUR BASIC STUDENT GROUPS

ADVANCED GROUP

Advanced students have already completed some of the grade-level material. They make rapid progress and become bored with repetition. They may or may not have been formally identified as gifted or talented in the area of mathematics.

SUGGESTED PLAN

1. Assess what these students already know.
2. Allow these students to "test out" of chapters or assignments.
3. Substitute challenging assignments for easier ones.
4. Modify instruction so that it is more complex or more in-depth.

GRADE LEVEL GROUP

Students achieving at grade level may have minor, occasional difficulties but they can be assisted to maintain their progress with extra practice and individual or group assistance on an ad hoc basis.

SUGGESTED PLAN

1. Assess what these students already know.
2. Progress through *Middle School Math* at the recommended pace and sequence.
3. On an ad hoc basis, review or provide additional practice as needed.

UNDERACHIEVING GROUP

These learners are not achieving at expected grade level but can, with a carefully designed program that provides targeted assistance. Systematic differentiation such as preteaching, reteaching, and additional instructional time should be planned for these students, as suggested in each chapter.

SUGGESTED PLAN

1. Assess what these students already know.
2. Provide additional scaffolding and the instructional variations suggested in this book.
3. Focus on the key concepts and present material systematically.
4. Vary the kinds of instruction so that students have several opportunities to understand.
5. Provide additional practice homework.

INTENSIVE NEEDS GROUP

Intensive needs students are those whose performance is two or more standard deviations below the mean on standardized measures. These students will probably already be eligible for special education services. This is a very small percentage of the general population.

SUGGESTED PLAN

1. Assess what these students already know.
2. Determine if these students have an IEP.
3. Refer students for special education testing or child study team discussion; enlist the help of specialists.
4. Carefully consider each student's most appropriate placement in mathematics.
5. Use the specific suggestions for underachieving learners.

Continued

more complex ones. Ample practice is provided. Challenge exercises are included throughout the pupil text. Activities provide students with models for conceptual understanding of the mathematical reasoning behind each key concept. Mathematical reasoning is stressed throughout each chapter. Vocabulary words, examples, and Getting Ready to Practice exercises are standard features of each chapter. Each lesson includes Mixed Review exercises so that students recall and use skills and understandings from previous chapters. These features were designed to help you meet the needs of the students in your class.

FOR STUDENTS WHO HAVE TROUBLE PAYING ATTENTION

Some students in your classroom may be formally identified as having Attention Deficit Hyperactivity Disorder (ADHD) or Attention Deficit Disorder (ADD). Others may exhibit the same learning challenges but may not be formally identified. Whether formally identified or not, students who have trouble paying attention generally share the following characteristics:

- Trouble paying attention is not just occasional. It occurs most or all of the time, across content areas, and is inappropriate for the age of the child.

- Forgetfulness, memory problems, losing things, disorganization

- Restlessness, fidgeting

- Socially inappropriate behavior such as excessive talking, interrupting others, and difficulty waiting their turn

These students may be very bright and capable in mathematics but have a hard time staying focused for long periods of time. They need to be taught strategies for organizing their work and keeping track of where they are. In general, students with attention problems need to be helped to develop coping strategies. The teacher should approach the student in a problem solving mode: "Let's find ways to help you concentrate and organize your work," rather than using one of the following strategies in a punitive way.

1. **Present the work in smaller chunks over smaller time periods** and then gradually increase expectations. If students have trouble completing long tests, for example, break the material into smaller quizzes and increase the length of the quizzes as the year progresses.

2. **Use cumulative review and practice.** Have students periodically review what they learned in previous chapters and provide additional practice if they have forgotten.

3. **Make it more obvious what the student should focus on.** For example, use the test generator to put only four problems on each page; use a large font; or use an index card or piece of cardboard with a hole cut out of the middle to place on the page so that the student can focus on one problem at a time. A pencil, finger, highlighter, or sticky paper can also be used by the student to keep track of which problem he or she is working on.

4. **Have students race against the clock.** For some students, racing against the clock to see how many problems can be completed accurately within a five-minute time period is more motivating than doing the same number of problems at their leisure. The time period can be extended gradually.

5. **Help students develop simple strategies for bringing work to and from class.** A two-pocket folder, where homework goes home in the left pocket and comes back in the right, is a simple way to keep track of assignments.

6. **Allow movement and schedule breaks.**

7. **Minimize distractions by seating students that are easily distracted near the teacher** and away from hallway noise. Tables with several students at a table are more distracting than rows of desks. When students are to work quietly, offer headphones to block out noise. Headphones can be set to play quiet music, "white noise," or can be used just as earplugs to help block out noise.

8. **Graphic organizers** such as Venn diagrams, tree diagrams, lists, outlines, tables, and charts can all provide structures for organizing and remembering information. Mental images, choral responses, or even hand signals can help students remember. Highlighters can be used to make sure that decimal points are lined up. Graph paper is excellent for keeping homework problems neat, even when a graph is not required.

9. **Keep instructions simple and clear, especially at the beginning of the year.** Establish routines (e.g., the week's homework is always due on Thursday; assignments are written in a specific place on the board; the last ten minutes of class is used to make sure everyone understands what homework is expected and how to do it). Students who know the routine find it easier to work independently.

FOR STUDENTS WHO HAVE TROUBLE UNDERSTANDING THE CONCEPTS

Success in mathematics, as in music, sports, or other areas, comes for most students only with hard work and persistent effort. Concepts may seem difficult at first, but with repeated teaching and practice virtually all students can master the mathematics they need to graduate from high school, access a variety of jobs, and lay the foundation for further study in mathematics or a related field.

Several strategies can help students make steady progress in mathematics. These include:

1. Focus on key mathematical concepts.

2. Review key concepts and skills from earlier lessons, chapters, or years.

3. Preteach key concepts and vocabulary.

4. Anticipate problem areas.

5. Provide scaffolding (guided practice) for students who need extra help.

6. Think out loud to show hidden steps.

7. Provide a sample problem to which students can return when they get stuck.

8. Break problems into simpler components.

9. Explicitly teach students a variety of problem solving strategies and help them select one that fits the situation.

10. Present concepts in a variety of ways: visually, verbally, concretely, abstractly, etc.

11. Encourage students to draw a picture or use a visual aid such as a number line, graph, or diagram.

12. Provide sufficient practice.

Finally, good teachers are perpetual students themselves. They are always looking for ways to deepen their understanding of mathematics and for good ways to explain and teach mathematics to others.

FOR ADVANCED STUDENTS

Occasionally students can demonstrate mastery of all the mathematics expected to be learned in a given grade level. Repeating previously learned material for a year is deadly to these students. It can make them dislike mathematics. For these students, moving them up a grade level for math is a simple and cost-effective solution.

Most advanced students, however, are advanced in some areas but not in others. They tend to learn quickly and need more instructional material, as well as more difficult material.

The student edition, teacher's edition, and ancillaries for this program provide challenging exercises that can be used when students have demonstrated competence in a particular area. These challenge exercises should be substituted for the easier exercises in a homework assignment or lesson. When they have the time and interest, all students should be encouraged to work the challenge exercises.

General strategies for differentiating the curriculum for advanced learners include:

1. **Vary the pacing.** Allow advanced students some flexibility in how they progress through the course. Students who can demonstrate mastery of the objectives for a given lesson or chapter can be working on challenge exercises. Advanced students may become fascinated with a particular aspect of mathematics and want to spend *more* time on it.

2. **Differentiate in terms of depth.** Encourage advanced students to delve more in depth into mathematics. Looking at the details and the patterns; studying the language of the discipline; and looking at trends, themes, properties, theorems, proofs, and unanswered questions can enrich the curriculum for advanced students.

3. **Differentiate in terms of complexity.** Advanced students may be ready to connect ideas across disciplines in ways characteristic of older students or adults. Encourage them to investigate relationships between mathematics and art, history, science, and music, and to look at the development of mathematics over time.

USING GROUPING TO BENEFIT ALL STUDENTS

Grouping advanced learners together for investigations of challenge problems can provide you with time to work more closely with a group of students who need help in a particular area. Alternatively, while students who need more help are working on additional reinforcement activities or practice, you can work with a group of advanced students on a challenge project. Groups can be organized and revised daily, weekly, or by lesson according to how proficient students are with the concepts and skills targeted for that day, week, or lesson. At times you may have only one student who is ready for a challenge problem; at other times the whole class may be ready. Flexible grouping is the key to ensuring that students do not become "tracked." Asking advanced students to report to the whole class on their progress on challenge problems can provide the opportunity for the whole class to engage in more abstract and theoretical thinking.

Adapting Curriculum and Instruction
for English Learners

English learners come to the classroom with all the variety of English speakers in regard to mathematics achievement. They may be at, behind, or ahead of grade expectations in mathematics. They may be gifted or eligible for special education services. They may have been born in the United States, or they may have arrived in this country very recently. They may speak one or more languages, and they may be literate in one or more languages other than English. They may be nearly fluent in English or have beginning or intermediate levels of understanding and production. They have in common one characteristic: They are all learning English.

With careful planning, teachers can maximize success for English learners in the mathematics classroom. Assessing each student's competencies in mathematics and English will form a basis for program planning.

ENGLISH LEARNERS

LOW MATHEMATICS ACHIEVEMENT		HIGH MATHEMATICS ACHIEVEMENT	

LOW READING ACHIEVEMENT

Who is this student?

Student may be new to the class, school, or country.

Student may have had inadequate schooling.

Student may have moved a lot.

Student may be unmotivated or have test anxiety.

Low reading achievement may be depressing mathematics scores.

Student may have gaps and holes in knowledge.

Student may need special education assistance.

What to do?

Examine cumulative folder for other testing, notes, etc.

Delay any testing for a week or two. Help student feel comfortable in the class during that period of time.

Administer mathematics achievement test and reading test, preferably in an individual setting.

Plan to assess this student at weekly intervals and closely monitor classroom work to determine if progress is being made.

Look at the English Learners suggestions in each chapter.

Who is this student?

Student has had good prior mathematics instruction.

Mathematics is an area where this student can excel.

Math achievement level may actually be higher than scores indicate. (Limited English reading skills affect mathematics achievement as well.)

Word problems will be especially difficult.

What to do?

Mathematics instruction should proceed at normal or near normal pace.

Student should be involved in a systematic English language development program and intensive reading program outside of mathematics class.

Spend part of each class period on mathematics vocabulary study.

Provide a bilingual dictionary or math glossary and a grade-level mathematics text in the home language for home use.

Look at the English Learners suggestions in each chapter for those that are most useful.

HIGH READING ACHIEVEMENT

Who is this student?

Student may have been designated as an English learner because oral skills lag behind reading skills.

Student may not test well in mathematics.

Most students can make rapid progress in mathematics; a few may have learning difficulties that require the help of a specialist.

What to do?

Assess mathematics achievement in a variety of ways.

Concentrate on developing oral fluency.

Focus on vocabulary specific to mathematics.

Use a student's reading ability to improve his or her math scores.

Who is this student?

May be a student who is ready for re-designation as a fluent English speaker.

May need extra study in academic vocabulary, *i.e.,* the specialized vocabulary of mathematics.

Given systematic instruction, this student should be able to achieve at or above grade level.

What to do?

Scan all of the suggestions for English learners in each chapter and progress through the ones the student needs as quickly as possible.

Monitor carefully to make sure this student continues to progress at a reasonable pace.

GETTING TO KNOW YOUR STUDENTS

Before school starts, check the cumulative folder on each student in your class to determine which ones are learning English. See if there is recent testing. Two types of testing are most useful: mathematics achievement and reading achievement levels. If no recent test information is available, you may instead administer a pre-course math test and ask English learners to write a dictated paragraph in English to assess their reading and writing skills. Use the chart on the facing page as a guide to understanding student assessment data.

SUGGESTIONS FOR MATHEMATICS TEACHERS OF ENGLISH LEARNERS

1. Allocate additional time for mathematics. Many students will be translating from English to their primary language and back again. The meaning of many words will not be immediately clear. When you ask questions, allow extra time for students to respond. Reading mathematics textbooks and understanding what is asked for in a word problem will be slower.

2. Use student's background knowledge. Some English learners will have developed substantial background in mathematics; others will have very little. Find out what students know and then build on that knowledge.

3. Reduce the amount and sophistication of the English language used. This may be done by reordering the lessons in each chapter to begin with key vocabulary, followed by problems with a minimum of written English, followed by at least one word problem each day. Choose word problems that don't rely on assumed background knowledge. Monitor and simplify the speech you use. Speak more slowly, avoid idioms and slang, be precise and concise, and use short sentences and simple vocabulary. Using hand gestures and pictures as well as words aids communication.

4. Introduce one concept per day. Keeping the focus of each day simple will aid students in understanding the point of the lesson. Focus on key concepts, and use mathematics instructional time well.

5. Use a variety of different methods for getting a point across. Presenting concepts verbally and visually, with concrete examples and in abstract mathematical symbols, and using pictures, graphs, diagrams, and charts will enhance the chance that students will understand at least one of the presentations. As you introduce a new word, rule, or property, write it down.

6. Provide opportunities for English learners to interact with their English-speaking peers. Students who are learning a language need to hear native speakers using the language, and they need opportunities to use their new mathematics vocabulary in their speech and in their writing.

7. Provide opportunities for English learners to discuss their understandings with each other, confirm the homework assignments, or ask questions of each other in whatever language they may have in common.

8. Allow English learners to demonstrate what they know in a variety of ways. When students first learn a language, they are usually shy about speaking. They generally understand spoken language before they can produce it. Students who have recently arrived from another country with good prior schooling may be able to read in English but not speak it. Allow students to point, nod, gesture, draw a picture, or work math problems without words as they learn English.

9. Extend mathematics instructional time through homework, an extra class period, summer school, or tutoring. Many of the language-related suggestions for English learners in this series can be carried out in collaboration with the language arts teacher.

10. Keep on hand picture dictionaries, foreign language dictionaries, multi-language math glossaries, and drawing materials.

SPECIFIC SUGGESTIONS

Prior to each chapter you will find suggestions to help you modify curriculum and instruction so that the content is accessible to English learners. You may want to collaborate with language arts teachers or other specialists, because many of the suggestions are well suited for discussion in a language arts class, English as a second language class, or in a tutorial. In these sections we will provide you suggestions and activities designed to (1) teach the vocabulary commonly used in mathematics; (2) explain mathematical concepts in a variety of ways; and (3) dissect the structure of word problems. Much of the vocabulary study in this book may be review for your students, and in that case, you should feel free to work as quickly as possible through the activities. For those students who need more systematic study, progressing through the activities as indicated will ensure that students have refreshed their understanding of basic terms prior to statewide testing that generally occurs toward the end of each school year. We recommend that if you have English learners in your classroom, you skim all the chapter suggestions for English learners so that you may use them as you need them.

NAEP: National Assessment of Educational Progress

The NAEP is used to assess student understanding of math across the nation. The chart below lists the topics assessed by the NAEP, and lessons and features from Middle School Math, Course 1 that address them.

NUMBER PROPERTIES AND OPERATIONS

1) **Number sense**	1.3, 3.1, 3.2, 3.3, 3.4, 4.3 Act., Ch. 5, 6.3 Act., 6.5 Act., 6.5, 7.1, 7.2 Act., 7.3, Ch. 8, 10.3, 11.1, 11.2 Act., 11.2, 13.1, Skills Rev. Handbook
2) **Estimation**	1.2 Act., 1.2, Ch. 3 Opener, 3.4, 3.5 Act., 3.5, 3.6 Prob. Solving, 3.6, 3.6 Tech. Act., 4.1, 4.3, 4.6, 6.1, 7.1, 7.3, 7.5, 8.7, 8.7 Tech. Act., Skills Rev. Handbook
3) **Number operations**	Ch. 1, Ch. 3, Ch. 4, 5.2 Prob. Solving, Ch. 6, Ch. 7, 8.5, 8.7 Prob. Solving, 8.7, 8.7 Tech. Act., Ch. 11, Skills Rev. Handbook
4) **Ratios and proportional reasoning**	2.3, 2.7, Ch. 8, 10.1
5) **Properties of number and operations**	1.6, 3.6, 4.1, 4.2, Ch. 5, 11.2 Act., 11.3 Act.

MEASUREMENT

1) **Measuring physical attributes**	1.5 (Exs. 45–47), Ch. 2, 3.2 Act., 3.2, 3.3, 3.5 Act., 4.2, 4.3, 4.7 Prob. Solving, 4.7, 5.6 Act., 5.6, 6.6, Ch. 6 Math in Sci., 7.4, 7.6, 8.2, 8.4, Ch. 9, Ch. 10, 11.5, Skills Rev. Handbook
2) **Systems of measurement**	2.1, 2.2, 2.3, 3.2 Act., 3.2, 4.1 (Ex. 38), 4.7 Prob. Solving, 4.7, 4.8, 6.6, 7.1 (Exs. 42–44), 7.6, 7.7, 7.7 Tech. Act., 8.2, 8.4, 10.1, 10.3 Tech. Act., 10.7, Skills Rev. Handbook

GEOMETRY

1) **Dimension and shape**	1.7, Ch. 9, Ch. 10, 11.6 Prob. Solving
2) **Transformation of shapes and preservation of properties**	8.4, 9.7, 9.8 Prob. Solving, 9.8, 10.1 Act., 10.2, 10.4, 11.6 Prob. Solving (Exs. 3–5), 11.6, 11.7, 11.7 Special Topic
3) **Relationships between geometric figures**	Chapter 9, Chapter 10
4) **Position and direction**	9.1, 9.3, 10.1, 10.4 Special Topic, 11.6 Prob. Solving, 11.6, 11.7
5) **Mathematical reasoning**	9.4 Act., 9.5 Act., 9.6, 9.8 Prob. Solving, 9.8, 11.7 Special Topic

DATA ANALYSIS AND PROBABILITY

1) **Data representation**	Ch. 2, 3.4, 4.5, 6.3, 8.5, 10.4, Ch. 12 Math in Sci., Ch. 13, Skills Rev. Handbook
2) **Characteristics of data sets**	2.8 Act., 2.8, 4.7, 11.5, 11.5 Tech. Act., 13.4, 13.5, 13.6, 13.7
3) **Experiments and samples**	This topic is covered in Grades 7 and 8.
4) **Probability**	5.2 Prob. Solving, Ch. 13

ALGEBRA

1) **Patterns, relations, and functions**	1.1, 4.5, 5.1 Act., 5.3 Act., 7.7 Prob. Solving, 8.7 Prob. Solving, 9.6 (Exs. 19–21), 9.8 Prob. Solving, 11.4, 11.7 Special Topic, 12.5 Act., 12.5, 12.6 Prob. Solving, 12.6
2) **Algebraic representations**	1.6, 1.7, 2.6, 3.6, 4.2, 4.8, 6.2, 8.3, 11.4, 11.6 Prob. Solving, 11.6, 11.7, Ch. 12
3) **Variables, expressions, and operations**	1.5 Act., 1.5, 1.7, 2.2, 3.6, 4.1 Tech. Act., 4.2, 4.3, 4.8, 6.2, 7.2, 8.3, 8.4, 8.7, 9.3, 9.4 Tech. Act., 10.1, 10.2, 10.3, 10.4, 10.7, 11.4, Ch. 12
4) **Equations and inequalities**	1.6, 2.2, 8.3, 8.4, 9.3, 9.4, 10.1, 10.2, 10.7, Ch. 12

NCTM: National Council of Teachers of Mathematics

The chart below lists the lessons and other features in the textbook that address the NCTM Standards.

CONTENT STANDARDS

1) Number and Operations Understand numbers, ways of representing numbers, relationships among numbers, and number systems; understand meanings of operations and how they relate to one another; compute fluently and make reasonable estimates.	1.1 through 1.6, 3.1, 3.3, 3.4, 3.5 Act., 3.5, 3.6 Tech. Act., 4.1 through 4.6, 5.1 Act., 5.2 Prob. Solving, 5.3 through 5.8, 6.1 through 6.5, 6.6 Prob. Solving, 7.1 through 7.5, 7.7, 8.1, 8.3, 8.5 Act., 8.5, 8.6, 8.7, 11.1 through 11.5, 12.1, 12.2 Act., 12.3
2) Algebra Understand patterns, relations, and functions; represent and analyze mathematical situations and structures using algebraic symbols; use mathematical models to represent and understand quantitative relationships; analyze change in various contexts.	1.1, 1.3, 1.5 Act., 1.5, 1.6, 2.2, 2.3 Prob. Solving, 2.3, 4.1 Tech. Act., 4.2, 4.3, 4.5, 5.1 Act., 5.3, 5.4, 5.5, 7.2, 7.7 Prob. Solving, 8.2, 8.3, 8.4, 8.7 Prob. Solving, 8.7, 9.4, 10.1 through 10.7, 11.4, 12.1 through 12.6
3) Geometry Analyze characteristics and properties of two- and three-dimensional geometric shapes and develop mathematical arguments about geometric relationships; specify locations and describe spatial relationships using coordinate geometry and other representational systems; apply transformations and use symmetry to analyze mathematical situations; use visualization, spatial reasoning, and geometric modeling to solve problems.	2.6, 9.1 through 9.8, 10.1 Act., 10.2, 10.4 Special Topic, 10.5, 10.6 Prob. Solving, 10.6, 10.7, 11.6 Prob. Solving, 11.6, 11.7, 11.7 Special Topic
4) Measurement Understand measurable attributes of objects and the units, systems, and processes of measurement; apply appropriate techniques, tools, and formulas to determine measurements.	2.1, 2.2, 3.2 Act., 3.2, 3.5 Act., 4.7, 4.8, 5.6 Act., 5.6, 6.6, 7.7, 7.7 Tech. Act., 8.1 Act., 8.2, 8.4, 9.2, 9.4 Tech. Act., 9.5 Act., Ch. 10
5) Data Analysis and Probability Formulate questions that can be addressed with data and collect, organize, and display relevant data to answer them; select and use appropriate statistical methods to analyze data; develop and evaluate inferences and predictions that are based on data; understand and apply basic concepts of probability.	2.4 through 2.8, Ch. 3 Opener, 11.5, 11.5 Tech. Act., 13.1 through 13.7

PROCESS STANDARDS

6) Problem Solving Build new mathematical knowledge through problem solving; solve problems that arise in mathematics and in other contexts; apply and adapt a variety of appropriate strategies to solve problems; monitor and reflect on the process of mathematical problem solving.	1.2 through 1.7, 2.3 Prob. Solving, 3.5 through 3.6, 4.1 through 4.2, 4.4, 4.6, 4.7 Prob. Solving, 4.8, 5.2 Prob. Solving, 5.2, 5.5, 6.1, 6.4 through 6.6, 7.3 through 7.5, 7.7 Prob. Solving, 7.7 Tech. Act., 8.3, 8.4, 8.6 through 8.7, 9.8 Prob. Solving, 10.1, 10.3, 10.4, 10.6 Prob. Solving, 11.3, 11.6 Prob. Solving, 12.6 Prob. Solving, 13.1 through 13.3
7) Reasoning and Proof Recognize reasoning and proof as fundamental aspects of mathematics; make and investigate mathematical conjectures; develop and evaluate mathematical arguments and proofs; select and use various types of reasoning and methods of proof.	1.5 Act., 5.1 Act., 6.6 Prob. Solving, 9.4 Act., 9.5 Act., 9.5
8) Communication Organize and consolidate their mathematical thinking through communication; communicate their mathematical thinking coherently and clearly to peers, teachers, and others; analyze and evaluate the mathematical thinking and strategies of others; use the language of mathematical ideas precisely.	2.8 Act., 9.1, 9.7, 13.4 through 13.6
9) Connections Recognize and use connections among mathematical ideas; understand how mathematical ideas interconnect and build on one another to produce a coherent whole; recognize and apply mathematics in contexts outside of mathematics.	1.7, 2.3, 2.5 Act., 2.8, Ch. 3 Opener, 5.2, 5.4, 9.4 Act., 9.4, 9.6, 11.6, 12.6
10) Representation Create and use representations to organize, record, and communicate mathematical ideas; select, apply, and translate among mathematical representations to solve problems; use representations to model and interpret physical, social, and mathematical phenomena.	1.2, 1.7, 2.3 through 2.6, 3.1, 3.4, 3.6, Ch. 3 Opener, 4.3 Act., 4.3, 4.5, 5.2 Prob. Solving, 5.3 Act., 5.7, 6.2, 6.3 Act., 7.2 Act., 7.2, 7.4 Act., 8.1 Act., 8.5 Act., 8.5, 9.1, 9.3, 9.5, 9.8 Prob. Solving, 9.8, 10.2, 10.3 Act., 10.5, 11.1 through 11.3, 11.6 Prob. Solving, 11.7, 11.7 Special Topic, 12.6, 12.6 Tech. Act., 13.2 through 13.3, 13.7

SCOPE AND SEQUENCE FOR MIDDLE SCHOOL MATH, COURSES 1–3

TOPICS	Middle School Math Course 1	Middle School Math Course 2	Middle School Math Course 3	IN COURSE 1, SEE THE FOLLOWING KEY PAGES:
NUMBERS AND THEIR OPERATIONS				
Whole Numbers and Decimals				
Whole number concepts	■	■	■	pp. 684–686
Whole number operations	▲■	■	■	pp. 5–9, 152, 687–691
Order of operations	▲■	▲■	▲■	pp. 21–24
Reading and writing decimals	●▲■	▲■	■	pp. 107–111, 113, 168, 532
Expanded form for whole numbers and decimals	▲■	●	■	pp. 108, 110, 532, 684
Rounding decimals	▲■	▲■	■	pp. 124–128
Comparing and ordering decimals	▲■	●▲■	■	pp. 118–121
Adding and subtracting decimals	●▲■	●▲■	▲■	pp. 136–140, 141, 157, 179, 698, 699
Multiplying and dividing decimals	●▲■	▲■	▲■	pp. 153–158, 163, 164–168, 169–173, 180–184, 190
Multiplying and dividing by powers of 10	●▲■	▲■	■	pp. 176–179, 690–691
Equivalent forms of decimals and fractions	●▲■	▲■	▲■	pp. 249–252, 253–256, 257, 628
Fractions and Mixed Numbers				
Meaning of a fraction or a mixed number	●▲■	▲■	■	pp. 226–227, 228, 244, 312, 700
Fractions as division	▲■	■	■	pp. 253–256, 350
Equivalent fractions including simplest form	●▲■	●▲■	●▲■	pp. 226–227, 228–232, 238–242, 266, 628
Equivalent forms of improper fractions and mixed numbers	▲■	▲■	▲■	pp. 244–248, 289, 290–294, 326–327
Common denominators	▲■	●▲■	▲■	pp. 239–242, 277–281
Comparing and ordering fractions	●▲■	●▲■	▲■	pp. 239–242
Equivalent forms of fractions and decimals	●▲■	▲■	▲■	pp. 249–252, 253–256, 257, 628
Adding and subtracting fractions, mixed numbers, and rational numbers	●▲■	●▲■	▲■	pp. 268–270, 271–275, 276, 277–281, 284–288, 289, 290–294, 295
Multiplying and dividing fractions, mixed numbers, and rational numbers	●▲■	●▲■	●▲■	pp. 313–317, 318–319, 320–325, 326–330, 333, 334–338, 339–343
Ratio, Proportion, and Percent				
Modeling ratios and percents	●▲	●▲■	■	pp. 373, 374, 383, 394, 395–398, 402
Writing and using ratios and rates	▲■	●▲■	●▲■	pp. 374–377, 379–382
Equivalent ratios	▲■	▲■	▲■	pp. 374–378, 383–384
Equivalent rates and unit rates	▲■	▲■	▲■	pp. 379–382
Unit price and comparison shopping	▲	▲■	■	pp. 380, 382
Deciding whether ratios form a proportion	▲	▲■	■	pp. 383, 385–386
Writing and solving proportions	▲■	●▲■	▲■	pp. 383–387, 388–391
Making a prediction in proportional situations	▲	▲■	▲■	pp. 89–91, 384–387

Symbol Key
● Explore ▲ Teach and Assess ■ Maintain and Apply

TOPICS	Middle School Math Course 1	Middle School Math Course 2	Middle School Math Course 3	IN COURSE 1, SEE THE FOLLOWING KEY PAGES:
Scale drawings, including map scales	▲■	●▲■	●▲■	pp. 68–71, 388–391, 477–479
Similar figures		●▲■	▲■	
Equivalent forms of percents, decimals, and fractions	●▲■	▲■	▲■	pp. 394, 395–398, 399–403, 406–410, 628
Percent of a number	●▲■	●▲■	▲■	pp. 406–410, 411
Percent equations		▲■	▲■	
Interest	▲	▲■	▲■	pp. 168, 408–410, 411
Consumer percent applications	▲■	▲■	■	pp. 407–409, 413, 415–417
Percent of change		●▲■	▲■	
Ratios in right triangles			▲■	
Trigonometric ratios			●▲■	

Estimation

TOPICS	Course 1	Course 2	Course 3	KEY PAGES
Estimation strategies	▲■	▲■	▲■	pp. 12–15, 124–128, 130–133, 138–139, 141, 154, 166, 267–270, 315–317, 327, 340–341, 407, 411, 686, 692, 693, 694, 695
Checking reasonableness	▲■	▲■	▲■	pp. 13, 15, 134–135, 138–139, 141, 154, 165–167, 181, 327, 340–341, 411
Estimating with whole numbers	●▲■	■	■	pp. 10–11, 12–15, 106, 686, 692, 693, 694, 695
Estimating with decimals	▲■	▲■		pp. 124–128, 130–133, 138–139, 141, 154, 165–167, 181
Estimating with fractions	▲■			pp. 267–270, 315–317, 327, 340–341
Estimating with ratio and percent	▲■			pp. 407, 409, 411

Integers

TOPICS	Course 1	Course 2	Course 3	KEY PAGES
Meaning of integers	▲	▲	▲	pp. 533, 534
Integers on a number line	▲■	●▲■	●▲■	pp. 533–536, 538–540, 544, 546
Absolute value of a number	▲■	▲■	▲■	pp. 539–540
Ordering integers	▲■	▲■	▲■	pp. 533–536
Adding and subtracting integers	●▲■	●▲■	▲■	pp. 537, 538–541, 542–543, 544–547, 559
Multiplying and dividing integers	●▲■	●▲■	▲■	pp. 550–553, 554–558, 559

Rational and Real Numbers

TOPICS	Course 1	Course 2	Course 3	KEY PAGES
Terminating and repeating decimals	▲■	▲	▲■	pp. 254–256, 372, 401
Showing that a number is rational		▲■	▲■	
Classifying real numbers as rational or irrational		▲■	▲■	
Ordering rational or irrational numbers		▲■	▲■	
Computing with rational numbers		▲■		
Evaluating square roots		▲■	●▲■	

Symbol Key

● Explore   ▲ Teach and Assess   ■ Maintain and Apply

TOPICS	Middle School Math Course 1	Middle School Math Course 2	Middle School Math Course 3	IN COURSE 1, SEE THE FOLLOWING KEY PAGES:
Using Exponents				
Exponential notation	▲■	▲■	▲■	pp. 16–19, 20, 21–25, 212, 216
Zero and negative exponents		▲	▲	
Scientific notation		▲■	▲■	
Properties of exponents			●▲■	
Computation involving powers			●▲■	
Number Properties				
Commutative Properties of Addition and Multiplication	▲■	▲■	▲■	pp. 137–139, 152, 155–156, 724
Associative Properties of Addition and Multiplication	▲■	▲■	▲■	pp. 137–139, 152, 155–156, 724
Distributive Property	▲■	▲	▲	pp. 159–162, 724
Properties of 0 and 1	▲	▲■	▲■	pp. 37, 39–40, 724
Cross Products Property	▲■	▲■	▲■	pp. 383–387, 388, 724
Number fact families and related equations	▲■	● ■	■	pp. 63, 385, 438, 477, 481, 511, 687
Number Theory				
Factors of a number	▲	●▲■	●▲■	pp. 214–218, 220
Divisibility tests	●▲■	▲■	■	pp. 213, 215–219
Prime and composite numbers	▲■	●▲■	●▲■	pp. 215–219
Prime factorization	▲■	▲■	▲■	pp. 216–219
Common factors and greatest common factor	▲■	▲■	●▲■	pp. 222–225
Multiples and least common multiple	▲■	●▲■	▲■	pp. 235–238, 239–240
MEASUREMENT				
Length, Weight, and Capacity				
Reading rulers and other measurement scales	●▲■	●▲■	■	pp. 55–59, 112, 113–117, 129, 185–186, 243, 244, 247, 267, 514–515
Customary units of length, weight, and capacity	●▲■	▲■		pp. 55–59, 243, 244, 247, 344–347, 514–515
Metric units of length, mass, and capacity	●▲■	●▲■		pp. 56–59, 112, 113–117, 187–190, 514
Benchmarks for customary and metric units	▲■	▲		pp. 57–59, 187–188, 190, 344–345, 347
Choosing an appropriate unit of measure	▲■	▲		pp. 56, 58–59, 187–190, 344–347
Rewriting customary measurements	▲■	▲■	■	pp. 55, 58, 350–354
Rewriting metric measurements	●▲■	●▲■	■	pp. 56, 58, 112, 113–117, 187, 190, 191–195
Perimeter				
Perimeter of polygons	▲■	▲■	●▲■	pp. 61–65, 66–67, 389–391, 702
Circumference of a circle	●▲■	▲■	●▲■	pp. 484, 485–488, 490
Comparison of similar figures	▲	● ■	● ■	pp. 389–391

Symbol Key

● Explore   ▲ Teach and Assess   ■ Maintain and Apply

TOPICS	Middle School Math Course 1	Middle School Math Course 2	Middle School Math Course 3	IN COURSE 1, SEE THE FOLLOWING KEY PAGES:
Area				
Square and rectangle	●▲■	●▲■	●▲■	pp. 61–65, 166–167, 330, 389–391, 475, 702
Triangle	●▲■	●▲■	●▲■	pp. 480–483
Parallelogram	●▲■	●▲■	▲■	pp. 475, 476–479, 480
Trapezoid		●▲■	▲■	
Circle	▲■	▲■	●▲■	pp. 491–495
Irregular figures	▲■	■	▲■	pp. 481–483, 492–494, 702
Comparison of similar figures	▲■	■	▲■	pp. 389–391, 492, 495
Surface Area				
Prism	●▲■	●▲■	▲■	pp. 504–505, 506–509
Cylinder		●▲■	▲■	
Pyramid			▲■	
Cone			▲■	
Volume				
Prism	▲■	●▲■	●▲■	pp. 510–513
Cylinder		▲■	▲■	
Pyramid		▲■	●▲■	
Cone			▲■	
Time and Temperature				
Finding elapsed time	▲■	■	■	pp. 298–301, 308–309
Rewriting units of time	■	■	■	p. 701
Temperature	■	■	■	pp. 52–53, 317, 555, 608
Indirect Measurement				
Scale drawings, including map scales	●▲■	●▲■	●▲■	pp. 68–71, 388–391, 477–479
Pythagorean Theorem		●▲■	●▲■	
Using similar triangles		▲■	▲■	
Ratios in right triangles			▲■	
Trigonometric ratios			●▲■	

Symbol Key

● Explore ▲ Teach and Assess ■ Maintain and Apply

TOPICS	Middle School Math Course 1	Middle School Math Course 2	Middle School Math Course 3	IN COURSE 1, SEE THE FOLLOWING KEY PAGES:
GEOMETRY				
Geometry of a Plane				
Points, lines, and planes	▲ ■	▲ ■	■	pp. 421–424, 434
Parallel lines	▲ ■	▲ ■	■	pp. 422–423
Angles formed by parallel lines and a transversal		▲ ■	▲ ■	
Naming, measuring, and drawing angles	▲ ■	● ▲ ■	● ▲ ■	pp. 425–428
Acute, right, obtuse, or straight angles	▲ ■	▲ ■	▲ ■	pp. 430, 432–433
Vertical angles	▲ ■	● ▲	▲ ■	pp. 431–433
Supplementary and complementary angles	▲ ■	▲ ■	▲ ■	pp. 431–433
Classifying triangles, quadrilaterals, and other polygons	▲ ■	▲ ■	▲ ■	pp. 436–440, 445–448, 449–453
Angle relationships in polygons	● ▲ ■	● ▲ ■	● ▲ ■	pp. 435, 437–440, 441, 444, 448
Congruent and similar figures	● ▲ ■	● ▲ ■	● ▲ ■	pp. 454–457, 501
Properties of similar figures		● ▲ ■	▲ ■	
Tilings of a plane (Tessellations)	▲	▲	▲	pp. 572–573
Using algebra to solve geometry problems	▲ ■	▲ ■	▲ ■	pp. 432–434, 438–440, 448, 476–478, 480–483, 510–513
Pythagorean Theorem		● ▲ ■	● ▲ ■	
Geometry of Space				
Polyhedrons and their parts	▲ ■	● ▲ ■	▲	pp. 500–503
Cones, cylinders, spheres, and their parts	▲ ■	● ▲ ■	▲ ■	pp. 500, 502–503
Surface area	● ▲ ■	● ▲ ■	▲ ■	pp. 504–505, 506–509
Volume	▲ ■	● ▲ ■	● ▲ ■	pp. 510–513
Views of a solid	■	▲	▲ ■	p. 517
Geometric Transformations				
Reflections, or flips	▲ ■	▲ ■	▲ ■	pp. 567–571
Rotations, or turns	▲ ■	● ▲ ■	▲ ■	pp. 567–571
Translations, or slides	▲ ■	▲ ■	▲ ■	pp. 562–566, 568–571
Line and rotational symmetry	● ▲ ■	● ▲ ■	▲ ■	pp. 460–463
Dilations			▲	
Coordinate Geometry				
Plotting ordered pairs	▲ ■	● ▲ ■	● ▲ ■	pp. 83–86, 452, 562–566, 571, 612–616
Graphing equations with two variables	▲ ■	▲ ■	● ▲ ■	pp. 612–616, 617
Recognizing linear and non-linear graphs	▲	▲	■	pp. 613–615

Symbol Key
● Explore   ▲ Teach and Assess   ■ Maintain and Apply

TOPICS	Middle School Math Course 1	Middle School Math Course 2	Middle School Math Course 3	IN COURSE 1, SEE THE FOLLOWING KEY PAGES:
Intercepts of a line		▲■	●▲■	
Slope of a line		●▲■	●▲■	
Graphing systems of equations			▲	
Transformations in a coordinate plane	▲■	▲■	●▲■	pp. 562–566, 567–571
Using a coordinate plane to represent data graphically	▲■	▲■	▲■	pp. 83–86, 612–616, 624–625
Graphing linear inequalities			●▲■	

Spatial Visualization

	Course 1	Course 2	Course 3	Key Pages
Visual patterns	▲■	▲■		pp. 348–349, 606, 608, 572–573
Visualizing plane and space figures	●▲■	●▲■	●▲■	pp. 60, 453, 458–459, 470–471, 472–473, 481–483, 488, 489, 492–495, 501–503, 504–505, 506–509, 517, 560–561

DATA ANALYSIS AND PROBABILITY
Statistics

	Course 1	Course 2	Course 3	Key Pages
Data in tables	●▲■	▲■	▲■	pp. 79–81, 84–86, 87, 127–128, 130, 133, 139, 140, 213, 243, 274, 319, 320, 333
Tallies	●▲■	▲■	●▲■	pp. 72–75, 78
Frequency table	●▲■	●▲■	●▲■	pp. 72–75, 78
Range of a set of data	▲■	▲■	▲■	pp. 94–96, 658, 660
Mean, median, and mode of a set of data	▲■	●▲■	●▲■	pp. 93–97, 555–557, 654–656
Quartiles of a set of data	▲	▲■	▲■	pp. 657–661
Using percents to help organize data	▲■	▲■	▲■	pp. 396, 398, 662
Evaluating methods of sampling		▲	▲	
Collecting data	●■	●■	●	pp. 75, 78, 625, 629

Graphs

	Course 1	Course 2	Course 3	Key Pages
Organizing data with a graph	▲■	■	▲■	pp. 79–82, 84–86, 653–656, 657–660, 662–665
Organizing data with a color-coded map	■	■	■	pp. 253, 280, 301
Bar graphs	▲■	▲■	▲■	pp. 79–82, 87, 126, 704
Histograms		●▲■	▲■	
Line graphs	▲■	▲■	▲■	pp. 83–86, 87, 649–650, 705
Circle graphs	▲■	▲■	▲■	pp. 88–91, 251, 277, 316, 396, 398, 493–495
Pictographs	■			pp. 177, 179, 706–707
Line plots	▲■	■	■	pp. 73–75
Scatter plots		●▲■	▲■	
Box-and-whisker plots	▲■	▲■	▲■	pp. 657–660

Symbol Key

● Explore   ▲ Teach and Assess   ■ Maintain and Apply

TOPICS	Middle School Math Course 1	Middle School Math Course 2	Middle School Math Course 3	IN COURSE 1, SEE THE FOLLOWING KEY PAGES:
Stem-and-leaf plots	▲■	▲■	▲■	pp. 653–656
Appropriate graphs	▲■	▲■	▲■	pp. 89, 91, 648–652, 662–665
Misleading graphs	●▲	▲	▲	pp. 648–652
Comparing different graphs of the same data	▲■	▲■	▲	pp. 91, 648–652, 662–665
Probability				
Finding outcomes	▲■	●▲	▲■	pp. 630–632, 634, 636–639, 642–643
Combinations and permutations	▲	●▲■	▲■	pp. 637–639, 640–641
Counting Principle		●▲■	▲■	
Simulating or conducting an experiment	●▲	●▲	●	pp. 629, 635
Probability of a simple event and its complement	▲■	●▲■	●▲■	pp. 630–634
Dependent and independent events	▲■	●▲■	●▲■	pp. 642–645
Comparison of theoretical and experimental probabilities	▲	▲	▲	p. 635
Odds	■	■	▲	p. 634
ALGEBRA				
Expressions				
Numerical expressions	●▲■	●▲■	●▲■	pp. 21–25, 28, 137–140, 159–162
Variable expressions	●▲■	●▲■	▲■	pp. 28–33, 54, 137, 139, 274, 321, 323, 551, 553, 583–586
Powers and square roots (exponents)	▲■	●▲■	●▲■	pp. 16–19, 20, 22–24, 30–32, 62, 491–495, 616
Order of operations	▲■	●▲■	▲■	pp. 21–24, 30–32
Simplifying expressions		▲■	●▲■	
Writing verbal phrases as algebraic expressions	▲■	▲■	▲■	pp. 583–586, 589–591, 592–595
Polynomials and standard form			▲■	
Computing with monomials and polynomials			●▲■	
Equations				
Checking a solution to an equation	▲■	●▲■	▲■	pp. 36, 589–591, 592–594, 598–601
Using mental math to solve	▲■	●▲■	▲■	pp. 37–40, 384–387
Using a letter to represent an unknown in an equation	▲■	▲■	▲■	pp. 36–40, 63–64, 384–387, 388, 431–432, 437–438, 476–479, 480–483, 510–513, 584–586, 589–591, 592–595, 598–601
Addition and subtraction equations	●▲■	●▲■	●▲■	pp. 36–40, 431–432, 437–438, 587, 588–591, 592–595
Multiplication and division equations	●▲■	●▲■	●▲■	pp. 36–40, 63–64, 384–388, 390, 476–479, 480–483, 510–513, 598–601

Symbol Key
● Explore   ▲ Teach and Assess   ■ Maintain and Apply

TOPICS	Middle School Math Course 1	Middle School Math Course 2	Middle School Math Course 3	IN COURSE 1, SEE THE FOLLOWING KEY PAGES:
Multi-step equations		●▲■	●▲■	
Equations with variables on both sides			●▲■	
Percent equations		▲■	▲■	
Solving equations involving fractions and decimals			▲■	
Equations whose solutions are square roots		▲■	▲■	
Writing verbal sentences as algebraic equations	▲■	▲■	▲■	pp. 584–586, 589–591, 592–595, 599–601
Formulating an equation from a problem situation	▲■	▲■	▲■	pp. 63, 384, 386–387, 388, 390, 584–586, 589–591, 592–595, 599–601
Translating an equation into words	▲■	▲	▲■	pp. 37–39, 586
Generating a formula	●▲	●▲	●	pp. 475–476, 480, 484–485
Using a formula	▲■	●▲■	●▲■	pp. 61–65, 154, 158, 160, 166, 168, 317, 408, 431–432, 437–438, 441, 474, 476–479, 480–483, 485–488, 491–494, 510–513, 607, 608, 616, 630
Equations with two variables	▲■	▲■	▲■	pp. 612–616, 617
Systems of equations		▲		

Inequalities

TOPICS	Course 1	Course 2	Course 3	KEY PAGES
Solving and graphing inequalities in one variable	▲	▲■	●▲■	pp. 602–603
Solving and graphing inequalities in two variables			▲■	
Checking the solution to a linear inequality			▲■	

Patterns and Functions

TOPICS	Course 1	Course 2	Course 3	KEY PAGES
Number patterns	●▲■	●▲■	●▲■	pp. 7–9, 176, 226–227, 348–349, 404–405, 550, 606–608, 610–611
Geometric patterns	▲■	▲■		pp. 19, 348–349, 405, 572–573, 606, 608
Making and using function tables	●▲■	▲■	●▲■	pp. 604, 605–609, 612–616
Writing a rule for a function	●▲■	▲■	●▲■	pp. 604, 606–609, 614–615
Evaluating a function	▲■	▲■	●▲■	pp. 605–608, 612–616
Graphing a function	▲■	▲■	●▲■	pp. 612–616

MODELS AND MANIPULATIVES
Set Models

TOPICS	Course 1	Course 2	Course 3	KEY PAGES
For representing fractions and ratios	▲■	▲■		pp. 232, 312, 374, 383, 395, 700
For multiplying	●▲	▲		pp. 314, 318

Area Models

TOPICS	Course 1	Course 2	Course 3	KEY PAGES
For representing decimals and fractions	●▲■	●▲■	●▲■	pp. 226–227, 228, 232, 239, 249, 312, 313, 394, 532, 700

TOPICS	Middle School Math Course 1	Middle School Math Course 2	Middle School Math Course 3	IN COURSE 1, SEE THE FOLLOWING KEY PAGES:
For adding and subtracting	●▲■	●▲■	▲■	pp. 271, 276, 289, 290, 292, 313
For multiplying and dividing	●▲■	●▲■	● ■	pp. 163, 164, 319, 320, 339, 341
For representing ratio, proportion, and percent	●▲■	● ■	■	pp. 373, 394, 396–398, 402
Number-Line Models				
For whole numbers	▲■	■		pp. 43, 685, 686, 688, 693
For decimals, fractions, or percents	▲■	▲■	▲■	pp. 118, 120, 124, 248, 401, 631
For integers	▲■	●▲■	●▲■	pp. 533–536, 538–540, 544, 546
For rational or irrational numbers		▲	▲	
For probability	▲	▲■		p. 631
For inequalities	▲	▲■	▲■	p. 603
Problem Solving Models				
Using a diagram	▲■	●▲■	▲■	pp. 43, 66–67, 70, 507
Using a graph	▲■	●▲■	▲■	pp. 560–561
Using a list or table	▲■	●▲■	●▲■	pp. 220–221, 223, 637
Using a model		●▲■	●▲■	pp. 458–459, 463
Using a verbal model	▲■	▲■	▲■	pp. 41–42, 44–45, 138, 159, 192, 272, 384, 386, 551, 589
Graphic Organizers				
Factor tree	▲■	▲■	▲■	pp. 216–219, 222
Tree diagram	▲■	●▲■	▲■	pp. 636–639, 642–645
Venn diagram	▲■	▲■	■	pp. 420, 445, 703
Concept map	▲	▲	▲	pp. 372, 395
Concept grid		▲	▲	
Flow chart	▲			pp. 582, 613
Manipulatives				
Algebra tiles	●▲	●▲	●▲	pp. 587, 588, 598
Base-ten pieces	●▲	●		pp. 107, 109, 136, 153
Compass and straightedge	●▲■	●▲■	●▲■	pp. 484, 493, 496–497
Geoboard	●			p. 373
Integer chips	●			pp. 537, 542–543
Number counters or tiles	●	●	●	pp. 92, 318
Number cubes	●	●	●	pp. 10–11, 28, 97, 129, 629

Symbol Key
● Explore   ▲ Teach and Assess   ■ Maintain and Apply

TOPICS	Middle School Math Course 1	Middle School Math Course 2	Middle School Math Course 3	IN COURSE 1, SEE THE FOLLOWING KEY PAGES:
Paper folding and cutting	● ▲ ■	●	●	pp. 226–227, 239, 435, 458–459, 460–461, 463, 475, 480, 489, 572–573
Protractor	● ▲ ■	● ▲ ■	■	pp. 426–429, 433, 435, 439, 444, 493, 495
Ruler	● ▲ ■	● ▲ ■	● ■	pp. 55–59, 112, 113–117, 129, 243, 244, 247, 267
Unit cubes		▲	●	

PROBLEM SOLVING
Making Decisions

TOPICS	Middle School Math Course 1	Middle School Math Course 2	Middle School Math Course 3	IN COURSE 1, SEE THE FOLLOWING KEY PAGES:
Choosing an operation	▲ ■	■	■	pp. 134, 182, 193, 340, 342, 696, 697
Choosing an appropriate form of a number	▲ ■	▲ ■	▲ ■	pp. 351, 406, 486–488
Choosing a computation method	● ▲ ■	■	■	pp. 39, 287, 354, 386, 402, 591
Checking reasonableness	▲ ■	● ▲ ■	▲ ■	pp. 134–135, 138

Using Strategies

TOPICS	Middle School Math Course 1	Middle School Math Course 2	Middle School Math Course 3	IN COURSE 1, SEE THE FOLLOWING KEY PAGES:
Using a problem-solving plan	▲ ■	▲ ■	▲ ■	pp. 41–45
Guess, Check, and Revise	▲ ■	▲ ■	▲ ■	pp. 34–35, 36, 39
Draw a Diagram or Graph	▲ ■	▲ ■	▲ ■	pp. 43, 66–67, 70, 507, 560–561
Perform an Experiment	● ▲ ■	▲ ■	● ▲ ■	pp. 185–186, 187
Make a List or Table	▲ ■	▲ ■	● ▲ ■	pp. 220–221, 223, 637
Work Backward	▲ ■	● ▲ ■	▲ ■	pp. 296–297, 301, 592
Solve a Related/Simpler Problem	▲ ■	● ▲ ■	▲ ■	pp. 348–349, 352, 404–405, 407
Make a Model	▲ ■	● ▲ ■	● ▲ ■	pp. 458–459, 463
Break into Parts	● ▲ ■	▲ ■	▲ ■	pp. 504–505, 506
Look for a Pattern	▲ ■	▲ ■	▲ ■	pp. 7–9, 610–611, 614–615
Act it Out	▲ ■	▲ ■	▲ ■	pp. 640–641, 645
Estimate	■	▲ ■		pp. 131–132, 135, 405, 407
Write an Equation		▲ ■	▲ ■	

USING TECHNOLOGY

TOPICS	Middle School Math Course 1	Middle School Math Course 2	Middle School Math Course 3	IN COURSE 1, SEE THE FOLLOWING KEY PAGES:
Calculator	▲ ■	▲ ■	● ▲ ■	pp. 20, 141, 257, 355, 411, 490, 559, 635
Graphing calculator	▲	▲	▲ ■	p. 617
Spreadsheet	▲ ■	▲	▲ ■	pp. 87, 158, 441
Internet	▲	▲	▲	p. 295

Symbol Key
● Explore   ▲ Teach and Assess   ■ Maintain and Apply

Help with Taking Notes

One of the most important tools for success in mathematics is organizing what you have learned. Writing down important information in a notebook helps you remember key concepts and skills. You can use your notebook as a reference when you do your homework or when you study for a test.

Taking Notes

Your textbook displays important ideas and definitions on a notebook. You'll want to include this information in your notes.

Notetaking Strategies

You'll find a different notetaking strategy at the beginning of each chapter. Within the chapter, you'll find helpful hints about taking notes.

Notebook Review

Your textbook includes frequent notebook reviews. These reviews help you use your notebook to check your understanding of important skills and concepts.

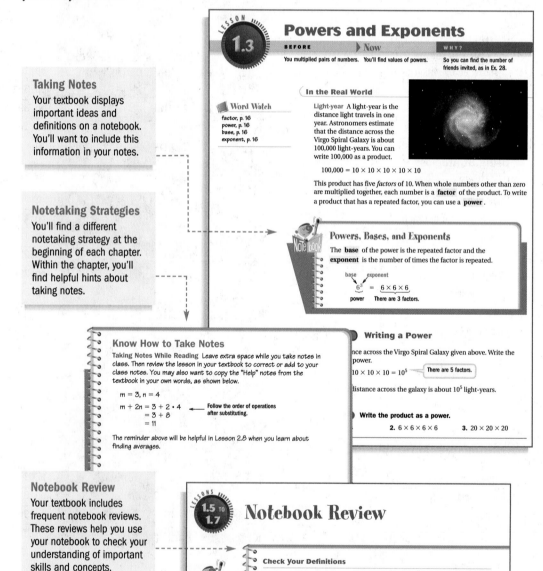

LESSON 1.3

Powers and Exponents

BEFORE	Now	WHY?
You multiplied pairs of numbers.	You'll find values of powers.	So you can find the number of friends invited, as in Ex. 28.

In the Real World

Word Watch
factor, p. 16
power, p. 16
base, p. 16
exponent, p. 16

Light-year A light-year is the distance light travels in one year. Astronomers estimate that the distance across the Virgo Spiral Galaxy is about 100,000 light-years. You can write 100,000 as a product.

$$100,000 = 10 \times 10 \times 10 \times 10 \times 10$$

This product has five *factors* of 10. When whole numbers other than zero are multiplied together, each number is a **factor** of the product. To write a product that has a repeated factor, you can use a **power** .

Powers, Bases, and Exponents

The **base** of the power is the repeated factor and the **exponent** is the number of times the factor is repeated.

$$\underset{\text{power}}{6^{3}} = \underset{\text{There are 3 factors.}}{6 \times 6 \times 6}$$

base   exponent

Writing a Power

...nce across the Virgo Spiral Galaxy given above. Write the ...power.

$$\dots 10 \times 10 \times 10 = 10^{5}$$ There are 5 factors.

...distance across the galaxy is about 10^5 light-years.

Write the product as a power.

2. $6 \times 6 \times 6 \times 6$ **3.** $20 \times 20 \times 20$

Know How to Take Notes

Taking Notes While Reading Leave extra space while you take notes in class. Then review the lesson in your textbook to correct or add to your class notes. You may also want to copy the "Help" notes from the textbook in your own words, as shown below.

$m = 3, n = 4$

$m + 2n = 3 + 2 \cdot 4$ ← Follow the order of operations after substituting.
$ = 3 + 8$
$ = 11$

The reminder above will be helpful in Lesson 2.8 when you learn about finding averages.

LESSONS 1.5 TO 1.7

Notebook Review

Check Your Definitions

variable, p. 29   equation, p. 36   solve, p. 37
variable expression, p. 29   solution, p. 36   verbal model, p. 41

Use Your Vocabulary

1. Copy and complete: The _?_ in the expression $x + 2$ is x.

Review the vocabulary definitions in ...

Help with Learning Mathematics

Your textbook helps you succeed in mathematics. Keep your eye out for notes that help you with reading mathematics, learning vocabulary terms, solving problems, using technology, and doing your homework. Some examples of the types of notes you'll see are shown below.

Help Notes
These notes help you understand and apply what you've learned.

Watch Out!
These notes help you avoid common errors.

Help with Homework
These notes tell you which textbook examples may help you with homework exercises, and let you know where to find extra help on the Internet.

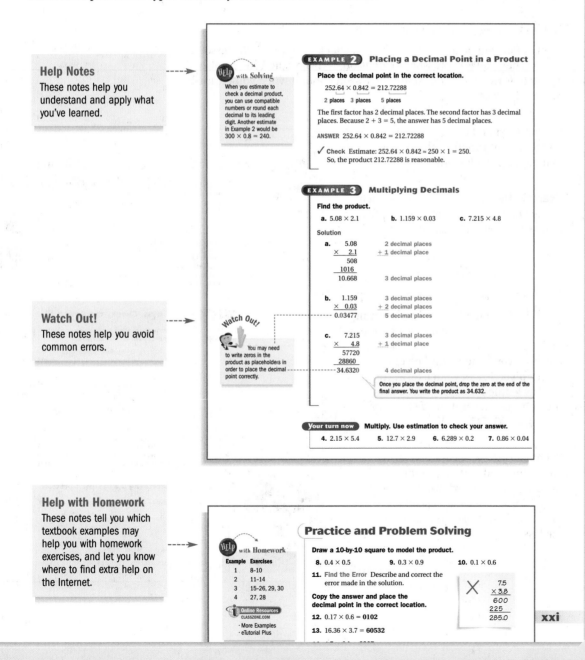

HELP with Solving
When you estimate to check a decimal product, you can use compatible numbers or round each decimal to its leading digit. Another estimate in Example 2 would be $300 \times 0.8 = 240$.

EXAMPLE 2 **Placing a Decimal Point in a Product**

Place the decimal point in the correct location.

$$252.64 \times 0.842 = 212.72288$$

2 places   3 places   5 places

The first factor has 2 decimal places. The second factor has 3 decimal places. Because $2 + 3 = 5$, the answer has 5 decimal places.

ANSWER $252.64 \times 0.842 = 212.72288$

✓ **Check** Estimate: $252.64 \times 0.842 \approx 250 \times 1 = 250$.
So, the product 212.72288 is reasonable.

EXAMPLE 3 **Multiplying Decimals**

Find the product.

a. 5.08×2.1 **b.** 1.159×0.03 **c.** 7.215×4.8

Solution

a.
$$\begin{array}{r} 5.08 \\ \times\ \ 2.1 \\ \hline 508 \\ 1016\ \ \\ \hline 10.668 \end{array}$$
2 decimal places
$+\ 1$ decimal place
3 decimal places

Watch Out!
You may need to write zeros in the product as placeholders in order to place the decimal point correctly.

b.
$$\begin{array}{r} 1.159 \\ \times\ \ 0.03 \\ \hline 0.03477 \end{array}$$
3 decimal places
$+\ 2$ decimal places
5 decimal places

c.
$$\begin{array}{r} 7.215 \\ \times\ \ 4.8 \\ \hline 57720 \\ 28860\ \ \\ \hline 34.6320 \end{array}$$
3 decimal places
$+\ 1$ decimal place
4 decimal places

Once you place the decimal point, drop the zero at the end of the final answer. You write the product as 34.632.

Your turn now Multiply. Use estimation to check your answer.

4. 2.15×5.4 **5.** 12.7×2.9 **6.** 6.289×0.2 **7.** 0.86×0.04

HELP with Homework

Example	Exercises
1	8-10
2	11-14
3	15-26, 29, 30
4	27, 28

Online Resources
CLASSZONE.COM
· More Examples
· eTutorial Plus

Practice and Problem Solving

Draw a 10-by-10 square to model the product.

8. 0.4×0.5 **9.** 0.3×0.9 **10.** 0.1×0.6

11. Find the Error Describe and correct the error made in the solution.

Copy the answer and place the decimal point in the correct location.

12. $0.17 \times 0.6 = 0102$

13. $16.36 \times 3.7 = 60532$

$$\begin{array}{r} \times\ \ 7.5 \\ \times\ 3.8 \\ \hline 600 \\ 225\ \ \\ \hline 285.0 \end{array}$$

xxi

T69

Reading Your Textbook

You need special skills to read a math textbook. These skills include *identifying the main idea, learning new vocabulary,* and *focusing on the important concepts* in a lesson. Most important, you need to *be an active reader.* You need to practice and apply the ideas you read about.

Identify the Main Idea

Even before you begin reading a lesson, check to see what the lesson is about. Then you'll know what to focus on in the lesson. You can also assess how well you understand the lesson content when you've finished reading the lesson.

Lesson Opener Look at the lesson opener for information about the main idea of the lesson.

Example Heads Use other clues, such as the heads that appear above examples, to identify the main idea.

Understand the Vocabulary

Reading mathematics involves learning and using new vocabulary terms. Refer to diagrams and worked-out examples to clarify your understanding of new terms. If you forget what a term you've already learned means, look back at previous lessons or use the Glossary on pages 725–747.

Vocabulary New vocabulary terms are highlighted within a lesson. In addition, the *Word Watch* at the beginning of the lesson lists the important vocabulary terms in the lesson.

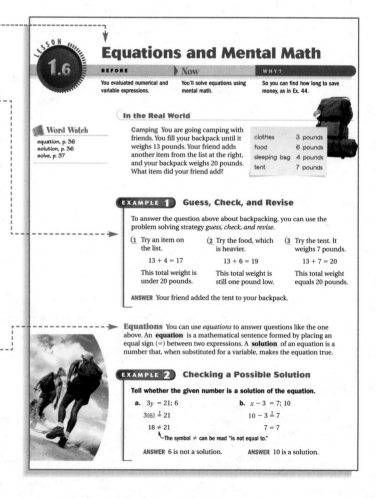

LESSON 1.6

Equations and Mental Math

BEFORE	Now	WHY?
You evaluated numerical and variable expressions.	You'll solve equations using mental math.	So you can find how long to save money, as in Ex. 44.

Word Watch
equation, p. 36
solution, p. 36
solve, p. 37

In the Real World

Camping You are going camping with friends. You fill your backpack until it weighs 13 pounds. Your friend adds another item from the list at the right, and your backpack weighs 20 pounds. What item did your friend add?

clothes	3 pounds
food	6 pounds
sleeping bag	4 pounds
tent	7 pounds

EXAMPLE 1 Guess, Check, and Revise

To answer the question above about backpacking, you can use the problem solving strategy *guess, check, and revise.*

① Try an item on the list.

$13 + 4 = 17$

This total weight is under 20 pounds.

② Try the food, which is heavier.

$13 + 6 = 19$

This total weight is still one pound low.

③ Try the tent. It weighs 7 pounds.

$13 + 7 = 20$

This total weight equals 20 pounds.

ANSWER Your friend added the tent to your backpack.

Equations You can use *equations* to answer questions like the one above. An **equation** is a mathematical sentence formed by placing an equal sign (=) between two expressions. A **solution** of an equation is a number that, when substituted for a variable, makes the equation true.

EXAMPLE 2 Checking a Possible Solution

Tell whether the given number is a solution of the equation.

a. $3y = 21;\ 6$

$3(6) \stackrel{?}{=} 21$

$18 \neq 21$

The symbol ≠ can be read "is not equal to."

b. $x - 3 = 7;\ 10$

$10 - 3 \stackrel{?}{=} 7$

$7 = 7$

ANSWER 6 is not a solution.   **ANSWER** 10 is a solution.

Know What's Important

Focus in on the important information in a lesson. Pay attention to highlighted vocabulary terms and definitions. Be on the lookout for definitions, properties, formulas, and other information displayed on a notebook. Make sure that you understand the worked-out examples.

Notebook Focus in on key ideas that are displayed on a notebook.

Worked-Out Examples Do the worked-out examples to make sure you know how to apply new concepts.

Be an Active Reader

As you read, keep a pencil in your hand and your notebook ready so that you can write down important information, practice new skills, and jot down questions to ask in class.

Use Your Notebook As you solve the examples yourself, you may find it helpful to draw a sketch in your notebook. Write down any questions you have so you can ask them in class.

Your Turn Now Solve the *Your turn now* exercises to check your understanding.

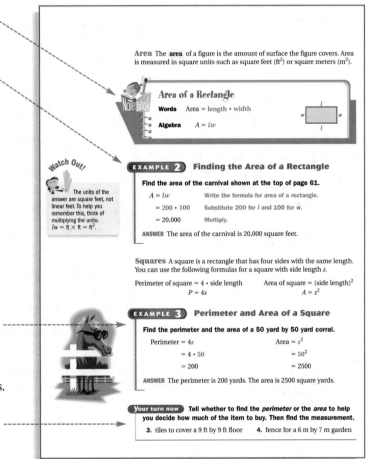

Area The **area** of a figure is the amount of surface the figure covers. Area is measured in square units such as square feet (ft^2) or square meters (m^2).

Area of a Rectangle

Words Area = length · width

Algebra $A = lw$

Watch Out!

The units of the answer are square feet, not linear feet. To help you remember this, think of multiplying the units: $lw = ft \times ft = ft^2$.

EXAMPLE 2 Finding the Area of a Rectangle

Find the area of the carnival shown at the top of page 61.

$A = lw$ Write the formula for area of a rectangle.

$= 200 \cdot 100$ Substitute 200 for l and 100 for w.

$= 20,000$ Multiply.

ANSWER The area of the carnival is 20,000 square feet.

Squares A square is a rectangle that has four sides with the same length. You can use the following formulas for a square with side length s.

Perimeter of square = 4 · side length   Area of square = (side length)^2

$P = 4s$ $A = s^2$

EXAMPLE 3 Perimeter and Area of a Square

Find the perimeter and the area of a 50 yard by 50 yard corral.

Perimeter = $4s$ Area = s^2

$= 4 \cdot 50$ $= 50^2$

$= 200$ $= 2500$

ANSWER The perimeter is 200 yards. The area is 2500 square yards.

Your turn now Tell whether to find the *perimeter* or the *area* to help you decide how much of the item to buy. Then find the measurement.

3. tiles to cover a 9 ft by 9 ft floor   **4.** fence for a 6 m by 7 m garden

Reading and Problem Solving

The language in your math textbook is precise. When you do your homework, be sure to read carefully. For example, the direction line below asks you to do three different things for each of the exercises: sketch, measure, and compare.

> **Estimation** **Sketch a line segment of the given length without using a ruler. Then use a ruler to check your estimate. How close was your estimate?**
>
> **21.** 6.5 cm   **22.** 45 mm   **23.** 0.01 m   **24.** 0.15 m

Reading Word Problems

Before you can solve a word problem, you need to read and understand it. You may find it useful to copy a word problem into your notebook. Then you can highlight important information, cross out unnecessary information, and organize your thinking.

> ~~A student went to the mall with 5 friends.~~ The student spent $6 on lunch, $17 on a new shirt, and $3 on some batteries. ~~On the way home from the mall, the student borrowed $2 from a friend.~~ How much money did the student spend at the mall?
>
> Spent: $ 6 on lunch
> $17 on shirt
> $ 3 on batteries
>
> To find how much money the student spent, add: $6 + $17 + $3 = $26

Make sure that you've solved a word problem completely. For example, to solve the word problem at the right, you need to calculate how much fencing you need. But to answer the question, you must determine how much money you will spend.

> You are buying fencing for a square rabbit pen. Its sides are 5 feet long. Fencing material costs $10 per foot. How much money will you spend?
>
> How much fencing: 4 x 5 feet = 20 feet
> How much money: $10 x 20 = $200

Additional Resources in Your Textbook

Your textbook contains many resources that you can use for reference when you are studying or doing your homework.

Skills Review Handbook Use the Skills Review Handbook on pages 684–707 to review material learned in previous courses.

Tables Refer to the tables on pages 721–724 if you need information about mathematical symbols, measures, formulas, and properties.

Glossary Use the Glossary on pages 725–747 to look up the meanings of math vocabulary terms. Each glossary entry also tells where in your book a term is covered in more detail.

Index Use the Index on pages 748–765 as a quick guide for finding out where a particular math topic is covered in the book.

Selected Answers Use the Selected Answers starting on page SA1 to check your work or to see whether you are on the right track in solving a problem.

Textbook Scavenger Hunt

Get some practice using your textbook. Use the additional resources described above to answer each question. Give page numbers to show where you found the answer to the question.

1 What is a scalene triangle?

2 Tell what each of these symbols means: $m\angle A$, $\approx$, $\overleftrightarrow{AB}$.

3 How many fluid ounces of water are there in one cup of water?

4 On what page or pages of the book is the commutative property of addition first discussed?

5 What is the boiling point of water in degrees Fahrenheit? in degrees Celsius?

6 What is a prime number?

7 On what page can you review the skill of making a Venn diagram?

8 On what page of the book can you find selected answers for Lesson 1.1?

9 What formula can you use to find the area of a parallelogram?

1. (4 × 1000) + (5 × 100) + (8 × 10) + (6 × 1); four thousand five hundred eighty-six

2. (5 × 10,000) + (4 × 100) + (2 × 10) + (3 × 1); fifty thousand, four hundred twenty-three

3. (9 × 100,000) + (1 × 10,000) + (8 × 1000) + (4 × 100) + (3 × 10) + (7 × 1); nine hundred eighteen thousand, four hundred thirty-seven

4. (3 × 1,000,000) + (5 × 100,000) + (4 × 10,000) + (6 × 100) + (9 × 10) + (2 × 1); three million five hundred forty thousand, six hundred ninety-two

Pre-Course Test

Number Sense and Operations

Whole Numbers *(Skills Review, pp. 684–687)*

Write the number in expanded form and in words. 1–4. See margin.

1. 4586 **2.** 50,423 **3.** 918,437 **4.** 3,540,692

Use a number line to order the numbers from least to greatest.

5. 3, 11, 14, 7, 6, 15
3, 6, 7, 11, 14, 15

6. 17, 11, 6, 0, 3, 5
0, 3, 5, 6, 11, 17

7. 6, 12, 17, 9, 3, 10, 13
3, 6, 9, 10, 12, 13, 17

Round the number to the place value of the red digit.

8. 18 20 **9.** 289 290 **10.** 945 900 **11.** 2575 2580

Operations with Whole Numbers *(Skills Review, pp. 688–691)*

Find the sum, difference, product, or quotient.

12. 655 + 348 1003 **13.** 3369 + 241 3610 **14.** 965 − 38 927 **15.** 4580 − 362 4218

16. 46 × 27 1242 **17.** 568 × 73 41,464 **18.** 6327 ÷ 9 703 **19.** 878 ÷ 22 39 R20

Estimating with Whole Numbers *(Skills Review, pp. 692–695)*

Estimate the sum, difference, product, or quotient. 20–27. Estimates may vary.

20. 441 + 333 + 789 1500 **21.** 67 + 72 + 69 210 **22.** 946 − 487 400 **23.** 5589 − 1377 4200

24. 246 × 318 75,000 **25.** 9333 × 65 630,000 **26.** 955 ÷ 89 10 **27.** 2521 ÷ 32 80

Find a low and high estimate for the product or quotient.

28. 858 × 29
16,000; 27,000

29. 9723 × 44
360,000; 500,000

30. 258 ÷ 7
30; 40

31. 95,661 ÷ 5
19,000; 20,000

Operations with Decimals and Fractions *(Skills Review, pp. 698–700)*

Find the sum or difference.

32. 19.6 + 34.7 54.3 **33.** 4.67 + 8.53 13.2 **34.** 12.55 − 9.39 3.16 **35.** 13.88 − 6.32 7.56

36. Alex has $12.38, Megan has $14.15, and Katherine has $28.55. How much do they have all together? $55.08

Write a fraction to represent the shaded region or part of a set.

37. $\frac{3}{4}$

38. $\frac{5}{6}$

50. Bottle Collection

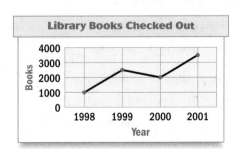

3rd Grade
4th Grade
5th Grade
6th Grade

= 4 bottles

Measurement

Units of Time *(Skills Review, p. 701)*

Copy and complete.

39. 6 hours 45 min = _?_ min 405

40. 4 days 6 hours = _?_ hours 102

41. 25 days = _?_ weeks _?_ days 3; 4

42. 32 days = _?_ weeks _?_ days 4; 4

Geometry

Perimeter and Area *(Skills Review, p. 702)*

Find the perimeter and area.

43.

16 units;
12 square units

44.

20 units;
13 square units

Data Analysis

Reading Bar Graphs and Line Graphs
(Skills Review, pp. 704–705)

In Exercises 45–47, use the bar graph.

45. Which fruit was the least favorite? oranges

46. Which fruit did 10 people vote for? grapes

47. Which fruit got 4 fewer votes than apples did? oranges

In Exercises 48 and 49, use the line graph.

48. In what year were the most books checked out? 2001

49. In what year were 2000 books checked out? 2000

Favorite Fruit

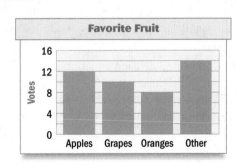

Library Books Checked Out

Pictographs *(Skills Review, pp. 706–707)*

50. Make a pictograph of the data in the table. See margin.

Grade	3rd	4th	5th	6th
Bottles collected	13	26	36	28

1. (6 × 1000) + (9 × 100) + (8 × 10) + (1 × 1); six thousand nine hundred eighty-one

2. (6 × 10,000) + (3 × 100) + (9 × 1); sixty thousand, three hundred nine

3. (8 × 100,000) + (1 × 10,000) + (7 × 1000) + (5 × 100) + (4 × 10) + (9 × 1); eight hundred seventeen thousand, five hundred forty-nine

4. (2 × 1,000,000) + (3 × 100,000) + (4 × 10,000) + (7 × 100) + (2 × 1); two million, three hundred forty thousand, seven hundred two

Pre-Course Practice

Number Sense and Operations

Whole Numbers *(Skills Review, pp. 684–687)*

Write the number in expanded form and in words. 1–4. See margin.

1. 6981   **2.** 60,309   **3.** 817,549   **4.** 2,340,702

Write the number in standard form.

5. $(2 × 100,000) + (6 × 1000) + (4 × 10)$ 206,040

6. seven hundred sixty-one thousand, twelve 761,012

Use a number line to order the numbers from least to greatest.

7. 9, 2, 12, 8, 16 2, 8, 9, 12, 16   **8.** 7, 0, 4, 6, 13 0, 4, 6, 7, 13   **9.** 7, 5, 16, 8, 12 5, 7, 8, 12, 16

Compare the numbers.

10. 12 and 17 12 < 17   **11.** 10 and 0 10 > 0   **12.** 17 and 1 17 > 1   **13.** 3 and 9 3 < 9

Round the number to the place value of the red digit.

14. 186 190   **15.** 2567 3000   **16.** 34,457 34,500   **17.** 49,598 50,000

In Exercises 18–19, copy and complete the number fact family.

18. $15 − 8 = 7$ $15 − \underline{?} = 8$ 7 $\underline{?} + 7 = 15$ 8 $7 + \underline{?} = \underline{?}$ 8; 15

19. $27 ÷ 3 = 9$ $9 × \underline{?} = 27$ 3 $27 ÷ \underline{?} = 3$ 9 $3 × \underline{?} = 27$ 9

20. Write a related division equation for $4 × 8 = 32$. 32 ÷ 4 = 8 or 32 ÷ 8 = 4

Operations with Whole Numbers *(Skills Review, pp. 688–691)*

Use a number line to add or subtract the numbers.

21. $9 + 7$ 16   **22.** $7 + 9$ 16   **23.** $6 − 4$ 2   **24.** $11 − 6$ 5

Find the sum or difference.

25. $39 + 17$ 56   **26.** $81 − 58$ 23   **27.** $172 − 45$ 127   **28.** $241 + 63$ 304

29. $446 + 278$ 724   **30.** $2298 + 197$ 2495   **31.** $878 − 199$ 679   **32.** $5430 − 186$ 5244

Find the product or quotient.

33. $294 × 64$ 18,816   **34.** $7694 × 58$ 446,252   **35.** $873 × 1,000$ 873,000   **36.** $8753 × 100,000$ 875,300,000

37. $4864 ÷ 8$ 608   **38.** $892 ÷ 13$ 68 R8   **39.** $2958 ÷ 34$ 87   **40.** $7675 ÷ 25$ 307

Estimating with Whole Numbers *(Skills Review, pp. 692–695)*

Estimate the sum. 41–44. Estimates may vary.

41. $321 + 538 + 689$ 1500   **42.** $845 + 311 + 196$ 1300   **43.** $83 + 78 + 81 + 77$ 320   **44.** $46 + 49 + 52 + 54$ 200

Find a low and high estimate for the difference.

45. $835 - 324$ 400; 600   **46.** $662 - 178$ 400; 600   **47.** $7654 - 2848$ 4000; 6000   **48.** $3879 - 1428$ 1000; 3000

Find a low and high estimate for the product.

49. 18×45 400; 1000   **50.** 783×42 28,000; 40,000   **51.** 671×562 300,000; 420,000   **52.** 8912×77 560,000; 720,000

Use compatible numbers to estimate the product.

53. 26×32 900   **54.** 499×33 15,000   **55.** 187×211 40,000   **56.** 1109×89 90,000

Find a low and high estimate for the quotient.

57. $243 \div 6$ 40; 50   **58.** $754 \div 7$ 100; 110   **59.** $3286 \div 5$ 600; 700   **60.** $5878 \div 6$ 900; 1000

Use compatible numbers to estimate the quotient.

61. $864 \div 88$ 10   **62.** $399 \div 27$ 16   **63.** $3806 \div 83$ 50   **64.** $6033 \div 21$ 300

Solving Problems Using Whole Numbers *(Skills Review, pp. 696–698)*

65. Anna collected 245 cans for recycling and Jim collected 382. How many cans did they collect in all?   627 cans

66. Last week a family spent $145 on groceries. This week they spent $183. How much more did they spend on groceries this week than last week? $38

67. There are 24 cans of soda in a case. You need 600 cans of soda for a school dance. How many cases do you need to buy?   25 cases

68. You buy a book for $8.95. How much change should you receive from a $10.00 bill? $1.05

Operations with Decimals and Fractions *(Skills Review, pp. 699–700)*

Find the sum or difference.

69. $3.87 + 9.63$ 13.5   **70.** $11.66 + 8.49$ 20.15   **71.** $19.1 - 11.7$ 7.4   **72.** $55.76 - 7.98$ 47.78

Write a fraction to represent the shaded region or part of a set.

73.  $\frac{5}{8}$ **74.**  $\frac{7}{10}$ **75.**  $\frac{1}{6}$

86.

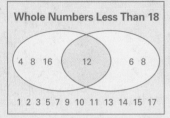

Whole Numbers Less Than 18

4 8 16   12   6 8

1 2 3 5 7 9 10 11 13 14 15 17

Measurement

Units of Time *(Skills Review, p. 701)*

Copy and complete.

76. 5 hours 15 min = _?_ min **315**

77. 18 days = _?_ weeks _?_ days **2; 4**

78. 50 hours = _?_ days _?_ hours **2; 2**

79. 310 sec = _?_ min _?_ sec **5; 10**

Geometry

Perimeter and Area *(Skills Review, p. 702)*

Find the perimeter.

80.

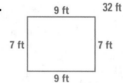

9 ft   32 ft

7 ft   7 ft

9 ft

81.

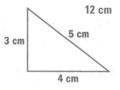

12 cm

3 cm   5 cm

4 cm

82.

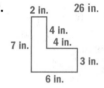

2 in.   26 in.

4 in.

7 in.   4 in.

   3 in.

6 in.

Find the area.

83.

21 square units

84.

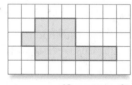

13 square units

85.

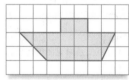

13 square units

Data Analysis

Venn Diagrams and Logical Reasoning *(Skills Review, p. 703)*

86. Draw a Venn diagram of the set of whole numbers less than 18 where set *A* consists of multiples of 4 and set *B* consists of multiples of 6. **See margin.**

87. Use the Venn diagram in Exercise 86. If a number is in set *A*, is it *always*, *sometimes*, or *never* in set *B*? **sometimes**

88. Use the Venn diagram in Exercise 86. If a number is prime, is it *always*, *sometimes*, or *never* in set *A*? **never**

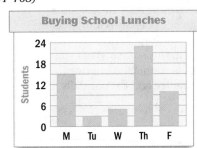

100. Where Students Like to Study

Table	
Desk	
Couch	
Floor	
Other	

= 4 students

Reading Bar Graphs and Line Graphs (*Skills Review, pp. 704–705*)

In Exercises 89–92, use the bar graph. It shows the number of students in a class who bought, rather than brought, lunch each day.

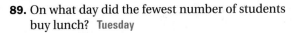

89. On what day did the fewest number of students buy lunch? Tuesday

90. On what day did 10 students buy lunch? Friday

91. On what day did 12 more students buy lunch than on Tuesday? Monday

92. Between what two days was there the least change in the number of students buying lunch? Tuesday and Wednesday

Buying School Lunches

In Exercises 93–96, use the line graph. It shows the temperature at different times of the day.

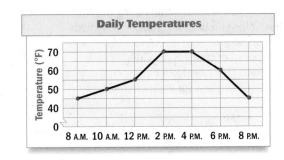

Daily Temperatures

93. When was the temperature the highest? the lowest? 2 P.M. and 4 P.M.; 8 A.M. and 8 P.M.

94. When were the recorded temperatures the same? 2 P.M. and 4 P.M.; 8 A.M. and 8 P.M.

95. Over what two-hour period did the temperature decrease the most? 6 P.M. to 8 P.M.

96. What is the difference between the highest and lowest temperature on the graph? 25°F

Pictographs (*Skills Review, pp. 706–707*)

In Exercises 97–99, use the pictograph. It shows an ice cream stand's cone sales for one day.

97. How many strawberry cones were sold? 60 strawberry cones

98. How many more chocolate than vanilla cones were sold? 48 cones

99. Which cone was ordered twice as often as mint? vanilla

100. Students at a school named their favorite place to study. Use the data in the table below to make a pictograph. See margin.

Monday's Cone Sales

Chocolate	
Vanilla	
Strawberry	
Mint	

= 24 cones

Where Students Like to Study				
At a table	At a desk	On a couch	On the floor	Other
36	22	16	20	10

Pre-Course Practice **xxxi**

Content and Assessment

Course Content

The authors have developed a sequence of lessons that include all the concepts and skills you need in this course. What you learn is connected to prior knowledge and to your daily life.

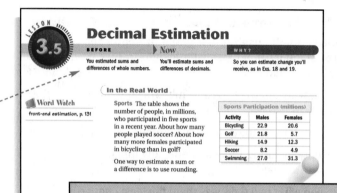

LESSON 3.5 — Decimal Estimation

BEFORE	Now	WHY?
You estimated sums and differences of whole numbers.	You'll estimate sums and differences of decimals.	So you can estimate change you'll receive, as in Exs. 18 and 19.

In the Real World

Word Watch
front-end estimation, p. 131

Sports The table shows the number of people, in millions, who participated in five sports in a recent year. About how many people played soccer? About how many more females participated in bicycling than in golf?

One way to estimate a sum or a difference is to use rounding.

Sports Participation (millions)		
Activity	Males	Females
Bicycling	22.9	20.6
Golf	21.8	5.7
Hiking	14.9	12.3
Soccer	8.2	4.9
Swimming	27.0	31.3

Test-Taking Practice

Each lesson includes test-taking practice that helps you become comfortable with different formats of test questions. Additional practice is provided on the Internet. There is also a chapter standardized test for each chapter.

Chapter Standardized Test

Test-taking Strategy **Make sure you understand the question before looking for the answer.**

Multiple Choice

1. Write *fourteen and fifteen ten-thousandths* as a decimal.
   A. 1.415 **B.** 14.15 **C.** 14.015 **D.** 14.0015

2. Complete the statement with the correct decimal: 2 and 21 hundredths meters equals ？ meters.
   F. 2.0 **G.** 2.0021 **H.** 2.021 **I.** 2.21

   ...rs is what decimal part of a...
   ...0.505 **C.** 0.055 **D.** 0.0055

   ...r is greater than 0.84 and less...
   ...0.82 **H.** 0.843 **I.** 0.847

   ...m manager lists the batting averages of four players on the team. Which list shows their batting averages in order from greatest to least?

8. Your friend buys a blouse for $28.95, a pair of sandals for $39.95, and a pair of shorts for $19.90. How much do the three items cost?
   F. $68.90 **G.** $78.80 **H.** $88.80 **I.** $88.85

9. What value of *x* makes the statement true?
   $5.6 + (0.3 + 4.9) = (5.6 + x) + 4.9$
   A. 0 **B.** 0.3 **C.** 4.9 **D.** 5.6

10. Evaluate the expression $x + 10.75 - 7.71$ when $x = 2.46$.
    F. 3.04 **G.** 4.5 **H.** 5.5 **I.** 16

Short Response

11. At a department store, you buy a sweater for $29.99, a notebook for $3.79, and a CD for $11.99. You give the cashier $50. About how much change should you expect? Explain your reasoning.

Extended Response

Year	Population
1960	2,479,015
1970	2,816,061
1980	2,966,850
1990	3,485,398
2000	3,694,820

...eral different years. ...e nearest hundred ...number as a decimal ...hen display your ...About how much did ...in millions, between ...000? Explain.

INTERNET
State Test Practice
CLASSZONE.COM

Test-Taking Practice

47. **Multiple Choice** Evaluate the expression $12.4 - 2.35 + 24.6$.
    A. 44.65 **B.** 39.35 **C.** 34.65 **D.** 34.75

48. **Short Response** You buy one video tape for $19.95 and rent one for $4.29. The sales tax is $1.45. How much change should you receive if you give the cashier $30? Explain how you solved the problem.

Test-Taking Skills and Strategies

At the end of each unit, you'll find pages that help you build and practice test-taking skills and strategies.

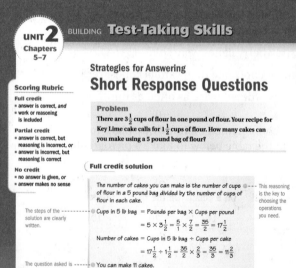

UNIT 2 Chapters 5–7 BUILDING **Test-Taking Skills**

Strategies for Answering
Short Response Questions

Scoring Rubric

Full credit
- answer is correct, *and*
- work or reasoning is included

Partial credit
- answer is correct, but reasoning is incorrect, *or*
- answer is incorrect, but reasoning is correct

No credit
- no answer is given, *or*
- answer makes no sense

Problem
There are $3\frac{1}{2}$ cups of flour in one pound of flour. Your recipe for Key Lime cake calls for $1\frac{1}{2}$ cups of flour. How many cakes can you make using a 5 pound bag of flour?

Full credit solution

The number of cakes you can make is the number of cups of flour in a 5 pound bag divided by the number of cups of flour in each cake.

— This reasoning is the key to choosing the operations you need.

The steps of the solution are clearly written.

Cups in 5 lb bag = Pounds per bag × Cups per pound
$$= 5 \times 3\frac{1}{2} = \frac{5}{1} \times \frac{7}{2} = \frac{35}{2} = 17\frac{1}{2}$$

Number of cakes = Cups in 5 lb bag ÷ Cups per cake
$$= 17\frac{1}{2} \div 1\frac{1}{2} = \frac{35}{2} \times \frac{2}{3} = \frac{35}{3} = 11\frac{2}{3}$$

The question asked is answered correctly.
You *can* make 11 cakes.

UNIT 1

Number Sense, Measurement, and Decimals

Chapter 1 Number Sense and Algebraic Thinking

- Write and evaluate numerical and variable expressions.
- Use a variety of strategies to predict, find, and check results.

Chapter 2 Measurement and Statistics

- Find lengths, perimeters, and areas in real-world situations.
- Use tables, graphs, and averages to organize and analyze data.

Chapter 3 Decimal Addition and Subtraction

- Name, write, order, and round decimals.
- Estimate and find sums and differences of decimals.
- Estimate and measure length.

Chapter 4 Decimal Multiplication and Division

- Multiply and divide by decimals and powers of ten.
- Use metric units of length, mass, and capacity.

From Chapter 4, p. 169
How much do sports cards cost?

UNIT RESOURCES

These resources are provided to help you prepare for the unit and to customize review materials:

 Chapter Resource Books
- Chapter 1
- Chapter 2
- Chapter 3
- Chapter 4

 Assessment Book
- Chapters 1–4, pp. 7–56

 Technology
- EasyPlanner CD-ROM
- Test and Practice Generator
- Electronic Lesson Presentations CD-ROM
- eTutorial CD-ROM

 Internet
- Classzone
- eEdition Plus Online
- eWorkbook Plus Online
- eTutorial Plus Online
- EasyPlanner Plus Online

ENGLISH LEARNER SUPPORT

- Spanish Study Guide
- Multi-Language Glossary
- Chapter Audio Summaries CDs
- Teacher's Edition
  Chapter 1, pp. 2E–2F
  Chapter 2, pp. 52E–52F
  Chapter 3, pp. 104E–104F
  Chapter 4, pp. 150E–150F

Pacing and Assignment Guide

Lesson	Les. Day	BASIC	AVERAGE	ADVANCED
1.1	Day 1	SRH p. 688 Exs. 1–4, 9–12; pp. 8–9 Exs. 16–31, 33–35, 37–45, 50, 51, 56–67, 72	pp. 8–9 Exs. 20–32, 35–41, 44–52, 60–73	pp. 8–9 Exs. 28–32, 35–39, 42–48, 51–55*, 60–63, 72, 73
1.2	Day 1	SRH p. 686 Exs. 1–5; pp. 14–15 Exs. 9–28, 33–38, 41, 43, 46–53, 55	pp. 14–15 Exs. 13–20, 25–34, 38–44, 46–51, 54, 55	pp. 14–15 Exs. 15–20, 27–45*, 47, 48, 54, 55
1.3	Day 1	pp. 18–19 Exs. 7–12, 14–25, 28–33, 38–40, 43–53	pp. 18–19 Exs. 7–13, 18–29, 34–41, 44–50, 53, 54	pp. 18–19 Exs. 10–13, 18–29, 36–42*, 44–48, 53, 54
1.4	Day 1	SRH p. 689 Exs. 1–4, 9–12; pp. 23–25 Exs. 9–27, 30–32, 36–42, 46, 55–63	pp. 23–25 Exs. 12–29, 33–39, 43–47, 54–64	pp. 23–25 Exs. 18–29, 33–35, 40–57*, 63, 64
1.5	Day 1	pp. 31–33 Exs. 13–18, 27, 29–31, 45, 59, 60, 64–67, 72	pp. 31–33 Exs. 13–18, 27, 29, 30, 45–47, 50–52, 63, 68–72	pp. 31–33 Exs. 15–18, 27, 30, 31, 45–52, 57*, 59–63, 72
	Day 2	pp. 31–33 Exs. 19–26, 28, 33–40, 46, 49, 51, 61, 62, 68–71	pp. 31–33 Exs. 13–18, 27, 29, 30, 45–47, 50–52, 63, 68–72	pp. 31–33 Exs. 21–26, 28, 32, 37–44, 53–56, 58*, 73
1.6	Day 1	SRH p. 696 Exs. 1–3, p. 697 Exs. 1–3; pp. 39–40 Exs. 15–27, 44–50	pp. 39–40 Exs. 18–27, 44–50, 61–65	pp. 39–40 Exs. 21–27, 48–53, 61–65
	Day 2	pp. 39–40 Exs. 28–43, 51–55, 61–70	pp. 39–40 Exs. 31–43, 51–56, 66–70	pp. 39–40 Exs. 34–44, 54–60*, 69, 70
1.7	Day 1	SRH p. 700 Exs. 1–6; pp. 44–45 Exs. 3–7, 15–21	pp. 44–45 Exs. 3–7, 15–21	pp. 44–45 Exs. 3–7, 15–21
	Day 2	pp. 44–45 Exs. 8, 9, 11–13, 22–26	pp. 44–45 Exs. 8–13, 22–26	pp. 44–45 Exs. 8–14*, 22–26
Review	Day 1	pp. 48–49 Exs. 1–68	pp. 48–49 Exs. 1–68	pp. 48–49 Exs. 1–68
Assess	Day 1	Chapter 1 Test	Chapter 1 Test	Chapter 1 Test

YEARLY PACING   Chapter 1 Total – **12 days**   Chapter 1 Total – **12 days**   Remaining – **148 days**

*Challenge Exercises   EP = Extra Practice   SRH = Skills Review Handbook   EC = Extra Challenge

BLOCK SCHEDULE

DAY 1	DAY 2	DAY 3	DAY 4	DAY 5	DAY 6
1.1 pp. 8–9 Exs. 20–32, 35–41, 44–52, 60–73	**1.3** pp. 18–19 Exs. 7–13, 18–29, 34–41, 44–50, 53, 54	**1.5** pp. 31–33 Exs. 13–30, 32–40, 45–48, 50–52, 54–56, 59–63, 68–73	**1.6** pp. 39–40 Exs. 18–27, 31–56, 61–70	**1.7** pp. 44–45 Exs. 3–13, 15–26	**Review** pp. 48–49 Exs. 1–68
1.2 pp. 14–15 Exs. 13–20, 25–34, 38–44, 46–51, 54, 55	**1.4** pp. 23–25 Exs. 12–29, 33–39, 43–47, 54–64				**Assess** Chapter 1 Test

YEARLY PACING   Chapter 1 Total – **6 days**   Chapter 1 Total – **6 days**   Remaining – **74 days**

Support Materials

📘 CHAPTER RESOURCE BOOK

CHAPTER SUPPORT

Tips for New Teachers	p. 1	Parents as Partners	p. 3

LESSON SUPPORT

	1.1	1.2	1.3	1.4	1.5	1.6	1.7
Lesson Plans (regular and block)	p. 7	p. 16	p. 25	p. 33	p. 43	p. 53	p. 62
Technology Activities & Keystrokes				p. 36	p. 45		
Activity Support Masters		p. 18					
Activity Masters				p. 35		p. 55	
Practice (3 levels)	p. 9	p. 19	p. 27	p. 37	p. 46	p. 56	p. 64
Study Guide	p. 12	p. 22	p. 30	p. 40	p. 49	p. 59	p. 67
Real-World Problem Solving	p. 14				p. 51		
Challenge Practice	p. 15	p. 24	p. 32	p. 42	p. 52	p. 61	p. 69

REVIEW

Games Support Masters	pp. 5, 70	Cooperative Project with Rubric	p. 74
Chapter Review Games and Activities	p. 71	Extra Credit Project with Rubric	p. 76
Real-Life Project with Rubric	p. 72	Cumulative Practice	p. 78
		Resource Book Answers	A1

📘 ASSESSMENT

Quizzes	p. 7	Alternative Assessments with Rubrics	p. 16
Chapter Tests (3 levels)	p. 9	Unit Test	p. 51
Standardized Test	p. 15	Cumulative Test	p. 53

🖥 TRANSPARENCIES

	1.1	1.2	1.3	1.4	1.5	1.6	1.7
Warm-Up / Daily Homework Quiz	✔	✔	✔	✔	✔	✔	✔
Notetaking Guide	✔	✔	✔	✔	✔	✔	✔
Teacher Support							✔
English/Spanish Problem Solving			✔	✔			
Answer Transparencies	✔	✔	✔	✔	✔	✔	✔

💻 TECHNOLOGY

- EasyPlanner CD-ROM
- Test and Practice Generator
- Electronic Lesson Presentations
- eTutorial CD-ROM
- Chapter Audio Summaries CDs
- Classzone.com
- eEdition Plus Online
- eWorkbook Plus Online
- eTutorial Plus Online
- EasyPlanner Plus Online

ADDITIONAL RESOURCES

- Worked-Out Solution Key
- Notetaking Guide
- Practice Workbook
- Tutor Place
- Professional Development Book
- Activities Book
- Poster Package
- Spanish Study Guide
- English/Spanish Chapter Reviews
- Multi-Language Glossary

Math Background and Teaching Strategies

Lesson 1.1

MATH BACKGROUND

INVERSE OPERATIONS Addition and subtraction are inverse operations because one operation can "undo" the other operation. A sum results from addition; a difference results from subtraction. Multiplication and division are inverse operations. A product results from multiplication; a quotient results from division.

TEACHING STRATEGIES

Emphasize the need for proper alignment of numbers when adding or subtracting. Keeping digits in proper places helps prevent errors.

Multiplying a 2-digit, 3-digit or 4-digit number by a 2-digit or 3-digit number requires an understanding of place value. To multiply 234 by 36, encourage students to think of 234 as 2 hundreds 3 tens and 4 ones and 36 as 3 tens and 6 ones.

Have students practice labeling division problems with dividend, divisor, and quotient before teaching students how to solve them. This helps students to learn which number represents each part of the problem.

Lesson 1.2

MATH BACKGROUND

ESTIMATES Explain that estimation can be used when you don't need an exact answer or to check computation. Number pairs whose sum is 10 or a multiple of 10 are compatible numbers for addition. When estimating sums, you can replace a pair of addends with compatible numbers before adding. Another way to estimate sums is to add the leading digits. Tens and hundreds are compatible numbers for subtraction because they are easy to subtract. Another way to estimate differences is to subtract the leading digits. To estimate products, you can multiply leading digits or you can round factors to the nearest multiple of 10. If one factor is a single digit, this factor should not be rounded. You can use multiples of 10 (such as 30, 300, or 3000) to help you estimate quotients. You can also use compatible numbers, where one number is a factor of the other, to estimate quotients.

TEACHING STRATEGIES

A number line can help students round numbers when estimating sums or differences.

Example $245 + 295 + 266 = \underline{\ ?\ }$

Draw a number line from 240 to 300. Have students find each of the addends on the number line.

```
     245        266         295
◄──┬──●──┬──┬──●──┬──┬──┬──●──┬──►
  240 250 260 270 280 290 300
```

Ask students to name the ten that is closest to each addend. Then have students estimate the sum as $250 + 300 + 270 = 820$.

Lesson 1.3

MATH BACKGROUND

REPEATED MULTIPLICATION Exponents represent repeated multiplication. For example, the **power** 2^4 means $2 \times 2 \times 2 \times 2$. The 2 is the factor to be multiplied, called the **base**, and the 4 is the **exponent**, which tells how many times the base is to be multiplied. This expression can be read as "2 to the fourth power." To **square** a number means to apply the exponent 2 to a base. To **cube** of a number means to apply the exponent 3 to a base.

TEACHING STRATEGIES

Write the first three rows of these "power towers" on an overhead transparency or on the board.

2	5	10
2×2	5×5	10×10
$2 \times 2 \times 2$	$5 \times 5 \times 5$	$10 \times 10 \times 10$
$2 \times 2 \times 2 \times 2$	$5 \times 5 \times 5 \times 5$	$10 \times 10 \times 10 \times 10$

Have students write the exponential form and evaluate each row. Ask questions such as, what is the product of 4 factors of 2? Of 2 factors of 5? Of 3 factors of 10?

Lesson 1.4

MATH BACKGROUND

ORDER OF OPERATIONS Expressions that contain numbers and symbols for operations are **numerical expressions**. They often also contain **grouping symbols**, such as parentheses or fraction bars. The operations in these expressions are carried out in a universally agreed-upon order to ensure that the expression will have the same value for everyone.

TEACHING STRATEGIES

Before students use parentheses in calculations, they need to be clear about the order of operations without parentheses. Start by reviewing the rules for evaluating an expression such as $12 + 4 \div 4 \times 2 - 1$. Discuss evaluating the expression using the standard order of operations to get 13. Then show students how parentheses can affect that order by asking them to evaluate $(12 + 4) \div (4 \times 2) - 1$ to get 1.

Lesson 1.5

MATH BACKGROUND

VARIABLES A variable represents a quantity that can have different values. A variable can be used in an expression to stand for a range of possible values or a variable can be used in an equation to represent a specific unknown quantity. A third use of variables is as placeholders in statements that are always true.

VARIABLE EXPRESSIONS An **expression** consists of a combination of numbers, operation symbols, and grouping symbols such as parentheses. An expression that also contains one or more variables is an **algebraic expression**. To evaluate a variable expression, substitute a number for the variable and evaluate the resulting numerical expression.

TEACHING STRATEGIES

Make a list of at least five different variables that relate to school. Possibilities include: s = number of sixth grade classes, f = number of fifth grade classes, t = the number of teachers in a class, b = the number of boys in a class, g = the number of girls in a class, and so on. Have students write expressions such as $t + b + g$ to represent the number of teachers, boys, and girls in a class.

Lesson 1.6

MATH BACKGROUND

EQUATIONS The power of algebra lies in its language and tools. An **equation**, which is a statement showing that two expressions or values are equal, enables us to describe relationships accurately and concisely.

Examples $5 + 2 = 7$ $12 = 4a$ $y = 8$ $4 = 16 - (9 + c)$

TEACHING STRATEGIES

Students will learn later that inverse operations can be used to solve equations. Here, they use the problem solving strategy Guess, Check, and Revise, and mental math to solve equations.

Give several examples of solving by using successive replacements for the variable. Stress that the goal is to arrive at a true statement about numbers.

Lesson 1.7

MATH BACKGROUND

Solving "word" problems is often a challenge. Having a general plan and a list of possible strategies to use are tools that can help solve problems. A problem solving plan includes reading comprehension to understand the problem, the ability to decide upon an appropriate strategy and the ability to carry out the chosen strategy, and a check of the reasonableness of the solution in the context of the original problem.

TEACHING STRATEGIES

Write on the board the words *Understand, Analyze, Plan, Estimate, Solve,* and *Examine*. Discuss the meanings of the terms in the context of solving a specific problem. Encourage students to see that to solve a problem they need first to understand the problem, then to analyze the problem to find what information they have and what they want to find out, and finally to plan how to solve the problem. When possible, they should estimate the answer before solving the problem. Finally, they should examine the answer to see if it makes sense.

Differentiating Instruction

At the start of each chapter, we will outline modifications of curriculum and instruction designed to address the unique needs of Underachieving Students, English Learners, and Advanced Learners. Underachievers are those whose mathematics achievement is below grade level who need strategic and sustained assistance in order to be successful in mathematics. English Learners are those who are not yet fluent in English. Advanced Learners are those whose mathematics achievement is above grade level. Each class of students is different, and you may find your whole class benefits from some of these suggestions. Most of the activities for Underachievers and English Learners would best be done in a second class period, as homework, or in a tutorial, since both groups of students need increased instructional time in mathematics. Some of the activities, particularly those involving vocabulary development, would fit nicely into a language arts period. The activities for Advanced Learners in these pages and throughout the text are meant as substitutes for easier problems in the text.

Strategies for Underachievers

ASSESS STUDENT ACHIEVEMENT

CONCEPT REVIEW This chapter includes a review of concepts that students should have already learned, such as knowledge of basic facts (through 12) and the ability to perform the algorithms for the four basic operations of addition, subtraction, multiplication, and division. Teachers are encouraged to review the math test results available for each student from the previous year. End-of-year tests that are in the mathematics book the student used, as well as any standardized testing or mathematics portfolios that might be available, can be utilized. Teachers may want to administer a chapter pretest to see if there are any common areas of weakness among students, and, if so, the prior year's textbook and ancillaries would provide ample teaching suggestions and practice exercises. Many students, especially those not in year-round schools, will simply have forgotten over the summer and will require just enough explanation and exercises to refresh their memories. Some students, however, will have gaps in their knowledge base. For those students, the teacher can select relevant portions of the prior year's textbook or problems in the ancillaries for review. Ideally, students who need extra help should be scheduled for an extra period of mathematics or tutorial help.

REVIEW PREVIOUSLY LEARNED CONCEPTS

ALGORITHMS A review of basic algorithms of addition, subtraction, multiplication, and division will be beneficial for many students. Discussing the vocabulary associated with these algorithms, such as "sum," "difference," "product," and "quotient," is necessary for students to communicate effectively.

PROVIDE SUFFICIENT PRACTICE

A few students need just a couple of examples in order to understand and remember a mathematical concept or procedure. Most students need more practice. Practice should be varied, so that students are assigned exercises that range from easy to difficult and so students must apply what they have learned to a variety of settings. Throughout this book, opportunities for additional practice are indicated. For keystone concepts such as order or operations and introduction of variables, provide sufficient practice, specifically targeting areas of common error, before moving on to new concepts.

Strategies for English Learners

VOCABULARY DEVELOPMENT

Common English words and specialized mathematical terms are vital to understanding and expressing mathematical concepts. By the middle grades, most native

English speakers have developed a full vocabulary of common English words, as well as mathematical terms and concepts. Words that express temporal relationships, such as *first, second, third, before* and *after, yesterday, today* and *tomorrow*; words that describe shapes, such as *circle, triangle, square*; and words that describe the relationships of objects in space such as *over, under,* and *between*, are commonly understood by fluent English speakers in the middle grades. But for the English learner, these words may represent large stumbling blocks as these students try to understand mathematical concepts, decide what is asked for in a word problem, and express their thinking in mathematics.

MATHEMATICS VOCABULARY Plan to spend some time each day developing vocabulary related to mathematics. You might start with your English learners by reading the 500 most common words in the English language. Several such lists are readily available. These common words can form the basis of vocabulary study done outside math class, in language arts, or in a tutorial.

WORDS AND SYMBOLS Mathematical notation can be confusing at this stage. Review with students words and symbols related to the four basic operations: $+$, $-$, $\times$, and $\div$.

Add, addition, sum, plus, total, all, $+$

Subtract, subtraction, difference, take away, minus, left over, $-$

Multiply, multiplication, times, product, factor, prime, common multiple, exponent

$5(5)$ $5 \cdot 5$ 5×5 5^2

Divide, divisor, dividend, quotient, factor, common divisor

$16 \div 4$ $\dfrac{16}{4}$ $4)\overline{16}$

Strategies for Advanced Learners

INCREASE DEPTH AND COMPLEXITY

Since advanced students tend to move more quickly through the instructional material than other students, the challenge problems in this Teacher's Edition can be substituted for easier problems. Encourage advanced students throughout the year to delve more deeply into mathematics content that interests them and to find connections between the mathematics in this course and the content of other courses, such as science, language arts, music, art, and social studies.

The following ideas and challenge problems may be used for extensions throughout Chapter 1.

In **Lesson 1.1**, you may wish to have students explore famous patterns, such as the Fibonacci Sequence and Pascal's Triangle. You also may wish to challenge students with problems such as the following.

- **Challenge** The difference between two whole numbers is 7, and their product is 30. Find the sum of the two numbers. 13

- **Challenge** The sum of the first ten counting numbers divided by sum of the first and tenth counting numbers is what number? The sum of the first twenty counting numbers divided by sum of the first and twentieth counting numbers is what number? The sum of the first thirty counting numbers divided by sum of the first and thirtieth counting numbers is what number? What do you think are the next the next three numbers in the pattern? 5; 10; 15; The next three numbers are 20, 25, 30.

In **Lesson 1.3**, you may wish to have students memorize the perfect squares through 20^2. Also in Lesson 1.3, students can be encouraged to explore looping patterns involving exponents by working problems such as the following.

- **Challenge** Investigate the pattern for the units digit for powers of 2. What is the units digit for 2^{12} and for 2^{30}? Note that the units digits repeat in cycles of 4 (2, 4, 8, 6, and so on) from 2^1 on, so divide the exponent by 4 and look at the remainder. If the remainder is 0, the units digit will be 6; if the remainder is 1, the units digit will be 2, and so on. For 2^{12}, the units digit is 6; for 2^{30}, the units digit is 4.

To challenge advanced learners in **Lesson 1.5**, you can integrate variables and the order of operations to create challenging problems that require multiple steps to solve.

- **Challenge** If $a \cdot b = 150$, and $a = 50$, find $a + b$. 53

- **Challenge** If $a \# b$ means $a^b - ab + b^a$, find $3 \# 2$.
  $3^2 - 3 \cdot 2 + 2^3 = 9 - 6 + 8 = 11$

Differentiating Instruction: Teaching Resources

Differentiating Practice

McDougal Littell *Middle School Mathematics* offers teachers a wide variety of practice for all levels of students. Pictured on these pages are facsimiles of the Level A, Level B, Level C, and Challenge Practice pages from the *Chapter 1 Resource Book*, pages from the *Practice Workbook*, and the *Test and Practice Generator*.

RESOURCE BOOK

The *Chapter Resource Books* contain three levels of practice, A (Basic), B (Average), and C (Advanced), for each lesson in the textbook. Also included is a page of Challenge practice for each lesson for your most advanced students.

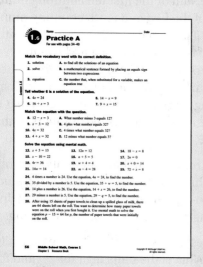

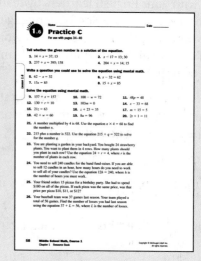

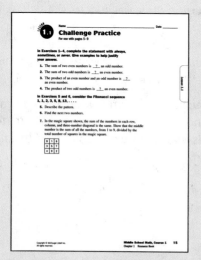

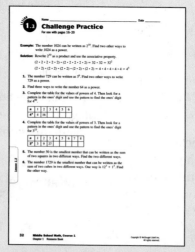

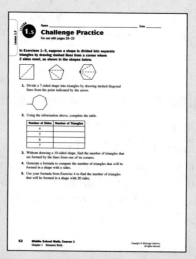

PRACTICE WORKBOOK

The *Practice Workbook* contains the average B-level practice for each lesson reformatted in workbook form to allow students to show their work for each exercise.

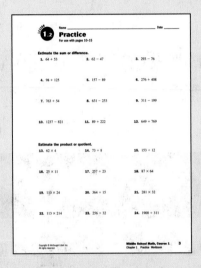
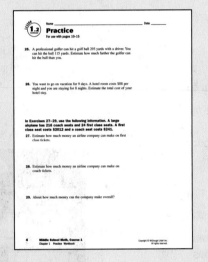
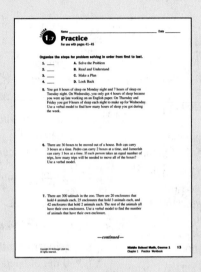

TEST AND PRACTICE GENERATOR CD-ROM

The *Test and Practice Generator* allows you to create practice worksheets for each lesson using both static and algorithmic exercises.

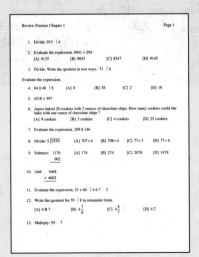
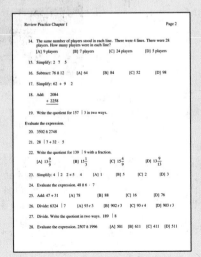
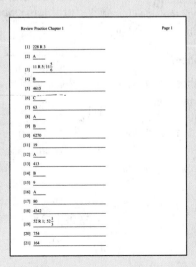

MAIN IDEAS

In this chapter, students compute and estimate with whole numbers. They evaluate powers and use the order of operations to evaluate expressions, including expressions that contain variables. Students also solve equations using mental math and learn a problem-solving plan.

PREREQUISITE SKILLS

The key skills reviewed in the games on these pages are:

- Adding, subtracting, multiplying, and dividing whole numbers
- Comparing whole numbers
- Completing number fact families

Additional practice with prerequisite skills can be found in the Review What You Need to Know exercises on page 4. Additional resources for reviewing prerequisite skills are:

- Skills Review Handbook, pp. 684–707
- Tutor Place
- eTutorial Plus Online

MANAGING THE GAMES

Tips for Success

In Whole Number Ride, caution students to double-check the sign before they compute. They may want to write down the results for pairs of spaces in order to compare them.

Reflecting on the Games

When discussing Stop and Think Question 2, ask students why $18 - 9$ is *not* one of the facts they can list. If the other player is on 9, you cannot move there.

Number Sense and Algebraic Thinking

BEFORE

In previous courses you've...

- Performed whole number operations
- Completed number fact families

Now

In Chapter 1 you'll study...

- Estimating with whole numbers
- Order of operations
- Evaluating variable expressions
- Equations and mental math
- Using a problem solving plan

WHY?

So you can solve real-world problems about...

- cheetahs, p. 9
- biking, p. 12
- weather, p. 31
- volleyball, p. 40

 Internet Preview
CLASSZONE.COM

- eEdition Plus Online
- eWorkbook Plus Online
- eTutorial Plus Online
- State Test Practice
- More Examples

Chapter Warm-Up Games

Review skills you need for this chapter in these quick games. Work with a partner.

BRAIN GAME

Key Skill:
Performing whole number operations

Find your way from the entrance to the Ferris wheel. Begin at the entrance. Find the sum, difference, product, or quotient. Then move one space along a path to a space that has a greater value.

Move along the following path from the entrance to $42 \div 7$ to $35 \div 5$ to $64 \div 8$ to $54 \div 6$ to $32 - 9$ to 5×5 to $7 + 19$ to $60 \div 2$ to $41 - 9$ to 6×8 to 11×5 to 9×7 to the Ferris wheel.

Bumper Cars

9	15	5	4
18	3	10	20
6	24	8	2

Key Skill:
Number facts

Materials:
One paper clip for each player

Place your paper clips on different numbers. Take turns following the directions below. **Check work.**

• Move one space in any direction to a new number. State one number fact using your old and new numbers. For example, if you move from 9 to 3, you could state these facts: $3 + 9$, $9 - 3$, 3×9, or $9 \div 3$.

• If the value of your number fact matches the number on which the other player is located, you may bump the player to any number except yours. Two players can never be on the same number at the same time. The first player to bump the other player 3 times wins.

Stop *and* Think

1. **Writing** Suppose you wanted to move from the Ferris wheel to the entrance in *Whole Number Ride*. How would you rewrite the rules of the game? **Change the last rule to move one space along a path to a space that has a lesser value.**

2. **Critical Thinking** List all the number facts you could make in *Bumper Cars* that would bump a player from the number 9. **$5 + 4$, $6 + 3$**

CHAPTER 1 Getting Ready to Learn

Review What You Need to Know

Using Vocabulary **Match the word with its correct symbol.**

1. sum B   **2.** difference C   **3.** product D   **4.** quotient A

A. ÷   **B.** +   **C.** −   **D.** ×

5. Tell whether the following statement is *true* or *false:* In a division sentence, the divisor is divided by the dividend. false

Identify the place value of the red digit. *(p. 684)*

6. 27 tens   **7.** 56 tens   **8.** 197 ones   **9.** 813 hundreds

Round the number to the red digit. *(p. 686)*

10. 16 20   **11.** 31 30   **12.** 257 300   **13.** 1909 1900

Find the sum, difference, product, or quotient. *(p. 687)*

14. $7 + 8$ 15   **15.** $6 + 5$ 11   **16.** $13 - 4$ 9   **17.** $11 - 3$ 8

18. 7×3 21   **19.** 9×5 45   **20.** $24 \div 4$ 6   **21.** $16 \div 2$ 8

Word Watch

Review Words

whole number, p. 684
place value, p. 684
round, p. 686
sum, p. 689
difference, p. 689
product, p. 690
quotient, p. 691
dividend, p. 691
divisor, p. 691

You should include material that appears on a notebook like this in your own notes.

Know How to Take Notes

Keeping a Notebook Some useful items to put in your mathematics notebook include the following:

- vocabulary
- rules and properties
- worked-out examples
- symbols
- formulas

When you copy examples, include reminders about important details.

Lesson 1.1 Whole Number Operations

$$\begin{array}{r} 1 \\ 134 \\ + 49 \\ \hline 183 \end{array}$$
Remember to line up the ones, the tens, and so on.

$$\begin{array}{r} 5\ 11\ 14 \\ \cancel{624} \\ - 259 \\ \hline 365 \end{array}$$
Remember to regroup so you can subtract.

In Lesson 1.5, you will see how a reminder can help you to relate a previous lesson to a new situation.

Whole Number Operations

BEFORE	▶ Now	WHY?
You learned basic number facts.	You'll add, subtract, multiply, and divide whole numbers.	So you can find the cost of music lessons, as in Example 3.

Activity **You can use addition skills to complete a magic square.**

In a *magic square*, the numbers in each row, column, and diagonal add up to the same magic number. Follow the steps below to complete the magic square.

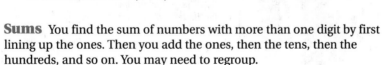

① Add the three numbers in the first row. **15**

② Add the three numbers in the second column. **15**

③ Add the three numbers along a diagonal. **15**

④ What is the magic number? **15**

⑤ Copy and complete the magic square. Explain how you found the missing numbers.
7, 4; *Sample answer:* For column one: 15 − (8 + 3) = 4; for column three: 15 − (6 + 2) = 7

Sums You find the sum of numbers with more than one digit by first lining up the ones. Then you add the ones, then the tens, then the hundreds, and so on. You may need to regroup.

HELP with Review

Need help with place value? See p. 684.

EXAMPLE 1 **Adding Whole Numbers**

a. To find the sum 49 + 36, first you line up the numbers on the ones' place. Next you add the ones. Then you add the tens.

$$
\begin{array}{r}
\overset{1}{4}9 \\
+\ 36 \\
\hline
85
\end{array}
$$
9 + 6 = 15. Regroup the 15 ones as 1 ten and 5 ones.

b. To find the sum 954 + 78, you line up the numbers on the ones' place. Next you add the ones, then the tens, then the hundreds.

$$
\begin{array}{r}
\overset{11}{9}54 \\
+\ 78 \\
\hline
1032
\end{array}
$$
← **4 + 8 = 12. Regroup the 12 ones as 1 ten and 2 ones.**
1 + 5 + 7 = 13. Regroup the 13 tens as 1 hundred and 3 tens.

Lesson 1.1 Whole Number Operations **5**

---

① PLAN

SKILL CHECK
1. 23 + 45 = _?_   68
2. 76 − 35 = _?_   41
3. 12 × 4 = _?_   48
4. 36 ÷ 3 = _?_   12

LESSON OBJECTIVE

Add, subtract, multiply, and divide whole numbers.

PACING

Suggested Number of Days
Basic Course: 1 day
Average Course: 1 day
Advanced Course: 1 day
Block: 0.5 block with 1.2

TEACHING RESOURCES

For a complete list of Teaching Resources, see page 2B.

TRANSPARENCY

Warm-Up Exercises for this lesson are available on a transparency.

② TEACH

MOTIVATING THE LESSON

Magic squares are a good method of getting students to review addition and subtraction skills. Give students additional magic squares to solve.

ACTIVITY

Goal Use addition to complete a magic square.

Key Discovery Each row, column, or diagonal of a magic square adds up to the same number.

 **with Solving**

You can check your answer to a subtraction problem by adding. For Example 2:

$$\begin{array}{r} 1\ 1 \\ 168 \\ +\ 36 \\ \hline 204 \end{array}$$

EXAMPLE 2 **Subtracting Whole Numbers**

To find the difference of 204 and 36, you line up the numbers on the ones' place. Next you subtract the ones, then the tens, and so on.

$$\begin{array}{r} 1\ 9\ 14 \\ 20\!\!\!/4 \\ -\ 36 \\ \hline 168 \end{array}$$

You need more ones to subtract 6, so regroup.
204 = 100 + 90 + 14.

Your turn now Find the sum or difference.

1. 95 + 37 **132**   **2.** 406 + 95 **501**   **3.** 82 − 49 **33**   **4.** 500 − 315 **185**

EXAMPLE 3 **Multiplying Whole Numbers**

Music Lessons Your music lessons cost $25 per week. How much will you pay for 12 weeks of lessons?

Solution You need to find the product 25 × 12.

$$\begin{array}{r} 25 \\ \times\ 12 \\ \hline 50 \\ 25 \\ \hline 300 \end{array}$$

Start the partial product for the tens' digit in the tens' column.

First multiply 25 by the ones' digit, 2.
Then multiply 25 by the tens' digit, 1.
Add the partial products.

ANSWER You will pay $300 for 12 weeks of music lessons.

EXAMPLE 4 **Dividing Whole Numbers**

To find the quotient of 592 and 7, you use long division. The dividend is 592 and the divisor is 7.

Align the 8 in the tens' column.

$$\begin{array}{r} 84\ \text{R4} \\ 7\overline{)592} \\ 56\downarrow \\ \hline 32 \\ 28 \\ \hline 4 \end{array}$$

Divide 59 by 7, because 7 is more than 5.
Multiply: 8 × 7 = 56.
Subtract: 59 − 56 = 3. Bring down the 2.
Repeat the process.
The remainder is 4.

Your turn now Find the product or quotient.

5. 29 × 31 **899**   **6.** 140 × 15 **2100**   **7.** 721 ÷ 6 **120 R1**   **8.** 418 ÷ 21 **19 R19**

UNITED STATES
OF AMERICA

EXAMPLE 5 **Finding Patterns**

Sports The Summer Olympics were held in 1988, 1992, 1996, and 2000. Describe the pattern. Then find the next two years in the pattern.

Solution

Look to see how each number is related to the preceding number. Each year after 1988 is 4 more than the preceding year.

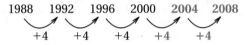

1988   1992   1996   2000   2004   2008
    +4   +4   +4   +4   +4

ANSWER The next two years in the pattern are 2004 and 2008.

Your turn now Describe the pattern. Then find the next two numbers.

9. 1, 4, 7, 10, ? , ?   add 3; 13, 16   **10.** 55, 50, 45, 40, ? , ?
                                                subtract 5; 35, 30
11. 3, 6, 12, 24, ? , ?   **12.** 320, 160, 80, 40, ? , ?
   multiply by 2; 48, 96   divide by 2; 20, 10

1.1 Exercises
More Practice, p. 708

INTERNET
eWorkbook Plus
CLASSZONE.COM

Getting Ready to Practice

Vocabulary Match the word with its meaning.

1. difference C   **A.** the result of adding two or more numbers

2. quotient B   **B.** the result of dividing one number by another

3. sum A   **C.** the result of subtracting one number from another

4. product D   **D.** the result of multiplying two or more numbers

Find the sum, difference, product, or quotient.

5. 45 + 36 81   **6.** 76 − 39 37   **7.** 24 × 18 432   **8.** 78 ÷ 5 15 R3

9. 802 − 19 783 **10.** 305 + 97 402 **11.** 607 ÷ 11 55 R2 **12.** 56 × 34 1904

Describe the pattern. Then find the next two numbers.

13. 60, 50, 40, 30, ? , ?   **14.** 1, 3, 9, 27, ? , ?
   subtract 10; 20, 10   multiply by 3; 81, 243
15. **Tickets** A ticket to the theater costs $26. If you buy 6 tickets, how much do you pay? $156

Lesson 1.1   Whole Number Operations   **7**

Example 5 Elections to the U.S. Congress were held in 1992, 1994, 1996, 1998, 2000, and 2002. Describe the pattern. Then find the next two election years in the pattern. Each year is 2 more than the preceding year. The next two years in the pattern are 2004 and 2006.

Differentiating Instruction

• **Advanced Students** Challenge your better students to come up with their own patterns. Ask them for a verbal description and for the next two numbers in their patterns.

• **Alternative Teaching Strategy** Have students analyze some patterns in numbers by finding products of a constant factor and successive terms. For example, to find the pattern in 1, 2, 4, 8, multiply the first term by 2 to get the second term, multiply the second term by 2 to get the third term, and so on.

 CONCEPT CHECK

When you add or subtract whole numbers, why do you sometimes need to use regrouping? In addition when you get more than 9 ones or more than 9 tens, you need to regroup. In subtraction, when you need more ones or more tens, you need to regroup.

 DAILY PUZZLER

Two whole numbers have a product of 120 and a difference of 2. What are the numbers? 12 and 10

③ APPLY

ASSIGNMENT GUIDE

Basic Course
Day 1: SRH p. 688 Exs. 1–4,
9–12; pp. 8–9 Exs. 16–31,
33–35, 37–45, 50, 51,
56–67, 72

Average Course
Day 1: pp. 8–9 Exs. 20–32,
35–41, 44–52, 60–73

Advanced Course
Day 1: pp. 8–9 Exs. 28–32,
35–39, 42–48, 51–55*,
60–63, 72, 73

Block
pp. 8–9 Exs. 20–32, 35–41,
44–52, 60–73 (with 1.2)

EXTRA PRACTICE

• Student Edition, p. 708
• Chapter 1 Resource Book,
  pp. 9–11
• Test and Practice Generator

TRANSPARENCY

Even-numbered answers are available on transparencies.

HOMEWORK CHECK

When you review students' homework for this lesson, go over the following exercises to check understanding of key concepts.
Basic: 17, 23, 27, 33, 40
Average: 20, 26, 27, 35, 40
Advanced: 29, 30, 36, 37, 43

TEACHING TIP

Exercises 51–52 should help students understand the relationship between addition and multiplication and the relationship between multiplication and division.

 with Homework

Example	Exercises
1	16–31, 37–47
2	16–31, 37–47
3	16–32, 40–47
4	16–31, 37–47
5	33–36

 **Online Resources**
CLASSZONE.COM
· More Examples
· eTutorial Plus

33. subtract 2; 22, 20

34. multiply by 2; 80, 160

Practice and Problem Solving

Find the sum, difference, product, or quotient.

A **16.** 37 + 46 83   **17.** 54 − 38 16   **18.** 402 × 5 2010   **19.** 58 ÷ 3 19 R1

20. 281 − 72 209   **21.** 164 + 72 236   **22.** 725 ÷ 6 120 R5   **23.** 15 × 40 600

24. 226 + 175 401   **25.** 812 − 125 687   **26.** 63 × 25 1575   **27.** 634 ÷ 11 57 R7

28. 600 − 472 128   **29.** 399 + 214 613   **30.** 7296 ÷ 3 2432   **31.** 249 × 31 7719

32. Find the Error Describe and correct the error made at the right. The partial product for the tens' digit was not started in the tens' column.

$$\begin{array}{r} 27 \\ \times\ 15 \\ \hline 135 \\ 27 \\ \hline 405 \end{array}$$

Describe the pattern. Then find the next two numbers.

33. 30, 28, 26, 24, _?_ , _?_

34. 5, 10, 20, 40, _?_ , _?_

35. 4, 12, 20, 28, _?_ , _?_ add 8; 36, 44

36. 64, 32, 16, 8, _?_ , _?_ divide by 2; 4, 2

37. Test Scores The scores on your first two math tests were 78 and 91. By how much did your score improve? 13

38. Shopping A shirt costs $18 and a wallet costs $25. Find the total cost. $43

39. Road Trip Your family made 3 rest stops each day during a road trip. There was a total of 42 rest stops. How many days did the trip take? 14 days

Decide Tell whether the statement is *true* or *false*. If it is false, change the underlined word to make the statement true.

40. The <u>sum</u> of 92 and 13 is 105. true   **41.** The <u>difference</u> of 15 and 5 is 75. false; product

42. The <u>product</u> of 26 and 3 is 23. false; difference   **43.** The <u>quotient</u> of 64 and 4 is 16. true

Mental Math Find the missing digit in the problem.

B **44.**
$$\begin{array}{r} 75 \\ +\ 2\ ? \\ \hline 102 \end{array}$$ 7

45.
$$\begin{array}{r} 8\ ? \\ -\ 36 \\ \hline 45 \end{array}$$ 1

46.
$$\begin{array}{r} 2\ ?5 \\ \times\ \ 3 \\ \hline 645 \end{array}$$ 1

47. $\ ?\,)\overline{102}$ 17 6

48. Explain In the magic square shown, the sum of the numbers in each row, column, and four-number diagonal is the same. Copy and complete the magic square.

4	14	15 ?	1
9	7 ?	6	12
5	11	10	8 ?
16	2	3	13 ?

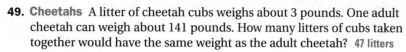

49. Cheetahs A litter of cheetah cubs weighs about 3 pounds. One adult cheetah can weigh about 141 pounds. How many litters of cubs taken together would have the same weight as the adult cheetah? **47 litters**

50. Look for a Pattern A one-minute phone call costs 13 cents. A two-minute call costs 26 cents. A three-minute call costs 39 cents. Describe the pattern. If this pattern continues, what is the cost of a four-minute call? a five-minute call? **multiply the number of minutes by 13; 52 cents, 65 cents**

Critical Thinking You find the product of 67 and 5 to be 335.

C **51.** How can you use addition to check if you are correct? **Add 67 five times.**

52. How can you use division to check if you are correct? **Divide 335 by either 67 or 5.**

Challenge You have $7, your cousin has $9, and your two friends each have $11. You use all of this money to buy tickets for carnival rides. Each ticket costs $2.

53. How many tickets can you buy? **19 tickets**

54. Can you split the tickets evenly among all of you? Explain. **No; there are 4 people and 19 is not evenly divisible by 4.**

55. If the tickets cost $3, how many tickets can you buy? Can you split the tickets evenly? **12 tickets; yes**

Mixed Review

Round the number to the red digit. *(p. 686)*

56. 32 **30**   **57.** 89 **90**   **58.** 951 **1000**   **59.** 344 **300**

60. 988 **1000**   **61.** 1384 **1000**   **62.** 7199 **7000**   **63.** 4511 **5000**

Basic Skills **Find the sum, difference, product, or quotient.**

64. 4×8 **32**   **65.** $11 - 7$ **4**   **66.** $14 \div 2$ **7**   **67.** $9 + 2$ **11**

68. $6 + 6$ **12**   **69.** 9×3 **27**   **70.** $13 - 8$ **5**   **71.** $30 \div 6$ **5**

Test-Taking Practice

72. Multiple Choice You have 28 boxes of apples. Each box has 26 apples. Which choice has a value equal to the total number of apples? **C**

    A. $28 + 26$ **B.** $28 - 26$ **C.** 28×26 **D.** $28 \div 26$

73. Multiple Choice You buy 245 plums. There are 35 plums per bag. How many bags of plums do you buy? **G**

    F. 5   **G.** 7   **H.** 31   **I.** 35

■ **Cheetahs**
A cheetah cub at birth is about 12 inches long from its nose to the end of its tail. An adult cheetah can be about 90 inches long. Is the adult cheetah *less than*, *equal to*, or *greater than* 7 times as long as the cub?

greater than

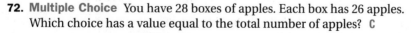

INTERNET
State Test Practice
CLASSZONE.COM

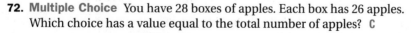

ASSESSMENT RESOURCES
For more assessment resources, see:
• Assessment Book
• Test and Practice Generator

MINI-QUIZ

1. $82 - 48 = \underline{?}$ **34**

2. $532 \div 8 = \underline{?}$ **66 R4**

3. $341 \times 21 = \underline{?}$ **7161**

4. $365 + 920 = \underline{?}$ **1285**

Describe the pattern. Then find the next two numbers.

5. 5, 12, 19, 26, $\underline{?}$, $\underline{?}$ **Each number is 7 more than the preceding number; 33, 40.**

6. 4, 12, 36, 108, $\underline{?}$, $\underline{?}$ **Each number is three times the preceding number; 324, 972.**

7. You want to save $150 to buy a bicycle. You can save $5 per week. How many weeks will it take? **30 weeks**

5 FOLLOW-UP

RETEACHING/REMEDIATION

• Study Guide in Chapter 1 Resource Book, pp. 12–13
• Tutor Place, Whole Numbers and Decimals Cards 1, 5, 7, 10, 11
• eTutorial Plus Online
• Student Edition, p. 708
• Lesson Practice in Chapter 1 Resource Book, pp. 9–11

CHALLENGE/ENRICHMENT

• Challenge Practice in Chapter 1 Resource Book, p. 15
• Teacher's Edition, p. 2F

ENGLISH LEARNER SUPPORT

• Spanish Study Guide
• Multi-Language Glossary
• Chapter Audio Summaries CDs

9

- Students will use a number cube to estimate a sum, difference, product, or quotient close to a target number.
- This activity leads into the study of estimation in Lesson 1.2. Estimation is a useful technique in checking the reasonableness of answers.

MATERIALS

Each student or group of students will need a number cube. See also the Activity Support Master in the *Chapter 1 Resource Book*.

RECOMMENDED TIME

Work activity: 10 min
Discuss results: 5 min

GROUPING

Students can work individually or in groups of two. If students work in groups, they can discuss the best position to place the number they roll on the number cube.

TEACH

TIPS FOR SUCCESS

Students may find it difficult to choose which squares to fill in as they roll the number cube. Point out that this is an open-ended activity with no one right answer. Doing the activity more than once may help students to better develop their number sense.

1.2 Hands-on Activity

GOAL
Use estimation to find a sum, difference, product, or quotient close to a target number.

MATERIALS
· number cube

Hitting the Target

You can use estimation to solve problems where you want to come close to some exact number.

Explore Form a sum that is close to the target number 100.

1 Sketch four squares arranged as shown at the right. Roll the number cube and place the result in one of the blank boxes.

It will be hard to get close to 100 with a 1 in the tens' column, so put the 1 here.

2 Roll again and place the result in another blank box.

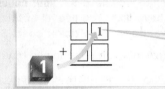

Putting the 6 in the tens' column will help you get close to 100.

3 Roll two more times to complete the diagram. Then find the sum. Compare it with the target number 100.

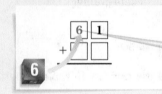

Your turn now Refer to the target game shown above.

1. Is it possible to rearrange the digits to get closer to the target sum? If so, how would you rearrange them? Yes. *Sample answer:* Change 34 to 43.

2. Repeat Steps 1–3 above to form another sum that is close to the target. Is it possible to rearrange your digits to get closer to the target sum? If so, how would you rearrange them? Answers may vary.

NCTM CURRICULUM STANDARDS
Standard 1: Understand how operations are related; Make reasonable estimates
Standard 6: Apply/adapt strategies to solve problems

KEY DISCOVERY

Students can estimate a sum, product, difference, or quotient.

ASSESSMENT

1. Estimate the sum of 42 and 36. How would you rearrange the digits so that the sum is closer to 100? *Sample answer:* 80; $42 + 63 = 105$

2. Estimate the product of 21 and 9. How would you rearrange the digits so that the product is closer to 100? *Sample answer:* 180; $12 \times 9 = 108$

6. A good answer should include these points.
- A good target number would be less than or equal to 30.
- 1 should not be considered as a possibility for the divisor.

Explore **Form a product that is close to the target number 200.**

① Copy the diagram at the right. Think about some possible products that would get you close to 200.

② Roll the number cube and place the result in one of the blank boxes.

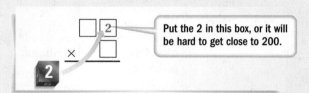

> Put the 2 in this box, or it will be hard to get close to 200.

③ Roll two more times to complete the diagram. Then find the product. Compare it with the target number 200.

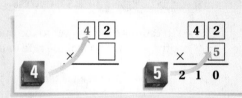

Your turn now **Refer to the target game shown above.**

3. Is it possible to rearrange the digits to get closer to the target product? If so, how would you rearrange them? Yes. *Sample answer:* $52 \times 4 = 208$.

4. Repeat Steps 1–3 above to form another product close to the target. Is it possible to rearrange your digits to get closer to the target product? If so, how would you rearrange them? Answers may vary.

Stop and Think

5. **Critical Thinking** Use the diagram at the right to play "target difference." Use a target number of 50. How would you arrange the digits 5, 1, 6, and 3? *Sample answer:* $65 - 13$.

6. **Writing** Write instructions telling how to play "target quotient" using the diagram at the right. What would be a good target number? Explain.
See margin.

SKILL CHECK
Round to the nearest ten.

1. 76   80
2. 183   180
3. 305   310

LESSON OBJECTIVE

Round to estimate with whole numbers.

PACING

Suggested Number of Days
Basic Course: 1 day
Average Course: 1 day
Advanced Course: 1 day
Block: 0.5 block with 1.1

TEACHING RESOURCES

For a complete list of Teaching Resources, see page 2B.

 TRANSPARENCY

Warm-Up Exercises for this lesson are available on a transparency.

2 TEACH

MOTIVATING THE LESSON

Estimating is a useful real-world skill. Expand on the biking example by having students do similar exercises using different maps.

TIPS FOR NEW TEACHERS

Make sure students understand the difference between rounding to a place value and rounding to the leading digit. See Tips for New Teachers in the *Chapter 1 Resource Book*.

LESSON 1.2

Whole Number Estimation

BEFORE — You calculated using whole numbers.

▶ **Now** — You'll round to estimate with whole numbers.

WHY? — So you can estimate traveling time, as in Example 1.

In the Real World

 **Word Watch**

leading digit, p. 13
compatible numbers, p. 13

Biking The map shows the time it takes to bike from place to place. About how long does it take to bike from the trailhead to the swinging bridge and then to the waterfall?

When you round to estimate a sum or difference, you should round the numbers to the same place value.

EXAMPLE 1 **Estimating Sums**

To estimate the answer to the question above about biking, round the time for each part of the ride to the same place value. Then add.

$$
\begin{array}{r} 28 \\ +114 \\ \hline \end{array}
\quad \textbf{Round each number to the nearest ten.} \quad
\begin{array}{r} 30 \\ +110 \\ \hline 140 \end{array}
$$

Round 28 up to 30.
Round 114 down to 110.

ANSWER It takes about 140 minutes to bike from the trailhead to the swinging bridge and then to the waterfall.

EXAMPLE 2 **Estimating Differences**

Use the map shown above. The travel time from the swinging bridge, past the waterfall, to the trailhead is 208 minutes. Estimate how much time it takes to bike from the waterfall to the trailhead.

Solution

$$
\begin{array}{r} 208 \\ -114 \\ \hline \end{array}
\quad \textbf{Round each number to the nearest hundred.} \quad
\begin{array}{r} 200 \\ -100 \\ \hline 100 \end{array}
$$

Round 208 down to 200.
Round 114 down to 100.

ANSWER It takes about 100 minutes to bike from the waterfall to the trailhead.

NCTM CURRICULUM STANDARDS
Standard 1: Make reasonable estimates
Standard 6: Solve problems in math and other contexts
Standard 10: Use representations to solve problems

Your turn now **Estimate the sum or difference.** Estimates may vary.

Your turn now **Estimate the sum or difference.** Estimates may vary.

1. $27 + 64$ 90   **2.** $59 + 623$ 700   **3.** $180 + 914$ 1100

4. $91 - 49$ 40   **5.** $612 - 83$ 500   **6.** $804 - 623$ 200

Using Leading Digits When you round to estimate a product, you should round the numbers to the place value of their *leading digits*. The **leading digit** of a whole number is the first digit at the left.

HELP with **Solving**

You can estimate an answer if you do not need an exact answer. You can also estimate to check whether a given answer is reasonable.

EXAMPLE 3 Estimating Products

Estimate to tell whether the given answer is reasonable.

a. $191 \times 11; 2101$

$200 \times 10 = 2000$ Round both numbers to the leading digit.

ANSWER The answer is reasonable because 2000 is close to 2101.

b. $1127 \times 4; 6508$

$1000 \times 4 = 4000$ Round 1127 to its leading digit.
Don't round the single digit.

ANSWER The answer is not reasonable because 4000 is not close to 6508.

Quotients When you estimate a quotient, you should look for compatible numbers. **Compatible numbers** are numbers that will make the calculation easier.

EXAMPLE 4 Estimating Quotients

Estimate the quotient $469 \div 59$.

$469 \div 59 \approx 469 \div 60$ Round the divisor to its leading digit.

$\approx 480 \div 60$ Replace the dividend with a number that is compatible with 60 and close to 469.

$= 8$ Divide. The quotient $469 \div 59$ is about 8.

HELP with **Reading**

The symbol $\approx$ can be read "is about equal to."

Your turn now **Estimate the product or quotient.** Estimates may vary.

7. 12×79 800   **8.** 879×31 27,000   **9.** 193×4 800

10. $191 \div 18$ 10   **11.** $213 \div 68$ 3   **12.** $972 \div 4$ 250

Example 1 Estimate the length of the longest path from school to playground. **about 140 ft**

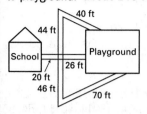

Example 2 Use the map above. Estimate the difference between the longest and shortest paths from school to playground. **about 90 ft**

Example 3 Estimate to tell if the answer is reasonable.
a. $295 \times 11 = 3140$
$300 \times 10 = 3000$; the answer is reasonable.
b. $989 \times 6 = 7250$
$1000 \times 6 = 6000$; the answer is not reasonable.

Example 4 Estimate the quotient $342 \div 71$. **5**

Differentiating Instruction

Alternative Teaching Strategy
Students may want to use multiplication and guess-and-check to estimate a quotient. In Example 4, they can round the divisor to 60. Then find 60×1, 60×2, 60×3, and so on, until they get close to the dividend.

 CONCEPT CHECK

Explain how to estimate the product of 195 and 28. **Round both numbers to the leading digit, or 200×30. Then multiply to get 6000.**

DAILY PUZZLER

Ten times the product of a number and 5 is 300. Find the number. **6**

ASSIGNMENT GUIDE

Basic Course
Day 1: SRH p. 686 Exs. 1–5;
pp. 14–15 Exs. 9–28, 33–38,
41, 43, 46–53, 55

Average Course
Day 1: pp. 14–15 Exs. 13–20,
25–34, 38–44, 46–51, 54, 55

Advanced Course
Day 1: pp. 14–15 Exs. 15–20,
27–45*, 47, 48, 54, 55

Block
pp. 14–15 Exs. 13–20, 25–34,
38–44, 46–51, 54, 55
(with 1.1)

HOMEWORK CHECK

When you review students' homework for this lesson, go over the following exercises to check understanding of key concepts.
Basic: 9, 11, 23, 24, 34
Average: 15, 16, 27, 31, 33
Advanced: 19, 30, 32, 33, 41

TEACHING TIP

For Exercises 17–20, students need to realize that there are different ways of rounding, that there is not just one correct estimate. For example, in Exercise 18 one student might estimate 879 + 94 as 900 + 100, while another might use 880 + 90.

Getting Ready to Practice

Vocabulary **Tell whether the numbers are compatible for division. If not, find a dividend compatible with the divisor.**

1. 16 ÷ 4 yes   **2.** 154 ÷ 20 no; 160   **3.** 7180 ÷ 90 no; 7200

Round each number to the given place value. Then estimate the sum or difference.

4. 33 + 87 (tens) 30, 90; 120   **5.** 624 − 139 (hundreds) 600, 100; 500

6. 2114 − 872 (hundreds)
2100, 900; 1200   **7.** 3899 + 5782 (thousands)
4000, 6000; 10,000

8. Guided Problem Solving Hot dogs come in packages of 48. You buy 11 packages for a cookout. Estimate how many hot dogs you buy.

    ① What operation do you use to find the number of hot dogs?
       multiplication

    ② Round each number to an appropriate place value.
       50, 10

    ③ Estimate the total number of hot dogs.
       500 hotdogs

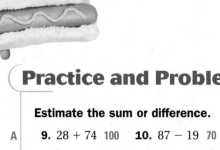

Practice and Problem Solving

Estimate the sum or difference. 9–20. Estimates may vary.

A **9.** 28 + 74 100   **10.** 87 − 19 70   **11.** 309 − 188 100 **12.** 285 + 307 600

13. 914 − 482 400 **14.** 682 + 297 1000 **15.** 78 + 233 300   **16.** 427 − 18 410

17. 618 − 89 500   **18.** 879 + 94 1000 **19.** 1129 + 403 1500   **20.** 2015 − 398 1600

Estimate the product or quotient. 21–32. Estimates may vary.

21. 38 × 2 80   **22.** 24 ÷ 5 5   **23.** 39 ÷ 4 10   **24.** 59 × 3 180

25. 702 ÷ 7 100   **26.** 21 × 31 600   **27.** 12 × 89 900   **28.** 63 ÷ 19 3

29. 123 × 41 4800 **30.** 498 ÷ 11 50   **31.** 597 ÷ 28 20   **32.** 287 × 12 3000

33. School Carnival Each student who went to a school carnival received 7 free game tickets. You know that 1337 free tickets were given out to students. About how many students went to the carnival?
about 200 students

34. Population Colby has 1811 residents. Arletta has 1227 residents. About how many more people live in Colby than in Arletta?
about 600 residents

HELP with Homework

Example	Exercises
1	9–20, 41, 42
2	9–20, 34, 41
3	21–32
4	21–32, 33

Online Resources
CLASSZONE.COM
· More Examples
· eTutorial Plus

Estimate to tell whether the given answer is reasonable.

B **35.** 9024 − 7182; 1842 yes **36.** 1104 + 4018; 6122 no **37.** 2912 ÷ 52; 560 no

38. 210 × 391; 82,110 yes **39.** 1982 × 35; 6937 no **40.** 6104 − 3971; 3133
no

North Carolina The map shows the direct distances in miles between cities in North Carolina.

41. The total distance from Greensboro to Raleigh to Charlotte is 198 miles. Estimate the distance from Raleigh to Charlotte. *Sample answer:* about 130 mi

42. Is it a longer drive from Greensboro to Raleigh to Charlotte, or from Greensboro to Charlotte to Raleigh?
from Greensboro to Charlotte to Raleigh

C **43.** **Painting** You are painting a fence and you don't want to make a second trip to the store for more paint. Should your estimate of the area each can of paint can cover be *high* or *low*? Explain. Low. Sample answer: You
want to be sure you have enough paint.

44. **Critical Thinking** You want to know whether 5 hours is enough time to read a book for class. To be sure you finish, should your estimate of the number of pages you can read per hour be *high* or *low*? Explain.
See margin.

45. **Challenge** Explain why you should not round down a single digit number when you estimate a product. *Sample answer:* Rounding a
single digit number down would give you a multiplier of zero.

Map: VIRGINIA, Greensboro, 68 miles, 83 miles, Raleigh, Charlotte, NORTH CAROLINA, SOUTH CAROLINA

Mixed Review

Find the sum or difference. *(Lesson 1.1)*

46. 429 − 52 377 **47.** 3011 − 947 **48.** 64 + 38 102 **49.** 629 + 85 714
2064

Basic Skills **Find the product.**

50. 9 × 7 63 **51.** 8 × 8 64 **52.** 12 × 6 72 **53.** 11 × 11 121

Test-Taking Practice

54. **Short Response** You are mailing 19 packages. It costs between $9 and $12 to mail each package. Estimate the total cost. Explain your method.
See margin.

55. **Multiple Choice** There are 8393 people at a football game. There are 5423 people sitting on the home team's side of the stadium. About how many people are sitting on the visiting team's side? D

A. 13,000 **B.** 12,000 **C.** 8000 **D.** 3000

15

SKILL CHECK
1. $3 \times 3 \times 3 \times 3 = \underline{?}$ 81
2. $5 \times 5 \times 5 = \underline{?}$ 125
3. $2 \times 2 \times 2 \times 2 = \underline{?}$ 16

LESSON OBJECTIVE
Find values of powers.

PACING
Suggested Number of Days
Basic Course: 1 day
Average Course: 1 day
Advanced Course: 1 day
Block: 0.5 block with 1.4

TEACHING RESOURCES
For a complete list of Teaching Resources, see page 2B.

 TRANSPARENCY
Warm-Up Exercises for this lesson are available on a transparency.

2 TEACH

MOTIVATING THE LESSON
Ask students if they like mathematical shortcuts, such as multiplication for repeated addition. Tell them they are about to learn a shortcut for repeated multiplication.

TIPS FOR NEW TEACHERS
Stress that the exponent of a power makes the product of the factors increase rapidly. Use 10 as an example. See Tips for New Teachers in the *Chapter 1 Resource Book.*

LESSON **1.3**

Powers and Exponents

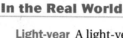

BEFORE	▶ Now	WHY?
You multiplied pairs of numbers.	You'll find values of powers.	So you can find the number of friends invited, as in Ex. 28.

 **Word Watch**
factor, p. 16
power, p. 16
base, p. 16
exponent, p. 16

In the Real World

Light-year A light-year is the distance light travels in one year. Astronomers estimate that the distance across the Virgo Spiral Galaxy is about 100,000 light-years. You can write 100,000 as a product.

$$100{,}000 = 10 \times 10 \times 10 \times 10 \times 10$$

This product has five *factors* of 10. When whole numbers other than zero are multiplied together, each number is a **factor** of the product. To write a product that has a repeated factor, you can use a **power**.

Powers, Bases, and Exponents

The **base** of the power is the repeated factor and the **exponent** is the number of times the factor is repeated.

$$\underset{\text{power}}{\underbrace{6}^{\,3}} \quad = \quad \underset{\text{There are 3 factors.}}{\underbrace{6 \times 6 \times 6}}$$

base ↗   exponent ↖

EXAMPLE 1 **Writing a Power**

Use the distance across the Virgo Spiral Galaxy given above. Write the distance as a power.

$$10 \times 10 \times 10 \times 10 \times 10 = 10^5$$ ◁ There are 5 factors.

ANSWER The distance across the galaxy is about 10^5 light-years.

Your turn now Write the product as a power.
1. $8 \times 8 \times 8$ 8^3 **2.** $6 \times 6 \times 6 \times 6$ 6^4 **3.** $20 \times 20 \times 20$ 20^3

NCTM CURRICULUM STANDARDS
Standard 1: Understand relationships among numbers; Understand meanings of operations
Standard 2: Understand patterns

Reading Powers When powers have an exponent of 2, the base is "squared." When powers have an exponent of 3, the base is "cubed."

3^2 is read "3 to the **second** power," or "3 **squared**."

4^3 is read "4 to the **third** power," or "4 **cubed**."

2^5 is read "2 to the **fifth** power."

EXAMPLE 2 Finding the Value of a Power

a. Find the value of five cubed.

$$5^3 = 5 \times 5 \times 5 \qquad \text{Write 5 as a factor three times.}$$

$$= 125 \qquad \text{Multiply.}$$

b. Find the value of two to the sixth power.

$$2^6 = 2 \times 2 \times 2 \times 2 \times 2 \times 2 \qquad \text{Write 2 as a factor six times.}$$

$$= 64 \qquad \text{Multiply.}$$

EXAMPLE 3 Powers in Real-World Problems

Telephone Calls You need to contact members of your softball league. You call 4 members in the morning. Those 4 people each call 4 more people in the afternoon. That night, those additional people each call 4 others. How many people are called that night?

Solution

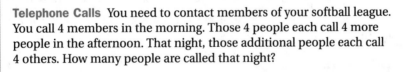

$$4 \qquad \times \qquad 4 \qquad \times \qquad 4 \qquad = 4^3 = 64$$

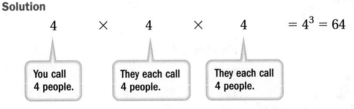

| You call 4 people. | They each call 4 people. | They each call 4 people. |

ANSWER That night, 64 people are called.

Your turn now Write the power as a product. Then find the value.

4. 11^2 **5.** 5^4 **6.** 1^7 **7.** 6^2

8. 7 squared $7 \times 7 = 49$ **9.** 3 to the fourth power
$3 \times 3 \times 3 \times 3 = 81$

4. $11 \times 11 = 121$

5. $5 \times 5 \times 5 \times 5 = 625$

6. $1 \times 1 \times 1 \times 1 \times 1 \times 1 \times 1 = 1$

7. $6 \times 6 = 36$

③ APPLY

ASSIGNMENT GUIDE

Basic Course
Day 1: pp. 18–19 Exs. 7–12, 14–25, 28–33, 38–40, 43–53

Average Course
Day 1: pp. 18–19 Exs. 7–13, 18–29, 34–41, 44–50, 53, 54

Advanced Course
Day 1: pp. 18–19 Exs. 10–13, 18–29, 36–42*, 44–48, 53, 54

Block
pp. 18–19 Exs. 7–13, 18–29, 34–41, 44–50, 53, 54 (with 1.4)

EXTRA PRACTICE

• Student Edition, p. 708
• Chapter 1 Resource Book, pp. 27–29
• Test and Practice Generator

② TRANSPARENCY

Even-numbered answers are available on transparencies.

HOMEWORK CHECK

When you review students' homework for this lesson, go over the following exercises to check understanding of key concepts.
Basic: 7, 11, 15, 18, 28
Average: 10, 12, 18, 20, 28
Advanced: 11, 13, 27, 28, 41

TEACHING TIP

For Exercises 14–27, encourage students to write the power as a product before doing each of these exercises.

MATH REASONING

For Exercise 28, a tree diagram may be a good organizer to help students find the value of the power.

Getting Ready to Practice

Vocabulary Tell whether what is highlighted in red is a *power*, a *base*, or an *exponent*. Then find the value of the power.

1. 3^3 base; 27   **2.** 9^2 power; 81   **3.** 1^4 exponent; 1

Which power is equal to the given product or power?

4. $2 \times 2 \times 2$ B   **A.** 2^2 **B.** 2^3 **C.** 3^2 **D.** 3^3

5. 5 squared B   **A.** 5^4 **B.** 5^2 **C.** 4^5 **D.** 2^5

6. **Classroom Seating** A classroom has 6 rows of seats. Each row has 6 seats. How many seats are in the classroom? Write your answer as a power. Then find the value of the power. $6^2 = 36$ seats

Practice and Problem Solving

with Homework

Example	Exercises
1	7–12
2	13–27, 29
3	28, 41

Online Resources
CLASSZONE.COM
· More Examples
· eTutorial Plus

Write the product as a power.

7. 8×8 8^2 **8.** $12 \times 12 \times 12$ 12^3 **9.** $9 \times 9 \times 9 \times 9$ 9^4

10. $4 \times 4 \times 4 \times 4 \times 4$ 4^5 **11.** $7 \times 7 \times 7 \times 7$ 7^4 **12.** $3 \times 3 \times 3 \times 3$ 3^4

13. **Find the Error** Describe and correct the error in the solution.
Sample answer: 4^3 means $4 \times 4 \times 4$, not 4×3; $4 \times 4 \times 4 = 64$.

$$4^3 = 4 \times 3$$
$$= 12$$

Find the value of the power.

14. 7^2 49   **15.** 12^2 144   **16.** 6^3 216   **17.** 100^2 10,000

18. 3^5 243   **19.** 2^5 32   **20.** 10^4 10,000   **21.** 1^6 1

22. 4 squared   16   **23.** 8 squared   64   **24.** 2 cubed   8   **25.** 10 cubed   1000

26. two to the seventh power   128   **27.** 10 to the sixth power   1,000,000

28. **Invitations** On Monday, you invited 2 friends to your party. On Tuesday, each friend invited 2 other friends. On Friday, each of those friends invited 2 more friends. How many people were invited on Friday? Write your answer as a power. Then find the value of the power. $2^3 = 8$

29. **Critical Thinking** Find the value of 1^8, 1^9, and 1^{10}. What can you say about the value of any power of 1? 1, 1, 1; the value is 1.

Tell which power has a greater value.

B **30.** 2^3 or 3^2 3^2 **31.** 4^3 or 6^2 4^3 **32.** 1^4 or 3^3 3^3 **33.** 10^3 or 13^2 10^3

34. 10^2 or 8^3 8^3 **35.** 5^3 or 1^5 5^3 **36.** 3^4 or 11^2 11^2 **37.** 24^5 or 25^5 25^5

Tiling **You are covering a plant stand with tiles that measure 1 inch by 1 inch. The plant stand measures 6 inches by 6 inches.**

38. How many square tiles do you need? Write your answer as a power. Then find the value.
$6^2 = 36$; 36 tiles

39. Suppose another stand measures 8 inches by 8 inches. How many tiles will you need to cover it? 64 tiles

40. **Geometry** Draw the next two figures in the pattern shown. Then copy and complete the table.

Number of small squares	1	4	9	?	?
Written as a power	1^2	2^2	?	?	?

16 25
3^2 4^2 5^2

C **41.** Find the total number of people called in Example 3 on page 17.
84 people

42. **Challenge** Write 256 as a power in three different ways.
16^2, 4^4, 2^8

Mixed Review

Find the next two numbers in the pattern. *(Lesson 1.1)*

43. 20, 17, 14, 11, _?_, _?_ 8, 5   **44.** 1, 2, 4, 8, _?_, _?_ 16, 32

Estimate the sum, difference, product, or quotient. *(Lesson 1.2)*

45. $157 + 38$ 200   **46.** $672 - 484$ 190   **47.** 72×5 350   **48.** $179 \div 18$ 10

Basic Skills **Identify the place value of the red digit.**

49. 98 tens   **50.** 1264 thousands   **51.** 9035 hundreds   **52.** 72,406 ten thousands

Test-Taking Practice

53. Multiple Choice Which power has a value of 25? C

A. 2^3 **B.** 2^5 **C.** 5^2 **D.** 5^3

54. Multiple Choice You stack boxes so that they are 7 high, 7 wide, and 7 long. How many boxes do you stack? H

F. 21   **G.** 49   **H.** 343   **I.** 2401

ASSESSMENT RESOURCES

For more assessment resources, see:
- Assessment Book
- Test and Practice Generator

MINI-QUIZ

Write the product as a power.
1. $6 \times 6 \times 6 \times 6 \times 6$ 6^5
2. $4 \times 4 \times 4$ 4^3

Find the value of the power.
3. 5^4 **625**
4. 4^5 **1024**
5. 1^7 **1**
6. 10^4 **10,000**
7. three to the fourth power **81**
8. 7 cubed **343**

Tell which power has the greater value.
9. 2^7 or 4^3 2^7
10. 10^3 or 25^2 10^3

5 FOLLOW-UP

RETEACHING/REMEDIATION
- Study Guide in Chapter 1 Resource Book, pp. 30–31
- eTutorial Plus Online
- Student Edition, p. 708
- Lesson Practice in Chapter 1 Resource Book, pp. 27–29

CHALLENGE/ENRICHMENT
- Challenge Practice in Chapter 1 Resource Book, p. 32
- Teacher's Edition, p. 2F

ENGLISH LEARNER SUPPORT
- Spanish Study Guide
- Multi-Language Glossary
- Chapter Audio Summaries CDs

CALCULATOR

Finding Values of Powers

GOAL Use a calculator to find values of expressions that involve powers.

Example **You can use the power key ⌃ to evaluate powers.**

A *byte* is a term used to describe a small unit of information stored in a computer's memory. For example, it takes one byte to store one character, such as a number or a letter. A *kilobyte* is defined as 2^{10} bytes. If a computer file is storing one kilobyte of data, how many characters can it be storing?

Solution

To find the value of 2^{10}, use the power key ⌃.

Keystrokes	Display
2 ⌃ 10 =	1024

ANSWER One kilobyte is equal to 1024 bytes, so the file can be storing 1024 characters.

HELP with Technology

The keystrokes shown here may not be the same as on your calculator. See your calculator's instruction manual for alternative keystrokes.

Your turn now **Use a calculator to find the value of the power.**

1. 5^8 390,625 **2.** 3^{12} 531,441 **3.** 4^{10} 1,048,576 **4.** 7^7 823,543

5. 41^4 2,825,761 **6.** 15^3 3375 **7.** 24^6 191,102,976 **8.** 96^5 8,153,726,976

9. 348^3 42,144,192 **10.** 832^2 692,224 **11.** 145^4 442,050,625 **12.** 627^2 393,129

13. twenty-seven cubed 19,683 **14.** eighty-four squared 7056

15. nineteen to the fifth power 2,476,099 **16.** twenty-four to the third power 13,824

Recall from the example that a computer uses one byte of memory to store one character of data.

17. A megabyte is defined as 2^{20} bytes. If a disk can store one megabyte of data, how many characters can it store? 1,048,576

18. A gigabyte is defined as 2^{26} bytes. If a disk can store one gigabyte of data, how many characters can it store? 67,108,864

NCTM CURRICULUM STANDARDS
Standard 1: Understand meanings of operations
Standard 6: Solve problems in math and other contexts

Order of Operations

LESSON 1.4

BEFORE
You found values with one operation.

Now
You'll evaluate expressions using the order of operations.

WHY?
So you can calculate the cost of wrapping gifts, as in Ex. 46.

PLAN

SKILL CHECK
1. $12 - 3 + 5 = \underline{?}$ 14
2. $22 + 8 - 13 = \underline{?}$ 17
3. $9 + 15 - 14 = \underline{?}$ 10

Word Watch

numerical expression, p. 21
grouping symbols, p. 21
evaluate, p. 21
order of operations, p. 21

Expressions A **numerical expression** represents a particular value. It consists of numbers and operations to be performed. An expression can also involve **grouping symbols**, as shown below.

$$7 + (11 - 2)$$

Operations in parentheses are done first.

$$\frac{3 + 7}{9 - 4}$$

A fraction bar groups the numerator separate from the denominator.

You **evaluate** an expression by finding its value. To make sure everyone gets the same result, mathematicians use the **order of operations**.

Order of Operations

Note book

1. Evaluate expressions inside grouping symbols.
2. Evaluate powers.
3. Multiply and divide from left to right.
4. Add and subtract from left to right.

Watch Out!

In part (a) of Example 1, divide *before* multiplying because the division is on the left. In part (b), subtract *before* adding because the subtraction is on the left.

EXAMPLE 1 **Using the Order of Operations**

a. $14 - 2 \times 5 = 14 - 10$ First multiply 2 and 5.

$\qquad = 4$ Then subtract 10 from 14.

b. $11 - 8 + 2 = 3 + 2$ First subtract 8 from 11.

$\qquad = 5$ Then add 3 and 2.

c. $16 + 4 \div 2 - 6 = 16 + 2 - 6$ First divide 4 by 2.

$\qquad = 18 - 6$ Next add 16 and 2.

$\qquad = 12$ Then subtract 6 from 18.

LESSON OBJECTIVE
Use the order of operations.

PACING
Suggested Number of Days
Basic Course: 1 day
Average Course: 1 day
Advanced Course: 1 day
Block: 0.5 block with 1.3

TEACHING RESOURCES
For a complete list of Teaching Resources, see page 2B.

TRANSPARENCY
Warm-Up Exercises for this lesson are available on a transparency.

TEACH

MOTIVATING THE LESSON
Ask students to suggest real-world activities that require an order of operations, such as putting on socks and then shoes.

TIPS FOR NEW TEACHERS
A mnemonic for remembering the order of operations is *Please Excuse My Dear Aunt Sally*, where *P* is parentheses, *E* is exponents, *M* is multiply, *D* is divide, *A* is add, and *S* is subtract. See Tips for New Teachers in the *Chapter 1 Resource Book*.

NCTM CURRICULUM STANDARDS
Standard 1: Understand how operations are related; Compute fluently
Standard 6: Solve problems in math and other contexts

Lesson 1.4   Order of Operations   **21**

NOTETAKING

Students may have trouble remembering the order of operations. Suggest that they list the order in their notebooks for reference.

Differentiating **Instruction**

Less Proficient Students For students who are having difficulty evaluating expressions like $9 - 2 \times 2$, suggest that they add parentheses to show the correct order of operations, $9 - (2 \times 2)$.

 CONCEPT CHECK

Evaluate $36 \div 3 \times 6 + (10 - 4)$.
78

 DAILY PUZZLER

Insert parentheses to make the statement true.
$48 \div 4 \times 4 + 8 \div 2 + 2 = 5$
$48 \div (4 \times 4) + 8 \div (2 + 2) = 5$

EXAMPLE 2 Powers and Grouping Symbols

a. $4 + 2^3 = 4 + 8$ First evaluate the power.

$\qquad = 12$ Then add.

b. $(3 + 1) \times 5 = 4 \times 5$ First evaluate inside grouping symbols.

$\qquad = 20$ Then multiply.

c. $\dfrac{8 + 6}{5 - 3} = \dfrac{14}{2}$ Evaluate the numerator and the denominator.

$\qquad = 7$ Then divide.

Your turn now Evaluate the expression.

1. $9 - 7 + 3$ **5**
2. $8 + 4 \times 3$ **20**
3. $24 - 8 \times 2 + 9$ **17**
4. $21 - 4^2$ **5**
5. $4 \times (6 - 1)$ **20**
6. $(24 - 8) \times 2 + 9$ **41**
7. $6 + 1 \times 5^2$ **31**
8. $\dfrac{11 + 19}{3}$ **10**
9. $\dfrac{2 + 18}{9 - 4}$ **4**

What do you think?

Science

■ **Aquarium**

The Florida Aquarium in Tampa offers a tour called DolphinQuest. If the cost is $15 per adult and $10 per person under the age of 13, how much would it cost for you to go with 2 adults and 4 friends who are 11 years old?

Sample answer: **$70**

EXAMPLE 3 Solving Multi-Step Problems

Aquarium Your class is visiting an aquarium. Admission is $16 per adult and $9 per student. There are 3 adults and 34 students. What is the total cost of admission?

Solution

1 Multiply to find the cost of admission for the **adults**.

$\qquad$ 3 adults $\times$ $16 per adult = **$48**

2 Multiply to find the cost of admission for the **students**.

$\qquad$ 34 students $\times$ $9 per student = **$306**

3 Add the **adult** cost and the **student** cost.

$\qquad$ $48 + $306 = **$354**

ANSWER The total cost of admission is $354.

Your turn now Use the situation in Example 3.

10. If 4 more adults decide to go on the trip, what will be the new total cost of admission? **$418**

1.4 Exercises
More Practice, p. 708

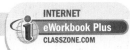
INTERNET
eWorkbook Plus
CLASSZONE.COM

Getting Ready to Practice

1. Vocabulary Parentheses and fraction bars are examples of ? .

grouping symbols

Evaluate the expression.

2. $9 - 8 + 5$ 6

3. $10 - 4 \div 2$ 8

4. 4×3^2 36

5. $4 \times (6 \div 3)$ 8

6. $3 \times (7 - 5) + 4$ 10

7. $\frac{20}{2 + 8}$ 2

8. Guided Problem Solving A compact disc club charges $6 per CD for your first 5 CDs and $10 per CD for your next 4 CDs. If you complete the offer, how much money will you spend?

(1 What is the total cost for the first 5 CDs? $30

(2 What is the total cost for the next 4 CDs? $40

(3 How much money will you spend altogether? $70

Practice and Problem Solving

HELP with Homework

Example	Exercises
1	9–14, 28, 29
2	15–26
3	27, 46, 47

Online Resources
CLASSZONE.COM
· More Examples
· eTutorial Plus

Evaluate the expression.

A

9. $7 - 5 + 1$ 3

10. $6 + 3 - 4$ 5

11. $9 \times 2 \div 3$ 6

12. $4 + 2 \times 3$ 10

13. $9 - 2 \times 4$ 1

14. $7 + 7 \div 7$ 8

15. $8 + 4^2$ 24

16. 5×10^3 5000

17. $12 \div (11 - 5)$ 2

18. $(2 + 8) \times 3$ 30

19. $\frac{24}{13 - 5}$ 3

20. $\frac{8 + 6}{7}$ 2

21. $10 - 4 \times 1 + 7$ 13

22. $18 \div 3 - 1 \times 4$ 2

23. $6 \times (7 - 5) \div 3$ 4

24. $(8 \div 2) + 2 \times 6$ 16

25. $\frac{4^3}{2 + 6}$ 8

26. $\frac{40 - 4}{6 + 3}$ 4

27. Writing You buy 3 pens for $4 each using your $30 gift card. Find the amount of money you have left to spend on the gift card. Then explain how you solved the problem.

$18; multiply $4 by 3. Subtract the product from $30.

Lesson 1.4   Order of Operations   23

3 APPLY

ASSIGNMENT GUIDE

Basic Course
Day 1: SRH p. 689 Exs. 1–4, 9–12; pp. 23–25 Exs. 9–27, 30–32, 36–42, 46, 55–63

Average Course
Day 1: pp. 23–25 Exs. 12–29, 33–39, 43–47, 54–64

Advanced Course
Day 1: pp. 23–25 Exs. 18–29, 33–35, 40–57*, 63, 64

Block
pp. 23–25 Exs. 12–29, 33–39, 43–47, 54–64 (with 1.3)

EXTRA PRACTICE
• Student Edition, p. 708
• Chapter 1 Resource Book, pp. 37–39
• Test and Practice Generator

TRANSPARENCY
Even-numbered answers are available on transparencies.

HOMEWORK CHECK
When you review students' homework for this lesson, go over the following exercises to check understanding of key concepts.
Basic: 10, 13, 18, 20, 27
Average: 12, 14, 23, 25, 46
Advanced: 14, 19, 25, 46, 47

COMMON ERROR
Some students may have difficulty with Exercise 21. Remind them that because multiplication is done before subtraction, this problem is equivalent to $10 - (4 \times 1) + 7$.

28. *Sample answer:* According to the order of operations, you divide before you add;

$6 + 12 \div 3 = 6 + 4 = 10.$

29. *Sample answer:* in order from left to right; The same rule applies: multiply and divide in order from left to right.

---

28. Find the Error Describe and correct the error in the solution.

$$\begin{aligned} 6 + 12 \div 3 &= 18 \div 3 \\ &= 6 \end{aligned}$$

29. Critical Thinking If the only operations in an expression are addition and subtraction, in what order do you perform the operations? What if the only operations are multiplication and division?

Tell whether the statement is *true* or *false*. If it is false, find the correct answer.

30. $8 + 3 \times 4 = 44$ **31.** $18 - 15 \div 3 = 1$ **32.** $4 \times (12 + 4) = 64$ true
     false; 20   false; 13

33. $15 - 2 + 11 = 24$ **34.** $72 - 6 + 4 = 62$ **35.** $3^2 \times 6 \div 3 = 18$ true
     true   false; 70

Estimation Match the expression with its closest estimate.

36. $150 - 3 \times 21$ C   **A.** 100

37. $10 + 3 \times 29$ A   **B.** 20

38. $5 + 102 \div 4$ D   **C.** 90

39. $12 \times 8 \div 4$ B   **D.** 30

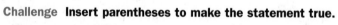

Technology Use a calculator to evaluate the expression.

40. $190 - 16 \times 7 + 45$ **41.** $162 \div 18 + 14 \times 12$ **42.** $84 - 78 \div 6 + 5$ 76
     123   177

43. $378 \div 3^2 - 7 \times 4$ 14   **44.** $11 \times 23 + 5 - 91$ **45.** $5^3 - 39 \div 3 + 2$ 114
                             167

46. Gifts You buy 3 rolls of gift wrap for $7 each, 4 rolls of ribbon for $3 each, and 5 packs of gift cards for $4 each. What is the total cost? $53

47. Seating One side of a movie theater has 20 rows with 4 seats per row. The other side has 18 rows with 6 seats per row. How many seats are there altogether?   188 seats

Challenge Insert parentheses to make the statement true.

48. $12 + 4 \times 4 = 64$ **49.** $8 - 2 \times 6 \div 3^2 = 4$ **50.** $5 + 9 \div 4 - 1 = 8$
     $(12 + 4) \times 4 = 64$ $(8 - 2) \times 6 \div 3^2 = 4$ $5 + 9 \div (4 - 1) = 8$

51. $2 \times 9 - 4 + 3 = 13$ **52.** $48 \div 8 - 2 + 6 = 4$ **53.** $3 \times 3 + 9 \div 9 = 4$
     $2 \times (9 - 4) + 3 = 13$ $48 \div (8 - 2 + 6) = 4$ $3 \times (3 + 9) \div 9 = 4$

54. Band Competition Your school band of 50 members is competing in a band competition. Each band member needs $10 for food. The band also rents 2 buses for $225 each. The cost of the buses will be split evenly among the band members. Write an expression for the total cost per student. Then find the total cost per student.

$10 + (2 \times 225) \div 50 = \$19$

Mixed Review

55. You pay $42 for 6 cases of fruit juice. How much does the juice cost per case? *(Lesson 1.1)* **$7**

Write the power as a product. Then find the value. *(Lesson 1.3)*

56. 10^2 **57.** 4^4 **58.** 7^3 **59.** 1^5
$10 \times 10 = 100$ $4 \times 4 \times 4 \times 4 = 256$

58. $7 \times 7 \times 7 = 343$

59. $1 \times 1 \times 1 \times 1 \times 1 = 1$

Basic Skills   **Order the numbers from least to greatest.**

60. 99, 19, 90, 9   **61.** 414, 41, 4, 404   **62.** 555, 50, 510, 505
     9, 19, 90, 99   4, 41, 404, 414   50, 505, 510, 555

Test-Taking Practice

63. Multiple Choice What is the first step in evaluating $3 + 5 \times 8 - 7$? **B**

A. $3 + 5$ **B.** 5×8 **C.** $8 - 7$ **D.** $3 + 7$

64. Multiple Choice Evaluate the expression $6 + 18 \div 3^2$. **F**

F. 8   **G.** 31   **H.** 42   **I.** 64

BRAIN GAME

Solve the Riddle

Match each numbered expression in the first column with the letter of the expression in the second column that has the same value. Then replace the number in each box with its matching letter to find the answer to the riddle.

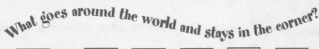
What goes around the world and stays in the corner?

| 3 | 4 | 1 | 3 | 5 | 2 |

1. $3 + 2 \div 1 - 4$ **T**

2. $4 - 2 + 9 \div 3$ **P**

3. $8 \div (1 \times 2) - 2$ **A**

4. $7 + (8 - 4 \times 2)$ **S**

5. $1 + 3 \times 4 - 3$ **M**

A STAMP

R. $(8 - 4 + 2) \div 2$

S. $0 + (15 - 1) \div 2$

T. $10 - (4 + 3) - 2$

E. $2 \times (12 - 8) + 5$

P. $(10 \div 5) \times 4 - 3$

M. $(7 - 4) \times 3 + 1$

A. $11 - 6 - (12 \div 4)$

---

4 ASSESS

ASSESSMENT RESOURCES
For more assessment resources, see:
- Assessment Book
- Test and Practice Generator

MINI-QUIZ
Evaluate the expression.

1. $8 - 4 + 5$ **9**

2. $56 \div 8 \times 2$ **14**

3. $4 + 3^3$ **31**

4. $24 \div (3 \times 2)$ **4**

5. $18 - 6 \times 2 + 7$ **13**

6. $\dfrac{2^4}{3 + 5}$ **2**

7. $4^2 + (8 + 2) - 9$ **17**

Tell whether the statement is *true* or *false*. If it is false, find the correct answer.

8. $24 - 6 \times 2 + 3 = 39$ **false; 15**

9. $15 + 4 - 5 \times 2 = 9$ **true**

10. $13 \times 2 - 2 + 3^2 = 1$ **false; 33**

5 FOLLOW-UP

RETEACHING/REMEDIATION
- Study Guide in Chapter 1 Resource Book, pp. 40–41
- eTutorial Plus Online
- Student Edition, p. 708
- Lesson Practice in Chapter 1 Resource Book, pp. 37–39

CHALLENGE/ENRICHMENT
- Challenge Practice in Chapter 1 Resource Book, p. 42
- Teacher's Edition, p. 2F

ENGLISH LEARNER SUPPORT
- Spanish Study Guide
- Multi-Language Glossary
- Chapter Audio Summaries CDs

LESSONS 1.1 TO 1.4

Notebook Review

Review the vocabulary definitions in your notebook.

Copy the review examples in your notebook. Then complete the exercises.

Check Your Definitions

leading digit, p. 13	base, p. 16	grouping symbols, p. 21
compatible numbers, p. 13	exponent, p. 16	evaluate, p. 21
factor, p. 16	numerical expression, p. 21	order of operations, p. 21
power, p. 16		

Use Your Vocabulary

1. Copy and complete: When using the order of operations, you multiply and ? from left to right before you add and ? from left to right. **divide; subtract**

2. Identify the base and the exponent in the power 9^5. **base: 9; exponent: 5**

1.1–1.2 Can you find exact answers and estimates?

Review **EXAMPLE** Find the exact answer.

a.
$$\begin{array}{r} \overset{1\,1}{986} \\ +\ 57 \\ \hline 1043 \end{array}$$

b.
$$\begin{array}{r} \overset{2\,9\,16}{3\cancel{0}\cancel{6}} \\ -\ 47 \\ \hline 259 \end{array}$$

c.
$$\begin{array}{r} 75 \\ \times\ 42 \\ \hline 150 \\ 300 \\ \hline 3150 \end{array}$$

d.
$$\begin{array}{r} 94\ \text{R1} \\ 8)\overline{753} \\ 72 \\ \hline 33 \\ 32 \\ \hline 1 \end{array}$$

 Find the sum, difference, product, or quotient.

3. $746 + 389$ **1135**   4. $921 - 467$ **454**   5. 65×23 **1495**   6. $451 \div 7$ **64 R3**

 Review **EXAMPLE** Use rounding or compatible numbers to estimate.

a. $431 + 278 \approx 400 + 300 = 700$ **Round to the same place value.**

b. $136 - 49 \approx 140 - 50 = 90$ **Round to the same place value.**

c. $191 \times 43 \approx 200 \times 40 = 8000$ **Round to the leading digit.**

d. $182 \div 21 \approx 180 \div 20 = 9$ **Round the divisor to the leading digit. Find a compatible dividend.**

Estimate the sum, difference, product, or quotient. Estimates may vary.

7. $123 + 68$ **190**   8. $882 - 407$ **470**   9. 87×13 **900**   10. $341 \div 5$ **68**

1.3–1.4 Can you find values of powers and expressions?

 EXAMPLE

$2^4 = 2 \times 2 \times 2 \times 2 = 16$ Write 2 as a factor four times. Multiply.

✓ **Find the value of the power.**   **11.** 5^2 25   **12.** 4 cubed 64

 EXAMPLE

$28 \div (9 - 5) + 3^2 = 28 \div 4 + 3^2$ Evaluate inside grouping symbols.

$= 28 \div 4 + 9$ Evaluate powers.

$= 7 + 9$ Multiply and divide from left to right.

$= 16$ Add and subtract from left to right.

✓ **Evaluate the expression.**   **13.** $4^2 + 18 \div 6$ **14.** $2 \times (3 + 8) - 14$
                                                    19   8

Stop and Think about Lessons 1.1–1.4

15. Estimation Will your estimate of a sum be high or low if you round both numbers up? if you round both numbers down? Explain.

15. High; low; if both numbers are rounded up, the estimate will be greater than the actual sum. If both numbers are rounded down, the estimate will be less than the actual sum.

Review Quiz 1

Find the sum, difference, product, or quotient.

1. $29 + 35$ 64   **2.** $90 - 34$ 56   **3.** 32×18 576   **4.** $124 \div 8$
                                                                                        15 R4

Estimate the sum, difference, product, or quotient. Estimates may vary.

5. $284 - 48$ 230   **6.** 147×5 750   **7.** $1004 + 678$ 1700   **8.** $163 \div 4$ 40

Find the value of the power.

9. 10^2 100   **10.** 7^3 343   **11.** 2^6 64   **12.** 10^5 100,000

Evaluate the expression.

13. $9 + 7 \times 4$ 37   **14.** $27 \div 3^2 + 5$ 8   **15.** $3 \times (32 - 7)$ 75

16. Phone Card Your phone card has 404 minutes on it. You use 189 minutes. Estimate how many minutes your card has left.

about 200 min

PLAN

EXPLORE THE CONCEPT

- Students will use symbols to represent quantities that may vary.
- This activity leads into the concept of a variable as the question mark is replaced by a letter in Lesson 1.5.

MATERIALS

Each group will need a number cube.

RECOMMENDED TIME

Work activity: 10 min
Discuss results: 5 min

GROUPING

Students should work in groups of two.

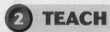 **TEACH**

TIPS FOR SUCCESS

Students will evaluate these expressions more successfully if they remember the order of operations.

 **CLOSE**

🔍 KEY DISCOVERY

A symbol can be used to represent a quantity that has different values.

ASSESSMENT

Evaluate for 1, 2, 3, 4, 5, and 6.
1. $4 \cdot \underline{?} - 2$ 2, 6, 10, 14, 18, 22
2. $120 \div \underline{?}$ 120, 60, 40, 30, 24, 20

1.5 **Hands-on Activity**

GOAL Use symbols to represent quantities that may vary.

MATERIALS · number cube

Representing Quantities

When an unknown quantity might have several different values, you can use a symbol to represent the quantity.

Explore **Roll a number cube to choose values for an unknown quantity.**

		Player 1	Player 2
1	Start with an expression.	$2 \times \boxed{?} - 1$	$4 \times \boxed{?}$
2	Roll the number cube.	**5**	**3**
3	Replace the unknown with the number you roll.	$2 \times 5 - 1$	4×3
4	Evaluate the expression.	9	12

Your turn now **Work with a partner. Use each expression once.**

1. Take turns choosing an expression below and evaluating it following steps 2 through 4 above. Add the values from all your turns to get your score. The player with the highest score is the winner. **Answers may vary.**

   A. $3 \times \boxed{?} - 2$ **B.** $3 + \boxed{?}$ **C.** $17 - 2 \times \boxed{?}$ **D.** $6 \times \boxed{?} \div 3$

   E. $60 \div \boxed{?}$ **F.** $5 \times \boxed{?} - 4$ **G.** $8 \times \boxed{?} - 5$ **H.** $180 \div (3 \times \boxed{?})$

Stop and Think

2. **Critical Thinking** How many different values are possible for each expression when you use a number cube to choose values for the unknown quantity? **6**

3. **Writing** For any given expression, does rolling a high number like 5 always result in a greater value than rolling a low number like 2? Explain.
   No. Sample answer: If 5 is a divisor or being subtracted, it will produce a quotient or difference that is less than if 2 is the divisor or being subtracted.

NCTM CURRICULUM STANDARDS
Standard 2: Analyze situations using algebraic symbols
Standard 7: Investigate mathematical conjectures

Variables and Expressions

BEFORE	▶ **Now**	**WHY?**
You evaluated numerical expressions.	You'll evaluate expressions that involve variables.	So you can find distance traveled while rafting, as in Ex. 45.

(**In the Real World**

Dog's Age The following *rule of thumb* is a useful way to compare the age of an adult dog to the age of a human.

> *Multiply the dog's age by 4 and then add 15.*

Call this the dog's age in "dog years." How many dog years old is a dog that is 4 years old? 6 years old? 10 years old? In Example 2 on page 30 you will use a variable expression to find out.

Variable Expressions A **variable** is a symbol, usually a letter, that represents one or more numbers. A **variable expression** consists of numbers, variables, and the operations to be performed. To evaluate a variable expression, substitute a number for each variable and evaluate the resulting numerical expression.

EXAMPLE 1 **Evaluating Expressions**

a. Evaluate $4 + t$, when $t = 2$.

$4 + t = 4 + 2$ Substitute 2 for t.

$ = 6$ Add.

b. Evaluate $x \div 8$, when $x = 16$.

$x \div 8 = 16 \div 8$ Substitute 16 for x.

$ = 2$ Divide.

Your turn now   Evaluate the expression.

1. $s + 9$, when $s = 7$ **16**

2. $13 - r$, when $r = 5$ **8**

3. $x - 3$, when $x = 8$ **5**

4. $m \div 4$, when $m = 32$ **8**

Lesson 1.5   Variables and Expressions   **29**

Multiplication and Variables To avoid confusion between the multiplication symbol $\times$ and the variable x, you should express multiplication with variables in one of the following ways.

multiplication dot	parentheses	no symbol
$3 \cdot x$	$3(x)$	$3x$

EXAMPLE 2 **Evaluating Multiplication Expressions**

To answer the questions about dog years at the top of page 29, evaluate the expression $4y + 15$ when $y = 4$, $y = 6$, and $y = 10$.

① Choose values for y (age in years).	② Substitute for y in the expression $4y + 15$.	③ Evaluate the expression to find the age in dog years.
4	$4 \cdot 4 + 15$	31
6	$4 \cdot 6 + 15$	39
10	$4 \cdot 10 + 15$	55

ANSWER A 4-year-old dog is 31 dog years old. A 6-year-old dog is 39 dog years old. A 10-year-old dog is 55 dog years old.

EXAMPLE 3 **Expressions with Two Variables**

Evaluate the expression when $x = 8$ and $y = 2$.

a. $x + y = 8 + 2$ Substitute 8 for x and 2 for y.

      $= 10$ Add.

b. $x - y^2 = 8 - 2^2$ Substitute 8 for x and 2 for y.

      $= 8 - 4$ Evaluate the power.

      $= 4$ Subtract.

 **with Notetaking**

You may want to include part (b) of Example 3 in your notebook as a reminder to use the order of operations when evaluating a variable expression.

Your turn now Evaluate the expression when $m = 10$ and $n = 5$.

5. $3m$ 30   **6.** $11n$ 55   **7.** $2n + 4$ 14   **8.** $25 - 2m$ 5

9. $m - n$ 5   **10.** $m + 3n$ 25   **11.** $26 - n^2$ 1   **12.** $n + 9 - m$ 4

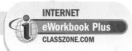
INTERNET
eWorkbook Plus
CLASSZONE.COM

Getting Ready to Practice

1. **Vocabulary** Identify the variable in the expression $5a - 2$. *a*

2. What operation is represented by the dot in $10 + 7 \cdot x$? *multiplication*

3. **Find the Error** Describe and correct the error in evaluating $3t$ when $t = 2$.
   Sample answer: 3(2) means to multiply 3 and 2.
   $3t = 3(2) = 6$

   $$\begin{array}{l} 3t = 3(2) \\ = 32 \end{array}$$

Evaluate the expression when $m = 9$ and $n = 3$.

4. $n + 8$ 11
5. $7m$ 63
6. $n \div 1$ 3
7. $14 - n$ 11
8. $m - n$ 6
9. $m + n$ 12
10. $m \div n$ 3
11. $m + 2n$ 15

12. **Boots** Let h represent your height in inches while barefoot. You can use the expression $2 + h$ to represent your height while wearing boots with 2-inch heels. Use the expression to find how tall you are while wearing boots if you are 53 inches tall while barefoot. 55 in.

Practice and Problem Solving

with Homework

Example	Exercises
1	13–18, 27, 29–31
2	19–26, 28
3	32–44

Online Resources
CLASSZONE.COM
· More Examples
· eTutorial Plus

Evaluate the expression.

A
13. $9 + x$, when $x = 7$ 16
14. $t + 5$, when $t = 8$ 13
15. $y - 7$, when $y = 13$ 6
16. $12 - n$, when $n = 3$ 9
17. $w \div 4$, when $w = 20$ 5
18. $18 \div s$, when $s = 3$ 6
19. $r \cdot 9$, when $r = 5$ 45
20. $6m$, when $m = 10$ 60
21. $16 - a^2$, when $a = 3$ 7
22. $d^2 - 8$, when $d = 5$ 17
23. $5 + 12 \div u$, when $u = 6$ 7
24. $8 \div w + 5$, when $w = 2$ 9
25. $2c - 5$, when $c = 4$ 3
26. $13 + 4z$, when $z = 11$ 57

27. **Weather** You can use the expression $n \div 5$ to estimate how far, in miles, you are from lightning. The variable n represents the number of seconds from when you see the lightning to when you hear thunder. How far away is the lightning when $n = 20$?
   4 mi

ASSIGNMENT GUIDE
Basic Course
Day 1: pp. 31–33 Exs. 13–18, 27, 29–31, 45, 59, 60, 64–67, 72
Day 2: pp. 31–33 Exs. 19–26, 28, 33–40, 46, 49, 51, 61, 62, 68–71
Average Course
Day 1: pp. 31–33 Exs. 13–18, 27, 29, 30, 45–47, 50–52, 63, 68–72
Day 2: pp. 31–33 Exs. 19–26, 28, 32–40, 48, 54–56, 59–62, 73
Advanced Course
Day 1: pp. 31–33 Exs. 15–18, 27, 30, 31, 45–52, 57*, 59–63, 72
Day 2: pp. 31–33 Exs. 21–26, 28, 32, 37–44, 53–56, 58*, 73
Block
pp. 31–33 Exs. 13–30, 32–40, 45–48, 50–52, 54–56, 59–63, 68–73

EXTRA PRACTICE
• Student Edition, p. 708
• Chapter 1 Resource Book, pp. 46–48
• Test and Practice Generator

TRANSPARENCY
Even-numbered answers are available on transparencies.

HOMEWORK CHECK
When you review students' homework for this lesson, go over the following exercises to check understanding of key concepts.
Basic: 13, 21, 24, 29, 37
Average: 15, 22, 25, 30, 38
Advanced: 17, 23, 26, 32, 43

45. 18 mi; *Sample answer:* The rate, *r*, is 6 miles per hour and the time, *t*, is 3 hours. Substitute these values into the expression $r \cdot t$ and multiply.

48. *Sample answer:* Substitute 7 for *u* and 9 for *w*. Then multiply 2 by 7, and 5 by 9. Then add the products.

$2 \cdot 7 + 5 \cdot 9 = 14 + 45 = 59$

Recreation

Rafting

Sections of whitewater river are rated on a scale of 1 to 6. A rating of 1 means the current is slow and it's easy to raft. A rating of 6 means it's too dangerous to raft. What rating would you give to a river section that is rafted only by expert rafters? Explain. *Sample answer:* 5; It would be difficult to raft, but a challenge for expert rafters.

28. Dog Years Your dog is five years old. You can estimate a dog's age in dog years by using the expression $4y + 15$, where *y* represents the dog's age. How old is your dog in dog years? **35 years old**

Geometry **The perimeter of a figure is the sum of the lengths of its sides. Find the perimeter of the triangle when $x = 3$ feet.**

29. 12 ft, 4 ft, 5 ft, *x*   **30.** 11 ft, 4 ft, 4 ft, *x*   **31.** 14 ft, 6 ft, 5 ft, *x*

32. Find the Error Describe and correct the error in evaluating $6y + x$, when $x = 3$ and $y = 5$.

$$\begin{aligned} 6y + x &= 6 \cdot 3 + 5 \\ &= 18 + 5 \\ &= 23 \end{aligned}$$

Sample answer: 3 was substituted for *y* and 5 for *x*. It should be just the opposite. $6y + x = 6 \cdot 5 + 3 = 30 + 3 = 33$

Evaluate the expression when $x = 6$ and $y = 3$.

33. $x + y$ 9   **34.** $x - y$ 3   **35.** $x \div y$ 2   **36.** $x \cdot y$ 18

37. $4x - y$ 21   **38.** $x + 5y$ 21   **39.** $y + 2x$ 15   **40.** $3y - x$ 3

41. $2x \cdot y$ 36   **42.** $y + 18 \div x$ 6   **43.** $x - 18 \div y^2$ 4   **44.** $y - 2 + x^2$ 37

Extended Problem Solving **In Exercises 45–47, use the expression $r \cdot t$ to find how far you travel while rafting. The variable r is your speed, in miles per hour. The variable t is hours traveled.**

45. Explain How far do you travel if you raft at a speed of 6 miles per hour for 3 hours? Explain how you found your answer. **See margin.**

46. Calculate How far does your friend travel if she rafts at a speed of 8 miles per hour for 2 hours? **16 mi**

47. Compare Who travels *faster*, you or your friend? Who travels *farther*? **my friend; me**

48. Writing Explain how to evaluate the expression $2u + 5w$ when $u = 7$ and $w = 9$. **See margin.**

Evaluate the expression when $x = 6$, $y = 5$, and $z = 2$.

49. $x - z + y$ 9   **50.** $x \div z + y$ 8   **51.** $y \cdot (x - z)$ 20   **52.** $x + 2y + z$ 18

53. $x^2 + z - y$ 33   **54.** $x + y^2 - z$ 29   **55.** $xy - z$ 28   **56.** $x + yz$ 16

Challenge Use the table to find a rule that relates each number and its result. Write a variable expression to represent the rule for *n*.

57. *Sample answer:* Add 5 to the number to get the result; 9; $n + 5$.

57.

Number	Result
1	6
2	7
3	8
4	?
n	?

58. *Sample answer:* Multiply the number by 2 and add 1; 11; $2n + 1$.

58.

Number	Result
2	5
3	7
4	9
5	?
n	?

Mixed Review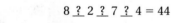

Evaluate the expression. *(Lesson 1.4)*

59. $8 + 6 \times 3$ **26**   **60.** $(24 - 6) \div 3$ **6** **61.** $18 - 3 \times 5$ **3**   **62.** $1 + 2^3$ **9**

Choose a Strategy Use a strategy from the list to solve the following problem. Explain your choice of strategy.

63. ×; +; ×; *sample answer:* Guess, Check, and Revise; It is the best choice of strategies of those listed.

63. Use the symbols $+$, $-$, $\times$, or $\div$ to make the following statement true. You may use a symbol more than once.

$$8 \; \underline{?} \; 2 \; \underline{?} \; 7 \; \underline{?} \; 4 = 44$$

Problem Solving Strategies
- Guess, Check, and Revise
- Make a List
- Draw a Diagram
- Work Backward

Basic Skills Tell whether the statement is *true* or *false*. If it is false, find the correct answer.

64. $9 \times 5 = 54$ false; 45   **65.** $7 + 4 = 11$ true   **66.** $10 \div 5 = 5$ false; 2   **67.** $17 - 8 = 9$ true

68. $8 + 6 = 14$ true   **69.** $48 \div 8 = 7$ false; 6   **70.** $13 - 5 = 6$ false; 8   **71.** $3 \times 7 = 21$ true

Test-Taking Practice

72. **Multiple Choice** You can stuff 8 envelopes per minute. The expression $8x$ represents the number of envelopes you can stuff in x minutes. Which expression represents the number of envelopes you can stuff in 16 minutes? **C**

A. $8 + 16$ **B.** $16 - 8$ **C.** $8 \cdot 16$ **D.** $16 \div 8$

73. $172; The number of weeks, *w*, is 14 and the amount you started with, *x*, is $32. Substitute 14 for *w* and 32 for *x* in the expression $10w + x$. Multiply 10 and 14, and then add $32 to get $172.

73. **Short Response** You have some money saved, and you plan to save an additional $10 per week to pay for a school trip. You can model this situation with the expression $10w + x$, where w is the number of weeks and x is the amount of money you start with. How much money will you have after 14 weeks if you start with $32? Explain how you found your answer.

4 ASSESS

ASSESSMENT RESOURCES
For more assessment resources, see:
- Assessment Book
- Test and Practice Generator

MINI-QUIZ
Evaluate the expression.
1. $y + 8$ for $y = 5$ **13**
2. $16 \div x$ for $x = 2$ **8**
3. $14 - a + 3$ for $a = 5$ **12**
4. $24 \div s + 6$ for $s = 4$ **12**
5. $20 - x^3$ for $x = 2$ **12**

Evaluate the expression for $x = 4$ and $y = 5$.
6. $y - x$ **1**
7. $2x - y$ **3**
8. $y - 12 \div x$ **2**
9. $x \cdot y^2$ **100**
10. $3xy$ **60**

5 FOLLOW-UP

RETEACHING/REMEDIATION
- Study Guide in Chapter 1 Resource Book, pp. 49–50
- eTutorial Plus Online
- Student Edition, p. 708
- Lesson Practice in Chapter 1 Resource Book, pp. 46–48

CHALLENGE/ENRICHMENT
- Challenge Practice in Chapter 1 Resource Book, p. 52
- Teacher's Edition, p. 2F

ENGLISH LEARNER SUPPORT
- Spanish Study Guide
- Multi-Language Glossary
- Chapter Audio Summaries CDs

Guess, Check, and Revise is an appropriate strategy for students to use when they do not have enough information. It allows them to try different numbers until they find a solution. An advantage to using this strategy is that students will learn that guessing is a useful and acceptable technique in mathematics. They will learn to analyze their first result so that their next attempts are "educated" guesses.

2 TEACH

GUIDING STUDENTS' WORK

Students may have difficulty with the order of operations when checking the guess in Step 3. Remind them that to simplify an expression, multiplication is done before addition. Be sure students understand why the number of notes cards rather than the number of calendars should be increased.

EXTRA EXAMPLES

Example Faeza paid the $60 bill for pizzas and soda. In all, 12 pizzas and sodas were purchased. A pizza costs $7 and a soda costs $1. How many pizzas and how many sodas were purchased? **8 pizzas and 4 sodas**

1.6 Problem Solving Strategies

- Draw a Diagram
- Make a List
- Make a Table
- Work Backward
- **Guess, Check, and Revise**
- Look for a Pattern
- Act It Out

Guess, Check, and Revise

Problem You are selling note cards and calendars to raise money for a class trip. So far, you have sold 18 items worth a total of $159. A box of note cards costs $10, and a calendar costs $7. How many of each item have you sold?

1 Read and Understand

Read the problem carefully.

You want to know how many of the 18 items you sold were note cards and how many were calendars.

2 Make a Plan

Decide on a strategy to use.

Guess two whole numbers whose sum is 18. *Check* whether the value of the 18 items is $159. *Revise* your guess as needed.

3 Solve the Problem

Reread the problem and guess an answer.

Guess: Try 9 boxes of note cards and 9 calendars.

Check: $9 \times \$10 + 9 \times \$7 = \$153$

$\qquad$ $153 is less than $159.

Revise: Try more note cards.

Guess: Try 10 boxes of note cards and 8 calendars.

Check: $10 \times \$10 + 8 \times \$7 = \$156$

$\qquad$ $156 is less than $159, but closer.

Revise: Try still more note cards.

Guess: Try 11 boxes of note cards and 7 calendars.

Check: $11 \times \$10 + 7 \times \$7 = \$159$

ANSWER You have sold 11 boxes of note cards and 7 calendars.

4 Look Back

Check that your answer meets all the conditions of the problem. You have sold 18 items, because $11 + 7 = 18$. Their value is $159, because $11 \times \$10 + 7 \times \$7 = \$159$.

NCTM CURRICULUM STANDARDS
Standard 1: Compute fluently
Standard 6: Solve problems in math and other contexts;
$\qquad$ Apply/adapt strategies to solve problems

Practice the Strategy

Use the strategy *guess, check, and revise*.

1. **Flowers** Your teacher spent $55 on tulips and daffodils. A pot of tulips costs $5, and a pot of daffodils costs $4. If your teacher bought 12 pots, how many pots of each kind of flower did your teacher buy?
7 pots of tulips and 5 pots of daffodils

2. **Fundraising** You are selling note cards and calendars for a school fundraiser. You have sold 15 items worth a total of $117. A box of note cards costs $10, and a calendar costs $7. How many of each item have you sold?
4 boxes of notes cards and 11 calendars

3. **Quizzes** A math quiz is worth 100 points. There are 13 problems on the quiz. Some problems are worth 5 points, and the rest are worth 12 points. How many of each kind of problem are on the quiz? 8 questions worth 5 points and 5 questions worth 12 points

4. **Number Sense** The product of two whole numbers is 1122. Their difference is 1. Find both numbers. 33 and 34

5. **Ropes** A rope is 33 feet long. You cut the rope into two pieces so that one piece is 3 feet longer than the other. Find the length of the longer piece. 18 ft

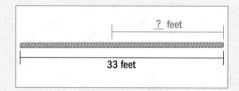

6. **Order of Operations** Use the symbols $+$, $-$, $\times$, or $\div$ to make the following statement true. You may use a symbol more than once. $\times$, $+$, $\times$

$$4 \; \underline{?} \; 5 \; \underline{?} \; 6 \; \underline{?} \; 10 = 80$$

Mixed Problem Solving

Use any strategy to solve the problem.

7. **CD Players** You are saving money to buy a CD player that costs $160. So far, you have saved $100. If you save $20 more each month, in how many months will you have exactly $160? 3 months

8. **Sweaters** A shop sells sweaters in small, medium, and large. Each size is available in red, blue, black, and white. How many different kinds of sweaters does the shop need to keep in stock? 12 kinds of sweaters

9. **Rules** Use the table to find one rule that relates each number in Column A with the corresponding number in Column B. $A - 6 = B$

Column A	Column B
11	5
10	4
9	3
8	2
7	1

10. **Computers** Your family plans to buy a computer for $980, plus a sales tax of $49. The first payment will be $150, and the rest of the cost will be paid in 3 equal payments. Find the amount of each equal payment. $293

COMMON ERROR

In Exercises 1–6, students may forget to check that their answer meets all of the conditions of the problem. Remind them that this is a necessary step.

MATH REASONING

For Exercise 4, students should understand that if two numbers have a difference of one, they are consecutive. They should reason that if their first choice of consecutive numbers gives them a product that is too high, and their second choice gives them a product that is too low, then their third choice should be a pair of numbers between the first two choices.

SUGGESTED STRATEGIES

You may wish to suggest the following strategies for the problems in the Mixed Problem Solving:
- Exercise 7: Make a Table, Look for a Pattern
- Exercise 8: Draw a Diagram, Make a List
- Exercise 9: Guess, Check, and Revise, Look for a Pattern
- Exercise 10: Make a Table, Look for a Pattern

LESSON OBJECTIVE

Solve equations using mental math.

PACING

Suggested Number of Days
Basic Course: 2 days
Average Course: 2 days
Advanced Course: 2 days
Block: 1 block

TEACHING RESOURCES

For a complete list of Teaching
Resources, see page 2B.

 TRANSPARENCY

Warm-Up Exercises for this lesson
are available on a transparency.

2 TEACH

MOTIVATING THE LESSON

Have students write a problem like
the camping example, exchange it
with a partner, and then solve the
problem they receive.

 LESSON **1.6**

Equations and Mental Math

BEFORE	▶ Now	WHY?
You evaluated numerical and variable expressions.	You'll solve equations using mental math.	So you can find how long to save money, as in Ex. 44.

In the Real World

Word Watch

equation, p. 36
solution, p. 36
solve, p. 37

Camping You are going camping with friends. You fill your backpack until it weighs 13 pounds. Your friend adds another item from the list at the right, and your backpack weighs 20 pounds. What item did your friend add?

clothes	3 pounds
food	6 pounds
sleeping bag	4 pounds
tent	7 pounds

EXAMPLE 1 **Guess, Check, and Revise**

To answer the question above about backpacking, you can use the problem solving strategy *guess, check, and revise.*

(1) Try an item on the list.

$13 + 4 = 17$

This total weight is under 20 pounds.

(2) Try the food, which is heavier.

$13 + 6 = 19$

This total weight is still one pound low.

(3) Try the tent. It weighs 7 pounds.

$13 + 7 = 20$

This total weight equals 20 pounds.

ANSWER Your friend added the tent to your backpack.

Equations You can use *equations* to answer questions like the one above. An **equation** is a mathematical sentence formed by placing an equal sign (=) between two expressions. A **solution** of an equation is a number that, when substituted for a variable, makes the equation true.

EXAMPLE 2 **Checking a Possible Solution**

Tell whether the given number is a solution of the equation.

a. $3y = 21;\ 6$

$3(6) \stackrel{?}{=} 21$

$18 \neq 21$

The symbol $\neq$ can be read "is not equal to."

ANSWER 6 is not a solution.

b. $x - 3 = 7;\ 10$

$10 - 3 \stackrel{?}{=} 7$

$7 = 7$

ANSWER 10 is a solution.

NCTM CURRICULUM STANDARDS
Standard 1: Understand meanings of operations
Standard 2: Represent situations using algebraic symbols
Standard 6: Apply/adapt strategies to solve problems

Solving Equations To **solve** an equation, you find all the solutions of the equation. To solve simple equations using mental math, you can think of the equation as a question.

HELP with Notetaking

In your notes on *Equations and Mental Math*, you may want to include examples showing equations rewritten as questions, like the ones in Example 3.

EXAMPLE 3 **Using Mental Math to Solve Equations**

Equation	→	Question	→	Solution	→	Check
a. $y - 8 = 4$		What number minus 8 equals 4?		12		$12 - 8 = 4$
b. $10x = 90$		10 times what number equals 90?		9		$10 \cdot 9 = 90$
c. $n \div 4 = 7$		What number divided by 4 equals 7?		28		$28 \div 4 = 7$

Mental Math When you do mental math, keep in mind the following rules that will help you to solve some equations that involve a 0 or a 1.

Operations Involving 0 and 1

Adding 0 The sum of any number and 0 is that number.

Multiplying by 0 The product of any number and 0 is 0.

Multiplying by 1 The product of any number and 1 is that number.

EXAMPLE 4 **Mental Math with 0 and 1**

Equation	→	Question	→	Solution	→	Check
a. $y + 2 = 2$		What number plus 2 equals 2?		0		$0 + 2 = 2$
b. $6 \cdot x = 6$		6 times what number equals 6?		1		$6 \cdot 1 = 6$

Your turn now Solve the equation using mental math.

1. $x + 10 = 24$ 14   **2.** $13n = 13$ 1   **3.** $35y = 0$ 0

4. $9x = 54$ 6   **5.** $y - 6 = 11$ 17   **6.** $18 \div n = 9$ 2

TIPS FOR NEW TEACHERS
Help students see why the question mark is used above the equal sign in Example 2. Encourage them to use this device in connection with the Guess, Check, and Revise strategy to solve equations. See Tips for New Teachers in the *Chapter 1 Resource Book*.

EXTRA EXAMPLES

Example 1 You want to buy 32 ounces of sliced meat. The butcher initially weighs out 14 ounces. How many more ounces of meat should he add, 12 ounces, 14 ounces, or 18 ounces? **18 oz**

Example 2 Tell whether the number is a solution of the equation.
a. $5y = 30$; 6 **yes**
b. $x + 8 = 15$; 10 **no**

Example 3 Use mental math to solve the equations.
a. $x + 12 = 17$ **5**
b. $6y = 24$ **4**
c. $n \div 8 = 10$ **80**

Example 4 Use mental math to solve the equations.
a. $x + 4 = 4$ **0**
b. $3y = 3$ **1**

MATH REASONING

Students should be able to reason that if the product of any two numbers is 0, then at least one of the numbers must be 0. Ask them to consider several examples that verify this statement.

EXAMPLE 5 **Solving Problems Using Mental Math**

Salmon Migration You are 100 miles upstream from the sea. Salmon migrating upstream have been spotted 41 miles from the sea. Use mental math to solve the equation $d + 41 = 100$ to find the distance d, in miles, between you and the salmon.

Solution

Think of the equation as a question.

Equation	d	$+$	41	$=$	100
Question	What number	plus	41	equals	100?
Solution	59	plus	41	equals	100.

ANSWER The distance between you and the salmon is 59 miles.

1.6 **Exercises**
More Practice, p. 708

Getting Ready to Practice

1. **Vocabulary** The number 9 is the ? of the equation $x - 5 = 4$. **solution**

Tell whether 5 is a solution of the equation.

2. $t + 2 = 7$
   5 is a solution.
3. $16 - k = 11$
   5 is a solution.
4. $15 \div m = 5$
   5 is not a solution.
5. $4y = 20$
   5 is a solution.

Solve the equation using mental math.

6. $4 + z = 12$ **8** 7. $x - 2 = 1$ **3** 8. $6r = 24$ **4** 9. $w \div 2 = 5$ **10**

10. $17 - y = 9$ **8** 11. $c + 8 = 21$ **13** 12. $56 \div m = 7$ **8** 13. $3t = 27$ **9**

14. **Sports** The table shows three major league baseball players and their home run totals as of June 11 of a recent season. Solve the equations in the table to find the number of home runs, x, that each player needed to hit in order to reach 40 home runs.

Player	Home Runs	Equation	
Barry Bonds	32	$x + 32 = 40$	8
Luis Gonzalez	26	$x + 26 = 40$	14
Manny Ramirez	21	$x + 21 = 40$	19

Practice and Problem Solving

HELP with Homework

Example	Exercises
1	44
2	15-23
3	24-39
4	40-43
5	54, 55

Online Resources
CLASSZONE.COM
· More Examples
· eTutorial Plus

Tell whether the given number is a solution of the equation.

A

15. $7 + x = 10$; 3
  3 is a solution.

16. $y - 3 = 7$; 4
  4 is not a solution.

17. $9 - r = 8$; 2
  2 is not a solution.

18. $m + 2 = 6$; 4
  4 is a solution.

19. $4c = 32$; 9
  9 is not a solution.

20. $4y = 4$; 1
  1 is a solution.

21. $10s = 77$; 7
7 is not a solution.

22. $30 \div x = 10$; 10
  10 is not a solution.

23. $48 \div r = 6$; 8
  8 is a solution.

Match the equation with the question.

24. $6 - n = 2$ D

A. What number minus 2 equals 6?

25. $n - 2 = 6$ A

B. 2 times what number equals 12?

26. $2n = 12$ B

C. 12 times what number equals 6?

27. $12n = 6$ C

D. 6 minus what number equals 2?

Solve the equation using mental math.

28. $8 + y = 10$ 2

29. $s - 5 = 9$ 14

30. $14 - z = 1$ 13

31. $d + 3 = 11$ 8

32. $2w = 16$ 8

33. $27 \div r = 9$ 3

34. $m \div 6 = 7$ 42

35. $5w = 45$ 9

36. $c + 6 = 13$ 7

37. $23 - t = 10$ 13

38. $22 - n = 17$ 5

39. $x + 9 = 20$ 11

40. $36h = 36$ 1

41. $35 + a = 35$ 0

42. $3f = 0$ 0

43. Find the Error Describe and
correct the error in solving the
equation $5x = 5$.

The 0 in the second line should be 1.
$5x = 5$
$5(1) = 5$ So, 1 is the solution.

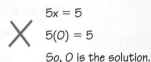
$5x = 5$
$5(0) = 5$
So, 0 is the solution.

B

44. Guess, Check, and Revise You are saving money to buy a camera that
costs $195. So far, you have saved $87. If you save $9 more each week,
in how many weeks will you have exactly $195? **12 weeks**

 Choose a Method Tell whether the given number is a solution of
the equation. Then tell whether you used *mental math*, *paper and
pencil*, or *a calculator* to get each answer. **Methods will vary.**

45. $y - 9 = 2$; 12
12 is not a solution.

46. $10 + x = 25$; 15
  15 is a solution.

47. $14t = 122$; 8
  8 is not a solution.

48. $3x + 2 = 32$; 9
9 is not a solution.

49. $16y + 6 = 300$; 18
  18 is not a solution.

50. $32 - 4r = 8$; 6
  6 is a solution.

51. $9r = 63$; 7
  7 is a solution.

52. $110n = 1980$; 19
  19 is not a solution.

53. $3380 \div w = 13$; 26
  26 is not a solution.

54. Computer Games You earned 300 points playing a computer game.
Your goal is to reach 500 points. Solve the equation $p + 300 = 500$
to find the number of points, p, you need to reach your goal. **200 points**

Lesson 1.6   Equations and Mental Math   **39**

③ APPLY

ASSIGNMENT GUIDE
Basic Course
Day 1: SRH p. 696 Exs. 1-3,
p. 697 Exs. 1-3; pp. 39-40
Exs. 15-27, 44-50
Day 2: pp. 39-40 Exs. 28-43,
51-55, 61-70
Average Course
Day 1: pp. 39-40 Exs. 18-27,
44-50, 61-65
Day 2: pp. 39-40 Exs. 31-43,
51-56, 66-70
Advanced Course
Day 1: pp. 39-40 Exs. 21-27,
48-53, 61-65
Day 2: pp. 39-40 Exs. 34-44,
54-60*, 69, 70
Block
pp. 39-40 Exs. 18-27, 31-56,
61-70

EXTRA PRACTICE
• Student Edition, p. 708
• Chapter 1 Resource Book,
pp. 56-58
• Test and Practice Generator

TRANSPARENCY
Even-numbered answers are available on transparencies.

HOMEWORK CHECK
When you review students' homework
for this lesson, go over the following
exercises to check understanding of
key concepts.
Basic: 15, 28, 40, 44, 54
Average: 18, 34, 41, 44, 55
Advanced: 21, 37, 42, 44, 55

MATH REASONING
Exercises 48-50 foreshadow solving
equations with multiple steps. Ask
students to describe how they would
check each solution.

39

④ ASSESS

ASSESSMENT RESOURCES

For more assessment resources, see:
- Assessment Book
- Test and Practice Generator

MINI-QUIZ

Tell whether the given number is a solution to the equation.

1. $3 + y = 8$; 5 yes

2. $12 \div x = 3$; 6 no

Solve the equation using mental math.

3. $8 - a = 2$ 6

4. $32 \div s = 4$ 8

5. $7x = 0$ 0

6. $24y = 24$ 1

7. $21 + x = 30$ 9

8. So far, you have 650 points playing a computer game. Solve the equation $650 + p = 1000$ to find the number of points, p, you need to reach 1000 points.
350 points

⑤ FOLLOW-UP

RETEACHING/REMEDIATION

- Study Guide in Chapter 1 Resource Book, pp. 59–60
- eTutorial Plus Online
- Student Edition, p. 708
- Lesson Practice in Chapter 1 Resource Book, pp. 56–58

CHALLENGE/ENRICHMENT

- Challenge Practice in Chapter 1 Resource Book, p. 61
- Teacher's Edition, p. 2F

ENGLISH LEARNER SUPPORT

- Spanish Study Guide
- Multi-Language Glossary
- Chapter Audio Summaries CDs

55. Baby-sitting You make $7 an hour baby-sitting. You need to earn $420. Solve the equation $7h = 420$ to find the number of hours, h, you need to baby-sit. 60 h

56. Volleyball Your gym class is split up into teams of 6 students for a volleyball tournament. There are 48 students in the class. Choose the equation you can use to find how many teams, t, you have. Then solve the equation using mental math. B; 8

A. $t + 6 = 48$ **B.** $6t = 48$

C. $t \div 48 = 6$ **D.** $t - 6 = 48$

Challenge Tell whether the equation has *no solution*, *one solution*, or *many solutions*. Use examples to explain your answer.

57. $0 \cdot x = 0$ **58.** $x \cdot 0 = 8$

59. $1 \cdot x = x$ **60.** $0 + x = 0$

57. many solutions; $0 \cdot 4 = 0$; $0 \cdot 9 = 0$; $0 \cdot 26 = 0$

58. no solution; $6 \cdot 0 = 0$, $23 \cdot 0 = 0$, $74 \cdot 0 = 0$

59. many solutions; $1 \cdot 6 = 6$, $1 \cdot 9 = 9$, $1 \cdot 25 = 25$

60. one solution; $0 + 0 = 0$

Mixed Review

61. You know that 717 children and 489 adults went to your school fair. Estimate the total number of people who went to the fair. *(Lesson 1.2)*
about 1200 people

Evaluate the expression when $y = 3$. *(Lesson 1.5)*

62. $15 - y$ 12   **63.** $8 \cdot y$ 24   **64.** $y + 9$ 12   **65.** $18 \div y$ 6

Basic Skills Tell which expression has the greater value.

66. $8 + 4$ or $20 \div 4$ **67.** $15 - 6$ or $20 \div 2$ **68.** 3×8 or $9 + 9$ 3 × 8
    8 + 4   20 ÷ 2

Test-Taking Practice

INTERNET
State Test Practice
CLASSZONE.COM

69. Multiple Choice You earn $15 each time you mow your neighbor's lawn. Solve the equation $d \div 4 = 15$ to find the amount of money d, in dollars, you earn by mowing the lawn 4 times. D

A. 11   **B.** 19   **C.** 21   **D.** 60

70. Multiple Choice Your friend can read 2 pages per minute in her library book. She read 20 pages last night. Solve the equation $m \cdot 2 = 20$ to find the number of minutes, m, she spent reading. F

F. 10   **G.** 20   **H.** 22   **I.** 40

A Problem Solving Plan

BEFORE
You used the strategy *guess, check,* and *revise.*

▶ **Now**
You'll use a 4-step plan to solve many kinds of problems.

WHY?
So you can find how many ways to pay a toll, as in Ex. 4.

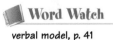 **Word Watch**
verbal model, p. 41

In the Real World

Shopping You went to the mall with $29 and came home with $3. Later, you made a list of how much you spent on each item, but you didn't have a receipt for the food. How much did you spend on food?

CD	$8
yo-yo	$3
sunglasses	$5
food	?

EXAMPLE 1 **Understanding and Planning**

To solve the problem about spending money, first make sure you understand the problem. Then make a plan for solving the problem.

Read and Understand

What do you know?

You started with $29. Now you have $3.

You bought a CD for $8, a yo-yo for $3, and sunglasses for $5.

What do you want to find out?

How much did you spend on food?

Make a Plan

How can you relate what you know to what you want to find out?

Write a *verbal model* to describe how the values in this problem are related. A **verbal model** uses words to describe ideas and then uses math symbols to relate the words.

$$\begin{array}{c} \text{Money spent} \\ \text{on food} \end{array} = \begin{array}{c} \text{Money spent} \\ \text{at the mall} \end{array} - \begin{array}{c} \text{Money spent on CD,} \\ \text{yo-yo, and sunglasses} \end{array}$$

 **Your turn now** Use the information at the top of the page.

1. How can you figure out how much you spent at the mall?
Subtract $3 from $29.

2. How can you figure out how much you spent for items besides food?
Add $8, $3, and $5.

Lesson 1.7   A Problem Solving Plan   **41**

---

1 PLAN

SKILL CHECK
1. $127 + 89 = \underline{?}$ 216
2. $213 - 76 = \underline{?}$ 137
3. $23 \times 14 = \underline{?}$ 322
4. $174 \div 6 = \underline{?}$ 29

LESSON OBJECTIVE
Use a problem solving plan.

PACING
Suggested Number of Days
Basic Course: 2 days
Average Course: 2 days
Advanced Course: 2 days
Block: 1 block

TEACHING RESOURCES
For a complete list of Teaching Resources, see page 2B.

 **TRANSPARENCY**
Warm-Up Exercises for this lesson are available on a transparency.

2 TEACH

MOTIVATING THE LESSON
Have students discuss real-world experiences where they used a plan to solve a problem.

TIPS FOR NEW TEACHERS
Help students solve real-world problems by telling them to always follow the plan on page 42. See Tips for New Teachers in the *Chapter 1 Resource Book.*

Example 1 You want to read a 48-page chapter in a book in 7 days. You plan to read 5 pages a day for six days and finish the chapter on the seventh day. How many pages will you have to read on the seventh day?

a. What do you know? **You want to read 48 pages in 7 days. You read 5 pages a day for 6 days.**

b. What do you want to find out? **how many pages you will have to read on the seventh day**

Example 2 Write a verbal model to help solve the problem in Extra Example 1. Then solve the problem. **total number of pages read = 6 days × 5 pages per day + number of pages on the seventh day;**
$48 = 6 \cdot 5 + n$
$48 = 30 + n$
$18 = n$

 NOTETAKING

To stress the importance of the Problem Solving Plan, have students copy it into their notebooks. Students should add the What do you know?, What do you want to find out?, How can you relate what you know to what you want to find out? questions at the appropriate points in the plan to help clarify what they are doing at each step.

TEACHING TIP

Ask students to always check their results with the original problem. They can estimate the reasonableness of their answer quickly, then verify the exact answer.

EXAMPLE 2 **Solving and Looking Back**

To solve the problem at the top of page 41 about spending money, you need to carry out the plan from Example 1 and then check the answer.

Solve the Problem

Write a verbal model to relate the amount of money spent on food to the dollar values you are given at the top of page 41.

Money spent on food	=	Money spent at the mall	−	Money spent on CD, yo-yo, and sunglasses
	=	$(29 - 3)$	−	$(8 + 3 + 5)$
	=	26	−	16
	=	10		

ANSWER You spent $10 on food at the mall.

Look Back

Make sure your answer is reasonable. Add the money you spent on each item to what you had left. This should be equal to the amount of money you had when you started.

$$8 + 3 + 5 + 10 + 3 = 29 \checkmark$$

Your turn now **Use Example 2 above.**

3. If you came home with $5 instead of $3, how much did you spend on food at the mall? **$8**

Problem Solving Plan

1. **Read and Understand** Read the problem carefully. Identify the question and any important information.

2. **Make a Plan** Decide on a problem solving strategy.

3. **Solve the Problem** Use the problem solving strategy to answer the question.

4. **Look Back** Check that your answer is reasonable.

Here is a list of some common problem solving strategies.

Guess, Check, and Revise
Draw a Diagram
Perform an Experiment
Make a List
Make a Table
Work Backward
Solve a Related Problem
Solve a Simpler Problem
Make a Model
Break into Parts
Draw a Graph
Look for a Pattern
Act It Out

EXAMPLE 3 **Draw a Diagram**

The mall is 12 miles from your home. Your school is one third of the way from your home to the mall. The library is one fourth of the way from the school to the mall. How far is the library from home?

Solution

Read and Understand Your school and the library are between your home and the mall, which are 12 miles apart. You need to find the distance between your home and the library.

Make a Plan Draw a diagram showing the relationships between the different locations. Use the diagram to solve the problem.

Solve the Problem Draw a number line and mark the locations.

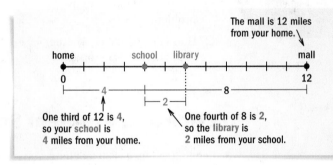

ANSWER From the diagram you can see that the library is
$4 + 2 = 6$ miles from your home.

Look Back The mall is 12 miles from your home and the library is between them. Because 6 is less than 12, the answer is reasonable.

Your turn now **The map shows the distances between four cities.**

4. How many different routes are possible from City A to City D without backtracking? **4**

5. What is the longest route from City A to City D?
   City A to City B to City C to City D

6. What is the longest route from City C to City B?
   City C to City D to City B

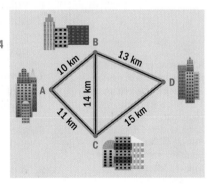

Example 3 Use the diagram below to find the shortest path in minutes to the pool.

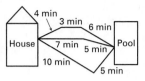

The three paths take $4 + 3 + 6 = 13$ minutes; $7 + 5 = 12$ minutes, and $10 + 5 = 15$ minutes. Choose the path that takes 12 minutes.

MULTIPLE REPRESENTATIONS

You can use the diagram below to represent miles in Example 3.

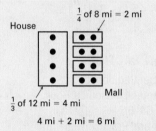

$\frac{1}{3}$ of 12 mi = 4 mi

4 mi + 2 mi = 6 mi

TRANSPARENCY

A support transparency is available for Example 3.

CONCEPT CHECK

Your telephone bill is $19 per month plus an additional $7 for each 100 minutes of local calls. Use a verbal model to determine the telephone bill for 300 minutes. **bill = monthly charge + 7 × the number of 100 minute units in 300 minutes; bill = 19 + 7 × (300 ÷ 100); bill = 19 + 7 × 3 = 40; the bill is $40.**

DAILY PUZZLER

There are 6 teams in your bowling league. Each team plays each other team once. How many total games are played? **15 games**

43

EXTRA PRACTICE

- Student Edition, p. 708
- Chapter 1 Resource Book, pp. 64–66
- Test and Practice Generator

 **TRANSPARENCY**

Even-numbered answers are available on transparencies.

HOMEWORK CHECK

When you review students' homework for this lesson, go over the following exercises to check understanding of key concepts.
Basic: 3, 4, 6, 7, 8
Average: 3, 5, 6, 7, 8
Advanced: 4, 5, 7, 8, 9

 COMMON ERROR

In Exercise 10, make certain all students understand why 5 buses are needed rather than 4 buses even though $4\frac{14}{70}$ is closer to 4 than to 5.

1–2. See Additional Answers beginning on page AA1.

44

1.7 Exercises
More Practice, p. 708

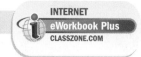
Getting Ready to Practice

1, 2. See margin.

1. **Vocabulary** Explain the four steps of the problem solving plan.

2. **Guided Problem Solving** A conductor on a train has run out of quarters and has to make change using only dimes and nickels. What are all the ways that the conductor can make 40 cents in change?

   ① What are you trying to find?

   ② How can a table like the one at the right help you to solve the problem?

   ③ Use the table to solve the problem.

   ④ How can you check whether your answer is reasonable?

Number of dimes	Number of nickels	Total value
?	?	?
?	?	?
?	?	?
?	?	?
?	?	?

Practice and Problem Solving

9. **Sample answer:** Have 6 people represent adults. Give each of these people $12. Have 4 people represent children. Give each of these people $7. Put all of the money together and count it to find the total cost.

3. **Fencing** A fence is 30 feet long. You need to place a fence post at both ends of the fence and every 5 feet along the fence. Draw a diagram to find how many posts you need. **7 posts**

4. **Tollbooths** The toll at a tollbooth is 45 cents for each car. Use a table to find all the different ways you can pay the toll exactly if you can use quarters, dimes, and nickels. **8 ways**

5. **Cell Phone** You pay $49 for a cell phone and $19 per month for phone service. Use a verbal model to find your total cost after 12 months. **$277**

6. **Video Game** You share the cost of buying a new video game with Alice, Omar, and Celine. You want to decide the order in which each person gets to try the game. Make a list to show all the different possible orders. **24 different orders**

7. **Number Sense** The product of two whole numbers is 24. Their sum is 10. Find the two numbers. Begin by making a list of pairs of whole numbers whose product is 24. **6 and 4**

B 8. **Museum** Tickets to a science museum cost $12 per adult and $7 per child. Find the total cost for a group of 6 adults and 4 children. **$100**

9. **Writing** Explain how you could find the total cost in Exercise 8 by acting out the problem with a group of people using play money.

10. *Sample answer:* The remainder shows that 4 buses are not enough. Five buses will be needed to carry all of the passengers.

10. Find the Error Describe and correct the error in the solution at the right to the problem below.

Your school is sending 177 people on a field trip. Each bus can carry 40 passengers. How many buses are needed?

$$\begin{array}{r} 4 \text{ R}17 \\ 40\overline{)177} \\ 160 \\ \hline 17 \end{array}$$

So, 4 buses are needed.

11. Amusement Park You buy 20 tickets. You ride the Ferris wheel for 4 tickets and you visit the house of mirrors for 3 tickets. After you ride the roller coaster, you have 7 tickets left. How many tickets did you use to ride the roller coaster? **6 tickets**

12. Basketball You get 1 point for making a free throw, 3 points for making a long 3-point shot, and 2 points for making other shots. What are all the different ways you can score 6 points? **7 ways**

13. Waiting Lines John is second in a line of 11 people. There are 5 people between Lauren and Franco. There are 2 people between Franco and John. How many people are there between Lauren and John? How many people are ahead of Lauren in line? **8 people; 10 people**

c 14. Challenge You forgot the three-digit access code for your garage door. The first digit is 3 and the last two digits are odd numbers. How many different access codes are possible? **25 different codes are possible;**
Sample answer: **There are 5 possible odd digits: 1, 3, 5, 7, or 9. Make a list of the possible combinations.**

Mixed Review

Write the product as a power. *(Lesson 1.3)*

15. 17×17 17^2 **16.** $11 \times 11 \times 11$ 11^3 **17.** $8 \times 8 \times 8 \times 8$ 8^4

Solve the equation using mental math. *(Lesson 1.6)*

18. $x + 9 = 14$ **5**   **19.** $6w = 48$ **8**   **20.** $c \div 2 = 9$ **18**   **21.** $n - 3 = 7$ **10**

26. 126 seats; $1449; divide the number of seats by 2 and then multiply the quotient by $23.

Basic Skills   **Round the number to the red digit.**

22. 2562 **2600**   **23.** 17,608 **20,000**   **24.** 148,563 **149,000**   **25.** 924,375 **900,000**

Test-Taking Practice

26. Extended Response The balcony section of a theater has 9 rows of seats. Each row has 14 seats. A ticket for a balcony seat costs $23. How many seats are in the balcony section of the theater? If half of the tickets for balcony seats are sold, how much money is raised from tickets for balcony seats? Explain how you found your answer.
See margin.

Lesson 1.7   A Problem Solving Plan   **45**

4 ASSESS

ASSESSMENT RESOURCES

For more assessment resources, see:
• Assessment Book
• Test and Practice Generator

MINI-QUIZ

1. Tickets to the school talent show cost $3 for adults and $2 for students. Find the total ticket cost for 25 adults and 80 children. **$235**

2. In football, you get 6 points for making a touchdown, 1 point for kicking the "extra point" after the touchdown, 3 points for making a field goal, and 2 points for a safety. What are the different ways you can score 10 points? **touchdown + extra point + field goal, touchdown + 2 safeties, 2 field goals + 2 safeties, 5 safeties**

3. The ice cream parlor offers 6 flavors of ice cream and 4 toppings. How many different ice cream cones are available? **24 cones**

5 FOLLOW-UP

RETEACHING/REMEDIATION

• Study Guide in Chapter 1 Resource Book, pp. 67–68
• eTutorial Plus Online
• Student Edition, p. 708
• Lesson Practice in Chapter 1 Resource Book, pp. 64–66

CHALLENGE/ENRICHMENT

• Challenge Practice in Chapter 1 Resource Book, p. 69
• Teacher's Edition, p. 2F

ENGLISH LEARNER SUPPORT

• Spanish Study Guide
• Multi-Language Glossary
• Chapter Audio Summaries CDs

Notebook Review

LESSONS 1.5 TO 1.7

Review the vocabulary definitions in your notebook.

Copy the review examples in your notebook. Then complete the exercises.

Check Your Definitions

variable, p. 29   equation, p. 36   solve, p. 37
variable expression, p. 29   solution, p. 36   verbal model, p. 41

Use Your Vocabulary

1. Copy and complete: The __?__ in the expression $x + 2$ is x. variable

2. **Writing** Is 5 a solution of the equation $3n = 15$? Why or why not?
Yes; because $3 \cdot 5 = 15$.

1.5 Can you evaluate variable expressions?

Review

EXAMPLE Evaluate $t + 17$ when $t = 4$.

$t + 17 = 4 + 17 = 21$ Substitute 4 for t. Then add.

 Evaluate when $y = 6$. **3.** $19 + y$ 25   **4.** $y \div 3$ 2   **5.** $18 - 2 \cdot y$ 6

1.6 Can you solve equations using mental math?

Review

EXAMPLE To solve $4n = 40$, ask "4 times what number equals 40?"

ANSWER The solution is 10, because $4 \cdot 10 = 40$.

 Solve the equation. **6.** $r - 1 = 5$ 6 **7.** $7m = 7$ 1   **8.** $40 \div c = 5$ 8

1.7 Can you use a problem solving plan?

Review

EXAMPLE You pay $50 for a gym membership and $3 per visit. What is your total cost for 20 visits?

Understand and Plan Find the total cost by using a verbal model.

Solve Total cost = Membership cost + Cost for visits

$\qquad = \$50 + \$3 \cdot 20$

$\qquad = \$110$

Look Back $\$50 + \$3 \cdot 20 = \$50 + \$60 = \$110$ ✓

 9. What is your total cost if you make 30 visits to the gym? $140

Brain Game
The equations and their solutions along the correct path are as follows.
START $8x = 16$ (solution: 2);
$3x = 3$ (solution: 1);
$9 \div x = 3$ (solution: 3);
$4 + x = 5$ (solution: 1);
$7 - x = 2$ (solution: 5);
$2 + x = 4$ (solution: 2);
$x + 1 = 7$ (solution: 6);
$9 - x = 4$ (solution: 5); FINISH

Stop and Think about Lessons 1.5–1.7

10. **Mental Math** Is $x \cdot 0 = 12$ true for any value of x? Explain. No; any number times 0 is always 0.

11. Sample answer: It helps you to make sure your answer is reasonable.

11. **Writing** Explain why *looking back* at your answer is an important part of the problem solving plan.

Review Quiz 2

Evaluate the expression when $a = 12$ and $b = 3$.

1. $15 - a$ 3
2. $a \div 6$ 2
3. $3 + 5 \cdot b$ 18
4. $9 - 6 \div b$ 7
5. $7b$ 21
6. $a + b$ 15

Solve the equation using mental math.

7. $r - 1 = 2$ 3
8. $5 + z = 25$ 20
9. $y \div 3 = 7$ 21
10. $12m = 72$ 6

11. **Food** You are ordering a pizza. You have a choice of three toppings: mushrooms, pepperoni, or peppers. How many different pizzas can you order if you select exactly two different toppings? 3 pizzas

To find your way across the river, solve the equations using mental math.

- If the solution is 1 or 6, go to the right.
- If the solution is 2 or 5, go down.
- If the solution is 3, go up.
- If the solution is 4, go to the left.

Write down each equation you solve and its solution. See margin.

River Crossing

START $8x = 16$

$4 + x = 5$ $7 - x = 2$ $8 - x = 4$
$3x = 3$ $9 \div x = 3$ $2 + x = 4$ $3x = 9$
$2x = 6$ $x + 3 = 7$ $x + 1 = 7$ $9 - x = 4$
$1 + x = 4$ $6 - x = 3$ $3 + x = 8$ FINISH

Chapter Review

Vocabulary

leading digit, p. 13
compatible numbers, p. 13
factor, p. 16
power, p. 16
base, p. 16
exponent, p. 16

numerical expression, p. 21
grouping symbols, p. 21
evaluate, p. 21
order of operations, p. 21
variable, p. 29

variable expression, p. 29
equation, p. 36
solution, p. 36
solve, p. 37
verbal model, p. 41

Vocabulary Review

Copy and complete the statement.

1. To make sure that everyone always gets the same result, you evaluate expressions using the ?. **order of operations**

2. A ? has a base and an exponent. **power**

3. The ? of a power is the repeated factor. **base**

4. A ? is a symbol, usually a letter, that represents one or more numbers. **variable**

5. A mathematical sentence formed by placing an equals sign (=) between two expressions is an ?. **equation**

6. When a number is substituted for a variable, it is a ? of the equation if it makes the equation true. **solution**

Review Questions

Find the sum, difference, product, or quotient. *(Lesson 1.1)*

7. $928 + 185$ **1113**

8. $64 - 27$ **37**

9. 15×35 **525**

10. $216 \div 9$ **24**

11. $471 \div 6$ **78 R3**

12. 36×12 **432**

13. $551 - 138$ **413**

14. $157 + 3094$ **3251**

Describe the pattern. Then find the next two numbers. *(Lesson 1.1)*

15. 9, 18, 27, 36, ?, ? **add 9; 45, 54**

16. 40, 80, 160, 320, ?, ? **multiply by 2; 640, 1280**

17. 67, 57, 47, 37, ?, ? **subtract 10; 27, 17**

Estimate the sum, difference, product, or quotient. *(Lesson 1.2)* **Estimates may vary.**

18. $149 - 53$ **100**

19. $286 + 109$ **400**

20. 39×88 **3600**

21. $411 \div 18$ **20**

22. $635 \div 8$ **80**

23. 592×3 **1800**

24. $2120 + 791$ **2900**

25. $715 - 296$ **400**

26. Population About how many people are living in a town with 3411 households if there are about 3 people per household? *(Lesson 1.2)* **about 10,500 people**

Find the value of the power. *(Lesson 1.3)*

27. 7^3 343   **28.** 10^5 100,000   **29.** 5^4 625   **30.** 1^{100} 1

31. 13^2 169   **32.** 9^3 729   **33.** 50 squared 2500   **34.** 8 cubed 512

Evaluate the expression. *(Lesson 1.4)*

35. $20 - 3 \times 5$ 5   **36.** $11 - 9 + 2$ 4   **37.** $8 - 6 \div 3$ 6   **38.** $4 \times (9 - 7) + 6$ 14

39. 8×10^4 80,000   **40.** $9 + 4 \div 4$ 10   **41.** $\frac{9 + 3}{4}$ 3   **42.** 3×5^2 75

43. $\frac{6^2}{5 + 7}$ 3   **44.** $(13 - 6) \times 4$ 28   **45.** $8 \times (4 - 1) \div 6$ 4   **46.** $\frac{55 - 6}{1 + 6}$ 7

Evaluate the expression. *(Lesson 1.5)*

47. $x + 4$, when $x = 6$ 10   **48.** $19 - y$, when $y = 12$ 7   **49.** $48 - m$, when $m = 39$ 9

50. $22r$, when $r = 3$ 66   **51.** $s \div 9$, when $s = 63$ 7   **52.** $3n + 7$, when $n = 8$ 31

Evaluate the expression when $x = 3$ and $y = 5$. *(Lesson 1.5)*

53. $5 \cdot x$ 15   **54.** $y + 9$ 14   **55.** $75 \div x$ 25   **56.** $3y - 2$ 13

57. **Statues** You can represent the total height of a statue standing on an 18 inch platform using the expression $18 + h$, where h is the statue's height in inches. What is the total height of the statue and the platform if the statue is 48 inches tall? *(Lesson 1.5)* 66 in.

58. **Trains** The length of a train with an engine and three cars can be represented by the expression $n + 3c$, where n is the length, in feet, of the engine and c is the length, in feet, of a car. What is the train's total length if the engine is 64 feet long and a car is 90 feet long? *(Lesson 1.5)* 334 ft

Solve the equation using mental math. *(Lesson 1.6)*

59. $9x = 45$ 5   **60.** $n - 3 = 10$ 13   **61.** $8 + y = 8$ 0   **62.** $21 \div n = 3$ 7

63. $x \div 10 = 6$ 60   **64.** $y + 16 = 20$ 4   **65.** $19 - x = 15$ 4   **66.** $3n = 45$ 15

67. **Phones** To make a phone call, you pay \$2 for the first 20 minutes, then 10 cents per minute. What is the total cost of a 32-minute phone call? *(Lesson 1.7)* \$3.20

68. **Highways** Exits 1 through 4 are in order on a highway. Exit 4 is 27 miles from Exit 1. Exit 2 is 12 miles from Exit 3 and 16 miles from Exit 4. How many miles is Exit 3 from Exit 1? *(Lesson 1.7)*

23 mi

C H A P T E R

1

Chapter Test

Find the sum, difference, product, or quotient.

1. $85 + 47$ 132

2. $435 - 18$ 417

3. 24×31 744

4. $492 \div 6$ 82

5. $613 - 174$ 439

6. $283 + 197$ 480

7. $527 \div 11$ 47 R10

8. 16×32 512

Nutrition **The table shows the protein content of several foods in a 160-gram serving.**

9. Find the total amount of protein in a fish sandwich and one serving of tuna salad. 43 g

10. How many more grams of protein are in one serving of roasted turkey than in one serving of fried chicken? 7 g

Food	Protein Content
fish sandwich	17 grams
roasted turkey	34 grams
tuna salad	26 grams
fried chicken	27 grams

Estimate the sum, difference, product, or quotient. Estimates may vary.

11. $86 + 19$ 110

12. $91 - 24$ 70

13. 19×32 600

14. $272 \div 7$ 40

15. $534 - 18$ 510

16. $279 + 316$ 600

17. $375 \div 18$ 20

18. 4×523 2000

Find the value of the power.

19. 7^2 49

20. 4 cubed 64

21. 2^5 32

22. 3^4 81

Evaluate the expression.

23. $14 - 8 \div 2$ 10

24. $4 + 3 \times 6$ 22

25. $36 \div (2 + 7)$ 4

26. $15 - 3^2$ 6

27. $(24 \div 4) \times 3$ 18

28. $2 + 5 \times 4 - 13$ 9

Evaluate the variable expression when $x = 5$.

29. $9 + x$ 14

30. $x - 3$ 2

31. $x \cdot 7$ 35

32. $23 - x$ 18

33. $x + 16$ 21

34. $45 \div x$ 9

Solve the equation using mental math.

35. $9 + x = 15$ 6

36. $11 - z = 7$ 4

37. $10t = 90$ 9

38. $n - 3 = 12$ 15

39. $c + 7 = 21$ 14

40. $y \div 5 = 35$ 175

41. **Environment** You are going to plant trees in your neighborhood. You can choose from apple, maple, oak, poplar, and spruce. Make a list to show how many ways you can plant three different trees. 10 ways

Chapter Standardized Test

Test-Taking Strategy Have a positive attitude during any test so that you can gain confidence and stay focused on each question.

16. 19 packages. *Sample answer:* You need a total of $38 \times 2 = 76$ party favors. To find the number of packages needed, divide 76 by 4.

Multiple Choice

1. Find the sum $934 + 357$. **C**

   A. 577   **B.** 1223   **C.** 1291   **D.** 1381

2. Find the difference $623 - 197$. **F**

   F. 426   **G.** 516   **H.** 710   **I.** 820

3. Which expression has a value of 322? **C**

   A. $481 - 129$ **B.** $138 + 194$
   C. 14×23 **D.** $657 \div 3$

4. Estimate the sum $198 + 328$. **H**

   F. 300   **G.** 400   **H.** 500   **I.** 600

5. Estimate the cost per sandwich if you pay $53 for 11 sandwiches. **C**

   A. \$3   **B.** \$4   **C.** \$5   **D.** \$6

6. Which power has a value of 9? **G**

   F. 2^3 **G.** 3^2 **H.** 9^2 **I.** 6^3

7. What is the value of 7^3? **D**

   A. 21   **B.** 49   **C.** 283   **D.** 343

8. What is the value of $5 \times 5 \times 5$? **G**

   F. 25   **G.** 125   **H.** 625   **I.** 3125

9. Evaluate the expression $12 - 3 \times 2$. **B**

   A. 3   **B.** 6   **C.** 9   **D.** 18

10. Evaluate the expression $\frac{14 + 7}{7 - 4}$. **H**

   F. 1   **G.** 3   **H.** 7   **I.** 11

11. Which expression has a value of 8 when $x = 4$? **B**

   A. $8 - x$ **B.** $2x$ **C.** $36 \div x$ **D.** $x + 6$

12. Evaluate $x \cdot 3 + 7$ when $x = 2$. **H**

   F. 11   **G.** 12   **H.** 13   **I.** 20

13. What is the solution of the equation $7x = 28$? **C**

   A. 2   **B.** 3

   C. 4   **D.** 7

14. Which equation has a solution of 5? **F**

   F. $40 \div x = 8$ **G.** $20 - x = 5$
   H. $x + 8 = 14$ **I.** $5x = 30$

15. You need to deliver 75 plants for a florist. You delivered 25 plants. Solve the equation $x + 25 = 75$ to find how many more plants you need to deliver. **C**

   A. 3   **B.** 45   **C.** 50   **D.** 100

Short Response

16. There are 4 party favors in a package. How many packages do you need to buy if you want to give 2 party favors to everyone in a group of 38 people? Explain. **See margin.**

Extended Response

17. At a restaurant, you can choose from four omelet fillings: cheese, peppers, tomatoes, mushrooms. Use a problem solving plan to find how many different omelets you can choose that use exactly three different fillings. Show your work.

17. 4 different omelets; Make a list of all the possible omelets, choosing 3 fillings at a time. The list will contain 24 omelets. Eliminate any duplicates (omelets that have the same fillings).

REGULAR SCHEDULE

Lesson	Les. Day	BASIC	AVERAGE	ADVANCED
2.1	Day 1	pp. 58–60 Exs. 9–16, 32–35, 45–50	pp. 58–60 Exs. 9–16, 32–38, 46–49	pp. 58–60 Exs. 10–16, 31–36, 47–49
	Day 2	pp. 58–60 Exs. 17–30, 37–41, 51	pp. 58–60 Exs. 21–31, 41–43, 50–52	pp. 58–60 Exs. 21–28, 37–44*, 51, 52
2.2	Day 1	SRH p. 702 Exs. 1–6; pp. 64–65 Exs. 6–10, 14–17, 28, 33–41	pp. 64–65 Exs. 6–10, 27–29, 37–40	pp. 64–65 Exs. 8–10, 18, 27–29, 35–38, 41
	Day 2	pp. 64–65 Exs. 11–13, 19–24, 26, 31, 32, 42	pp. 64–65 Exs. 11–26, 31–36, 41, 42	pp. 64–65 Exs. 12–17, 19–26, 29–32*, 42
2.3	Day 1	EP p. 708 Exs. 9–11; pp. 70–71 Exs. 7–16, 19, 20, 24–31	pp. 70–71 Exs. 7–20, 23–31	pp. 70–71 Exs. 9–13, 16–26, 30, 31, EC: TE p. 52D*
2.4	Day 1	pp. 74–75 Exs. 5–10, 12–14, 18–24	pp. 74–75 Exs. 5–15, 17–24	pp. 74–75 Exs. 5–19*, 24
2.5	Day 1	SRH p. 704 Exs. 1–3; pp. 81–82 Exs. 5–8, 10, 14–23	pp. 81–82 Exs. 5–12, 16–20, 23, 24	pp. 81–82 Exs. 5–13*, 16–18, 23, 24
2.6	Day 1	SRH p. 705 Exs. 1–4; pp. 85–86 Exs. 8–18, 25–31	pp. 85–86 Exs. 8–23, 25–31	pp. 85–86 Exs. 11–26*, 30, 31
2.7	Day 1	SRH p. 706 Exs. 1–2, p. 707 Ex. 1; pp. 90–91 Exs. 6–10, 12–19, 26–35	pp. 90–91 Exs. 6–24, 26–29, 32–35	pp. 90–91 Exs. 8–11, 14–25*, 28, 29, 34, 35
2.8	Day 1	SRH p. 685 Exs. 1–3, p. 691 Exs. 1–4; pp. 95–97 Exs. 6–11, 14, 15, 17–20, 22, 26–29, 34–41	pp. 95–97 Exs. 6–12, 14–19, 21–24, 26–31, 34–38, 41, 42	pp. 95–97 Exs. 10–22, 25–36*, 41, 42
Review	Day 1	pp. 100–101 Exs. 1–33	pp. 100–101 Exs. 1–33	pp. 100–101 Exs. 1–33
Assess	Day 1	Chapter 2 Test	Chapter 2 Test	Chapter 2 Test

YEARLY PACING	Chapter 2 Total – **12 days**	Chapters 1–2 Total – **24 days**	Remaining – **136 days**

*Challenge Exercises   EP = Extra Practice   SRH = Skills Review Handbook   EC = Extra Challenge

BLOCK SCHEDULE

DAY 1	DAY 2	DAY 3	DAY 4	DAY 5	DAY 6
2.1 pp. 58–60 Exs. 9–16, 21–38, 41–43, 46–52	**2.2** pp. 64–65 Exs. 6–29, 31–42	**2.3** pp. 70–71 Exs. 7–20, 23–31 **2.4** pp. 74–75 Exs. 5–15, 17–24	**2.5** pp. 81–82 Exs. 5–12, 16–20, 23, 24 **2.6** pp. 85–86 Exs. 8–23, 25–31	**2.7** pp. 90–91 Exs. 6–24, 26–29, 32–35 **2.8** pp. 95–97 Exs. 6–12, 14–19, 21–24, 26–31, 34–38, 41, 42	**Review** pp. 100–101 Exs. 1–33 **Assess** Chapter 2 Test

YEARLY PACING	Chapter 2 Total – **6 days**	Chapters 1–2 Total – **12 days**	Remaining – **68 days**

Support Materials

📖 CHAPTER RESOURCE BOOK

CHAPTER SUPPORT

Tips for New Teachers	p. 1	Parents as Partners	p. 3

LESSON SUPPORT

	2.1	2.2	2.3	2.4	2.5	2.6	2.7	2.8
Lesson Plans (regular and block)	p. 5	p. 13	p. 23	p. 31	p. 39	p. 48	p. 57	p. 65
Technology Activities & Keystrokes						p. 50		p. 67
Activity Support Masters								
Activity Masters		p. 15						
Practice (3 levels)	p. 7	p. 16	p. 25	p. 33	p. 41	p. 51	p. 59	p. 70
Study Guide	p. 10	p. 19	p. 28	p. 36	p. 44	p. 54	p. 62	p. 73
Real-World Problem Solving		p. 21			p. 46			
Challenge Practice	p. 12	p. 22	p. 30	p. 38	p. 47	p. 56	p. 64	p. 75

REVIEW

Chapter Review Games and Activities	p. 76	Extra Credit Project with Rubric	p. 81
Real-Life Project with Rubric	p. 77	Cumulative Practice	p. 83
Cooperative Project with Rubric	p. 79	Resource Book Answers	A1

📖 ASSESSMENT

Quizzes	p. 18	Alternative Assessments with Rubrics	p. 27
Chapter Tests (3 levels)	p. 20	Unit Test	p. 51
Standardized Test	p. 26	Cumulative Test	p. 53

📑 TRANSPARENCIES

	2.1	2.2	2.3	2.4	2.5	2.6	2.7	2.8
Warm-Up / Daily Homework Quiz	✔	✔	✔	✔	✔	✔	✔	✔
Notetaking Guide	✔	✔	✔	✔	✔	✔	✔	✔
Teacher Support		✔				✔		
English/Spanish Problem Solving				✔	✔	✔		✔
Answer Transparencies	✔	✔	✔	✔	✔	✔	✔	✔

💻 TECHNOLOGY

- EasyPlanner CD-ROM
- Test and Practice Generator
- Electronic Lesson Presentations
- eTutorial CD-ROM
- Chapter Audio Summaries CDs
- Classzone.com
- eEdition Plus Online
- eWorkbook Plus Online
- eTutorial Plus Online
- EasyPlanner Plus Online

ADDITIONAL RESOURCES

- Worked-Out Solution Key
- Notetaking Guide
- Practice Workbook
- Tutor Place
- Professional Development Book
- Activities Book
- Poster Package
- Spanish Study Guide
- English/Spanish Chapter Reviews
- Multi-Language Glossary

Math Background and Teaching Strategies

Lesson 2.1

MATH BACKGROUND

CUSTOMARY AND METRIC SYSTEMS The metric system is based upon the decimal numeration system. It is easier to convert within the metric system than in the customary system where relationships between units must be memorized.

TEACHING STRATEGIES

It is very important to have students estimate a measurement before they make it. Discuss the benchmark units introduced in the lesson. Explain that using benchmarks will help students improve their estimates of customary and metric lengths.

Lesson 2.2

MATH BACKGROUND

PERIMETER AND AREA The distance around a figure is called the **perimeter**. Thus, to find the perimeter of any shape, add the lengths of all sides. **Area**, the number of square units needed to cover a plane figure, is found by multiplying two linear dimensions. The formula $A = lw$ can be used to find the area of a rectangle.

TEACHING STRATEGIES

You might want to use physical models—oaktag rectangles and unit squares—to discuss area. After students count unit squares to find area, have them measure dimensions and use multiplication to find the same area. Use rectangles of different dimensions.

Lesson 2.3

MATH BACKGROUND

SCALE DRAWINGS A scale drawing has the same shape but not the same size as the object it represents. A **scale**, or *scale factor*, is the ratio of the measurement on a scale drawing to the measurement of the real object.

TEACHING STRATEGIES

On grid paper have students draw a simple shape, such as a triangle or rectangle. After their shape is complete, have them draw a larger or smaller shape that is similar to the first. This can be done on a grid of the same size or a different size. After students have completed pictures of different sizes, have them compare the ratios of the lengths of corresponding segments.

Lesson 2.4

MATH BACKGROUND

FREQUENCY TABLES A frequency table is a way to show how often an item, a number, or a range of numbers occurs. When you are counting responses to a question, a frequency table helps you to keep track of each response.

LINE PLOTS Line plots are useful displays of data along a numeric scale. To make a line plot, a number line is drawn and an X is made above the corresponding value on the line for every data element.

TEACHING STRATEGIES

Have students work in groups to complete a chart to list the possible sums when rolling 2 number cubes. Before students complete 100 rolls, have them predict which sum or sums they expect to obtain most often and least often and why. Most likely is 7, because there are 6 ways to obtain 7; least likely are 2 and 12, because there is only 1 way to obtain each sum. Ask each group to make a frequency table to organize the results of their 100 rolls and then use the frequency table to make a line plot.

Lesson 2.5

MATH BACKGROUND

BAR GRAPHS A bar graph uses the length of solid bars to compare data. To compare two sets of data, a **double bar graph** can be made.

TEACHING STRATEGIES

Help students generate and organize some data about themselves. Introduce the activity by letting the students know that you would like to know more about their interests. Have them write the name of their favorite sport on squares of paper—one color for the boys and another for the girls. Then ask the students how the data can be organized. Students may suggest reading the responses and sorting them into piles according to sport, then counting them.

Make piles of the different responses, combining the boys' and girls' responses. If there are many different sports mentioned, group some of them with small numbers into an "Other" pile.

Ask: "How many students chose [name of sport]? How many chose [name of sport]?" Students should count the responses in each pile and make a chart of the numbers. Guide students through the construction of a bar graph on the display board, using the combined data. Finally, as an extension, have students separate the squares for each sport into two piles, one for boys and one for girls, to construct a double bar graph.

Lesson 2.6

MATH BACKGROUND

LINE GRAPHS A line graph is used when there is a numeric value associated with equally spaced points along a continuous number scale. Points are plotted to represent two related pieces of data and a line is drawn to connect the points. Line graphs are appropriate for data that shows change over time.

TEACHING STRATEGIES

Bring in several examples of line graphs from newspapers, news magazines, and Internet sites that can be shared with the class. You might want to make an overhead transparency of some of the graphs.

Lesson 2.7

MATH BACKGROUND

CIRCLE GRAPHS A **circle graph** is used when data have been broken into parts and you wish to compare the ratio of each part to the whole.

TEACHING STRATEGIES

Have pairs of students come up with topics that could be represented by a circle graph. Ask pairs to share their topic with the class and ask the class members if they agree that a circle graph would be appropriate in each case.

Lesson 2.8

MATH BACKGROUND

DESCRIBING NUMERICAL DATA Two types of measures are often used to summarize numerical data: measures of central tendency and measures of variability. Three common measures of central tendency are the **mode**, **median**, and **mean**. A measure of simple variability is the **range**.

The mode is the most frequently occurring value in a set of data; the median is the middle value; the mean is the average calculated by a adding together all the values in the data set and dividing by the number of values. The range is the difference between the smallest and largest values.

TEACHING STRATEGIES

Use the following example to introduce the concepts of mean, median, and mode.

The following numbers show the number of miles driven by five families who came to a reunion.

$$5, 120, 36, 36, 97, 509, 247$$

Have the students put the numbers in order. Then work with students to find the range (504), the mode (36), the median (97), and the mean (150).

Differentiating Instruction

Strategies for Underachievers

USE SCAFFOLDING

"Scaffolding" is a pedagogical technique designed to help students build the understanding they need for solving complex and multi-step problems. This involves breaking down word problems so that they can be solved by a step-by-step approach. Example 1 on page 79 shows students how to set up a bar graph in a step-by-step format. Example 2 reemphasizes constructing a bar graph while explaining double bar graphs to students. Throughout the course, when students are having difficulty with a particular type of problem, simplify and break down what they are asked to do. You might first ask them to tell you aloud what they are being asked to solve, what information they already know, and what they can tell from the information they are given. Often, simply stating what they know helps students clarify their thinking. This process of breaking complex problems down to separate, simpler parts will allow underachieving students better access to grade level problems.

Example Exercise 27 on Page 65 asks students to estimate whether a bag of fertilizer is enough to cover a lawn; it also asks for students to explain their answers.

- You may first wish to ask students to restate this problem in their own words.
- Then ask them to decide which operation or formula they would need to find the area of the lawn.
- Then have students tell you how they would determine if the bag of fertilizer is sufficient to cover the lawn.
- They then may show a number sentence and explain their conclusion and their reasoning.
- You may also wish to give students some sentence starters or other prompts to help them to write their explanations.

PROVIDE CONCRETE EXAMPLES

USING SCALES When working with scale drawings, scale factors, or ratios, you may wish to use concrete examples, such as maps, architectural plans or drawings, model kits of cars, and so on, to show students real-life applications of scale. You may then wish to engage students in a discussion of where they might have used scales, such as in doll clothing, model airplanes, or tree houses.

PROVIDE SUFFICIENT PRACTICE

Some students need just a couple of examples in order to understand and remember a mathematical concept or procedure. Most students need more practice. Practice should be varied, so that students are assigned exercises that range from easy to difficult and so students must apply what they have learned to a variety of settings.

CONCEPT RETENTION

REPEATED INSTRUCTION When students who have had a difficult time with a concept finally seem to understand it, do not assume it will be retained. Return to this concept repeatedly during the school year. Each lesson of this book contains an exercise section entitled "Mixed Review." Assigning these problems to students can help to reinforce concepts taught in previous lessons; this can also help teachers to check to see what concepts and skills students retain and what they have forgotten. In addition, students may only know what skill to use in solving a problem when that particular skill is the focus of the lesson being taught. For example, in Lesson 2.3, students may understand the concept of scale drawing, but later in Chapter 2, they may not understand that the concept of scale must be applied to axes for bar graphs or to wedges in circle graphs.

Strategies for English Learners

VOCABULARY DEVELOPMENT

FORMULAS Certain letters are commonly used in formulas to mean specific things. Review with your English learners common abbreviations used in mathematics formulas. These may be in capitals or lowercase and include:

distance (d)	length (l)
rate (r)	width (w)
time (t)	circumference (C)
perimeter (P)	radius (r)
area (A)	degrees Fahrenheit (F)
base (b)	degrees Celsius (C)
height (h)	

Note that some letters stand for more than one thing, and students will need to look at the context to understand the abbreviation. Students should also memorize which abbreviations use capital letters and which use lowercase letters.

NAMING UNITS English learners may need to learn or review the commonly used abbreviations for units of length. Keep customary and metric units separate. Common customary unit abbreviations include in. (with the period), ft, yd, and mi; common metric unit abbreviations include mm, cm, m, and km. You may wish to have students create a glossary of abbreviations in their notebooks.

Strategies for Advanced Learners

ASSESS STUDENT ACHIEVEMENT

This would be a good point at which to assess which students complete the review activities quickly, complete their homework with few errors, and seem ready to move at a faster pace. Advanced students may be able to move very quickly through the first three chapters. You may wish to give them the Chapter Tests from Chapters 2 and 3. This will help you and the student determine which concepts and skills have already been mastered. If students can demonstrate mastery, substitute the challenge problems in the book or the Teacher's Edition for homework problems that are too easy. Also consider having advanced learners work on a small research project on their own on a mathematics topic that interests them.

INCREASE DEPTH AND COMPLEXITY

Students may wish to explore some of the cross-curricular links in chapters and learn more about subjects that incorporate the mathematics in the chapter. For example, as students work through Chapter 2, they could explore survey questions which are cross-curricular in nature, such as election questions for Social Studies, genetics questions such as eye color for Science, or measurable athletic performance questions for Physical Education. Students can then survey the entire class or grade, and they could then write a written report in English Language Arts class.

As advanced students complete challenge problems, other students may show an interest in the problems as well. Encourage all students who show an interest to try these challenge problems. Decide beforehand upon a policy regarding credit given for completion of challenge problems.

The following problem can be used with **Lesson 2.3**:

- **Challenge** Use a piece of grid paper to complete a scale drawing of the perimeter of the classroom and items within the classroom, such as the teacher's desk, students' desks, and other items which are integral parts of the classroom. Check work.

In **Lesson 2.8**, introduce students to the term, "outlier," which means a datum that is significantly greater or less than the rest of the data and, as a result, skews the mean of the whole set of data.

- **Challenge** These are the salaries for a small company: $20,000, $22,000, $22,000, $25,000, $100,000. Find the mean of this data. Is this a typical salary? Why or why not? The mean of these salaries is $37,800; it is not typical because a salary between $20,000 and $25,000 would better describe what the "average" worker earns.

Differentiating Instruction: Teaching Resources

Differentiating Assessment

McDougal Littell *Middle School Mathematics* offers a wide variety of assessment. This includes Level A, Level B, and Level C Chapter Tests, Standardized Tests, Cumulative Tests, and Quizzes from the *Assessment Book*, Daily Homework Quizzes from the *Warm-Up Transparencies*, and the *Test and Practice Generator*.

ASSESSMENT BOOK

The *Assessment Book* contains two quizzes, three levels of chapter tests, A (Basic), B (Average), and C (Advanced), and a standardized test for each chapter in the textbook. Also included are cumulative tests and unit tests.

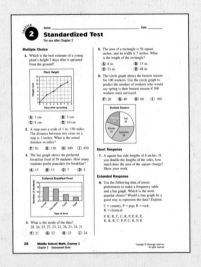
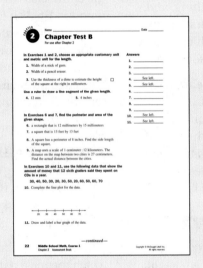
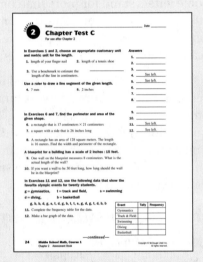
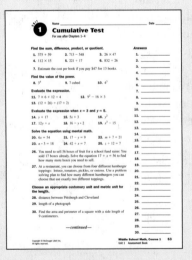
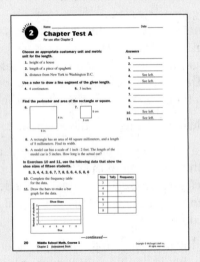
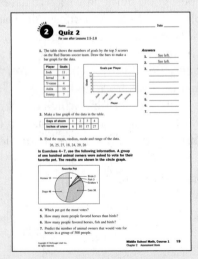

WARM-UP TRANSPARENCIES WITH DAILY HOMEWORK QUIZ

The *Warm-Up Transparencies with Daily Homework Quiz* contains a daily homework quiz for each lesson in the textbook. Each quiz appears with a set of warm-up exercises.

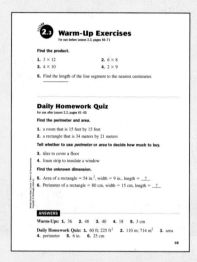

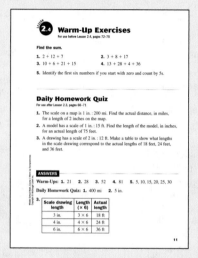

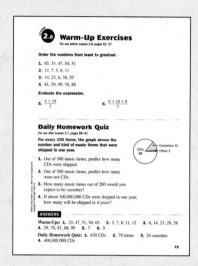

TEST AND PRACTICE GENERATOR CD-ROM

The *Test and Practice Generator* can be used to create numerous quizzes and tests for each lesson and for each chapter using both static and algorithmic exercises.

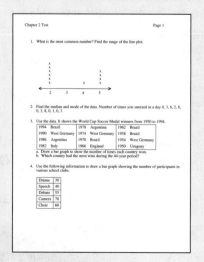

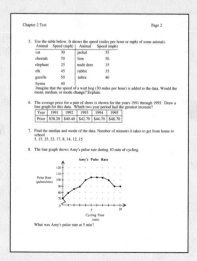

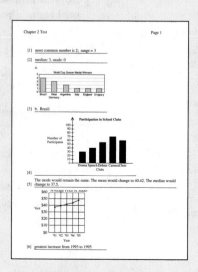

MAIN IDEAS

In this chapter, students measure lengths and find the perimeter and area of geometric figures. They also find actual lengths from scale drawings. They create and interpret frequency tables and line plots, and display data in bar graphs. They plot points in the first quadrant to make line graphs. Students also interpret circle graphs, and describe data using mean, median, mode, and range.

PREREQUISITE SKILLS

The key skills reviewed in the game on these pages are:
- Finding a data point on a graph
- Interpreting the data on a graph
- Estimating whole numbers
- Comparing data from a graph

Additional practice with prerequisite skills can be found in the Review What You Need to Know exercises on page 54. Additional resources for reviewing prerequisite skills are:
- Skills Review Handbook, pp. 684–707
- Tutor Place
- eTutorial Plus Online

MANAGING THE GAME

Tips for Success

Students should read the horizontal axis on the bar graph carefully so they realize that each value should be multiplied by 1000.

Reflecting on the Game

In Stop and Think Question 2, students should be able to see that the temperature graph has a cyclic nature to it and that the temperature rises or falls at a fairly even rate. Encourage them to find similar data for your region to determine how the graph of the average monthly temperature there looks.

CHAPTER 2

Measurement and Statistics

BEFORE

In previous courses you've...
- Interpreted data displays
- Used measurements in problems

Now

In Chapter 2 you'll study...
- Metric and customary units of length
- Area and perimeter
- Making scale drawings
- Making data displays
- Finding mean, median, and mode

WHY?

So you can solve real-world problems about...
- rock climbing, p. 59
- weather, p. 75
- in-line skating, p. 82
- sea turtles, p. 96

Internet Preview
CLASSZONE.COM
- eEdition Plus Online
- eWorkbook Plus Online
- eTutorial Plus Online
- State Test Practice
- More Examples

Chapter Warm-Up Game

Review skills you need for this chapter in this quick game.

Key Skill: Interpreting data displays

DESERT MATH

HOW TO PLAY

1 **USE** the data displays to answer each question. Then match each answer with a value and a letter from the table.
- What is the average temperature in July in Saguaro National Park? **86, M**
- Estimate the difference between the average July and January temperatures. **36, T**
- What is the approximate area of the Sonoran Desert? **120,000, V**
- The Chihuahuan Desert is about how many times as large as the Mojave Desert? **8, N**

Match your Answer	
5 A	8 N
180,000 Z	200,000 M
120,000 V	50 U
86 M	36 T
160,000 X	120 C

2 **FIND** the least and greatest values among your answers. The letters associated with these values spell a two letter abbreviation for a state known for its beautiful deserts. **NV**

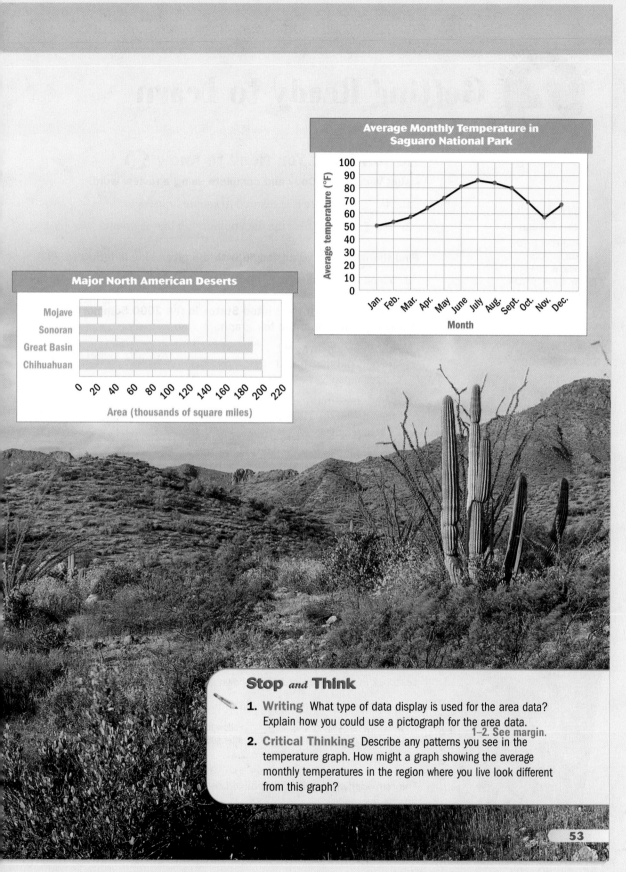

Major North American Deserts

Mojave
Sonoran
Great Basin
Chihuahuan

0 20 40 60 80 100 120 140 160 180 200 220

Area (thousands of square miles)

Average Monthly Temperature in Saguaro National Park

Average temperature (°F)

100
90
80
70
60
50
40
30
20
10
0

Jan. Feb. Mar. Apr. May June July Aug. Sept. Oct. Nov. Dec.

Month

Stop *and* Think

1. Writing What type of data display is used for the area data? Explain how you could use a pictograph for the area data.

1–2. See margin.

2. Critical Thinking Describe any patterns you see in the temperature graph. How might a graph showing the average monthly temperatures in the region where you live look different from this graph?

53

CHAPTER RESOURCES

These resources are provided to help you prepare for the chapter and to customize review materials:

Chapter 2 Resource Book
- Tips for New Teachers, pp. 1–2
- Lesson Plan, pp. 5, 13, 23, 31, 39, 48, 58, 65
- Lesson Plan for Block Scheduling, pp. 6, 14, 24, 32, 40, 49, 59, 66

Technology
- EasyPlanner CD-ROM
- Test and Practice Generator
- Electronic Lesson Presentations CD-ROM
- eTutorial CD-ROM

Internet
- Classzone
- eEdition Plus Online
- eWorkbook Plus Online
- eTutorial Plus Online
- EasyPlanner Plus Online

ENGLISH LEARNER SUPPORT
- Spanish Study Guide
- Multi-Language Glossary
- Chapter Audio Summaries CDs
- Teacher's Edition, pp. 52E–52F

1. **Bar graph.** *Sample answer:* Use a symbol for each 20 thousand square miles and show one symbol for the Mojave desert, 6 symbols for the Sonoran desert, $9\frac{1}{2}$ symbols for the Great Basin desert, and 10 symbols for the Chihuahuan desert.

2. The average monthly temperature rose from January through July, fell from July through November, and then rose again from November to December; answers may vary.

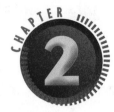

PREPARE

DIAGNOSIS/REMEDIATION

Review What You Need to Know
The Review What You Need to Know exercises can help you diagnose whether students have the following skills needed in Chapter 2:

- Vocabulary (Exs. 1-2)
- Find the perimeter of a triangle (Exs. 3-4)
- Read a bar graph (Exs. 5-7)
- Evaluate expressions (Exs. 8-11)

Chapter 2 Resource Book

- Study Guide (Lessons 2.1-2.8)

Tutor Place

NOTETAKING STRATEGIES

Students who take notes usually do so in class. Most students do not think of taking notes while reading. The strategy presented on this page not only points out that this is a useful practice, but also offers students a way to self-correct their class notes as they take notes while reading. Further suggestions for keeping a notebook can be found on page 94.

For more support on notetaking, see:

- Notetaking Guide Workbook
- Notetaking Transparencies

CHAPTER 2 Getting Ready to Learn

Review What You Need to Know

Using Vocabulary **Copy and complete using a review word.**

1. The _?_ of a figure is measured in square units. **area**

2. In a _?_, you connect the data points with line segments. **line graph**

Word Watch

Review Words

perimeter, p. 702
area, p. 702
data, p. 704
bar graph, p. 704
line graph, p. 705

Find the perimeter of a triangle with the given side lengths. *(p. 702)*

3. 5 feet, 2 feet, 6 feet **13 ft**

4. 10 inches, 10 inches, 10 inches **30 in.**

The medal count for the United States in the 2000 Summer Olympics is shown in the bar graph. *(p. 704)*

5. About how many gold medals did the United States receive? **about 39 gold medals**

6. About how many silver medals did the United States receive? **about 25 silver medals**

7. About how many medals did the United States receive in all? **about 96 medals**

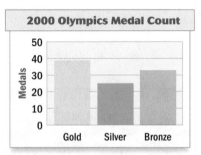

Evaluate the expression when $x = 8$ and $y = 2$. *(p. 29)*

8. $2x$ **16**

9. $4y$ **8**

10. $x + y$ **10**

11. $2x - y$ **14**

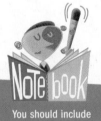

You should include material that appears on a notebook like this in your own notes.

Know How to Take Notes

Taking Notes While Reading Leave extra space while you take notes in class. Then review the lesson in your textbook to correct or add to your class notes. You may also want to copy the "Help" notes from the textbook in your own words, as shown below.

$m = 3, n = 4$

$$m + 2n = 3 + 2 \cdot 4$$
$$= 3 + 8$$
$$= 11$$

← **Follow the order of operations after substituting.**

The reminder above will be helpful in Lesson 2.8 when you learn about finding averages.

Measuring Length

BEFORE	▶ **Now**	**WHY?**
You used a ruler to draw straight lines.	You'll measure length using customary and metric units.	So you can find lengths, such as lengths of animals in Exs. 9 and 10.

PLAN

SKILL CHECK

1. $8 \times 12 =$ _?_   96
2. $1760 \times 4 =$ _?_   7040
3. $288 \div 36 =$ _?_   8
4. $723 \div 3 =$ _?_   241

LESSON OBJECTIVE

Measure length using customary and metric units.

PACING

Suggested Number of Days
Basic Course: 2 days
Average Course: 2 days
Advanced Course: 2 days
Block: 1 block

TEACHING RESOURCES

For a complete list of Teaching Resources, see page 52B.

TRANSPARENCY

Warm-Up Exercises for this lesson are available on a transparency.

TEACH

MOTIVATING THE LESSON

Extend the Activity by having students measure other objects using paper clips and little finger widths.

ACTIVITY

Goal Use paper clips and finger widths to estimate length.

Key Discovery Different units can be used to measure length.

Word Watch

inch, p. 55
foot, p. 55
yard, p. 55
mile, p. 55
millimeter, p. 56
centimeter, p. 56
meter, p. 56
kilometer, p. 56

Activity You can use many different units to measure length.

① Look at your math book and estimate the length in "paper clips."
Sample answer: 8 paper clips

② Using paper clips, measure the length of your book. How does the result compare to your estimate?
Sample answer: 8 paper clips; the result is the same as the estimate.

③ Look at your math book and estimate the width in "little fingers."
Sample answer: 15 little fingers

④ Using your little finger, measure the width of your book. How does the result compare to your estimate?
Sample answer: 20 little fingers; the result is greater than the estimate.

Count the last clip if half or more of it is used.

Customary Units A small paper clip is about one inch long. An **inch** (in.) is a customary unit of length. Three other customary units of length are the **foot** (ft), the **yard** (yd), and the **mile** (mi). Inches, feet, yards, and miles are related to each other.

$$1 \text{ ft} = 12 \text{ in.} \qquad 1 \text{ yd} = 3 \text{ ft} = 36 \text{ in.} \qquad 1 \text{ mi} = 1760 \text{ yd} = 5280 \text{ ft}$$

EXAMPLE 1 **Using Customary Units of Length**

Find the length of the caterpillar to the nearest inch.

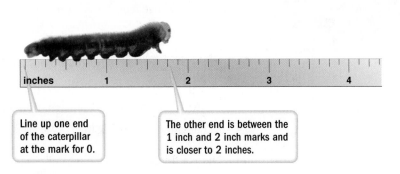

Line up one end of the caterpillar at the mark for 0.

The other end is between the 1 inch and 2 inch marks and is closer to 2 inches.

ANSWER The caterpillar is about 2 inches long.

NCTM CURRICULUM STANDARDS
Standard 4: Understand the units of measurement; Understand the processes of measurement; Apply proper tools to find measures

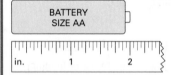
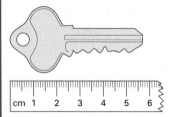
 HELP *with Vocabulary*

The Latin prefixes *milli-* (thousand) and *centi-* (hundred) are used to form units less than a meter. The Greek prefix *kilo-* (thousand) is used to form a unit greater than a meter.

Metric Units Your little finger is about one centimeter wide. The commonly used metric units of length are the **millimeter** (mm), the **centimeter** (cm), the **meter** (m), and the **kilometer** (km). Here are some common metric unit relationships.

$$1 \text{ cm} = 10 \text{ mm} \qquad 1 \text{ m} = 100 \text{ cm} = 1000 \text{ mm} \qquad 1 \text{ km} = 1000 \text{ m}$$

EXAMPLE 2 Using Metric Units of Length

Find the length of the seashell to the nearest millimeter.

Line up one end of the shell at the mark for 0.

The other end lines up with 40 mm + 5 mm, or 45 mm.

1 cm is equal to 10 mm, so the 4 represents 40 mm.

ANSWER The seashell is about 45 millimeters long.

EXAMPLE 3 Choosing Appropriate Units

Choose an appropriate customary unit and metric unit for the length.

a. distance from Boston to Chicago **b.** height of a full grown tree

Solution

a. The distance from Boston to Chicago is much greater than one yard or one meter. So, you should use miles or kilometers.

b. The height of a full grown tree is much greater than one inch or one centimeter, and much less than one mile or one kilometer. So, you should use feet, yards, or meters.

Your turn now **Measure the object to the nearest whole unit.**

1. length of your math book (inches) *Sample answer: about 10 in.*

2. width of your math book (centimeters) *Sample answer: about 20 cm*

3. height of your desk (feet) *Sample answer: about 3 ft*

Choose an appropriate customary unit and metric unit for the length.

4. height of a two year old child **feet; meters**

5. width of a baseball card **inches; centimeters**

Example 4 Estimate the width of your calculator in inches. Use a paper clip as a benchmark Then measure to check your estimate.

Sample answer: about 3 in.

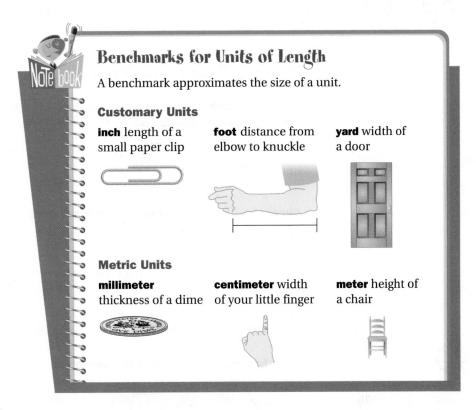

Benchmarks for Units of Length

A benchmark approximates the size of a unit.

Customary Units

inch length of a small paper clip

foot distance from elbow to knuckle

yard width of a door

Metric Units

millimeter thickness of a dime

centimeter width of your little finger

meter height of a chair

Differentiating Instruction

Alternative Teaching Strategy
Have students create their own set of benchmarks for units of length with various objects in the classroom, like pencils or desks. Then have students use their benchmarks to estimate lengths.

CONCEPT CHECK

The width of your mathematics book is approximately 8 "paper clips". What is the approximate width in customary units? **about 8 in.**

DAILY PUZZLER

Copy the triangle and place the digits 1 through 9, with one at each vertex and two along each side, so that the sum along each side is 17.

EXAMPLE 4 **Estimating Length Using Benchmarks**

Estimate the height, in meters, of the door below. Then measure to check your estimate.

1 To estimate, imagine how high the door is in "chairs."

2 To check your estimate, measure the door with a meter stick.

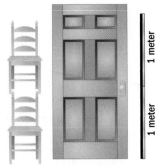

1 meter

1 meter

ANSWER The door is about 2 "chairs" high, which is about 2 meters. The height of the door is just over 2 meters.

HELP with Solving

You can use your own height as a benchmark when estimating.

2.1 Exercises

More Practice, p. 709

Getting Ready to Practice

Vocabulary **Copy and complete the statement with the appropriate customary unit or metric unit.**

1. 1 yd = 3 ? ft   **2.** 1 cm = 10 ? mm   **3.** 1 m = 100 ? cm   **4.** 1 ft = 12 ? in.

5. Measure the length of your math notebook to the nearest millimeter, to the nearest centimeter, and to the nearest inch. *Answers may vary.*

Choose an appropriate customary unit and metric unit for the length.

6. height of a flagpole *feet or yards; meters*   **7.** length of a river *miles; kilometers*

8. Use a benchmark to estimate the length of your pencil in inches. Then measure to check your estimate. *Sample answer:* 4 paper clips; 4 in.

Practice and Problem Solving

HELP with Homework

Example	Exercises
1	9-10, 15-16
2	11-14
3	17-24
4	25-30

Online Resources
CLASSZONE.COM
· More Examples
· eTutorial Plus

Find the length of the animal to the nearest inch.

A **9.**

2 in.

10.

1 in.

Find the length of the line segment to the nearest millimeter and to the nearest centimeter.

11.

38 mm; 4 cm

12.

23 mm; 2 cm

Draw a line segment of the given length. 13–16. Check drawings.

13. 12 centimeters   **14.** 48 millimeters

15. 5 inches   **16.** 8 inches

Choose an appropriate customary unit and metric unit for the length.

17. length of a marathon *miles; kilometers*   **18.** thickness of a CD *inches; millimeters*

19. length of a diving board *feet; meters*   **20.** length of a computer screen *inches; centimeters*

21. length of a clarinet *inches; centimeters*   **22.** distance to the moon *miles; kilometers*

23. length of a bike *feet; meters*   **24.** height of a building *feet or yards; meters*

Estimation **Use a benchmark to estimate the length in the given unit. Then measure to check your estimate.** 25–30. Sample answers are given.

25. height of a stove (feet)
3 elbow to knuckle units; 3 ft

26. length of a bed (feet)
7 elbow to knuckle units; 7 ft

27. width of a television (inches)
26 paper clips; 26 in.

28. length of a spoon (inches)
4 paper clips; 4 in.

29. height of a lamp (centimeters)
45 little fingers; 45 cm

30. length of a shoe (centimeters)
20 little fingers 20 cm

31. **Find the Error** Your friend says that the length of the eraser is about 3 inches. Describe and correct the error. *Sample answer:* The left end of the eraser is not lined up at the mark for 0. The length of the eraser is about 2 inches.

The length of the eraser is about 3 inches.

Tell whether the statement is reasonable. If it is not, change the unit of measure so that it is reasonable.

B 32. A driveway is 14 *feet* wide.
reasonable

33. A cat is 12 *inches* long.
reasonable

34. A bike path is 8 *millimeters* long.
not reasonable; kilometers

35. A book is 10 *meters* thick.
not reasonable; millimeters

36. **Rock Climbing** The height of the person in the photo at the left is 6 feet. Estimate the height of the rock that the person is climbing.
40 ft

Geometry **Without using a ruler, draw a square with the given side length. Then use a ruler to check your drawing.** 37–40. Check drawings.

37. 6 centimeters

38. 4 inches

39. 7 inches

40. 70 millimeters

41. **Writing** Do you need an actual measurement or an estimate to determine whether a table will fit through a doorway? Explain.
41–44. See margin.

42. **Critical Thinking** A line segment is 6 centimeters long, to the nearest centimeter. Give 5 possible lengths of the line segment in millimeters.

C 43. **Explain** Choose a benchmark that could be used for a mile. Explain how you would use that benchmark to measure a distance near where you live.

44. **Challenge** You have bought a case that is 15 centimeters tall to protect your electronic game. To the nearest centimeter, your game is also 15 centimeters tall. Assuming that the case is wide enough, can you be sure that your game will fit completely into the case? Why or why not?

 Nature

■ **Rock Climbing**

Some rock climbers practice on rock climbing walls. A variety of "holds" are placed on rock climbing walls to help the climbers grip the wall with their hands and feet as they climb. About how far should one hold be placed from the next for a beginning climber of your height?
Sample answer: about 5 ft

For more assessment resources, see:
• Assessment Book
• Test and Practice Generator

MINI-QUIZ

Choose an appropriate customary and metric unit for the length.

1. length of a flute **inches or centimeters**

2. height of an elephant **feet, yards, or meters**

3. Use a benchmark to estimate the height of a paperback book in centimeters. Then measure to check your estimate. **Sample answer: about 17 cm**

Tell whether the statement is reasonable. If not, change the unit of measurement so that it is reasonable.

4. A computer mouse is 11 meters long. **not reasonable; centimeters**

5. A refrigerator is 5 feet high. **reasonable**

⑤ FOLLOW-UP

RETEACHING/REMEDIATION

• Study Guide in Chapter 2 Resource Book, pp. 10–11
• eTutorial Plus Online
• Extra Practice, p. 709
• Lesson Practice in Chapter 2 Resource Book, pp. 7–9

CHALLENGE/ENRICHMENT

• Challenge Practice in Chapter 2 Resource Book, p. 12
• Teacher's Edition, p. 52F

ENGLISH LEARNER SUPPORT

• Spanish Study Guide
• Multi-Language Glossary
• Chapter Audio Summaries CDs

Mixed Review

Evaluate the expression when $t = 4$ and $u = 6$. *(Lesson 1.5)*

45. $4t$ 16   **46.** u^2 36   **47.** $2t + u$ 14   **48.** $2u - t$ 8

Choose a Strategy Use a strategy from the list to solve the following problem. Explain your choice of strategy.

> **Problem Solving Strategies**
> • Guess, Check, and Revise
> • Draw a Diagram
> • Make a List
> • Act It Out

49. The *perimeter* of a figure is the distance around the figure. A triangle with two equal sides has a perimeter of 32 inches. The third side is 4 inches shorter than each of the other sides. Find the lengths of the sides.

49. 12 in., 12 in., and 8 in.; *Sample answer:* I used Guess, Check, and Revise because I thought guessing the lengths of the sides and then checking to see if they worked was the easiest strategy to use.

Basic Skills   Copy and complete the number fact family.

50. $\underline{?} \times 2 = 18$ 9 $9 \times \underline{?} = 18$ 2 $18 \div \underline{?} = 2$ 9 $\underline{?} \div 2 = 9$ 18

Test-Taking Practice 📝

INTERNET
State Test Practice
CLASSZONE.COM

51. Multiple Choice Which item is likely to be measured in meters? C

   A. thimble   **B.** leaf   **C.** sofa   **D.** freeway

52. Multiple Choice Which measure is closest to the length of the item? H

   F. 5 cm   **G.** 53 mm   **H.** 58 mm   **I.** 6 cm

BRAIN GAME

Optical Illusions

Which line segment is longer?

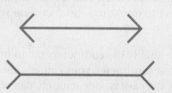

The segments are the same length.

Which person is the tallest?

The persons are all the same height.

LESSON 2.2

Perimeter and Area

BEFORE ▸ **Now** **WHY?**

You found the square of a number. | You'll use formulas to find perimeter and area. | So you can find measurements, such as poster areas in Ex. 28.

In the Real World

Word Watch

perimeter, p. 61
area, p. 62

Carnival A carnival is going to be held in your school's parking lot. How much rope is needed to enclose the carnival? To answer this question, you can find the carnival's *perimeter*.

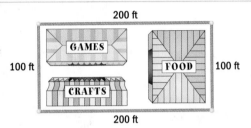

200 ft

GAMES

FOOD

100 ft   100 ft

CRAFTS

200 ft

The **perimeter** of a figure is the distance around the figure. Perimeter is measured in linear units such as feet, inches, or meters.

Perimeter of a Rectangle

Words Perimeter = 2 • length + 2 • width

Algebra $P = 2l + 2w$

l
w w
l

EXAMPLE 1 **Finding the Perimeter of a Rectangle**

To answer the real-world question above, find the perimeter.

$P = 2l + 2w$ — Write the formula for perimeter of a rectangle.

$= 2 \cdot 200 + 2 \cdot 100$ — Substitute 200 for l and 100 for w.

$= 400 + 200$ — Multiply.

$= 600$ — Add.

ANSWER The amount of rope needed to enclose the carnival is 600 feet.

Your turn now **Find the perimeter of the rectangle described.**

1. length = 9 m, width = 5 m **28 m**
2. length = 20 in., width = 12 in. **64 in.**

NCTM CURRICULUM STANDARDS
Standard 2: Represent situations using algebraic symbols
Standard 4: Understand measurable attributes of objects; Apply proper formulas to find measures

---

① PLAN

SKILL CHECK
1. $2 \cdot 18 + 2 \cdot 12 = \underline{?}$ 60
2. $23 \times 15 = \underline{?}$ 345
3. $32^2 = \underline{?}$ 1024

LESSON OBJECTIVE
Use formulas to find perimeter and area.

PACING
Suggested Number of Days
Basic Course: 2 days
Average Course: 2 days
Advanced Course: 2 days
Block: 1 block

TEACHING RESOURCES
For a complete list of Teaching Resources, see page 52B.

TRANSPARENCY
Warm-Up Exercises for this lesson are available on a transparency.

② TEACH

MOTIVATING THE LESSON
Give students diagrams of rectangles, squares, and other figures. Have students use rulers to find the distance around each figure.

TIPS FOR NEW TEACHERS
To help students distinguish between perimeter and area, discuss a variety of real-world examples. See Tips for New Teachers in the *Chapter 2 Resource Book*.

61

Area The **area** of a figure is the amount of surface the figure covers. Area is measured in square units such as square feet (ft^2) or square meters (m^2).

Area of a Rectangle

Words Area = length · width

Algebra $A = lw$

Watch Out!

The units of the answer are square feet, not linear feet. To help you remember this, think of multiplying the units: $lw = \text{ft} \times \text{ft} = \text{ft}^2$.

EXAMPLE 2 Finding the Area of a Rectangle

Find the area of the carnival shown at the top of page 61.

$A = lw$	Write the formula for area of a rectangle.
$= 200 \cdot 100$	Substitute 200 for l and 100 for w.
$= 20,000$	Multiply.

ANSWER The area of the carnival is 20,000 square feet.

Squares A square is a rectangle that has four sides with the same length. You can use the following formulas for a square with side length s.

Perimeter of square = 4 · side length
$$P = 4s$$

Area of square = (side length)^2
$$A = s^2$$

EXAMPLE 3 Perimeter and Area of a Square

Find the perimeter and the area of a 50 yard by 50 yard corral.

Perimeter = $4s$	Area = s^2
$= 4 \cdot 50$	$= 50^2$
$= 200$	$= 2500$

ANSWER The perimeter is 200 yards. The area is 2500 square yards.

Your turn now Tell whether to find the *perimeter* or the *area* to help you decide how much of the item to buy. Then find the measurement.

3. tiles to cover a 9 ft by 9 ft floor
area; 81 ft^2

4. fence for a 6 m by 7 m garden
perimeter; 26 m

EXAMPLE 4 **Solving for an Unknown Dimension**

 Algebra **Write and solve an equation to find the width of a rectangle whose area is 195 square centimeters and whose length is 15 centimeters.**

 with Review

Need help with thinking of a related equation? See page 687.

$A = lw$	Write the formula for the area of a rectangle.
$195 = 15w$	Substitute the known values for A and l.
$w = 195 \div 15$	Write the related division equation.
$w = 13$	Divide.

ANSWER The width of the rectangle is 13 centimeters.

Your turn now **Write and solve an equation to find the length.**

5. Area of rectangle = 91 in.², width = 7 in., length = _?_ $91 = l \cdot 7$; 13 in.

6. Perimeter of square = 132 cm, side length = _?_ $132 = 4s$; 33 cm

CONCEPT CHECK

Explain how the formulas for the perimeter and area of a square can be derived from the formulas for the perimeter and area of a rectangle. **In the formulas, substitute s for l and w. $P = 2l + 2w$ becomes $P = 2s + 2s$, or $P = 4s$; $A = lw$ becomes $A = s \cdot s$, or $A = s^2$.**

DAILY PUZZLER

Find the perimeter of a square that has an area of 36 square centimeters. **24 cm**

2.2 Exercises

More Practice, p. 709

INTERNET
eWorkbook Plus
CLASSZONE.COM

Getting Ready to Practice

1. **Vocabulary** The _?_ of a rectangle is the sum of twice its length and twice its width. The _?_ of a rectangle is the product of its length and its width. **perimeter; area**

Find the perimeter and the area of the rectangle or square.

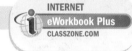

2.
3 m
6 m
$P = 18$ m; $A = 18$ m²

3.
2 ft
7 ft
$P = 18$ ft; $A = 14$ ft²

4.
10 in.
10 in.
$P = 40$ in.; $A = 100$ in.²

5. **Guided Problem Solving** You plan to use 64 feet of fencing to form a square pen for your dog. How long will each side be?

   (1 Decide whether 64 feet is the perimeter or the area of the pen. **perimeter**

   (2 Write an equation to represent this situation. **$64 = 4s$**

   (3 Solve the equation to find the length of each side of the pen. **16 ft**

29. *Sample answer:* One rectangle
has sides of length 3 and 5,
while the second rectangle has
sides of length 2 and 6.

18. *Sample answer:*
Perimeter is not measured
in square units. The final
answer should be 20 feet.

■ **Gymnastics**

Where should a gymnast
start and end a tumbling
run to make it as long as
possible and still stay
within the boundary lines
on the mat shown at the
right? **The gymnast
should start at one corner
and end in the diagonally
opposite corner.**

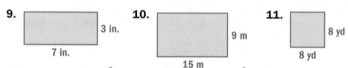

HELP with Homework

Example	Exercises
1	6–18
2	6–17
3	11–12, 19–20
4	21–24

ⓘ **Online Resources**
CLASSZONE.COM
· More Examples
· eTutorial Plus

Practice and Problem Solving

Tell whether the measure could represent a *perimeter* or an *area*.

A 6. 15 yd perimeter   **7.** 10 in.² area   **8.** 56 cm² area

Find the perimeter and the area of the rectangle or square.

9. [rectangle 7 in. by 3 in.]   **10.** [rectangle 15 m by 9 m]   **11.** [square 8 yd by 8 yd]

$P = 20$ in; $A = 21$ in.² $P = 48$ m; $A = 135$ m² $P = 32$ yd; $A = 64$ yd²

12. a square that is 15 cm by 15 cm   **13.** a rectangle that is 19 ft by 17 ft
   $P = 60$ cm; $A = 225$ cm² $P = 72$ ft; $A = 323$ ft²

Home Improvement **Tell whether you would use *perimeter* or *area*
to help you decide how much of the item to buy.**

14. fringe for the edges of a rug   **15.** paint for a ceiling area
      perimeter
16. carpeting to cover a floor area   **17.** lace to trim the edges of a pillow
                                                  perimeter

18. Find the Error Describe and correct the error in the solution.

✗ Perimeter = 2 · 6 + 2 · 4
      = 12 + 8
      = 20 square feet

[rectangle 6 ft by 4 ft]

Gymnastics **The mat at the right is used for
performing gymnastics floor routines. The
gymnast must stay within the white lines.**

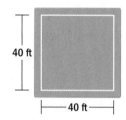
[square 40 ft by 40 ft]

19. How much space does the gymnast
   have to perform in? 1600 ft

20. What is the length of tape needed to
   mark off the white lines? 160 ft

ⓧⓨ **Algebra** **Write and solve an equation to find the unknown dimension.**

B 21. Area of rectangle = 42 in.², width = 3 in., length = ? $42 = l \cdot 3$; 14 in.

22. Area of rectangle = 132 m², length =12 m, width = ? $132 = 12w$; 11 m

23. Perimeter of square = 100 ft, side length = ? $100 = 4s$; 25 ft

24. Perimeter of square = 56 cm, side length = ? $56 = 4s$; 14 cm

25. A square has a side length of 8 inches. A rectangle has a length of
   16 inches and a width of 8 inches. Compare the areas of the figures.
   The square has an area of 64 square inches and the rectangle has an area of 128
   square inches. The area of the rectangle is twice the area of the square.

26. Writing Find both the perimeter and area of a 5 inch by 5 inch square using the formulas for a square and for a rectangle. Compare the results.

See margin.

27. Estimation You are fertilizing a lawn that is 32 feet by 50 feet. Your bag of fertilizer will cover 1500 square feet. Do you have enough? Explain.

See margin.

28. Movie Posters At one time, 14 inch by 22 inch movie posters were made with a blank rectangle at the top for printing dates and locations. Collectors often find these posters with the blank rectangle trimmed off to form a 14 inch by 17 inch poster. How much area was trimmed off?

70 in.²

29. Describe Describe two different rectangles with a perimeter of 16.

See margin.

30. Challenge Your rectangular property is 42 yards long and covers
C 1302 square yards of land. How much fencing is needed to enclose it?

146 yd

Each figure below is made of rectangles and squares. Find its area.

31.

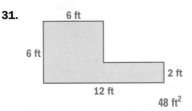

48 ft²

32.

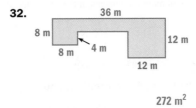

272 m²

Mixed Review

Find the value of the power. *(Lesson 1.3)*

33. 4^3 64

34. 3^5 243

35. 10^3 1000

36. 6^4 1296

Find the length of the segment to the nearest centimeter. *(Lesson 2.1)*

37. ————————— 3 cm

38. ————————— 4 cm

Basic Skills Use front-end estimation to estimate the sum.

39–40. Estimates may vary.

39. $254 + 503 + 739$ 1490

40. $127 + 182 + 569$ 880

26. $P = 20$ in.; $A = 25$ in.²; The perimeter and area are the same no matter which formula is used.

27. No; a low estimate for the area of the lawn is $30 \cdot 50 = 1500$ square feet, which is exactly the area the fertilizer will cover.

Test-Taking Practice

INTERNET
State Test Practice
CLASSZONE.COM

41. Short Response Use estimation to decide which figure has a greater area, a square that is 87 inches by 87 inches or a rectangle that is 198 inches by 61 inches. Explain your reasoning. **The rectangle.**

Sample answer: $90 \times 90 = 8100$ and $200 \times 60 = 12,000$.

42. Multiple Choice How much trim do you need if you want to sew trim along each edge of a 54 inch by 102 inch tablecloth? **B**

A. 156 in.   **B.** 312 in.   **C.** 312 in.²   **D.** 5508 in.²

4 ASSESS

ASSESSMENT RESOURCES

For more assessment resources, see:
• Assessment Book
• Test and Practice Generator

MINI-QUIZ

Find the perimeter and area.

1. a room that is 15 feet by 15 feet
60 ft; 225 ft²

2. a rectangle that is 34 meters by 21 meters **110 m; 714 m²**

Tell whether to use *perimeter* or *area* to decide how much to buy.

3. tiles to cover a floor **area**

4. foam strip to insulate a window
perimeter

Find the unknown dimension.

5. Area of a rectangle = 54 in.²,
width = 9 in., length = _?_ **6 in.**

6. Perimeter of a rectangle = 80 cm,
width = 15 cm, length = _?_
25 cm

5 FOLLOW-UP

RETEACHING/REMEDIATION

• Study Guide in Chapter 2 Resource Book, pp. 19–20
• Tutor Place, Geometry and Measurement Cards 11, 12, 14
• eTutorial Plus Online
• Extra Practice, p. 709
• Lesson Practice in Chapter 2 Resource Book, pp. 16–18

CHALLENGE/ENRICHMENT

• Challenge Practice in Chapter 2 Resource Book, p. 22
• Teacher's Edition, p. 52F

ENGLISH LEARNER SUPPORT

• Spanish Study Guide
• Multi-Language Glossary
• Chapter Audio Summaries CDs

Guess, Check, and Revise
Make a List
Make a Table
Work Backward
Draw a Diagram
Break into Parts
Look for a Pattern

① PLAN

STRATEGY BACKGROUND

Drawing a Diagram is appropriate when the words in the problem suggest a visual representation. Measurement and geometry problems are obvious applications of this strategy, but it is also useful for problems in logic, number theory, and probability. The strategy allows you to overview the problem with one glance, and this may lead to other strategies that you may not have considered.

② TEACH

GUIDING STUDENTS' WORK

You may need to remind students that the perimeter of a rectangle can be found by adding twice the length and twice the width. Remind them also that the order of operations includes doing multiplication before addition in Step 3.

EXTRA EXAMPLES

Example You cut a round pizza with 3 straight cuts. What is the greatest number of pieces you could have made? **7 pieces**

Draw a Diagram

Problem You have 18 yards of wire fence to enclose a community garden. What are the different ways you can fence off the area as a rectangle with whole number dimensions?

① Read and Understand

Read the problem at least twice.

You need to find all the rectangles with whole number dimensions and a perimeter of 18 yards.

② Make a Plan

Decide on a strategy to use.

You can draw diagrams of rectangles that have a perimeter of 18 yards.

③ Solve the Problem

Reread the problem and draw diagrams.

Choose a width and draw a rectangle with that width and a length that produces a perimeter of 18 yards.

$$2 \cdot 8 + 2 \cdot 1 = 18$$

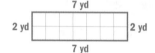

$$2 \cdot 7 + 2 \cdot 2 = 18$$

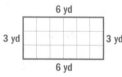

$$2 \cdot 6 + 2 \cdot 3 = 18$$

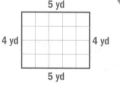

$$2 \cdot 5 + 2 \cdot 4 = 18$$

ANSWER The possible dimensions for the community garden are 8 yards by 1 yard, 7 yards by 2 yards, 6 yards by 3 yards, and 5 yards by 4 yards.

④ Look Back

Check to make sure that you found all the possibilities. The next width to try would be 5 yards, but this has already been covered by the rectangle that is 5 yards by 4 yards.

NCTM CURRICULUM STANDARDS
Standard 2: Use models to understand relationships
Standard 6: Solve problems in math and other contexts
Standard 10: Use representations to solve problems

Practice the Strategy

Use the strategy _draw a diagram_.

1. **Archaeology** You find an old piece of pottery at a construction site. You have 16 yards of rope to enclose the area around it. Find the different ways you can enclose the area as a rectangle with whole number dimensions. **7 yd by 1 yd, 6 yd by 2 yd, 5 yd by 3 yd, 4 yd by 4 yd**

2. **Lawn Care** You would like to cover your backyard with grass. The backyard is 45 feet by 25 feet. A square patio in one corner that is 15 feet by 15 feet will not be covered by grass. What is the total area that you would like to cover with grass? **900 ft²**

3. **Measurement** How can you use the rods shown below to measure a length of 1 centimeter? **See margin.**

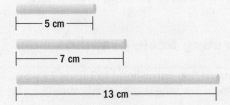

4. **Remodeling** You want to cover an area in your kitchen that is 6 feet by 7 feet with blue square tiles that measure 1 foot by 1 foot. Around the tiled area, you would like to arrange a single line of red square tiles of the same size. How many tiles of each color will you need? **42 blue tiles and 30 red tiles**

5. **Bus Stops** The Youth Center is halfway from your house to the movie theater, which is 8 miles from your house. There is a bus stop three quarters of the way from the theater to the Youth Center. How far is the bus stop from the Youth Center? **1 mi**

Mixed Problem Solving

Use any strategy to solve the problem.

6. **Book Covers** You want to start a business selling textbook covers. You will offer small, medium, and large covers in black, red, and blue. How many different types of covers will you be offering? **9 types of covers**

7. **Missing Number** What number belongs in the blank? **6**

$$(\underline{\text{?}} \times 4) \div 2 + 17 = 29$$

8. **Number Pairs** Two numbers have a sum of 45. If you subtract one number from the other, the difference is 7. What are the two numbers? **19 and 26**

9. **Riddles** Use the riddle below to name a correct animal that would gain you admission to a dance. **See margin.**

> These animals will
> get you through: elk, yak, dog.
> These animals will
> never do: horse, mouse, frog.

10. **Movie Tickets** A movie theater charges $6 for a matinee and $9 for all other shows. In one day, the movie theater sold 400 matinee tickets and 500 other tickets. How much money did the theater make from ticket sales that day? **$6900**

Lesson 2.3   Scale Drawings   **67**

③ APPLY

TRANSPARENCY

Even-numbered answers are available on transparencies.

TEACHING TIP

To simulate Exercise 1, give students a 16-inch length of string and a piece of grid paper, where 1 inch of string equals 1 yard of rope. To simulate Exercise 2, encourage students to draw diagrams on grid paper.

MATH REASONING

For Exercise 3, students should be able to reason that one solution is to draw a segment that is 14 centimeters from two 7-centimeter segments and then superimpose the segment of 13 centimeters. They should reason that it then becomes a subtraction problem that can be represented by the equation $1 = 2(7) - 13$.

SUGGESTED STRATEGIES

You may wish to suggest the following strategies for the problems in the Mixed Problem Solving:

- Exercise 6: Make a List, Make a Table, Draw a Diagram
- Exercise 7: Guess, Check, and Revise, Work Backward
- Exercise 8: Guess, Check, and Revise
- Exercise 9: Look for a Pattern
- Exercise 10: Make a Table, Look for a Pattern

3. _Sample answer:_ Place the 5 centimeter rod end to end with the 7 centimeter rod to make a 12 centimeter rod. Use the difference between this combination and the 13 centimeter rod to measure 1 centimeter.

9. any animal name that has three letters in it, such as "cat"

LESSON OBJECTIVE

Use scale drawings to find actual length.

PACING

Suggested Number of Days
Basic Course: 1 day
Average Course: 1 day
Advanced Course: 1 day
Block: 0.5 block with 2.4

TEACHING RESOURCES

For a complete list of Teaching Resources, see page 52B.

 TRANSPARENCY

Warm-Up Exercises for this lesson are available on a transparency.

2 TEACH

MOTIVATING THE LESSON

Expand the Activity by having students use actual road maps.

ACTIVITY

Goal Use a map to find actual distances.

Key Discovery The scale on a map can be used to change map distances to actual distances.

LESSON 2.3

Scale Drawings

BEFORE	▶ Now	WHY?
You used rulers to find the actual lengths of objects.	You'll use scale drawings to find actual lengths.	So you can use a map to find distances, as in Exs. 19–21.

 **Word Watch**

scale drawing, p. 68
scale, p. 68

Activity **You can use a map to find an actual distance.**

Use the map to find the distance you will canoe.

1. Measure the distance, in centimeters, between the lodge and the dam.
   2 cm

2. The note in the corner of the map reads 1 cm : 2 km, so a distance of 1 cm on the map represents 2 km on the lake. What distance does your measurement represent? **4 km**

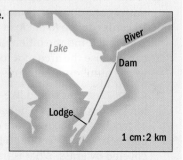

The map in the activity is a *scale drawing*. A **scale drawing** is the same shape as the original object, but not the same size. The **scale** tells how the drawing's dimensions and the actual dimensions are related.

EXAMPLE 1 **Interpreting Scale Drawings**

Canoes Find the actual lengths that correspond to 1 inch, 2 inches, and 3 inches on the scale drawing. How long is the actual canoe?

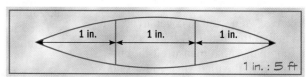

Solution

Make a table. The scale on the drawing is 1 in. : 5 ft. Each inch on the drawing represents 5 feet on the canoe.

Scale drawing length (inches)	Length × 5	Actual canoe length (feet)
1	1 × 5	5
2	2 × 5	10
3	3 × 5	15

ANSWER The actual canoe is 15 feet long.

NCTM CURRICULUM STANDARDS
Standard 2: Use models to understand relationships
Standard 9: Apply math in contexts outside of mathematics
Standard 10: Use representations to solve problems

HELP with **Reading**

The standard way to write a scale is *scale model : actual object*.

EXAMPLE 2 **Using a Scale to Find Actual Lengths**

Catalogs A catalog pictures a necklace that appears smaller than the actual necklace. The scale is 3 cm : 9 cm. If the length of the necklace in the picture is 18 centimeters, how long is the actual necklace?

Solution

Find the relationship between the known length and the scale.

picture : actual

$\times$? $\begin{pmatrix} 3 \text{ cm} : 9 \text{ cm} \\ 18 \text{ cm} : \underline{?} \text{ cm} \end{pmatrix}$ Ask, "3 times what number equals 18?"

Because $3 \times 6 = 18$, you **multiply by 6** to find the actual length.

$\begin{pmatrix} 3 \text{ cm} : 9 \text{ cm} \\ 18 \text{ cm} : 54 \text{ cm} \end{pmatrix} \times 6$

ANSWER The actual necklace is 54 centimeters long.

EXAMPLE 3 **Finding Lengths for a Model**

Models You are building a model boat with a scale of 1 in. : 2 ft. The actual boat is 18 feet long. How long do you make your model?

Solution

Find the relationship between the known length and the scale.

model : actual

$\begin{pmatrix} 1 \text{ in.} : 2 \text{ ft} \\ \underline{?} \text{ in.} : 18 \text{ ft} \end{pmatrix} \times$?   Ask, "2 times what number equals 18?"

Because $2 \times 9 = 18$, you **multiply by 9** to find the length of the model: 1 in. $\times 9 = 9$ in.

ANSWER You make your model 9 inches long.

Your turn now **Refer to Examples 1–3.**

1. Find the length of the canoe in Example 1 using the scale 1 in. : 6 ft.
   18 ft

2. Find the actual length of the necklace in Example 2 if the necklace in the picture is 21 centimeters long. **63 cm**

3. Find the length of your model in Example 3 if the scale is 1 in. : 3 ft.
   6 in.

EXTRA EXAMPLES

Example 1 A scale drawing of a porpoise is shown below. How long is the actual porpoise?

1 in.:4 ft

about 6 ft long

Example 2 A catalog shows a picture of a porcelain doll that is larger than the actual doll. The scale is 4 in. : 3 in. If the height of the doll in the picture is 8 inches, what is the height of the actual doll? **6 in.**

Example 3 You are building a model train with a scale of 12 in. : 88 ft. The length of an actual boxcar is 44 feet. How long is your model? **6 in.**

CONCEPT CHECK

Explain the meaning of the scale in a map or scale drawing. **The scale tells how the dimensions in the map or drawing are related to the actual distances or dimensions.**

 DAILY PUZZLER

Suppose a photocopier enlarges an image using a scale of 1 : 2. How many times do you have to enlarge each image to get an image that is 8 times the size of original? **3 times**

ASSIGNMENT GUIDE

Basic Course
Day 1: EP p. 708 Exs. 9–11;
pp. 70–71 Exs. 7–16, 19, 20,
24–31

Average Course
Day 1: pp. 70–71 Exs. 7–20,
23–31

Advanced Course
Day 1: pp. 70–71 Exs. 9–13,
16–26, 30, 31, EC: TE p. 52D*

Block
pp. 70–71 Exs. 7–20, 23–31
(with 2.4)

EXTRA PRACTICE

• Student Edition, p. 709
• Chapter 2 Resource Book,
pp. 25–27
• Test and Practice Generator

TRANSPARENCY

Even-numbered answers are available on transparencies.

HOMEWORK CHECK

When you review students' homework for this lesson, go over the following exercises to check understanding of key concepts.
Basic: 7, 8, 11, 13, 15
Average: 8, 9, 11, 14, 17
Advanced: 9, 10, 12, 16, 17

MATH REASONING

In Exercises 13–16, students should be able to reason that if the actual length is given, they should *divide* to get the length of the scale model.

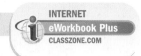

2.3 Exercises

More Practice, p. 709

Getting Ready to Practice

1. Vocabulary Tell what the scale 1 in.: 40 mi means.
Each inch on the scale drawing represents 40 miles on the actual object.

The scale on a scale drawing is 1 cm: 12 m. Find the length on the drawing for the given actual length.

2. 24 meters 2 cm **3.** 36 meters 3 cm **4.** 72 meters 6 cm **5.** 120 meters
10 cm

6. Eiffel Tower A model of the Eiffel Tower is 20 centimeters tall. Use the scale 5 cm: 80 m to approximate the height of the actual Eiffel Tower.
320 m

Practice and Problem Solving

with **Homework**

Example	Exercises
1	7–10
2	7–12
3	13–17

Online Resources
CLASSZONE.COM
· More Examples
· eTutorial Plus

Maps **The scale on a map is 1 in.: 150 mi. Find the actual distance, in miles, for the given length on the map.**

A **7.** 2 inches 300 mi **8.** 4 inches 600 mi **9.** 5 inches 750 mi **10.** 7 inches 1050 mi

Find the actual length for the length labeled in the photo.

11.

6 cm
1 cm : 2 cm
3 cm

12.

30 cm
1 cm : 10 cm
3 cm

Models **A model collection uses the scale 1 in.: 16 ft. Find the length of the model, in inches, for the given actual length.**

13. 32 feet 2 in.   **14.** 64 feet 4 in.   **15.** 112 feet 7 in.   **16.** 144 feet 9 in.

B **17. Find the Error** Describe and correct the error in the solution.

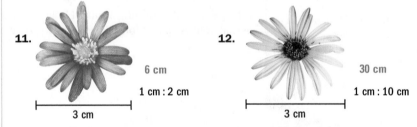

The scale is 2 in.: 5 ft. The actual length is 20 feet.

$$\times 10 \left(\begin{array}{c} 2:5 \\ 20:50 \end{array} \right) \times 10$$

The length of the model is 50 inches.

17. Sample answer: The actual length of 20 ft corresponds to 5 feet in the scale. So you should multiply 2 in. by 4, and the length of the model is 8 in.

$$\times 4 \left(\begin{array}{c} 2:5 \\ 8:20 \end{array} \right) \times 4$$

The length of the model is 8 inches.

18. Draw a Diagram Using the scale 1 in. : 10 ft, make a scale drawing of a dance floor that is 30 ft by 40 ft. Use your drawing to find the distance from one corner of the dance floor to the opposite corner.
Check drawings. The diagram should be a rectangles 30 in. by 40 in.; 50 ft.

■ **Lighthouses**

The earliest lighthouses were nothing more than bonfires constructed on hillsides so boat pilots could see them. How does the height of a lighthouse influence how effective it is?

Sample answer: The taller the lighthouse, the farther away its light can be seen.

INTERNET
State Test Practice
CLASSZONE.COM

Extended Problem Solving The map shows part of Washington, D.C.

19. Measurement How many centimeters apart are the U.S. Capitol and the White House on the map? **5 cm**

20. Find the actual distance for the situation in Exercise 19. **2500 m**

21. Estimation Estimate the shortest distance from Union Station to the Washington Monument via the two other red landmarks. **4500 m**

Map labels: Union Station, White House, Washington Monument, U.S. Capitol, **1 cm : 500 m**

Lighthouses The Port Austin Reef Lighthouse is 60 feet tall. Use the height of the model given to complete the scale. How many times taller than the model is the actual lighthouse?

C 22. height: 10 inches
scale: 2 in.: _?_ ft
12; 72 times taller

23. height: 6 inches
scale: 2 in.: _?_ ft **20; 120 times taller**

Mixed Review

Tell whether the statement is reasonable. If it is not, change the unit of measure so that it is reasonable. *(Lesson 2.1)*

24. A bed is 7 *miles* long.
not reasonable; feet

25. A computer keyboard is 18 *inches* long.
reasonable

26. Find the perimeter and area of a 4 ft by 6 ft rectangle. *(Lesson 2.2)*
$P = 20$ ft; $A = 24$ ft^2

Basic Skills **Order the numbers from least to greatest.**

27. 3, 0, 8, 4, 16, 1
0, 1, 3, 4, 8, 16

28. 12, 3, 7, 6, 17, 21
3, 6, 7, 12, 17, 21

29. 22, 25, 14, 11, 23
11, 14, 22, 23, 25

Test-Taking Practice

30. Multiple Choice Find the actual length of the classroom. The scale is 1 cm : 2 m. **B**

A. 9 m   **B.** 6 m

C. 3 m   **D.** 1 m

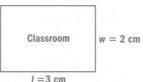

Classroom, $w = 2$ cm, $l = 3$ cm

31. Multiple Choice An architect constructs a model of a building that will be 120 feet tall. If every 2 inches on the model represents 5 feet on the building, how tall will the architect's model be? **H**

F. 300 in.   **G.** 60 in.   **H.** 48 in.   **I.** 24 in.

④ ASSESS

ASSESSMENT RESOURCES

For more assessment resources, see:
• Assessment Book
• Test and Practice Generator

MINI-QUIZ

1. The scale on a map is 1 in. : 200 mi. Find the actual distance, in miles, for a length of 2 inches on the map. **400 mi**

2. A model has a scale of 1 in. : 15 ft. Find the length of the model, in inches, for an actual length of 75 ft. **5 in.**

3. A drawing has a scale of 2 in. : 12 ft. Make a table to show what lengths in the scale drawing correspond to the actual lengths of 18 feet, 24 feet, and 36 feet.

Scale drawing length	Length (× 6)	Actual length
3 in.	3 × 6	18 ft
4 in.	4 × 6	24 ft
6 in.	6 × 6	36 ft

⑤ FOLLOW-UP

RETEACHING/REMEDIATION

• Study Guide in Chapter 2 Resource Book, pp. 28–29
• eTutorial Plus Online
• Extra Practice, p. 709
• Lesson Practice in Chapter 2 Resource Book, pp. 25–27

CHALLENGE/ENRICHMENT

• Challenge Practice in Chapter 2 Resource Book, p. 30
• Teacher's Edition, p. 52F

ENGLISH LEARNER SUPPORT

• Spanish Study Guide
• Multi-Language Glossary
• Chapter Audio Summaries CDs

Lesson 2.3   Scale Drawings   **71**

71

Frequency Tables and Line Plots

BEFORE	Now	WHY?
You read data from a table and drew number lines.	You'll create and interpret frequency tables and line plots.	So you can organize data, such as orchestra members in Ex. 8.

In the Real World

Word Watch

data, p. 72
frequency table, p. 72
line plot, p. 73

Art Projects Students in an art class were given the choice of doing a painting, a sculpture, or a drawing as their project this quarter. Which type of project was chosen most often?

One way to organize **data** , or information, is to use a *frequency table*. A **frequency table** lists the number of times each item occurs in a data set.

Student Choices for Art Projects	
painting	sculpture
painting	painting
painting	drawing
sculpture	sculpture
drawing	sculpture
painting	painting

EXAMPLE 1 Making a Frequency Table

To find which type of art project was chosen most often, you can make a frequency table.

Use a tally mark for each time that project was chosen.

The frequency is the number of tally marks.

Art project	Tally	Frequency
painting	IIII I	6
sculpture	IIII	4
drawing	II	2

ANSWER A painting project was chosen most often.

Your turn now

1. The data at the top of the page could have been recorded in a frequency table as the information was gathered. Explain how this could be done and why this might be a better way to record the data.
   See margin.

2. Make a frequency table of the letters that occur in the word "Mississippi." Which letters occur most often? **See margin for table.**
   The letters I and S occur most often.

Line Plots When the items or categories being tallied are numbers, a *line plot* can be used to visually display the data. A **line plot** uses X marks above a number line to show the frequencies.

Need help with number lines? See p. 685.

HELP with **Review**

EXAMPLE 2 Making a Line Plot

Summer Reading The frequency table shows how many books the students in a class read during summer vacation.

a. Make a line plot of the data.

b. Use the line plot to find the total number of students.

Books read	Tally	Frequency
1	IIII	5
2	IIII	5
3	IIII I	6
4	II	2
5		0
6	IIII	4

c. Use the line plot to find how many students read four or more books.

Solution

a.

The number line includes the different numbers of books read.

The X marks above the number line show the frequencies.

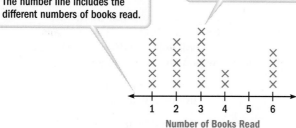

Number of Books Read

b. There are 22 X marks in all, so the total number of students is 22.

c. The total number of X marks above the numbers 4, 5, and 6 is six, so six students read four or more books.

Your turn now The following data show the numbers of letters in students' names. Use the data in Exercises 3–5.

6, 5, 4, 4, 5, 3, 9, 8, 6, 4, 3, 4, 7, 5, 4, 3, 8, 4, 9, 3

3. Make a frequency table of the data. 3, 4. See margin.

4. Make a line plot of the data.

5. Choose one of the displays and use it to find out whether more students have names with 3 letters or names with 7 or more letters. Which display did you choose and how did you use it to answer the question?

5. More have names with 7 or more letters. *Sample answer:* Line plot; counted the number of x's above the 3, and the number of x's above 7, 8, and 9 to find that there are more x's above the names with 7 or more letters.

Example 1 Make a frequency table for the data.

Students' Favorite Colors		
red	green	red
green	green	green
red	red	green
green	white	red

Color	Tally	Frequency
red	IIII	5
green	IIII I	6
white	I	1

Example 2 The frequency table shows how many siblings each student has.

Siblings	Tally	Frequency
1	IIII II	7
2	IIII	5
3	III	3

a. Make a line plot of the data.

Number of Siblings

b. How many students have 3 siblings? **3 students**

CONCEPT CHECK

Explain how the number of tally marks in a row of a frequency table is related to the number of X marks above a number in a line plot for the same data. **The number of tallies matches the number of X marks.**

DAILY PUZZLER

Sandy ate 100 pumpkin seeds in 5 days. Each day, she ate 6 more seeds than on the previous day. How many pumpkin seeds did Sandy eat on the first day? **8 seeds**

1–4. See Additional Answers beginning on page AA1.

③ APPLY

ASSIGNMENT GUIDE

Basic Course
Day 1: pp. 74–75 Exs. 5–10, 12–14, 18–24

Average Course
Day 1: pp. 74–75 Exs. 5–15, 17–24

Advanced Course
Day 1: pp. 74–75 Exs. 5–19*, 24

Block
pp. 74–75 Exs. 5–15, 17–24 (with 2.3)

EXTRA PRACTICE

• Student Edition, p. 709
• Chapter 2 Resource Book, pp. 33–35
• Test and Practice Generator

 TRANSPARENCY

Even-numbered answers are available on transparencies.

HOMEWORK CHECK

When you review students' homework for this lesson, go over the following exercises to check understanding of key concepts.
Basic: 5, 6, 7, 9, 10
Average: 5, 6, 9, 10, 11
Advanced: 5, 6, 8, 10, 11

TEACHING TIP

Some students may have difficulty with Exercise 8, since the data is not numerical. Suggest that they list the letters in alphabetical order and that they carefully count the repetitions of each letter. Suggest also that they recount each letter to make certain that their results are correct.

2, 3, 5, 8–10, 12, 14, 17, 24. See Additional Answers beginning on page AA1.

74

Getting Ready to Practice

1. **Vocabulary** When creating a frequency table, you count the number of tally marks to find the _?_ for each category. **frequency**

Bicycles **In Exercises 2–4, use the list below showing the numbers of bicycles owned by families of class members.**

2, 3, 1, 0, 1, 1, 3, 1, 2, 1, 2, 3, 2, 1, 4, 0, 1, 4, 2, 6, 0

2. Make a frequency table.   3. Make a line plot.
2–3. See margin.

4. What number of bicycles is owned by exactly two families? How can you find this answer using the frequency table? using the line plot?
4 bicycles; look for the 2 in the Frequency column; look for 2 x's above the numbers.

Practice and Problem Solving

Volunteer Fire Department **The frequency table shows the calls a small volunteer fire department responded to in one year.**

A 5. Copy and complete the frequency table. **See margin.**

6. Which type of call occurred most often? least often? **other fires; rescues**

Type of call	Tally	Frequency
building fires	ЖЖ I	?
other fires	ЖЖ ЖЖ II	?
hazardous materials	ЖЖ II	?
rescues	III	?
false alarms	ЖЖ II	?
mutual aid	IIII	?

7. How many calls were responded to that year? **39 calls**

8. **Music** An orchestra has four sections: woodwinds (W), percussion (P), brass (B), and strings (S). The data below show the section each member of one particular orchestra belongs to. Make a frequency table and use it to find which section of the orchestra is the largest. **See margin.**

P, S, B, W, S, S, B, S, W, S, S, W, S, S, B, S, W, S, B, S, W, S, W,
S, B, W, S, W, S, S, B, S, B, S, S, S, B, S, B, W, B, S, P, S, B, S

Make a frequency table and a line plot of the set of data. Then tell which item occurs most often and which item occurs least often.

9. Point values of a team's shots during the first half of a basketball game:

2, 2, 1, 3, 2, 2, 1, 3, 2, 2, 1, 2, 3, 2, 2, 1, 2, 1, 2, 1, 1
2 occurs most often and 3 occurs least often. See margin.

10. Number of weeks class members attended summer camp:

4, 0, 1, 2, 8, 2, 4, 4, 8, 5, 6, 4, 6, 6, 4, 0, 6, 8, 4, 4, 8, 4, 4, 4, 8, 4
4 occurs most often and 3 and 7 occur least often. See margin.

with Homework

Example Exercises
1   5–12
2   9–11

Online Resources
CLASSZONE.COM
· More Examples
· eTutorial Plus

11. Writing Compare the frequency table and the line plot you created in Exercise 10 on page 74. Describe one way in which each type of display is more helpful or easier to use than the other type. **See margin.**

Weather Use the calendar and codes at the right.

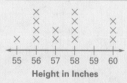
SUNNY PARTLY CLOUDY CLOUDY RAINY

B 12. Make a frequency table of the types of weather. **See margin.**

13. How many more days were either cloudy or partly cloudy than were sunny? **4 days**

14. Explain How many days didn't have rain? Give two ways to find the answer. **See margin.**

15. Can you make a line plot of the weather data? Explain. **See margin.**

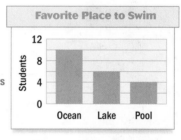

C 16. Challenge Use Example 2 on page 73. Find the total number of books read by all the students in the class over the summer. **65 books**

17. Birthdays Gather data on the birth months of your classmates and of the United States presidents. Make a line plot of each data set and compare the data. **Check line plots of birth months of classmates. See margin for art.**

11. *Sample answer:* The frequency table is easier to use to find the number of occurrences. The line plot is easier to use to see the items that occurred most or least often.

15. No. *Sample answer:* The items being tallied are not numbers so a line plot cannot be used to display the data.

Mixed Review

Use the bar graph. *(p. 704)*

18. How many of the students surveyed chose the ocean? **10 students**

19. How many more students chose a lake than a pool? **2 more students**

Favorite Place to Swim

| | | |
| Students | Ocean | Lake | Pool |

Basic Skills **Identify the first six numbers if you start with zero and count using the given increment.**

20. count by 4s
0, 4, 8, 12, 16, 20

21. count by 7s
0, 7, 14, 21, 28, 35

22. count by 25s
0, 25, 50, 75, 100, 125

23. count by 20s
0, 20, 40, 60, 80, 100

Test-Taking Practice

24. Extended Response The list below gives the number of students in each homeroom class in a school. Make a frequency table and a line plot of the data. Use each display to determine which class size is most common and how many classes have fewer than 25 students. Explain your steps. **See margin for table and art. A class size of 26 is most common; four classes have fewer than 25 students.**

24, 28, 26, 24, 23, 26, 24, 25, 27, 26, 25, 26

---

④ ASSESS

ASSESSMENT RESOURCES

For more assessment resources, see:
• Assessment Book
• Test and Practice Generator

MINI-QUIZ

1. The list below shows the heights, in inches, of the players on a soccer team. Make a frequency table and a line plot of the data.

56, 58, 55, 56, 60, 57, 58, 60, 57, 58, 56, 58, 60, 56

Height (in.)	Tally	Frequency
55	I	1
56	IIII	4
57	II	2
58	IIII	4
59		0
60	III	3

```
        ×       ×
        ×       ×
    ×   ×   ×       ×
×   ×   ×   ×       ×
+---+---+---+---+---+---+
55  56  57  58  59  60
      Height in Inches
```

⑤ FOLLOW-UP

RETEACHING/REMEDIATION

• Study Guide in Chapter 2 Resource Book, pp. 36–37
• eTutorial Plus Online
• Extra Practice, p. 709
• Lesson Practice in Chapter 2 Resource Book, pp. 33–35

CHALLENGE/ENRICHMENT

• Challenge Practice in Chapter 2 Resource Book, p. 38
• Teacher's Edition, p. 52F

ENGLISH LEARNER SUPPORT

• Spanish Study Guide
• Multi-Language Glossary
• Chapter Audio Summaries CDs

LESSONS 2.1 TO 2.4

Notebook Review

Review the vocabulary definitions in your notebook.

Copy the review examples in your notebook. Then complete the exercises.

Check Your Definitions

inch, p. 55	centimeter, p. 56	scale drawing, p. 68
foot, p. 55	meter, p. 56	scale, p. 68
yard, p. 55	kilometer, p. 56	data, p. 72
mile, p. 55	perimeter, p. 61	frequency table, p. 72
millimeter, p. 56	area, p. 62	line plot, p. 73

Use Your Vocabulary

1. Writing Define area and perimeter. See margin.

2.1–2.2 Can you find perimeter and area?

 EXAMPLE Use a ruler to find the length of the rectangle in centimeters. Then find the perimeter and the area.

$$P = 2l + 2w \qquad A = lw$$
$$= 2 \cdot 3 + 2 \cdot 2 \qquad = 3 \cdot 2$$
$$= 10 \text{ cm} \qquad = 6 \text{ cm}^2$$

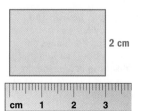

2 cm

 2. Find the perimeter and the area of a 7 inch by 7 inch square.
$P = 28$ in.; $A = 49$ in.

3. Estimate then measure the length of this sentence in inches.
4 in.; 4 in.

2.3 Can you use a scale?

 EXAMPLE The length of a wall on a scale drawing is 192 millimeters. Find the actual length if the scale on the drawing is 8 mm : 2 m.

$\times 24 \left(\begin{array}{l} 8\text{ mm} : 2\text{ m} \\ 192\text{ mm} : \underline{\ ?\ }\text{ m} \end{array} \right.$ You multiply by 24, so the actual length is 48 m.

☑ **Find the actual length of the wall in the Example above using the given scale.**

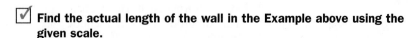

4. 3 mm : 1 m **5.** 4 mm : 2 m **6.** 12 mm : 4 m **7.** 6 mm : 6 m
64 m   96 m   64 m   192 m

2.4 Can you make a frequency table and a line plot?

Review

EXAMPLE The list below shows the numbers of pets that students in a class have. Make a frequency table and a line plot of the data.

2, 0, 1, 3, 0, 2, 1, 1, 0, 3, 3, 1, 4, 0, 1, 1, 0, 0, 2, 1, 0

Pets owned	Tally	Frequency
0	JHT II	7
1	JHT II	7
2	III	3
3	III	3
4	I	1

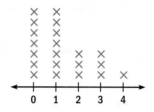

8. Make a frequency table and a line plot of the data.

12, 11, 10, 15, 14, 12, 13, 10, 11, 13, 15, 15, 13, 11, 12 See margin.

Stop and Think about Lessons 2.1–2.4

9. Critical Thinking Describe a situation in which it is okay to estimate a measurement rather than find the actual measurement. See margin.

10. Writing Compare a frequency table and a line plot. How are they alike? How are they different? See margin.

8.

Number	Tally	Frequency
10	II	2
11	III	3
12	III	3
13	III	3
14	I	1
15	III	3

9. A good situation for an estimate will be one in which an exact measurement is not needed, such as the distance between a city in California and a city in New York.

10. Frequency tables and line plots are similar in that they both tell how frequent a number occurs. They are different in that the frequency table makes it easier to see the number of occurrences, whereas the line plot makes it easier to see which item occurred most or least often.

Review Quiz 1

7.

Height	Tally	Frequency
50	I	1
51		0
52	III	3
53	II	2
54	II	2

50 51 52 53 54
Height in Inches

Review Quiz 1

1. Estimate the length of the line segment in millimeters. Then measure to check. 43 mm

Choose an appropriate customary unit and metric unit for the length.

2. height of a Ferris wheel feet; meters

3. length of a calculator inches; centimeters

Find the perimeter and the area of the rectangle described.

4. length = 4 ft, width = 2 ft
P = 12 ft; A = 8 ft²

5. length = 7 m, width = 5 m
P = 24 m; A = 35 m²

6. Titanic The scale for a model of the Titanic is 1 cm : 6 m. The model is 45 centimeters long. About how long was the actual Titanic? 270 m

7. Make a frequency table and a line plot of the following data showing the heights, in inches, of several teenagers. See margin.

52, 53, 52, 50, 54, 54, 53, 52

PLAN

EXPLORE THE CONCEPT

- Students will collect and display data.
- Relate the shaded boxes in this activity to the bars in Example 1 on page 79.

MATERIALS

Each student needs graph paper. A support transparency is available for this activity.

RECOMMENDED TIME

Work activity: 10 min
Discuss results: 5 min

GROUPING

This activity is best done individually.

TEACH

TIPS FOR SUCCESS

Students may feel more comfortable if they first create a frequency table using tally marks.

CLOSE

KEY DISCOVERY

A modified frequency table can be used to display data.

ASSESSMENT

1. Make a modified frequency table of the following data. 2, 6, 0, 4, 6, 4, 9, 4, 6, 0, 2, 3, 5, 4

2, 3. See Additional Answers beginning on page AA1.

78

2.5 **Hands-on Activity**

GOAL Collect and display data.

MATERIALS · graph paper

Collecting and Organizing Data

You can make a modified frequency table to display data.

Explore Display data you collect from a phone book in a modified frequency table.

1 Look at the last digit of 25 telephone numbers from a telephone book.

2 List the digits on graph paper. Beside each digit, shade one box for each telephone number that ends with that digit.

Kristine 34 Wrentham 555-0108
Kristine 16 Oakland 555-0198
L J 81 Ten Hills.................................555-0149
LaNell 515 Coolidge 555-0181
Lodish 64 Stetson 555-0190
Lois 36 Georgia 555-0120
Lucy 6 Lucerne.................................555-0185
M C 80 Highland 555-0189
M D 85 Melrose 555-0125
Mae 414 Bowdoin 555-0194
Mark 73 Winthrop 555-0191
Martin 7 Norcross 555-0144
Mary J 34 Foster 555-0134
Mary R, Dr 61 Franklin.....................555-0117
Melissa 652 Shawmut 555-0148
Mervyn 80 Park 555-0114
Mildred 54 Orleans...........................555-0132
Natalie 28 St Germain 555-0138
P 133 Marlborough 555-0153
Pamela 591 Fisher............................555-0164
Pat 77 Moreland...............................555-0177
Patricia 25 Broadway 555-0173
Patrick 88 Liberty 555-0165
Patrick 84 Central.............................555-0109
Ruth 22 Haskell 555-0167

Last digit	Tally	Frequency
0	𝍸𝍸	2
1	𝍸𝍸	2
2	𝍸	1
3	𝍸𝍸	2
4	𝍸𝍸𝍸𝍸𝍸	5
5	𝍸𝍸𝍸	3
6		0
7	𝍸𝍸𝍸	3
8	𝍸𝍸𝍸𝍸	4
9	𝍸𝍸𝍸	3

3 telephone numbers end in 5.

Your turn now Use the data from Steps 1 and 2 above.

1. Which digit was the last digit most often? least often? 4; 6

2. Make another modified frequency table using the sixth digit of the telephone number. See margin.

Stop and Think

3. **Writing** Describe how the display you made in Exercise 2 can help you compare frequencies. See margin.

NCTM CURRICULUM STANDARDS
Standard 5: Collect, organize, and display data; Develop inferences that are based on data
Standard 9: Use connections among mathematical ideas

LESSON 2.5

Bar Graphs

BEFORE	**Now**	**WHY?**
You organized and displayed data using frequency tables.	You'll display data using bar graphs.	So you can visualize data, such as the soccer records in Ex. 8.

Word Watch

bar graph, p. 79
double bar graph, p. 80

In the Real World

Zoo Animals Two hundred sixth and seventh grade students were asked to name their favorite zoo animal. The results are shown in the table. How can you represent this data visually?

A **bar graph** is a type of graph in which the lengths of the bars are used to represent and compare data. A numerical scale is used to determine the lengths of the bars.

Favorite Zoo Animal

Zoo animal	Students
lion	43
giraffe	19
monkey	55
elephant	49
other	34

with Review

Need help with reading a bar graph? See page 704.

EXAMPLE 1 **Making a Bar Graph**

You can display the data from the table above in a bar graph.

① Choose a numerical scale.

Start the scale at 0. The greatest data value is 55, so end the scale at a value greater than 55, such as 60. Use equal increments along the scale, such as increments of 10.

② Draw and label the graph.

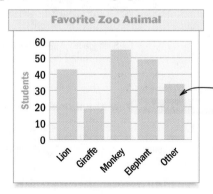

Favorite Zoo Animal

Use the scale to decide how long to make the bar for each data value.

NCTM CURRICULUM STANDARDS
Standard 5: Collect, organize, and display data
Standard 10: Create representations to communicate mathematical ideas

Example 1 Make a bar graph.

Favorite pet	Students
cat	8
bird	6
dog	12

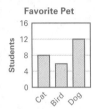

Favorite Pet

Example 2 Make a double bar graph of the data.

Favorite pet	Sixth Grade	Seventh Grade
cat	8	16
bird	15	8
dog	10	15

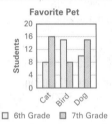

Favorite Pet

☐ 6th Grade ☐ 7th Grade

 CONCEPT CHECK

Explain how to make a bar graph.
Choose a numerical scale starting at 0 and ending higher than the highest data value. Use equal increments and spacing along the scale. Draw and label the graph.

 DAILY PUZZLER

A person has 7 pets. Some are cats and the rest are dogs. The pets eat 32 biscuits. Each cat eats 4 biscuits and each dog eats 5. How many cats and how many dogs are there? **3 cats and 4 dogs**

1. See Additional Answers beginning on page AA1.

Double Bar Graphs A **double bar graph** is a bar graph that shows two sets of data on the same graph. The two bars for each category are drawn next to each other.

EXAMPLE 2 Making a Double Bar Graph

Zoo Animals Make a double bar graph of the zoo animal data in the table at the right.

Favorite zoo animal	Sixth grade	Seventh grade
lion	19	24
giraffe	13	6
monkey	29	26
elephant	21	28
other	15	19

① First draw one set of bars using the sixth grade data, as shown below. The greatest data value in the table is 29, so end the scale at 30.

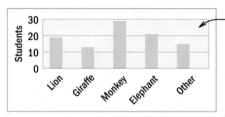

Leave room for the seventh grade bars.

② Then draw the seventh grade bars next to the sixth grade bars and shade them a different color. Add a title and a key.

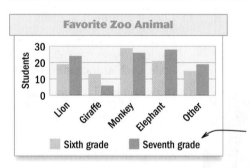

Make a key to show what each color represents.

Your turn now **Make a double bar graph of the data.** See margin.

1.

Favorite Sports					
Sport	basketball	swimming	gymnastics	hockey	track
Watching	593	260	370	175	250
Participating	570	319	197	197	209

1. *Sample answer:* Start the scale at 0 and end at a value greater than the greatest data value. Use equal increments along the scale.

INTERNET
eWorkbook Plus
CLASSZONE.COM
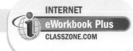

Getting Ready to Practice

1. Vocabulary Explain how to choose a scale for a bar graph. **See Margin.**

A survey asked the question, "What is the most important thing kids can do to protect the environment?" The results are shown in the table.

Activity	Responses
Recycle	834
Buy environmentally friendly products	358
Write your elected representatives	221
Raise money	401
Plant trees	480

2. Choose a scale for a bar graph of the data. *Sample answer:* 0 to 900, with increments of 100.

3. Draw and label the bar graph. See margin.

4. "Recycle" had about 4 times the number of responses as which other activity? Write your elected representatives

Practice and Problem Solving

Make a bar graph of the data. 5, 6. See margin.

A 5.

Mountain Ranges of the World	
Range	Peaks (over 6000 m)
Kunlun	228
St. Elias	1
Tien Shan	40
Andes	84

6.

Maximum Life Span of Animals in Captivity	
Animal	Life Span (years)
lion	30
giraffe	36
monkey	37
asian elephant	77

Make a double bar graph of the data. 7, 8. See margin.

7.

Cost of Food (cents per pound)		
Food	1990	2000
apples	77	82
chicken	86	108
ice cream	254	366
eggs	100	96
spaghetti	85	88

8.

Major Indoor Soccer League National Conference 2000–2001		
Team	Wins	Losses
Kansas City	14	26
Toronto	21	19
Detroit	13	27
Milwaukee	24	16
Wichita	18	21

9. Use your graph from Exercise 7 to decide which of the foods had the greatest price increase from 1990 to 2000. **ice cream**

 HELP with Homework

Example	Exercises
1	5, 6
2	7, 8

Online Resources
CLASSZONE.COM
· More Examples
· eTutorial Plus

ASSIGNMENT GUIDE

Basic Course
Day 1: SRH p. 704 Exs. 1–3; pp. 81–82 Exs. 5–8, 10, 14–23

Average Course
Day 1: pp. 81–82 Exs. 5–12, 16–20, 23, 24

Advanced Course
Day 1: pp. 81–82 Exs. 5–13*, 16–18, 23, 24

Block
pp. 81–82 Exs. 5–12, 16–20, 23, 24 (with 2.6)

EXTRA PRACTICE

• Student Edition, p. 709
• Chapter 2 Resource Book, pp. 41–43
• Test and Practice Generator

 TRANSPARENCY

Even-numbered answers are available on transparencies.

HOMEWORK CHECK

When you review students' homework for this lesson, go over the following exercises to check understanding of key concepts.
Basic: 5, 6, 7, 8, 10
Average: 5, 6, 7, 8, 11
Advanced: 5, 6, 7, 8, 12

NOTETAKING

Students may have trouble remembering all the steps needed to make a double bar graph in Exercises 7 and 8. Encourage them to write the necessary steps in their notebooks for reference.

3, 5–8. See Additional Answers beginning on page AA1.

4 ASSESS

ASSESSMENT RESOURCES

For more assessment resources, see:
- Assessment Book
- Test and Practice Generator

MINI-QUIZ

1. Make a double bar graph.

Online purchase	Females (millions)	Males (millions)
books	9	1
CDs/videos	7	16
computers	5	8
travel	4	15

Online Purchases

□ Females   □ Males

5 FOLLOW-UP

RETEACHING/REMEDIATION

- Study Guide in Chapter 2 Resource Book, pp. 44–45
- Tutor Place, Whole Numbers and Decimals Card 20
- eTutorial Plus Online
- Extra Practice, p. 709
- Lesson Practice in Chapter 2 Resource Book, pp. 41–43

CHALLENGE/ENRICHMENT

- Challenge Practice in Chapter 2 Resource Book, p. 47
- Teacher's Edition, p. 52F

ENGLISH LEARNER SUPPORT

- Spanish Study Guide
- Multi-Language Glossary
- Chapter Audio Summaries CDs

13, 18. See Additional Answers beginning on page AA1.

82

---

10. *Sample answer:* In either case, the bars will be shorter and the differences between them will seem less.

11. *Sample answer:* If the greatest data value in the scale is much greater than the actual greatest data value and the increments are too large, the differences in the bars will seem to be less than they really are.

12. *Sample answer:* The advantages are it takes less room and you can see the totals for each category easily. The disadvantages are it is difficult to compare the two results and difficult to determine the amount represented by the top bar.

INTERNET
 State Test Practice
CLASSZONE.COM

B 10. Movie Ticket Prices Describe how the appearance of the graph will change if the scale goes from 0 to 40 in increments of 10 or from 0 to 200 in increments of 50.

11. Writing How might the scale of a bar graph affect how the bar graph is interpreted? See margin.

In-line Skating The stacked bar graph shows the results of a survey about how people use in-line skates.

C 12. Compare and Contrast What are the advantages and disadvantages of a stacked bar graph? See margin.

13. Challenge Draw the stacked bar graph as a double bar graph. See margin.

Movie Ticket Prices

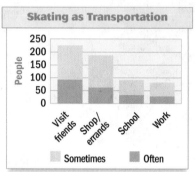
Skating as Transportation
□ Sometimes   ■ Often

Mixed Review

Solve the equation using mental math. *(Lesson 1.6)*

14. $x + 2 = 15$ 13 **15.** $10 - x = 6$ 4 **16.** $3x = 24$ 8 **17.** $72 \div x = 9$ 8

18. Make a frequency table and a line plot of the following scores for a 10 point quiz: 9, 10, 6, 7, 7, 8, 9, 8, 9, 6, 7, 9, 8, 7, 7, 9. *(Lesson 2.4)* See margin.

Basic Skills **Tell how much change you should receive if you pay for an item of the given price with a $10 bill.**

19. $5.25 $4.75 **20.** $3.75 $6.25 **21.** $7.75 $2.25 **22.** $6.50 $3.50

Test-Taking Practice

23. Multiple Choice Choose the best increment for the numerical scale of a bar graph showing the data values 53, 31, 25, 13, and 46. B

A. 1   **B.** 10   **C.** 50   **D.** 100

24. Short Response Explain how to make a double bar graph of favorite school subjects from a graph showing favorites for sixth graders and a graph showing favorites for seventh graders. *Sample answer:* Make a new graph by drawing the bars for each subject from each of the two graphs next to each other.

Coordinates and Line Graphs

BEFORE | ▶ **Now** | **WHY?**

You plotted points on number lines and made bar graphs. | You'll plot points on coordinate grids and make line graphs. | So you can visualize change, as with the Internet data in Ex. 21.

① PLAN

SKILL CHECK

Plot 3, 5, 9, and 10 on a number line.

1 2 3 4 5 6 7 8 9 10

📓 **Word Watch**

ordered pair, p. 83
coordinates, p. 83
line graph, p. 84

Coordinates The graph below shows a point on a coordinate grid. Each point is described by an **ordered pair** of numbers. The numbers are the **coordinates** of the point.

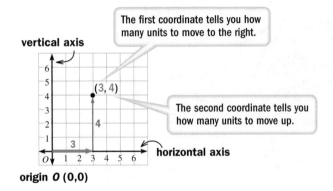

The first coordinate tells you how many units to move to the right.

vertical axis

(3, 4)

The second coordinate tells you how many units to move up.

horizontal axis

origin O (0,0)

LESSON OBJECTIVE

Plot points on coordinate grids and make line graphs.

PACING

Suggested Number of Days
Basic Course: 1 day
Average Course: 1 day
Advanced Course: 1 day
Block: 0.5 block with 2.5

TEACHING RESOURCES

For a complete list of Teaching Resources, see page 52B.

🖉 **TRANSPARENCY**

Warm-Up Exercises for this lesson are available on a transparency.

EXAMPLE 1 **Graphing Points**

a. Graph the point (4, 3) on a coordinate grid.

Start at (0, 0). Move **4** units to the right and **3** units up.

(4, 3)

b. Graph the point (0, 2) on a coordinate grid.

Start at (0, 0). Move **0** units to the right and **2** units up.

(0, 2)

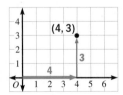
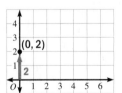

1–4. See margin.

Your turn now Graph the points on the same coordinate grid.

1. (1, 0)   **2.** (2, 1)   **3.** (3, 2)   **4.** (5, 5)

5. In Exercises 1–4, the first coordinate is the number of days after a seed was planted. The second coordinate is the plant's height in centimeters. How high was the plant after 3 days? **2 cm**

② TEACH

MOTIVATING THE LESSON

Bring in line graphs from magazines and newspapers to show their usefulness in the real world.

TIPS FOR NEW TEACHERS

Relate the horizontal and vertical axes to number lines that intersect at 0, or the origin. See Tips for New Teachers in the *Chapter 2 Resource Book*.

NCTM CURRICULUM STANDARDS

Standard 3: Specify locations using coordinate geometry
Standard 5: Collect, organize, and display data
Standard 10: Use representations to model phenomena

1–4. See Additional Answers beginning on page AA1.

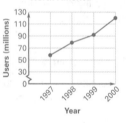
84

Line Graphs A **line graph** represents data using points connected by line segments. Line graphs are often used to show change over time. You can make a break at the beginning of the scale to focus on the interval where the data fall.

 History

■ **Radio Stations**

In 1950 there were 2144 AM radio stations and 691 FM radio stations. How many more total radio stations were there in 1998 than in 1950?

7620 more total radio stations

EXAMPLE 2 Making a Line Graph

Radio Stations **Make a line graph of the radio station data below. Data were collected at the end of each year.**

AM Radio Stations						
Year	1993	1994	1995	1996	1997	1998
AM stations	4994	4913	4150	4857	4762	4793

Solution

To make a line graph of the data, think of each column in the table as an ordered pair: **(year, AM stations)**.

① Choose a scale. Use a break in the scale for AM stations to focus on values from 4000 to 5000.

② Graph each point.

③ Draw line segments to connect the points.

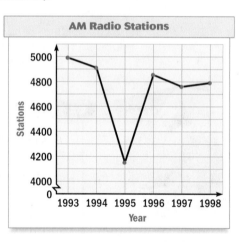

Your turn now In Exercise 6, use the graph above.

6. During which year was the increase in the number of AM stations the greatest? How can you tell that from the graph? **1995; The segment from 1995 to 1996 is the steepest of the segments showing increase.**

7. Make a line graph of the number of FM radio stations.
See margin.

Year	1993	1994	1995	1996	1997	1998
FM stations	4971	5109	5730	5419	5542	5662

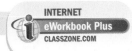

eWorkbook Plus
CLASSZONE.COM

③ **APPLY**

ASSIGNMENT GUIDE

Basic Course
Day 1: SRH p. 705 Exs. 1–4;
pp. 85–86 Exs. 8–18, 25–31

Average Course
Day 1: pp. 85–86 Exs. 8–23,
25–31

Advanced Course
Day 1: pp. 85–86 Exs. 11–26*,
30, 31

Block
pp. 85–86 Exs. 8–23, 25–31
(with 2.5)

Getting Ready to Practice

Vocabulary **Choose the letter that shows the location of the item on the coordinate grid.**

1. point (2, 1) *C*   **2.** origin *O*

3. point (0, 3) *E*   **4.** vertical axis *F*

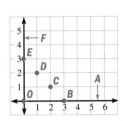

Television **Use the data in the table.**

5. Tell which number you would skip to after a break in the minutes scale and where you would end the scale.
160; 200

6. Make a line graph of the data.
See margin.

7. Did teenagers watch more television each year? Explain. No. *Sample answer:* They watched less television from 1992 to 1996, and then more television from 1996 to 2000.

| Teenager TV Viewing ||
Year	Minutes each day
1992	190
1994	185
1996	169
1998	178
2000	184

Practice and Problem Solving

Graph the points on the same coordinate grid. 8–15. See margin.

A **8.** (6, 3)   **9.** (2, 7)   **10.** (0, 0)   **11.** (4, 0)

12. (1, 8)   **13.** (0, 6)   **14.** (9, 0)   **15.** (5, 5)

16. Birds Make a line graph of the data. After a break in the scale for species, number the scale from 80 to 94 using increments of 2.
See margin.

| Endangered or Threatened Bird Species in the U.S. ||||||||||
Year	1992	1993	1994	1995	1996	1997	1998	1999	2000
Species	84	88	90	91	90	93	93	89	93

Make a line graph of the data. 17–20. See margin.

17.

Hour (A.M.)	7	8	9	10
Cars in lot	1	4	15	17

18.

Hour (P.M.)	1	2	3	4
Tickets sold	81	90	103	120

19.

Year	1998	2000	2002
Students	1253	1425	1310

20.

Day of fair	1	3	5
Dollars raised	105	198	380

EXTRA PRACTICE

• Student Edition, p. 709
• Chapter 2 Resource Book, pp. 51–53
• Test and Practice Generator

④ **TRANSPARENCY**

Even-numbered answers are available on transparencies. Support transparencies are available for Exercises 6 and 8–22.

HOMEWORK CHECK

When you review students' homework for this lesson, go over the following exercises to check understanding of key concepts.
Basic: 8, 11, 13, 16, 17
Average: 9, 12, 14, 18, 20
Advanced: 14, 15, 16, 19, 20

Ⓧ **COMMON ERROR**

In Exercises 8–15, students often confuse the order of the coordinates when graphing points. Suggest the mnemonic (*h*, *v*) to help them associate the first coordinate with a *horizontal* move and the second coordinate with a *vertical* move.

6, 8–20. See Additional Answers beginning on page AA1.

HELP
with Homework

Example	Exercises
1	8–15
2	16–20

Online Resources
CLASSZONE.COM
· More Examples
· eTutorial Plus

ASSESSMENT RESOURCES

For more assessment resources, see:
- Assessment Book
- Test and Practice Generator

MINI-QUIZ

1. Make a line graph of the U.S. population data shown below.

Year	Population (millions)
1960	181
1970	205
1980	228
1990	250
2000	276

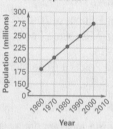

U.S. Population

RETEACHING/REMEDIATION

- Study Guide in Chapter 2 Resource Book, pp. 54–55
- eTutorial Plus Online
- Extra Practice, p. 709
- Lesson Practice in Chapter 2 Resource Book, pp. 51–53

CHALLENGE/ENRICHMENT

- Challenge Practice in Chapter 2 Resource Book, p. 56
- Teacher's Edition, p. 52F

ENGLISH LEARNER SUPPORT

- Spanish Study Guide
- Multi-Language Glossary
- Chapter Audio Summaries CDs

21, 22, 26. See Additional Answers beginning on page AA1.

B **21. Internet** Make a line graph of the data below. Use it to estimate the number of countries connected to the Internet in 1995. **See margin for art. about 125 countries**

Year	1988	1990	1992	1994	1996	1998	2000
Countries connected	8	22	43	81	165	200	214

Fitness During exercise, most people's heart rate should be between the minimum and maximum recommended rates shown.

Recommended Heart Rate (beats per minute)		
Age	Minimum	Maximum
20	130	160
30	124	152
40	117	144
50	111	136
60	104	128

22. Make a double line graph. Use a different color for the minimum rates and the maximum rates. Include a key. **See margin.**

23. Estimate the minimum rate for a 25-year-old. **127 beats per minute**

C **24. Challenge** Why is a line graph not appropriate for displaying the data?

Date in January	1	2	3	4	5	6	7	8
Daily snowfall (inches)	6	20	0	3	8	0	1	10

Sample answer: The data does not show a trend, or change over time.

Mixed Review

25. The scale on a map is 2 in. : 15 mi. Explain what this means. *(Lesson 2.3)* **2 inches on the map represents 15 miles on the ground.**

26. You sent 2 postcards on Monday, 13 on Tuesday, 0 on Wednesday, and 1 on Thursday. Make a bar graph of the data. *(Lesson 2.5)* **See margin.**

Basic Skills **Find the sum or difference.**

27. $3 + 8 + 7$ **18**   **28.** $2 + 13 + 8 + 7$ **30**   **29.** $200 - 125$ **75**

Test-Taking Practice

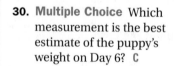

INTERNET
State Test Practice
CLASSZONE.COM

30. Multiple Choice Which measurement is the best estimate of the puppy's weight on Day 6? **C**

A. 11 oz   **B.** 12 oz

C. 13 oz   **D.** 14 oz

31. Multiple Choice Which ordered pair represents point *Z* above? **H**

F. (1, 10)   **G.** (10, 2)   **H.** (2, 10)   **I.** (10, 1)

Growth of Puppy

Creating Data Displays

GOAL Use a spreadsheet to create data displays.

Example You can create bar graphs, line graphs, and other types of data displays using a spreadsheet program.

The table shows the population of the United States from 1996 to 2000. Make a bar graph.

Solution

1 Enter the data in the first two columns of the spreadsheet. Use an apostrophe in front of each year ('1996). Highlight the data in cells A2:B6 and insert a chart. Select *column* chart as the chart type.

2 Choose chart options, such as the title, gridlines, and a legend (key).

3 Double click on a feature to change its formatting. For example, use a population scale from 0 to 300,000 in increments of 50,000.

	A	B
1	Year	Population (thousands)
2	1996	265,229
3	1997	267,784
4	1998	270,248
5	1999	272,691
6	2000	276,059

A2:B6 in Step 1 refers to the rectangle of cells whose opposite corners are A2 and B6.

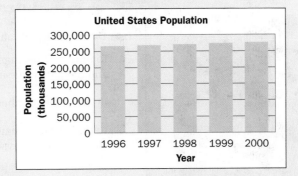

Your turn now Use the data below. 1, 2. See margin.

1. Make a *double* bar graph of the data. Follow Steps 1–3 above, but highlight three columns of data.

2. Make a double line graph of the data. Follow the steps in the Example, but enter the years without apostrophes, and select a *scatter plot* that connects points with lines as the type of chart. Show *major* gridlines for both axes. The population scale doesn't have to start at 0.

	A	B	C
1	Year	Male population (thousands)	Female population (thousands)
2	1996	129,504	135,724
3	1997	130,783	137,001
4	1998	132,030	138,218
5	1999	133,277	139,414
6	2000	134,979	141,080

NCTM CURRICULUM STANDARDS
Standard 5: Collect, organize, and display data
Standard 10: Create representations to communicate mathematical ideas

Lesson 2.6   Coordinates and Line Graphs   **87**

① PLAN

LEARN THE METHOD
- Students will use a spreadsheet to create data displays.
- To practice using a spreadsheet to draw line graphs, have students redo Example 2 on p. 84.

② TEACH

TIPS FOR SUCCESS
Point out that the year column in the spreadsheet becomes the horizontal axis, while the population column becomes the vertical axis.

EXTRA EXAMPLES

Example Make a bar graph.

Year	CD sales (millions)
1995	$9377
1996	$9935
1997	$9915
1998	$11,416
1999	$12,816

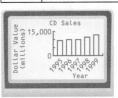

③ CLOSE

ASSESSMENT

1. Make a line graph for the CD data in the Extra Example.

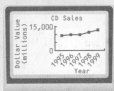

1, 2. See Additional Answers beginning on page AA1.

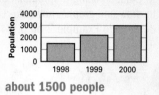

 **LESSON 2.7**

Circle Graphs

BEFORE	Now	WHY?
You made and interpreted bar graphs and line graphs.	You'll interpret circle graphs and make predictions.	So you can predict costs, as in Exs. 17–19.

In the Real World

Roller Coasters A group of teenagers are asked what they think about roller coasters. Their answers are shown in the *circle graph* at the right. How many of them think roller coasters are great?

A **circle graph** is a graph that represents data as parts of a circle. The entire circle represents all of the data. You can make conclusions about the data in a circle graph based on the size of each section.

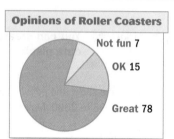

Opinions of Roller Coasters

Not fun 7
OK 15
Great 78

EXAMPLE 1 **Interpreting a Circle Graph**

Use the circle graph above.

a. To find out how many of the teenagers think roller coasters are great, find the data value in the section labeled "Great."

ANSWER The number who think roller coasters are great is 78.

b. To find out how many of the teenagers do not think roller coasters are great, add the values in the "OK" and the "Not fun" sections: $15 + 7 = 22$.

ANSWER The number who do not think roller coasters are great is 22.

Your turn now The circle graph shows how many people out of 100 prefer each of four types of space materials for a paperweight.

1. Which type of paperweight is least popular? **Man-made satellite**

2. How many of the people do not prefer a meteor? **78 people**

3. Yes. *Sample answer:* 45 out of 100 people prefer moon rock, which is more than the numbers who prefer any other type.

3. Is it reasonable to say that moon rock is the most popular choice? Explain.

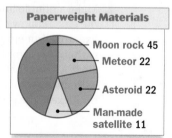

Paperweight Materials

Moon rock 45
Meteor 22
Asteroid 22
Man-made satellite 11

HELP with Reading

Writing down key facts as you read a problem can help you solve it. In Example 2, you know: 100 students were surveyed, 38 of them like vanilla ice cream, and 300 students will be at the party.

EXAMPLE 2 Using a Graph

Ice Cream The circle graph shows the favorite ice cream flavors of 100 students. About 300 students will attend an ice cream party. Predict how many students will ask for vanilla ice cream.

Vanilla 38 Chocolate 40 Strawberry 22

Solution

Find the relationship between the number of students surveyed and the number of students who will attend the party: $100 \times 3 = 300$.

Multiply the number of students who prefer vanilla by 3 to predict the number of students who will ask for vanilla at the party: $38 \times 3 = 114$.

ANSWER About 114 students will ask for vanilla ice cream at the party.

Your turn now Use the circle graph in Example 2.

4. Predict the number of students who will ask for strawberry ice cream at an ice cream party for 200 students. **44 students**

2.7 **Exercises**
More Practice, p. 709

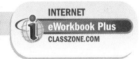

INTERNET
eWorkbook Plus
CLASSZONE.COM

Getting Ready to Practice

Vocabulary **Which type of graph is best suited for the purpose?**

1. comparing separate categories C   **A.** circle graph

2. comparing part of a data set to the entire set A   **B.** line graph

3. showing change over time B   **C.** bar graph

Population **The circle graph shows the population of the United States, in millions, in 2000.**

4. Which age group was the smallest?

5. How can you tell from the graph that about half the population was under 35 years old?

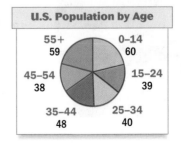

U.S. Population by Age

55+ 59   0–14 60   15–24 39   25–34 40   35–44 48   45–54 38

5. Look at the sections for ages from 0 to 34. They make up about half of the circle, which means they make up about half of the population.

Lesson 2.7   Circle Graphs   **89**

EXTRA EXAMPLES

Example 1 The circle graph displays data from a survey of 100 people.

Attendance at Professional Games

Basketball 25
Baseball 35
Football 20
Hockey 10
Soccer 6
Other 4

a. How many people are likely to attend a soccer game?
6 people

b. How many people are not likely to attend a baseball, basketball, or football game?
20 people

Example 2 The graph shows the favorite pizza of 100 students. About 500 students are in the school. Predict how many students chose cheese pizza.
240 students

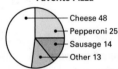

Favorite Pizza

Cheese 48
Pepperoni 25
Sausage 14
Other 13

CONCEPT CHECK

Use the graph in Extra Example 2 to predict how many students like pepperoni pizza if there are 400 students in the school. **100 students**

DAILY PUZZLER

In a survey of 36 teenagers taken at a mall, 22 said they were going to a record store, 17 were going to a clothing store, and 2 were going to neither of these. How many teenagers were going to both kinds of store?
5 teenagers

ASSIGNMENT GUIDE

Basic Course
Day 1: SRH p. 706 Exs. 1–2,
p. 707 Ex. 1; pp. 90–91
Exs. 6–10, 12–19, 26–35

Average Course
Day 1: pp. 90–91 Exs. 6–24,
26–29, 32–35

Advanced Course
Day 1: pp. 90–91 Exs. 8–11,
14–25*, 28, 29, 34, 35

Block
pp. 90–91 Exs. 6–24, 26–29,
32–35 (with 2.8)

EXTRA PRACTICE

- Student Edition, p. 709
- Chapter 2 Resource Book,
  pp. 59–61
- Test and Practice Generator

 TRANSPARENCY

Even-numbered answers are available on transparencies.

HOMEWORK CHECK

When you review students' homework for this lesson, go over the following exercises to check understanding of key concepts.
Basic: 6, 9, 10, 12, 16
Average: 7, 10, 11, 13, 17
Advanced: 8, 11, 15, 17, 19

TEACHING TIP

In Exercises 12–15, emphasize the usefulness of circle graphs to make predictions. Ask students to predict how many home runs Cal Ripkin, Jr. might have gotten in any number of seasons.

20, 29. See Additional Answers beginning on page AA1.

HELP with Homework

Example	Exercises
1	6–11
2	12–19

 **Online Resources**
CLASSZONE.COM
· More Examples
· eTutorial Plus

Practice and Problem Solving

Tell which section of the circle graph below fits the description.

A **6.** It represents about half the data. **C**

7. It represents the least data value. **A**

8. It represents the greatest data value. **C**

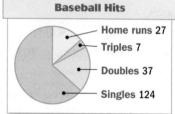

Geography **The circle graph shows the amount of Earth's surface, in millions of square kilometers, that is covered by each ocean.**

9. Which ocean covers the least area? **Arctic Ocean**

10. Which ocean covers the greatest area? **Pacific Ocean**

11. What is the total area of the five oceans? **335 million km²**

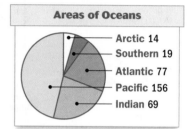
Areas of Oceans
Arctic 14
Southern 19
Atlantic 77
Pacific 156
Indian 69

Predict **The circle graph shows the types of hits by Cal Ripken, Jr., in one season. In Exercises 12–15, predict the number of hits he might have gotten in 4 seasons.**

12. singles
496 singles
13. doubles
148 doubles
14. triples
28 triples
15. home runs
108 home runs
16. Predict the total number of hits Cal Ripken, Jr., might have gotten in 3 seasons. **585 hits**

Baseball Hits
Home runs 27
Triples 7
Doubles 37
Singles 124

Marine Mammals **The circle graph shows the total amount of money spent to feed the three types of mammals at an aquarium for one year.**

17. Predict how much money will be spent to feed the sea otters for four years. **$160,000**

B 18. There are 4 sea lions. About how much does it cost to feed one sea lion for one year? **about $2500**

19. There are 7 harbor seals. About how much does it cost to feed one harbor seal for one year? **about $1900**

Yearly Food Costs
Sea lions $10,000
Harbor seals $13,300
Sea otters $40,000

Favorite Season A group of people voted for their favorite season. The results are shown in the circle graph.

20. Use the data to make a bar graph. *See margin.*

21. Which season got the most votes? Which graph did you use to decide? *fall; bar graph*

22. On which graph can you see that spring and summer combined got slightly more than half the votes? *circle graph*

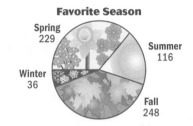

Favorite Season

Spring 229
Summer 116
Winter 36
Fall 248

Movies The graph shows the amounts 100 people paid to rent a movie.

23. How many people out of 300 would you expect to pay $4 or less? *276 people*

24. Writing Explain how a bar graph of the data would be similar to the circle graph.
C

25. Challenge Is a line graph a good choice to represent the data? Why or why not?

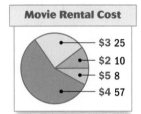

Movie Rental Cost

$3 25
$2 10
$5 8
$4 57

24. *Sample answer:* The longest bar and the largest section are both at $4 and the shortest bar and smallest section are both at $5.

25. No; the data does not show change over time.

Mixed Review

Evaluate the expression. *(Lesson 1.4)*

26. $\dfrac{2+8}{5}$ 2

27. $(8+3+7) \div 3$ 6

28. $\dfrac{5+11+8+12}{4}$ 9

29. Graph the point (0, 8) on a coordinate grid. *(Lesson 2.6)* See margin.

Basic Skills Find the quotient.

30. $255 \div 5$ 51 **31.** $468 \div 3$ 156 **32.** $1250 \div 25$ 50 **33.** $4725 \div 21$ 225

Test-Taking Practice

The circle graph shows students' favorite school lunches.

34. Multiple Choice How many more students chose hot lunches than homemade lunches? **B**

A. 10 **B.** 12 **C.** 14 **D.** 18

35. Multiple Choice Which is a possible value for the number of students who chose the salad? **G**

F. 22 **G.** 99 **H.** 250 **I.** 258

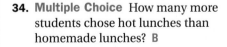

Types of Lunches

Hot 264
Homemade 252
Salad ?
Sandwich 465

ASSESSMENT RESOURCES

For more assessment resources, see:
- Assessment Book
- Test and Practice Generator

MINI-QUIZ

For every 100 items, the graph shows the number and kind of music items that were shipped in one year.

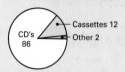

CD's 86
Cassettes 12
Other 2

1. Of 500 music items, predict how many CDs were shipped. **430 CDs**

2. Out of 500 music items, predict how many were not CDs. **70 items**

3. How many music items out of 200 would you expect to be cassettes? **24 cassettes**

4. If about 100,000,000 CDs were shipped in one year, how many will be shipped in 4 years? **400,000,000 CDs**

5 FOLLOW-UP

RETEACHING/REMEDIATION

- Study Guide in Chapter 2 Resource Book, pp. 62–63
- eTutorial Plus Online
- Extra Practice, p. 709
- Lesson Practice in Chapter 2 Resource Book, pp. 59–61

CHALLENGE/ENRICHMENT

- Challenge Practice in Chapter 2 Resource Book, p. 64
- Teacher's Edition, p. 52F

ENGLISH LEARNER SUPPORT

- Spanish Study Guide
- Multi-Language Glossary
- Chapter Audio Summaries CDs

PLAN

EXPLORE THE CONCEPT
- Students will use numbers to describe a set of data.
- This activity leads to the study of mean, median, and mode in Lesson 2.8.

MATERIALS
Each student or group of students will need counters or coins.

RECOMMENDED TIME
Work activity: 10 min
Discuss results: 5 min

GROUPING
This activity can be done individually or in groups of two.

TEACH

DISCUSSION
A class discussion of Exercise 3 will be worthwhile as students are led to realize that at different times different values can be considered "typical" for different data sets.

CLOSE

KEY DISCOVERY
Different values can be considered typical for different data sets.

ASSESSMENT
1. Find the middle number in the following stack heights.
7, 8, 4, 5, 10, 9, 6 **7**
2. Which of the numbers in the data set in Exercise 1 is typical of the data set? **7**

1–3. See Additional Answers beginning on page AA1.

2.8 **Hands-on Activity**

GOAL
Use numbers to describe a set of data.

MATERIALS
· counters or coins

Finding Typical Data Values

Explore Use counters to find values to describe a set of data.

1 Create five stacks of counters with the heights 8, 3, 7, 5, and 7. Arrange the stacks in a row from shortest to tallest.

2 Find a typical height of a stack of counters.

> The height of the middle stack is 7 counters.

> The most common stack height is 7 counters.

3 Make the stacks the same height by moving counters.

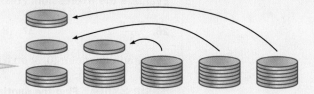

> 6 is also a typical height of a stack of counters.

Your turn now Repeat Steps 1–3 above to find three values to describe the data set. 1–3. See margin.

1. stack heights: 2, 7, 5, 9, 9, 5, 5
2. stack heights: 2, 8, 6, 2, 7

Stop and Think

3. **Critical Thinking** Do you think all three values you found to describe the data could be considered "typical" for the data set in Exercise 1? for the data set in Exercise 2? Why or why not?

NCTM CURRICULUM STANDARDS
Standard 5: Develop inferences that are based on data
Standard 8: Use the language of math to express ideas

LESSON 2.8

Mean, Median, and Mode

BEFORE	▶ **Now**	**WHY?**
You represented data using graphs.	You'll describe data using mean, median, mode, and range.	So you can find the best average, as in Exs. 13 and 14.

Word Watch

mean, p. 93
median, p. 93
mode, p. 93
range, p. 94

In the Real World

Astronauts In the Apollo space program, each lunar landing mission had one lunar module pilot. The ages of the pilots are listed below. What is the average age?

Apollo mission	11	12	13	14	15	16	17
Pilot's age	39	37	36	40	41	36	37

There are three types of averages used to describe a data set.

Averages

The **mean** of a data set is the sum of the values divided by the number of values.

The **median** of a data set is the middle value when the values are written in numerical order. If a data set has an even number of values, the median is the mean of the two middle values.

The **mode** of a data set is the value that occurs most often. A data set can have one mode, more than one mode, or no mode.

EXAMPLE 1 Finding a Mean

To find the mean of the ages for the Apollo pilots given above, add their ages. Then divide by 7, the number of pilots.

$$\text{Mean} = \frac{39 + 37 + 36 + 40 + 41 + 36 + 37}{7} = \frac{266}{7} = 38$$

ANSWER The mean of the Apollo pilots' ages is 38 years.

Lesson 2.8 Mean, Median, and Mode **93**

---

1 PLAN

SKILL CHECK
1. $24 + 38 + 31 + 27 + 33 + 25 + 39 = \underline{?}$ **217**
2. Divide the answer to Exercise 1 by 7. **31**

LESSON OBJECTIVE
Describe data using mean, median, mode, and range.

PACING
Suggested Number of Days
Basic Course: 1 day
Average Course: 1 day
Advanced Course: 1 day
Block: 0.5 block with 2.7

TEACHING RESOURCES
For a complete list of Teaching Resources, see page 52B.

TRANSPARENCY
Warm-Up Exercises for this lesson are available on a transparency.

2 TEACH

MOTIVATING THE LESSON
Demonstrate to students how often mean, median, and mode are used in the real world by bringing numerous examples of their use to class.

TIPS FOR NEW TEACHERS
Ask students for their ages and discuss the idea of a typical age for the students in your class. See Tips for New Teachers in the *Chapter 2 Resource Book*.

 **Science**

■ **Astronauts**

An astronaut's weight on Earth is 139 pounds. The same astronaut weighs about 23 pounds on the moon. How many more pounds does the astronaut weigh on Earth than on the moon?

116 more pounds

1. mean = 14, median = 13, mode = 23, range = 19

2. mean = 25, median = 26, no mode, range = 11

3. mean = 7, median = 7, modes = 4 and 8, range = 11

4. mean = 88, median = 80, mode = 80, range = 79

 with **Notetaking**

Be sure your notes include an example where there is an even number of data values, as in Example 3. Make note of the fact that the median is the mean of the two middle numbers.

Range The **range** of a data set is the difference between the greatest value and the least value.

EXAMPLE 2 **Finding Median, Mode, and Range**

Astronauts **Find the median, mode(s), and range of the pilots' ages from the top of page 93.**

Put the ages in order from least to greatest.

36   36   37   37   39   40   41

Median: The middle number is 37, so the median is 37.

Mode: Both 36 and 37 occur twice. There are two modes, 36 and 37.

Range: Range = Oldest age − Youngest age = $41 - 36 = 5$

EXAMPLE 3 **Choosing the Best Average**

Music The minutes that students practice a musical instrument each week are listed below. Choose the best average(s) for the data.

30   30   50   90   100   120   150   630

Solution

Mean: $1200 \div 8 = 150$

The mean is greater than all but two data values.

Median: $(90 + 100) \div 2 = 95$

Mode: The mode is 30. It is the least data value.

ANSWER The mean and the mode are not typical of the data. The median best represents the data.

Your turn now Find the mean, median, mode(s), and range.

1. 10, 23, 13, 23, 4, 9, 16

2. 27, 23, 30, 26, 19

3. 8, 13, 8, 4, 11, 4, 2, 6

4. 91, 150, 80, 71, 74, 81, 80, 77

5. Choose the best average(s) to represent the data in Exercise 4.

median and mode

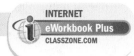
INTERNET
eWorkbook Plus
CLASSZONE.COM

Getting Ready to Practice

1. Vocabulary The _?_ of a data set is the difference between the greatest and the least values. The _?_ of a data set is the middle value when the values are written in numerical order. **range; median**

Find the mean, median, mode(s), and range of the data.

2. 2, 3, 1, 1, 3   **3.** 10, 8, 9, 8, 5   **4.** 13, 8, 11, 7, 5, 10

5. Guided Problem Solving The ages of the counselors at a camp are listed below. What is a typical age?

    21, 49, 23, 25, 23, 21, 21, 25

    1 Find the mean, median, and mode(s) of the ages.
        mean = 26, median = 23, mode = 21
    2 Decide whether each average represents a typical age.

    3 Choose the average that best represents the data. **median**

Answers (left margin)

2. mean = 2, median = 2, modes = 1 and 3, range = 2

3. mean = 8, median = 8, mode = 8, range = 5

4. mean = 9, median = 9, no mode, range = 8

5. Step 2: The mean is a little higher than the typical age; the median represents the data well; the mode is a little lower than the typical age.

Practice and Problem Solving

 with Homework

Example	Exercises
1	6–11, 15
2	6–12, 15
3	13, 14, 16

 Online Resources
CLASSZONE.COM
· More Examples
· eTutorial Plus

Find the mean, median, mode(s), and range of the data.

6. 7, 9, 12, 5, 12   mean = 9, median = 9, mode = 12, range = 7
7. 5, 11, 9, 5, 25   mean = 11, median = 9, mode = 5, range = 20
8. 14, 10, 9, 7, 14, 16, 14   mean = 12, median = 14, mode = 14, range = 9
9. 42, 37, 25, 33, 25, 18, 37   See margin.
10. 26, 22, 10, 12, 16, 28   mean = 19, median = 19, no mode, range = 18
11. 30, 60, 10, 30, 30, 50, 80, 30   See margin.

12. Find the Error Your friend found the median and the mode of a data set. Describe and correct your friend's error(s). **See margin.**

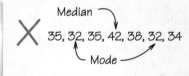

Answers (left margin)

9. mean = 31, median = 33, modes = 25 and 37, range = 24

11. mean = 40, median = 30, mode = 30, range = 70

12. *Sample answer:* The data are not listed in numerical order, so neither the median nor the mode can be easily found. The data in order are 32, 32, 34, 35, 35, 38, 42. The median is 35 and the modes are 32 and 35.

Writing Find the mean, median, and mode(s). Then choose the best average(s) to represent a typical score. Explain your choice.

13. Bowling scores: 180, 170, 190, 200, 130, 30, 180, 160   13, 14. See margin.

14. Math test scores: 70, 71, 97, 71, 62, 94, 95

15. Basketball The data show the heights, in inches, of the players on the Seattle Storm team at one time. Find the mean, median, mode(s), and range of the data.   mean = 73, median = 73, mode = 77, range = 10

    77, 76, 67, 77, 76, 68, 73, 77, 70, 72, 70

---

3 APPLY

ASSIGNMENT GUIDE

Basic Course
Day 1: SRH p. 685 Exs. 1–3, p. 691 Exs. 1–4; pp. 95–97 Exs. 6–11, 14, 15, 17–20, 22, 26–29, 34–41

Average Course
Day 1: pp. 95–97 Exs. 6–12, 14–19, 21–24, 26–31, 34–38, 41, 42

Advanced Course
Day 1: pp. 95–97 Exs. 10–22, 25–36*, 41, 42

Block
pp. 95–97 Exs. 6–12, 14–19, 21–24, 26–31, 34–38, 41, 42 (with 2.7)

EXTRA PRACTICE

• Student Edition, p. 709
• Chapter 2 Resource Book, pp. 70–72
• Test and Practice Generator

TRANSPARENCY

Even-numbered answers are available on transparencies.

HOMEWORK CHECK

When you review students' homework for this lesson, go over the following exercises to check understanding of key concepts.
Basic: 6, 7, 10, 11, 14
Average: 8, 9, 10, 12, 14
Advanced: 10, 12, 13, 15, 16

 COMMON ERROR

Exercise 12 highlights a common error, namely picking the middle number as the mean before putting the data in numerical order. Caution students about making this error.

13, 14. See Additional Answers beginning on page AA1.

TEACHING TIP

For Exercises 22–25, it may be helpful to ask students to first order the data sets and estimate the mean. This should help them understand whether the mean that is given is reasonable.

16. **Sea Turtles** Find the mean, median, and mode(s) of the data. What is the best average to use to represent the most typical length?

mean = 45, median = 39, mode = 30; median

Adult Sea Turtle Lengths			
Type of turtle	Length (inches)	Type of turtle	Length (inches)
Kemps Ridley	30	Loggerhead	48
Olive Ridley	30	Black	39
Leatherback	96	Flatback	39
Green	48	Hawksbill	30

In Exercises 17 and 18, find the mode(s) of the data.

17. green, red, green, blue, blue, green, green, red, red, blue, green, red
green

18. left, right, straight, right, left, right, straight, left, right, left, straight
left and right

19. **Explain** For Exercises 17 and 18, is there a mean? a median? Explain.
No; no; the data sets are not numerical.

Find the mean of the data.

20. 142, 131, 135, 148, 139 139

21. 796, 849, 833, 840, 827, 836, 843
832

22. No; 19; the mean given is greater than any of the data.

23. No; 8; the mean given is too close to the least data value.

25. No; 16; the mean given is too close to the greatest data value.

30. No; *Sample answer:* The temperatures on some days could have been much higher or much lower than the average, in which case they would not be near freezing.

31. A good answer should include these two points for each of the three averages.
· The data set listed should actually have the average given.
· The context should make it very clear that the given average is most descriptive of the data set.

Number Sense Tell whether the mean is reasonable. If it is not reasonable, then find the correct mean. Explain your reasoning.

22. 13, 16, 9, 21, 25, 30; Mean: 32

23. 5, 11, 4, 11, 7, 7, 10, 8, 9; Mean: 5

24. 6, 4, 3, 8, 9, 12, 13, 9; Mean: 8
yes

25. 9, 12, 13, 8, 33, 15, 22; Mean: 30

Tell whether the statement is *true* or *false*.

26. The mode is always one of the numbers in a data set. true

27. The mean can be one of the numbers in a data set. true

28. The median is always one of the numbers in a data set. false

29. A data set always has a mode. false

30. **Writing** The average of the temperatures at noon on Inauguration Day from 1957 to 1997 was 36°F. Do you think the temperature was near freezing (32°F) for every inauguration from 1957 to 1997? Explain.

31. **Critical Thinking** Find a data set for a situation where the best average is the mean. Repeat this exercise for the median and the mode(s).

Challenge Use the given mean or median of the data to find the missing number.

32. 14, 24, _?_, 18, 30; 29
Mean: 23

33. 40, 28, 16, 18, 37, 20, _?_, 35; 24
Median: 26

Mixed Review

The graph shows the results of a survey of 100 people. *(Lesson 2.7)*

Favorite Hot Dog Topping

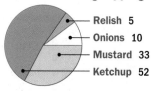

- Relish 5
- Onions 10
- Mustard 33
- Ketchup 52

34. How many more people prefer ketchup than mustard? **19 more people**

35. Predict how many people out of 500 would prefer relish. **25 people**

Choose a Strategy **Use a strategy from the list to solve the following problem. Explain your choice of strategy.**

Problem Solving Strategies
- Guess, Check, and Revise
- Draw a Diagram
- Work Backward
- Make a Model

36. An elevator in a building starts on the ground floor, which is numbered 1. It rises 6 floors, descends 4 floors, rises 15 floors, and descends 12 floors. Which floor is the elevator on?

36. Floor 6. *Sample answer:* I used Draw a Diagram because I could easily keep track of what floor the elevator was on after each rise and descent.

37. thirty-five

38. one hundred twenty-six

39. six hundred seven

40. one thousand five hundred seventy-eight

Basic Skills **Write the number in words.**

37. 35   **38.** 126   **39.** 607   **40.** 1578

Test-Taking Practice

41. Multiple Choice Which number is *not* the mean, median, mode, or range of the data set 4, 3, 15, 11, 3, 8, 7, 5? **B**

    A. 3   **B.** 5   **C.** 6   **D.** 7

42. Short Response Paint for your garage should be applied when the temperature is at or above 60°F. If the average temperature for a week is 65°F, could you have painted every day of that week? Explain.
Sample answer: Yes. It is possible that all the temperatures could all have been clustered tightly around 65° F.

BRAIN GAME

Lucky Sevens

Each person rolls a number cube seven times and records the result for each roll. After the seventh roll, calculate the median and mode(s) of the results.

The person with the highest median gets one point and the person with the highest mode gets one point. If you tie, play another round.

Play the game three times. Total your scores to see who has the most points.
Answers may vary.

---

4 ASSESS

ASSESSMENT RESOURCES

For more assessment resources, see:
- Assessment Book
- Test and Practice Generator

MINI-QUIZ

Find the mean, median, mode(s), and range of the data.

1. 18, 22, 13, 15, 28, 10, 13
    mean: 17; median: 15; mode: 13; range: 18

2. 30, 40, 30, 50, 60, 90, 70, 110
    mean: 60; median: 55; mode: 30; range: 80

Find the mean, median, and mode(s). Then choose the best average(s) to represent a typical value.

3. Heights of students in inches: 47, 49, 55, 53, 56 **mean: 52; median: 53; mode: none; mean**

4. Project grades: 80, 84, 95, 84, 98, 98, 94, 71 **mean: 88; median: 89; modes: 84, 98; median**

5 FOLLOW-UP

RETEACHING/REMEDIATION

- Study Guide in Chapter 2 Resource Book, pp. 73–74
- Tutor Place, Whole Numbers and Decimals Card 19
- eTutorial Plus Online
- Extra Practice, p. 709
- Lesson Practice in Chapter 2 Resource Book, pp. 70–72

CHALLENGE/ENRICHMENT

- Challenge Practice in Chapter 2 Resource Book, p. 75
- Teacher's Edition, p. 52F

ENGLISH LEARNER SUPPORT

- Spanish Study Guide
- Multi-Language Glossary
- Chapter Audio Summaries CDs

ADDITIONAL RESOURCES

The following resources are available to help review the materials in Lessons 2.5–2.8.

 Chapter 2 Resource Book
- Lesson Practice
- Study Guide

 Assessment Book
- Chapter 2 Quiz 2

 Technology
- Test and Practice Generator
- eTutorial CD-ROM

 Internet
- Classzone
- eWorkbook Plus Online
- eTutorial Plus Online

ENGLISH LEARNER SUPPORT

- Spanish Study Guide
- Multi-Language Glossary
- Chapter Audio Summaries CDs

3. *Sample answer:* **Start the scale at 0 and end the scale at 14, using equal increments of 2.**

4.

5.

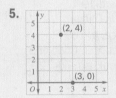

LESSONS 2.5 TO 2.8

Notebook Review

Note book

Review the vocabulary definitions in your notebook.

Copy the review examples in your notebook. Then complete the exercises.

Check Your Definitions

bar graph, p. 79	line graph, p. 84	mode, p. 93
double bar graph, p. 80	circle graph, p. 88	range, p. 94
ordered pair, p. 83	mean, p. 93	
coordinates, p. 83	median, p. 93	

Use Your Vocabulary

1. **Copy and complete:** The first coordinate in the _?_ (6, 0) tells you how many units to move to the right to graph the point. **ordered pair**

2. **Writing** Explain how to find the mean of a set of data.
Add the values and divide by the number of values.

2.5–2.6 Can you make a bar graph and a line graph?

 Review

EXAMPLE Choose appropriate scales and make graphs of the data.

a. Make a bar graph of the data for games won.

b. Make a line graph of the data for male soccer players.

Team	Games won
Bears	14
Cardinals	11
Otters	9
Eagles	13

Year	Male	Female
1995	7691	4285
1996	8626	5251
1997	8303	5348
1998	8232	4935

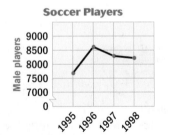

3. Describe another appropriate scale for the data in the bar graph.
3–5. See margin.
4. Make a line graph of the data above for female soccer players.
5. Graph the points (2, 4) and (3, 0) on the same coordinate grid.

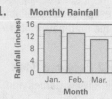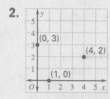
2.7–2.8 Can you read a circle graph and find averages?

EXAMPLE The graph shows the shoreline lengths, in kilometers, of the Great Lakes and their islands. Find the mean, median, mode(s), and range.

Mean: $\dfrac{6157 + 4385 + 1400 + 2670 + 1168}{5}$

= 3156 km

Median: The middle number is 2670 km.

Mode: Each number occurs only once, so there is no mode.

Range: 6157 − 1168 = 4989 km

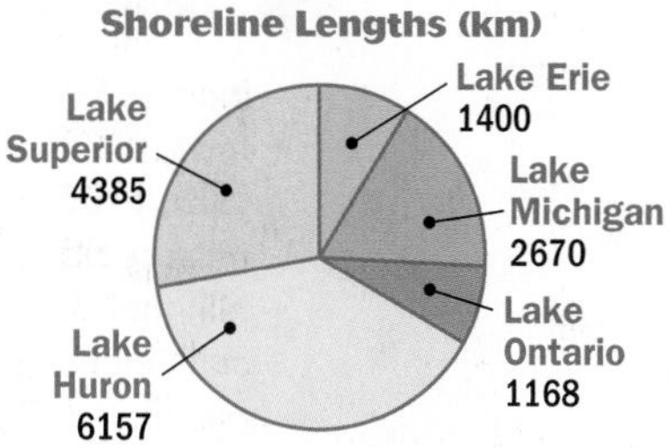

Shoreline Lengths (km)

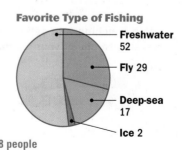

Lake Superior 4385
Lake Erie 1400
Lake Michigan 2670
Lake Huron 6157
Lake Ontario 1168

☑ **6.** Use the graph above. Which lake has the least amount of shoreline?
Lake Ontario

7. Find the mean, median, mode(s), and range: 45, 39, 82, 45, 39, 50.
mean = 50, median = 45, modes = 39 and 45, range = 43

Stop and Think about Lessons 2.5–2.8

8. Writing Explain how to choose the scale for a bar graph. 8–9. See margin.

9. Critical Thinking Explain why the mean of a data set may not represent the data very well.

8. *Sample answer:* Start the scale at 0 and end the scale at a value greater than the greatest data value, using equal increments along the scale.

9. *Sample answer:* Data values that are much less or much greater than most of the other data values can make the mean less or greater than the average that best represents the data.

3. mean = 9, median = 9, mode = 11, range = 14; The mean and the median represent the data best.

Review Quiz 2

1. Make a bar graph of the data in the table at the right.
1, 2. See margin.

Monthly Rainfall			
Month	**Jan.**	**Feb.**	**Mar.**
Rainfall (inches)	14	13	11

2. Graph the points (4, 2), (0, 3), and (1, 0) on the same coordinate grid.

3. Find the mean, median, mode(s), and range of the data. Choose the best average(s) to represent the data. See margin.

11, 17, 5, 7, 11, 3

Fishing **The graph shows the results of a survey of 100 people who like fishing.**

Favorite Type of Fishing

Freshwater 52
Fly 29
Deep-sea 17
Ice 2

4. What type of fishing is the most popular? the least popular?
freshwater fishing; ice fishing

5. Predict the number of people who would prefer deep-sea fishing in a group of 400 people who like fishing. 68 people

Chapter Review

 **Vocabulary**

inch, p. 55	area, p. 62	coordinates, p. 83
foot, p. 55	scale drawing, p. 68	line graph, p. 84
yard, p. 55	scale, p. 68	circle graph, p. 88
mile, p. 55	data, p. 72	mean, p. 93
millimeter, p. 56	frequency table, p. 72	median, p. 93
centimeter, p. 56	line plot, p. 73	mode, p. 93
meter, p. 56	bar graph, p. 79	range, p. 94
kilometer, p. 56	double bar graph, p. 80	
perimeter, p. 61	ordered pair, p. 83	

Vocabulary Review

1. Give three examples of customary units of length. **Answer should include any three of the following: inch, foot, yard, mile.**

2. Give three examples of metric units of length. **Answer should include any three of the following: millimeter, centimeter, meter, kilometer.**

Tell whether the statement is *true* or *false*.

3. The perimeter of a figure is a measure of how much surface the figure covers. **false**

4. A line graph is often used to represent data that changes over time. **true**

Copy and complete the statement.

5. The first ? in the ordered pair (3, 5) is 3. **coordinate**

6. The ? of a data set is the sum of the values divided by the number of values. **mean**

7. The ? of a data set is the middle value when the values are written in numerical order. If a data set has an even number of values, the ? is the ? of the two middle values. **median; median; average**

8. The ? of a data set is the value that occurs most often. **mode**

Review Questions

Choose an appropriate customary unit and metric unit for the length. *(Lesson 2.1)*

9. length of a canoe oar
   feet; meters

10. height of a skyscraper
    feet, meters

11. length of the Colorado river
    miles; kilometers

Use a benchmark to estimate the length of the object in inches. Then measure to check your estimate. *(Lesson 2.1)*

12.
    paper clip; 2 in.

13.
    paper clip; 3 in.

Score	Tally	Frequency
71	IIII	4
72	IIII	4
73	I	1
74		0
75	II	2
76	I	1
77		0
78	III	3
79	II	2
80	IIII	4
81	IIII	4

Review Questions

Use a benchmark to estimate the length of the line segment in centimeters. Then find the length of the line segment to the nearest millimeter and to the nearest centimeter. *(Lesson 2.1)* **14–15. Estimates may vary.**

14. ――――――――
4 little fingers; 43 mm; 4 cm

15. ―――――――
3 little fingers; 35 mm; 4 cm

Find the perimeter and the area of the figure described. *(Lesson 2.2)*

16. a rectangle that is 12 cm by 4 cm
$P = 32$ cm; $A = 48$ cm^2

17. a square that is 9 yd by 9 yd
$P = 36$ yd; $A = 81$ yd^2

Models **An airplane model uses the scale 1 in. : 32 in.** *(Lesson 2.3)*

18. If the actual airplane is 512 inches long, how long is the model? **16 in.**

19. If a stripe on the model is 8 inches long, how long is the actual stripe? **256 in.**

Marching Band **The data show the scores for a band competition.** *(Lesson 2.4)*
71, 81, 72, 81, 72, 80, 78, 75, 71, 78, 80, 73, 76, 78, 81, 72, 75, 79, 80, 79, 72, 71, 80, 81, 71
20, 21. See margin.

20. Make a frequency table of the data.

21. Make a line plot of the data.

22. **Bike Riding** The table below shows how many miles you rode your bike each day of one week. Make a bar graph of the data. *(Lesson 2.5)* **See margin.**

Day	Sun.	Mon.	Tues.	Wed.	Thur.	Fri.	Sat.
Distance (miles)	5	2	0	2	3	0	4

Graph the points on the same coordinate grid. *(Lesson 2.6)* **23–27. See margin for art.**

23. (7, 1) **24.** (0, 8) **25.** (3, 7) **26.** (4, 0)

27. **Butter Prices** The table at the right shows prices of butter, in cents per pound. Make a line graph of the data. *(Lesson 2.6)*

Year	1996	1997	1998	1999
Price	217	246	318	227

The circle graph shows the number of wins, losses, and ties for a hockey team in one season. *(Lesson 2.7)*

28. How many games were played? **82 games**

29. How many more wins than ties were there? **20 more wins**

30. Predict the number of wins for 2 seasons. **78 wins**

Hockey Games
Ties 19
Wins 39
Losses 24

Find the mean, median, mode(s), and range of the data. *(Lesson 2.8)*

31. Prices of portable CD players (dollars): 70, 180, 110, 100, 200, 100, 80
mean = 120, median = 100, mode = 100, range = 130

32. Ages of houses in a neighborhood (years): 28, 20, 28, 26, 20, 63, 23, 24
mean = 29, median = 25, modes = 20 and 28, range = 43

33. Choose the best average(s) to represent the data in Exercise 32. Explain.
Median. *Sample answer:* It is the closest to most of the data.

21.

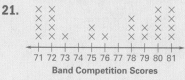
71 72 73 74 75 76 77 78 79 80 81
Band Competition Scores

22.

Bike Riding
Distance (miles) / Day

23–26.
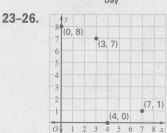
(0, 8), (3, 7), (7, 1), (4, 0)

27.
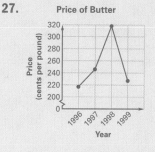
Price of Butter
Price (cents per pound) / Year

6.

Roll	Tally	Frequency
1	III	3
2	JHT I	6
3	IIII	4
4	JHT II	7
5	II	2
6	III	3

7.
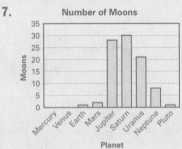

8–13.
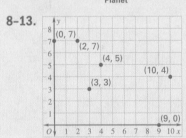

Chapter Test

Choose an appropriate customary unit and metric unit for the length.

1. distance between Earth and the sun miles; kilometers

2. height of a waterfall feet or yards; meters

3. Use a ruler to draw a line segment that is 4 inches long. **Check drawings.**

4. Measure to find the length, in centimeters, of one side of the square shown at the right. Then find its perimeter and its area.
2 cm; *P* = 8 cm; *A* = 4 cm²

5. A scale drawing uses a scale of 1 in. : 3 yd. A distance on the drawing is 12 inches. What is the actual distance? **36 yd**

6. The rolls of a number cube are given. Make a frequency table of the data.

2, 3, 6, 4, 5, 4, 4, 4, 3, 2, 5, 3, 6, 6, 4, 1, 1, 2, 3, 2, 4, 2, 1, 4, 2 **See margin.**

7. Astronomy The table at the right shows the number of moons that orbit each of the planets in our solar system. Make a bar graph of the data.
See margin.

Planet	Number of moons
Mercury	0
Venus	0
Earth	1
Mars	2
Jupiter	28
Saturn	30
Uranus	21
Neptune	8
Pluto	1

Graph the points on the same coordinate grid. 8–13. See margin.

8. (10, 4)   **9.** (4, 5)

10. (0, 7)   **11.** (2, 7)

12. (9, 0)   **13.** (3, 3)

Theater Seats **The circle graph shows the number of seats available in a theater.**

14. How many seats are in the theater? **976 seats**

15. How many more Orchestra seats than Mezzanine seats are there? **10 more seats**

16. How many Mezzanine Box tickets will be sold if a show sells out for 5 performances? **160 tickets**

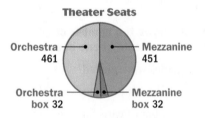
Theater Seats
Orchestra 461
Mezzanine 451
Orchestra box 32
Mezzanine box 32

In Exercises 17 and 18, find the mean, median, mode(s), and range.

17. Monthly allowances: 40, 20, 32, 80, 28, 20, 20, 28, 20 mean = 32, median = 28, mode = 20, range = 60

18. Ages of grandchildren: 2, 3, 4, 6, 7, 2, 9, 7 mean = 5, median = 5, modes = 2 and 7, range = 7

19. In Exercise 17, which is the best average to represent the data? **mean**

Chapter Standardized Test

Test-taking Strategy Go through the test and do the easiest questions first. Then go back through the test and do the questions that are more difficult.

ADDITIONAL RESOURCES

 Assessment Book
• Standardized Chapter Test, p. 26

 Test and Practice Generator

Multiple Choice

1. Which of the following ordered pairs corresponds to point *L* on the coordinate grid? **A**

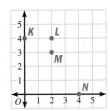

   A. (2, 4)   **B.** (4, 0)   **C.** (0, 4)   **D.** (2, 3)

2. Which unit of measure would *not* be used to measure the length of a snake? **I**

   F. millimeters   **G.** centimeters

   H. inches   **I.** kilometers

3. A map uses a scale of 1 in. : 200 mi. The distance between two cities on the map is 4 inches. What is the actual distance in miles? **D**

   A. 50   **B.** 200   **C.** 204   **D.** 800

4. What is the best estimate of the length of the line segment, in inches? **G**

_____

   F. 1   **G.** 2   **H.** 3   **I.** 6

5. A rectangle has an area of 40 square centimeters. The width of the rectangle is 5 centimeters. What is the length of the rectangle, in centimeters? **A**

   A. 8   **B.** 10   **C.** 15   **D.** 200

6. The data below are the siblings in your friends' families. How many X marks would you put above the 2 on a line plot?

   2, 0, 1, 2, 3, 4, 5, 3, 1, 1, 0, 2 **I**

   F. 6   **G.** 5   **H.** 4   **I.** 3

7. Which of the scales is the most appropriate for the data set: 16, 31, 82, 105? **B**

   A. 0–100, increments of 10

   B. 0–120, increments of 20

   C. 0–120, increments of 50

   D. 0–200, increments of 200

8. Your scores on six science tests were 95, 84, 82, 90, 93, and 84. What is the range? **G**

   F. 11   **G.** 13   **H.** 84   **I.** 88

Short Response

9. Use the graph below to help you predict how many students walk to school out of a group of 300 students. Show your work.
   See margin.

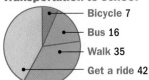

Transportation to School
- Bicycle 7
- Bus 16
- Walk 35
- Get a ride 42

Extended Response

10. Find the mean, median, and mode(s) of the weekly grocery bills: $155, $150, $60, $158, and $162. Which is the best average to represent the data? Explain. **See margin.**

9. 105 students; the total number of students represented by the graph is 7 + 16 + 35 + 42 = 100. So 35 × 3 = 105 students walk to school out of a group of 300 students.

10. Mean = 137, median = 155, no mode. *Sample answer:* Median; it is closest to the middle of the data set.

Pacing and Assignment Guide

REGULAR SCHEDULE

Lesson	Les. Day	BASIC	AVERAGE	ADVANCED
3.1	Day 1	SRH p. 684 Exs. 5–8; pp. 109–111 Exs. 12–19, 21–35, 40–47, 50, 54–60	pp. 109–111 Exs. 12–33, 36–41, 44–52, 54–60	pp. 109–111 Exs. 14–20, 23–33, 37, 41, 44–55*, 60
3.2	Day 1	pp. 115–117 Exs. 6–19, 21, 22, 27–33	pp. 115–117 Exs. 6–20, 23–25, 27–33	pp. 115–117 Exs. 8–20, 23–28*, 32, 33
3.3	Day 1	SRH p. 685 Exs. 4–9; pp. 120–121 Exs. 6–21, 24, 25, 27, 32–38	pp. 120–121 Exs. 9–29, 32–38	pp. 120–121 Exs. 10–15, 19–26, 29–33*, 37, 38
3.4	Day 1	SRH p. 686 Exs. 6–10; pp. 127–128 Exs. 11–21 odd, 23–26, 32–39, 43, 48–59	pp. 127–128 Exs. 10–22 even, 27–32, 35–45, 49–55, 58–60	pp. 127–128 Exs. 12, 13, 18–22, 29–33, 36–48*, 51–54, 59, 60
3.5	Day 1	SRH p. 692 Exs. 1–3, p. 693 Exs. 1–4; pp. 132–133 Exs. 6–14, 19–22, 27, 28, 31–39	pp. 132–133 Exs. 10–29, 31–40	pp. 132–133 Exs. 12–19, 23–36*, 40
3.6	Day 1	SRH p. 698 Exs. 1–3; pp. 139–140 Exs. 9–31 odd, 33–36, 41–47	pp. 139–140 Exs. 10–20 even, 21–27, 30–39, 41–44, 47, 48	pp. 139–140 Exs. 13–20, 24–26, 28, 29, 31–34, 37–42*, 47, 48
Review	Day 1	pp. 144–145 Exs. 1–58	pp. 144–145 Exs. 1–58	pp. 144–145 Exs. 1–58
Assess	Day 1	Chapter 3 Test	Chapter 3 Test	Chapter 3 Test

YEARLY PACING   Chapter 3 Total – **8 days**   Chapters 1–3 Total – **32 days**   Remaining – **128 days**

*Challenge Exercises   EP = Extra Practice   SRH = Skills Review Handbook   EC = Extra Challenge

BLOCK SCHEDULE

DAY 1	DAY 2	DAY 3	DAY 4
3.1 pp. 109–111 Exs. 12–33, 36–41, 44–52, 54–60 **3.2** pp. 115–117 Exs. 6–20, 23–25, 27–33	**3.3** pp. 120–121 Exs. 9–29, 32–38 **3.4** pp. 127–128 Exs. 10–22 even, 27–32, 35–45, 49–55, 58–60	**3.5** pp. 132–133 Exs. 10–29, 31–40 **3.6** pp. 139–140 Exs. 10–20 even, 21–27, 30–39, 41–44, 47, 48	**Review** pp. 144–145 Exs. 1–58 **Assess** Chapter 3 Test

YEARLY PACING   Chapter 3 Total – **4 days**   Chapters 1–3 Total – **16 days**   Remaining – **64 days**

Support Materials

📖 CHAPTER RESOURCE BOOK

CHAPTER SUPPORT

Tips for New Teachers	p. 1	Parents as Partners	p. 3

LESSON SUPPORT

	3.1	3.2	3.3	3.4	3.5	3.6
Lesson Plans (regular and block)	p. 5	p. 15	p. 23	p. 33	p. 42	p. 52
Technology Activities & Keystrokes					p. 44	
Activity Support Masters	p. 7					p. 7
Activity Masters			p. 25	p. 35		
Practice (3 levels)	p. 9	p. 17	p. 26	p. 36	p. 45	p. 54
Study Guide	p. 12	p. 20	p. 29	p. 39	p. 49	p. 57
Real-World Problem Solving			p. 31			p. 59
Challenge Practice	p. 14	p. 22	p. 32	p. 41	p. 51	p. 60

REVIEW

Games Support Masters	p. 61	Cooperative Project with Rubric	p. 65
Chapter Review Games and Activities	p. 62	Extra Credit Project with Rubric	p. 67
Real-Life Project with Rubric	p. 63	Cumulative Practice	p. 69
		Resource Book Answers	A1

📖 ASSESSMENT

Quizzes	p. 29	Alternative Assessments with Rubrics	p. 38
Chapter Tests (3 levels)	p. 31	Unit Test	p. 51
Standardized Test	p. 37	Cumulative Test	p. 53

🖨 TRANSPARENCIES

	3.1	3.2	3.3	3.4	3.5	3.6
Warm-Up / Daily Homework Quiz	✔	✔	✔	✔	✔	✔
Notetaking Guide	✔	✔	✔	✔	✔	✔
Teacher Support	✔	✔	✔	✔		✔
English/Spanish Problem Solving			✔		✔	✔
Answer Transparencies	✔	✔	✔	✔	✔	✔

💻 TECHNOLOGY

- EasyPlanner CD-ROM
- Test and Practice Generator
- Electronic Lesson Presentations
- eTutorial CD-ROM
- Chapter Audio Summaries CDs
- Classzone.com
- eEdition Plus Online
- eWorkbook Plus Online
- eTutorial Plus Online
- EasyPlanner Plus Online

ADDITIONAL RESOURCES

- Worked-Out Solution Key
- Notetaking Guide
- Practice Workbook
- Tutor Place
- Professional Development Book
- Activities Book
- Poster Package
- Spanish Study Guide
- English/Spanish Chapter Reviews
- Multi-Language Glossary

Math Background and Teaching Strategies

Lesson 3.1

MATH BACKGROUND

DECIMALS Decimal numbers are an extension of base-ten notation to include numbers between whole numbers. Just as with whole numbers, a digit in any place has a value 10 times the value of the digit one place to the right.

TEACHING STRATEGIES

Students may have trouble reading a decimal number. The biggest confusion seems to come with the use of the word *and*. It is best to reserve this word to denote the decimal point, trying not to use it when reading a whole number. Use examples like the ones shown here to give students practice in reading decimal numbers.

Read 125 as "one hundred twenty-five."

Read 100.25 as "one hundred and twenty-five hundredths."

Read 0.12 as "twelve hundredths."

Lesson 3.2

MATH BACKGROUND

METRIC SYSTEM The metric system is based on powers of 10, such as 10, 100, and 1000. Converting within the metric system is done by multiplying and dividing by powers of 10.

Prefixes in the metric system have consistent meanings:

Prefix	Meaning
milli-	one thousandth
centi-	one hundredth
kilo-	one thousand

TEACHING STRATEGIES

To practice measuring in centimeters and millimeters, have students work in groups of 3 or 4. Pass out centimeter rulers. Have students measure the length of their math books in centimeters. Make sure that students line up the correct end of the ruler with the math book. Then give each group 5–10 small objects. Have students take turns measuring each object, first to the nearest centimeter, then to the nearest millimeter. Then give students the opportunity to measure several objects so they gain proficiency in using a centimeter ruler.

Lesson 3.3

MATH BACKGROUND

The concept of comparing and ordering whole numbers can be smoothly transferred to comparing and ordering decimals. If you know how to compare two decimals, you also know how to put a group of decimals in order, since to write decimals from least to greatest, you need to first compare the numbers two at a time.

TEACHING STRATEGIES

Students can compare and order decimals by locating them on a number line or by comparing the digits by place value. Tell students they can compare and order decimals just as they compare and order whole numbers. When comparing decimals by examining the digits, it is helpful to write them one above the other with the decimal points aligned.

Lesson 3.4

MATH BACKGROUND

Rounding and estimating with decimals follow procedures similar to those used when rounding and estimating with whole numbers.

TEACHING STRATEGIES

When rounding a decimal number, students should find the place value to which they need to round and then look at the digit one place to the right of this. They should then round as they would for a whole number. Alternately, a number line provides a visual method of rounding numbers.

Example Rounded to the nearest tenth, 8.03 is 8.0.

Lesson 3.5

MATH BACKGROUND

ROUNDING For many decimal computations, rough estimates can be made easily by rounding the numbers to whole numbers. In almost all cases, a goal should be to have the estimates contain the correct number of digits to the left of the decimal point.

FRONT-END ESTIMATION Decimal sums can be estimated using the front-end digits of the decimals. In addition, front-end estimation always gives a sum less than the actual sum. To improve the estimate, use rounding with the remaining digits to get an estimate that is closer to the actual sum.

TEACHING STRATEGIES

To estimate sums and differences with decimal numbers, have students first round each decimal to the nearest whole number and then add the rounded numbers. Begin by selecting problems for which estimates are not terribly difficult and work through them with the students.

Examples

$3.806 + 133.02 + 55.2233 \rightarrow 4 + 133 + 55 = 192$

$545.9 - 11.123 \rightarrow 546 - 11 = 535$

Lesson 3.6

MATH BACKGROUND

ADDING AND SUBTRACTING DECIMALS The rules for adding and subtracting decimals are the same as the ones for adding and subtracting whole numbers. The skill is to be sure that the place values line up, which is achieved by lining up the decimal points. The **Commutative** and **Associative Properties of Addition** hold for both whole numbers and decimals.

ALGEBRAIC EXPRESSIONS Evaluating expressions involving decimals follows the same pattern as evaluating expressions involving whole numbers.

TEACHING STRATEGIES

An easy way to be sure students always line up digits properly is to have them use a place-value chart or a piece of notebook paper turned sideways. You can demonstrate the use of this technique to the class by using an overhead projector.

Examples

Find $4.513 + 8.5 + 13.65$.

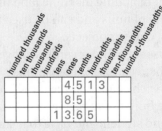

2 6.6 6 3

When you add, the decimal points line up.

Find $18.46 - 3.6$.

1 4.8 6

When you subtract, the decimal points line up.

3 Differentiating Instruction

Strategies for Underachievers

PROVIDE TOOLS FOR CONCRETE LEARNING

MANIPULATIVES Many students, especially concrete learners, learn better if they are able to see, touch, and manipulate objects that represent the concept being taught. Chapter 3 provides many opportunities for you to reach these learners.

In Lessons 3.1, 3.4, and 3.6, these students should be shown the concepts using base-ten blocks. Each student should have his/her own set to manipulate.

In Lesson 3.2, students can create out of oak tag or card stock their own metric and customary rulers to use in measuring. Students who are not yet proficient at reading the markings on rulers can create individual rulers for each unit. For example, they can create a centimeter ruler that not only has lines and numbers for the number of centimeters but also has lines 1 millimeter apart that students will label as 2.1 cm, 2.2 cm, for example. Students can create a meter stick out of adding machine tape that can be labeled with a variety of units and can be used to measure circumferences of circular objects.

In Lesson 3.3, create a class set of index cards with whole and decimal numbers on them carried out to various place values. Distribute a card to each student in the class. Call on a student to come to the front of the class and display his/her card. Call on a second student and have that student place him/herself appropriately to the right or left of the first student to begin to create a human number line. As each is called on to come to the front of the class, he/she should place him/herself appropriately on the number line. Additionally, when finished, students can place their numbers proportionally on a large paper number line on the wall. You may wish to include multiple classes in this activity, each class having a distinct set of number cards.

VOCABULARY DEVELOPMENT

Provide a teacher-created or a student-created word bank for lessons that are rich in mathematics vocabulary. In Lesson 3.1, some students will need a word bank of place value vocabulary to be able to write out numbers in words.

SEPARATE CONFUSING ELEMENTS

Some students grasp a concept with one or two examples, but some students need many more. If students are confused about place value relationships that they are learning in this chapter, select a few examples and spend extra time on them. For example, 2.3 (two and three tenths) is equal 2.30 (two and thirty hundredths) or 2.300 (two and three hundred thousandths). This will lay the foundation of equivalences for comparing decimal numbers and for future computation problems involving decimals. Encourage students to ask questions, and as they are solving a problem, circulate around the room to see their work. Have students sufficiently practice one kind of problem before going on to the next type. Do not introduce multiple confusing concepts on the same day—in fact, space them over several days in order to ensure that students understand one concept before going on to the next. As part of a general weekly or monthly review, include an appropriate problem or two to remind students of concepts that they found to be particularly difficult.

Strategies for English Learners

VOCABULARY DEVELOPMENT

While the mathematics teacher is helping students learn the language of the discipline, the language arts teacher can be helping students learn common English words used in describing relationships between things. Many of these words can be paired as opposites, and students can be encouraged to find synonyms for each word in the pair. Some common English words expressing relationships between things are: all, alone, and, also, both, common, always, each, every, more, main, most, much (more than), greater (greater than), less (less than), same (same as), equal (equal to), different, small, smaller, smallest, large, larger, largest, light, lighter, lightest, heavy, heavier, heaviest, short, shorter, shortest, long, longer, longest, tall, taller, tallest, little, main, big, bigger, biggest, missing, none, many, few, some, other, past, round, several, left/right, top/bottom, up/down, on (on top of)/under (underneath), in/out, under/over, start/finish, above/below, close or near/far, closest or nearest/farthest, middle, first, next, last, most often, least often, once, twice, never, often, seldom, almost, this, these, together, separate, opposite, whole, part, group.

Strategies for Advanced Learners

INCREASE DEPTH AND COMPLEXITY

SCIENCE Students may continue to explore cross-curricular links in Chapter 3. Throughout Chapter 3, it would be appropriate to plan a co-curricular unit with the science teacher consisting of lessons about measurement tools. In science class, students could explore measurement using graduated cylinders, balances, heights of plants, and so on.

As advanced students complete challenge problems and activities, other students may show an interest in them as well. Encourage all students who show an interest to try these problems and activities. Decide beforehand upon a policy regarding credit given for completion of the problems and activities.

The following ideas and challenge problems may be used for extensions throughout Chapter 3:

In **Lesson 3.1**, advanced students may be ready to explore the relationship between decimal place value and base-ten fractions.

- **Challenge** Notice that 0.001 (one thousandth) is equal to $\frac{1}{1000}$ (one one-thousandth). Give other examples.

  $0.01 = \frac{1}{100}$; $0.1 = \frac{1}{10}$; $0.0001 = \frac{1}{10,000}$

Supply grid paper, metric rulers and meter sticks for this activity for use with **Lesson 3.2**.

- **Challenge** Complete a scale drawing of the classroom, including floor, walls, windows, and so on, using the scale of 1 cm = 1 m. Check work.

Provide students with sheets of grid paper and rulers to complete this activity for use with **Lesson 3.4**. You may wish to provide an example or template for students to model. You may also wish to make copies of created puzzles for other class members to solve. You may wish to set parameters for this activity, such as number of clues, size of puzzle, and difficulty level expected.

- **Challenge** Create a cross-number puzzle (similar to a crossword puzzle) with solution key. Check work.

In connection with **Lesson 3.5**, you may wish to bring in or have students collect grocery receipts. Cut off the totals from these receipts and use them in the following challenge activity.

- **Challenge** You have $100 to spend on groceries. Do you have enough money to pay for the groceries? Check work.

In connection with **Lesson 3.6**, have students collect catalogs containing items they might wish to have.

- **Challenge** Go on an imaginary catalog shopping-spree with $1,000. You must order at least 10 items but no more than 25. Spend as close to $1,000 as you can without going over because you cannot keep any remaining cash. Check work.

Differentiating Instruction: Teaching Resources

Differentiating Alternate Assessment

McDougal Littell *Middle School Mathematics* offers teachers a wide variety of alternative assessment for all levels of students. Pictured here are facsimiles of the alternative assessment pages from the *Assessment Book*, and the various types of chapter projects available in the *Chapter 3 Resource Book*.

ASSESSMENT BOOK

The *Assessment Book* contains two pages of alternative assessment for each chapter in the textbook.

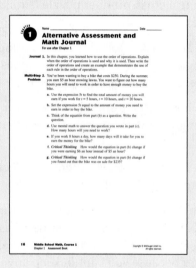

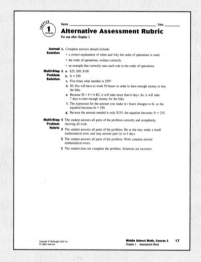

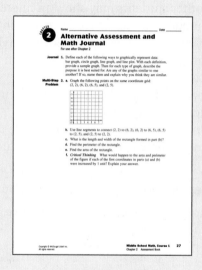

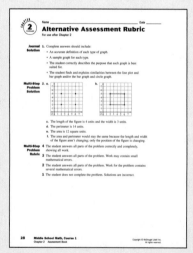

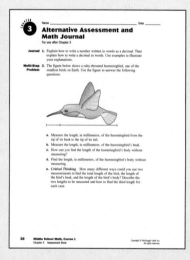

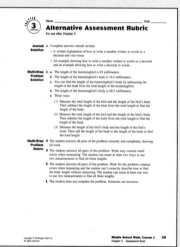

RESOURCE BOOK

The *Chapter Resource Books* contain three different projects for each chapter: Real Life, Cooperative, and Independent Extra Credit. Each project is accompanied by a scoring rubric. Shown below are the three projects for Chapter 3 with their rubrics. A complete discussion of rubrics is available in the *Professional Development Book*.

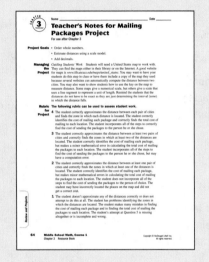

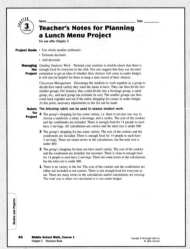

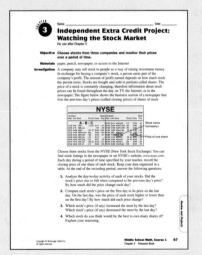

OVERVIEW

MAIN IDEAS

In this chapter, students explore decimals. They begin with place values to hundred-thousandths, and they model decimals using money and metric lengths. Then they order decimals using a number line, and round decimals. Finally, they find the sum or difference of two decimals or of a decimal and a whole number.

PREREQUISITE SKILLS

The key skills reviewed in the games on these pages are:

- Rounding 3-digit numbers to the nearest 10 or nearest 100
- Adding or subtracting 3-digit numbers
- Comparing 3-digit numbers

Additional practice with prerequisite skills can be found in the Review What You Need to Know exercises on page 106. Additional resources for reviewing prerequisite skills are:

- Skills Review Handbook, pp. 684–707
- Tutor Place
- eTutorial Plus Online

MANAGING THE GAMES

Tips for Success

For students who have trouble starting the second game, suggest that they write two columns:

Will not pass	Will pass
100–250	0–99
400–500	251–399
650–800	501–649
900–1000	801–899

Then ask them to compare the sums and differences they find to the ranges in each of these columns.

CHAPTER 3

Decimal Addition and Subtraction

BEFORE

In previous chapters you've...

- Rounded whole numbers
- Added and subtracted whole numbers

Now

In Chapter 3 you'll study...

- Measuring metric lengths
- Rounding decimals
- Estimating sums and differences of decimals
- Adding and subtracting decimals

WHY?

So you can solve real-world problems about...

- fossils, p. 113
- volcanoes, p. 121
- skateboarding, p. 127
- mountains, p. 133

Internet Preview
CLASSZONE.COM

- eEdition Plus Online
- eWorkbook Plus Online
- eTutorial Plus Online
- State Test Practice
- More Examples

Chapter Warm-Up Games

Review skills you need for this chapter in these quick games.

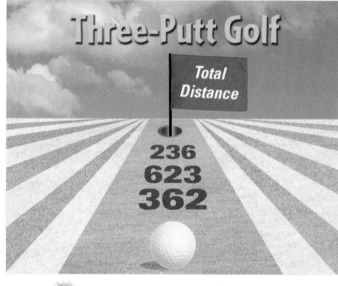

Three-Putt Golf

Total Distance

236
623
362

BRAIN GAME

Key Skill:
Rounding whole numbers

- The numbers above represent distances in centimeters.

- Choose one of the numbers to be your first putt. Choose another number and round it to the nearest 10. The result is your second putt. Round the remaining number to the nearest 100 for your third putt.

- Add your three putts to find your total distance. Then use the same numbers but pick a different order of putts. Try to raise your total distance.

Check work.

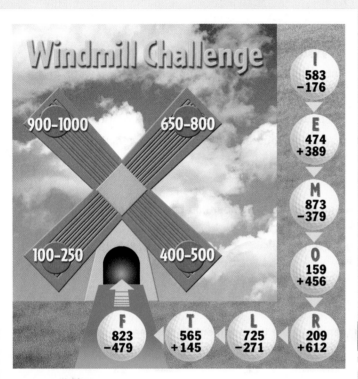

Windmill Challenge

Spoke	Range
	900–1000
	650–800
	100–250
	400–500

I
583
−176

E
474
+389

M
873
−379

O
159
+456

F
823
−479

T
565
+145

L
725
−271

R
209
+612

BRAIN GAME

Key Skill:
Adding and subtracting whole numbers

- Find the sum or difference associated with each golf ball. A golf ball passes through the windmill only if its sum or difference does not fall into any of the ranges on the spokes of the windmill.

- Once you know which golf balls can pass through the windmill, order their sums and differences from least to greatest. The corresponding letters spell out a cry that you might hear on a miniature golf course.
  See margin.

1. 1263; 1182. *Sample answer:* I found all possible combinations.

2. No; an estimate might be in the range but the actual answer might not be in the range, or vice versa.

Stop *and* Think

1. **Writing** What is the greatest distance you can get in *Three-Putt Golf*? What is the least? Explain how you know.

2. **Critical Thinking** In *Windmill Challenge*, are there any sums or differences for which you could use estimation rather than an exact calculation? Explain.

105

Reflecting on the Games

Extend the second game by forming groups of three students. One student is the "judge," a second student writes a 3-digit number, and the third student selects one spoke of the windmill. Then each member (except the judge) finds another number such that the sum or difference of the two numbers falls into the range indicated by the windmill spoke. The judge tells which student has the first correct answer, and that student is the judge for the next round.

CHAPTER RESOURCES

These resources are provided to help you prepare for the chapter and to customize review materials:

Chapter 3 Resource Book
- Tips for New Teachers, pp. 1–2
- Lesson Plan, pp. 6, 15, 23, 33, 42, 52
- Lesson Plan for Block Scheduling, pp. 7, 16, 24, 34, 43, 53

Technology
- EasyPlanner CD-ROM
- Test and Practice Generator
- Electronic Lesson Presentations CD-ROM
- eTutorial CD-ROM

Internet
- Classzone
- eEdition Plus Online
- eWorkbook Plus Online
- eTutorial Plus Online
- EasyPlanner Plus Online

ENGLISH LEARNER SUPPORT

- Spanish Study Guide
- Multi-Language Glossary
- Chapter Audio Summaries CDs
- Teacher's Edition, pp. 104E–104F

Review What You Need to Know
The Review What You Need to Know exercises can help you diagnose whether students have the following skills needed in Chapter 3:
- Vocabulary (Exs. 1–4)
- Graphing and ordering numbers (Exs. 5–6)
- Estimating sums and differences (Exs. 7–10)
- Measuring segments (Exs. 11–13)

 Chapter 3 Resource Book
- Study Guide (Lessons 3.1–3.6)

 Tutor Place

NOTETAKING STRATEGIES

Writing down questions to ask in class is most likely a new concept for students. To demonstrate to students how useful this strategy is, ask them to recall the times they had a question while doing homework only to have forgotten to ask it in class the next day. Point out that by writing down their question, students will surely remember to ask it. Further suggestions for keeping a notebook can be found on pages 107 and 126.

For more support on notetaking, see:
- Notetaking Guide Workbook
- Notetaking Transparencies

CHAPTER 3 Getting Ready to Learn

Review What You Need to Know

Using Vocabulary Copy and complete using a review word.

1. A ? is a metric unit of length longer than a centimeter. meter

2. A ? is a metric unit of length shorter than a centimeter. millimeter

3. When you ? the number 125 to the nearest ten, the answer is 130. round

4. The ? of 17 and 9 is 8. difference

Word Watch

Review Words

millimeter (mm), p. 56
centimeter (cm), p. 56
meter (m), p. 56
number line, p. 685
round, p. 686
sum, p. 689
difference, p. 689

Graph the numbers on a number line to order them from least to greatest. (p. 685)

5. 5, 19, 16, 9, 12, 6, 13
    5, 6, 9, 12, 13, 16, 19

6. 10, 7, 3, 2, 15, 11, 17
    2, 3, 7, 10, 11, 15, 17

Estimate the sum or difference. (p. 12) Estimates may vary.

7. 16 + 27 50   **8.** 34 + 79 110   **9.** 81 − 42 40   **10.** 65 − 17 50

Find the length of the line segment to the nearest centimeter. (p. 55)

11. ——————
2 cm

12. ————————
3 cm

13. ————
1 cm

You should include material that appears on a notebook like this in your own notes.

Know How to Take Notes

Write Questions About Homework As you complete your homework assignments, write down in your notebook any questions you want to ask the teacher. An example is shown below.

Chapter 1 Whole Number Estimation

1. 39 → 40   2. 345 → 350   Am I right to round
   + 160 → + 160   − 171 → − 170   up? Ask in class
      200   180   tomorrow.

In Lesson 3.4, you may have questions like the one above when you round decimals. Use answers to such questions and corrected homework assignments to study for quizzes and tests.

Decimals and Place Value

BEFORE	▶ **Now**	**WHY?**
You learned how to read and write whole numbers.	You'll read and write decimals.	So you can read decimals, such as the race times in Example 3.

Word Watch

decimal, p. 108

Activity You can use base-ten pieces to model numbers.

The diagram below shows the values of the base-ten pieces.

1 one (1 whole)   1 tenth   1 hundredth

Use base-ten pieces to complete the statement.

1. 1 one = _?_ tenths 10   **2.** 1 one = _?_ hundredths 100

3. 1 tenth = _?_ hundredths 10   **4.** 30 tenths = _?_ ones 3

5. 40 hundredths = _?_ tenths 4   **6.** 2 ones and 5 tenths = _?_ tenths 25

EXAMPLE 1 **Expressing a Number in Different Ways**

a. Write 20 hundredths using only tenths.

20 hundredths

2 × 10 hundredths

2 × 1 tenth

2 tenths

> **Think of 10 hundredths as 1 tenth.**
>
>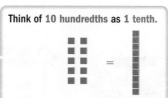

b. Write 1 one and 4 tenths using only tenths.

1 one and 4 tenths

10 tenths and 4 tenths

14 tenths

> Use the fact that **1 one** equals **10 tenths.**

HELP with Notetaking

You might want to record relationships between base-ten pieces in your notebook, such as 1 one = 10 tenths.

Your turn now Copy and complete the statement.

1. 500 hundredths = _?_ tenths 50   **2.** 4 ones and 9 tenths = _?_ tenths 49

NCTM CURRICULUM STANDARDS
Standard 1: Understand ways of representing numbers
Standard 10: Create representations to communicate mathematical ideas

Lesson 3.1   Decimals and Place Value   **107**

---

1 PLAN

SKILL CHECK
Give the place value of the indicated digit.
1. 64**13**   hundreds
2. 13,2**0**5   tens
3. 17,**3**24   thousands

LESSON OBJECTIVE
Read and write decimals.

PACING
Suggested Number of Days
Basic Course: 1 day
Average Course: 1 day
Advanced Course: 1 day
Block: 0.5 block with 3.2

TEACHING RESOURCES
For a complete list of Teaching Resources, see page 104B.

**TRANSPARENCY**
Warm-Up Exercises for this lesson are available on a transparency. A support transparency is available for the Activity and Example 1.

2 TEACH

MOTIVATING THE LESSON
Relate decimals to money by reminding students that 1 penny = $.01, 1 nickel = $.05, 1 dime = $.10, and 1 quarter = $.25.

ACTIVITY
Goal Use base-ten pieces to model numbers.

Key Discovery Ones, tenths, and hundredths are related to each other by place value just as hundreds, tens, and ones are related to each other.

107

A **decimal** is a number that is written using the base-ten place-value system. Each place value is ten times the place value to its right.

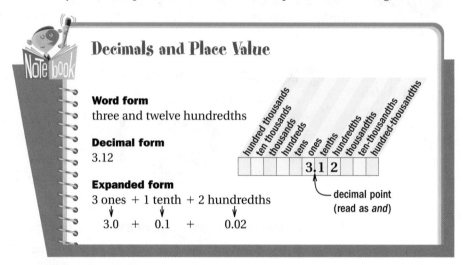

Decimals and Place Value

Word form
three and twelve hundredths

Decimal form
3.12

Expanded form
3 ones + 1 tenth + 2 hundredths
3.0 + 0.1 + 0.02

hundred thousands | ten thousands | thousands | hundreds | tens | ones | tenths | hundredths | thousandths | ten-thousandths | hundred-thousandths

3.1 2

decimal point (read as *and*)

EXAMPLE 2 **Writing Decimals**

Swimming A timer at your swim meet says your time was twenty-eight and six tenths seconds. Write your time as a decimal.

twenty-eight and six tenths

28.6 seconds

> The word *and* indicates the decimal point.

EXAMPLE 3 **Reading Decimals**

Auto Racing Helio Castroneves won the 2001 Indianapolis 500. His best lap time was 41.0238 seconds. Write his time in words.

41.0238

> You read a decimal according to the last place value.

forty-one and two hundred thirty-eight <u>ten-thousandths</u> seconds

Your turn now

3. Write *twenty-five and seven hundred-thousandths* as a decimal.
   25.00007
4. Write 5.029 in words.
   five and twenty-nine thousandths
5. Write 706.25 in words.
   seven hundred six and twenty-five hundredths

INTERNET
eWorkbook Plus
CLASSZONE.COM

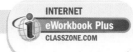

Getting Ready to Practice

Vocabulary **Name the place value of the 3 in the decimal.**

1. 1.038
hundredths

2. 16.329 tenths

3. 4.61093
hundred thousandths

4. 564.0732
thousandths

5. Find the Error Describe and correct the error in the solution.

5. *Sample answer:* There is no *and* after "hundred," so the number should have a zero to the left of the decimal point. The answer should be 0.412.

 four hundred twelve thousandths = 400.012

Write the number as a decimal.

6. five and eighteen hundredths 5.18 **7.** six and nine thousandths 6.009

Write the decimal in words.

8. 0.45
forty-five
hundredths

9. 8.0014
eight and fourteen
ten-thousandths

10. 7.0009
seven and nine
ten-thousandths

11. 24.006
twenty-four
and six thousandths

Practice and Problem Solving

with Homework

Example	Exercises
1	12–15
2	16–25, 33–37
3	20, 26–32

Online Resources
CLASSZONE.COM
· More Examples
· eTutorial Plus

Copy and complete the statement.

A **12.** 4 tenths = ? hundredths 40

13. 70 tenths = ? ones 7

14. 200 hundredths = ? tenths = ? ones 20; 2

15. 1 one and 5 tenths = ? tenths = ? hundredths 15; 150

Match the number with its decimal form.

16. twenty and four hundred five ten-thousandths C   **A.** 20.045

17. twenty and forty-five ten-thousandths D   **B.** 20.00045

18. twenty and forty-five hundred-thousandths B   **C.** 20.0405

19. twenty and forty-five thousandths A   **D.** 20.0045

20. Model A: three tenths, 0.3;
Model B: thirty hundredths, 0.30; yes;
Sample answer: Since 30 hundredths is equal to 3 tenths, they represent the same amount.

20. Writing Write the numbers modeled in words and as decimals. Do the models represent the same amount? Explain.

Model A   **Model B**

ASSIGNMENT GUIDE
Basic Course
Day 1: SRH p. 684 Exs. 5–8;
pp. 109–111 Exs. 12–19,
21–35, 40–47, 50, 54–60

Average Course
Day 1: pp. 109–111 Exs. 12–33,
36–41, 44–52, 54–60

Advanced Course
Day 1: pp. 109–111 Exs. 14–20,
23–33, 37, 41, 44–55*, 60

Block
pp. 109–111 Exs. 12–33,
36–41, 44–52, 54–60
(with 3.2)

EXTRA PRACTICE
- Student Edition, p. 710
- Chapter 3 Resource Book,
  pp. 9–11
- Test and Practice Generator

 TRANSPARENCY

Even-numbered answers are available on transparencies. A support transparency is available for Exercise 20.

HOMEWORK CHECK

When you review students' homework for this lesson, go over the following exercises to check understanding of key concepts.
Basic: 12, 14, 16, 26, 34
Average: 14, 15, 17, 27, 36
Advanced: 15, 18, 20, 30, 37

Alternative Teaching Strategy
If students are having difficulty reading and writing decimals in Exercises 21–31, have them work in pairs. One student should read a decimal aloud while the other student writes the decimal in words. Students should switch roles for each exercise.

 COMMON ERROR

Some students may have difficulty with Exercises 21–25 because they do not understand that "and" represents the decimal point. Refer back to the arrow in Example 3 that points from the decimal point to the word "and" to emphasize this.

TEACHING TIP

For Exercises 34–37, you may wish to have actual coins to demonstrate the correct answers. For example, in Exercise 35, show that 1 nickel = 5 pennies, that 4 nickels = 4 • 5 pennies = 20 pennies = 0.20 dollars.

COMMON ERROR

In Exercises 38–41, students may not write their answers as decimals. For example, they may write the answer to Exercise 40 as 4.0 + 2 + 5. Remind them that when expanding a decimal, they must show the decimal form of each place.

26. ninety-nine hundredths

27. four and sixteen hundredths

28. three hundred sixty-seven thousandths

29. seventeen and twenty-two thousandths

30. eight and ninety-three ten-thousandths

31. ten and two hundred fifty-five ten-thousandths

45. See Additional Answers beginning on page AA1.

110

Sports

■ **Turbojets**

The *Spirit of Australia's* record speed was about 318 kilometers per hour, which is much faster than the maximum speed of some cruise ships, which is about 42 kilometers per hour. About how many times faster can the *Spirit of Australia* go than some cruise ships?
about 8 times faster

Write the number as a decimal.

21. thirty and fifteen hundredths 30.15

22. fifty-eight and twenty-seven thousandths 58.027

23. seven hundred five thousandths 0.705

24. two hundred seventy-eight ten-thousandths 0.0278

25. eighty-six and one hundred forty-three ten-thousandths 86.0143

Write the decimal in words. 26–31. See margin.

26. 0.99   27. 4.16   28. 0.367

29. 17.022   30. 8.0093   31. 10.0255

32. **Turbojets** The *Spirit of Australia* set a record for the fastest water vehicle. This turbojet was timed at 317.58 kilometers per hour. Write this speed in words. **three hundred seventeen and fifty-eight hundredths kilometers per hour**

33. **Bridges** The main section of the Akachi-Kaikyo bridge in Japan is about one and ninety-nine hundredths kilometers long. Write this length as a decimal. **1.99 km**

Money Write the amount as a decimal part of a dollar.

34. 1 quarter   35. 4 nickels   36. 89 pennies   37. 7 dimes
    $0.25 $0.20 $0.89 $0.70

Copy and complete the expanded form of the decimal.

38. 8.6 = 8.0 + _?_ 0.6

39. 5.392 = 5.0 + 0.3 + _?_ + _?_ 0.09; 0.002

40. 4.25 = 4.0 + _?_ + _?_ 0.2; 0.05

41. 0.1472 = 0.1 + 0.04 + _?_ + _?_ 0.007; 0.0002

Gemstones The table shows the weights of several different gemstones at a jewelry store.

42. Write the weight of the topaz in words. **sixty-five hundredths carats**

43. Write the weight of the emerald in words. **one and five hundredths carats**

44. Which gems weigh less than 1 carat? **amethyst, topaz, sapphire**

Gemstone	Weight (carats)
amethyst	0.48
diamond	1.29
emerald	1.05
topaz	0.65
sapphire	0.50

45. Sketch a base-ten model to represent the weight of the diamond. **See margin.**

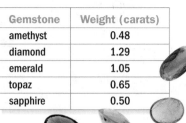

Write the decimal described.

46. one tenth more than 20.8 20.9

47. one hundredth less than 14.77 14.76

48. one tenth less than 34.7 34.6

49. one hundredth more than 85.29 85.30

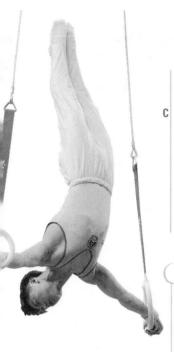

Gymnastics The table shows the scores for men's gymnastics teams at the Olympics.

C

50. Write China's score in words. **See margin.**

51. Which team's score is between 230 and 230.1? **Russia**

52. Which team's score is closest to 229? **United States**

Team	Score
China	231.919
Ukraine	230.306
Russia	230.019
Japan	229.857
United States	228.983

53. Challenge Sketch a model of 1 ten using ones' pieces. How many ones' pieces did you need? How many tenths' pieces would you need to make the model? How many hundredths' pieces? **See margin.**

Mixed Review

54. Out of 40 students, 4 said they check their e-mail less than once a week, 10 said once a week, 8 said twice a week, 12 said once a day, and 6 said several times a day. Make a bar graph of the data. *(Lesson 2.5)*

See margin.

Choose a Strategy Use a strategy from the list to solve the problem in Exercise 55. Explain your choice of strategy.

> *Problem Solving Strategies*
> ▪ Guess, Check, and Revise
> ▪ Draw a Diagram
> ▪ Make a List

55. The booths at a carnival are 6 feet wide and spaced 4 feet apart. What is the maximum number of booths you can fit in a row that is 50 feet long?

Basic Skills Write the number in words.

56. 5078   **57.** 4,027,000   **58.** 15,400,000

Test-Taking Practice

59. Multiple Choice A marathon race is about twenty-six and two tenths miles long. Which decimal equals this distance? **D**

A. 26.002 mi   **B.** 26.02 mi   **C.** 26.10 mi   **D.** 26.2 mi

60. Multiple Choice The moon revolves around Earth once every 27.3217 days. How do you write this number in words? **G**

F. twenty-seven and three thousand seven thousandths

G. twenty-seven and three thousand two hundred seventeen ten-thousandths

H. two hundred seventy-three and two hundred seventeen thousandths

I. twenty-seven hundred and three thousand two hundred seventeen ten-thousandths

---

Margin notes (left column):

50. two hundred thirty-one and nine hundred nineteen thousandths

55. 5; *Sample answer:* I chose Draw a Diagram because it was easy to draw and label booths and spaces until the length is about 50 feet.

56. five thousand seventy-eight

57. four million, twenty-seven thousand

58. fifteen million, four hundred thousand

INTERNET
State Test Practice
CLASSZONE.COM

Right sidebar:

4 ASSESS

ASSESSMENT RESOURCES

For more assessment resources, see:
• Assessment Book
• Test and Practice Generator

MINI-QUIZ

Rewrite each number in the given form.

1. Write 420 thousandths using only hundredths. **42 hundredths**

2. Write the number fifteen and six hundred forty-eight thousandths as a decimal. **15.648**

3. Write the decimal 3.0079 in words. **three and seventy-nine ten-thousandths**

5 FOLLOW-UP

RETEACHING/REMEDIATION

• Study Guide in Chapter 3 Resource Book, pp. 12–13
• Tutor Place, Whole Numbers and Decimals Cards 1, 2
• eTutorial Plus Online
• Extra Practice, p. 710
• Lesson Practice in Chapter 3 Resource Book, pp. 9–11

CHALLENGE/ENRICHMENT

• Challenge Practice in Chapter 3 Resource Book, p. 14
• Teacher's Edition, p. 104F

ENGLISH LEARNER SUPPORT

• Spanish Study Guide
• Multi-Language Glossary
• Chapter Audio Summaries CDs

53–54. See Additional Answers beginning on page AA1.

PLAN

EXPLORE THE CONCEPT

- Students will measure lengths in different metric units.
- This activity leads into the use of decimals in metric measurement in Lesson 3.2.

MATERIALS

Students will need a metric ruler and a meter stick. A support transparency is available for this activity.

RECOMMENDED TIME

Work activity: 10 min
Discuss results: 5 min

GROUPING

Students can work individually or in groups of two.

TIPS FOR SUCCESS

Be sure students understand that the unlabeled marks on a metric ruler represent millimeters.

KEY DISCOVERY

Metric units of length are related in much the same way that decimal place values are related.

ASSESSMENT

1. Convert 13 millimeters to centimeters and millimeters.
   13 mm = 10 mm + 3 mm = 1 cm + 3 mm

2. Convert 2 meters + 28 centimeters to centimeters. **228 cm**

2–3. See Additional Answers beginning on page AA1.

112

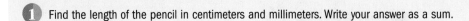

3.2 Hands-on **Activity**

GOAL
Express lengths in different metric units.

MATERIALS
- metric ruler
- meter stick

Using Different Metric Units

You can express the same length using different metric units.

Explore **Measure the pencil in different units.**

1 Find the length of the pencil in centimeters and millimeters. Write your answer as a sum.

Line up one end of the pencil with the zero mark on the ruler.

Look at where the tip of the pencil lines up with the tick marks on the ruler.

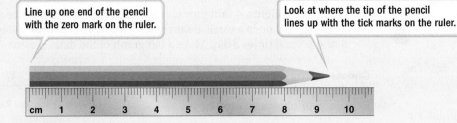

The length of the pencil is 9 cm + 4 mm.

2 Find the length of the pencil in millimeters. Use the fact that there are 10 millimeters in 1 centimeter.

9 cm + 4 mm = (10 × 9) mm + 4 mm = 94 mm

Your turn now

1. Copy and complete the table by measuring different objects in your classroom as described above.

Object	Measurement 1	Measurement 2
length of a pencil	9 cm + 4 mm	94 mm
length of a notebook	_?_ cm + _?_ mm	_?_ mm
height of a desk	_?_ m + _?_ cm	_?_ cm
width of a door	_?_ m + _?_ cm	_?_ cm

Answers may vary.

Stop *and* **Think** 2–3. See margin.

2. **Writing** The length of a pen is 112 millimeters. Explain how you can find the length in centimeters and millimeters without measuring.

3. **Critical Thinking** For any height given in centimeters, how can you find the height in meters and centimeters without measuring?

NCTM CURRICULUM STANDARDS
Standard 4: Understand the units of measurement; Understand the systems of measurement; Apply proper tools to find measures

LESSON 3.2

Measuring Metric Lengths

BEFORE	Now	WHY?
You measured lengths to the nearest whole metric unit.	You'll use decimals to express metric measurements.	So you can measure lengths precisely, as with the otter in Ex. 17.

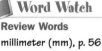

Word Watch

Review Words

millimeter (mm), p. 56
centimeter (cm), p. 56
meter (m), p. 56

In the Real World

Fossils Scientists study fossils to learn about plants and animals that lived in prehistoric times. The size of a fossil can help a scientist figure out what type of plant or animal it came from. A scientist finds a dinosaur tooth that is about 3 centimeters long. What is a more precise measurement for the tooth?

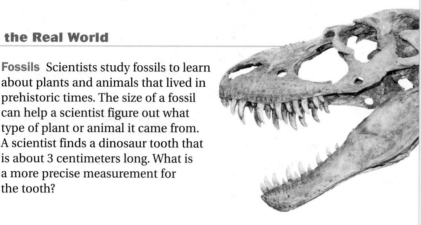

EXAMPLE 1 **Writing Measurements as Decimals**

To answer the question above about dinosaur teeth, use a metric ruler and write your answer as a decimal number of centimeters.

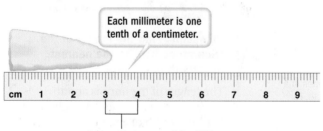

Each millimeter is one tenth of a centimeter.

1 centimeter = 10 millimeters

From the metric ruler you can see that 2 millimeters is 2 tenths of a centimeter. The length is about 3 and 2 tenths centimeters.

ANSWER The length of the dinosaur tooth is about 3.2 centimeters.

Your turn now Write the length of the line segment as a decimal number of centimeters.

1. 2.6 cm

2. 3.3 cm

Lesson 3.2   Measuring Metric Lengths   **113**

---

1 PLAN

SKILL CHECK

1. 200 cm = _?_ m   2
2. 6 m = _?_ mm   6000
3. 350 mm = _?_ cm   35

LESSON OBJECTIVE

Use decimals to express metric measurement.

PACING

Suggested Number of Days
Basic Course: 1 day
Average Course: 1 day
Advanced Course: 1 day
Block: 0.5 block with 3.1

TEACHING RESOURCES

For a complete list of Teaching Resources, see page 104B.

TRANSPARENCY

Warm-Up Exercises for this lesson are available on a transparency. A support transparency is available for Examples 1–3.

2 TEACH

MOTIVATING THE LESSON

Have students measure the segments in this lesson in customary units. Then ask them if they would rather work with the fractional parts of an inch or the decimal parts of a centimeter.

TIPS FOR NEW TEACHERS

Students can become familiar with metric lengths by measuring various objects in the classroom. See Tips for New Teachers in the *Chapter 3 Resource Book*.

MULTIPLE REPRESENTATIONS

Students should become familiar with the idea that the expressions "67 millimeters," "6 and 7 tenths cm," "6.7 cm," and "0.067 m" all represent the same measurement.

 COMMON ERROR

Some rulers have a space between the left edge of the ruler and the zero mark. Be sure students align the zero mark with the edge of the object they are measuring.

 CONCEPT CHECK

Which statement is correct? c

a. One millimeter is one hundredth of a centimeter.

b. One millimeter is one hundredth of a meter.

c. One centimeter is one hundredth of a meter.

 DAILY PUZZLER

The length of a library table is 35 and 2 tenths centimeters longer than 2 meters. How long is the library table in meters? in centimeters? 2.352 m; 235.2 cm

114

Metric Units of Length

millimeter (mm)	centimeter (cm)	meter (m)
1 mm = 0.1 cm	1 cm = 10 mm	1 m = 1000 mm
1 mm = 0.001 m	1 cm = 0.01 m	1 m = 100 cm
		1 m = 0.001 km

 with Review

Need help with metric units of length? See p. 55.

 with Solving

It takes more of a smaller unit of length to equal a measurement written in a larger unit of length. For example, it takes 300 cm to equal 3 m.

EXAMPLE 2 **Measuring in Centimeters**

Find the length of the line segment to the nearest tenth of a centimeter.

6 and 7 tenths centimeters

ANSWER The length of the line segment is about 6.7 centimeters.

EXAMPLE 3 **Measuring in Meters**

Dinosaurs Find the length of the triceratops horn to the nearest hundredth of a meter.

The length of the horn is about 25 centimeters. Because 1 centimeter is 1 hundredth of a meter, 25 centimeters is 25 hundredths of a meter.

ANSWER The length of the triceratops horn is about 0.25 meter.

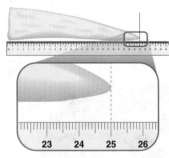

Your turn now Find the length of the line segment to the given unit.

3. to the nearest tenth of a centimeter

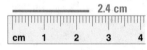
2.4 cm

4. to the nearest hundredth of a meter

0.038 m

3.2 Exercises

More Practice, p. 710

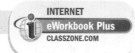
INTERNET
eWorkbook Plus
CLASSZONE.COM

Getting Ready to Practice

Vocabulary Copy and complete the statement.

1. 1 centimeter = _?_ meter 0.01

2. 1 millimeter = _?_ centimeter 0.1

3. 1 meter = _?_ centimeters 100

4. 1 centimeter = _?_ millimeters 10

5. Guided Problem Solving The wingspan of the Blue Metalmark butterfly is more than 2 centimeters. Write the wingspan as a decimal number of centimeters.

(1 How many millimeters longer than 2 centimeters is the wingspan? 4 mm

(2 What part of a centimeter is this? 0.4

(3 Write the wingspan of the butterfly in centimeters. 2.4 cm

cm   1   2   3

Practice and Problem Solving

with Homework

Example	Exercises
1	6–12
2	13–16
3	17–19

Online Resources
CLASSZONE.COM
· More Examples
· eTutorial Plus

Copy and complete the statement.

A

6. 3 and 8 tenths centimeters = _?_ centimeters 3.8

7. 5 and 2 hundredths meters = _?_ meters 5.02

8. 1 and 35 hundredths meters = _?_ meters 1.35

9. 12 and 4 thousandths meters = _?_ meters 12.004

10. Pancakes The height of a stack of pancakes is nine and one tenth centimeters. Write this measurement in decimal form. 9.1 cm

11. Desks The width of a library desk is eighty-eight hundredths of a meter. Write this measurement in decimal form. 0.88 m

12. Multiple Choice What is the length of the goldfish? B

A. 4.6 meters

B. 4.6 centimeters

C. 4.4 centimeters

D. 44 millimeters

cm   1   2   3   4   5

Lesson 3.2 · Measuring Metric Lengths   **115**

TEACHING TIP

In Exercise 13, point out to students that the measurement associated with the letter *E* should be 9.0 cm to show that the length is measured to the nearest tenth of a centimeter.

13. Write the measurement for each letter to the nearest tenth of a centimeter.

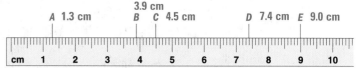

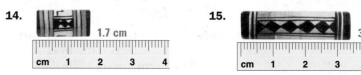

Find the length of the object to the nearest tenth of a centimeter.

14.

1.7 cm

15.

3.4 cm

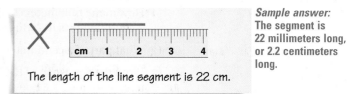

16. Find the Error Describe and correct the error in the measurement.

The length of the line segment is 22 cm.

Sample answer:
The segment is 22 millimeters long, or 2.2 centimeters long.

17. Sea Otters Use the meter stick to find the length of the sea otter to the nearest hundredth of a meter. **0.96 m**

Instruments **Write the length to the nearest hundredth of a meter.**

18. The length of an electronic keyboard is 85 centimeters. **0.85 m**

19. A guitar case is 14 centimeters longer than a meter. **1.14 m**

20. Writing Your friend claims that measuring to the nearest tenth of a centimeter is the same as measuring to the nearest thousandth of a meter. Do you agree or disagree? Explain. **See margin.**

Estimation **Sketch a line segment of the given length without using a ruler. Then use a ruler to check your estimate. How close was your estimate?** Answers may vary.

21. 6.5 cm   **22.** 45 mm   **23.** 0.01 m   **24.** 0.15 m

What do you think?

? Science

■ **Sea Otters**

Sea otters will dive 35 meters to find clams, crabs, snails, and starfish to eat! What distance in your school is about 35 meters?

Answers may vary.   B

20. *Sample answer:* I agree because a tenth of a centimeter is the same as a millimeter, which is one thousandth of a meter.

C 25. **Snowboards** Use the meter stick to give the measure of the snowboard to the nearest thousandth of a meter. **1.372 m**

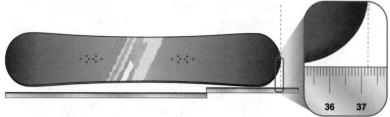

26. **Challenge** You measure an object to the nearest centimeter and the result is 4 centimeters. You then measure the same object to the nearest tenth of a centimeter. What results are possible? Explain. *Sample answer:* **The results can be anywhere from 3.5 centimeters to 4.4 centimeters because all numbers from 3.5 to 4.4 are rounded to 4.**

Mixed Review

27. The scale on a scale drawing is 1 cm : 5 m. If your room is 10 meters long, how long is it on the scale drawing? *(Lesson 2.3)* **2 cm**

28. 3. *Sample answer:* I used Guess, Check, and Revise because I tried different numbers raised to the fourth power and kept changing the number until I got 81.

Choose a Strategy Use a strategy from the list to solve the problem in Exercise 28. Explain your choice of strategy.

28. Your friend is thinking of a number between 1 and 10, and this number raised to the fourth power is 81. What is your friend's number?

> **Problem Solving Strategies**
> - Guess, Check, and Revise
> - Draw a Diagram
> - Look for a Pattern
> - Solve a Simpler Problem

Basic Skills Tell whether the number in red is *less than*, *greater than*, or *equal to* the value of the expression.

29. 3×6; 24
    greater than

30. $48 \div 6$; 7
    less than

31. $18 - 17$; 1
    equal to

Test-Taking Practice

32. **Multiple Choice** In the 1996 Summer Olympics, Joanna Stone threw a javelin 54 centimeters more than 58 meters. Which choice represents the distance she threw the javelin as a decimal number of meters? **C**

    A. 5.458 meters   **B.** 54.58 meters

    C. 58.54 meters   **D.** 585.4 centimeters

33. **Multiple Choice** What is the length of the line segment to the nearest tenth of a centimeter? **H**

    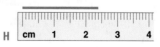

    F. 240 mm   **G.** 24 cm   **H.** 2.4 cm   **I.** 2.4 mm

Lesson 3.2   Measuring Metric Lengths   **117**

---

4 **ASSESS**

ASSESSMENT RESOURCES

For more assessment resources, see:
- Assessment Book
- Test and Practice Generator

MINI-QUIZ

1. Measure the length of the title "Mixed Review" on page 117 to the nearest tenth of a centimeter. **3.6 cm**

2. The seat of a chair is exactly 43 centimeters from the floor. Write that distance in millimeters. **430 mm**

5 **FOLLOW-UP**

RETEACHING/REMEDIATION
- Study Guide in Chapter 3 Resource Book, pp. 20–21
- eTutorial Plus Online
- Extra Practice, p. 710
- Lesson Practice in Chapter 3 Resource Book, pp. 17–19

CHALLENGE/ENRICHMENT
- Challenge Practice in Chapter 3 Resource Book, p. 22
- Teacher's Edition, p. 104F

ENGLISH LEARNER SUPPORT
- Spanish Study Guide
- Multi-Language Glossary
- Chapter Audio Summaries CDs

LESSON OBJECTIVE

Compare and order decimals.

PACING

Suggested Number of Days
Basic Course: 1 day
Average Course: 1 day
Advanced Course: 1 day
Block: 0.5 block with 3.4

TEACHING RESOURCES

For a complete list of Teaching Resources, see page 104B.

 TRANSPARENCY

Warm-Up Exercises for this lesson are available on a transparency. A support transparency is available for Example 2.

2 TEACH

MOTIVATING THE LESSON

Show students different amounts of money in coins. Ask students to put the amounts in order from least to greatest.

TIPS FOR NEW TEACHERS

Be sure students understand how to line up decimal numbers on the decimal points when comparing or ordering decimals. See Tips for New Teachers in the *Chapter 3 Resource Book.*

LESSON 3.3

Ordering Decimals

BEFORE | **Now** | **WHY?**

You compared and ordered whole numbers. | You'll compare and order decimals. | So you can order data such as ages of volcanoes in Ex. 25.

In the Real World

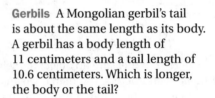

Word Watch

Review Words
number line, p. 685

Gerbils A Mongolian gerbil's tail is about the same length as its body. A gerbil has a body length of 11 centimeters and a tail length of 10.6 centimeters. Which is longer, the body or the tail?

10.6 cm   11 cm

EXAMPLE 1 **Comparing Metric Lengths**

To answer the real-world question above, use a metric ruler. The tail length, 10.6 centimeters, is to the left of the body length, 11 centimeters.

You can say: $10.6 < 11$ or $11 > 10.6$

                  is less than   *is greater than*

tail   body
length   length

HELP with Reading

Less than and *greater than* symbols always point to the lesser number.

ANSWER The gerbil's body is longer than its tail.

EXAMPLE 2 **Ordering Decimals on a Number Line**

Order the numbers from least to greatest: 3.1, 3.28, 3.06, 3, 3.15.

Graph each number on a number line. Begin by marking tenths from 3.0 to 3.3. Then mark hundredths by dividing each tenth into ten sections.

The numbers on a number line increase from left to right.

3   3.06   3.1   3.15   3.28

3.0   3.1   3.2   3.3

ANSWER An ordered list of the numbers is 3, 3.06, 3.1, 3.15, and 3.28.

Your turn now Use the number line in Example 2.

1. Order the numbers from least to greatest: 3.2, 3.29, 3.04, and 3.17.
3.04, 3.17, 3.2, 3.29

2. Write three numbers that are greater than 3.2 and less than 3.25.
Sample answer: 3.21, 3.27, 3.29

NCTM CURRICULUM STANDARDS
Standard 1: Understand numbers; Understand ways of representing numbers; Understand relationships among numbers

Comparing Decimals When you graph decimals on a number line to compare them, the greater number is farther to the right. You can also compare decimals by looking at their place values.

Steps for Comparing Decimals

1. Write the decimals in a column, lining up the decimal points.

2. If necessary, write zeros to the right of the decimals so that all decimals have the same number of decimal places.

3. Compare place values from left to right.

EXAMPLE 3 **Comparing Decimals**

Copy and complete the statement with <, >, or =.

a. 5.796 ? 5.802

5.796 — The ones' digits are the same.
5.802 — The tenths' digits are different: 7 < 8.

ANSWER 5.796 < 5.802

b. 2.94 ? 2.9

2.94 — The ones' and tenths' digits are the same.
2.90 — Write a zero.
The hundredths' digits are different: 4 > 0.

ANSWER 2.94 > 2.9

EXAMPLE 4 **Ordering Decimals**

Order the gerbils from heaviest to lightest.

The digits are the same through the tenths' place. Compare hundredths, then thousandths if necessary: 77.0250, 77.0212, 77.0113, and 77.0033.

ANSWER The gerbils, from heaviest to lightest, are Scruff, Fluff, Edgar, and Scamp.

Gerbil	Weight (grams)
Edgar	77.0113
Fluff	77.0212
Scamp	77.0033
Scruff	77.0250

Your turn now **Copy and complete the statement with <, >, or =.**

3. 7.54 ? 7.45 >   **4.** 8.5 ? 8.50 =   **5.** 0.409 ? 0.411 <

Example 1 Which is greater, the length of the word "Metric" or the length of the word "Lengths" in the title of Example 1? "Lengths" is longer than "Metric."

Example 2 Order from greatest to least: 14.10, 14.5, 14.56, 14.03, 14.51. **14.56, 14.51, 14.5, 14.10, 14.03**

Example 3 Use <, >, or =.
a. 13.5 ? 13.52 <
b. 10.513 ? 10.509 >

Example 4 Order from shortest to longest.

Pencil	Length (cm)
Blue	17.58
Red	17.54
Green	17.57
Gray	17.62

red, green, blue, gray

VISUALIZE

For Example 2 students can imagine that they are looking at the number line with stronger and stronger magnifying lenses. This can help them realize that for any two neighboring marks on a number line, they can always imagine dividing that interval into ten smaller intervals.

CONCEPT CHECK

Suppose the decimals 15.35, 107.216, 6.057, and 15.821 are lined up vertically so they can be compared and ordered. Which digits would be aligned under the "3" in 15.35? **2, 0, 8**

DAILY PUZZLER

What two letters come next in this pattern?
HTTHTO.THT
T for ten-thousandths and H for hundred-thousandths

119

ASSIGNMENT GUIDE

Basic Course
Day 1: SRH p. 685 Exs. 4–9;
pp. 120–121 Exs. 6–21, 24,
25, 27, 32–38

Average Course
Day 1: pp. 120–121 Exs. 9–29,
32–38

Advanced Course
Day 1: pp. 120–121 Exs. 10–15,
19–26, 29–33*, 37, 38

Block
pp. 120–121 Exs. 9–29, 32–38
(with 3.4)

TRANSPARENCY

Even-numbered answers are available on transparencies. A support transparency is available for the exercises in this lesson.

HOMEWORK CHECK

When you review students' homework for this lesson, go over the following exercises to check understanding of key concepts.
Basic: 6, 9, 15, 16, 24
Average: 9, 10, 15, 17, 24
Advanced: 12, 15, 21, 23, 24

Differentiating Instruction

Advanced Students As a challenge for Exercises 27–29, write all student responses to each exercise on the board and ask students to put the responses in order from least to greatest.

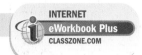
Getting Ready to Practice

Vocabulary Copy and complete the statement using a decimal that is graphed in red on the number line.

7.2　　7.3　　7.4　　7.5　　7.6

1. 7.41 is less than ? . 7.55　　　　**2.** 7.33 is greater than ? . 7.24

3. ? is between 7.33 and 7.41. 7.38　　**4.** 7.41 is between 7.33 and ? . 7.55

5. Telephone Calls Order the following list of telephone call costs from least to greatest: $3.70, $3.29, $3.07, $3.92, $2.79, and $3.79.
　　　　$2.79, $3.07, $3.29, $3.70, $3.79, $3.92

Practice and Problem Solving

Copy and complete the statement with <, >, or =.

6. 2.8 ? 2.6 >　　　　**7.** 7.1 ? 6.9 >　　　　**8.** 8.5 ? 9.4 <

9. 1.21 ? 1.12 >　　　**10.** 4.82 ? 4.94 <　　　**11.** 9.50 ? 9.05 >

12. 8.7 ? 8.70 =　　　**13.** 4.40 ? 4.4 =　　　**14.** 42.1 ? 4.21 >

15. Explain Will a book that is 27.36 centimeters tall stand upright in a bookcase whose shelves are 27.4 centimeters apart? Explain.
　　　　Yes; since 27.36 < 27.4, the book will stand upright.

Order the numbers from least to greatest.

16. 5.34, 5.12, 5.43
5.12, 5.34, 5.43
17. 9.07, 9.06, 9.1
9.06, 9.07, 9.1
18. 4.3, 4.25, 4.31
4.25, 4.3, 4.31

19. 0.9, 1.1, 0.1, 1.5
0.1, 0.9, 1.1, 1.5
20. 7.4, 7.9, 7, 6.9
6.9, 7, 7.4, 7.9
21. 1.2, 1.05, 1.15, 0.98
0.98, 1.05, 1.15, 1.2

22. 2.94, 2.904, 2.844, 2.899, 2.894 2.844, 2.894, 2.899, 2.904, 2.94

23. 0.055, 0.555, 0.55, 0.065, 0.56 0.055, 0.065, 0.55, 0.555, 0.56

24. Milk Prices The average cost of a gallon of milk in various cities is given below. Order the costs from least to greatest.
　　　　　　$2.08, $2.61, $2.62, $2.84, $3.07, $8.40

with **Homework**

Example	Exercises
1	15
2	16–21
3	6–14
4	16–24

Online Resources
CLASSZONE.COM
· More Examples
· eTutorial Plus

Los Angeles	Rio De Janeiro	London	Paris	Hong Kong	Sydney
$3.07	$2.61	$2.08	$2.84	$8.40	$2.62

25. Volcanoes The table shows the ages, in millions of years, of four Hawaiian volcanoes. Order the volcanoes from youngest to oldest. *Mauna Kea, Haleakala, West Maui, West Molokai*

Hawaiian Volcano Ages (millions of years)				
Volcano	Mauna Kea	West Maui	West Molokai	Haleakala
Age	0.375	1.32	1.9	0.75

26. Critical Thinking If the price of every item in a store goes up by the same amount, does the order of least expensive item to most expensive item change? Why or why not? **No. *Sample answer:* If all prices increase by the same amount, the differences remain the same so the order remains the same.**

 Algebra **Find a value of *n* that makes the statement true.**
Answers may vary.
27. $8.3 < n$ and $n < 9$ **8.7** **28.** $0.5 < n$ and $n < 1$ **0.9** **29.** $3.6 < n$ and $n < 3.7$ **3.65**

Challenge **In Exercise 30, use only the digits 0 and 1.**

C **30.** Write all the different decimals of the form ⬚ . ⬚ ⬚ .
0.00, 0.11, 1.01, 1.10, 1.00, 0.10, 0.01, 1.11
31. Order the decimals you wrote in Exercise 30 from least to greatest.
0.00, 0.01, 0.10, 0.11, 1.00, 1.01, 1.10, 1.11

Mixed Review

32. The heights, in feet, of newly planted trees are given below. Find the mean, median, mode, and range of the data. *(Lesson 2.8)* **5; 5; 4 and 5; 4**
4, 5, 7, 5, 3, 4, 6, 5, 4, 5, 6, 4, 7

33. Write the number *twenty-eight and sixteen ten-thousandths* as a decimal. *(Lesson 3.1)* **28.0016**

Basic Skills **Round the number to the place value of the red digit.**

34. 2**7**13 **2700**   **35.** 1**0**6,503 **107,000**   **36.** **1**,970,241 **2,000,000**

Test-Taking Practice

37. Multiple Choice Order the decimals from least to greatest: 0.3454, 0.4345, 0.3354, and 0.3345. **C**

A. 0.4345, 0.3454, 0.3354, 0.3345   **B.** 0.3354, 0.3345, 0.4345, 0.3454

C. 0.3345, 0.3354, 0.3454, 0.4345   **D.** 0.3354, 0.3454, 0.3345, 0.4345

38. Multiple Choice In a competition, four of the participants have completed their performances. Their scores are 9.61, 9.66, 9.64, and 9.60. Which score will enable the last participant to win the competition? **F**

F. 9.67   **G.** 9.65   **H.** 9.62   **I.** 9.06

What do you think?

Science

Volcanoes

Lanai is another Hawaiian volcano. It is 1.28 million years old. How does the age of Lanai compare with the ages of the other volcanoes in Exercise 25?

It is between Haleakala and West Maui in age.

INTERNET
State Test Practice
CLASSZONE.COM

④ ASSESS

ASSESSMENT RESOURCES

For more assessment resources, see:
• Assessment Book
• Test and Practice Generator

MINI-QUIZ

1. Complete each statement with <, >, or =.
a. 8.7 _?_ 9 **<**
b. 13.5 _?_ 13.500 **=**
c. 27 _?_ 26.47 **>**
d. 34.57 _?_ 34.5 **>**
e. 7.3529 _?_ 7.3551 **<**

2. Order the numbers from least to greatest.
22.56, 22.55, 22.5, 22.555, 22.48
22.48, 22.5, 22.55, 22.555, 22.56

⑤ FOLLOW-UP

RETEACHING/REMEDIATION

• Study Guide in Chapter 3 Resource Book, pp. 29–30
• Tutor Place, Whole Numbers and Decimals Cards 3, 4
• eTutorial Plus Online
• Extra Practice, p. 710
• Lesson Practice in Chapter 3 Resource Book, pp. 26–28

CHALLENGE/ENRICHMENT

• Challenge Practice in Chapter 3 Resource Book, p. 32
• Teacher's Edition, p. 104F

ENGLISH LEARNER SUPPORT

• Spanish Study Guide
• Multi-Language Glossary
• Chapter Audio Summaries CDs

LESSONS 3.1 TO 3.3 Notebook Review

Review the vocabulary definitions in your notebook.

Copy the review examples in your notebook. Then complete the exercises.

Check Your Definitions

decimal, p. 108	centimeter (cm), p. 56	number line, p. 685
millimeter (mm), p. 56	meter (m), p. 56	

Use Your Vocabulary

1. Copy and complete: The decimal 2.06 is read "two and six _?_." **hundredths**

2. **Writing** Explain the role of the decimal point in a decimal.
   Sample answer: It separates the whole number part from the decimal part.

3.1–3.2 Can you measure and write decimal lengths?

 EXAMPLE Write the length of the line segment as a decimal number of centimeters.

ANSWER The length is 7.6 centimeters.

☑ **Write the length in words and as a decimal.**

3. Find the length of this sentence to the nearest tenth of a centimeter.
   eleven and two tenths centimeters; 11.2 cm
4. Find the height of this book to the nearest hundredth of a meter.
   twenty-six hundredths meter; 0.26 m

3.3 Can you compare and order decimals?

 EXAMPLE Which is greater, 8.4 or 8.42?

8.40
8.42 —— The first two digits are the same.
The hundredths' digits are different: 2 > 0.

ANSWER 8.42 > 8.4

☑ **Copy and complete the statement with <, >, or =.**

5. 6.54 _?_ 6.45 **>**   6. 2.536 _?_ 2.541 **<**   7. 9.7 _?_ 9.70 **=**

8. Order the numbers from least to greatest: 0.91, 0.94, 0.09, 0.082, 0.75.
   0.082, 0.09, 0.75, 0.81, 0.94

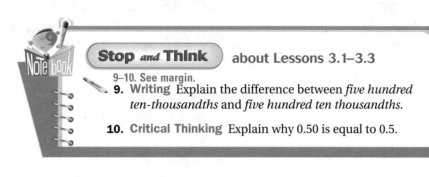

Stop and Think about Lessons 3.1–3.3

9–10. See margin.
9. **Writing** Explain the difference between *five hundred ten-thousandths* and *five hundred ten thousandths*.

10. **Critical Thinking** Explain why 0.50 is equal to 0.5.

Review Quiz 1

Write the decimal in words.

1. six and fifty-two hundredths

2. seventeen and seventeen thousandths

3. one thousand two hundred thirty-four ten-thousandths

1. 6.52   2. 17.017   3. 0.1234

4. Write the number *eight and seven hundred fifty-two thousandths* as a decimal. **8.752**

5. Find the length of the line segment to the nearest tenth of a centimeter.

5.8 cm

6. Order the numbers from least to greatest: 11.21, 11.02, 11.20, 11, 11.041.
   11, 11.02, 11.041, 11.19, 11.21

Copy and complete the statement with <, >, or =.

7. 5.02 ? 5.21 <   8. 24.632 ? 24.236 >   9. 38.9 ? 38.90 =

10. **Body Temperature** If normal body temperature is about 98.6°F, is a temperature of 98.06°F *above* or *below* normal? **below**

What Number Am I?

I have two digits to the left of my decimal point and two digits to the right of my decimal point. My hundredths' digit is two times my tenths' digit. When 1 is subtracted from my tens' digit, the answer is 5. I have a 2 as my tenths' digit. My ones' digit is greater than 0 and less than my tenths' digit. What number am I? **61.24**

Round to the place value indicated.

1. 1843; hundreds   1800
2. 765; tens   770
3. 596; tens   600

LESSON OBJECTIVE

Round decimals.

PACING

Suggested Number of Days
Basic Course: 1 day
Average Course: 1 day
Advanced Course: 1 day
Block: 0.5 block with 3.3

TEACHING RESOURCES

For a complete list of Teaching Resources, see page 104B.

 **TRANSPARENCY**

Warm-Up Exercises for this lesson are available on a transparency.

2 TEACH

MOTIVATING THE LESSON

Tell students they already know how to round decimals. It is the same as rounding whole numbers.

TIPS FOR NEW TEACHERS

Have students use different ways to identify the digit in the place to be rounded and the digit to its right. For example, have them underline the digit to be rounded and circle the digit to its right. See Tips for New Teachers in the *Chapter 3 Resource Book.*

Rounding Decimals

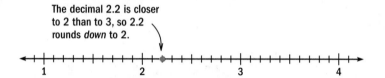

BEFORE	▶ Now	WHY?
You rounded whole numbers.	You'll round decimals.	So you can read large numbers, such as the salaries in Example 4.

 **Word Watch**

Review Words
leading digit, p. 13
round, p. 686

Number Lines A number line can help you picture how to round a decimal.

The decimal 2.2 is closer to 2 than to 3, so 2.2 rounds *down* to 2.

EXAMPLE 1   **Using a Number Line to Round**

Use a number line to round 3.87 to the nearest tenth.

The decimal 3.87 is closer to 3.9 than to 3.8.

ANSWER The decimal 3.87 rounds up to 3.9.

Your turn now   Use a number line to round the decimal as specified.

1. 1.3 (nearest one) 1   **2.** 2.8 (nearest one) 3
3. 3.74 (nearest tenth) 3.7   **4.** 3.86 (nearest tenth) 3.9

Using a Rule On a number line, you round a decimal by deciding which number it is closer to. The same idea applies when you use the rule below.

Rounding Decimals

To round a decimal to a given place value, look at the digit in the place to the right.

• If the digit is 4 or less, round down.

• If the digit is 5 or greater, round up.

NCTM CURRICULUM STANDARDS
Standard 1: Understand relationships among numbers
Standard 10: Use representations to communicate mathematical ideas

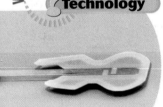

Watch Out!

In rounding problems like part (d) of Example 2, do not drop the final zero. Keep it to mark the place value you rounded to.

What do you think?

Technology

■ **Music**

This tiny guitar was created as a fun way to demonstrate technology for making very small objects. If the size of most human cells is 0.00003937 inch, which is larger, the guitar or the cell?
the guitar

EXAMPLE 2 **Rounding Decimals**

Round the decimal to the place value of the red digit.

a. 3.23 ——→ 3.2   The digit to the right of 2 is 3, so round down.

b. 6.485 ——→ 6.49   The digit to the right of 8 is 5, so round up.

c. 2.83619 ——→ 2.836   The digit to the right of 6 is 1, so round down.

d. 5.961 ——→ 6.0   The digit to the right of 9 is 6, so round up.

Your turn now **Round the decimal as specified.**

5. 5.29 (nearest tenth) 5.3   **6.** 7.096 (nearest hundredth) 7.10

7. 6.48 (nearest one) 6   **8.** 3.9876 (nearest thousandth)
                                                        3.988

Rounding Small Numbers You can round a very small number to the place value of its leading digit to help make it easier to understand. In a decimal, the leading digit is the first nonzero digit at the left.

EXAMPLE 3 **Rounding to the Leading Digit**

Music A guitar was created that is 0.0003937 inch long. Round the length of the guitar to the place value of the leading digit.

Solution

The first nonzero digit at the left of 0.0003937 is 3, and it is in the ten-thousandths' place. You should round the length to the nearest ten-thousandth.

    0.000**3**937   3 is in the ten-thousandths' place.

Because 9 is to the right of the ten-thousandths' place, round 3 up to 4.

ANSWER The length of the guitar rounded to the place value of the leading digit is 0.0004 inch.

Your turn now **Round the decimal to the leading digit.**

9. 0.058 0.06   **10.** 0.0091 0.009   **11.** 0.0952 0.10   **12.** 0.006192
                                                                     0.006

Example 4 Round each quarterly sales figure to the nearest hundred thousand. Then write each rounded amount as a decimal number of millions.
a. First quarter: $2,457,390
   $2,500,000; $2.5 million
b. Second quarter: $3,127,640
   $3,100,000; $3.1 million
c. Third quarter: $9,124,852
   $9,100,000; $9.1 million
d. Fourth quarter: $10,429,448
   $10,400,000; $10.4 million

Differentiating Instruction

Less Proficient Students
Suggest to students who are having difficulty identifying the correct place to round to that they write the decimal in a place-value chart as was done in Lesson 3.1, page 108. This will help them to identify not only the place they are rounding to, but also whether to round up or down.

 CONCEPT CHECK

To round a number to the nearest hundredth, which place value do you inspect? What determines whether you will round up or round down?
To round a number to the nearest hundredth, look at the digit in the thousandths place. If that digit is 4 or less, round down. If that digit is 5 or more, round up.

 DAILY PUZZLER

Find two decimals that have different digits in their thousandths place but that are equal if they are rounded to the tenths, hundredths, or thousandths place. *Sample answer:* 0.1235 and 0.1241

EXAMPLE 4 **Using Decimals for Large Numbers**

Sports The average annual salaries for some positions in major league baseball in a recent year are shown below. Round each salary to the nearest hundred thousand. Then write each rounded salary as a decimal number of millions. Display your results in a bar graph.

Position:	Average Salary:	Round:	Write in millions:
First Base	$4,996,933	$5,000,000	$5.0 million
Outfield	$3,480,792	$3,500,000	$3.5 million
Pitcher	$3,064,021	$3,100,000	$3.1 million
Catcher	$2,767,726	$2,800,000	$2.8 million

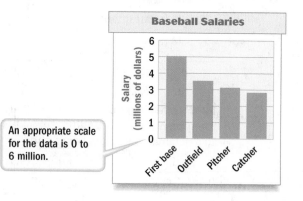

An appropriate scale for the data is 0 to 6 million.

3.4 **Exercises**

More Practice, p. 710

More Practice, p. 710

INTERNET
eWorkbook Plus
CLASSZONE.COM

Getting Ready to Practice

Vocabulary Identify the leading digit of the decimal. Then round to the place value of the leading digit.

1. 0.024 2; 0.02   **2.** 0.0078 7; 0.008   **3.** 0.00149 1; 0.001   **4.** 0.000485 4; 0.0005

HELP with Notetaking

As you work on the exercises, remember to write down any questions you want to ask your teacher.

Round the decimal as specified.

5. 8.21 (nearest tenth) 8.2   **6.** 1.159 (nearest hundredth) 1.16

7. 10.6289 (nearest thousandth) 10.629 **8.** 1.498 (nearest one) 1

9. Round the number 8,438,100 to the nearest hundred thousand. Then write the rounded number as a decimal number of millions. 8,400,000; 8.4 million

Practice and Problem Solving

with Homework

Example	Exercises
1	10–13
2	14–22, 32
3	23–30
4	33–36

Online Resources
CLASSZONE.COM

· More Examples
· eTutorial Plus

32. *Sample answer:* The answer should be 10.0 because a zero should have been kept in the tenths' place to indicate the place value to which the number was rounded.

33. 15,900,000; 15.9 million

34. 6,500,000; 6.5 million

35. 10,000,000; 10.0 million

36. 15,000,000; 15.0 million

A

Use a number line to round the decimal as specified.

10. 5.3 (nearest one) 5

11. 9.5 (nearest one) 10

12. 3.76 (nearest tenth) 3.8

13. 1.41 (nearest tenth) 1.4

Round the decimal as specified.

14. 9.41 (nearest one) 9

15. 2.59 (nearest one) 3

16. 8.087 (nearest tenth) 8.1

17. 8.981 (nearest tenth) 9.0

18. 6.999 (nearest hundredth) 7.00

19. 3.902 (nearest hundredth) 3.90

20. 2.5634 (nearest thousandth) 2.563

21. 7.2961 (nearest thousandth) 7.296

22. Writing After sharing a pizza, you and two friends divide the cost by three. You each owe $2.666666. Explain how to round this to the nearest dime. *Sample answer:* A dime is 0.10 of a dollar, so round to the nearest tenth, or $2.70.

Round the decimal to the place value of the leading digit.

23. 0.0263 0.03

24. 0.0588 0.06

25. 0.0092 0.009

26. 0.006178 0.006

27. 0.00019 0.0002

28. 0.000231 0.0002

29. 0.00009888 0.00010

30. 0.0000177 0.00002

31. Skateboarding The table shows the scores of 4 skateboarders after three rounds of a skateboarding competition. Why is it not reasonable to round the scores to the nearest one? Explain. *Sample answer:* because many of the scores would round to 81

	Round 1	Round 2	Round 3
Rob	80.7	84.4	80.8
Ruth	83.3	78.6	81.1
Kenny	81.2	83.6	80.6
Jessica	82.7	79.2	80.9

32. Find the Error Describe and correct the error in the form of the answer. See margin.

 Round to the nearest tenth.

9.95 ⟶ 10

Round the number to the nearest hundred thousand. Then write the rounded number as a decimal number of millions.

33. 15,925,000

34. 6,549,000

35. 9,987,260

36. 14,962,000

Technology A calculator will sometimes give long decimals. Round the number on the calculator display to the nearest hundredth.

B

37. 1.285714286 1.29

38. 1.076923077 1.08

39. 1.714285714 1.71

Lesson 3.4   Rounding Decimals   **127**

ASSIGNMENT GUIDE

Basic Course
Day 1: SRH p. 686 Exs. 6–10; pp. 127–128 Exs. 11–21 odd, 23–26, 32–39, 43, 48–59

Average Course
Day 1: pp. 127–128 Exs. 10–22 even, 27–32, 35–45, 49–55, 58–60

Advanced Course
Day 1: pp. 127–128 Exs. 12, 13, 18–22, 29–33, 36–48*, 51–54, 59, 60

Block
pp. 127–128 Exs. 10–22 even, 27–32, 35–45, 49–55, 58–60 (with 3.3)

EXTRA PRACTICE

• Student Edition, p. 710
• Chapter 3 Resource Book, pp. 36–38
• Test and Practice Generator

 TRANSPARENCY

Even-numbered answers are available on transparencies. A support transparency is available for Exercises 10–13.

HOMEWORK CHECK

When you review students' homework for this lesson, go over the following exercises to check understanding of key concepts.
Basic: 11, 17, 19, 24, 34
Average: 12, 18, 27, 32, 35
Advanced: 13, 20, 29, 32, 36

 COMMON ERROR

In Exercise 32, stress that when rounding, the number of digits shown indicates which place the number has been rounded to. Thus, 10, 10.0, and 10.00 all represent different degrees of rounding.

ASSESSMENT RESOURCES

For more assessment resources, see:
- Assessment Book
- Test and Practice Generator

MINI-QUIZ

Round each number to the indicated place value.

1. Round 12.087 to the nearest hundredth. **12.09**

2. Round 35.951 to the nearest tenth. **36.0**

3. Round 0.0509 to its leading digit. **0.05**

4. Round 20.501745 to the nearest ten-thousandth. **20.5017**

5. Round 4,575,428 to the nearest hundred thousand. Then write the rounded number as a decimal number of millions. **4,600,000; 4.6 million**

5 **FOLLOW-UP**

RETEACHING/REMEDIATION
- Study Guide in Chapter 3 Resource Book, pp. 39–40
- Tutor Place, Whole Numbers and Decimals Card 16
- eTutorial Plus Online
- Extra Practice, pp. 710
- Lesson Practice in Chapter 3 Resource Book, pp. 36–38

CHALLENGE/ENRICHMENT
- Challenge Practice in Chapter 3 Resource Book, p. 41
- Teacher's Edition, p. 104F

ENGLISH LEARNER SUPPORT
- Spanish Study Guide
- Multi-Language Glossary
- Chapter Audio Summaries CDs

41–46. See Additional Answers beginning on page AA1.

128

What do you think?

Biology

■ **Hair**

An average person's head typically has 100,000 hairs on it. Suppose the girl in the picture measures a strand of her hair and finds it is 8 inches long. If all of her hair was one continuous strand, about how long would it be? **800,000 in.**

INTERNET
State Test Practice
CLASSZONE.COM

60. Ashley: 138, Ellie: 137, Alina: 137, Julie: 137, Dionne: 136; Ashley: 137.5, Alina: 137.45, Julie: 137.35, Ellie: 136.7, Dionne: 136.35; *Sample answer:* ranking the divers without rounding the scores so that no ties result

40. Hair The width of a human hair is about 0.00389763 inch. Explain why it is not reasonable to round the width to the nearest hundredth. Find a reasonable estimate for the width. *Sample answer:* because the width would be 0.00 inch; 0.004 in.

Tourism **The table shows the total number of people that visited the state parks of five states in one year.** 41–42. See margin.

41. Round each number to the nearest hundred thousand. Then write the rounded number as a decimal number of millions.

42. Display your results in a bar graph.

State	Visitors
California	76,736,000
Illinois	41,891,000
New York	61,960,000
Ohio	60,220,000
Washington	48,138,000

Number Sense **Find three decimals that round to the number.**
43–46. See margin.

43. 4   **44.** 15   **45.** 3.4   **46.** 8.7

47. Challenge In Exercise 43, you are asked to find three decimals that round to 4. How many answers are possible? Explain.
Sample answer: There are infinitely many possible answers because there are infinitely many possible decimal places.

Mixed Review

Estimate the sum or difference. (Lesson 1.2) Estimates may vary.

48. 136 + 75 **220**   **49.** 418 + 397 **800**   **50.** 572 − 269 **300**   **51.** 343 − 27 **310**

Copy and complete the statement with <, >, or =. (Lesson 3.3)

52. 0.79 ? 0.9 **<**   **53.** 0.05 ? 0.05000 **=**   **54.** 3.037 ? 3.073 **<**

Basic Skills **Find the product or quotient.**

55. 214 × 9 **1926**   **56.** 125 × 10 **1250**   **57.** 345 ÷ 3 **115**   **58.** 270 ÷ 10 **27**

Test-Taking Practice

59. Multiple Choice You record the weight of a package weighing 14.57 pounds to the nearest pound. What weight do you record? **D**

A. 10 pounds   **B.** 14 pounds   **C.** 14.5 pounds   **D.** 15 pounds

60. Short Response The table shows the scores of 5 divers in a school diving competition. Round the scores to the nearest one and order them from greatest to least, to find each diver's rank. Then rank the divers without rounding the scores. Which method is more reasonable to rank the divers? Explain.

Diver	Score
Dionne	136.35
Ashley	137.5
Ellie	136.7
Alina	137.45
Julie	137.35

3.5 Hands-on **Activity**

GOAL
Develop number sense skills for adding decimals.

MATERIALS
· metric ruler
· number cube
· colored pencils or markers

Targeting a Sum of 10

You can use number sense skills to choose values that come close to a target without going over. When these values are ones and tenths, you can use a metric ruler to help you.

Explore **Use a metric ruler to come close to 10 centimeters without going over.**

1. Draw a line segment that is 10 centimeters long.

2. Roll a number cube. Decide whether you want the number rolled to represent whole centimeters or tenths of centimeters. Draw a segment of this length below the line segment you drew in Step 1.

 = 6.0 centimeters

3. Repeat Step 2 six more times. Begin each line segment where the last one ended and alternate colors. Try to get as close to 10 centimeters as you can without going over. Measure to see how close you came after seven rolls.

 = 0.3 centimeters

Your turn now **Use the steps above.**

1. Follow the steps to create a segment that is as close to 10 centimeters long as possible without going over. Record the length you choose for each roll. **Answers may vary.**

Stop and Think

2. **Writing** In Exercise 1, could you choose different lengths for some rolls so that your sum comes closer to 10 centimeters? Explain. **Answers may vary.**

NCTM CURRICULUM STANDARDS
Standard 1: Understand ways of representing numbers; Make reasonable estimates
Standard 4: Apply proper tools to find measures

Lesson 3.5 Decimal Estimation **129**

---

1 **PLAN**

EXPLORE THE CONCEPT
• Students will develop number sense skills for adding decimals.
• This activity leads into a study of decimal estimation in Lesson 3.5. Decimal estimation has many uses in the real world.

MATERIALS
Each student will need a metric ruler, number cube, and colored pencils or markers. A support transparency is available for this activity.

RECOMMENDED TIME
Work activity: 10 min
Discuss results: 5 min

GROUPING
Students should do this activity individually.

2 **TEACH**

ALTERNATIVE STRATEGY
This can be done as a class activity, allowing students to discuss whether each number should be a whole centimeter or tenths of a centimeter.

3 **CLOSE**

KEY DISCOVERY
Using number sense is a useful skill when estimating decimal sums.

ASSESSMENT
1. You roll three 5s, one 6, and four 7s. Can you create a segment between 9 and 10 cm? **Yes;**
$5 + 0.5 + 0.5 + 0.6 + 0.7 + 0.7 + 0.7 + 0.7 = 9.4$

SKILL CHECK

Estimate to the nearest 10.

1. $317 + 42$ **360**

2. $241 + 88$ **330**

3. $462 - 77$ **380**

4. $355 - 119$ **240**

LESSON OBJECTIVE

Estimate sums and differences of decimals.

PACING

Suggested Number of Days
Basic Course: 1 day
Average Course: 1 day
Advanced Course: 1 day
Block: 0.5 block with 3.6

TEACHING RESOURCES

For a complete list of Teaching Resources, see page 104B.

 TRANSPARENCY

Warm-Up Exercises for this lesson are available on a transparency.

 TEACH

MOTIVATING THE LESSON

Example 3 provides a good motivator for this lesson. Present the situation to students before they open their books and ask them to offer solutions.

TIPS FOR NEW TEACHERS

Be sure students understand that different methods of estimating may give different values. See Tips for New Teachers in the *Chapter 3 Resource Book*.

LESSON **3.5**

Decimal Estimation

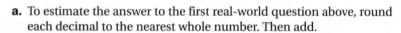

BEFORE	▶ Now	WHY?
You estimated sums and differences of whole numbers.	You'll estimate sums and differences of decimals.	So you can estimate change you'll receive, as in Exs. 18 and 19.

In the Real World

 **Word Watch**

front-end estimation, p. 131

Sports The table shows the number of people, in millions, who participated in five sports in a recent year. About how many people played soccer? About how many more females participated in bicycling than in golf?

One way to estimate a sum or a difference is to use rounding.

Sports Participation (millions)		
Activity	**Males**	**Females**
Bicycling	22.9	20.6
Golf	21.8	5.7
Hiking	14.9	12.3
Soccer	8.2	4.9
Swimming	27.0	31.3

EXAMPLE 1   Estimating Sums and Differences

a. To estimate the answer to the first real-world question above, round each decimal to the nearest whole number. Then add.

$$
\begin{array}{r}
8.2 \longrightarrow 8 \\
+\ 4.9 \longrightarrow +5 \\
\hline
13
\end{array}
$$

    Round 8.2 down to 8.
    Round 4.9 up to 5.

ANSWER About 13 million people played soccer.

b. To estimate the answer to the second real-world question above, round each decimal to the nearest whole number. Then subtract.

$$
\begin{array}{r}
20.6 \longrightarrow 21 \\
-\ 5.7 \longrightarrow -6 \\
\hline
15
\end{array}
$$

    Round 20.6 up to 21.
    Round 5.7 up to 6.

ANSWER About 15 million more females participated in bicycling than in golf.

Your turn now   Use the information provided at the top of the page.

1. Estimate the total number of people who participated in hiking.
27 million

2. Estimate how many more males participated in swimming than in golf.   5 million

NCTM CURRICULUM STANDARDS
Standard 1: Understand relationships among numbers; Make reasonable estimates
Standard 6: Solve problems in math and other contexts

EXAMPLE 2 Predicting Results

Shopping You buy a T-shirt that costs $9.21. You give the clerk $20.00. Estimate your change. Is this estimate *high* or *low*?

$$\begin{array}{ccc} \$20.00 & & \$20 \\ -\ \$9.21 & \longrightarrow & -\ \$9 \\ \hline & & \$11 \end{array}$$ Round 9.21 down to 9.

ANSWER Your change is about $11. This estimate is high because you subtracted too little by rounding $9.21 down to $9.

Front-End Estimation You can also estimate sums using **front-end estimation**. You add the front-end digits to get a low estimate. Then you use the remaining digits to adjust the sum and get a closer estimate.

EXAMPLE 3 Using Front-End Estimation

Groceries You have $10 to buy bread, milk, and cereal. If you have enough money, you would like to buy popcorn. The prices of these items are shown. Do you have enough money to buy popcorn?

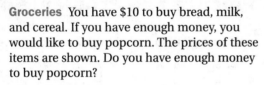

Grocery List
bread $1.79
milk $2.18
cereal $3.34
popcorn $3.65

Solution

Find the sum of all the prices, including the price of the popcorn.

(1 Add the front-end digits: the dollars.

$$\begin{array}{r} \$1.79 \\ \$2.18 \\ \$3.34 \\ +\ \$3.65 \\ \hline \$9 \end{array}$$

(2 Estimate the sum of the remaining digits: the cents.

$$\begin{array}{r} \$1.79 \\ \$2.18 \rightarrow \$1 \\ \$3.34 \\ +\ \$3.65 \rightarrow \$1 \\ \hline \$2 \end{array}$$

(3 Add your results.

$$\begin{array}{r} \$9 \\ +\ \$2 \\ \hline \$11 \end{array}$$

ANSWER You do not have enough money to buy popcorn.

 Your turn now Use front-end estimation to estimate the sum.

3. 6.42 + 7.64 + 3.94 + 2.21 **20**   **4.** 8.59 + 1.37 + 2 + 6.12 **18**

5. How can you estimate the difference in Example 2 so that your answer is a low estimate? *Sample answer:* Subtract $10 from $20.

Lesson 3.5   Decimal Estimation   **131**

 CONCEPT CHECK

When shopping for a list of items, how can you get a good estimate of what the total will be? **Add the front-end digits (the dollars) to get a low estimate. Then use the remaining digits (the cents) to adjust the sum and get a closer estimate.**

 DAILY PUZZLER

Each of two items cost between $2 and $3. The estimated difference in the costs is $.99 more than the exact difference. What are the costs of the items? **$2.50 and $2.49**

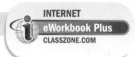

Getting Ready to Practice

1. **Vocabulary** Identify the front-end digits of $1.12 and $5.86. **1 and 5**

Use rounding to estimate the sum or difference.

2. 2.6 + 8.9 **12**   3. 12.43 + 5.8 **18**   4. 15.5 − 14.7 **1**

5. **Guided Problem Solving** A table is 73.66 centimeters tall. An iguana cage on the table is 76.2 centimeters tall. Estimate to decide whether they will fit beneath a shelf that is 157.16 centimeters off the floor.

   ① Draw a diagram of the situation. **Check drawings.**

   ② Estimate the height of the table and the cage combined. **150 cm**

   ③ Compare the combined heights to the height of the shelf.
   150 centimeters is less than 157.16 centimeters,
   so they will fit beneath the shelf.

Practice and Problem Solving

Use rounding to estimate the sum or difference.

A 6. 9.7 + 8.4 **18**   7. 8.3 + 3.8 **12**   8. 9.3 − 6.9 **2**

   9. 7.2 − 4.6 **2**   10. 10.64 + 7.49 **18**   11. 2.25 + 0.93 **3**

   12. 12.81 − 1.92 **11**   13. 10.72 − 2.85 **8**   14. 15.99 + 3.4 **19**

   15. 12.38 + 12.8 **25**   16. 20.2 − 10.31 **10**   17. 9.1 − 8.98 **0**

Critical Thinking Estimate the change you will receive and tell whether the estimate is *high* or *low*. Explain.

18. You buy several postcards totaling $3.82. You give the clerk $10.00.
$6.00; low; $3.82 was rounded up.

19. You buy a bag of pretzels for $1.15. You give the cashier $5.00.
$4.00; high; $1.15 was rounded down.

Use front-end estimation to estimate the sum.

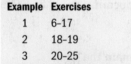
HELP with Homework

Example	Exercises
1	6–17
2	18–19
3	20–25

20. 4.79 + 5.16 + 8.08 **18**   21. 6.23 + 4.75 + 3.91 **15**   22. 4.5 + 8.92 + 9.21 **23**

23. 6.46 + 3.22 + 2.58 **12**   24. 5.55 + 7.19 + 4.49 **17**   25. 6.31 + 2.5 + 1.93 **11**

B 26. **Find the Error** Describe and correct the error in the estimate.

Sample answer:
The sum of the front-end digits is $5, not $6. The correct estimate is $5 + $1 = $6.

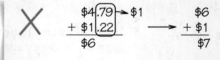

What do you think?

? Geography

■ **Mountains**

Most climbers of Mount Everest will start from the Everest Base Camp, which is about 3.2 miles high. About how far do they climb from the base camp to the top?
about 2.3 mi

40. Using rounding, the total cost is about $25. Using front-end estimation, the cost is about $24 + $2 = $26. Front-end estimation is a better method because it is closer to the exact sum. You want to use the method that gives an estimate closer to the exact sum and that is less likely to give an underestimate.

INTERNET

State Test Practice
CLASSZONE.COM

Extended Problem Solving The *Seven Summits* are the highest mountain peaks on each of the seven continents. The heights of the summits are shown in the table. Use the table in Exercises 27–29. 27–30. See margin.

Mountain	Height (miles)
Mount Elbrus (Europe)	3.5
Mount Kosciusko (Australia)	1.38
Mount Aconcagua (South America)	4.33
Mount Everest (Asia)	5.50
Mount Kilimanjaro (Africa)	3.7
Mount McKinley (North America)	3.85
Vinson Massif (Antarctica)	3.04

27. Order the heights of the mountains from least to greatest. Then find the median of the heights.

28. Estimate the mean of the heights. Is your estimate *high* or *low*? Explain.

29. **Critical Thinking** Which is a better estimate of the average height, the *median* or the *mean*? Explain.

30. **Challenge** How can you use rounding to overestimate the sum of two numbers? the difference of two numbers? How can you use rounding to underestimate the sum of two numbers? the difference of two numbers? Explain and show examples.

Mixed Review

Evaluate the expression when $x = 2$ and $y = 3$. *(Lesson 1.5)*

31. $x + 14$ 16   **32.** $9y$ 27   **33.** $x + y$ 5   **34.** $y + x \cdot y$ 9

Round the decimal as specified. *(Lesson 3.4)*

35. 17.8023 (nearest thousandth) 17.802   **36.** 4.79663 (nearest hundredth) 4.80

Basic Skills **Find the sum or difference.**

37. $10.75 + $1.25   **38.** $9.80 + $4.20   **39.** $2.85 - $1.35
$12.00 $14.00 $1.50

Test-Taking Practice

40. **Extended Response** You have $25 to buy prizes for a game. The table shows the prizes and their prices. Use rounding to estimate the total cost and decide if this estimate is *high* or *low*. Then use front-end estimation to find the total cost. Which method is better when you have a fixed amount of money to spend? Explain. See margin.

Prize	Price
yo-yo	$1.48
bear	$9.46
sunglasses	$1.07
magic tricks	$5.91
set of books	$8.00

Lesson 3.5   Decimal Estimation   **133**

4 ASSESS

ASSESSMENT RESOURCES

For more assessment resources, see:
• Assessment Book
• Test and Practice Generator

MINI-QUIZ

Round each value to the nearest whole number to estimate each sum or difference.

1. $5.73 + 12.84 + 3.15$ **22**

2. $25.33 - 9.82$ **15**

3. $14 - 7.61$ **6**

4. In Exercise 3, is the estimate *high* or *low*? Explain. **The estimate is low. The number 7.61 was rounded up to 8, so the estimate subtracted a larger number than the exact value.**

5. For $2.25 + 6.87 + 3.72 + 4.09$, what sum do you get from adding just the front-end digits? What adjustment do you get from adding just the remaining digits? **15; 2**

5 FOLLOW-UP

RETEACHING/REMEDIATION

• Study Guide in Chapter 3 Resource Book, pp. 49–50
• Tutor Place, Whole Numbers and Decimals Card 17
• eTutorial Plus Online
• Extra Practice, p. 710
• Lesson Practice in Chapter 3 Resource Book, pp. 46–48

CHALLENGE/ENRICHMENT

• Challenge Practice in Chapter 3 Resource Book, p. 51
• Teacher's Edition, p. 104F

ENGLISH LEARNER SUPPORT

• Spanish Study Guide
• Multi-Language Glossary
• Chapter Audio Summaries CDs

133

PLAN

STRATEGY BACKGROUND

Check Reasonableness is a strategy that is applied to any potential solution for a problem. The strength of the strategy is that it is a real-world appraisal of whether an answer is possible and appropriate. Students will realize that the strategy is not a way to generate an answer, but a way to check a trial answer.

TEACH

GUIDING STUDENTS' WORK

In Step 3, students can write the quotient as 5 R25, as $5\frac{25}{30}$, or even 5.833... . In each case, the whole number 5 refers to the number of complete picture frames that can be made.

Draw a Diagram
Guess, Check, and Revise
Make a Table
Make a List
Check Reasonableness
Work Backward
Look for a Pattern

Check Reasonableness

Problem You would like to construct wooden photo frames. You need 50 centimeters of wood for each frame. You have a total of 275 centimeters of wood. How many photo frames can you make?

① Read and Understand

Read the problem carefully.

Your answer should be a whole number of photo frames.

② Make a Plan

Decide on a strategy to use.

To solve this problem, you need to choose the operation, carry out the operation, and then check the reasonableness of the answer.

③ Solve the Problem

Reread the problem and choose an operation.

You need to divide to find the number of times 50 centimeters goes into 275 centimeters.

$$\begin{array}{r} 5\ R25 \\ 50\overline{)275} \\ \underline{250} \\ 25 \end{array}$$

Evaluate the reasonableness of 5 R25.

→ 5   R25 ←

5 whole picture frames   **25 centimeters left over**

You cannot make a complete photo frame with 25 centimeters, so you need to round down to 5.

ANSWER You can make 5 photo frames.

EXTRA EXAMPLES

Example Each framed photo is hung by attaching a 90 mm length of wire on the back of the frame. You have 425 mm of wire. How many photos can you hang?

$$\begin{array}{r} 4\ R65 \\ 90\overline{)425} \\ \underline{360} \\ 65 \end{array}$$

You can attach wire to 4 frames. To check the reasonableness of the solution, use the compatible numbers 90 and 450: $450 \div 90 = 5$. This is an overestimate because $450 > 425$. So the answer 4 is reasonable.

④ Look Back

Check the reasonableness of your solution using estimation. Using compatible numbers, you get $300 \div 50 = 6$. This is an overestimate, because 300 is greater than 275. Your answer is reasonable.

NCTM CURRICULUM STANDARDS
Standard 6: Solve problems in math and other contexts; Apply/adapt strategies to solve problems; Reflect on the process of problem solving

Practice the Strategy

Solve the problems and *check for reasonableness.*

1. **Medals** You are putting ribbons on medals for a sports competition. Each medal needs 25 inches of ribbon. You have 16 feet of ribbon. How many medals can you decorate with ribbon? **7 medals**

2. **Frames** You would like to construct wooden photo frames. You need 40 centimeters of wood for each frame and you have a total of 140 centimeters of wood. How many photo frames can you make? **3 frames**

3. **Buses** You are helping the science teacher plan a field trip to the natural history museum. There are 105 students signed up for the field trip. Each bus can hold 45 students. How many buses do you recommend reserving? **3 buses**

4. **Books** A bookstore needs to mail 225 books. The boxes they will use can hold 12 books each. How many boxes will the bookstore need to mail all of the books? **19 boxes**

5. **Gifts** You have $55 to buy three birthday gifts. The prices of three possible gifts and an estimate of the tax are listed below. Will you have enough money? **no**

Birthday Gifts

CD	$17.99
Book	$12.25
Game	$24.75
Tax	$4.50

Mixed Problem Solving

Use any strategy to solve the problem.

6. **Decorating** You are arranging furniture in a 10 foot by 8 foot room. You have a 6 foot by 6 foot rug. You want to place a 4 foot by 3 foot desk against a wall, but not on the rug. Is this possible? Why or why not? **Yes; put the rug in one of the corners.**

7. **Locks** You can remember the three numbers for a lock, but you can't remember their order. One possibility is shown below. What are the other possibilities? **652, 265, 256, 526, 562**

8. **Supplies** You spent $17 on construction paper and envelopes. If a box of envelopes costs $3 and a package of construction paper costs $4, how many boxes of envelopes and packages of construction paper did you buy? **See margin.**

9. **Shopping** You spend half of your money at the first store in the mall, $5 in the second store, and $7 in the third store. At this point, you have $3 left. How much money did you start with? **$30**

---

③ **APPLY**

 TRANSPARENCY
Even-numbered answers are available on transparencies.

TEACHING TIP
For Exercises 1–4, students can write a list of multiples for the divisor in each problem. Then they can use that list to find the whole-number part of the quotient.

ⓧ **COMMON ERROR**
For Exercises 1 and 2, and the problem on page 134, the answer "rounds down" the quotient to the previous integer. Students who continue that pattern in Exercises 3 and 4 will be incorrect, because those problems require the student to "round up" to the next integer.

SUGGESTED STRATEGIES
You may wish to suggest the following strategies for the problems in the Mixed Problem Solving:
- Exercise 6: Draw a Diagram
- Exercise 7: Make a List, Guess, Check, and Revise
- Exercise 8: Guess, Check, and Revise, Make a Table
- Exercise 9: Guess, Check, and Revise, Work Backward

8. **3 boxes of envelopes and 2 packages of construction paper**

SKILL CHECK

1. $231 + 157 = \underline{\ ?\ }$ 388
2. $388 + 279 = \underline{\ ?\ }$ 667
3. $573 - 381 = \underline{\ ?\ }$ 192
4. $604 - 367 = \underline{\ ?\ }$ 237

LESSON OBJECTIVE

Add and subtract decimals.

PACING

Suggested Number of Days
Basic Course: 1 day
Average Course: 1 day
Advanced Course: 1 day
Block: 0.5 block with 3.5

TEACHING RESOURCES

For a complete list of Teaching Resources, see page 104B.

 TRANSPARENCY

Warm-Up Exercises for this lesson are available on a transparency. A support transparency is available for the Activity.

2 TEACH

MOTIVATING THE LESSON

Expand upon the activity by having students use base-ten pieces to model decimal subtraction.

ACTIVITY

Goal Add decimals.

Key Discovery Base-ten pieces can help you with regrouping when you add decimals.

LESSON 3.6

Adding and Subtracting Decimals

BEFORE	▶ Now	WHY?
You added and subtracted whole numbers.	You'll add and subtract decimals.	So you can find account balances, as in Example 4.

📓 Word Watch

commutative property of addition, p. 137
associative property of addition, p. 137

Activity You can use base-ten pieces to model decimal addition.

To find the sum of 1.15 and 0.95, combine the pieces.

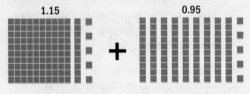

(1) Model the numbers using base-ten pieces.

(2) Combine the pieces.

(3) Trade 10 tenths for 1 one and 10 hundredths for 1 tenth.

$$1.15 + 0.95 = 2.1$$

2.1

Use base-ten pieces to find the sum.

1. $2.1 + 0.9$ 3.0   **2.** $1.5 + 0.8$ 2.3   **3.** $2.23 + 1.89$ 4.12

To add and subtract decimals, line up the decimal points. Then add or subtract as with whole numbers and bring down the decimal point.

 HELP with Solving

You can add zeros following the last digit to the right of the decimal point to help you line up the decimal points.

EXAMPLE 1 Adding and Subtracting Decimals

a. $9.8 + 2.12$

$$\begin{array}{r} 9.80 \\ +\ 2.12 \\ \hline 11.92 \end{array}$$

b. $8 - 1.65$

$$\begin{array}{r} 8.00 \\ -\ 1.65 \\ \hline 6.35 \end{array}$$

NCTM CURRICULUM STANDARDS
Standard 6: Solve problems in math and other contexts
Standard 10: Create representations to communicate mathematical ideas

EXAMPLE 2 Evaluating Algebraic Expressions

Evaluate 20 − x when x = 4.71.

$$20 - x = 20 - 4.71 \qquad \text{Substitute 4.71 for } x.$$
$$= 15.29$$

Your turn now Evaluate the expression when x = 5.82 and y = 9.1.

1. $4.7 + x$ 10.52   **2.** $12.56 - y$ 3.46   **3.** $y - x$ 3.28

EXAMPLE 3 Using Mental Math to Add Decimals

Bakery Find the total cost for a sweet roll that costs $1.30, two hard rolls that cost $1.20 each, and a coffee cake that costs $3.70.

List the prices:	Rearrange the prices and group pairs of prices.	
$1.30	$1.30	
$1.20	$3.70	→ $5
$1.20	$1.20	→ $2.40 → $7.40
$3.70	$1.20	

ANSWER The bakery goods will cost $7.40.

Mental Math In Example 3, you rearranged numbers and grouped them. The properties that allow you to do this are shown below.

Properties of Addition

Commutative Property You can add numbers in any order.

    Numbers $2 + 5 = 5 + 2$ **Algebra** $a + b = b + a$

Associative Property The value of a sum does not depend on how the numbers are grouped.

    Numbers $(2 + 5) + 4 = 2 + (5 + 4)$

    Algebra $(a + b) + c = a + (b + c)$

Your turn now Tell which property is illustrated. Then find the sum.

4. $9.3 + 2.9 = 2.9 + 9.3$
commutative property; 12.2

5. $(6.4 + 4.8) + 5.2 = 6.4 + (4.8 + 5.2)$
associative property; 16.4

EXTRA EXAMPLES

Example 1 Find the sum and the difference.
a. $3.286 + 4.51$ **7.796**
b. $15 - 2.08$ **12.92**

Example 2 Evaluate $15.5 - y$ when $y = 12.719$. **2.781**

Example 3 Use mental math to find the total cost of two notebooks at $1.45 each, two pads at $.55 each, and one box of pencils at $2.75. **The total cost is $6.75.**

MULTIPLE REPRESENTATIONS
Base-ten pieces can help students understand the regrouping that occurs when they add decimals.

MATH REASONING
Just as students use specific numbers to calculate $2 + 5$ and $5 + 2$ and explore the pattern of the Commutative Property of Addition, they can look at specific examples such as $5 - 2$ and $2 - 5$ to see that there cannot be a commutative property for subtraction.

HELP with **Reading**

The *balance* in an account is the amount of money in the account. When you *deposit* money, you add to the balance. When you *withdraw* money, you take away from the balance.

EXAMPLE 4 Writing a Model

Banking You have a balance of $141.82 in an account. You withdraw $30 and then deposit a check for $41.93. What is the new balance?

Solution

Write a verbal model to help you find the new balance.

New balance = Beginning balance − Withdrawal + Deposit

$= 141.82 - 30 + 41.93$ Substitute.

$= 111.82 + 41.93$ Subtract.

$= 153.75$ Add.

ANSWER The new balance is $153.75.

✓ **Check** Use estimation to check that your answer is reasonable. Round $141.82 to $142 and $41.93 to $42. Because $142 - 30 + 42 = 154$, the answer is reasonable.

3.6 **Exercises**

More Practice, p. 710

INTERNET
eWorkbook Plus
CLASSZONE.COM

Getting Ready to Practice

1. **Vocabulary** According to the ? property, you can add numbers in any order. **commutative**

Find the sum or difference.

2. $3.6 + 1.89$ **5.49**   3. $6.54 + 12.1$ **18.64**   4. $9.8 - 7.96$ **1.84**   5. $4 - 0.25$ **3.75**

Tell which property is illustrated.

6. $3.8 + 4.1 = 4.1 + 3.8$
commutative property

7. $(3.1 + 2.1) + 9 = 3.1 + (2.1 + 9)$
associative property

8. **Guided Problem Solving** The Metro heavy rail system in Washington, D.C., has 198.7 miles of track. Cleveland's RTA has 46.7 miles of track. Boston's MBTA has 107.7 miles of track. How many more miles of track does the Metro have than the RTA and the MBTA combined?

(**1** Write a verbal model of the problem.
Number of miles = Metro miles − (RTA miles + MBTA miles)
(**2** Use the model to solve the problem.
See margin.
(**3** Check your answer using estimation.
$200 - (50 + 100) = 200 - 150 = 50$, so the answer is reasonable.

8. Step 2:
Number of miles
$= 198.7 - (46.7 + 107.7)$
$= 198.7 - 154.4$
$= 44.3$

HELP with Homework

Example	Exercises
1	9–20
2	21–26
3	27–30
4	31–32

Online Resources
CLASSZONE.COM
· More Examples
· eTutorial Plus

What do you think?

Sports

■ **Orienteering**

On a map an orienteer is using, the scale is 1 cm : 100 m. If the map of the course is 20 cm tall and 30 cm wide, what is the actual area of the course?
6,000,000 m²

Practice and Problem Solving

Find the sum or difference.

A

9. $5.56 + 3.7$ 9.26
10. $2.88 + 6.7$ 9.58
11. $16.2 + 8.34$ 24.54
12. $18.4 + 1.6$ 20.0

13. $4.091 + 5.87$ 9.961
14. $3.781 + 4.19$ 7.971
15. $5.56 - 2.3$ 3.26
16. $7.42 - 3.2$ 4.22

17. $6.18 - 1.71$ 4.47
18. $9.14 - 6.64$ 2.5
19. $4 - 1.24$ 2.76
20. $8 - 6.68$ 1.32

Algebra Evaluate the expression when $x = 2.4$ and $y = 8.75$.

21. $4.52 + x$ 6.92
22. $y + 7.5$ 16.25
23. $y - 3.01$ 5.74

24. $6.48 - x$ 4.08
25. $x + y$ 11.15
26. $y - x$ 6.35

Mental Math Tell which property is being illustrated. Then use mental math to evaluate the expression in red.

27. $(9.5 + 4.9) + 5.1 = 9.5 + (4.9 + 5.1)$ associative property; 19.5

28. $4.2 + (2.8 + 11.95) = (4.2 + 2.8) + 11.95$ associative property; 18.95

29. $1.5 + (1.74 + 3.5) = 1.5 + (3.5 + 1.74)$ commutative property; 6.74

30. $(3.7 + 8.9) + 6.3 = (8.9 + 3.7) + 6.3$ commutative property; 18.9

Estimation Solve the problem. Use estimation to check that your answer is reasonable.

31. Dining Out Your meal at a restaurant costs $5.29. Your guest's meal costs $4.95. You give the cashier $15 for the two meals. How much change should you get? **$4.76**

32. Banking You have $98 in your savings account. You withdraw $5.50 and deposit $22.75. What is the new balance? **$115.25**

Orienteering In Exercises 33 and 34, use the table at the right.
In the sport of orienteering, people use maps and compasses to find their way from point to point along an unfamiliar outdoor course. The table shows the average of the best scores of the top five women orienteers in the world at one time.

Orienteer	Average of Best Scores
Simone Luder	1422.75
Hanne Staff	1394.5
Reeta Kolkkala	1373.75
Vroni Koenig-Salmi	1371.25
Heather Monro	1362.5

B

33. How much greater was Simone Luder's score than the next best score? **28.25**

34. Find the range of the scores. **60.25**

Lesson 3.6 Adding and Subtracting Decimals **139**

3 APPLY

ASSIGNMENT GUIDE

Basic Course
Day 1: SRH p. 698 Exs. 1–3; pp. 139–140 Exs. 9–31 odd, 33–36, 41–47

Average Course
Day 1: pp. 139–140 Exs. 10–20 even, 21–27, 30–39, 41–44, 47, 48

Advanced Course
Day 1: pp. 139–140 Exs. 13–20, 24–26, 28, 29, 31–34, 37–42*, 47, 48

Block
pp. 139–140 Exs. 10–20 even, 21–27, 30–39, 41–44, 47, 48 (with 3.5)

EXTRA PRACTICE

• Student Edition, p. 710
• Chapter 3 Resource Book, pp. 54–56
• Test and Practice Generator

TRANSPARENCY

Even-numbered answers are available on transparencies.

HOMEWORK CHECK

When you review students' homework for this lesson, go over the following exercises to check understanding of key concepts.
Basic: 9, 15, 21, 27, 31
Average: 14, 24, 27, 30, 31
Advanced: 17, 25, 29, 31, 32

Differentiating Instruction

Advanced Students You may wish to challenge students by giving them exercises like Exercises 21–26, which involve more than two variables.

ASSESSMENT RESOURCES

For more assessment resources, see:
- Assessment Book
- Test and Practice Generator

MINI-QUIZ

1. Find each sum or difference.
   a. $23 - 13.57$ **9.43**
   b. $31.05 - 19.68$ **11.37**
   c. $8.07 + 19.1$ **27.17**
   d. $53.176 + 23.05$ **76.226**

2. What is the value of $17 - x$ when $x = 15.01$? When $x = 3.788$? **1.99; 13.212**

3. Your sister owes you $7.50. She pays you $5.75 and then borrows $2.30. What does she owe you now? **$4.05**

⑤ FOLLOW-UP

RETEACHING/REMEDIATION

- Study Guide in Chapter 3 Resource Book, pp. 57–58
- Tutor Place, Whole Numbers and Decimals Cards 6, 18
- eTutorial Plus Online
- Extra Practice, p. 710
- Lesson Practice in Chapter 3 Resource Book, pp. 54–56

CHALLENGE/ENRICHMENT

- Challenge Practice in Chapter 3 Resource Book, p. 60
- Teacher's Edition, p. 104F

ENGLISH LEARNER SUPPORT

- Spanish Study Guide
- Multi-Language Glossary
- Chapter Audio Summaries CDs

41. See Additional Answers beginning on page AA1.

Geometry Find the perimeter of the triangle.

35.
21 cm   7.5 cm
6 cm
7.5 cm

36.
21.45 mm   9.1 mm
6.5 mm
5.85 mm

37.
12.3 m 3.075 m   4.1 m
5.125 m

38. **Critical Thinking** Follow the order of operations to evaluate the expressions $(9.5 - 3.5) - 3.2$ and $9.5 - (3.5 - 3.2)$. Based on your results, decide whether subtraction is associative.
2.8; 9.2; subtraction is not associative.

Astronauts On a space shuttle mission, astronauts are allowed 1.5 pounds of personal items. The table shows the weights of some possible items.

Item	Weight (pounds)
2 rolls of pennies	1.12
5 golf balls	0.506
watch	0.09
college sweatshirt	0.75
whistle	0.125
camera	0.625

39. If an astronaut decides to bring 2 rolls of pennies and a watch on the mission, what other item from the list could the astronaut bring? **whistle**

40. **Challenge** What is the maximum number of different items an astronaut could bring from the list? What are they? What is their total weight? **4; 5 golf balls, watch, whistle, and either the college sweatshirt or the camera**

Mixed Review

41. Make a frequency table of the data. *(Lesson 2.4)* **See margin.**
   2, 3, 5, 9, 4, 1, 0, 2, 3, 4, 5, 6, 7, 8, 1, 3, 5, 9, 1, 3, 5, 6, 4, 5, 1

42. **Camping** According to the graph, which camping activity was favored by the least number of people surveyed? *(Lesson 2.7)* **Hiking**

Favorite Camping Activities

Canoeing   Campfire
Hiking   Swimming

Basic Skills Find the product.

43. $12 \cdot 14$ **168**
44. $30 \cdot 15$ **450**
45. $54 \cdot 16$ **864**
46. $23 \cdot 74$ **1702**

Test-Taking Practice

47. **Multiple Choice** Evaluate the expression $12.4 - 2.35 + 24.6$. **C**
   A. 44.65   **B.** 39.35   **C.** 34.65   **D.** 34.75

48. **Short Response** You buy one video tape for $19.95 and rent one for $4.29. The sales tax is $1.45. How much change should you receive if you give the cashier $30? Explain how you solved the problem.
$4.31; Add 19.95, 4.29, and 1.45; then subtract this sum from 30.00.

CALCULATOR

Technology Activity

Adding and Subtracting Decimals

GOAL Use a calculator to add and subtract decimals.

Example You can add and subtract decimals using the ➕ and ➖ keys.

A national collegiate triathlon championship consists of a 0.932 mile swim, a 24.9 mile bike ride, and a 6.21 mile run. What is the total length of the triathlon?

Solution

When using a calculator to add and subtract decimals, you do not have to worry about lining up the decimal points.

Keystrokes

0 . 932 ➕ 24 . 9 ➕ 6 . 21 =

Display

| 32.042 |

ANSWER The triathlon is 32.042 miles long.

✓ **Check** Round 0.932 to 1, 24.9 to 25, and 6.21 to 6. Because 1 + 25 + 6 = 32, the answer is reasonable.

Your turn now Use a calculator to evaluate the expression.

1. 6.705 + 0.68 7.385
2. 9.83 − 5.846 3.984
3. 12.753 − 4.1 8.653

4. 9.32 − 7.3 − 0.02 2
5. 6.942 + 3.3 − 5.39 4.852
6. 20.87 − 9.7 + 3.42 14.59

7. Geometry A triangle has side lengths of 4.5 inches, 6.2 inches, and 9.4 inches. What is the perimeter of the triangle? 20.1 in.

8. Body Temperature To convert a temperature in kelvins (K) to degrees Celsius (°C), you subtract 273.15. Normal body temperature is 310.15K. What is normal body temperature in degrees Celsius? 37°C

9. Triathlon A national triathlon championship for athletes who are 11 to 14 years old consists of a 0.114 mile swim, a 6.2 mile bike ride, and a 1.2 mile run. What is the total length of the triathlon? 7.514 mi

---

NCTM CURRICULUM STANDARDS
Standard 1: Understand numbers
Standard 6: Solve problems in math and other contexts

Lesson 3.6   Adding and Subtracting Decimals   **141**

LEARN THE METHOD

- Students will use a calculator to add and subtract decimals.
- As shown in Lesson 3.6, lining up decimal points is important. The equivalent operation on a calculator is pushing the decimal point key at the correct time.

2 TEACH

TIPS FOR SUCCESS

Some students incorrectly press the 0 key instead of the decimal point; other students might forget to press the "+" or "−" key between the numbers. You can have students check each other as they keyboard numbers and symbols.

EXTRA EXAMPLES

Example Use a calculator to add: 1.312 + 2.057 + 0.058
3.427

3 CLOSE

ASSESSMENT

Use a calculator to evaluate each expression.

1. 13.078 − 8.57 + 6.051
10.559

2. 10.95 + 16.305 − 5.06
22.195

LESSONS 3.4 TO 3.6 Notebook Review

Notebook

Review the vocabulary definitions in your notebook.

Copy the review examples in your notebook. Then complete the exercises.

Check Your Definitions

front-end estimation, p. 131   commutative property of addition, p. 137   associative property of addition, p. 137

Use Your Vocabulary

1. When you add front-end digits, is your estimate *high* or *low*? low

2. Name the property that allows you to add two numbers in any order.
commutative property

3.4–3.5 Can you round and estimate answers?

 EXAMPLE

a. Round to estimate difference.

$$
\begin{array}{rl}
16.7 & \rightarrow \quad 17 \quad \text{Round up.} \\
-\ 6.2 & \rightarrow -\ 6 \quad \text{Round down.} \\
\hline
& \quad\quad 11
\end{array}
$$

b. Use front-end estimation to the estimate the sum.

$$
\begin{array}{r}
9.67 \\
8.39 \\
+\ 4.2 \\
\hline
21
\end{array}
\quad
\begin{array}{r}
21 \\
+\ 1 \\
\hline
22
\end{array}
$$

☑ **Round the decimal as specified.**

3. 5.643 (nearest tenth) 5.6   **4.** 3.0465 (nearest thousandth) 3.047

☑ **Round to estimate the sum or difference.**

5. 3.5 + 6.8 11   **6.** 9.7 − 2.83 7   **7.** 1.42 + 3.59 + 7.98 + 4.06
17

3.6 Can you add and subtract decimals?

 EXAMPLE

a. 2.8 1 4.63

$$
\begin{array}{r}
2.80 \\
+\ 4.63 \\
\hline
7.43
\end{array}
$$
Line up the decimal points.

b. 7.61 2 5.438

$$
\begin{array}{r}
7.610 \\
-\ 5.438 \\
\hline
2.172
\end{array}
$$
Add a zero.

☑ **Add or subtract.**   **8.** 6.568 + 9.73   **9.** 12.35 − 4.062
16.298   8.288

Stop *and* **Think** about Lessons 3.4–3.6

10. Estimation When estimating a sum of decimals, explain how adjusting the sum of the leading digits alters the estimate. It increases the estimate and makes it more accurate

11. Writing Explain why you line up the decimal points when you add or subtract decimals. *Sample answer:* With the decimal points lined up, you add digits with the same place value.

Review Quiz 2

Round the decimal as specified.

1. 5.687 (nearest tenth) 5.7

2. 6.7591 (nearest hundredth) 6.76

3. 2.1295 (nearest thousandth) 2.130

4. 4.987 (nearest one) 5

Use rounding to estimate the sum or difference.

5. 6.75 + 4.17 11

6. 15.6 + 17.82 34

7. 9.15 − 3.67 5

8. 32.14 − 14.8 17

9. Buying Music You want to buy 2 CDs and 2 cassette tapes. The CDs cost $16.59 and $17.65. The cassette tapes cost $8.32 and $7.54. Use front-end estimation to estimate the total cost of your purchase.

about $50

Find the sum or difference.

10. 3.17 + 9.07
12.24

11. 5.42 + 8.93
14.35

12. 4.176 + 7.523
11.699

13. 1.39 + 14.6
15.99

14. 7.65 − 1.982
5.668

15. 13.657 − 9.4
4.257

16. 6 − 1.03 4.97

17. 9 − 7.39 1.61

18. Box Office Over a weekend, Movie A earned $14.85 million while Movie B earned $9.6 million. How much more did Movie A earn?

$5.25 million

Decimal Challenge

Complete each box with a digit from 0 to 9 and use each digit exactly once. Find the greatest possible sum, the greatest possible difference, the least possible sum, and the least possible difference. *Sample answers:* 97.531 + 86.420 = 183.951; 98.765 − 10.234 = 88.531; 10.578 + 23.469 = 34.047; 20.543 − 19.876 = 0.667

ADDITIONAL RESOURCES

The following resources are available to help review the materials in this chapter.

 Chapter 3 Resource Book
- Chapter Review Games and Activities, p. 62
- Cumulative Practice, Chs. 1–3

English/Spanish Chapter Reviews and Tests

Chapter Audio Summaries CDs

eTutorial CD-ROM

eWorkbook Plus Online

eTutorial Plus Online

Chapter Review

Vocabulary

decimal, p. 108
front-end estimation, p. 131

commutative property of addition, p. 137

associative property of addition, p. 137

Vocabulary Review

1. Write 15.368 in words.
   fifteen and three hundred sixty-eight thousandths

2. Copy and complete: When you add the front-end digits and estimate the sum of the remaining digits, you are using __?__.
   front-end estimation

3. Tell which property is illustrated:
   $6.51 + 7.21 = 7.21 + 6.51$. **commutative property**

4. Tell which property is illustrated:
   $(4.3 + 6.2) + 9.8 = 4.3 + (6.2 + 9.8)$.
   associative property

Review Questions

Write the number as a decimal. *(Lesson 3.1)*

5. twelve and two tenths **12.2**

6. nine and thirty-six hundredths **9.36**

7. six and eleven thousandths **6.011**

8. two hundred seven ten-thousandths **0.0207**

Copy and complete the statement. *(Lesson 3.2)*

9. 4 and 4 tenths meters = __?__ meters **4.4**

10. 7 and 28 hundredths meters = __?__ meters **7.28**

Measure the line segment to the nearest tenth of a centimeter. *(Lesson 3.2)*

11. **3.5 cm**

12. **2.7 cm**

Order the numbers from least to greatest. *(Lesson 3.3)*

13. 17.12, 17.02, 17.21, 17.20
    17.02, 17.12, 17.20, 17.21

14. 1.301, 1.310, 1.133, 3.011, 1.033
    1.033, 1.133, 1.301, 1.310, 3.011

40. Athens: $1.50; Hong Kong:
    $1.60; London: $.70; Los
    Angeles: $1.50; Mexico City:
    $1.10; Paris: $1.90

41. $.68, $1.13, $1.49, $1.50,
    $1.62, $1.85; Paris; London

Review Questions

Copy and complete the statement with <, >, or =. *(Lesson 3.3)*

15. 8.2 ? 7.3 >   **16.** 5.6 ? 5.1 >   **17.** 10.2 ? 13.5 <   **18.** 23.7 ? 32.7 <

19. 5.30 ? 5.3 =   **20.** 3.401 ? 3.41 <   **21.** 6.21 ? 6.215 <   **22.** 7.196 ? 7.1960 =

Round the decimal as specified. *(Lesson 3.4)*

23. 0.0068 (leading digit) 7

24. 10.226 (nearest tenth) 10.2

25. 1.606 (nearest hundredth) 1.61

26. 4.8873 (nearest thousandth) 4.887

Use rounding to estimate the sum or difference. *(Lesson 3.5)*

27. 7.5 + 3.8 12   **28.** 8.4 + 9.9 18   **29.** 6.7 − 2.8 4   **30.** 7.4 − 3.6 3

31. 5.38 + 6.65 12   **32.** 17.84 + 3.54 22   **33.** 12.71 − 3.54 9   **34.** 9.2 − 5.81 3

Use front-end estimation to estimate the sum. *(Lesson 3.5)*

35. 5.6 + 7.2 + 9.3 + 4.8 27

36. 1.02 + 3.7 + 0.8 + 6.4 12

37. 3.61 + 1.5 + 7.3 + 5.34 18

38. 3.51 + 6.30 + 9.49 + 4.72 24

39. Exercise You are exercising on a treadmill. You walk for 1.2 miles, jog for 3.7 miles, then walk for another 0.9 mile. Your goal is to walk and jog for a total of 6 miles. How much farther must you walk or jog? *(Lesson 3.6)* 0.2 mi

Food **The table shows the costs of a 24 ounce loaf of wheat bread in selected cities.** *(Lessons 3.3, 3.4, 3.6)*

City	Cost
Athens	$1.50
Hong Kong	$1.62
London	$0.68
Los Angeles	$1.49
Mexico City	$1.13
Paris	$1.85

40. Round each cost to the nearest dime. **See margin.**

41. Order the costs from least to greatest. In which city is wheat bread most expensive? least expensive?
See margin.

42. How much more does wheat bread cost in Hong Kong than in Mexico City? $0.49

Find the sum or difference. *(Lesson 3.6)*

43. 3.9 + 2.08 5.98   **44.** 4.61 + 1.015 5.625   **45.** 0.8 + 6.47 7.27   **46.** 5.372 + 3.87 9.242

47. 9.173 − 1.03 8.143   **48.** 8.32 − 2.161 6.159   **49.** 7 − 2.195 4.805   **50.** 7.62 − 4.7 2.92

Evaluate the expression when $x = 9.37$ and $y = 4.16$. *(Lesson 3.6)*

51. $15 - x$ 5.63   **52.** $2.8 + x$ 12.17   **53.** $y + 3.2$ 7.36   **54.** $6.8 - y$ 2.64

55. $3.287 + x$ 12.657   **56.** $y - 3.1$ 1.06   **57.** $5.816 - y$ 1.656   **58.** $x + y$ 13.53

Chapter Test

1. Write the number *eighteen and six thousandths* as a decimal. 18.006

2. Write 0.12 in words. twelve hundredths

3. Write 220.0022 in words. two hundred twenty and twenty-two ten-thousandths

Copy and complete the statement.

4. 6 and 4 tenths centimeters = _?_ centimeters 6.4

5. 5 and 28 hundredths meters = _?_ meters 5.28

Copy and complete the statement with <, >, or =.

6. 3.07 _?_ 3.009 >

7. 13.76 _?_ 13.760 =

8. 25.853 _?_ 25.883 <

9. 5.5912 _?_ 5.5921 <

Order the numbers from least to greatest.

10. 6.2, 6.04, 6.16, 6.02, 6.1, 6.056
6.02, 6.04, 6.056, 6.1, 6.16, 6.2

11. 0.056, 0.49, 0.509, 0.0487, 0.005
0.005, 0.0487, 0.056, 0.49, 0.509

Round the decimal as specified.

12. 10.0962 (nearest tenth) 10.1

13. 14.925 (nearest hundredth) 14.93

14. 0.5691 (nearest thousandth) 0.569

15. 0.00291 (leading digit) 0.003

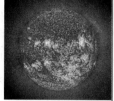

16. **Astronomy** The diameter of the Sun is about 1,392,000 kilometers. Round the diameter to the nearest hundred thousand. Then write the rounded diameter as a decimal number of millions. 1,400,000; 1.4 million

Use rounding to estimate the sum or difference.

17. 6.9 + 0.8 8

18. 12.4 + 10.7 23

19. 15.2 − 9.9 5

20. 5.7 − 2.8 3

Use front-end estimation to estimate the sum.

21. 4.39 + 1.84 + 5.62 + 9.1 21

22. 2.07 + 1.74 + 1.24 + 2.88 8

Find the sum or difference.

23. 18.79 + 3.6 22.39

24. 10.29 + 19.71 30

25. 6.073 − 5.02 1.053

26. 7.5 − 1.54 5.96

27. Tell which property is illustrated: (10 + 2.9) + 7.1 = 10 + (2.9 + 7.1). associative property

28. **Computers** Your computer's hard drive has 20 gigabytes of memory, and you are currently using 5.93 gigabytes. How much memory is available on your computer? 14.07 gigabytes

Chapter Standardized Test

Test-taking Strategy Make sure you understand the question before looking for the answer.

Multiple Choice

1. Write *fourteen and fifteen ten-thousandths* as a decimal. **D**

   A. 1.415   **B.** 14.15   **C.** 14.015   **D.** 14.0015

2. Complete the statement with the correct decimal: 2 and 21 hundredths meters equals _?_ meters. **I**

   F. 2.0   **G.** 2.0021   **H.** 2.021   **I.** 2.21

3. 55 centimeters is what decimal part of a meter? **A**

   A. 0.55   **B.** 0.505   **C.** 0.055   **D.** 0.0055

4. Which number is greater than 0.84 and less than 0.845? **H**

   F. 0.8   **G.** 0.82   **H.** 0.843   **I.** 0.847

5. A baseball team manager lists the batting averages of four players on the team. Which list shows their batting averages in order from greatest to least? **D**

   A. 0.298, 0.336, 0.283, 0.332
   B. 0.336, 0.332, 0.283, 0.298
   C. 0.283, 0.298, 0.332, 0.336
   D. 0.336, 0.332, 0.298, 0.283

6. Round 4.658 to the nearest hundredth. **G**

   F. 4.6   **G.** 4.66   **H.** 4.67   **I.** 4.7

7. You buy a new carpet on sale for $829.99. The regular price for the carpet is $1483.99. What is the best estimate of the total amount you save? **B**

   A. $300   **B.** $700   **C.** $1000   **D.** $2200

8. Your friend buys a blouse for $28.95, a pair of sandals for $39.95, and a pair of shorts for $19.90. How much do the three items cost? **H**

   F. $68.90   **G.** $78.80   **H.** $88.80   **I.** $88.85

9. What value of x makes the statement true? **B**

   $$5.6 + (0.3 + 4.9) = (5.6 + x) + 4.9$$

   A. 0   **B.** 0.3   **C.** 4.9   **D.** 5.6

10. Evaluate the expression $x + 10.75 - 7.71$ when $x = 2.46$. **H**

   F. 3.04   **G.** 4.5   **H.** 5.5   **I.** 16

Short Response

11. At a department store, you buy a sweater for $29.99, a notebook for $3.79, and a CD for $11.99. You give the cashier $50. About how much change should you expect? Explain your reasoning. **See margin.**

Extended Response

12. The population of Los Angeles has grown rapidly in the last 50 years. The table shows the population of Los Angeles in several different years. Round the data to the nearest hundred thousand. Write each number as a decimal number of millions. Then display your results in a bar graph. About how much did the population grow, in millions, between the years 1960 and 2000? Explain. **See margin for art. The population grew by about 1.2 million between 1960 and 2000. The population was about 2.5 million in 1960 and about 3.7 million in 2000.**

Year	Population
1960	2,479,015
1970	2,816,061
1980	2,966,850
1990	3,485,398
2000	3,694,820

ADDITIONAL RESOURCES

 Assessment Book
  • Standardized Chapter Test, p. 37

 Test and Practice Generator

11. About $4. *Sample answer:* You spent about $30 + $4 + $12 = $46. Since $50 − $46 = $4, that is about how much change you should expect.

12. a. 1960: 2,500,000; 1970: 2,800,000; 1980: 3,000,000; 1990: 3,500,000; 2000: 3,700,000

c. Population Growth in Los Angeles

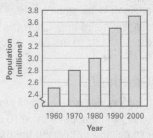

EXPLORE THE CONCEPT

- Students make and interpret bar graphs.
- Bar graphs were studied in Lesson 2.5. Mean was studied in Lesson 2.8.
- The bear population can be estimated by counting the number of females with cubs each year.

SCIENCE BACKGROUND

Conservation biologists and other scientists monitor the populations of various species of animals by collecting and analyzing data. The grizzly bears of Yellowstone National Park are monitored to see how the bears are adjusting to the park conditions.

GROUPING

Students can do the activity individually, or in groups of three so they can discuss patterns in the data.

② **TEACH**

TIPS FOR SUCCESS

For Exercises 1–3, you may want students to do the bar graphs in groups of three. Have one student make the bar graph showing the number of female bears, another student can do the bar graph of the cub data, and the third student can record patterns the group notices between the graphs.

GUIDING STUDENTS' WORK

For Exercises 1–3, suggest students label the horizontal axis from 1970 to 2000 by 2s, and the vertical axis from 0 to 40 by 5s. For Exercises 4–6, suggest labeling the vertical axis in tenths from 1.5 to 2.5.

1–2. See Additional Answers beginning on page AA1.

EXPLORING MATH IN SCIENCE

The Grizzlies of Yellowstone

Monitoring the Grizzlies

The grizzly bears of Yellowstone National Park used to feed on garbage dumps in the park. When the dumps were closed in 1967, the amount of food available to the grizzlies was reduced. At first many grizzlies did not survive. For a number of years, scientists have been monitoring the grizzly population of Yellowstone to see how the bears are adjusting to more natural conditions.

The population is hard to count because the bears live in remote places and avoid humans. One way to estimate the total population is to count how many female bears are sighted with a new litter of cubs each year.

Grizzly Bear Counts in Yellowstone National Park					
Year	Females	Cubs	Year	Females	Cubs
1974	15	26	1988	19	41
1976	17	32	1990	25	58
1978	9	19	1992	25	60
1980	12	23	1994	20	47
1982	11	20	1996	33	72
1984	17	31	1998	35	70
1986	25	48	2000	37	72

The table above shows how many female bears with new litters were sighted and the total number of new cubs for even-numbered years from 1974 to 2000. Use the table for Exercises 1–3.

1. Use the data to make a bar graph showing the number of female bears with new litters. Put years on the horizontal axis and put the number of females on the vertical axis.   1–2. See margin.

2. Use the cub data to make a bar graph similar to the one you made in Exercise 1.

3. What patterns do you notice in these two graphs?

Sample answer: As the number of females increased, the number of cubs increased; both the number of females and the number of cubs increased over the years.

Comparing Litter Sizes

Female grizzlies usually have two cubs in a litter but sometimes have as many as four. The table below shows the average litter size for the grizzlies in Yellowstone in different years. Because the numbers are averages, some of them are decimals.

Average Litter Sizes			
Year	Average Litter Size	Year	Average Litter Size
1974	1.7	1988	2.2
1976	1.9	1990	2.3
1978	2.1	1992	2.4
1980	1.9	1994	2.4
1982	1.8	1996	2.2
1984	1.8	1998	2.0
1986	1.9	2000	2.0

4. In what year(s) was the average litter size the greatest? In what year(s) was it the least? What was the difference between the greatest and least average litter sizes? **1992 and 1994; 1974; 0.7**

5. Make a bar graph of the data. What patterns, if any, do you notice about the data? Did the litter size increase over time? **See margin.**

6. **Critical Thinking** Based on the three graphs you have made, do you think the bears in Yellowstone are making a successful recovery after the closing of the garbage dumps? Explain your reasoning.
Yes. *Sample answer:* **There are more females and cubs in 2000 than in 1974.**

Project IDEAS

- **Predict** Based on the data given, how many females with new litters do you think were sighted in 2002? How many new cubs?
  about 38; about 75
- **Report** Find out more about Yellowstone Park. What other animals live there? Present your findings to the class. **A good answer will include the names of several animals other than the grizzly bear and a good presentation.**
- **Research** Find out more about the grizzly bear. What kinds of food does it eat? What climates does it live in? Do grizzlies hibernate? Present your findings to the class.
  A good answer will include well-documented research.
- **Career** The scientists who monitor the grizzlies are called conservation biologists. Find out what other kinds of work conservation biologists do. Present your findings to the class.
  A good answer will include well-documented research and a good presentation.

INTERNET
Project Support
CLASSZONE.COM

REFLECTING ON THE ACTIVITY

The data in the activity supports the belief that grizzly bears have adjusted well to the natural conditions in Yellowstone National Park.

PROJECT IDEAS

For additional information on the Project Ideas and for suggestions for more projects, go to classzone.com

④ ASSESS

The rubric below can be used to assess the project on the pupil pages. For more information on rubrics, see the Professional Development Book.

1 The student fully achieves the mathematical and project goals. The graphs are drawn and labeled correctly. All questions are answered. All work is complete and accurate.

2 The student substantially achieves the mathematical and project goals. There may be small errors in the graphs or in the answers to the questions. There may be some minor misunderstanding of content, errors in computation, or weakness in presentation.

3 The student partially achieves the mathematical and project goals. Some graphs may not have been done, or some of the questions may not have been answered. Some of the work may be incomplete, misdirected, or unclear.

4 The student makes little progress toward accomplishing the goals of the project due to a lack of understanding or effort. The student did not draw the graphs or did not answer the questions.

5. See Additional Answers beginning on page AA1.

Pacing and Assignment Guide

REGULAR SCHEDULE

Lesson	Les. Day	BASIC	AVERAGE	ADVANCED
4.1	Day 1	SRH p. 694 Exs. 13-20; pp. 156-157 Exs. 9-11, 16-21, 30-33, 39	pp. 156-157 Exs. 9-15, 30-33, 42-47	pp. 156-157 Exs. 10-15, 30-33, 39, 40, 42-44, 52
	Day 2	pp. 156-157 Exs. 12-14, 22-29, 34-36, 42-52	pp. 156-157 Exs. 20-29, 34-40, 48-53	pp. 156-157 Exs. 22-29, 34-38, 41*, 46-48, 53
4.2	Day 1	EP p. 708 Exs. 29-32; pp. 161-162 Exs. 7-12, 20, 21, 38, 40, 44-49	pp. 161-162 Exs. 7-14, 20, 21, 34-36, 38-40, 45-48	pp. 161-162 Exs. 11-19, 35, 40, 46-49, 53, 54
	Day 2	pp. 161-162 Exs. 13-18, 22-27, 32-35, 37, 50-54	pp. 161-162 Exs. 15-19, 22-33, 37, 52-54	pp. 161-162 Exs. 20-25, 30-33, 36-38, 41-43*
4.3	Day 1	SRH p. 690 Exs. 5-10; pp. 167-168 Exs. 8-14, 31-38	pp. 167-168 Exs. 8-14, 33-38, 45-51, 54	pp. 167-168 Exs. 10-14, 33-42, 49, 54
	Day 2	pp. 167-168 Exs. 15-23, 27-29, 39, 40, 45-54	pp. 167-168 Exs. 15-32, 39-43, 55	pp. 167-168 Exs. 18-30, 43-48*, 55
4.4	Day 1	SRH p. 691 Exs. 5-8; pp. 171-173 Exs. 9-23, 28-31, 34, 35, 38-40, 42-45, 49-65	pp. 171-173 Exs. 9-11, 16-29, 32-36, 40-47, 51-62, 66	pp. 171-173 Exs. 10, 11, 20-29, 32-37, 40-50*, 55-58, 65, 66
4.5	Day 1	SRH p. 690 Exs. 11-16, p. 706 Exs. 3-7; pp. 178-179 Exs. 12-28, 30-33, 36-39, 42-54	pp. 178-179 Exs. 12-33, 36-39, 42-51, 54, 55	pp. 178-179 Exs. 12-15, 22-29, 34-41*, 44-48, 54, 55
4.6	Day 1	SRH p. 695 Exs. 17-22; pp. 182-184 Exs. 11-29 odd, 31-33, 37-47, 55-57, 63-74	pp. 182-184 Exs. 12-30 even, 31-38, 41-54, 58-60, 64-68, 71-75	pp. 182-184 Exs. 15-18, 27-38, 43-53, 56-62*, 65-70, 74, 75
4.7	Day 1	EP p. 709 Exs. 2-4; pp. 189-190 Exs. 8-26, 30-33, 38-49	pp. 189-190 Exs. 8-20, 24-35, 39-45, 48, 49	pp. 189-190 Exs. 12-23, 27-29, 33-43*, 48, 49
4.8	Day 1	pp. 193-195 Exs. 7-23, 41, 44	pp. 193-195 Exs. 7-27, 50-55	pp. 193-195 Exs. 9-14, 18-27, 47-55*
	Day 2	pp. 193-195 Exs. 26-38, 48-51, 53-59 odd, 60-62	pp. 193-195 Exs. 28-39, 41-45, 56-62	pp. 193-195 Exs. 30-46, 62
Review	Day 1	pp. 198-199 Exs. 1-79	pp. 198-199 Exs. 1-79	pp. 198-199 Exs. 1-79
Assess	Day 1	Chapter 4 Test	Chapter 4 Test	Chapter 4 Test

YEARLY PACING   Chapter 4 Total – **14 days**   Chapters 1–4 Total – **46 days**   Remaining – **114 days**

*Challenge Exercises   EP = Extra Practice   SRH = Skills Review Handbook   EC = Extra Challenge

BLOCK SCHEDULE

DAY 1	DAY 2	DAY 3	DAY 4	DAY 5	DAY 6	DAY 7
4.1 pp. 156-157 Exs. 9-40, 42-53	**4.2** pp. 161-162 Exs. 7-40, 45-48, 52-54	**4.3** pp. 167-168 Exs. 8-43, 45-51, 54, 55	**4.4** pp. 171-173 Exs. 9-11, 16-29, 32-36, 40-47, 51-62, 66 **4.5** pp. 178-179 Exs. 12-33, 36-39, 42-51, 54, 55	**4.6** pp. 182-184 Exs. 12-30 even, 31-38, 41-54, 58-60, 64-68, 71-75 **4.7** pp. 189-190 Exs. 8-20, 24-35, 39-45, 48, 49	**4.8** pp. 193-195 Exs. 7-39, 41-45, 50-62	**Review** pp. 198-199 Exs. 1-79 **Assess** Chapter 4 Test

YEARLY PACING   Chapter 4 Total – **7 days**   Chapters 1–4 Total – **23 days**   Remaining – **57 days**

Support Materials

📖 CHAPTER RESOURCE BOOK

CHAPTER SUPPORT

| Tips for New Teachers | p. 1 | | | Parents as Partners | | | p. 3 | |

LESSON SUPPORT

	4.1	4.2	4.3	4.4	4.5	4.6	4.7	4.8
Lesson Plans (regular and block)	p. 8	p. 18	p. 27	p. 36	p. 47	p. 55	p. 63	p. 71
Technology Activities & Keystrokes	p. 10							p. 73
Activity Support Masters			p. 29					
Activity Masters		p. 20						
Practice (3 levels)	p. 11	p. 21	p. 30	p. 38	p. 49	p. 57	p. 65	p. 74
Study Guide	p. 14	p. 24	p. 33	p. 41	p. 52	p. 60	p. 68	p. 77
Real-World Problem Solving	p. 16			p. 43				
Challenge Practice	p. 17	p. 26	p. 35	p. 44	p. 54	p. 62	p. 70	p. 79

REVIEW

Games Support Masters	pp. 5, 45	Cooperative Project with Rubric	p. 83
Chapter Review Games and Activities	p. 80	Extra Credit Project with Rubric	p. 85
Real-Life Project with Rubric	p. 81	Cumulative Practice	p. 87
		Resource Book Answers	A1

📖 ASSESSMENT

Quizzes	p. 40	Alternative Assessments with Rubrics	p. 49
Chapter Tests (3 levels)	p. 42	Unit Test	p. 51
Standardized Test	p. 48	Cumulative Test	p. 53

📑 TRANSPARENCIES

	4.1	4.2	4.3	4.4	4.5	4.6	4.7	4.8
Warm-Up / Daily Homework Quiz	✔	✔	✔	✔	✔	✔	✔	✔
Notetaking Guide	✔	✔	✔	✔	✔	✔	✔	✔
Teacher Support	✔		✔				✔	
English/Spanish Problem Solving		✔		✔	✔	✔		
Answer Transparencies	✔	✔	✔	✔	✔	✔	✔	✔

💻 TECHNOLOGY

- EasyPlanner CD-ROM
- Test and Practice Generator
- Electronic Lesson Presentations
- eTutorial CD-ROM
- Chapter Audio Summaries CDs
- Classzone.com
- eEdition Plus Online
- eWorkbook Plus Online
- eTutorial Plus Online
- EasyPlanner Plus Online

ADDITIONAL RESOURCES

- Worked-Out Solution Key
- Notetaking Guide
- Practice Workbook
- Tutor Place
- Professional Development Book
- Activities Book
- Poster Package
- Spanish Study Guide
- English/Spanish Chapter Reviews
- Multi-Language Glossary

Math Background and Teaching Strategies

Lesson 4.1

MATH BACKGROUND

MULTIPLICATION The **Commutative** and **Associative Properties of Multiplication** apply to whole numbers and decimals. When multiplying a decimal by a whole number, the number of decimal places in the product is the same as the number of decimal places in the decimal factor. Rounding the decimal factor to a whole number and finding the product of the two whole numbers is one way to check whether or not the product obtained with the original factors is reasonable.

TEACHING STRATEGIES

When students are learning to multiply decimals, the use of estimation to check the reasonableness of a product is important. Pose the following problem to the class: Judy fills 4 containers with 2.8 liters of juice. How many liters of juice does she have in all? Have the students estimate by asking questions involving estimation: Could the answer be more than 12 liters? Could it be 8 liters? Then ask students to use any method to find an exact answer.

Lesson 4.2

MATH BACKGROUND

The **Distributive Property of Multiplication over Addition** establishes that for numbers a, b, and c,

$$a(b + c) = ab + ac.$$

By extension, multiplication also distributes over subtraction:

$$a(b - c) = ab - ac.$$

TEACHING STRATEGIES

Explain to students that the Distributive Property gives them the opportunity to break apart a multiplication problem to make two simpler problems. Give them examples that will help them see that the Distributive Property can help them find sums or differences very easily.

Examples

$$
\begin{aligned}
9(43) &= 9 \times (40 + 3) \\
&= 9 \times 40 + 9 \times 3 \\
&= 360 + 27 \\
&= 387
\end{aligned}
$$

$$
\begin{aligned}
6 \times 99 &= 6 \times (100 - 1) \\
&= (6 \times 100) - (6 \times 1) \\
&= 600 - 6 \\
&= 594
\end{aligned}
$$

Lesson 4.3

MATH BACKGROUND

There is one important rule to remember when multiplying decimals: ***The number of decimal places in the product must equal the total number of decimal places in the factors.*** The justification of this rule can be based upon area models as shown in the text.

TEACHING STRATEGIES

One point where students might need help is in understanding the importance of showing all zeros in a product in order to help them correctly place the decimal point. Work through several examples with students.

Lesson 4.4

MATH BACKGROUND

DIVISION When you divide a decimal by a whole number, the quotient has as many digits to the right of the decimal points as the dividend has. Thus, you can place the decimal point in the quotient directly above the decimal point in the dividend and divide as if the numbers were whole numbers.

TEACHING STRATEGIES

It is easier for students to decide where the decimal point belongs in a quotient if they use graph paper or paper with vertical rules to help them align digits when dividing. If they work carefully, the decimal point in the quotient will align with the decimal point in the dividend.

Lesson 4.5

MATH BACKGROUND

POWERS OF 10 The powers of 10 are $10^1 = 10$, $10^2 = 100$, $10^3 = 1000$, and so on. Thus, the positive exponent of a power of 10 will always be the same as the number of zeros in the standard form. When you multiply a decimal by a power of 10, the decimal point moves to the right the number of places designated by the exponent.

$2.435 \times 10^1 = 24.35$ Moves 1 place right.
$2.435 \times 10^2 = 243.5$ Moves 2 places right.
$2.435 \times 10^3 = 2435$ Moves 3 places right.

When you divide a decimal by a power of 10, the decimal point moves to the left—the opposite direction—the number of places designated by the exponent.

$2.435 \div 10^1 = 0.2435$ Moves 1 place left.
$2.435 \div 10^2 = 0.02435$ Moves 2 places left.
$2.435 \div 10^3 = 0.002435$ Moves 3 places left.

TEACHING STRATEGIES

Work through the following examples with the students.

$23.42 \times 10 = 234.2$	Multiply—move to the right.
$23.42 \div 10 = 2.342$	Divide—move to the left.
$0.04 \times 1000 = 40$	Multiply—move to the right. Add zeros as needed.
$0.040 \div 1000 = 0.00004$	Divide—move to the left. Add zeros as needed.

Lesson 4.6

MATH BACKGROUND

To change a division problem like $45.36 \div 1.2$ to $453.6 \div 12$, where the divisor is a whole number, begin by multiplying 1.2 by 10. To ensure that the quotient will not change, also multiply the dividend 45.36 by 10.

TEACHING STRATEGIES

Ask students how they might find the quotient $4.32 \div 1.8$. Remind them that multiplying 1.8 by 10 will changes the divisor to 18 and explain that they should also multiply 4.32 by 10 so the quotient will not change. Thus,

$$4.32 \div 1.8 = 43.2 \div 18.$$

Lesson 4.7

MATH BACKGROUND

METRIC MEASURES Within the metric system, the gram is the fundamental unit of mass, and the liter is the fundamental unit of capacity. Since the metric system is a base-ten system, other units are related to the gram and the liter by powers of 10.

TEACHING STRATEGIES

Use common objects to help students get a feel for metric units of mass and capacity. For example, a paper clip and a math book can help students understand how a gram compares to a kilogram. Similarly, an eyedropper and a liter bottles can help students understand how a milliliter compares to a liter.

Lesson 4.8

MATH BACKGROUND

Because the metric system is a base-ten system, you simply need to multiply or divide by powers of 10 to convert between units. The relationships are:

1. The prefix *kilo-* means 1000 times the basic unit.

2. The prefix *centi-* means $\frac{1}{100}$ of the basic unit.

3. The prefix *milli-* means $\frac{1}{1000}$ of the basic unit.

TEACHING STRATEGIES

Give examples of measures such as 50 meters and ask what you need to do to change the measure to centimeters. Then ask what you need to do to change the measure to kilometers. Give enough examples so that students know that to change to a smaller unit, they should multiply by a positive power of 10 and that to change to a larger unit, they should divide by a positive power of 10.

Differentiating Instruction

Strategies for Underachievers

MANIPULATIVES AND TOOLS FOR CONCRETE LEARNING

Many students, especially concrete learners, learn better if they are able to see, touch, and manipulate objects that represent the concept being taught. Chapter 4 provides many opportunities for you to reach these learners.

In Lesson 4.1, these students should be shown how to multiply a decimal number by a whole number, using base-ten blocks. Each student should have his/her own set to manipulate. In Lesson 4.3, when multiplying a decimal by a decimal, and in Lesson 4.6, when using long division, grid paper is an excellent tool to help students to organize and keep neat their work, thereby reducing careless errors. In Lessons 4.7 and 4.8, students should be given ample opportunities to hold, feel, weigh, and measure the mass of objects in order to develop a connection to the actual sizes of grams, meters, and so on.

VOCABULARY DEVELOPMENT

Provide a teacher-created or a student-created word bank for lessons that are rich in mathematics vocabulary. In Lessons 4.7 and 4.8, some students will need a word bank and chart of the metric prefixes and should have access to this whenever they are converting between units.

THINKING OUT LOUD

VERBALIZING PROCEDURES Sometimes mathematical procedures become so automatic to adults that they do not even realize all the steps they have taken. For example, in Exercise 28 on page 182, there are several steps that students need to learn explicitly. Teachers can talk through their own thinking while solving the problem. After students become familiar with their teacher's thinking, they should be asked to express their own thinking out loud. This gives the teacher an excellent opportunity to determine where students may be confused. Long division problems, such as this problems involving decimals, involve many distinct steps, all of which students must complete correctly.

Example Divide 6.2 by 0.7. Round the answer to the nearest tenth, if necessary.

Solution (The teacher should think out loud for the class.) "I know that I have to divide by a whole number, so I multiply 0.7 by 10 to get a divisor of 7. I know that I must also multiply the dividend 6.2 by 10, so the new dividend is 62. The problem is now 62 ÷ 7. I must write the decimal point to the right of the 2, in case I need to add zeroes to the dividend. Also, at this time, I will write the decimal point in the quotient directly above the decimal point in the dividend. Now, I am ready to divide. Since 7 × 8 = 56, I will write an 8 in the quotient to the left of the decimal point and above the 2 in the dividend. I subtract 56 from 62 to get a difference of 6. Since the remainder is not zero, I need to add a zero to the dividend to the right of the decimal point. I will then bring down this zero and divide 60 by 7, again getting 8. I will write this 8 to the right of the decimal point in the quotient, and I will subtract 56 from 60, getting 4. I know that in order to round to the nearest tenth, I divide out to the hundredths place to determine whether to round the tenths digit up or to leave it as is. So I need to add another zero to the dividend, which I will bring down and divide 40 by 7, getting 5. I will write the 5 to the right of 8.8 in the quotient, making 8.85. Now I need to round my quotient to the nearest tenth. Since the number in the hundredths place is 5, I must round the quotient 8.85 to 8.9."

Note the number of steps and amount of vocabulary that are needed to solve just one long division problem. All students will need to practice these types of problems. If students have to explain what steps they are taking it will help you to determine where they are making mistakes. Having students communicate mathematically with good math vocabulary will help them with responses to open-response or open-ended problems as well.

Strategies for English Learners

DISSECT WORD PROBLEMS

In many contexts, including on standardized tests, students will need to be able to decipher word problems.

Word problems are particularly difficult for English learners. Providing a bilingual dictionary and additional time helps English learners improve their scores on word problems. Fortunately, most word problems follow a standard format, and there are clues provided by "signal words," words that signal what will follow or what came before. Most word problems also contain numbers, and usually you must do something with the numbers to solve the problems. Analyzing the units in a problem can provide a clue as to the answer that is needed. English learners often use these strategies without thinking about them, although when they encounter a difficult word problem, they may use the strategies overtly.

Examine the following example with your students.

TRAVEL It takes you 2.5 hours by train to get to a neighboring city. The train travels at a constant speed of 40 miles per hour. How far away is the neighboring city?

Point out the following features:

Heading (optional) *TRAVEL*	A word or short phrase at the beginning gives you a clue about the problem but is not usually needed to solve the problem.
First sentence *It takes you 2.5 hours by train to get to a neighboring city.*	Sometimes the first sentence is a background sentence that provides more context, but usually it provides the first fact or number you will need to work with, in this case *2.5 hours*.
Second sentence *The train travels at a constant speed of 40 miles per hour.*	The second sentence usually gives you the second fact or number you will be working with, in this case *40 miles per hour*.
Third sentence *How far away is the neighboring city?*	The last sentence or two sentences often contain either a command verb, or one of the following words or phrases: *who, what, when, where, why, how many, how much, which, how long, how far*. These signal words are usually followed closely by a description of what you are supposed to provide in your answer. In this case you are to answer *how far away is the neighboring city?*

Strategies for Advanced Learners

INCREASE DEPTH AND COMPLEXITY

Students may be intrigued by the fact that division by certain divisors creates repeating decimals in the quotient. Students who are comfortable with the division algorithm can proceed with the following challenge activity for use with **Lesson 4.4**.

- **Challenge** Have students complete various division exercises using the numbers 3, 6, 9, and 11 as divisors. Be certain that the dividends are not multiples of the divisors. Students may enjoy starting with dividing the counting numbers by 9 and investigating the patterns that occur. $1 \div 9 = 0.111...$, $2 \div 9 = 0.222...$, and so on. They can then investigate the patterns created by the other divisors. Students who still need an extra challenge can investigate division by 7, 13, and 14. Division by 6 could introduce an interesting investigation into how a supermarket charges for individual items that are priced at 6 for $1.00. Check work.

At the completion of **Chapter 4** students can do the following challenge activity.

- **Challenge** Have students investigate the real-world application of multiplication and division of decimal numbers. One interesting topic could be Olympic or World records in sports that involve times or distances using decimal places. Students could use their multiplication and division skills to find unit rates. For example, if an athlete runs 100 meters in 9.8 seconds, how long does it take that athlete to run 1 meter or 200 meters at that same rate? Students should consider if this rate is reasonable and can research the 100-meter and 200-meter records and compare them. Check work.

Differentiating Instruction: Teaching Resources

Differentiating Review, Reteaching, and Remediation

McDougal Littell *Middle School Mathematics* offers teachers a wide variety of reteaching and remediation resources. Pictured here are facsimiles of various pages from the *Notetaking Guide*, the Study Guide pages from the *Chapter 4 Resource Book*, and remediation cards from *Tutor Place*.

NOTETAKING GUIDE

The *Notetaking Guide* easily allows students to take notes on and review each lesson in the textbook by using guided examples and Your Turn Now exercises. The *Notetaking Guide* is available on transparencies also.

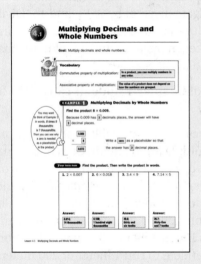
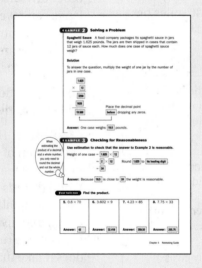

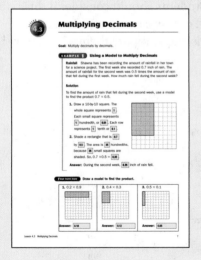
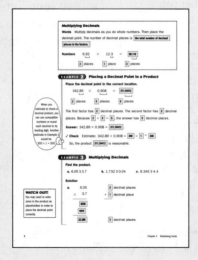
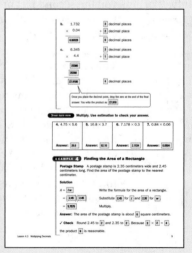

RESOURCE BOOK

The *Chapter Resource Books* contain Study Guide pages with reteaching examples and exercises for each lesson in the textbook. Pictured below are Study Guide pages from the *Chapter 4 Resource Book*. (The Study Guide pages are also available in Spanish in the *Spanish Study Guide*.)

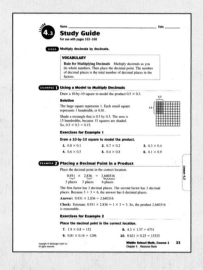

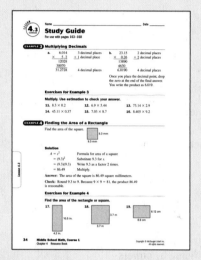

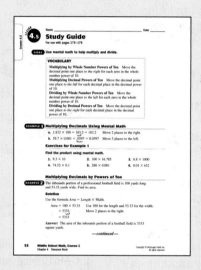

TUTOR PLACE

Tutor Place helps students practice and master essential topics. Instruction is provided by 104 cards containing examples and two sets of practice exercises. Answers are provided in a handy answer key.

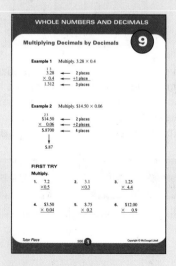

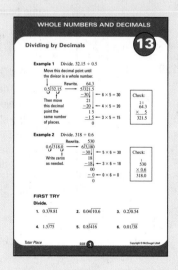

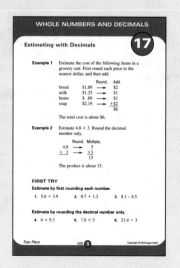

OVERVIEW

MAIN IDEAS

In this chapter, students continue to investigate decimals. They start by using the distributive property and area models to develop skill in multiplying with decimals. They explore multiplying and dividing by powers of 10 and then explore dividing decimals by whole numbers or by other decimals. Students also use metric measurements for mass, capacity, and length.

PREREQUISITE SKILLS

The key skills reviewed in the game on these pages are:
- Multiplying and dividing whole numbers
- Finding the quotient and remainder for a division problem
- Estimating products and quotients

Additional practice with prerequisite skills can be found in the Review What You Need to Know exercises on page 152. Additional resources for reviewing prerequisite skills are:
- Skills Review Handbook, pp. 684–707
- Tutor Place
- eTutorial Plus Online

MANAGING THE GAME

Tips for Success

Be sure students understand the conditions stated on each space of the game board before they begin to play.

Reflecting on the Game

As a follow-up to Stop and Think Question 2, ask students which spaces require exact products or quotients and which do not.

4 Decimal Multiplication and Division

BEFORE

In previous chapters you've...

- **Multiplied and divided whole numbers**
- **Added and subtracted decimals**

Now

In Chapter 4 you'll study...

- **Multiplying and dividing decimals**
- **Multiplying and dividing by powers of ten**
- **Measuring mass and capacity**

WHY?

So you can solve real-world problems about...

- car washes, p. 159
- sports cards, p. 169
- ice hockey, p. 179
- mountain climbing, p. 189

Internet Preview
CLASSZONE.COM

- eEdition Plus Online
- eWorkbook Plus Online
- eTutorial Plus Online
- State Test Practice
- More Examples

Chapter Warm-Up Game

Review skills you need for this chapter in this game. Work with a partner.

Key Skills:
- Multiplying and dividing whole numbers
- Estimating products and quotients

OPERATION COVER-UP

MATERIALS

- 1 deck of *Operation Cover-up* cards

- 2 *Operation Cover-up* game boards

PREPARE Each player uses his or her own game board. Players share the deck of cards. First shuffle the deck, then place it face down between the two players. On each turn, each player should follow the steps on the next page. Wait until both players are done before beginning the next turn.

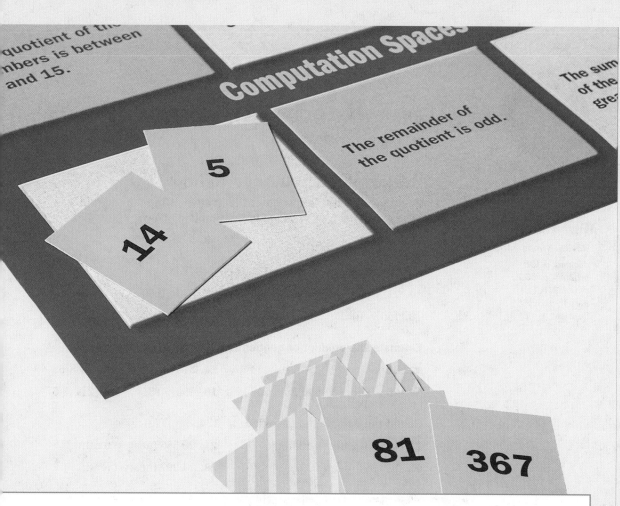

Computation Spaces

...quotient of the ...bers is between ...and 15.

The remainder of the quotient is odd.

The sum of the... of the... gre...

5

14

81 367

1 **DRAW** 2 cards. Each card has a number.

2 **DECIDE** whether the numbers form a product or a quotient that satisfies one of the conditions on a space on your game board.

3 **COVER** the space with your cards. If your numbers do not satisfy any of the conditions that are uncovered, discard them.

HOW TO WIN Be the first player to cover all 6 spaces on your game board, or be the player with the most spaces covered when you run out of cards. **Check work.**

1. *Sample answer:* I would estimate and then compute.

Stop *and* Think

1. **Writing** What strategies do you recommend for someone playing this game? For example, do you recommend that players estimate before computing? Or should players compute before estimating?

2. **Critical Thinking** Explain why you don't need to perform an exact computation to determine that the product of two numbers is between 5000 and 15,000.
Sample answer: The range between 5000 and 15,000 is great, so an exact answer would not be necessary.

151

CHAPTER RESOURCES

These resources are provided to help you prepare for the chapter and to customize review materials:

 Chapter 4 Resource Book
- Tips for New Teachers, pp. 1–2
- Lesson Plan, pp. 8, 18, 27, 36, 47, 55, 63, 71
- Lesson Plan for Block Scheduling, pp. 9, 19, 28, 37, 48, 56, 64, 72

 Technology
- EasyPlanner CD-ROM
- Test and Practice Generator
- Electronic Lesson Presentations CD-ROM
- eTutorial CD-ROM

 Internet
- Classzone
- eEdition Plus Online
- eWorkbook Plus Online
- eTutorial Plus Online
- EasyPlanner Plus Online

ENGLISH LEARNER SUPPORT

- Spanish Study Guide
- Multi-Language Glossary
- Chapter Audio Summaries CDs
- Teacher's Edition, pp. 150E–150F

Getting Ready to Learn

Review What You Need to Know

Using Vocabulary Tell whether the number is the *divisor*, *quotient*, or *dividend* in the problem shown.

$$4\overline{)52} \quad \frac{13}{}$$

1. 52 dividend   **2.** 13 quotient   **3.** 4 divisor

Find the product or quotient. *(pp. 690–691)*

4. 71×100 7100 **5.** 6×1000 6000 **6.** 95×1000 95,000 **7.** 138×100 13,800

8. $150 \div 10$ 15 **9.** $1640 \div 10$ 164 **10.** $2300 \div 100$ 23 **11.** $500 \div 100$ 5

Estimate the product or quotient. *(p. 12)* 12–19. Estimates may vary.

12. 32×46 1500 **13.** 119×11 1200 **14.** 315×4 1500 **15.** 78×62 4800

16. $25 \div 8$ 3 **17.** $36 \div 5$ 7 **18.** $158 \div 83$ 2 **19.** $211 \div 67$ 3

Round the decimal as specified. *(p. 124)*

20. 1.068 (nearest hundredth) 1.07 **21.** 28.556 (nearest tenth) 28.6

22. 5.21354 (nearest thousandth) 5.214 **23.** 14.997 (nearest tenth) 15.0

Word Watch

Review Words

decimal, p. 108
product, p. 690
dividend, p. 691
divisor, p. 691
quotient, p. 691

You should include material that appears on a notebook like this in your own notes.

Know How to Take Notes

Previewing the Chapter Before you start a lesson or chapter, look at what you are about to learn. Find familiar words and write them down. Then list what you already know about the words and topics you see.

Multiply Whole Numbers

$$\begin{array}{r} 25 \\ \times 12 \\ \hline 50 \\ 25 \\ \hline 300 \end{array}$$ ← Line up the partial products correctly.

Decimal

8.256

tenths ↗   ↑   ↖ thousandths

hundredths

Commutative Property of Addition

$3 + 5 = 5 + 3$

Associative Property of Addition

$12 + (3 + 5) = (12 + 3) + 5$

The notes above will help you prepare for Lessons 4.1 – 4.3. You should review other topics, such as division, to prepare for Lessons 4.4 – 4.8.

Multiplying Decimals and Whole Numbers

BEFORE	**Now**	**WHY?**
You multiplied whole numbers by whole numbers.	You'll multiply decimals and whole numbers.	So you can find the length of a race, as in Example 2.

Activity **You can use base-ten pieces to multiply.**

With base-ten pieces, *one hundredth* is represented by ▪ = 0.01, and *one tenth* is represented by ▪▪▪▪▪▪▪▪▪▪ = 0.1.

① Model 1 × 0.04.

▪▪▪▪

This is one row of 4 hundredths.

② Model 2 × 0.04.

▪▪▪▪
▪▪▪▪

③ Model 3 × 0.04.

▪▪▪▪
▪▪▪▪
▪▪▪▪

1 × 0.04 = 0.04   2 × 0.04 = 0.08   3 × 0.04 = 0.12

Use a model to find the product.

1. 3 × 0.02 0.06   **2.** 3 × 0.2 0.6   **3.** 4 × 0.03 0.12   **4.** 4 × 0.3 1.2

5. How do the number of decimal places in your answers to Exercises 1–4 compare to the number of decimal places in the factors? They are the same.

1. 0.015; 5 thousandths times 3 is 15 thousandths.

2. 0.096; 24 thousandths times 4 is 96 thousandths.

3. 8.4; 1 and 2 tenths times 7 is 8 and 4 tenths.

4. 11.80; 2 and 36 hundredths times 5 is 11 and 80 hundredths.

 with Solving

You may want to think of Example 1 in words. *7 times 6 thousandths is 42 thousandths.* Then you can see why a zero is needed as a placeholder in the product.

Multiplying with Decimals When you multiply a decimal and a whole number, the number of decimal places in the product is the same as the number of decimal places in the decimal factor.

EXAMPLE 1 **Multiplying Decimals by Whole Numbers**

Find the product 7 × 0.006.

Because 0.006 has 3 decimal places, the answer will have 3 decimal places.

$$
\begin{array}{r}
0.006 \\
\times \quad 7 \\
\hline
0.042
\end{array}
$$

Write a zero as a placeholder so that the answer has 3 decimal places.

Your turn now **Find the product. Then write the product in words.**

1. 3 × 0.005   **2.** 4 × 0.024   **3.** 1.2 × 7   **4.** 2.36 × 5
1–4. See margin.

Lesson 4.1 Multiplying Decimals and Whole Numbers **153**

What do you think?

Sports

■ **Iditarod Race**

Fourteen teams competed in the 2001 Junior Iditarod race in Alaska. The musher (or driver) for each team of dogs was between the ages of 14 and 17. If each team had 7–10 dogs, estimate how many dogs participated in the race. **between 98 and 140 dogs**

Counting Zeros You need to include the zeros at the *end* of a product in order to count the decimal places correctly. Once you place the decimal point, however, you can drop any zeros that occur at the end of the answer, as in Example 2 below.

EXAMPLE 2 Solving a Problem

Junior Iditarod Race In the 2001 Junior Iditarod race, one team completed the race in about 18 hours over two days. The team's average rate was 8.875 miles per hour. About how long was the race? Round to the nearest mile.

Solution

Use the formula *Distance = Rate × Time*.

$$
\begin{array}{r}
8.875 \\
\times \quad 18 \\
\hline
71000 \\
8875 \quad \\
\hline
159.750
\end{array}
$$

Place the decimal point before dropping any zeros.

ANSWER The race was about 160 miles long.

EXAMPLE 3 Checking for Reasonableness

Use estimation to check that the answer to Example 2 is reasonable.

$$\text{Distance} = 8.875 \times 18$$
$$\approx 9 \times 18 \qquad \text{Round 8.875 to its leading digit.}$$
$$= 162$$

ANSWER Because 160 is close to 162, the distance is reasonable.

Your turn now **Find the product.**

5. 0.9×50 **45**   **6.** 1.505×8 **12.04**   **7.** 3.14×75 **235.5**   **8.** 6.25×22 **137.5**

Use estimation to check that the answer is reasonable.

9. 3.254×18; 58.572 **yes**   **10.** 12.706×3; 381.18 **no**

11. Explain why the answer 84 is *not* reasonable for the product 3×2.8. *Sample answer:* It is very far from the estimate of $3 \times 3 = 9$.
12. Explain why the answer 1.06 *is* reasonable for the product 2×0.53. *Sample answer:* It is very close to the estimate of $2 \times 0.5 = 1$.

Properties of Multiplication You used properties of addition in Lesson 3.6. Similar properties for multiplication are shown below.

Properties of Multiplication

Commutative Property In a product, you can multiply numbers in any order.

Numbers $2 \times 6.5 = 6.5 \times 2$ **Algebra** $a \cdot b = b \cdot a$

Associative Property The value of a product does not depend on how the numbers are grouped.

Numbers $(2 \times 6.5) \times 4 = 2 \times (6.5 \times 4)$

Algebra $(a \cdot b) \cdot c = a \cdot (b \cdot c)$

EXAMPLE 4 **Using Properties of Multiplication**

Tell whether the *commutative* or *associative* property of multiplication allows you to rewrite the problem as shown. Explain your choice.

a. $5 \times 3.25 \times 2 = 3.25 \times 5 \times 2$

The order of the numbers has changed, so this is an example of the commutative property of multiplication.

b. $(3.25 \times 5) \times 2 = 3.25 \times (5 \times 2)$

The numbers that are grouped have changed, so this is an example of the associative property of multiplication.

4.1 Exercises

More Practice, p. 711

INTERNET
eWorkbook Plus
CLASSZONE.COM

5. 0.6; 3 times 2 tenths is 6 tenths.

6. 5.4; 6 times 9 tenths is 5 and 4 tenths.

7. 15.82; 3 and 164 thousandths times 5 is 15 and 82 hundredths.

8. 125.1; 2 and 78 hundredths times 45 is 125 and 1 tenth.

Getting Ready to Practice

1. Vocabulary Which property does $(2 \cdot 8) \cdot 9 = 2 \cdot (8 \cdot 9)$ illustrate?
associative property of multiplication

Copy the answer and place the decimal point in the correct location.

2. $34 \times 1.6 = $ **544**   **3.** $15 \times 1.04 = $ **1560**   **4.** $7.841 \times 3 = $ **23523**
54.4   15.60   23.523

Find the product. Then write the product in words.

5. 3×0.2 **6.** 6×0.9 **7.** 3.164×5 **8.** 2.78×45

Example 4 Tell whether the commutative or associative property of multiplication allows you to rewrite the problem as shown. Explain your choice.

a. $(1.25 \times 2) \times 5 = 1.25 \times (2 \times 5)$ The numbers that are grouped have changed, so this is an example of the associative property of multiplication.

b. $2 \times 1.25 \times 5 = 1.25 \times 2 \times 5$ The order of the numbers has changed, so this is an example of the commutative property of multiplication.

Differentiating Instruction

Less Proficient Students Ask less capable students to list the commutative and associative properties of addition in algebraic form alongside the corresponding properties of multiplication. Then ask the students to give numerical examples involving decimals and whole numbers for all four properties.

 CONCEPT CHECK

When you multiply a decimal and a whole number, how is the number of decimal places in the product related to the number of decimal places in the decimal factor? The number of decimal places in the product is the same as the number of decimal places in the decimal factor.

 DAILY PUZZLER

Which is greater, $(1 - 0.5)(1 - 0.7)(1 - 0.9)$ or $(1 - 0.6)(1 - 0.8)(1 - 1.0)$? $(1 - 0.5)(1 - 0.7)(1 - 0.9)$ is greater.

155

ASSIGNMENT GUIDE

Basic Course
Day 1: SRH p. 694 Exs. 13–20;
pp. 156–157 Exs. 9–11,
16–21, 30–33, 39
Day 2: pp. 156–157 Exs. 12–14,
22–29, 34–36, 42–52

Average Course
Day 1: pp. 156–157 Exs. 9–15,
30–33, 42–47
Day 2: pp. 156–157 Exs. 20–29,
34–40, 48–53

Advanced Course
Day 1: pp. 156–157 Exs. 10–15,
30–33, 39, 40, 42–44, 52
Day 2: pp. 156–157 Exs. 22–29,
34–38, 41*, 46–48, 53

Block
pp. 156–157 Exs. 9–40, 42–53

EXTRA PRACTICE

- Student Edition, p. 711
- Chapter 4 Resource Book,
  pp. 11–13
- Test and Practice Generator

 TRANSPARENCY

Even-numbered answers are available on transparencies. A support transparency is available for Exercises 5, 6, and 9–11.

HOMEWORK CHECK

When you review students' homework for this lesson, go over the following exercises to check understanding of key concepts.
Basic: 9, 17, 28, 30, 34
Average: 10, 20, 28, 31, 34
Advanced: 11, 26, 29, 32, 35

HELP with Homework

Example	Exercises
1	9–27
2	12–27, 30–33
3	16–27, 34, 35
4	28, 29

Online Resources
CLASSZONE.COM
· More Examples
· eTutorial Plus

9. 0.8; 4 times 2 tenths is 8 tenths.

10. .18; 6 times 3 hundredths is 18 hundredths.

11. 0.06; 2 times 3 hundredths is 6 hundredths.

15. *Sample answer:* There should be four decimal places in the answer and there are only three. Add a zero before the 112 and place the decimal point correctly. The correct product is 0.0112.

Practice and Problem Solving

A **Use a model to find the product. Then write the product in words.**

9. 4×0.2 **10.** 6×0.03 **11.** 2×0.03
9–11. See margin.

Copy the answer and place the decimal point in the correct location.

12. $27 \times 5.34 = \mathbf{14418}$ **13.** $9 \times 0.873 = \mathbf{7857}$ **14.** $2.03 \times 5 = \mathbf{1015}$
         144.18   7.857   10.15

15. **Find the Error** Describe and correct the error in the solution.
See margin.

$$\begin{array}{r} 0.0028 \\ \times \quad 4 \\ \hline 00.112 \end{array}$$

Find the product. Use estimation to check your answer.

16. 6×3.5 21   **17.** 9×2.17 19.53   **18.** 0.008×9 0.072   **19.** 5.31×18 95.58

20. 0.29×82 23.78   **21.** 0.32×55 17.6   **22.** 7.25×34 246.5 **23.** 3.072×8
                                                     24.576

24. 9.426×3 **25.** 2.125×15 **26.** 52×0.088 **27.** 18×0.005
     28.278   31.875   4.576   0.09

Copy and complete each statement. Tell whether you used the *commutative* or *associative* property of multiplication.

28. $2 \times 79 \times 0.5 = 79 \times \underline{?} \times 0.5$ **29.** $(0.4 \times 83) \times 5 = 0.4 \times (\underline{?} \times 5)$
    2; commutative   83; associative

Shopping **Find the amount you would spend in the situation.**

30. You want to buy balloons for a friend's birthday. The balloons cost $1.50 each. You buy 6 balloons. $9

31. Each ticket for a rock concert costs $48.35. You buy 7 tickets. $338.45

32. It costs $.12 to make a photocopy. You make 84 photocopies. $10.08

33. A paintbrush costs $3.79. You buy 11 of them. $41.69

B **Number Sense** **Use estimation to explain why the statement is false.**

34. The product of 5 and 0.85 is more than 5.
Sample answer: $5 \times 1 = 5$, which is greater than the actual product.

35. The product of 24 and 1.107 is less than 24.
Sample answer: 24×1 is 24, which is less than the actual product.

36. **Bottled Water** A beverage company packages spring water in bottles that hold 1.5 liters. How many liters of water are in a case that contains 8 bottles? How many liters are in a case that contains 12 bottles?   12 L;
                                                        18 L

37. **Writing** Explain why you can drop the zero at the end of the products in your answers to Exercise 36. Why might you need to keep the final zero in the product for a situation involving money?
Sample answers: It does not change the answer in any way or have any effect on the value of the number; if there is a digit in the tenths place, there must be a digit in the hundredths place for money.

38. Armor The table at the right shows the heights of three suits of armor. Change the heights from centimeters to inches. Use the fact that 1 cm ≈ 0.3937 in. **72.8345; 42.9133; 25.1968**

Type of Armor	Adult	Child	Dog
Height (cm)	185	109	64
Height (in.)	?	?	?

 Algebra **Evaluate the variable expression.**

39. $120x + 3$, when $x = 0.1$ **15**

40. $7 + 16x$, when $x = 4.2$ **74.2**

C 41. Challenge Use estimation to find a decimal that when multiplied by 18 gives a product between 24 and 30. *Sample answer:* **1.5**

Mixed Review

Evaluate the expression. (*Lesson 1.4*)

42. $104 \times 5 + 2 \times 7$ **534** **43.** $5 \times (36 \div 3)$ **60** **44.** $28 - 2 \times 3^2$ **10**

Use front-end estimation to estimate the sum. (*Lesson 3.5*) **45–47. Estimates may vary.**

45. $3.64 + 8.22 + 2.15$ **14** **46.** $7.1 + 2.83 + 2.15$ **12** **47.** $1.7 + 6.1 + 3.28$ **11**

Choose a Strategy **Use a strategy from the list to solve the following problem. Explain your choice of strategy.**

48. You are at an awards dinner and have a choice of 3 dinner entrees, 2 side dishes, and 2 desserts. You can choose only one of each. How many different meals can you select?

> **Problem Solving Strategies**
> ▪ Draw a Diagram
> ▪ Make a List
> ▪ Make a Table
> ▪ Find a Pattern

48. 12 meals. *Sample answer:* I used the strategy draw a diagram because a tree diagram shows all of the possibilities and makes it easy to count the number of different meals.

Basic Skills **Write the place value of the red digit.**

49. 320,840 **hundred** **50.** 340,875 **hundred thousand** **51.** 1,263,920 **ten thousand**

Test-Taking Practice

52. Multiple Choice Tracy bought 39 basketball tickets that cost $19.25 each. What is the best estimate of the amount Tracy spent? **C**

A. $600   **B.** $700   **C.** $800   **D.** $900

53. Short Response Kari works five days per week and four hours per day. If she earns $9.75 per hour, how much does she earn per week? Explain how you found your answer.

53. $195. *Sample answer:* Multiply 4×5 to find the total number of hours she works each week. Multiply that product times $9.75 to find the amount she earns per week.

ASSESSMENT RESOURCES

For more assessment resources, see:
- Assessment Book
- Test and Practice Generator

MINI-QUIZ

1. Evaluate 0.057×7. **0.399**

2. A car averaged 52.755 miles per hour for 4 hours. How far did the car travel? **211.02 mi**

3. A student calculated that $39.75 \times 41 = 1629.75$. Is that answer reasonable? **$40 \times 40 = 1600$, so the answer is reasonable.**

4. Tell whether the associative or commutative property of multiplication lets you rewrite each problem.
  a. $2.5 \times 17 \times 4 = 17 \times 2.5 \times 4$ **commutative**
  b. $1.25 \times (4 \times 7.8) = (1.25 \times 4) \times 7.8$ **associative**

RETEACHING/REMEDIATION

- Study Guide in Chapter 4 Resource Book, pp. 14–15
- Tutor Place, Whole Numbers and Decimals Cards 8, 17
- eTutorial Plus Online
- Extra Practice, p. 711
- Lesson Practice in Chapter 4 Resource Book, pp. 11–13

CHALLENGE/ENRICHMENT

- Challenge Practice in Chapter 4 Resource Book, p. 17
- Teacher's Edition, p. 150F

ENGLISH LEARNER SUPPORT

- Spanish Study Guide
- Multi-Language Glossary
- Chapter Audio Summaries CDs

① PLAN

LEARN THE METHOD

- Students will use a spreadsheet to multiply decimals by whole numbers.
- Students can use a spreadsheet to check the accuracy of the products they found for Exercises 30–33 in Lesson 4.1.

GROUPING

This activity can be done in groups of two. During the activity, one student can enter the data in the spreadsheet while the other student reads the data from the book.

② TEACH

DISCUSSION

As students work through Step 1, you may wish to ask them how the cell number relates to its location in the spreadsheet. In Steps 3 and 4, stress that the formulas are entered in the cells and not the dollar amounts shown in the sample spreadsheet.

EXTRA EXAMPLES

Example Suppose the biologist saves 3% of each week's earnings. Write an expression to calculate each week's savings.
B1 * B3 * 0.03

③ CLOSE

ASSESSMENT

1. Find the weekly and yearly earnings for a plumber's assistant who works 32 hours per week and earns $13.50 per hour. **$432; $22,464**

Technology Activity

SPREADSHEET

Multiplying Decimals by Whole Numbers

GOAL Use a spreadsheet to multiply decimals by whole numbers.

Example You can enter formulas in a spreadsheet to multiply numbers.

A biologist works 40 hours a week and earns $22.18 an hour. How much does the biologist earn in one week? How much does the biologist earn in one year?

Solution

Create a spreadsheet like the one shown below.

① Enter the number of hours worked in cell B1.

② Enter the hourly wage in cell B3.

③ To find the biologist's weekly earnings, use a formula to multiply the number of hours worked by the hourly wage.

④ To find the biologist's yearly earnings, use a formula to multiply the weekly earnings by the number of weeks in a year.

	A	B
1	Hours per week:	40
2		
3	Dollars per hour:	$22.18
4		
5	Weekly earnings:	$887.20
6		
7	Yearly earnings:	$46,134.40

In cell B5, enter the formula = B1*B3.

In cell B7, enter the formula = B5*52.

ANSWER The biologist earns $887.20 a week and $46,134.40 a year.

Your turn now Use a spreadsheet to find the person's weekly and yearly earnings.

1. A programmer works 56 hours a week and earns $26.33 an hour. **$1474.48; $76,672.96**

2. A hairdresser works 50 hours a week and earns $18.89 an hour. **$944.50; $49,114.00**

3. A doctor works 40 hours a week and earns $35.21 an hour. **$1408.40; $73,236.80**

4. A babysitter works 12 hours a week and earns $6.50 an hour. **$78; $4056**

NCTM CURRICULUM STANDARDS
Standard 1: Understand meanings of operations
Standard 2: Understand patterns
Standard 6: Solve problems in math and other contexts

LESSON 4.2

The Distributive Property

BEFORE

You used order of operations to evaluate expressions.

▶ **Now**

You'll use the distributive property to evaluate expressions.

WHY?

So you can find the cost of a field trip, as in Ex. 6.

Word Watch

distributive property, p. 159

In the Real World

Car Wash Your class held a two-day car wash to raise money. The class washed 40 cars on the first day and 30 cars on the second day. The class charged $5 for each car. How much money did the class raise?

HELP with **Review**

Remember that 5(70) is another way to write 5×70.

EXAMPLE 1 Evaluating Expressions

Method 1 To answer the question above, first find the total number of cars washed. Then multiply to find the total amount raised.

Charge per car × Total number of cars washed $= 5(40 + 30)$

$$= 5(70)$$

$$= 350$$

Method 2 To answer the question above, first find the amount raised each day. Then add to find the total amount raised.

First day amount + Second day amount $= 5 \times 40 + 5 \times 30$

$$= 200 + 150$$

$$= 350$$

ANSWER Your class raised $350.

The methods used in Example 1 show the **distributive property**.

The Distributive Property

Words You can multiply a number and a sum by multiplying the number by each part of the sum and then adding these products. The same property applies with subtraction.

Numbers $3(4 + 6) = 3(4) + 3(6)$ $2(8 - 5) = 2(8) - 2(5)$

Algebra $a(b + c) = ab + ac$ $a(b - c) = ab - ac$

NCTM CURRICULUM STANDARDS
Standard 1: Understand how operations are related
Standard 2: Understand patterns
Standard 6: Solve problems in math and other contexts

Lesson 4.2   The Distributive Property   **159**

---

1 PLAN

SKILL CHECK
Use the order of operations.

1. $8(6 + 4)$		80
2. $8 \times 6 + 8 \times 4$		80
3. $(18 + 22)5$		200
4. $18 \times 5 + 22 \times 5$	200

LESSON OBJECTIVE

Use the distributive property.

PACING

Suggested Number of Days
Basic Course: 2 days
Average Course: 2 days
Advanced Course: 2 days
Block: 1 block

TEACHING RESOURCES

For a complete list of Teaching Resources, see page 150B.

TRANSPARENCY

Warm-Up Exercises for this lesson are available on a transparency.

2 TEACH

MOTIVATING THE LESSON

If any students have been involved in a fund-raiser like the car wash, ask them to describe the fund-raising effort.

TIPS FOR NEW TEACHERS

Have students include in their notebooks the algebraic forms of the distributive property, along with numerical examples. See Tips for New Teachers in the *Chapter 4 Resource Book*.

159

EXAMPLE 2 **Using the Distributive Property**

a. 2(50 + 6) = 2(50) + 2(6)
= 100 + 12
= 112

b. 10(8.6 − 2.4) = 10(8.6) − 10(2.4)
= 86 − 24
= 62

Your turn now Use the distributive property to evaluate.
1. 2(17 + 10) 54 **2.** 7(20 − 3) 119 **3.** 100(6.8 − 4) 280 **4.** 0.5(24 + 18) 21

EXAMPLE 3 **Evaluating Using Mental Math**

a. To find 6(87), rewrite 87.

6(87) = 6(90 − 3)
= 6(90) − 6(3)
= 540 − 18
= 522

b. To find 8(6.1), rewrite 6.1.

8(6.1) = 8(6 + 0.1)
= 8(6) + 8(0.1)
= 48 + 0.8
= 48.8

EXAMPLE 4 **Using a Formula**

Astronomy The Hubble Telescope orbits Earth at a rate of about 4.78 miles per second. How far does the telescope travel in 3 seconds?

Solution
Use the formula *Distance = Rate × Time*.

Distance = (4.78)3   Use 4.78 for the rate and 3 for the time.
= (5 − 0.22)3   Rewrite 4.78 as 5 − 0.22.
= (5)3 − (0.22)3   Use the distributive property.
= 15 − 0.66   Multiply.
= 14.34   Subtract.

ANSWER The telescope travels about 14.34 miles in 3 seconds.

Your turn now Use mental math to find the product.
5. 8(53) 424 **6.** 4(97) 388 **7.** 3(12.8) 38.4 **8.** 7(1.4) 9.8

What do you think?
Science

■ **Astronomy**

The Hubble Space Telescope is a satellite that takes photographs of outer space and sends them to Earth. The telescope was launched on April 24, 1990. Traveling at about 5 miles per second, how far does the telescope travel in 1 day? in 1 year?
432,000 mi; 157,680,000 mi

4.2 Exercises

More Practice, p. 711

INTERNET
eWorkbook Plus
CLASSZONE.COM

Getting Ready to Practice

1. **Vocabulary** Rewrite the expression $2(3.1 + 7.4)$ using the distributive property. $2(3.1) + 2(7.4)$

Copy and complete the statement using the distributive property.

2. $3(40 + 5) = 3(\underset{40}{\underline{?}}) + \underset{3}{\underline{?}}(5)$

3. $7(50 + 2) = 7(\underset{50}{\underline{?}}) + \underset{7}{\underline{?}}(2)$

4. $6(7 + 5.4) = 6(\underset{7}{\underline{?}}) + \underset{6}{\underline{?}}(5.4)$

5. $8(3.2 - 9) = 8(\underset{3.2}{\underline{?}}) - \underset{8}{\underline{?}}(9)$

6. **Field Trip** A class of 30 students is taking a field trip to a museum. The cost for each student is $9 for admission plus $5 more for the laser show. How much money is needed to pay for all the students to see the museum and the laser show? $420

Practice and Problem Solving

A **Use the distributive property to evaluate the expression.**

7. $4(80 + 3)$ 332

8. $6(7 + 50)$ 342

9. $2(39 - 10)$ 58

10. $15(2 + 9)$ 165

11. $6(8.2 + 3)$ 67.2

12. $8(3.1 + 5.7)$ 70.4

13. $10(4.8 + 2.7)$ 75

14. $14(8.1 - 6)$ 29.4

15. $3(90 + 0.6)$ 271.8

16. $9(7 - 0.11)$ 62.01

17. $7(13 - 0.02)$ 90.86

18. $12(3 + 0.4)$ 40.8

19. **Find the Error** Describe and correct the error in the solution. *Sample answer:* The 2 was distributed to the 32 and not to the 6. The solution should be $2(32 + 6) = 2(32) + 2(6) = 64 + 12 = 76$.

$$2(32 + 6) = 2(32) + 6$$
$$= 64 + 6$$
$$= 70$$

Copy and complete the statement.

20. $5(30 + 0.2) = 5(30) + \underset{5}{\underline{?}}(0.2)$

21. $7(40 + 8) = \underset{7}{\underline{?}}(40) + \underset{7}{\underline{?}}(8)$

22. $4(7.9) = 4(8 - \underset{0.1}{\underline{?}})$

23. $3(67) = 3(\underset{60}{\underline{?}} + 7)$

Use the distributive property and mental math to find the product.

24. $6(37)$ 222

25. $7(98)$ 686

26. $3(85)$ 255

27. $9(41)$ 369

28. $8(5.7)$ 45.6

29. $5(9.2)$ 46

30. $9(7.3)$ 65.7

31. $7(6.9)$ 48.3

B 32. Find the product $7(2.006)$ using the distributive property. 14.042

33. **Lunch Costs** For each day of school, you pay $2.50 for lunch and $.45 for milk. How much money do you spend in 5 days? $14.75

HELP with Homework

Example	Exercises
1	7–18, 33
2	7–23
3	22–32
4	33, 37

Online Resources
CLASSZONE.COM
· More Examples
· eTutorial Plus

---

3 **APPLY**

ASSIGNMENT GUIDE

Basic Course
Day 1: EP p. 708 Exs. 29–32; pp. 161–162 Exs. 7–12, 20, 21, 38, 40, 44–49
Day 2: pp. 161–162 Exs. 13–18, 22–27, 32–35, 37, 50–54

Average Course
Day 1: pp. 161–162 Exs. 7–14, 20, 21, 34–36, 38–40, 45–48
Day 2: pp. 161–162 Exs. 15–19, 22–33, 37, 52–54

Advanced Course
Day 1: pp. 161–162 Exs. 11–19, 35, 40, 46–49, 53, 54
Day 2: pp. 161–162 Exs. 20–25, 30–33, 36–38, 41–43*

Block
pp. 161–162 Exs. 7–40, 45–48, 52–54

EXTRA PRACTICE

- Student Edition, p. 711
- Chapter 4 Resource Book, pp. 21–23
- Test and Practice Generator

TRANSPARENCY

Even-numbered answers are available on transparencies.

HOMEWORK CHECK

When you review students' homework for this lesson, go over the following exercises to check understanding of key concepts.
Basic: 7, 11, 21, 25, 33
Average: 12, 17, 22, 28, 37
Advanced: 16, 19, 23, 31, 37

COMMON ERROR

In Exercises 7–18, many students will make the mistake exhibited in Exercise 19. Stress that both numbers inside the parentheses must be multiplied by the factor on the left.

4 ASSESS

ASSESSMENT RESOURCES

For more assessment resources, see:
- Assessment Book
- Test and Practice Generator

MINI-QUIZ

Find the product.

1. 7(50 + 9) **413**

2. 10(3.7 − 1.8) **19**

3. 8(97) **776**

4. (3.8)(6) **22.8**

5. A car travels an average of 24.7 miles per gallon of gas. How far can it travel on 8 gallons of gas? **197.6 mi**

5 FOLLOW-UP

RETEACHING/REMEDIATION

- Study Guide in Chapter 4 Resource Book, pp. 24–25
- eTutorial Plus Online
- Extra Practice, p. 711
- Lesson Practice in Chapter 4 Resource Book, pp. 21–23

CHALLENGE/ENRICHMENT

- Challenge Practice in Chapter 4 Resource Book, p. 26
- Teacher's Edition, p. 150F

ENGLISH LEARNER SUPPORT

- Spanish Study Guide
- Multi-Language Glossary
- Chapter Audio Summaries CDs

■ **U.S. Mint**

Coins are minted in Philadelphia and in Denver. Coins minted in Denver have a "D" on the front. Coins minted in Philadelphia have a "P" on the front. Do you think people in your class have coins from Denver or Philadelphia? Why?
Sample answer: Both since we are not closer to either city.

U.S. Mint **In Exercises 34–36, use the table. It shows what it cost to produce some U.S. coins in two different years.**

34. Evaluate the expression 50(2.0 − 1.6) to find how much more it cost to produce 50 dimes in 2000 than in 1995. **20¢**

35. Evaluate the expression 50(0.8 − 0.7) to find how much more it cost to produce 50 pennies in 2000 than in 1995. **5¢**

Coin	1995	2000
Penny	0.7¢	0.8¢
Nickel	2.74¢	3.0¢
Dime	1.6¢	2.0¢
Quarter	3.65¢	5.0¢

36. Write an expression to find how much more it cost to produce 50 nickels in 2000 than in 1995. Then evaluate the expression. **50(3.0 − 2.74); 13¢**

37. Geometry Use the formula $P = 2(l + w)$ to find the perimeter of a flower box with length 27 inches and width 6 inches. **66 in.**

Algebra **Use the distributive property to rewrite the expression.**
C For example, 2(x + 4) = 2x + 8.

38. 3(x + 7) **3x + 21**   **39.** 5(x + 5.2) **5x + 26**   **40.** 6(4 − x) **24 − 6x**

Challenge **Rewrite the expression as a product using parentheses.**

41. 4x + 4y **4(x + y)**   **42.** 0.9m − 0.9n **0.9(m − n)**   **43.** 5.5x − 5.5y + 5.5 **5.5(x − y + 1)**

Mixed Review

Order the numbers from least to greatest. *(Lesson 3.3)*

44. 2.1, 2.9, 2.8, 2.6 **2.1, 2.6, 2.8, 2.9**   **45.** 7.63, 7.06, 7.61, 7.6 **7.06, 7.6, 7.61, 7.63**   **46.** 0.5, 0.55, 0.05, 0.005 **0.005, 0.05, 0.5, 0.55**

Evaluate the expression when x = 3.1 and y = 5.62. *(Lesson 3.6)*

47. x + 2.83 **5.93**   **48.** x + y **8.72**   **49.** y − 3.092 **2.528**

Basic Skills **Round to the place value of the red digit.**

50. 63,498 **63,500**   **51.** 32,921 **30,000**   **52.** 204,238 **204,000**

Test-Taking Practice

53. Multiple Choice Which expression is equal to 4(2 + 6)? **D**

A. 2(4 + 6)   **B.** 4 × 2 × 6

C. 4 × 2 + 6   **D.** 4 × 2 + 4 × 6

54. Multiple Choice Which expression is equal to 2(4.9)? **G**

F. 2(4 + 9)   **G.** 2(4 + 0.9)   **H.** 2 × 4 × 9   **I.** 2(5 − 1)

GOAL
Use an area model to find the product of two decimals.

MATERIALS
- graph paper
- colored pencils

Multiplying Decimals Using Models

In this activity, you will use area models to multiply two decimals. The decimals will represent the length and width of a rectangle. The area of the rectangle will represent the product of the decimals.

Explore   Model 0.8 × 0.7 using an area model.

1 Start with a 10-by-10 square drawn on graph paper.

The whole square represents 1.

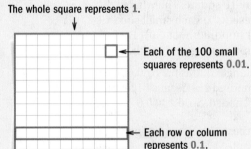

Each of the 100 small squares represents 0.01.

Each row or column represents 0.1.

2 Use a colored pencil to shade a rectangle that is 8 rows long by 7 columns wide.

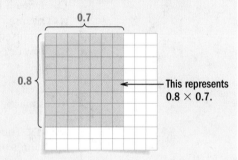

0.7

0.8

This represents 0.8 × 0.7.

3 The area of the rectangle represents the product 0.8 × 0.7. Count the number of squares in the shaded rectangle. Because each small square represents 0.01, 56 of the small squares represent 0.56, or fifty-six hundredths. So, 0.8 × 0.7 = 0.56.

Your turn now   Use a model to find the product.

1. 0.3 × 0.9 0.27   **2.** 0.4 × 0.4 0.16   **3.** 0.5 × 0.6 0.3   **4.** 0.7 × 0.3 0.21

5. In Step 3 above, is the product *greater than* or *less than* each of the numbers being multiplied? less than

Stop *and* **Think**

6. Critical Thinking Use a model to find the product 0.7 × 0.8. Is the result any different than the result in Step 3 above? Why or why not?
0.56; no. *Sample answer:* The commutative property of multiplication says that order does not matter.

NCTM CURRICULUM STANDARDS
Standard 1: Understand meanings of operations
Standard 10: Create representations to communicate ideas; Use representations to solve problems

Lesson 4.3   Multiplying Decimals   **163**

SKILL CHECK
Determine the number of decimal places in the answer.

1. 7×1.5 **1 decimal place**
2. 9.133×5 **3 decimal places**
3. 3×0.72 **2 decimal places**

LESSON OBJECTIVE

Multiply decimals by decimals.

PACING

Suggested Number of Days
Basic Course: 2 days
Average Course: 2 days
Advanced Course: 2 days
Block: 1 block

TEACHING RESOURCES

For a complete list of Teaching Resources, see page 150B.

 TRANSPARENCY

Warm-Up Exercises for this lesson are available on a transparency.

2 TEACH

MOTIVATING THE LESSON

Ask students to suggest animals other than a sloth that travel slowly, such as a snail. Have them write and answer their own question about the distance traveled by their animal in a portion of an hour.

LESSON 4.3

Multiplying Decimals

BEFORE	▶ Now	WHY?
You multiplied decimals by whole numbers.	You'll multiply decimals by decimals.	So you can find the distance traveled by a turtle, as in Ex. 30.

 **Word Watch**

Review Words
factor, p. 16

(**In the Real World**

Sloths The sloth is commonly referred to as the "slowest mammal on Earth." Its top speed on the ground is about 0.2 mile per hour. What is the farthest a sloth might go in 0.6 hour?

EXAMPLE 1 **Using a Model to Multiply Decimals**

To find how far a sloth might go in the question above, use a model to find the product 0.2×0.6.

① Draw a 10-by-10 square. The whole square represents 1. Each small square represents 1 hundredth, or 0.01. Each row or column represents 1 tenth, or 0.1.

② Shade a rectangle that is 0.2 by 0.6. The area is 12 hundredths, because 12 small squares are shaded. So, $0.2 \times 0.6 = 0.12$.

ANSWER The farthest a sloth might go in 0.6 hour is 0.12 mile.

Your turn now Draw a model to find the product.

1. 0.1×0.7 **0.07**
2. 0.3×0.8 **0.24**
3. 0.9×0.7 **0.63**

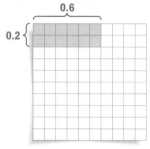 **Notebook**

Multiplying Decimals

Words Multiply decimals as you do whole numbers. Then place the decimal point. The number of decimal places is the total number of decimal places in the factors.

Numbers

3.14	$\times$	15.6	$=$	48.984
2 places		1 place		3 places

NCTM CURRICULUM STANDARDS
Standard 1: Compute fluently
Standard 2: Represent situations using algebraic symbols
Standard 10: Use representations to communicate ideas

HELP with **Solving**

When you estimate to check a decimal product, you can use compatible numbers or round each decimal to its leading digit. Another estimate in Example 2 would be 300 × 0.8 = 240.

EXAMPLE 2 **Placing a Decimal Point in a Product**

Place the decimal point in the correct location.

252.64 × 0.842 = 212.72288

2 places   **3 places**   **5 places**

The first factor has 2 decimal places. The second factor has 3 decimal places. Because 2 + 3 = 5, the answer has 5 decimal places.

ANSWER 252.64 × 0.842 = 212.72288

✓ **Check** Estimate: 252.64 × 0.842 ≈ 250 × 1 = 250.
So, the product 212.72288 is reasonable.

EXAMPLE 3 **Multiplying Decimals**

Find the product.

a. 5.08 × 2.1   **b.** 1.159 × 0.03   **c.** 7.215 × 4.8

Solution

a.   5.08   **2 decimal places**
   ×   2.1   **+ 1 decimal place**
      508
    1016
   10.668   **3 decimal places**

b.   1.159   **3 decimal places**
   × 0.03   **+ 2 decimal places**
   0.03477   **5 decimal places**

c.   7.215   **3 decimal places**
   ×   4.8   **+ 1 decimal place**
    57720
   28860
   34.6320   **4 decimal places**

> Once you place the decimal point, drop the zero at the end of the final answer. You write the product as 34.632.

 Watch Out!

You may need to write zeros in the product as placeholders in order to place the decimal point correctly.

Your turn now **Multiply. Use estimation to check your answer.**

4. 2.15 × 5.4 **11.61** **5.** 12.7 × 2.9 **36.83** **6.** 6.289 × 0.2 **1.2578** **7.** 0.86 × 0.04 **0.0344**

TIPS FOR NEW TEACHERS

As you discuss the rule for multiplying decimals with students, have them apply the rule to the products found in the exercises on page 163 and the product found in Example 1 on this page. See Tips for New Teachers in the *Chapter 4 Resource Book*.

EXTRA EXAMPLES

Example 1 Use an area model to find 0.9 × 0.8. **0.72**

Example 2 Tell how many decimal places will be in the product. Then write the product placing the decimal point in the correct location.
324.17 × 0.48 = 1556016
4 decimal places; 155.6016

Example 3 Find the product.
a. 7.03 × 4.6 **32.338**
b. 2.125 × 0.007 **0.014875**
c. 13.028 × 3.5 **45.598**

VISUALIZE

An area model like the one in Example 1 can help students visualize why (0.1)(0.1) = 0.01.

MULTIPLE REPRESENTATIONS

In Example 3, students should realize that 34.6320 and 34.632 are different representations of the same number.

 COMMON ERROR

Be sure students count decimal places from the right to the decimal point, and *not* from the left to the decimal point.

TRANSPARENCY

A support transparency is available for Example 1.

CONCEPT CHECK

How is the number of decimal places in a product related to the numbers of decimal places in the factors? **The number of decimal places in the product is equal to the sum of the number of decimal places in the factors.**

 DAILY PUZZLER

Find two decimal factors so that each has one decimal place but their product has no decimal places. *Sample answer: 2.5 × 2.4 = 6*

The American flag hanging from the Hoover Dam is known as Superflag.

EXAMPLE 4 **Finding the Area of a Rectangle**

American Flag One of the largest flags ever made is about 153.9 meters long and 68.6 meters wide. Find the area of the flag to the nearest hundred square meters.

Solution

$A = lw$	Write the formula for the area of a rectangle.
$= (153.9)(68.6)$	Substitute 153.9 for l and 68.6 for w.
$= 10,557.54$	Multiply.

ANSWER The area of the flag is about 10,600 square meters.

✓ **Check** Round 153.9 to 150 and 68.6 to 70. Because $150 \times 70 = 10,500$, the product 10,600 is reasonable.

Your turn now Find the area of the rectangle or square.

8. A square with side length 3.2 meters **10.24 m²**

9. A rectangle with length 8.1 inches and width 3.25 inches **26.325 in.²**

4.3 Exercises

More Practice, p. 711

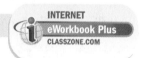

INTERNET
eWorkbook Plus
CLASSZONE.COM

Getting Ready to Practice

1. Vocabulary The number of decimal places in a product is equal to the ? of the number of decimal places in the factors. **sum**

Find the product.

2. 0.4×0.9 **0.36**　　**3.** 1.6×0.5 **0.8**　　**4.** 1.18×0.02 **0.0236**　　**5.** 3.74×4.2 **15.708**

Geometry Find the area of the rectangle or square.

6.
6.25 cm²
2.5 cm
2.5 cm

7.
17.325 ft²
2.75 ft
6.3 ft

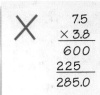
Practice and Problem Solving

11. *Sample answer:* The original problem has two decimal places so the answer should also have two decimal places. The solution should be

$$
\begin{array}{r}
7.5 \\
\times\ 3.8 \\
\hline
600 \\
225\ \ \\
\hline
28.50
\end{array}
$$

A **Draw a 10-by-10 square to model the product.**

8. 0.4×0.5 0.2

9. 0.3×0.9 0.27

10. 0.1×0.6 0.06

11. Find the Error Describe and correct the error made in the solution. **See margin.**

$$
\begin{array}{r}
7.5 \\
\times\ 3.8 \\
\hline
600 \\
225\ \ \\
\hline
285.0
\end{array}
$$

Copy the answer and place the decimal point in the correct location.

12. $0.17 \times 0.6 = $ **0102** 0.102

13. $16.36 \times 3.7 = $ **60532** 60.532

14. $4.7 \times 6.1 = $ **2867** 28.67

Multiply. Use estimation to check that the product is reasonable.

15. 0.3×0.6 0.18

16. 1.1×0.4 0.44

17. 3.72×0.8 2.976

18. 4.91×2.3 11.293

19. 3.052×4.7 14.3444

20. 2.05×5.8 11.89

21. 3.25×4.6 14.95

22. 1.08×0.45 0.486

23. 1.126×0.08 0.09008

24. 3.201×0.03 0.09603

25. 9.817×8.6 84.4262

26. 6.87×9.61 66.0207

Geometry **Find the area of the rectangle or square.**

27. 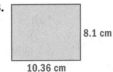 2.89 ft^2 1.7 ft 1.7 ft

28. 83.916 cm^2 8.1 cm 10.36 cm

29. Hair Growth Sophia's hair grows at a rate of about 0.5 inch per month. How much does Sophia's hair grow in 4.5 months? 2.25 in.

30. Animals A turtle is traveling at a speed of 4.015 meters per minute. How far does the turtle travel in 8.5 minutes? Round your answer to the nearest meter. 34 m

B **Number Sense** **Copy and complete the statement with <, >, or =.**

31. 64.2×1.12 ? 64 >

32. 2.2×0.12 ? 2.64 <

33. 32.5×0.01 ? 3.25 <

34. 0.505×10.1 ? 5.1005 =

Estimation **Check that the location of the decimal point in the product is reasonable. Correct the answer if necessary.**

35. 4.2×0.9; 37.8 no; 3.78

36. 32.06×11.94; 3.827964 no; 382.7964

37. 109.452×5.7; 623.8764 yes

38. 48.005×17.3; 83,0486.5 no; 830.4865

ASSIGNMENT GUIDE

Basic Course
Day 1: SRH p. 690 Exs. 5-10; pp. 167-168 Exs. 8-14, 31-38
Day 2: pp. 167-168 Exs. 15-23, 27-29, 39, 40, 45-54

Average Course
Day 1: pp. 167-168 Exs. 8-14, 33-38, 45-51, 54
Day 2: pp. 167-168 Exs. 15-32, 39-43, 55

Advanced Course
Day 1: pp. 167-168 Exs. 10-14, 33-42, 49, 54
Day 2: pp. 167-168 Exs. 18-30, 43-48*, 55

Block
pp. 167-168 Exs. 8-43, 45-51, 54, 55

EXTRA PRACTICE
• Student Edition, p. 711
• Chapter 4 Resource Book, pp. 30-32
• Test and Practice Generator

TRANSPARENCY
Even-numbered answers are available on transparencies. A support transparency is available for Exercises 8-10.

HOMEWORK CHECK
When you review students' homework for this lesson, go over the following exercises to check understanding of key concepts.
Basic: 8, 9, 12, 16, 27
Average: 10, 12, 22, 27, 29
Advanced: 10, 14, 25, 28, 30

TEACHING TIP
For Exercises 15, 16, 22, 23, and 24, note that the estimates of the products will be 0, since one of the factors rounds to 0.

167

④ ASSESS

ASSESSMENT RESOURCES

For more assessment resources, see:
- Assessment Book
- Test and Practice Generator

MINI-QUIZ

Find the product.
1. 0.6 × 0.8 **0.48**
2. 3.05 × 4.7 **14.335**
3. 4.257 × 0.02 **0.08514**
4. 13.85 × 6.8 **94.18**
5. A square has a side that is 0.31 meter long. Find the area of the square in square meters. **0.0961 m²**

⑤ FOLLOW-UP

RETEACHING/REMEDIATION

- Study Guide in Chapter 4 Resource Book, pp. 33–34
- Tutor Place, Whole Numbers and Decimals Cards 9, 17
- eTutorial Plus Online
- Extra Practice, p. 711
- Lesson Practice in Chapter 4 Resource Book, pp. 30–32

CHALLENGE/ENRICHMENT

- Challenge Practice in Chapter 4 Resource Book, p. 35
- Teacher's Edition, p. 150F

ENGLISH LEARNER SUPPORT

- Spanish Study Guide
- Multi-Language Glossary
- Chapter Audio Summaries CDs

45–48. See Additional Answers beginning on page AA1.

Delis In Exercises 39 and 40, use the table. It shows the prices of several foods. You buy 0.75 pound of ham, 0.5 pound of cheese, and 1.25 pounds of turkey.

Food	Price per pound
Ham	$5.49
Cheese	$4.79
Turkey	$4.25

39. Find the price of each item and the total amount you pay for these items. Round your result to the nearest cent. ham: $4.12; cheese: $2.40; turkey: $5.31; total: $11.83

40. **Decide** Can you buy 2.5 pounds of turkey if you have only $10? no

41. **Writing** Explain when you need to include a zero as a placeholder in a product. Give an example. See margin.

C **Critical Thinking** **Choose the correct response and explain your choice.**

42. When you multiply two decimals between 0 and 1, is the product *less than* or *greater than* both factors? See margin.

43. When you multiply a number greater than 1 by a number between 0 and 1, is the product *less than* or *greater than* the first number?
See margin.

44. **Challenge** The simple interest you might earn at a bank is found by the formula $I = Prt$, where I is the simple interest, P is the principal, r is the interest rate, and t is the time. What will the simple interest be when $P = \$200$, $r = 0.03$, and $t = 3.25$? $19.50

41. *Sample answer:* Use zero as a placeholder when the number of decimal places needed is greater than the number of digits in the product. For example, $0.2 \times 0.036 = 0.0072$, where the two zeros before the 7 were added to create four decimal places.

42. Less than. *Sample answer:* A model can be used to show that the number of squares shaded for the product is less than the number of squares shaded for either of the two numbers.

43. Less than. *Sample answer:* A model can be used to show that the number of squares shaded for the product is less than the number of squares shaded for either of the two numbers.

INTERNET
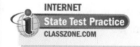
State Test Practice
CLASSZONE.COM

Mixed Review

Graph the points on the same coordinate grid. *(Lesson 2.6)* 45–48. See margin.

45. (2, 1)   46. (1, 4)   47. (0, 8)   48. (3, 0)

49. **Clothesline Length** In 1999, a clothesline loaded with clothes set a record at 15.02 miles long. Write the length of the clothesline in words. *(Lesson 3.1)* fifteen and two hundredths miles

Basic Skills **Divide.**

50. $3\overline{)798}$ 266   51. $4\overline{)1340}$ 335   52. $13\overline{)208}$ 16   53. $21\overline{)315}$ 15

Test-Taking Practice

54. **Multiple Choice** Find the product 4.769×2.8. D
   A. 133,532   **B.** 13,353.2   **C.** 133.532   **D.** 13.3532

55. **Short Response** Oranges cost $3.29 per pound. You buy 1.8 pounds for yourself and 2.3 pounds for your friend. How much do you spend on oranges to the nearest cent? Explain how you solved the problem. $13.49. *Sample answer:* Add 1.8 and 2.3 then multiply the sum by $3.29.

LESSON 4.4

Dividing by Whole Numbers

BEFORE
You multiplied decimals and whole numbers.

Now
You'll divide decimals by whole numbers.

WHY?
So you can schedule volunteers to work at a school fair, as in Ex. 28.

In the Real World

Word Watch

Review Words
dividend, p. 691
divisor, p. 691
quotient, p. 691

Sports Cards Your soccer team orders sports cards for each player. You buy a set of 8 cards for $9.92. How much did you pay for each card?

You can use the rule below to help you find how much you paid for each card.

Dividing a Decimal by a Whole Number

Words When dividing a decimal by a whole number, place the decimal point in the quotient above the point in the dividend.

Numbers

$$6)\overline{32.4} \quad \begin{array}{c} 5.4 \end{array}$$

Place the decimal point in the quotient above the point in 32.4.

EXAMPLE 1 Dividing a Decimal by a Whole Number

To answer the question above about sports cards, find $9.92 \div 8$.

1 Place the decimal point.

$$8)\overline{9.92}$$

2 Then divide.

$$\begin{array}{r} 1.24 \\ 8)\overline{9.92} \\ \underline{8} \\ 19 \\ \underline{16} \\ 32 \\ \underline{32} \\ 0 \end{array}$$

ANSWER You pay $1.24 for each sports card.

Your turn now Find the quotient.

1. $5)\overline{13.5}$ 2.7
2. $4)\overline{24.8}$ 6.2
3. $7)\overline{4.48}$ 0.64

Lesson 4.4   Dividing by Whole Numbers   **169**

---

1 PLAN

SKILL CHECK
1. $196 \div 7 = \underline{?}$ 28
2. $380 \div 5 = \underline{?}$ 76
3. $1989 \div 9 = \underline{?}$ 221

LESSON OBJECTIVE
Divide decimals by whole numbers.

PACING
Suggested Number of Days
Basic Course: 1 day
Average Course: 1 day
Advanced Course: 1 day
Block: 0.5 block with 4.5

TEACHING RESOURCES
For a complete list of Teaching Resources, see page 150B.

 TRANSPARENCY
Warm-Up Exercises for this lesson are available on a transparency.

2 TEACH

MOTIVATING THE LESSON
Bring in a variety of packets of sports cards that each list the price of the packet and the number of cards in it on the packaging. Ask students how they could determine which packet is the best value.

TIPS FOR NEW TEACHERS
Suggest that students use ruled paper to keep digits and decimal points aligned while dividing. See Tips for New Teachers in the *Chapter 4 Resource Book*.

MULTIPLE REPRESENTATIONS

In Example 2, students should understand that writing two additional zeros in the dividend is simply representing 14 as 14.00.

Differentiating Instruction

Alternative Strategy In Example 3, another way to approach rounding to the nearest thousandth is to divide until there is a digit in the thousandths place. Then, if the remainder is one half the divisor or greater, the thousandths' place digit of the quotient should be rounded up.

 CONCEPT CHECK

When you divide a decimal number by a whole number, where do you place the decimal point in the quotient? **The decimal point in the quotient is placed directly above the decimal point in the dividend.**

 DAILY PUZZLER

A softball player had 15 hits and her batting average was 0.250. She then had 15 more times at bat and her batting average increased to 0.280. How many new hits did she get?
6 hits

Writing Additional Zeros You may need to write additional zeros in the dividend to continue dividing. The zeros do not change the value of the dividend. For example, 14 = 14.0 = 14.00.

EXAMPLE 2 **Writing Additional Zeros**

Find the quotient 14 ÷ 8.

(1) Place the decimal point and begin dividing.

$$
\begin{array}{r}
1. \\
8\overline{)14.} \\
\underline{8} \\
6
\end{array}
$$

(2) Write additional zeros in the dividend as needed.

$$
\begin{array}{r}
1.75 \\
8\overline{)14.00} \\
\underline{8} \\
60 \\
\underline{56} \\
40 \\
\underline{40} \\
0
\end{array}
$$

ANSWER 14 ÷ 8 = 1.75

EXAMPLE 3 **Using Zeros as Placeholders**

Baseball A batting average is the number of hits divided by the number of times at bat. Find the batting average of a player who made 7 hits in 23 times at bat. Round your answer to the nearest thousandth.

Solution

$$
\begin{array}{r}
.3043 \\
23\overline{)7.0000} \\
\underline{6\,9} \\
10 \\
\underline{0} \\
100 \\
\underline{92} \\
80 \\
\underline{69} \\
11
\end{array}
$$

Write zeros in the dividend as needed.

You cannot divide 10 by 23, so put a zero in the quotient as a placeholder.

Stop when the quotient reaches the ten-thousandths' place.

ANSWER The player's batting average is 0.304.

 **with Solving**

To round to a given decimal place, divide until the quotient has one more decimal place than needed. Then round back.

Your turn now **Divide. Round to the nearest tenth if necessary.**

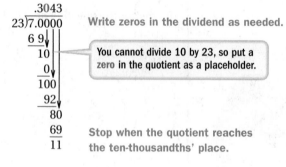

4. $4\overline{)26}$ **6.5**　　**5.** $8\overline{)10}$ **1.3**　　**6.** $8\overline{)49.92}$ **6.2**　　**7.** $12\overline{)29.37}$ **2.4**

INTERNET
eWorkbook Plus
CLASSZONE.COM

Getting Ready to Practice

Vocabulary Tell whether the number is the *divisor*, *quotient*, or *dividend* in the problem shown.

$$2)\overline{5.8} \quad 2.9$$

1. 2.9 quotient   **2.** 5.8 dividend   **3.** 2 divisor

Divide. Round to the nearest tenth if necessary.

4. $6)\overline{32.4}$ 5.4   **5.** $5)\overline{22}$ 4.4   **6.** $7)\overline{51}$ 7.3   **7.** $6)\overline{7.42}$ 1.2

8. Guided Problem Solving Use the table at the right.
Speedskater Hiroyasu Shimizu of Japan recorded the times shown for three 500 meter races during the 2000–2001 season. How do these times compare with his time of 34.65 seconds during a 500 meter race at the 2002 Winter Olympic Games?

Time (sec)
34.32
34.83
35.22

(1 Write an expression to find the mean of the times in the table.
$(34.32 + 34.83 + 35.22) \div 3$

(2 Evaluate the expression you wrote in Step 1. 34.79 sec

(3 Compare your answer to Step 2 with Hiroyasu's Olympic time of 34.65 seconds. *Sample answer:* His Olympic time is faster than his average time.

Practice and Problem Solving

A Copy the answer and place the decimal point in the correct location.

9. $49.5 \div 6 = \mathbf{825}$ **10.** $110.16 \div 9 = \mathbf{1224}$ **11.** $7 \div 4 = \mathbf{175}$
8.25   12.24   1.75

Divide. Round to the nearest tenth if necessary.

12. $9.5 \div 5$ 1.9   **13.** $14.8 \div 2$ 7.4   **14.** $11 \div 9$ 1.2   **15.** $2.2 \div 3$ 0.7

16. $11.6 \div 4$ 2.9   **17.** $21 \div 6$ 3.5   **18.** $7.42 \div 6$ 1.2   **19.** $33.6 \div 7$ 4.8

20. $43.2 \div 6$ 7.2   **21.** $31.75 \div 8$ 4.0   **22.** $44.16 \div 5$ 8.8   **23.** $20 \div 3$ 6.7

24. $8 \div 12$ 0.7   **25.** $28.46 \div 3$ 9.5   **26.** $34.92 \div 20$ 1.7   **27.** $24.61 \div 13$ 1.9

28. School Fair You are organizing volunteers to work at an exhibit at a science fair. You have 6 volunteers to cover a total of 27 hours. How many hours will each volunteer have to work? 4.5 h

29. Compact Discs Your favorite CD has a total running time of 44 minutes. If there are 12 songs on the CD, what is the mean length of a song? Round the answer to the nearest tenth. 3.7 min

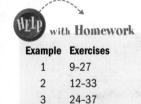
with Homework

Example Exercises
1   9-27
2   12-33
3   24-37

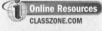
Online Resources
CLASSZONE.COM
· More Examples
· eTutorial Plus

ASSIGNMENT GUIDE

Basic Course
Day 1: SRH p. 691 Exs. 5-8; pp. 171-173 Exs. 9-23, 28-31, 34, 35, 38-40, 42-45, 49-65

Average Course
Day 1: pp. 171-173 Exs. 9-11, 16-29, 32-36, 40-47, 51-62, 66

Advanced Course
Day 1: pp. 171-173 Exs. 10, 11, 20-29, 32-37, 40-50*, 55-58, 65, 66

Block
pp. 171-173 Exs. 9-11, 16-29, 32-36, 40-47, 51-62, 66 (with 4.5)

EXTRA PRACTICE

- Student Edition, p. 711
- Chapter 4 Resource Book, pp. 38-40
- Test and Practice Generator

① TRANSPARENCY

Even-numbered answers are available on transparencies.

HOMEWORK CHECK

When you review students' homework for this lesson, go over the following exercises to check understanding of key concepts.
Basic: 9, 12, 20, 30, 34
Average: 10, 17, 24, 32, 36
Advanced: 11, 22, 29, 33, 37

TEACHING TIP

For Exercises 12-27, be sure students correctly identify the divisor and dividend when they rewrite the expression $a \div b$ in computational form.

What do you think?

Travel

■ **Sky Tram**

In Laon, France, an Automated People Mover (APM) connects the newer part of the city with the historic center. A one-way trip takes about 3 min. If the APM operates 13 hours per day 7 days a week, how many trips does it make in a week? **1820 trips**

Restaurant Bills **The number of people who eat together at a restaurant and the amount of the bill is given. Find the amount each person pays if the bill is divided equally.**

30. 6 people; bill is $47.10 **$7.85**   **31.** 4 people; bill is $39.20 **$9.80**

32. 8 people; bill is $102 **$12.75**   **33.** 7 people; bill is $80.50 **$11.50**

Batting Averages **Find the batting average of the player described. Round the answer to the nearest thousandth.**

34. 13 hits in 45 times at bat **0.289**   **35.** 8 hits in 26 times at bat **0.308**

36. 11 hits in 36 times at bat **0.306**   **37.** 9 hits in 29 times at bat **0.310**

B Algebra **Evaluate the variable expression. Round the answer to the nearest tenth.**

38. $5 \div x$, when $x = 3$ **1.7**   **39.** $6 \div x$, when $x = 14$ **0.4**

40. $23.51 \div x$, when $x = 7$ **3.4**   **41.** $89.34 \div x$, when $x = 25$ **3.6**

Number Sense **Copy and complete the statement using <, >, or =.**

42. $1.9 \div 2 \underline{?} 1$ **<**   **43.** $0.36 \div 1 \underline{?} 0.36$ **=**   **44.** $3 \div 9 \underline{?} 0.3$ **>**

45. **Sky Tram** There are 45 students waiting in line to take a tram car to the top of a mountain. Each car can take only 6 people at a time. How many cars will be needed to carry all the students? **8 tram cars**

46. **Shoe Sale** An advertisement for a sale at a shoe store says that when you buy 2 pairs of shoes for $24.95 each, you will get a third pair for free. What is the mean cost for a pair of shoes? **$8.32**

47. **Explain** A chemist is mixing different solutions. If 90 milliliters of a solution need to be divided equally into 8 test tubes, how much should go into each test tube? Does the answer need to be exact or could the chemist use an estimate? Explain your answer. **11.25 mL.** *Sample answer:* **An estimate can be used because the amount is so small.**

C 48. **Challenge** Sometimes items at a grocery store are priced in groups of items. For lunch, you only want one of each item. Find the total cost for a lunch that includes 1 bagel, 1 apple, 1 box of raisins, and 1 juice package. **$1.54**

Grocery Items	
6 Bagels	$2.88
5 Apples	$1.80
4 Boxes of raisins	$1.10
8 Juice packages	$3.40

Mixed Review

Find the value of the power. *(Lessons 1.3, 4.3)*

49. 10^1 10 **50.** 10^2 100 **51.** $(0.1)^2$ 0.01 **52.** $(0.01)^2$ 0.0001

Solve the equation using mental math. *(Lesson 1.6)*

53. $x - 4 = 5$ 9 **54.** $1 + x = 8$ 7 **55.** $24 \div x = 12$ 2 **56.** $3x = 0$ 0

Find the product. *(Lesson 4.3)*

57. 5.42×6.3 34.146 **58.** 1.8×0.04 0.072 **59.** 3.107×2.7 8.3889 **60.** 2.56×4.1 10.496

Basic Skills **Estimate the product.** 61–64. Estimates may vary.

61. 11×79 790 **62.** 2×101 200 **63.** 53×19 1000 **64.** 187×31 6000

Test-Taking Practice

INTERNET
State Test Practice
CLASSZONE.COM

65. **Multiple Choice** An industrial arts teacher wants to cut a board that is 8.52 meters long into 4 equal pieces. How long will each piece be? **B**

   A. 2 meters   **B.** 2.13 meters   **C.** 2.31 meters   **D.** 23.1 meters

66. **Multiple Choice** Four people go to a restaurant. The bill is $26.88. If they split the bill equally, how many dollars does each person pay? **H**

   F. $.15   **G.** $6.00   **H.** $6.72   **I.** $13.44

BRAIN GAME

Matching Cards

$0.2 \div 4 = 0.05$	$3.65 \div 5 = 0.73$
$1.8 \div 3 = 0.6$	$5.2 \div 10 = 0.52$
$9.6 \div 12 = 0.8$	$0.79 \div 100 = 0.0079$
$0.08 \div 2 = 0.04$	$4.8 \div 16 = 0.3$

Preparation Write the following quotients and division statements on separate index cards.

Quotients:

0.73	0.0079
0.04	0.3
0.6	0.05
0.52	0.8

Division Statements:

$0.2 \div 4$	$3.65 \div 5$
$1.8 \div 3$	$5.2 \div 10$
$9.6 \div 12$	$0.79 \div 100$
$0.08 \div 2$	$4.8 \div 16$

Game Shuffle and place the cards face down in a 4-by-4 grid.

- Flip over two cards.
- Keep the cards if you match a division statement and its quotient. Otherwise, flip the cards back over.
- The person with the most cards at the end wins the game.

---

4 ASSESS

ASSESSMENT RESOURCES

For more assessment resources, see:
- Assessment Book
- Test and Practice Generator

MINI-QUIZ

Find the quotient.

1. $84.91 \div 7$ **12.13**

2. $131 \div 8$ **16.375**

3. A baseball player had 6 hits in 29 times at bat. Find the player's batting average to the nearest thousandth. **0.207**

5 FOLLOW-UP

RETEACHING/REMEDIATION

- Study Guide in Chapter 4 Resource Book, pp. 41–42
- Tutor Place, Whole Numbers and Decimals Card 12
- eTutorial Plus Online
- Extra Practice, p. 711
- Lesson Practice in Chapter 4 Resource Book, pp. 38–40

CHALLENGE/ENRICHMENT

- Challenge Practice in Chapter 4 Resource Book, p. 44
- Teacher's Edition, p. 150F

ENGLISH LEARNER SUPPORT

- Spanish Study Guide
- Multi-Language Glossary
- Chapter Audio Summaries CDs

Notebook Review

LESSONS 4.1 TO 4.4

Review the vocabulary definitions in your notebook.

Copy the review examples in your notebook. Then complete the exercises.

Check Your Definitions

commutative property of multiplication, p. 155

associative property of multiplication, p. 155

distributive property, p. 159

Use Your Vocabulary

1. Copy and complete: The __?__ is illustrated by $a(b + c) = ab + ac$.
distributive property

4.1 Can you multiply decimals and whole numbers?

 EXAMPLE

$$\begin{array}{r} 3.81 \\ \times \quad 7 \\ \hline 26.67 \end{array}$$

2 decimal places

2 decimal places

 Multiply. **2.** 1.742×3 **3.** 0.05×12 0.6   **4.** 16×0.78 12.48
5.226

4.2 Can you use the distributive property?

 EXAMPLE $4(70 + 9) = 4(70) + 4(9)$ Use the distributive property.

$\qquad\qquad\qquad = 280 + 36$ Multiply.

$\qquad\qquad\qquad = 316$ Add.

☑ **Use the distributive property to evaluate the expression.**

5. $5(50 + 8)$ **6.** $8(30 - 7)$ **7.** $6(70 - 0.5)$ **8.** $10(9.7 + 5.6)$
290   184   417   153

4.3 Can you multiply decimals?

EXAMPLE

$$\begin{array}{r} 2.47 \\ \times \ 0.3 \\ \hline 0.741 \end{array}$$

2 decimal places

+ 1 decimal place

3 decimal places

☑ **Multiply.**   **9.** 1.4×0.3 **10.** 5.61×7.2 **11.** 0.213×0.4
0.42   40.392   0.0852

4.4 Can you divide decimals by whole numbers?

 EXAMPLE

$$\begin{array}{r} 2.8 \\ 5\overline{)14.0} \\ \underline{10}\downarrow \\ 4\,0 \\ \underline{4\,0} \\ 0 \end{array}$$

Place the decimal point.

Write and bring down zeros as needed.

☑ **Divide. Round to the nearest tenth if necessary.**

12. $3\overline{)21.9}$ 7.3   **13.** $5\overline{)32.64}$ 6.5   **14.** $4\overline{)13}$ 3.3   **15.** $105\overline{)22}$ 0.2

Stop and Think about Lessons 4.1–4.4

 16. Writing Explain how to use mental math to find the product 7(5.1).

17. Writing Explain how to find the number of decimal places in the product 0.92×2.4.

16. *Sample answer:* Write 5.1 as 5 + 0.1 and use the distributive property. So, 7(5 + 0.1) = 35 + 0.7 = 35.7.

17. Add the number of decimal places in each of the two factors to find the number of decimal places in the product. Because 2 + 1 = 3, the product has 3 decimal places.

Review Quiz 1

Multiply. Use estimation to check your answer.

1. 4.7×6 **2.** 0.6512×8 **3.** 4×2.083 **4.** 0.724×12
   28.2   5.2096   8.332   8.688
5. 2.9×2.4 **6.** 1.45×0.03 **7.** 6.08×3.7 **8.** 3.84×2.16
   6.96   0.0435   22.496   8.2944

9. Travel A car can travel about 27.5 miles on a gallon of gas. About how far can the car travel on 8 gallons of gas? 220 mi

Use the distributive property to evaluate the expression.

10. $8(20 + 7)$ 216   **11.** $10(7.6 - 3)$ 46   **12.** $4(9 + 1.5)$ 42

13. Use mental math to find the product 6(9.8). 58.8

14. Television One of the largest television sets in the world is in Tokyo, Japan. The screen has a length of 24.3 meters and a width of 45.7 meters. Find the area of the screen. 1110.51 m²

Divide. Round to the nearest tenth if necessary.

15. $6\overline{)31.78}$ 5.3   **16.** $5\overline{)44.21}$ 8.8   **17.** $9\overline{)4}$ 0.4   **18.** $8\overline{)15}$ 1.9

SKILL CHECK
1. $10^3 = $ _?_   1000
2. $10^2 = $ _?_   100
3. $10^4 = $ _?_   10,000

LESSON OBJECTIVE

Use mental math.

PACING

Suggested Number of Days
Basic Course: 1 day
Average Course: 1 day
Advanced Course: 1 day
Block: 0.5 block with 4.4

TEACHING RESOURCES

For a complete list of Teaching Resources, see page 150B.

 **TRANSPARENCY**

Warm-Up Exercises for this lesson are available on a transparency.

2 TEACH

MOTIVATING THE LESSON

Ask students the difference between multiplying 2.7 by 10 and by 0.1.

ACTIVITY

Goal Multiply by a power of 10.

Key Discovery Multiplying by a power of 10 moves the decimal point to the right or to the left.

TIPS FOR NEW TEACHERS

Be sure students understand that a decimal power of 10 is a number like 0.1, 0.01, 0.001, ...
See Tips for New Teachers in the *Chapter 4 Resource Book.*

LESSON 4.5

Multiplying and Dividing by Powers of Ten

BEFORE	▶ Now	WHY?
You multiplied and divided with decimals.	You'll use mental math to help multiply and divide.	So you can find the number of hockey players in Exs. 36–37.

Word Watch

Review Words

power, p. 16
exponent, p. 16

Activity   **What happens when you multiply by a power of ten?**

1–2. See margin.

1. Complete the table.
2. What do you notice about the movement of the decimal point when you multiply by whole number powers of 10? by decimal powers of 10?

Whole Number Powers of Ten	Decimal Powers of Ten
$10 \times 8.3 = $ _?_	$0.1 \times 8.3 = $ _?_
$100 \times 8.3 = $ _?_	$0.01 \times 8.3 = $ _?_
$1000 \times 8.3 = $ _?_	$0.001 \times 8.3 = $ _?_
$10,000 \times 8.3 = $ _?_	$0.0001 \times 8.3 = $ _?_

Step 1: $10 \times 8.3 = 83$
$0.1 \times 8.3 = 0.83$

$100 \times 8.3 = 830$
$0.01 \times 8.3 = 0.083$

$1000 \times 8.3 = 8300$
$0.001 \times 8.3 = 0.0083$

$10,000 \times 8.3 = 83,000$
$0.0001 \times 8.3 = 0.00083$

Step 2: *Sample answer:*
The decimal point is moved one place to the left for each decimal place in the decimal power of 10; the decimal point is moved one place to the right for each zero in the power of 10.

Notebook

Multiplying by Powers of Ten

Multiplying by Whole Number Powers of 10 Move the decimal point one place *to the right* for each zero in the whole number power of 10.

    Numbers $3.995 \times 100 = 3\,9\,9.5$

Multiplying by Decimal Powers of 10 Move the decimal point one place *to the left* for each decimal place in the decimal power of 10.

    Numbers $399.5 \times 0.001 = 0.3\,9\,9\,5$

 **with Solving**

When you move a decimal point to the right or left, you may need to write zeros as placeholders.

EXAMPLE 1   **Multiply Decimals Using Mental Math**

a. $0.05 \times 1000 = 0\,0\,5\,0. = 50$ Move 3 places to the right.

b. $95.38 \times 0.0001 = .0\,0\,9\,5\,3\,8 = 0.009538$ Move 4 places to the left.

Your turn now   Find the product using mental math.

1. 21.48×10
   214.8
2. 6.07×1000
   6070
3. 153.6×0.01
   1.536
4. 12×0.001
   0.012

NCTM CURRICULUM STANDARDS
Standard 1: Compute fluently
Standard 2: Understand patterns
Standard 10: Use representations to communicate ideas

EXAMPLE 2 Multiply Decimals by Powers of Ten

Bridges The graph shows the number of vehicles that crossed bridges during 2000. How many vehicles crossed the Golden Gate Bridge?

Vehicle Traffic in 2000		
Francis Scott Key Bridge (MD)	🚗 ı	1.09
Golden Gate Bridge (CA)	🚗 🚗 🚗 🚗 🚙	4.25
George Washington Bridge (NY)	🚗 🚗 🚗 🚗 🚗 🚗 🚗	5.34

🚗 = 10,000,000 vehicles

$4.25 \times 10{,}000{,}000 = 4\,2\,5\,0\,0\,0\,0\,0.$ **Move 7 places to the right.**

$= 42{,}500{,}000$

ANSWER In 2000, 42,500,000 vehicles crossed the Golden Gate Bridge.

Dividing by Powers of Ten

Dividing by Whole Number Powers of 10 Move the decimal point one place *to the left* for each zero in the whole number power of 10.

Numbers $35 \div 100 = 0.3\,5$

Dividing by Decimal Powers of 10 Move the decimal point one place *to the right* for each decimal place in the decimal power of 10.

Numbers $35 \div 0.001 = 3\,5\,0\,0\,0.$

EXAMPLE 3 Divide Decimals Using Mental Math

a. $508.3 \div 10 = 5\,0.8\,3 = 50.83$ **Move 1 place to the left.**

b. $508.3 \div 0.01 = 5\,0\,8\,3\,0. = 50{,}830$ **Move 2 places to the right.**

Your turn now Find the quotient using mental math.

5. $42.6 \div 100$
0.426

6. $509 \div 1000$
0.509

7. $5 \div 0.1$
50

8. $3.2 \div 0.001$
3200

Example 1 Multiply the decimals using mental math.
a. 0.001×4.53 **0.00453**
b. $2.75 \times 10{,}000$ **27,500**

Example 2 The graph shows the number of hours of music played by a radio station during a year. How many hours of music were played during the winter? **38,200 h**

Hours of Music

Spring		5.15
Summer		6.65
Fall		3.54
Winter		3.82

Ω = 10,000 hours

Example 3 Divide the decimals using mental math.
a. $72.7 \div 0.001$ **72,700**
b. $72.7 \div 10{,}000$ **0.00727**

 CONCEPT CHECK

How can you multiply or divide by a whole number power of 10? How can you multiply or divide by a decimal power of 10? **To multiply or divide by a whole number power of 10, move the decimal point one place to the right (to multiply) or to the left (to divide) for each zero in the power of 10. To multiply or divide by a decimal power of 10, move the decimal point one place to the left (to multiply) or to the right (to divide) for each decimal place in the decimal power of 10.**

DAILY PUZZLER

What number should 412,000 be multiplied by so the product is 0.000412? What number should 412,000 be divided by so the quotient is 0.000412? **0.000000001; 1,000,000,000**

177

ASSIGNMENT GUIDE

Basic Course
Day 1: SRH p. 690 Exs. 11–16,
p. 706 Exs. 3–7; pp. 178–179
Exs. 12–28, 30–33, 36–39,
42–54

Average Course
Day 1: pp. 178–179 Exs. 12–33,
36–39, 42–51, 54, 55

Advanced Course
Day 1: pp. 178–179 Exs. 12–15,
22–29, 34–41*, 44–48, 54,
55

Block
pp. 178–179 Exs. 12–33, 36–39,
42–51, 54, 55 (with 4.4)

EXTRA PRACTICE

- Student Edition, p. 711
- Chapter 4 Resource Book,
  pp. 49–51
- Test and Practice Generator

⊘ TRANSPARENCY

Even-numbered answers are available on transparencies.

HOMEWORK CHECK

When you review students' homework for this lesson, go over the following exercises to check understanding of key concepts.
Basic: 12, 17, 24, 28, 36
Average: 13, 19, 25, 29, 36
Advanced: 14, 25, 28, 29, 37

⊗ COMMON ERROR

Students often count zeros when multiplying or dividing by decimal powers of 10, and get incorrect answers in problems like those in Exercises 16–27. For multiplying or dividing by decimal powers of 10, students should count decimal *places*, not *zeros*.

178

Getting Ready to Practice

Vocabulary Use the numbers 10, 0.01, 100, and 0.1.

1. Which numbers are whole number powers of 10? 10, 100

2. Which numbers are decimal powers of 10? 0.01, 0.1

Find the product or quotient using mental math.

3. 7.58×10 75.8 **4.** 24.831×0.1 2.4831 **5.** 16.35×0.01 0.1635 **6.** 0.7×1000 700

7. $13.4 \div 10$ 1.34 **8.** $27.65 \div 100$ 0.2765 **9.** $5.21 \div 0.01$ 521 **10.** $3.108 \div 0.1$ 31.08

11. Weaving The width of a tapestry is 56.7 inches. The length of the tapestry is 100 inches. Find the area of the tapestry. 5670 in.²

Practice and Problem Solving

HELP with Homework

Example	Exercises
1	16–21, 28
2	36, 37
3	12–15, 22–27, 29

ⓘ **Online Resources**
CLASSZONE.COM
· More Examples
· eTutorial Plus

A **Match the expression with its quotient.**

12. $320.7 \div 100$ C **13.** $320.7 \div 10$ A **14.** $320.7 \div 0.01$ D **15.** $320.7 \div 0.1$ B

A. 32.07   **B.** 3207   **C.** 3.207   **D.** 32,070

Find the product or quotient using mental math.

16. 3.9×10 39   **17.** 7.434×100 743.4   **18.** 459.8×0.001 0.4598

19. $0.502 \times 10,000$ 5020 **20.** 4.9×0.1 0.49   **21.** 1000×0.01 10

22. $726.9 \div 1000$ 0.7269 **23.** $3.457 \div 100$ 0.03457 **24.** $82.93 \div 10$ 8.293

25. $12.57 \div 0.01$ 1257   **26.** $0.9813 \div 0.1$ 9.813   **27.** $0.31725 \div 0.001$ 317.25

28. Alaska In 1999, the population of Alaska was 0.62 million. Write the population as a whole number. 620,000

29. Microns A micron is a distance of 0.001 millimeter. An object has a length of 87.2 millimeters. How many microns long is it? 87,200 microns

xy **Algebra** **Evaluate the expression.**

B **30.** $8.3x$, when $x = 1000$ 8300   **31.** $3.75 \div x$, when $x = 0.01$ 375

32. $5 \div x + 0.02$, when $x = 100$ 0.07 **33.** $6 \div x + 34$, when $x = 0.01$ 634

34. $50 - 8x$, when $x = 0.001$ 49.992 **35.** $3.06x - 21.5$, when $x = 10$ 9.1

INTERNET

State Test Practice
CLASSZONE.COM

Ice Hockey The graph shows the number of people of different ages who played ice hockey in 2000.

36. Find the number of 12–17 year olds that played ice hockey in 2000. 441,000

Ice Hockey Players in 2000		
7-11 year olds		3.74
12-17 year olds		4.41
18-24 year olds		2.93

= 100,000 people

37. How many more 7–11 year olds played ice hockey in 2000 than 18–24 year olds? 81,000

Number Sense Copy and complete the statement using <, >, or =.

38. 532.4×0.001 ? 5.32 <

39. $12.22 \div 0.01$? 0.12 >

C **Challenge** Tell whether the statement is *true* or *false*.

40. When you divide a whole number by a whole number power of 10, the quotient is less than or equal to the dividend. true

41. When you divide a whole number by a decimal power of 10, the quotient is less than the dividend. false

Mixed Review

Find the sum or difference. *(Lesson 3.6)*

42. $5.5 + 4.8$ 10.3

43. $18.7 + 2.19$ 20.89

44. $6 - 3.4$ 2.6

45. $7.21 - 5.94$ 1.27

Find the product. *(Lesson 4.3)*

46. 7.5×6.8 51

47. 2.24×0.04 0.0896

48. 6.02×3.7 22.274

49. 9.114×5.3 48.3042

Basic Skills You give a salesclerk $15. Tell how much change you should receive for the given purchase amount.

50. $12 $3

51. $14.91 $0.09

52. $11.58 $3.42

53. $6.32 $8.68

Test-Taking Practice

54. Multiple Choice The price of one nail is $.01. If the price for a whole box of the nails is $36.80, how many nails does the box contain? C

A. 37   **B.** 368   **C.** 3680   **D.** 36,800

55. Multiple Choice What is the product 43.64×0.1? G

F. 0.4364   **G.** 4.364   **H.** 43.64   **I.** 436.4

LESSON OBJECTIVE

Divide by decimals.

PACING

Suggested Number of Days

Basic Course: 1 day
Average Course: 1 day
Advanced Course: 1 day
Block: 0.5 block with 4.7

TEACHING RESOURCES

For a complete list of Teaching Resources, see page 150B.

 TRANSPARENCY

Warm-Up Exercises for this lesson are available on a transparency.

② TEACH

MOTIVATING THE LESSON

Have students compare the answers to these three division problems:
20 ÷ 5   200 ÷ 50   2000 ÷ 500
Then ask them to compare the divisor and the dividend of the first problem to those in the other two.

TIPS FOR NEW TEACHERS

Be sure students understand that multiplying both the dividend and divisor by the same power of 10 does not change the quotient. See Tips for New Teachers in the *Chapter 4 Resource Book.*

180

LESSON 4.6 Dividing by Decimals

BEFORE	▶ Now	WHY?
You divided by whole numbers.	You'll divide by decimals.	So you can find the gas mileage of a car, as in Ex. 47.

In the Real World

 **Word Watch**

Review Words
dividend, p. 691
divisor, p. 691
quotient, p. 691

Pumpkins At a pumpkin patch you choose a pumpkin weighing 9.5 pounds and pay $4.75. What is the cost per pound of the pumpkin?

You will answer the question above in Example 3. You will need to divide by a decimal.

Dividing by a Decimal

Words When you divide by a decimal, multiply both the divisor and the dividend by a power of ten that will make the divisor a whole number.

Numbers $2.5\overline{)3.75}$ Multiply 2.5 and 3.75 by 10. $\longrightarrow$ $25\overline{)37.5}^{\,1.5}$

EXAMPLE 1   **Writing Divisors as Whole Numbers**

Rewrite the division problem so that the divisor is a whole number.

a. $1.83 ÷ 2.5$

$2.5\overline{)1.83}$ ← Multiply the divisor and dividend by 10.

ANSWER $18.3 ÷ 25$

b. $3 ÷ 0.15$

$0.15\overline{)300}$ ← Write zeros as placeholders.

Multiply the divisor and dividend by 100.

ANSWER $300 ÷ 15$

 **with Solving**

When you divide by a decimal with one decimal place, multiply the divisor and the dividend by 10. For a divisor with two decimal places, multiply by 100, and so on.

Your turn now   Rewrite the division problem so that the divisor is a whole number.

1. $0.7\overline{)5.6}$ $7\overline{)56}$ **2.** $3.8\overline{)4.56}$ $38\overline{)45.6}$ **3.** $0.14\overline{)0.84}$ $14\overline{)84}$ **4.** $0.038\overline{)171}$ $38\overline{)171,000}$

NCTM CURRICULUM STANDARDS

Standard 1: Understand how operations are related; Compute fluently

Standard 6: Solve problems in math and other contexts

EXAMPLE 2 **Using Zeros While Dividing**

Find the quotient.

a. $0.88 \div 1.6$

$$1.6 \overline{)0.88}$$

$$\begin{array}{r} .55 \\ 16\overline{)8.80} \\ \underline{8\ 0} \\ 80 \\ \underline{80} \\ 0 \end{array}$$

b. $30 \div 0.02$

$$0.02 \overline{)30.00}$$

> Sometimes you need to write zeros as placeholders in the quotient.

$$\begin{array}{r} 1500 \\ 2\overline{)3000} \\ \underline{2} \\ 10 \\ \underline{10} \\ 0 \end{array}$$

ANSWER $0.88 \div 1.6 = 0.55$

ANSWER $30 \div 0.02 = 1500$

EXAMPLE 3 **Solving Problems Involving Decimals**

To find the cost per pound of the pumpkin from page 180, you can divide the total cost of the pumpkin by the number of pounds.

Divide $4.75 by 9.5 pounds.

$$9.5 \overline{)4.75}$$ Multiply the divisor and dividend by 10.

$$\begin{array}{r} .5 \\ 95\overline{)47.5} \\ \underline{47\ 5} \\ 0 \end{array}$$

ANSWER Because money is represented with two decimal places, the pumpkin costs $.50 per pound.

✓ **Check** Estimate: $4.75 \div 9.5 \approx 5 \div 10 = 0.5$. So, the answer of $.50 per pound is reasonable.

Your turn now **Divide. Round to the nearest tenth if necessary.**

5. $0.2\overline{)0.99}$ **4.95**   **6.** $1.3\overline{)7.69}$ **5.9**   **7.** $0.28\overline{)25.5}$ **91.1**   **8.** $2.5\overline{)51}$ **20.4**

9. If you paid $10.17 for 3.4 pounds of dried fruit, what was the cost per pound? **$2.99**

ASSIGNMENT GUIDE

Basic Course
Day 1: SRH p. 695 Exs. 17–22;
pp. 182–184 Exs. 11–29 odd,
31–33, 37–47, 55–57, 63–74

Average Course
Day 1: pp. 182–184 Exs. 12–30
even, 31–38, 41–54, 58–60,
64–68, 71–75

Advanced Course
Day 1: pp. 182–184 Exs. 15–18,
27–38, 43–53, 56–62*,
65–70, 74, 75

Block
pp. 182–184 Exs. 12–30 even,
31–38, 41–54, 58–60, 64–68,
71–75 (with 4.7)

HOMEWORK CHECK

When you review students' homework for this lesson, go over the following exercises to check understanding of key concepts.
Basic: 11, 19, 31, 37, 39
Average: 12, 22, 32, 36, 42
Advanced: 15, 28, 33, 38, 45

TEACHING TIP

In Exercises 19–30, remind students that when they round the quotient to tenths, they need to determine what the digit in the hundredths' place is. Also remind them that they can add as many zeros to the dividend as necessary.

4.6 Exercises

More Practice, p. 711

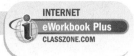

INTERNET
eWorkbook Plus
CLASSZONE.COM

Getting Ready to Practice

1. **Vocabulary** Identify the dividend and the divisor in the quotient $8.49 \div 0.3$. **dividend: 8.49, divisor: 0.3**

Rewrite the division problem so that the divisor is a whole number.

2. $3.1\overline{)12.8}$ $31\overline{)128}$　　3. $0.28\overline{)4.76}$ $28\overline{)476}$　4. $4.6\overline{)9.43}$ $46\overline{)94.3}$　5. $2.1\overline{)0.04}$
$21\overline{)0.4}$

Divide. Round to the nearest tenth if necessary.

6. $0.6\overline{)8.1}$ 13.5　　　7. $0.03\overline{)15}$ 500　　　8. $0.08\overline{)32.32}$ 404　　9. $3.2\overline{)6.56}$ 2.05

10. **Guided Problem Solving** A stack of books is 1.35 meters tall. Each book is about 0.09 meter thick. How many books are in the stack?

　(1 Do you need to *multiply* or *divide* to solve the problem? **divide**

　(2 Write an expression to find the number of books in the stack.
$1.35 \div 0.09$

　(3 Evaluate your expression. How many books are in the stack?
15 books

Practice and Problem Solving

A Rewrite the division problem so that the divisor is a whole number.

11. $9.1 \div 4.3$	12. $14.88 \div 0.93$	13. $7 \div 0.38$	14. $15 \div 0.2$
$91 \div 43$	$1488 \div 93$	$700 \div 38$	$150 \div 2$
15. $1.32 \div 0.55$	16. $17 \div 0.24$	17. $139 \div 3.2$	18. $7.67 \div 1.3$
$132 \div 55$	$1700 \div 24$	$1390 \div 32$	$76.7 \div 13$

Divide. Round to the nearest tenth if necessary.

19. $48 \div 0.6$ **80**　20. $45 \div 1.8$ **25**　21. $7.74 \div 0.9$ **8.6**　22. $1.18 \div 0.2$ **5.9**

23. $4.96 \div 1.6$ **3.1**　24. $20.3 \div 0.7$ **29**　25. $3.6 \div 2.4$ **1.5**　26. $3.48 \div 2.4$ **1.5**

27. $53 \div 0.7$ **75.7**　28. $6.2 \div 0.7$ **8.9**　29. $7.9 \div 3.5$ **2.3**　30. $199.1 \div 5.5$
36.2

Choose an Operation Solve. Explain why you chose the operation you used.

31. **Photos** You have a roll of 24 pictures developed and each picture is 15.24 centimeters long. How long will the pictures be if placed end-to-end? **365.76 cm. *Sample answer*. Multiplication will show how long the pictures are.**

32. **Clothing Costs** Your sweatshirt costs $29.99, your jeans cost $34.65, and your sneakers cost $45.50. How much does your outfit cost?
$110.14. *Sample answer*. Addition will will give the total cost of the outfit.

33. **Geometry** A rectangle has an area of 43.7 square centimeters. The length of the rectangle is 9.5 centimeters. Find the width. **See margin.**

33. **4.6 cm. *Sample answer*.** Division will give you the width of the rectangle.

 with Homework

Example	Exercises
1	11–18, 34
2	19–30, 39–46
3	31–33, 35–38

Online Resources
CLASSZONE.COM

· More Examples
· eTutorial Plus

B 34. Find the Error Describe and correct the error in rewriting the problem.

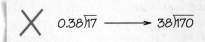

Sample answer: Both the divisor and the dividend should be multiplied by 100, so the rewritten problem should be 38)1700.

✗ COMMON ERROR

Exercises 52 and 53 require the use of the order of operations. Be on the lookout for students who add first and then divide.

Estimation Estimate the cost per pound of the fruit.

35. Apples: 7.1 pounds cost $7.85. **$1**

36. Bananas: 4.8 pounds cost $4.93. **$1**

37. Pears: 3.2 pounds cost $8.28. **$3**

38. Peaches: 4.5 pounds cost $6.75. **$1**

Divide. Round to the nearest tenth if necessary.

39. $0.09 \div 3$ 0.03   **40.** $8.69 \div 4.1$ 2.1   **41.** $40 \div 0.05$ 800   **42.** $90 \div 0.18$ 500

43. $97.2 \div 0.9$ 108   **44.** $2.16 \div 0.02$ 108   **45.** $21.3 \div 0.07$ 304.3   **46.** $5.34 \div 1.86$ 2.9

47. Cars Juan drives his car 470.8 miles and uses 14.5 gallons of gasoline. Find the gas mileage (miles divided by gallons) of Juan's car. Round your answer to the nearest tenth. **32.5 mi/gal**

48. Critical Thinking Why is it helpful to rewrite a division problem so that the divisor is a whole number? *Sample answer:* It makes it easy to know where to place the decimal point in the quotient.

49. Writing Write an addition, a subtraction, a multiplication, and a division problem with a solution of 3.5. *Sample answers:* 1.8 + 1.7 = 3.5, 7.1 − 3.6 = 3.5, 1.75 × 2 = 3.5, 10.5 ÷ 3 = 3.5

xy **Algebra Evaluate the expression when $x = 4.54$ and $y = 7.5$. Round to the nearest hundredth if necessary.**

50. $x \div y$ 0.61   **51.** $y \div x$ 1.65   **52.** $x + 3.15 \div y$ 4.96   **53.** $y + x \div 0.8$ 13.18

World Population Use the table below to answer Exercises 54 and 55. Round to the nearest tenth.

World Population (billions)								
Year	1650	1700	1750	1800	1850	1900	1950	2000
Population	0.51	0.63	0.79	0.97	1.26	1.66	2.56	6.08

54. How many times greater was the population in 2000 than in 1900?
3.7 times greater

55. How many times greater was the population in 1950 than in 1650?
5.0 times greater

Number Sense Copy and complete the statement using <, >, or =.

56. $13.42 \div 1.18$ _?_ $134.2 \div 118$ >   **57.** $6.857 \div 2.56$ _?_ $685.7 \div 256$ =

58. $43.75 \div 2.28$ _?_ $43.75 \div 22.8$ >   **59.** $21.74 \div 1.02$ _?_ $21.74 \div 0.102$ <

MINI-QUIZ

Divide. Round to the nearest tenth if necessary.

1. $0.0884 \div 0.17$ **0.52**

2. $2.49 \div 1.5$ **1.66**

3. $17 \div 0.025$ **680**

4. $7.595 \div 0.35$ **21.7**

5. A turkey drumstick weighs 1.5 pounds and costs $4.47. Find the cost per pound. **$2.98 per lb**

C 60. Amusement Parks The average price to enter an amusement park is $18.50. The park collects about $6.29 million just from entrance fees for the year. About how many people visited the park? **340,000 people**

Challenge Tell whether the statement is *always*, *sometimes*, or *never* true.

61. If the divisor is less than the dividend and greater than 0, the quotient is greater than 1. **always**

62. If the divisor is greater than the dividend, and the dividend is greater than 0, the quotient is less than 1. **always**

Mixed Review

Evaluate the expression. (Lesson 1.4)

63. $15 \div 5 \times 2$ **6**   **64.** $16 \div (2 + 6) \times 4$ **8**   **65.** $36 - 2^3$ **28**

66. Choose an appropriate customary and metric unit you might use to measure the height of a movie screen. (Lesson 2.1) **feet or meters**

Find the product. (Lesson 4.1)

67. 5×0.6 **3**   **68.** 0.02×2 **0.04**   **69.** 8.037×4 **32.148**   **70.** 0.89×21 **18.69**

Basic Skills The pictograph shows the results of a survey that asked students to choose their favorite fruit. Use the pictograph to answer the following questions.

71. Which fruit was most popular? How many students chose that fruit? **banana; 30 students**

72. Which two fruits had the same number of responses? **orange and watermelon**

73. Find the total number of students surveyed. **95 students**

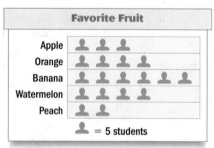

Test-Taking Practice

74. Multiple Choice What is the quotient $6.56 \div 0.4$? **B**

   A. 1.64   **B.** 16.4   **C.** 164   **D.** 1640

75. Short Response Write a division problem that has a quotient of 2.6. Explain how you found the divisor and the dividend.
Sample answer: 1.56 ÷ 0.6; multiplied 2.6 by 0.6 to find 1.56.

Guess, Check, and Revise
Draw a Diagram
Make a Table
Make a List
Perform an Experiment
Work Backward
Look for a Pattern

Perform an Experiment

Problem You have a 13 cm by 13 cm piece of cardboard. You want to fold it into a box. Which will hold more, a box that is 5 cm by 5 cm by 4 cm or a box that is 10 cm by 10 cm by 1.5 cm?

1 Read and Understand

Read the problem carefully.

The main idea of the problem is to compare the amounts that two different boxes can hold.

2 Make a Plan

Decide on a strategy to use.

One way to solve the problem is to perform an experiment. You will need stiff paper or cardboard, a metric ruler, scissors, tape, a metric measuring cup, and 250 milliliters (mL) of rice.

3 Solve the Problem

Reread the problem and perform an experiment.

First, cut out two squares of paper that measure 13 cm on each side.

Next, cut the corners out of the paper as shown below. Then fold along the dotted lines to form two boxes. Tape the edges.

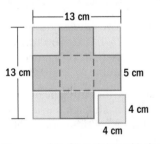
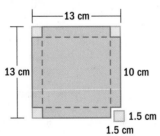

Then, carefully fill each box with rice. Use the metric measuring cup to measure how much rice each box holds.

ANSWER The first box holds 100 mL of rice while the second box holds 150 mL of rice.

4 Look Back

By performing an experiment, you found that two different sized boxes, created from the same size paper, hold different amounts of material.

NCTM CURRICULUM STANDARDS
Standard 6: Build knowledge through problem solving;
Solve problems in math and other contexts;
Apply/adapt strategies to solve problems

STRATEGY BACKGROUND
When students use the strategy Perform an Experiment, they often construct and use an object or objects to generate data. The experiment usually results in a comparison of measurable quantities such as volume or time.

GUIDING STUDENTS' WORK
In Step 3, after students pour rice into each container, they should be sure the top of the rice is level and it completely fills the container. Then they should pour the rice into a measuring cup to determine the amount of rice that was in the container. Also, help students to calculate the volume of each open box and use the relationship that 1 milliliter equals 1 cubic centimeter to see how the text came up with the exact values 100 milliliters and 150 milliliters.

EXTRA EXAMPLES

Example You have two 10 inches by 6 inches pieces of cardboard. Which will hold more sand, a box that is 8 inches by 4 inches by 1 inch or a box that is 7 inches by 3 inches by 1.5 inches? **The first box holds a little more sand than the second box.**

2. *Sample answer:* Beginning in the upper left corner, draw the square, then draw its diagonal, and then finish the triangle.

Lesson 4.7   Mass and Capacity   **185**

APPLY

 TRANSPARENCY

Even-numbered answers are available on transparencies.

TEACHING TIP

Exercise 4 should be done as a group activity. It requires popcorn, rice, sand, beans, or other solid material. If you used one of these materials for the problem on page 185, you can use it again here.

SUGGESTED STRATEGIES

You may wish to suggest the following strategies for the problems in the Mixed Problem Solving:

- Exercise 5: Draw a Diagram, Make a Table
- Exercise 6: Draw a Diagram, Guess, Check, and Revise
- Exercise 7: Guess, Check, and Revise
- Exercise 8: Make a Table, Perform an Experiment

Practice the Strategy

Use the strategy *perform an experiment*.

1. **Measurement** Compare the time it takes to do 10 jumping jacks to the time it takes to jump rope 10 times. Which activity takes you the least amount of time to complete? *Sample answer:* Jump rope 10 times.

2. **Drawing** Use examples to show whether the figure below can be drawn without lifting your pencil off the paper or retracing any segment. **See margin.**

3. **Toothpicks** There are 18 rectangles of different sizes formed by the toothpicks below. What is the least number of toothpicks that you can remove to have only 3 rectangles? **5 toothpicks**

4. **Popcorn** You can form a tube by taping together the edges of an $8\frac{1}{2}$ in. by 11 in. piece of paper. Predict which tube will hold more popcorn. Then experiment to test your prediction. **the shorter tube**

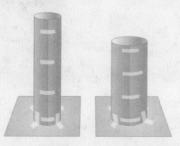

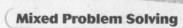

Mixed Problem Solving

Use any strategy to solve the problem.

5. **Puppy** You need to fence in a part of the backyard for the family puppy. The puppy will need an area of 100 square feet. What are the different ways you can fence off the area as a rectangle with whole number dimensions? **1 ft by 100 ft, 2 ft by 50 ft, 4 ft by 25 ft, 5 ft by 20 ft, 10 ft by 10 ft**

6. **Watchbands** You are cutting strips of leather for watchbands. Each watchband requires 8 inches of leather. You have 285 inches of leather. How many watchbands can you make? **35 watchbands**

7. **Mystery Numbers** Two whole numbers have a product of 575. If you subtract one number from the other, the difference is 2. What are the numbers? **23 and 25**

8. **Games** At a fair, you toss three bean bags at the target below. Each bean bag lands on the target. How many different point totals are possible? **4 different point totals**

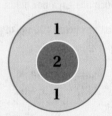

Mass and Capacity

BEFORE	**Now**	**WHY?**
You measured length using customary and metric units.	You'll use metric units of mass and capacity.	So you can analyze water usage, as in Exs. 27–29.

Word Watch

mass, p. 187
gram, p. 187
milligram, p. 187
kilogram, p. 187
capacity, p. 188
liter, p. 188
milliliter, p. 188
kiloliter, p. 188

 Activity Perform an experiment to measure *mass*.

① One person in the group holds a pen in one hand and a paper clip in the other hand. **Check work.**

② Another person adds paper clips until the first person feels that both hands hold the same amount. Record the number of paper clips. *Sample answer:* 12 paper clips

③ Every person in the group takes a turn estimating the pen's mass. Find the mean of the group's results. *Sample answer:* 12 paper clips

④ Based on the mean you found in Step 3, how many paper clips would you have in your hand for 10 pens? for 100 pens? *Sample answer:* 120 paper clips; 1200 paper clips

Units of Mass The **mass** of an object is the amount of matter it has. The **gram** (g) is a metric unit of mass. Two other metric units of mass are the **milligram** (mg) and the **kilogram** (kg).

milligram about the mass of a grain of sugar

gram about the mass of a small paper clip

kilogram about the mass of a book

HELP with **Notetaking**

As you preview this lesson, you may want to review what you learned about benchmarks for metric units of length in Lesson 2.1.

Grams, milligrams, and kilograms are related to each other.

$$1 \text{ g} = 1000 \text{ mg} \qquad 1 \text{ mg} = 0.001 \text{ g} \qquad 1 \text{ kg} = 1000 \text{ g}$$

EXAMPLE 1 **Choosing Units of Mass**

An item has a mass of 10.3 kilograms. Is it a *dog* or a *pencil*? Explain.

The mass of a book is about 1 kg, so 10.3 kg is the mass of about 10 books. The mass of a *dog* is closest to the mass of 10 books, so the item is a dog.

NCTM CURRICULUM STANDARDS
Standard 4: Understand measurable attributes of objects; Understand the units of measurement; Understand the systems of measurement

---

1 PLAN

SKILL CHECK
1. Which is longer, 1 millimeter or 1 centimeter? **1 cm**
2. Which is shorter, 1 meter or 1 kilometer? **1 m**

LESSON OBJECTIVE
Use metric mass and capacity.

PACING
Suggested Number of Days
Basic Course: 1 day
Average Course: 1 day
Advanced Course: 1 day
Block: 0.5 block with 4.6

TEACHING RESOURCES
For a complete list of Teaching Resources, see page 150B.

TRANSPARENCY
Warm-Up Exercises for this lesson are available on a transparency.

2 TEACH

MOTIVATING THE LESSON
Extend the Activity by having students use paper clips to measure the mass of other small objects.

ACTIVITY
Goal Measure mass.
Key Discovery You can use common objects to estimate mass.

TIPS FOR NEW TEACHERS
Be sure students understand that mass is to metric units as weight is to customary units. See Tips for New Teachers in the *Chapter 4 Resource Book*.

Units of Capacity **Capacity** measures the amount that a container can hold. The **liter** (L) is a metric unit of capacity. Two other metric units of capacity are the **milliliter** (mL) and the **kiloliter** (kL).

milliliter about the capacity of an eyedropper

liter about the capacity of a large bottle of water

kiloliter about the capacity of 5 bathtubs

Liters, milliliters, and kiloliters are related to each other.

$$1 \text{ L} = 1000 \text{ mL} \qquad 1 \text{ mL} = 0.001 \text{ L} \qquad 1 \text{ kL} = 1000 \text{ L}$$

EXAMPLE 2 **Choosing Units of Capacity**

Tell whether the most appropriate unit to measure the capacity of the item is *milliliters*, *liters*, or *kiloliters*.

a. bucket   **b.** teaspoon

Solution

a. The capacity of a bucket is closest to the capacity of a large bottle of water. You should use liters.

b. The capacity of a teaspoon is closest to the capacity of an eyedropper. You should use milliliters.

EXAMPLE 3 **Choosing Metric Units**

Choose an appropriate metric unit to measure the item.

a. mass of an eraser   **b.** capacity of a bottle of nail polish

Solution

a. The mass of an eraser is much greater than one milligram and less than one kilogram. So, you should use a gram.

b. The capacity of a bottle of nail polish is much less than one liter or one kiloliter. So, you should use a milliliter.

Your turn now **Choose an appropriate metric unit to measure the item.**

1. mass of a car **kilogram**   **2.** capacity of a thermos **liter**

Getting Ready to Practice

Vocabulary Tell whether the measurement is a *mass*, a *capacity*, or a *length*.

1. 30 mL capacity   **2.** 15 g mass   **3.** 20 mm length

Choose an appropriate metric unit to measure the item.

4. mass of a leaf   **5.** mass of a sofa   **6.** capacity of a pool
   milligram   kilogram   kiloliter

7. Ice Tea You want to determine how much ice tea will fit into a pitcher. Do you need to know the mass or the capacity of the pitcher? capacity

Practice and Problem Solving

Tell whether the measurement is a *mass*, a *capacity*, or a *length*.

A **8.** 10 L capacity   **9.** 0.68 kg mass   **10.** 7.5 mm length **11.** 9.2 mL capacity

12. 5.5 g mass   **13.** 2 m length   **14.** 80.4 mg mass **15.** 614 cm length

16. The mass of an item is 5 kg. Is the item a *shoelace*, a *plate*, or a *bicycle*?
   bicycle

17. Isaac is holding an object that has a mass of 5 grams. Is the object a *book*, a *nickel*, or a *feather*? nickel

18. Gail is describing an object that has a capacity of 1.9 liters. Is she describing a *refrigerator*, a *water pitcher*, or a *cereal bowl*? water pitcher

Mountain Climbing A mountain climber uses a piece of equipment called a *carabiner*. A carabiner is a small metal ring that attaches to the climber's ropes.

19. Do you think the mass of a carabiner should be measured in *milligrams*, *grams*, or *kilograms*? Explain your choice.

20. Do you think the mass of the climber should be measured in *milligrams*, *grams*, or *kilograms*? Explain your choice.

Choose an appropriate metric unit to measure the item.

B **21.** capacity of a sink   **22.** capacity of a lake   **23.** mass of a horse
      liter   kiloliter   kilogram
24. mass of a bubble   **25.** capacity of a glass   **26.** mass of a kick ball
      milligram   milliliter   gram

19. Grams. *Sample answer:* it is closest to the mass of a paper clip

20. Kilograms. *Sample answer:* it is closest to the mass of a book

Lesson 4.7 Mass and Capacity **189**

MINI-QUIZ

1. Here are three masses:
   I. 10 milligrams
   II. 1 kilogram
   III. 1 gram
   Match each item with a mass.
   a. bag of apples II
   b. plastic fork III
   c. sesame seed I

2. Tell whether the most appropriate unit to measure the capacity of the item is milliliters, liters, or kiloliters.
   a. bottle of catsup liters
   b. city water reservoir kiloliters
   c. motorcycle gas tank liters
   d. contact lens case milliliters

RETEACHING/REMEDIATION

• Study Guide in Chapter 4 Resource Book, pp. 68–69
• eTutorial Plus Online
• Extra Practice, p. 711
• Lesson Practice in Chapter 4 Resource Book, pp. 65–67

CHALLENGE/ENRICHMENT

• Challenge Practice in Chapter 4 Resource Book, p. 70
• Teacher's Edition, p. 150F

ENGLISH LEARNER SUPPORT

• Spanish Study Guide
• Multi-Language Glossary
• Chapter Audio Summaries CDs

INTERNET
State Test Practice
CLASSZONE.COM

Extended Problem Solving The table shows the amounts of water a person usually uses for certain activities.

Activity	Water used
showering	75.7
brushing teeth	3.8
washing hands	3.2

27. **Explain** Are the amounts measured in *liters* or *milliliters*? Explain your choice. See margin.

28. How much water do 4 people use if each person takes 1 shower, brushes their teeth 3 times, and washes their hands 5 times? 412.4 L

29. How much water is used in a week for 4 people to do the activities in Exercise 28? How would you express this amount in kiloliters?
    2886.8 L; 2.8868 kL

27. Liters. *Sample answer:* the amounts used would be closest to the capacity of a large bottle of water.

Copy and complete the statement.

30. 1000 mg = _?_ g 1   31. 1 kg = _?_ g 1000   32. 1 kL = _?_ L 1000

33. 6 kL = _?_ L 6000   34. 9 g = _?_ mg 9000   35. 4 mL = _?_ L 0.004

Challenge Use a benchmark to estimate the mass of a brick. Then estimate the number of bricks you would need to equal the mass of the object. The mass of the object is given. 36–37. Estimates may vary.

C 36. bag of cement; 24 kg
      3 kg; 8 bricks

37. sports car; about 1800 kg
    3 kg; 600 bricks

Mixed Review ↻

Round the decimal as specified. *(Lesson 3.4)*

38. 5.976 (nearest tenth) 6.0   39. 0.0929 (nearest thousandth) 0.093

Evaluate the expression. *(Lesson 4.5)*

40. 1.26×1000 41. $5.7 \div 100$ 42. $6.3 \div 0.1$ 43. 37.4×0.01
    1260   0.057   63   0.374

Basic Skills **Estimate the quotient.** 44–47. Estimates may vary.

44. $10\overline{)98}$ 10   45. $19\overline{)105}$ 5   46. $32\overline{)305}$ 10   47. $102\overline{)9982}$ 100

Test-Taking Practice

48. **Multiple Choice** Which measurement is most likely the capacity of a fish bowl? B

    A. 0.5 L   **B.** 3.8 L   **C.** 7.6 L   **D.** 20.5 L

49. **Multiple Choice** The mass of a piece of paper would most likely be expressed with which unit of measurement? G

    F. liters   **G.** milligrams   **H.** grams   **I.** kilograms

Changing Metric Units

LESSON 4.8

BEFORE
You learned metric units for length, mass, and capacity.

Now
You'll change from one metric unit of measure to another.

WHY?
So you can find the height of a sunflower in meters, as in Ex. 27.

📕 **Word Watch**

Review Words
meter, p. 56
gram, p. 187
liter, p. 188

Changing Units You can change from one unit to another in the metric system by multiplying or dividing by a power of 10.

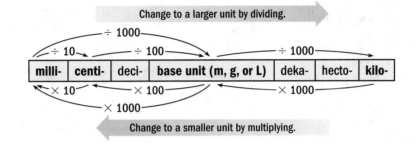

Change to a larger unit by dividing.

÷ 1000
÷ 10   ÷ 100   ÷ 1000

| milli- | centi- | deci- | base unit (m, g, or L) | deka- | hecto- | kilo- |

× 10   × 100   × 1000
× 1000

Change to a smaller unit by multiplying.

EXAMPLE 1 **Changing Units Using Multiplication**

Change 0.64 L to milliliters.

  ① Decide whether to multiply or divide.

  ② Select the power of 10.

ANSWER 0.64 L = 640 mL

Change to a smaller unit by multiplying.

mL ◄── × 1000 ── L

$0.64 \times 1000 = 640.$

EXAMPLE 2 **Changing Units Using Division**

Change 23.6 g to kilograms.

  ① Decide whether to multiply or divide.

  ② Select the power of 10.

ANSWER 23.6 g = 0.0236 kg

Change to a larger unit by dividing.

g ── ÷ 1000 ──► kg

$23.6 \div 1000 = 0.0236$

Your turn now **Copy and complete the statement.**

1. 230 g = _?_ kg
   0.23

2. 2.5 mL = _?_ L
   0.0025

3. 0.45 m = _?_ cm
   45

NCTM CURRICULUM STANDARDS
Standard 4: Understand the units of measurement; Understand the systems of measurement
Standard 6: Solve problems in math and other contexts

Lesson 4.8   Changing Metric Units   **191**

---

① PLAN

SKILL CHECK
How many places and in which direction does the decimal point move when a decimal is divided by 100? multiplied by 100?
2 places left; 2 places right

LESSON OBJECTIVE
Change one unit to another.

PACING
Suggested Number of Days
Basic Course: 2 days
Average Course: 2 days
Advanced Course: 2 days
Block: 1 block

TEACHING RESOURCES
For a complete list of Teaching Resources, see page 150B.

TRANSPARENCY
Warm-Up Exercises for this lesson are available on a transparency.

② TEACH

MOTIVATING THE LESSON
Ask students whether they multiply or divide when changing yards to feet. Then ask them whether they multiply or divide when changing inches to feet.

TIPS FOR NEW TEACHERS
Use an example to show students that when they use a larger unit they need fewer of those units to measure an object. See Tips for New Teachers in the *Chapter 4 Resource Book*.

192

Comparing Measures To compare measures that have different units, change one of them so that both measures have the *same* units.

EXAMPLE 3 Comparing Measures

Which is longer, 170 cm or 1.6 m?

Change 170 cm to meters so the units are the same for both measures.

$$170 \text{ cm} = (170 \div 100) \text{ m} \qquad 100 \text{ cm} = 1 \text{ m}$$
$$= 1.7 \text{ m}$$

Then compare the measures.

Because 1.7 m > 1.6 m, you know that 170 cm > 1.6 m.

ANSWER 170 cm is longer than 1.6 m.

HELP with Solving
You can change either unit to the other. In Example 3, you could have changed 1.6 meters to centimeters instead.

Your turn now Copy and complete the statement with <, >, or =.

4. 50 mm ? 3.5 cm   **5.** 450 mL ? 5 L   **6.** 0.01 kg ? 10 g
$\quad\quad\;>$ $\quad\quad\quad\quad\quad\;<$ $\quad\quad\quad\quad\quad\;=$

EXAMPLE 4 Using a Verbal Model

State Quarters A bank filled with state quarters has a mass of 2.3 kg. The bank's mass is 0.9 kg when empty. Given that a quarter has a mass of about 5.6 g, about how many quarters are in the bank?

Solution

(1 Write a verbal model to find the mass of the quarters in the bank.

Mass of quarters	=	Mass of full bank	−	Mass of empty bank
	=	2.3 kg	−	0.9 kg
	=	1.4 kg		

(2 Change the mass of the quarters to grams.

$$1.4 \text{ kg} = (1.4 \times 1000) \text{ g}$$
$$= 1400 \text{ g}$$

(3 Find the number of quarters by dividing the mass of the quarters by the mass of one quarter.

```
      250.
  56)14000.
     112
     280
     280
       0
```

ANSWER There are about 250 state quarters in the bank.

4.8 Exercises

More Practice, p. 711

INTERNET
eWorkbook Plus
CLASSZONE.COM

Getting Ready to Practice

1. **Vocabulary** Name the three base units for length, mass, and capacity in the metric system.   meter, gram, liter

2. To change from a smaller unit to a larger unit, do you *multiply* or *divide*?   divide

Copy and complete the statement.

3. 520 mg = _?_ g 0.52   4. 360 cm = _?_ m 3.6   5. 0.8 L = _?_ mL 800

6. **Guided Problem Solving** You are comparing lemonade mixes. Mix A will make four 2 liter pitchers of lemonade. Mix B will make twenty 500 milliliter glasses of lemonade. Which mix will make more lemonade?

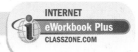

> ① Find the total number of liters of lemonade Mix A makes. **8 L**
>
> ② Find the total number of milliliters of lemonade Mix B makes. **10,000 mL**
>
> ③ Change the amount of lemonade Mix B makes to liters. **10 L**
>
> ④ Compare the two amounts. Which mix will make more lemonade?
> **Mix B**

Practice and Problem Solving

A **Tell whether you would *multiply* or *divide* to change the units.**

7. Change milliliters to liters.   divide
8. Change grams to milligrams.   multiply
9. Change meters to centimeters.   multiply
10. Change grams to kilograms.   divide

Copy and complete the statement.

11. To change from millimeters to centimeters, you divide by _?_.   10
12. To change from meters to kilometers, you divide by _?_.   1000
13. To change from kilograms to grams, you multiply by _?_.   1000
14. To change from liters to milliliters, you multiply by _?_.   1000

Copy and complete the statement.

15. 8 mm = _?_ cm 0.8   16. 0.04 L = _?_ mL 40   17. 255 g = _?_ kg 0.255
18. 6.25 g = _?_ mg 6250   19. 4 km = _?_ m 4000   20. 468 mL = _?_ L 0.468
21. 0.8 kg = _?_ g 800   22. 7.4 cm = _?_ mm 74   23. 8.1 kL = _?_ L 8100

with Homework

Example	Exercises
1	7–27
2	7–27
3	28–35
4	36–39

Online Resources
CLASSZONE.COM

· More Examples
· eTutorial Plus

Lesson 4.8   Changing Metric Units   **193**

③ **APPLY**

ASSIGNMENT GUIDE

Basic Course
Day 1: pp. 193–195 Exs. 7–23, 41, 44
Day 2: pp. 193–195 Exs. 26–38, 48–51, 53–59 odd, 60–62

Average Course
Day 1: pp. 193–195 Exs. 7–27, 50–55
Day 2: pp. 193–195 Exs. 28–39, 41–45, 56–62

Advanced Course
Day 1: pp. 193–195 Exs. 9–14, 18–27, 47–55*
Day 2: pp. 193–195 Exs. 30–46, 62

Block
pp. 193–195 Exs. 7–39, 41–45, 50–62

EXTRA PRACTICE

• Student Edition, p. 711
• Chapter 4 Resource Book, pp. 74–76
• Test and Practice Generator

③ TRANSPARENCY

Even-numbered answers are available on transparencies.

HOMEWORK CHECK

When you review students' homework for this lesson, go over the following exercises to check understanding of key concepts.
Basic: 7, 12, 26, 29, 36
Average: 9, 14, 25, 31, 37
Advanced: 10, 14, 26, 32, 38

⊗ COMMON ERROR

In Exercise 11, students often think that in changing from millimeters to centimeters, you divide by 100. Remind them that a centimeter is 10 times as long as a millimeter.

In Exercises 36–39, some students may choose grams and others may choose kilograms. Have students compare the results in Exercises 38 and 39 using each unit. Ask if using different units had any effect on the results. Finally, as a prelude to Exercise 40, ask students which unit of measure—grams or kilograms—would give the more accurate result.

Brain Game
Sample answer: Fill the 1 liter container. From the 1 liter container, fill the 300 milliliter container 3 times. There are now 100 milliliters left in the 1 liter container. Pour that into the pitcher. Fill the 1 liter container again. From the 1 liter container, fill the 300 milliliter container twice. There are now 400 milliliters left in the 1 liter container. Pour the 400 milliliters from the 1 liter container into the pitcher with the 100 milliliters to get 500 milliliters.

39. mean = 4.998 kg,
median = 5.25 kg,
mode = 2.72 kg.
Sample answer: Mean; it is closer to the middle of all the data.

43. The answer in square meters will be 1,000,000 times the answer in square kilometers.

24. How many grams are in 0.49 kilogram? 490 g

25. How many liters are in 750 milliliters? 0.75 L

26. **Lions** A grown male lion has a mass of about 18,000 grams. What is the mass of the lion in kilograms? 18 kg

27. **Flowers** A sunflower has a height of 64 centimeters. What is the sunflower's height in meters? 0.64 m

Copy and complete the statement with <, >, or =.

B 28. 308 g ? 0.4 kg <   **29.** 1.2 km ? 1300 m <   **30.** 1.3 kL ? 1300 L =

31. 70 mL ? 0.7 L <   **32.** 34.8 kg ? 3480 g >   **33.** 452 L ? 4600 mL >

Animals Tell which dimension is greater.

34. A butterfly has a wingspan of 77 millimeters and a height of 7 centimeters. Which is greater, *wingspan* or *height*? wingspan

35. An orangutan has an arm span of 2.1 meters and a height of 140 centimeters. Which is greater, *arm span* or *height*? arm span

Extended Problem Solving In Exercises 36–39, use the chart showing the masses of 6 bowling balls.

36. What common unit of mass could you use so that each mass is in the same unit?
Sample answer: kg

37. **Calculate** Change the masses in the table to the unit you chose in Exercise 36.
7.26 kg; 5.98 kg; 2.72 kg; 6.79 kg

38. **Compare** List the masses in order from least to greatest. 2.72 kg, 2.72 kg, 4.52 kg, 5.98 kg, 6.79 kg, 7.26 kg

39. **Decide** Find the mean, median, and mode(s) of the masses. Which averages best represent the data? Explain. See margin.

40. **Critical Thinking** Melissa and Jennifer each measure the width of a standard piece of paper. Melissa says the paper is 216 mm wide. Jennifer says the paper is 22 cm wide. Which measurement is more accurate? Explain your reasoning.
216 mm. *Sample answer:* A smaller unit is more accurate.

Bowling Balls
2.72 kg
7260 g
5,980,000 mg
2,720,000 mg
4.52 kg
6790 g

Comparing Areas In Exercises 41 and 42, use a square with side length 1.2 kilometers.

41. Find the area of the square in square kilometers. 1.44 km²

42. Find the side length of the square in meters and its area in square meters. 1200 m; 1,440,000 m²

43. Based on your answers to Exercises 41 and 42, how do square kilometers compare with square meters? See margin.

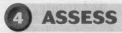

 Algebra **Suppose *x* represents a length in meters. Tell whether the expression represents the same length in the given unit.**

C **44.** $(100x)$ cm yes   **45.** $(x \div 1000)$ km yes **46.** $(x \div 1000)$ mm no

47. Challenge Every centimeter on a map of your town represents an actual distance of 200 meters. If you measure 8.5 centimeters on the map, how many kilometers does it represent? **1.7 km**

Mixed Review

Find the value of the power. *(Lesson 1.3)*

48. 3^3 27   **49.** 2^6 64   **50.** 10 squared 100 **51.** 4 cubed 64

Multiply. Use estimation to check that the product is reasonable.
(Lesson 4.3, 4.5)

52. 2.8×0.9 2.52 **53.** 0.5×4.8 2.4   **54.** 7.318×5.1 **55.** 6.94×4.7
                                                   37.3218   32.618
56. 1000×3.492 **57.** 0.01×458.7 **58.** 0.01×64.76 **59.** 100×31.6
        3492   4.587   0.6476   3160

Basic Skills **Order the numbers from least to greatest.**

60. 64, 78, 29, 32 29, 32, 64, 78   **61.** 105, 150, 101, 110 101, 105, 110, 150

Test-Taking Practice

62. Extended Response A 591 milliliter container of juice costs $1.25. A 1.89 liter container of the same juice costs $3.29. Find the cost per liter for each container of juice. Which container is the better buy? Explain how you found your answer. See margin.

62. The 591 milliliter container costs $2.12 per liter, the 1.89 liter container costs $1.74 per liter. The second container is a better buy. *Sample answer*: Change 591 milliliters to .591 liters. Then to find the price per liter for each container, take the price and divide it by the corresponding number of liters.

INTERNET
State Test Practice
CLASSZONE.COM

MINI-QUIZ

1. Change 2.8 liters to milliliters. **2800 mL**

2. Change 47.6 millimeters to centimeters. **4.76 cm**

3. Complete each statement with $<$, $>$, or $=$.
   a. 1200 mg _?_ 12 g $<$
   b. 50 m _?_ 0.05 km $=$
   c. 2005 L _?_ 2.05 kL $<$
   d. 0.15 m _?_ 1.5 cm $>$

4. A bank filled with quarters has a mass of 4.5 kilograms. The bank's mass is 0.86 kilograms when empty. Given that a quarter has a mass of about 5.6 grams, about how many quarters are in the bank? **650 quarters**

5 FOLLOW-UP

RETEACHING/REMEDIATION

• Study Guide in Chapter 4 Resource Book, pp. 77–78
• Tutor Place, Geometry and Measurement Cards 25, 26
• eTutorial Plus Online
• Extra Practice, p. 711
• Lesson Practice in Chapter 4 Resource Book, pp. 74–76

CHALLENGE/ENRICHMENT

• Challenge Practice in Chapter 4 Resource Book, p. 79
• Teacher's Edition, p. 150F

ENGLISH LEARNER SUPPORT

• Spanish Study Guide
• Multi-Language Glossary
• Chapter Audio Summaries CDs

Fruit Punch

You want to make some fruit punch, but your little sister has taken the measuring cup you need and she won't tell you where it is. You need to measure out 500 mL of water for the punch.

If you have a pitcher for the fruit punch, an unmarked 300 mL container, and an unmarked 1 L container, how can you measure out the right amount of water for the fruit punch?
See margin.

Lesson 4.8   Changing Metric Units   **195**

2. *Sample answer:* Multiply both the divisor and the dividend by a power of 10 that will make the divisor a whole number.

LESSON **4.5** TO **4.8**

Notebook Review

Notebook

Review the vocabulary definitions in your notebook.

Copy the review examples in your notebook. Then complete the exercises.

Check Your Definitions

mass, p. 187   kilogram, p. 187   milliliter, p. 188
gram, p. 187   capacity, p. 188   kiloliter, p. 188
milligram, p. 187   liter, p. 188

Use Your Vocabulary

1. Copy and complete: The kilogram is a measure of _?_ while the milliliter is a measure of _?_. **mass; capacity**

2. **Writing** Explain the first step needed to find the quotient $31.97 \div 2.78$. **See margin.**

4.5 Can you multiply and divide by powers of ten?

 EXAMPLE Evaluate using mental math.

a. $1357.25 \times 0.001 = 1.35725$ Move decimal point 3 places to the left.
$= 1.35725$

b. $46.9 \div 0.01 = 4690.$ Move decimal point 2 places to the right.
$= 4690$

☑ **Evaluate using mental math.**

3. 38.06×10 4. 459.1×0.01 5. $621.37 \div 10$ 6. $97.8 \div 0.001$
   380.6   4.591   62.137   97,800

4.6 Can you divide by decimals?

 EXAMPLE To divide $24 \div 0.03$, multiply the divisor and dividend by 100.

$$24 \div 0.03 \longrightarrow 0.03\overline{)24.00} \longrightarrow \begin{array}{r} 800 \\ 3\overline{)2400} \\ \underline{24} \\ 0 \end{array}$$

ANSWER $24 \div 0.03 = 800$

☑ **Divide. Round to the nearest tenth if necessary.**

7. $620 \div 0.58$ 8. $11.8 \div 0.27$ 9. $38 \div 1.6$ 10. $303.2 \div 0.5$
   1069.0   43.7   23.8   606.4

4.7 Can you use metric units of mass and capacity?

 EXAMPLE Choose an appropriate metric unit to measure the mass of a laptop computer.

ANSWER A kilogram is about the mass of this book and the mass of a laptop computer would be at least the same as this book. So, kilograms is an appropriate unit of measure for the mass of a laptop computer.

☑ **Choose an appropriate metric unit to measure the item.**

11. mass of a mouse gram

12. capacity of a coffee cup milliliter

4.8 Can you change metric units?

 EXAMPLE Copy and complete the statement.

a. 52 g = _?_ mg

52 × 1000 = 52,000

ANSWER 52 g = 52,000 mg

b. 36.8 mL = _?_ L

36.8 ÷ 1000 = 0.0368

ANSWER 36.8 mL = 0.0368 L

☑ **Copy and complete the statement.**

13. 24.5 L = _?_ kL
0.0245

14. 21.2 kg = _?_ g
21,200

15. 20 mm = _?_ cm
2

Stop *and* **Think** about Lessons 4.5–4.8

16. **Writing** How do you change from a smaller metric unit to a larger metric unit? How do you change from a larger to a smaller unit?
divide; multiply

Review Quiz 2

Find the product or quotient. Use mental math, if possible.

1. 4.56 × 100
456

2. 9.75 × 0.01
0.0975

3. 27.9 ÷ 0.09
310

4. 135 ÷ 2.5
54

5. 61.4 ÷ 0.04
1535

6. 36 ÷ 1.8
20

7. 50.8 ÷ 0.5
101.6

8. 0.748 ÷ 0.22
3.4

9. Is the capacity of a backpack measured in *liters* or *milliliters*? liters

Copy and complete the statement.

10. 10 L = _?_ mL
10,000

11. 7 cm = _?_ m
0.07

12. 5.02 g = _?_ kg
0.00502

4 Chapter Review

Vocabulary

commutative property of multiplication, p. 155
associative property of multiplication, p. 155
distributive property, p. 159

mass, p. 187
gram, p. 187
milligram, p. 187
kilogram, p. 187

capacity, p. 188
liter, p. 188
milliliter, p. 188
kiloliter, p. 188

Vocabulary Review

1. Which property allows you to write $3(70 + 0.8)$ as $3(70) + 3(0.8)$? **distributive property**

2. Give three examples of metric units used to measure mass. **milligram, gram, kilogram**

3. Give three examples of metric units used to measure capacity. **milliliter, liter, kiloliter**

Copy and complete the statement.

4. To change from milliliters to liters you divide by _?_. **1000**

5. To change from kilograms to grams you _?_ by 1000. **multiply**

Review Questions

Find the product. Use estimation to check your answer. (Lesson 4.1)

6. 5.61×7 **39.27**
7. 4.18×5 **20.9**
8. 12×0.324 **3.888**
9. 23×6.284 **144.532**
10. 0.85×6 **5.1**
11. 25.5×4 **102**
12. 18×7.89 **142.02**
13. 32×40.78 **1304.96**

14. **Employment** If you earn $8.75 an hour, how much will you be paid for 15 hours of work? (Lesson 4.1) **$131.25**

15. **Snow** If you charge $14.50 an hour to shovel snow and you worked 9 hours this week, how much did you earn? (Lesson 4.1) **$130.50**

Use the distributive property and mental math to find the product. (Lesson 4.2)

16. $5(43)$ **215**
17. $3(77)$ **231**
18. $8(6.1)$ **48.8**
19. $5(3.2)$ **16**
20. $3(16.2)$ **48.6**
21. $5(8.9)$ **44.5**
22. $10(1.8 + 2.3)$ **41**
23. $100(0.15 + 2.2)$ **235**

Multiply. Use estimation to check that the product is reasonable. (Lesson 4.3)

24. 1.2×6.4 **7.68**
25. 0.8×3.7 **2.96**
26. 7.04×0.3 **2.112**
27. 8.67×0.06 **0.5202**
28. 3.14×1.5 **4.71**
29. 6.1×0.007 **0.0427**
30. 3.475×0.08 **0.278**
31. 0.547×4.8 **2.6256**
32. 30.08×0.006 **0.18048**
33. 28.1×0.45 **12.645**
34. 12.34×0.56 **6.9104**
35. 9.63×0.41 **3.9483**

Review Questions

36. Fundraising A company will donate $.75 for every dollar raised by the company's employees in a marathon. If the employees raise $250, how much does the company donate? *(Lesson 4.1)* $187.50

Divide. Round to the nearest tenth if necessary. *(Lesson 4.4, 4.6)*

37. 21.6 ÷ 9 2.4   **38.** 28.2 ÷ 3 9.4   **39.** 48.23 ÷ 7 6.9   **40.** 18.24 ÷ 6 3.0

41. 77.36 ÷ 8 9.7   **42.** 82.44 ÷ 12 6.9   **43.** 45 ÷ 11 4.1   **44.** 30 ÷ 16 1.9

45. 7.9 ÷ 0.4 19.8   **46.** 8.5 ÷ 0.8 10.6   **47.** 6.2 ÷ 3.8 1.6   **48.** 9.9 ÷ 2.2 4.5

49. 22.5 ÷ 0.25 90   **50.** 3.35 ÷ 0.14 23.9   **51.** 44.82 ÷ 3.6 12.5   **52.** 28.49 ÷ 7.4 3.9

53. Tacos Eight tacos cost $10.80. How much does each taco cost? *(Lesson 4.4)* $1.35

54. Muffins Twelve muffins cost $5.49. How much does each muffin cost? $0.46
(Lesson 4.4)

Find the product or quotient using mental math. *(Lesson 4.5)*

55. 2.4 × 10 24   **56.** 6.318 × 100 631.8   **57.** 656.9 × 0.001 0.6569

58. 125 ÷ 1000 0.125   **59.** 8.147 ÷ 100 0.08147   **60.** 0.693 ÷ 0.1 6.93

61. Geometry A rectangle has an area of 6.72 square millimeters. The width of the rectangle is 2.1 millimeters. Find the length by dividing the area of the rectangle by its width. Check your answer. *(Lesson 4.6)* 3.2 mm

2.1 mm

l

Choose an appropriate metric unit to measure the item. *(Lesson 4.7)*

62. capacity of a tea kettle liter   **63.** mass of an ant milligram

64. mass of a train kilogram   **65.** capacity of a raindrop milliliter

66. capacity of Lake Michigan kiloliter   **67.** mass of a pen gram

Copy and complete the statement. *(Lesson 4.8)*

68. 647 mm = _?_ cm 64.7   **69.** 729 mL = _?_ L 0.729   **70.** 26 kg = _?_ g 26,000

71. 54.9 m = _?_ mm 54,900   **72.** 0.34 kL = _?_ L 340   **73.** 0.017 g = _?_ mg 17

74. 9.5 km = _?_ m 9500   **75.** 30 L = _?_ mL 30,000   **76.** 8 g = _?_ kg 0.008

List the measurements in each table from least to greatest. *(Lesson 4.8)*

77.

Table 1
2.7 mg
270 g
0.027 kg

2.7 mg, 0.027 kg, 270 g

78.

Table 2
13 mL
1.3 kL
130 L

13 mL, 130 L, 1.3 kL

79.

Table 3
8 cm
8000 mm
0.8 m

8 cm, 0.8 m, 8000 mm

CHAPTER 4

Chapter Test

Multiply. Use estimation to check that the answer is reasonable.

1. 5.8 × 3 **17.4** **2.** 9.2 × 17 **156.4** **3.** 2.692 × 100 **269.2** **4.** 3.115 × 8 **24.92**

5. 7.25 × 4.6 **33.35** **6.** 12.46 × 3.2 **39.872** **7.** 8.51 × 6.3 **53.613** **8.** 13.77 × 0.04 **0.5508**

Use mental math to find the product or quotient.

9. 13.77 × 1000 **13,770** **10.** 12.46 × 0.01 **0.1246** **11.** 1.5 ÷ 100 **0.015** **12.** 6.25 ÷ 0.1 **62.5**

13. **Auto Racing** The distance around the racetrack at Talladega Superspeedway in Alabama is about 2.66 miles. What is the total distance for 16 laps? 100 laps? **42.56 mi; 266 mi**

Tell whether the *commutative* or *associative* property of multiplication allows you to rewrite the problem as shown.

14. (3 × 7.2) × 2.1 = 3 × (7.2 × 2.1) **associative** **15.** 2 × 6.82 × 25 = 6.82 × 2 × 25 **commutative**

16. Use the distributive property and mental math to find the product 9(4.8). **43.2**

Divide. Round to the nearest tenth if necessary.

17. 28.95 ÷ 2 **14.5** **18.** 13.72 ÷ 4 **3.4** **19.** 9.4 ÷ 52 **0.2** **20.** 6 ÷ 16 **0.4**

21. 10 ÷ 0.8 **12.5** **22.** 3.24 ÷ 0.6 **5.4** **23.** 109.2 ÷ 0.15 **728** **24.** 22.54 ÷ 0.23 **98**

25. **Whales** Eight whales have been born at an aquarium. Their total mass is 1300 kilograms. Find the mean mass of the whales. **162.5 kg**

Copy and complete the statement.

26. 0.9 g = ? mg **900** **27.** 98 m = ? km **0.098** **28.** 3200 L = ? kL **3.2**

29. What do you think the mass of a desk lamp might be: 50 mg, 50 g, or 50 kg? Explain. **50 g.** *Sample answer:* It would be about the same as the weight of 50 paper clips.

Copy and complete the statement with <, >, or =.

30. 4300 L ? 4.39 kL **<** **31.** 215 kg ? 2150 g **>** **32.** 321 mm ? 3.21 cm **>**

33. **Soup** A can of soup contains 710 milligrams of sodium. How many grams of sodium are in the can? **0.71 g**

Chapter Standardized Test

Test-taking Strategy If you have time, check your work. Be sure to use a different method than you originally used. Otherwise, you might make the same mistake twice.

Multiple Choice

1. Estimate the product 4.8×3.2. **C**

   A. 0.15 **B.** 6 **C.** 15 **D.** 25

2. Which answer shows how $5(3 - 0.2)$ can be rewritten using the distributive property? **I**

   F. 5(2.8) **G.** $15 - 0.2$
   H. $15 - 0.1$ **I.** $15 - 1$

3. The cheerleaders sold school pennants for $2.50 each. How much money did they raise if they sold 240 pennants? **D**

   A. $60 **B.** $96 **C.** $240 **D.** $600

4. Which answer shows the quotient $14 \div 128$ rounded to the nearest hundredth? **I**

   F. 0.1 **G.** 0.10 **H.** 0.109 **I.** 0.11

5. Four friends divide the cost of a CD equally. The total cost is $17.60. How much does each person pay? **B**

   A. $4.04 **B.** $4.40 **C.** $4.44 **D.** $4.54

6. You pay $14.57 for 2.98 pounds of cheese at a supermarket. Estimate the price per pound. **H**

   F. Less than $2
   G. Between $2 and $3
   H. Between $4 and $5
   I. More than $7

7. What is the value of $0.608 \div 0.1$? **B**

   A. 0.0608 **B.** 6.08 **C.** 60.8 **D.** 608

8. What is the value of 4217.9×0.01? **G**

   F. 4.2179 **G.** 42.179
   H. 42,179 **I.** 421,790

9. Find the quotient $7.248 \div 0.24$. **D**

   A. 0.302 **B.** 3.02 **C.** 3.2 **D.** 30.2

10. Raul describes an object that has a mass of about 145 grams. Which object could he be describing? **F**

    F. a baseball **G.** a car
    H. a button **I.** a piano

11. A sports bottle holds 1.63 liters of water. What is the capacity in milliliters? **C**

    A. 0.00163 mL **B.** 163 mL
    C. 1630 mL **D.** 16,300 mL

Short Response

12. A rectangle has a length of 8.2 centimeters and an area of 20.5 square centimeters. What is the width of the rectangle? Explain how you found your answer. **2.5 cm; divide the area by the length to obtain the width; $20.5 \div 8.2 = 2.5$ cm.**

13. Tell how you would rewrite 24(9.8) using the distributive property. Explain why this may be helpful. $24(9.8) = 24(10 - 0.2)$. *Sample answer:* 24(10) and 24(0.2) are easy to find and then subtract.

Extended Response

14. You have a choice of two packages of pens to buy. One package contains 8 pens and costs $4.50. The other package has 12 pens and costs $6.25. Which package is the better buy? Explain your reasoning. **See margin.**

14. The package of 12 pens. *Sample answer:* Each pen in the package of 8 pens costs $.56 and each pen in the package of 12 pens costs $.52, which is less than $.56.

UNIT 1
Chapters
1–4

BUILDING **Test-Taking Skills**

Strategies for Answering
Multiple Choice Questions

You can use the problem solving plan on page 42 to solve any problem. If you have difficulty solving a problem involving multiple choice, you may be able to use one of the strategies below to choose the correct answer. You may also be able to use these strategies and others to check whether your answer to a multiple choice question is reasonable.

Strategy: Estimate the Answer

Problem 1

The operation you will use for this problem is multiplication because there are 3.5 times as many cups of sugar in 3.5 pounds of sugar as there are in 1 pound.

There are 2.25 cups of sugar in one pound of sugar. How many cups of sugar are in 3.5 pounds?

A. 1.75

B. 5.75

C. 7.875

D. 78.75

Estimate: $3.5 \times 2.25 \approx 4 \times 2 = 8$, so the correct answer is C.

Strategy: Use Visual Clues

Problem 2

The circle graph shows sales of CDs at a music store. What part of the total sales are pop or rock?

Look at the regions for pop and rock as though they were combined. The combined region is more than half the graph.

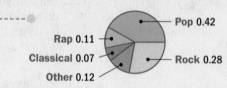

Pop 0.42
Rap 0.11
Classical 0.07
Rock 0.28
Other 0.12

F. 0.14

G. 0.28

H. 0.42

I. 0.7

0.7 is the only one of the given decimals that is greater than 0.5, so the correct answer is I.

Strategy: Use Number Sense

Notice that 0 is a factor in the product $(14.5 \times 3) \times 0$. Use the fact that the product of 0 and any number is 0.

Problem 3

Evaluate the expression $46.97 + (14.5 \times 3) \times 0$.

A. 46.97   B. 64.47   C. 90.47   D. 184.41

$46.97 + 0 = 46.97$, so the correct answer is A.

Eliminating Unreasonable Choices The strategies used to find the correct answers for Problems 1–3 can also be used to eliminate answer choices that are unreasonable or obviously incorrect.

Problem 4

Read the problem carefully. The length of the classroom is $12.2 + 2.6 = 14.8$ meters, not 2.6 meters. To find the area, use the formula $A = lw$.

A middle school classroom is 12.2 meters wide. The length is 2.6 meters more than the width. What is the area?

F. **31.72 square meters** — *Not* the correct answer: $14.8 \times 12.2 \approx 15 \times 12 = 180$.

G. **54 meters** — *Not* the correct answer: area is measured in *square* units.

H. **177.6 square meters** — *Not* the correct answer: the product 14.8×12.2 should end in 6, but it should have two decimal places.

I. **180.56 square meters** — I is the correct answer: $(12.2 + 2.6) \times 12.2 = 180.56$.

1. 2.75 m is greater than the length of the board.

2. $10 - 10$ has the least value, not the greatest value.

3. Perimeter is measured in linear units, not square units.

Watch Out!

Some answers may appear correct at first glance, but they may be incorrect answers you would find by making common errors.

Your turn now

Explain why the highlighted answer choice is unreasonable. 1–3. See margin.

1. A board that is 2.25 meters long is cut into 5 pieces of equal length. How many meters long is each piece?

   A. 0.25 m   B. 0.45 m   ✗C. 2.75 m   D. 11.5 m

2. Which expression has the greatest value when $x = 10$?

   F. $10x$ ✗G. $10 - x$ H. $8x + 3$ I. $x^2 + 5$

3. A rectangle is twice as long as it is wide. If the rectangle is 3.2 meters wide, what is its perimeter?

   A. 9.6 m   B. 19.2 m   C. 20.48 m   ✗D. 20.48 m^2

12. 1602 seats; in the first section, 22 rows times 45 seats per row is 990 seats. In the second section, 18 rows times 34 seats per row is 612 seats. The total number of seats is $990 + 612 = 1602$.

13. 420 mm; $420 = 4.2 \times 10^2$, so the enlarged image is 10^2 or 100 times the actual size of the ant.

15. The can; $\$2.58 \div 3 = \$.86$ and $\$64.48 \div (24 \times 3) \approx \$.90$ and $\$.86 < \$.90$.

16. More than; 5 more glasses; $15 \times 240 \text{ mL} = 3600 \text{ mL}$ of punch are poured in 15 glasses, and $(5000 - 3600) \div 240 = 5.8$, so 5 more glasses can be poured.

UNIT **1**
Chapters
1–4

PRACTICING **Test-Taking Skills**

Multiple Choice

1. A theater can hold 450 people. During a performance, an usher counted 17 empty seats. How many seats were occupied? **B**

   A. 143 seats   **B.** 433 seats

   C. 443 seats   **D.** 467 seats

2. Marissa puts 52 cards into stacks of 5 cards each. How many cards are left over? **F**

   F. 2 cards   **G.** 5 cards

   H. 8 cards   **I.** 10 cards

3. Eric collected 230 aluminum cans to be recycled. Molly collected 151 cans. Mark collected twice as many cans as Molly. Which expression represents the total number of cans collected for recycling? **C**

   A. $230 + 151 + 2$ **B.** $151 + 2 \times 230$

   C. $230 + 3 \times 151$ **D.** $2(230 + 151)$

4. A family drove 90 miles to attend a family reunion. After the reunion, they drove to a park. When they arrived at the park, they had traveled 110 miles. Solve the equation $90 + d = 110$ to find the distance d, in miles, from the reunion to the park. **G**

   F. 10   **G.** 20   **H.** 79   **I.** 200

5. Gary mows a field that is 120 yards by 75 yards. What is the area he mows? **D**

   A. 195 yards   **B.** 390 yards

   C. 8000 square yards   **D.** 9000 square yards

6. The expression $50x$ represents the distance, in miles, a monarch butterfly can travel in x days during migration. How far can the butterfly travel in 8 days? **H**

   F. 40 mi   **G.** 42 mi   **H.** 400 mi   **I.** 508 mi

7. The circle graph shows how often some students exercise. How many of the students exercise less frequently than once a week? **A**

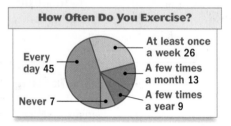

How Often Do You Exercise?
Every day 45 / At least once a week 26 / A few times a month 13 / A few times a year 9 / Never 7

   A. 29   **B.** 45   **C.** 55   **D.** 71

8. Lynann wants to buy a snorkel set for $17.88. She has $9.89. How much more money does Lynann need? **F**

   F. $7.99   **G.** $8.01   **H.** $8.99   **I.** $27.77

9. Sam bought the items shown. What is the best estimate of the total cost of the items? **C**

1 gallon of milk	$2.95
1 dozen eggs	$1.39
bag of bagels	$1.59

   A. $4   **B.** $5   **C.** $6   **D.** $7

10. Kendra bought a box of greeting cards for $12.25. Each card costs $.49. How many cards are in 4 boxes? **I**

   F. 25 cards   **G.** 50 cards

   H. 75 cards   **I.** 100 cards

11. A map of the Nile River has the scale 1 in. : 250 mi. If the length of the river on the map is about 16.5 inches, about how long is the actual river? **C**

   A. 250 miles   **B.** 1515 miles

   C. 4125 miles   **D.** 5175 miles

Short Response

12. An auditorium is divided into two sections. The first section contains 22 rows, and each row has 45 seats. The second section contains 18 rows, and each row has 34 seats. How many seats are in the auditorium? Explain your reasoning.
See margin.

13. An ant is about 4.2 millimeters long. An enlarged image of the ant is 0.42 meters long. Rewrite the enlarged length in millimeters. Then use a power of 10 to explain how the two sizes are related.
See margin.

14. Rosa's car can travel 27 miles per gallon of gas. How far can the car travel on 8 gallons of gas? Explain how you can use the distributive property to answer this question.

216 mi; 8(27) = 8(20 + 7) = 8(20) + 8(7) = 160 + 56 = 216.

Extended Response

18–19. See margin.

18. The students in Mr. Hanson's science class planted tree seedlings and are monitoring their growth. The table shows the height of each tree in inches.

Tree	Apple	Maple	Cedar	Oak
Height (inches)	7	15	20	29

Make a bar graph of the heights. Find the difference in height between the tallest and shortest trees. Is it easier to use the *table* or the *bar graph* to answer this question? Which two trees are closest in height? Is it easier to use the *table* or the *bar graph* to answer this question? Explain your answers.

19. A survey was sent to families asking how many times anyone in the family went to an amusement park in the past two years. Completed surveys were returned by 18 families and the results are shown at the right.

Make a frequency table and a line plot of the data. Compare and contrast the displays. Use each display to find the most common response. Use each display to determine how many of the responses were fewer than two times. Explain your steps.

SURVEY

How many trips has your family made to an amusement park in the past two years?

RESULTS

0	4	1	1	2	5	2	2	2
2	4	0	1	1	1	4	2	2

15. Tennis balls are sold in cans of 3 balls or in cases of 24 cans. Suppose a can of one brand of tennis balls costs $2.58 while a case of the same brand costs $64.48. Which has the lower cost per ball, the *can* or the *case*? Explain how you found your answer.
See margin.

16. Chang buys 5 liters of punch for a party. Fifteen glasses of punch are poured, with 240 mL in each glass. Is the remaining amount of punch *more than* or *less than* a liter? How many more 240 mL glasses could be poured? Explain your steps. *See margin.*

17. Beth's scores on her math quizzes are 78, 27, 81, 95, 83, and 95. Find the mean, median, and mode of the test scores. What is the best average to use to represent the most typical score? Explain your reasoning.
mean = 76.5, median = 82, mode = 95; median; there are the same number of scores above the median as below.

18.

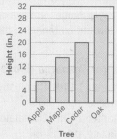

Growth of Tree Seedlings

22 in.; table; Maple and Cedar; bar graph; the exact numbers are given in the table, so it is easier to use to find differences in height; it is easy to see on the bar graph which trees are closest in height.

19.

Number of Trips to Amusement Park	Tally	Frequency
0	II	2
1	IIII	5
2	IIII II	7
3		0
4	III	3
5	I	1

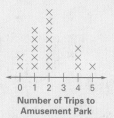

Number of Trips to Amusement Park

The displays show the same data; it is easier to find exact differences using the frequency table, but it is easier to use the line plot to find the most common response; 2 trips; 1 response; look for the greatest number in the frequency table and the most X's in the line plot; look for 1 tally mark in the frequency table and 1 X on the line plot.

UNIT 1
Chapters 1–4

PRACTICING **Test-Taking Skills**

Cumulative Practice for Chapters 1–4

Chapter 1

Multiple Choice **In Exercises 1–6, choose the letter of the correct answer.**

1. Brian puts 155 pencils in an empty box and Judy puts in 79 pencils. How many pencils are in the box? *(Lesson 1.1)* **B**

   A. 224   **B.** 234   **C.** 334   **D.** 344

2. Andy unloaded 121 bags of rice before lunch and another 286 bags of rice after lunch. About how many bags did he unload in all? *(Lesson 1.2)* **I**

   F. 100   **G.** 200   **H.** 300   **I.** 400

3. How can you write $6 \times 6 \times 6 \times 6$ as a power? *(Lesson 1.3)* **C**

   A. 6×4 **B.** 6^3 **C.** 6^4 **D.** 4^6

4. What is the value of 10^4? *(Lesson 1.3)* **I**

   F. 14   **G.** 40   **H.** 1000   **I.** 10,000

5. What is the value of $60 - (30 \div 5) \times 3$? *(Lesson 1.4)* **C**

   A. 2   **B.** 18   **C.** 42   **D.** 58

6. What is the value of the expression $2m + 8$ when $m = 9$? *(Lesson 1.5)* **G**

   F. 19   **G.** 26   **H.** 34   **I.** 37

7. **Short Response** Sam is the second oldest of 5 friends. Sarah is younger than Sam but she is older than Chris. Maria is the oldest. Scott is older than Sarah. Order the friends from youngest to oldest. *(Lesson 1.7)*
   Chris, Sarah, Scott, Sam, Maria

8. **Extended Response** Annabella works at a store and earns $8 an hour. One week she earned $88. *(Lessons 1.2, 1.6)*

   a. Which equation represents the number of hours h that Annabella worked that week: $8h = 88$ or $88h = 8$? **$8h = 88$**

   b. Solve the equation you chose in part (a). **11 h**

   c. Explain how you can estimate to check whether your answer is reasonable.
   Estimate 8(11) and compare to 88.

Chapter 2

Multiple Choice **In Exercises 9–14, choose the letter of the correct answer.**

9. Which item is likely to be measured in centimeters? *(Lesson 2.1)* **B**

   A. a grain of rice   **B.** a pencil

   C. a field   **D.** the equator

10. Which expression can be used to find the perimeter of a garden that is 15 feet long and 10 feet wide? *(Lesson 2.2)* **H**

    F. $2(10 \times 15)$ **G.** 10×15

    H. $2(15) + 2(10)$ **I.** $10 + 15$

11. Carmela makes a scale drawing of a room. The room is 33 feet long. She is using the scale 1 in. : 3 ft. How long is the room on the drawing? *(Lesson 2.3)* **C**

    A. 1 in.   **B.** 3 in.   **C.** 11 in.   **D.** 33 in.

12. Which is the best increment for the scale of a bar graph showing the data values 23, 34, 28, 33, 30, and 32? *(Lesson 2.5)* **G**

    F. 1   **G.** 5   **H.** 20   **I.** 30

13. Which point has coordinates (5, 2)? *(Lesson 2.6)* **B**

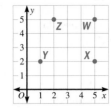

A. W **B.** X

C. Y **D.** Z

14. The graph shows the number of pets in a town. How many more dogs are there than hamsters? *(Lesson 2.7)* **G**

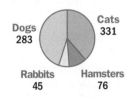

Dogs 283
Cats 331
Rabbits 45
Hamsters 76

F. 76   **G.** 207   **H.** 283   **I.** 359

15. Short Response The table shows the annual amount of snowfall in 7 countries. Explain how to find a reasonable estimate of the mean. How does your estimate compare to the median? *(Lesson 2.8)* **See margin.**

Snow Fall	
Country	**Feet**
Italy	42
Sweden	76
Russia	68
Malaysia	73
Bolivia	45
France	64
Canada	69

16. Extended Response A television show gets the following ratings over a 9 week period. *(Lessons 2.4, 2.5)*

Week	1	2	3	4	5	6	7	8	9
Rating	18	20	19	18	21	22	18	20	18

a. Make a line plot of the data. **See margin.**

b. Make a bar graph of the data. **See margin.**

c. Which one would you use to decide which rating is most common? Why?
The line plot; it shows the frequency of each rating.

Chapter 3

Multiple Choice **In Exercises 17–21, choose the letter of the correct answer.**

17. One yard is ninety-one and forty-four hundredths centimeters. Which measurement equals one yard? *(Lesson 3.1)* **C**

   A. 0.09144 cm   **B.** 91.044 cm

   C. 91.44 cm   **D.** 901.44 cm

18. Which measurement represents a length of 35 centimeters written to the nearest hundredth of a meter? *(Lesson 3.2)* **F**

   F. 0.35 m   **G.** 3.5 m   **H.** 35 m   **I.** 350 m

19. What is the greatest number in the list below? *(Lesson 3.3)* **D**

     5.05, 0.505, 5.5, 5.005, 5.505, 0.0505

   A. 0.0505   **B.** 5.005   **C.** 5.5   **D.** 5.505

20. Mark spent $39.90 on sneakers, $19.95 on a basketball, and $7.05 on a new hat. What is a good estimate of how much he spent? *(Lesson 3.5)* **H**

   F. less than $40   **G.** $40 to $50

   H. $50 to $70   **I.** $70 to $90

21. What is the value of $b - a$ when $a = 3.681$ and $b = 5.04$? *(Lesson 3.6)* **A**

   A. 1.359   **B.** 2.469   **C.** 2.641   **D.** 3.177

22. Short Response The recorded times, in seconds, for skiers in a slalom event were 48.37, 49.80, 49.60, 50.16, 49.92, 48.01, 49.61, and 49.34. Order the times from least to greatest and state the winning time. Explain why it does not make sense to round the times to the nearest whole number before ordering them. *(Lessons 3.3, 3.4)*
           See margin.

15. Round to find a sum and then use compatible numbers to divide the sum by 7; it is less than the median.

16. a.

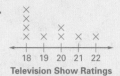

18 19 20 21 22
Television Show Ratings

b. See Additional Answers beginning on page AA1.

22. 48.01, 48.37, 49.34, 49.60, 49.61, 49.80, 49.92, 50.16; 48.01; many of the rounded times are the same and could not be ordered.

31. 7 yards for $10.08;
$8.45 ÷ 5 = $1.69 and
$10.08 ÷ 7 = $1.44, and
$1.44 < $1.69.

23. Extended Response The Ruiz family wants to spend an average of $200 a week on groceries. The table shows the actual amounts spent for 4 weeks.
(Lessons 3.5, 3.6)

Week 1	$188.99
Week 2	$202.89
Week 3	$185.66
Week 4	$210.34

a. Estimate the total amount spent. **$800**

b. Estimate the average amount spent per week. **$200**

c. Did the Ruiz family stay close to their weekly budget? Explain.
Yes, the estimate is exactly $200.

Chapter 4

Multiple Choice In Exercises 24–30, choose the letter of the correct answer.

24. What is the cost of a 5 pound bag of peanuts at $3.89 per pound?
(Lesson 4.1) **C**

A. $8.89   **B.** $15.05

C. $19.45   **D.** $1945

25. Which expression is equivalent to $5(2 + 0.6)$? *(Lesson 4.2)* **G**

F. $5 \times 2 + 0.6$ **G.** $5(2) + 5(0.6)$

H. $10 + 0.30$ **I.** $52 + 0.6$

26. What is the product of 24.5 and 0.07?
(Lesson 4.3) **B**

A. 0.1715   **B.** 1.715

C. 17.15   **D.** 171.5

27. What is the value of the quotient $0.0456 \div 0.01$? *(Lesson 4.5)* **H**

F. 0.000456   **G.** 0.0456

H. 4.56   **I.** 45.6

28. Pat biked 41.4 miles in 4.5 hours. What was his average rate in miles per hour?
(Lesson 4.6) **C**

A. 0.092   **B.** 0.92   **C.** 9.2   **D.** 92

29. What unit of measurement would most likely be used to express the mass of a whale? *(Lesson 4.7)* **I**

F. meters   **G.** milligrams

H. grams   **I.** kilograms

30. A tornado typically moves about 64,000 meters in an hour. How many kilometers is this? *(Lesson 4.8)* **B**

A. 0.064 km   **B.** 64 km

C. 640 km   **D.** 64,000,000 km

31. Short Response Michelle bought 5 yards of a fabric for $8.45 and 7 yards of another fabric for $10.08. Which fabric is the least expensive per yard? Explain. *(Lesson 4.4)*
See margin.

32. Extended Response A rectangle has a length of 10 centimeters and a width of 8 centimeters. *(Lesson 4.2)*

a. Use the formula for the perimeter of a rectangle to write an expression for the perimeter of this rectangle.
2(10) + 2(8)

b. Use the distributive property to rewrite the expression. **2(10 + 8)**

c. Show that both expressions give the same answer for the perimeter.
2(10) + 2(8) = 20 + 16 = 36 yards and 2(10 + 8) = 2(18) = 36 yards.

UNIT 2

Fraction Concepts and Operations

Chapter 5 Number Patterns and Fractions

- Use divisibility rules and find common factors and common multiples.
- Know the relationships between fractions and decimals.
- Use customary units of length.

Chapter 6 Addition and Subtraction of Fractions

- Estimate a sum or difference.
- Add and subtract fractions and mixed numbers to solve problems.
- Add and subtract measures of time.

Chapter 7 Multiplication and Division of Fractions

- Use multiplication and division to solve real-world problems.
- Estimate, change, and choose units of capacity and weight.
- Use patterns to predict outcomes and solve problems.

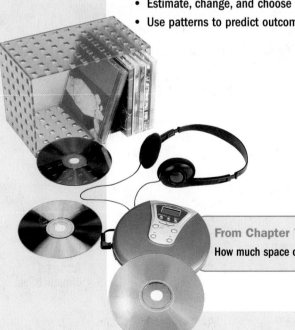

From Chapter 7, p. 315

How much space do you need for your CDs?

UNIT RESOURCES

These resources are provided to help you prepare for the unit and to customize review materials:

 Chapter Resource Books
- Chapter 5
- Chapter 6
- Chapter 7

 Assessment Book
- Chapters 5–7, pp. 57–95

 Technology
- EasyPlanner CD-ROM
- Test and Practice Generator
- Electronic Lesson Presentations CD-ROM
- eTutorial CD-ROM

 Internet
- Classzone
- eEdition Plus Online
- eWorkbook Plus Online
- eTutorial Plus Online
- EasyPlanner Plus Online

ENGLISH LEARNER SUPPORT

- Spanish Study Guide
- Multi-Language Glossary
- Chapter Audio Summaries CDs
- Teacher's Edition
  Chapter 5, pp. 210E–210F
  Chapter 6, pp. 264E–264F
  Chapter 7, pp. 310E–310F

209

Pacing and Assignment Guide

REGULAR SCHEDULE

Lesson	Les. Day	BASIC	AVERAGE	ADVANCED
5.1	Day 1	pp. 217–219 Exs. 13–28, 49–53, 56–58, 72–74	pp. 217–219 Exs. 13–28, 49–54, 68–75	pp. 217–219 Exs. 17–26, 49–55, 66–69, 74
	Day 2	pp. 217–219 Exs. 29–37, 39–47, 64–71	pp. 217–219 Exs. 29–48, 58–61, 64–67	pp. 217–219 Exs. 31–38, 43–48, 58–63*, 75
5.2	Day 1	pp. 224–225 Exs. 6–23, 25–27, 32–39	pp. 224–225 Exs. 5–28, 32–40	pp. 224–225 Exs. 5–11, 18–34*, 39, 40
5.3	Day 1	SRH p. 700 Exs. 7–12; pp. 231–232 Exs. 11–25 odd, 37–44	pp. 231–232 Exs. 10–24 even, 37–44	pp. 231–232 Exs. 14–25, 39–44
	Day 2	pp. 231–232 Exs. 26–36, 49–59	pp. 231–232 Exs. 26–36, 49–59	pp. 231–232 Exs. 28–36, 45–53*, 58, 59
5.4	Day 1	pp. 237–238 Exs. 9–27 odd, 31–44	pp. 237–238 Exs. 8–16 even, 17–28, 31–35, 38–45	pp. 237–238 Exs. 12–16, 21–31*, 34–37, 44, 45
5.5	Day 1	EP p. 710 Exs. 16–18; pp. 241–242 Exs. 7–23, 29–31, 36–46	pp. 241–242 Exs. 7–23, 28–34, 36–47	pp. 241–242 Exs. 11–19, 24–42*, 47
5.6	Day 1	EP p. 709 Ex. 1; pp. 247–248 Exs. 10–12, 13–27 odd, 29–37, 42–55	pp. 247–248 Exs. 10–12, 14–28 even, 29–40, 44–55	pp. 247–248 Exs. 11–16, 25–31, 34–49*, 54, 55
5.7	Day 1	EP p. 710 Exs. 3–7; pp. 251–252 Exs. 8–19, 24–27, 33–37, 39–42	pp. 251–252 Exs. 8–11, 16–28, 35–42	pp. 251–252 Exs. 8–22 even, 24–32*, 35–38, 41, 42
5.8	Day 1	pp. 255–256 Exs. 14–34, 39–52	pp. 255–256 Exs. 14–25, 30–37, 41–44, 48–53	pp. 255–256 Exs 16–21, 26–38*, 39–49 odd, 52, 53
Review	Day 1	pp. 260–261 Exs. 1–65	pp. 260–261 Exs. 1–65	pp. 260–261 Exs. 1–65
Assess	Day 1	Chapter 5 Test	Chapter 5 Test	Chapter 5 Test

YEARLY PACING   Chapter 5 Total – **12 days**   Chapters 1–5 Total – **58 days**   Remaining – **102 days**

*Challenge Exercises   EP = Extra Practice   SRH = Skills Review Handbook   EC = Extra Challenge

BLOCK SCHEDULE

DAY 1	DAY 2	DAY 3	DAY 4	DAY 5	DAY 6
5.1 pp. 217–219 Exs. 13–54, 58–61, 64–75	**5.2** pp. 224–225 Exs. 5–28, 32–40 **5.3** pp. 231–232 Exs. 10–24 even, 37–44	**5.3 cont.** pp. 231–232 Exs. 26–36, 49–59 **5.4** pp. 237–238 Exs. 8–16 even, 17–28, 31–35, 38–45	**5.5** pp. 241–242 Exs. 7–23, 28–34, 36–47 **5.6** pp. 247–248 Exs. 10–12, 14–28 even, 29–40, 44–55	**5.7** pp. 251–252 Exs. 8–11, 16–28, 35–42 **5.8** pp. 255–256 Exs. 14–25, 30–37, 41–44, 48–53	**Review** pp. 260–261 Exs. 1–65 **Assess** Chapter 5 Test

YEARLY PACING   Chapter 5 Total – **6 days**   Chapters 1–5 Total – **29 days**   Remaining – **51 days**

Support Materials

📖 CHAPTER RESOURCE BOOK

CHAPTER SUPPORT

Tips for New Teachers	p. 1			Parents as Partners			p. 3	

LESSON SUPPORT

	5.1	5.2	5.3	5.4	5.5	5.6	5.7	5.8
Lesson Plans (regular and block)	p. 5	p. 14	p. 22	p. 30	p. 39	p. 48	p. 58	p. 67
Technology Activities & Keystrokes						p. 50		p. 69
Activity Support Masters							p. 60	
Activity Masters				p. 32				
Practice (3 levels)	p. 7	p. 16	p. 24	p. 33	p. 41	p. 52	p. 61	p. 70
Study Guide	p. 10	p. 19	p. 27	p. 36	p. 44	p. 55	p. 64	p. 73
Real-World Problem Solving	p. 12				p. 46			
Challenge Practice	p. 13	p. 21	p. 29	p. 38	p. 47	p. 57	p. 66	p. 75

REVIEW

Chapter Review Games and Activities	p. 76		Extra Credit Project with Rubric	p. 81
Real-Life Project with Rubric	p. 77		Cumulative Practice	p. 83
Cooperative Project with Rubric	p. 79		Resource Book Answers	A1

📖 ASSESSMENT

Quizzes	p. 57		Alternative Assessments with Rubrics	p. 66
Chapter Tests (3 levels)	p. 59		Unit Test	p. 90
Standardized Test	p. 65		Cumulative Test	p. 92

📑 TRANSPARENCIES

	5.1	5.2	5.3	5.4	5.5	5.6	5.7	5.8
Warm-Up / Daily Homework Quiz	✔	✔	✔	✔	✔	✔	✔	✔
Notetaking Guide	✔	✔	✔	✔	✔	✔	✔	✔
Teacher Support						✔	✔	
English/Spanish Problem Solving					✔			
Answer Transparencies	✔	✔	✔	✔	✔	✔	✔	✔

💻 TECHNOLOGY

- EasyPlanner CD-ROM
- Test and Practice Generator
- Electronic Lesson Presentations
- eTutorial CD-ROM
- Chapter Audio Summaries CDs
- Classzone.com
- eEdition Plus Online
- eWorkbook Plus Online
- eTutorial Plus Online
- EasyPlanner Plus Online

ADDITIONAL RESOURCES

- Worked-Out Solution Key
- Notetaking Guide
- Practice Workbook
- Tutor Place
- Professional Development Book
- Activities Book
- Poster Package
- Spanish Study Guide
- English/Spanish Chapter Reviews
- Multi-Language Glossary

Math Background and Teaching Strategies

Lesson 5.1

MATH BACKGROUND

PRIME AND COMPOSITE NUMBERS A prime number is a counting number that has just two factors, itself and 1; all other counting numbers are composite. The **prime factorization** of a number is the number written as the product of its primes factors. The Fundamental Theorem of Arithmetic states that the prime factorization of a number is unique, except for the order in which the factors are written. A **factor tree** is a useful device for finding and displaying the prime factorization of a number.

TEACHING STRATEGIES

Discuss several examples to be sure students understand the distinction between finding all the factors of a number and finding the prime factorization of a number. For example, the factors of 24 are 1, 2, 3, 4, 6, 8, 12, and 24, while its prime factorization is $2^3 \times 3$.

Lesson 5.2

MATH BACKGROUND

The **Greatest Common Factor (GCF)** of two or more numbers is the largest number that is a divisor of all the numbers. It is sometimes called the Greatest Common Divisor. It can be used to simplify (or reduce) fractions. The GCF can be founding by listing all factors of each number or by using prime factorizations to find common prime factors.

TEACHING STRATEGIES

Listing all factors of each number is probably the easiest way for most students to find the GCF. One technique to help students determine if they have all factors is to pair factors that have the number as their product. Caution students that the GCF contains a common factor the least number of times it occurs in any of the numbers; that is, if 5 is a factor twice in two of the numbers and three times in a third number, it is a factor twice in the GCF.

Lesson 5.3

MATH BACKGROUND

EQUIVALENT FRACTIONS Two fractions are equivalent if they name the same amount. To get an equivalent fraction, you would multiply or divide the numerator and the denominator by the same nonzero number.

SIMPLEST FORM A fraction is in simplest form if the GCF of the numerator and the denominator is 1. To find the simplest form of a fraction, you can divide the numerator and the denominator by common factors until the only common factor is 1, or you can divide the numerator and denominator by the GCF.

TEACHING STRATEGIES

The general approach to a conceptual understanding of equivalent fractions is to have students use length models to generate different names for fractions.

Example

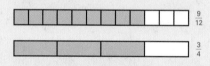

The model shows that $\frac{9}{12} = \frac{3}{4}$.

Lesson 5.4

MATH BACKGROUND

The **Least Common Multiple (LCM)** of two or more numbers is the smallest number that is a common multiple of the numbers.

TEACHING STRATEGIES

Some students might find the following method of finding the LCM easy to use.

1. Find the GCF of the numbers.

2. Multiply the original numbers together.

3. Divide the product of the original numbers by the GCF.

Example

Find the LCM of 15 and 12.

- Since $15 = 3 \times 5$ and $12 = 2 \times 2 \times 3$, the GCF is 3.
- Multiply the numbers: $15 \times 12 = 180$.
- Divide this product by the GCF, 3: $180 \div 3 = 60$.

The LCM of 15 and 12 is 60.

Lesson 5.5

MATH BACKGROUND

Comparing and ordering fractions is a useful skill in connection with customary measures, where fractions with denominators of 2, 3, 4, 8, 12, and 16 are likely to occur. One way to compare fractions is to write equivalent fractions that have a common denominator.

TEACHING STRATEGIES

Be sure students understand that when they order fractions by using equivalent fractions with a common denominator, they need only compare numerators. For students who learn from visual models, a number line can help them order fractions.

Lesson 5.6

MATH BACKGROUND

IMPROPER FRACTIONS These fractions have a numerator that is equal to or greater than the denominator. As opposed to proper fractions, improper fractions represent numbers equal to or greater than 1 and can be rewritten as a whole number or a mixed number. Mixed numbers, which have a whole-number part and a fractional part, can be rewritten as improper fractions.

Example

Order $\frac{3}{4}$, $\frac{1}{2}$, and $\frac{7}{8}$ from least to greatest.

Solution

Note that the LCD of the fractions is 8. Use a number line marked off in eighths.

Thus, $\frac{1}{2} < \frac{3}{4} < \frac{7}{8}$.

TEACHING STRATEGIES

Once students understand the meaning of each part of a fraction, they will find it easy to write an improper fraction as a mixed number. Be sure they understand that the denominator tells how many equal parts are in one whole unit. Dividing out all of the whole units gives the whole-number part of the number with the same value as the fraction. If there is a remainder from this division, it is the numerator of the proper-fraction part of a mixed number. Explain to students that they already know the denominator: It is the denominator of the original improper fraction.

Lessons 5.7 and 5.8

MATH BACKGROUND

CHANGING DECIMALS TO FRACTIONS Changing a decimal to a fraction is a straightforward process of writing the decimal as a fraction with the appropriate denominator. If the decimal has one digit to the right of the decimal point, the fraction has a denominator of 10; if the decimal has two digits to the right of the decimal point, the denominator is 100, and so on. Often the resulting fraction can be simplified.

CHANGING FRACTIONS TO DECIMALS To change a fraction to a decimal, divide the numerator by the denominator, using the process of writing 0s to the right of the decimal point. The result of changing a fraction to a decimal will be either a **terminating decimal** or a **repeating decimal**.

TEACHING STRATEGIES

As an introduction to Lesson 5.7, have students choose five amounts of money between 1¢ and $1 and write each as a decimal on the chalkboard. Then ask students to think of the amounts as fractions of 100 pennies and to write a fraction in simplest form for each decimal they listed.

For Lesson 5.8, have students shade in familiar fractions on a 10×10 grid. The grid translates any fraction to a base-ten fraction. So, the fraction can easily be written as a decimal.

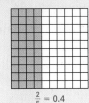

$\frac{2}{5} = 0.4$

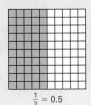

$\frac{1}{2} = 0.5$

5 Differentiating Instruction

Strategies for Underachievers

ANTICIPATE PROBLEM AREAS WITH VOCABULARY

VOCABULARY Students may be overwhelmed by all of the new vocabulary in this chapter. Vocabulary should be presented in such a way that students can build upon previously learned terms. Students must first understand what a "multiple" is before they can understand the concepts of "common multiple" and then "least common multiple." Likewise, students must first understand "factor" before "common factor" and "greatest common factor." You might suggest that students create a graphic organizer or notes cards for organizing and learning this vocabulary. If using note cards, you may want to have student color code cards related to the same topic. For example, one color group might include all of the following terms whose root word is "factor": "factor," "prime factorization," "factor tree," "common factor," "greatest common factor." Other color groups could include terms related to "fraction" and to "multiple" and to "decimal."

STUDENT INVESTIGATION INTO PRIME NUMBERS

Students may better retain knowledge of key prime numbers if they generate these prime numbers using the Sieve of Eratosthenes. If you are not familiar with this device, you may demonstrate it as follows. Provide each student with a 10×10 array of the whole numbers from 1 to 100. To start, tell them that 1 is neither prime nor composite. Have them draw a triangle around it to distinguish its uniqueness. Next, have students circle 2 as the first prime number. Then, have students draw a neat diagonal line through all the numbers (except 2) that are multiples of 2. Ask students what these numbers have in common and to describe any patterns they see. Next, circle the next number that is not crossed out, which is 3, the next prime number. Continue to draw a diagonal line through all the multiples of 3. This would be a good time to remind students of the divisibility rule for 3. Have students check some of the numbers crossed out as "multiples of 3"

against the divisibility rule for 3 to show that the rule really does work. Again ask students what these numbers have in common and to describe any patterns they see. Continue this pattern by circling 5 and crossing out all its multiples. This sieve will eventually "sift" out all of the prime numbers less than or equal to 100. While in actuality, it is not necessary to try any prime number beyond 10, since $10 \cdot 10 = 100$, you should allow students to discover this on their own while attempting to complete the sieve. Students who are not likely to be neat in completing this activity should keep an ongoing list of the prime numbers as they are circled. At the end of this activity, all students should have a list of all the prime numbers that are less than 100.

ALTERNATIVE TEACHING METHOD

Some students may be more successful at finding the GCF and LCM by the "Upside-down Division" method, which works in the following way, using the numbers 28 and 42.

Step 1 Write the numbers in the following way:

$$|\,28, 42$$

Step 2 Divide by any common factor of 28 and 42. Let's start with 2, a likely student choice.

$$2\,|\,28, 42$$
$$|\,14, 21$$

Step 3 If the resulting numbers are not yet relatively prime, divide by a common factor of 14 and 21. This will be 7 in this example.

$$2\,|\,28, 42$$
$$7\,|\,14, 21$$
$$2, 3$$

Step 4 Since 2 and 3 are relatively prime, we can now find the GCF and LCM. The GCF will be the product of the divisors—in this case, $2 \cdot 7$, which is 14. The LCM will be the product $2 \cdot 7 \cdot 2 \cdot 3$, which is 84.

Strategies for English Learners

VOCABULARY STUDY

In Chapter 4, we suggested that teachers review action verbs with students. These verbs, such as *solve, find, test, classify,* and *choose,* tell students what to do. Interrogative pronouns often provide a similar signal. Have English learners look for problems in this chapter that start with one of the following: *how, how many, how much, what, which,* and so on. In word problems, these pronouns are usually followed by a noun, and the sentence ends in a question mark. Then have students write their own word problems beginning with an interrogative pronoun. When students recognize this basic and common type of phrase, they can more easily determine what is asked for in word problems.

Strategies for Advanced Learners

DIFFERENTIATE IN TERMS OF DEPTH

DIVISIBILITY In **Lesson 5.1**, *most* students can easily see why the divisibility rules for 2, 5, and 10 work. The rules for 3 and 9, however, are more complicated.

- **Challenge** Once advanced students have figured out *how* the rules for 3 and 9 work, challenge them to figure out *why* these rules work. This is not an easy investigation and could keep interested, motivated students busy for a long time. Check work.

Use this challenge in connection with **Activity 5.3.**

- **Challenge** How can you fold paper to model fractions with denominators of 6, 12, 18, and 24? 6: Fold the paper into thirds in one direction and into halves the other way; 12: Fold the paper into thirds in one direction and into fourths the other way; 18: Fold the paper into sixths in one direction and into thirds the other way; 24: Fold the paper into sixths in one direction and into fourths the other way.

Use this challenge as an ongoing project for **Chapter 5.**

- **Challenge** There are 200 lockers in your school, numbered from 1 through 200 consecutively. The lockers are all closed to begin. Student #1 walks down the corridor and opens all the lockers that are numbered with a multiple of 1, thereby all the lockers are opened. Student #2 then walks down the corridor and changes the status (closed lockers are opened; open lockers are closed) of all the lockers that are numbered with a multiple of 2 (note that in the case of Student #2, this only involves closing lockers). Student #3 then walks down the corridor and changes the status of all the lockers that are numbered with a multiple of 3. By the end of this scenario, 200 students will have walked down the corridor, in numerical order, with each student changing the status of those lockers that are numbered with a number that is a multiple of the student's number. At that point, which of the lockers are open? More importantly, why are these lockers open? The open lockers are 1, 4, 9, 16, 25, 36, 49, 64, 81, 100, 121, 144, 169, and 196. These numbers are the perfect squares; perfect squares are the only numbers with an odd number of factors; likewise, open lockers are those which have had their status changed an odd number of times.

Differentiating Instruction: Teaching Resources

Differentiating Technology

McDougal Littell *Middle School Mathematics* offers teachers a wide variety of technology, ranging from calculator activities in the *Chapter Resource Books* to the *Test and Practice Generator CD-ROM* to interactive, online resources and products accessed at Classzone.com.

CLASSZONE.COM

Classzone.com provides helpful online resources for students and teachers, including More Examples, Vocabulary Support, and State Test Practice. Classzone.com is also the access point for the following online products: *eEdition Plus Online*, an interactive, online version of the textbook; *eWorkbook Plus Online*, an interactive practice workbook correlated to the textbook; *eTutorial Plus Online*, an Internet tutorial that makes it easier than ever to help students master skills and concepts; and *EasyPlanner Plus Online*, an online resource with teacher tools and a lesson planner.

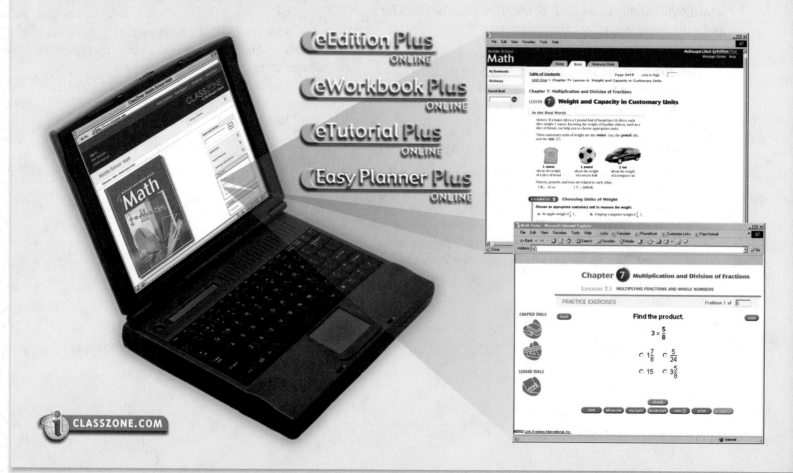

TEST AND PRACTICE GENERATOR CD-ROM

The *Test and Practice Generator* can be used to create numerous practice sheets and quizzes for each lesson and tests for each chapter using both static and algorithmic exercises. Information about creating and editing questions is provided.

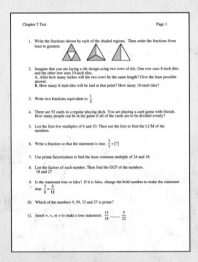

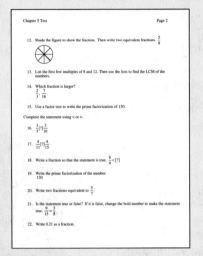

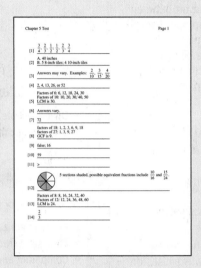

RESOURCE BOOK

The *Chapter Resource Books* contain technology activities that are different from the activities given in the textbook. Also included, where appropriate, are calculator keystrokes that can be used to do the technology activities and exercises that appear in the textbook and in the *Chapter Resource Books*.

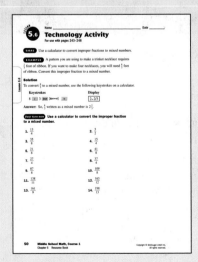

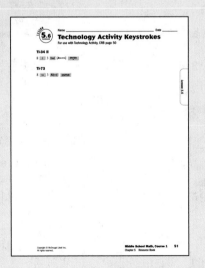

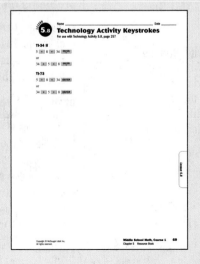

MAIN IDEAS

In this chapter, students investigate prime factorization and fractions. They relate prime factorization to the greatest common factor and to the least common multiple of pairs of numbers. With fractions, students use area models to find equivalent fractions, and then they order fractions. Students also convert between mixed numbers and improper fractions, and rewrite decimals as fractions or mixed numbers. Finally, they rewrite fractions as decimals and explore repeating decimals.

PREREQUISITE SKILLS

The key skills reviewed in the games on these pages are:
- Dividing whole numbers
- Ordering decimals
- Understanding place value

Additional practice with prerequisite skills can be found in the Review What You Need to Know exercises on page 212. Additional resources for reviewing prerequisite skills are:
- Skills Review Handbook, pp. 684–707
- Tutor Place
- eTutorial Plus Online

MANAGING THE GAMES

Tips for Success

If students have difficulty ordering the quotients in Follow the Clues, encourage them to add as many zeros as necessary so that all quotients have the same number of digits to the right of the decimal point.

CHAPTER

5

Number Patterns and Fractions

BEFORE

In previous chapters you've...
- Divided whole numbers
- Ordered decimals

Now

In Chapter 5 you'll study...
- Prime factorization
- Equivalent fractions
- Comparing and ordering fractions and mixed numbers
- Writing decimals as fractions and fractions as decimals

WHY?

So you can solve real-world problems about...
- marching bands, p. 217
- chess, p. 231
- baseball bats, p. 246
- fishing, p. 256

Internet Preview
CLASSZONE.COM
- eEdition Plus Online
- eWorkbook Plus Online
- eTutorial Plus Online
- State Test Practice
- More Examples

Chapter Warm-Up Games

Review skills you need for this chapter in these quick games.

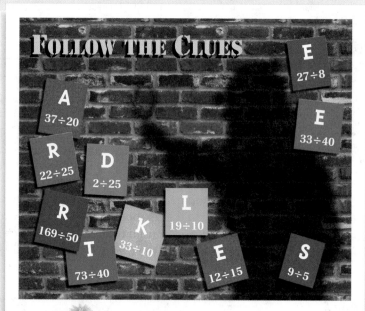

FOLLOW THE CLUES

E 27÷8
A 37÷20
E 33÷40
R 22÷25
D 2÷25
R 169÷50
K 33÷10
L 19÷10
T 73÷40
E 12÷15
S 9÷5

BRAIN GAME

Key Skills:
- Dividing whole numbers
- Ordering decimals

- Each clue shown above contains an expression and a letter. Evaluate the expression on each clue.

- Order your answers from least to greatest. Write the letters associated with the answers in the same order. These letters spell out the name of the type of hat Sherlock Holmes wears.

A = 1.85; R = 0.88; D = 0.08; R = 3.38; T = 1.825; K = 3.3; L = 1.9; E = 0.8; S = 1.8; E = 0.825; E = 3.375; DEERSTALKER

If a number cannot be evenly divided by 3, what are all the possible values for the remainder? **1 or 2** What are all the possible remainders if a number cannot be divided evenly by 4? **1, 2, or 3** Make a general statement about the remainder when a number cannot be divided evenly by a whole number *n*. **If a number cannot be divided evenly by a whole number *n*, then the remainder can be any positive integer less than *n*.**

CHAPTER RESOURCES

These resources are provided to help you prepare for the chapter and to customize review materials:

Chapter 5 Resource Book
- Tips for New Teachers, pp. 1–2
- Lesson Plan, pp. 5, 14, 22, 30, 39, 48, 58, 67
- Lesson Plan for Block Scheduling, pp. 6, 15, 23, 31, 40, 49, 59, 68

Technology
- EasyPlanner CD-ROM
- Test and Practice Generator
- Electronic Lesson Presentations CD-ROM
- eTutorial CD-ROM

Internet
- Classzone
- eEdition Plus Online
- eWorkbook Plus Online
- eTutorial Plus Online
- EasyPlanner Plus Online

ENGLISH LEARNER SUPPORT
- Spanish Study Guide
- Multi-Language Glossary
- Chapter Audio Summaries CDs
- Teacher's Edition, pp. 210E–210F

MYSTERY NUMBERS

A I am a one digit number. I divide evenly into 27 but I do not divide into 30. What number am I?

B I am a two digit number. I can be divided evenly by 5. The sum of my two digits is 12. What number am I?

C I am a two digit number. My tens digit is 7. I can be divided evenly by 12. What number am I?

D I am a two digit number. I can be divided evenly by 7. If you switch my digits, I grow by 18. What number am I?

A – 8   B – 67   C ÷ 9   D ÷ 5

?   ?   ?   ?

BRAIN GAME

Key Skills:
- Understanding place value
- Dividing whole numbers

- Use the clues to find the mystery numbers.
- Use the mystery numbers to evaluate the expressions above.
- The values of the expressions, written in the order shown, give the year in which Sir Arthur Conan Doyle published the first Sherlock Holmes story.

A = 9; B = 75; C = 72; D = 35; A − 8 = 1; B − 67 = 8; C ÷ 9 = 8; D ÷ 5 = 7; 1887

1. No; some of the estimates would have been the same and then the order could not be determined.

2. A good answer will include a two-digit number with clearly written clues.

Stop *and* Think

1. **Critical Thinking** In *Follow the Clues,* could you figure out the hidden word by using estimation rather than exact division? Why or why not?

2. **Writing** Pick a two digit number. Write a few clues about it like the ones in *Mystery Numbers.* Then see if someone else can guess the number.

211

PREPARE

DIAGNOSIS/REMEDIATION

Review What You Need to Know
The Review What You Need to Know exercises can help you diagnose whether students have the following skills needed in Chapter 5:

- Vocabulary (Exs. 1–4)
- Write fractions shown by models (Exs. 5–6)
- Write products as powers (Exs. 7–10)
- Estimate and then measure a length (Ex. 11)
- Use a number line to order decimals (Exs. 12–14)

 Chapter 5 Resource Book
- Study Guide (Lessons 5.1–5.8)

 Tutor Place

NOTETAKING STRATEGIES

Including an example of the use of each vocabulary term is an important part of notetaking. Such examples help students to place the vocabulary term into the correct context when reading their notes at a later date. Visual learners should be encouraged to include a diagram that models a vocabulary term whenever possible. Further suggestions for keeping a notebook can be found on page 228.

For more support on notetaking, see:
- Notetaking Guide Workbook
- Notetaking Transparencies

CHAPTER 5 Getting Ready to Learn

Review What You Need to Know

Using Vocabulary **Copy and complete using a review word.**

Word Watch

Review Words
factor, p. 16
inch, p. 55
foot, p. 55
yard, p. 55
fraction p. 700
numerator, p. 700
denominator, p. 700

1. 12 inches = 1 $\underline{?}$ foot **2.** 3 feet = 1 $\underline{?}$ yard **3.** 36 $\underline{?}$ = 1 yard **inches**

4. The numbers 6 and 4 are $\underline{?}$ of 24. **factors**

Write the fraction shown by the model. *(p. 700)*

5. $\dfrac{9}{16}$

6. $\dfrac{3}{10}$

Write the product as a power. *(p. 16)*

7. $5 \times 5 \times 5 \times 5$ 5^4 **8.** $10 \times 10 \times 10$ 10^3 **9.** 11×11 11^2

10. Estimate the length of the straw to the nearest inch. Then measure to check your estimate. *(p. 55)* **Estimates may vary; 4.75 in.**

Use a number line to order the decimals from least to greatest. *(p. 118)*

11. 1.4, 1.8, 1.5, 1.6, 1.7, 2
1.4, 1.5, 1.6, 1.7, 1.8, 2

12. 2.7, 2.07, 2.77, 2.71, 2.17
2.07, 2.17, 2.7, 2.71, 2.77

13. 3.28, 2.83, 3.82, 8.23, 2.38
2.38, 2.83, 3.28, 3.82, 8.23

14. 7.24, 7.31, 7.03, 7.26, 7.17
7.03, 7.17, 7.24, 7.26, 7.31

You should include material that appears on a notebook like this in your own notes.

Know How to Take Notes

Learning Vocabulary You need to learn the complete and accurate meanings of vocabulary words. Copy the words from each lesson's Word Watch in your notebook with a definition and an example.

Vocabulary for Lesson 1.3

Factor - a whole number other than zero that is multiplied by another whole number to give a product.

Example

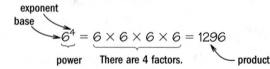

exponent
base
$6^4 = 6 \times 6 \times 6 \times 6 = 1296$
power   There are 4 factors.   product

As you work through Chapter 5, include new vocabulary in your notes.

5.1 Hands-on Activity

GOAL
Use number sense to test whether 2, 3, 6, and 9 are factors of a number.

MATERIALS
- paper
- pencil

Divisibility Rules

You can use rules to decide whether certain numbers are factors of another number. For example, 2 is a factor of a number if the number is even.

Explore Copy and complete the table to decide if 3 is a factor of each number.

1. Decide whether 3 is a factor of 18.

   Because $18 = 6 \times 3$, you know 3 is a factor of 18.

2. Add the digits in the number 18: $1 + 8 = 9$.

3. Decide whether 3 is a factor of the sum from Step 2.

   Because $9 = 3 \times 3$, you know 3 is a factor of 9.

4. Repeat Steps 1–3 for all the numbers in the first column of the table. *See table.*

Number	Is 3 a factor?	Sum of digits	Is 3 a factor of the sum?
18	Yes	9	Yes
60	? Yes	? 6	? No
80	? No	? 8	? No
99	? Yes	? 18	? Yes
315	? Yes	? 9	? Yes
329	? No	? 14	? No

Your turn now Use the table above.

1. Decide whether 2 is a factor of each number in the first column.
   yes; yes; yes; no; no; no

2. Follow the steps above to create another table that shows which of the numbers have 9 as a factor. *See margin.*

Stop and Think

3. **Writing** Look back at the tables you made. Write a rule that tells you whether 3 is a factor of a given number. Write a similar rule for 9. *See margin.*

4. **Critical Thinking** If 2 and 3 are factors of a number, is 6 always a factor of the number? Explain. Yes. *Sample answer:* Since $2 \times 3 = 6$, if 2 and 3 are both factors of a number then 6 is also a factor.

Lesson 5.1 Prime Factorization **213**

---

1 PLAN

EXPLORE THE CONCEPT
- Students will use number sense to test whether 2, 3, 6, and 9 are factors of a number.
- This activity introduces the divisibility rules for 2, 3, 6, and 9, which are given in Lesson 5.1.

MATERIALS
Each student or group of students will need paper and pencil.

RECOMMENDED TIME
Work activity: 15 min
Discuss results: 5 min

GROUPING
This activity is best done individually.

2 TEACH

TIPS FOR SUCCESS
Be sure students understand that one number is a factor of another number if there is a remainder of 0 when the second number is divided by the first.

3 CLOSE

KEY DISCOVERY
If the sum of the digits of a number is divisible by 3, then the number is divisible by 3.

ASSESSMENT
1. Use the digits 2, 3, 5, and 7 no more than once for each number to write two 3-digit numbers that are divisible by 3. *Sample answer:* 237, 537

2–3. See Additional Answers beginning on page AA1.

SKILL CHECK
Find the quotient.

1. $45 \div 9$ 5

2. $108 \div 6$ 18

Evaluate the expression.

3. $2 \times 3 \times 5^2$ 150

4. $2^3 \times 3^2 \times 5$ 360

LESSON OBJECTIVE

Write whole numbers as the product of prime factors.

PACING

Suggested Number of Days
Basic Course: 2 days
Average Course: 2 days
Advanced Course: 2 days
Block: 1 block

TEACHING RESOURCES

For a complete list of Teaching Resources, see page 210B.

 TRANSPARENCY

Warm-Up Exercises for this lesson are available on a transparency.

2 TEACH

MOTIVATING THE LESSON

Have students count the number of desks in the room. Ask them to suggest possible arrangements of the desks into rows with an equal number of desks in each row.

LESSON 5.1

Prime Factorization

BEFORE	Now	WHY?
You found products of whole numbers.	You'll write whole numbers as the product of prime factors.	So you can arrange groups, such as the dancers in Example 1.

 Word Watch

divisible, p. 214
prime number, p. 215
composite number, p. 215
prime factorization, p. 216
factor tree, p. 216

In the Real World

Dancers A dance teacher is planning a dance for a show. The dancers will be arranged in rows with the same number of dancers in each row. Can a group of 12 dancers or a group of 14 dancers be arranged in more ways?

EXAMPLE 1 **Finding Factors**

To answer the question above, list all the factors of 12 and 14 by writing each number as a product of two numbers in as many ways as possible.

12 : 1×12 14 : 1×14
       2×6 **Stop when** 2×7
       3×4 **a pair of**
       4×3 **factors repeats.** 7×2

The factors of 12   The factors of 14
are 1, 2, 3, 4, 6, and 12.   are 1, 2, 7, and 14.

ANSWER A group of 12 dancers can be arranged in more ways than a group of 14 dancers, because 12 has more factors than 14.

Divisibility A number is **divisible** by another number if that other number is a factor of the first. Divisibility rules can help you find factors.

 Notebook

Divisibility Rules for 2, 3, 5, 6, 9, and 10

A whole number is divisible by:

- **2** if the number is even.
- **3** if the sum of its digits is divisible by 3.
- **5** if it ends with 5 or 0.

- **6** if it is even and divisible by 3.
- **9** if the sum of its digits is divisible by 9.
- **10** if it ends with 0.

NCTM CURRICULUM STANDARDS
Standard 1: Understand relationships among numbers
Standard 9: Grasp connections among math ideas; Understand how math ideas build on one another

EXAMPLE 2

Using Divisibility Rules

Test 150 for divisibility by 2, 3, 5, 6, 9, and 10.

150 is even, so it is divisible by 2.

$1 + 5 + 0 = 6$, and 6 is divisible by 3, but not by 9. So, 150 is divisible by 3, but it is not divisible by 9.

150 ends with 0, so it is divisible by 5 and by 10.

150 is even and divisible by 3, so it is divisible by 6.

ANSWER 150 is divisible by 2, 3, 5, 6, and 10, but not by 9.

Your turn now List all the factors of the number.

1. 8 1, 2, 4, 8
2. 9 1, 3, 9
3. 15 1, 3, 5, 15
4. 18 1, 2, 3, 6, 9, 18

Test the number for divisibility by 2, 3, 5, 6, 9, and 10.

5. 100
6. 456
7. 783
8. 1584

5. 100 is divisible by 2, 5, and 10, but not by 3, 6, or 9.

6. 456 is divisible by 2, 3, and 6, but not by 5, 9, or 10.

7. 783 is divisible by 3 and 9, but not by 2, 5, 6, or 10.

8. 1584 is divisible by 2, 3, 6, and 9, but not by 5 or 10.

Primes and Composites

A **prime number** is a whole number greater than 1 whose only factors are 1 and itself. A **composite number** is a whole number greater than 1 that has factors other than 1 and itself. The number 1 is neither prime nor composite.

EXAMPLE 3 **Classifying as Prime or Composite**

HELP with **Solving**

Another way to tell if a number is composite is to use divisibility rules. For example, 51 is divisible by 3. So, 3 is a factor of 51 and 51 is composite.

Tell whether the number is *prime* or *composite*.

a. 51
b. 59

Solution

a. List the factors of 51: 1, 3, 17, 51.

ANSWER The number 51 is composite. It has factors other than 1 and itself.

b. List the factors of 59: 1, 59.

ANSWER The number 59 is prime. Its only factors are 1 and itself.

Your turn now Tell whether the number is *prime* or *composite*.

9. 11 prime
10. 13 prime
11. 14 composite
12. 35 composite

TIPS FOR NEW TEACHERS

You can introduce finding factors by helping students find all the different-shaped rectangles that have a particular area. Explain that the dimensions are the factors and the area is the product. See Tips for New Teachers in the *Chapter 5 Resource Book*.

EXTRA EXAMPLES

Example 1 Sports teams will march in a parade, arranged so the same number of athletes is in each row. Which team can be arranged in more ways, a team with 30 members or a team with 28 members? A team of 30 members can be arranged in more ways, because 30 has more factors than 28.

Example 2 Test 210 for divisibility by 2, 3, 5, 6, 9, and 10. 210 is divisible by 2, 3, 5, 6, and 10.

Example 3 Tell whether the number is *prime* or *composite*.
a. 67 prime
b. 65 composite

MATH REASONING

Point out to students that the divisibility rule for 6 is different from the other rules in that it is a rule based on logic and reasoning rather than one based on observations.

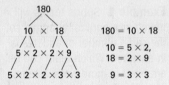

Prime Factorization Writing the **prime factorization** of a number means writing the number as the product of prime numbers. You can use a diagram called a **factor tree** to write a factorization of a number. To write the prime factorization, continue factoring until only prime factors appear in the product.

EXAMPLE 4 **Writing a Prime Factorization**

Write the prime factorization of 180.

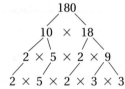

Only prime and composite numbers are used in a factor tree. So, the number 1 is not used in a factor tree.

180   Write the original number.

10 × 18   Factor 180 as 10 times 18.

2 × 5 × 2 × 9   Factor 10 and 18.

2 × 5 × 2 × 3 × 3   Factor 9.

ANSWER The prime factorization of 180 is $2^2 \times 3^2 \times 5$.

✓ **Check** Use multiplication to check your answer.
$2^2 \times 3^2 \times 5 = 4 \times 9 \times 5 = 180$

5.1 Exercises

More Practice, p. 712

INTERNET
eWorkbook Plus
CLASSZONE.COM

Getting Ready to Practice

1. *Sample answer:* All even numbers are divisible by 2.

2. *Sample answer:* A number is divisible by 3 if the sum of its digits is divisible by 3.

3. *Sample answer:* A number is divisible by 5 if it ends in a 5 or a 0.

4. *Sample answer:* A number is divisible by 6 if it is even and is divisible by 3.

Vocabulary Write the divisibility rule for the number in your own words.

1. 2   **2.** 3   **3.** 5   **4.** 6

Vocabulary Tell whether the number is *prime*, *composite*, or *neither*.

5. 4 composite   **6.** 9 composite   **7.** 5 prime   **8.** 1 neither

Copy and complete the factor tree. Then write the prime factorization.

9–11. See margin.

9.
42
? × ?
2 × ? × 7

10.
68
2 × ?
? × 2 × ?

11.
81
? × 9
? × 3 × ? × 3

12. Exercise A fitness instructor needs to arrange 80 people in her class in equal rows. Can she arrange them in rows of 6? no

Online Resources
CLASSZONE.COM
· More Examples
· eTutorial Plus

16. 1, 2, 3, 4, 6, 9, 12, 18, 36

17. 1, 2, 4, 5, 10, 20, 25, 50, 100

18. 1, 2, 3, 4, 6, 9, 12, 18, 27, 36, 54, 108

Music

■ **Marching Band**

At Ohio State University, being the band member that dots the "i" as the band spells "Ohio" on the football field is a big honor. The first time anyone dotted the "i" was October 10, 1936. 46 years earlier, on May 3rd, Ohio State University had played its first football game. What year was that? **1890**

Practice and Problem Solving

List all the factors of the number.

A **13.** 14 1, 2, 7, 14   **14.** 27 1, 3, 9, 27   **15.** 19 1, 19   **16.** 36
                                                                            16–18. See margin.
17. 100   **18.** 108   **19.** 121 1, 11, 121   **20.** 91 1, 7, 13, 91

Test the number for divisibility by 2, 3, 5, 6, 9, and 10. 21–28. See margin.

21. 140   **22.** 144   **23.** 282   **24.** 315

25. 1578   **26.** 4860   **27.** 8745   **28.** 9990

Tell whether the number is *prime* or *composite*.

29. 7 prime   **30.** 19 prime   **31.** 28 composite   **32.** 15 composite

33. 37 prime   **34.** 43 prime   **35.** 49 composite   **36.** 97 prime

37. Summer Camp There are 117 students going to summer camp. Can the campers be divided into small groups of equal size with at least 2 campers in each group? Explain. **Yes.** *Sample answer:* **117 is divisible by 3.**

38. Find the Error Describe and correct the error in the prime factorization. **The number 1 is not used in prime factorization. So the prime factorization should be 2×3^2.**

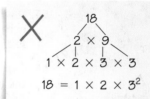

$$18 = 1 \times 2 \times 3^2$$

Write the prime factorization of the number.

39. 39 3×13 **40.** 55 5×11 **41.** 63 $3^2 \times 7$ **42.** 48 $2^4 \times 3$

43. 54 2×3^3 **44.** 88 $2^3 \times 11$ **45.** 150 $2 \times 3 \times 5^2$ **46.** 165 $3 \times 5 \times 11$

B **47. Marching Band** You are planning a half-time show for your school's marching band. There are 75 musicians in the band, and you want to divide them into groups of equal size to make different formations. Which of the following group sizes are possible? **A and B**

A.   **B.**   **C.**

---

③ **APPLY**

ASSIGNMENT GUIDE
Basic Course
Day 1: pp. 217–219 Exs. 13–28, 49–53, 56–58, 72–74

Day 2: pp. 217–219 Exs. 29–37, 39–47, 64–71

Average Course
Day 1: pp. 217–219 Exs. 13–28, 49–54, 68–75

Day 2: pp. 217–219 Exs. 29–48, 58–61, 64–67

Advanced Course
Day 1: pp. 217–219 Exs. 17–26, 49–55, 66–69, 74

Day 2: pp. 217–219 Exs. 31–38, 43–48, 58–63*, 75

Block
pp. 217–219 Exs. 13–54, 58–61, 64–75

EXTRA PRACTICE

· Student Edition, p. 712
· Chapter 5 Resource Book, pp. 7–9
· Test and Practice Generator

 TRANSPARENCY

Even-numbered answers are available on transparencies.

HOMEWORK CHECK

When you review students' homework for this lesson, go over the following exercises to check understanding of key concepts.
Basic: 13, 21, 29, 39, 44
Average: 15, 23, 31, 38, 45
Advanced: 17, 25, 33, 38, 46

 COMMON ERROR

In Exercises 13–20, remind students to include both 1 and the number itself as factors.

21–28. See Additional Answers beginning on page AA1.

MATH REASONING

Exercise 48 will help dispel a common incorrect notion that many students have; namely, that there is only one factor tree for a given number. Stress to students that there is only one prime factorization for a given number, but that a number of different factor trees might lead to that prime factorization.

75. *Sample answer:*

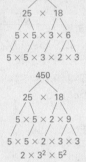

450
25 × 18
5 × 5 × 3 × 6
5 × 5 × 3 × 2 × 3

450
25 × 18
5 × 5 × 2 × 9
5 × 5 × 2 × 3 × 3
$2 \times 3^2 \times 5^2$

48. *Sample answer:* The methods are the same, but different factors were used in the first factorization. The results were exactly the same.

48. Writing A student made the factor tree at the right by looking for a prime factor at each step. Make a different factor tree for 140. Compare and contrast the methods and the results.

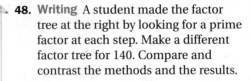

140
2 × 70
2 × 2 × 35
2 × 2 × 5 × 7

Number Sense Tell whether the statement is *true* or *false*.

49. Any number that is divisible by 6 is divisible by 2. true

50. Any number that is divisible by 5 is divisible by 10. false

51. All prime numbers are odd. false

52. All multiples of 3 are composite. false

Extended Problem Solving In Exercises 53–55, you are planning relay races. Information about the races is given at the right.

53. Mental Math What are the possible team sizes? How many teams would there be for each team size? 2, 3, 4, or 6; 24, 16, 12, or 8

54. Decide You want exactly 6 teams in each race. Which team sizes from Exercise 53 are still possible? 2 or 4

55. Explain You want to have a runoff among the winning teams. What team size from Exercise 54 should you use if you want 4 teams in the runoff? Explain.

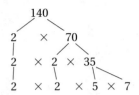

Relay Races

48 students participating

Teams of equal size

Maximum team size: 6 students

55. *Sample answer:* 6; if there are 6 students per team, there will be 8 teams, or 4 pairs of teams. In the first round of races, 4 teams will win and 4 will lose. So there will be 4 teams left for the runoff.

Find the least number that is divisible by the given numbers.

56. 2, 6, and 9 18

57. 2, 3, and 5 30

58. 3, 5, and 9 45

59. 6, 9, and 10 90

60. Find a number between 30 and 40 that is composite and has prime factors that add up to 12. 35

61. Cryptography To keep e-mail and other electronic information private, cryptographers use large numbers that are difficult to factor. Use a calculator to find the prime factorization of the number 3551. 53 × 67

62. Critical Thinking Why is a number that is divisible by 3 and 5 always divisible by 15, when a number that is divisible by 2 and 6 isn't necessarily divisible by 12? *Sample answer:* 3 is not a factor of 5, while 2 is a factor of 6.

63. Challenge Twin primes are pairs of prime numbers whose difference is 2. An example is 3 and 5. Find the next 4 pairs of twin primes.
5 and 7, 11 and 13, 17 and 19, 29 and 31

Mixed Review

Use the distributive property to evaluate the expression.
(Lesson 4.2)

64. $7(40 + 8)$ 336   **65.** $8(30 + 7)$ 296   **66.** $5(50 - 8)$ 210   **67.** $4(60 - 6)$ 216

Divide. Round to the nearest tenth if necessary. *(Lesson 4.4)*

68. $8.6 \div 2$ 4.3   **69.** $96.3 \div 3$ 32.1   **70.** $36.8 \div 16$ 2.3   **71.** $5.9 \div 2$ 3.0

Basic Skills   Solve the following problems.

72. You would like to buy a pair of jeans for $35. You have $23. How much more money do you need? **$12**

73. Your sister has 87 stickers. Her friend gives her 16 more. How many stickers does she have? **103 stickers**

Test-Taking Practice

74. Multiple Choice Which of the following numbers is a composite number? **C**

   A. 11   **B.** 17   **C.** 20   **D.** 23

75. Short Response The factor tree at the right is not complete. Copy and complete the factor tree in two different ways. Then write the prime factorization of 450. **See margin.**

450
25×18

Which Telephone Number?

Joey has a list of five telephone numbers on a slip of paper, but his hamster ate a part of this paper that had all the names next to the numbers. Now he wants to call Paul, and he does not know which of the five numbers to dial. He does remember the following facts about Paul's number:

1. It is divisible by 9.
2. It is divisible by 2.
3. It is not divisible by 10.
4. It is not divisible by 4.

Ignoring the hyphens, which telephone number could be Paul's? **642-3174**

835-6257
555-6902
903-1248
420-2730
642-3174

The strategy Make a List or Table provides two useful kinds of information. Students can use the list to find the total number of possibilities for a problem, and they can also use the list to identify patterns or properties of the entries on the list. Before making a list, students should always take time to think about the heading or headings for the list.

2 TEACH

GUIDING STUDENTS' WORK

In Step 3, students must use the information in the problem to know what entries they should write in the left column. The problem says that there are no more than 5 rows, and the number of rows must be a factor of 30. The factors of 30 are 1, 2, 3, 5, 6, 10, 15, and 30, so the first four numbers 1, 2, 3, 5 are all the possible values for the first column.

EXTRA EXAMPLES

Example You have 50 posters. Each poster is a square, and you want to use some of the posters in a square display. How many different sizes of displays are possible?

Rows	Columns	No. of posters in the display
1	1	1
2	2	4
3	3	9
4	4	16
5	5	25
6	6	36
7	7	49

7 different displays are possible.

5.2 Problem Solving Strategies

- Draw a Diagram
- Guess, Check, and Revise
- Look for a Pattern
- Work Backward
- **Make a List or Table**
- Perform an Experiment
- Check Reasonableness

Make a List or Table

Problem You are displaying student art work for a show. You have 30 pieces to display. You will arrange them in alphabetical order across the rows. How many different possibilities for a rectangular display are there if you want no more than 5 rows of posters?

1 Read and Understand

Read the problem carefully.

You want to find all of the ways to make a rectangle with 30 art pieces.

2 Make a Plan

Decide on a strategy to use.

One way to solve a problem is to make a list or a table of all of the possibilities.

3 Solve the Problem

Reread the problem and make a list or table.

You know that your display will have 30 art pieces. You also know that you will have no more than 5 rows of art pieces. List all of the whole number factors of 30 less than or equal to 5. Column headings help you organize rows and columns for your display.

Rows	Columns	Display
1	30	30
2	15	30
3	10	30
5	6	30

The table allows you to see how many columns you will have for each number of rows.

ANSWER There are 4 different possibilities for a display of 30 pieces of student art.

4 Look Back

Check to make sure that you used all possibilities of whole number factors of 30 less than or equal to 5. You could also draw a diagram of each situation.

NCTM CURRICULUM STANDARDS
Standard 1: Understand relationships among numbers
Standard 6: Apply/adapt strategies to solve problems
Standard 10: Create representations to communicate ideas

Practice the Strategy

Use the strategy _make a list or table_.

1. **Science Fair** You have entered the school science fair with an experiment. The guidelines allocate 40 square feet per participant. How many possibilities for a rectangular space with whole number dimensions are there? **4 possibilities**

2. **Coins** Copy and extend the table to find all the ways you can combine change to get 25 cents. **See margin.**

Pennies	Nickels	Dimes	Quarters
25	0	0	0
20	1	0	0
15	2	0	0
15	0	1	0

3. **Change** You purchase a magazine and are going to receive a dollar in change. How many different ways can you receive the change if it's given in quarters only, in nickels only, or in quarters and nickels? **5 ways**

4. **Fundraising** You sell $60 worth of merchandise to raise money for a school club. You sell candles for $5 and candleholders for $6. In how many ways could you have earned $60? **3 ways**

5. **Code Words** You and a friend decide to send letters in a secret code. How many different three-letter code words can you make using the letters _A_, _B_, and _C_ if repetition of the letters is _not_ permitted? **6 code words**

Mixed Problem Solving

Use any strategy to solve the problem.

6. **Find the Number** What number belongs in the blank? **11**

$$(121 \div \underline{\ ?\ }) \times 4 + 8 = 52$$

7. **Photos** You want to display photos of friends on a bulletin board. Assuming adjacent sides of the photos overlap and each corner must be tacked, what is the least number of tacks you need to display six rectangular photos of the same size and shape? **12 tacks**

8. **Find the Rule** Use the table to find a rule that relates the number and its result.

2 times the number plus 2 gives the result.

Number	Result
4	10
5	12
6	14
7	16
8	18

9. **Trip** You are planning a trip to the beach for seventeen friends. Four parents volunteer to drive and each car will hold four friends. Will four cars be enough? Why or why not? **No; the cars will only hold 20 people and they need to hold 21 people.**

Greatest Common Factor

LESSON 5.2

BEFORE	Now	WHY?
You found all the factors of a number.	You'll find the greatest common factor of two or more numbers.	So you can divide large groups evenly, as in Ex. 23.

In the Real World

Word Watch
common factor, p. 222
greatest common factor (GCF), p. 222

Gardening You are dividing a garden into sections. You have 64 marigolds and 120 petunias. You want each section to have the same number of each type of flower, and you want to use all of the flowers. What is the greatest number of sections you can have?

A whole number that is a factor of two or more nonzero whole numbers is a **common factor** of the numbers. The largest of the common factors is the **greatest common factor (GCF)**.

EXAMPLE 1   **Finding the GCF of Two Numbers**

The greatest number of sections that you can have in the garden described above is the GCF of 64 and 120. Two methods for finding the GCF are shown.

Method 1: List all the factors of 64 and 120.

Factors of 64: 1, 2, 4, 8, 16, 32, 64

Factors of 120: 1, 2, 3, 4, 5, 6, 8, 10, 12, 15, 20, 24, 30, 40, 60, 120

The common factors are 1, 2, 4, and 8. The GCF is 8.

Method 2: Write the prime factorization of 64 and 120. Then find the product of the common prime factors.

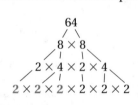

$$
\begin{array}{c}
64 \\
8 \times 8 \\
2 \times 4 \times 2 \times 4 \\
2 \times 2 \times 2 \times 2 \times 2 \times 2
\end{array}
\qquad
\begin{array}{c}
120 \\
10 \times 12 \\
2 \times 5 \times 2 \times 6 \\
2 \times 5 \times 2 \times 2 \times 3
\end{array}
$$

The common prime factors are 2, 2, and 2. The GCF is 2^3, or 8.

ANSWER The greatest number of sections that you can have is 8.

NCTM CURRICULUM STANDARDS
Standard 6: Build knowledge through problem solving
Standard 9: Grasp how mathematical ideas interconnect; Understand how math ideas build on one another

Example 1 Find the GCF of 90 and 102. **6**

Example 2 Find the GCF of 60, 90, and 175. **5**

Example 3 This chart shows what each of three people spent on gifts. If each gift cost the same, what is the most that each gift could cost?

Person	Spent
1	$72
2	$60
3	$84

The most each gift could cost is $12.

Finding the Greatest Common Factor (GCF)

Method 1: List all the factors of each number. Then find the greatest factor that is common to all numbers.

Method 2: Write the prime factorization of each number. Then find the product of the prime factors the numbers have in common.

EXAMPLE 2 Finding the GCF of Three Numbers

Find the GCF of 12, 21, and 30.

Factors of 12: 1, 2, 3, 4, 6, 12
Factors of 21: 1, 3, 7, 21
Factors of 30: 1, 2, 3, 5, 6, 10, 15, 30

ANSWER The GCF of 12, 21, and 30 is 3.

EXAMPLE 3 Making a List

Tours Three groups will take the Cave of the Winds tour of Niagara Falls. The amount they will spend on tickets is given at the right. If each ticket is the same price, what is the most a ticket could cost?

	Amount
Group 1	$27
Group 2	$45
Group 3	$72

Solution

Find the GCF of the amounts spent by listing the factors.

Factors of 27: 1, 3, 9, 27
Factors of 45: 1, 3, 5, 9, 15, 45
Factors of 72: 1, 2, 3, 4, 6, 8, 9, 12, 18, 24, 36, 72

The common factors are 1, 3, and 9.

ANSWER The most a ticket could cost is $9.

 NOTETAKING
This chapter contains a great deal of new vocabulary. Students' notes for this lesson should include both the meaning of GCF and the fast way to calculate the GCF along with specific examples.

 CONCEPT CHECK
How can you use a prime factorization to find the GCF of two or more numbers? **Write the prime factorization of each number. Then find the product of the factors that are common to all the numbers.**

 DAILY PUZZLER
The GCF of 756 and a second number is 252. What is the smallest possible value for the other number? **252**

Your turn now Find the GCF of the numbers.

1. 14, 35   7   **2.** 16, 36   4   **3.** 42, 72   6

4. 4, 6, 8   2   **5.** 12, 24, 30   6   **6.** 24, 48, 72   24

ASSIGNMENT GUIDE

Basic Course
Day 1: pp. 224–225 Exs. 6–23, 25–27, 32–39

Average Course
Day 1: pp. 224–225 Exs. 5–28, 32–40

Advanced Course
Day 1: pp. 224–225 Exs. 5–11, 18–34*, 39, 40

Block
pp. 224–225 Exs. 5–28, 32–40 (with 5.3)

EXTRA PRACTICE

- Student Edition, p. 712
- Chapter 5 Resource Book, pp. 16–18
- Test and Practice Generator

 TRANSPARENCY

Even-numbered answers are available on transparencies.

HOMEWORK CHECK

When you review students' homework for this lesson, go over the following exercises to check understanding of key concepts.
Basic: 6, 10, 14, 18, 23
Average: 5, 7, 11, 18, 23
Advanced: 5, 8, 19, 21, 23

 COMMON ERROR

Students often omit a factor when they list the factors of a number, as illustrated in Exercise 5. Suggest to students that they check their lists by pairing factors whose product is the given number. In this case, 14 should be paired with 2 as a factor of 28.

5.2 Exercises

More Practice, p. 712

INTERNET
eWorkbook Plus
CLASSZONE.COM

Getting Ready to Practice

Vocabulary **Find the GCF of the numbers using the factors listed.**

1. GCF of 18 and 32 **2**
  Factors of 18: 1, 2, 3, 6, 9, 18
  Factors of 32: 1, 2, 4, 8, 16, 32

2. GCF of 21 and 39 **3**
  Factors of 21: 1, 3, 7, 21
  Factors of 39: 1, 3, 13, 39

3. Use factor trees to find the GCF of 15 and 45. **15**

4. **Guided Problem Solving** For your school's fair, you make 42 magnets and 36 key chains with your school's mascot on them. You want to display them in rows of equal size, but you do not want to mix the items. What is the greatest number of items you can have in a row? How many rows of each item will there be?

  ① Find the GCF of 42 and 36. **6**

  ② Divide to find the number of rows of magnets. **7 rows**

  ③ Divide to find the number of rows of key chains. **6 rows**

Practice and Problem Solving

A **5.** **Find the Error** Describe and correct the error in finding the GCF of 28 and 42.
The factor of 14 is not included in the factors of 28. So the GCF is 14.

> Factors of 28: 1, 2, 4, 7, 28
> Factors of 42: 1, 2, 3, 6, 7, 14, 21, 42
> The GCF is 7.

Find the GCF of the numbers by listing the factors.

6. 10, 28 **2**   **7.** 24, 84 **12**   **8.** 16, 48 **16**   **9.** 11, 44 **11**

Find the GCF of the numbers using factor trees.

10. 12, 54 **6**   **11.** 32, 40 **8**   **12.** 20, 75 **5**   **13.** 36, 90 **18**

Find the GCF of the numbers using either method.

14. 9, 42 **3**   **15.** 8, 28 **4**   **16.** 12, 25 **1**   **17.** 15, 52 **1**
18. 12, 21, 30 **3**   **19.** 16, 40, 88 **8**   **20.** 30, 75, 120 **15** **21.** 13, 65, 117 **13**

22. **Parades** A group of 45 singers will march behind a group of 30 clowns in a parade. You want to arrange the two groups in rows with the same number of people in each row, but without mixing the groups. What is the greatest number of people you can have in each row? **15 people**

with Homework

Example	Exercises
1	5–17, 22
2	18–21
3	23

Online Resources
CLASSZONE.COM
· More Examples
· eTutorial Plus

■ **History Museums**

An African elephant, such as the one on display at the National Museum of Natural History in Washington, D.C., can weigh in the vicinity of 14,000 pounds. The average mid-size sedan weighs about 3300 pounds. How many times more does the African elephant weigh than the average mid-size sedan? **about 4 times more**

24. **19 groups.** *Sample answer:* The first group will be divided into 3 smaller groups, the second will be divided into 7, and the third into 9 for a total of 19 smaller groups.

28. **Yes.** *Sample answer:* The lesser number is a factor of itself and the greater number, so it is the GCF of the numbers.

History Museums In Exercises 23 and 24, use the information below.
A museum has three groups of people scheduled for tours. The groups have 48, 112, and 144 people. The tour guides want to divide the groups into smaller groups of equal size, without mixing any of the groups.

23. What is the greatest number of people each group can have? **16 people**

24. **Explain** How many groups of people will there be? Explain. **See margin.**
B

Tell whether the statement is *always*, *sometimes*, or *never* true.

25. The GCF of two numbers is one of the two numbers. **sometimes**

26. The GCF of two numbers is greater than one of the numbers. **never**

27. The GCF of two prime numbers is 1. **always**

C 28. **Critical Thinking** If one number is a factor of another number, will the GCF always be the lesser number? Explain. **See margin.**

Challenge Find the GCF of the numbers.

29. 658, 770 **14**   30. 279, 414 **9**   31. 372, 582 **6**

Mixed Review

32. Order the numbers 1.26, 1.02, 1.6, 0.96, 1, 0.1, and 1.216 from least to greatest. *(Lesson 3.3)* **0.1, 0.96, 1, 1.02, 1.216, 1.26, 1.6**

Evaluate the expression using mental math. *(Lesson 4.5)*

33. $0.05 \div 100$ **0.0005**   34. $3.46 \div 0.01$ **346**   35. $0.9 \div 0.001$ **900**

Basic Skills   **What fraction is shown by the model?**

36. $\frac{1}{3}$ 37. $\frac{3}{8}$ 38. $\frac{1}{6}$

Test-Taking Practice

39. **Multiple Choice** What is the greatest common factor of 14 and 26? **A**

   A. 2   **B.** 7   **C.** 14   **D.** 182

40. **Short Response** Ashley has 27 violet marbles, 54 blue marbles, and 72 white marbles. She wants to divide the marbles into groups so that each group has the same number of each color marble. What is the greatest number of groups that Ashley can make? Explain.

   9 groups; 9 is the GCF of 27, 54, and 72.

MINI-QUIZ

Find the GCF for each group of numbers.

1. 45, 105 **15**

2. 36, 54, 90 **18**

3. 72, 120, 280 **8**

4. 56, 196, 252 **28**

5. An antiques dealer has 35 rings and 75 pins to display. The display should have equal sized rows, and pins and rings should not appear in the same row. How many items should appear in each row? How many rows will there be for each item? **Each row should have 5 items. There should be 7 rows of rings and 15 rows of pins.**

① PLAN

EXPLORE THE CONCEPT

- Students will use models to find equivalent fractions.
- In this activity students use paper folding to model fractions and identify equivalent fractions. These models for equivalent fractions are used again at the beginning of Lesson 5.3.

MATERIALS

Each student will need two sheets of paper.

RECOMMENDED TIME

Work activity: 10 min
Discuss results: 5 min

GROUPING

This activity is best done individually.

② TEACH

TIPS FOR SUCCESS

To fold a paper in thirds, as required in Explore 2, some students may need to use a ruler to mark the fold lines. This will help them accurately model thirds and ninths.

ALTERNATIVE STRATEGY

For Explore 1, start with circular disks of paper and fold the disks into halves, fourths, and eighths.

5.3 Hands-on **Activity**

GOAL
Use models to find equivalent fractions.

MATERIALS
- paper
- pencil

Modeling Equivalent Fractions

You can use paper models to represent fractions in more than one way.

Explore 1 Model the fraction $\frac{1}{2}$ in different ways.

① Fold a piece of paper in half. Then unfold the paper and draw a line along the fold. Shade one half as shown.

② Refold the paper. Then fold it in half again in the same direction. Unfold the paper and draw a line along each new fold.

Copy and complete the statement: $\frac{1}{2} = \frac{?}{4}$. **2**

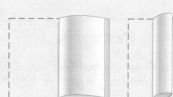

③ Fold the paper in half in the other direction. Then unfold the paper and draw a line along the new fold.

Copy and complete the statement: $\frac{1}{2} = \frac{?}{8}$. **4**

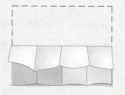
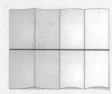

Your turn now Use the fractions in Steps 1–3 above.

1. Describe a pattern in the numerators of the fractions above. Do you see the same pattern in the denominators? **The pattern is 1, 2, 4 and each number is 2 times the previous number; yes.**
2. Use your answers to Exercise 1 to help you copy and complete the following fractions.

$$\frac{1}{2} = \frac{2}{4} = \frac{4}{8} = \frac{?}{16} \quad \textbf{8}$$

NCTM CURRICULUM STANDARDS
Standard 1: Understand numbers
Standard 10: Create representations to communicate mathematical ideas

KEY DISCOVERY

When a part of a whole can be represented with two or more fractions, those fractions are equivalent.

Explore 2 Model the fraction $\frac{1}{3}$ in different ways.

1 Fold a piece of paper in thirds. Then unfold the paper and draw a line along each fold. Shade one third as shown.

2 Refold the paper. Then fold it in thirds again in the same direction. Unfold the paper and draw a line along each new fold.

Copy and complete the

statement: $\frac{1}{3} = \frac{?}{9}$. **3**

3 Fold the paper in thirds in the other direction. Then unfold the paper and draw a line along each new fold.

Copy and complete the

statement: $\frac{1}{3} = \frac{?}{27}$. **9**

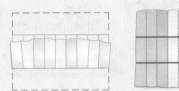

ASSESSMENT

1. Fold a piece of paper in fourths and then in eighths. Complete the statement: $\frac{3}{4} = \frac{?}{8}$. **6**

2. Fold a piece of paper in ninths and then in twenty-sevenths. Complete the statement: $\frac{5}{9} = \frac{?}{27}$. **15**

Your turn now Use the fractions in Steps 1–3 above.

3. Copy and complete the following fractions.

$\frac{1}{3} = \frac{3}{9} = \frac{9}{27} = \frac{?}{81}$ **27**

Stop and Think

4. **Writing** Describe a method you could use to find three fractions with different numerators and denominators that all represent the same fraction. *Sample answer:* Multiply the numerator and denominator of the first fraction by the same number. Repeat with each new fraction.

Lesson 5.3 Equivalent Fractions **227**

SKILL CHECK

Evaluate the expression.

1. $\dfrac{2 \times 5}{3 \times 5}$ $\dfrac{10}{15}$

2. $\dfrac{3 \times 6}{4 \times 6}$ $\dfrac{18}{24}$

3. $\dfrac{20 \div 5}{45 \div 5}$ $\dfrac{4}{9}$

4. $\dfrac{32 \div 16}{48 \div 16}$ $\dfrac{2}{3}$

LESSON OBJECTIVE

Write equivalent fractions.

PACING

Suggested Number of Days
Basic Course: 2 days
Average Course: 2 days
Advanced Course: 2 days
Block: 0.5 block with 5.2
0.5 block with 5.4

TEACHING RESOURCES

For a complete list of Teaching Resources, see page 210B.

 TRANSPARENCY

Warm-Up Exercises for this lesson are available on a transparency.

2 TEACH

MOTIVATING THE LESSON

Have other models of fractions equivalent to $\frac{1}{3}$ ready for discussion after presenting the equivalence $\frac{1}{3} = \frac{4}{12}$ at the beginning of the lesson. Ask students to sketch other such equivalent models.

LESSON 5.3 Equivalent Fractions

BEFORE	▶ Now	WHY?
You wrote equivalent decimals.	You'll write equivalent fractions.	So you can simplify fractions, such as the survey responses in Example 3.

 **Word Watch**

fraction, p. 228
equivalent fractions, p. 228
simplest form, p. 229

Fractions Recall that a **fraction** is a number of the form $\frac{a}{b}$, where $b \neq 0$.

$$\dfrac{a}{b} \quad \begin{array}{l} \longleftarrow \text{numerator} \\ \longleftarrow \text{denominator} \end{array}$$

A fraction can represent part of a whole, as shown below.

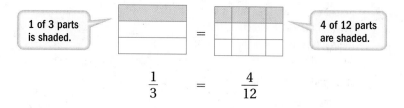

1 of 3 parts is shaded.   =   4 of 12 parts are shaded.

$$\dfrac{1}{3} \qquad = \qquad \dfrac{4}{12}$$

The fractions above are **equivalent** because they represent the same number. As you may have noticed in the activity, you can write equivalent fractions by multiplying or dividing the numerator and denominator by the *same* number.

HELP with Notetaking

In your notebook, you might want to record models of the equivalent fractions shown in Example 1.

EXAMPLE 1 **Writing Equivalent Fractions**

Write two fractions that are equivalent to $\frac{1}{3}$.

$\dfrac{1}{3} = \dfrac{1 \times 2}{3 \times 2} = \dfrac{2}{6}$ Multiply the numerator and denominator by 2.

$\dfrac{1}{3} = \dfrac{1 \times 3}{3 \times 3} = \dfrac{3}{9}$ Multiply the numerator and denominator by 3.

ANSWER The fractions $\frac{2}{6}$ and $\frac{3}{9}$ are equivalent to $\frac{1}{3}$.

Your turn now Write two fractions that are equivalent to the given fraction. 1–4. Answers may vary.

1. $\dfrac{1}{2}$ $\dfrac{2}{4}, \dfrac{3}{6}$

2. $\dfrac{1}{4}$ $\dfrac{2}{8}, \dfrac{3}{12}$

3. $\dfrac{3}{5}$ $\dfrac{6}{10}, \dfrac{9}{15}$

4. $\dfrac{2}{3}$ $\dfrac{4}{6}, \dfrac{6}{9}$

NCTM CURRICULUM STANDARDS
Standard 1: Understand numbers; Understand relationships among numbers
Standard 2: Understand patterns

EXAMPLE 2 Completing Equivalent Fractions

Complete the equivalent fraction.

a. $\dfrac{3}{5} = \dfrac{12}{?}$

b. $\dfrac{16}{24} = \dfrac{?}{12}$

$$\overset{3\,\times\,4}{\underset{5\,\times\,4}{\dfrac{3}{5} = \dfrac{12}{20}}}$$

You multiply 3 by 4 to get 12, so multiply the denominator by 4.

$$\overset{16\,\div\,2}{\underset{24\,\div\,2}{\dfrac{16}{24} = \dfrac{8}{12}}}$$

You divide 24 by 2 to get 12, so divide the numerator by 2.

Your turn now Copy and complete the statement.

5. $\dfrac{2}{5} = \dfrac{6}{?}$ 15

6. $\dfrac{4}{7} = \dfrac{?}{21}$ 12

7. $\dfrac{15}{20} = \dfrac{3}{?}$ 4

8. $\dfrac{18}{27} = \dfrac{?}{3}$ 2

Simplifying A fraction is in **simplest form** if its numerator and denominator have a greatest common factor of 1. To *simplify* a fraction, divide its numerator and denominator by their greatest common factor.

EXAMPLE 3 Simplifying Fractions

Movies In a survey of 16 middle school students, 12 said that comedy was their favorite type of movie. Write this as a fraction in simplest form.

Solution

Write "12 out of 16" as a fraction. Then simplify.

$\dfrac{12}{16} = \dfrac{3 \times 4}{4 \times 4}$ Use the GCF to write the numerator and denominator as products.

$= \dfrac{3 \times \cancel{4}^{\,1}}{4 \times \cancel{4}_{\,1}}$ Divide the numerator and denominator by the GCF.

$= \dfrac{3}{4}$ Simplest form

ANSWER The fraction, in simplest form, of students who said comedy was their favorite type of movie is $\dfrac{3}{4}$.

Your turn now Write the fraction in simplest form.

9. $\dfrac{5}{25}$ $\dfrac{1}{5}$

10. $\dfrac{8}{24}$ $\dfrac{1}{3}$

11. $\dfrac{14}{21}$ $\dfrac{2}{3}$

12. $\dfrac{15}{35}$ $\dfrac{3}{7}$

Lesson 5.3   Equivalent Fractions   **229**

Example 4 You spent an hour last weekend reading and responding to e-mails. Write a fraction in simplest form to describe each amount of time.

a. You spent 5 minutes on e-mails with a cousin. $\frac{1}{12}$ h

b. You spent 45 minutes on e-mails with a classmate. $\frac{3}{4}$ h

c. You spent 10 minutes on e-mails with a school club. $\frac{1}{6}$ h

 CONCEPT CHECK

When is a fraction in simplest form? A fraction is in simplest form when the greatest common factor of the numerator and denominator is 1.

 DAILY PUZZLER

How can you use the digits 1, 2, 3, 4, 6, 8 to write three equivalent fractions? Use each digit exactly once. $\frac{1}{2} = \frac{3}{6} = \frac{4}{8}$

EXAMPLE 4 **Applying Fractions**

Homework You spent an hour on homework last night. Write a fraction in simplest form to describe the amount of time you spent on each subject.

a. You spent 15 minutes on literature. $\frac{15}{60} = \frac{1 \times \cancel{15}^{1}}{4 \times \cancel{15}_{1}} = \frac{1}{4}$ hour

b. You spent 25 minutes on math. $\frac{25}{60} = \frac{5 \times \cancel{5}^{1}}{12 \times \cancel{5}_{1}} = \frac{5}{12}$ hour

c. You spent 20 minutes on science. $\frac{20}{60} = \frac{1 \times \cancel{20}^{1}}{3 \times \cancel{20}_{1}} = \frac{1}{3}$ hour

5.3 Exercises

More Practice, p. 712

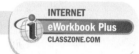
INTERNET
eWorkbook Plus
CLASSZONE.COM

Getting Ready to Practice

Vocabulary Tell whether the fraction is in simplest form. If not, simplify it.

1. $\frac{1}{2}$ yes

2. $\frac{2}{3}$ yes

3. $\frac{3}{9}$ no; $\frac{1}{3}$

4. $\frac{4}{10}$ no; $\frac{2}{5}$

Which fraction is not equivalent to the given fraction?

5. $\frac{1}{8}$ A **A.** $\frac{2}{9}$ **B.** $\frac{2}{16}$ **C.** $\frac{3}{24}$ **D.** $\frac{5}{40}$

6. $\frac{2}{5}$ B **A.** $\frac{10}{25}$ **B.** $\frac{5}{20}$ **C.** $\frac{20}{50}$ **D.** $\frac{40}{100}$

7. $\frac{16}{40}$ D **A.** $\frac{8}{20}$ **B.** $\frac{4}{10}$ **C.** $\frac{2}{5}$ **D.** $\frac{1}{4}$

8. $\frac{12}{36}$ A **A.** $\frac{1}{24}$ **B.** $\frac{1}{3}$ **C.** $\frac{2}{6}$ **D.** $\frac{4}{12}$

9. Beads You are using the beads below to make a bracelet. Write fractions in simplest form to describe the portion of beads that are each color.

blue: $\frac{5}{18}$; orange: $\frac{1}{2}$; green: $\frac{2}{9}$

Practice and Problem Solving

Write two fractions that are equivalent to the given fraction.

10–17. Answers may vary.

A **10.** $\frac{1}{5}$ $\frac{2}{10}, \frac{3}{15}$ **11.** $\frac{1}{10}$ $\frac{2}{20}, \frac{3}{30}$ **12.** $\frac{3}{7}$ $\frac{6}{14}, \frac{9}{21}$ **13.** $\frac{3}{5}$ $\frac{6}{10}, \frac{9}{15}$

14. $\frac{3}{11}$ $\frac{6}{22}, \frac{9}{33}$ **15.** $\frac{9}{20}$ $\frac{18}{40}, \frac{27}{60}$ **16.** $\frac{4}{25}$ $\frac{8}{50}, \frac{12}{75}$ **17.** $\frac{3}{100}$ $\frac{6}{200}, \frac{9}{300}$

Copy and complete the statement.

18. $\frac{4}{5} = \frac{?}{20}$ 16   **19.** $\frac{7}{9} = \frac{35}{?}$ 45   **20.** $\frac{18}{30} = \frac{6}{?}$ 10   **21.** $\frac{20}{25} = \frac{?}{5}$ 4

22. $\frac{6}{7} = \frac{18}{?}$ 21   **23.** $\frac{9}{11} = \frac{?}{66}$ 54   **24.** $\frac{44}{52} = \frac{?}{13}$ 11   **25.** $\frac{28}{49} = \frac{4}{?}$ 7

Tell whether the fraction is in simplest form. If not, simplify it.

26. $\frac{7}{14}$ no; $\frac{1}{2}$ **27.** $\frac{9}{27}$ no; $\frac{1}{3}$ **28.** $\frac{9}{32}$ yes   **29.** $\frac{13}{64}$ yes

30. $\frac{15}{48}$ no; $\frac{5}{16}$ **31.** $\frac{40}{45}$ no; $\frac{8}{9}$ **32.** $\frac{24}{77}$ yes   **33.** $\frac{50}{175}$ no; $\frac{2}{7}$

34. Buying Lunch There are 30 people in a class and 21 of them buy lunch at school. Write the portion of the class that buys lunch at school as a fraction in simplest form. $\frac{7}{10}$

Chess A chessboard is shown at the right.

35. Write a fraction in simplest form that represents the portion of the squares on the board that are shaded purple. $\frac{1}{2}$

36. Write a fraction in simplest form that represents the portion of the board covered by one player's chess pieces. $\frac{1}{4}$

 **Algebra** Find the value of x.

B **37.** $\frac{x}{8} = \frac{25}{40}$ 5   **38.** $\frac{x}{42} = \frac{1}{6}$ 7   **39.** $\frac{12}{x} = \frac{2}{9}$ 54   **40.** $\frac{7}{x} = \frac{49}{70}$ 10

Geometry What fraction of the large rectangle's area is shaded red? Write the answer in simplest form.

41. 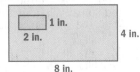 $\frac{1}{16}$ **42.** 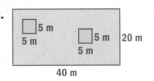 $\frac{1}{16}$

Lesson 5.3 · Equivalent Fractions   **231**

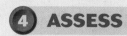
MINI-QUIZ

1. Write two fractions equivalent to the given fraction.

   a. $\frac{4}{9}$ *Sample answer:* $\frac{8}{18}, \frac{12}{27}$

   b. $\frac{1}{15}$ *Sample answer:* $\frac{2}{30}, \frac{3}{45}$

2. Complete the equivalent fraction.

   a. $\frac{5}{40} = \frac{?}{8}$ 1

   b. $\frac{2}{11} = \frac{10}{?}$ 55

3. In a survey of 30 students, 9 said they took public transportation to school. Write this as a fraction in simplest form. $\frac{3}{10}$

 FOLLOW-UP

RETEACHING/REMEDIATION

• Study Guide in Chapter 5 Resource Book, pp. 27–28
• Tutor Place, Fractions Cards 1–3
• eTutorial Plus Online
• Extra Practice, p. 712
• Lesson Practice in Chapter 5 Resource Book, pp. 24–26

CHALLENGE/ENRICHMENT

• Challenge Practice in Chapter 5 Resource Book, p. 29
• Teacher's Edition, p. 210F

ENGLISH LEARNER SUPPORT

• Spanish Study Guide
• Multi-Language Glossary
• Chapter Audio Summaries CDs

Critical Thinking Tell whether the statement is *always*, *sometimes*, or *never* true.

43. An equivalent fraction has a smaller denominator than the original fraction. sometimes

44. A fraction in simplest form has a smaller denominator than an equivalent fraction that is not in simplest form. always

Challenge Write the fraction in simplest form.

C **45.** $\frac{76}{104}$ $\frac{19}{26}$
46. $\frac{180}{222}$ $\frac{30}{37}$
47. $\frac{95}{245}$ $\frac{19}{49}$
48. $\frac{207}{270}$ $\frac{23}{30}$

Mixed Review

Find the GCF of the numbers. *(Lesson 5.2)*

49. 12, 34 2
50. 14, 42 14
51. 36, 40 4
52. 18, 36, 90 18

Choose a Strategy Use a strategy from the list to solve the following problem. Explain your choice of strategy.

53. The denominator of a fraction is 8 more than the numerator. The denominator is also 3 times the numerator. Find the fraction.

> **Problem Solving Strategies**
> ■ Guess, Check, and Revise
> ■ Make a Table
> ■ Solve a Simpler Problem
> ■ Look for a Pattern

53. $\frac{4}{12}$. *Sample answer:* I used Make a Table to solve the problem so I could keep track of the numerators and denominators and their relationships.

Basic Skills **Find the product.**

54. 10×12 120
55. 100×12 1200
56. 1000×12 12,000
57. $10,000 \times 12$ 120,000

Test-Taking Practice

58. Multiple Choice Which fraction model does *not* equal $\frac{2}{3}$? D

A.

B.

C.

D.

59. Multiple Choice Alaska and Hawaii are not part of the 48 contiguous states in the United States. What fraction of the 50 states are not part of the 48 contiguous states? I

F. $\frac{46}{48}$
G. $\frac{48}{50}$
H. $\frac{2}{48}$
I. $\frac{1}{25}$

232 Chapter 5 Number Patterns and Fractions

LESSONS 5.1 TO 5.3

Notebook Review

Review the vocabulary definitions in your notebook.

Copy the review examples in your notebook. Then complete the exercises.

Check Your Definitions

divisible, p. 214

prime number, p. 215

composite number, p. 215

prime factorization, p. 216

factor tree, p. 216

common factor, p. 222

greatest common factor (GCF), p. 222

fraction, p. 228

equivalent fractions, p. 228

simplest form, p. 229

Use Your Vocabulary

1. Copy and complete: A _?_ is a whole number greater than 1 whose only factors are 1 and itself. **prime number**

2. Copy and complete: The factors of 9 are 1, _?_, and _?_. So, 9 is a _?_.
3, 9, composite number

5.1–5.2 Can you use divisibility rules and find factors?

 Review

EXAMPLE Test 574 for divisibility by 2, 3, 5, 6, 9, and 10.

574 is even, so it is divisible by 2.

$5 + 7 + 4 = 16$, which is not divisible by 3 or 9, so 574 is not either.

574 does not end with 0 or 5, so it is not divisible by 5 or 10.

574 is not divisible by 6 because it is not divisible by 3.

✓ **Test the number for divisibility by 2, 3, 5, 6, 9, and 10.** See margin.

3. 49   **4.** 252   **5.** 396   **6.** 1402

Review

EXAMPLE Find the greatest common factor (GCF) of 90 and 126.

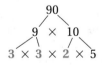

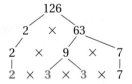

ANSWER The GCF of 90 and 126 is $2 \times 3 \times 3$, or 18.

✓ **Find the GCF.**   **7.** 48, 84 **12**   **8.** 54, 81 **27**

ADDITIONAL RESOURCES

The following resources are available to help review the materials in Lessons 5.1–5.3.

Chapter 5 Resource Book
- Lesson Practice
- Study Guide

Assessment Book
- Chapter 5 Quiz 1

Technology
- Test and Practice Generator
- eTutorial CD-ROM

Internet
- Classzone
- eWorkbook Plus Online
- eTutorial Plus Online

ENGLISH LEARNER SUPPORT

- Spanish Study Guide
- Multi-Language Glossary
- Chapter Audio Summaries CDs

3. 49 is not divisible by 2, 3, 5, 6, 9, or 10.

4. 252 is divisible by 2, 3, 6, and 9, but not by 5 or 10.

5. 396 is divisible by 2, 3, 6, and 9, but not by 5 or 10.

6. 1402 is divisible by 2, but not by 3, 5, 6, 9, or 10.

5.3 Can you simplify fractions?

EXAMPLE Use the GCF to write the fraction in simplest form.

a. $\dfrac{6}{24} = \dfrac{1 \times \cancel{6}^1}{4 \times \cancel{6}_1} = \dfrac{1}{4}$ GCF is 6.   **b.** $\dfrac{15}{33} = \dfrac{5 \times \cancel{3}^1}{11 \times \cancel{3}_1} = \dfrac{5}{11}$ GCF is 3.

☑ **Write the fraction in simplest form.**

9. $\dfrac{3}{21}$ $\dfrac{1}{7}$ **10.** $\dfrac{18}{27}$ $\dfrac{2}{3}$ **11.** $\dfrac{10}{32}$ $\dfrac{5}{16}$ **12.** $\dfrac{20}{45}$ $\dfrac{4}{9}$

Stop *and* Think   about Lessons 5.1–5.3

13. Critical Thinking Why is it helpful to know divisibility rules when finding factors of a number? *Sample answer:* You can use the rules to quickly determine a factor of a number.

14. Writing Write two numbers whose GCF is 8. Explain how you found the answer. *Sample answer:* 8 and 16; multiplied 8 by two different numbers.

Review Quiz 1

1. 54 is divisible by 2, 3, 6, and 9, but not by 5 or 10; composite.

2. 77 is not divisible by 2, 3, 5, 6, 9, or 10; composite.

3. 405 is divisible by 3, 5, and 9, but not by 2, 6, or 10; composite.

4. 1270 is divisible by 2, 5, and 10, but not by 3, 6, or 9; composite.

Test the number for divisibility by 2, 3, 5, 6, 9, and 10. Then tell whether the number is *prime* or *composite*.

1. 54   **2.** 77   **3.** 405   **4.** 1270

Write the prime factorization of the number.

5. 34 2×17 **6.** 48 $2^4 \times 3$ **7.** 164 $2^2 \times 41$ **8.** 840 $2^3 \times 3 \times 5 \times 7$

Find the GCF of the numbers.

9. 7, 56 7   **10.** 10, 21 1   **11.** 42, 90 6   **12.** 8, 40, 54 2

13. Field Trip Three science classes go on a field trip to an observatory. The classes spend $75, $54, and $96 for student admission. Find the greatest possible student admission price for the observatory. $3

14. Copy and complete: $\dfrac{6}{11} = \dfrac{?}{55}$. 30

Write the fraction in simplest form.

15. $\dfrac{6}{45}$ $\dfrac{2}{15}$ **16.** $\dfrac{10}{110}$ $\dfrac{1}{11}$ **17.** $\dfrac{14}{50}$ $\dfrac{7}{25}$ **18.** $\dfrac{39}{130}$ $\dfrac{3}{10}$

Least Common Multiple

BEFORE	▶ Now	WHY?
You found greatest common factors.	You'll find least common multiples.	So you can coordinate schedules, as with the soccer games in Ex. 7.

 **Word Watch**

multiple, p. 235
common multiple, p. 235
least common multiple
(LCM), p. 236

In the Real World

Ferry Boats Two ferry boats leave a loading platform at the same time. One of the ferry boats returns to the loading platform every 25 minutes. The other returns every 30 minutes. In the next 300 minutes, when will they return at the same time?

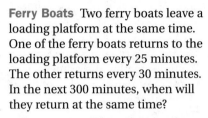

You can use *multiples* to answer the question above. A **multiple** of a number is the product of the number and any nonzero whole number.

> The three dots show that the pattern continues forever.

Multiples of 2: 2, 4, 6, 8, 10, 12, 14, . . .

A multiple shared by two or more numbers is a **common multiple**.

EXAMPLE 1 **Finding a Common Multiple**

You can use common multiples to answer the question above about ferry boats. Begin by writing the multiples of 25 and 30. Then identify common multiples through 300.

Multiples of 25: 25, 50, 75, 100, 125, **150**, 175, 200, 225, 250, 275, **300**

Multiples of 30: 30, 60, 90, 120, **150**, 180, 210, 240, 270, **300**

The common multiples of 25 and 30 are 150 and 300.

ANSWER The ferry boats will return to the loading platform at the same time in 150 minutes and in 300 minutes.

Your turn now **Find two common multiples of the numbers.**

1–4. Answers may vary.

1. 2, 3 6, 12   **2.** 3, 5 15, 30   **3.** 8, 10 40, 80   **4.** 6, 18 18, 36

5. A cuckoo clock has birds that pop out of their nests every 6 minutes and dancers that pop out every 15 minutes. Suppose that the birds and dancers have just popped out at the same time. When will this happen again in the next 60 minutes? in 30 min and in 60 min

---

NCTM CURRICULUM STANDARDS
Standard 1: Understand relationships among numbers
Standard 2: Understand patterns
Standard 9: Grasp connections among mathematical ideas

Lesson 5.4   Least Common Multiple   **235**

Example 1 Two security guards leave their office at the same time. One returns every 20 minutes, while the other returns every 35 minutes. In the next 360 minutes, when will they both return to the office at the same time? **The guards will return at the same time in 140 minutes and in 280 minutes.**

Example 2 Find the LCM of 15 and 18. **90**

Example 3 Use prime factorization to find the LCM of 20 and 42. **420**

 NOTETAKING

Students' notes should include both the meaning of LCM and the fastest way to calculate the LCM.

Advanced Students Ask advanced students to describe how they can calculate the LCM of two numbers using their GCF.

 CONCEPT CHECK

How can you describe the LCM of several numbers in terms of the prime factorization of each number? **Find the product of the prime factors, using each prime factor the greatest number of times it is a factor of any of the numbers.**

 DAILY PUZZLER

The LCM of 252 and a second number is 504. What is the largest possible value for the second number? What is the smallest possible positive value? **504, 8**

236

Finding the Least Common Multiple (LCM)

The **least common multiple** of two or more numbers is the smallest of the common multiples. Below are two methods to find the LCM.

Method 1: Start listing the multiples of each number. Then find the smallest of the common multiples.

Method 2: Write the prime factorizations of the numbers. Multiply together the prime factors, using each prime factor the greatest number of times it is a factor of any of the numbers.

 HELP with **Solving**

If the only common factor of two numbers is 1, then their least common multiple is the product of the two numbers.

EXAMPLE 2 **Finding the LCM**

Find the LCM of 9 and 12.

Multiples of 9: 9, 18, 27, **36**, 45, 54, . . .

Multiples of 12: 12, 24, **36**, 48, . . .

ANSWER The LCM of 9 and 12 is 36.

EXAMPLE 3 **Using Prime Factorization**

Find the LCM of 42 and 60 using prime factorization.

(1) Write the prime factorizations. Circle any common factors.

$42 = ⟨2⟩ × ⟨3⟩ × 7$

$60 = ⟨2⟩ × 2 × ⟨3⟩ × 5$

(2) Multiply together the prime factors, using each circled factor the greatest number of times it occurs in either factorization.

$2 × 2 × 3 × 5 × 7 = 420$

ANSWER The LCM of 42 and 60 is 420.

Your turn now Find the LCM of the numbers.

6. 8, 12 24　　　　**7.** 7, 8, 14 56　　　　**8.** 50, 90 450

Getting Ready to Practice

Vocabulary **List the first three multiples of the number.**

1. 7 7, 14, 21   **2.** 8 8, 16, 24   **3.** 11 11, 22, 33   **4.** 16 16, 32, 48

Use the prime factorizations to find the LCM of the numbers.

5. $32 = 2 \times 2 \times 2 \times 2 \times 2$ 96
$24 = 2 \times 2 \times 2 \times 3$

6. $48 = 2 \times 2 \times 2 \times 2 \times 3$ 336
$56 = 2 \times 2 \times 2 \times 7$

7. **Guided Problem Solving** You bring the drinks for your soccer team every sixth game. Every third game is a home game. When will you first bring the drinks to a home game? If there are 20 games in a season, how many times will you bring the drinks to a home game this season?

(1 List the multiples of 6 and 3. 6, 12, 18, 24, 30, 36, …; 3, 6, 9, 12, 15, 18, 21, …

(2 Find the common multiples of 6 and 3 from 1 to 20. 6, 12, 18

(3 Use the results of Step 2 to answer the questions being asked.
game 6; 3 times

Practice and Problem Solving

16. Each prime factor, 2 and 3, should be used the greatest number of times it occurs in either factorization. So the LCM should be $2 \times 2 \times 2 \times 3 \times 3$ or 72.

HELP with Homework

Example	Exercises
1	8–15, 25
2	8–15, 25
3	16–25

Online Resources
CLASSZONE.COM
· More Examples
· eTutorial Plus

Find the LCM of the numbers by listing multiples.

A **8.** 3, 7 21   **9.** 5, 8 40   **10.** 6, 10 30   **11.** 10, 12 60

12. 3, 6, 9 18   **13.** 4, 8, 16 16   **14.** 2, 3, 5 30   **15.** 4, 9, 24 72

16. **Find the Error** Describe and correct the error in finding the LCM of 24 and 36.

$24 = 2 \times 2 \times 2 \times 3$
$36 = 2 \times 2 \times 3 \times 3$

The LCM of 24 and 36 is $2 \times 2 \times 3 = 12$.

Find the LCM of the numbers using prime factorization.

17. 21, 28 84   **18.** 30, 42 210   **19.** 22, 36 396   **20.** 32, 40 160

21. 27, 45 135   **22.** 56, 64 448   **23.** 60, 72 360   **24.** 50, 75 150

25. **Writing** A store gives every 20th customer a $20 gift certificate. Every 75th customer gets a $75 gift certificate. Which customer will be the first to receive both types of gift certificates? Explain how you found your answer. 300th customer; find the LCM of 20 and 75.

3 APPLY

ASSIGNMENT GUIDE
Basic Course
Day 1: pp. 237–238 Exs. 9–27 odd, 31–44

Average Course
Day 1: pp. 237–238 Exs. 8–16 even, 17–28, 31–35, 38–45

Advanced Course
Day 1: pp. 237–238 Exs. 12–16, 21–31*, 34–37, 44, 45

Block
pp. 237–238 Exs. 8–16 even, 17–28, 31–35, 38–45 (with 5.3)

EXTRA PRACTICE
• Student Edition, p. 712
• Chapter 5 Resource Book, pp. 33–35
• Test and Practice Generator

TRANSPARENCY
Even-numbered answers are available on transparencies.

HOMEWORK CHECK
When you review students' homework for this lesson, go over the following exercises to check understanding of key concepts.
Basic: 9, 13, 17, 19, 25
Average: 10, 14, 18, 22, 25
Advanced: 12, 14, 16, 23, 25

COMMON ERROR
In Exercises 17–24, some students may multiply all the prime factors, but they may not use each prime factor the greatest number of times it is a factor in any of the numbers. Refer those students to Example 3.

MINI-QUIZ

1. Find two common multiples, each less than 1000, for the numbers 24 and 180. **360, 720**

Find the LCM for each pair of numbers.

2. 9 and 15 **45**

3. 16 and 20 **80**

4. Write the prime factorization of 70 and 175. Use the prime factorizations to find the LCM of 70 and 175. **70 = 2 · 5 · 7 and 175 = 5² · 7, so the LCM is 2 · 5² · 7 = 350.**

B 26. Insects A cricket and a grasshopper are in a jumping contest. The cricket jumps three inches every jump and the grasshopper jumps four inches every jump. Name 4 points where the cricket and the grasshopper will both land. How many jumps will it take each of them to land at these points? **12 in., 24 in., 36 in., 48 in.; cricket: 4, 8, 12, and 16 jumps, grasshopper: 3, 6, 9, and 12 jumps**

Number Sense **Find a pair of numbers that matches the description.**

27. The LCM of two prime numbers is 51. **3 and 17**

28. The LCM of two numbers is 48. Their sum is 19. **3 and 16**

29. The LCM of two numbers is 16. Their product is 64. **4 and 16**

C 30. Challenge Find the GCF and the LCM of 6 and 12. How does the product of the GCF and the LCM compare to the product of 6 and 12? Try several pairs of numbers. What does this suggest about the product of two whole numbers and the product of their GCF and LCM? **GCF: 6, LCM: 12; they are the same.** *Sample answer:* **The product of two whole numbers equals the product of their GCF and LCM.**

Mixed Review

31. Write *two and fifty-six thousandths* as a decimal. *(Lesson 3.1)* **2.056**

Find the quotient. *(Lesson 4.6)*

32. $20.44 \div 0.56$ **36.5**   **33.** $13.08 \div 0.24$ **54.5**   **34.** $1.76 \div 5.5$ **0.32**   **35.** $1.8 \div 7.2$ **0.25**

Write two fractions that are equivalent to the given fraction. *(Lesson 5.3)* **36–39. Answers may vary.**

36. $\frac{1}{8}$ $\frac{2}{16}, \frac{3}{24}$ **37.** $\frac{3}{10}$ $\frac{6}{20}, \frac{9}{30}$ **38.** $\frac{5}{12}$ $\frac{10}{24}, \frac{15}{36}$ **39.** $\frac{12}{17}$ $\frac{24}{34}, \frac{36}{51}$

Basic Skills **Copy and complete the statement with <, >, or =.**

40. 416 ? 419 **<**   **41.** 680 ? 68 **>**   **42.** 32 ? 352 **<**   **43.** 36 ? 390 **<**

Test-Taking Practice

44. Multiple Choice What is the least common multiple of 10 and 3? **C**

A. 1   **B.** 13   **C.** 30   **D.** 60

45. Short Response Pencils come in packages of 10. Rulers come in packages of 8. Hannah wants exactly one pencil for every ruler. What is the smallest number of packages of each she will need to buy? Explain how you found your answer. **40 packages; find the LCM of 10 and 8.**

Ordering Fractions

BEFORE
You compared and ordered decimals.

▶ **Now**
You'll compare and order fractions.

WHY?
So you can compare measures, such as sizes of wrenches in Example 3.

Word Watch

least common denominator (LCD), p. 239

 You can use models to compare $\frac{3}{4}$ and $\frac{7}{8}$.

(1) Fold one piece of paper into fourths and another piece of paper into eighths as shown.

(2) Shade $\frac{3}{4}$ of the first piece and $\frac{7}{8}$ of the second piece.

(3) Compare the shaded regions. Because the shaded region for $\frac{3}{4}$ is smaller than the shaded region for $\frac{7}{8}$, you can see that $\frac{3}{4} < \frac{7}{8}$.

Use models to copy and complete the statement with <, >, or =.

1. $\frac{1}{2} \underline{?} \frac{1}{4}$ >   2. $\frac{1}{4} \underline{?} \frac{1}{3}$ <   3. $\frac{2}{4} \underline{?} \frac{2}{3}$ <   4. $\frac{3}{4} \underline{?} \frac{2}{3}$ >

Least Common Denominator You can use models to compare fractions or you can use the *least common denominator* to write equivalent fractions. The **least common denominator (LCD)** of two or more fractions is the least common multiple of the denominators.

EXAMPLE 1 **Comparing Fractions Using the LCD**

Compare $\frac{5}{6}$ and $\frac{7}{9}$.

(1) Find the LCD: Because the LCM of 6 and 9 is 18, the LCD is 18.

(2) Use the LCD to write equivalent fractions.

$$\frac{5}{6} = \frac{5 \times 3}{6 \times 3} = \frac{15}{18} \qquad\qquad \frac{7}{9} = \frac{7 \times 2}{9 \times 2} = \frac{14}{18}$$

(3) Compare: Because 15 > 14, you know that $\frac{15}{18} > \frac{14}{18}$. So, $\frac{5}{6} > \frac{7}{9}$.

HELP with Solving
You can use any common denominator to compare two fractions, but it is usually easiest to use the LCD.

NCTM CURRICULUM STANDARDS
Standard 1: Understand relationships among numbers
Standard 2: Use models to understand relationships
Standard 6: Solve problems in math and other contexts

Lesson 5.5   Ordering Fractions   **239**

---

1 PLAN

SKILL CHECK
1. Order 0.5, 0.45, 0.54, 0.445, and 0.4 from least to greatest. **0.4, 0.445, 0.45, 0.5, 0.54**

LESSON OBJECTIVE
Compare and order fractions.

PACING
Suggested Number of Days
Basic Course: 1 day
Average Course: 1 day
Advanced Course: 1 day
Block: 0.5 block with 5.6

TEACHING RESOURCES
For a complete list of Teaching Resources, see page 210B.

TRANSPARENCY
Warm-Up Exercises for this lesson are available on a transparency.

2 TEACH

MOTIVATING THE LESSON
Have pairs of students check each others' work in the Activity.

ACTIVITY
Goal Fold paper to model halves, thirds, fourths, and eighths.
Key Discovery You can use an area model to compare fractions.

TIPS FOR NEW TEACHERS
Give examples to show that the LCD is the LCM of the numbers in the denominators. See Tips for New Teachers in the *Chapter 5 Resource Book*.

EXAMPLE 2 **Ordering Fractions**

Order the fractions $\frac{3}{10}$, $\frac{2}{5}$, $\frac{1}{4}$ from least to greatest.

(**1** Find the LCD: Because the LCM of 10, 5, and 4 is 20, the LCD is 20.

(**2** Use the LCD to write equivalent fractions.

$$\frac{3}{10} = \frac{3 \times 2}{10 \times 2} = \frac{6}{20} \qquad \frac{2}{5} = \frac{2 \times 4}{5 \times 4} = \frac{8}{20} \qquad \frac{1}{4} = \frac{1 \times 5}{4 \times 5} = \frac{5}{20}$$

(**3** Compare: Because $\frac{5}{20} < \frac{6}{20}$, you know that $\frac{1}{4} < \frac{3}{10}$.

Because $\frac{6}{20} < \frac{8}{20}$, you know that $\frac{3}{10} < \frac{2}{5}$.

ANSWER The fractions, from least to greatest, are $\frac{1}{4}$, $\frac{3}{10}$, and $\frac{2}{5}$.

Your turn now **Order the fractions from least to greatest.**

1. $\frac{7}{12}$, $\frac{5}{9}$, $\frac{2}{3}$, $\frac{5}{9}$, $\frac{7}{12}$, $\frac{2}{3}$ **2.** $\frac{1}{3}$, $\frac{2}{9}$, $\frac{3}{7}$, $\frac{2}{9}$, $\frac{1}{3}$, $\frac{3}{7}$ **3.** $\frac{1}{5}$, $\frac{3}{10}$, $\frac{7}{15}$

3. $\frac{1}{5}$, $\frac{3}{10}$, $\frac{7}{15}$

EXAMPLE 3 **Ordering Fractions to Solve a Problem**

Wrench Sizes You are making repairs to your bicycle. You grab a $\frac{1}{2}$ inch wrench from the toolbox, then realize it is too small. Should you try a $\frac{5}{8}$ inch wrench or a $\frac{7}{16}$ inch wrench?

Solution

Order the fractions from least to greatest.

(**1** Find the LCD: Because the LCM of 2, 8, and 16 is 16, the LCD is 16.

(**2** Use the LCD to write equivalent fractions.

$$\frac{1}{2} = \frac{1 \times 8}{2 \times 8} = \frac{8}{16} \qquad \frac{5}{8} = \frac{5 \times 2}{8 \times 2} = \frac{10}{16} \qquad \frac{7}{16}$$

(**3** Order the fractions: The fractions, from least to greatest, are $\frac{7}{16}$, $\frac{1}{2}$, and $\frac{5}{8}$.

ANSWER You should try the $\frac{5}{8}$ inch wrench.

5.5 Exercises

More Practice, p. 712

INTERNET
eWorkbook Plus
CLASSZONE.COM

Getting Ready to Practice

1. Vocabulary What is a *least common denominator*? the least common multiple of the denominators

Find the LCD. Then copy and complete the statement with <, >, or =.

2. $\frac{5}{7}$ _?_ $\frac{6}{7}$ 7; <   **3.** $\frac{1}{3}$ _?_ $\frac{1}{6}$ 6; >   **4.** $\frac{9}{21}$ _?_ $\frac{3}{7}$ 21; =   **5.** $\frac{3}{5}$ _?_ $\frac{3}{4}$ 20; <

6. Shoes The heights of the heels on three pairs of shoes in a catalog are $\frac{1}{2}$ inch, $\frac{3}{8}$ inch, and $\frac{3}{4}$ inch. Order the heights from least to greatest.

$\frac{3}{8}$ in., $\frac{1}{2}$ in., $\frac{3}{4}$ in.

Practice and Problem Solving

Copy and complete the statement with <, >, or =.

A **7.** $\frac{5}{9}$ _?_ $\frac{2}{9}$ >   **8.** $\frac{2}{11}$ _?_ $\frac{4}{11}$ <   **9.** $\frac{3}{7}$ _?_ $\frac{4}{11}$ >   **10.** $\frac{2}{5}$ _?_ $\frac{6}{15}$ =

11. $\frac{1}{6}$ _?_ $\frac{1}{8}$ >   **12.** $\frac{2}{3}$ _?_ $\frac{5}{7}$ <   **13.** $\frac{5}{8}$ _?_ $\frac{2}{3}$ <   **14.** $\frac{5}{6}$ _?_ $\frac{3}{4}$ >

15. $\frac{8}{18}$ _?_ $\frac{4}{9}$ =   **16.** $\frac{11}{15}$ _?_ $\frac{7}{9}$ <   **17.** $\frac{3}{4}$ _?_ $\frac{5}{7}$ >   **18.** $\frac{5}{18}$ _?_ $\frac{4}{15}$ >

19. Photo Albums You have two photo albums. One is $\frac{13}{16}$ inch thick, and the other is $\frac{7}{8}$ inch thick. Which one is thicker? $\frac{7}{8}$ in. album

Order the fractions from least to greatest. 20–27. See margin.

20. $\frac{6}{11}, \frac{8}{11}, \frac{5}{11}$ **21.** $\frac{3}{4}, \frac{2}{3}, \frac{5}{8}$ **22.** $\frac{7}{9}, \frac{5}{6}, \frac{13}{18}$ **23.** $\frac{9}{10}, \frac{17}{20}, \frac{4}{5}$

24. $\frac{8}{14}, \frac{11}{28}, \frac{3}{7}$ **25.** $\frac{5}{9}, \frac{3}{4}, \frac{7}{12}$ **26.** $\frac{7}{10}, \frac{14}{25}, \frac{1}{2}$ **27.** $\frac{3}{8}, \frac{11}{24}, \frac{4}{9}$

28. Writing Write and solve a real-world problem that involves ordering three fractions. Make one of the denominators a multiple of the others. A good answer should include three fractions in a scenario such as ordering lengths of material given in fractions of a yard.

29. Gold Jewelry made of 14 carat gold is 14 parts gold and 10 parts other metals, or $\frac{14}{24}$ gold. You are looking at three bracelets that are $\frac{1}{2}, \frac{5}{12}$, and $\frac{2}{3}$ gold. Which bracelet contains the most gold?

The bracelet containing $\frac{2}{3}$ gold.

Margin answers

20. $\frac{5}{11}, \frac{6}{11}, \frac{8}{11}$

21. $\frac{5}{8}, \frac{2}{3}, \frac{3}{4}$

22. $\frac{13}{18}, \frac{7}{9}, \frac{5}{6}$

23. $\frac{4}{5}, \frac{17}{20}, \frac{9}{10}$

24. $\frac{11}{28}, \frac{3}{7}, \frac{8}{14}$

25. $\frac{5}{9}, \frac{7}{12}, \frac{3}{4}$

26. $\frac{1}{2}, \frac{14}{25}, \frac{7}{10}$

27. $\frac{3}{8}, \frac{4}{9}, \frac{11}{24}$

 **with Homework**

Example	Exercises
1	7–19
2	20–27
3	28–29

Online Resources
CLASSZONE.COM
· More Examples
· eTutorial Plus

Lesson 5.5   Ordering Fractions   **241**

---

3 APPLY

ASSIGNMENT GUIDE

Basic Course
Day 1: EP p. 710 Exs. 16–18; pp. 241–242 Exs. 7–23, 29–31, 36–46

Average Course
Day 1: pp. 241–242 Exs. 7–23, 28–34, 36–47

Advanced Course
Day 1: pp. 241–242 Exs. 11–19, 24–42*, 47

Block
pp. 241–242 Exs. 7–23, 28–34, 36–47 (with 5.6)

EXTRA PRACTICE

• Student Edition, p. 712
• Chapter 5 Resource Book, pp. 41–43
• Test and Practice Generator

TRANSPARENCY

Even-numbered answers are available on transparencies.

HOMEWORK CHECK

When you review students' homework for this lesson, go over the following exercises to check understanding of key concepts.
Basic: 7, 11, 20, 22, 29
Average: 8, 12, 20, 22, 29
Advanced: 11, 19, 26, 28, 29

TEACHING TIP

In Exercise 29, it may be easier for students to use the approach described in the Differentiating Instruction note on page 240, noting that one fraction is $\frac{1}{2}$, one fraction is less than $\frac{1}{2}$, and one fraction is greater than $\frac{1}{2}$.

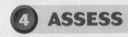

4 ASSESS

ASSESSMENT RESOURCES

For more assessment resources, see:
- Assessment Book
- Test and Practice Generator

MINI-QUIZ

Rewrite each fraction using the LCD. Then order the original fractions from least to greatest.

1. $\frac{3}{7}$ and $\frac{2}{5}$ $\frac{3}{7} = \frac{15}{35}, \frac{2}{5} = \frac{14}{35};$ $\frac{2}{5}, \frac{3}{7}$

2. $\frac{2}{3}, \frac{5}{12}, \frac{1}{6}$ $\frac{2}{3} = \frac{8}{12}, \frac{5}{12} = \frac{5}{12},$ $\frac{1}{6} = \frac{2}{12}; \frac{1}{6}, \frac{5}{12}, \frac{2}{3}$

3. A ream of paper contains 500 sheets. You need to add paper to a printer, but $\frac{1}{2}$ a ream is too much paper. Should you try $\frac{3}{8}$ of a ream or $\frac{3}{5}$ of a ream? $\frac{3}{8}$ of a ream

5 FOLLOW-UP

RETEACHING/REMEDIATION

- Study Guide in Chapter 5 Resource Book, pp. 44–45
- Tutor Place, Fractions Card 4
- eTutorial Plus Online
- Extra Practice, p. 712
- Lesson Practice in Chapter 5 Resource Book, pp. 41–43

CHALLENGE/ENRICHMENT

- Challenge Practice in Chapter 5 Resource Book, pp. 47
- Teacher's Edition, p. 210F

ENGLISH LEARNER SUPPORT

- Spanish Study Guide
- Multi-Language Glossary
- Chapter Audio Summaries CDs

242

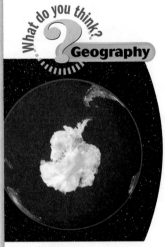

What do you think?

Geography

■ **Continents**

The continent of Antarctica, seen here from space, is almost completely covered in ice. If all of Antarctica's ice sheets melted at once, the Earth's oceans would rise about 60 meters everywhere! About how many feet would the oceans rise? **about 196.85 ft**

34. Australia, Europe, Antarctica, South America, North America, Africa, Asia

35. Compare the denominators. *Sample answer:* The fraction with the greater denominator is the smaller fraction because 2 of 7 equal parts is less than 2 of 5 of the same sized parts.

INTERNET

State Test Practice

CLASSZONE.COM

Continents The table shows the fraction of Earth's total land area covered by each continent. Which continent has the greater land area?

Continent	Africa	Antarctica	Asia	Australia	Europe	North America	South America
Fraction of Land Area	$\frac{1}{5}$	$\frac{1}{10}$	$\frac{3}{10}$	$\frac{1}{20}$	$\frac{7}{100}$	$\frac{4}{25}$	$\frac{3}{25}$

B **30.** Asia or Africa **Asia**

31. North America or Africa **Africa**

32. Europe or Australia **Europe**

33. South America or Antarctica **South America**

34. Order the continents from smallest to largest. **See margin.**

C **35.** **Challenge** How could you compare two fractions whose numerators are the same, such as $\frac{2}{7}$ and $\frac{2}{5}$, without changing them to equivalent fractions with the same denominator? Explain your reasoning.

See margin.

Mixed Review

Copy and complete the statement. *(Lesson 4.8)*

36. 10 mg = $\underline{\ ?\ }$ g **0.01**   **37.** 12 kg = $\underline{\ ?\ }$ g **12,000**   **38.** 15 L = $\underline{\ ?\ }$ kL **0.015**

Write the fraction in simplest form. *(Lesson 5.3)*

39. $\frac{7}{28}$ $\frac{1}{4}$ **40.** $\frac{12}{20}$ $\frac{3}{5}$ **41.** $\frac{16}{40}$ $\frac{2}{5}$ **42.** $\frac{10}{42}$ $\frac{5}{21}$

Basic Skills Find the difference.

43. $286 - 149$ **137** **44.** $507 - 376$ **131** **45.** $3200 - 1798$ **1402** **46.** $2050 - 1271$ **779**

Test-Taking Practice

47. **Extended Response** Jeff uses a different paintbrush for each color of a painting. For the red paint, he uses a $\frac{7}{16}$ inch paintbrush. For the blue paint, he uses a $\frac{3}{8}$ inch paintbrush. For the green paint, he uses a $\frac{1}{4}$ inch paintbrush. Is the red or green paintbrush larger? Is the blue or green paintbrush larger? Order the paintbrushes from smallest to largest. Show your work.

red $\left(\frac{7}{16} > \frac{4}{16}\right)$; blue $\left(\frac{6}{16} > \frac{4}{16}\right)$; green, blue, red $\left(\frac{4}{16} < \frac{6}{16} \text{ and } \frac{6}{16} < \frac{7}{16}\right)$

5.6 Hands-on Activity

GOAL
Read fractions of an inch on a ruler and express them numerically.

MATERIALS
· ruler

Measuring Fractions of an Inch

The marks on a ruler represent different fractions of an inch.

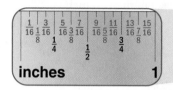

Explore   Use a ruler to tell how many fourths are in 1 inch.

1   Count the number of fourths in 1 inch.

2   Write the result of Step 1 as a fraction:

$1 \text{ inch} = \dfrac{4}{4} \text{ inch}.$

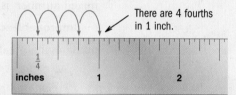

There are 4 fourths in 1 inch.

Your turn now   Follow Steps 1 and 2 above to copy and complete the table.

1.

Measure	Whole	Halves	Fourths	Eighths	Sixteenths
1 in.	$\dfrac{1}{1}$	$\dfrac{?}{2}$ 2	$\dfrac{4}{4}$	$\dfrac{?}{8}$ 8	$\dfrac{?}{16}$ 16
2 in.	$\dfrac{2}{1}$	$\dfrac{?}{2}$ 4	$\dfrac{?}{4}$ 8	$\dfrac{?}{8}$ 16	$\dfrac{?}{16}$ 32
$2\dfrac{1}{4}$ in.	——	——	$\dfrac{?}{4}$ 9	$\dfrac{?}{8}$ 18	$\dfrac{?}{16}$ 36

Stop and Think

2. Writing How many eighths are in $2\dfrac{5}{8}$ inches? Explain how you can answer this without actually using a ruler. *Sample answer:* Change 2 to $\dfrac{16}{8}$ and add it to $\dfrac{5}{8}$.

NCTM CURRICULUM STANDARDS
Standard 4: Understand the units of measurement; Apply proper techniques to find measures

Lesson 5.6   Mixed Numbers and Improper Fractions   **243**

SKILL CHECK
Evaluate the expression.

1. $4 \times 2 + 1$ **9**
2. $3 \times 4 + 2$ **14**
3. $6 \times 7 + 3$ **45**
4. Divide 26 by 5.   **5 R1**
5. Divide 33 by 7.   **4 R5**

LESSON OBJECTIVE

Rewrite mixed numbers and improper fractions.

PACING

Suggested Number of Days
Basic Course: 1 day
Average Course: 1 day
Advanced Course: 1 day
Block: 0.5 block with 5.5

TEACHING RESOURCES

For a complete list of Teaching Resources, see page 210B.

TRANSPARENCY

Warm-Up Exercises for this lesson are available on a transparency. A support transparency is available for Example 1.

2 TEACH

MOTIVATING THE LESSON

Provide students with rulers and ask them how many eighths of an inch are in several measures between 1 inch and 3 inches.

LESSON 5.6

Mixed Numbers and Improper Fractions

BEFORE	▶ Now	WHY?
You wrote equivalent fractions.	You'll rewrite mixed numbers and improper fractions.	So you can compare lengths, such as the pole vault records in Ex. 36.

Word Watch

mixed number, p. 244
improper fraction, p. 244
proper fraction, p. 245

Measuring Inches You can use a ruler to measure lengths to the nearest half, fourth, eighth, or sixteenth of an inch.

The length of the line segment is $2\frac{5}{8}$ inches, or $\frac{21}{8}$ inches.

The number $2\frac{5}{8}$, read as "two and five eighths," is a *mixed number*. A **mixed number** is the sum of a whole number part and a fraction part. An **improper fraction**, such as $\frac{21}{8}$, is any fraction in which the numerator is greater than or equal to the denominator.

EXAMPLE 1   Measuring to a Fraction of an Inch

Industrial Arts You need to measure a piece of wood for a birdhouse. Write the length as a mixed number and as an improper fraction.

Solution

First write the length as a mixed number: $3\frac{3}{4}$ inches.

Then count fourths to write the length as an improper fraction: $\frac{15}{4}$ inches.

There are 15 fourths in $3\frac{3}{4}$.

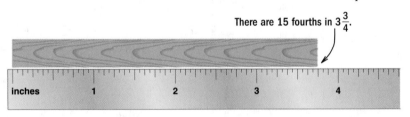

Your turn now   **Draw a line segment that has the given length.**

1–2. Check drawings.

1. $\frac{15}{2}$ in.
2. $6\frac{1}{4}$ in.

NCTM CURRICULUM STANDARDS
Standard 1: Understand ways of representing numbers
Standard 4: Apply proper techniques to find measures;
Apply proper tools to find measures

Rewriting Mixed Numbers In the activity on page 243, you may have seen that 1 whole can be written in different forms. You can use these forms of 1 to help you write mixed numbers as improper fractions.

$$1 = \frac{1}{1} \qquad 1 = \frac{2}{2} \qquad 1 = \frac{3}{3} \qquad 1 = \frac{4}{4} \qquad 1 = \frac{5}{5}$$

Watch Out!

In Example 2, don't forget to add the fraction part, $\frac{3}{5}$, after you write the whole part as a fraction.

EXAMPLE 2 Rewriting Mixed Numbers

Write $4\frac{3}{5}$ as an improper fraction.

$$4\frac{3}{5} = \frac{20 + 3}{5} \qquad \text{1 whole} = \frac{5}{5}, \text{ so 4 wholes} = \frac{4 \times 5}{5}, \text{ or } \frac{20}{5}.$$

$$= \frac{23}{5} \qquad \text{Simplify the numerator.}$$

Rewriting Improper Fractions You can also write an improper fraction as a mixed number. First divide the numerator by the denominator, and then put the remainder over the denominator. Make sure that the fraction part is a **proper fraction**, which is a fraction in which the numerator is less than the denominator.

EXAMPLE 3 Rewriting Improper Fractions

Write $\frac{16}{3}$ as a mixed number.

① Divide 16 by 3.

$$\begin{array}{r} 5\,\text{R1} \\ 3\overline{)16} \\ \underline{15} \\ 1 \end{array}$$

After you divide, $\frac{1}{3}$ still remains.

② Write the mixed number. $5 + \frac{1}{3} = 5\frac{1}{3}$

Your turn now Write the mixed number as an improper fraction.

3. $3\frac{2}{3}$ $\frac{11}{3}$ **4.** $2\frac{1}{4}$ $\frac{9}{4}$ **5.** $4\frac{5}{6}$ $\frac{29}{6}$

Write the improper fraction as a mixed number.

6. $\frac{22}{5}$ $4\frac{2}{5}$ **7.** $\frac{34}{13}$ $2\frac{8}{13}$ **8.** $\frac{41}{12}$ $3\frac{5}{12}$

TIPS FOR NEW TEACHERS
Be sure students recognize mixed numbers and improper fractions. Then introduce the ideas that a mixed number can always be written as an improper fraction and that an improper fraction can be written either as a whole number or a mixed number. See Tips for New Teachers in the *Chapter 5 Resource Book*.

EXTRA EXAMPLES

Example 1 On the ruler on page 244, look at the point that is three-eighths of an inch longer than 2 inches.
a. Write the length as a mixed number. $2\frac{3}{8}$ in.
b. Write the length as an improper fraction. $\frac{19}{8}$ in.

Example 2 Write $5\frac{2}{7}$ as an improper fraction. $\frac{37}{7}$

Example 3 Write $\frac{23}{10}$ as a mixed number. $2\frac{3}{10}$

VISUALIZE

Some students might find rectangles or circles useful for visualizing mixed numbers and improper fractions, as illustrated below. The shaded region can be written as $1\frac{1}{2}$ or $\frac{6}{4}$ or $\frac{3}{2}$.

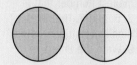

What do you think?

Sports

■ **Baseball bats**

Baseball bats come in many different weights. To find out which bat size is best for you, divide your height, in inches, by 3. Then add 6. This is the weight, in ounces, of a baseball bat that is appropriate for you. What is the best bat weight for you? **Weights will vary.**

Comparing Numbers To compare and order mixed numbers and improper fractions, begin by writing them all in the same form.

EXAMPLE 4 Ordering Numbers

Baseball Bats The widths of three baseball bats are $2\frac{5}{8}$, $2\frac{3}{4}$, and $\frac{9}{4}$ inches. Order the widths from least to greatest.

Solution

① Write all of the widths as improper fractions.

$$2\frac{5}{8} = \frac{16+5}{8} = \frac{21}{8} \qquad 2\frac{3}{4} = \frac{8+3}{4} = \frac{11}{4} \qquad \frac{9}{4}$$

② Rewrite all of the widths using the LCD, 8.

$$\frac{21}{8} \qquad \frac{11}{4} = \frac{11 \times 2}{4 \times 2} = \frac{22}{8} \qquad \frac{9}{4} = \frac{9 \times 2}{4 \times 2} = \frac{18}{8}$$

③ Compare the fractions.

Because $\frac{18}{8} < \frac{21}{8}$ and $\frac{21}{8} < \frac{22}{8}$, you know that $\frac{9}{4} < 2\frac{5}{8}$ and $2\frac{5}{8} < 2\frac{3}{4}$.

ANSWER The widths, from least to greatest, are $\frac{9}{4}$, $2\frac{5}{8}$, and $2\frac{3}{4}$ inches.

 **5.6 Exercises**

More Practice, p. 712

INTERNET
eWorkbook Plus
CLASSZONE.COM

Getting Ready to Practice

1. **Vocabulary** Explain what it means for a fraction to be an improper fraction. **A fraction is improper if its numerator is greater than or equal to its denominator.**

Copy and complete the statement.

2. $6\frac{1}{2} = \frac{?}{2}$ **13**   3. $3\frac{1}{4} = \frac{?}{4}$ **13**   4. $\frac{17}{3} = 5\frac{?}{3}$ **2**   5. $\frac{11}{4} = 2\frac{?}{4}$ **3**

Copy and complete the statement with <, >, or =.

6. $\frac{7}{4} \underline{\;?\;} 1\frac{1}{4}$ **>**   7. $3\frac{2}{3} \underline{\;?\;} \frac{11}{3}$ **=**   8. $5\frac{2}{5} \underline{\;?\;} \frac{28}{5}$ **<**   9. $2\frac{4}{7} \underline{\;?\;} \frac{20}{7}$ **<**

Practice and Problem Solving

Measurement Use a ruler to measure the candle to the end of its wick. Write the answer as a mixed number and as an improper fraction.

A **10.**

$1\frac{3}{4}$ in.; $\frac{7}{4}$ in.

11.

$2\frac{1}{8}$ in.; $\frac{17}{8}$ in.

12. Draw a line segment that has a length of $\frac{11}{4}$ inches. **Check drawings.**

Write the mixed number as an improper fraction.

13. $4\frac{1}{2}$ $\frac{9}{2}$ **14.** $1\frac{5}{8}$ $\frac{13}{8}$ **15.** $3\frac{2}{5}$ $\frac{17}{5}$ **16.** $5\frac{3}{4}$ $\frac{23}{4}$

17. $7\frac{2}{3}$ $\frac{23}{3}$ **18.** $1\frac{9}{10}$ $\frac{19}{10}$ **19.** $10\frac{1}{2}$ $\frac{21}{2}$ **20.** $12\frac{1}{4}$ $\frac{49}{4}$

Write the improper fraction as a mixed number.

21. $\frac{8}{3}$ $2\frac{2}{3}$ **22.** $\frac{25}{6}$ $4\frac{1}{6}$ **23.** $\frac{18}{5}$ $3\frac{3}{5}$ **24.** $\frac{15}{4}$ $3\frac{3}{4}$

25. $\frac{13}{2}$ $6\frac{1}{2}$ **26.** $\frac{22}{3}$ $7\frac{1}{3}$ **27.** $\frac{12}{7}$ $1\frac{5}{7}$ **28.** $\frac{33}{4}$ $8\frac{1}{4}$

Order the numbers from least to greatest.

29. $\frac{7}{2}, 2\frac{3}{4}, 3$ $2\frac{3}{4}, 3, \frac{7}{2}$ **30.** $\frac{23}{5}, \frac{19}{4}, 4\frac{1}{2}$ $4\frac{1}{2}, \frac{23}{5}, \frac{19}{4}$ **31.** $5, \frac{41}{8}, \frac{17}{3}, 5\frac{1}{6}$

$5, \frac{41}{8}, 5\frac{1}{6}, \frac{17}{3}$

Write 1 as a fraction using the given denominator.

B **32.** 4 $\frac{4}{4}$ **33.** 6 $\frac{6}{6}$ **34.** 10 $\frac{10}{10}$ **35.** 14 $\frac{14}{14}$

36. Pole Vaulting The pole vault records for four different schools are shown in the table. Which school's record is the highest? **Perry**

School	Oakmont	Chester	Central	Perry
Pole vault height (feet)	$\frac{49}{3}$	$16\frac{3}{8}$	$\frac{33}{2}$	$16\frac{9}{16}$

Critical Thinking Find a mixed number that is between the numbers.

37–40. Answers may vary.

C **37.** $1\frac{3}{5}, \frac{11}{5}$ $1\frac{4}{5}$ **38.** $\frac{9}{2}, 5$ $4\frac{3}{4}$ **39.** $3, \frac{27}{8}$ $3\frac{1}{4}$ **40.** $5\frac{4}{9}, \frac{29}{5}$ $5\frac{1}{2}$

41. Challenge Your friend is thinking of an improper fraction that is more than 2 and less than $2\frac{1}{4}$. The sum of the numerator and the denominator is 19. What is your friend's number? $\frac{13}{6}$

46. fourteen and one tenth

47. twenty-three and five tenths

48. sixty-four and ninety-two hundredths

49. seventy-eight and fifteen hundredths

INTERNET
State Test Practice
CLASSZONE.COM

Mixed Review

Evaluate the expression. *(Lesson 1.5)*

42. $20 \div x$, when $x = 2$ 10

43. $x - 2$, when $x = 21$ 19

44. $15 - x + 4$, when $x = 3$ 16

45. $3x + y$, when $x = 4$ and $y = 6$ 18

Write the decimal in words. *(Lesson 3.1)*

46. 14.1

47. 23.5

48. 64.92

49. 78.15

Basic Skills **Round the number to the place value of the red digit.**

50. 8701 9000

51. 9900 10,000

52. 2457 2500

53. 4391 4390

Test-Taking Practice

54. **Multiple Choice** Which mixed number is equivalent to $\frac{17}{5}$? D

   A. $1\frac{2}{5}$

   B. $2\frac{1}{5}$

   C. $3\frac{1}{5}$

   D. $3\frac{2}{5}$

55. **Multiple Choice** A jewelry box is $4\frac{5}{8}$ inches wide. Write this mixed number as an improper fraction. H

   F. $\frac{20}{8}$ inches

   G. $\frac{32}{8}$ inches

   H. $\frac{37}{8}$ inches

   I. $\frac{37}{5}$ inches

BRAIN GAME

What Does it Say?

To find the saying below, write the improper fractions as mixed numbers. Find the mixed number below the number line and write the corresponding letter in the blank above the improper fraction.

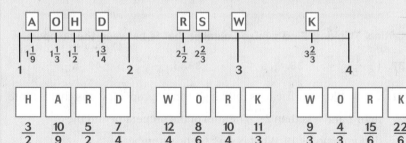

A	O	H	D		R	S	W		K	
$1\frac{1}{9}$	$1\frac{1}{3}$	$1\frac{1}{2}$	$1\frac{3}{4}$		$2\frac{1}{2}$	$2\frac{2}{3}$			$3\frac{2}{3}$	
1				2			3			4

H	A	R	D	W	O	R	K	W	O	R	K	S
$\frac{3}{2}$	$\frac{10}{9}$	$\frac{5}{2}$	$\frac{7}{4}$	$\frac{12}{4}$	$\frac{8}{6}$	$\frac{10}{4}$	$\frac{11}{3}$	$\frac{9}{3}$	$\frac{4}{3}$	$\frac{15}{6}$	$\frac{22}{6}$	$\frac{8}{3}$

LESSON 5.7

Changing Decimals to Fractions

BEFORE
You wrote decimals and fractions.

Now
You'll write a decimal as a fraction.

WHY?
So you can find the miles you've gone on a road trip, as in Ex. 7.

Word Watch

Review Words

simplest form, p. 229
mixed number, p. 244

Activity You can use models to write decimals as fractions.

(1) Draw a model for 0.25. Each small square represents one hundredth. The shaded part represents twenty-five hundredths.

$$0.25 = \frac{25}{100}$$

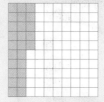

(2) Draw a model for 0.3. Each column represents one tenth. The shaded part represents three tenths.

$$0.3 = \frac{3}{10}$$

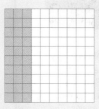

Use a model to write the decimal as a fraction.

1. 0.15 $\frac{3}{20}$
2. 0.35 $\frac{7}{20}$
3. 0.4 $\frac{2}{5}$
4. 0.5 $\frac{1}{2}$

HELP with Solving

With practice, you will learn to recognize the fraction form of several common decimals. Here are some examples.

$0.5 = \frac{1}{2}$ $0.2 = \frac{1}{5}$

$0.25 = \frac{1}{4}$ $0.125 = \frac{1}{8}$

$0.75 = \frac{3}{4}$ $0.4 = \frac{2}{5}$

You can use decimal place value to help you write a decimal as a fraction in simplest form.

one tenth	**one hundredth**	**one thousandth**
$0.1 = \frac{1}{10}$	$0.01 = \frac{1}{100}$	$0.001 = \frac{1}{1000}$

EXAMPLE 1 Writing Decimals as Fractions

Write the decimal as a fraction in simplest form.

a. $0.8 = \frac{8}{10}$ Write eight tenths as a fraction.

$= \frac{4}{5}$ Simplify.

b. $0.36 = \frac{36}{100}$ Write thirty-six hundredths as a fraction.

$= \frac{9}{25}$ Simplify.

NCTM CURRICULUM STANDARDS
Standard 1: Understand ways of representing numbers
Standard 10: Use representations to communicate mathematical ideas

Lesson 5.7   Changing Decimals to Fractions   **249**

CONCEPT CHECK

How can you write a decimal as a mixed number or fraction? Write the whole-number part. Write the decimal as a fraction with a power of ten as the denominator. Write the fraction in simplest form, and write it next to the whole-number part.

DAILY PUZZLER

Using each of the digits 5, 6, and 7 exactly once, what is the greatest mixed number that you can write? What is the least mixed number?

greatest: $7\frac{5}{6}$; least: $5\frac{6}{7}$

250

■ **Planets**

What do you think? **Science**

The length of a planet's year is the time it takes to revolve once about the Sun. The closer the planet is to the Sun, the shorter its year. The length of Jupiter's year is 4330.6 Earth days. Saturn's year is 10,747 Earth days. Which is closer to the Sun?

Jupiter

EXAMPLE 2 **Writing Decimals as Mixed Numbers**

Planets The length of a planet's day is the time it takes the planet to rotate once about its axis. Write each length as a mixed number in simplest form.

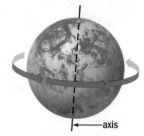

←— axis

a. Length of day on Saturn: 10.5 hours

b. Length of day on Jupiter: 9.92 hours

Solution

a. $10.5 = 10\frac{5}{10}$ Write ten and five tenths as a mixed number.

   $= 10\frac{1}{2}$ Simplify.

ANSWER The length of a day on Saturn is $10\frac{1}{2}$ hours.

b. $9.92 = 9\frac{92}{100}$ Write nine and ninety-two hundredths as a mixed number.

   $= 9\frac{23}{25}$ Simplify.

ANSWER The length of a day on Jupiter is $9\frac{23}{25}$ hours.

EXAMPLE 3 **Decimals with Zeros**

Write the decimal as a fraction or mixed number in simplest form.

a. $2.04 = 2\frac{4}{100}$ Write two and four hundredths as a mixed number.

   $= 2\frac{1}{25}$ Simplify.

b. $0.608 = \frac{608}{1000}$ Write six hundred eight thousandths as a fraction.

   $= \frac{76}{125}$ Simplify.

Your turn now Write the decimal as a fraction or mixed number in simplest form.

1. 0.4 $\frac{2}{5}$ **2.** 1.82 $1\frac{41}{50}$ **3.** 2.005 $2\frac{1}{200}$ **4.** 0.405 $\frac{81}{200}$

5.7 Exercises
More Practice, p. 712

INTERNET
eWorkbook Plus
CLASSZONE.COM

Getting Ready to Practice

1. Vocabulary Explain how you know a fraction is in simplest form.
When the GCF of the numerator and denominator is 1.

2. Find the Error Describe and correct the error in the solution. **0.7 should be written as $\frac{7}{10}$.**

$$\times \quad 0.7 = \frac{7}{100}$$

Copy and complete the statement.

3. $0.27 = \frac{?}{100}$ **27**   **4.** $2.3 = 2\frac{3}{?}$ **10**   **5.** $6.2 = 6\frac{?}{10}$ **2**   **6.** $5.23 = 5\frac{23}{?}$ **100**

7. Road Trip At your first stop during a road trip, you record the distance you've traveled as 128.4 miles. How could you write this distance as a mixed number in simplest form? **Write a mixed number with the whole number being 128 and the fraction $\frac{4}{10}$ which simplifies to $\frac{2}{5}$.**

Practice and Problem Solving

Write the number as a decimal and as a fraction or mixed number.

A 8. nine tenths $0.9; \frac{9}{10}$ **9.** fifty-three hundredths $0.53; \frac{53}{100}$

10. two and seven tenths $2.7; 2\frac{7}{10}$ **11.** three and eleven hundredths
$3.11; 3\frac{11}{100}$

Write the decimal as a fraction or mixed number in simplest form.

12. 0.16 $\frac{4}{25}$ **13.** 0.72 $\frac{18}{25}$ **14.** 5.9 $5\frac{9}{10}$ **15.** 9.3 $9\frac{3}{10}$

16. 4.06 $4\frac{3}{50}$ **17.** 3.01 $3\frac{1}{100}$ **18.** 0.902 $\frac{451}{500}$ **19.** 0.806 $\frac{403}{500}$

20. 0.039 $\frac{39}{1000}$ **21.** 0.025 $\frac{1}{40}$ **22.** 6.036 $6\frac{9}{250}$ **23.** 9.401 $9\frac{401}{1000}$

In Exercises 24–26, use the graph.
The graph shows the portion of space in a mall occupied by different types of stores. The portions are written as decimals.

24. Which type of store occupies the least space in the mall? the most?
furniture; clothing

25. Use the circle graph to order the types of stores by the portion of space they occupy. **clothing, food, gifts, electronics, furniture**

26. Write the decimals from Exercise 25 as fractions in order from least to greatest. $\frac{12}{25}, \frac{19}{100}, \frac{9}{50}, \frac{1}{10}, \frac{1}{20}$

Mall Space by Store Type

Clothing 0.48
Food 0.19
Gifts 0.18
Electronics 0.10
Furniture 0.05

HELP with Homework

Example	Exercises
1	8–9, 12–13, 24–26
2	10–11, 14–15
3	16–23

Online Resources
CLASSZONE.COM
· More Examples
· eTutorial plus

---

③ APPLY

ASSIGNMENT GUIDE

Basic Course
Day 1: EP p. 710 Exs. 3–7;
pp. 251–252 Exs. 8–19,
24–27, 33–37, 39–42

Average Course
Day 1: pp. 251–252 Exs. 8–11,
16–28, 35–42

Advanced Course
Day 1: pp. 251–252 Exs. 8–22
even, 24–32*, 35–38, 41, 42

Block
pp. 251–252 Exs. 8–11, 16–28,
35–42 (with 5.8)

EXTRA PRACTICE

• Student Edition, p. 712
• Chapter 5 Resource Book,
pp. 61–63
• Test and Practice Generator

TRANSPARENCY

Even-numbered answers are available on transparencies.

HOMEWORK CHECK

When you review students' homework for this lesson, go over the following exercises to check understanding of key concepts.
Basic: 8, 10, 12, 14, 16
Average: 9, 10, 17, 20, 25
Advanced: 8, 12, 14, 18, 26

COMMON ERROR

In Exercises 20–22, some students ignore the zero in the tenths place and think 0.039, for example, means thirty-nine hundredths. Encourage students to start the problem by counting the decimal digits and determining the denominator for the fraction.

Lesson 5.7   Changing Decimals to Fractions   **251**

251

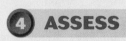

4 ASSESS

ASSESSMENT RESOURCES

For more assessment resources, see:
- Assessment Book
- Test and Practice Generator

MINI-QUIZ

Write the decimal as a fraction or mixed number in simplest form.

1. 0.12 $\frac{3}{25}$

2. 3.05 $3\frac{1}{20}$

3. 0.5 $\frac{1}{2}$

4. 0.432 $\frac{54}{125}$

5. Here are the lengths of two segments. Rewrite each length as a mixed number in simplest form.

  a. 8.48 in. $8\frac{12}{25}$ in.

  b. 7.4 in. $7\frac{2}{5}$ in.

5 FOLLOW-UP

RETEACHING/REMEDIATION

- Study Guide in Chapter 5 Resource Book, pp. 64–65
- Tutor Place, Fractions Card 5
- eTutorial Plus Online
- Extra Practice, p. 712
- Lesson Practice in Chapter 5 Resource Book, pp. 61–63

CHALLENGE/ENRICHMENT

- Challenge Practice in Chapter 5 Resource Book, p. 66
- Teacher's Edition, p. 210F

ENGLISH LEARNER SUPPORT

- Spanish Study Guide
- Multi-Language Glossary
- Chapter Audio Summaries CDs

B 27. Honeybee A bee has a length of approximately 0.4708 inch. Write the bee's length as a fraction in simplest form. $\frac{1177}{2500}$ in.

28. Rainfall The normal monthly precipitation for New Orleans is 4.50 inches in April and 3.05 inches in October. Write the difference of these amounts as a mixed number in simplest form. $1\frac{9}{20}$ in.

Challenge Write the decimal as an improper fraction in simplest form.

C 29. 2.37 $\frac{237}{100}$ **30.** 6.95 $\frac{139}{20}$ **31.** 9.86 $\frac{493}{50}$ **32.** 5.34 $\frac{267}{50}$

Mixed Review

Divide. Round your answer to the nearest tenth, if necessary.
(Lesson 4.4)

33. 8 ÷ 11 0.7   **34.** 6 ÷ 12 0.5   **35.** 3 ÷ 5 0.6   **36.** 5 ÷ 9 0.6

37. Order the fractions $\frac{5}{6}, \frac{1}{2}, \frac{11}{36}$, and $\frac{13}{18}$ from least to greatest. *(Lesson 5.5)*
$\frac{11}{36}, \frac{1}{2}, \frac{13}{18}, \frac{5}{6}$

Choose a Strategy Use a strategy from the list to solve the following problem. Explain your choice of strategy.

> **Problem Solving Strategies**
> - Guess, Check, and Revise
> - Draw a Diagram
> - Perform an Experiment
> - Work Backward

38. You have 2 rectangular concert tickets that are both the same size. How many ways can you arrange them face up and next to each other to form a rectangle with twice the area of one of the tickets? 4 ways. *Sample answer:* I used Draw a Diagram because I could see all of the different arrangements.

Basic Skills Copy and complete the statement.

39. 5 hours = ? minutes 300

40. 367 minutes = ? hours ? minutes 6, 7

Test-Taking Practice

41. Multiple Choice Which fraction is equivalent to the decimal 0.24? C

A. $\frac{1}{24}$ **B.** $\frac{3}{25}$ **C.** $\frac{6}{25}$ **D.** $\frac{12}{25}$

42. Multiple Choice A survey at a middle school said that 0.65 of the sixth grade students named basketball as their favorite sport. Which fraction represents the decimal 0.65? G

F. $\frac{3}{5}$ **G.** $\frac{13}{20}$ **H.** $\frac{7}{10}$ **I.** $\frac{3}{4}$

INTERNET
State Test Practice
CLASSZONE.COM

LESSON 5.8

Changing Fractions to Decimals

BEFORE
You wrote decimals as fractions.

▶ **Now**
You'll write fractions as decimals.

WHY?
So you can order numbers, such as the lengths of the fish in Ex. 34.

Word Watch

terminating decimal, p. 254
repeating decimal, p. 254

In the Real World

= States with lighthouses

Lighthouses At one time, 31 out of the 50 states in the United States had lighthouses. This can be written as the fraction $\frac{31}{50}$. How can you write this fraction as a decimal?

EXAMPLE 1 Writing a Fraction as a Decimal

To answer the question above about lighthouses, write the fraction $\frac{31}{50}$ as a decimal by dividing 31 by 50.

$$
\begin{array}{r}
0.62 \\
50\overline{)31.00} \\
\underline{30\ 0} \\
1\ 00 \\
\underline{1\ 00} \\
0
\end{array}
$$

← The remainder is 0.

ANSWER The quotient is 0.62, so 0.62 of the states had lighthouses.

Writing a Fraction as a Decimal

Words To write a fraction as a decimal, divide the numerator by the denominator.

Numbers $\frac{1}{4}$ means $1 \div 4$ **Algebra** $\frac{a}{b}$ means $a \div b$ ($b \neq 0$)

Your turn now Write the fraction as a decimal.

1. $\frac{1}{2}$ 0.5   **2.** $\frac{4}{5}$ 0.8   **3.** $\frac{1}{4}$ 0.25   **4.** $\frac{3}{8}$ 0.375

NCTM CURRICULUM STANDARDS
Standard 1: Understand ways of representing numbers; Understand relationships among numbers; Compute fluently

Lesson 5.8   Changing Fractions to Decimals   **253**

---

① PLAN

SKILL CHECK

1. 24 − 21 _?_   3
2. 100 − 96 _?_   4

Write the mixed number as an improper fraction.

3. $4\frac{3}{5}$ $\frac{23}{5}$ **4.** $7\frac{5}{9}$ $\frac{68}{9}$

LESSON OBJECTIVE

Write fractions as decimals.

PACING

Suggested Number of Days
Basic Course: 1 day
Average Course: 1 day
Advanced Course: 1 day
Block: 0.5 block with 5.7

TEACHING RESOURCES

For a complete list of Teaching Resources, see page 210B.

 TRANSPARENCY

Warm-Up Exercises for this lesson are available on a transparency.

② TEACH

MOTIVATING THE LESSON

Have students repeat Example 1 for the 19 states without lighthouses.

TIPS FOR NEW TEACHERS

When students convert a fraction to a decimal, be sure they use the numerator as the dividend and the denominator as the divisor. See Tips for New Teachers in the *Chapter 5 Resource Book*.

253

EXAMPLE 2 Writing a Mixed Number as a Decimal

Write $2\frac{1}{8}$ as a decimal.

(1) Divide 1 by 8.

$$\begin{array}{r} 0.125 \\ 8\overline{)1.000} \\ \underline{8} \\ 20 \\ \underline{16} \\ 40 \\ \underline{40} \\ 0 \end{array}$$ ← The remainder is 0.

(2) Add the whole number and the decimal.

$$2 + 0.125 = 2.125$$

ANSWER The mixed number $2\frac{1}{8}$, written as a decimal, is 2.125.

HELP with Solving

With practice, you will learn to recognize the decimal form of several common fractions. Here are some examples.

$\frac{1}{2} = 0.5$ $\frac{1}{5} = 0.2$

$\frac{1}{4} = 0.25$ $\frac{1}{3} = 0.\overline{3}$

$\frac{1}{10} = 0.1$ $\frac{1}{8} = 0.125$

Types of Decimals A decimal is called a **terminating decimal** when it has a final digit, such as 0.125 in Example 2. A decimal is called a **repeating decimal** when one or more digits repeat forever. A repeating decimal can be written with a bar over the digits that repeat.

One digit repeats:	Two digits repeat:	Three digits repeat:
$0.3333... = 0.\overline{3}$	$2.010101... = 2.\overline{01}$	$0.4205205... = 0.4\overline{205}$

EXAMPLE 3 Repeating Decimals

a. Write $\frac{7}{6}$ as a decimal.

$$\begin{array}{r} 1.166... \\ 6\overline{)7.000} \\ \underline{6} \\ 1\,0 \\ \underline{6} \\ 40 \\ \underline{36} \\ 40 \\ \underline{36} \\ 4 \end{array}$$ The digit 6 repeats.

ANSWER $\frac{7}{6} = 1.1\overline{6}$

b. Write $1\frac{5}{33}$ as a decimal.

$$\begin{array}{r} 0.1515... \\ 33\overline{)5.0000} \\ \underline{3\,3} \\ 1\,70 \\ \underline{1\,65} \\ 50 \\ \underline{33} \\ 170 \\ \underline{165} \\ 5 \end{array}$$ The digits 1 and 5 repeat.

ANSWER $1\frac{5}{33} = 1.\overline{15}$

Your turn now Write the fraction or mixed number as a decimal.

5. $5\frac{2}{5}$ **5.4** **6.** $3\frac{5}{8}$ **3.625** **7.** $\frac{2}{3}$ **0.$\overline{6}$** **8.** $3\frac{2}{11}$ **3.$\overline{18}$**

Getting Ready to Practice

Vocabulary Is the decimal *repeating* or *terminating*?

1. 0.875
terminating

2. $0.2\overline{3}$
repeating

3. $4.2\overline{27}$
repeating

4. 0.700
terminating

Rewrite the repeating decimal using bar notation.

5. 0.111111 . . .
$0.\overline{1}$

6. 3.727272 . . .
$3.\overline{72}$

7. 8.040404 . . .
$8.\overline{04}$

8. 0.466666 . . .
$0.4\overline{6}$

Write the fraction or mixed number as a decimal.

9. $\frac{2}{5}$ 0.4

10. $\frac{9}{20}$ 0.45

11. $2\frac{3}{4}$ 2.75

12. $1\frac{1}{6}$ $1.1\overline{6}$

13. Dog Biscuits You buy $\frac{2}{3}$ pound of dog biscuits at a pet store. If the
scale gives a decimal weight to the nearest hundredth, what should
the scale read? 0.67 lb

Practice and Problem Solving

Write the next four decimal places of the repeating decimal.

A 14. $0.0\overline{5}$
0.055555...

15. $0.3\overline{8}$
0.388888...

16. $3.4\overline{12}$
3.4121212...

17. $0.4\overline{915}$
0.49159159...

Write the fraction or mixed number as a decimal.

18. $\frac{3}{10}$ 0.3

19. $\frac{4}{5}$ 0.8

20. $3\frac{1}{4}$ 3.25

21. $2\frac{21}{25}$ 2.84

22. $\frac{9}{5}$ 1.8

23. $\frac{15}{4}$ 3.75

24. $\frac{1}{6}$ $0.1\overline{6}$

25. $\frac{5}{18}$ $0.2\overline{7}$

26. $\frac{8}{3}$ $2.\overline{6}$

27. $5\frac{8}{9}$ $5.\overline{8}$

28. $1\frac{6}{11}$ $1.\overline{54}$

29. $\frac{7}{12}$ $0.58\overline{3}$

HELP with Homework

Example	Exercises
1	18-19, 22-23
2	20-21, 31-32
3	14-17, 24-30

Online Resources
CLASSZONE.COM
· More Examples
· eTutorial Plus

Gardening **Write the number as a fraction or mixed number and as
a decimal.**

30. A flower petal is two thirds inch long. $\frac{2}{3}$; $0.\overline{6}$

31. A carnation's stem is one and three fourths feet long. $1\frac{3}{4}$; 1.75

32. A plant must be planted in a hole that is two and one half inches deep.
$2\frac{1}{2}$; 2.5

B 33. Watermelons About $\frac{23}{25}$ of a watermelon is water. Write this fraction
as a decimal. Then find what portion of a watermelon is *not* water.
0.92; 0.08

ASSIGNMENT GUIDE
Basic Course
Day 1: pp. 255–256 Exs. 14–34, 39–52
Average Course
Day 1: pp. 255–256 Exs. 14–25, 30–37, 41–44, 48–53
Advanced Course
Day 1: pp. 255–256 Exs 16–21, 26–38*, 39–49 odd, 52, 53
Block
pp. 255–256 Exs. 14–25, 30–37, 41–44, 48–53
(with 5.7)

EXTRA PRACTICE
• Student Edition, p. 712
• Chapter 5 Resource Book, pp. 70–72
• Test and Practice Generator

② TRANSPARENCY
Even-numbered answers are available on transparencies.

HOMEWORK CHECK
When you review students' homework for this lesson, go over the following exercises to check understanding of key concepts.
Basic: 14, 18, 20, 23, 31
Average: 15, 19, 20, 30, 31
Advanced: 16, 19, 21, 30, 32

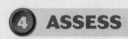
MINI-QUIZ

1. In a textbook, 17 of 25 pages in a chapter have pictures. Write $\frac{17}{25}$ as a decimal. **0.68**

Write each fraction or mixed number as a decimal.

2. $4\frac{7}{8}$ **4.875**

3. $2\frac{5}{9}$ **2.5̄**

4. $\frac{15}{11}$ **1.3̄6̄**

5. $\frac{22}{5}$ **4.4**

RETEACHING/REMEDIATION

• Study Guide in Chapter 5 Resource Book, pp. 73–74
• Tutor Place, Fractions Cards 5, 6
• eTutorial Plus Online
• Extra Practice, p. 712
• Lesson Practice in Chapter 5 Resource Book, pp. 70–72

CHALLENGE/ENRICHMENT

• Challenge Practice in Chapter 5 Resource Book, p. 75
• Teacher's Edition, p. 210F

ENGLISH LEARNER SUPPORT

• Spanish Study Guide
• Multi-Language Glossary
• Chapter Audio Summaries CDs

34. Fishing On a fishing trip, you catch five fish. The lengths, in inches, of the fish are given below. Order the lengths from least to greatest.

$$13\frac{3}{16} \qquad 13.25 \qquad \frac{55}{4} \qquad 13\frac{3}{8} \qquad 13.1 \quad 13.1, 13\frac{3}{16}, 13.25, 13\frac{3}{8}, \frac{55}{4}$$

Critical Thinking Tell whether the statement is *true* or *false*.

35. If the numerator of a fraction is greater than the denominator, then the decimal is greater than 1. **true**

36. If the denominator of a fraction is a factor of the numerator, then the fraction is not in simplest form. **true**

C **37. Predict** Write $\frac{1}{11}$, $\frac{2}{11}$, and $\frac{3}{11}$ as decimals. Based on your results, what would be the decimal equivalents of $\frac{4}{11}$ and $\frac{5}{11}$? **0.0̄9̄, 0.1̄8̄, 0.2̄7̄; 0.3̄6̄, 0.4̄5̄**

38. Challenge Write $\frac{1}{7}$ as a decimal. How many digits repeat? **0.1̄42857̄; 6**

Mixed Review

Round the decimal as specified. *(Lesson 3.4)*

39. 0.45 (nearest tenth) **0.5**

40. 0.689 (nearest hundredth) **0.69**

41. 1.9999 (nearest thousandth) **2.000**

42. 6.9135 (nearest one) **7**

Choose an appropriate metric unit to measure the item. *(Lesson 4.7)*

43. mass of a mouse **grams**

44. capacity of a water tank **kiloliters**

45. mass of an ant **milligrams**

Write the prime factorization using a factor tree. *(Lesson 5.1)*

46. 38 **2 × 19**

47. 68 **$2^2 \times 17$**

48. 200 **$2^3 \times 5^2$**

49. 504 **$2^3 \times 3^2 \times 7$**

Basic Skills **Estimate the sum.** **Estimates may vary.**

50. 488 + 310 + 845 **1600**

51. 1987 + 5006 + 2640 **10,000**

Test-Taking Practice

INTERNET
State Test Practice
CLASSZONE.COM

52. Multiple Choice Which decimal is equivalent to the fraction $\frac{21}{40}$? **B**

A. 0.053   **B.** 0.525   **C.** 1.905   **D.** 5.25

53. Multiple Choice Janet got a hit $\frac{7}{27}$ of her times at bat. Write this as a decimal rounded to the nearest thousandth. **G**

F. 0.258   **G.** 0.259   **H.** 0.260   **I.** 0.369

CALCULATOR

5.8

Decimals and Fractions

GOAL Use a calculator to convert fractions to decimals.

 Example You can write fractions as decimals using a calculator.

On January 29, 2001, the New York Stock Exchange began reporting all stock prices as decimals instead of fractions and mixed numbers. If the value of a stock was listed as \$34$\frac{5}{8}$ before the conversion, how would this value be listed after the conversion?

Solution

To convert a mixed number to a decimal, divide the numerator of the fraction by the denominator and add the whole number part.

Keystrokes

5 ÷ 8 + 34 =

Display

34.625

Since dollar amounts are given in cents, round your answer to the nearest hundredth.

ANSWER After the conversion, the value of this stock would be listed as \$34.63.

 **with Technology**

If your calculator follows the order of operations, you can instead type

34 + 5 ÷ 8 =

to get the answer.

4. 0.62
8. 18.23
12. 67.18

 Your turn now Write the fraction or mixed number as a decimal. Round to the nearest hundredth if necessary.

4, 8, 12. See margin.

1. $\frac{5}{6}$ 0.83
2. $\frac{1}{8}$ 0.13
3. $\frac{5}{16}$ 0.31
4. $\frac{99}{160}$

5. $5\frac{3}{8}$ 5.38
6. $4\frac{11}{20}$ 4.55
7. $13\frac{7}{18}$ 13.39
8. $18\frac{9}{40}$

9. $29\frac{3}{16}$ 29.19
10. $45\frac{9}{32}$ 45.28
11. $50\frac{41}{50}$ 50.82
12. $67\frac{23}{125}$

13. **Stocks** A stock was listed as \$13$\frac{3}{8}$ before the conversion to decimals. How was it listed after the conversion? \$13.38

NCTM CURRICULUM STANDARDS
Standard 1: Understand ways of representing numbers; Understand relationships among numbers

---

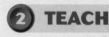 **PLAN**

LEARN THE METHOD

- Students will use a calculator to convert fractions to decimals.
- In Lesson 5.8, students changed a fraction to a decimal by dividing the numerator of the fraction by its denominator. This activity shows students how to use a calculator to convert a mixed number to a decimal.

2 TEACH

ALTERNATIVE STRATEGY

When converting mixed numbers to decimals, students can simply use their calculators to convert the fractional part to a decimal and then append the whole number part to the resulting quotient.

EXTRA EXAMPLES

Example Convert the decimal to a fraction and convert the fraction to a decimal.

a. 10.8 $10\frac{4}{5}$

b. $6\frac{13}{50}$ 6.26

 **CLOSE**

ASSESSMENT

1. A business envelope is $9\frac{1}{2}$ inches by $4\frac{1}{8}$ inches. Convert the measurements to decimals. **9.5 in. by 4.125 in.**

2. A nail polish bottle is 3.625 inches tall. Convert the decimal to a fraction. $3\frac{5}{8}$ **in.**

257

1. Multiples of 6: 6, 12, 18, 24, 30, 36, 42, 48, 54, 60, 66, 72, 78, 84, 90, 96; multiples of 8: 8, 16, 24, 32, 40, 48, 56, 64, 72, 80, 88, 96; no; the LCM of 6 and 8 is 24, not 48.

 LESSONS **5.4** TO **5.8**

Notebook Review

 NoTebook

Review the vocabulary definitions in your notebook.

Copy the review examples in your notebook. Then complete the exercises.

Check Your Definitions

multiple, p. 235

common multiple, p. 235

least common multiple (LCM), p. 236

least common denominator (LCD), p. 239

mixed number, p. 244

improper fraction, p. 244

proper fraction, p. 245

terminating or repeating decimal, p. 254

Use Your Vocabulary

1. List the multiples, through 100, of 6 and 8. Is 48 the LCM? **See margin.** Why or why not?

2. Copy and complete: A $\underline{\ ?\ }$ has digits that repeat forever. **repeating decimal**

5.4–5.5 Can you use the LCM to order fractions?

Review

EXAMPLE Order the fractions $\frac{2}{3}$, $\frac{2}{9}$, and $\frac{3}{5}$ from least to greatest.

(**1** The LCM of 3, 9, and 5 is 45. Use this to write equivalent fractions.

$$\frac{2}{3} = \frac{30}{45} \qquad \frac{2}{9} = \frac{10}{45} \qquad \frac{3}{5} = \frac{27}{45} \qquad \frac{10}{45} < \frac{27}{45} \text{ and } \frac{27}{45} < \frac{30}{45}$$

(**2** Order: The fractions, from least to greatest, are $\frac{2}{9}$, $\frac{3}{5}$, and $\frac{2}{3}$.

 3. Order the fractions $\frac{7}{10}$, $\frac{7}{25}$, $\frac{2}{5}$, and $\frac{3}{10}$ from least to greatest. $\frac{7}{25}, \frac{3}{10}, \frac{2}{5}, \frac{7}{10}$

5.6 Can you rewrite improper fractions and mixed numbers?

Review

EXAMPLE **a.** Write $2\frac{7}{8}$ as an improper fraction.

$$2\frac{7}{8} = \frac{16 + 7}{8} = \frac{23}{8}$$

b. Write $\frac{19}{8}$ as a decimal.

$$19 \div 8 = 2.375$$

 Compare the numbers.

4. $1\frac{1}{4}$ and $\frac{5}{3}$ $1\frac{1}{4} < \frac{5}{3}$

5. $\frac{7}{2}$ and $3\frac{1}{8}$ $\frac{7}{2} > 3\frac{1}{8}$

5.7–5.8 Can you rewrite decimals and fractions?

EXAMPLE

a. Write 2.08 as a mixed number.

$$2.08 = 2\frac{8}{100}$$

$$= 2\frac{2}{25}$$

b. Write $\frac{7}{9}$ as a decimal.

$$\begin{array}{r} 0.77\ldots \\ 9\overline{)7.00} \\ \underline{6\,3} \\ 70 \\ \underline{63} \\ 7 \end{array} \qquad \frac{7}{9} = 0.\overline{7}$$

☑ **6.** Write 0.65 as a fraction. $\frac{13}{20}$ **7.** Write $2\frac{13}{20}$ as a decimal. **2.65**

Stop *and* **Think**   about Lessons 5.4–5.8

8. Writing Describe both methods for finding the least common multiple. When would you use each method? **See margin.**

9. Critical Thinking When comparing a mixed number to an improper fraction, is it always necessary to write both numbers in the same form? Explain. **See margin.**

8. Find the smallest of all of the common multiples; use the prime factorization and multiply together the prime factors, using each the greatest number of times it is a factor of any of the numbers. *Sample answer:* Use prime factorization if the numbers are large and list multiples if the numbers are small.

9. Yes. *Sample answer:* It is hard to compare them in different forms.

Review Quiz 2

Find the LCM of the numbers.

1. 4, 11   44   **2.** 4, 14   28   **3.** 21, 72   504   **4.** 4, 6, 10   60

5. Order the fractions $\frac{9}{28}, \frac{3}{14}, \frac{1}{4}$ from least to greatest. $\frac{3}{14}, \frac{1}{4}, \frac{9}{28}$

Copy and complete the statement with <, >, or =.

6. $3\frac{2}{5}$? $\frac{16}{5}$ >   **7.** $1\frac{17}{28}$? $\frac{13}{7}$ <   **8.** $\frac{28}{15}$? $1\frac{4}{5}$ >   **9.** $2\frac{1}{11}$? $\frac{45}{22}$ >

10. Write $\frac{31}{8}$ as a mixed number.   **11.** Write $2\frac{3}{14}$ as an improper fraction.
$3\frac{7}{8}$ $\frac{31}{14}$

12. Write $3\frac{4}{15}$ as a decimal. Does it terminate or repeat? $3.2\overline{6}$; **repeat**

Write the decimal as a fraction or mixed number in simplest form.

13. 0.56 $\frac{14}{25}$ **14.** 0.409 $\frac{409}{1000}$ **15.** 1.03 $1\frac{3}{100}$ **16.** 1.88 $1\frac{22}{25}$

8. 45 is divisible by 3, 5, and 9, but not by 2, 6, or 10.

9. 150 is divisible by 2, 3, 5, 6, and 10, but not by 9.

10. 522 is divisible by 2, 3, 6, and 9, but not by 5 or 10.

11. 430 is divisible by 2, 5, and 10, but not by 3, 6, or 9.

12. 780 is divisible by 2, 3, 5, 6, and 10, but not by 9.

13. 1464 is divisible by 2, 3, and 6, but not by 5, 9, or 10.

14. 1515 is divisible by 3 and 5, but not by 2, 6, 9, or 10.

15. 2970 is divisible by 2, 3, 5, 6, 9, and 10.

Chapter Review

Vocabulary

divisible, p. 214
prime number, p. 215
composite number, p. 215
prime factorization, p. 216
factor tree, p. 216
common factor, p. 222
greatest common factor (GCF), p. 222

fraction, p. 228
equivalent fractions, p. 228
simplest form, p. 229
multiple, p. 235
common multiple, p. 235
least common multiple (LCM), p. 236

least common denominator (LCD), p. 239
mixed number, p. 244
improper fraction, p. 244
proper fraction, p. 245
terminating or repeating decimal, p. 254

Vocabulary Review

1. What is a *common multiple*?
   a multiple shared by two or more numbers

2. What does it mean when one number is divisible by another number?
   the other number is a factor of the first

3. Give three examples of a prime number. What makes them prime?
   Sample answer: 2, 3, 5; their only factors are 1 and itself.

4. Give three examples of a composite number. What makes them composite?
   Sample answer: 4, 8, 9; they have factors other than 1 and itself.

Copy and complete the statement.

5. Two fractions are _?_ if they represent the same number. **equivalent**

6. A fraction is in _?_ if its numerator and denominator have a GCF of 1. **simplest form**

7. The numerator of a _?_ is less than the denominator. **proper fraction**

Review Questions

Test the number for divisibility by 2, 3, 5, 6, 9, and 10. *(Lesson 5.1)* 8–15. See margin.

8. 45	**9.** 150	**10.** 522	**11.** 430
12. 780	**13.** 1464	**14.** 1515	**15.** 2970

Write the prime factorization of the number. *(Lesson 5.1)*

16. 32 2^5	**17.** 80 $2^4 \times 5$	**18.** 74 2×37	**19.** 108 $2^2 \times 3^3$
20. 250 2×5^3	**21.** 207 $3^2 \times 23$	**22.** 327 3×109	**23.** 441 $3^2 \times 7^2$

Find the GCF of the numbers. *(Lesson 5.2)*

24. 6, 45 3

25. 8, 68 4

26. 21, 75 3

27. 25, 70 5

28. 16, 192 16

29. 18, 405 9

30. 24, 60, 72 12

31. 13, 78, 104 13

Tell whether the fraction is in simplest form. If not, simplify it. *(Lesson 5.3)*

32. $\frac{7}{35}$ no; $\frac{1}{5}$

33. $\frac{36}{96}$ no; $\frac{3}{8}$

34. $\frac{11}{98}$ yes

35. $\frac{22}{62}$ no; $\frac{11}{31}$

36. Groceries Your friend has a carton of one dozen eggs. The carton falls to the ground and three eggs break. What fraction of the eggs does your friend have left? Write your answer in simplest form. *(Lesson 5.3)* $\frac{3}{4}$

Find the LCM of the numbers. *(Lesson 5.4)*

37. 4, 10 20

38. 9, 16 144

39. 4, 38 76

40. 35, 45 315

41. 8, 52 104

42. 10, 100 100

43. 4, 5, 8 40

44. 6, 9, 24 72

45. Watches Ana sets her watch to beep every 15 minutes. Sam sets his watch to beep every 20 minutes. If they just set their watches, after how many minutes will the watches beep at the same time? *(Lesson 5.4)* 60 min

Copy and complete the statement with <, >, or =. *(Lesson 5.5)*

46. $\frac{2}{3}$? $\frac{4}{7}$ >

47. $\frac{5}{6}$? $\frac{7}{9}$ >

48. $\frac{3}{5}$? $\frac{5}{8}$ <

49. $\frac{5}{9}$? $\frac{7}{12}$ <

Order the fractions from least to greatest. *(Lesson 5.5)* 52. $\frac{1}{8}, \frac{7}{48}, \frac{1}{6}, \frac{3}{16}$ 53. $\frac{1}{72}, \frac{1}{24}, \frac{1}{18}, \frac{1}{12}$

50. $\frac{1}{7}, \frac{9}{56}, \frac{1}{8}$ $\frac{1}{8}, \frac{1}{7}, \frac{9}{56}$

51. $\frac{5}{28}, \frac{1}{4}, \frac{3}{14}$ $\frac{5}{28}, \frac{3}{14}, \frac{1}{4}$

52. $\frac{1}{6}, \frac{7}{48}, \frac{3}{16}, \frac{1}{8}$

53. $\frac{1}{72}, \frac{1}{24}, \frac{1}{18}, \frac{1}{12}$

Rewrite the number as an improper fraction or mixed number. *(Lesson 5.6)*

54. $\frac{15}{7}$ $2\frac{1}{7}$

55. $4\frac{1}{5}$ $\frac{21}{5}$

56. $3\frac{4}{7}$ $\frac{25}{7}$

57. $\frac{23}{9}$ $2\frac{5}{9}$

Write the decimal as a fraction or mixed number in simplest form. *(Lesson 5.7)*

58. 0.34 $\frac{17}{50}$

59. 4.8 $4\frac{4}{5}$

60. 2.05 $2\frac{1}{20}$

61. 0.605 $\frac{121}{200}$

Write the fraction or mixed number as a decimal. *(Lesson 5.8)*

62. $\frac{7}{8}$ 0.875

63. $3\frac{2}{5}$ 3.4

64. $5\frac{4}{9}$ $5.\overline{4}$

65. $\frac{17}{8}$ 2.125

CHAPTER

5 Chapter Test

1. Is the number 83 *prime* or *composite*? prime

2. Test 116 for divisibility by 2, 3, 5, 6, 9, and 10. 116 is divisible by 2, but not by 3, 5, 6, 9, or 10.

Write the prime factorization of the number.

3. 28 $2^2 \times 7$

4. 96 $2^5 \times 3$

5. 125 5^3

6. 340 $2^2 \times 5 \times 17$

Find the GCF of the numbers.

7. 8, 52 4

8. 5, 16 1

9. 7, 56 7

10. 16, 48, 88 8

11. Write two fractions that are equivalent to $\frac{5}{6}$. *Sample answer:* $\frac{10}{12}, \frac{15}{18}$

Write the fraction in simplest form.

12. $\frac{4}{20}$ $\frac{1}{5}$

13. $\frac{22}{34}$ $\frac{11}{17}$

14. $\frac{15}{60}$ $\frac{1}{4}$

15. $\frac{14}{42}$ $\frac{1}{3}$

16. **Bagels** You are buying bagels. You buy 3 blueberry, 6 plain, 5 cinnamon raisin, and 1 honey grain. Find the fraction of the bagels that are cinnamon raisin. Write your answer in simplest form. $\frac{1}{3}$

Find the LCM of the numbers.

17. 6, 15 30

18. 10, 14 70

19. 5, 18 90

20. 4, 10, 15 60

21. **Sports** A baseball player pitches every fifth day. An opposing player pitches every fourth day. The two pitchers just pitched on the same day. After how many days will they pitch on the same day again? 20 days

22. **Agriculture** A farmer plants a variety of crops on his land. He plants $\frac{1}{12}$ of the land with corn, $\frac{1}{4}$ with soybeans, $\frac{3}{8}$ with wheat, and $\frac{3}{16}$ with potatoes. Which crop takes up the most land? the least land? wheat; corn

23. Order the numbers $\frac{17}{5}$, $3\frac{3}{10}$, $\frac{15}{4}$, $3\frac{1}{2}$ from least to greatest. $3\frac{3}{10}, \frac{17}{5}, 3\frac{1}{2}, \frac{15}{4}$

24. **Water** About three hundredths of Earth's water is fresh water. Write this number as a decimal and as a fraction. $0.03; \frac{3}{100}$

Rewrite the number as specified.

25. $1\frac{7}{10}$ (fraction) $\frac{17}{10}$

26. 4.3 (fraction) $\frac{43}{10}$

27. $3\frac{5}{9}$ (decimal) $3.\overline{5}$

28. $\frac{22}{3}$ (mixed number) $7\frac{1}{3}$

Chapter Standardized Test

Test-Taking Strategy Look for choices that are obviously not the right answer and eliminate them first.

ADDITIONAL RESOURCES

Assessment Book
- Standardized Chapter Test, p. 65

Test and Practice Generator

12. $\frac{95}{2}$; $47\frac{1}{2}$; yes; the GCF of the numerator and denominator is 1.

Multiple Choice

1. Which number is a prime number? **C**

   A. 62   **B.** 87   **C.** 109   **D.** 129

2. Which number is divisible by 2, 3, 5, 6, 9, and 10? **H**

   F. 120   **G.** 150   **H.** 180   **I.** 600

3. Which number is *not* a multiple of 7? **D**

   A. 98   **B.** 112   **C.** 147   **D.** 163

4. What is the GCF of 20 and 35? **F**

   F. 5   **G.** 7   **H.** 10   **I.** 15

5. What is the LCM of 15 and 45? **B**

   A. 15   **B.** 45   **C.** 90   **D.** 139

6. **Tile Designs** A square tile has a side length of 14 centimeters. A rectangular tile has a length of 20 centimeters. If the tiles are laid out in a line in two separate rows of the same tiles, at what point will the rows be the same length? **G**

   F. at 120 cm   **G.** at 140 cm

   H. at 210 cm   **I.** at 320 cm

7. Which fraction is equivalent to $\frac{7}{15}$? **A**

   A. $\frac{70}{150}$ **B.** $\frac{14}{45}$ **C.** $\frac{28}{80}$ **D.** $\frac{56}{140}$

8. Which fractions are in order from least to greatest? **G**

   F. $\frac{5}{16}, \frac{3}{8}, \frac{1}{4}, \frac{9}{16}$ **G.** $\frac{1}{4}, \frac{5}{16}, \frac{3}{8}, \frac{9}{16}$

   H. $\frac{3}{8}, \frac{9}{16}, \frac{1}{4}, \frac{5}{16}$ **I.** $\frac{9}{16}, \frac{1}{4}, \frac{3}{8}, \frac{5}{16}$

9. Which number is equal to $3\frac{3}{4}$? **D**

   A. $\frac{9}{4}$ **B.** $\frac{10}{4}$ **C.** $\frac{13}{4}$ **D.** $\frac{15}{4}$

10. Which number is equal to 2.08? **F**

    F. $2\frac{2}{25}$ **G.** $2\frac{1}{8}$ **H.** $2\frac{1}{4}$ **I.** $2\frac{8}{25}$

11. Which statement is *false*? **C**

    A. $1\frac{11}{12} > 1.9$ **B.** $\frac{27}{10} < 2\frac{7}{9}$

    C. $\frac{23}{8} > 2.88$ **D.** $3\frac{5}{6} > 3\frac{4}{5}$

Short Response

12. Use the digits 2, 5, and 9 to write a fraction of the greatest possible value. Write this fraction as a mixed number. Is the fraction part in simplest form? Explain. **See margin.**

Extended Response

13. List all the pairs of factors of 60 and write the prime factorization. Describe a relationship between the prime factors and any pair of factors.
    1×60, 2×30, 4×15, 5×12, 6×10; $2^2 \times 3 \times 5$.

    Sample answer: for each factor in a pair except 1, at least one of the prime factors is also a factor of it.

Pacing and Assignment Guide

REGULAR SCHEDULE

Lesson	Les. Day	BASIC	AVERAGE	ADVANCED
6.1	Day 1	SRH p. 692 Exs. 7–9; pp. 269–270 Exs. 11–22, 27, 28, 31, 36–48	pp. 269–270 Exs. 11–18, 23–34, 38–49	pp. 269–270 Exs. 12–22, 27–37*, 42, 43, 48, 49
6.2	Day 1	EP p. 712 Exs. 25–29; pp. 273–275 Exs. 7–18, 23–25, 29–32, 35–37, 40–49	pp. 273–275 Exs. 11–28, 31–38, 42–50	pp. 273–275 Exs. 15–44*, 49, 50
6.3	Day 1	EP p. 712 Exs. 30–33; pp. 279–281 Exs. 7–21 odd, 39–41, 46, 55–57	pp. 279–281 Exs. 7–22, 36–41, 50–53	pp. 279–281 Exs. 15–22, 34–36, 38, 47–49*, 57
	Day 2	pp. 279–281 Exs. 8–22 even, 23, 25–38, 50–54	pp. 279–281 Exs. 23–35, 44–46, 54–58	pp. 279–281 Exs. 23–32, 39–43, 50–54, 58
6.4	Day 1	EP p. 712 Exs. 20–24; pp. 287–288 Exs. 14–21, 28, 29, 34–36, 45, 50–55	pp. 287–288 Exs. 14–21, 34–36, 44, 45, 47, 58–62	pp. 287–288 Exs. 16–21, 34–36, 47, 56, 57, 62
	Day 2	pp. 287–288 Exs. 22–25, 27, 30–33, 37–43, 56–62	pp. 287–288 Exs. 22–33, 37–43, 46, 50–57, 63	pp. 287–288 Exs. 22–27, 32, 33, 37–44, 46, 48–53*, 63
6.5	Day 1	pp. 292–294 Exs. 10–18, 35–38, 41–44, 60–64	pp. 292–294 Exs. 10–18, 35–38, 43–46, 55–58	pp. 292–294 Exs. 10–18, 35–38, 57–59, 64
	Day 2	pp. 292–294 Exs. 19–24, 26–34, 45–51, 55–59, 65	pp. 292–294 Exs. 19–34, 39, 40, 49–52, 59–65	pp. 292–294 Exs. 21–34, 40–45, 49–54*, 65
6.6	Day 1	pp. 300–301 Exs. 11–16, 26–28, 37–43	pp. 300–301 Exs. 11–16, 26–29, 39–43	pp. 300–301 Exs. 11–16, 26–32*, 43
	Day 2	pp. 300–301 Exs. 17–25, 31–36	pp. 300–301 Exs. 17–25, 31–38	pp. 300–301 Exs. 17–25, 33–38
Review	Day 1	pp. 304–305 Exs. 1–46	pp. 304–305 Exs. 1–46	pp. 304–305 Exs. 1–46
Assess	Day 1	Chapter 6 Test	Chapter 6 Test	Chapter 6 Test

YEARLY PACING   Chapter 6 Total – **12 days**   Chapters 1–6 Total – **70 days**   Remaining – **90 days**

*Challenge Exercises   EP = Extra Practice   SRH = Skills Review Handbook   EC = Extra Challenge

BLOCK SCHEDULE

DAY 1	DAY 2	DAY 3	DAY 4	DAY 5	DAY 6
6.1 pp. 269–270 Exs. 11–18, 23–34, 38–49 **6.2** pp. 273–275 Exs. 11–28, 31–38, 42–50	**6.3** pp. 279–281 Exs. 7–41, 44–46, 50–58	**6.4** pp. 287–288 Exs. 14–47, 50–63	**6.5** pp. 292–294 Exs. 10–40, 43–46, 49–52, 55–65	**6.6** pp. 300–301 Exs. 11–29, 31–43	**Review** pp. 304–305 Exs. 1–46 **Assess** Chapter 6 Test

YEARLY PACING   Chapter 6 Total – **6 days**   Chapters 1–6 Total – **35 days**   Remaining – **45 days**

Support Materials

📖 CHAPTER RESOURCE BOOK

CHAPTER SUPPORT

Tips for New Teachers	p. 1	Parents as Partners	p. 3

LESSON SUPPORT

	6.1	6.2	6.3	6.4	6.5	6.6
Lesson Plans (regular and block)	p. 7	p. 15	p. 25	p. 34	p. 43	p. 51
Technology Activities & Keystrokes						p. 55
Activity Support Masters						p. 53
Activity Masters				p. 36		
Practice (3 levels)	p. 9	p. 17	p. 27	p. 37	p. 45	p. 57
Study Guide	p. 12	p. 20	p. 30	p. 40	p. 48	p. 60
Real-World Problem Solving			p. 32			p. 62
Challenge Practice	p. 14	p. 22	p. 33	p. 42	p. 50	p. 63

REVIEW

Games Support Masters	pp. 5, 23	Cooperative Project with Rubric	p. 67
Chapter Review Games and Activities	p. 64	Extra Credit Project with Rubric	p. 69
Real-Life Project with Rubric	p. 65	Cumulative Practice	p. 71
		Resource Book Answers	A1

📖 ASSESSMENT

Quizzes	p. 68	Alternative Assessments with Rubrics	p. 77
Chapter Tests (3 levels)	p. 70	Unit Test	p. 90
Standardized Test	p. 76	Cumulative Test	p. 92

📽 TRANSPARENCIES

	6.1	6.2	6.3	6.4	6.5	6.6
Warm-Up / Daily Homework Quiz	✔	✔	✔	✔	✔	✔
Notetaking Guide	✔	✔	✔	✔	✔	✔
Teacher Support						
English/Spanish Problem Solving			✔	✔	✔	
Answer Transparencies	✔	✔	✔	✔	✔	✔

💻 TECHNOLOGY

- EasyPlanner CD-ROM
- Test and Practice Generator
- Electronic Lesson Presentations
- eTutorial CD-ROM
- Chapter Audio Summaries CDs
- Classzone.com
- eEdition Plus Online
- eWorkbook Plus Online
- eTutorial Plus Online
- EasyPlanner Plus Online

ADDITIONAL RESOURCES

- Worked-Out Solution Key
- Notetaking Guide
- Practice Workbook
- Tutor Place
- Professional Development Book
- Activities Book
- Poster Package
- Spanish Study Guide
- English/Spanish Chapter Reviews
- Multi-Language Glossary

Math Background and Teaching Strategies

Lesson 6.1

MATH BACKGROUND

ROUNDING FRACTIONS AND MIXED NUMBERS Proper fractions can be rounded to the nearest half. If a fraction is between 0 and $\frac{1}{2}$ but closer to 0 than to $\frac{1}{2}$, it rounds to 0. If the fraction is closer to $\frac{1}{2}$, it rounds to $\frac{1}{2}$. Similarly, a fraction between $\frac{1}{2}$ and 1 rounds down to $\frac{1}{2}$ or up to 1. The fraction part of a mixed number rounds in the same way; so the mixed number rounds down to the whole number part if the fraction is between 0 and $\frac{1}{2}$ and up to the next whole number if the fraction is equal to $\frac{1}{2}$ or between $\frac{1}{2}$ and 1.

TEACHING STRATEGIES

To introduce the lesson, draw a number line on the board that is divided into fractions. Have students come to the board and place a fraction on the number line. Then have students in the class determine if the fraction is closer to 0, $\frac{1}{2}$, or 1.

Lesson 6.2

MATH BACKGROUND

ADDING AND SUBTRACTING FRACTIONS You can introduce the addition and subtraction of fractions with like denominators by explaining to students that it is similar to adding and subtracting with whole numbers, except that the sum or difference is written over the common denominator. When the denominators of fractions are the same, you can say the fractions have the same name; so 3 eighths plus 4 eighths equals 7 eighths.

TEACHING STRATEGIES

Adding and subtracting fractions with common denominators should not be difficult for most students. One pitfall to be aware of is that some students might try to add or subtract denominators as well as numerators. Students also need to know how to simplify answers by reducing fractions or, in the case of a sum, rewriting an improper fraction as a mixed number.

Lesson 6.3

MATH BACKGROUND

Adding or subtracting fractions with different denominators requires the initial step of rewriting one or both fractions so that the two have a common denominator.

TEACHING STRATEGIES

You can use visual models to introduce the concept of adding and subtracting fractions with unlike denominators.

Example To find the sum $\frac{1}{3} + \frac{1}{4}$, place the following fraction models on the board or an overhead transparency.

So, $\frac{1}{3} + \frac{1}{4} = \frac{4}{12} + \frac{3}{12} = \frac{7}{12}$

Lesson 6.4

MATH BACKGROUND

The sequence of lessons in Chapter 6 shows how arithmetic skills can be built upon previously learned skills. First, students learn to add and subtract fractions with the same denominator. Next they use this skill as a part of the process of adding and subtracting fractions with different denominators. In this lesson, they use these skills in adding and subtracting mixed numbers, where whole-number parts and fraction parts are added separately. The next lesson extends this process to renaming mixed numbers in subtraction.

TEACHING STRATEGIES

Distribute copies of the shapes shown below to the students.

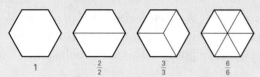

These shapes can be used to show whole and fractional parts. If the hexagon represents 1, then two trapezoids can be put together to represent $\frac{2}{2}$ or 1, three rhombuses can be put together to represent $\frac{3}{3}$ or 1, and six equilateral triangles can be used to show $\frac{6}{6}$ or 1. Also have students observe that a trapezoid can be replaced with 3 triangles and a rhombus can be replaced with 2 triangles. Have students work in small groups and use the shapes to model $2\frac{1}{3}$, $3\frac{1}{2}$, $1\frac{1}{6}$, and so on. Ask students if they can put the shapes together to show a sum such as $2\frac{1}{2} + 3\frac{2}{3}$.

Lesson 6.5

MATH BACKGROUND

SUBTRACTING MIXED NUMBERS When subtracting mixed numbers, it may be necessary to rename in order to subtract the fractional parts. Relate this concept to the need to rename when subtracting whole numbers, as when subtracting 28 from 72. Once the number being subtracted from has been renamed, the subtraction process is the same as in the previous lesson.

TEACHING STRATEGIES

Again, stress the use of the vertical format for students to use to show their work. This format, with all steps written down, helps students eliminate careless errors and helps you diagnose problem areas.

Lesson 6.6

MATH BACKGROUND

ADDING AND SUBTRACTING MEASURES OF TIME

Measures of length, weight, and time that involve several units are called **compound denominate numbers**. Computing with such numbers is similar to computing with mixed numbers in that parts of the numbers are added or subtracted separately. The results may also need to be simplified, just as the results with mixed numbers sometime need to be simplified.

ELAPSED TIME The time interval between two events is elapsed time. Determining elapsed time is a useful skill related to many everyday activities such as cooking, figuring arrival and departure times, exercising, and so on.

TEACHING STRATEGIES

One way to find elapsed time is to use a number line.

```
       8:30 A.M.                            12:15 P.M.
   ├──────┼──────┼──────┼──────┼──────┼──────┼──────→
  8:00 A.M.  9:00 A.M.  10:00 A.M.  11:00 A.M.  Noon  1:00 P.M.
       ├──────────────── 3 h 45 min ────────────┤
```

Another way to determine elapsed time is to subtract.

$$
\begin{array}{l}
1 \text{ h } 90 \text{ min} \\
2 \text{ h } 30 \text{ min} \\
\underline{-\ 1 \text{ h } 45 \text{ min}} \\
45 \text{ min}
\end{array}
\qquad
\begin{array}{l}
3 \text{ h } 45 \text{ min} \\
\underline{+\ 4 \text{ h } 50 \text{ min}} \\
7 \text{ h } 95 \text{ min} = 7 \text{ h} + 1 \text{ h} + 35 \text{ min} \\
\phantom{7 \text{ h } 95 \text{ min} } = 8 \text{ h } 35 \text{ min}
\end{array}
$$

Provide students with copies of airline schedules or have them use the Internet to obtain information on flights to 5 or 6 different locations in the United States. Have students calculate the elapsed time between flights from one location to another.

Differentiating Instruction

Strategies for Underachievers

PHYSICAL MODELING

Divide the class into 4 equal groups (as nearly as possible). Have each group brainstorm many ways to visually represent $\frac{1}{4}$. Give each group a sheet of easel paper to draw their representations. When they are done, tape their papers to the wall for the entire class to see them. Discuss the results with the class.

Next, give each group its own individual fraction to represent. You may wish to set up these groups by ability and give stronger groups more difficult fractions.

When you feel that your groups are developing a solid, concrete foundation of what a fraction represents, you may now want to compare proper fractions according their proximate size relating to 0, $\frac{1}{2}$, or 1. Students may need to see many examples before developing a deep understanding of this concept. It is unlikely that students will develop this understanding by looking at numerical representations only. Another tool which may help anchor this concept of proximity to 0, $\frac{1}{2}$, or 1, is a customary ruler.

Continue the use of physical models into the lessons on adding and subtracting fractions with like denominators. Students will be able to see concretely that $\frac{1}{5} + \frac{2}{5} = \frac{3}{5}$, not $\frac{3}{10}$, as in the example below.

Notice that 3 regions are shaded, and that each region is still the same, original size, which is $\frac{1}{5}$, and that the sum is clearly $\frac{3}{5}$.

With unlike denominators, you may wish to use a circle to show a simpler sum, such as $\frac{1}{4} + \frac{3}{8}$. The circle should be first divided into fourths with one-fourth being shaded. Then you may wish to ask students how to divide the circle so that one could represent $\frac{3}{8}$. Students should see

that they can simply divide each section in half to create 8 equal sections. You may point out that pizzas and pies are frequently cut into eighths in this way. Then shade three of the eighths. Next point out that the shaded $\frac{1}{4}$ can also be described as $\frac{2}{8}$. Add these two shaded areas together to get a sum of $\frac{5}{8}$.

These same models for addition can be easily adapted for subtraction. You may wish to describe subtraction problems as "take away" problems.

Underachieving students may benefit by using fraction bar sets for the duration of this chapter to increase their conceptual understanding of fractions. If you do not have fraction bars, you may use $\frac{1}{2}$-inch graph paper to create them. Cut out bars that are 12 squares long and 2 squares wide. Shade these bars individually to represent halves, thirds, fourth, sixths, and twelfths.

PROVIDE SCAFFOLDING

MULTI-STEP PROBLEMS Many problems involving fractions require students to complete a number of steps in a particular order. Advanced students not only remember the steps, they know when and how to use shortcuts, they understand why they are doing what they are doing, and know when the order of steps does or does not matter. Underachieving students may not fully understand any shortcuts, and trying to apply them will only lead to great confusion.

Less proficient students may need extra help understanding why they take each step. When students seem overwhelmed by a multi-step problem, or if they seem to be oversimplifying a multi-step problem such as subtracting fractions with unlike denominators, have them play "The 'Why' Game". See if they can come up with a reason for each of the steps that they take when solving a problem. Have them give a reason in their own words for the work that they have done.

Strategies for English Learners

DISSECT WORD PROBLEMS

This chapter has more word problems and fewer strictly numerical problems than other chapters, so it may be more difficult for English learners to read. You can minimize the amount of reading required and focus on the mathematics by making sure that students know key phrases and by presenting problems in a predictable format. For example, the following phrase occurs in some of the problems in this chapter:

Estimate how much . . .

In several places in this chapter, the questions are organized so that the basic sentence structure remains consistent, and the student must come up with the same type of answer each time even though the particular facts of the problem change.

Strategies for Advanced Learners

DIFFERENT INSTRUCTION IN TERMS OF COMPLEXITY

After discussing Lesson 6.4, give advanced students recipes that contain several fractions. Challenge these students to adjust these recipes to serve twice the number of people, three times the number of people, and so on. Since they will have not yet studied multiplication of fractions, students can complete these problems using multiple additions.

CROSS-CURRICULAR CONNECTION

In Physical Education classes, students might participate in field events, such as the long jump or shot put. Have students measure their attempts in fractional units and find the differences between their attempts and high school records for these events.

Advanced students enjoy doing number puzzles. Here is a number puzzle you can use with **Lesson 6.4**:

- **Challenge** The sum of two mixed numbers is $5\frac{4}{5}$. The difference of the numbers is $1\frac{2}{5}$. Both numbers have a denominator of 5. Find the numbers. $3\frac{3}{5}$ and $2\frac{1}{5}$

The following problem can be used with Lesson 6.5:

- **Challenge** A bowling lane is 62 feet $10\frac{3}{16}$ inches long and $3\frac{5}{12}$ feet wide. How much longer is the lane than it is wide? 59 ft $5\frac{3}{16}$ in.

Differentiating Instruction: Teaching Resources

Differentiating Enrichment and Activities

McDougal Littell *Middle School Mathematics* offers teachers enrichment for all levels of students. Pictured on these pages are facsimiles of the Real-World Problem Solving pages, Chapter Review Games, and Chapter Projects from the *Chapter 6 Resource Book* and a number of activities from the *Special Activities Book*. Also available is the *Poster Package* containing large, full-color posters, one for each unit.

RESOURCE BOOK

The *Chapter Resource Books* contain Real-World Problem Solving activities for various lessons in the textbook, Chapter Review Games for a motivating review of each chapter, and Chapter Projects with rubrics that apply the mathematics of the chapter.

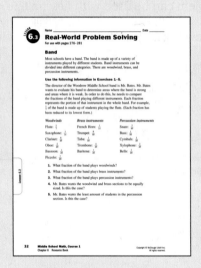

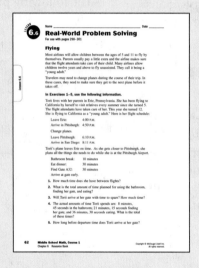

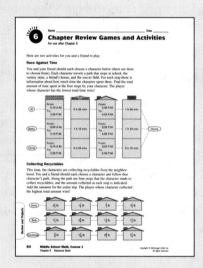

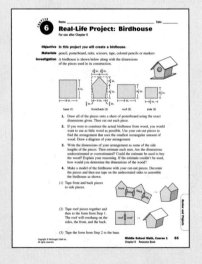

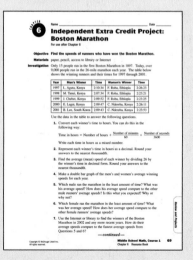

SPECIAL ACTIVITIES BOOK

The *Special Activities Book* contains numerous activities including activities for the start of school, activities for substitute teachers, activities for use before holiday breaks, and short change-of-pace activities.

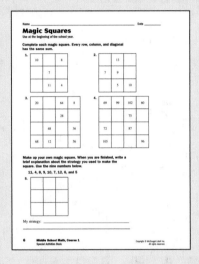

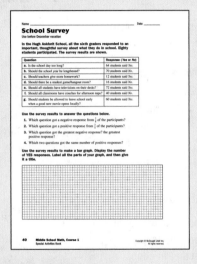

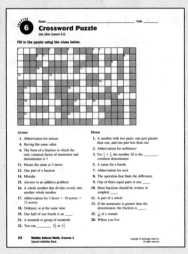

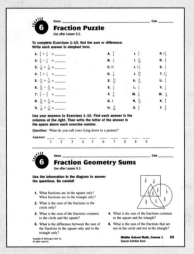

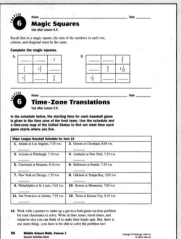

MAIN IDEAS

In this chapter, students estimate sums and differences of fractions and mixed numbers. They also add and subtract fractions and mixed numbers. Finally, students will add and subtract measures of time.

PREREQUISITE SKILLS

The key skills reviewed in the game on these pages are:

- Comparing fractions and mixed numbers
- Naming equivalent fractions

Additional practice with prerequisite skills can be found in the Review What You Need to Know exercises on page 266. Additional resources for reviewing prerequisite skills are:

- Skills Review Handbook, pp. 684–707
- Tutor Place
- eTutorial Plus Online

MANAGING THE GAME

Tips for Success

Since students play this game in pairs, have them ask their partner to explain why two cards match or why they do not match. This will help students review what they know about fractions.

Reflecting on the Game

Stop and Think Question 1 can help students generalize about the quantitative relationship between the numerator and nominator of an improper fraction.

CHAPTER 6

Addition and Subtraction of Fractions

BEFORE

In previous chapters you've...

- **Compared and ordered fractions**
- **Changed between mixed numbers and fractions**

Now

In Chapter 6 you'll study...

- **Estimating sums and differences of fractions and mixed numbers**
- **Adding and subtracting fractions and mixed numbers**
- **Measuring time**

WHY?

So you can solve real-world problems about...

- **the Appalachian Trail, p. 280**
- **volcanoes, p. 286**
- **horses, p. 291**
- **the Tour de France, p. 298**

Internet Preview
CLASSZONE.COM

- **eEdition Plus Online**
- **eWorkbook Plus Online**
- **eTutorial Plus Online**
- **State Test Practice**
- **More Examples**

Chapter Warm-Up Game

Review skills you need for this chapter in this game. Work with a partner.

Key Skill:
Comparing fractions and mixed numbers

JUNGLE FRACTIONS

If you want to be amazed, take a walk through the tangled vegetation jungle. This matching game involves some amazing facts about jungle animals.

MATERIALS

16 jungle cards

PREPARE The 16 jungle cards consist of 8 fact cards and 8 number cards. Each fact card contains a fraction or mixed number that is equivalent to a fraction on one of the number cards. Shuffle all 16 jungle cards together. Arrange the cards face down in 4 rows.

Some toucans have bills that are about $\frac{1}{3}$ the length of their bodies.

$$\frac{20}{60}$$

CHAPTER RESOURCES

These resources are provided to help you prepare for the chapter and to customize review materials:

 Chapter 6 Resource Book
- Tips for New Teachers, pp. 1–2
- Lesson Plan, pp. 7, 15, 25, 34, 43, 51
- Lesson Plan for Block Scheduling, pp. 8, 16, 26, 35, 44, 52

 Technology
- EasyPlanner CD-ROM
- Test and Practice Generator
- Electronic Lesson Presentations CD-ROM
- eTutorial CD-ROM

Internet
- Classzone
- eEdition Plus Online
- eWorkbook Plus Online
- eTutorial Plus Online
- EasyPlanner Plus Online

ENGLISH LEARNER SUPPORT

- Spanish Study Guide
- Multi-Language Glossary
- Chapter Audio Summaries CDs
- Teacher's Edition, pp. 264E–264F

1 **REVEAL** 2 cards and read them aloud.

2 **DECIDE** whether the numbers on the 2 cards are equivalent. If they are, you may keep the cards. Otherwise, turn them back over.

3 **REMEMBER** where the cards are so you can find equivalent number pairs on future turns.

HOW TO WIN The player who collects the most cards wins.

Stop and Think

1. **Writing** Suppose you get a number card with an improper fraction on it. What can you predict about the numerator and the denominator in the mixed number on the matching fact card? Explain.
   The numerator will be different, but the denominator will be the same.
2. **Critical Thinking** As you learned in *Jungle Fractions*, a spider monkey's tail is $\frac{7}{12}$ of the monkey's total length. Sketch a visual model to illustrate this fact. Based on your model, would you say that a spider monkey is about twice as long as its tail? Explain your thinking.

Check drawings; yes; $\frac{7}{12}$ is about $\frac{1}{2}$.

265

DIAGNOSIS/REMEDIATION

Review What You Need to Know
The Review What You Need to Know exercises can help you diagnose whether students have the following skills needed in Chapter 6:

- Vocabulary (Exs. 1–4)
- Convert units of time (Exs. 5–8)
- Find sums and differences (Exs. 9–12)
- Write equivalent fractions (Exs. 13–16)
- Find least common multiples (Exs. 17–20)

 Chapter 6 Resource Book
- Study Guide (Lessons 6.1–6.6)

 Tutor Place

NOTETAKING STRATEGIES

When creating their outline of the chapter, students should use the headings associated with each example. In Lesson 6.1, these are Rounding Fractions, Rounding Mixed Numbers, Estimating a Difference, and Estimating a Sum. The Notebook boxes in Lessons 6.2–6.5 should also be part of the outline. Further suggestions for keeping a notebook can be found on page 278.

For more support on notetaking, see:
- Notetaking Guide Workbook
- Notetaking Transparencies

CHAPTER 6 Getting Ready to Learn

Word Watch

Review Words

fraction, p. 228
equivalent fractions, p. 228
simplest form, p. 229
least common multiple (LCM), p. 236
mixed number, p. 244
improper fraction, p. 244
whole number, p. 684

Review What You Need to Know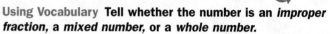

Using Vocabulary Tell whether the number is an *improper fraction*, a *mixed number*, or a *whole number*.

1. $3\frac{1}{8}$ mixed number

2. $\frac{3}{2}$ improper fraction

3. 6 whole number

4. $\frac{5}{4}$ improper fraction

Copy and complete the statement. *(p. 701)*

5. 2 hours = ? min 120

6. 4 min = ? sec 240

7. 400 sec = ? min ? sec 6; 40

8. 250 min = ? hours ? min 4; 10

Find the sum or difference. *(p. 136)*

9. $7.2 + 4.9$ 12.1

10. $2.43 + 16.7$ 19.13

11. $10.8 - 8.9$ 1.9

12. $51.0 - 2.57$ 48.43

Copy and complete the statement. *(p. 228)*

13. $\frac{3}{6} = \frac{1}{?}$ 2

14. $\frac{2}{3} = \frac{?}{12}$ 8

15. $\frac{2}{5} = \frac{10}{?}$ 25

16. $\frac{6}{16} = \frac{?}{8}$ 3

Find the least common multiple of the numbers. *(p. 235)*

17. 3 and 5 15

18. 8 and 10 40

19. 4 and 12 12

20. 6 and 7 42

NoTebook

You should include material that appears on a notebook like this in your own notes.

Know How to Take Notes

Writing a Summary To summarize a chapter in your notes, first create an outline of the chapter using the headings from the lesson. Then fill in the outline with concepts and examples from the lesson.

Lesson 5.3 Equivalent Fractions

Write two fractions that are equivalent to $\frac{2}{5}$.

$$\frac{2}{5} = \frac{2 \times 3}{5 \times 3} = \frac{6}{15}$$

$$\frac{2}{5} = \frac{2 \times 4}{5 \times 4} = \frac{8}{20}$$

You can use this tool to summarize each lesson in Chapter 6.

Fraction Estimation

BEFORE	▶ Now	WHY?
You estimated with whole numbers and decimals.	You'll estimate with fractions and mixed numbers.	So you can estimate the length of a rocket, as in Ex. 30.

📖 Word Watch

Review Words
fraction, p. 228
mixed number, p. 244
round, p. 686

In the Real World

Geckos The world's smallest adult reptile is a dwarf gecko that is about $\frac{5}{8}$ inch in body length. From the ruler, you can tell that $\frac{5}{8}$ is closer to $\frac{1}{2}$ than to 1.

inches   1

One way to round fractions is to compare the numerator and the denominator. Fractions are usually rounded to the nearest half. Mixed numbers are usually rounded to the nearest whole number.

EXAMPLE 1 Rounding Fractions

Round the fraction.

a. $\frac{1}{8} \approx 0$ Because 1 is much less than 8, round $\frac{1}{8}$ to 0.

b. $\frac{5}{9} \approx \frac{1}{2}$ Because 5 is about half of 9, round $\frac{5}{9}$ to $\frac{1}{2}$.

c. $\frac{6}{7} \approx 1$ Because 6 is almost as great as 7, round $\frac{6}{7}$ to 1.

EXAMPLE 2 Rounding Mixed Numbers

Round the mixed number.

a. $4\frac{1}{3} \approx 4$ Because $\frac{1}{3}$ is less than $\frac{1}{2}$, round $4\frac{1}{3}$ down to 4.

b. $5\frac{3}{4} \approx 6$ Because $\frac{3}{4}$ is greater than $\frac{1}{2}$, round $5\frac{3}{4}$ up to 6.

 with Solving

If the fraction or mixed number that you are rounding is halfway between two numbers, you usually round to the greater number.

Your turn now Round the fraction or mixed number.

1. $\frac{1}{4}$ $\frac{1}{2}$ **2.** $\frac{5}{6}$ 1   **3.** $2\frac{9}{16}$ 3   **4.** $5\frac{3}{7}$ 5

NCTM CURRICULUM STANDARDS
Standard 1: Understand numbers
Standard 6: Make reasonable estimates

Lesson 6.1   Fraction Estimation   **267**

---

1 PLAN

SKILL CHECK
Estimate the sum or difference.

1.	$71 + 47$	120
2.	$6.15 + 8.92$	15
3.	$392 - 127$	300
4.	$7.775 - 4.393$	4

LESSON OBJECTIVE
Estimate with fractions and mixed numbers.

PACING
Suggested Number of Days
Basic Course: 1 day
Average Course: 1 day
Advanced Course: 1 day
Block: 0.5 block with 6.2

TEACHING RESOURCES
For a complete list of Teaching Resources, see page 264B.

🔺 **TRANSPARENCY**
Warm-Up Exercises for this lesson are available on a transparency.

2 TEACH

MOTIVATING THE LESSON
Have students with pets estimate the length of their pet to the nearest inch.

TIPS FOR NEW TEACHERS
Ask students how they would round various fractions in terms of their distance from $0, \frac{1}{2}$, or 1.
See Tips for New Teachers in the *Chapter 6 Resource Book*.

Example 1 Round the fraction.
a. $\frac{1}{7}$ 0 **b.** $\frac{9}{16}$ $\frac{1}{2}$ **c.** $\frac{4}{5}$ 1

Example 2 Round.
a. $3\frac{1}{4}$ 3 **b.** $6\frac{7}{8}$ 7

Example 3 Estimate the difference $7\frac{4}{5} - 2\frac{1}{6}$. 6

Example 4 You need $\frac{3}{4}$ cup of sugar for one recipe and $1\frac{1}{3}$ cups of sugar for another recipe. You want to know how much sugar you need.
a. Should your estimate be *high* or *low*? **high**
b. Estimate the amount of sugar you need. $2\frac{1}{2}$ c

CONCEPT CHECK

Estimate $3\frac{1}{4} + 2\frac{7}{8}$. 6

DAILY PUZZLER

Estimate the sum of *x* and $6\frac{7}{8}$ if *x* is a number between 2 and $2\frac{1}{2}$. 9

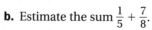
Visual Arts

■ **Costumes**

The lead actress in a play needs three costumes. Suppose each costume requires $9\frac{7}{8}$ yards of fabric.

Estimate how many yards will be used to make all 3 costumes.
about 30 yds

EXAMPLE 3 **Estimating a Difference**

Estimate the difference $6\frac{1}{4} - 1\frac{5}{6}$.

$6\frac{1}{4} - 1\frac{5}{6} \approx 6 - 2$ Round each mixed number.

$= 4$ Find the difference.

Real-World Estimates In some situations, you may want to round the numbers so that you get an estimate that is high or low.

EXAMPLE 4 **Estimating a Sum**

Costumes You need $\frac{1}{5}$ yard of ribbon for one costume and $\frac{7}{8}$ yard for another costume. You want to know how much ribbon you need.

a. Should your estimate of the amount of ribbon be *high* or *low*?

b. Estimate the amount of ribbon you need.

Solution

a. Your estimate of the amount of ribbon you need should be high so that you will not run out of ribbon before finishing the costumes.

b. Estimate the sum $\frac{1}{5} + \frac{7}{8}$.

$\frac{1}{5} + \frac{7}{8} \approx \frac{1}{2} + 1$ Round each fraction up to get a high estimate.

$= 1\frac{1}{2}$ Find the sum.

ANSWER You will need about $1\frac{1}{2}$ yards of ribbon.

Your turn now   Estimate the sum or difference. **5–8. Estimates may vary.**

5. $\frac{7}{8} + \frac{4}{5}$ 2 **6.** $\frac{9}{16} - \frac{1}{6}$ $\frac{1}{2}$ **7.** $3\frac{1}{5} - 2\frac{7}{10}$ 0 **8.** $1\frac{5}{6} + 2\frac{1}{2}$ 5

9. An empty ice chest weighs $4\frac{1}{3}$ pounds. You put $3\frac{3}{5}$ pounds of ice into the chest. Estimate how much the ice chest now weighs. **8 lb**

INTERNET
eWorkbook Plus

CLASSZONE.COM

Getting Ready to Practice

1. **Vocabulary** ? are usually rounded to the nearest half. Mixed numbers are usually rounded to the nearest ? . **Fractions; whole number**

Round the fraction or mixed number.

2. $\frac{4}{9}$ $\frac{1}{2}$

3. $\frac{1}{6}$ 0

4. $1\frac{3}{8}$ 1

5. $3\frac{5}{7}$ 4

Estimate the sum or difference. 6–9. Estimates may vary.

6. $\frac{11}{12} + \frac{3}{4}$ 2

7. $2\frac{7}{8} + 4\frac{1}{6}$ 7

8. $5\frac{3}{10} - 1\frac{1}{8}$ 4

9. $\frac{4}{7} - \frac{1}{5}$ $\frac{1}{2}$

10. **Long Lines** You wait in line for $1\frac{1}{3}$ hours for a mountain ride and $1\frac{4}{5}$ hours for a water ride. Estimate how many hours you wait in line.

3 h

Practice and Problem Solving

Round the fraction or mixed number.

A 11. $\frac{4}{5}$ 1

12. $\frac{7}{10}$ $\frac{1}{2}$

13. $3\frac{1}{2}$ 4

14. $4\frac{3}{8}$ 4

Estimate the sum or difference. 15–26. Estimates may vary.

15. $\frac{1}{6} + \frac{1}{5}$ 0

16. $\frac{6}{7} + \frac{13}{15}$ 2

17. $\frac{2}{7} - \frac{1}{5}$ 0

18. $\frac{9}{10} - \frac{1}{3}$ 1

19. $\frac{9}{16} + \frac{7}{12}$ 1

20. $\frac{4}{9} - \frac{3}{8}$ 0

21. $2\frac{7}{10} + 2\frac{5}{14}$ 5

22. $1\frac{5}{6} + 3\frac{5}{12}$ 5

23. $8\frac{11}{20} - 3\frac{3}{5}$ 5

24. $7\frac{2}{15} - 2\frac{1}{18}$ 5

25. $4\frac{8}{9} - 1\frac{1}{2}$ 3

26. $1\frac{3}{17} + 2\frac{1}{2}$ 4

27. **Muffins** You have $5\frac{5}{8}$ cups of flour. You use $1\frac{1}{3}$ cups of flour to make blueberry muffins. Estimate how much flour you have left. 5 c

28. **Paint** You need $4\frac{1}{4}$ gallons of paint for one room and $3\frac{1}{3}$ gallons for another room. Estimate how much paint you need. 7 gal

29. **Writing** In Exercise 28, tell whether it is better to have a *low* or *high* estimate of the answer. Explain your choice. high estimate; so that you will not run out of paint

HELP
with Homework

Example	Exercises
1	11–12
2	13–14
3	15–28
4	15–29

Online Resources

CLASSZONE.COM

· More Examples
· eTutorial Plus

3 **APPLY**

ASSIGNMENT GUIDE

Basic Course
Day 1: SRH p. 692 Exs. 7–9; pp. 269–270 Exs. 11–22, 27, 28, 31, 36–48

Average Course
Day 1: pp. 269–270 Exs. 11–18, 23–34, 38–49

Advanced Course
Day 1: pp. 269–270 Exs. 12–22, 27–37*, 42, 43, 48, 49

Block
pp. 269–270 Exs. 11–18, 23–34, 38–49 (with 6.2)

EXTRA PRACTICE

• Student Edition, p. 713
• Chapter 6 Resource Book, pp. 9–11
• Test and Practice Generator

TRANSPARENCY

Even-numbered answers are available on transparencies.

HOMEWORK CHECK

When you review students' homework for this lesson, go over the following exercises to check understanding of key concepts.
Basic: 11, 13, 15, 18, 20
Average: 11, 14, 16, 23, 27
Advanced: 12, 14, 17, 27, 28

TEACHING TIP

In Exercises 23–26, remind students to first round each mixed number up or down to the nearest whole number. Then add (or subtract) the whole numbers.

4 ASSESS

ASSESSMENT RESOURCES

For more assessment resources, see:
- Assessment Book
- Test and Practice Generator

MINI-QUIZ

Round the fraction or mixed number.

1. $\frac{1}{8}$ 0   **2.** $\frac{7}{9}$ 1   **3.** $3\frac{3}{5}$ 4

Estimate the sum or difference.

4. $\frac{1}{4} + \frac{7}{8}$ 1   **5.** $\frac{7}{8} - \frac{1}{4}$ 1

6. $3\frac{1}{3} - 1\frac{1}{4}$ 2   **7.** $5\frac{1}{4} + 1\frac{5}{8}$ 7

8. You need $2\frac{3}{4}$ yards of fabric to make one T-shirt and $3\frac{1}{8}$ yards of fabric to make a second T-shirt. About how many yards do you need in all? **6 yd**

5 FOLLOW-UP

RETEACHING/REMEDIATION
- Study Guide in Chapter 6 Resource Book, pp. 12–13
- eTutorial Plus Online
- Extra Practice, p. 713
- Lesson Practice in Chapter 6 Resource Book, pp. 9–11

CHALLENGE/ENRICHMENT
- Challenge Practice in Chapter 6 Resource Book, p. 14
- Teacher's Edition, p. 264F

ENGLISH LEARNER SUPPORT
- Spanish Study Guide
- Multi-Language Glossary
- Chapter Audio Summaries CDs

34–35. See Additional Answers beginning on page AA1.

270

What do you think?

Science

■ **Rockets**

The Saturn V rocket was used to land the first man on the moon on July 20, 1969. Laying flat, the bottom of the rocket is about 33 feet tall. About how many times as tall as you is the bottom of the rocket?
Sample answer: about 6 times as tall

INTERNET
State Test Practice
CLASSZONE.COM

B 30. Rockets Estimate the total length of the Saturn V rocket shown below.

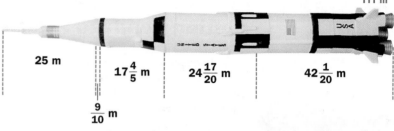

111 m

25 m $17\frac{4}{5}$ m $24\frac{17}{20}$ m $42\frac{1}{20}$ m

$\frac{9}{10}$ m

Tell whether the answer is a *high estimate* or a *low estimate*.

31. $3\frac{7}{11} + 8\frac{6}{7} \approx 13$ high   **32.** $2\frac{1}{6} + 4\frac{2}{9} \approx 8$ high   **33.** $10\frac{4}{5} - 3\frac{1}{8} \approx 6$ low

C 34. Explain Suppose you round $\frac{3}{4}$ down to $\frac{1}{2}$, and your friend rounds $\frac{3}{4}$ up to 1. Explain why both answers are reasonable. See margin.

35. Challenge Describe a real-world situation in which you would always round two mixed numbers down before estimating the sum. See margin.

Mixed Review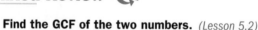

Find the GCF of the two numbers. *(Lesson 5.2)*

36. 6 and 14 2   **37.** 5 and 15 5   **38.** 7 and 13 1   **39.** 12 and 18 6

Write the mixed number as an improper fraction. *(Lesson 5.6)*

40. $7\frac{1}{2}$ $\frac{15}{2}$ **41.** $2\frac{2}{3}$ $\frac{8}{3}$ **42.** $4\frac{9}{10}$ $\frac{49}{10}$ **43.** $8\frac{1}{4}$ $\frac{33}{4}$

Basic Skills **Find the sum or difference.**

44. $178 + 304$ 482   **45.** $627 + 385$ 1012   **46.** $375 - 168$ 207   **47.** $926 - 349$ 577

Test-Taking Practice

48. Multiple Choice You run $3\frac{3}{4}$ miles on Friday and $2\frac{1}{3}$ miles on Monday to prepare for a track meet. Estimate the total number of miles you run. C

A. 3 miles   **B.** 4 miles   **C.** 6 miles   **D.** 8 miles

49. Short Response You have $2\frac{1}{4}$ yards of fabric and buy $3\frac{7}{8}$ yards more. You use 5 yards to decorate your room. Estimate the total amount of fabric you have left. Show your steps.
1 yd; step 1: 2 + 4 = 6, step 2: 6 − 5 = 1

LESSON 6.2

Fractions with Common Denominators

BEFORE

You estimated the sums and differences of fractions.

▶ **Now**

You'll find actual sums and differences of fractions.

WHY?

So you can analyze a school survey, as in Exs. 35–37.

Word Watch

Review Words

mixed number, p. 244
improper fraction, p. 244

Activity You can use a model to add two fractions.

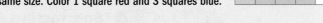

① Draw a rectangle divided into 5 squares of the same size. Color 1 square red and 3 squares blue.

② Copy and complete the following statement with the correct numbers:

$$\frac{\overset{1}{?\ \text{red squares}}}{\underset{5}{?\ \text{total squares}}} + \frac{\overset{3}{?\ \text{blue squares}}}{\underset{5}{?\ \text{total squares}}} = \frac{\overset{4}{?\ \text{colored squares}}}{\underset{5}{?\ \text{total squares}}}$$

Use a model to find the sum.

1. $\frac{2}{9} + \frac{5}{9}$ $\frac{7}{9}$

2. $\frac{1}{8} + \frac{3}{8}$ $\frac{1}{2}$

Adding Fractions with Common Denominators

Words To add two fractions with a common denominator, write the sum of the numerators over the denominator.

Numbers $\frac{2}{7} + \frac{4}{7} = \frac{6}{7}$

Algebra $\frac{a}{c} + \frac{b}{c} = \frac{a+b}{c}$

HELP with Review

Need help with rewriting improper fractions as mixed numbers? See p. 244.

EXAMPLE 1 Adding Fractions

$\frac{3}{5} + \frac{4}{5} = \frac{3+4}{5}$ Add the numerators.

$= \frac{7}{5}$ Simplify the numerator.

$= 1\frac{2}{5}$ Rewrite the improper fraction as a mixed number.

Your turn now Find the sum. Simplify if possible.

1. $\frac{1}{9} + \frac{7}{9}$ $\frac{8}{9}$

2. $\frac{1}{8} + \frac{5}{8}$ $\frac{3}{4}$

3. $\frac{5}{7} + \frac{6}{7}$ $1\frac{4}{7}$

4. $\frac{9}{10} + \frac{3}{10}$ $1\frac{1}{5}$

NCTM CURRICULUM STANDARDS
Standard 1: Understand meanings of operations
Standard 10: Use representations to communicate mathematical ideas

Lesson 6.2   Fractions with Common Denominators   **271**

① PLAN

SKILL CHECK
Rewrite as a mixed number.

1. $\frac{14}{9}$ $1\frac{5}{9}$

2. $\frac{19}{8}$ $2\frac{3}{8}$

Simplify the fraction.

3. $\frac{6}{9}$ $\frac{2}{3}$

4. $\frac{10}{24}$ $\frac{5}{12}$

LESSON OBJECTIVE

Find actual sums and differences of fractions.

PACING

Suggested Number of Days
Basic Course: 1 day
Average Course: 1 day
Advanced Course: 1 day
Block: 0.5 block with 6.1

TEACHING RESOURCES

For a complete list of Teaching Resources, see page 264B.

 **TRANSPARENCY**

Warm-Up Exercises for this lesson are available on a transparency.

② TEACH

MOTIVATING THE LESSON

Expand the Activity by having students do more exercises.

ACTIVITY

Goal Use a model to add fractions.

Key Discovery To add fractions with like denominators, add the numerators.

Step 2. See Additional Answers beginning on page AA1.

Subtracting with Common Denominators

Words To subtract two fractions with a common denominator, write the difference of the numerators over the denominator.

Numbers $\frac{5}{9} - \frac{1}{9} = \frac{4}{9}$ **Algebra** $\frac{a}{c} - \frac{b}{c} = \frac{a-b}{c}$

 with **Review**

Need help with writing fractions in simplest form? See p. 228.

EXAMPLE 2 Subtracting Fractions

$\frac{7}{10} - \frac{3}{10} = \frac{7-3}{10}$ Subtract the numerators.

$= \frac{4}{10}$ Simplify the numerator.

$= \frac{2}{5}$ Simplify the fraction.

EXAMPLE 3 Using a Verbal Model

Cookies A recipe for oatmeal cookies uses $\frac{5}{8}$ cup of raisins. You have only $\frac{3}{8}$ cup of raisins. How many more cups of raisins do you need?

Solution

Amount you need	=	Amount for recipe	−	Amount you have	
	=	$\frac{5}{8}$	−	$\frac{3}{8}$	Substitute amounts you know.
	=	$\frac{2}{8}$			Subtract the fractions.
	=	$\frac{1}{4}$			Simplify.

ANSWER You need $\frac{1}{4}$ cup of raisins.

Your turn now Find the difference. Simplify if possible.

5. $\frac{2}{3} - \frac{1}{3}$ $\frac{1}{3}$ 6. $\frac{7}{8} - \frac{5}{8}$ $\frac{1}{4}$ 7. $\frac{5}{12} - \frac{1}{12}$ $\frac{1}{3}$ 8. $\frac{8}{9} - \frac{5}{9}$ $\frac{1}{3}$

Hands-on *Activity*

GOAL
Use models to subtract mixed numbers by renaming.

MATERIALS
· colored pencils

Using Models to Subtract

Sometimes you need to rename mixed numbers when you subtract.

Explore Use models to find $3\frac{1}{4} - 1\frac{3}{4}$.

1 Draw a model of $3\frac{1}{4} - 1\frac{3}{4}$.

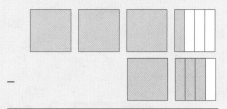

2 You can't subtract $\frac{3}{4}$ from $\frac{1}{4}$.
Redraw the model so that
you rename $3\frac{1}{4}$ as $2\frac{5}{4}$.

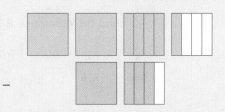

3 Use the model to find the difference.
$3\frac{1}{4} - 1\frac{3}{4} = 1\frac{2}{4}$, or $1\frac{1}{2}$

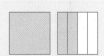

Your turn now Use models to find the difference. Simplify if possible.

1. $3\frac{1}{3} - 1\frac{2}{3}$ $1\frac{2}{3}$ **2.** $5\frac{1}{5} - 3\frac{4}{5}$ $1\frac{2}{5}$ **3.** $6\frac{1}{6} - 4\frac{5}{6}$ $1\frac{1}{3}$ **4.** $4\frac{3}{8} - 3\frac{7}{8}$ $\frac{1}{2}$

Stop *and* **Think**

5. Writing Explain why you must rename to find $8\frac{2}{5} - 4\frac{3}{5}$.

Then explain how to rename $8\frac{2}{5}$. The fraction in the first mixed number is less than the fraction in the second mixed number. You cannot subtract 3 from 2, so think of 8 as $7 + \frac{5}{5}$. Then $8\frac{2}{5}$ becomes $7\frac{7}{5}$.

---

1 PLAN

EXPLORE THE CONCEPT
• Students will use models to subtract mixed numbers.
• In Example 1 on page 290, students will use a model to rename a fraction.

MATERIALS
Each student will need colored pencils.

RECOMMENDED TIME
Work activity: 10 min
Discuss results: 5 min

GROUPING
Students should work individually.

2 TEACH

TIPS FOR SUCCESS
Emphasize that renaming fractions makes the whole-number part of a fraction decrease by 1.

3 CLOSE

 KEY DISCOVERY
Before subtracting, you may need to rename a mixed number so that the fraction part is an improper fraction.

ASSESSMENT
Use models to find the difference.
1. $4\frac{1}{8} - 1\frac{3}{4}$ $2\frac{3}{8}$
2. $3\frac{1}{8} - 2\frac{5}{8}$ $\frac{1}{2}$

SKILL CHECK

Find the sum or difference.

1. $\dfrac{9}{14} - \dfrac{3}{7}$ $\dfrac{3}{14}$

2. $\dfrac{4}{5} - \dfrac{7}{10}$ $\dfrac{1}{10}$

3. $\dfrac{4}{5} + \dfrac{7}{10}$ $1\dfrac{1}{2}$

4. $\dfrac{3}{8} + \dfrac{5}{6}$ $1\dfrac{5}{24}$

LESSON OBJECTIVE

Subtract mixed numbers by renaming.

PACING

Suggested Number of Days
Basic Course: 2 days
Average Course: 2 days
Advanced Course: 2 days
Block: 1 block

TEACHING RESOURCES

For a complete list of Teaching Resources, see page 264B.

TRANSPARENCY

Warm-Up Exercises for this lesson are available on a transparency.

2 TEACH

MOTIVATING THE LESSON

Models are a good learning tool for visual learners. Have students draw models like those at the beginning of the lesson to show the renaming of other mixed numbers.

LESSON 6.5

Subtracting Mixed Numbers by Renaming

BEFORE	**Now**	**WHY?**
You subtracted mixed numbers without renaming.	You'll subtract mixed numbers by renaming.	So you can study the lengths of snakes, as in Exs. 49–51.

Renaming When you subtract mixed numbers, as in Example 1, you may need to *rename* the first mixed number.

 Word Watch

Review Words

least common denominator (LCD), p. 239
mixed number, p. 244

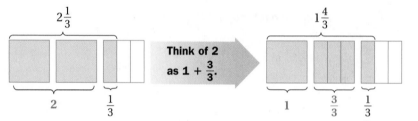

EXAMPLE 1   Subtracting Mixed Numbers

Find the difference $2\dfrac{1}{3} - 1\dfrac{2}{3}$.

You can't subtract $\dfrac{2}{3}$ from $\dfrac{1}{3}$. Think of $2\dfrac{1}{3}$ as $1 + \dfrac{3}{3} + \dfrac{1}{3}$.

$$
\begin{array}{rcl}
2\dfrac{1}{3} & = & 1\dfrac{4}{3} \qquad \text{Rename } 2\dfrac{1}{3} \text{ as } 1\dfrac{4}{3}. \\[2mm]
-1\dfrac{2}{3} & = & -1\dfrac{2}{3} \\[1mm]
\hline
 & & \dfrac{2}{3} \qquad \text{Subtract.}
\end{array}
$$

Subtracting Mixed Numbers

1. Rewrite the fractions using the LCD.
2. Rename if necessary.
3. Subtract. Simplify if possible.

Your turn now   Find the difference. Simplify if possible.

1. $6\dfrac{2}{7} - 4\dfrac{3}{7}$ $1\dfrac{6}{7}$ **2.** $3\dfrac{1}{4} - 1\dfrac{3}{4}$ $1\dfrac{1}{2}$ **3.** $6\dfrac{3}{8} - 3\dfrac{7}{8}$ $2\dfrac{1}{2}$ **4.** $2\dfrac{3}{5} - \dfrac{4}{5}$ $1\dfrac{4}{5}$

NCTM CURRICULUM STANDARDS
Standard 1: Understand numbers; Understand meanings of operations
Standard 6: Solve problems in math and other contexts

Renaming a Whole Number Sometimes you need to rename a whole number as a mixed number. To do this, rename one whole part as a fraction equal to 1.

EXAMPLE 2 **Subtracting from a Whole Number**

Find the difference $5 - 3\frac{1}{7}$.

Think of 5 as $4 + 1$, or $4 + \frac{7}{7}$.

$$
\begin{array}{rcl}
5 & = & 4\frac{7}{7} \qquad \text{Rename 5 as } 4\frac{7}{7}. \\
-3\frac{1}{7} & = & -3\frac{1}{7} \\
\hline
& & 1\frac{6}{7} \qquad \text{Subtract.}
\end{array}
$$

EXAMPLE 3 **Solving Subtraction Problems**

Horses The height of a horse is measured from its shoulders, as shown in the figure. How much taller is the Clydesdale than the Shetland?

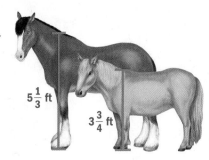

$5\frac{1}{3}$ ft

$3\frac{3}{4}$ ft

Solution
You need to find the difference $5\frac{1}{3} - 3\frac{3}{4}$. Use the LCD, 12.

$$
\begin{array}{rcccl}
5\frac{1}{3} & = & 5\frac{4}{12} & = & 4\frac{16}{12} \qquad \text{Rename } 5\frac{4}{12} \text{ as } 4\frac{16}{12}. \\
-3\frac{3}{4} & = & -3\frac{9}{12} & = & -3\frac{9}{12} \\
\hline
& & & & 1\frac{7}{12} \qquad \text{Subtract.}
\end{array}
$$

ANSWER The Clydesdale is $1\frac{7}{12}$ feet taller than the Shetland.

■ Horses

Horse heights are measured in hands and inches, where 1 hand = 4 inches. Suppose a horse is 15 hands tall. How tall is the horse in inches? **60 in.**

Your turn now **Find the difference. Simplify if possible.**

5. $3 - 2\frac{1}{2}$ $\frac{1}{2}$

6. $8 - 5\frac{3}{8}$ $2\frac{5}{8}$

7. $6\frac{1}{4} - 2\frac{3}{5}$ $3\frac{13}{20}$

8. $10\frac{2}{3} - 7\frac{5}{6}$ $2\frac{5}{6}$

292

③ APPLY

ASSIGNMENT GUIDE

Basic Course
Day 1: pp. 292–294 Exs. 10–18, 35–38, 41–44, 60–64
Day 2: pp. 292–294 Exs. 19–24, 26–34, 45–51, 55–59, 65

Average Course
Day 1: pp. 292–294 Exs. 10–18, 35–38, 43–46, 55–58
Day 2: pp. 292–294 Exs. 19–34, 39, 40, 49–52, 59–65

Advanced Course
Day 1: pp. 292–294 Exs. 10–18, 35–38, 57–59, 64
Day 2: pp. 292–294 Exs. 21–34, 40–45, 49–54*, 65

Block
pp. 292–294 Exs. 10–40, 43–46, 49–52, 55–65

EXTRA PRACTICE

- Student Edition, p. 713
- Chapter 6 Resource Book, pp. 45–47
- Test and Practice Generator

 TRANSPARENCY

Even-numbered answers are available on transparencies.

HOMEWORK CHECK

When you review students' homework for this lesson, go over the following exercises to check understanding of key concepts.
Basic: 10, 15, 20, 24, 26
Average: 10, 12, 16, 21, 26
Advanced: 11, 17, 22, 30, 36

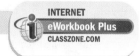
INTERNET
eWorkbook Plus
CLASSZONE.COM

6.5 Exercises
More Practice, p. 713

Getting Ready to Practice

Vocabulary Copy and complete the equivalent mixed number.

1. $2\frac{1}{6} = 1\frac{?}{6}$ 7
2. $4\frac{3}{5} = ?\frac{8}{5}$ 3
3. $5\frac{1}{3} = ?\frac{4}{3}$ 4
4. $3\frac{4}{7} = 2\frac{?}{7}$ 11

Find the difference. Simplify if possible.

5. $4\frac{1}{6} - 2\frac{5}{6}$ $1\frac{1}{3}$
6. $3\frac{5}{8} - \frac{7}{8}$ $2\frac{3}{4}$
7. $6 - 4\frac{1}{4}$ $1\frac{3}{4}$
8. $5 - \frac{2}{7}$ $4\frac{5}{7}$

9. Unicycles Members of a unicycle club are taking a two day trip. The trip is a total of $16\frac{1}{4}$ miles. If they travel $6\frac{1}{2}$ miles on the first day, how far will they travel on the second day? $9\frac{3}{4}$ mi

Practice and Problem Solving

A 10. What renaming do the models represent? $2\frac{3}{4} = 1\frac{7}{4}$

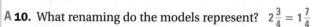

Find the difference.

11. $5\frac{3}{8} - 2\frac{7}{8}$ $2\frac{1}{2}$
12. $6\frac{1}{4} - 1\frac{3}{4}$ $4\frac{1}{2}$
13. $5\frac{4}{7} - \frac{6}{7}$ $4\frac{5}{7}$
14. $9\frac{2}{5} - 7\frac{4}{5}$ $1\frac{3}{5}$

15. $4 - 1\frac{7}{8}$ $2\frac{1}{8}$
16. $9 - 4\frac{3}{10}$ $4\frac{7}{10}$
17. $10 - \frac{8}{15}$ $9\frac{7}{15}$
18. $7 - \frac{5}{6}$ $6\frac{1}{6}$

19. $3\frac{1}{7} - 1\frac{1}{2}$ $1\frac{9}{14}$
20. $4\frac{1}{5} - 3\frac{2}{3}$ $\frac{8}{15}$
21. $5\frac{1}{2} - 4\frac{3}{4}$ $\frac{3}{4}$
22. $8\frac{1}{3} - \frac{7}{9}$ $7\frac{5}{9}$

23. Roads A road sign says that you are $1\frac{3}{4}$ miles from Exit 1 and $3\frac{1}{2}$ miles from Exit 2. How far is Exit 2 from Exit 1? $1\frac{3}{4}$ mi

24. Pogo Sticks Your friend can jump 5 inches high on a pogo stick. You can jump $3\frac{2}{3}$ inches high. How much higher can your friend jump? $1\frac{1}{3}$ in.

25. Find the Error Describe and correct the error in the solution. See margin.

$$4\frac{2}{5} - 1\frac{4}{5} = 4\frac{7}{5} - 1\frac{4}{5}$$
$$= 3\frac{3}{5}$$

---

25. *Sample answer:*

$4\frac{2}{5}$ should be renamed as $3\frac{7}{5}$; the solution should be

$4\frac{2}{5} - 1\frac{4}{5} = 3\frac{7}{5} - 1\frac{4}{5}$
$= 2\frac{3}{5}$.

HELP with Homework

Example	Exercises
1	10–14; 25–33, 40
2	15–18, 24, 34–39
3	19–23; 26–33

Online Resources
CLASSZONE.COM
· More Examples
· eTutorial Plus

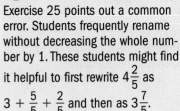

COMMON ERROR

Exercise 25 points out a common error. Students frequently rename without decreasing the whole number by 1. These students might find it helpful to first rewrite $4\frac{2}{5}$ as $3 + \frac{5}{5} + \frac{2}{5}$ and then as $3\frac{7}{5}$.

Number Sense Tell whether you need to rename the whole part and the fraction in the first mixed number to subtract. Explain.

26–33. See margin.

26. $6\frac{1}{4} - 3\frac{1}{2}$ 27. $7\frac{1}{2} - 2\frac{5}{6}$ 28. $8\frac{7}{10} - \frac{3}{10}$ 29. $8\frac{4}{7} - 3\frac{5}{7}$

30. $5 - 2\frac{1}{3}$ 31. $4\frac{2}{5} - 3$ 32. $7\frac{5}{8} - 6\frac{1}{6}$ 33. $9\frac{2}{3} - 4\frac{3}{4}$

34. **Blue Crabs** A fisherman catches a blue crab that is $2\frac{1}{3}$ inches wide. Blue crabs that are less than 5 inches wide are returned to the water. How much wider must the crab be before it will be 5 inches wide? $2\frac{2}{3}$ in.

Mental Math Find the difference using mental math.

B 35. $6 - 5\frac{3}{4}$ $\frac{1}{4}$ 36. $8 - 7\frac{2}{3}$ $\frac{1}{3}$ 37. $4 - 3\frac{7}{8}$ $\frac{1}{8}$ 38. $3 - 2\frac{5}{7}$ $\frac{2}{7}$

39. **Hockey** A professional ice hockey goal is 4 feet tall. You buy a hockey goal that is $3\frac{2}{3}$ feet tall. How much taller is the professional goal? $\frac{1}{3}$ ft

40. **Critical Thinking** When subtracting mixed numbers, how do you know whether you need to rename? See margin.

26. Yes; you cannot subtract $\frac{1}{2}$ from $\frac{1}{4}$.

27. Yes; you cannot subtract $\frac{5}{6}$ from $\frac{1}{2}$.

28. No; you can subtract $\frac{3}{10}$ from $\frac{7}{10}$.

29. Yes; you cannot subtract $\frac{5}{7}$ from $\frac{4}{7}$.

30. Yes; you cannot subtract $\frac{1}{3}$ from 0.

31. No; you can subtract 0 from $\frac{2}{5}$.

32. No; you can subtract $\frac{1}{6}$ from $\frac{5}{8}$.

33. Yes; you cannot subtract $\frac{3}{4}$ from $\frac{2}{3}$.

 Algebra Evaluate the expression when $x = 3\frac{5}{6}$ and $y = 6\frac{1}{4}$.

41. $5\frac{1}{6} - x$ $1\frac{1}{3}$ 42. $x - 1\frac{7}{8}$ $1\frac{23}{24}$ 43. $8\frac{1}{5} - y$ $1\frac{19}{20}$ 44. $y - 2\frac{3}{4}$ $3\frac{1}{2}$

45. $8 - x$ $4\frac{1}{6}$ 46. $4 - x$ $\frac{1}{6}$ 47. $7 - y$ $\frac{3}{4}$ 48. $10 - y$ $3\frac{3}{4}$

Snakes In Exercises 49–51, use the table at the right. It shows the lengths of four snakes at a zoo exhibit.

49. How much longer is the green water snake than the southern ringneck snake? $21\frac{3}{4}$ in.

50. How much longer is the checkered garter snake than the northern brown snake? $8\frac{1}{6}$ in.

51. The glossy crayfish snake is one half inch shorter than the checkered garter snake. How long is the glossy crayfish snake? $19\frac{1}{2}$ in.

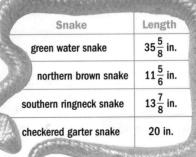

Snake	Length
green water snake	$35\frac{5}{8}$ in.
northern brown snake	$11\frac{5}{6}$ in.
southern ringneck snake	$13\frac{7}{8}$ in.
checkered garter snake	20 in.

C 52. **Writing** You are subtracting a mixed number from a whole number. Describe how to find the fraction you should use when you rename the whole number. See margin.

TEACHING TIP

In Exercises 45–48, students may need extra practice renaming a whole number as another whole number plus a fraction. Use an example such as $3 = 2 + \frac{4}{4}$ and tell students to think of the whole number as a mixed number with the fraction part having the same denominator as the fraction being subtracted.

40. *Sample answer:* When you can't subtract the fraction in the second mixed number from the fraction in the first mixed number, then you need to rename.

52. *Sample answer:* The fraction should have the same numerator and denominator as the denominator in the mixed number being subtracted.

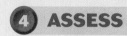
For more assessment resources, see:
- Assessment Book
- Test and Practice Generator

MINI-QUIZ

Find the difference.

1. $6\frac{3}{8} - 3\frac{7}{8}$ $2\frac{1}{2}$

2. $6 - 3\frac{1}{10}$ $2\frac{9}{10}$

3. $7\frac{3}{4} - 2\frac{7}{8}$ $4\frac{7}{8}$

4. Town A is $3\frac{1}{4}$ miles from Town B. Town B is $2\frac{7}{8}$ miles from Town C. How much further is it from Town A to Town B than from Town B to Town C? $\frac{3}{8}$ mi

5. Evaluate $6 - x$ when $x = 2\frac{3}{4}$. $3\frac{1}{4}$

5 FOLLOW-UP

RETEACHING/REMEDIATION

- Study Guide in Chapter 6 Resource Book, pp. 48–49
- Tutor Place, Fractions Card 14
- eTutorial Plus Online
- Extra Practice, p. 713
- Lesson Practice in Chapter 6 Resource Book, pp. 45–47

CHALLENGE/ENRICHMENT

- Challenge Practice in Chapter 6 Resource Book, p. 50
- Teacher's Edition, p. 264F

ENGLISH LEARNER SUPPORT

- Spanish Study Guide
- Multi-Language Glossary
- Chapter Audio Summaries CDs

294

Challenge Some of the tallest trees in Massachusetts can be found in the Mohawk Trail State Forest.

53. A White Pine is $47\frac{3}{10}$ feet taller than an American Basswood, which is $7\frac{7}{10}$ feet shorter than a Northern Red Oak. If the Northern Red Oak is 119 feet tall, how tall is the White Pine? $158\frac{3}{5}$ ft

54. **Explain** A White Ash is $13\frac{4}{5}$ feet shorter than the White Pine in Exercise 53. Is it *taller* or *shorter* than the Northern Red Oak in Exercise 53? How much taller or shorter? Explain your method.

taller; $25\frac{4}{5}$ ft; draw a picture

Mixed Review

Find the sum. *(Lesson 6.4)*

55. $3\frac{7}{9} + 1\frac{1}{3}$ $5\frac{1}{9}$ 56. $4\frac{2}{5} + 4\frac{7}{10}$ $9\frac{1}{10}$ 57. $1\frac{7}{12} + 2\frac{1}{6}$ $3\frac{3}{4}$ 58. $7\frac{5}{6} + 5\frac{1}{2}$ $13\frac{1}{3}$

Choose a Strategy Use a strategy from the list to solve the following problem. Explain your choice of strategy.

> **Problem Solving Strategies**
> - Guess, Check, and Revise
> - Draw a Diagram
> - Make a Table
> - Solve a Simpler Problem

59. 3.3 m. *Sample answer:* I used Draw a Diagram because the picture helped me see what I needed to find.

59. The perimeter of a triangle is 9.8 meters. One side of the triangle is 3.2 meters. The other two sides have the same length. Find the length of the other two sides.

Basic Skills   Copy and complete the statement.

60. 8 minutes = ? seconds   480   61. 290 min = ? hours ? min   4; 50

62. 343 sec = ? min ? sec   5; 43   63. 11 hours = ? minutes   660

Test-Taking Practice

64. **Multiple Choice** What is the value of the expression $6\frac{2}{3} - 5\frac{3}{4}$?   B

   A. $\frac{1}{12}$ B. $\frac{11}{12}$ C. $1\frac{1}{12}$ D. $1\frac{11}{12}$

65. **Multiple Choice** A jar contains $2\frac{1}{2}$ cups of honey. You pour $1\frac{3}{5}$ cups into a bowl. How many cups of honey are left in the jar?   I

   F. $\frac{1}{10}$ cup   G. $\frac{2}{3}$ cup   H. $\frac{3}{5}$ cup   I. $\frac{9}{10}$ cup

Technology Activity

Using the Internet

GOAL Use the Internet to find information.

 Example **You can use an Internet search engine to find information about paper sizes.**

Some common paper sizes are U.S. letter (11 in. $\times$ $8\frac{1}{2}$ in.) and European A4. What

are the dimensions of A4 paper? How does this size compare to the U.S. letter size?

Solution

Choose a search engine. Type in the key words and phrases that are likely to generate a list of Web sites that give the dimensions of A4 paper, in inches. Then examine the list of sites until you find the information you need.

Find the difference in length and in width of the paper sizes.

"paper sizes", A4, inches, fraction	Search

Paper size	Dimensions (length by width)
A4	$11\frac{2}{3}$ in. $\times$ $8\frac{1}{4}$ in.

difference in length

$$11\frac{2}{3} \quad \text{(A4)}$$
$$\underline{-11} \quad \text{(U.S. letter)}$$
$$\frac{2}{3}$$

difference in width

$$8\frac{1}{2} = 8\frac{2}{4} \quad \text{(U.S. letter)}$$
$$-8\frac{1}{4} = -8\frac{1}{4} \quad \text{(A4)}$$
$$\frac{1}{4}$$

ANSWER The A4 size is $\frac{2}{3}$ inch longer, and the U.S. letter size is $\frac{1}{4}$ inch wider.

Your turn now **Use the Internet to find information about the paper sizes. Then find the difference in length and in width.**

1. A5 and A4   **2.** B5 and A5   **3.** legal and letter

 **with Technology**

Your search engine may have special features to help make a search more precise. Read its Help section for alternative search methods.

1. The A4 size is $2\frac{3}{8}$ inches wider and $3\frac{5}{12}$ inches longer.

2. The B5 size is $1\frac{1}{8}$ inches wider and $1\frac{5}{8}$ inches longer.

3. The two sizes are the same width, and the U.S. legal size is 3 inches longer.

Lesson 6.5   Subtracting Mixed Numbers by Renaming   **295**

Work Backward is an appropriate strategy for students to use when they need information that will lead to a known result. Students are told the result and asked to determine what led to the result. To use this strategy, students start with the result and retrace steps backward. An advantage of this strategy is that it makes sense to students.

2 TEACH

GUIDING STUDENTS' WORK

You may need to remind students to be sure to use the opposite arithmetic operation when retracing their steps. You may want to practice naming the opposite operation: the opposite of multiplication is division; the opposite of addition is subtraction; the opposite of doubling is taking one half, and so on.

EXTRA EXAMPLES

Example You have $320 in your savings account. You started with $100 and then saved $10 per week. How many weeks did you save? **22 weeks**

6.6 Problem Solving Strategies

- Guess, Check, and Revise
- Draw a Diagram
- Perform an Experiment
- Make a List
- Work Backward
- Make a Table
- Look for a Pattern

Work Backward

Problem Your friend is playing a video game and pauses to take a break. After the break, you continue the game and double the current score by crossing a rickety bridge. Next you earn 30 points twice for collecting treasure. Then you lose 15 points for slipping while climbing a mountain. You finish with 155 points. How many points did your friend have right before the break?

1 Read and Understand

Read the problem carefully.

- You have 155 points at the end of the game.
- You want to know how many points your friend had before the break.

2 Make a Plan

Decide on a strategy to use.

One way to solve the problem is to work backward. To do this, start with the end result and retrace your steps.

3 Solve the Problem

Reread the problem and work backward.

You have 155 points at the end of the video game.

You lost 15 points on a mountain, so add 15 points to 155.

- Total points + Points lost on mountain = $155 + 15 = 170$

You gained 30 points twice for treasure, so subtract 60 points from 170.

- $170 -$ Points for collecting treasure $= 170 - 60 = 110$

You doubled your score at a bridge, so find half of 110 points.

- $110 \div 2 = 55$

ANSWER Your friend had 55 points before the break.

4 Look Back

Start with 55 points and check to be sure that your final score is 155.

$155 \stackrel{?}{=} 55 \times 2 + 2 \times 30 - 15$

$155 \stackrel{?}{=} 110 + 60 - 15$

$155 = 155$

NCTM CURRICULUM STANDARDS

Standard 1: Understand how operations are related

Standard 6: Apply/adapt strategies to solve problems

Standard 7: Use types of reasoning/methods of proof

Practice the Strategy

Use the strategy *work backward*.

1. **Agility Course** Your dog has a total of 335 points after 4 agility course events. The dog earned 77 points in the last event, 95 points in the third event, and 84 points in the second event. How many points did your dog earn in the first event? **79 points**

2. **Lunch** You have $4.25 at the end of a school day. You spent $2.75 for lunch. After lunch, a friend gave you $1.50 that he owed you. How much money did you have before lunch? **$5.50**

3. **Number Sense** What number belongs in the blank? **60**

   $(\underline{\ ?\ } \div 5) \times 9 + 42 = 150$

4. **Street Maps** To get from the bus stop to the park, you walk 2 blocks north, then 3 blocks west, and then 1 block north. Which point on the map below represents the bus stop? **D**

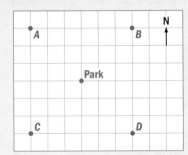

5. **Calendars** Today is Tuesday. You had a track meet 3 days ago. Your friend's party was 8 days before the track meet. Your piano recital was 2 days before the party. On which day of the week was the recital? **Wednesday**

Mixed Problem Solving

Use any strategy to solve the problem.

6. **Sandwiches** Your friend can make 3 sandwiches per minute. You can make 2 sandwiches per minute. How many more sandwiches can your friend make than you in 10 minutes? **10 sandwiches**

7. **Number Puzzle** Remove only one number from each row so that the sum of the remaining numbers in each row is the same. **Row 1: remove 8; Row 2: remove 3; Row 3: remove 6**

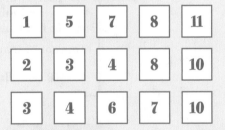

8. **Skateboarding** The mean score for your skateboarding run is 92.5. Three of the four judges gave you scores of 92, 89, and 95. What score did the fourth judge give you? **94**

9. **Patios** The floor area of a patio is 48 square yards. You paint a 2 yard by 2 yard square at each corner of the floor using red paint. You paint the rest of the floor white. What area of the floor is white? **32 yd²**

TEACHING TIP
You may want to have students write a verbal problem to go with the equation in Exercise 3. This should help them understand how to work backwards from a result.

MATH REASONING
For Exercise 5, students should be able to reason that one way to work backwards is to count every 7 days as a week so that each group of 7 previous days will fall on a Tuesday. They can use this fact to work through the problem more quickly.

SUGGESTED STRATEGIES
You may wish to suggest the following strategies for the problems in the Mixed Problem Solving:
- Exercise 6: Make a Table, Look for a Pattern
- Exercise 7: Guess, Check, and Revise, Perform an Experiment
- Exercise 8: Guess, Check, and Revise, Work Backward
- Exercise 9: Draw a Diagram, Work Backward

SKILL CHECK
1. $32 + 60 = \underline{?}$ 92
2. $25 + 60 = \underline{?}$ 85
3. $82 - 48 = \underline{?}$ 34
4. $105 - 57 = \underline{?}$ 48

LESSON OBJECTIVE
Add and subtract measures of time.

PACING
Suggested Number of Days
Basic Course: 2 days
Average Course: 2 days
Advanced Course: 2 days
Block: 1 block

TEACHING RESOURCES
For a complete list of Teaching Resources, see page 264B.

 TRANSPARENCY
Warm-Up Exercises for this lesson are available on a transparency.

2 TEACH

MOTIVATING THE LESSON
Give students other examples where they need to add or subtract times.

TIPS FOR NEW TEACHERS
Point out the similarity to rewriting and renaming when students add and subtract mixed numbers. See Tips for New Teachers in the *Chapter 6 Resource Book.*

LESSON 6.6 Measures of Time

BEFORE	▶ Now	WHY?
You added and subtracted fractions and mixed numbers.	You'll add and subtract measures of time.	So you can study time zones, as in Exs. 26 and 27.

In the Real World

 **Word Watch**
elapsed time, p. 299

Tour de France Lance Armstrong won the 2001 Tour de France in 86 hours, 17 minutes, and 28 seconds. Jan Ullrich finished 6 minutes and 44 seconds later. What was Jan Ullrich's time?

When you add or subtract measures of time, use the information below.

1 hour (h) = 60 minutes (min)

1 minute (min) = 60 seconds (sec)

EXAMPLE 1   Adding Measures of Time

To answer the real-world question above, add 6 minutes and 44 seconds to 86 hours, 17 minutes, and 28 seconds.

```
   86 h  17 min  28 sec
+         6 min  44 sec
   86 h  23 min  72 sec
```
Add the hours, the minutes, and the seconds.

Think of 72 sec as 1 min 12 sec. Then add 1 min to 23 min.

ANSWER Jan Ullrich's time was 86 hours, 24 minutes, and 12 seconds.

EXAMPLE 2   Subtracting Measures of Time

```
  11 h  17 min
−  8 h  42 min
```

 Think of 11 h 17 min as 10 h 77 min.

```
  10 h  77 min    Rename.
−  8 h  42 min
   2 h  35 min    Subtract.
```

 **Your turn now**   Add or subtract the measures of time.

1.
```
   5 h  29 min   8 sec
+  2 h  45 min  33 sec
   8 h  14 min  41 sec
```

2.
```
   3 min  26 sec
−  1 min  40 sec
   1 min  46 sec
```

NCTM CURRICULUM STANDARDS
Standard 4: Understand the units of measurement; Apply proper techniques to find measures
Standard 6: Solve problems in math and other contexts

Elapsed Time The amount of time between a start time and an end time is called **elapsed time**. To find elapsed time, think about the number of hours that pass, then the number of minutes that pass.

EXAMPLE 3 **Finding Elapsed Time**

Winter Solstice The winter solstice occurs on the day with the least amount of daylight. Suppose that on this day, the sun rises at 7:15 A.M. and sets at 4:22 P.M. How long does the daylight last?

Solution

Break the problem into parts.

① Find the elapsed time from 7:15 A.M. to 12:00 P.M.

7:15 A.M.		11:15 A.M.		12:00 P.M.
	4 h →		45 min →	

② Find the elapsed time from 12:00 P.M. to 4:22 P.M.

12:00 P.M.		4:00 P.M.		4:22 P.M.
	4 h →		22 min →	

③ Add the two elapsed times.

$$\begin{array}{r} 4\text{ h }\ 45\text{ min} \\ +\ 4\text{ h }\ 22\text{ min} \\ \hline 8\text{ h }\ 67\text{ min} \end{array}$$

Think of 67 min as 1 h 7 min. Then add 1 h to 8 h.

ANSWER The daylight lasts for 9 hours and 7 minutes.

Watch Out!

You can't always subtract two times to find elapsed time. For example, to find the elapsed time from 8:00 A.M. to 4:25 P.M., you can't compute 4 h 25 min − 8 h. You need to break the problem into parts.

Your turn now Find the elapsed time.

3. 6:00 A.M. to 11:00 A.M. **5 h**   **4.** 7:30 A.M. to 11:45 A.M. **4 h 15 min**

5. 11:45 A.M. to 2:15 P.M. **2 h 30 min**   **6.** 8:50 P.M. to 3:30 A.M. **6 h 40 min**

7. Your bus leaves Glenwood Station at 9:23 A.M. and arrives at Park Station at 10:08 A.M. How long is the bus ride? **45 min**

EXTRA EXAMPLES

Example 1 A triathlon athlete had the following times for her events: 23 minutes, 18 minutes 25 seconds, and 1 minute 45 seconds. What was her total time? **43 min 10 sec**

Example 2 Subtract.
$$\begin{array}{r} 13\text{ h }18\text{ min} \\ -\ 7\text{ h }39\text{ min} \\ \hline 5\text{ h }39\text{ min} \end{array}$$

Example 3 A seed germinates between the hours of 6:30 A.M. and 7:14 P.M., when it sprouts. Find the elapsed time. **12 h 44 min**

VISUALIZE

Ask students to use the clock in the classroom to help them visualize how to find elapsed time.

CONCEPT CHECK

Find the elapsed time from 9:30 A.M. to 4:45 P.M. **7 h 15 min**

DAILY PUZZLER

A clock lets you know the hour by striking a gong. If it takes 5 seconds to strike 6 o'clock, how many seconds will it take to strike 10 o'clock? **9 sec**

300

ASSIGNMENT GUIDE

Basic Course
Day 1: pp. 300–301 Exs. 11–16, 26–28, 37–43
Day 2: pp. 300–301 Exs. 17–25, 31–36

Average Course
Day 1: pp. 300–301 Exs. 11–16, 26–29, 39–43
Day 2: pp. 300–301 Exs. 17–25, 31–38

Advanced Course
Day 1: pp. 300–301 Exs. 11–16, 26–32*, 43
Day 2: pp. 300–301 Exs. 17–25, 33–38

Block
pp. 300–301 Exs. 11–29, 31–43

EXTRA PRACTICE

• Student Edition, p. 713
• Chapter 6 Resource Book, pp. 57–59
• Test and Practice Generator

 TRANSPARENCY

Even-numbered answers are available on transparencies.

HOMEWORK CHECK

When you review students' homework for this lesson, go over the following exercises to check understanding of key concepts.
Basic: 12, 14, 17, 21, 23
Average: 12, 15, 18, 22, 24
Advanced: 13, 19, 23, 24, 25

 COMMON ERROR

In Exercises 21 and 22, caution students that the first time is before noon and the second time is after noon. Stress that they should count from the A.M. time to noon and then count from noon to the P.M. time.

 **Exercises**
More Practice, p. 713

Getting Ready to Practice

Vocabulary Copy and complete the statement.

1. 120 min = _?_ h 2
2. 3 min = _?_ sec 180
3. 300 sec = _?_ min 5
4. 4 h = _?_ min 240

Add or subtract the measures of time.

5. 4 h 24 min
− 2 h 48 min
1 h 36 min

6. 3 min 35 sec
+ 2 min 50 sec
6 min 25 sec

7. 1 h 25 min 52 sec
+ 5 h 5 min 30 sec
6 h 31 min 22 sec

Find the elapsed time.

8. 7:00 A.M. to 10:00 A.M. 3 h
9. 9:30 P.M. to 2:45 A.M. 5 h 15 min

10. Snorkeling You went snorkeling from 9:30 A.M. to 11:15 A.M. How long did you snorkel? 1 h 45 min

Practice and Problem Solving

Add or subtract the measures of time.

A 11. 2 h 50 min
+   35 min
3 h 25 min

12. 4 h 38 min
+ 3 h 22 min
8 h

13. 3 h 12 min 53 sec
+ 2 h 20 min 42 sec
5 h 33 min 35 sec

14. 4 h 25 min
− 1 h 31 min
2 h 54 min

15. 5 h 10 min
− 2 h 55 min
2 h 15 min

16. 3 h 2 min
−   58 min 12 sec
2 h 3 min 48 sec

Find the elapsed time.

17. 1:00 P.M. to 3:00 P.M. 2 h
18. 2:30 A.M. to 6:35 A.M. 4 h 5 min
19. 5:10 A.M. to 9:45 A.M. 4 h 35 min
20. 1:45 P.M. to 10:50 P.M. 9 h 5 min
21. 9:30 A.M. to 5:20 P.M. 7 h 50 min
22. 11:20 A.M. to 8:15 P.M. 8 h 55 min

 **with Homework**

Example	Exercises
1	11–16, 23
2	11–16, 24
3	17–22, 25

Online Resources
CLASSZONE.COM
· More Examples
· eTutorial Plus

23. Baseball The first game of a baseball double-header lasts 2 hours and 35 minutes. The second game lasts 3 hours and 45 minutes. How long is the double-header? 6 h and 20 min

24. Trains The first part of a train ride lasts 3 hours. The second part lasts 1 hour and 8 minutes. How much longer is the first part? 1 h and 52 min

B 25. Meteors You watch a meteor shower from 11:50 P.M. to 1:25 A.M. How long do you watch the meteor shower? 1 h 35 min

Time Zones The map shows four standard time zones in the United States. Each time zone differs from the next by one hour.

26. If it is 12:30 P.M. in Chicago, what time is it in Denver? **11:30 A.M.**

27. **Decide** Your plane leaves New York at 9:10 A.M., Eastern Standard Time. The flight lasts 5 hours and 30 minutes. Will you land in Los Angeles by 1:00 P.M., Pacific Standard Time? **yes**

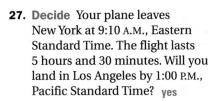

Los Angeles (Pacific)   Denver (Mountain)   Chicago (Central)   New York (Eastern)

28. **Working Backward** You are playing a role in a school play that begins at 7:30 P.M. It takes you 15 minutes to get into costume, 35 minutes to do your makeup, and 20 minutes to fix your hair. By what time should you start getting ready? **6:20 P.M.**

29. **Writing** A movie starts at 7:50 P.M. and runs for 135 minutes. At what time does the movie end? Show how you found your answer. **10:05 P.M.**

30. **Challenge** You use your cell phone from 11:57 A.M. to 1:23 P.M. Before the call, you had 941 free minutes left on your calling plan for the month. How much free calling time, in hours, do you have left after the call? Write your answer as a mixed number. $14\frac{1}{4}$ **h**

Mixed Review

Test the number for divisibility by 6. *(Lesson 5.1)*

31. 42 **yes**   32. 64 **no**   33. 261 **no**   34. 5800 **no**

Find the difference. *(Lesson 6.5)*

35. $6\frac{5}{8} - 5\frac{7}{8}$ $\frac{3}{4}$ 36. $8 - 3\frac{4}{7}$ $4\frac{3}{7}$ 37. $4\frac{1}{6} - 2\frac{5}{9}$ $1\frac{11}{18}$ 38. $6\frac{1}{4} - 1\frac{7}{10}$ $4\frac{11}{20}$

Basic Skills **Find the product.**

39. 4×80 **320**   40. 9×500 **4500**   41. 6×300 **1800**   42. 7×1000 **7000**

Test-Taking Practice

INTERNET
State Test Practice
CLASSZONE.COM

43. **Extended Response** The first part of a plane trip lasts 3 hours and 49 minutes. The second part lasts 2 hours and 14 minutes. You have a 50 minute break between flights. How long does the whole trip last? How much longer is the first part than the second part? Explain.

    6 h 53 min; 1 h 35 min; subtract the second time from the first time

Lesson 6.6   Measures of Time   **301**

4 ASSESS

ASSESSMENT RESOURCES
For more assessment resources, see:
• Assessment Book
• Test and Practice Generator

MINI-QUIZ
Add or subtract the measures of time.

1. 3 h 45 min + 32 min
   4 h 17 min

2. 6 h 32 min + 2 h 48 min
   9 h 20 min

3. 5 h 18 min − 2 h 31 min
   2 h 47 min

4. 9 h 22 min 24 sec − 4 h 18 min 52 sec   **5 h 3 min 32 sec**

Find the elapsed time.

5. 4:00 P.M. to 7:30 P.M.
   3 h 30 min

6. 8:30 A.M. to 2:45 P.M.
   6 h 15 min

7. You visit the zoo from 11:15 A.M. to 3:22 P.M. Find the elapsed time.   **4 h 7 min**

5 FOLLOW-UP

RETEACHING/REMEDIATION
• Study Guide in Chapter 6 Resource Book, pp. 60–61
• eTutorial Plus Online
• Extra Practice, p. 713
• Lesson Practice in Chapter 6 Resource Book, pp. 57–59

CHALLENGE/ENRICHMENT
• Challenge Practice in Chapter 6 Resource Book, p. 63
• Teacher's Edition, p. 264F

ENGLISH LEARNER SUPPORT
• Spanish Study Guide
• Multi-Language Glossary
• Chapter Audio Summaries CDs

LESSONS 6.4 TO 6.6 Notebook Review

Review the vocabulary definitions in your notebook.

Copy the review examples in your notebook. Then complete the exercises.

Check Your Definitions

simplest form, p. 229

least common denominator, p. 239

mixed number, p. 244

elapsed time, p. 299

Use Your Vocabulary

1. **Writing** Explain why the mixed number $3\frac{1}{3}$ is equivalent to the mixed number $2\frac{4}{3}$. *Sample answer:* 3 can be rewritten as $2\frac{3}{3}$, so $3\frac{1}{3}$ is equal to $2\frac{4}{3}$.

2. Copy and complete: The amount of time between a start time and an end time is called ? . **elapsed time**

6.4–6.5 Can you add and subtract mixed numbers?

 EXAMPLE Find the sum.

$$3\frac{7}{8} \quad = \quad 3\frac{7}{8} \quad = \quad 3\frac{7}{8}$$
$$+\,4\frac{3}{4} \quad = \quad +\,4\frac{3\times2}{4\times2} \quad = \quad +\,4\frac{6}{8} \qquad \text{Rewrite using the LCD, 8.}$$
$$7\frac{13}{8}, \text{ or } 8\frac{5}{8} \qquad \text{Add. Think of } 7\frac{13}{8} \text{ as } 7 + 1\frac{5}{8}.$$

 EXAMPLE Find the difference.

$$9\frac{2}{9} \quad = \quad 8\frac{11}{9} \qquad \text{Rename } 9\frac{2}{9} \text{ as } 8\frac{11}{9}.$$
$$-\,4\frac{5}{9} \quad = \quad -\,4\frac{5}{9}$$
$$4\frac{6}{9}, \text{ or } 4\frac{2}{3} \qquad \text{Subtract and simplify.}$$

☑ **Find the sum or difference.**

3. $1\frac{4}{7} + 7\frac{1}{7}$ $8\frac{5}{7}$ **4.** $2\frac{5}{12} + 6\frac{7}{8}$ $9\frac{7}{24}$ **5.** $8\frac{17}{28} - 3\frac{1}{4}$ $5\frac{5}{14}$ **6.** $9\frac{8}{9} - 4\frac{2}{9}$ $5\frac{2}{3}$

7. $5\frac{1}{4} - 2\frac{2}{3}$ $2\frac{7}{12}$ **8.** $11\frac{1}{5} - 8\frac{1}{3}$ $2\frac{13}{15}$ **9.** $6 - 4\frac{5}{8}$ $1\frac{3}{8}$ **10.** $3 - 1\frac{3}{5}$ $1\frac{2}{5}$

6.6 Can you add and subtract measures of time?

Review

EXAMPLE Find the elapsed time from 9:40 A.M. to 5:35 P.M.

2 h 20 min Find the elapsed time from 9:40 A.M. to 12:00 P.M.
+ 5 h 35 min Find the elapsed time from 12:00 P.M. to 5:35 P.M.
7 h 55 min Add the elapsed times.

✓ **Find the elapsed time.**

11. 7:45 A.M. to
2:00 P.M.
6 h 15 min

12. 5:30 P.M. to
1:45 A.M.
8 h 15 min

Stop *and* **Think**   about Lessons 6.4–6.6

13. Critical Thinking How is adding and subtracting measures of
time similar to adding and subtracting mixed numbers?
Sample answer: sometimes you have to rename

Review Quiz 2

Find the sum or difference.

1. $9\frac{3}{5} + 7\frac{1}{5}$ $16\frac{4}{5}$ **2.** $3\frac{9}{17} + 11$ $14\frac{9}{17}$ **3.** $5\frac{3}{8} + 2\frac{1}{6}$ $7\frac{13}{24}$ **4.** $2\frac{3}{10} + 8\frac{3}{4}$ $11\frac{1}{20}$

5. $9\frac{5}{7} - 3\frac{2}{7}$ $6\frac{3}{7}$ **6.** $10\frac{11}{12} - 4\frac{3}{4}$ $6\frac{1}{6}$ **7.** $5\frac{1}{3} - 1\frac{4}{9}$ $3\frac{8}{9}$ **8.** $6 - 2\frac{1}{8}$ $3\frac{7}{8}$

9. Sleep A baby sleeps from 10:18 A.M. to 12:05 P.M., from 4:10 P.M. to
5:25 P.M., and from 9:36 P.M. to 6:10 A.M. Find the total sleep time.
11 h 36 min

Magic Square

In the magic square at the right,
the sum of each row, column,
and diagonal is the same. Copy
and complete the magic square.

Chapter Review

 **Vocabulary**

fraction, p. 228
simplest form, p. 229

least common
   denominator, p. 239
mixed number, p. 244

improper fraction, p. 244
elapsed time, p. 299
round, p. 686

Vocabulary Review

Copy and complete the statement.

1. You usually round fractions to the nearest __?__ and __?__ to the nearest whole number. **half; mixed numbers**

2. If the sum of two fractions is an __?__, you rewrite it as a mixed number. **improper fraction**

3. The amount of time between a start time and an end time is called __?__. **elapsed time**

4. To add or subtract fractions and mixed numbers with different denominators, you first need to find the __?__. **LCD**

Review Questions

Estimate the sum or difference. *(Lesson 6.1)* **5–13. Estimates may vary.**

5. $\frac{8}{9} + \frac{4}{7}$ $1\frac{1}{2}$

6. $\frac{1}{6} + \frac{7}{8}$ 1

7. $\frac{11}{12} - \frac{1}{5}$ 1

8. $\frac{9}{10} - \frac{4}{9}$ $\frac{1}{2}$

9. $1\frac{5}{6} + 10\frac{1}{4}$ 12

10. $11\frac{4}{5} + 8\frac{3}{4}$ 21

11. $6\frac{1}{12} - 3\frac{5}{16}$ 3

12. $9\frac{1}{3} - 2\frac{8}{11}$ 6

13. Concert A music concert features two singers. The first singer performs for $1\frac{3}{4}$ hours, and the second singer performs for $2\frac{2}{3}$ hours. Estimate the total number of hours of singing at the concert. *(Lesson 6.1)* **5 h**

Find the sum or difference. *(Lessons 6.2, 6.3)*

14. $\frac{3}{9} + \frac{5}{9}$ $\frac{8}{9}$

15. $\frac{5}{6} + \frac{5}{6}$ $1\frac{2}{3}$

16. $\frac{3}{5} - \frac{1}{5}$ $\frac{2}{5}$

17. $\frac{9}{10} - \frac{3}{10}$ $\frac{3}{5}$

18. $\frac{7}{12} + \frac{3}{4}$ $1\frac{1}{3}$

19. $\frac{1}{3} + \frac{4}{15}$ $\frac{3}{5}$

20. $\frac{2}{3} - \frac{1}{4}$ $\frac{5}{12}$

21. $\frac{7}{10} - \frac{3}{5}$ $\frac{1}{10}$

22. Bike Relay You and a friend are competing in a two part bike relay. You bike $\frac{4}{5}$ mile in the first part. Your friend bikes $\frac{2}{3}$ mile in the second part. How many miles long is the bike relay? *(Lesson 6.3)* $1\frac{7}{15}$ mi

23. Candles You light a candle that is $\frac{5}{6}$ inch tall. The candle melts to $\frac{3}{4}$ inch tall. What is the decrease in height? *(Lesson 6.3)* $\frac{1}{12}$ in.

Find the sum or difference. *(Lessons 6.4, 6.5)*

24. $9\frac{1}{8} + 4\frac{5}{8}$ $13\frac{3}{4}$ **25.** $6\frac{3}{7} + 1\frac{5}{7}$ $8\frac{1}{7}$ **26.** $8\frac{3}{4} + 1\frac{1}{2}$ $10\frac{1}{4}$ **27.** $3\frac{2}{3} + \frac{1}{7}$ $3\frac{17}{21}$

28. $7\frac{3}{8} + 5\frac{5}{6}$ $13\frac{5}{24}$ **29.** $6\frac{4}{5} + 4\frac{7}{10}$ $11\frac{1}{2}$ **30.** $14\frac{3}{4} - 6\frac{1}{4}$ $8\frac{1}{2}$ **31.** $5\frac{3}{5} - 1\frac{1}{6}$ $4\frac{13}{30}$

32. $5\frac{1}{3} - 2\frac{5}{12}$ $2\frac{11}{12}$ **33.** $4\frac{7}{9} - 1\frac{8}{9}$ $2\frac{8}{9}$ **34.** $8 - 2\frac{7}{9}$ $5\frac{2}{9}$ **35.** $6 - \frac{3}{10}$ $5\frac{7}{10}$

36. Arm Span Your cousin's arm span is $3\frac{3}{4}$ feet. Your arm span is $1\frac{1}{8}$ feet wider. How wide is your arm span? *(Lesson 6.4)* $4\frac{7}{8}$ ft

37. Bass Fishing The winner of a bass fishing contest caught 14 pounds of bass. The runner-up caught $12\frac{11}{16}$ pounds of bass. How many more pounds did the winner catch than the runner-up? *(Lesson 6.5)* $1\frac{5}{16}$ lb

Add or subtract the measures of time. *(Lesson 6.6)*

38.   6 h 31 min
      + 7 h 32 min
      ‾‾‾‾‾‾‾‾‾‾‾‾‾‾
       14 h 3 min

39.   3 h 14 min 25 sec
      + 1 h 25 min 42 sec
      ‾‾‾‾‾‾‾‾‾‾‾‾‾‾‾‾‾‾‾‾‾‾‾
       4 h 40 min 7 sec

40.   9 h 10 min
      − 4 h 55 min
      ‾‾‾‾‾‾‾‾‾‾‾‾‾‾
       4 h 15 min

Find the elapsed time. *(Lesson 6.6)*

41. 5:00 A.M. to 7:00 A.M. 2 h

42. 1:40 P.M. to 8:00 P.M. 6 h 20 min

43. 10:30 P.M. to 4:45 A.M. 6 h 15 min

44. 6:00 A.M. to 3:00 P.M. 9 h

45. Flights The first part of a flight lasts 2 hours and 38 minutes. The second part lasts 3 hours and 26 minutes. What is the total flight time? *(Lesson 6.6)* 6 h 4 min

46. Movies A movie starts at 9:45 P.M. and ends at 12:20 A.M. How long is the movie? *(Lesson 6.6)* 2 h 35 min

Chapter Test

Estimate the sum or difference. 1–4. Estimates may vary.

1. $\frac{1}{8} + \frac{17}{20}$ 1

2. $\frac{7}{12} - \frac{2}{11}$ $\frac{1}{2}$

3. $6\frac{3}{10} - 3\frac{9}{16}$ 2

4. $3\frac{1}{6} + 5\frac{3}{8}$ 8

Find the sum or difference.

5. $\frac{5}{7} + \frac{1}{7}$ $\frac{6}{7}$

6. $\frac{3}{5} + \frac{4}{5}$ $1\frac{2}{5}$

7. $\frac{7}{10} - \frac{3}{10}$ $\frac{2}{5}$

8. $\frac{7}{12} - \frac{1}{12}$ $\frac{1}{2}$

9. $\frac{5}{6} + \frac{5}{8}$ $1\frac{11}{24}$

10. $\frac{7}{16} + \frac{1}{4}$ $\frac{11}{16}$

11. $\frac{2}{3} - \frac{1}{6}$ $\frac{1}{2}$

12. $\frac{4}{5} - \frac{1}{4}$ $\frac{11}{20}$

13. Banquet At a banquet, chicken, vegetarian, and beef dinners are served. The chef knows that $\frac{1}{4}$ of the guests order chicken and $\frac{1}{3}$ order beef. What fraction of the guests order meat dinners? $\frac{5}{12}$ of the guests

Find the sum or difference.

14. $2\frac{5}{7} + 8\frac{1}{7}$ $10\frac{6}{7}$

15. $7\frac{1}{4} + 2\frac{1}{8}$ $9\frac{3}{8}$

16. $6\frac{7}{15} + 3\frac{4}{5}$ $10\frac{4}{15}$

17. $4\frac{7}{10} + 5\frac{3}{10}$ 10

18. $7\frac{2}{3} - 4\frac{1}{8}$ $3\frac{13}{24}$

19. $12\frac{7}{10} - 8\frac{1}{2}$ $4\frac{1}{5}$

20. $8\frac{1}{6} - 4\frac{5}{9}$ $3\frac{11}{18}$

21. $5 - 1\frac{3}{5}$ $3\frac{2}{5}$

22. Helmets Your friend's bicycle helmet weighs $23\frac{1}{2}$ ounces. Your helmet weighs $43\frac{1}{5}$ ounces. Estimate how much more your helmet weighs. Then find the exact answer.

19 oz; $19\frac{7}{10}$ oz

Add or subtract the measures of time.

23.
$$\begin{array}{r} 4\text{ h }35\text{ min} \\ +\quad 45\text{ min} \\ \hline 5\text{ h }20\text{ min} \end{array}$$

24.
$$\begin{array}{r} 9\text{ h }20\text{ min }52\text{ sec} \\ -\ 2\text{ h }42\text{ min }\ 4\text{ sec} \\ \hline 6\text{ h }38\text{ min }48\text{ sec} \end{array}$$

Find the elapsed time.

25. 1:50 P.M. to 3:35 P.M. 1 h 45 min

26. 6:38 A.M. to 10:05 A.M. 3 h 27 min

27. 4:45 A.M. to 2:15 P.M. 9 h 30 min

28. 7:25 P.M. to 12:30 A.M. 5 h 5 min

29. Video You use 2 hours and 48 minutes of a 6 hour videotape to record your sister's school play. How much time is left on the tape? 3 h 12 min

Chapter Standardized Test

Test-Taking Strategy During a test, make notes, sketches, or graphs on a separate piece of paper. Remember to keep your answer sheet neat.

ADDITIONAL RESOURCES

 Assessment Book
• Standardized Chapter Test, p. 76

 Test and Practice Generator

Multiple Choice

1. Estimate the sum $\frac{9}{10} + \frac{4}{7}$. **C**

A. $\frac{1}{2}$ **B.** 1   **C.** $1\frac{1}{2}$ **D.** 2

2. Estimate the difference $7\frac{1}{6} - 3\frac{7}{8}$. **F**

F. 3   **G.** 6   **H.** 10   **I.** 11

3. To find the sum $\frac{1}{6} + \frac{3}{4}$, use the LCD, $\underline{\ ?\ }$. **D**

A. $\frac{3}{4}$ **B.** $\frac{11}{12}$ **C.** 6   **D.** 12

4. Find the difference $\frac{9}{10} - \frac{3}{10}$. **H**

F. $\frac{3}{10}$ **G.** $\frac{1}{2}$ **H.** $\frac{3}{5}$ **I.** $\frac{7}{10}$

5. Find the sum $\frac{7}{9} + 2\frac{1}{4}$. **A**

A. $3\frac{1}{36}$ **B.** $2\frac{35}{36}$ **C.** $3\frac{1}{12}$ **D.** $3\frac{1}{6}$

6. The sum $2\frac{5}{8} + 4\frac{3}{4}$ is between which numbers? **H**

F. 5 and 6   **G.** 6 and 7
H. 7 and 8   **I.** 8 and 9

7. Which expression has the least value? **A**

A. $3\frac{1}{4} + 2\frac{1}{4}$ **B.** $8\frac{1}{3} - 1\frac{1}{2}$

C. $6\frac{1}{4} + 1$ **D.** $12\frac{2}{5} - 5$

8. Find the difference $10 - 4\frac{1}{7}$. **G**

F. $5\frac{1}{7}$ **G.** $5\frac{6}{7}$ **H.** $6\frac{1}{7}$ **I.** $6\frac{6}{7}$

9. Which expression do you need to rename? **C**

A. $3\frac{1}{6} - 1\frac{1}{6}$ **B.** $9\frac{5}{7} - 2\frac{2}{7}$

C. $8\frac{1}{4} - 4\frac{3}{4}$ **D.** $7\frac{5}{12} - 5$

10. Which has the shortest elapsed time? **I**

F. 9:30 A.M. to 1:00 P.M.
G. 7:00 A.M. to 11:45 A.M.
H. 5:15 P.M. to 9:00 P.M.
I. 11:30 P.M. to 2:45 A.M.

11. A train leaves Carline at 11:45 A.M. and arrives in Trenton 3 hours and 50 minutes later. At what time does the train arrive? **C**

A. 2:35 P.M.   **B.** 3:30 P.M.
C. 3:35 P.M.   **D.** 3:50 P.M.

Short Response 12–13. See margin.

12. A baseball game begins at 6:00 P.M. It takes you 15 minutes to get to the bus stop and another 50 minutes to get to the stadium. What time should you leave home? Explain.

Extended Response

13. The perimeter of a triangle is $17\frac{1}{6}$ feet. The lengths of two of the sides are $6\frac{2}{3}$ feet and $4\frac{3}{4}$ feet. Find the length of the third side. Show your steps.

12. 4:55 P.M. *Sample answer:* You need to leave $15 + 50 = 65$ minutes before the game starts. Since the elapsed time between 4:55 and 6:00 is 65 minutes, you need to leave at 4:55 P.M.

13. $6\frac{2}{3} + 4\frac{3}{4} = 11\frac{5}{12}$, $17\frac{1}{6} - 11\frac{5}{12} = 5\frac{3}{4}$ ft

EXPLORE THE CONCEPT

- Students make and interpret line graphs, which were studied in Lesson 2.6.
- The number of daylight hours in a city varies during the year.

SCIENCE BACKGROUND

In the Northern Hemisphere the summer solstice is in June and the winter solstice is in December. Since Anchorage is closer to the North Pole than Miami, the number of hours of daylight is much greater there at the summer solstice and much less there at the winter solstice.

GROUPING

Students can do the activity individually, but it may be helpful to do the activity in groups of four so they can compare line graphs and discuss how they interpreted the graphs.

2 TEACH

TIPS FOR SUCCESS

If students work in groups of four, ask one student to graph the Miami data, another to graph the Anchorage data, a third to record the patterns in the Miami line graph, and a fourth to record the patterns in the Anchorage line graph. Have the whole group discuss their results.

GUIDING STUDENTS' WORK

For Exercises 1–3, students may be confused about how to find the difference between the sunset and sunrise times. Encourage them to count from sunrise to noon, and then from noon to sunset.

1–2, 5. See Additional Answers beginning on page AA1.

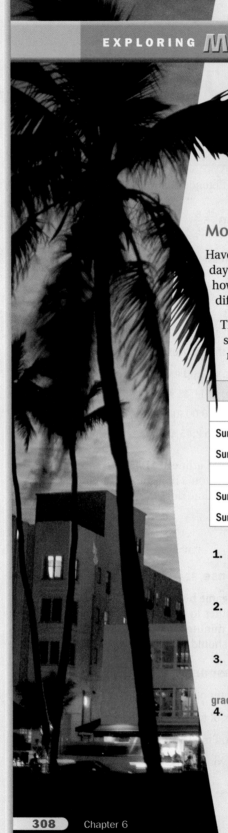

EXPLORING **MATH** IN **SCIENCE**

Measuring the Day

Monthly Variation

Have you ever noticed that the sun rises and sets at different times each day? Using the data given below and on page 309, you will determine how much the number of daylight hours varies through the year in two different cities in the United States.

The table below gives the time of the sunrise and the time of the sunset in Miami, Florida. The data are for the twenty-first of each month during 2002. The times given are Eastern Standard Time.

Sunrise and Sunset in Miami, Florida						
	Jan.	**Feb.**	**Mar.**	**Apr.**	**May**	**June**
Sunrise	7:08 A.M.	6:51 A.M.	6:24 A.M.	5:53 A.M.	5:33 A.M.	5:30 A.M.
Sunset	5:56 P.M.	6:18 P.M.	6:33 P.M.	6:47 P.M.	7:03 P.M.	8:15 P.M.
	July	**Aug.**	**Sept.**	**Oct.**	**Nov.**	**Dec.**
Sunrise	5:42 A.M.	5:57 A.M.	6:09 A.M.	6:23 A.M.	6:43 A.M.	7:03 A.M.
Sunset	7:13 P.M.	6:51 P.M.	6:18 P.M.	5:48 P.M.	5:30 P.M.	5:35 P.M.

1. Find the elapsed time from sunrise to sunset for each month. Record your results in a table. The elapsed time describes the number of daylight hours during the day. **See margin.**

2. Use your table from Exercise 1 to make a line graph. Put the months on the horizontal axis. Put number of daylight hours on the vertical axis. Use a scale from 5 hours to 20 hours in half hour increments.
See margin.

3. **Interpret** What patterns do you see in your line graph? During which month or months does Miami have the greatest number of daylight hours? the least number of daylight hours? **The elapsed time gradually increases and then gradually decreases; June; December.**

4. The summer solstice occurs on the day with the greatest number of daylight hours. The winter solstice occurs on the day with the least number of daylight hours. Find the difference between the number of daylight hours on the summer solstice and the number of daylight hours on the winter solstice. This difference describes Miami's seasonal variation in daylight hours. **4 h 13 min**

Regional Variation

The length of time between sunrise and sunset varies not only due to the time of the year, but also due to location on the globe.

Anchorage, Alaska, is much closer to the North Pole than Miami, Florida. The table below gives the sunrise and sunset times for Anchorage for the twenty-first of each month in 2002. The times given are Alaska Standard Time.

North Pole

Florida

Alaska

Sunrise and Sunset in Anchorage, Alaska

	Jan.	Feb.	Mar.	Apr.	May	June
Sunrise	9:45 A.M.	8:24 A.M.	6:57 A.M.	5:20 A.M.	3:58 A.M.	3:20 A.M.
Sunset	4:37 P.M.	6:03 P.M.	7:17 P.M.	8:38 P.M.	9:56 P.M.	10:42 P.M.

	July	Aug.	Sept.	Oct.	Nov.	Dec.
Sunrise	4:05 A.M.	5:24 A.M.	6:41 A.M.	7:58 A.M.	9:22 A.M.	10:14 A.M.
Sunset	10:05 P.M.	8:40 P.M.	7:02 P.M.	5:29 P.M.	4:09 P.M.	3:41 P.M.

5. Find the elapsed time from sunrise to sunset for each month. Record your results in a table. Then plot these data on the graph you made in Exercise 2. **See margin.**

6. Interpret Compare the graphs for the two cities. How are they alike? How are they different? When do the summer and winter solstices occur for each city? How does Anchorage's seasonal variation in daylight hours compare with Miami's? **The elapsed time increases from January to June and then decreases from June to December; the increase and decrease is much greater in Anchorage than in Miami; June and December; it is much greater in Anchorage.**

Project IDEAS

- **Report** Find information about the daylight patterns at the North Pole and at the equator. Present your findings to the class. **A good answer will include clearly presented information.**
- **Research** Find information about daylight-saving time. Why do people use daylight-saving time? How does its use affect sunrise and sunset times? Present your findings. **To have more daylight in the evening; sunrise and sunset are each pushed back 1 hour.**
- **Predict** Make a prediction about how the number of daylight hours where you live changes over the year. Describe how you might check your prediction. **A good answer will include clearly presented information.**
- **Career** Meteorologists study weather and other natural occurrences, such as the sunrise and sunset. Find out what kinds of work meteorologists do. Present your findings to the class. **A good answer will include well-documented research and a clear presentation.**

INTERNET
Project Support
CLASSZONE.COM

---

③ APPLY

REFLECTING ON THE ACTIVITY

While the number of daylight hours in a given city varies throughout the year, the way the number of hours varies is similar from one city to the next.

PROJECT IDEAS

For additional information on the Project Ideas and for suggestions for more projects, go to classzone.com

④ ASSESS

The rubric below can be used to assess the projects on the pupil page. For more information on rubrics, see the Professional Development Book.

4 The student fully achieves the mathematical and project goals. The graphs are drawn and labeled correctly. All graphs are interpreted correctly. All work is complete and accurate.

3 The student substantially achieves the mathematical and project goals. There may be small errors in the graphs, or small errors in the answers to the questions. There may be some minor mis-understanding of content, errors in computation, or weakness in presentation.

2 The student partially achieves the mathematical and project goals. One of the graphs may not have been done correctly, or some of the questions may not have been answered. Some of the work may be incomplete, misdirected, or unclear.

1 The student makes little progress toward accomplishing the goals of the project because of a lack of understanding or lack of effort. The student did not do the graphs or did not answer the questions.

Pacing and Assignment Guide

REGULAR SCHEDULE

Lesson	Les. Day	BASIC	AVERAGE	ADVANCED
7.1	Day 1	EP p. 712 Exs. 43–47; pp. 316–317 Exs. 11–30, 35–39, 42, 48–59	pp. 316–317 Exs. 15–26, 31–44, 48–53, 57–59	pp. 316–317 Exs. 17–26, 31–47*, 50–55, 59
7.2	Day 1	EP p. 712 Exs. 16–19; pp. 323–325 Exs. 10–14, 19–22, 37–39, 52–57	pp. 323–325 Exs. 10–12, 17–22, 40–45, 54–57	pp. 323–325 Exs. 10, 15–22, 40–46, 52–55
	Day 2	pp. 323–325 Exs. 23–31, 36, 43–47, 60–62	pp. 323–325 Exs. 27–36, 46–50, 61–63	pp. 323–325 Exs. 29–36, 47–51*, 58–63
7.3	Day 1	EP p. 712 Exs. 38–42; pp. 328–330 Exs. 11–22, 27–33, 36–41, 48–53	pp. 328–330 Exs. 19–26, 29–37, 40–46, 49–54	pp. 328–330 Exs. 21–28, 31–35, 38–50*, 53, 54
7.4	Day 1	pp. 336–338 Exs. 10–20, 26–29, 34–39, 42–54, 58–70	pp. 336–338 Exs. 14–25, 30–56, 60–65, 69–71	pp. 336–338 Exs. 16–25, 32–57*, 60–65, 70, 71
7.5	Day 1	pp. 341–343 Exs. 7–15, 22–29, 32–37, 39–45, 50–57	pp. 341–343 Exs. 7–17, 22–25, 30–48, 50–52, 56–58	pp. 341–343 Exs. 7–11, 18–25, 28–51*, 56–58
7.6	Day 1	EP p. 711 Exs. 36–41; pp. 346–347 Exs. 7–20, 24–27, 31–41	pp. 346–347 Exs. 7–17, 21–29, 31–42	pp. 346–347 Exs. 7–17, 21–35*, 40–42
7.7	Day 1	SRH p. 701 Exs. 1–6; pp. 353–354 Exs. 12–21, 28–31, 33–44, 50–60	pp. 353–354 Exs. 15–24, 28–35, 39–48, 50–55, 59–61	pp. 353–354 Exs. 15–21, 25–32, 36–41, 45–55*, 60, 61
Review	Day 1	pp. 358–359 Exs. 1–55	pp. 358–359 Exs. 1–55	pp. 358–359 Exs. 1–55
Assess	Day 1	Chapter 7 Test	Chapter 7 Test	Chapter 7 Test
YEARLY PACING		Chapter 7 Total – **10 days**	Chapters 1–7 Total – **80 days**	Remaining – **80 days**

*Challenge Exercises   EP = Extra Practice   SRH = Skills Review Handbook   EC = Extra Challenge

BLOCK SCHEDULE

DAY 1	DAY 2	DAY 3	DAY 4	DAY 5
7.1 pp. 316–317 Exs. 15–26, 31–44, 48–53, 57–59 **7.2** pp. 323–325 Exs. 10–12, 17–22, 40–45, 54–57	**7.2 cont.** pp. 323–325 Exs. 27–36, 46–50, 61–63 **7.3** pp. 328–330 Exs. 19–26, 29–37, 40–46, 49–54	**7.4** pp. 336–338 Exs. 14–25, 30–56, 60–65, 69–71 **7.5** pp. 341–343 Exs. 7–17, 22–25, 30–48, 50–52, 56–58	**7.6** pp. 346–347 Exs. 7–17, 21–29, 31–42 **7.7** pp. 353–354 Exs. 15–24, 28–35, 39–48, 50–55, 59–61	**Review** pp. 358–359 Exs. 1–55 **Assess** Chapter 7 Test

| YEARLY PACING | Chapter 7 Total – **5 days** | Chapters 1–7 Total – **40 days** | Remaining – **40 days** |

Support Materials

📖 CHAPTER RESOURCE BOOK

CHAPTER SUPPORT

| Tips for New Teachers | p. 1 | Parents as Partners | p. 3 |

LESSON SUPPORT	7.1	7.2	7.3	7.4	7.5	7.6	7.7
Lesson Plans (regular and block)	p. 5	p. 13	p. 22	p. 30	p. 38	p. 50	p. 58
Technology Activities & Keystrokes					p. 40		p. 60
Activity Support Masters		p. 15					
Activity Masters					p. 42		
Practice (3 levels)	p. 7	p. 16	p. 24	p. 32	p. 43	p. 52	p. 62
Study Guide	p. 10	p. 19	p. 27	p. 35	p. 46	p. 56	p. 65
Real-World Problem Solving					p. 48		p. 67
Challenge Practice	p. 12	p. 21	p. 29	p. 37	p. 49	p. 57	p. 68

REVIEW

Chapter Review Games and Activities	p. 69	Extra Credit Project with Rubric	p. 74
Real-Life Project with Rubric	p. 70	Cumulative Practice	p. 76
Cooperative Project with Rubric	p. 72	Resource Book Answers	A1

📖 ASSESSMENT

Quizzes	p. 79	Alternative Assessments with Rubrics	p. 88
Chapter Tests (3 levels)	p. 81	Unit Test	p. 90
Standardized Test	p. 87	Cumulative Test	p. 92

🖨 TRANSPARENCIES

	7.1	7.2	7.3	7.4	7.5	7.6	7.7
Warm-Up / Daily Homework Quiz	✔	✔	✔	✔	✔	✔	✔
Notetaking Guide	✔	✔	✔	✔	✔	✔	✔
Teacher Support		✔		✔		✔	
English/Spanish Problem Solving		✔	✔		✔		
Answer Transparencies	✔	✔	✔	✔	✔	✔	✔

💻 TECHNOLOGY

- EasyPlanner CD-ROM
- Test and Practice Generator
- Electronic Lesson Presentations
- eTutorial CD-ROM
- Chapter Audio Summaries CDs
- Classzone.com
- eEdition Plus Online
- eWorkbook Plus Online
- eTutorial Plus Online
- EasyPlanner Plus Online

ADDITIONAL RESOURCES

- Worked-Out Solution Key
- Notetaking Guide
- Practice Workbook
- Tutor Place
- Professional Development Book
- Activities Book
- Poster Package
- Spanish Study Guide
- English/Spanish Chapter Reviews
- Multi-Language Glossary

Math Background and Teaching Strategies

Lessons 7.1 through 7.3

MATH BACKGROUND

When you multiply any number (whole number, fraction, mixed number) by a fraction less than 1, the product is less than that number because you are only looking for a part of it.

TEACHING STRATEGIES

Suppose there are 18 students in your class, and that in a survey two-thirds of them say they like using a word processor better than writing by hand. How many students prefer using a word processor? Since not all of the students prefer using a word processor, you know that the number who do is less than 18. To solve this problem you would multiply $\frac{2}{3} \times 18$.

USING A MODEL You can find $\frac{2}{3} \times 18$ by drawing a picture.

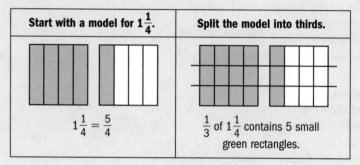

So, $\frac{2}{3} \times 18 = 12$. (Point out that $12 < 18$.)

TEACHING STRATEGIES

On the board, draw a circle divided into sections that are $\frac{1}{2}$, $\frac{1}{4}$, $\frac{1}{8}$, and $\frac{1}{16}$ of the circle as shown at the right. Shade each section with a different color of chalk but do not label the sections. Ask students what fraction of the circle each colored section models. Then ask questions such as "What is $\frac{1}{4}$ of the orange section?" Students then draw pictures and work together to answer the questions.

In a bike race, suppose $\frac{1}{3}$ of the course is paved road. If the course is $1\frac{1}{4}$ miles long, what length is paved road? To solve the problem, you need to multiply $\frac{1}{3} \times 1\frac{1}{4}$. Draw this diagram.

Start with a model for $1\frac{1}{4}$.	Split the model into thirds.
$1\frac{1}{4} = \frac{5}{4}$	$\frac{1}{3}$ of $1\frac{1}{4}$ contains 5 small green rectangles.

Each small shaded rectangle is $\frac{1}{12}$ of a large rectangle. So, $\frac{1}{3} \times 1\frac{1}{4} = \frac{5}{12}$. $\left(\text{Point out that } \frac{5}{12} < 1\frac{1}{4}.\right)$

Lesson 7.4

MATH BACKGROUND

Reciprocals are number pairs that have a product of 1. To find the reciprocal of any fraction, you just flip it over. If you have a whole number or mixed number, rewrite it as a fraction first and then flip that fraction upside down.

TEACHING STRATEGIES

USING AN ALGORITHM Suppose you have $\frac{3}{4}$ yard of fabric. Into how many $\frac{3}{8}$-yard pieces can you cut the fabric? To solve this problem, divide $\frac{3}{4}$ by $\frac{3}{8}$. The first step involves using the reciprocal.

Multiply the dividend by the divisor's reciprocal. $\rightarrow$ $\frac{3}{4} \div \frac{3}{8}$ $\rightarrow$ $\frac{3}{4} \times \frac{8}{3} = \frac{24}{12}$

Write the product in simplest form. $\rightarrow$ $\frac{24}{12} = \frac{24 \div 12}{12 \div 12} = \frac{2}{1}$ $\rightarrow$ 2

So, two $\frac{3}{8}$-yard pieces can be cut from $\frac{3}{4}$ yard of fabric.

Lesson 7.5

MATH BACKGROUND

To find the number of halves in 3 wholes, you can either

divide 3 by $\frac{1}{2}$ or multiply 3 by 2. This is true because dividing by a fraction is the same as multiplying by the reciprocal of that fraction. You can use what you know about dividing fractions to divide mixed numbers.

TEACHING STRATEGIES

Suppose you have a shelf that is $3\frac{1}{8}$ feet long and you want to know how many $\frac{3}{4}$-foot long boxes you can put on the shelf.

You need to determine how many $\frac{3}{4}$-foot lengths are in $3\frac{1}{8}$ feet, or $3\frac{1}{8} \div \frac{3}{4}$.

Write the mixed number as a fraction.

$$3\frac{1}{8} \div \frac{3}{4} = \left(\frac{24}{8} + \frac{1}{8}\right) \div \frac{3}{4} = \frac{25}{8} \div \frac{3}{4}$$

Multiply by the reciprocal of the divisor.

$$\frac{25}{8} \div \frac{3}{4} = \frac{25}{8} \times \frac{4}{3} = \frac{100}{24}$$

Write the product in simplest form.

$$\frac{100}{24} = \frac{96}{24} + \frac{4}{24} = 4 + \frac{1}{6} = 4\frac{1}{6}$$

Since the number of boxes must be a whole number, four $\frac{3}{4}$-foot-long boxes can be stored on a shelf that is $3\frac{1}{8}$ feet long.

REASONING Write these four expressions on the board: $1\frac{1}{2} \div 1\frac{3}{4}$, $1\frac{3}{4} \div 1\frac{1}{2}$, $12 \div \frac{2}{3}$, and $\frac{2}{3} \div 12$. As you ask the following questions, have students decide whether the answer will be *greater than 1* or *less than 1*, and which expression could be used to find the answer. Then have them calculate the quotient.

- How many one and one halves are in one and three fourths?
- How many one and three fourths are in one and one half?
- How many twelves are in two thirds?

Lesson 7.6

MATH BACKGROUND

Note the use of the unit fluid ounces (fl oz) in the lesson. While ounce (oz) is a unit of weight (16 oz = 1 lb), the fluid ounce is a unit of capacity (8 fl oz = 1 c). For water, as well as for most other liquids, fluid ounces and ounces are equivalent, and the "fl" is sometimes omitted from the abbreviation (for example, "8 oz = 1 cup"). To be correct, we use ounce for weight only

and fluid ounce for capacity. For liquids that weigh considerably more or less than water, the difference between ounces and fluid ounces is significant.

TEACHING STRATEGIES

Display pictures of the following items: a bathtub, 1 cup (8 ounces), 1 pint carton, 1 quart container, and 1 gallon container. Ask students, "Which is a more reasonable measure of the capacity of the bathtub, 2 quarts or 25 gallons?" Since 2 quarts are less than 1 gallon, this would not be enough to fill a bathtub; much more would be needed. A more reasonable measure of the capacity of the bathtub is 25 gallons.

Display a picture of a basket of fruit or bring in a basket filled with fruits. Ask, "Which is the most reasonable measure of the weight of the basket of fruit, 10 ounces, 10 pounds, or 10 tons?" Since 10 ounces would be about the weight of 10 slices of bread and 10 tons would be about the weight of 10 cars, the most reasonable weight must be 10 pounds.

Lesson 7.7

MATH BACKGROUND

Students will review the customary units of length, capacity, and weight, converting among customary units. To convert between units of length, units of capacity, or units of weight, students must know the unit equivalencies and then decide whether to multiply or divide.

TEACHING STRATEGIES

Ask students, "How do you decide when to multiply or divide in changing feet to inches, feet to yards, miles to yards, feet to miles, yards to miles, or yards to feet?"

Have students picture replacing one of the units with several of the other units. For example, to change yards to feet, use the fact that 1 yard = 3 feet. So if you have 5 yards, you can replace each of these yards with 3 feet.

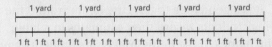

If you were changing from feet to yards, you would do the opposite type of replacement: given 15 feet, you would make groups of 3 feet and then replace each group with 1 yard. Since 15 divided by 3 is 5 groups, 15 feet = 3 yards. This method works for units of capacity and weight as well.

Differentiating Instruction

Strategies for Underachievers

PROVIDE AND CREATE MANIPULATIVES AND TOOLS FOR CONCRETE LEARNING

Many students, especially concrete learners, learn better if they are able to see, touch, and manipulate objects that represent the concept being taught. Chapter 7 provides many opportunities for you to reach these learners.

MANIPULATIVES In Lesson 7.1, Hands-on Activity 7.2, and Lesson 7.2, you may want to provide students with fraction tiles for them to manipulate when showing multiplication of fractions and whole numbers. The use of tiles allows students to quickly build several examples of these operations. This helps students gain a concrete grasp of how to find these products before they move on to using an algorithm.

Hands-on Activity 7.4 can be adapted for Underachieving students by starting with a ruler marked with increments of only $\frac{1}{4}$ inch. You may wish to draw the following table for students to complete.

Dividend	Divisor	Quotient	Dividend	Multiplier	Product
2	$\div \frac{1}{4}$	$= 8$	2	$\times \frac{4}{1}$	$= 8$
$\frac{3}{4}$	$\div \frac{1}{4}$	$= ?$	$\frac{3}{4}$	$\times \frac{4}{1}$	$= ?$
$1\frac{1}{2}$	$\div \frac{1}{4}$	$= ?$	$1\frac{1}{2}$	$\times \frac{4}{1}$	$= ?$

Depending upon the level of understanding of your students, you may also wish to complete a similar table using $\frac{3}{4}$ as the divisor.

In Lesson 7.7, to reach all students, you may wish to provide them with numerous items whose weight can be estimated. It is a good idea to pass the items around the room, having students record their estimates in a table that lists the names of the items. Make sure students have labeled their weights; stress that giving an answer without a unit label is unacceptable. Now choose individual students to come to the front of the classroom and weigh the items on a balance or a scale. Students should compare their estimates to the actual weights of the items. This activity will help you determine whether your students have a grasp of the relative weights of objects. After several of the objects have been weighed, you might wish to pass the remaining ones around the room again, allowing students to change their estimates if they wish to do so.

USE SCAFFOLDING

Because many of the concepts in this chapter require students to execute multiple steps, you may first wish to provide review, practice, and reinforcement of previously-learned concepts that students will need.

ESTIMATION In Example 4 of Lesson 7.1 on page 315, students are shown the use of compatible numbers to make an estimate. You may wish to take some time to review *compatible numbers* and *multiples* before beginning the estimation problems in Exercises 6–8 and 27–34. Students who have not mastered their multiplication facts will need a table to assist them.

UNIT CONVERSIONS In Lesson 7.7, many students will need a table of conversions. For some students, you may wish to provide a table that instructs them when to multiply and when to divide to make a conversion.

USE A GRAPHIC ORGANIZER

VISUAL AID When multiplying or dividing with mixed numbers, students may benefit from creating a graphic organizer to detail the many steps they must follow. For multiplying two mixed numbers, you might wish to provide students with a graphic "hamburger" organizer like the one shown below, which instructs them on how to fill in each portion.

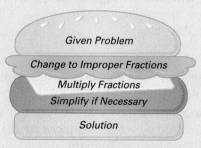

Given Problem

Change to Improper Fractions

Multiply Fractions
Simplify if Necessary

Solution

You can also create a "double hamburger" organizer with one more "patty" for division of mixed numbers, adding the step of changing a division problem to the equivalent problem of multiplying by the reciprocal of the divisor. (You can create "veggieburger" organizers for the vegetarians in your class!)

Strategies for English Learners

DISSECT WORD PROBLEMS

The last sentence of a word problem usually contains a verb that issues a command. It orders the reader to do something. Almost always it is followed by an additional description of what the person is to do, as in "Solve the following equation," with *solve* being the command, and *the following equation* identifying what is to be solved. These command verbs are signals to the student that explain what the student is to do in the word problem.

COMMAND VERBS The following command verbs were compiled from sample standardized test problems, word problems found in mathematics textbooks, and state standards:

Apply, approximate, assume, calculate, choose, circle, classify, compute, convert, create, decide, demonstrate, describe, design, determine, draw, establish, estimate, explain, extend, extrapolate, find, fit, identify, interpolate, interpret, investigate, make, mark, model, order, organize, perform, predict, prove, recognize, read, represent, round, select, show, sketch, solve, transform, translate, use, verify, visualize

Ask students to group the words into categories, such as words that tell you to pick from a list, words that tell you to calculate something, and so on. Allow students to make up their own categories. It is important here to let students express and discuss what they think these terms mean. Many of the words would fit into more than one category depending on the context. For example, the term *draw* can be used in the following ways: Draw a picture; Draw a conclusion. These are very different requests, and students need to know both meanings. Through discussion, students can expose the different meanings of words and expand their concepts of what words mean. Watch for the tendency of students to confuse words that sound or look similar, for example *make* and *mark*. Encourage students to write new words in their journal, accompanied by a picture or an explanation in their primary language. Use a dictionary and thesaurus to provide additional meanings of words, as well as synonyms and antonyms.

Strategies for Advanced Learners

PROVIDE DIFFERENTIATED INSTRUCTION IN TERMS OF DEPTH

Students who have a firm grasp of customary and metric units may wish to extend Technology Activity 7.7 by investigating objects that are labeled in both customary and metric units, such as many consumer goods. They should find some items that are measured only in customary units or only in metric units, and then convert these measurements to the other system. Students will need access to a calculator for this activity. Have students write a short report discussing how to convert from customary to customary, metric to metric, customary to metric, and metric to customary. Instruct them to include some of their thoughts on the ease and practicality of using each of these measurement systems.

USE CROSS-CURRICULAR CONNECTIONS

You may wish to develop a cross-curricular unit with the Social Studies, Science, and Language Arts teachers surrounding the topic of the history of measurement in various civilizations.

The following problem can be used with **Lesson 7.4**:

- **Challenge** Complete the puzzle below by finding the values of w, x, y, and z. $w = \frac{225}{2}, x = \frac{225}{4}, y = 45, z = 15$

$$w \times \frac{1}{2} = x, x \times \frac{4}{5} = y, y \times \frac{1}{3} = z, z \times \frac{3}{4} = \frac{45}{4}$$

To check students' mathematical reasoning regarding multiplication and division of fractions and mixed numbers, use the following problem with **Lesson 7.5**:

- **Challenge** Complete each statement with *sometimes*, *always*, or *never*.
  - **A.** The product of two mixed numbers is __?__ greater than 1. always
  - **B.** The product of a mixed number and 0 is __?__ greater than 1. never
  - **C.** The reciprocal of a mixed number is __?__ less than 1. always
  - **D.** A whole number divided by a mixed number is __?__ greater than 1. sometimes

Differentiating Instruction: Teaching Resources

Differentiating Teacher Materials

McDougal Littell *Middle School Mathematics* offers a wide variety of materials to help with professional development and teaching. These resources can be found in this *Teacher's Edition*, in the *Professional Development Book*, in the *Chapter Resource Books*, and in the multi-language resources.

PROFESSIONAL DEVELOPMENT BOOK

The *Professional Development Book* contains ideas for in-service workshops, professional articles, mathematical background notes, bulletin board ideas, teacher tips, and a reprint of the Parents as Partners pages from the Chapter Resource Books. (Parents as Partners is also available in Spanish in the *Spanish Study Guide*.)

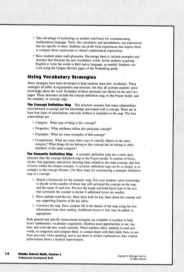

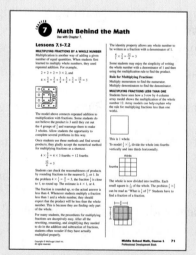

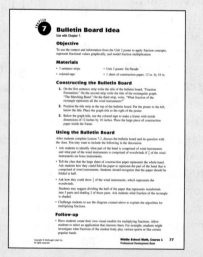

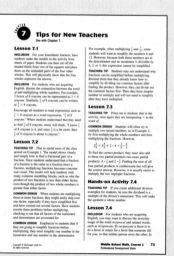

RESOURCE BOOK

Each *Chapter Resource Book* contains a section of tips for new teachers and a section on parental involvement. There is also a lesson plan page for both a regular schedule course and a block schedule course for each lesson in the textbook.

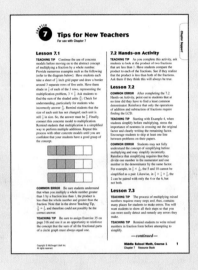
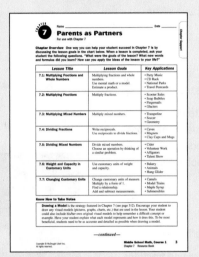
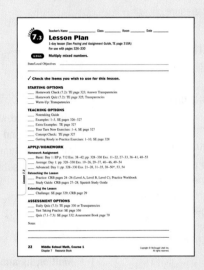

MULTI-LANGUAGE RESOURCES

A number of resources are available to help students acquiring English. These include a *Spanish Study Guide, English/Spanish Chapter Reviews and Tests, Chapter Audio Summaries,* and a *Multi-Language Glossary.*

MAIN IDEAS

In this chapter students **multiply and divide** with **fractions and mixed numbers**. The concepts are introduced by using an area model for multiplying fractions and a ruler model for dividing fractions. Students also explore **customary units** for **weight**, **capacity**, and **length**, including **changing units** of measure.

PREREQUISITE SKILLS

The key skills reviewed in the games on these pages are:

- writing improper fractions as mixed numbers
- ordering mixed numbers
- finding parts of whole numbers

Additional practice with prerequisite skills can be found in the Review What You Need to Know exercises on page 312. Additional resources for reviewing prerequisite skills are:

- Skills Review Handbook, pp. 684–707
- Tutor Place
- eTutorial Plus Online

MANAGING THE GAMES

Tips for Success

In the first game, suggest students use a calculator to compare the fractional parts of the mixed numbers when placing them in order. In the second game, remind students that "of" in the formula indicates multiplication.

Reflecting on the Games

When discussing Stop and Think Exercise 1, ask students to focus on the reasoning by applying it to fractions such as $\frac{5}{6}$ and $\frac{3}{2}$. Point out that even though $5 > 3$ and $6 > 2$, $\frac{5}{6}$ cannot be greater than $\frac{3}{2}$ because $\frac{5}{6} < 1$ and $\frac{3}{2} > 1$. For Exercise 2, ask students to calculate all of the possible total distances. There are six.

CHAPTER 7

Multiplication and Division of Fractions

Chapter Warm-Up Games

Review skills you need for this chapter in these quick games.

BEFORE

In previous chapters you've...

- Modeled and written fractions
- Compared and ordered fractions and mixed numbers
- Added and subtracted fractions

Now

In Chapter 7 you'll study...

- Multiplying and dividing fractions and mixed numbers
- Using customary units

WHY?

So you can solve real-world problems about...

- national parks, p. 316
- glaciers, p. 324
- soccer, p. 328
- caves, p. 335
- camels, p. 351

Internet Preview
CLASSZONE.COM

- eEdition Plus Online
- eWorkbook Plus Online
- eTutorial Plus Online
- State Test Practice
- More Examples

MIXED Number Race

| A $\frac{44}{7}$ | T $\frac{49}{6}$ | N $\frac{28}{3}$ | R $\frac{34}{5}$ | O $\frac{17}{2}$ | M $\frac{23}{4}$ | H $\frac{67}{8}$ | A $\frac{71}{9}$ |

BRAIN GAME

Key Skills:
- Writing fractions as mixed numbers
- Ordering mixed numbers

- Write the improper fractions as mixed numbers. Then order the mixed numbers from least to greatest. **See margin.**

- The letters associated with the numbers will spell out the name of a town in ancient Greece whose name is used for a modern track and field event. **MARATHON**

Chapter 7 Resource Book
- Tips for New Teachers, pp. 1–2
- Lesson Plan, pp. 5, 13, 22, 30, 38, 50, 58
- Lesson Plan for Block Scheduling, pp. 6, 14, 23, 31, 39, 51, 59

Technology
- EasyPlanner CD-ROM
- Test and Practice Generator
- Electronic Lesson Presentations CD-ROM
- eTutorial CD-ROM

Internet
- Classzone
- eEdition Plus Online
- eWorkbook Plus Online
- eTutorial Plus Online
- EasyPlanner Plus Online

ENGLISH LEARNER SUPPORT

- Spanish Study Guide
- Multi-Language Glossary
- Chapter Audio Summaries CDs
- Teacher's Edition, pp. 310E–310F

Brain Game (p. 310)

$\frac{44}{7} = 6\frac{2}{7}; \frac{49}{6} = 8\frac{1}{6}; \frac{28}{3} = 9\frac{1}{3};$

$\frac{34}{5} = 6\frac{4}{5}; \frac{17}{2} = 8\frac{1}{2}; \frac{23}{4} = 5\frac{3}{4};$

$\frac{67}{8} = 8\frac{3}{8}; \frac{71}{9} = 7\frac{8}{9}; 5\frac{3}{4}, 6\frac{2}{7}, 6\frac{4}{5},$

$7\frac{8}{9}, 8\frac{1}{6}, 8\frac{3}{8}, 8\frac{1}{2}, 9\frac{1}{3}$

Key Skill:
Finding parts of whole numbers

In the triple jump, athletes perform a hop, a step, and a jump. In this game you will complete a mathematical triple jump.

- Choose one of the following numbers to be your hop, one to be your step, and one to be your jump: 24, 36, 48. Use each number once.

- Use the fractions in the formula above. Find the given parts of the hop, step, and jump numbers you chose. Then add these results to find your total distance. Your goal is to get the greatest distance possible. **Check work.**

1. *Sample answer:* $\frac{71}{9}$ is actually less than $\frac{67}{8}$, because $\frac{71}{9} = 7\frac{8}{9}$ and $\frac{67}{8} = 8\frac{3}{8}$. While it is true that 71 > 67, ninths are actually less than eighths.

2. 29; 25; to find the greatest total distance, find $\frac{1}{3}$ of the greatest number, $\frac{1}{4}$ of the next greatest number, and $\frac{1}{6}$ of the least number; reverse this to find the least total distance.

Stop *and* Think

1. **Writing** In *Mixed Number Race*, a student thinks that $\frac{71}{9}$ is greater than $\frac{67}{8}$ because 71 is greater than 67 and 9 is greater than 8. What is wrong with the student's reasoning?

2. **Critical Thinking** What is the greatest total distance you can get in *Triple Jump*? What is the least total distance? Explain how you know.

311

Review What You Need to Know
The Review What You Need to Know exercises can help you diagnose whether students have the following skills needed in Chapter 7:
- Vocabulary (Exs. 1–2)
- Estimate quotients (Exs. 3–5)
- Convert metric units (Exs. 6–8)
- Write mixed numbers as improper fractions (Exs. 9–12)
- Round to the nearest whole number (Exs. 13–16)

 Chapter 7 Resource Book
- Study Guide (Lessons 7.1–7.7)

 Tutor Place

NOTETAKING STRATEGIES

Students use visual models throughout the chapter to help them understand multiplication and division of fractions and mixed numbers. Suggest that students use graph paper to help them draw any models they wish to include in their notebooks. Remind students to label their diagrams clearly to show the product or quotient being modeled. Further suggestions for keeping a notebook can be found on page 313.

For more support on notetaking, see:
- Notetaking Guide Workbook
- Notetaking Transparencies

Getting Ready to Learn

Review What You Need to Know ⟲

Using Vocabulary Copy and complete using a review word.

1. _?_ measures the amount that a container can hold. **Capacity**

2. Two numbers that go together nicely to make a calculation easier are called _?_. **compatible numbers**

Estimate the quotient. *(p. 12)* 3–5. **Estimates may vary.**

3. $47 \div 8$ 6   4. $186 \div 22$ 9   5. $342 \div 48$ 7

Copy and complete the statement. *(p. 191)*

6. $16 \text{ kg} = \underline{?} \text{ g}$ 16,000   7. $25 \text{ L} = \underline{?} \text{ mL}$ 25,000   8. $150 \text{ cm} = \underline{?} \text{ m}$ 1.5

Write the mixed number as an improper fraction. *(p. 244)*

9. $4\frac{1}{6}$ $\frac{25}{6}$ 10. $6\frac{2}{3}$ $\frac{20}{3}$ 11. $2\frac{5}{6}$ $\frac{17}{6}$ 12. $1\frac{3}{4}$ $\frac{7}{4}$

Round to the nearest whole number. *(p. 267)*

13. $\frac{7}{8}$ 1   14. $1\frac{2}{9}$ 1   15. $7\frac{1}{4}$ 7   16. $2\frac{8}{11}$ 3

You should include material that appears on a notebook like this in your own notes.

Know How to Take Notes

Drawing a Model When you take notes, include the visual models that are used in the lesson. Seeing the models can help you to understand and remember what you have learned. Below are some fraction models.

$\frac{5}{8}$ $\frac{9}{20}$ $1\frac{2}{5}$

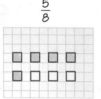   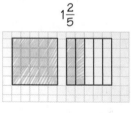

5 out of 8 objects   9 out of 20 parts   1 whole and $\frac{2}{5}$ of 1 whole

In Lessons 7.1 and 7.2, you will use models to multiply by a fraction.

Multiplying Fractions and Whole Numbers

BEFORE	▶ Now	WHY?
You multiplied decimals and whole numbers.	You'll multiply fractions and whole numbers.	So you can interpret data shown in a circle graph, as in Ex. 35.

Word Watch

Review Words
compatible numbers, p. 13
whole number, p. 684

Activity

You can use repeated addition to multiply a fraction by a whole number.

① The product $6 \times \frac{2}{3}$ can be written as the sum $\frac{2}{3} + \frac{2}{3} + \frac{2}{3} + \frac{2}{3} + \frac{2}{3} + \frac{2}{3}$.

Show that the sum is equal to $\frac{6 \times 2}{3}$.

$\frac{2}{3} + \frac{2}{3} + \frac{2}{3} + \frac{2}{3} + \frac{2}{3} + \frac{2}{3} = \frac{12}{3} = \frac{6 \times 2}{3}$

② Write a rule for multiplying a fraction by a whole number. Then try another product to check your rule. **See margin.**

In the activity, you may have become aware of the following rule by thinking about multiplication as repeated addition.

Step 2. Multiply the whole number times the numerator of the fraction and keep the denominator. *Sample answer.*

$3 \times \frac{3}{4} = \frac{3 \times 3}{4} = \frac{9}{4}$
$= \frac{3}{4} + \frac{3}{4} + \frac{3}{4}.$

Multiplying Fractions by Whole Numbers

Words To multiply a fraction by a whole number, multiply the numerator of the fraction by the whole number and write the product over the original denominator. Simplify if possible.

Numbers $2 \times \frac{3}{7} = \frac{6}{7}$ **Algebra** $a \cdot \frac{b}{c} = \frac{a \cdot b}{c}$

HELP with Notetaking

When you write the rule for multiplying fractions by whole numbers in your notebook, you may want to include a model like the one in the activity.

EXAMPLE 1   **Multiply Fractions by Whole Numbers**

$6 \times \frac{3}{4} = \frac{6 \times 3}{4}$ Multiply the numerator by the whole number.

$= \frac{18}{4}$

$= \frac{9}{2}$, or $4\frac{1}{2}$ Simplify.

NCTM CURRICULUM STANDARDS
Standard 1: Understand meanings of operations; Understand how operations are related; Make reasonable estimates

Lesson 7.1   Multiplying Fractions and Whole Numbers   **313**

---

1 PLAN

SKILL CHECK
Simplify.

1. $\frac{8}{10}$ $\frac{4}{5}$ **2.** $\frac{10}{4}$ $2\frac{1}{2}$

3. $\frac{6}{4}$ $1\frac{1}{2}$ **4.** $\frac{15}{3}$ 5

LESSON OBJECTIVE
Multiply fractions and whole numbers.

PACING
Suggested Number of Days
Basic Course: 1 day
Average Course: 1 day
Advanced Course: 1 day
Block: 0.5 block with 7.2

TEACHING RESOURCES
For a complete list of Teaching Resources, see page 310B.

TRANSPARENCY
Warm-Up Exercises for this lesson are available on a transparency.

2 TEACH

MOTIVATING THE LESSON
Before starting the Activity, ask students to use rectangles to model $2 \times \frac{3}{5}$ as $\frac{3}{5} + \frac{3}{5}$. Then discuss the fact that $\frac{3}{5} + \frac{3}{5}$ is the same as $\frac{2 \times 3}{5}$ as a lead-in to the Activity.

Activity

Goal Develop a rule for multiplying a fraction by a whole number.

Key Discovery To multiply a fraction by a whole number, multiply the numerator by the whole number and write that product over the denominator.

TIPS FOR NEW TEACHERS

Be sure students know how to write improper fractions as mixed numbers when simplifying products. See Tips for New Teachers in the *Chapter 7 Resource Book*.

EXTRA EXAMPLES

Example 1 $\frac{3}{8} \times 10 = \underline{?}$. $3\frac{3}{4}$

Example 2 Multiply.

a. $\frac{2}{9} \times 3$ $\frac{2}{3}$

b. $\frac{12}{5} \times 4$ $9\frac{3}{5}$

Example 3 You are buying 16 cans of cat food. You want $\frac{3}{8}$ of the cans to be chicken flavored. How many chicken flavored cans should you buy? 6

NOTETAKING

Notebook entries for this lesson should include specific examples as well as the general pattern of multiplying whole numbers and fractions.

Common Error

Some students may multiply both numerator and denominator by the whole number. Have these students simplify their answer to see that it is incorrect to do this.

HELP with Solving

You can find the product the same way whether the whole number is written on the left or on the right. In part (a) of Example 2, $\frac{3}{8} \times 2 = 2 \times \frac{3}{8} = \frac{3}{4}$.

EXAMPLE 2 Multiply Whole Numbers by Fractions

a. $\frac{3}{8} \times 2 = \frac{6}{8}$

$= \frac{3}{4}$

b. $\frac{4}{3} \times 2 = \frac{8}{3}$

$= 2\frac{2}{3}$

Your turn now **Find the product. Simplify if possible.**

1. $3 \times \frac{3}{10}$ $\frac{9}{10}$ **2.** $9 \times \frac{3}{8}$ $3\frac{3}{8}$ **3.** $\frac{6}{5} \times 7$ $8\frac{2}{5}$ **4.** $\frac{5}{6} \times 3$ $2\frac{1}{2}$

5. Look at the results in Example 2. Then predict whether the product will be *greater than 2* or *less than 2* when 2 is multiplied by $\frac{13}{8}$. greater than 2

Using Mental Math You can sometimes find the product of a whole number and a fraction using mental math or a model, as in Example 3.

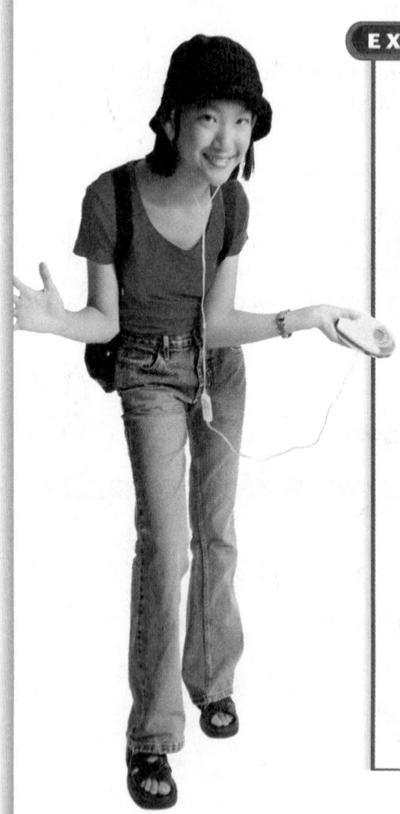

EXAMPLE 3 Using Mental Math or a Model

Party Music You are choosing 18 CDs to bring to a party. You want $\frac{2}{3}$ of the CDs to have dance music. How many dance music CDs should you choose?

Solution

The number of dance music CDs you should choose is $\frac{2}{3}$ *of* 18, or $\frac{2}{3} \times 18$. You can use a model or mental math to find this product.

Method 1 Use a model. Draw 18 circles. Divide them into three equal parts. Circle two of the three parts.

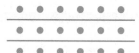

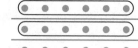

Method 2 Use mental math. Think: $\frac{1}{3}$ of 18 is 6, because $18 \div 3 = 6$. So, $\frac{2}{3}$ of 18 is 12, because $2 \times 6 = 12$.

ANSWER You should choose 12 dance music CDs to bring to the party.

EXTRA EXAMPLES

Example 4 You need to clear space on a shelf to make room for 15 notebooks. Each notebook is $\frac{7}{8}$ inch wide. Estimate how much space you need for the notebooks. **about 14 in.**

EXAMPLE 4 **Estimating a Product**

CD Rack You have 15 CDs and each CD case is $\frac{3}{8}$ inch wide. Estimate how wide a space you need on your CD rack to fit your 15 CDs.

$\text{Space} = \frac{3}{8} \times 15$ Multiply width of a CD case by number of cases.

$\approx \frac{3}{8} \times 16$ Replace 15 with a number compatible with 8.

$= 6$ Think: $\frac{1}{8}$ of 16 is 2, so $\frac{3}{8}$ of 16 is 6.

ANSWER You need a space that is about 6 inches wide.

Your turn now **Use mental math.**

6. Find $\frac{3}{4}$ of 28. **21**   **7.** Find $36 \times \frac{2}{9}$. **8**   **8.** Estimate $\frac{3}{4} \times 25$. **18**

CONCEPT CHECK

How do you multiply a fraction by a whole number? **Multiply the numerator of the fraction by the whole number. Write that product over the denominator of the fraction. Write the result as a simplified fraction or mixed number.**

DAILY PUZZLER

The product of a fraction and a whole number is 3. The product of another fraction and another whole number is also 3. If the two whole numbers are 4 and 9, what are the two fractions? $\frac{3}{4}$ and $\frac{1}{3}$

7.1 **Exercises**

More Practice, p. 714

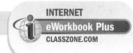

INTERNET
eWorkbook Plus
CLASSZONE.COM

Getting Ready to Practice

1. **Vocabulary** Is 9 compatible with 36 in the product $\frac{7}{9} \times 36$? **yes**

Find the product. Simplify if possible.

2. $5 \times \frac{2}{7}$ $1\frac{3}{7}$ **3.** $\frac{7}{4} \times 2$ $3\frac{1}{2}$ **4.** $\frac{1}{2} \times 8$ **4**   **5.** $24 \times \frac{5}{8}$ **15**

Use compatible numbers to estimate the product.

6. $\frac{5}{6} \times 23$ **20**   **7.** $\frac{2}{7} \times 15$ **4**   **8.** $39 \times \frac{3}{4}$ **30**   **9.** $18 \times \frac{3}{10}$ **6**

10. **Guided Problem Solving** Each student needs $\frac{3}{4}$ pound of sand for an experiment. About how much sand is needed for 21 students?

    1 Write an expression for what you need to find. $\frac{3}{4} \times 21$

    2 Choose a compatible number to substitute for 21. **20**

    3 Use mental math to estimate the answer. **about 15 lb of sand**

③ APPLY

ASSIGNMENT GUIDE

Basic Course
Day 1: EP p. 712 Exs. 43–47;
pp. 316–317 Exs. 11–30,
35–39, 42, 48–59

Average Course
Day 1: pp. 316–317 Exs. 15–26,
31–44, 48–53, 57–59

Advanced Course
Day 1: pp. 316–317 Exs. 17–26,
31–47*, 50–55, 59

Block
pp. 316–317 Exs. 15–26,
31–44, 48–53, 57–59
(with 7.2)

EXTRA PRACTICE

- Student Edition, p. 714
- Chapter 7 Resource Book, pp. 7–9
- Test and Practice Generator

⟳ TRANSPARENCY

Even-numbered answers are available on transparencies.

HOMEWORK CHECK

When you review students' homework for this lesson, go over the following exercises to check understanding of key concepts.
Basic: 11, 15, 19, 23, 27
Average: 15, 18, 23, 25, 31
Advanced: 17, 21, 24, 25, 32

HELP with Homework

Example	Exercises
1	11–26
2	11–26
3	19–24
4	27–34

ⓘ Online Resources
CLASSZONE.COM
· More Examples
· eTutorial Plus

37. High; yes. *Sample answer:* if the rack is too large, it will still hold all of the CDs; however, if it is too small, it will not hold all of them.

What do you think? **History**

■ **National Parks**

The Statue of Liberty National Monument has a total area of 58.38 acres. Its land consists of Liberty Island and Ellis Island. The official area of Liberty Island is 10.38 acres and of Ellis Island is 27.5 acres. About how many acres of the park are under water?
about 20.5 acres

Practice and Problem Solving

A Find the product.

11. $6 \times \frac{3}{7}$ $2\frac{4}{7}$ **12.** $3 \times \frac{3}{10}$ $\frac{9}{10}$ **13.** $\frac{3}{2} \times 5$ $7\frac{1}{2}$ **14.** $\frac{4}{3} \times 4$ $5\frac{1}{3}$

15. $2 \times \frac{5}{12}$ $\frac{5}{6}$ **16.** $6 \times \frac{2}{9}$ $1\frac{1}{3}$ **17.** $\frac{1}{6} \times 15$ $2\frac{1}{2}$ **18.** $\frac{5}{8} \times 6$ $3\frac{3}{4}$

19. $\frac{1}{5} \times 30$ 6 **20.** $\frac{5}{6} \times 12$ 10 **21.** $70 \times \frac{4}{7}$ 40 **22.** $40 \times \frac{9}{10}$ 36

Find the amount.

23. Number of minutes in $\frac{2}{3}$ of an hour   **40 min**

24. Cost of $\frac{3}{4}$ pound of nuts at \$8 per pound   **\$6**

25. Distance run if you run 10 times around a $\frac{1}{4}$ mile track   **$2\frac{1}{2}$ mi**

26. Distance walked in a week if you walk $\frac{1}{2}$ mile each day   **$3\frac{1}{2}$ mi**

Estimation **Identify the closest whole number that is compatible with the denominator of the fraction. Then estimate the answer.**

27. $\frac{1}{4}$ of 19 **20; 5**   **28.** $\frac{1}{7}$ of 47 **49; 7**   **29.** $\frac{2}{5}$ of 28 **30; 12**   **30.** $\frac{5}{8}$ of 43 **40; 25**

31. $\frac{7}{8} \times 46$ **48; 42**   **32.** $\frac{8}{9} \times 83$ **81; 72**   **33.** $32 \times \frac{2}{3}$ **33; 22**   **34.** $53 \times \frac{2}{11}$ **55; 10**

B 35. **National Parks** The total land area in the National Park system is about 78 million acres. Estimate the land area for each category shown in the circle graph.
Parks: 48 million acres; Preserves: 21 million acres; Recreation areas: 3 million acres; Monuments and other: 3 million acres

Land in National Park System

Parks $\frac{16}{25}$ — Preserves $\frac{7}{25}$ — Recreation areas $\frac{1}{25}$ — Monuments and other $\frac{1}{25}$

36. **Predict** Predict whether the product of 24 and each of the following fractions is *less than 24* or *greater than 24*: $\frac{2}{3}, \frac{5}{3}, \frac{1}{2}, \frac{3}{2}, \frac{3}{8}, \frac{9}{8}$.
Then find the product to check your answer.   less than, greater than, less than, greater than, less than, greater than; 16, 40, 12, 36, 9, 27

37. **Critical Thinking** Is the estimate in Example 4 on page 315 *high* or *low*? Is that appropriate for the situation? Explain.   See margin.

38. **Postcard Collections** You and a friend exchanged travel postcards. You gave your friend $\frac{1}{6}$ of a collection of 54 cards. Your friend gave you $\frac{2}{9}$ of a collection of 63 cards. How many cards do you each have now?
You have 59 cards and your friend has 58 cards.

Use the commutative and associative properties to find the product.

39. $\left(4 \times \frac{5}{7}\right) \times 35$ 100   **40.** $15 \times 8 \times \frac{2}{3}$ 80   **41.** $\frac{2}{9} \times 11 \times 18$ 44

C Measurement Use the formula $F = \frac{9}{5}C + 32$, where F is the temperature in degrees Fahrenheit (°F) and C is the temperature in degrees Celsius (°C). Write the temperature in degrees Fahrenheit.

42. 0°C   32°F   **43.** 35°C   95°F   **44.** 100°C   212°F

Challenge Use the part of a set to find the size of the whole set.

45. $\frac{1}{3}$ of a set is 8.   24   **46.** $\frac{3}{4}$ of a set is 9.   12   **47.** $\frac{5}{6}$ of a set is 10.   12

Mixed Review

Multiply. Use estimation to check your answer. *(Lesson 4.3)*

48. 18.7×4.2
     78.54

49. 2.63×0.51
     1.3413

50. 0.034×6.8
     0.2312

51. 0.74×0.059
     0.04366

Round the fraction to the nearest half. *(Lesson 6.1)*

52. $\frac{9}{10}$ 1   **53.** $\frac{5}{12}$ $\frac{1}{2}$ **54.** $\frac{4}{7}$ $\frac{1}{2}$ **55.** $\frac{1}{9}$ 0

Basic Skills **Write a fraction to represent the shaded region.**

56.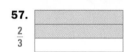
$\frac{3}{5}$

57.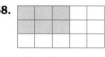
$\frac{2}{3}$

58.
$\frac{6}{15}$ or $\frac{2}{5}$

Test-Taking Practice

59. **Extended Response** You plan to make 6 times a chili recipe and 6 times a guacamole recipe. The chili recipe calls for $\frac{2}{3}$ cup of chopped tomatoes and the guacamole recipe calls for $\frac{3}{4}$ cup. One small tomato makes about $\frac{1}{2}$ cup of chopped tomatoes. Will 12 small tomatoes be enough? Explain your reasoning. *See margin.*

59. No. *Sample answer:*
12 small tomatoes make $\frac{1}{2} \times 12 = 6$ c chopped. Because $6 \times \frac{2}{3} = 4$ c for chili and $6 \times \frac{3}{4} = 4\frac{1}{2}$ c for guacamole, you need $8\frac{1}{2}$ c total, and $8\frac{1}{2}$ c > 6c. Alternatively, $6 \times \left(\frac{2}{3} + \frac{3}{4}\right)$ c is greater than 6 c because $\frac{2}{3} + \frac{3}{4} > 1$.

INTERNET
State Test Practice
CLASSZONE.COM

EXPLORE THE CONCEPT

- Students will use tiles or graph paper to form rectangles that model products of fractions.
- This activity leads into the computational skill of multiplying a fraction by a fraction, which is introduced in Lesson 7.2.

MATERIALS

Each student or group of students will need at least 35 tiles and graph paper. See also the Activity master in the *Chapter 7 Resource Book*.

RECOMMENDED TIME

Work activity: 15 min
Discuss results: 5 min

GROUPING

Students can work individually or in groups of two. If they work in pairs, they can discuss how to arrange their objects in rows and columns.

 TRANSPARENCY

A support transparency is available for this activity.

TIPS FOR SUCCESS

Be sure students understand that the parts of each model they make need to be the same size.

DISCUSSION

As students work through Step 1, you may wish to ask them why the tiles are arranged to form a 2 by 3 rectangle. **The 3 columns represent the denominator of $\frac{1}{3}$ and the 2 rows represent the denominator of $\frac{1}{2}$.**

318

7.2 Hands-on **Activity**

GOAL
Understand how to model the product of two fractions.

MATERIALS
- tiles (plastic counters, pennies, squares of paper)
- graph paper

Modeling Products of Fractions

In this activity, you will model products of fractions in two ways. To create a model for the product $\frac{1}{3} \times \frac{1}{2}$, you need to find $\frac{1}{3}$ *of* $\frac{1}{2}$ of a whole.

Explore 1 Model $\frac{1}{3} \times \frac{1}{2}$ using a rectangle of tiles.

1 Make a 2 by 3 rectangle of tiles to model halves and thirds.

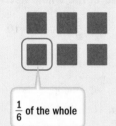

$\frac{1}{6}$ of the whole

2 Each row is $\frac{1}{2}$ of the tiles.

Each column is $\frac{1}{3}$ of the tiles.

$\frac{1}{2}$ $\frac{1}{3}$

3 Now, select $\frac{1}{2}$ of the tiles.

$\frac{1}{2}$

4 Next, find $\frac{1}{3}$ of $\frac{1}{2}$ of the tiles.

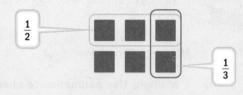

$\frac{1}{3} \times \frac{1}{2} = \frac{1}{6}$

Your turn now **Model the product using the given size rectangle of tiles.**

1. $\frac{1}{4} \times \frac{3}{4}$, 4 by 4 rectangle $\frac{3}{16}$ 2. $\frac{1}{2} \times \frac{3}{4}$, 2 by 4 rectangle $\frac{3}{8}$ 3. $\frac{3}{5} \times \frac{4}{7}$, 5 by 7 rectangle $\frac{12}{35}$

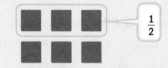 4. **Writing** Explain how you can decide what size rectangle of tiles to use to create a model for the product $\frac{1}{3} \times \frac{5}{6}$. **Look at the denominators to find the dimensions. In this case, use a 3 by 6 rectangle.**

NCTM CURRICULUM STANDARDS
Standard 1: Understand meanings of operations
Standard 10: Use representations to communicate mathematical ideas

🔍 **KEY DISCOVERY**

The product of two fractions is the product of the numerators divided by the product of the denominators.

ASSESSMENT

1. Model the product using the given size rectangle of tiles: $\frac{1}{8} \times \frac{3}{4}$, 8 by 4 rectangle $\frac{3}{32}$

2. Model the product on graph paper. $\frac{2}{5} \times \frac{2}{5}$ $\frac{4}{25}$

Explore 2 Model $\frac{1}{3} \times \frac{1}{2}$ on graph paper.

1 Draw a 2 by 3 rectangle on graph paper to model halves and thirds. There are 6 small squares, so each square is $\frac{1}{6}$ of the rectangle.

2 Shade $\frac{1}{2}$ of the rectangle.

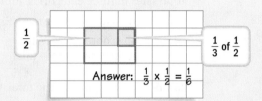

$\frac{1}{2}$ $\frac{1}{3}$ of $\frac{1}{2}$

Answer: $\frac{1}{3} \times \frac{1}{2} = \frac{1}{6}$

3 Then select $\frac{1}{3}$ of the $\frac{1}{2}$.

Your turn now Model the product on graph paper.

5. $\frac{1}{4} \times \frac{3}{4}$ $\frac{3}{16}$ **6.** $\frac{1}{2} \times \frac{3}{4}$ $\frac{3}{8}$ **7.** $\frac{3}{5} \times \frac{4}{7}$ $\frac{12}{35}$

8. Copy and complete the table. Use the model shown above and the ones you drew in Exercises 5–7.

Product	$\frac{1}{3} \times \frac{1}{2} = \frac{?}{?}$	$\frac{1}{4} \times \frac{3}{4} = \frac{?}{?}$	$\frac{1}{2} \times \frac{3}{4} = \frac{?}{?}$	$\frac{3}{5} \times \frac{4}{7} = \frac{?}{?}$
Number of squares in large rectangle you drew	6	? 16	? 8	? 35
Product of denominators	? 6	? 16	? 8	? 35
Number of squares in small rectangle you selected	1	? 3	? 3	? 12
Product of numerators	? 1	? 3	? 3	? 12

Stop and Think

9. Critical Thinking Use the information in your table to suggest a method for finding the product of two fractions without using a model. **Multiply the numerators and multiply the denominators.**

10. Number Sense For each product in the table, compare the answer to each of the fractions being multiplied. Is the answer *greater than* or *less than* the first fraction? the second fraction? Explain why this happens. **Less than; less than. *Sample answer:* You are finding part of a part which is smaller than either part.**

LESSON OBJECTIVE

Multiply fractions.

PACING

Suggested Number of Days
Basic Course: 2 days
Average Course: 2 days
Advanced Course: 2 days
Block: 0.5 block with 7.1
0.5 block with 7.3

TEACHING RESOURCES

For a complete list of Teaching Resources, see page 310B.

 **TRANSPARENCY**

Warm-Up Exercises for this lesson are available on a transparency. A support transparency is available for Example 1.

2 TEACH

MOTIVATING THE LESSON

Show students that the rule for multiplying a fraction by a whole number could be written as $\frac{a}{1} \cdot \frac{b}{c} = \frac{a \cdot b}{1 \cdot c}$. Then ask what the rule for multiplying $\frac{a}{b}$ by $\frac{c}{d}$ might be. $\frac{a \cdot c}{b \cdot d}$

Multiplying Fractions

LESSON 7.2

BEFORE	▶ Now	WHY?
You multiplied a fraction by a whole number.	You'll multiply fractions.	So you can find distances in a relay race, as in Exercise 35.

In the Real World

Word Watch

Review Words
factor, p. 16
common factor, p. 222
simplest form, p. 229

Scooter Sales The table shows the fraction of a sporting goods store's total sales in three categories. John, a salesperson at the store, made $\frac{2}{3}$ of the push scooter sales. What fraction of the total sales is this?

Fraction of Total Sales	
push scooters	$\frac{1}{5}$
in-line skates	$\frac{1}{10}$
bicycles	$\frac{3}{5}$

John's sales are $\frac{2}{3}$ of $\frac{1}{5}$ of the total. When you find part *of* a part, you are multiplying two fractions.

EXAMPLE 1 **Using a Model to Multiply Fractions**

To answer the question above about John's sales, you can use a model to find $\frac{2}{3}$ *of* $\frac{1}{5}$, or $\frac{2}{3} \times \frac{1}{5}$.

① Draw a 3 by 5 rectangle to model thirds and fifths. Each small square is $\frac{1}{15}$ of the whole.

② Shade $\frac{1}{5}$ of the rectangle.

③ Select $\frac{2}{3}$ of the shaded rectangle.

ANSWER Two of the 15 squares are selected, so $\frac{2}{3} \times \frac{1}{5} = \frac{2}{15}$.

John's push scooter sales are $\frac{2}{15}$ of the store's total sales.

Your turn now Draw a model to find the product. 1–3. Check drawings.

1. $\frac{1}{2} \times \frac{1}{5}$ $\frac{1}{10}$

2. $\frac{2}{3} \times \frac{2}{5}$ $\frac{4}{15}$

3. $\frac{3}{4} \times \frac{5}{7}$ $\frac{15}{28}$

NCTM CURRICULUM STANDARDS
Standard 1: Understand meanings of operations
Standard 2: Represent situations using algebraic symbols
Standard 10: Use representations to communicate ideas

Using a Rule Look back at the model of the product $\frac{2}{3} \times \frac{1}{5}$ in Example 1 to see how the model is related to the rule below.

$$\frac{\text{area of selected rectangle}}{\text{area of whole rectangle}} = \frac{2 \times 1}{3 \times 5} = \frac{\text{product of the numerators}}{\text{product of the denominators}}$$

Multiplying Fractions

Words product of fractions = $\dfrac{\text{product of the numerators}}{\text{product of the denominators}}$

Numbers $\dfrac{3}{4} \times \dfrac{5}{8} = \dfrac{15}{32}$ **Algebra** $\dfrac{a}{b} \cdot \dfrac{c}{d} = \dfrac{a \cdot c}{b \cdot d}$

EXAMPLE 2 **Multiplying Two Fractions**

$\dfrac{2}{5} \times \dfrac{4}{3} = \dfrac{2 \times 4}{5 \times 3}$ Use the rule for multiplying fractions.

$= \dfrac{8}{15}$ Multiply. The product is in simplest form.

EXAMPLE 3 **Evaluating an Algebraic Expression**

xy Algebra **Evaluate the expression** $\frac{1}{3}n$ **when** $n = \frac{2}{7}$.

$\dfrac{1}{3}n = \dfrac{1}{3} \times \dfrac{2}{7}$ Substitute $\frac{2}{7}$ for n.

$= \dfrac{1 \times 2}{3 \times 7}$ Use the rule for multiplying fractions.

$= \dfrac{2}{21}$ Multiply. The product is in simplest form.

HELP with Solving
Notice in Example 3 that the product of $\frac{1}{3}$ and $\frac{2}{7}$ is less than either fraction.

Your turn now In Exercises 4–7, find the value.

4. Find the product $\frac{1}{3} \times \frac{1}{6}$. $\frac{1}{18}$ **5.** Find the product $\frac{3}{7} \times \frac{1}{4}$. $\frac{3}{28}$

6. Evaluate $\frac{3}{4}n$ when $n = \frac{3}{5}$. $\frac{9}{20}$ **7.** Evaluate $\frac{2}{3}x$ when $x = \frac{4}{9}$. $\frac{8}{27}$

8. Is the product in Example 2 less than both fractions? no

TIPS FOR NEW TEACHERS
Check students as they complete the exercises to make sure that they multiply numerators by numerators and denominators by denominators when they find the product of two fractions. See Tips for New Teachers in the *Chapter 7 Resource Book*.

EXTRA EXAMPLES

Example 1 Draw an area model and use it to find $\frac{3}{5} \times \frac{1}{4}$.

$\frac{3}{5} \times \frac{1}{4} = \frac{3}{20}$

Example 2 Multiply $\frac{2}{7}$ by $\frac{6}{5}$.
$\frac{12}{35}$

Example 3 Evaluate the expression $\frac{3}{4}m$ when $m = \frac{5}{7}$.
$\frac{15}{28}$

VISUALIZE

When students visualize or draw area models such as the one for Example 1, be sure they understand that the dimensions of the rectangle correspond to the denominators of the fractions being multiplied.

MULTIPLE REPRESENTATIONS

Students should understand that $\frac{a}{b} \times \frac{c}{d}$ and $\frac{a \times c}{b \times d}$ are two different representations of the same value.

Simplifying First When you multiply fractions, it is sometimes easier to simplify before carrying out the multiplication.

EXAMPLE 4 **Simplifying Before Multiplying**

 with Solving

To simplify in Example 4, find the greatest factor of 8 that is also a factor of 12 or 15.

$$\frac{1}{12} \times \frac{8}{15} = \frac{1 \times 8}{12 \times 15} \qquad \text{Use the rule for multiplying fractions.}$$

$$= \frac{1 \times \overset{2}{\cancel{8}}}{\underset{3}{\cancel{12}} \times 15} \qquad \text{4 is a factor of 8 and 12. Divide 8 and 12 by 4.}$$

$$= \frac{1 \times 2}{3 \times 15} \qquad \text{Rewrite.}$$

$$= \frac{2}{45} \qquad \text{Multiply.}$$

You can use the rule for multiplying fractions to find the product of three or more fractions. You may be able to divide by more than one common factor when you simplify.

EXAMPLE 5 **Multiplying Three Fractions**

Watch Out!

Rewrite the fraction after dividing out common factors. You will be less likely to make an error when you multiply.

$$\frac{1}{6} \times \frac{3}{4} \times \frac{2}{5} = \frac{1 \times 3 \times 2}{6 \times 4 \times 5} \qquad \text{Use the rule for multiplying fractions.}$$

$$= \frac{1 \times \overset{1}{\cancel{3}} \times \overset{1}{\cancel{2}}}{\underset{2}{\cancel{6}} \times \underset{2}{\cancel{4}} \times 5} \qquad \begin{array}{l}\text{3 is a factor of 3 and 6. Divide 3 and 6 by 3.}\\\text{2 is a factor of 2 and 4. Divide 2 and 4 by 2.}\end{array}$$

$$= \frac{1 \times 1 \times 1}{2 \times 2 \times 5} \qquad \text{Rewrite.}$$

$$= \frac{1}{20} \qquad \text{Multiply.}$$

Your turn now Multiply. Write the answer in simplest form.

9. $\frac{3}{8} \times \frac{5}{9}$ $\frac{5}{24}$

10. $\frac{6}{7} \times \frac{2}{3}$ $\frac{4}{7}$

11. $\frac{5}{16} \times \frac{8}{15}$ $\frac{1}{6}$

12. $\frac{1}{2} \times \frac{3}{5} \times \frac{1}{6}$ $\frac{1}{20}$

13. $\frac{3}{7} \times \frac{5}{9} \times \frac{7}{10}$ $\frac{1}{6}$

14. $\frac{2}{5} \times \frac{1}{4} \times \frac{10}{11}$ $\frac{1}{11}$

15. Look at the rule for multiplying fractions on page 321. Use algebraic symbols to write a rule for multiplying three fractions.

$$\frac{a}{b} \cdot \frac{c}{d} \cdot \frac{e}{f} = \frac{a \cdot c \cdot e}{b \cdot d \cdot f}$$

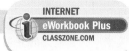

INTERNET
eWorkbook Plus
CLASSZONE.COM

Getting Ready to Practice

1. **Vocabulary** How can you tell whether a fraction is in simplest form? *if the GCF of the numerator and denominator is 1*

2. Draw a model to find the product $\frac{2}{3} \times \frac{4}{5}$. $\frac{8}{15}$

3. Find $\frac{3}{5}$ of $\frac{1}{2}$. $\frac{3}{10}$

4. Find $\frac{1}{6}$ of $\frac{6}{11}$. $\frac{1}{11}$

5. Find $\frac{7}{8}$ of $\frac{4}{5}$. $\frac{7}{10}$

 Algebra **Evaluate the expression when** $x = \frac{3}{4}$.

6. $\frac{1}{5}x$ $\frac{3}{20}$

7. $\frac{8}{9}x$ $\frac{2}{3}$

8. $\frac{3}{4}x$ $\frac{9}{16}$

9. **Find the Error** Describe and correct the error in the solution.
The GCF of 3 and 9 is 3, and 9 divided by 3 is 3, not 2. The solution is $\frac{5}{12}$.

$$\times \quad \frac{3}{4} \times \frac{5}{9} = \frac{\overset{1}{\cancel{3}} \times 5}{4 \times \underset{2}{\cancel{9}}} = \frac{5}{8}$$

Practice and Problem Solving

A 10. Draw a model to find the product $\frac{3}{5} \times \frac{1}{4}$. Use the model to explain why the product is less than 1. $\frac{3}{20}$. *Sample answer:* A part of a part is less than either part.

Find the product.

11. $\frac{1}{3} \times \frac{4}{7}$ $\frac{4}{21}$

12. $\frac{1}{3} \times \frac{1}{3}$ $\frac{1}{9}$

13. $\frac{3}{4} \times \frac{1}{4}$ $\frac{3}{16}$

14. $\frac{7}{8} \times \frac{1}{2}$ $\frac{7}{16}$

15. $\frac{1}{2} \times \frac{3}{10}$ $\frac{3}{20}$

16. $\frac{4}{5} \times \frac{6}{7}$ $\frac{24}{35}$

17. $\frac{2}{5} \times \frac{2}{9}$ $\frac{4}{45}$

18. $\frac{6}{5} \times \frac{3}{7}$ $\frac{18}{35}$

Algebra **Evaluate the expression when** $x = \frac{1}{5}$.

19. $\frac{1}{7}x$ $\frac{1}{35}$

20. $\frac{7}{10}x$ $\frac{7}{50}$

21. $\frac{6}{11}x$ $\frac{6}{55}$

22. **Soap Bubbles** You and a friend want to make one half of a batch of soap bubble solution. How much dishwashing liquid do you need? $\frac{1}{8}$ c

SOAP BUBBLE SOLUTION

1 cup warm water

$\frac{1}{4}$ cup dishwashing liquid

1 teaspoon salt

Combine all ingredients.
Mix well until salt dissolves.

323

36. $\frac{1}{12}$; $\frac{1}{15}$ in.;

Sample answer: The answer is reasonable because $\frac{1}{15}$ is much less than $\frac{4}{5}$.

46. $\frac{1}{80}$; 800 glaciers.

Sample answer: Estimate the product of $\frac{1}{80}$ and 67,000 by rounding 67,000 to 64,000, a number compatible with 80.

Find the product.

23. $\frac{1}{4} \times \frac{8}{15}$ $\frac{2}{15}$

24. $\frac{1}{2} \times \frac{4}{7}$ $\frac{2}{7}$

25. $\frac{2}{3} \times \frac{3}{8}$ $\frac{1}{4}$

26. $\frac{6}{1} \times \frac{1}{6}$ 1

27. $\frac{7}{9} \times \frac{9}{14}$ $\frac{1}{2}$

28. $\frac{3}{7} \times \frac{7}{9}$ $\frac{1}{3}$

29. $\frac{5}{8} \times \frac{24}{25}$ $\frac{3}{5}$

30. $\frac{11}{10} \times \frac{5}{22}$ $\frac{1}{4}$

31. $\frac{3}{4} \times \frac{5}{6} \times \frac{1}{2}$ $\frac{5}{16}$

32. $\frac{2}{3} \times \frac{3}{5} \times \frac{7}{10}$ $\frac{7}{25}$

33. $\frac{5}{8} \times \frac{3}{10} \times \frac{16}{21}$ $\frac{1}{7}$

34. $\frac{7}{8} \times \frac{4}{15} \times \frac{3}{14}$ $\frac{1}{20}$

35. **Sports** Two teams of four students are running a relay race. The total distance of the race is $\frac{1}{2}$ mile. The teams are tied $\frac{3}{4}$ of the way through the race. At this point, how far have the teams run? $\frac{3}{8}$ mi

36. **Fingernails** Healthy fingernails grow about $\frac{4}{5}$ inch per year. A month is what fraction of a year? Use that result to find how much healthy fingernails grow per month. Is your answer reasonable? Explain.
See margin.

B Number Sense **Copy and complete the statement using <, >, or =.**

37. $\frac{3}{8} \times \frac{4}{5} \underline{?} 1$ <

38. $1 \times \frac{2}{3} \underline{?} \frac{2}{3}$ =

39. $\frac{3}{8} \times \frac{5}{5} \underline{?} \frac{3}{8}$ =

40. $\frac{1}{3} \times \frac{4}{3} \underline{?} \frac{1}{3}$ >

41. $\frac{1}{3} \times \frac{4}{3} \underline{?} \frac{4}{3}$ <

42. $\frac{1}{3} \times \frac{3}{4} \underline{?} \frac{1}{3}$ <

Evaluate the expression.

43. $\frac{2}{3} + \frac{1}{3} \times \frac{3}{4}$ $\frac{11}{12}$

44. $\frac{5}{6} - \frac{1}{6} \times \frac{1}{2}$ $\frac{3}{4}$

45. $\frac{1}{2} \times \left(\frac{3}{5}\right)^2$ $\frac{9}{50}$

46. **Glaciers** The World Glacier Inventory contains data from over 67,000 glaciers around the world. About $\frac{1}{50}$ of the glaciers are in North America. About $\frac{5}{8}$ of these are in the Queen Elizabeth Islands in Northern Canada. What fraction of the glaciers are in the Queen Elizabeth Islands? Estimate the number of glaciers in the Queen Elizabeth Islands to the nearest hundred. Explain your steps.

What do you think? **Science**

 Glaciers

A glacier is a large mass of ice that flows over land. Glaciers are often between 300 and 10,000 feet thick. Is a glacier thicker than your school is tall? **Answers may vary.**

C Find the product.

47. $\frac{7}{24} \times \frac{18}{13} \times \frac{16}{21}$ $\frac{4}{13}$ **48.** $\frac{48}{77} \times \frac{33}{52} \times \frac{7}{18}$ $\frac{2}{13}$ **49.** $\frac{36}{49} \times \frac{25}{54} \times \frac{21}{40}$ $\frac{5}{28}$

50. Basketball This season the school basketball team played $\frac{3}{7}$ of their games at night and $\frac{4}{7}$ of their games during the day. They won $\frac{3}{4}$ of their night games and $\frac{1}{2}$ of their day games. What fraction of their games did they win during the season? Explain how you found your answer.

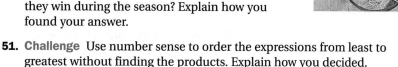

51. Challenge Use number sense to order the expressions from least to greatest without finding the products. Explain how you decided.

$\frac{17}{32} \times \frac{7}{12}$ $\qquad$ $\frac{7}{12} \times \frac{13}{27}$ $\qquad$ $\frac{18}{19} \times \frac{7}{12}$ $\qquad$ $\frac{7}{12} \times \frac{1}{2}$ $\qquad$ $\frac{7}{12} \times \frac{2}{21}$

Mixed Review

Copy and complete the statement. *(Lesson 5.6)*

52. $4\frac{2}{5} = \frac{?}{5}$ 22   **53.** $5\frac{1}{3} = \frac{16}{?}$ 3   **54.** $\frac{17}{6} = ?\frac{5}{6}$ 2   **55.** $\frac{25}{7} = 3\frac{?}{7}$ 4

Use compatible numbers to estimate the product. *(Lesson 7.1)*

56. $\frac{2}{5} \times 31$ 12   **57.** $\frac{5}{8} \times 18$ 10   **58.** $40 \times \frac{5}{6}$ 35   **59.** $28 \times \frac{2}{3}$ 18

Basic Skills Use clustering to estimate the sum.   60–61. Estimates may vary.

60. $28 + 33 + 31 + 27 + 30 + 32$
180

61. $209 + 195 + 211 + 193 + 198$
1000

Test-Taking Practice

INTERNET

State Test Practice
CLASSZONE.COM

62. Multiple Choice Which product is equal to $\frac{3}{5}$? D

A. $\frac{1}{5} \times \frac{2}{5}$ **B.** $\frac{3}{7} \times \frac{7}{10}$ **C.** $\frac{5}{6} \times \frac{9}{25}$ **D.** $\frac{5}{6} \times \frac{18}{25}$

63. Short Response A town is building a new school that will be about $\frac{1}{2}$ of a block wide and about $\frac{2}{3}$ of a block long. Draw a rectangle to represent one block and model the area of the school on the rectangle. Then give the area of the school in square blocks.

Check drawings; $\frac{1}{3}$ square blocks.

50. $\frac{17}{28}$. *Sample answer:*
Multiply $\frac{3}{7}$ and $\frac{3}{4}$ to find the fraction of night games won and multiply $\frac{4}{7}$ and $\frac{1}{2}$ to find the number of day games won. Add the products to find the answer.

51. $\frac{7}{12} \times \frac{2}{21}, \frac{7}{12} \times \frac{13}{27},$
$\frac{7}{12} \times \frac{1}{2}, \frac{17}{32} \times \frac{7}{12}, \frac{18}{19} \times \frac{7}{12}.$

Sample answer: All of the products contain a factor of $\frac{7}{12}$, so compare the other factors to find the order.

4 ASSESS

ASSESSMENT RESOURCES

For more assessment resources, see:
• Assessment Book
• Test and Practice Generator

MINI-QUIZ

Find each product.

1. $\frac{2}{3} \times \frac{4}{5}$ $\frac{8}{15}$

2. $\frac{3}{7} \times \frac{2}{11}$ $\frac{6}{77}$

3. $\frac{5}{12} \times \frac{6}{7}$ $\frac{5}{14}$

4. $\frac{4}{15} \times \frac{3}{8} \times \frac{1}{5}$ $\frac{1}{50}$

5. A rectangle has length $\frac{3}{5}$ inch and width w inches. Find the area of the rectangle if $w = \frac{7}{8}$ inch.
$\frac{21}{40}$ in.^{2}

5 FOLLOW-UP

RETEACHING/REMEDIATION

• Study Guide in Chapter 7 Resource Book, pp. 19–20
• Tutor Place, Fractions Card 15
• eTutorial Plus Online
• Extra Practice, p. 714
• Lesson Practice in Chapter 7 Resource Book, pp. 16–18

CHALLENGE/ENRICHMENT

• Challenge Practice in Chapter 7 Resource Book, p. 21
• Teacher's Edition, p. 310F

ENGLISH LEARNER SUPPORT

• Spanish Study Guide
• Multi-Language Glossary
• Chapter Audio Summaries CDs

LESSON OBJECTIVE

Multiply mixed numbers.

PACING

Suggested Number of Days
Basic Course: 1 day
Average Course: 1 day
Advanced Course: 1 day
Block: 0.5 block with 7.2

TEACHING RESOURCES

For a complete list of Teaching Resources, see page 310B.

 TRANSPARENCY

Warm-Up Exercises for this lesson are available on a transparency.

② **TEACH**

MOTIVATING THE LESSON

Tell students that altering recipes involves the concept in the Activity.

ACTIVITY

Goal Use a diagram to see how to multiply fractions and mixed numbers.

Key Discovery To multiply a fraction by a mixed number, first write the mixed number in fraction form.

Multiplying Mixed Numbers

BEFORE	Now	WHY?
You multiplied fractions.	You'll multiply mixed numbers.	So you can find areas, such as the area of a trampoline in Example 3.

 Word Watch

Review Words
mixed number, p. 244
improper fraction, p. 244

 Activity You can use a picture of measuring cups to find $\frac{1}{2} \times 1\frac{1}{3}$.

① Draw a picture of $1\frac{1}{3}$ cups.

② Replace 1 cup with three $\frac{1}{3}$ cups.

There are now four $\frac{1}{3}$ cups, or $\frac{4}{3}$ cups.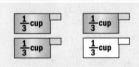

③ Circle $\frac{1}{2}$ of $\frac{4}{3}$. There are $\frac{2}{3}$ selected,

so $\frac{1}{2} \times 1\frac{1}{3} = \frac{2}{3}$.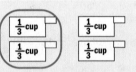

Draw a picture to find the product.   **1.** $\frac{2}{3} \times 1\frac{1}{2}$ 1   **2.** $\frac{1}{2} \times 2\frac{2}{3}$ $1\frac{1}{3}$

1–2. Check drawings.

In the activity, $1\frac{1}{3}$ is shown as $\frac{4}{3}$. When finding a product involving a mixed number, it is helpful to first write all the numbers in fraction form.

EXAMPLE 1 **Multiplying with Mixed Numbers**

HELP with **Solving**

In part (b) of Example 1, the whole number 3 was rewritten as the fraction $\frac{3}{1}$ (read "3 wholes"). You could instead have left the 3 in whole number form and multiplied as in Lesson 7.1.
$\frac{7}{4} \times 3 = \frac{21}{4}$

a. $\frac{5}{8} \times 1\frac{2}{3} = \frac{5}{8} \times \frac{5}{3}$ Write $1\frac{2}{3}$ as an improper fraction.

$= \frac{5 \times 5}{8 \times 3}$ Use the rule for multiplying fractions.

$= \frac{25}{24}$, or $1\frac{1}{24}$ Multiply. The answer is in simplest form.

b. $1\frac{3}{4} \times 3 = \frac{7}{4} \times \frac{3}{1}$ Write $1\frac{3}{4}$ and 3 as improper fractions.

$= \frac{7 \times 3}{4 \times 1}$ Use the rule for multiplying fractions.

$= \frac{21}{4}$, or $5\frac{1}{4}$ Multiply. The answer is in simplest form.

NCTM CURRICULUM STANDARDS
Standard 1: Understand how operations are related; Compute fluently
Standard 6: Solve problems in math and other contexts

TIPS FOR NEW TEACHERS

Be sure students know how to write mixed numbers as improper fractions and vice versa. See Tips for New Teachers in the *Chapter 7 Resource Book*.

EXAMPLE 2 Simplifying Before Multiplying

$$2\frac{2}{9} \times 4\frac{4}{5} = \frac{20}{9} \times \frac{24}{5}$$ Write $2\frac{2}{9}$ and $4\frac{4}{5}$ as improper fractions.

$$= \frac{\overset{4}{\cancel{20}} \times \overset{8}{\cancel{24}}}{\underset{3}{\cancel{9}} \times \underset{1}{\cancel{5}}}$$ Use the rule for multiplying fractions. Divide out common factors.

$$= \frac{4 \times 8}{3 \times 1}$$ Rewrite.

$$= \frac{32}{3}, \text{ or } 10\frac{2}{3}$$ Multiply. The answer is in simplest form.

✓ **Check** Round $2\frac{2}{9}$ to 2 and $4\frac{4}{5}$ to 5. Because $2 \times 5 = 10$, the product $10\frac{2}{3}$ is reasonable.

Your turn now Multiply. Write the answer in simplest form.

1. $2\frac{1}{3} \times \frac{5}{6}$ $1\frac{17}{18}$ **2.** $5 \times 2\frac{2}{5}$ 12 **3.** $3\frac{1}{3} \times 2\frac{1}{4}$ $7\frac{1}{2}$ **4.** $3\frac{1}{4} \times 2\frac{3}{5}$ $8\frac{9}{20}$

EXAMPLE 3 Multiplying to Solve Problems

Trampoline Olympic trampoliners get points deducted from their scores if they land outside a rectangle called the *jump zone*. The jump zone measures $7\frac{1}{21}$ feet by $3\frac{1}{2}$ feet. What is the area of the jump zone?

Solution

Area = Length × Width   Write formula for area of a rectangle.

$$= 7\frac{1}{21} \times 3\frac{1}{2}$$ Substitute for length and width.

$$= \frac{148}{21} \times \frac{7}{2}$$ Write $7\frac{1}{21}$ and $3\frac{1}{2}$ as improper fractions.

$$= \frac{\overset{74}{\cancel{148}} \times \overset{1}{\cancel{7}}}{\underset{3}{\cancel{21}} \times \underset{1}{\cancel{2}}}$$ Use the rule for multiplying fractions. Divide out common factors.

$$= \frac{74}{3}, \text{ or } 24\frac{2}{3}$$ Multiply. The answer is in simplest form.

ANSWER The area of the jump zone is $24\frac{2}{3}$ square feet.

■ **Trampoline**

Trampoline became an Olympic sport in 2000. A trampoliner jumps to heights of up to 30 feet. If a trampoliner is 5 feet 6 inches tall, about how many times her height could she jump?

about $5\frac{1}{2}$ times

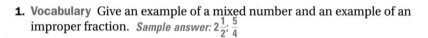
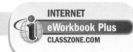
Getting Ready to Practice

1. **Vocabulary** Give an example of a mixed number and an example of an improper fraction. *Sample answer:* $2\frac{1}{2}$; $\frac{5}{4}$

Tell whether you can simplify before multiplying. If so, tell how.

2. $\frac{7}{3} \times \frac{3}{2}$
Yes; divide 3 into 3 and 3.

3. $\frac{5}{2} \times \frac{5}{3}$
no

4. $\frac{3}{2} \times \frac{15}{13}$
no

5. $\frac{18}{25} \times \frac{10}{9}$
Yes; divide 9 into 18 and 9, and divide 5 into 25 and 10.

Multiply. Write the answer in simplest form.

6. $\frac{5}{8} \times 2\frac{1}{4}$ $1\frac{13}{32}$

7. $3\frac{2}{5} \times 10$ 34

8. $3\frac{4}{7} \times 2\frac{1}{3}$ $8\frac{1}{3}$

9. $1\frac{5}{6} \times 1\frac{13}{22}$ $2\frac{11}{12}$

10. **Soccer** An indoor soccer goal is $6\frac{1}{2}$ feet high. An outdoor soccer goal is $1\frac{3}{13}$ times as high as an indoor goal. How high is an outdoor goal? Estimate to check that your answer is reasonable. 8 ft

Practice and Problem Solving

A Find the product.

11. $1\frac{5}{6} \times \frac{1}{2}$ $\frac{11}{12}$

12. $\frac{3}{4} \times 2\frac{1}{4}$ $1\frac{11}{16}$

13. $2 \times 5\frac{2}{3}$ $11\frac{1}{3}$

14. $1\frac{2}{5} \times 4$ $5\frac{3}{5}$

15. $1\frac{1}{6} \times 2\frac{1}{2}$ $2\frac{11}{12}$

16. $3\frac{2}{3} \times 3\frac{1}{2}$ $12\frac{5}{6}$

17. $1\frac{2}{5} \times 2\frac{1}{3}$ $3\frac{4}{15}$

18. $7 \times \frac{4}{9}$ $3\frac{1}{9}$

19. $1\frac{1}{6} \times 8$ $9\frac{1}{3}$

20. $2\frac{1}{3} \times \frac{3}{5}$ $1\frac{2}{5}$

21. $1\frac{1}{2} \times 1\frac{1}{3}$ 2

22. $1\frac{4}{5} \times 2\frac{1}{3}$ $4\frac{1}{5}$

23. $\frac{1}{6} \times 6\frac{3}{4}$ $1\frac{1}{8}$

24. $2\frac{2}{3} \times 5\frac{2}{5}$ $14\frac{2}{5}$

25. $\frac{5}{8} \times 36$ $22\frac{1}{2}$

26. $6 \times 2\frac{2}{9}$ $13\frac{1}{3}$

Estimation Use rounding to estimate the product.

27. $4\frac{5}{8} \times 3\frac{1}{3}$ 15

28. $6 \times 5\frac{7}{8}$ 36

29. $3\frac{2}{3} \times 3\frac{4}{5}$ 16

30. $2\frac{1}{8} \times 1\frac{2}{9}$ 2

Geometry Find the area of the rectangle.

31.
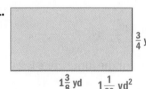
$\frac{3}{4}$ yd
$1\frac{3}{8}$ yd $1\frac{1}{32}$ yd²

32.
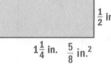
$\frac{1}{2}$ in.
$1\frac{1}{4}$ in. $\frac{5}{8}$ in.²

Projects **In Exercises 33 and 34, the students in a class are presenting their research projects. There are 20 students in the class. Each student will give an oral report that lasts about $3\frac{1}{2}$ minutes.**

33. How much time will it take for all 20 reports to be presented? **70 min**

34. A 15 minute presentation by the teacher was recorded on a $1\frac{1}{2}$ hour videotape. Can all the oral reports be recorded on that same videotape? **yes**

35. **Find the Error** Describe and correct the error in the solution.

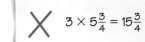
$$3 \times 5\frac{3}{4} = 15\frac{3}{4}$$

B **Find the product.**

36. $3\frac{5}{7} \times 8\frac{4}{5}$ $32\frac{24}{35}$ **37.** $4\frac{3}{8} \times 2\frac{1}{15}$ $9\frac{1}{24}$ **38.** $6\frac{5}{7} \times 1\frac{5}{9}$ $10\frac{4}{9}$ **39.** $1\frac{1}{9} \times 13\frac{1}{8}$ $14\frac{7}{12}$

40. **Writing** Look back at Example 4 on page 315 of Lesson 7.1. Explain how you can use this approach to estimate the product of a fraction and a mixed number. Describe the steps you would use to estimate $\frac{5}{8} \times 42\frac{2}{5}$. First, round the mixed number to a number compatible with the denominator of the fraction. Then multiply. $\frac{5}{8} \times 40 = 25$

41. **Critical Thinking** Jason is estimating $5\frac{1}{2} \times 2\frac{1}{2}$. Would he get a better estimate if he calculated 6×3 or 5×3? Explain your answer. See margin.

42. **Number Sense** Denise found the product $3 \times 6\frac{1}{4}$ mentally by calculating $(3 \times 6) + \left(3 \times \frac{1}{4}\right)$. Use the distributive property to show why Denise's method works. $3 \times 6\frac{1}{4} = 3\left(6 + \frac{1}{4}\right) = 3 \times 6 + 3 \times \frac{1}{4}$

43. **Miniature Books** The Morgan Library in New York City owns a miniature book *Book of Hours* that dates back to around 1535. The front cover measures $2\frac{4}{5}$ inches by $1\frac{9}{10}$ inches. What is the area of the front cover? $5\frac{8}{25}$ in.²

C **Measurement** **In Exercises 44–46, one "Smoot" equals $5\frac{7}{12}$ feet. The length of the Harvard Bridge is $364\frac{2}{5}$ Smoots plus one ear.**

44. Find the number of feet in 360 Smoots. **2010 ft**

45. Use rounding to estimate the number of feet in $4\frac{2}{5}$ Smoots. **24 ft**

46. Use Exercises 44 and 45 to estimate the length of the bridge in feet. **2034 ft**

47. **Challenge** Find the product $3\frac{12}{17} \times \frac{34}{45} \times 18 \times 1\frac{1}{24}$. $52\frac{1}{2}$

35. $5\frac{3}{4}$ must be changed to an improper fraction and then multiplied by 3. The solution should be $3 \times \frac{23}{4} = \frac{69}{4} = 17\frac{1}{4}$.

What do you think?

Measurement

■ **Measuring in Smoots**

In 1958, Massachusetts Institute of Technology student Oliver Reed Smoot, Jr., was used as a unit of measure to determine the length of the Harvard Bridge in Boston.
(See Brain Game, p. 330.)

Lesson 7.3 Multiplying Mixed Numbers **329**

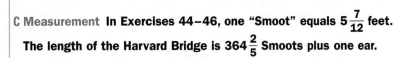

COMMON ERROR

In Exercises 11–26, some students use multiplication twice (i.e., they rewrite $1\frac{5}{6}$ as $\frac{6 \times 1 \times 5}{6}$) instead of using multiplication and addition $\left(1\frac{5}{6} = \frac{6 \times 1 + 5}{6}\right)$. Be sure students can explain and justify each step in writing mixed numbers as improper fractions.

MATH REASONING

In Exercises 27–30, ask students to state whether their estimates are overestimates or underestimates.

41. 5×3. *Sample answer:* With 5×3, one factor is rounded up and one is rounded down, so the estimate will be better.

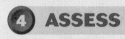

ASSESS

ASSESSMENT RESOURCES

For more assessment resources, see:
- Assessment Book
- Test and Practice Generator

MINI-QUIZ

Find each product.

1. $2\frac{2}{3} \times 4$ $10\frac{2}{3}$

2. $\frac{2}{5} \times 2\frac{3}{5}$ $1\frac{1}{25}$

3. $3\frac{3}{4} \times 5\frac{5}{9}$ $20\frac{5}{6}$

4. The door to a building is $3\frac{3}{8}$ feet by $8\frac{1}{3}$ feet. What is the area of the door? $28\frac{1}{8}$ ft²

FOLLOW-UP

RETEACHING/REMEDIATION

- Study Guide in Chapter 7 Resource Book, pp. 27–28
- Tutor Place, Fractions Card 18
- eTutorial Plus Online
- Extra Practice, p. 714
- Lesson Practice in Chapter 7 Resource Book, pp. 24–26

CHALLENGE/ENRICHMENT

- Challenge Practice in Chapter 7 Resource Book, p. 29
- Teacher's Edition, p. 310F

ENGLISH LEARNER SUPPORT

- Spanish Study Guide
- Multi-Language Glossary
- Chapter Audio Summaries CDs

Brain Game
1–4. See Additional Answers beginning on page AA1.

Mixed Review

Find the elapsed time. *(Lesson 6.6)*

48. 6:20 P.M. to 1:35 A.M. **7 h 15 min**   **49.** 9:15 A.M. to 3:42 P.M. **6 h 27 min**

Choose a Strategy **Use a strategy from the list to solve Exercise 50. Explain your choice of strategy.**

50. After spending $1 for bus fare and $4 for lunch and then earning $3, you have $6. How much money did you start with?

50. $8. *Sample answer:* I used work backward because we know what we have left and need to work backward to find what we had.

51. the number of groups

52. the size of each group

> **Problem Solving Strategies**
> - Guess, Check, and Revise
> - Draw a Diagram
> - Work Backward
> - Look for a Pattern

Basic Skills   **Use the division equation 48 ÷ 6 = 8. The 48 tells you the total number of people who are being split into groups.**

51. If the 6 tells you the size of each group, what does the 8 tell you?

52. If the 6 tells you the number of equal groups, what does the 8 tell you?

Test-Taking Practice

INTERNET
State Test Practice
CLASSZONE.COM

53. Multiple Choice In the race shown, how many miles are on the road? **B**

$1\frac{1}{4}$ mi

bike path · road

$\frac{2}{3}$ of race · $\frac{1}{3}$ of race

A. $\frac{1}{4}$ mi   **B.** $\frac{5}{12}$ mi   **C.** $1\frac{1}{4}$ mi   **D.** $1\frac{5}{12}$ mi

54. Short Response A recipe makes 12 muffins. Your pan will hold a total of 18 muffins. Will your pan hold $1\frac{1}{2}$ times the recipe? Explain.

Yes. *Sample answer:* $1\frac{1}{2}$ times 12 is 18, and the pan will hold 18 muffins.

BRAIN GAME

Making Up Your Own Unit of Measure

1. Choose a student in your group to be a unit of measure. Then decide on a name for the unit.

1–4. See margin.

2. Use your unit to measure the length and the width of your classroom. Describe your method of measuring. If the length and width were not a whole number of units, how did you measure the fractional parts?

3. Calculate the area of your classroom in your units.

4. Compare the area you calculated to the areas calculated by other groups. How do you account for any differences?

That's about $7\frac{1}{16}$ Amandas long.

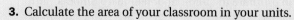

Notebook Review

Review the vocabulary definitions in your notebook.

Copy the review examples in your notebook. Then complete the exercises.

Check Your Definitions

compatible numbers, p. 13	common factor, p. 222	improper fraction, p. 244
factor, p. 16	simplest form, p. 229	whole number, p. 684
	mixed number, p. 244	

Use Your Vocabulary

1. Copy and complete: to multiply mixed numbers, rewrite them as _?_ .   *improper fractions*

7.1 Can you multiply a fraction and a whole number?

 EXAMPLE   **a.** Find $4 \times \frac{2}{9}$.   **b.** Estimate $\frac{3}{5} \times 31$.

a. $4 \times \frac{2}{9} = \frac{4 \times 2}{9} = \frac{8}{9}$ Multiply the numerator by the whole number.

b. $\frac{3}{5} \times 31 \approx \frac{3}{5} \times 30$ Replace 31 with a number compatible with 5.

$= 18$ Think: $\frac{1}{5}$ of 30 is 6, so $\frac{3}{5}$ of 30 is 18.

☑ **Estimate. Then find the product.**

2. $\frac{1}{6} \times 19$ 3; $3\frac{1}{6}$ 3. $\frac{3}{4} \times 11$ 9; $8\frac{1}{4}$ 4. $15 \times \frac{3}{8}$ 6; $5\frac{5}{8}$ 5. $30 \times \frac{2}{7}$ 8; $8\frac{4}{7}$

7.2–7.3 Can you multiply fractions and mixed numbers?

 EXAMPLE $3\frac{1}{8} \times 3\frac{3}{5} = \frac{25}{8} \times \frac{18}{5}$ Write $3\frac{1}{8}$ and $3\frac{3}{5}$ as fractions.

$= \frac{\overset{5}{\cancel{25}} \times \overset{9}{\cancel{18}}}{\underset{4}{\cancel{8}} \times \underset{1}{\cancel{5}}}$ Use rule for multiplying fractions. Divide out common factors.

$= \frac{45}{4}$, or $11\frac{1}{4}$ Multiply.

✓ **Check** Estimate: $3\frac{1}{8} \times 3\frac{3}{5} \approx 3 \times 4 = 12$. So, $11\frac{1}{4}$ is reasonable.

☑ **Find the product.**

6. $\frac{2}{5} \times \frac{5}{7}$ $\frac{2}{7}$ 7. $\frac{2}{3} \times 7$ $4\frac{2}{3}$ 8. $3 \times 1\frac{3}{4}$ $5\frac{1}{4}$ 9. $7\frac{1}{5} \times 3\frac{1}{8}$ $22\frac{1}{2}$

10. The product will be less than the whole number if the fraction is less than one and greater than the whole number if the fraction is greater then one (an improper fraction).

10. Number Sense When you multiply a nonzero whole number by a fraction, how can you tell if the product will be less than or greater than the whole number?

Review Quiz 1

Find the product.

1. $5 \times \frac{3}{4}$ $3\frac{3}{4}$ **2.** $\frac{5}{6} \times 42$ 35   **3.** $\frac{1}{8} \times \frac{2}{9}$ $\frac{1}{36}$ **4.** $\frac{3}{5} \times \frac{7}{10}$ $\frac{21}{50}$

5. $\frac{3}{4} \times \frac{2}{7} \times \frac{4}{5}$ $\frac{6}{35}$ **6.** $7 \times 2\frac{3}{7}$ 17   **7.** $2\frac{2}{3} \times \frac{3}{4}$ 2   **8.** $2\frac{6}{7} \times 4\frac{1}{12}$ $11\frac{2}{3}$

Estimate the product.

9. $19 \times \frac{2}{9}$ 4   **10.** $26 \times \frac{5}{9}$ 15   **11.** $1\frac{7}{8} \times 7$ 14   **12.** $4\frac{1}{4} \times 6\frac{7}{8}$ 28

13. Paperback Books The front cover of a paperback book measures $5\frac{5}{16}$ inches by 8 inches. What is the area of the front cover? $42\frac{1}{2}$ in.²

Brain Game

Equation 1: $\frac{3}{4}, \frac{1}{2}$;

Equation 2: $2\frac{2}{5}, \frac{2}{3}$;

Equation 3: $\frac{5}{6}, \frac{3}{5}$;

Equation 4: $2\frac{1}{4}, 3\frac{1}{3}$;

NICE WORK

BrAiN GAME

Fill in the Fractions

Copy the equations. To read a secret message, find pairs of numbers that make the equations true and fill in their letters. Use each number once. **See margin.**

| ? | × | ? | = | $\frac{3}{8}$ |

| ? | × | ? | = | $1\frac{3}{5}$ |

| ? | × | ? | = | $\frac{1}{2}$ |

| ? | × | ? | = | $7\frac{1}{2}$ |

First Column

$C = \frac{5}{6}$

$E = 2\frac{1}{4}$

$I = 2\frac{2}{5}$

$N = \frac{3}{4}$

Second Column

$K = 3\frac{1}{3}$

$O = \frac{2}{3}$

$R = \frac{3}{5}$

$W = \frac{1}{2}$

7.4 Hands-on **Activity**

GOAL
Understand how to divide by a fraction.

MATERIALS
· ruler

Modeling Fraction Division

In this activity, you will use a ruler and patterns to explore fraction division.

Explore **Model dividing by $\frac{3}{8}$. Use a table to look for a pattern.**

1 Use a ruler to find the quotient $3 \div \frac{3}{8}$.

> $\frac{3}{8}$ inch fits into 3 inches 8 times, so $3 \div \frac{3}{8} = 8$.

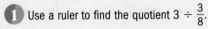
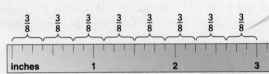

2 Copy the table below. Use a ruler to complete the left side. Then complete the right side.

Dividend	Divisor	Quotient	Dividend	Multiplier	Product
3	÷ $\frac{3}{8}$	= 8	3	× $\frac{8}{3}$	= 8
$\frac{3}{4}$	÷ $\frac{3}{8}$	= **? 2**	$\frac{3}{4}$	× $\frac{8}{3}$	= **? 2**
$\frac{3}{8}$	÷ $\frac{3}{8}$	= **? 2**	$\frac{3}{8}$	× $\frac{8}{3}$	= **? 2**

3 For each dividend, compare the product to the quotient. $3 \div \frac{3}{8} = 8$ and $3 \times \frac{8}{3} = 8$.

Your turn now **Use a ruler to find the quotient. Then find the product.**

1. $3 \div \frac{3}{4}$; $3 \times \frac{4}{3}$ 4; 4
2. $\frac{3}{4} \div \frac{1}{8}$; $\frac{3}{4} \times 8$ 6; 6
3. $\frac{3}{8} \div \frac{3}{16}$; $\frac{3}{8} \times \frac{16}{3}$ 2; 2

Stop and Think   5. Multiply $\frac{3}{4}$ by the reciprocal of $\frac{3}{16}$. $\frac{3}{4} \div \frac{3}{16} = 4$; $\frac{3}{4} \times \frac{16}{3} = 4$.

4. Critical Thinking Describe how the divisor and the multiplier are related in the table shown above and in Exercises 1–3. They are reciprocals.

5. Writing Explain how you could use multiplication to find the quotient $\frac{3}{4} \div \frac{3}{16}$. Try your method. Use a ruler to check your result.

NCTM CURRICULUM STANDARDS
Standard 1: Understand meanings of operations; Understand how operations are related
Standard 10: Use representations to communicate ideas

1 PLAN

EXPLORE THE CONCEPT
- Students use a ruler to help understand division of fractions.
- This activity leads into the computational skill of dividing a fraction by a fraction, which is introduced in Lesson 7.4.

MATERIALS
Each student will need a ruler with inches marked off in eighths.

RECOMMENDED TIME
Work activity: 10 min
Discuss results: 5 min

GROUPING
Students can work individually.

TRANSPARENCY
A support transparency is available for this activity.

2 TEACH

TIPS FOR SUCCESS
Students should use a ruler marked off in eighths of an inch, rather than sixteenths, as it will be easier to read.

3 CLOSE

KEY DISCOVERY
The quotient $\frac{a}{b} \div \frac{c}{d}$ has the same value as the product $\frac{a}{b} \times \frac{d}{c}$.

ASSESSMENT
1. The quotient $\frac{7}{8} \div \frac{3}{4}$ has the same value as the product $\frac{7}{8} \times \frac{p}{q}$. Find the value of $\frac{p}{q}$. $\frac{4}{3}$

LESSON OBJECTIVE

Use reciprocals to divide.

PACING

Suggested Number of Days
Basic Course: 1 day
Average Course: 1 day
Advanced Course: 1 day
Block: 0.5 block with 7.5

TEACHING RESOURCES

For a complete list of Teaching
Resources, see page 310B.

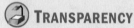 **TRANSPARENCY**

Warm-Up Exercises for this lesson
are available on a transparency.

2 TEACH

MOTIVATING THE LESSON

Before students read the first
paragraph, ask them to describe any
patterns in the multiplications.

TIPS FOR NEW TEACHERS

Be sure students know how to
write improper fractions as mixed
numbers. See Tips for New
Teachers in the *Chapter 7
Resource Book.*

LESSON 7.4

Dividing Fractions

BEFORE	▶ Now	WHY?
You multiplied fractions.	You'll use reciprocals to divide fractions.	So you can solve problems involving rates, as in Example 2.

 **Word Watch**

reciprocal, p. 334

Reciprocals For each pair of fractions being multiplied, the numerator and denominator of the product are equal, so the product is 1. Notice the relationship between the two fractions in each pair.

$$\frac{5}{3} \times \frac{3}{5} = \frac{15}{15} = 1 \qquad\qquad \frac{1}{12} \times \frac{12}{1} = \frac{12}{12} = 1$$

Two numbers, such as $\frac{5}{3}$ and $\frac{3}{5}$, whose product is 1 are **reciprocals**.

Every number except 0 has a reciprocal. To find it, write the number as a fraction, and then switch the numerator and the denominator.

EXAMPLE 1   Writing Reciprocals

	Original number	Fraction	Reciprocal	Check
a.	$\frac{4}{7}$	$\frac{4}{7}$	$\frac{7}{4}$	$\frac{4}{7} \times \frac{7}{4} = \frac{28}{28} = 1$
b.	10	$\frac{10}{1}$	$\frac{1}{10}$	$10 \times \frac{1}{10} = \frac{10}{10} = 1$
c.	$1\frac{3}{8}$	$\frac{11}{8}$	$\frac{8}{11}$	$1\frac{3}{8} \times \frac{8}{11} = \frac{88}{88} = 1$

Your turn now   Write the reciprocal of the number.

1. $\frac{1}{2}$ $\frac{2}{1}$ or 2
2. 6 $\frac{1}{6}$
3. 1 $\frac{1}{1}$ or 1
4. $1\frac{2}{5}$ $\frac{5}{7}$

In the activity on page 333, you may have become aware of the following rule for dividing by a fraction.

Dividing Fractions

Words To divide by a fraction, multiply by its reciprocal.

Numbers $\frac{2}{3} \div \frac{3}{4} = \frac{2}{3} \times \frac{4}{3}$ **Algebra** $\frac{a}{b} \div \frac{c}{d} = \frac{a}{b} \cdot \frac{d}{c}$

NCTM CURRICULUM STANDARDS

Standard 1: Understand how operations are related; Compute fluently
Standard 6: Solve problems in math and other contexts

Howe Caverns, New York

EXAMPLE 2 **Dividing Two Fractions**

Caves An underground boat ride at Howe Caverns in New York is $\frac{1}{4}$ mile long. Find the average rate of travel when the ride takes $\frac{1}{3}$ hour.

Rate = Distance ÷ Time — Write the formula.

$= \frac{1}{4} \div \frac{1}{3}$ — Use $\frac{1}{4}$ for the distance and $\frac{1}{3}$ for the time.

$= \frac{1}{4} \times \frac{3}{1}$ — Multiply by the reciprocal of the divisor.

$= \frac{1 \times 3}{4 \times 1}$ — Use the rule for multiplying fractions.

$= \frac{3}{4}$ — Multiply.

ANSWER The boat's average rate of travel is $\frac{3}{4}$ mile per hour.

EXAMPLE 3 **Dividing a Fraction and a Whole Number**

a. How can you share $\frac{3}{4}$ pound of a food equally among 6 people?

b. How many people does 6 cups serve, if $\frac{3}{4}$ cup serves one person?

Solution

a. Divide $\frac{3}{4}$ by 6.

$\frac{3}{4} \div 6 = \frac{3}{4} \div \frac{6}{1}$ ← *Write 6 as a fraction.*

$= \frac{3}{4} \times \frac{1}{6}$

$= \frac{\overset{1}{\cancel{3}} \times 1}{4 \times \underset{2}{\cancel{6}}}$

$= \frac{1}{8}$

ANSWER Each person gets $\frac{1}{8}$ pound.

b. Divide 6 by $\frac{3}{4}$.

$6 \div \frac{3}{4} = \frac{6}{1} \div \frac{3}{4}$

$= \frac{6}{1} \times \frac{4}{3}$

$= \frac{\overset{2}{\cancel{6}} \times 4}{1 \times \underset{1}{\cancel{3}}}$

$= 8$

ANSWER 6 cups serve 8 people.

Watch Out!

When dividing, be sure to take the reciprocal of the divisor, not the dividend. You can multiply to check your work. In Example 3, $\frac{1}{8} \times 6 = \frac{3}{4}$ and $8 \times \frac{3}{4} = 6$, so the divisions are correct.

Your turn now Divide. Write the answer in simplest form.

5. $\frac{5}{8} \div \frac{4}{3}$ $\frac{15}{32}$

6. $\frac{7}{10} \div \frac{1}{2}$ $1\frac{2}{5}$

7. $\frac{9}{10} \div 3$ $\frac{3}{10}$

8. $12 \div \frac{2}{3}$ 18

Lesson 7.4   Dividing Fractions   **335**

ASSIGNMENT GUIDE

Basic Course
Day 1: pp. 336–338 Exs. 10–20, 26–29, 34–39, 42–54, 58–70

Average Course
Day 1: pp. 336–338 Exs. 14–25, 30–56, 60–65, 69–71

Advanced Course
Day 1: pp. 336–338 Exs. 16–25, 32–57*, 60–65, 70, 71

Block
pp. 336–338 Exs. 14–25, 30–56, 60–65, 69–71 (with 7.5)

EXTRA PRACTICE

- Student Edition, p. 714
- Chapter 7 Resource Book, pp. 32–34
- Test and Practice Generator

 TRANSPARENCY

Even-numbered answers are available on transparencies.

HOMEWORK CHECK

When you review students' homework for this lesson, go over the following exercises to check understanding of key concepts.
Basic: 10, 19, 26, 34, 39
Average: 14, 23, 25, 32, 40
Advanced: 16, 24, 25, 36, 41

INTERNET
eWorkbook Plus
CLASSZONE.COM

Getting Ready to Practice

Vocabulary Tell whether the two numbers are reciprocals.

1. $\frac{3}{10}$ and $\frac{5}{3}$ no   **2.** $1\frac{1}{2}$ and $\frac{2}{3}$ yes   **3.** 8 and $\frac{1}{8}$ yes   **4.** 1 and 1 yes

Rewrite the division expression as an equivalent multiplication expression. Then evaluate the expression. 5–8. See margin.

5. $\frac{9}{2} \div \frac{3}{4}$ **6.** $\frac{5}{8} \div \frac{1}{3}$ **7.** $\frac{2}{3} \div 4$ **8.** $3 \div \frac{6}{5}$

9. Guided Problem Solving How many decorative magnets can you make with 12 inches of magnetic tape if each magnet uses $\frac{5}{8}$ inch of tape?

   ① Write a division expression. $12 \div \frac{5}{8}$

   ② Use multiplication by the reciprocal to find the quotient. $19\frac{1}{5}$

   ③ Explain how to interpret the quotient to answer the question. $\frac{1}{5}$
   Sample answer: You can only make 19 magnets because you cannot make $\frac{1}{5}$ of a magnet.

Practice and Problem Solving

A **Write the reciprocal of the number.**

10. $\frac{4}{5}$ $\frac{5}{4}$ **11.** $\frac{3}{7}$ $\frac{7}{3}$ **12.** $\frac{9}{4}$ $\frac{4}{9}$ **13.** $\frac{1}{3}$ $\frac{3}{1}$ or 3

14. 12 $\frac{1}{12}$ **15.** 10 $\frac{1}{10}$ **16.** $2\frac{1}{7}$ $\frac{7}{15}$ **17.** $3\frac{1}{2}$ $\frac{2}{7}$

18. Explain How can you check whether two numbers are reciprocals? Find their product, which should be 1.

Mental Math Copy and complete the statement.

19. $\frac{8}{5} \times \underline{?} = 1\frac{5}{8}$ **20.** $\underline{?} \times 7 = 1\frac{1}{7}$ **21.** $3 \times \frac{1}{3} = \underline{?}$ 1   **22.** $\frac{7}{6} \times \frac{6}{7} = \underline{?}$ 1

23. $6 \div \frac{1}{5} = 6 \times \underline{?} = \underline{?}$ 5, 30   **24.** $4 \div \frac{1}{6} = \underline{?} \times \underline{?} = \underline{?}$ 4, 6, 24

25. Find the Error
Describe and correct the error in the solution.
The dividend must be multiplied by the reciprocal of the divisor.

$$\bcancel{\frac{3}{4} \div \frac{1}{8} = \frac{4}{3} \times \frac{1}{8} = \frac{4}{24} = \frac{1}{6}}$$

The solution should be $\frac{3}{4} \div \frac{1}{8} = \frac{3}{4} \times \frac{8}{1} = 6$.

Margin answers:

5. $\frac{9}{2} \times \frac{4}{3} = 6$

6. $\frac{5}{8} \times \frac{3}{1} = 1\frac{7}{8}$

7. $\frac{2}{3} \times \frac{1}{4} = \frac{1}{6}$

8. $3 \times \frac{5}{6} = 2\frac{1}{2}$

 **with Homework**

Example	Exercises
1	10–22
2	25–31, 38
3	23–24, 32–37, 39–41

Online Resources
CLASSZONE.COM
· More Examples
· eTutorial Plus

Find the quotient.

26. $\frac{1}{3} \div \frac{2}{3}$ $\frac{1}{2}$ **27.** $\frac{7}{8} \div \frac{3}{5}$ $1\frac{11}{24}$ **28.** $\frac{5}{2} \div \frac{3}{4}$ $3\frac{1}{3}$ **29.** $\frac{7}{5} \div \frac{1}{10}$ 14

30. $\frac{2}{9} \div \frac{1}{4}$ $\frac{8}{9}$ **31.** $\frac{1}{12} \div \frac{5}{24}$ $\frac{2}{5}$ **32.** $8 \div \frac{4}{5}$ 10   **33.** $\frac{25}{9} \div 5$ $\frac{5}{9}$

34. $\frac{1}{8} \div 4$ $\frac{1}{32}$ **35.** $\frac{3}{10} \div 6$ $\frac{1}{20}$ **36.** $5 \div \frac{20}{7}$ $1\frac{3}{4}$ **37.** $3 \div \frac{10}{9}$ $2\frac{7}{10}$

38. How many $\frac{1}{4}$ cup scoops can you get from $\frac{7}{8}$ cup of tuna salad?
$3\frac{1}{2}$ scoops

39. Travel Rate You drive 15 miles in $\frac{1}{3}$ hour. Find your average rate of travel in miles per hour. 45 mi/h

40. Writing Write and solve a problem that can be represented by $\frac{3}{8} \div 6$.
See margin.

Extended Problem Solving It takes you $\frac{9}{16}$ pound of clay to make a teacup and $\frac{7}{8}$ pound of clay to make a mug.

41. Calculate How many teacups can you make with 5 pounds of clay? How many mugs can you make with 5 pounds of clay? 8 teacups; 5 mugs

B **42. Compare** Which uses more clay, a teacup or a mug?
a mug

43. Decide If you have a certain amount of clay, would you be able to make more teacups or more mugs? Explain how you know.
See margin.

Number Sense Copy and complete the statement using <, >, or =. Explain how you can tell without actually finding the quotient.
44–47. See margin.

44. $\frac{4}{9} \div 1$? $\frac{4}{9}$ **45.** $\frac{3}{5} \div 4$? $\frac{3}{5}$ **46.** $4 \div \frac{2}{3}$? 4   **47.** $6 \div \frac{3}{2}$? 6

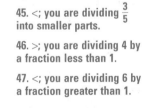

ⓧⓎ **Algebra Evaluate the expression when $p = \frac{1}{3}$, $q = \frac{5}{9}$, and $r = 3$.**

48. $p \div q$ $\frac{3}{5}$ **49.** $q \div p$ $1\frac{2}{3}$ **50.** $(p \div q) \div r$ $\frac{1}{5}$ **51.** $p \div (q \div r)$ $1\frac{4}{5}$

52. Interpret Use your results from Exercises 48–51. Can you conclude that fraction division is commutative? associative? Explain.
no; no; order changes the quotient

53. You earn \$8 for $\frac{2}{3}$ hour of work. Find your hourly rate of pay. \$12 per hour

54. Critical Thinking Use the diagram. Explain why you can find $3 \div \frac{1}{4}$ by multiplying 3×4.
3 divided into fourths creates 12 fourths which is the same as 3×4.

MINI-QUIZ

1. Write the reciprocal.
   a. $\frac{1}{7}$ 7 **b.** $2\frac{3}{5}$ $\frac{5}{13}$
   c. 1 1

2. The area of a rectangle is $\frac{8}{15}$ square foot. If the width is $\frac{4}{5}$ foot, what is the length? $\frac{2}{3}$ ft

3. How many people can be served by 4 pizzas if each person eats $\frac{4}{5}$ of a pizza? 5 people

4. How can you share $\frac{4}{5}$ of a pizza equally among 4 people? Each person gets $\frac{1}{5}$.

5 FOLLOW-UP

RETEACHING/REMEDIATION
- Study Guide in Chapter 7 Resource Book, pp. 35–36
- Tutor Place, Fractions Cards 16, 17
- eTutorial Plus Online
- Extra Practice, p. 714
- Lesson Practice in Chapter 7 Resource Book, pp. 32–34

CHALLENGE/ENRICHMENT
- Challenge Practice in Chapter 7 Resource Book, p. 37
- Teacher's Edition, p. 310F

ENGLISH LEARNER SUPPORT
- Spanish Study Guide
- Multi-Language Glossary
- Chapter Audio Summaries CDs

56. 10; 0.1. *Sample answer:* Dividing by a power of 10 is the same as multiplying by the reciprocal of the power of 10.

57. 6, 2; 4, 3. *Sample answer:* The chart shows that dividing 3 by a fraction is the same as multiplying 3 by the denominator 4 and then multiplying by the reciprocal of the numerator. This is the same as multiplying by the reciprocal of the fraction.

**INTERNET
State Test Practice**
CLASSZONE.COM

55. Construction Nine acres of land are being divided into $\frac{3}{4}$ acre lots to build new houses. How many lots are there? What happens to the number of lots if the number of acres of land needed per lot is doubled?
12 lots; cut in half

C **56. Writing** Copy and complete the statements. Then explain how dividing by a power of 10 follows the rule for dividing by a fraction.

Dividing by the decimal 0.1 has the same effect as multiplying by ?.
Dividing by 10 has the same effect as multiplying by the decimal ?.
See margin.

57. Challenge In Exercise 54, a model is used to show why $3 \div \frac{1}{4} = 3 \times 4$.

Use models to find $3 \div \frac{2}{4}$ and $3 \div \frac{3}{4}$.

Copy and complete the chart. Use the results to explain why you can divide by multiplying by the reciprocal.
See margin.

$3 \div \frac{1}{4} = 12 = 3 \times 4$

$3 \div \frac{2}{4} = \underline{?} = 3 \times 4 \times \frac{1}{?}$

$3 \div \frac{3}{4} = \underline{?} = 3 \times 4 \times \frac{1}{?}$

Mixed Review

Estimate the quotient. *(Lesson 1.2)* 58–61. Estimates may vary.

58. $569 \div 8$ 70 **59.** $145 \div 18$ 8 **60.** $253 \div 42$ 6 **61.** $308 \div 59$ 5

Find the product. *(Lessons 7.2, 7.3)*

62. $\frac{3}{5} \times \frac{1}{9}$ $\frac{1}{15}$ **63.** $\frac{7}{2} \times \frac{6}{7}$ 3 **64.** $8 \times 2\frac{1}{2}$ 20 **65.** $2\frac{2}{3} \times 1\frac{5}{6}$ $4\frac{8}{9}$

Basic Skills **You are given the price of an item. Determine the amount of change you will receive if you give the clerk a $20 bill.**

66. $7.50 $12.50 **67.** $14.78 $5.22 **68.** $.97 $19.03 **69.** $12.39 $7.61

Test-Taking Practice

70. Multiple Choice You have 4 pounds of trail mix. You put it in bags so that there is $\frac{2}{3}$ pound in each bag. How many bags do you fill? D

A. 2 **B.** $2\frac{2}{3}$ **C.** 3 **D.** 6

71. Multiple Choice Three gold prospectors pan $\frac{7}{8}$ ounce of gold from a stream. They split their gold into equal shares. Which choice shows each prospector's share? G

F. $\frac{1}{8}$ ounce **G.** $\frac{7}{24}$ ounce **H.** $\frac{1}{3}$ ounce **I.** $\frac{7}{12}$ ounce

LESSON 7.5

Dividing Mixed Numbers

BEFORE You divided fractions.

▶ **Now** You'll divide mixed numbers.

WHY? So you can plan schedules, such as audition times in Exs. 43–45.

Word Watch

Review Words

compatible numbers, p. 13
mixed number, p. 244
improper fraction, p. 244

Modeling Division You can use a model to find the quotient $3\frac{1}{3} \div \frac{2}{3}$. Begin by drawing a model for $3\frac{1}{3}$. Then divide the model into groups of $\frac{2}{3}$.

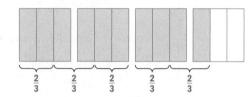

There are 5 groups of $\frac{2}{3}$. So, $3\frac{1}{3} \div \frac{2}{3} = 5$.

You can also find the quotient $3\frac{1}{3} \div \frac{2}{3}$ using paper and pencil, as in part (a) of Example 1. First you have to rewrite the mixed number as an improper fraction. In the model above, you can see that $3\frac{1}{3} = \frac{10}{3}$.

EXAMPLE 1 Dividing a Mixed Number

a. $3\frac{1}{3} \div \frac{2}{3} = \frac{10}{3} \div \frac{2}{3}$ Write $3\frac{1}{3}$ as an improper fraction.

$= \frac{10}{3} \times \frac{3}{2}$ Multiply by the reciprocal of the divisor.

$= \frac{\overset{5}{\cancel{10}} \times \overset{1}{\cancel{3}}}{\underset{1}{\cancel{3}} \times \underset{1}{\cancel{2}}}$ Use the rule for multiplying fractions.
   Divide out common factors.

$= 5$ Multiply.

b. $2\frac{5}{8} \div 6 = \frac{21}{8} \div \frac{6}{1}$ Write $2\frac{5}{8}$ and 6 as improper fractions.

$= \frac{21}{8} \times \frac{1}{6}$ Multiply by the reciprocal of the divisor.

$= \frac{\overset{7}{\cancel{21}} \times 1}{8 \times \underset{2}{\cancel{6}}}$ Use the rule for multiplying fractions.
   Divide out common factors.

$= \frac{7}{16}$ Multiply.

NCTM CURRICULUM STANDARDS
Standard 1: Understand how operations are related;
   Compute fluently
Standard 6: Solve problems in math and other contexts

Lesson 7.5   Dividing Mixed Numbers   **339**

---

① PLAN

SKILL CHECK
Write the reciprocal.

1. $\frac{2}{3} \quad \frac{3}{2}$ **2.** $\frac{1}{6} \quad \frac{6}{1}$

3. $1\frac{1}{4} \quad \frac{4}{5}$ **4.** $20 \quad \frac{1}{20}$

LESSON OBJECTIVE
Divide mixed numbers.

PACING
Suggested Number of Days
Basic Course: 1 day
Average Course: 1 day
Advanced Course: 1 day
Block: 0.5 block with 7.4

TEACHING RESOURCES
For a complete list of Teaching Resources, see page 310B.

TRANSPARENCY
Warm-Up Exercises for this lesson are available on a transparency.

② TEACH

MOTIVATING THE LESSON
Draw the model given on this page on an overhead projector. Ask students to help.

TIPS FOR NEW TEACHERS
Be sure students know how to write reciprocals of unit fractions, mixed numbers, and whole numbers. See Tips for New Teachers in the *Chapter 7 Resource Book.*

Watch Out!

When you divide by a mixed number, first you rewrite it as an improper fraction. Then don't forget to multiply by the *reciprocal* of the improper fraction.

EXAMPLE 2 **Dividing by a Mixed Number**

$$6\frac{3}{5} \div 2\frac{1}{4} = \frac{33}{5} \div \frac{9}{4}$$ Write $6\frac{3}{5}$ and $2\frac{1}{4}$ as improper fractions.

$$= \frac{33}{5} \times \frac{4}{9}$$ Multiply by the reciprocal of the divisor.

$$= \frac{\overset{11}{\cancel{33}} \times 4}{5 \times \cancel{9}_{3}}$$ Use the rule for multiplying fractions. Divide out common factors.

$$= \frac{44}{15}, \text{ or } 2\frac{14}{15}$$ Multiply.

✓ **Check** Round $2\frac{1}{4}$ to 2 and replace $6\frac{3}{5}$ with the compatible number 6. The answer is reasonable because it is close to the estimate $6 \div 2 = 3$.

Your turn now **Divide. Use estimation to check your answer.**

1. $9\frac{1}{6} \div 5 \quad 1\frac{5}{6}$
2. $6\frac{2}{3} \div \frac{8}{9} \quad 7\frac{1}{2}$
3. $\frac{7}{8} \div 3\frac{1}{4} \quad \frac{7}{26}$
4. $12\frac{1}{2} \div 3\frac{3}{4} \quad 3\frac{1}{3}$

5. Which quotient in Exercises 1–4 is less than 1? $\frac{7}{8} \div 3\frac{1}{4}$, or $\frac{7}{26}$

EXAMPLE 3 **Choosing an Operation**

Cider Forty pounds of apples make about $3\frac{1}{2}$ gallons of cider. About how many pounds of apples are needed to make 1 gallon of cider?

Solution

① Choose the operation by thinking about a similar whole number problem: If 40 pounds of apples made 4 gallons of cider, you would *divide* 40 by 4. So, *divide* 40 by $3\frac{1}{2}$.

② Divide.
$$40 \div 3\frac{1}{2} = \frac{40}{1} \div \frac{7}{2}$$

$$= \frac{40}{1} \times \frac{2}{7}$$

$$= \frac{40 \times 2}{1 \times 7}$$

$$= \frac{80}{7}, \text{ or } 11\frac{3}{7}$$

ANSWER You need about $11\frac{3}{7}$ pounds of apples to make 1 gallon of cider.

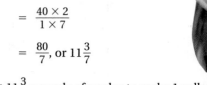
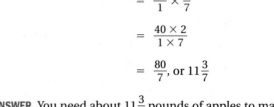
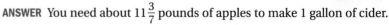

7.5 Exercises

More Practice, p. 714

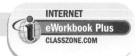

INTERNET
eWorkbook Plus
CLASSZONE.COM

Getting Ready to Practice

1. Vocabulary Find the reciprocal of the mixed number $2\frac{3}{8}$. $\frac{8}{19}$

Write the reciprocal of the divisor. Then find the quotient. Use estimation to check your answer.

2. $5\frac{1}{4} \div \frac{7}{8}$ $\frac{8}{7}$; 6

3. $\frac{5}{6} \div 4\frac{2}{7}$ $\frac{7}{30}$; $\frac{7}{36}$

4. $8\frac{1}{2} \div 3\frac{3}{4}$ $\frac{4}{15}$; $2\frac{4}{15}$

5. $14 \div 2\frac{2}{3}$ $\frac{3}{8}$; $5\frac{1}{4}$

6. Volunteer Work If you split $5\frac{1}{2}$ hours of volunteer work equally over the next three weeks, how much time will you volunteer each week? $1\frac{5}{6}$ h

Practice and Problem Solving

HELP with Homework

Example	Exercises
1	7-8, 10-14, 22
2	9, 15-21, 23-27
3	28-31

Online Resources
CLASSZONE.COM
· More Examples
· eTutorial Plus

A 7. What division problem involving a mixed number is represented by the model? What is the quotient?

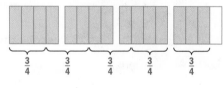

$\frac{3}{4}$ $\frac{3}{4}$ $\frac{3}{4}$ $\frac{3}{4}$ $\frac{3}{4}$

$3\frac{3}{4} \div \frac{3}{4}$; 5

8. Sketch a model similar to Exercise 7 for $2\frac{4}{5} \div \frac{2}{5}$. Find the quotient.
Check model; 7.

9. Decide Are $3\frac{2}{5}$ and $3\frac{5}{2}$ reciprocals? Why or why not?
No. *Sample answer:* Mixed numbers must be converted to improper fractions before the reciprocal can be found.

Find the quotient.

10. $7\frac{1}{5} \div \frac{2}{5}$ 18

11. $8\frac{2}{3} \div \frac{2}{9}$ 39

12. $4\frac{7}{8} \div \frac{13}{16}$ 6

13. $2\frac{1}{10} \div 3$ $\frac{7}{10}$

14. $3\frac{4}{7} \div 5$ $\frac{5}{7}$

15. $\frac{5}{9} \div 4\frac{1}{6}$ $\frac{2}{15}$

16. $\frac{3}{8} \div 2\frac{1}{4}$ $\frac{1}{6}$

17. $5 \div 3\frac{1}{8}$ $1\frac{3}{5}$

18. $11 \div 2\frac{4}{9}$ $4\frac{1}{2}$

19. $15 \div 2\frac{1}{7}$ 7

20. $4\frac{1}{4} \div 2\frac{1}{2}$ $1\frac{7}{10}$

21. $2\frac{5}{6} \div 5\frac{1}{6}$ $\frac{17}{31}$

22. Recipes You have only a $\frac{1}{4}$ cup measure. How many times must you fill the $\frac{1}{4}$ cup measure for a recipe that uses $2\frac{1}{4}$ cups of milk? 9 times

23. Packaging You are stacking books in a box that is 12 inches high. Each book is $1\frac{1}{4}$ inches thick. How many books can you fit in the box in a single stack? 9 books

3 APPLY

ASSIGNMENT GUIDE
Basic Course
Day 1: pp. 341–343 Exs. 7–15, 22–29, 32–37, 39–45, 50–57
Average Course
Day 1: pp. 341–343 Exs. 7–17, 22–25, 30–48, 50–52, 56–58
Advanced Course
Day 1: pp. 341–343 Exs. 7–11, 18–25, 28–51*, 56–58
Block
pp. 341–343 Exs. 7–17, 22–25, 30–48, 50–52, 56–58 (with 7.4)

EXTRA PRACTICE
• Student Edition, p. 714
• Chapter 7 Resource Book, pp. 43–45
• Test and Practice Generator

TRANSPARENCY
Even-numbered answers are available on transparencies.

HOMEWORK CHECK
When you review students' homework for this lesson, go over the following exercises to check understanding of key concepts.
Basic: 7, 9, 10, 23, 28
Average: 8, 9, 11, 25, 30
Advanced: 8, 9, 22, 25, 30

COMMON ERROR
In Exercises 15-21, some students may try to combine the steps of writing the mixed number as an improper fraction and writing its reciprocal. This can lead to errors. Encourage students to do the two steps separately.

30. $7\frac{1}{2}$ days. *Sample answer:* Use division because you are finding the number of times an equal daily portion fits into the bag.

34. greater than 1; $1\frac{1}{11}$

35. greater than 1; 8

36. less than 1; $\frac{4}{5}$

37. less than 1; $\frac{9}{10}$

38. The operation chosen should be multiplication instead of division. If it were a division problem, the reciprocal of the divisor should be used, not the reciprocal of the dividend. The correct answer is $2\frac{1}{3} \times \frac{3}{4} = \frac{7}{3} \times \frac{3}{4} = \frac{21}{12} = 1\frac{3}{4}$ cups.

Estimation **Estimate the quotient.** 24–27. Estimates may vary.

24. $15\frac{1}{3} \div 2\frac{2}{3}$ 5   25. $28\frac{9}{10} \div 5\frac{1}{4}$ 6   26. $18\frac{3}{5} \div 1\frac{11}{12}$ 9   27. $20 \div 3\frac{1}{7}$ 5

Choose the Operation **Solve. Explain why you chose the operation you used.**

28. **Books** One book is $2\frac{11}{16}$ inches thick. Another book is $1\frac{3}{8}$ inches thick. Will the books fit beside each other on a shelf that has a 4 inch space?
No. *Sample answer:* Use addition to find the total amount of space needed.

29. **Twins** Twin babies weigh $7\frac{1}{2}$ and $6\frac{5}{16}$ pounds. How much more does the heavier baby weigh than the lighter baby?
$1\frac{3}{16}$ lb. *Sample answer:* Use subtraction to find the difference in weights.

30. **Dog Food** If a bag contains 20 cups of dog food and you feed your dog $2\frac{2}{3}$ cups per day, how many days can you feed your dog from this bag?
See margin.

31. **Alligators** An alligator has a total length of $11\frac{3}{4}$ feet. The length of the alligator's tail is one half of its total length. How long is the tail?
$5\frac{7}{8}$ ft. *Sample answer:* Use multiplication by $\frac{1}{2}$ to find half *of* the total length.

B **Describe the pattern. Then find the next two numbers in the pattern.**

32. $25, 5, 1, \frac{1}{5}, \underline{?}, \underline{?}$
divide by 5; $\frac{1}{25}, \frac{1}{125}$

33. $\frac{1}{2}, \frac{1}{4}, \frac{1}{8}, \frac{1}{16}, \underline{?}, \underline{?}$
divide by 2; $\frac{1}{32}, \frac{1}{64}$

Critical Thinking **Predict whether the value of the expression $4\frac{4}{5} \div x$ will be *greater than 1* or *less than 1* for the given value of x. Then evaluate the expression.**

34. $x = 4\frac{2}{5}$ 35. $x = \frac{3}{5}$ 36. $x = 6$ 37. $x = 5\frac{1}{3}$

38. **Find the Error** A recipe calls for $2\frac{1}{3}$ cups of broth. A cook is making $\frac{3}{4}$ of the recipe. Describe and correct any errors in finding the amount of broth needed.

$$2\frac{1}{3} \div \frac{3}{4} = \frac{7}{3} \div \frac{3}{4}$$
$$\times$$
$$= \frac{3}{7} \times \frac{3}{4}$$
$$= \frac{9}{28} \text{ cup}$$

39. **Football** Your football team gains $3\frac{1}{2}$, 5, $4\frac{1}{2}$, 8, and $6\frac{1}{2}$ yards on five consecutive plays. Find the mean number of yards gained for the plays.
$5\frac{1}{2}$ yd

Evaluate the expression.

40. $\left(6\frac{3}{4} \div \frac{3}{8}\right) \times 1\frac{1}{2}$ 27   41. $4\frac{3}{8} \div 5 + 1\frac{3}{10}$ $2\frac{7}{40}$ 42. $7\frac{1}{6} - 2\frac{1}{4} \div 3\frac{6}{7}$ $6\frac{7}{12}$

Extended Problem Solving **Talent show auditions are scheduled to last about $3\frac{3}{4}$ hours. There are 31 acts to be viewed.** 43–45. See margin.

43. Represent Write an expression that represents the amount of time, in hours, for one act if each act is allowed the same amount of time.

44. Estimate Use a pair of compatible numbers to estimate the value of the expression you wrote in Exercise 43.

45. Interpret How many whole minutes should be allowed for each act?

 Algebra **Evaluate the expression for $x = \frac{5}{8}$ and $y = 2\frac{1}{2}$.**

C **46.** $\frac{2x}{y}$ $\frac{1}{2}$ **47.** $y + \frac{2}{x}$ $5\frac{7}{10}$ **48.** $\frac{x}{4 - y}$ $\frac{5}{12}$

49. Challenge A movie theater is open from 12:30 P.M. to 1:00 A.M. The length of each movie being shown at the theater is $2\frac{1}{4}$ hours. How many movies can be shown on each screen during one day? Does your answer change if there is a 15 minute break between movies? Explain.
See margin.

Mixed Review

50. Use a benchmark to estimate the length of a fork in inches. Then measure to check your estimate. *(Lesson 2.1)* Check estimates.

Find the sum or difference. *(Lessons 6.4, 6.5)*

51. $6\frac{4}{7} + 2\frac{5}{7}$ $9\frac{2}{7}$ **52.** $3\frac{2}{3} + 4\frac{3}{4}$ $8\frac{5}{12}$ **53.** $7 - 3\frac{4}{9}$ $3\frac{5}{9}$ **54.** $5\frac{1}{4} - 2\frac{7}{10}$ $2\frac{11}{20}$

Basic Skills **Copy and complete the statement.**

55. 5 weeks 3 days = ? days 38   **56.** 265 min = ? hours ? min 4, 25

Test-Taking Practice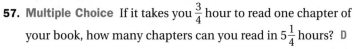

57. Multiple Choice If it takes you $\frac{3}{4}$ hour to read one chapter of your book, how many chapters can you read in $5\frac{1}{4}$ hours? D

A. $3\frac{15}{16}$ **B.** $4\frac{1}{2}$ **C.** 6   **D.** 7

58. Short Response How many shelves that are $1\frac{1}{2}$ feet long can you cut from a board that is $4\frac{3}{4}$ feet long? Is there wood left over? Explain.
See margin.

Margin (left column):

43. $3\frac{3}{4} \div 31$

44–45. Answers may vary.

44. $\frac{1}{8}$ h

45. about 8 min

49. 5 movies; no. *Sample answer:* There is time left over if 5 movies that are $2\frac{1}{4}$ hours long are shown, and the time is enough to allow a 15 minute break between each of 5 movies.

58. 3 shelves; yes. *Sample answer:* $4\frac{3}{4} \div 1\frac{1}{2}$ is $3\frac{1}{6}$, so there is enough wood left for $\frac{1}{6}$ of a shelf.

INTERNET
State Test Practice
CLASSZONE.COM

 **ASSESS**

ASSESSMENT RESOURCES

For more assessment resources, see:
• Assessment Book
• Test and Practice Generator

MINI-QUIZ

Find each quotient.

1. $4\frac{7}{8} \div 6\frac{1}{2}$ $\frac{3}{4}$

2. $3\frac{3}{10} \div \frac{3}{5}$ $5\frac{1}{2}$

3. $2\frac{5}{8} \div 3$ $\frac{7}{8}$

4. A recipe calls for $2\frac{1}{2}$ ounces of vanilla to flavor $6\frac{1}{4}$ pints of yogurt. About how many ounces of vanilla are needed for 1 pint of yogurt? $\frac{2}{5}$ oz

 **FOLLOW-UP**

RETEACHING/REMEDIATION
• Study Guide in Chapter 7 Resource Book, pp. 46–47
• Tutor Place, Fractions Card 18
• eTutorial Plus Online
• Extra Practice, p. 714
• Lesson Practice in Chapter 7 Resource Book, pp. 43–45

CHALLENGE/ENRICHMENT
• Challenge Practice in Chapter 7 Resource Book, p. 49
• Teacher's Edition, p. 310F

ENGLISH LEARNER SUPPORT
• Spanish Study Guide
• Multi-Language Glossary
• Chapter Audio Summaries CDs

PLAN

SKILL CHECK

1. Is the gram a measure of mass or capacity? **mass**

2. Is the liter a measure of mass or capacity? **capacity**

LESSON OBJECTIVE

Use customary units of weight and capacity.

PACING

Suggested Number of Days
Basic Course: 1 day
Average Course: 1 day
Advanced Course: 1 day
Block: 0.5 block with 7.7

TEACHING RESOURCES

For a complete list of Teaching Resources, see page 310B.

 TRANSPARENCY

Warm-Up Exercises for this lesson are available on a transparency. A support transparency is available for this lesson.

2 TEACH

MOTIVATING THE LESSON

Bring in actual examples of benchmarks for students to handle.

TIPS FOR NEW TEACHERS

Use common objects other than those in the examples on pages 344 and 345 to determine how familiar students are with customary units of weight and capacity. See Tips for New Teachers in the *Chapter 7 Resource Book*.

LESSON 7.6

Weight and Capacity in Customary Units

BEFORE ▶ **Now** **WHY?**

You used metric units of mass and capacity.

You'll use customary units of weight and capacity.

So you can estimate weights, such as that of a hang glider in Ex. 24.

In the Real World

 **Word Watch**

ounce (oz), p. 344
pound (lb), p. 344
ton (T), p. 344
fluid ounce (fl oz), p. 345
cup (c), p. 345
pint (pt), p. 345
quart (qt), p. 345
gallon (gal), p. 345

Bakery If a baker slices a 1 pound loaf of bread into 16 slices, each slice weighs 1 ounce. Knowing the weight of familiar objects, such as a slice of bread, can help you to choose appropriate units.

Three customary units of weight are the **ounce** (oz), the **pound** (lb), and the **ton** (T).

1 ounce
about the weight of a slice of bread

1 pound
about the weight of a soccer ball

1 ton
about the weight of a compact car

Ounces, pounds, and tons are related to each other.

1 lb = 16 oz   1 T = 2000 lb

EXAMPLE 1 **Choosing Units of Weight**

Choose an appropriate customary unit to measure the weight.

a. An apple weighs $6\frac{1}{4}$ _?_.

b. A laptop computer weighs $6\frac{1}{4}$ _?_.

Solution

a. An apple weighs $6\frac{1}{4}$ *ounces*, because it is heavier than a slice of bread and lighter than a soccer ball.

b. A laptop computer weighs $6\frac{1}{4}$ *pounds*, because it is heavier than a soccer ball and much lighter than a compact car.

Your turn now Choose an appropriate customary unit to measure the weight of the item.

1. golf ball **ounces**   **2.** blue whale **tons**   **3.** bicycle **pounds**

NCTM CURRICULUM STANDARDS
Standard 4: Understand measurable attributes of objects; Understand the units of measurement; Understand the systems of measurement

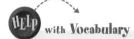 **HELP with Vocabulary**

Notice that there are two types of ounces: the fluid ounce (fl oz) used for measuring capacity and the ounce (oz) used for measuring weight.

Capacity Five customary units of capacity are the **fluid ounce** (fl oz), the **cup** (c), the **pint** (pt), the **quart** (qt), and the **gallon** (gal).

1 fluid ounce   **1 cup**   **1 pint**   **1 quart**   **1 gallon**

The units of capacity are related to each other.

1 c = 8 fl oz   1 pt = 2 c   1 qt = 2 pt   1 gal = 4 qt

EXAMPLE 2 **Choosing Units of Capacity**

Choose an appropriate customary unit to measure the capacity.

a. large mug   **b.** water cooler

Solution

a. A large mug holds about as much as a pint-sized milk carton does. You can use pints or one of the smaller units, fluid ounces or cups.

b. A water cooler holds much more than a gallon jug does. You can use gallons or quarts, but you wouldn't use the smaller units.

EXAMPLE 3 **Choosing Customary Units**

What does each measure describe about an empty glass aquarium?

a. 55 gal   **b.** 45 lb

Solution

a. A gallon is a measure of capacity, so 55 gallons describes the amount of water the aquarium can hold.

b. A pound is a measure of weight, so 45 pounds describes how much the empty aquarium weighs.

Your turn now   Choose an appropriate customary unit to measure.

4. capacity of a teakettle cups

5. capacity of a juice glass fluid ounces

6. weight of a toad ounces

Lesson 7.6   Weight and Capacity in Customary Units   **345**

EXTRA EXAMPLES

Example 1 Choose an appropriate customary unit to measure the weight.
a. A refrigerator weighs $\frac{1}{5}$? . ton
b. A banana weighs $2\frac{1}{2}$? . ounces

Example 2 Choose an appropriate customary unit to measure the capacity.
a. a hiking canteen quart
b. a bottle of sunscreen fluid ounce

Example 3 What does each measure describe about a large bowl?
a. 6.5 lb A pound is a measure of weight, so 6.5 lb describes how much the bowl weighs.
b. 4.8 qt A quart is a measure of capacity, so 4.8 qt describes how much the bowl can hold.

 CONCEPT CHECK

When would you use an ounce, pound, or ton as a unit of measurement and when would you use a fluid ounce, cup, pint, quart, or gallon? **You would use an ounce, pound, or ton when measuring weight and you would use a fluid ounce, cup, pint, quart, or gallon when measuring capacity.**

DAILY PUZZLER

To serve each of 20 campers an 8-ounce glass of milk, a counselor used up all of two containers of milk. What were the capacities of the containers? **1 gal and 1 qt**

345

7.6 **Exercises**
More Practice, p. 714

Getting Ready to Practice

Vocabulary **Order the units from least to greatest.**

1. Units of capacity: pints, gallons, cups, quarts, fluid ounces
   fluid ounces, cups, pints, quart, gallons
2. Units of weight: tons, ounces, pounds ounces, pounds, tons

Choose an appropriate customary unit to measure the item.

3. weight of a gorilla pounds
4. weight of a slipper ounces
5. capacity of a soup bowl cups
6. capacity of a kitchen sink gallons

Practice and Problem Solving

A **Match the object with its correct weight.**

7. wrecking ball B
8. kitten C
9. cellular phone A

A. $3\frac{1}{2}$ ounces
B. $3\frac{1}{2}$ tons
C. $3\frac{1}{2}$ pounds

10. **Animals** Choose an appropriate customary unit to measure the weight
    of each type of animal in the picture at the left. dog: pounds; cat: pounds;
    birds: ounces

**Choose an appropriate customary unit to measure the capacity
of the item.**

11. bathtub gallons
12. serving spoon
    fluid ounces
13. cream pitcher cups

**Copy and complete the statement using *fluid ounces*, *pints*, or
gallons.**

14. The capacity of a water bottle is $1\frac{1}{4}$? . pints

15. The amount of water in a carnival dunking booth is 400 ? . gallons

16. The amount of water you can hold in the palm of your hand is $\frac{3}{4}$? .
    fluid ounces

17. The capacity of a punch bowl is 24 ? . pints

Tell whether the measurement is a *weight*, a *capacity*, or a *length*.

18. 7 quarts capacity
19. $2\frac{7}{8}$ pounds weight
20. 15 inches length

21. $1\frac{1}{2}$ pints capacity
22. 4 ounces weight
23. 7 fluid ounces capacity

with **Homework**

Example	Exercises
1	7–10, 24
2	11–17
3	18–23

Online Resources
CLASSZONE.COM
· More Examples
· eTutorial Plus

B 24. Hang Glider Choose the best estimate for the weight of a hang glider.

    A. 70 oz   **B.** 70 lb   **C.** 700 lb   **D.** 7 T   B

Decide **Is the capacity of the given object *less than* a quart, *about equal to* a quart, or *more than* a quart? Explain.** *25–27. See margin.*

25. bathroom sink   **26.** bottle of cough syrup   **27.** ice cube tray

28. Compare Order the empty containers from smallest to largest by height, by capacity, and by weight. If you can't, explain why not. *See margin.*

    glass vase   **plastic bowl**   **paper cup**

C 29. Critical Thinking Give a different benchmark than the one pictured for each customary unit of weight and capacity on pages 344 and 345. *See margin.*

30. Challenge Have a family member tape over the weight or capacity measurement on the labels of various containers around your home. Estimate the hidden measurements. Then uncover the labels to see how close each estimate was to the actual measurement. *Check work.*

Mixed Review

Copy and complete the statement. *(Lesson 4.8)*

31. 76 cm = _?_ mm 760   **32.** 8.5 kg = _?_ g 8500   **33.** 175 mL = _?_ L 0.175

Write the fraction as a decimal. *(Lesson 5.8)*

34. $\frac{5}{8}$ 0.625   **35.** $\frac{3}{40}$ 0.075   **36.** $\frac{5}{6}$ $0.8\overline{3}$ **37.** $\frac{2}{9}$ $0.\overline{2}$

Basic Skills **Use multiplication to check if the answer is correct.**

38. 267 ÷ 6 = 41 R1 no   **39.** 2851 ÷ 9 = 316 R3   **40.** 928 ÷ 23 = 40 R8 yes
                                        no

Test-Taking Practice

41. Multiple Choice Which object is unlikely to be weighed in ounces? C

    A. bagel   **B.** screwdriver   **C.** piano   **D.** ear of corn

42. Short Response One pound of margarine measures 2 cups. You measure 2 cups of breakfast cereal and record its weight. Do you think the breakfast cereal also weighs one pound? Explain your reasoning.
No. *Sample answer:* The capacity, 2 cups, is the same, but the weight depends on what material is used to fill the 2 cups. The cereal would weigh less than a pound, because cereal is lighter than margarine.

Margin notes (left column):

25. More than. *Sample answer*: A bathroom sink is larger than a quart milk carton.

26. Less than. *Sample answer*: A bottle of cough syrup is smaller than a quart milk carton.

27. Less than. *Sample answer*: I tried pouring water and found that it took only about half of a quart to fill a tray.

28. Plastic bowl, glass vase, paper cup; glass vase, paper cup, plastic bowl; weights cannot be determined.

29. *Sample answer:*
1 ounce: 5 quarters;
1 pound: loaf of bread;
1 ton: ten 200 lb men;
1 fluid ounce: 2 tablespoons;
1 cup: small glass; 1 pint: tall glass; 1 quart: large mayonnaise jar; 1 gallon: 2 rectangular cartons of ice cream

INTERNET

State Test Practice
CLASSZONE.COM

347

One of the strengths of the strategy Solve a Related Problem is that it lets students who are good at seeing numerical patterns use that skill to solve geometric problems. Conversely, students who are good at visualization can use this ability to solve related numerical problems.

2 TEACH

GUIDING STUDENTS' WORK

Be sure students understand that a *row* with 2 more triangles is added each time, not just 2 more triangles. After discussing Step 4, ask students how many small triangle side lengths will be in the sixth shape.

EXTRA EXAMPLES

Example Find the pattern and draw the fifth diagram.

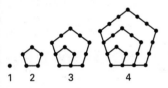

The numbers of dots formed are 1, 5, 12, 22, ... The pattern is: add 4 dots, add 7 dots, add 10 dots, ... For the next pattern, add 13 dots to the 22 dots, resulting in 35 dots.

7.7 Problem Solving Strategies

Guess, Check, and Revise
Draw a Diagram
Perform an Experiment
Make a List or Table
Solve a Related Problem
Work Backward
Make a Model

Solve a Related Problem

Problem A friend builds the four shapes below and then challenges you to find the pattern and build the fifth shape.

1 Read and Understand

Read the problem carefully.

Be sure to pay attention to both the number and the arrangement of small triangles.

2 Make a plan

Decide on a strategy to use.

One way to solve the problem is to solve a related problem.

3 Solve the Problem

Reread the problem and solve a related problem.

Count the number of small triangles in the shapes to form a number pattern. Then solve the related problem of continuing the number pattern.

Shape:	1st	2nd	3rd	4th	5th
Number of small triangles:	1	4	9	16	?

$$+3 \quad +5 \quad +7 \quad +?$$

The 5th shape will have $16 + 9 = 25$ small triangles.

ANSWER A row with 2 more triangles is added each time. Add a row of 9 small triangles to the bottom of the 4th shape to create the 5th shape.

4 Look Back

To check, you can think about the pattern another way and count small triangle side lengths along each edge.

NCTM CURRICULUM STANDARDS
Standard 2: Understand patterns
Standard 6: Solve problems in math and other contexts; Apply/adapt strategies to solve problems

Practice the Strategy

Use the strategy *solve a related problem*.

1. **Refreshments** You need to decide how many hot dogs to bring for a cookout with 30 students. Based on a party you had, you figure that 10 hot dogs serve 6 students. Describe how this problem is related to the scale drawing problems in Lesson 2.3. Then solve the problem. *See margin.*

2. **Art Project** Your art teacher gives you the pattern below as the beginning for a design. Use a related problem to help describe the pattern. Find the next two figures in the pattern. *See margin.*

3. **Building Shapes** You and a friend take turns adding on tiles as shown. Use a related problem to find the shapes you and your friend will build in the next two turns. *See margin.*

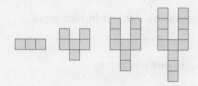

4. **Money** In the old English system of money, 12 pence = 1 shilling and 20 shillings = 1 pound. How is adding money in this system related to adding units of time? Express the sum of the two amounts shown using as few of these coins as possible.

   1 pound, 19 shillings, 10 pence
   2 shillings, 8 pence

   Sample answer: You need to regroup the smaller amounts to make larger amounts; 2 pounds, 2 shillings, 6 pence.

Mixed Problem Solving

Use any strategy to solve the problem.

5. **Tests** An 11 question English test is worth 100 points. If vocabulary questions are worth 5 points and short answer questions are worth 20 points, how many of each type are on the test?
   8 vocabulary questions and 3 short answer questions

6. **Crafts** For a craft project, you have colored straws that measure 5 inches, 9 inches, and 11 inches. How can you use these straws to measure 3 inches? *See margin.*

7. **Find the Number** What number belongs in the blank? 20

   $$(\underline{\ ?\ } \times 9) \div 2 + 6 - 45 = 51$$

8. **Spinner** The spinner at the right has 5 equal sections. You spin the spinner two times. How many possible results are there from the two spins?
   25 possible results

9. **Pictures** You are framing a picture that is $8\frac{1}{2}$ inches by 11 inches. The frame is $\frac{3}{4}$ inch wide and will cover $\frac{1}{4}$ inch along each edge of the picture. What will be the dimensions of the framed picture?
   $9\frac{1}{2}$ in. by 12 in.

Lesson 7.7   Changing Customary Units   **349**

③ APPLY

 TRANSPARENCY

Even-numbered answers are available on transparencies.

MATH REASONING

In Exercise 4, students should also be able to relate adding (and subtracting) using the old English money system to adding (and subtracting) compound denominate numbers, such as lengths expressed in inches, feet, and yards or capacities expressed in gallons, quarts, pints, and cups.

SUGGESTED STRATEGIES

You may wish to suggest the following strategies for the problems in the Mixed Problem Solving:
- Exercise 5: Guess, Check, and Revise, Make a List or Table
- Exercise 6: Draw a Diagram, Make a Model
- Exercise 7: Guess, Check, and Revise, Work Backward
- Exercise 8: Make a List or Table
- Exercise 9: Draw a Diagram

1. *Sample answer:* You can use a proportion to solve the problem; 50 hot dogs.

2–3. See Additional Answers beginning on page AA1.

6. *Sample answer:* Place the 5 inch straw and the 9 inch straw end to end to make a 14 inch straw. Use the difference between this combination and the 11 inch straw to measure 3 inches.

LESSON OBJECTIVE

Change customary units of measure.

PACING

Suggested Number of Days
Basic Course: 1 day
Average Course: 1 day
Advanced Course: 1 day
Block: 0.5 block with 7.6

TEACHING RESOURCES

For a complete list of Teaching Resources, see page 310B.

TRANSPARENCY

Warm-Up Exercises for this lesson are available on a transparency.

2 TEACH

MOTIVATING THE LESSON

Bring in actual objects so students can see the relationships in the table.

TIPS FOR NEW TEACHERS

Stress the relationships in the table on this page. See Tips for New Teachers in the *Chapter 7 Resource Book*.

LESSON **7.7**

Changing Customary Units

BEFORE	▶ Now	WHY?
You learned the customary units of measure.	You'll change customary units of measure.	So you can interpret measures, such as weight of a submersible in Ex. 39.

Word Watch

Review Words
inch (in.), p. 55
foot (ft), p. 55
yard (yd), p. 55
mi (mi), p. 55

Changing Customary Units You can multiply and divide using the relationships below to change from one customary unit to another.

Length	Weight	Capacity
1 ft = 12 in.	1 lb = 16 oz	1 c = 8 fl oz
1 yd = 3 ft = 36 in.	1 T = 2000 lb	1 pt = 2 c
1 mi = 1760 yd = 5280 ft		1 qt = 2 pt
		1 gal = 4 qt

EXAMPLE 1   Changing Units Using Multiplication

Change 3 ft 7 in. to inches.

3 ft 7 in. = 3 ft + 7 in.	Write the measure as a sum.
$= (3 \times 12)$ in. $+ 7$ in.	Change the feet to inches.
$= 36$ in. $+ 7$ in.	Multiply.
$= 43$ in.	Add.

Watch Out!

There should always be more of the smaller unit and fewer of the larger unit. So, you *multiply* by 12 to change feet to inches and you *divide* by 16 to change ounces to pounds.

EXAMPLE 2   Changing Units Using Division

Change 35 oz to pounds. Express the answer in two ways.

There are 16 oz in a pound, so divide 35 by 16.

$$\begin{array}{r} 2\ \text{R}3 \\ 16)\overline{35} \\ \underline{32} \\ 3 \end{array}$$

← You can interpret the remainder as 3 oz.

← You can also interpret the remainder as $\frac{3}{16}$ lb, because the remaining division $3 \div 16$ can be written as $\frac{3}{16}$.

ANSWER There are 2 lb 3 oz in 35 oz. This can also be written as $2\frac{3}{16}$ lb.

Your turn now   Copy and complete the statement.

1. 2 mi 480 yd = _?_ yd   4000   2. 26 fl oz = _?_ c $3\frac{1}{4}$ 3. $7\frac{1}{2}$ T = _?_ lb   15,000

NCTM CURRICULUM STANDARDS
Standard 1: Understand how operations are related
Standard 4: Understand the units of measurement;
Understand the systems of measurement

Multiplying by a Form of 1 You can also change units without deciding whether to multiply or divide. Instead, you always multiply by a fraction that is equal to 1. For example, 1 gal = 4 qt, so $\frac{4 \text{ qt}}{1 \text{ gal}} = 1$.

 **with Solving**

To get the correct unit in the answer, choose the form of 1 that has the unit you are changing to in the numerator and the unit you are changing from in the denominator.

EXAMPLE 3 Multiplying by a Form of 1

Change $2\frac{1}{4}$ ft to yards.

$2\frac{1}{4} \text{ ft} = \frac{9 \text{ ft}}{4}$ Write the measurement in fraction form.

$= \frac{9 \text{ ft}}{4} \times \frac{1 \text{ yd}}{3 \text{ ft}}$ Multiply by a form of 1. Use $\frac{1 \text{ yd}}{3 \text{ ft}}$.

$= \frac{\overset{3}{\cancel{9 \text{ ft}}} \times 1 \text{ yd}}{4 \times \cancel{3 \text{ ft}}_{1}}$ Divide out "ft" so you are left with "yd."

$= \frac{3}{4} \text{ yd}$

What do you think? **Science**

EXAMPLE 4 Finding a Relationship

Camels If a camel is very thirsty, it can drink 30 gallons of water in 10 minutes. How many cups of water is that?

Solution

(1) Find the relationship between gallons and cups. Use the three relationships 1 gal = 4 qt, 1 qt = 2 pt, and 1 pt = 2 c.

$\frac{1 \text{ gal}}{4 \text{ qt}} \times \frac{1 \text{ qt}}{2 \text{ pt}} \times \frac{1 \text{ pt}}{2 \text{ c}} = \frac{1 \text{ gal} \times 1 \text{ qt} \times 1 \text{ pt}}{4 \text{ qt} \times 2 \text{ pt} \times 2 \text{ c}} = \frac{1 \text{ gal}}{16 \text{ c}}$

So, 1 gallon = 16 cups.

(2) Multiply 30 gal by a form of 1 that relates gallons and cups.

$30 \text{ gal} \times \frac{16 \text{ c}}{1 \text{ gal}} = \frac{30 \text{ gal} \times 16 \text{ c}}{1 \text{ gal}} = 480 \text{ c}$

ANSWER A very thirsty camel can drink 480 cups of water in 10 minutes.

■ **Camels**

A camel's foot can be as big as a large plate. About how many inches across is a large plate? How does having such big feet help the camel to travel in the desert?

Your turn now Copy and complete the statement.

4. $\frac{5}{8} \text{ yd} = \underline{\ ?\ } \text{ in.}$ $22\frac{1}{2}$ **5.** $2\frac{3}{8} \text{ lb} = \underline{\ ?\ } \text{ oz}$ 38   **6.** $28 \text{ fl oz} = \underline{\ ?\ } \text{ qt}$ $\frac{7}{8}$

12 in. *Sample answer:* The camel's big feet make it easier to walk on the sand by distributing its weight evenly so it doesn't sink into the sand while it walks.

Lesson 7.7   Changing Customary Units   **351**

EXTRA EXAMPLES

Example 1 Change 3 yd 2 ft to feet. **11 ft**

Example 2 Change 23 fluid ounces to cups. Express the answer in two ways. **2 c 7 fl oz, $2\frac{7}{8}$ c**

Example 3 Change $2\frac{3}{5}$ T to pounds. **5200 lb**

Example 4 A student lives 14 miles from school. How many inches is that? **887,040 in.**

📖 **NOTETAKING**

Be sure students record the measurement equivalents given in the chart on page 350 in their notebooks. Students should also include benchmarks in their notes to give themselves a visual idea of the measures.

VISUALIZE

For Example 1, ask students to visualize (or sketch) three 1-foot rulers and 7 more inches. Then they can label each foot as 12 inches and find the total number of inches represented.

Differentiating Instruction

Alternative Teaching Strategy
For Example 2, students can use a calculator to express 35 ounces in ounces and pounds. By calculating that 35 ÷ 16 = 2.1875, they can tell that the whole number of pounds is 2. Then, by calculating that 0.1875 × 16 = 3, they find that the "extra" number of ounces is 3.

Example 5 A punchbowl set consists of a large punchbowl, a large pitcher, and glasses. The capacity of the punchbowl is 3 gal 3 qt and the capacity of the pitcher is 2 qt.

a. Find the total capacity of the punchbowl and pitcher. **4 gal 1 qt**

b. Find the difference in the capacities of the bowl and the pitcher. **3 gal 1 qt**

MATH REASONING

Students should understand that the addition and subtraction process in Example 5 follows the same reasoning as adding and subtracting mixed numbers.

 CONCEPT CHECK

Describe how you can change a measurement from one unit to another unit. Give examples.

Sample answer: Multiply the measurement by a fraction that is equal to 1. For example, to change 6 quarts to gallons, multiply by $\frac{1 \text{ gal}}{4 \text{ qt}}$: $\frac{6 \text{ qt}}{1} \times \frac{1 \text{ gal}}{4 \text{ qt}} = 1\frac{1}{2}$ gal.

To change $1\frac{1}{2}$ gal to quarts, multiply by $\frac{4 \text{ qt}}{1 \text{ gal}}$:

$1\frac{1}{2}$ gal $= \frac{3 \text{ gal}}{2} \times \frac{4 \text{ qt}}{1 \text{ gal}} = 6$ qt.

DAILY PUZZLER

How many feet per second are you moving in a car that is traveling at 60 miles per hour? **88 ft per sec**

Solving a Related Problem To add or subtract customary units, think about how you added and subtracted units of time in Lesson 6.6. You will set up the problem and rename units in the same way.

EXAMPLE 5 Adding and Subtracting Measures

Model Trains A steam locomotive on a large model train has a length of 3 ft 2 in. The length of a passenger car is 1 ft 11 in.

a. How long is a model train with the locomotive and one passenger car?

b. What is the difference in the lengths of the two cars?

The model locomotive shown is $26\frac{3}{8}$ in. long. It is built to a scale of 1 in. : 32 in.

Solution

a. Add. Then rename the sum.

$$
\begin{array}{r}
3 \text{ ft} \quad 2 \text{ in.} \\
+ 1 \text{ ft} \quad 11 \text{ in.} \\
\hline
4 \text{ ft} \quad 13 \text{ in.}
\end{array}
$$

Rename 4 ft 13 in. as 5 ft 1 in.

b. Rename. Then subtract.

Rename one of the feet as 12 in.

$$
\begin{array}{rcl}
3 \text{ ft} \quad 2 \text{ in.} & \longrightarrow & 2 \text{ ft} \quad 14 \text{ in.} \\
- 1 \text{ ft} \quad 11 \text{ in.} & & - 1 \text{ ft} \quad 11 \text{ in.} \\
\hline
& & 1 \text{ ft} \quad 3 \text{ in.}
\end{array}
$$

ANSWER The train is 5 ft 1 in. long.   **ANSWER** The difference is 1 ft 3 in.

7.7 Exercises

More Practice, p. 714

INTERNET
eWorkbook Plus
CLASSZONE.COM

Getting Ready to Practice

Vocabulary Copy and complete the statement.

1. $1 = \dfrac{8 \text{ fl oz}}{? \text{ c}}$ 1   **2.** $1 = \dfrac{? \text{ mi}}{1760 \text{ yd}}$ 1   **3.** $1 = \dfrac{1 \text{ lb}}{? \text{ oz}}$ 16   **4.** $1 = \dfrac{? \text{ qt}}{1 \text{ gal}}$ 4

Copy and complete the statement.

5. 1 mi 6000 ft = 2 mi _?_ ft 720

6. 5 qt 1 pt = _?_ qt 3 pt 4

7. 2 T 300 lb = _?_ lb 4300

8. 99 in. = _?_ yd _?_ in., or _?_ yd
2, 27, 2.75

In Exercises 9–10, change the measurement to the specified unit.

9. 17 yards to feet **51 ft**

10. $1\frac{1}{3}$ cups to quarts $\frac{1}{3}$ qt

11. Find the sum and the difference of 6 lb 3 oz and 4 lb 15 oz.
11 lb 2 oz; 1 lb 4 oz

Practice and Problem Solving

with Homework

Example	Exercises
1	12–28
2	12–28
3	19–28
4	29–31
5	32–38

Online Resources
CLASSZONE.COM

· More Examples
· eTutorial Plus

A Copy and complete the statement.

12. 3 lb 7 oz = ? oz 55 **13.** 4 yd 1 ft = ? ft 13 **14.** 5 c 6 fl oz = ? fl oz 46

15. 64 in. = ? ft ? in. **16.** 64 in. = ? ft $5\frac{1}{3}$ **17.** 30 qt = ? gal $7\frac{1}{2}$
5, 4

18. Amusement Park You must be more than 50 inches tall to go on a certain ride. You are 4 feet 3 inches tall. Are you allowed on the ride?
yes

Change the measurement to the specified unit.

19. 6 T to pounds **20.** 2 mi to yards 3520 yd **21.** 10 pt to quarts 5 qt
12,000 lb

22. 24 fl oz to cups 3 c **23.** 45 in. to feet $3\frac{3}{4}$ ft **24.** 4500 lb to tons $2\frac{1}{4}$ T

25. $\frac{5}{8}$ lb to ounces 10 oz **26.** $40\frac{1}{2}$ in. to yards **27.** $8\frac{1}{2}$ c to pints $4\frac{1}{4}$ pt
$1\frac{1}{8}$ yd

28. Maple Syrup One taphole in a maple tree typically yields enough sap in a year to produce $\frac{1}{3}$ gallon of syrup. How many quarts of syrup is that? $1\frac{1}{3}$ qt

Change the measurement to the specified unit.

29. $1\frac{3}{4}$ qt to cups 7 c **30.** $3\frac{1}{2}$ gal to pints 28 pt **31.** 48 fl oz to quarts $1\frac{1}{2}$ qt

32. Find the Error Describe and correct the error in the solution. **There are 16 oz in 1 lb, so 13 oz should be 19 oz. The correct answer is 1 lb 11 oz.**

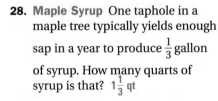

$$\begin{array}{r} 4\text{ lb }3\text{ oz} \\ -\ 2\text{ lb }8\text{ oz} \end{array} \longrightarrow \begin{array}{r} 3\text{ lb }13\text{ oz} \\ -\ 2\text{ lb }\ 8\text{ oz} \\ \hline 1\text{ lb }\ 5\text{ oz} \end{array}$$

Find the sum or difference.

33.
$$\begin{array}{r} 6\text{ ft }7\text{ in.} \\ +\ 5\text{ ft }8\text{ in.} \\ \hline 12\text{ ft }3\text{ in.} \end{array}$$

34.
$$\begin{array}{r} 10\text{ lb }9\text{ oz} \\ +\ 11\text{ lb }8\text{ oz} \\ \hline 22\text{ lb }1\text{ oz} \end{array}$$

35.
$$\begin{array}{r} 4\text{ gal }1\text{ qt} \\ +\ 2\text{ gal }3\text{ qt} \\ \hline 7\text{ gal} \end{array}$$

36.
$$\begin{array}{r} 17\text{ yd }1\text{ ft} \\ -\ 14\text{ yd }2\text{ ft} \\ \hline 2\text{ yd }2\text{ ft} \end{array}$$

37.
$$\begin{array}{r} 9\text{ T }397\text{ lb} \\ -\ 2\text{ T }478\text{ lb} \\ \hline 6\text{ T }1919\text{ lb} \end{array}$$

38.
$$\begin{array}{r} 7\text{ c }3\text{ fl oz} \\ -\ 1\text{ c }5\text{ fl oz} \\ \hline 5\text{ c }6\text{ fl oz} \end{array}$$

Submersibles ALVIN is an underwater vehicle used for research.

B 39. ALVIN weighs 35,200 pounds. What is its weight in tons? $17\frac{3}{5}$ T

40. Technology ALVIN can dive to depths as great as 14,764 feet. What is its depth limit in miles? Round to the nearest tenth of a mile. 2.8 mi

Science

■ **Submersibles**

ALVIN can carry a load of 1500 lb. Certain standard equipment weighs 339 lb. If the three people it carries weigh a total of 480 lb, about how many pounds of load are available for the researchers' equipment and samples? What decimal part of the 1500 lb load is that?

681 lb; 0.454

ASSIGNMENT GUIDE

Basic Course
Day 1: SRH p. 701 Exs. 1–6; pp. 353–354 Exs. 12–21, 28–31, 33–44, 50–60

Average Course
Day 1: pp. 353–354 Exs. 15–24, 28–35, 39–48, 50–55, 59–61

Advanced Course
Day 1: pp. 353–354 Exs. 15–21, 25–32, 36–41, 45–55*, 60, 61

Block
pp. 353–354 Exs. 15–24, 28–35, 39–48, 50–55, 59–61 (with 7.6)

HOMEWORK CHECK

When you review students' homework for this lesson, go over the following exercises to check understanding of key concepts.
Basic: 12, 16, 19, 29, 33
Average: 15, 18, 20, 30, 34
Advanced: 15, 18, 25, 31, 36

COMMON ERROR

In Exercises 33–35, students may rename the sum incorrectly. This may be especially true in Exercise 35, where the renamed sum has no quarts. Refer students to the chart on page 350 and Example 5.

MINI-QUIZ

1. Change 29 feet to yards. Write your answer in yards and feet. **9 yd 2 ft**

2. Change 35 feet to yards. Write your answer in yards. $11\frac{2}{3}$ **yd**

3. Change 2 lb 5 oz to ounces. **37 oz**

4. Change $1\frac{3}{4}$ lb to ounces. **28 oz**

5. How many fluid ounces is 14 qt? **448 fl oz**

6. A flat roof is at a height of 26 ft 9 in. The chimney extends another 5 ft 11 in.
   a. What is the difference in the two heights? **20 ft 10 in.**
   b. How high is the top of the chimney? **32 ft 8 in.**

42–47. Sample answers are given.

42. I chose mental math because it is easy to find $1\frac{1}{2}$ times 2000.

43. I chose paper and pencil because it is hard to find $\frac{7}{8}$ times 5280 mentally.

44. I chose paper and pencil because it is hard to divide $2\frac{1}{2}$ by 2 mentally.

45. I chose paper and pencil because it is hard to multiply $1\frac{2}{3}$ by 8 mentally.

46. I chose mental math because it is easy to multiply $2\frac{5}{12}$ by 12 mentally.

47. I chose paper and pencil because it is hard to divide 280 by 16 mentally.

INTERNET
State Test Practice
CLASSZONE.COM

41. Estimation Hank Aaron hit a record 755 home runs in his career. The distance around a baseball diamond is 360 feet. Estimate how many miles Hank Aaron ran after hitting home runs. **about 50 mi**

Choose a Method Choose *mental math* or *paper and pencil* to copy and complete the statement with <, >, or =. Explain your choice.

42–47. See margin for explanations.

42. 3645 lb _?_ $1\frac{1}{2}$ T **>**   **43.** $\frac{7}{8}$ mi _?_ 4875 ft **<**   **44.** $2\frac{1}{2}$ pt _?_ $1\frac{1}{4}$ qt **=**

45. $1\frac{2}{3}$ c _?_ $13\frac{1}{3}$ fl oz **=**   **46.** $2\frac{5}{12}$ ft _?_ 30 in. **<**   **47.** 280 oz _?_ 17 lb **>**

C 48. Geometry Find the perimeter of the figure. **736 in.**

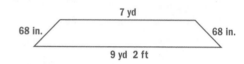

49. Challenge About 6 gallons of ice cream and related frozen desserts are eaten per person per year in the United States. How many fluid ounces per person per day is that? Round to the nearest whole number. **2 fl oz**

Mixed Review

Find the next two numbers in the pattern. *(Lesson 1.1)*

50. 94, 87, 80, 73, _?_, _?_ **66, 59**   **51.** 729, 243, 81, 27, _?_, _?_ **9, 3**

Find the quotient. *(Lessons 7.4, 7.5)*

52. $\frac{5}{9} \div \frac{10}{27}$ $1\frac{1}{2}$ **53.** $3\frac{1}{9} \div 5$ $\frac{28}{45}$ **54.** $2\frac{3}{4} \div 2\frac{2}{7}$ $1\frac{13}{64}$ **55.** $\frac{1}{10} \div 7\frac{3}{5}$ $\frac{1}{76}$

Basic Skills Copy and complete the statement.

56. $\frac{4}{5} = \frac{20}{?}$ **25**   **57.** $\frac{3}{11} = \frac{?}{22}$ **6**   **58.** $\frac{42}{18} = \frac{?}{3}$ **7**   **59.** $\frac{16}{36} = \frac{4}{?}$ **9**

Test-Taking Practice

60. Multiple Choice Which of the following is *not* equivalent to 64 inches? **D**

   A. $1\frac{7}{9}$ yd   **B.** 5 ft 4 in.   **C.** $5\frac{1}{3}$ ft   **D.** $5\frac{1}{4}$ ft

61. Multiple Choice You can buy drinks in three sizes: 12 fluid ounces, $\frac{1}{2}$ pint, 2 cups. Which choice shows these sizes from greatest to least? **G**

   F. 12 fl oz, $\frac{1}{2}$ pt, 2 c   **G.** 2 c, 12 fl oz, $\frac{1}{2}$ pt

   H. 12 fl oz, 2 c, $\frac{1}{2}$ pt   **I.** $\frac{1}{2}$ pt, 2 c, 12 fl oz

7.7

CALCULATOR

Technology Activity

Changing Units

GOAL Use a calculator to change between metric units and customary units.

Example **The calculator memory can help you change units.**

You plan to take the Marine Drive along the coast of Nova Scotia in Canada. The distance is given as 340 kilometers, but you want to know the distance in miles.

Solution

To change metric units to customary units, use the relationships shown in the table.

Length	Capacity	Weight
1 mm ≈ 0.0394 in.	1 mL ≈ 0.0338 fl oz	1 g ≈ 0.0353 oz
1 m ≈ 3.28 ft	1 L ≈ 1.06 qt	1 kg ≈ 2.2 lb
1 km ≈ 0.621 mi	1 kL ≈ 264 gal	

To change between kilometers and miles, use the fact that 1 km ≈ 0.621 mi. You will use 0.621 any time you change between these units, so store this value in memory.

Keystrokes

0.621 [STO ▶] [=]

Display

[0.621]

To change to miles, you would multiply $340 \text{ km} \times \dfrac{0.621 \text{ mi}}{1 \text{ km}}$, so *multiply* by the value in memory. (To change miles to kilometers, you would *divide* by the value in memory.)

Keystrokes

340 [×] [2nd] [RCL] [=] [=]

Display

[211.14]

ANSWER The Marine Drive is about 211 miles long.

HELP with Technology

Many calculator keys have two uses. The use shown by the label above the key is called the second function. For this use, press [2nd] before pressing the key. To recall a value, some calculators use [RCL], the second function of [STO ▶].

Your turn now Find each value to the nearest whole number.

1.

Length
127 km = _?_ mi
_?_ km = 34 mi
1388 km = _?_ mi

79; 55; 862

2.

Capacity
500 mL = _?_ fl oz
_?_ mL = 6 fl oz
1600 mL = _?_ fl oz

17; 178; 54

3.

Weight
12 kg = _?_ lb
50 kg = _?_ lb
_?_ kg = 77 lb

26; 110; 35

Lesson 7.7   Changing Customary Units   **355**

---

① PLAN

LEARN THE METHOD

- Students will use a calculator to change from metric units to customary units and vice versa.
- Have students convert the given numbers in Exercises 12–17 on page 353 to appropriate metric units.

② TEACH

TIPS FOR SUCCESS

As students complete the exercises, encourage them to decide in advance whether they will multiply or divide by the appropriate conversion factor.

EXTRA EXAMPLES

Example Complete using the relationship 2.54 cm = 1 in.
a. 35 cm = _?_ in. **13.8**
b. _?_ cm = 50 in. **127**

③ CLOSE

ASSESSMENT

Find each to the nearest whole number.

1. a. 28 mL = _?_ fl oz **1**
   b. _?_ mL = 47 fl oz **1391**

2. a. _?_ g = 310 oz **8782**
   b. 450 g = _?_ oz **16**

LESSONS 7.4 TO 7.7

Notebook Review

Review the vocabulary definitions in your notebook.

Copy the review examples in your notebook. Then complete the exercises.

Check Your Definitions

reciprocal, p. 334	ton, p. 344	pint, p. 345
ounce, p. 344	fluid ounce, p. 345	quart, p. 345
pound, p. 344	cup, p. 345	gallon, p. 345

Use Your Vocabulary

1. Copy and complete: A number times its __?__ is equal to 1. **reciprocal**

7.4–7.5 Can you divide fractions and mixed numbers?

 EXAMPLE $9 \div 4\frac{2}{3} = \frac{9}{1} \div \frac{14}{3}$ Write 9 and $4\frac{2}{3}$ as improper fractions.

$$= \frac{9}{1} \times \frac{3}{14}$$ Multiply by the reciprocal of the divisor.

$$= \frac{27}{14}, \text{ or } 1\frac{13}{14}$$ Find the product.

✓ **Check** Estimate: $9 \div 4\frac{2}{3} \approx 10 \div 5 = 2$. So, $1\frac{13}{14}$ is reasonable.

 Find the quotient.

2. $\frac{5}{6} \div \frac{7}{10}$ $1\frac{4}{21}$ 3. $\frac{4}{7} \div 5$ $\frac{4}{35}$ 4. $\frac{3}{8} \div 2\frac{2}{5}$ $\frac{5}{32}$ 5. $6\frac{3}{4} \div 1\frac{3}{4}$ $3\frac{6}{7}$

7.6–7.7 Can you use customary units?

 EXAMPLE Copy and complete the statement.

a. $25 \text{ oz} = \underline{?} \text{ lb } \underline{?} \text{ oz} = \underline{?} \text{ lb}$ **b.** $53 \text{ fl oz} = \underline{?} \text{ pt}$

$25 \div 16 = 1 \text{ R}9$ $53 \text{ fl oz} = 53 \text{ fl oz} \times \frac{1 \text{ c}}{8 \text{ fl oz}} \times \frac{1 \text{ pt}}{2 \text{ c}}$

So, $25 \text{ oz} = 1 \text{ lb } 9 \text{ oz} = 1\frac{9}{16} \text{ lb}$. $= \frac{53 \text{ pt}}{16}, \text{ or } 3\frac{5}{16} \text{ pt}$

In Exercises 6–8, copy and complete the statement.

6. $\frac{3}{8} \text{ T} = \underline{?} \text{ lb}$ **750**   7. $3\frac{1}{2} \text{ pt} = \underline{?} \text{ gal}$ $\frac{7}{16}$ 8. $4 \text{ ft } 10 \text{ in.} = \underline{?} \text{ in.}$ **58**

9. Find the sum and the difference of 5 yd 1 ft and 2 yd 2 ft.   **8 yd; 2 yd 2 ft**

10. Choose an appropriate customary unit to measure a baby's weight.   **pounds**

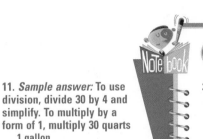

11. *Sample answer:* To use division, divide 30 by 4 and simplify. To multiply by a form of 1, multiply 30 quarts by $\frac{1 \text{ gallon}}{4 \text{ quarts}}$ and simplify.

The methods are similar in that you end up dividing by 4 in both.

11. Critical Thinking You can change 30 quarts to gallons by using division or by multiplying by a form of 1. Describe the steps for each method. Then explain how the two methods are similar.

Review Quiz 2

Find the quotient.

1. $\frac{2}{15} \div \frac{3}{10}$ $\frac{4}{9}$

2. $7 \div \frac{4}{5}$ $8\frac{3}{4}$

3. $2\frac{5}{8} \div 3$ $\frac{7}{8}$

4. $6\frac{3}{5} \div 2\frac{4}{9}$ $2\frac{7}{10}$

Copy and complete the statement using an appropriate customary unit.

5. weight of a bulldozer = 15 ? tons

6. capacity of a thermos = 32 ? ounces

Copy and complete the statement.

7. 5500 lb = ? T ? lb 2; 1500

8. $2\frac{2}{3}$ yd = ? in. 96

9. 22 c = ? qt $5\frac{1}{2}$

10. Electronics Your television weighs 19 pounds 8 ounces. Your stereo weighs 20 pounds 12 ounces. Can you safely place your television and your stereo on a shelf that holds 40 pounds? Explain.

No. *Sample answer:* The total weight of the two is 40 pounds 4 ounces, which is greater than 40 pounds.

A Pattern of Measures

For each box in which the measures are equal, list the number shown in red. Work in order across the rows. The numbers you list form a pattern. Look for the pattern and then predict the next two numbers. 2, 9, 6, 13, 10, 17, 14; 21, 18

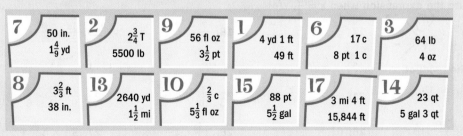

Chapter Review

 **Vocabulary**

reciprocal, p. 334	ton, p. 344	pint, p. 345
ounce, p. 344	fluid ounce, p. 345	quart, p. 345
pound, p. 344	cup, p. 345	gallon, p. 345

Vocabulary Review

Tell whether the statement is *true* or *false*.

1. The number 0 has no reciprocal. **true**

2. The number 1 has no reciprocal. **false**

3. The reciprocal of $1\frac{1}{3}$ is $\frac{4}{3}$. **false**

4. The reciprocal of $\frac{1}{5}$ is 5. **true**

5. The unit *pint* is used to measure weight. **false**

6. The unit *ounce* is used to measure capacity. **false**

7. 4 quarts = 1 gallon **true**

8. 1000 pounds = 1 ton **false**

9. 1 yard = 36 inches **true**

10. 1 cup = 2 pints **false**

Review Questions

Use compatible numbers to estimate the product. *(Lesson 7.1)*

11. $\frac{1}{3} \times 20$ **7**

12. $35 \times \frac{1}{6}$ **6**

13. $42 \times \frac{7}{8}$ **35**

14. $\frac{5}{12} \times 35$ **15**

15. Basketball You practice dribbling a basketball for $\frac{3}{4}$ hour each day. How much time do you practice dribbling in a week? *(Lesson 7.1)* **$5\frac{1}{4}$ h**

Evaluate the expression when $x = \frac{3}{4}$. *(Lesson 7.2)*

16. $\frac{8}{9}x$ **$\frac{2}{3}$**

17. $\frac{4}{15}x$ **$\frac{1}{5}$**

18. $\frac{7}{12}x$ **$\frac{7}{16}$**

19. $\frac{12}{23}x$ **$\frac{9}{23}$**

Find the product. *(Lessons 7.2, 7.3)*

20. $\frac{4}{7} \times \frac{3}{5}$ **$\frac{12}{35}$**

21. $\frac{1}{12} \times \frac{2}{3}$ **$\frac{1}{18}$**

22. $\frac{3}{10} \times \frac{6}{5}$ **$\frac{9}{25}$**

23. $\frac{7}{9} \times \frac{3}{4} \times \frac{2}{5}$ **$\frac{7}{30}$**

24. $2 \times 5\frac{1}{6}$ **$10\frac{1}{3}$**

25. $6\frac{2}{5} \times \frac{3}{16}$ **$1\frac{1}{5}$**

26. $2\frac{1}{4} \times 1\frac{2}{3}$ **$3\frac{3}{4}$**

27. $3\frac{2}{7} \times 4\frac{2}{3}$ **$15\frac{1}{3}$**

28. Flying Billboards A flying billboard measures $6\frac{2}{3}$ yards by 15 yards. What is the area of the billboard? *(Lesson 7.3)* **100 yd²**

Estimate the product or quotient. *(Lessons 7.3, 7.5)*

29. $3\frac{3}{4} \times 2\frac{2}{7}$ **8**

30. $6\frac{9}{10} \times 4$ **28**

31. $11\frac{1}{2} \div 1\frac{7}{8}$ **6**

32. $26 \div 5\frac{1}{3}$ **5**

Find the quotient. *(Lessons 7.4, 7.5)*

33. $\frac{2}{9} \div \frac{2}{3}$ $\frac{1}{3}$

34. $\frac{5}{12} \div 10$ $\frac{1}{24}$

35. $14 \div \frac{7}{8}$ **16**

36. $\frac{21}{4} \div \frac{1}{6}$ $31\frac{1}{2}$

37. $4\frac{2}{5} \div 4$ $1\frac{1}{10}$

38. $8\frac{3}{4} \div \frac{5}{8}$ **14**

39. $\frac{9}{10} \div 2\frac{1}{2}$ $\frac{9}{25}$

40. $5\frac{5}{8} \div 3\frac{3}{5}$ $1\frac{9}{16}$

41. Sub Sandwiches How many sub sandwiches that are $4\frac{1}{2}$ inches long can be cut from a sub that is 60 inches long? Is any left over? Explain. *(Lesson 7.5)* **13; yes; 60 divided by $4\frac{1}{2}$ is $13\frac{1}{3}$, so there is $\frac{1}{3}$ of a sandwich left over.**

Choose an appropriate customary unit of weight. *(Lesson 7.6)*

42. elephant **tons**

43. bowling ball **pounds**

44. refrigerator **pounds**

45. scoop of ice cream **ounces**

46. Blender The capacity of the blender shown at the right is $1\frac{1}{2}$ of some unit. Is that unit *fluid ounces, quarts,* or *gallons?* *(Lesson 7.6)* **quarts**

Copy and complete the statement. *(Lesson 7.7)*

47. $2\frac{3}{4}$ lb = ? oz **44**

48. 86 in. = ? yd ? in. **2, 14**

49. 48 fl oz = ? qt $1\frac{1}{2}$

50. 8 gal 3 qt = ? qt **35**

51. Trucks A pickup truck weighs about $1\frac{7}{8}$ tons. How many pounds does it weigh? *(Lesson 7.7)* **3750 lb**

Add or subtract. *(Lesson 7.7)*

52.
```
  2 ft  10 in.
+ 4 ft   5 in.
```
7 ft 3 in.

53.
```
  8 qt  1 pt
+ 3 qt  1 pt
```
12 qt

54.
```
  6 c  1 fl oz
- 2 c  7 fl oz
```
3 c 2 fl oz

55.
```
  14 lb   8 oz
-  9 lb  13 oz
```
4 lb 11 oz

Chapter Test

Find the product.

1. $10 \times \frac{4}{15}$ $2\frac{2}{3}$

2. $\frac{1}{5} \times \frac{2}{9}$ $\frac{2}{45}$

3. $\frac{5}{12} \times \frac{3}{7}$ $\frac{5}{28}$

4. $\frac{1}{6} \times \frac{3}{8} \times \frac{2}{5}$ $\frac{1}{40}$

5. $3\frac{1}{4} \times 2$ $6\frac{1}{2}$

6. $4\frac{5}{8} \times \frac{8}{11}$ $3\frac{4}{11}$

7. $5\frac{1}{2} \times 3\frac{1}{3}$ $18\frac{1}{3}$

8. $1\frac{2}{9} \times 1\frac{7}{11}$ 2

Estimate the product or quotient.   9–12. Estimates may vary.

9. $\frac{1}{7} \times 65$ 9

10. $\frac{5}{8} \times 41$ 25

11. $6 \times 7\frac{2}{3}$ 48

12. $9\frac{1}{2} \div 3\frac{1}{8}$ 3

13. **Trains** A train has 50 cars. $\frac{3}{5}$ of the cars are carrying grain.
How many cars are carrying grain? **30 cars**

14. Evaluate the expression $\frac{3}{8}x$ when $x = \frac{5}{7}$. $\frac{15}{56}$

Find the quotient.

15. $\frac{5}{6} \div \frac{4}{9}$ $1\frac{7}{8}$

16. $\frac{1}{7} \div \frac{7}{12}$ $\frac{12}{49}$

17. $8 \div \frac{2}{5}$ 20

18. $\frac{3}{10} \div 9$ $\frac{1}{30}$

19. $2\frac{5}{8} \div 7$ $\frac{3}{8}$

20. $6\frac{3}{5} \div \frac{3}{4}$ $8\frac{4}{5}$

21. $\frac{1}{12} \div 3\frac{1}{4}$ $\frac{1}{39}$

22. $10\frac{1}{2} \div 2\frac{3}{4}$ $3\frac{9}{11}$

23. Is the capacity of a teacup measured in *fluid ounces*, *pints*, or *quarts*? **fluid ounces**

Music Use the instruments shown.

24. An English horn is how many times
as long as a flute? $1\frac{1}{6}$ **times as long**

25. Change each length to inches.
English horn: $31\frac{1}{2}$ **in.; flute: 27 in.**

26. Copy and complete the statement
using *ounces*, *pounds*, or *tons*:
A flute weighs about $15\frac{1}{2}$?. **ounces**

$2\frac{5}{8}$ ft

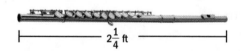
$2\frac{1}{4}$ ft

Copy and complete the statement.

27. 8 yd = ? ft 24

28. $7\frac{1}{2}$ gal = ? pt 60

29. 19 fl oz = ? c ? fl oz 2, 3

30. 5000 lb = ? T $2\frac{1}{2}$

31. 5 lb 3 oz − 3 lb 8 oz = ? lb ? oz 1, 11

Chapter Standardized Test

Test-Taking Strategy If you are struggling to answer a particular question and find you are becoming very anxious or frustrated, then leave that question and go on.

Multiple Choice

1. A weather update on the news lasts $\frac{2}{15}$ hour. How many minutes does the update last? **D**

A. 2 min **B.** 4 min **C.** 6 min **D.** 8 min

2. What is the value of the expression $\frac{7}{3}n$ when $n = \frac{9}{10}$? **H**

F. $1\frac{7}{10}$ **G.** $\frac{61}{30}$ **H.** $2\frac{1}{10}$ **I.** $2\frac{3}{10}$

3. A lemonade recipe calls for $\frac{2}{3}$ cup of lemon juice. How much lemon juice do you need to make $1\frac{1}{2}$ times the recipe? **B**

A. $\frac{3}{4}$ cup **B.** 1 cup

C. $1\frac{1}{3}$ cups **D.** $\frac{3}{2}$ cups

4. How many pieces of ribbon that are $\frac{1}{8}$ yard long can you cut from $\frac{3}{4}$ yard of ribbon? **H**

F. 2 **G.** 4 **H.** 6 **I.** 8

5. A magic show is scheduled to last $2\frac{3}{4}$ hours. Each of the 6 magicians in the show is given the same amount of time. How long does each magician have? **B**

A. $\frac{5}{12}$ h **B.** $\frac{11}{24}$ h **C.** $\frac{1}{2}$ h **D.** $\frac{3}{4}$ h

6. Which of the following is not a unit of capacity? **F**

F. ounce **G.** cup **H.** pint **I.** gallon

7. Which measurement could be the weight of a bar of soap? **C**

A. $4\frac{3}{4}$ T **B.** $4\frac{3}{4}$ lb **C.** $4\frac{3}{4}$ oz **D.** $4\frac{3}{4}$ fl oz

8. What is the sum of 17 feet 7 inches and 11 feet 9 inches? **H**

F. 5 ft 10 in. **G.** 28 ft 4 in.

H. 29 ft 4 in. **I.** 29 ft 6 in.

9. Which of the following statements is false? **A**

A. $2\frac{1}{2}$ qt > 5 pt **B.** 3 gal < 25 pt

C. 2 pt > 30 fl oz **D.** $5\frac{1}{4}$ c = 42 fl oz

Short Response

10. The diagram shows the dimensions of the pages in a magazine. Estimate the area of each page. Explain your steps. See margin.

Extended Response

11. A quilt pattern uses squares with sides that are $4\frac{1}{2}$ inches long, not including seams. Sue wants to reduce each side to $\frac{2}{3}$ of the length on the pattern. What are the dimensions of a reduced square? How many reduced squares does she need to sew together to make a 1 foot by 1 foot square? Explain your steps. See margin.

ADDITIONAL RESOURCES

Assessment Book
- Standardized Chapter Test, p. 87

Test and Practice Generator

10. *Sample answer:* 88 in.^{2}; round $10\frac{13}{16}$ inches to 11 inches and round $8\frac{1}{4}$ inches to 8 inches. Then $11 \times 8 = 88$ square inches.

11. 3 inches by 3 inches; 16. *Sample answer:* Sue would need to sew four squares on each edge to make a 1 foot by 1 foot square. So she would need $4 \times 4 = 16$ squares to make a 1 foot by 1 foot square.

USING RUBRICS

The rubric given on the pupil page is a sample of a three-level rubric. Other rubrics may contain four, five, or six levels. For more information on rubrics, see the Professional Development Book.

TEST-TAKING TIP

Caution students, especially advanced students, to show all of the steps they perform when solving a short response question. Some students may do part of their calculations mentally and then neglect to write down enough information to receive full credit. Encourage students to "think like a reviewer" who is scoring their work, asking themselves if they have shown all of the important information.

 COMMON ERROR

Students can become so focused on doing all of the necessary computations and getting a solution for a short response question that they fail to answer the question posed. Remind students to quickly read the problem again after completing their computations. Stress that the result of their calculations is not always the answer to the question.

VISUALIZE

Suggest that students use a sketch, similar to the factor trees they used in Chapter 5, to show how many cups of flour are in a 5 pound bag. Starting with a "5 pound" square at the top, they should draw five smaller "1 pound" squares in a row below it. Below each "1 pound" square they should draw three smaller "1 cup" squares and a "$\frac{1}{2}$ cup" small square. Students can then divide some of the "1 cup" squares into "$\frac{1}{2}$ cup" squares and finish by circling all of the possible "1 cup" and "$\frac{1}{2}$ cup" pairs in their diagram to solve the problem.

362

UNIT 2 Chapters 5–7

BUILDING **Test-Taking Skills**

Strategies for Answering
Short Response Questions

Scoring Rubric

Full credit
- answer is correct, *and*
- work or reasoning is included

Partial credit
- answer is correct, but reasoning is incorrect, *or*
- answer is incorrect, but reasoning is correct

No credit
- no answer is given, *or*
- answer makes no sense

Problem
There are $3\frac{1}{2}$ cups of flour in one pound of flour. Your recipe for Key Lime cake calls for $1\frac{1}{2}$ cups of flour. How many cakes can you make using a 5 pound bag of flour?

Full credit solution

The number of cakes you can make is the number of cups of flour in a 5 pound bag divided by the number of cups of flour in each cake.

This reasoning is the key to choosing the operations you need.

The steps of the solution are clearly written.

Cups in 5 lb bag = Pounds per bag × Cups per pound

$$= 5 \times 3\frac{1}{2} = \frac{5}{1} \times \frac{7}{2} = \frac{35}{2} = 17\frac{1}{2}$$

Number of cakes = Cups in 5 lb bag ÷ Cups per cake

$$= 17\frac{1}{2} \div 1\frac{1}{2} = \frac{35}{2} \times \frac{2}{3} = \frac{35}{3} = 11\frac{2}{3}$$

The question asked is answered correctly.

You can make 11 cakes.

Partial credit solution

There are $17\frac{1}{2}$ cups of flour in a 5 pound bag.

The reasoning and calculations are correct.

The answer makes no sense. You cannot make a fractional number of cakes.

$$17\frac{1}{2} \div 1\frac{1}{2} = \frac{35}{2} \times \frac{2}{3} = \frac{35}{3} = 11\frac{2}{3}$$

You can make $11\frac{2}{3}$ cakes.

Partial credit solution

Without explanation, the reasoning behind this calculation is unclear.

$$\frac{35}{2} \times \frac{2}{3} = \frac{35}{3} = 11\frac{2}{3}$$

You can make 11 cakes.

The answer is correct.

No credit solution

The wrong operations have been chosen. ---- $\left(5 + 3\frac{1}{2}\right) \times 1\frac{1}{2} = 8\frac{1}{2} \times 1\frac{1}{2} = \frac{17}{2} \times \frac{3}{2} = \frac{51}{4} = 12\frac{3}{4}$

You can make 12 cakes. ---------------------- The answer is not correct.

Your turn now

Score each solution to the short response question below as *full credit, partial credit,* or *no credit*. Explain your reasoning.

1–3. See margin.

Problem Rina weighed $7\frac{1}{4}$ pounds at birth. She gained an average of $\frac{1}{24}$ pound per day for the first 30 days and an average of $1\frac{1}{4}$ pounds per month for the next 5 months. What was Rina's weight in pounds at six months?

Watch Out!

If a problem involves measurements, don't forget to include units with your solutions.

1. No credit; the wrong operations have been chosen and the answer is not correct.

2. Full credit; the reasoning is correct, the steps are clearly written, and the question is answered correctly.

3. Full credit; the reasoning is correct, the steps are clearly written, and the question is answered correctly.

1. $7\frac{1}{4} + \frac{2}{3} + 1\frac{1}{4} = 9\frac{1}{6}$; Rina's weight at six months was $9\frac{1}{6}$ pounds.

2. Rina gained $30 \times \frac{1}{24} = \frac{30}{24} = \frac{5}{4}$ pounds in her first 30 days and $5 \times 1\frac{1}{4} = \frac{5}{1} \times \frac{5}{4} = \frac{25}{4}$ pounds in the next 5 months. At six months she weighed $7\frac{1}{4} + \frac{5}{4} + \frac{25}{4} = 7\frac{31}{4} = 14\frac{3}{4}$ pounds.

3. Rina's total weight gain was $30 \times \frac{1}{24} + 5 \times 1\frac{1}{4}$, or $7\frac{1}{2}$ pounds, so her weight at six months was $7\frac{1}{4} + 7\frac{1}{2} = 14\frac{3}{4}$ pounds.

3. 12 in.; 23 pieces; the greatest common factor of 60, 96, and 120 is 12, so the greatest possible length is 12 inches; she can cut (60 ÷ 12) + (96 ÷ 12) + (120 ÷ 12) = 23 pieces.

4. Kaylene and Roger; lower; Kaylene's score was $\frac{23}{25} = 0.92$ which is the same as Roger's score; Devon's score was $\frac{9}{10} = 0.9 < 0.92$.

5. Yes; the perimeter of the triangle is $5\frac{1}{2} + 3\frac{7}{8} + 2\frac{1}{4} = 11\frac{5}{8}$ inches, which is less that 1 foot or 12 inches, so the piece of yarn will fit around the triangle.

6. $2\frac{3}{4}$ in.; the nail is longer than the width of the door, so the door is $3\frac{5}{8} - \frac{7}{8} = 2\frac{3}{4}$ inches wide.

8. 6 in.; she has $5 - 4\frac{5}{6} = \frac{1}{6}$ yard extra, which is $\frac{1}{6}(36) = 6$ inches.

9. 15 columns; $56 ÷ 3\frac{1}{2} = 16$, so 16 columns without space can be created. To create 15 columns, $15\left(3\frac{1}{2}\right) = 52.5$ inches are needed. If fourteen $\frac{1}{4}$ inch spaces are added, another 3.5 inches are needed for a total of 52.5 + 3.5 = 56 inches.

10. $22\frac{1}{2}$ c; 6 quarts is 6(32) = 192 fluid ounces and 192 − 12 = 180 fluid ounces are left, which is 180 ÷ 8 = $22\frac{1}{2}$ cups.

Short Response

1. Suppose you earn $4.75 per hour and work 3.5 hours each day, 4 days per week. What is your weekly salary? Explain how you found your answer. **$66.50; you work 3.5 × 4 = 14 hours and make $4.75 × 14 = $66.50.**

2. A 3.5 pound bag of oranges costs $2.99. Individual oranges are sold at $.89 per pound. Which is the better buy? Explain your reasoning. **The 3.5 pound bag; each pound in the bag costs $2.99 ÷ 3 ≈ $.85 < $.89.**

3. Sandra has three boards, as shown.

Board	1	2	3
Length (inches)	60	96	120

She needs to cut the boards into short pieces of the same length. What is the greatest possible length that she can use for the short pieces? How many pieces of that length will she have altogether after cutting the boards? Show your steps. **See margin.**

4. Kaylene's score on a quiz was $\frac{23}{25}$. Roger's score was 0.92, and Devon's score was $\frac{9}{10}$. Which two students received the same score? Was the third score *higher* or *lower* than the other two scores? Explain. **See margin.**

5. The sides of a triangular design are $5\frac{1}{2}$ inches, $3\frac{7}{8}$ inches, and $2\frac{1}{4}$ inches long. Is a one foot piece of yarn long enough to fit around the design? Explain. **See margin.**

6. A $3\frac{5}{8}$ inch nail is driven through a wooden door. The nail extends beyond the door by $\frac{7}{8}$ inch. How thick is the door? Explain how you found your answer. **See margin.**

7. Twelve students tried out for speaking parts in the school play. Two thirds of these students will get speaking parts. How many of the students who tried out for a speaking part will *not* get one? Explain how you found your answer. **4 students; if two thirds get a part, then one third do not, and one third of 12 is 4.**

8. Alice needed $4\frac{5}{6}$ yards of ribbon for a project. She bought 5 yards of ribbon. How many extra inches of ribbon did Alice buy? Show your steps. **See margin.**

9. A bulletin board is 56 inches wide. How many $3\frac{1}{2}$ inch columns can be created if $\frac{1}{4}$ inch is left between columns? Explain how you found your answer. **See margin.**

10. Katie poured 12 fluid ounces of juice from a full 6 quart container. How many cups were left in the container? Explain how you found your answer. **See margin.**

11. Sammy has 4 pounds 8 ounces of trail mix. He wants to make snack bags of the mix that are $\frac{3}{8}$ pound each. How many bags can he make? Show your steps. **See margin.**

12. The circle graph shows the results of a survey that asked people about the amount of sleep they usually get.

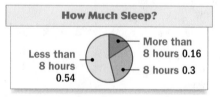

How Much Sleep?

Less than 8 hours 0.54
More than 8 hours 0.16
8 hours 0.3

Write each decimal as a fraction and show that the fractions add up to 1. Explain why the fractions must add up to 1. **See margin.**

11. 12 bags; 4 pounds 8 ounces is $4\frac{1}{2}$ pounds, and $4\frac{1}{2} \div \frac{3}{8} = 12$, which is the number of bags that can be made.

12. $0.16 = \frac{4}{25}$; $0.54 = \frac{27}{50}$; $0.3 = \frac{3}{10}$; $\frac{4}{25} + \frac{27}{50} + \frac{3}{10} = \frac{8}{50} + \frac{27}{50} + \frac{15}{50} = \frac{50}{50} = 1$; the circle graph shows all possible results.

Multiple Choice

13. Mr. Washington wants to divide his class of 30 students into groups of the same size with none left over. Which number of groups would *not* be possible? **B**

A. 3   **B.** 4   **C.** 5   **D.** 6

14. A mark on the side of a pier shows that the water is $4\frac{7}{8}$ feet deep. When the tide is high, the depth increases by $2\frac{1}{4}$ feet. About how deep is the water when the tide is high? **H**

F. 2 feet   **G.** 3 feet

H. 7 feet   **I.** 8 feet

15. Yesterday, Jerome spent $1\frac{3}{4}$ hours skateboarding, while Alisha played basketball for $\frac{17}{10}$ hours. Yolanda jogged for $1\frac{4}{5}$ hours, while Miguel played soccer for $\frac{3}{2}$ hours. Who devoted the most time to his or her activity? **D**

A. Alisha   **B.** Miguel

C. Jerome   **D.** Yolanda

16. An adult has 206 bones. Of these, 106 are in the feet, ankles, wrists, and hands. What fraction of the bones are in the feet, ankles, wrists, and hands? **G**

F. $\frac{1}{2}$ **G.** $\frac{53}{103}$ **H.** $\frac{6}{11}$ **I.** $\frac{11}{20}$

Extended Response

17. The table below shows the number of minutes of commercials on three stations for a certain number of minutes of viewing time.

Channel	A	B	C
Minutes of commercials	22	29	14
Viewing time (minutes)	90	120	60

Channel A; it was easier to compare using decimals because you can just look at the places and tell which is the greatest.

Use fractions to decide which channel showed commercials for the greatest portion of the viewing time. Then use decimals to answer this question. Compare and contrast the two methods.

18. Megan left her house at 7:30 A.M. She walked to the bus stop in 14 minutes. The bus ride to the city took 57 minutes. Then she spent 8 minutes walking to her office. Did she arrive at the office before 9 A.M.? Explain.

Yes; it took her $14 + 57 + 8 = 79$ minutes to get to the office, and 79 minutes after 7:30 A.M. is 8:49 A.M.

19. Nick is planning a party. He invites 24 guests. He wants to serve at least 2 cups of fruit punch to each guest. He plans to fill a $3\frac{1}{2}$ gallon punch bowl. Will he have enough punch? Explain your answer.   Yes; he will serve at least $24 \times 2 = 48$ cups of punch, which is 3 gallons.

ADDITIONAL RESOURCES

The following resources are available to help review the materials in this unit:

Chapter Resource Books
- Chapter 5 CRB, Cumulative Practice, pp. 83–84
- Chapter 6 CRB, Cumulative Practice, pp. 71–72
- Chapter 7 CRB, Cumulative Practice, pp. 76–77

Assessment Book
- Unit Test, pp. 90–91
- Cumulative Test, pp. 92–95

PRACTICING **Test-Taking Skills**

UNIT 2
Chapters 5–7

Cumulative Practice for Chapters 5–7

Chapter 5

Multiple Choice In Exercises 1–11, choose the letter of the correct answer.

1. Which number is prime? *(Lesson 5.1)* **B**

   A. 10   **B.** 41   **C.** 63   **D.** 77

2. What is the prime factorization of 96? *(Lesson 5.1)* **G**

   F. $1 \times 2^5 \times 3$ **G.** $2^5 \times 3$

   H. $4^2 \times 6$ **I.** 2×48

3. You have boards of lengths 80 inches and 128 inches. You divide the boards into pieces of the same length. Find the greatest possible length you can use. *(Lesson 5.2)* **C**

   A. 4 in.   **B.** 8 in.   **C.** 16 in.   **D.** 32 in.

4. Which fraction is *not* equivalent to $\frac{24}{40}$? *(Lesson 5.3)* **I**

   F. $\frac{3}{5}$ **G.** $\frac{6}{10}$ **H.** $\frac{12}{20}$ **I.** $\frac{4}{5}$

5. Which fraction is the simplest form of $\frac{16}{48}$? *(Lesson 5.3)* **A**

   A. $\frac{1}{3}$ **B.** $\frac{2}{6}$ **C.** $\frac{4}{12}$ **D.** $\frac{8}{24}$

6. What is the LCM of 40 and 18? *(Lesson 5.4)* **I**

   F. 24   **G.** 120   **H.** 160   **I.** 360

7. Which list of fractions is arranged in order from least to greatest? *(Lesson 5.5)* **A**

   A. $\frac{1}{3}, \frac{3}{8}, \frac{3}{5}, \frac{5}{6}$ **B.** $\frac{1}{3}, \frac{3}{8}, \frac{5}{6}, \frac{3}{5}$

   C. $\frac{1}{3}, \frac{3}{5}, \frac{3}{8}, \frac{5}{6}$ **D.** $\frac{5}{6}, \frac{3}{5}, \frac{3}{8}, \frac{1}{3}$

8. Which improper fraction is equivalent to $7\frac{5}{8}$? *(Lesson 5.6)* **H**

   F. $\frac{47}{8}$ **G.** $\frac{56}{8}$ **H.** $\frac{61}{8}$ **I.** $\frac{61}{5}$

9. How can $\frac{22}{3}$ be written as a mixed number? *(Lesson 5.6)* **B**

   A. $2\frac{2}{3}$ **B.** $7\frac{1}{3}$ **C.** $7\frac{2}{3}$ **D.** $8\frac{1}{3}$

10. Val has recorded 0.4 of the school concert on a cassette tape. What fraction of the concert has she recorded? *(Lesson 5.7)* **G**

   F. $\frac{1}{4}$ **G.** $\frac{2}{5}$ **H.** $\frac{3}{5}$ **I.** $\frac{3}{4}$

11. Which decimal is equivalent to $\frac{5}{9}$? *(Lesson 5.8)* **C**

   A. $0.\overline{4}$ **B.** 0.5 **C.** $0.\overline{5}$ **D.** 1.8

12. **Short Response** Judy has 126 pencil boxes stacked in piles of equal size. What are all the possible pile sizes? Explain how you found your answer. *(Lesson 5.1)* **2, 3, 6, 7, 9, 14, 18, 21, 42, or 63; make a list of all of the factors of 126.**

13. **Extended Response** Today every eighth customer at a restaurant will get a free sandwich, and every sixth customer will get a free drink. *(Lesson 5.4)*

   a. Which customers will be the first three to get free sandwiches? **eighth, sixteenth, and twenty-fourth**

   b. Which customers will be the first three to get free drinks? **sixth, twelfth, and eighteenth**

   c. Which customer will be the first to get both a free drink and a free sandwich? **twenty-fourth**

22. $\frac{21}{50}$; looked for the sections labeled museum and added the fractions, $\frac{1}{10} + \frac{8}{25} = \frac{21}{50}$.

23a. $7\frac{1}{2}$ c; $36 = 18 \times 2$, so multiply $3\frac{3}{4} \times 2$.

Test-Taking Skills

Chapter 6

Multiple Choice In Exercises 14–21, choose the letter of the correct answer.

14. Which number is the best estimate of the sum $3\frac{6}{7} + 4\frac{1}{8}$? *(Lesson 6.1)* **B**

A. 7 **B.** 8 **C.** 9 **D.** 11

15. Which number is the best estimate of the difference $10\frac{7}{8} - 5\frac{1}{6}$? *(Lesson 6.1)* **H**

F. 3 **G.** 4 **H.** 6 **I.** 7

16. The Tylers canned $\frac{11}{12}$ bushel of potatoes yesterday. They canned $\frac{5}{12}$ bushel of potatoes today. How much more did they can yesterday than today? *(Lesson 6.2)* **B**

A. $\frac{5}{12}$ bushel **B.** $\frac{1}{2}$ bushel

C. $\frac{2}{3}$ bushel **D.** $1\frac{1}{3}$ bushels

17. Find the difference $\frac{13}{14} - \frac{5}{7}$. *(Lesson 6.3)* **F**

F. $\frac{3}{14}$ **G.** $\frac{3}{7}$ **H.** $1\frac{1}{7}$ **I.** $1\frac{9}{14}$

18. Find the sum $4\frac{2}{3} + 1\frac{7}{9}$. *(Lesson 6.4)* **C**

A. $5\frac{4}{9}$ **B.** $5\frac{3}{4}$ **C.** $6\frac{4}{9}$ **D.** $6\frac{5}{9}$

19. One hiking trail is $6\frac{1}{10}$ miles long. Another hiking trail is $3\frac{4}{5}$ miles long. How much longer is the first trail? *(Lesson 6.5)* **F**

F. $2\frac{3}{10}$ miles **G.** $2\frac{4}{5}$ miles

H. $3\frac{3}{5}$ miles **I.** $3\frac{7}{10}$ miles

20. On Saturday David spent 1 hour and 30 minutes on homework. On Sunday he spent 1 hour and 45 minutes on homework. How much time did David spend on homework altogether? *(Lesson 6.6)* **C**

A. 1 h 15 min **B.** 2 h 15 min

C. 3 h 15 min **D.** 3 h 45 min

21. The Lions plan to arrive at the field at 7:15 A.M. for the baseball playoff. Their game begins at 10:05 A.M. How long will they have to wait until their game starts? *(Lesson 6.6)* **I**

F. 1 h 15 min **G.** 1 h 20 min

H. 2 h 45 min **I.** 2 h 50 min

22. Short Response The graph shows the results of a survey about favorite places to visit in a city. What fraction of the people surveyed prefer to go to a museum when they visit the city? Explain how you found your answer. *(Lesson 6.3)* **See margin.**

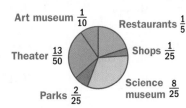

Art museum $\frac{1}{10}$ Restaurants $\frac{1}{5}$

Theater $\frac{13}{50}$ Shops $\frac{1}{25}$

Parks $\frac{2}{25}$ Science museum $\frac{8}{25}$

23. Extended Response A bagel recipe calls for $3\frac{3}{4}$ cups of flour to make 18 bagels. Bob wants to make 36 bagels. *(Lessons 6.4, 6.5)*

a. How much flour does Bob need to make 36 bagels? Explain how you found your answer. **See margin.**

b. Bob has $1\frac{2}{3}$ cups of flour. How much more flour does he need? Explain how you found your answer.
$5\frac{5}{6}$ c; subtract $1\frac{2}{3}$ from $7\frac{1}{2}$.

33. 2475 calories; you biked for
$\frac{3}{4} + 1\frac{1}{2} + 3\frac{1}{4} = 5\frac{1}{2}$ hours
and burned $5\frac{1}{2} \times 450 =$
2475 calories.

Chapter 7

Multiple Choice In Exercises 24–32, choose the letter of the correct answer.

24. Which number is *not* a reasonable estimate of the product $\frac{5}{6} \times 35$? *(Lesson 7.1)* **D**

A. 25 **B.** 30 **C.** 35 **D.** 42

25. What is the value of $\frac{3}{4}n$ when $n = \frac{5}{6}$?
(Lesson 7.2) **G**

F. $\frac{8}{15}$ **G.** $\frac{5}{8}$ **H.** $\frac{4}{5}$ **I.** $\frac{5}{6}$

26. What is the area of a rectangular pen that is $2\frac{1}{2}$ yards long and $1\frac{2}{3}$ yards wide?
(Lesson 7.3) **B**

A. $4\frac{1}{6}$ yd **B.** $4\frac{1}{6}$ yd^2

C. $8\frac{1}{3}$ yd **D.** $8\frac{1}{3}$ yd^2

27. Find the quotient $\frac{4}{5} \div \frac{2}{3}$. *(Lesson 7.4)* **I**

F. $\frac{2}{15}$ **G.** $\frac{8}{15}$ **H.** $\frac{5}{6}$ **I.** $1\frac{1}{5}$

28. Find the quotient $4 \div \frac{3}{8}$. *(Lesson 7.4)* **C**

A. $\frac{3}{32}$ **B.** $1\frac{1}{2}$ **C.** $10\frac{2}{3}$ **D.** $11\frac{1}{3}$

29. Sharon uses $11\frac{1}{2}$ cups of flour to make 4 loaves of bread. How many cups of flour does she use for each loaf? *(Lesson 7.5)* **G**

F. $2\frac{1}{2}$ cups **G.** $2\frac{7}{8}$ cups

H. $3\frac{1}{8}$ cups **I.** $4\frac{1}{8}$ cups

30. Find the quotient $4\frac{1}{5} \div 1\frac{3}{4}$. *(Lesson 7.5)* **B**

A. $2\frac{14}{37}$ **B.** $2\frac{2}{5}$ **C.** $4\frac{4}{15}$ **D.** $7\frac{7}{20}$

31. Which measurement could be the weight of an apple? *(Lesson 7.6)* **F**

F. 4 oz **G.** 4 qt **H.** 4 lb **I.** 4 T

32. What is the difference between 12 feet 7 inches and 4 feet 9 inches?
(Lesson 7.7) **A**

A. 7 ft 10 in. **B.** 8 ft 1 in.

C. 8 ft 2 in. **D.** 16 ft 16 in.

33. **Short Response** You burn about 450 calories per hour biking. You biked $\frac{3}{4}$ hour on Friday, $1\frac{1}{2}$ hours on Saturday, and $3\frac{1}{4}$ hours on Sunday. How many calories did you burn on those days? Explain. *(Lesson 7.3)*
See margin.

34. **Extended Response** Use the recipe below. *(Lessons 7.1, 7.7)*

Onion Dip

Serves 2

$\frac{1}{4}$ cup sour cream

$\frac{1}{2}$ teaspoon lemon juice

1 tablespoon onion soup mix

---

a. Explain how to increase the recipe to serve 14 people. multiply by 7

b. How many teaspoons of lemon juice will you need if you increase the recipe to serve 14 people? $3\frac{1}{2}$ teaspoons

c. How many pints of sour cream will you need if you increase the recipe to serve 14 people? $\frac{7}{8}$ pint

Proportions, Percent, and Geometry

Chapter **8** Ratio, Proportion, and Percent

- Use ratios, rates, proportions, and percents to solve problems.
- Know the relationships between fractions, decimals, and percents.

Chapter **9** Geometric Figures

- Draw, name, classify, and measure angles.
- Draw, name, and use symbols to represent geometric figures.
- Relate, classify, and know the properties of two-dimensional figures.

Chapter **10** Geometry and Measurement

- Estimate, find, and relate areas of two-dimensional figures.
- Know the properties of, classify, and draw solid figures.
- Draw circle graphs.

From Chapter 8, p. 374

How many cellos are in a school orchestra?

UNIT RESOURCES

These resources are provided to help you prepare for the unit and to customize review materials:

 Chapter Resource Books
- Chapter 8
- Chapter 9
- Chapter 10

 Assessment Book
- Chapters 8–10, pp. 96–134

 Technology
- EasyPlanner CD-ROM
- Test and Practice Generator
- Electronic Lesson Presentations CD-ROM
- eTutorial CD-ROM

 Internet
- Classzone
- eEdition Plus Online
- eWorkbook Plus Online
- eTutorial Plus Online
- EasyPlanner Plus Online

ENGLISH LEARNER SUPPORT

- Spanish Study Guide
- Multi-Language Glossary
- Chapter Audio Summaries CDs
- Teacher's Edition
  Chapter 8, pp. 370E–370F
  Chapter 9, pp. 418E–418F
  Chapter 10, pp. 472E–472F

CHAPTER 8

Pacing and Assignment Guide

REGULAR SCHEDULE

Lesson	Les. Day	BASIC	AVERAGE	ADVANCED
8.1	Day 1	EP p. 712 Exs. 56-60; pp. 376-378 Exs. 11, 12, 17-21, 27-30	pp. 376-378 Exs. 11, 12, 17-22, 29-32, 39-42	pp. 376-378 Exs. 11, 12, 17-21, 31-33*, 35-39
	Day 2	pp. 376-378 Exs. 13-16, 23-26, 34-42	pp. 376-378 Exs. 13-16, 23-28, 34-37, 43	pp. 376-378 Exs. 13-16, 23-30, 42, 43
8.2	Day 1	pp. 381-382 Exs. 7-13, 15-19, 21-26, 29-35	pp. 381-382 Exs. 7-14, 17-27, 29-32, 35, 36	pp. 381-382 Exs. 7-14, 17-30*, 35, 36
8.3	Day 1	EP p. 708 Exs. 42-49; pp. 386-387 Exs. 12-24, 28-31, 33-39, 43-47	pp. 386-387 Exs. 14-23, 27-34, 37-41, 43-48	pp. 386-387 Exs. 14-17, 22-37, 39-44*, 47, 48
8.4	Day 1	EP p. 709 Exs. 5-10; pp. 390-391 Exs. 4-9, 19-25	pp. 390-391 Exs. 4-9, 19-25	pp. 390-391 Exs. 4-9, 19-23
	Day 2	pp. 390-391 Exs. 10-16, 26-29	pp. 390-391 Exs. 10-17, 26-28	pp. 390-391 Exs. 10-18*, 28, 29
8.5	Day 1	EP p. 711 Exs. 24-27; pp. 397-398 Exs. 8-18, 34-37	pp. 397-398 Exs. 8-18, 28-30, 40, 41	pp. 397-398 Exs. 8-18, 28-31*
	Day 2	pp. 397-398 Exs. 19-30, 38-40	pp. 397-398 Exs. 19-27, 34-39	pp. 397-398 Exs. 19-27, 32-35*, 40, 41
8.6	Day 1	EP p. 710 Exs. 10-15; pp. 402-403 Exs. 8-15, 28, 30-40	pp. 402-403 Exs. 8-15, 28, 30-35, 45-50	pp. 402-403 Exs. 12-15, 30-33, 36-40, 45-50
	Day 2	pp. 402-403 Exs. 16-27, 43, 45-55	pp. 402-403 Exs. 16-24, 29, 36-43, 53-55	pp. 402-403 Exs. 16-29, 41-44*, 55
8.7	Day 1	EP p. 714 Exs. 5-8; pp. 409-410 Exs. 7-12, 20, 30-35, 43-49	pp. 409-410 Exs. 7-10, 18-20, 33-35, 43-51	pp. 409-410 Exs. 11-18, 27-29, 33-35, 43-45
	Day 2	pp. 409-410 Exs. 13-18, 21-29, 37-40, 50	pp. 409-410 Exs. 11-14, 21-29, 36-41	pp. 409-410 Exs. 19-26, 36-42*, 50, 51
Review	Day 1	pp. 414-415 Exs. 1-42	pp. 414-415 Exs. 1-42	pp. 414-415 Exs. 1-42
Assess	Day 1	Chapter 8 Test	Chapter 8 Test	Chapter 8 Test

YEARLY PACING   Chapter 8 Total – **14 days**   Chapters 1–8 Total – **94 days**   Remaining – **66 days**

*Challenge Exercises   EP = Extra Practice   SRH = Skills Review Handbook   EC = Extra Challenge

BLOCK SCHEDULE

DAY 1	DAY 2	DAY 3	DAY 4	DAY 5	DAY 6	DAY 7
8.1 pp. 376-378 Exs. 11-32, 34-37, 39-43	**8.2** pp. 381-382 Exs. 7-14, 17-27, 29-32, 35, 36 **8.3** pp. 386-387 Exs. 14-23, 27-34, 37-41, 43-48	**8.4** pp. 390-391 Exs. 4-17, 19-28	**8.5** pp. 397-398 Exs. 8-30, 34-41	**8.6** pp. 402-403 Exs. 8-24, 28-43, 45-50, 53-55	**8.7** pp. 409-410 Exs. 7-14, 18-29, 33-41, 43-51	**Review** pp. 414-415 Exs. 1-42 **Assess** Chapter 8 Test

YEARLY PACING   Chapter 8 Total – **7 days**   Chapters 1–8 Total – **47 days**   Remaining – **33 days**

Support Materials

📖 CHAPTER RESOURCE BOOK

CHAPTER SUPPORT

Tips for New Teachers	p. 1	Parents as Partners	p. 3

LESSON SUPPORT

	8.1	8.2	8.3	8.4	8.5	8.6	8.7
Lesson Plans (regular and block)	p. 7	p. 16	p. 25	p. 33	p. 42	p. 50	p. 61
Technology Activities & Keystrokes						p. 52	p. 63
Activity Support Masters	p. 9						
Activity Masters		p. 18		p. 35			
Practice (3 levels)	p. 10	p. 19	p. 27	p. 36	p. 44	p. 54	p. 64
Study Guide	p. 13	p. 22	p. 30	p. 39	p. 47	p. 57	p. 67
Real-World Problem Solving						p. 59	p. 69
Challenge Practice	p. 15	p. 24	p. 32	p. 41	p. 49	p. 60	p. 70

REVIEW

Games Support Masters	p. 5	Cooperative Project with Rubric	p. 74
Chapter Review Games and Activities	p. 71	Extra Credit Project with Rubric	p. 76
Real-Life Project with Rubric	p. 72	Cumulative Practice	p. 78
		Resource Book Answers	A1

📖 ASSESSMENT

Quizzes	p. 96	Alternative Assessments with Rubrics	p. 105
Chapter Tests (3 levels)	p. 98	Unit Test	p. 129
Standardized Test	p. 104	Cumulative Test	p. 131

📑 TRANSPARENCIES

	8.1	8.2	8.3	8.4	8.5	8.6	8.7
Warm-Up / Daily Homework Quiz	✔	✔	✔	✔	✔	✔	✔
Notetaking Guide	✔	✔	✔	✔	✔	✔	✔
Teacher Support		✔		✔		✔	
English/Spanish Problem Solving	✔	✔			✔		✔
Answer Transparencies	✔	✔	✔	✔	✔	✔	✔

💻 TECHNOLOGY

- EasyPlanner CD-ROM
- Test and Practice Generator
- Electronic Lesson Presentations
- eTutorial CD-ROM
- Chapter Audio Summaries CDs
- Classzone.com
- eEdition Plus Online
- eWorkbook Plus Online
- eTutorial Plus Online
- EasyPlanner Plus Online

ADDITIONAL RESOURCES

- Worked-Out Solution Key
- Notetaking Guide
- Practice Workbook
- Tutor Place
- Professional Development Book
- Activities Book
- Poster Package
- Spanish Study Guide
- English/Spanish Chapter Reviews
- Multi-Language Glossary

8 Math Background and Teaching Strategies

Lesson 8.1

MATH BACKGROUND

RATIOS A **ratio** is an ordered pair of numbers, written as a to b, $a:b$, or $\frac{a}{b}$, with $b \neq 0$. All fractions are ratios, and the terminology of *numerator* and *denominator* is used for ratios as well as for fractions. Consequently, to find equivalent ratios, you can multiply or divide the numerator and denominator by a nonzero number. To compare ratios, you write the ratios as decimals.

TEACHING STRATEGIES

Give each student a copy of an illustration that contains two green buttons, one pink button, three black buttons, and three white buttons. Ask the students to suggest as many different ratios among the groups of buttons as they can think of within a limited amount of time. You may wish to model a response, such as *There are 2 green buttons to 1 pink button. This is the ratio 2:1.* Have students write some of their ratios on the board.

Lesson 8.2

MATH BACKGROUND

RATES A **rate** is a ratio of two measures that have different units. Rates such as miles per gallon, kilometers per hour, dollars per hour, cents per ounce, and people per square mile are examples of **unit rates**.

TEACHING STRATEGIES

Ask students to give expressions they might have heard that include the word *per*, such as "miles per gallon." Explain that these rates all have 1 unit in the denominator. Ask students what they might do to find a unit rate from a given rate such as $17.50 for 10 gallons. Conversely ask how they might use a unit rate such as $7.50 per hour to find the amount earned in 10 hours.

Lesson 8.3

MATH BACKGROUND

PROPORTIONS A **proportion** is an equation showing that two ratios are equivalent. In general $\frac{a}{b} = \frac{c}{d}$ is a proportion if and only if $ad = bc$. In the proportion, $\frac{a}{b} = \frac{c}{d}$, a and d are the **extreme** terms and b and c are the **mean** terms. The products ad and bc are called **cross products**. The cross product property can be used to solve proportions.

TEACHING STRATEGIES

You will need the following materials: copies of the design below, poster board, rulers, and colored pencils or markers. Have students work in pairs and create an enlargement of the design below.

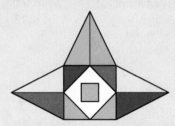

Students should begin by choosing a ratio for their enlargement. Have students measure the design and set up proportions to find the new dimensions. For example, if the enlargement is 5 to 1, then one proportion might be $\frac{5}{1} = \frac{x \text{ cm}}{3 \text{ cm}}$. By solving the proportions, students will find the lengths they need to make their enlargements.

Lesson 8.4

MATH BACKGROUND

SCALE DRAWINGS The scale in a scale drawing is a ratio, and the lengths of segments in the drawing are proportional to corresponding lengths in the actual object. The use of the scale may result in an enlargement or a reduction.

PERIMETER AND AREA IN SCALE DRAWINGS In a scale drawing, the ratio of the perimeters is equal to the scale. Thus, if $a:b$ is the scale, then the ratio of the perimeters is also $a:b$. By contrast, the ratio of the areas is the square of the scale. Thus, if $a:b$ is the scale, then the ratio of the areas is $a^2:b^2$.

TEACHING STRATEGIES

Have students draw a small rectangle, such as 2 grids by 4 grids, on grid paper. Then ask them to choose a scale, such as 3 grids to 1 grid and draw an enlargement of the rectangle. Students can count grid lines and grid squares to ascertain that the ratio of the perimeters is the same as the scale and that the ratio of the areas is the square of the scale.

Lesson 8.5

MATH BACKGROUND

PERCENTS A **percent** is a ratio that compares a number to 100. The percent symbol, %, represents the denominator of 100. Percents between 0% and 100% represent fractions or decimals between 0 and 1. Percents equal to or greater than 100% represent improper fractions, whole numbers, or decimals equal to or greater than 1.00.

TEACHING STRATEGIES

Have students work in small groups. You will need several collections of coins that add up to $1. Give each group 10 to 20 coins that add up to $1. Have them work together to find at least 5 combinations of coins that equal less than $1 and express the amounts in as many ways as possible.

Lesson 8.6

MATH BACKGROUND

An ability to use percents, decimals, and fractions interchangeably is important. Fractions can be changed to decimals by dividing the numerator by the denominator and those decimals can be changed to percents by moving the decimal point two places to the right. Conversely, percents can be changed to decimals by moving the decimal point two places to the left and those decimals can be converted to fractions by writing them as a whole number over the appropriate power of 10.

TEACHING STRATEGIES

For this activity students will need a copy of the tangram puzzle at the right. Have students work in pairs. Give each pair a copy of the tangram puzzle and ask them to work together to decide how each labeled part can be expressed as a fraction of the 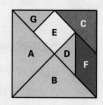 whole and as a percent of the whole. A: $\frac{1}{4}$ or 25%; B: $\frac{1}{4}$ or 25%; C: $\frac{1}{8}$ or $12\frac{1}{2}$%; D: $\frac{1}{16}$ or $6\frac{1}{4}$%; E: $\frac{1}{8}$ or $12\frac{1}{2}$%; F: $\frac{1}{8}$ or $12\frac{1}{2}$%; G: $\frac{1}{16}$ or $6\frac{1}{4}$% Ask each pair to find ways to check their work.

Sample answer: Add the fractions to see if they equal 1 and the percents to see if they equal 100%. Have students check with each other to make sure that they both understand the process.

Lesson 8.7

MATH BACKGROUND

SIMPLE INTEREST Interest is the amount of money that someone pays to borrow money or earns when providing money. The amount of money borrowed or invested is called the **principal**. The **interest rate** is the percent charged or paid during a given period of time. To find the amount of simple interest, you can use this formula: Interest (I) = principal (p) · annual rate of interest (r) · time in years (t).

TEACHING STRATEGIES

For this activity, you will need the following materials: poster board, markers, and pictures of clothing cut from magazines. Have the students work in small groups to create a clothing sale sign showing prices that are percentages off the regular price. For example, pictures of shirts might be under a sign saying "Take 30% off!" while skirts might be shown under a sign marked "Save 15%." With each sale sign should be several pictures with price tags, such as a shirt for $22.99. After all the groups are finished, have students walk through the room and "shop" at each sale. Have them see how quickly they can estimate the discount on each item by estimating the percent off the regular price.

Differentiating Instruction

Strategies for Underachievers

REVIEW PREVIOUSLY LEARNED CONCEPTS

A review of writing equivalent fractions will be beneficial for many students. Give examples of the procedure used in Lesson 5.3 to find equivalent fractions and to simplify fractions. Compare this procedure to writing a ratio in simplest form in Lesson 8.1, to finding a unit rate in Lesson 8.2, and to solving a proportion in Lesson 8.3.

USE ALTERNATIVE METHODS

In Lesson 8.3, some students may have difficulty visualizing cross products within a proportion. You may wish to present an alternate way to draw the arrows to show the cross products. One way to do that may be to draw a straight arrow along the diagonals, passing through the equal sign.

$$\frac{40}{56} \diagdown \frac{5}{7}$$

$$40 \cdot 7 = 56 \cdot 5$$

USE CONCRETE REPRESENTATTION

In Lesson 8.5, you might anticipate difficulty with student understanding that 40% is not only equal to "40 out of 100" but that it is also equal to "4 out of 10" or "2 out of 5." You may wish to guide these students through the following activity. Have each student take three "100 Squares." With the first square, have students shade 40 squares out of the 100. Take the second square and have students draw thick lines around 10 groups of 10 squares each; then have them shade 4 of these sections. With the third square, have them draw thick lines around 5 groups of 20 squares each; then have them shade 2 of these sections. In all three cases, students should see that 40 squares were shaded. Guide them to conclude that "40 out of 100" = 0.40 = 0.4 = 40%, and that "4 out of 10" = 0.40 = 0.4 = 40%, and that "2 out of 5" = 0.40 = 0.4 = 40%. Note that when shading the squares, it would be helpful if students shaded complete columns or complete rows.

USE LEARNING AIDS

In Lesson 8.6, some students will have difficulty memorizing the table on page 401. These students should be given a teacher-generated table of the common equivalencies and have access to it at all times.

Strategies for English Learners

DISSECT WORD PROBLEMS

Word problems are a big challenge for English learners. For an English learner, a word problem can look something like the first two lines of Lewis Carroll's "Jabberwocky," where the only words you know are *and, the, did, in, all,* and *were.*

In some cases the teacher can turn the "word" problem into a "picture" problem:

Word problem:　If a 10-ounce bottle of shampoo costs $3.45, how much will a 15-ounce bottle cost? This is a ratio problem that students can set up in the following way: $\frac{3.45}{10} = \frac{x}{15}$

Picture problem:

In many contexts, however, including standardized tests, students will need to be able to decipher word problems. Fortunately, most word problems follow a standard format and there are clues provided by "signal words," words of high frequency that signal what will follow or what came before. Most word problems also contain numbers, and usually you must do something with the numbers to solve the problems. Analyzing the units in a problem can provide a clue to the answer that is needed.

Strategies for Advanced Learners

INCREASE DEPTH AND COMPLEXITY

Lesson 8.2 on unit rates naturally extends into an exploration of unit pricing in supermarkets. You may wish to have some students and their parents compare unit prices of items based upon different quantities, different brands, or different stores in order to determine the best buy. Students can create a display or a report, complete with some overall conclusions, regarding unit pricing.

In Lesson 8.6, some students who quickly memorize the more basic percent, decimal, and fraction equivalencies may be challenged to memorize the equivalencies for sixths, eighths, and ninths.

Here is an activity to use in connection with **Lesson 8.6**.

- **Challenge** Randomly select a paragraph from a newspaper or magazine and count the number of occurrences of each letter in the alphabet. Keep an organized frequency table. Find the total number of letters, the fractional part of the paragraph made up by each letter, and the percent of the time each letter appears. Compare results with other students who have chosen different paragraphs to see if you can make any conclusions about the frequency of vowels versus consonants, and about the most common and least common letters. Check work.

Use this activity in connection with finding discounts in **Lesson 8.7**.

- **Challenge** Find newspaper advertisements showing sale prices involving a certain percent discount. Find what the sale prices of the items will be. Show that if an item is on sale for 25% off, and if you have a coupon for an additional 25% off of the sale price, that this is not the same as receiving 50% off the original price. Explain the difference. Check work. *Sample answer:* Getting 25% off on a $100 item means the buyer pays $75. Getting 25% off this price means the buyer saves another $75 • 0.25, or $18.75, and pays $56.25 for the item. Getting 50% off would mean the buyer pays just $50 for the $100 item.

USE CROSS-CURRICULAR CONNECTIONS

In conjunction with Lesson 8.4, you may wish to work with a Technology Educator/Industrial Arts Teacher to develop a scale drawing of a car, a house, or some other real-world object. Students could cut out a picture of their chosen object from a magazine and then decide what scale factor connects the photograph to the actual real-world object. Students could brainstorm what occupations would require a strong knowledge of scale drawings.

Differentiating Instruction: Teaching Resources

Differentiating Practice

McDougal Littell *Middle School Mathematics* offers teachers a wide variety of practice for all levels of students. Pictured on these pages are facsimiles of the Level A, Level B, Level C, and Challenge Practice pages from the *Chapter 8 Resource Book*, pages from the *Practice Workbook*, and the *Test and Practice Generator*.

RESOURCE BOOK

The *Chapter Resource Books* contain three levels of practice, A (Basic), B (Average), and C (Advanced), for each lesson in the textbook. Also, included is a page of Challenge practice for each lesson for your most advanced students.

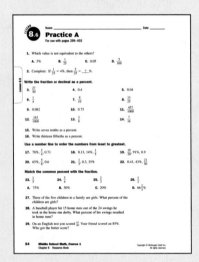

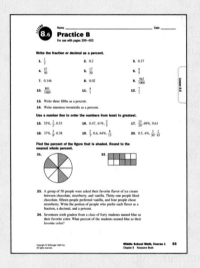

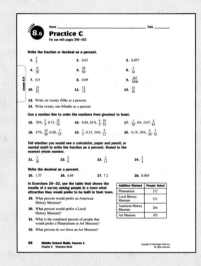

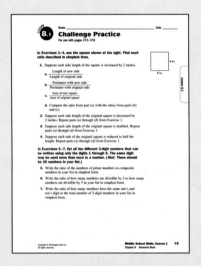

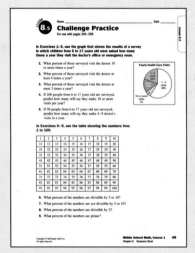

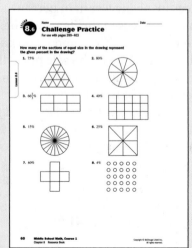

PRACTICE WORKBOOK

The *Practice Workbook* contains the average B-level practice for each lesson reformatted in workbook form to allow students to show their work for each exercise.

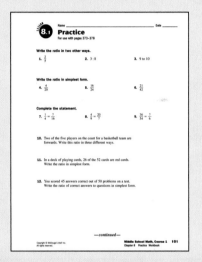

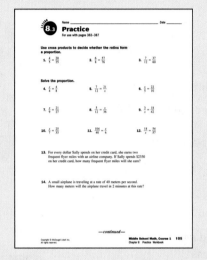

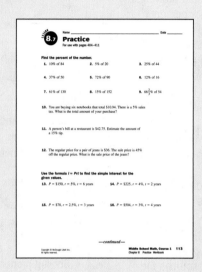

TEST AND PRACTICE GENERATOR CD-ROM

The *Test and Practice Generator* allows you to create practice worksheets for each lesson using both static and algorithmic exercises.

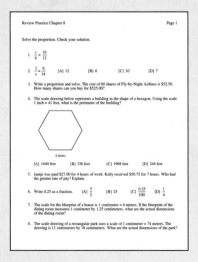

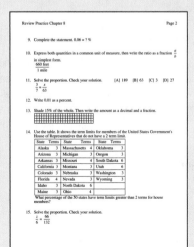

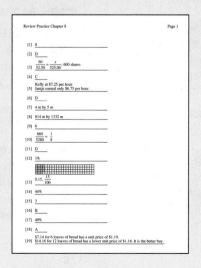

OVERVIEW

MAIN IDEAS

In this chapter students study ratios, rates, proportions, and percents. They simplify and find equivalent ratios and rates, and they calculate and use unit rates. They solve proportions formed by pairs of equal ratios or rates, and they apply proportions to work with scale drawings. Students also investigate percent. They write fractions and decimals as percents, they use percents in circle graphs, and they find a percent of a number in problems involving discounts, tax, and simple interest.

PREREQUISITE SKILLS

The key skill reviewed in the game on these pages is:

• Comparing and ordering fractions and decimals

Additional practice with prerequisite skills can be found in the Review What You Need to Know exercises on page 372. Additional resources for reviewing prerequisite skills are:

• Skills Review Handbook, pp. 684–707
• Tutor Place
• eTutorial Plus Online

MANAGING THE GAME

Tips for Success

If students have difficulty ordering two fractions, or ordering a fraction and a decimal, encourage them to write both numbers as decimals.

Reflecting on the Game

Extend the game by adding some new cards to the deck, using repeating decimals such as 0.111... and 0.181818... As before, be sure each decimal card has a matching card with an equivalent fraction $\left(\dfrac{1}{9}, \dfrac{2}{11}\right)$ on it.

Ratio, Proportion, and Percent

BEFORE

In previous chapters you've...

• Compared and ordered fractions and decimals
• Found perimeters and areas

Now

In Chapter 8 you'll study...

• Writing ratios and rates
• Solving proportions
• Working with percents
• Changing between percents, decimals, and fractions

WHY?

So you can solve real-world problems about...

• space, p. 379
• kangaroos, p. 387
• school murals, p. 389
• volleyball, p. 399

Internet Preview
CLASSZONE.COM

• eEdition Plus Online
• eWorkbook Plus Online
• eTutorial Plus Online
• State Test Practice
• More Examples

Chapter Warm-Up Game

Review skills you need for this chapter in this game. Work with a partner.

Key Skill:
Comparing fractions and decimals

NUMBER CHALLENGE

MATERIALS

• 1 deck of *Number Challenge* cards

PREPARE Deal half the cards to each player. Place your cards face down in front of you in a pile. On each turn, follow the steps on the next page.

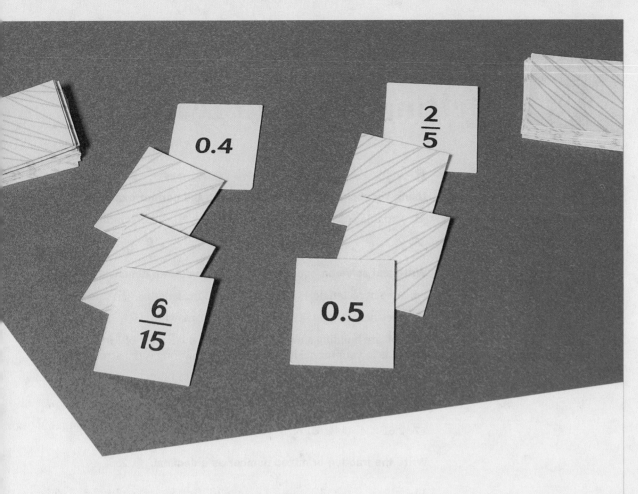

CHAPTER RESOURCES

These resources are provided to help you prepare for the chapter and to customize review materials:

 Chapter 8 Resource Book
- Tips for New Teachers, pp. 1–2
- Lesson Plan, pp. 7, 16, 25, 33, 42, 50, 61
- Lesson Plan for Block Scheduling, pp. 8, 17, 26, 34, 43, 51, 62

 Technology
- EasyPlanner CD-ROM
- Test and Practice Generator
- Electronic Lesson Presentations CD-ROM
- eTutorial CD-ROM

Internet
- Classzone
- eEdition Plus Online
- eWorkbook Plus Online
- eTutorial Plus Online
- EasyPlanner Plus Online

ENGLISH LEARNER SUPPORT

- Spanish Study Guide
- Multi-Language Glossary
- Chapter Audio Summaries CDs
- Teacher's Edition, pp. 370E–370F

1 COMPARE Turn over the top cards from your piles. The player with the greater number collects the cards and puts them on the bottom of his or her pile.

2. A good answer will include three pairs of cards, with one card in each pair a decimal and the other an equivalent fraction.

2 CHALLENGE If the two cards have the same value, each player places two new cards face down on the cards played in Step 1. Then repeat Step 1.

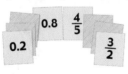

HOW TO WIN Collect all the cards, or collect the greater number of cards after a set period of time.

Stop and Think

1. 2.25 and $\frac{222}{100}$; yes

1. **Critical Thinking** Which cards have the greatest value in this game? If you have all of these cards, is there any way you can lose?

2. **Extension** Design six new cards to add to the deck. The cards may be either decimals or fractions, but make sure that each card has a matching card with an equivalent number on it.

371

CHAPTER 8 Getting Ready to Learn

Review What You Need to Know

Using Vocabulary **Match the word with the correct example.**

1. variable C   **2.** equation B   **3.** solution A

A. 2   **B.** $x + 3 = 5$ **C.** x

Write and solve an equation to find the unknown dimension. *(p. 61)*

4. Area of rectangle = 12 in.², width = 3 in., length = _?_ $12 = 3l$; 4 in.

5. Area of rectangle = 96 m², length = 12 m, width = _?_ $96 = 12w$; 8 m

6. You are building a model playground with a scale of 1 in. : 2 ft. The slide in your model is 6 inches long. How long is the actual slide? *(p. 68)* 12 ft

Find the product. Simplify if possible. *(pp. 153, 313)*

7. 2.61×4 10.44   **8.** 6.78×9 61.02   **9.** $\frac{3}{8} \times 24$ 9   **10.** $9 \times \frac{4}{3}$ 12

Write the fraction or mixed number as a decimal. *(p. 253)*

11. $\frac{3}{4}$ 0.75   **12.** $\frac{8}{9}$ $0.\overline{8}$ **13.** $3\frac{1}{5}$ 3.2   **14.** $2\frac{1}{8}$ 2.125

Word Watch

Review Words

variable, p. 29
equation, p. 36
solution, p. 36
area, p. 62
scale drawing, p. 68
scale, p. 68
decimal, p. 108
fraction, p. 228
simplest form, p. 229

You should include material that appears on a notebook like this in your own notes.

Know How to Take Notes

Drawing a Concept Map You can draw a diagram called a concept map to show connections among key ideas. Here is a concept map showing some forms of numbers.

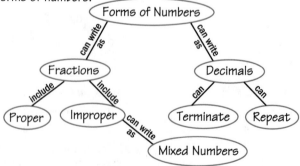

In Lesson 8.5, you will work with percents, fractions, and decimals. Then you will be able to add percents to a concept map showing forms of numbers.

Hands-on Activity

GOAL
Compare the areas of figures on a geoboard.

MATERIALS
· geoboard
· colored rubber bands

Comparing Areas

In this activity, you will use a geoboard to write fractions that compare areas.

 Explore   Compare areas of figures using a geoboard.

Use a geoboard that is 5 pegs long by 5 pegs wide. The smallest square you can make with 4 pegs is called a *unit square*.

1 Use a blue rubber band to make a square around the entire geoboard.

2 Use a red rubber band to make a square that is 3 pegs long by 3 pegs wide.

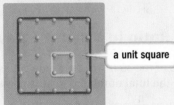

a unit square

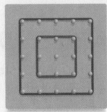

3 Copy and complete the statement at the right to write a fraction that compares the number of unit squares in each figure.

$$\frac{\text{Unit squares in red square}}{\text{Unit squares in blue square}} = \frac{?}{?} \quad \frac{4}{16}$$

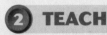

Your turn now   Add the given rectangle to your geoboard from **Steps 1 and 2 above. Then copy and complete the statement.**

1. green rectangle:
3 pegs long by 2 pegs wide

$$\frac{\text{Unit squares in green rectangle}}{\text{Unit squares in red square}} = \frac{?}{?} \quad \frac{2}{4}$$

2. purple rectangle:
4 pegs long by 3 pegs wide

$$\frac{\text{Unit squares in purple rectangle}}{\text{Unit squares in blue square}} = \frac{?}{?} \quad \frac{6}{16}$$

Stop and Think

3. Critical Thinking How could you write the fractions you wrote in Step 3 above and in Exercises 1 and 2 in another way? Explain.

They can all be written in simplest form. *Sample answer:* The fraction in Step 3 can be written as $\frac{1}{4}$.

NCTM CURRICULUM STANDARDS
Standard 4: Understand the units of measurement
Standard 10: Create representations to communicate mathematical ideas

---

1 **PLAN**

EXPLORE THE CONCEPT
• Students use a geoboard to compare areas.
• This activity leads to writing ratios and equivalent ratios in Lesson 8.1.

MATERIALS
Each student or group of students will need a geoboard and colored rubber bands. See also the Activity master in the *Chapter 8 Resource Book*.

RECOMMENDED TIME
Work activity: 10 min
Discuss results: 5 min

GROUPING
Students can work individually or in groups of two. If students work in groups, they can discuss the Critical Thinking issues in Exercise 3.

2 **TEACH**

ALTERNATIVE STRATEGY
if geoboards art not available, this activity can be done on an overhead.

3 **CLOSE**

 KEY DISCOVERY

Fractions can be used to compare areas, and a fraction can sometimes be rewritten as an equivalent fraction.

ASSESSMENT
1. Write the fraction
$$\frac{\text{unit squares in red square}}{\text{units squares in purple rectangle}}.$$
$\frac{4}{6}$ or $\frac{2}{3}$

373

LESSON OBJECTIVE

Write ratios and equivalent ratios.

PACING

Suggested Number of Days
Basic Course: 2 days
Average Course: 2 days
Advanced Course: 2 days
Block: 1 block

TEACHING RESOURCES

For a complete list of Teaching Resources, see page 370B.

 TRANSPARENCY

Warm-Up Exercises for this lesson are available on a transparency.

2 TEACH

MOTIVATING THE LESSON

Have students in the school band estimate what instruments are what fraction of the band.

TIPS FOR NEW TEACHERS

Be sure students can find the GCF of two numbers, which they can use to write ratios in simplest form. See Tips for New Teachers in the *Chapter 8 Resource Book*.

LESSON 8.1

Ratios

BEFORE   ▶ **Now**   **WHY?**

You wrote fractions and equivalent fractions.

You'll write ratios and equivalent ratios.

So you can write a ratio of ingredients in a recipe, as in Ex. 19.

In the Real World

 Word Watch

ratio, p. 374
equivalent ratio, p. 375

School Orchestras In some school orchestras, all of the instruments are stringed: violins, violas, cellos, and double basses. How can you compare the numbers of instruments in the orchestra?

18 violins   8 violas   6 cellos   3 double basses

One way to compare the numbers of instruments is to use a *ratio*. The **ratio** of a number a to a nonzero number b is the quotient when a is divided by b. You can write the ratio of a to b as $\frac{a}{b}$, as $a : b$, or as "a to b."

EXAMPLE 1   Writing a Ratio in Different Ways

In the orchestra shown above, 8 of the 35 instruments are violas. The ratio of the number of violas to the total number of instruments,

$\frac{\text{Violas}}{\text{Total instruments}}$, can be written as $\frac{8}{35}$, as 8 : 35, or as 8 to 35.

1. $\frac{18}{35}$, 18 : 35, 18 to 35

EXAMPLE 2   Writing Ratios in Simplest Form

Use the diagram above. Write the ratio of the number of double basses to the number of cellos in simplest form.

$$\frac{\text{Double basses}}{\text{Cellos}} = \frac{3}{6} = \frac{1 \times \cancel{3}^{1}}{2 \times \cancel{3}_{1}} = \frac{1}{2}$$

ANSWER The ratio is $\frac{1}{2}$, or 1 to 2, so there is 1 double bass for every 2 cellos.

Your turn now   In Exercises 1 and 2, write the ratio in three ways.

1. violins to total instruments   **2.** violas to double basses $\frac{8}{3}$, 8 : 3, 8 to 3
    See margin.
3. Write the ratio of the number of cellos to the number of violins in simplest form. $\frac{1}{3}$

NCTM CURRICULUM STANDARDS
Standard 1: Understand numbers; Understand ways of representing numbers; Understand relationships among numbers

HELP with **Review**

Need help with equivalent fractions? See p. 228.

Writing Equivalent Ratios You can multiply or divide the numerator and denominator of a ratio by the same number to get an **equivalent ratio** .

EXAMPLE 3 Writing an Equivalent Ratio

Complete the statement $\frac{5}{15} = \frac{?}{60}$ to write equivalent ratios.

Solution

Think about the denominators of the two fractions.

$$\overset{5 \times 4}{\overset{\frown}{\frac{5}{15} = \frac{20}{60}}}\underset{15 \times 4}{}$$

> You multiplied 15 by 4 to get 60, so multiply 5 by 4 also.

ANSWER $\frac{5}{15} = \frac{20}{60}$

Writing Ratios as Decimals Writing ratios as decimals may make it easier to compare the ratios.

EXAMPLE 4 Comparing Ratios Using Decimals

Football Allen completes $\frac{3}{4}$ of his pass attempts. Mike completes 7 out of every 10 pass attempts. Who has the better record?

Solution

Write each ratio as a decimal. Then compare the decimals.

Allen: $\frac{3}{4} = 0.75$ Mike: 7 out of 10 $= \frac{7}{10} = 0.7$

ANSWER Because 0.75 > 0.7, Allen has the better record.

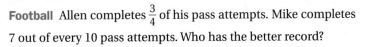

Your turn now   Copy and complete the statement.

4. $\frac{2}{3} = \frac{?}{15}$ 10   **5.** $\frac{7}{?} = \frac{35}{50}$ 10   **6.** $\frac{20}{32} = \frac{5}{?}$ 8

Copy and complete the statement using <, >, or =.

7. $\frac{5}{20}$ _?_ $\frac{4}{10}$ <   **8.** $\frac{3}{5}$ _?_ 18 out of 30   =   **9.** 2:4 _?_ 7:35   >

 CONCEPT CHECK

What can you do to a ratio to get an equivalent ratio? **You can multiply or divide the numerator and denominator of a ratio by the same (nonzero) number to get an equivalent ratio.**

DAILY PUZZLER

A ratio is equivalent to 3:8. When the ratio is written as a fraction, the sum of the numerator and denominator is 121. What is the ratio? **33:88**

ASSIGNMENT GUIDE

Basic Course
Day 1: EP p. 712 Exs. 56–60;
pp. 376–378 Exs. 11, 12,
17–21, 27–30
Day 2: pp. 376–378 Exs. 13–16,
23–26, 34–42

Average Course
Day 1: pp. 376–378 Exs. 11, 12,
17–22, 29–32, 39–42
Day 2: pp. 376–378 Exs. 13–16,
23–28, 34–37, 43

Advanced Course
Day 1: pp. 376–378 Exs. 11, 12,
17–21, 31–33*, 35–39
Day 2: pp. 376–378 Exs. 13–16,
23–30, 42, 43

Block
pp. 376–378 Exs. 11–32, 34–37,
39–43

EXTRA PRACTICE
- Student Edition, p. 715
- Chapter 8 Resource Book,
  pp. 10–12
- Test and Practice Generator

TRANSPARENCY

Even-numbered answers are available on transparencies.

HOMEWORK CHECK

When you review students' homework for this lesson, go over the following exercises to check understanding of key concepts.
Basic: 11, 12, 14, 16, 23
Average: 11, 14, 16, 18, 24
Advanced: 11, 15, 18, 20, 25

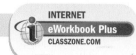
Getting Ready to Practice

1. Vocabulary Write the ratio $\frac{5}{12}$ in two other ways. **5 : 12, 5 to 12**

Write the ratio in simplest form.

2. $\frac{6}{15}$ $\frac{2}{5}$

3. $\frac{8}{20}$ $\frac{2}{5}$

4. $\frac{20}{75}$ $\frac{4}{15}$

5. $\frac{12}{3}$ **4**

6. 9 was multiplied by 2 to get 18, so 7 needs to be multiplied by 2 to get the numerator. The answer should be $\frac{7}{9} = \frac{14}{18}$.

6. Find the Error Describe and correct the error in writing an equivalent ratio.

$$\times \quad \frac{7}{9} = \frac{?}{18} \longrightarrow \frac{7}{9} = \frac{16}{18}$$

Copy and complete the statement.

7. $\frac{4}{5} = \frac{?}{10}$ **8**

8. $\frac{?}{7} = \frac{6}{21}$ **2**

9. $\frac{5}{6} = \frac{15}{?}$ **18**

10. $\frac{24}{?} = \frac{8}{9}$ **27**

Practice and Problem Solving

with Homework

Example	Exercises
1	11, 17
2	12, 18–22
3	13–16
4	23–25

Online Resources
CLASSZONE.COM
· More Examples
· eTutorial Plus

A 11. Write the ratio 13 to 20 in two other ways. $\frac{13}{20}$, 13 : 20

12. Write the ratio 10 : 15 in simplest form. **2 : 3**

Copy and complete the statement.

13. $\frac{3}{8} = \frac{?}{24}$ **9**

14. $\frac{7}{10} = \frac{14}{?}$ **20**

15. $\frac{2}{?} = \frac{22}{33}$ **3**

16. $\frac{?}{2} = \frac{5}{10}$ **1**

17. Keyboards On the keyboard shown, 31 of the 76 keys are black. Write this ratio in three different ways.
$\frac{31}{76}$, 31 : 76, 31 to 76

18. Pets A survey says that 28 out of 42 people have a pet. Write this ratio in simplest form. $\frac{2}{3}$

19. Party Punch A recipe for party punch suggests mixing 64 fluid ounces of cranberry juice with 128 fluid ounces of orange juice. Write the ratio of cranberry juice to orange juice in the punch in simplest form. $\frac{1}{2}$

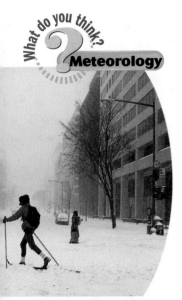

CROSS-CURRICULUM

Music After finding the ratio in Exercise 17, have students research other keyboard instruments to find their ratio of black keys to total keys.

 COMMON ERROR

In Exercise 28, students may read the problem as "number of sopranos" to "number of singers." Be sure they understand how to calculate the number of "other singers."

What do you think?

Meteorology

Average Temperatures **Use the average December temperatures for the cities shown to write the ratio described in simplest form.**

20. $\dfrac{\text{Number of temperatures over 68°F}}{\text{Total number of temperatures}}$ $\dfrac{1}{6}$

21. $\dfrac{\text{Number of temperatures over 33°F}}{\text{Total number of temperatures}}$ $\dfrac{2}{3}$

22. $\dfrac{\text{Number of temperatures over 33°F}}{\text{Number of temperatures under 33°F}}$ $\dfrac{2}{1}$

City	Temperature
Washington, D.C.	39°F
Miami Beach, FL	70°F
Dallas, TX	48°F
Sacramento, CA	45°F
Helena, MT	21°F
Chicago, IL	30°F

Baseball **A *batting average* is the ratio of the number of hits to the number of times at bat. Who has the better batting average?**

23. Carl: 20 to 50 *Joel* **24.** Sara: 0.305 *Sara* **25.** John: 0.258 *John*

Joel: $\dfrac{9}{20}$ Miranda: $\dfrac{21}{70}$ Mike: $\dfrac{19}{75}$

■ **Average Temperatures**

Average temperatures can be helpful in predicting future temperatures. Which city in the table above is closest to your city or town? Use the table to predict your city or town's average temperature in December. **Answers may vary.**

Extended Problem Solving **A chorus has 68 singers. The graph shows that it includes tenors, basses, altos, and sopranos.**

B 26. Find the total number of tenors, basses, and altos in the chorus. 34

27. **Describe** Find the number of sopranos in the chorus. Describe your method.
27–28. See margin.

28. **Interpret** Write the ratio of the number of sopranos to the number of other singers in simplest form. What does the ratio mean?

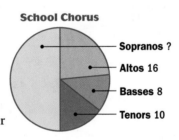

School Chorus

Sopranos ?
Altos 16
Basses 8
Tenors 10

27, 34. *Sample answer:* Subtract the number of altos, basses, and tenors from the total number of singers.

28. 1 : 1; the number of sopranos is the same as the number of other singers.

Summer Camp **In Exercises 29 and 30, use the table. The ratio of the number of counselors to the number of campers is constant.**

29. Write the ratio of counselors to campers in simplest form. $\frac{1}{8}$

30. Copy and complete the table.

Counselors	2	3	4	5
Campers	16	24	?	?

32 40

31. Rewrite both fractions with the least common denominator. The fraction with the greatest numerator is the larger fraction.

C 31. **Critical Thinking** Explain how you could use common denominators to rewrite two ratios in order to compare them.

32. **Geometry** Write the ratio of the perimeter to the area for a square that is 8 meters by 8 meters. $\frac{32}{64}$ or $\frac{1}{2}$

33. **Challenge** Find two numbers that form a ratio equivalent to 2 : 3 that have a sum of 10. 4 and 6

Lesson 8.1 Ratios **377**

④ ASSESS

ASSESSMENT RESOURCES

For more assessment resources, see:
- Assessment Book
- Test and Practice Generator

MINI-QUIZ

1. There are 47 seats and 15 of them are empty. Write the ratio of empty seats to total seats in three ways. $\frac{15}{47}$, 15:47, 15 to 47

2. Simplify 12:40. **3:10**

3. Complete $\frac{?}{15} = \frac{15}{45}$. $\frac{5}{15} = \frac{15}{45}$

4. On a math test, Julio was correct on 16 of the 20 items and Jason was correct on $\frac{9}{10}$ of the items.

   Who got more items correct? How many more? **Jason; 2 more than Julio**

⑤ FOLLOW-UP

RETEACHING/REMEDIATION

- Study Guide in Chapter 8 Resource Book, pp. 13–14
- Tutor Place, Ratio, Proportion, and Percent Cards 1, 6
- eTutorial Plus Online
- Extra Practice, p. 715
- Lesson Practice in Chapter 8 Resource Book, pp. 10–12

CHALLENGE/ENRICHMENT

- Challenge Practice in Chapter 8 Resource Book, p. 15
- Teacher's Edition, p. 370F

ENGLISH LEARNER SUPPORT

- Spanish Study Guide
- Multi-Language Glossary
- Chapter Audio Summaries CDs

37. See Additional Answers beginning on page AA1.

Mixed Review ↻

Copy and complete the statement. *(Lesson 4.8)*

34. 787 mm = _?_ cm   **35.** 16 kL = _?_ L   **36.** 2.6 kg = _?_ g
     78.7   16,000   2600

Choose a Strategy Use a strategy from the list to solve the following problem. Explain your choice of strategy.
See margin.

Problem Solving Strategies
- Guess, Check, and Revise
- Make a List or Table
- Perform an Experiment
- Solve a Related Problem

37. Find the next two figures in the pattern.

Basic Skills   Divide.

38. 4.2 ÷ 7 **0.6**   **39.** 60 ÷ 1.2 **50**   **40.** 1.36 ÷ 3.4 **0.4**   **41.** 0.497 ÷ 7.1 **0.07**

Test-Taking Practice ✏️

INTERNET
State Test Practice
CLASSZONE.COM

42. Multiple Choice A farmer plants corn on 24 acres of a 48 acre field. What is another way to write this ratio? **C**

   A. $\frac{1}{3}$ **B.** $\frac{3}{8}$ **C.** $\frac{1}{2}$ **D.** $\frac{2}{3}$

43. Multiple Choice Which ratio is equivalent to 2:3? **H**

   F. 7:9   **G.** 3:4   **H.** 6:9   **I.** 12:27

BRAIN GAME

Ratio Puzzlers

- The number of cats in a neighborhood is 4 more than the number of dogs and the ratio of cats to dogs is 3:2. How many cats are there in the neighborhood? **12 cats**

- If the ratio of cats to fish in the neighborhood is 3:4, how many fish are there in the neighborhood? **16 fish**

Rries

LESSON 8.2

BEFORE
You wrote ratios and equivalent ratios.

▶ **Now**
You'll write rates, equivalent rates, and unit rates.

WHY?
So you can find the rate of the water over Niagara Falls in Ex. 19.

Word Watch
rate, p. 379
unit rate, p. 379

In the Real World

Space The International Space Station orbits Earth at an average *rate* of 15 miles every 3 seconds. How long will it take the Station to travel 150 miles?

A **rate** is a ratio of two measures that have different units, such as $\frac{15 \text{ mi}}{3 \text{ sec}}$. A **unit rate** is a rate with a denominator of 1.

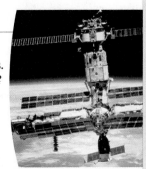

EXAMPLE 1 Writing an Equivalent Rate

To answer the question above, write an *equivalent rate* that has 150 miles in the numerator.

$$\overset{15 \times 10}{\overbrace{}}$$
$$\frac{15 \text{ mi}}{3 \text{ sec}} = \frac{150 \text{ mi}}{30 \text{ sec}}$$
$$\underset{3 \times 10}{\underbrace{}}$$

> You multiplied 15 mi by 10 to get 150 mi, so multiply 3 sec by 10 also.

ANSWER It will take the Space Station 30 seconds to travel 150 miles.

EXAMPLE 2 Writing a Unit Rate

Write the Space Station's average rate of $\frac{15 \text{ mi}}{3 \text{ sec}}$ as a unit rate.

$$\overset{15 \div 3}{\overbrace{}}$$
$$\frac{15 \text{ mi}}{3 \text{ sec}} = \frac{5 \text{ mi}}{1 \text{ sec}}$$
$$\underset{3 \div 3}{\underbrace{}}$$

> You divided 3 sec by 3 to get 1 sec, so divide 15 mi by 3 also.

with Reading
The word *per* is often used to express division in unit rates, such as miles per second.

ANSWER The Space Station's average unit rate is 5 miles per second.

Your turn now Copy and complete the statement.

1. $\frac{5 \text{ lb}}{\$10} = \frac{20 \text{ lb}}{?}$ $\$40$

2. $\frac{35 \text{ mi}}{6 \text{ h}} = \frac{?}{12 \text{ h}}$ 70 mi

3. $\frac{32 \text{ oz}}{\$8} = \frac{?}{\$1}$ 4 oz

NCTM CURRICULUM STANDARDS
Standard 2: Understand relations
Standard 4: Understand the units of measurement; Apply proper techniques to find measures

Lesson 8.2   Rates   **379**

---

① PLAN

SKILL CHECK
1. $8 \div 20 = \underline{?}$ 0.4
2. $6 \div 25 = \underline{?}$ 0.24
3. $3.75 \times 5 = \underline{?}$ 18.75
4. $5.8 \times 3 = \underline{?}$ 17.4

LESSON OBJECTIVE
Write rates, equivalent rates, and unit rates.

PACING
Suggested Number of Days
Basic Course: 1 day
Average Course: 1 day
Advanced Course: 1 day
Block: 0.5 block with 8.3

TEACHING RESOURCES
For a complete list of Teaching Resources, see page 370B.

 TRANSPARENCY
Warm-Up Exercises for this lesson are available on a transparency.

② TEACH

MOTIVATING THE LESSON
Discuss with students situations involving rates of speed that are within their experience.

TIPS FOR NEW TEACHERS
Be sure students understand that since a rate is a ratio involving two different units, they must include units with both numerator and denominator. See Tips for New Teachers in the *Chapter 8 Resource Book*.

379

Example 1 A communications satellite orbits Earth at an average rate of 24 miles in 4 seconds. How long will it take the satellite to travel 120 miles? **20 sec**

Example 2 Write the communications satellite's average rate of $\frac{24 \text{ mi}}{4 \text{ sec}}$ as a unit rate. $\frac{6 \text{ mi}}{1 \text{ sec}}$

Example 3 There are about 39.37 inches in a meter. About how many inches are in 4 meters? **about 157.48 in.**

Example 4 A 16 ounce sports drink costs $2.40. A 30 ounce drink costs $3.60. Which size is the better buy? Explain.
$\frac{\$2.40}{16} = \$.15$ per ounce and
$\frac{\$3.60}{30} = \$.12$ per ounce.
Since $.12 < $.15, the 30 ounce drink is the better buy.

 TRANSPARENCY

Support transparencies are available for Example 3.

 CONCEPT CHECK

How can you calculate the unit price for an item? **Divide the cost of the item by the number of units. The result, or cost per unit for the item, is the unit price.**

 DAILY PUZZLER

A car travels 30 miles in 30 minutes. What is its unit rate in miles per hour? Miles per minute? Feet per second? **60 miles per hour; 1 mile per minute; 88 feet per second**

EXAMPLE 3 **Using a Unit Rate**

Measurement There are 2.54 centimeters in 1 inch. How many centimeters are in 3 inches?

Solution

Write an equivalent rate that has 3 inches in the denominator.

$$\overset{2.54 \times 3}{\overbrace{\frac{2.54 \text{ cm}}{1 \text{ in.}} = \frac{7.62 \text{ cm}}{3 \text{ in.}}}}$$
$$\underset{1 \times 3}{\underbrace{}}$$

> You multiplied 1 in. by 3 to get 3 in., so multiply 2.54 cm by 3 also.

ANSWER There are 7.62 centimeters in 3 inches.

EXAMPLE 4 **Comparing Unit Rates**

At the Movies A 12 ounce tub of popcorn costs $3. A 20 ounce tub of popcorn costs $4. Which size is the better buy? Explain.

Solution

The rates for the two sizes are $\frac{\$3}{12 \text{ oz}}$ and $\frac{\$4}{20 \text{ oz}}$. Find the *unit price* for each tub of popcorn by finding the cost for 1 ounce of popcorn.

12 ounce tub	**20 ounce tub**
$\overset{3 \div 12}{\overbrace{\frac{\$3}{12 \text{ oz}} = \frac{\$.25}{1 \text{ oz}}}}$ $\underset{12 \div 12}{\underbrace{}}$	$\overset{4 \div 20}{\overbrace{\frac{\$4}{20 \text{ oz}} = \frac{\$.20}{1 \text{ oz}}}}$ $\underset{20 \div 20}{\underbrace{}}$

Compare the unit prices: $.20 < $.25.

ANSWER Because the unit price for the 20 ounce tub is less than the unit price for the 12 ounce tub, the 20 ounce size is the better buy.

Your turn now **Decide which size is the better buy. Explain.**

4. 5 lb bag; the unit price for the 3 pound bag is $.75 and the unit price for the 5 pound bag is $.70.

4. A 3 pound bag of apples costs $2.25.
A 5 pound bag of apples costs $3.50.

Getting Ready to Practice

Vocabulary Tell whether the rate is written as a unit rate.

1. 2 feet per second unit rate

2. 76 words in 2 minutes
not a unit rate

Tell whether the rates are *equivalent* or *not equivalent*.

3. $\dfrac{32 \text{ Calories}}{2 \text{ h}}$ and $\dfrac{64 \text{ Calories}}{4 \text{ h}}$
equivalent

4. $\dfrac{60 \text{ words}}{3 \text{ min}}$ and $\dfrac{25 \text{ words}}{1 \text{ min}}$
not equivalent

5. Bottled Water A factory produces an average of 45,000 liters of bottled water per hour. How many liters will the factory produce in 4 hours?
180,000 L

6. Guided Problem Solving On average, a Ruby-throated Hummingbird beats its wings about 3000 times in 60 seconds. A Giant Hummingbird beats its wings an average of about 180 times in 15 seconds. Which bird beats its wings faster?

(1 Find the unit rate for the Ruby-throated Hummingbird. 50 times in 1 second

(2 Find the unit rate for the Giant Hummingbird.
12 times in 1 second

(3 Compare the unit rates.
The Ruby-throated Hummingbird beats its wings faster.

Giant Hummingbird

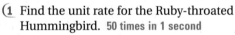
Ruby-throated Hummingbird

Practice and Problem Solving

Copy and complete the statement.

A 7. $\dfrac{\$4}{3 \text{ oz}} = \dfrac{\$16}{?}$ 12 oz

8. $\dfrac{40 \text{ gal}}{8 \text{ h}} = \dfrac{20 \text{ gal}}{?}$ 4 h

9. $\dfrac{54 \text{ mi}}{9 \text{ h}} = \dfrac{?}{3 \text{ h}}$ 18 mi

Write the unit rate.

10. $\dfrac{220 \text{ mi}}{4 \text{ h}}$ $\dfrac{55 \text{ mi}}{1 \text{ h}}$

11. $\dfrac{81 \text{ m}}{27 \text{ sec}}$ $\dfrac{3 \text{ m}}{1 \text{ sec}}$

12. $\dfrac{\$15}{12 \text{ muffins}}$ $\dfrac{\$1.25}{1 \text{ muffin}}$

Tell whether the rates are *equivalent* or *not equivalent*.

13. $\dfrac{8 \text{ lb}}{\$4}$ and $\dfrac{12 \text{ lb}}{\$3}$ not equivalent

14. $\dfrac{42 \text{ calls}}{3 \text{ h}}$ and $\dfrac{28 \text{ calls}}{2 \text{ h}}$ equivalent

Write the rate and unit rate. 15–18. See margin.

15. 20 words in 5 minutes

16. 48 students for 24 computers

17. 160 miles in 4 hours

18. 250 pages in 5 chapters

Margin answers

15. $\dfrac{20 \text{ words}}{5 \text{ min}}$; $\dfrac{4 \text{ words}}{1 \text{ min}}$

16. $\dfrac{48 \text{ students}}{24 \text{ computers}}$; $\dfrac{2 \text{ students}}{1 \text{ computer}}$

17. $\dfrac{160 \text{ mi}}{4 \text{ h}}$; $\dfrac{40 \text{ mi}}{1 \text{ h}}$

18. $\dfrac{250 \text{ pages}}{5 \text{ chapters}}$; $\dfrac{50 \text{ pages}}{1 \text{ chapter}}$

with Homework

Example	Exercises
1	7–9, 13–14
2	10–12, 15–18
3	19–20
4	25–26

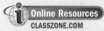
Online Resources
CLASSZONE.COM
· More Examples
· eTutorial Plus

3 APPLY

ASSIGNMENT GUIDE

Basic Course
Day 1: pp. 381–382 Exs. 7–13, 15–19, 21–26, 29–35

Average Course
Day 1: pp. 381–382 Exs. 7–14, 17–27, 29–32, 35, 36

Advanced Course
Day 1: pp. 381–382 Exs. 7–14, 17–30*, 35, 36

Block
pp. 381–382 Exs. 7–14, 17–27, 29–32, 35, 36 (with 8.3)

EXTRA PRACTICE

• Student Edition, p.715
• Chapter 8 Resource Book, pp. 19–21
• Test and Practice Generator

TRANSPARENCY

Even-numbered answers are available on transparencies.

HOMEWORK CHECK

When you review students' homework for this lesson, go over the following exercises to check understanding of key concepts.
Basic: 7, 10, 16, 19, 25
Average: 8, 11, 17, 19, 26
Advanced: 7, 12, 18, 20, 26

MINI-QUIZ

1. Water is filling a storage tank at an average rate of 25 gallons in 5 minutes. Write this as a unit rate. **5 gal per minute**

2. There are 30.48 centimeters in a foot. How many centimeters are in 5 feet? **152.4 cm**

3. A 3 ounce tube of toothpaste costs $.75. A 15 ounce tube costs $6.00. Which size is the better buy? Explain. **The unit rate for the 3 oz size is $.25 per ounce. The unit rate for the 15 oz size is $.40 per ounce. Since $.25 < $.40, the 3 oz size is the better buy.**

5 FOLLOW-UP

RETEACHING/REMEDIATION
- Study Guide in Chapter 8 Resource Book, pp. 22–23
- Tutor Place, Ratio, Proportion, and Percent Card 2
- eTutorial Plus Online
- Extra Practice, p. 715
- Lesson Practice in Chapter 8 Resource Book, pp. 19–21

CHALLENGE/ENRICHMENT
- Challenge Practice in Chapter 8 Resource Book, p. 24
- Teacher's Edition, p. 370F

ENGLISH LEARNER SUPPORT
- Spanish Study Guide
- Multi-Language Glossary
- Chapter Audio Summaries CDs

What do you think?
Geography

■ **Niagara Falls**

The Niagara Falls consist of the American Falls, the Bridal Veil Falls, and the Canadian Falls, or Horseshoe Falls, shown above. The Canadian Falls are about 170 feet high. How high are the Canadian Falls, to the nearest meter, if 1 foot equals 0.3048 meter? **52 m**

23. $\dfrac{2.54 \text{ cm}}{1 \text{ in.}}$

24. $\dfrac{1.61 \text{ km}}{1 \text{ mi}}$

25. 18 oz box; the unit price for the 18 ounce box is about $.22 and the unit price for the 12 ounce box is $.25.

INTERNET
State Test Practice
CLASSZONE.COM

19. Niagara Falls On average, 700,000 gallons of water flow over the Canadian Falls every second. How many gallons flow over the Canadian Falls in 30 seconds? **21,000,000 gal**

20. Gardening You work in a local park removing weeds. You earn $7.50 per hour. How much do you earn for working 6 hours? **$45**

Write the unit rate.

B **21.** $\dfrac{6.63 \text{ lb}}{3 \text{ kg}}$ $\dfrac{2.21 \text{ lb}}{1 \text{ kg}}$ **22.** $\dfrac{56.7 \text{ g}}{2 \text{ oz}}$ $\dfrac{28.35 \text{ g}}{1 \text{ oz}}$ **23.** $\dfrac{10.16 \text{ cm}}{4 \text{ in.}}$ **24.** $\dfrac{8.05 \text{ km}}{5 \text{ mi}}$

23–24. See margin.

25. Explain A 12 ounce box of cereal costs $3. An 18 ounce box costs $4. Which box is the better buy? Explain. **See margin.**

26. Decide Your friend purchases 26 bagels for $10.40. You purchase 39 bagels at a price of 3 bagels for $1. Which purchase is the better buy? **3 bagels for $1**

C **27. Critical Thinking** Would the result have been different in Example 2 on page 379 if you used the rate $\dfrac{150 \text{ mi}}{30 \text{ sec}}$ to find the unit rate? Explain.
No; the unit rate for both rates is $\dfrac{5 \text{ mi}}{1 \text{ sec}}$.

28. Challenge An office has two paper shredders, A and B. On average, shredder A shreds 1100 pounds of paper in 5 hours. On average, shredder B shreds 4.4 pounds of paper per minute. Which machine is faster? **shredder B**

Mixed Review

29. Find the length of a rectangle whose area is 24 square meters and whose width is 4 meters. *(Lesson 2.2)* **6 m**

30. Find the least common multiple of 21 and 27. *(Lesson 5.4)* **189**

Basic Skills **Find the greatest common factor of the numbers.**

31. 16, 40 **8**   **32.** 36, 81 **9**   **33.** 18, 72 **18**   **34.** 20, 56 **4**

Test-Taking Practice

35. Multiple Choice On average, a car gets 20 miles per gallon. At this rate, how many gallons will the car use to travel 80 miles? **C**

A. 2.8 gallons   **B.** 3.5 gallons   **C.** 4.0 gallons   **D.** 4.6 gallons

36. Multiple Choice Denise works for 3 hours and earns $24. At this rate, how much does Denise earn in 1 hour? **G**

F. $16   **G.** $8   **H.** $6   **I.** $4

LESSON 8.3

Solving Proportions

BEFORE You solved equations.

▶ Now You'll write and solve proportions.

WHY? So you can predict water use, as in Ex. 29.

Word Watch

proportion, p. 383
cross products, p. 383

Proportions and Equivalent Ratios A **proportion** is an equation you write to show that two ratios are equivalent. The proportion below shows that the ratios in the pictures are equivalent.

Ratio: 2 out of 3   Ratio: 8 out of 12   Proportion

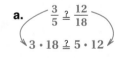   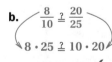 $\dfrac{2}{3} = \dfrac{8}{12}$

If you multiply the numerator of each ratio by the denominator of the other ratio, you'll find the *cross products*. For the proportion $\dfrac{a}{b} = \dfrac{c}{d}$, where b and d are nonzero, the **cross products** are ad and bc. The cross products for the proportion above are $2 \cdot 12$ and $3 \cdot 8$.

Cross Products Property

Words In a proportion, the cross products are equal.

Algebra

$\dfrac{a}{b} = \dfrac{c}{d}$, where b and d are nonzero.

$ad = bc$

Numbers

$3 \cdot 8 = 4 \cdot 6$

EXAMPLE 1   **Checking a Proportion**

Use cross products to decide whether the ratios form a proportion.

a. $\dfrac{3}{5} \overset{?}{=} \dfrac{12}{18}$

$3 \cdot 18 \overset{?}{=} 5 \cdot 12$

$54 \neq 60$

The cross products are not equal, so the ratios do not form a proportion.

b. $\dfrac{8}{10} \overset{?}{=} \dfrac{20}{25}$

$8 \cdot 25 \overset{?}{=} 10 \cdot 20$

$200 = 200 \checkmark$

The cross products are equal, so the ratios form a proportion.

HELP with Reading

The proportion $\dfrac{3}{5} = \dfrac{12}{18}$ in part (a) of Example 1 is read "3 is to 5 as 12 is to 18."

NCTM CURRICULUM STANDARDS
Standard 1: Understand how operations are related
Standard 2: Understand relations
Standard 6: Solve problems in math and other contexts

Lesson 8.3   Solving Proportions   **383**

---

① PLAN

SKILL CHECK
Which products are equal?
1. $12 \times 4, 5 \times 11, 16 \times 3$
   $12 \times 4 = 16 \times 3$
2. $11 \times 9, 10 \times 10, 4 \times 25$
   $10 \times 10 = 4 \times 25$
3. $4 \times 8, 9 \times 4, 16 \times 2$
   $4 \times 8 = 16 \times 2$

LESSON OBJECTIVE
Write and solve proportions.

PACING
Suggested Number of Days
Basic Course: 1 day
Average Course: 1 day
Advanced Course: 1 day
Block: 0.5 block with 8.2

TEACHING RESOURCES
For a complete list of Teaching Resources, see page 370B.

TRANSPARENCY
Warm-Up Exercises for this lesson are available on a transparency.

② TEACH

MOTIVATING THE LESSON
Provide groups of students with a large number of small squares of two different colors. Have each group create an arrangement of squares in which 2 out of every 3 are one color and the rest are the other color. Have each group compare their arrangement with another group's.

383

Solving Proportions To solve a proportion, you find the value of any missing part. One way to solve a proportion is to use mental math.

EXAMPLE 2 Solving Using Mental Math

Solve the proportion $\dfrac{4}{12} = \dfrac{20}{x}$.

Solution

Method 1 Use equivalent ratios.

$$\overset{4 \times 5}{\dfrac{4}{12} = \dfrac{20}{x}}_{12 \times 5}$$

> You multiplied 4 by 5 to get 20, so multiply 12 by 5 also.

$12 \times 5 = 60$, so $x = 60$.

Method 2 Use cross products.

$$\dfrac{4}{12} = \dfrac{20}{x}$$

$$4x = 240$$

$$x = 60$$

> Ask, "4 times what number equals 240?"

ANSWER The solution is 60.

Your turn now Solve the proportion.

1. $\dfrac{n}{4} = \dfrac{6}{24}$ 1
2. $\dfrac{25}{10} = \dfrac{5}{k}$ 2
3. $\dfrac{30}{x} = \dfrac{6}{11}$ 55
4. $\dfrac{10}{4} = \dfrac{s}{12}$ 30

EXAMPLE 3 Solving Using a Verbal Model

Boating You are on a riverboat trip. You travel 5 miles in 3 hours. At that same rate, how long will it take you to travel 20 miles?

Solution

Use a proportion. Let t represent the total time of the 20 mile trip.

$$\dfrac{\text{Distance traveled}}{\text{Time traveled}} = \dfrac{\text{Total distance}}{\text{Total time}} \qquad \text{Write a verbal model.}$$

$$\dfrac{5 \text{ mi}}{3 \text{ h}} = \dfrac{20 \text{ mi}}{t \text{ h}} \qquad \text{Substitute values.}$$

$$\dfrac{5}{3} = \dfrac{20}{t} \qquad \text{Write the cross products. They are equal.}$$

$$5t = 60$$

$$t = 12 \qquad \text{Solve using mental math.}$$

ANSWER It will take you 12 hours to travel 20 miles.

What do you think?

Travel

■ **Boating**

The tour boat in the photo is traveling on the Moselle River in Germany. The tour boat can carry 250 passengers. About how many classes of students at your school would fit on the boat?

Answers may vary.

 with **Review**

Need help writing a related equation? See p. 63.

EXAMPLE 4 **Solving Using a Related Equation**

Solve the proportion $\frac{30}{12} = \frac{x}{18}$.

Solution

$$\frac{30}{12} = \frac{x}{18}$$ Write the cross products.
They are equal.

$$540 = 12x$$

$$540 \div 12 = x$$ Write the related division equation.

$$45 = x$$ Divide.

ANSWER The solution is 45.

Your turn now Solve the proportion.

5. $\frac{x}{15} = \frac{10}{6}$ 25

6. $\frac{30}{y} = \frac{50}{60}$ 36

7. $\frac{70}{21} = \frac{a}{6}$ 20

8. $\frac{32}{20} = \frac{40}{m}$ 25

8.3 Exercises

More Practice, p. 715

INTERNET
eWorkbook Plus
CLASSZONE.COM

Getting Ready to Practice

1. Vocabulary The cross products for the proportion $\frac{3}{8} = \frac{9}{x}$ are ? and ? .
3x, 72

Use cross products to decide whether the ratios form a proportion.

2. $\frac{3}{4} \stackrel{?}{=} \frac{9}{12}$ yes

3. $\frac{10}{16} \stackrel{?}{=} \frac{5}{8}$ yes

4. $\frac{6}{14} \stackrel{?}{=} \frac{8}{20}$ no

5. $\frac{30}{6} \stackrel{?}{=} \frac{20}{15}$ no

6. Which equation is related to the equation $8x = 112$? C

A. $x = 112 + 8$ **B.** $x = 112 - 8$ **C.** $x = 112 \div 8$

Solve the proportion.

7. $\frac{1}{6} = \frac{5}{x}$ 30

8. $\frac{2}{5} = \frac{r}{20}$ 8

9. $\frac{n}{28} = \frac{2}{7}$ 8

10. $\frac{40}{z} = \frac{15}{3}$ 8

11. Literature In Jonathan Swift's book *Gulliver's Travels*, Gulliver's body height and the height of a Lilliputian are "in the proportion of twelve to one." If a Lilliputian is 6 inches tall, how tall is Gulliver? 72 in.

Lesson 8.3 Solving Proportions **385**

 CONCEPT CHECK

How can you test whether two ratios can form a proportion? **Find the cross products, which are the products of each numerator with the other ratio's denominator. If the cross products are equal, then the ratios can form a proportion.**

 DAILY PUZZLER

The numbers 5, 6, and 30 are three of the four numbers in a proportion. How many numbers can you find that could be the fourth number in the proportion? What are the numbers? Explain. **There are three values for the fourth number, 1, 25, and 36. The proportions are** $\frac{5}{30} = \frac{1}{6}$, $\frac{5}{6} = \frac{25}{30}$, **and** $\frac{5}{6} = \frac{30}{36}$.

ASSIGNMENT GUIDE

Basic Course
Day 1: EP p. 708 Exs. 42–49;
pp. 386–387 Exs. 12–24,
28–31, 33–39, 43–47

Average Course
Day 1: pp. 386–387 Exs. 14–23,
27–34, 37–41, 43–48

Advanced Course
Day 1: pp. 386–387 Exs. 14–17,
22–37, 39–44*, 47, 48

Block
pp. 386–387 Exs. 14–23, 27–34,
37–41, 43–48 (with 8.2)

EXTRA PRACTICE

- Student Edition, p. 715
- Chapter 8 Resource Book,
  pp. 27–29
- Test and Practice Generator

TRANSPARENCY

Even-numbered answers are available on transparencies.

HOMEWORK CHECK

When you review students' homework for this lesson, go over the following exercises to check understanding of key concepts.
Basic: 12, 16, 24, 28, 31
Average: 14, 17, 27, 29, 31
Advanced: 13, 22, 27, 30, 32

TEACHING TIP

In Exercises 12–15, students can check their answers by using a calculator to convert each fraction to a decimal.

---

 with Homework

Example	Exercises
1	12–15
2	16–23, 28–30, 33–36
3	31–32
4	24–27, 33–36

Online Resources
CLASSZONE.COM
· More Examples
· eTutorial Plus

Practice and Problem Solving

Use cross products to decide whether the ratios form a proportion.

A 12. $\frac{9}{21} \stackrel{?}{=} \frac{3}{7}$ yes   **13.** $\frac{3}{8} \stackrel{?}{=} \frac{15}{40}$ yes   **14.** $\frac{3}{2} \stackrel{?}{=} \frac{12}{10}$ no   **15.** $\frac{4}{5} \stackrel{?}{=} \frac{16}{21}$ no

Solve the proportion.

16. $\frac{3}{6} = \frac{x}{2}$ 1   **17.** $\frac{m}{8} = \frac{8}{64}$ 1   **18.** $\frac{5}{z} = \frac{25}{10}$ 2   **19.** $\frac{12}{18} = \frac{2}{p}$ 3

20. $\frac{12}{28} = \frac{3}{c}$ 7   **21.** $\frac{9}{x} = \frac{27}{30}$ 10   **22.** $\frac{a}{5} = \frac{99}{55}$ 9   **23.** $\frac{5}{6} = \frac{n}{120}$ 100

24. $\frac{9}{6} = \frac{h}{14}$ 21   **25.** $\frac{12}{r} = \frac{8}{20}$ 30   **26.** $\frac{24}{36} = \frac{10}{x}$ 15   **27.** $\frac{t}{4} = \frac{45}{18}$ 10

28. **Distance** You travel about 60 miles on 2 gallons of gasoline. About how far do you travel on 1 gallon of gasoline? **30 mi**

29. **Water Use** You use about 50 gallons of water per day. About how much water do you use per week? **350 gal**

30. **Currency** The value of 5 U.S. dollars is about 19 Malaysian ringgits. What is the value in U.S. dollars of 95 ringgits?
25 U.S. dollars

Use a verbal model to write a proportion. Then solve the proportion.

31. **Quiz Grades** You and a friend got the same grade on your quizzes. You got 6 out of 8 questions correct. If your friend's quiz had 12 questions, how many did your friend get correct? **9 questions**

32. **E-mail** Four out of 10 students surveyed in a class have their own e-mail accounts. If there are 40 students in the class, how many would you expect to have their own e-mail accounts? **16 students**

Choose a Method Tell whether you would solve the proportion using *mental math* or a *related equation*. Then solve the proportion.

33–36. Methods may vary.

33. mental math; 6

34. related equation; 25

35. related equation; 33

36. mental math; 25

B 33. $\frac{x}{14} = \frac{3}{7}$ **34.** $\frac{10}{12} = \frac{m}{30}$ **35.** $\frac{6}{y} = \frac{8}{44}$ **36.** $\frac{20}{100} = \frac{5}{w}$

Copy and complete the table using proportions.

37.

Games played	6	9	?	15
Total cost	8	12	16	?

12 ... 20

38.

Servings	4	10	16	?
Number of cups	10	?	40	55

22 ... 25

39. Kangaroos Hannah and Juan are trying to estimate the distance a kangaroo will cover in 6 hops if it covers 40 feet in 2 hops.

Hannah
$$\frac{2}{40} = \frac{6}{x}$$

Juan
$$\frac{2}{6} = \frac{40}{x}$$

Are both methods correct? Use cross products to check. **yes**

C 40. Writing Six out of 10 students in your school saw a movie last weekend. There are 480 students in your school. Is there enough information to find the number of students in your school who *did not* see a movie last weekend? Explain. **See margin.**

41. Critical Thinking In Example 2 on page 384, you use either equivalent ratios or cross products to solve the proportion. Explain how you can use equivalent ratios to solve Example 4 on page 385. **See margin.**

42. Challenge A flea with a length of 3 millimeters can jump a distance of 33 centimeters. If the jumping ability of a human is proportional to the jumping ability of a flea, how far can a human jump who is 180 centimeters tall? **19,800 cm**

40. Yes. *Sample answer:* Use the proportion $\frac{6}{10} = \frac{x}{480}$ to find the number of students who did see the movie and subtract this number from the total number of students.

41. *Sample answer:* Since multiplying 12 by $1\frac{1}{2}$ gives 18, multiply 30 by $1\frac{1}{2}$ to find the unknown value, 45.

Mixed Review

43. A puppy's weight is greater than 3.5 pounds and less than 3.55 pounds. Give a possible weight. *(Lesson 3.3)* *Sample answer:* **3.52 lb**

44. A boulder has a weight of $8\frac{1}{2}$ tons. How many pounds does it weigh? *(Lesson 7.7)* **17,000 lb**

Basic Skills Find the perimeter and the area of the figure described.

45. a rectangle that is 14 cm by 3 cm
34 cm; 42 cm²

46. a square that is 8 ft by 8 ft
32 ft; 64 ft²

Test-Taking Practice

47. 50 hens. *Sample answer:* Solve the proportion $\frac{10 \text{ hens}}{7 \text{ eggs}} = \frac{x \text{ hens}}{35 \text{ eggs}}$.
$10 \cdot 35 = 7 \cdot x$, $x = 50$ hens

47. Short Response A farmer has 10 hens that produce a total of 7 eggs each day. Use a proportion to find the number of hens it would take to produce 35 eggs each day. Describe the steps you took to solve the problem. **See margin.**

48. Multiple Choice At a health food store, 8 ounces of curry powder cost $8.99. At that rate, find the cost of 12 ounces of curry powder. **C**

A. $4.00   **B.** $12.99   **C.** $13.49   **D.** $20.99

Lesson 8.3   Solving Proportions   **387**

4 ASSESS

ASSESSMENT RESOURCES
For more assessment resources, see:
• Assessment Book
• Test and Practice Generator

MINI-QUIZ

1. Find each pair of cross products and decide whether the ratios form a proportion.
 a. $\frac{4}{14} \stackrel{?}{=} \frac{14}{36}$ $4 \times 36 \neq 14 \times 14$; **no**
 b. $\frac{6}{15} \stackrel{?}{=} \frac{13}{32}$ $6 \times 32 \neq 13 \times 15$; **no**

2. On a car trip you have traveled 225 miles in 5 hours. At that same rate, how long will it take you to travel 315 miles? **7 h**

3. Solve each proportion.
 a. $\frac{x}{14} = \frac{18}{42}$ **6**
 b. $\frac{14}{x} = \frac{21}{12}$ **8**

5 FOLLOW-UP

RETEACHING/REMEDIATION
• Study Guide in Chapter 8 Resource Book, pp. 30–31
• Tutor Place, Ratio, Proportion, and Percent Cards 3–5
• eTutorial Plus Online
• Extra Practice, p. 715
• Lesson Practice in Chapter 8 Resource Book, pp. 27–29

CHALLENGE/ENRICHMENT
• Challenge Practice in Chapter 8 Resource Book, p. 32
• Teacher's Edition, p. 370F

ENGLISH LEARNER SUPPORT
• Spanish Study Guide
• Multi-Language Glossary
• Chapter Audio Summaries CDs

LESSON 8.4 Proportions and Scale Drawings

BEFORE	▶ Now	WHY?
You used mental math to find the actual length of an object.	You'll use proportions to find measures of objects.	So you can find the height of the Statue of Liberty in Ex. 3.

In the Real World

 **Word Watch**

Review Words
scale drawing, p. 68
scale, p. 68

Soap Box Derby You are building a car for a Soap Box Derby race. In the *scale drawing* of the Derby car shown below, the car has a length of 2.8 inches. What is the actual length of the Derby car?

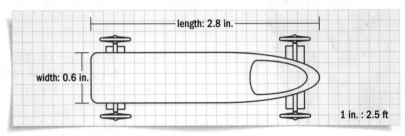

The *scale* of 1 in. : 2.5 ft on the drawing is a ratio that means 1 inch on the drawing represents an actual distance of 2.5 feet on the car.

$$\frac{1 \text{ in.}}{2.5 \text{ ft}} \quad \begin{array}{l} \longleftarrow \text{Measure on drawing} \\ \longleftarrow \text{Actual measure} \end{array}$$

EXAMPLE 1 Using a Scale Drawing

To find the actual length of the car above, write and solve a proportion. Let x represent the Derby car's actual length in feet.

$\dfrac{1 \text{ in.}}{2.5 \text{ ft}} = \dfrac{\text{Length on drawing}}{\text{Actual length}}$	Write a proportion.
$\dfrac{1 \text{ in.}}{2.5 \text{ ft}} = \dfrac{2.8 \text{ in.}}{x \text{ ft}}$	Substitute values.
$1 \cdot x = (2.5)(2.8)$	The cross products are equal.
$x = 7$	Multiply.

ANSWER The actual length of the Derby car is 7 feet.

Your turn now Use the scale drawing shown above.

1. Find the actual width of the Derby car. **1.5 ft**

2. If the actual wheelbase of the Derby car is 5.5 feet, what is the wheelbase of the car in the scale drawing? **2.2 in.**

NCTM CURRICULUM STANDARDS
Standard 2: Represent situations using algebraic symbols
Standard 4: Apply proper techniques to find measures
Standard 6: Solve problems in math and other contexts

Perimeter and Area The ratio of the perimeter of a scale drawing to the actual perimeter is related to the scale. So is the ratio of the areas.

HELP with **Review**

Need help with finding the perimeter and area of a rectangle? See p. 61.

EXAMPLE 2 Finding Ratios of Perimeters

School Murals A finished mural is to be 20 feet by 10 feet. Your scale drawing of the mural is shown below.

a. What is the perimeter of the drawing? of the mural?

b. Find the ratio of the drawing's perimeter to the mural's perimeter. How is this ratio related to the scale?

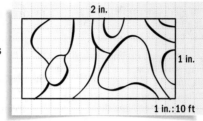

2 in.

1 in.

1 in.:10 ft

Solution

a. Perimeter of drawing: $P = 2l + 2w = 2(2) + 2(1) = 6$ in.

Perimeter of mural: $P = 2l + 2w = 2(20) + 2(10) = 60$ ft

b. $\dfrac{\text{Perimeter of drawing}}{\text{Perimeter of mural}} = \dfrac{6 \text{ in.}}{60 \text{ ft}} = \dfrac{1 \text{ in.}}{10 \text{ ft}}$

ANSWER The ratio of the perimeters is the same as the scale.

EXAMPLE 3 Finding Ratios of Areas

Use the information from Example 2. Find the ratio of the drawing's area to the mural's area. How is this ratio related to the scale?

Solution

Area of drawing: $A = lw = 2 \cdot 1 = 2$ in.^{2}

Area of mural: $A = lw = 20 \cdot 10 = 200$ ft^2

$\dfrac{\text{Area of drawing}}{\text{Area of mural}} = \dfrac{2 \text{ in.}^2}{200 \text{ ft}^2} = \dfrac{1 \text{ in.}^2}{100 \text{ ft}^2} = \dfrac{1 \cdot 1 \text{ in.}^2}{10 \cdot 10 \text{ ft}^2}$

ANSWER The ratio of the areas, 1^2 in.^{2}: 10^2 ft^2, is the square of the scale.

Your turn now A scale drawing of another mural has a length of 5 cm and a width of 3 cm. The scale of the drawing is 1 cm : 2 m.

3. What is the ratio of the perimeters of the drawing and the mural? $\dfrac{1 \text{ cm}}{2 \text{ m}}$

4. What is the ratio of the areas of the drawing and the mural? $\dfrac{1 \text{ cm}^2}{4 \text{ m}^2}$

Example 1 Use the scale drawing in Example 1. Suppose the length of the front axle in the drawing is 0.8 in. What is the actual length of the front axle? **2 ft**

Example 2 A mural is to be 18 feet by 12 feet. A scale drawing is 6 inches by 4 inches.
a. What is the perimeter of the mural? Of the drawing? **60 ft, 20 in.**
b. Find the ratio of the drawing's perimeter to the mural's perimeter. How is this ratio related to the scale? **The ratio of the perimeters, $\dfrac{1 \text{ in.}}{3 \text{ ft}}$, is the same as the scale.**

Example 3 Use the information for Extra Example 2. Find the ratio of the drawing's area to the mural's area. How is this ratio related to the scale? **The ratio of the areas, $\dfrac{1 \text{ in.}^2}{9 \text{ ft}^2}$, is the square of the scale.**

 CONCEPT CHECK

How can you use a scale drawing to find a measurement of the full size object? **Write a proportion using a measurement from the scale drawing, the scale, and the unknown measurement. Then solve the proportion for the unknown measurement.**

 DAILY PUZZLER

An architect prepared two scale drawings of a city park, one using a scale of 1 in. : 25 ft and the other using a scale of 1 cm : 50 ft. On the first drawing, the main entrance is 1.25 in. wide. What is the width of the entrance on the second scale drawing? **0.625 cm**

ASSIGNMENT GUIDE

Basic Course
Day 1: EP p. 709 Exs. 5–10;
   pp. 390–391 Exs. 4–9, 19–25
Day 2: pp. 390–391 Exs. 10–16,
   26–29

Average Course
Day 1: pp. 390–391 Exs. 4–9,
   19–25
Day 2: pp. 390–391 Exs. 10–17,
   26–28

Advanced Course
Day 1: pp. 390–391 Exs. 4–9,
   19–23
Day 2: pp. 390–391 Exs. 10–18*,
   28, 29

Block
pp. 390–391 Exs. 4–17, 19–28

EXTRA PRACTICE

- Student Edition, p. 715
- Chapter 8 Resource Book,
  pp. 36–38
- Test and Practice Generator

TRANSPARENCY

Even-numbered answers are available on transparencies. A support transparency is available for Exercises 10–11.

HOMEWORK CHECK

When you review students' homework for this lesson, go over the following exercises to check understanding of key concepts.
Basic: 4, 6, 10, 11, 14
Average: 4, 7, 11, 12, 15
Advanced: 5, 8, 12, 14, 15

---

11. A good answer should include the use of the ratio $\frac{1}{2}$ in proportions to find the width and length of the enlarged rectangle. For Rectangle 1, the enlarged rectangle will be 8 cm × 4 cm. For Rectangle 2, the enlarged rectangle will be 6 cm × 10 cm. For Rectangle 3, the enlarged rectangle will be 12 cm × 12 cm.

12. Rectangle 1 perimeters are 12 cm and 24 cm, and the areas are 8 cm² and 32 cm². Rectangle 2 perimeters are 16 cm and 32 cm, and the areas are 15 cm² and 60 cm². Rectangle 3 perimeters are 24 cm and 48 cm, and the areas are 36 cm² and 144 cm².

 **with Homework**

Example	Exercises
1	4–9
2	10–16
3	10–16

Online Resources
CLASSZONE.COM
· More Examples
· eTutorial Plus

13. For all rectangles, the ratio of the perimeters is $\frac{1\text{ cm}}{2\text{ cm}}$ and the ratio of the areas is $\frac{1\text{ cm}^2}{4\text{ cm}^2}$. The ratio of the perimeters is the same as the scale, and the ratio of the areas is the square of the scale.

 8.4 Exercises
More Practice, p. 715

Getting Ready to Practice

1 in. to 5 ft; $\frac{1\text{ in.}}{5\text{ ft}}$

1. **Vocabulary** Express the scale 1 in. : 5 ft as a ratio in two other ways.

2. A scale drawing has a scale of 1 in. : 6 ft. The actual length of the object is 48 feet. Choose the proportion you can use to find the length of the drawing. Then find the length. B; 8 in.

   A. $\dfrac{1\text{ in.}}{6\text{ ft}} = \dfrac{48\text{ ft}}{\text{Length of drawing}}$ **B.** $\dfrac{1\text{ in.}}{6\text{ ft}} = \dfrac{\text{Length of drawing}}{48\text{ ft}}$

3. **Statue of Liberty** The model shown has a scale of about 1 in. : 20 ft. Copy and complete the proportion below to find the combined height of the actual Statue of Liberty and the pedestal. about 300 ft

   $$\dfrac{1\text{ in.}}{20\text{ ft}} = \dfrac{\text{Height of model}}{\text{Height of actual monument}}$$

15 in.

Practice and Problem Solving

A scale drawing of a very small object is larger than the object. The scale of a drawing is 2 cm : 9 mm. Find the unknown measure.

A   4. length on drawing = 6 cm;   5. width of object = 45 mm;
      length of object = ? 27 mm   width on drawing = ? 10 cm

A map uses a scale of 1 in. : 50 mi. Find the actual distance for the given distance on the map.

6. 3 inches 150 mi   7. 8 inches 400 mi   8. 0.5 inch 25 mi   9. 4.5 inches 225 mi

Geometry In Exercises 10–13, use the table.

10. Choose one of the rectangles. Use a metric ruler to draw the rectangle. Check drawings.

11. **Describe** Enlarge your rectangle so that 2 centimeters on the new rectangle represents 1 centimeter on the original rectangle. Describe your method. 11–13. See margin.

Rectangle 1	4 cm × 2 cm
Rectangle 2	3 cm × 5 cm
Rectangle 3	6 cm × 6 cm

12. Find the perimeters and areas of the original and enlarged rectangles.

13. **Interpret** Write the ratio of the perimeters and the ratio of the areas. Explain how these ratios are related to the scale.

Landscape Architects A landscape architect is designing a garden for a city park. The drawing has a scale of 1 cm : 5 m. Use the drawing in Exercises 14–16.

B 14. Find the actual dimensions of the garden. **15 m × 20 m**

15. Find the ratio of the drawing's perimeter to the garden's perimeter. $\dfrac{1\ cm}{5\ m}$

16. Find the ratio of the drawing's area to the garden's area. $\dfrac{1\ cm^2}{25\ m^2}$

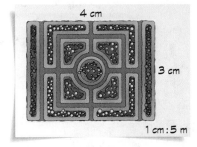
4 cm
3 cm
1 cm : 5 m

17. No; no. *Sample answer:* Since 12 inches = 1 foot, the number 12 should be squared to find the number of square inches in 1 square foot. Similarly, since 3 ft = 1 yard, the number 3 should be squared to find the number of square feet in 1 square yard.

C 17. Critical Thinking Are there 12 square inches in 1 square foot? Are there 3 square feet in 1 square yard? Why or why not? Explain.

18. Challenge If a scale drawing has the scale $a : b$, write algebraic expressions for the ratio of the perimeters and for the ratio of the areas. $\dfrac{a}{b},\ \dfrac{a^2}{b^2}$

Mixed Review

19. Choose an appropriate customary unit to measure the weight of a dining table. *(Lesson 7.6)* **pounds**

Solve the proportion. *(Lesson 8.3)*

20. $\dfrac{5}{4} = \dfrac{x}{16}$ **20**   **21.** $\dfrac{2}{3} = \dfrac{22}{a}$ **33**   **22.** $\dfrac{6}{y} = \dfrac{9}{21}$ **14**   **23.** $\dfrac{10}{n} = \dfrac{25}{40}$ **16**

Basic Skills Use mental math to find the quotient.

24. $1.5 \div 10$ **0.15**   **25.** $71 \div 10$ **7.1**   **26.** $230 \div 100$ **2.3**   **27.** $68 \div 100$ **0.68**

Test-Taking Practice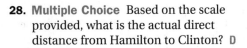

28. Multiple Choice Based on the scale provided, what is the actual direct distance from Hamilton to Clinton? **D**

Clinton
2 cm
Hamilton
1 cm : 15 km

A. 2 km   **B.** 15 km

C. 17 km   **D.** 30 km

29. Multiple Choice A model airplane uses the scale 2 in. : 15 ft. The model's length is 20 inches. What is the actual length of the airplane? **H**

F. 30 in.   **G.** 100 in.   **H.** 150 ft   **I.** 400 ft

4 ASSESS

ASSESSMENT RESOURCES
For more assessment resources, see:
• Assessment Book
• Test and Practice Generator

MINI-QUIZ
A mural is 12 ft by 4 ft, and a scale drawing of it is 6 in. by 2 in.
1. What are the perimeter and area of the mural? **32 ft; 48 ft²**
2. What are the perimeter and area of the drawing? **16 in.; 12 in.²**
3. What is the ratio of the perimeters? How is this related to the scale? **2 ft : 1 in.; the ratio is the same as the scale.**
4. What is the ratio of the areas? How is this related to the scale? **4 ft² : 1 in.²; the ratio is the square of the scale.**

5 FOLLOW-UP

RETEACHING/REMEDIATION
• Study Guide in Chapter 8 Resource Book, pp. 39–40
• Tutor Place, Ratio, Proportion, and Percent Card 6
• eTutorial Plus Online
• Extra Practice, p. 715
• Lesson Practice in Chapter 8 Resource Book, pp. 36–38

CHALLENGE/ENRICHMENT
• Challenge Practice in Chapter 8 Resource Book, p. 41
• Teacher's Edition, p. 370F

ENGLISH LEARNER SUPPORT
• Spanish Study Guide
• Multi-Language Glossary
• Chapter Audio Summaries CDs

LESSONS **8.1** TO **8.4**

Notebook Review

Review the vocabulary definitions in your notebook.

Copy the review examples in your notebook. Then complete the exercises.

Check Your Definitions

scale drawing, p. 68   equivalent ratio, p. 375   proportion, p. 383
scale, p. 68   rate, p. 379   cross products, p. 383
ratio, p. 374   unit rate, p. 379

Use Your Vocabulary

1. Copy and complete: A $\underline{\ ?\ }$ is a ratio of two measures that have different units. **rate**

2. Copy and complete: A proportion is an equation you write to show that two $\underline{\ ?\ }$ are $\underline{\ ?\ }$. **ratios, equivalent**

3. What are the cross products for the proportion $\frac{2}{x} = \frac{4}{6}$? **12 and 4x**

8.1–8.3 Can you use ratios, rates, and proportions?

 Review

EXAMPLE Solve the proportion.

a. $\frac{3}{4} = \frac{x}{12}$

Use equivalent ratios.

$$\begin{array}{c} 3 \times 3 \\ \frac{3}{4} = \frac{x}{12} \\ 4 \times 3 \end{array}$$

> You multiplied 4 by 3 to get 12, so multiply 3 by 3 also.

$3 \times 3 = 9$, so $x = 9$.

b. $\frac{10}{4} = \frac{x}{14}$

Use cross products and a related equation.

$$\frac{10}{4} = \frac{x}{14}$$

$$140 = 4x$$

$$140 \div 4 = x$$

$$35 = x$$

 4. Copy and complete to write an equivalent rate: $\frac{20 \text{ in.}}{9 \text{ sec}} = \frac{100 \text{ in.}}{?}$. **45 sec**

5. Copy the statement: 8 out of 12 $\underline{\ ?\ }$ $\frac{7}{9}$. Then write the ratios as decimals and use <, >, or = to complete the statement. **<; $0.\overline{6} < 0.\overline{7}$**

6. Four pounds of tomatoes cost $10. Find the unit price. **$2.50**

7. Solve the proportion $\frac{x}{4} = \frac{18}{6}$. **12**

8.4 Can you find measurements with scale drawings?

Review **EXAMPLE** A map uses a scale of 1 in. : 75 mi. On the map, two cities are 2 inches apart. What is the actual distance between the cities?

$$\frac{1 \text{ in.}}{75 \text{ mi}} = \frac{\text{Distance on map}}{\text{Actual distance}}$$ Write a proportion.

$$\frac{1 \text{ in.}}{75 \text{ mi}} = \frac{2 \text{ in.}}{x \text{ mi}}$$ Substitute values.

$$1 \cdot x = 75 \cdot 2$$ The cross products are equal.

$$x = 150$$ Multiply.

ANSWER The actual distance between the cities is 150 miles.

 8. A model uses the scale 2 in. : 5 ft. The length of the model is 50 inches. What is the actual length? **125 ft**

Stop and Think about Lessons 8.1–8.4

 9. Writing Compare a rate with a unit rate. How are they alike? How are they different? Explain. **See margin.**

9. *Sample answer:* They both are ratios of measures that have different units. A rate can have a denominator other than 1, but a unit rate must have a denominator of 1.

Review Quiz 1

Match the ratio with an equivalent ratio.

1. 5 to 30 **B**   **2.** 12 : 4 **A**   **3.** 24 to 18 **D**   **4.** 9 : 72 **C**

A. 3 to 1   **B.** $\frac{1}{6}$ **C.** 1 : 8   **D.** 4 to 3

5. Shopping A 32 ounce carton of juice costs \$3.20. A 16 ounce carton of juice costs \$1.92. Which carton is the better buy? Explain. **32 oz carton; the unit price for the 32 ounce carton is \$.10 and the unit price for the 16 ounce carton is \$.12.**

Solve the proportion.

6. $\frac{4}{21} = \frac{x}{84}$ **16**   **7.** $\frac{25}{z} = \frac{100}{84}$ **21**   **8.** $\frac{36}{g} = \frac{8}{10}$ **45**   **9.** $\frac{n}{30} = \frac{8}{12}$ **20**

10. Geometry Use a metric ruler to make a scale drawing of the rectangle shown using the scale 5 cm : 1 cm. Then find the ratio of the area of the original rectangle to the area of the enlarged rectangle.

1 cm

2 cm

Check drawings, the dimensions of the drawing will be 10 cm × 5 cm; $\frac{1 \text{ cm}^2}{25 \text{ cm}^2}$.

Lessons 8.1–8.4   Notebook Review   **393**

1 PLAN

EXPLORE THE CONCEPT

- Students make models to represent percents.
- This activity leads to writing percents in different forms in Lesson 8.5.

MATERIALS

Each student will need graph paper.

RECOMMENDED TIME

Work activity: 10 min
Discuss results: 5 min

GROUPING

Students can work individually.

 **TRANSPARENCY**

A support transparency is available for this Activity.

2 TEACH

DISCUSSION

As students work through Step 3, you may wish to ask them if it makes a difference which 25 small squares are shaded.

3 CLOSE

 **KEY DISCOVERY**

A 10 × 10 grid can be used to model a fraction as a percent.

ASSESSMENT

1. How can you model 75%? Make a 10 × 10 grid on graph paper. Shade 75 squares.

4. See Additional Answers beginning on page AA1.

394

8.5 Hands-on **Activity**

GOAL
Use models to represent percents.

MATERIALS
- graph paper
- colored pencils

Modeling Percents

In this activity, you will make models to represent *percents*. A percent is a ratio that compares a number to 100. The symbol for percent is %.

Explore — **Model 25%.**

1 On graph paper, make a border to form a 10 × 10 grid that contains 100 squares.

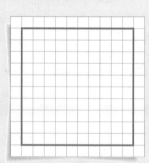

2 Each of the small squares in the grid represents $\frac{1}{100}$ of the grid.

$$\frac{1}{100} = 1\%$$

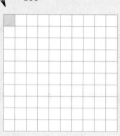

3 To model 25%, shade 25 squares. The shaded portion represents 25%, the decimal 0.25, and the fraction $\frac{25}{100} = \frac{1}{4}$.

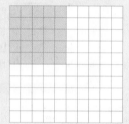

Your turn now — Write the percent, decimal, and fraction for the model.

1.
2.
3.

1. 43%, 0.43, $\frac{43}{100}$

2. 66%, 0.66, $\frac{66}{100} = \frac{33}{50}$

3. 90%, 0.90, $\frac{90}{100} = \frac{9}{10}$

4. Use graph paper to make a model that represents 80%. See margin.

 Stop and Think

5. Shade all squares in a 10 × 10 grid; use two 10 × 10 grids and shade all squares in one grid and 50 squares in the second grid; use two 10 × 10 grids and shade all squares in both grids.

5. Critical Thinking How could you model 100%? 150%? 200%?

394 Chapter 8 Ratio, Proportion, and Percent

NCTM CURRICULUM STANDARDS
Standard 1: Understand ways of representing numbers
Standard 10: Use representations to communicate mathematical ideas

Understanding Percent

BEFORE	▶ Now	WHY?
You wrote ratios and rates.	You'll write percents as decimals and fractions.	So you can analyze a survey on computer use, as in Exs. 25–27.

Word Watch

percent, p. 395

Modeling Percents A **percent** is a ratio that compares a number to 100. The word *percent* means "per hundred," or "out of 100." The symbol for percent is %.

There are 100 marbles shown at the right, and 43 out of 100 are blue. You can represent this ratio using a percent, a decimal, or a fraction.

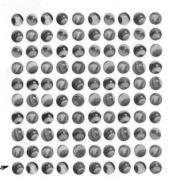

Each marble represents 1% of the group of 100 marbles.

Percent	Decimal	Fraction
43%	0.43	$\frac{43}{100}$

EXAMPLE 1 **Writing Ratios in Different Forms**

In the diagram above, 7 out of the 100 marbles are red. Write this ratio as a percent, a decimal, and a fraction.

Percent: 7%   **Decimal:** 0.07   **Fraction:** $\frac{7}{100}$

EXAMPLE 2 **Writing Percents**

Write the number in words and as a percent.

a. $\frac{9}{100}$ **b.** 0.39   **c.** $\frac{32.5}{100}$ **d.** 3, or $\frac{300}{100}$

Solution

a. nine hundredths, or 9%

b. thirty-nine hundredths, or 39%

c. thirty-two and five tenths hundredths, or 32.5%

d. three-hundred hundredths, or 300%

HELP with Notetaking

In your notes, you may want to include percents in a concept map about forms of numbers, like the concept map shown on page 372.

Your turn now **Write the number as a percent, decimal, and fraction.**

29%, 0.29, $\frac{29}{100}$

1. 29 hundredths   **2.** 3 hundredths   **3.** 100 hundredths

3%, 0.03, $\frac{3}{100}$ 100%, 1.00, $\frac{100}{100} = 1$

NCTM CURRICULUM STANDARDS
Standard 1: Understand ways of representing numbers
Standard 10: Use representations to communicate mathematical ideas

---

1 PLAN

SKILL CHECK

1. $\frac{7}{10} = \frac{?}{100}$ 70

2. $\frac{1}{4} = \frac{?}{100}$ 25

3. $\frac{4}{5} = \frac{?}{100}$ 80

OBJECTIVE
Write percents as decimals and fractions.

PACING
Suggested Number of Days
Basic Course: 2 days
Average Course: 2 days
Advanced Course: 2 days
Block: 1 block

TEACHING RESOURCES
For a complete list of Teaching Resources, see page 370B.

 TRANSPARENCY
Warm-Up Exercises for this lesson are available on a transparency.

2 TEACH

MOTIVATING THE LESSON
Discuss with students whether a quiz with 3 out of 4 correct would be a better score than a quiz with 8 out of 10 correct.

TIPS FOR NEW TEACHERS
Be sure students understand that 100% represents 1. See Tips for New Teachers in the *Chapter 8 Resource Book*.

Example 1 In a bag, 19 out of 100 marbles are green. Write this as a percent, a decimal, and a fraction. **19%; 0.19; $\frac{19}{100}$**

Example 2 Write the number in words and as a percent.

a. $\frac{76.3}{100}$ seventy-six-point-three hundredths; **76.3%**

b. 7, or $\frac{700}{100}$ seven hundred hundredths; **700%**

c. 0.08 eight hundredths; **8%**

d. $\frac{41}{100}$ forty-one hundredths; **41%**

Example 3

a. Write 72% as a fraction. **72% = $\frac{18}{25}$**

b. Write 30.7% as a decimal. **30.7% = 0.307**

Example 4 Refer to the circle graph in Example 4.

a. What percent of the people did not respond "Owner's bed"? **58%**

b. What percent of the people responded "Dog house" or "Owner's bed"? **72%**

CONCEPT CHECK

How can you write a percent as a decimal or as a fraction? **To write a percent as a decimal, divide the value by 100. To write a percent as a fraction, rewrite the percent using a denominator of 100. Then simplify if possible.**

DAILY PUZZLER

A fraction uses the number 16 in its numerator or denominator. When the fraction is written as a percent, its value is 25% What are two values for the fraction? **$\frac{4}{16}$, $\frac{16}{64}$**

Writing Percents as Decimals and Fractions

To write a percent as a *decimal*:

Divide the value by 100. $57\% = 57 \div 100 = 0.57$

To write a percent as a *fraction*:

Rewrite the percent using a denominator of 100. Simplify if possible. $35\% = \frac{35}{100} = \frac{7}{20}$

EXAMPLE 3 Writing Percents in Different Forms

a. Write 64.5% as a decimal.

$64.5\% = 64.5 \div 100 = 0.645$

b. Write 80% as a fraction.

$80\% = \frac{80}{100} = \frac{4}{5}$

Circle Graphs Circle graphs are often used to represent the results of a survey. The parts of a circle graph together represent a total of 100%.

EXAMPLE 4 Circle Graphs with Percents

Survey In a survey, 100 dog owners were asked where their dogs sleep. The results are shown as percents.

a. What percent of the people responded "Other"?

b. What percent of the people did *not* respond "Dog bed"?

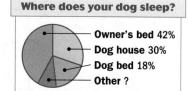

Where does your dog sleep?

- Owner's bed 42%
- Dog house 30%
- Dog bed 18%
- Other ?

Solution

a. The circle graph represents 100%. The sum of the percents given is $42\% + 30\% + 18\% = 90\%$, so the "Other" part is $100\% - 90\% = 10\%$.

b. The percent of people who did not respond "Dog bed" is $100\% - 18\% = 82\%$.

Your turn now Write the percent as a decimal and a fraction.

4. 5% **5.** 75% **6.** 20% **7.** 3.5%

$0.05, \frac{5}{100} = \frac{1}{20}$ $0.75, \frac{75}{100} = \frac{3}{4}$ $0.20, \frac{20}{100} = \frac{1}{5}$ $0.035, \frac{3.5}{100} = \frac{7}{200}$

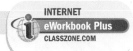
INTERNET
eWorkbook Plus
CLASSZONE.COM

③ APPLY

ASSIGNMENT GUIDE

Basic Course
Day 1: EP p. 711 Exs. 24–27;
pp. 397–398 Exs. 8–18, 34–37
Day 2: pp. 397–398 Exs. 19–30,
38–40

Average Course
Day 1: pp. 397–398 Exs. 8–18,
28–30, 40, 41
Day 2: pp. 397–398 Exs. 19–27,
34–39

Advanced Course
Day 1: pp. 397–398 Exs. 8–18,
28–31*
Day 2: pp. 397–398 Exs. 19–27,
32–35*, 40, 41

Block
pp. 397–398 Exs. 8–30, 34–41

Getting Ready to Practice

6. 48%, 0.48, $\frac{48}{100} = \frac{12}{25}$

11. forty-two hundredths, 42%,
12. six hundredths, 6%
13. fifty-seven hundredths, 57%
14. seventy-four hundredths, 74%
15. twenty-eight hundredths, 28%
16. nineteen hundredths, 19%
17. two-hundred hundredths, 200%
18. fifty-two-point-eight hundredths, 52.8%

1. **Vocabulary** When you write a percent as a fraction, you rewrite the percent using a denominator of _?_. **100**

Write the number in words and as a percent.

2. $\frac{11}{100}$ eleven hundredths, 11% **3.** $\frac{81}{100}$ eighty-one hundredths, 81% **4.** 0.04 four hundredths, 4% **5.** 0.63 sixty-three hundredths, 63%

6. Write *forty-eight hundredths* as a percent, a decimal, and a fraction.
See margin.

7. **Walking to School** In one town, 20 out of 100 students walk to school. What percent of students walk to school? **20% of the students**

Practice and Problem Solving

HELP with Homework

Example	Exercises
1	8–10, 23–24
2	11–18
3	19–22
4	25–27

Online Resources
CLASSZONE.COM
· More Examples
· eTutorial Plus

Each small square in the model represents 1% $\left(\text{or } \frac{1}{100}\right)$. **Represent the number of shaded squares as a percent, decimal, and fraction.**

A 8.

9.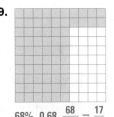

10.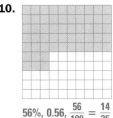

15%, 0.15, $\frac{15}{100} = \frac{3}{20}$

68%, 0.68, $\frac{68}{100} = \frac{17}{25}$

56%, 0.56, $\frac{56}{100} = \frac{14}{25}$

Write the number in words and as a percent. 11–18. See margin.

11. 0.42   **12.** 0.06   **13.** 0.57   **14.** 0.74

15. $\frac{28}{100}$ **16.** $\frac{19}{100}$ **17.** $\frac{200}{100}$ **18.** $\frac{52.8}{100}$

Match the percent with its equivalent decimal or fraction.

19. 34% B   **20.** 40% C   **21.** 85% D   **22.** 17% A

A. 0.17   **B.** $\frac{17}{50}$ **C.** 0.4   **D.** $\frac{17}{20}$

23. **Exercise** Of 100 people surveyed, 36 said they exercise daily. Write this result as a percent, a decimal, and a fraction. 36%, 0.36, $\frac{36}{100} = \frac{9}{25}$

24. **Explain** On a necklace of 100 beads, 45 of the beads are round. The rest of the beads are rectangular. What percent of the beads are round? What percent are rectangular? How did you find your answers?
45%; 55%. *Sample answer:* $\frac{45}{100}$ is 45%; subtracted 45 from 100 to get 55%.

EXTRA PRACTICE
- Student Edition, p. 715
- Chapter 8 Resource Book, pp. 44–46
- Test and Practice Generator

 TRANSPARENCY

Even-numbered answers are available on transparencies.

HOMEWORK CHECK

When you review students' homework for this lesson, go over the following exercises to check understanding of key concepts.
Basic: 8, 11, 19, 23, 25
Average: 8, 12, 20, 23, 26
Advanced: 10, 13, 21, 24, 27

 COMMON ERROR

In Exercise 11, be sure students use a hyphen in "forty-two hundredths" to distinguish it from "forty two-hundredths," which would be $\frac{40}{200}$.

4 ASSESS

ASSESSMENT RESOURCES

For more assessment resources, see:
- Assessment Book
- Test and Practice Generator

MINI-QUIZ

1. At a dog show, 18 of the 100 dogs won a ribbon. Write that ratio as a percent, a decimal, and a fraction. **18%; 0.18; $\frac{9}{50}$**

2. Write each number in the given form or forms.
   a. Write 0.58 in words and as a percent. **fifty-eight hundredths; 58%**
   b. Write 23.8% as a decimal. **0.238**
   c. Write 40% as a fraction. **$\frac{2}{5}$**
   d. Write $\frac{2}{100}$ in words and as a percent. **two hundredths; 2%**

5 FOLLOW-UP

RETEACHING/REMEDIATION
- Study Guide in Chapter 8 Resource Book, pp. 47–48
- Tutor Place, Ratio, Proportion, and Percent Cards 7–9
- eTutorial Plus Online
- Extra Practice, p. 715
- Lesson Practice in Chapter 8 Resource Book, pp. 44–46

CHALLENGE/ENRICHMENT
- Challenge Practice in Chapter 8 Resource Book, p. 49
- Teacher's Edition, p. 370F

ENGLISH LEARNER SUPPORT
- Spanish Study Guide
- Multi-Language Glossary
- Chapter Audio Summaries CDs

398

Computer Use The graph shows the results of a survey in which people from 10 to 14 years old were asked how many days a week they use their computer.

B **25. Critical Thinking** What percent of those surveyed use their computers 4 or more days a week? Explain. **See margin.**

26. What percent of those surveyed use their computers 1 day or less? **19%**

27. Rewrite the percents for all four sections as decimals and as fractions. **See margin.**

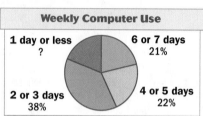

Weekly Computer Use

1 day or less ?
6 or 7 days 21%
2 or 3 days 38%
4 or 5 days 22%

Number Sense Copy and complete the statement using <, >, or =.

28. 50% ? 0.05   **>**   **29.** 14% ? $\frac{1.4}{100}$ **>**   **30.** 0.4 ? 40%   **=**

Challenge The ratio of students who play soccer to all students is given. Find the percent of students who do *not* play soccer.

C **31.** 40 out of 100   **60%**   **32.** 110 out of 200   **45%**   **33.** 60 out of 300   **80%**

25. 43%; add 22% for 4 or 5 days to 21% for 6 or 7 days to get 43%.

27. 1 day or less: 0.19, $\frac{19}{100}$;

2 or 3 days: 0.38, $\frac{38}{100} = \frac{19}{50}$;

4 or 5 days: 0.22, $\frac{22}{100} = \frac{11}{50}$;

6 or 7 days: 0.21, $\frac{21}{100}$

Mixed Review

Sample answer: $\frac{6}{10}, \frac{9}{15}$

34. Write two fractions that are equivalent to $\frac{3}{5}$. *(Lesson 5.3)*

35. A basketball game begins at 6:30 P.M. and ends at 8:45 P.M. How long does the game last? *(Lesson 6.6)* **2 h 15 min**

Basic Skills Order the numbers from least to greatest.

36. 2.4, 1.7, 2.9   **37.** 1.57, 4.1, 3.8   **38.** 5.3, 3.5, 5.03   **39.** 9.2, 9, 9.4
1.7, 2.4, 2.9   **1.57, 3.8, 4.1**   **3.5, 5.03, 5.3**   **9, 9.2, 9.4**

Test-Taking Practice

INTERNET
State Test Practice
CLASSZONE.COM

41. 42%. *Sample answer:* Add the number of students who will be singing and the number who will be playing an instrument and subtract that sum from 100.

40. Multiple Choice Write 47 out of 100 as a percent.   **B**
   A. 4.7%   **B.** 47%   **C.** 470%   **D.** 4700%

41. Short Response Out of 100 students surveyed about the Spring Music Festival, 36 said they will play an instrument, 22 said they will sing, 19 said they will run the equipment, and the rest said they will be in the audience. What percent of the students will *not* be singing or playing an instrument? Show how you found the answer.

LESSON 8.6

Percents, Decimals, and Fractions

BEFORE	▶ Now	WHY?
You wrote percents as fractions and decimals.	You'll write fractions and decimals as percents.	So you can find the percent of Earth that is desert in Ex. 28.

Word Watch
Review Words
decimal, p. 108
fraction, p. 228
percent, p. 395

In the Real World

Volleyball In a volleyball game, a player's serves must land in a certain region to be playable. What percent of serves did Maria get "in" for today's games? What percent did she get "in" so far this season?

You can use the fraction of Maria's serves that she got "in" to find the percent that she got "in." To do this, you write an equivalent fraction with a denominator of 100.

Serving Record

Maria	Serves "in"	Total serves
Today	4	10
Season	17	25

EXAMPLE 1 Writing Fractions as Percents

To answer the questions above, first write each record as a fraction. Then write an equivalent fraction with a denominator of 100 to find the percent.

a. $\dfrac{4}{10}$ ← serves "in" today
       ← total serves today

$$4 \times 10$$

$$\frac{4}{10} = \frac{40}{100}$$

$$10 \times 10$$

$$\frac{40}{100} = 40\%$$

ANSWER Maria got 40% of her serves "in" today.

b. $\dfrac{17}{25}$ ← serves "in" this season
        ← total serves this season

$$17 \times 4$$

$$\frac{17}{25} = \frac{68}{100}$$

$$25 \times 4$$

$$\frac{68}{100} = 68\%$$

ANSWER Maria got 68% of her serves "in" so far this season.

Your turn now Write the fraction as a percent.

1. $\dfrac{3}{4}$ 75%   **2.** $\dfrac{7}{10}$ 70%   **3.** $\dfrac{7}{20}$ 35%   **4.** $\dfrac{9}{50}$ 18%

NCTM CURRICULUM STANDARDS
Standard 1: Understand ways of representing numbers; Understand relationships among numbers
Standard 6: Solve problems in math and other contexts

Lesson 8.6   Percents, Decimals, and Fractions   **399**

---

① PLAN

SKILL CHECK
Write an equivalent fraction with a denominator of 100.

1. $\dfrac{3}{5}$ $\dfrac{60}{100}$

2. 0.15 $\dfrac{15}{100}$

3. 47% $\dfrac{47}{100}$

4. 0.07 $\dfrac{7}{100}$

5. 153% $\dfrac{153}{100}$

LESSON OBJECTIVE

Write fractions and decimals as percents.

PACING

Suggested Number of Days
Basic Course: 2 days
Average Course: 2 days
Advanced Course: 2 days
Block: 1 block

TEACHING RESOURCES

For a complete list of Teaching Resources, see page 370B.

 TRANSPARENCY

Warm-Up Exercises for this lesson are available on a transparency.

② TEACH

MOTIVATING THE LESSON

Describe a basketball game in which one player made 3 out of 4 free throws and another made 10 out of 15. Ask students how they might decide which player did better at free throw shooting. Some students might suggest using percents.

EXAMPLE **2** **Writing Decimals as Percents**

Write the decimal as a percent.

a. $0.06 = \frac{6}{100}$ 0.06 is six hundredths.

$= 6\%$

b. $0.6 = \frac{6}{10}$ 0.6 is six tenths.

$= \frac{60}{100}$ Multiply the numerator and denominator by 10 to get a denominator of 100.

$= 60\%$

c. $0.025 = \frac{25}{1000}$ 0.025 is twenty-five thousandths.

$= \frac{2.5}{100}$ Divide the numerator and denominator by 10 to get a denominator of 100.

$= 2.5\%$

HELP with Solving

Remember that you can divide by 10 by moving the decimal point 1 place to the left. In part (c) of Example 2, $25 \div 10 = 2.5$.

Using Decimals If the denominator of a fraction is not a factor of 100, it may be easiest to write the fraction as a decimal first.

EXAMPLE **3** **Using Decimals to Write Percents**

Field Trip You have attended 5 out of 8 Science Club meetings. You must attend at least 60% of the meetings to go on a trip. Can you go?

Solution

$\frac{5}{8} = 0.625$ Divide 5 by 8 to write the fraction as a decimal.

$= \frac{625}{1000}$ 0.625 is 625 thousandths.

$= \frac{62.5}{100}$ Divide the numerator and denominator by 10 to get a denominator of 100.

$= 62.5\%$

ANSWER Because 62.5% > 60%, you can go on the field trip.

Your turn now **Write the decimal or fraction as a percent.**

5. 0.3 **30%**   **6.** 0.105 **10.5%**   **7.** $\frac{3}{8}$ **37.5%**   **8.** $\frac{9}{40}$ **22.5%**

Common Percents, Decimals, and Fractions

Fifths	Fourths	Thirds
$20\% = 0.2 = \frac{1}{5}$	$25\% = 0.25 = \frac{1}{4}$	$33\frac{1}{3}\% = 0.\overline{3} = \frac{1}{3}$
$40\% = 0.4 = \frac{2}{5}$	$50\% = 0.5 = \frac{1}{2}$	$66\frac{2}{3}\% = 0.\overline{6} = \frac{2}{3}$
$60\% = 0.6 = \frac{3}{5}$	$75\% = 0.75 = \frac{3}{4}$	
$80\% = 0.8 = \frac{4}{5}$		

EXAMPLE 4 **Using Common Relationships**

Order the numbers $\frac{3}{4}$, 80%, and 0.71 from least to greatest.

Write the numbers as decimals and graph them on a number line.

0.71 $\frac{3}{4} = 0.75$ $80\% = 0.8$

0.70 0.72 0.74 0.76 0.78 0.80 0.82

ANSWER An ordered list of the numbers is 0.71, $\frac{3}{4}$, and 80%.

 8.6 Exercises

More Practice, p. 715

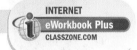
INTERNET
eWorkbook Plus
CLASSZONE.COM

Getting Ready to Practice

1. Vocabulary What commonly used percent is equal to 0.6? **60%**

Match the decimal or fraction with its equivalent percent.

2. 0.17 **D**   **3.** 0.05 **E**   **4.** $\frac{17}{50}$ **A**   **5.** 0.5 **B**   **6.** $\frac{3}{5}$ **C**

A. 34%   **B.** 50%   **C.** 60%   **D.** 17%   **E.** 5%

7. Sewing A survey asked 50 students if they sew. Eighteen students responded "yes." What percent of the students surveyed do *not* sew?
64% do not sew

Lesson 8.6   Percents, Decimals, and Fractions   **401**

MATH REASONING

Students should be able to reverse the procedures in Examples 1 and 2 to write a percent as a fraction or as a decimal.

EXTRA EXAMPLES

Example 4 Order the numbers $\frac{5}{6}$, 82%, and 0.88 from least to greatest. **An ordered list of numbers is 82%, $\frac{5}{6}$, 0.88.**

 TRANSPARENCY

A support transparency is available for Example 4.

NOTETAKING

Have students copy the Common Percents, Decimals, and Fractions table into their notebooks. Then ask students to add the percent and decimal equivalents for $\frac{1}{8}$, $\frac{3}{8}$, $\frac{5}{8}$, and $\frac{7}{8}$ to their lists.

 CONCEPT CHECK

How can you write a fraction or a decimal as a percent? **To write a fraction or a decimal as a percent, write the number as a fraction with a denominator of 100.**

 DAILY PUZZLER

One fraction is 200% of a second fraction, and the sum of the fractions can be written as 0.75. Find the two fractions. **$\frac{1}{4}$, $\frac{1}{2}$**

ASSIGNMENT GUIDE

Basic Course
Day 1: EP p. 710 Exs. 10–15; pp. 402–403 Exs. 8–15, 28, 30–40
Day 2: pp. 402–403 Exs. 16–27, 43, 45–55

Average Course
Day 1: pp. 402–403 Exs. 8–15, 28, 30–35, 45–50
Day 2: pp. 402–403 Exs. 16–24, 29, 36–43, 53–55

Advanced Course
Day 1: pp. 402–403 Exs. 12–15, 30–33, 36–40, 45–50
Day 2: pp. 402–403 Exs. 16–29, 41–44*, 55

Block
pp. 402–403 Exs. 8–24, 28–43, 45–50, 53–55

EXTRA PRACTICE

- Student Edition, p. 715
- Chapter 8 Resource Book, pp. 54–56
- Test and Practice Generator

 TRANSPARENCY

Even-numbered answers are available on transparencies. A support transparency is available for Exercises 22–27.

HOMEWORK CHECK

When you review students' homework for this lesson, go over the following exercises to check understanding of key concepts.
Basic: 8, 12, 16, 20, 22
Average: 9, 13, 17, 20, 23
Advanced: 15, 19, 21, 25, 41

22–27. See Additional Answers beginning on page AA1.

HELP with **Homework**

Example	Exercises
1	8–11, 20–21, 28
2	12–15
3	16–19, 29
4	22–27, 41

 **Online Resources**
CLASSZONE.COM
· More Examples
· eTutorial Plus

Practice and Problem Solving

Write the fraction or decimal as a percent.

A **8.** $\frac{1}{2}$ 50% **9.** $\frac{13}{20}$ 65% **10.** $\frac{3}{50}$ 6% **11.** $\frac{7}{25}$ 28%

12. 0.92 92% **13.** 0.2 20% **14.** 0.02 2% **15.** 0.084 8.4%

16. $\frac{261}{1000}$ 26.1% **17.** $\frac{587}{1000}$ 58.7% **18.** $\frac{1}{8}$ 12.5% **19.** $\frac{3}{200}$ 1.5%

20. Write two fifths as a percent. 40%

21. Write nine tenths as a percent. 90%

Use a number line to order the numbers from least to greatest.
22–27. See margin.

22. 68%, $\frac{67}{100}$, 0.64 **23.** $\frac{1}{4}$, 15%, 0.16 **24.** $\frac{17}{20}$, 82%, 0.88

25. 50%, 0.77, $\frac{7}{10}$, $\frac{2}{3}$ **26.** $\frac{4}{5}$, 0.72, 79%, $\frac{3}{4}$ **27.** $\frac{1}{3}$, 33%, 34%, 0.3

28. **Deserts** Deserts cover about $\frac{1}{5}$ of Earth's land surface. What percent of Earth's land surface is desert? 20%

29. **Soccer** A survey at the Roosevelt Middle School said $\frac{11}{40}$ of the sixth grade students named soccer as their favorite sport. What percent of the sixth grade students named soccer as their favorite sport? 27.5%

Geometry **Find the percent of the figure that is shaded. Round to the nearest whole percent.**

B **30.** 67% **31.** 56%

Choose a Method **Tell whether you would use a *calculator*, *paper and pencil*, or *mental math* to write the fraction as a percent. Round to the nearest whole percent.**

32–35. Methods may vary.
32. mental math; 30%
33. mental math; 36%
34. calculator; 29%
35. calculator; 44%

32. $\frac{3}{10}$ **33.** $\frac{9}{25}$ **34.** $\frac{2}{7}$ **35.** $\frac{4}{9}$

Write the decimal as a percent.

36. 1.25 125% **37.** 3.5 350% **38.** 8.2 820% **39.** 0.004 0.4%

40. **Mental Math** Copy and complete: If $\frac{3}{20}$ = 15%, then $\frac{6}{20}$ = ? %. 30

41. Quiz Scores On their math quiz papers, John's score is written as
"$\frac{22}{25}$ correct," Sam's score is "0.87 correct," and Vince's score is
"84.5% correct." Who received the highest score? the lowest score?

John; Vince

42. Writing What percent of a meter is 5 centimeters? What percent of a
meter is 5 millimeters? Explain how you found your answers. **See margin.**

Babies' Names **In Exercises 43 and 44, use the information below.**
In the United States in 2000, Michael and Matthew represented about
2.9% of all the names for newborn males. Madison and Ashley
represented about 1.9% of all the names for newborn females.

C 43. Out of 1000 male babies born in the year 2000, about how many have
the name Michael or Matthew? **29**

44. Challenge Out of 1000 female babies born in the year 2000, about how
many *do not* have the name Madison or Ashley? **981**

Mixed Review

45. A giant anteater eats 9000 ants in 3 hours. Find the unit rate.
(Lesson 8.2) $\frac{3000 \text{ ants}}{1 \text{ h}}$

Write the percent as a decimal and a fraction. *(Lesson 8.5)*

46. 2% $0.02; \frac{1}{50}$ **47.** 37% $0.37; \frac{37}{100}$ **48.** 75% $0.75; \frac{3}{4}$ **49.** 96% $0.96; \frac{24}{25}$

Choose a Strategy **Use a strategy from
the list to solve the following problem.
Explain your choice of strategy.**

> **Problem Solving Strategies**
> ▪ Guess, Check, and Revise
> ▪ Make a List or Table
> ▪ Work Backward
> ▪ Solve a Related Problem

50. On a shopping trip, you spend $10.75
at one store. At another store, you
spend $16.30. You have $4.35 left.
How much did you start with? $31.40. *Sample answer:* I used Work
Backward because I started with what
was left and added the amounts spent.

Basic Skills **Find the product.**

51. $2 \times 7.5 \times 10$
150
52. $4 \times 50 \times 0.7$
140
53. 0.3×6.25
1.875
54. 0.005×10
0.05

Test-Taking Practice

55. Extended Response A rectangle is 10 meters long and 4 meters wide.
You create a new rectangle by multiplying the length and width by 2.
Find the area of each rectangle. Write a fraction that compares the area
of the small rectangle to the area of the large rectangle. What percent of
the large rectangle can be covered by the small rectangle?

$10 \times 4 = 40 \text{ m}^2, 20 \times 8 = 160 \text{ m}^2; \frac{40}{160} = \frac{1}{4}; \frac{1}{4} = 25\%$

42. 5%; 0.5%.
Sample answer:
5 centimeters is $\frac{5}{100}$ of
a meter which is 5%;
5 millimeters is $\frac{5}{1000}$ of
a meter, or $\frac{0.5}{100}$ of a meter,
which is 0.5%.

ASSESSMENT RESOURCES

For more assessment resources, see:
• Assessment Book
• Test and Practice Generator

MINI-QUIZ

1. Write each number as a percent.
  a. $\frac{9}{10}$ 90% **b.** $\frac{18}{40}$ 45%
  c. 0.1 10% **d.** 0.04 4%

2. Order $\frac{2}{5}$, 0.28, 37% from least
to greatest. 0.28, 37%, $\frac{2}{5}$

3. A club has 20 members, and 13
are at a meeting. The club's rules
say that 60% of the members
must be present to vote. Can the
members vote during the meeting?
Explain. Yes; $\frac{13}{20} = 65\%$ and
65% > 60%.

5 FOLLOW-UP

RETEACHING/REMEDIATION

• Study Guide in Chapter 8
  Resource Book, pp. 57–58
• Tutor Place, Ratio, Proportion,
  and Percent Cards 9, 10
• eTutorial Plus Online
• Extra Practice, p. 715
• Lesson Practice in Chapter 8
  Resource Book, pp. 54–56

CHALLENGE/ENRICHMENT

• Challenge Practice in Chapter 8
  Resource Book, p. 60
• Teacher's Edition, p. 370F

ENGLISH LEARNER SUPPORT

• Spanish Study Guide
• Multi-Language Glossary
• Chapter Audio Summaries CDs

403

1 PLAN

STRATEGY BACKGROUND

The purpose of the strategy Solve a Simpler Problem is to use smaller numbers or simpler diagrams to identify a pattern that can then be applied to the original problem. Several examples of simpler problems need to be considered to make sure that the pattern observed in one case does in fact extend to other cases and is applicable to the original problem.

2 TEACH

GUIDING STUDENTS' WORK

To help students see the pattern in the simpler problem, have them solve two other simpler problems: finding the sum after 4 days and finding the sum after 8 days. Then have students move to Step 4 to check another example.

EXTRA EXAMPLES

Example Find the sum $2 + 4 + 6 + ... + 200$. The same pattern as the one in the given example can be used. The number of pairs is 50 and the sum for each pair is 202. The total is $(50)(202) = 10,100$.

8.7 Problem Solving Strategies

- Guess, Check, and Revise
- Draw a Diagram
- Perform an Experiment
- Make a List or Table
- Solve a Simpler Problem
- Work Backward
- Solve a Related Problem

Solve a Simpler Problem

Problem Your school is collecting money for a local charity. The first day, 1 dollar bill is placed in a jar. The second day, 2 dollar bills are added to the jar. The third day, 3 dollar bills are added to the jar, and so on. How much money will be in the jar after 100 days?

① Read and Understand

Read the problem carefully.

You need to know the total number of dollar bills in the jar to know the value.

② Make a Plan

Decide on a strategy to use.

Solve a simpler problem using fewer days. Look for a method you can then use with 100 days.

③ Solve the Problem

Reread the problem and solve a simpler problem.

First, find the total amount of money after only 6 days. Pair numbers to help find the total. What do you notice?

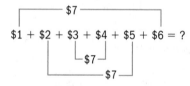

$$\$1 + \$2 + \$3 + \$4 + \$5 + \$6 = ?$$

The number of pairs is 3, which is half the number of days. The sum of each pair is $7, which is the sum of the first and last numbers. So, the amount after 6 days is 3($7) = $21.

Now apply this method to find $1 + $2 + ⋯ + $99 + $100, the amount of money in the jar after 100 days. There will be 50 pairs of numbers, each with a sum of $101.

ANSWER You will have collected $5050 after 100 days because 50($101) = $5050.

④ Look Back

To help you find the total or check a method for finding the total, you may want to try a second small number, such as 10 days.
$$\$1 + \$2 + \$3 + \$4 + \$5 + \$6 + \$7 + \$8 + \$9 + \$10 = 5(\$11) = \$55$$

NCTM CURRICULUM STANDARDS
Standard 2: Understand patterns
Standard 6: Solve problems in math and other contexts;
Apply/adapt strategies to solve problems

Practice the Strategy

Use the strategy *solve a simpler problem.*

1. **Lockers** The lockers at a city pool are numbered from 1 to 150. How many lockers from 1 to 50 will have a 2 in the number? How many lockers from 1 to 150 will have a 2 in the number? **14; 33**

2. **Estimation** You are buying a present for a friend. You spend $15.20 for a gift, $3.75 for a card, $6.90 for wrapping paper, and $2.05 for ribbon. Will $25 be enough money to buy all these items? Explain how you can use estimation to solve the problem. Then solve the problem. **See margin.**

3. **Large Sums** Find the sum of the first 100 odd whole numbers. **10,000**

$$1 + 3 + 5 + \cdots + 199 = \underline{\;?\;}$$

4. **Food Drive** Your class has collected 210 cans for a food drive. All the cans are the same size. You want to stack the cans in rows so that each row has 1 more can than the row above it, as shown below. If you put 20 cans in the bottom row, will you have enough cans so that you'll have 1 can in the top row? **yes**

5. **Ones' Digits** If you evaluate the power 8^{12}, what will the ones' digit be? **6**

Mixed Problem Solving

Use any strategy to solve the problem.

6. **Stained Glass** You are creating a stained glass border using the pattern below. What will be the shape of the 23rd figure in the pattern? **circle**

7. **School Supplies** You bought pencils and pens for $36. Packages of pencils cost $3. Packages of pens cost $5. How many packages of each type did you buy?
See margin.

8. **Paper** You have 20 rectangular pieces of colored paper that each measure 1 inch by 2 inches. Is it possible to arrange them to form a 5 inch by 8 inch rectangle with no gaps or overlaps? If so, show one possible arrangement. **Yes; see margin for art.**

9. **Dining Out** At a restaurant, you have a choice of a poultry dish, a vegetable, and a type of potato. How many different meals are possible? **18 different meals**

Daily Specials

Your choice of:

POULTRY
• Chicken or Turkey •

VEGETABLE
• Beans, Broccoli, or Zucchini •

POTATOES
• Mashed, Scalloped, or Baked •

MATH REASONING

To find the number of odd whole numbers in Exercise 3, students can use the expression $2n - 1$ and notice that for $n = 1, 2, 3, \ldots, 100$ the value of $2n - 1$ is $1, 3, 5, \ldots, 199$. Since n takes on 100 values, the number of odd whole numbers from 1 to 199 is 100.

SUGGESTED STRATEGIES

You may wish to suggest the following strategies for the problems in the Mixed Problem Solving:

• Exercise 6: Draw a Diagram; Make a List or Table; Make a Model
• Exercise 7: Guess, Check, and Revise; Make a List or Table
• Exercise 8: Draw a Diagram; Make a Model
• Exercise 9: Draw a Diagram; Make a List or Table

2. No; round each amount and add; $15.20 + $3.75 + $6.90 + $2.05 = $27.90, so $25 is not enough money.

7. 2 packages of pencils and 6 packages of pens, or 7 packages of pencils and 3 packages of pens

8. *Sample:*

LESSON OBJECTIVE

Multiply to find a percent of a number.

PACING

Suggested Number of Days
Basic Course: 2 days
Average Course: 2 days
Advanced Course: 2 days
Block: 1 block

TEACHING RESOURCES

For a complete list of Teaching Resources, see page 370B.

 TRANSPARENCY

Warm-Up Exercises for this lesson are available on a transparency.

 **TEACH**

MOTIVATING THE LESSON

Ask students if they have used a copier to reduce a photo. Ask how they might calculate the size of the reduced photo if they know the size of the original and the reduction percent.

1–4. Explanations may vary.

1. 24; change 50% to $\frac{1}{2}$ and multiply.

2. 9; change 20% to $\frac{1}{5}$ and multiply.

3. 4.5; change 9% to 0.09 and multiply.

4. 3.6; change 10% to 0.1 and multiply.

LESSON
8.7

Finding a Percent of a Number

BEFORE	▶ **Now**	**WHY?**
You multiplied whole numbers by decimals and fractions.	You'll multiply to find a percent of a number.	So you can estimate a tip, as in Ex. 22.

📓 **Word Watch**

interest, p. 408
principal, p. 408
annual interest rate, p. 408
simple interest, p. 408

Step 3. *Sample answer:* a, d; b, c; a and d were easier to find by changing the percents to fractions because the denominator of the fraction easily divides into 72. b and c were easier to find by changing the percents to decimals because the fractions were not easy to use.

🔵 **HELP** with **Notetaking**

You may want to include Example 1 in your notes to illustrate when a fraction or when a decimal may be the more convenient form of a percent to use. In part (a), $\frac{3}{4}$ is compatible with 60.

In part (b), you can multiply by 0.1 easily using mental math.

Activity You can change a percent to a fraction or a decimal to find a percent of a number.

Recall that "of" means "multiply." To find 50% of 8, find $\frac{1}{2} \times 8$ or 0.5×8.

① Write the percent as a fraction and multiply to find the percent of the number.

a. 25% of 72   **b.** 10% of 72   **c.** 62% of 72   **d.** $33\frac{1}{3}$% of 72
        18              $7\frac{1}{5}$ or 7.2 $44\frac{16}{25}$ or 44.64   24

② Write the percents in Step 1 as decimals to find the percent of the number.

③ Compare Steps 1 and 2. Which answers were easier to find by changing the percents to fractions? Which answers were easier to find by changing the percents to decimals? Explain.

Finding a Percent of a Number The activity above suggests two ways to find a percent of a number.

• Change the percent to a fraction and multiply by the number.

• Change the percent to a decimal and multiply by the number.

EXAMPLE 1 Finding a Percent of a Number

a. Find 75% of 60. Use a fraction.   **b.** Find 10% of 74. Use a decimal.

$$75\% \text{ of } 60 = \frac{3}{4} \times 60$$

$$= \frac{180}{4}$$

$$= 45$$

ANSWER 75% of 60 is 45.

$$10\% \text{ of } 74 = 0.1 \times 74$$

$$= 7.4$$

ANSWER 10% of 74 is 7.4.

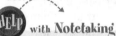 **Your turn now** Find the percent of the number. Explain your method.

1. 50% of 48   **2.** 20% of 45   **3.** 9% of 50   **4.** 10% of 36
                                                            1–4. See margin.

NCTM CURRICULUM STANDARDS
Standard 1: Make reasonable estimates
Standard 2: Represent situations using algebraic symbols
Standard 6: Solve problems in math and other contexts

ACTIVITY

Goal Students find a percent of a number by changing the percent to a fraction or a decimal before multiplying.

Key Discovery You can find a percent of a number by multiplying.

EXAMPLE 2 **Finding a Discount**

Sneaker Sale The regular price of a pair of sneakers is $40. The sale price is 25% off the regular price. What is the sale price?

(1 Find the discount. $\quad$ 25% of $40 = \frac{1}{4} \times \$40 = \$10$

(2 Subtract the discount $\quad$ $\$40 - \$10 = \$30$
from the regular price.

ANSWER The sale price of the sneakers is $30.

EXAMPLE 3 **Finding the Sales Tax**

Feeding Your Dog You are buying dog food that costs $8.50. There is a 6% sales tax. What is the total amount of your purchase?

(1 Find the sales tax. $\quad$ 6% of $8.50 = 0.06 \times \$8.50 = \$.51$

(2 Add the sales tax to the $\quad$ $\$8.50 + \$.51 = \$9.01$
cost of the item.

ANSWER The total amount of your purchase is $9.01.

What do you think?

Animals

Feeding Your Dog

In 2000, there were about 60,000,000 dogs in United States households. That year, about $7,300,000,000 was spent on dog food. About how much was spent on each dog? **about $120**

EXAMPLE 4 **Solving a Simpler Problem**

Leaving a Tip Your bill in a restaurant is $23.78. You want to leave a tip of about 15%. Use simpler percents and mental math to estimate the amount of the tip.

(1 Round the bill to the nearest dollar. $\quad$ $\$23.78 \approx \$24.00$

(2 Find 10% of the bill. $\quad$ $0.1 \times \$24 = \$2.40$

(3 Find 5% of the bill. $\quad$ $\frac{1}{2} \times \$2.40 = \$1.20$
It is half of 10% of the bill.

(4 Add the partial tips. $\quad$ $\$2.40 + \$1.20 = \$3.60$

ANSWER A 15% tip for a $23.78 bill is about $3.60.

Your turn now **Find the cost described.**

5. A book's regular price is $19.95. Find the cost after a 20% discount. **$15.96**

6. The price of a cat toy is $9.50. Find the cost with a sales tax of 8%. **$10.26**

CONCEPT CHECK

Describe two ways to find a percent of a number. **Change the percent to a fraction and multiply by the number; change the percent to a decimal and multiply by the number.**

 DAILY PUZZLER

What is 75% of $\frac{2}{5}$ of 0.68? Write your result as a percent, a decimal, and a fraction. **20.4%, 0.204, $\frac{51}{250}$**

Simple Interest When you save money at a bank, you *earn interest*. When you borrow money, you *pay interest*. **Interest** is the amount paid for the use of money. The amount you save or borrow is the **principal**. The **annual interest rate** is the percent of the principal you earn or pay per year.

Simple Interest Formula

Interest paid only on the principal is **simple interest**.

Words $\dfrac{\text{Simple}}{\text{interest}}$ = Principal · $\dfrac{\text{Annual}}{\text{interest rate}}$ · $\dfrac{\text{Time}}{\text{in years}}$

Algebra $I = Prt$

EXAMPLE 5   **Finding Simple Interest**

Savings You deposit $75 in an account. The annual interest rate is 4%. How much simple interest will you earn on that money in 1 year?

$I = Prt$ Write the simple interest formula.

$= 75\,(0.04)(1)$ Substitute values. Write 4% as a decimal.

$= 3$ Multiply.

ANSWER You will earn $3 in simple interest in 1 year.

 **8.7** **Exercises**
More Practice, p. 715

INTERNET
eWorkbook Plus
CLASSZONE.COM

Getting Ready to Practice

1. **Vocabulary** What does each variable in the formula $I = Prt$ represent?
   I = simple interest; P = principal; r = annual interest rate; t = time in years

Find the percent of the number.

2. 60% of 60 **36**   3. 45% of 20 **9**   4. 85% of 12 **10.2**   5. 40% of 150 **60**

6. **Leaving a Tip** Your bill in a restaurant is $29.87. Use mental math to estimate a tip of 15%. **$4.50**

HELP with Homework

Example	Exercises
1	7–19
2	20, 27–29, 38
3	21, 38
4	22, 36
5	23–26

Online Resources
CLASSZONE.COM
· More Examples
· eTutorial Plus

Practice and Problem Solving

Find the percent of the number.

A **7.** 50% of 84 42 **8.** 25% of 80 20 **9.** 10% of 100 10 **10.** 11% of 4 0.44

11. 75% of 72 54 **12.** 60% of 15 9 **13.** 18% of 45 8.1 **14.** 83% of 20 16.6

15. 31% of 120 37.2 **16.** 65% of 150 97.5 **17.** $33\frac{1}{3}$% of 63 21 **18.** $66\frac{2}{3}$% of 9 6

19. Find the Error Describe and correct the error in the solution.

$$\times \quad 1\% \text{ of } 400 = \frac{1}{10} \times 400 = \frac{400}{10} = 40$$

1% is $\frac{1}{100}$.
The answer should be
$\frac{1}{100} \times 400 = \frac{400}{100} = 4$.

20. Theater Your class is going to a play. Tickets are usually $20, but because of a group discount, each ticket will be 12% cheaper. How much will each ticket cost? $17.60

21. Video Games You are buying a video game that costs $50. There is a 5% sales tax. What is the total amount of your purchase? $52.50

22. Pizza You and your friends are eating at a pizza shop after school. The bill is $17.53. You want to leave about 15% for a tip. Estimate the amount of the tip. $2.70

Algebra Find the simple interest I = Prt for the given values.

23. $P = \$275$, $r = 4\%$, $t = 5$ years $55 **24.** $P = \$320$, $r = 3\%$, $t = 4$ years $38.40

25. $P = \$84$, $r = 2\%$, $t = 3$ years $5.04 **26.** $P = \$112$, $r = 2.5\%$, $t = 2$ years $5.60

Mental Math A pair of jeans costs $32. Use mental math to find the discount described.

B **27.** a 10% discount $3.20 **28.** a 25% discount $8.00 **29.** a 40% discount $12.80

Estimation Estimate the percent of the number. 30–35. Estimates may vary.

30. 11% of 400 40 **31.** 75% of 804 600 **32.** 48% of 7.9 4

33. 19% of 205 40 **34.** 6% of 62 3 **35.** 89% of 80.1 72

36. Writing Explain how you can use mental math to estimate the amount of a 20% tip on a restaurant bill of $43.72. *Sample answer: Round $43.72 to $44.00 and find 10% of $44.00, which is $4.40. 20% is two times $4.40, or $8.80.*

37. Critical Thinking If you know that 20% of a number is 16, how can you use this information to find 40% of the number? 60% of the number?
double the answer; triple the answer

38. Clothing A sweater is on sale for 25% off. There is a 7% sales tax. If the regular price is $56, how much will you pay for the sweater? $44.94

3 APPLY

ASSIGNMENT GUIDE
Basic Course
Day 1: EP p. 714 Exs. 5–8;
pp. 409–410 Exs. 7–12, 20,
30–35, 43–49
Day 2: pp. 409–410 Exs. 13–18,
21–29, 37–40, 50

Average Course
Day 1: pp. 409–410 Exs 7–10,
18–20, 33–35, 43–51
Day 2: pp. 409–410 Exs. 11–14,
21–29, 36–41

Advanced Course
Day 1: pp. 409–410 Exs. 11–18,
27–29, 33–35, 43–45
Day 2: pp. 409–410 Exs. 19–26,
36–42*, 50, 51

Block
pp. 409–410 Exs. 7–14, 18–29,
33–41, 43–51

EXTRA PRACTICE
• Student Edition, p. 715
• Chapter 8 Resource Book,
pp. 64–66
• Test and Practice Generator

 TRANSPARENCY
Even-numbered answers are available on transparencies.

HOMEWORK CHECK
When you review students' homework for this lesson, go over the following exercises to check understanding of key concepts.
Basic: 7, 20, 21, 22, 23
Average: 8, 21, 22, 24, 27
Advanced: 11, 21, 25, 29, 36

409

MINI-QUIZ

1. What is 81% of 30? **24.3**
2. Find the sales tax and total cost on a purchase of $12.50 if the sales tax is 4%. **$.50, $13.00**
3. Find the discount and sale price if the sale price is 22% off a regular price of $21.50. **$4.73, $16.77**
4. Find the amount of simple interest if the principal is $400, the interest rate is 4.5%, and the period is 3 years. **$54.00**

5 FOLLOW-UP

RETEACHING/REMEDIATION

- Study Guide in Chapter 8 Resource Book, pp. 67–68
- Tutor Place, Ratio, Proportion, and Percent Card 11
- eTutorial Plus Online
- Extra Practice, p. 715
- Lesson Practice in Chapter 8 Resource Book, pp. 64–66

CHALLENGE/ENRICHMENT

- Challenge Practice in Chapter 8 Resource Book, p. 70
- Teacher's Edition, p. 370F

ENGLISH LEARNER SUPPORT

- Spanish Study Guide
- Multi-Language Glossary
- Chapter Audio Summaries CDs

Extended Problem Solving Use this information in Exercises 39–41.
A sporting goods store offers a package of hockey equipment for 20% less than the cost of the same items sold separately. The costs of the items are shown in the table. You already have a helmet.

Item	Price
helmet	$46
shoulder pads	$58
shin guards	$46
elbow pads	$30
skates	$110

39. Find the total of the costs without the helmet. Then add 6% sales tax. **$244; $258.64**

40. Find the cost of all the equipment. Then find the cost of this package after the 20% discount. Then add 6% sales tax. **$290; $232; $245.92**

41. **Compare** Which will cost you less: buying the package or buying just the equipment you don't have? **buying the package**

C 42. **Challenge** On June 15, you deposited $120 in an account with an annual interest rate of 4%. It is now December 15 of the same year. How much simple interest has your money earned in that time? **$2.40**

Mixed Review

Find the mean, median, mode(s), and range. *(Lesson 2.8)*

43. 4, 7, 5, 26, 10, 8, 10 **10; 8; 10; 22**   44. 3, 6, 1, 9, 10, 9, 8, 3, 16, 5 **7; 7; 3 and 9; 15**

45. An engineer looks at a blueprint of a bridge that has a scale of 1 cm : 20 m. On the blueprint, the span of the bridge is 35 centimeters. What is the actual span of the bridge? *(Lesson 8.4)* **700 m**

Basic Skills Find the sum or difference.

46. 8.8 + 54 **62.8**   47. 1.45 + 7.8 **9.25**   48. 0.79 − 0.48 **0.31**   49. 58 − 45.3 **12.7**

INTERNET
State Test Practice
CLASSZONE.COM

Test-Taking Practice

50. **Multiple Choice** You have a stamp collection with 120 stamps. The circle graph shows the percent of stamps from each country. How many of your stamps are from Canada? **C**

Stamp Collection
- United States 50%
- Canada 20%
- Mexico 15%
- France 10%
- China 5%

A. 6 stamps   B. 18 stamps

C. 24 stamps   D. 60 stamps

51. **Short Response** You have a coupon for a 15% discount off any item in a store. You'll pay 5% sales tax on the discounted price. How much will you pay for a shirt whose regular price is $16.50? Explain how you found your answer. **$14.73; find the discounted price and then find the sales tax on that amount.**

CALCULATOR

8.7 Technology Activity

Finding a Percent of a Number

GOAL Use a calculator to find a percent of a number.

Example You deposit $100 in an account with an annual interest rate of 5.25%. How much simple interest will you earn on that money in 7 years?

You can use the percent feature, **2nd** [%], to find a percent of a number. The percent feature can often be found above the left parenthesis key, **(**.

Solution

Use the formula for simple interest $I = Prt$ with $P = \$100$, $r = 5.25\%$, and $t = 7$ years.

Keystrokes	Display
100 **×** 5.25 **2nd** [%] **×** 7 **=**	**36.75**

ANSWER You will earn $36.75 interest.

✓ **Check** Round 5.25% to 5%. Because $100 × 5\% × 7 = 35$, the answer is reasonable.

 **HELP** with **Technology**

The percent key changes a percent to a decimal by dividing by 100 for you. For example,

5.25 **2nd** [%]

is displayed as 0.0525.

Your turn now Use a calculator to find the answer.

1. 8% of 90 7.2
2. 14% of 173 24.22
3. 57% of 13.7 7.809
4. 3.5% of 8 0.28
5. 24.3% of 99 24.057
6. 7.28% of 205 14.924

7. **Simple Interest** You deposit $75 in an account with an annual interest rate of 6.5%. How much simple interest will you earn on that money in 4 years? $19.50

8. **Sales Tax** You are buying a CD that costs $14.95. The sales tax is 7%. What is the amount of tax that you owe? What is the total amount of your purchase? $1.05; $16.00

9. **Discount** A store is having a 35% off sale. If an item was originally priced $49.50, what will you pay for it now, not including sales tax? $32.18

NCTM CURRICULUM STANDARDS
Standard 1: Understand ways of representing numbers
Standard 6: Solve problems in math and other contexts

Lesson 8.7 Finding a Percent of a Number **411**

LESSONS 8.5 TO 8.7

Notebook Review

Review the vocabulary definitions in your notebook.

Copy the review examples in your notebook. Then complete the exercises.

Check Your Definitions

percent, p. 395
interest, p. 408

principal, p. 408
annual interest rate, p. 408

simple interest, p. 408

Use Your Vocabulary

1. Copy and complete: Interest paid only on the _?_ is simple interest. **principal**

8.5–8.6 Can you use percents?

 EXAMPLE Write the decimal or fraction as a percent.

a. $0.63 = \frac{63}{100} = 63\%$

b. $\frac{1}{8} = 0.125 = \frac{125}{1000} = \frac{12.5}{100} = 12.5\%$

 2. Write 16% as a decimal and a fraction. $0.16, \frac{16}{100} = \frac{4}{25}$

Write the decimal or fraction as a percent.

3. 0.7 **70%** **4.** 0.24 **24%** **5.** $\frac{6}{25}$ **24%** **6.** $\frac{7}{8}$ **87.5%**

8.7 Can you find a percent of a number?

EXAMPLE You are buying a pair of in-line skates that cost $48.50. The sales tax is 6%. What is the total amount of your purchase?

(1) Find the sales tax. 6% of $48.50 = $0.06 \times $48.50 = $2.91

(2) Add the tax to the cost. $48.50 + $2.91 = $51.41

 Find the percent of the number.

7. 25% of 400 **100** **8.** 60% of 105 **63** **9.** 10% of 24 **2.4** **10.** 85% of 130 **110.5**

11. You deposit $150 in a savings account. The annual interest rate is 6%. How much simple interest will you earn on that money in 1 year? **$9**

Stop *and* Think about Lessons 8.5–8.7

12. Writing Describe the process of finding a percent of a number. What might you consider to make the computation easier?

Review Quiz 2

Write the percent as a decimal and a fraction.

1. 43% $0.43, \frac{43}{100}$ **2.** 97% $0.97, \frac{97}{100}$ **3.** 2% $0.02, \frac{2}{100} = \frac{1}{50}$ **4.** 12% $0.12, \frac{12}{100} = \frac{3}{25}$

Write the fraction or decimal as a percent.

5. $\frac{27}{100}$ 27%   **6.** 0.82 82%   **7.** 0.7 70%   **8.** $\frac{3}{5}$ 60%

9. Order the numbers 34%, $\frac{8}{25}$, and 0.37 from least to greatest. $\frac{8}{25}$, 34%, 0.37

10. Internet Use You spend a total of 15 hours on the Internet during a 2 week period. You research a school project 60% of that time. How many hours do you spend researching the project?   9 h

Find the simple interest *I* = *Prt* for the given values.

11. $P = \$375$, $r = 7\%$, $t = 3$ years   **12.** $P = \$215$, $r = 3\%$, $t = 5$ years
$78.75 $32.25

13. Leaving a Tip Your bill in a restaurant is $28.70. You want to leave about 20% for a tip. Estimate the amount of the tip. $6

BRAIN GAME

Target 203

Your goal is to find sums of the percents of the given numbers. Is it possible to get a sum as great as 203?   yes

1. Choose any blue percent and any purple number. Find this percent of the number you have selected.

2. Repeat Step 1 until you have selected each number and each percent once. Organize your results.

3. Add your products together. How close are you to 203? What can you do differently to get a sum closer to 203?
Answers may vary.

Chapter Review

 Vocabulary

ratio, p. 374	proportion, p. 383	principal, p. 408
equivalent ratio, p. 375	cross products, p. 383	annual interest rate,
rate, p. 379	percent, p. 395	p. 408
unit rate, p. 379	interest, p. 408	simple interest, p. 408

Vocabulary Review

Tell whether the statement is *true* or *false*.

1. The ratios $\frac{4}{7}$ and $\frac{16}{21}$ are equivalent. **false**

2. A rate is a ratio of two measures that have different units. **true**

3. A percent is a ratio that compares a number to 100. **true**

Copy and complete the statement.

4. A __?__ is a rate that has a denominator of 1.
  unit rate

5. In the proportion $\frac{a}{b} = \frac{c}{d}$, ad and bc are __?__.
  cross products

6. In the proportion $\frac{a}{b} = \frac{c}{d}$, ad is equal to __?__. **bc**

Review Questions

Copy and complete the statement. *(Lesson 8.1)*

7. $\frac{2}{3} = \frac{6}{?}$ **9**

8. $\frac{6}{7} = \frac{?}{21}$ **18**

9. $\frac{?}{9} = \frac{16}{36}$ **4**

10. $\frac{4}{?} = \frac{8}{30}$ **15**

Amusement Parks The graph shows the favorite amusement park rides for a group of students. Write the given ratio in simplest form. *(Lesson 8.1)*

11. bumper cars votes to roller coaster votes $\frac{1}{2}$

12. water slide votes to total students surveyed $\frac{2}{7}$

13. Ferris wheel votes to water slide votes $\frac{1}{4}$

14. **Auto Racing** A racecar travels 110 miles using 22 gallons of fuel. Find the unit rate. *(Lesson 8.2)* $\frac{5 \text{ mi}}{1 \text{ gal}}$

15. **Travel** You are traveling from New York City to Charlotte, North Carolina, a distance of about 540 miles. Find the unit rate if it takes you 9 hours to make the trip. *(Lesson 8.2)* $\frac{60 \text{ mi}}{1 \text{ h}}$

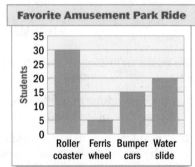

Favorite Amusement Park Ride

Solve the proportion. *(Lesson 8.3)*

16. $\frac{x}{4} = \frac{21}{12}$ 7

17. $\frac{8}{g} = \frac{24}{27}$ 9

18. $\frac{6}{10} = \frac{9}{y}$ 15

19. $\frac{12}{10} = \frac{b}{25}$ 30

20. Science A desk that weighs 90 pounds on Earth would weigh about 15 pounds on the moon. If a rock weighs 450 pounds on Earth, how much would it weigh on the moon? *(Lesson 8.3)* **75 lb**

In Exercises 21 and 22, use the scale drawing shown. *(Lesson 8.4)*

21. The scale drawing of a parking lot uses the scale 1 in. : 25 ft. What are the actual dimensions of the parking lot? **175 ft × 75 ft**

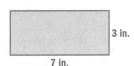

3 in.

7 in.

22. Find the ratio of the scale drawing's area to the parking lot's area. $\frac{1 \text{ in.}^2}{625 \text{ ft}^2}$

Write the number in words and as a percent. *(Lesson 8.5)*

23. $\frac{34}{100}$
thirty-four hundredths, 34%

24. $\frac{16}{100}$
sixteen hundredths, 16%

25. 0.05
five hundredths, 5%

26. 0.65
sixty-five hundredths, 65%

Write the percent as a decimal and a fraction. *(Lesson 8.5)*

27. 64% 0.64, $\frac{64}{100} = \frac{16}{25}$

28. 26% 0.26, $\frac{26}{100} = \frac{13}{50}$

29. 90% 0.90, $\frac{90}{100} = \frac{9}{10}$

30. 8% 0.08, $\frac{8}{100} = \frac{2}{25}$

Write the decimal or fraction as a percent. *(Lesson 8.6)*

31. 0.4 40%

32. $\frac{4}{5}$ 80%

33. $\frac{10}{16}$ 62.5%

34. 0.425 42.5%

35. Order the numbers from least to greatest. *(Lesson 8.6)*

$\frac{1}{3}$, 25%, 0.2, 40%, $\frac{3}{5}$, 0.35   0.2, 25%, $\frac{1}{3}$, 0.35, 40%, $\frac{3}{5}$

Find the percent of the number. *(Lesson 8.7)*

36. 80% of 110 88

37. 4% of 300 12

38. 36% of 75 27

39. $66\frac{2}{3}$% of 600 400

40. Taxi Ride You take a taxi ride and your fare comes to $12.80. You want to give the driver a 15% tip. Estimate the amount of the tip. *(Lesson 8.7)* **$1.95**

41. Money You deposit $115 into a savings account with an annual interest rate of 5%. How much simple interest will you earn on that money in 3 years? *(Lesson 8.7)* **$17.25**

42. On Sale What is the cost of a $36 pair of jeans after a 20% discount, not including sales tax? *(Lesson 8.7)* **$28.80**

CHAPTER 8 Chapter Test

Online Shopping The graph shows the number of people in a survey who chose different reasons for using online shopping. Write the ratios in Exercises 1 and 2 in simplest form.

Reasons for Online Shopping

Discounts 48
Free gifts 25
Free shipping 27

1. discounts responses to total number of shoppers surveyed $\frac{12}{25}$

2. free shipping responses to discounts responses $\frac{9}{16}$

3. Write the ratio $\frac{2}{5}$ in two other ways. 2 : 5, 2 to 5

4. **Phones** You pay $3.36 for a 14 minute phone call. Find the unit rate. $\frac{\$.24}{1 \text{ min}}$

Solve the proportion.

5. $\frac{x}{4} = \frac{21}{12}$ 7

6. $\frac{18}{81} = \frac{2}{n}$ 9

7. $\frac{r}{10} = \frac{4}{8}$ 5

8. $\frac{6}{j} = \frac{10}{25}$ 15

9. **Currency** Six U.S. dollars are worth about 804 Japanese yen. How many Japanese yen is one U.S. dollar worth? 134 yen

10. **Bikes** A model of a bike has a scale of 1 in. : 2 ft. The length of the model is 3.5 inches. What is the actual length of the bike? 7 ft

Write the decimal or fraction as a percent.

11. 0.36 36%

12. 0.08 8%

13. $\frac{23}{100}$ 23%

14. $\frac{2}{25}$ 8%

15. Write *fifty-five percent* as a fraction. $\frac{55}{100} = \frac{11}{20}$

16. **Flowers** One sixth of your flower garden is tulips, 0.195 is marigolds, and 18% is roses. Order these numbers from least to greatest. $\frac{1}{6}$, 18%, 0.195

17. **Geography** In the United States, 23 of the 50 states border an ocean. What percent of the states border an ocean? 46%

18. Find 40% of 85. 34

19. Find 75% of 60. 45

20. Find 12% of 150. 18

21. Find 88% of 1000. 880

Restaurant Bill A restaurant bill totals $45.80. Use mental math to estimate the tip described.

22. 10% $4.60

23. 20% $9.20

24. 15% $6.90

25. 25% $11.50

Chapter Standardized Test

Test-Taking Strategy As you take a test, avoid spending too much time on any one question. Go on to another question and come back later if time permits.

ADDITIONAL RESOURCES

 Assessment Book
• Standardized Chapter Test, p. 104

 Test and Practice Generator

12. *Sample answer:* $\frac{3}{4} = \frac{36}{48}$; yes;

4 and 36 can change places, or 3 and 48 can change places and the cross products will still be the same.

Multiple Choice

1. Which ratio is equivalent to $\frac{20}{8}$? C

   A. $\frac{10}{5}$ B. $\frac{30}{14}$ C. $\frac{60}{24}$ D. $\frac{14}{4}$

2. Solve the proportion $\frac{7}{3} = \frac{x}{21}$. I

   F. 28   G. 35   H. 42   I. 49

3. You deposit $140 in a savings account. The annual interest rate is 4%. How much simple interest will you earn on that money in 2 years? C

   A. $5.60   B. $7.60   C. $11.20   D. $16.80

4. You buy a model boat kit for $15 and an extra motor for $5.50. There is a 6% sales tax. What is the total amount of your purchase? I

   F. $15.90   G. $20.50   H. $21.40   I. $21.73

5. Your bill in a restaurant is $29.97. You want to leave a tip of about 20%. What is a good estimate for the tip? C

   A. $4.50   B. $5   C. $6   D. $8

6. An elephant walks 60 miles in 12 hours. What is the unit rate? G

   F. 4 miles per hour

   G. 5 miles per hour

   H. 6 miles per hour

   I. 48 miles per hour

7. Write 0.27 as a percent. C

   A. 0.27%   B. 2.7%   C. 27%   D. 270%

8. A school fair raises a total of $24,478. If 25% of this amount goes to a particular charity, how much will the charity receive? F

   F. $6119.50   G. $6120.50

   H. $18,358.50   I. $30,597.50

9. A car is 4 feet tall and 8 feet long. If the scale of a model of the car is 4 in. : 1 ft, how long is the model? B

   A. 8 in.   B. 32 in.   C. 16 ft   D. 32 ft

10. The regular price of a pair of hiking boots is $65. If the boots are on sale for 40% off, how much will you save off the regular price?

    F. $25   G. $26   H. $39   I. $45   G

11. 20%. *Sample answer:* Divide 16 by 80 and change the decimal to a percent.

Short Response

11. Doreen has a collection of 80 baseball caps. Sixteen of the caps are blue. What percent of the caps are blue? Explain how you found your answer.

12. Write a proportion using the numbers 4, 36, 3, and 48. Is there more than one proportion that you can write? Explain.

    See margin.

Extended Response

13. Store A has a jacket that is regularly $36, on sale for 15% off. The same jacket at Store B is regularly $40, on sale for 20% off. You pay 5% sales tax on the discounted price at either store. Find the cost of the jacket at Store A and then at Store B. Which jacket is the better buy? Explain.

    $36 jacket. *Sample answer:* It is on sale for $30.60 (with tax, $32.13) while the $40 jacket is on sale for $32 (with tax, $33.60).

Pacing and Assignment Guide

REGULAR SCHEDULE

Lesson	Les. Day	BASIC	AVERAGE	ADVANCED
9.1	Day 1	pp. 423–424 Exs. 8–28, 33–39	pp. 423–424 Exs. 8–19, 22–29, 33–39	pp. 423–424 Exs. 10–22, 25–35*, 39
9.2	Day 1	pp. 428–429 Exs. 12–19, 29–34	pp. 428–429 Exs. 12–19, 29–34	pp. 428–429 Exs. 12–17, 29–36
	Day 2	pp. 428–429 Exs. 23–27, 35–42	pp. 428–429 Exs. 22–28, 35–42	pp. 428–429 Exs. 20–28, 39–42, EC: TE p. 418F*
9.3	Day 1	pp. 433–434 Exs. 15–21, 29–31, 42–46	pp. 433–434 Exs. 15–21, 32–37, 42–45	pp. 433–434 Exs. 17–21, 31–37, 42–45
	Day 2	pp. 433–434 Exs. 22–28, 33–37, 47–50	pp. 433–434 Exs. 22–31, 38–40, 46–50	pp. 433–434 Exs. 22–30, 38–41*, 48–50
9.4	Day 1	pp. 439–440 Exs. 11–17, 20–29, 32–36, 40–47	pp. 439–440 Exs. 11–21, 26–38, 40–42, 45–48	pp. 439–440 Exs. 11–22, 26–31, 34–42*, 47, 48
9.5	Day 1	pp. 447–448 Exs. 8–14, 27–31	pp. 447–448 Exs. 8–14, 27–32	pp. 447–448 Exs. 10–14, 22–27*, 34
	Day 2	pp. 447–448 Exs. 15–22, 32–34	pp. 447–448 Exs. 15–25, 33–35	pp. 447–448 Exs. 15–21, 28–31, 35
9.6	Day 1	pp. 451–453 Exs. 8–12, 14–21, 27–33	pp. 451–453 Exs. 8–16, 19–24, 27–29, 32–34	pp. 451–453 Exs. 10–14, 17–29*, 33, 34
9.7	Day 1	pp. 456–457 Exs. 6–10, 18, 22–24	pp. 456–457 Exs. 6–9, 16–20, 22, 23	pp. 456–457 Exs. 7–9, 14–18, 27
	Day 2	pp. 456–457 Exs. 11–15, 25–28	pp. 456–457 Exs. 11–15, 24–28	pp. 456–457 Exs. 11–13, 19–23*, 28
9.8	Day 1	pp. 462–463 Exs. 5–11, 14–16, 19–31	pp. 462–463 Exs. 5–11, 14–17, 19–26, 29–32	pp. 462–463 Exs. 5–8, 12–26*, 30–32
Review	Day 1	pp. 464–467 Exs. 1–34	pp. 464–467 Exs. 1–34	pp. 464–467 Exs. 1–34
Assess	Day 1	Chapter 9 Test	Chapter 9 Test	Chapter 9 Test

YEARLY PACING   Chapter 9 Total – **14 days**   Chapters 1–9 Total – **108 days**   Remaining – **52 days**

*Challenge Exercises   EP = Extra Practice   SRH = Skills Review Handbook   EC = Extra Challenge

BLOCK SCHEDULE

DAY 1	DAY 2	DAY 3	DAY 4	DAY 5	DAY 6	DAY 7
9.1 pp. 423–424 Exs. 8–19, 22–29, 33–39 **9.2** pp. 428–429 Exs. 12–19, 29–34	**9.2 cont.** pp. 428–429 Exs. 22–28, 35–42 **9.3** pp. 433–434 Exs. 15–21, 32–37, 42–45	**9.3 cont.** pp. 433–434 Exs. 22–31, 38–40, 46–50 **9.4** pp. 439–440 Exs. 11–21, 26–38, 40–42, 45–48	**9.5** pp. 447–448 Exs. 8–25, 27–35	**9.6** pp. 451–453 Exs. 8–16, 19–24, 27–29, 32–34 **9.7** pp. 456–457 Exs. 6–9, 16–20, 22, 23	**9.7 cont.** pp. 456–457 Exs. 11–15, 24–28 **9.8** pp. 462–463 Exs. 5–11, 14–17, 19–26, 29–32	**Review** pp. 464–467 Exs. 1–34 **Assess** Chapter 9 Test

YEARLY PACING   Chapter 9 Total – **7 days**   Chapters 1–9 Total – **54 days**   Remaining – **26 days**

Support Materials

📖 CHAPTER RESOURCE BOOK

CHAPTER SUPPORT

Tips for New Teachers	p. 1	Parents as Partners	p. 3

LESSON SUPPORT

	9.1	9.2	9.3	9.4	9.5	9.6	9.7	9.8
Lesson Plans (regular and block)	p. 5	p. 13	p. 23	p. 32	p. 41	p. 50	p. 60	p. 68
Technology Activities & Keystrokes				p. 34		p. 52		
Activity Support Masters					p. 43			
Activity Masters			p. 25					
Practice (3 levels)	p. 7	p. 15	p. 26	p. 35	p. 44	p. 54	p. 62	p. 70
Study Guide	p. 10	p. 18	p. 29	p. 38	p. 47	p. 57	p. 65	p. 73
Real-World Problem Solving		p. 20						p. 75
Challenge Practice	p. 12	p. 21	p. 31	p. 40	p. 49	p. 59	p. 67	p. 76

REVIEW

Games Support Masters	p. 22	Cooperative Project with Rubric	p. 80
Chapter Review Games and Activities	p. 77	Extra Credit Project with Rubric	p. 82
Real-Life Project with Rubric	p. 78	Cumulative Practice	p. 84
		Resource Book Answers	A1

📖 ASSESSMENT

Quizzes	p. 107	Alternative Assessments with Rubrics	p. 116
Chapter Tests (3 levels)	p. 109	Unit Test	p. 129
Standardized Test	p. 115	Cumulative Test	p. 131

📑 TRANSPARENCIES

	9.1	9.2	9.3	9.4	9.5	9.6	9.7	9.8
Warm-Up / Daily Homework Quiz	✔	✔	✔	✔	✔	✔	✔	✔
Notetaking Guide	✔	✔	✔	✔	✔	✔	✔	✔
Teacher Support		✔	✔					✔
English/Spanish Problem Solving		✔	✔				✔	✔
Answer Transparencies	✔	✔	✔	✔	✔	✔	✔	✔

💻 TECHNOLOGY

- EasyPlanner CD-ROM
- Test and Practice Generator
- Electronic Lesson Presentations
- eTutorial CD-ROM
- Chapter Audio Summaries CDs
- Classzone.com
- eEdition Plus Online
- eWorkbook Plus Online
- eTutorial Plus Online
- EasyPlanner Plus Online

ADDITIONAL RESOURCES

- Worked-Out Solution Key
- Notetaking Guide
- Practice Workbook
- Tutor Place
- Professional Development Book
- Activities Book
- Poster Package
- Spanish Study Guide
- English/Spanish Chapter Reviews
- Multi-Language Glossary

Math Background and Teaching Strategies

Lesson 9.1

MATH BACKGROUND

SETS OF POINTS A **line** is a straight set of **points** with no endpoints. Since any two points determine a line, you can use the two points, along with the symbol ↔ to name the line. A **ray** has one endpoint and continues indefinitely in one direction. You name a ray with its endpoint and one other point on the ray along with the symbol →. A **segment** has two endpoints and includes all of the points between those two endpoints. To name a segment, use the endpoints along with the symbol ‾. A **plane** is a flat surface that extends indefinitely in all directions. **Parallel lines** are lines that are in the same plane and never cross because they are always the same distance apart. **Intersecting lines** are lines that do cross.

TEACHING STRATEGIES

Have students discuss what they already know about lines, points, segments, rays, and parallel and intersecting lines. Draw several figures on the board and have the students identify points, lines, segments, rays, parallel lines, and intersecting lines. Ask students how they know that two lines are parallel. *Sample answer: The lines are always the same distance apart, so they never meet.* Ask students how they know that two lines are intersecting. *Sample answer: The lines cross; they have one point in common.*

Lesson 9.2

MATH BACKGROUND

ANGLES An **angle** is the union of two rays with a common endpoint called the **vertex**. You can name an angle by using a point on one ray, the vertex, and a point on the other ray, along with the symbol ∠. An angle can be thought of as a rotation around a point, and the size of the angle is the measure in **degrees** (°) of how far one side is rotated from the other side. 0° is no rotation, 90° is a right-angle rotation, and 180° is straight-angle rotation.

TEACHING STRATEGIES

Before students use a protractor, have them draw angles and use the corner of an index card to decide whether their angles measure less than 90°, about 90°, or more than 90°.

Lesson 9.3

MATH BACKGROUND

An **acute** angle measures less than 90°. A **right** angle measures exactly 90°. An **obtuse** angle measures more than 90° and less than 180°. A **straight** angle measures exactly 180°. If the sum of the measures of two angles is 180°, then the two angles are **supplementary**. If the sum of the measures of two angles is 90°, then the angles are **complementary**.

TEACHING STRATEGIES

If available, use a demonstration clock with movable hands to introduce the four types of angles described on the first page of the lesson. Ask students to tell you how to position the hands to show angles suggested by the class.

Lesson 9.4

MATH BACKGROUND

CLASSIFYING TRIANGLES A triangle that has one right angle is a **right triangle**, a triangle with an obtuse angle is an **obtuse triangle**, and a triangle in which all three angles are acute is an **acute triangle**. Triangles can also be classified according to side lengths.

Triangle	Name
All sides of equal length	equilateral triangle
At least two sides of equal length	isosceles triangle
All three sides of different length	scalene triangle

TEACHING STRATEGIES

As an extension of Hands-on Activity 9.4, provide the students with copies of an equilateral triangle, a scalene triangle, and an isosceles triangle. Have the students mark the vertices on each triangle with a point, and label the angles 1, 2, and 3. Direct the students to cut out the triangles and tear off the corners of each triangle. Have them draw a straight line, mark a point on it, and place the angles formed by the torn corners of one triangle adjacent to each other with the three marked vertices meeting at the point. Students should realize that the type of triangle does not affect the sum of the angle measures.

Lesson 9.5

MATH BACKGROUND

QUADRILATERALS Many quadrilaterals can be classified in more than one way. For example, a square is defined as a quadrilateral with four sides of equal length and four right angles. However, a square can also be classified as a parallelogram because it satisfies the definition of parallelogram.

TEACHING STRATEGIES

One way to help students memorize terminology and classify quadrilaterals that belong to two or more groups is to use the Venn diagram shown below.

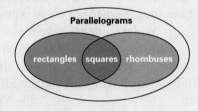

Lesson 9.6

MATH BACKGROUND

POLYGONS A **polygon** is a closed figure whose sides are all segments. A **diagonal** of a polygon is a segment with endpoints that are two non-adjacent vertices. **Regular polygons** have equal side lengths and equal angle measures.

TEACHING STRATEGIES

Investigating examples of shapes that are and are not polygons is an effective way to encourage students to look at properties and distinguish the properties that define a polygon from those that do not.

Lesson 9.7

MATH BACKGROUND

SIMILARITY **Similar figures** are figures that have the same shape, but not necessarily the same size. Two similar polygons have corresponding angles that have the same measure and corresponding sides that are proportional.

CONGRUENCE Figures that have the same shape *and* size are **congruent**. If two figures are congruent, then all the corresponding parts of the two figures are congruent.

TEACHING STRATEGIES

For this activity students will need a large piece of construction paper, a ruler, and a protractor. Have students work in pairs. Have each pair draw a large triangle with sides of different lengths. Have them measure and record the measure of each angle; also have them record the length of each side. Then ask each pair to draw a segment within the triangle parallel to one side of the triangle. Have them measure and record the lengths of the sides and the measures of the angles of the smaller triangle they have formed. Have students repeat this process again, to create three similar triangles. Then have each pair of students compare the angle measures of the three triangles and the lengths of the corresponding sides. If they have measured carefully, corresponding angles should be equal and corresponding sides should have the same ratio.

Lesson 9.8

MATH BACKGROUND

SYMMETRY If you can fold a figure so that is has two parts that match exactly, that figure has **line symmetry**. The fold line is called the **line of symmetry**.

TEACHING STRATEGIES

Some of the letters of our alphabet are symmetrical. Write all of the capital letters on a handout for students. Ask them to identify the letters with one or more lines of symmetry.

Differentiating Instruction

Strategies for Underachievers

ANTICIPATE PROBLEMS WITH VOCABULARY

VOCABULARY One of the most important keys to student success in geometry is mastery of the many important vocabulary terms. Beginning with Lesson 9.1, students should write all the geometry vocabulary terms in a personal glossary. With each new lesson in Chapter 9, they should add to this glossary. Students should also draw diagrams or pictures for each entry, when appropriate.

You might suggest that students create a graphic organizer or note cards for organizing and learning the vocabulary. You may want to have students color code note cards related to the same topic. For example, one color group might contain all the vocabulary terms related to triangles, such as "equilateral," "right," and so on. Additionally, some vocabulary terms may belong in more than one color group; these should be placed in each group. Creating multiple note cards for some terms will only help to reinforce student understanding.

To help students with vocabulary terms in Lesson 9.6 that relate to polygons, it might be helpful to connect the prefixes to uses of the same prefix in the real world. Here are some examples:

triangle : 3 sides	tricycle : 3 wheels
quadrilateral : 4 sides	quadruplet : 4 in a group
pentagon : 5 sides	Pentagon : 5-sided building in Washington, D.C.
hexagon : 6 sides	hexameter : line of poetry with 6 beats
octagon : 8 sides	octopus : 8 tentacles

The word "corresponding" may be difficult to define; it may be more effective to simply *show* students the concept of "corresponding." If your students are seated in rows, call upon the second student in one row and ask who is seated in the "corresponding" seat in another row. Repeat this questioning with several students until you are comfortable that all students understand the concept.

Then connect the idea of students in "corresponding" seats to "corresponding" parts of polygons. Further, a term that is similar in meaning to "corresponding" is "matching," and you may wish to have some students substitute this word for "corresponding."

USE CROSS-CURRICULAR CONNECTIONS

It may be useful to work with a Language Arts teacher to tackle the new vocabulary in this chapter. In addition to defining these terms, which you will do in the math classroom, these terms also provide a good list of spelling words. In a Language Arts class, students typically write sentences that contain spelling words; this activity will help to reinforce student understanding of these new terms.

PROVIDE TOOLS FOR CONCRETE LEARNING

In Lesson 9.2, it is important for students to be able to accurately use a protractor. You may wish to choose a protractor that has only a single scale and whose edge represents the 0° line. When students have mastered using the single scale protractor, then decide whether it is appropriate to introduce the protractor with both inner and outer scales. If students are having difficulty reading their protractor correctly, teach them the "90° rule." The "90° rule" states that if an angle can be covered by the corner of a sheet of paper when aligning the corner to the vertex of the angle, then the angle is less than 90°. Likewise, if it is not possible to cover the angle in the same manner, then the angle is greater than 90°. Connect this to choosing the correct scale on the protractor.

CONGRUENT FIGURES In Lesson 9.7, students should be provided with actual cutouts of congruent figures. They can turn and flip these figures to learn that two figures can still be congruent even though their positions or orientations may be different. Students can also draw congruent figures in different positions or orientations on dot paper to reinforce this concept. Another useful manipulative to demonstrate this concept is the geoboard. A good tool to show the concept of similarity can be the overhead projector. Adjusting and moving the projector or transparency will alter the size of the image, but the shape of the image remains the same as that of the original.

In Lesson 9.8, to help students with the concept of symmetry, you might have them use a reflecting tool, which will allow them to see an image and its reflection simultaneously.

USE SCAFFOLDING

In Hands-on Activity 9.5, it is important that students have enough time to thoroughly complete this investigation. Some students, however, will require a lot of time to simply trace the figures and to copy the table. For these students, you should provide a sheet of paper with the figures and table on it that are ready to use.

Strategies for English Learners

VOCABULARY DEVELOPMENT

NUMBERS Latin and Greek names for numbers have influenced many English mathematical words. Put these words for cardinal numbers on the board and ask students to think of English words that appear to be related to the Latin or Greek names.

English	Latin	Greek
one	unus, una, unum	
two	duo, duae	
three	tres, tria	
four	quattor	tetra
five	quinque	pente
six	sex	hex
seven	septum	hepta
eight	octo	okto
nine	novem	
ten	decem	deka

Strategies for Advanced Learners

USE CROSS-CURRICULAR CONNECTIONS

You may wish to work with an Art teacher to develop some ideas for designs to investigate line symmetry, as discussed in Lesson 9.8. You may wish to consider designs that relate to the current season or an approaching holiday. You may also want to consider team or product logos for this activity.

INCREASE DEPTH AND COMPLEXITY

LINES OF SYMMETRY You may wish to have some students further investigate lines of symmetry in polygons with an increasing number of sides. Students should look for patterns in drawing and counting lines of symmetry. Be sure that they consider polygons with both odd and even numbers of sides. To carry this activity further, students can investigate the lines of symmetry in a circle. Students can prepare a written or oral presentation of their discoveries.

Use the following activity in connection with **Lesson 9.1**.

- **Challenge** Sketch the figure described. Draw two points, A and B. Sketch segment AB. Draw a line, t, that intersects segment AB at point C. Draw a line, s, that intersects segment AB at point B and is parallel to line t.
  Sample:

Use the following activity in connection with **Lesson 9.5**.

- **Challenge** Use your protractor to draw a neat, accurate triangle with angle measures of 42°, 58°, and 80°.
  Check drawings.

Differentiating Instruction: Teaching Resources

Differentiating Assessment

McDougal Littell *Middle School Mathematics* offers a wide variety of assessment. This includes Level A, Level B, and Level C Chapter Tests, Standardized Tests, Cumulative Tests, and Quizzes from the *Assessment Book*, Daily Homework Quizzes from the *Warm-Up Transparencies*, and the *Test and Practice Generator*.

ASSESSMENT BOOK

The *Assessment Book* contains two quizzes, three levels of chapter tests, A (Basic), B (Average), and C (Advanced), and a standardized test for each chapter in the textbook. Also included are cumulative tests and unit tests.

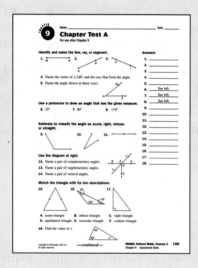

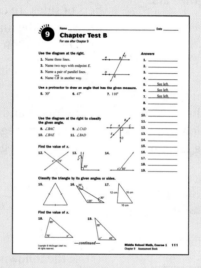

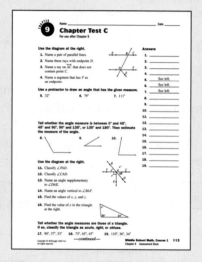

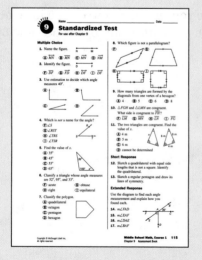

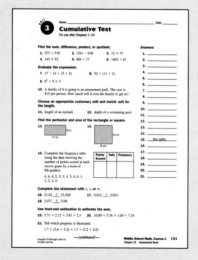

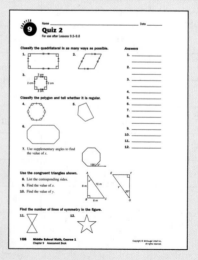

WARM-UP TRANSPARENCIES WITH DAILY HOMEWORK QUIZ

The *Warm-Up Transparencies with Daily Homework Quiz* contains a daily homework quiz for each lesson in the textbook. Each quiz appears with a set of warm-up exercises.

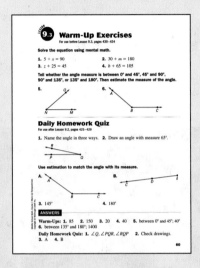

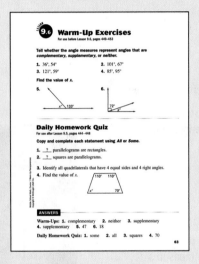

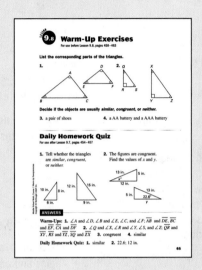

TEST AND PRACTICE GENERATOR CD-ROM

The *Test and Practice Generator* can be used to create numerous quizzes and tests for each lesson and for each chapter using both static and algorithmic exercises.

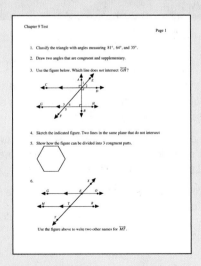

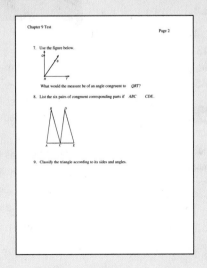

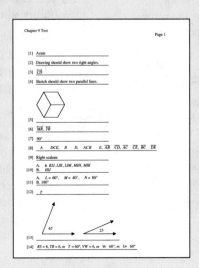

Geometric Figures

9

OVERVIEW

MAIN IDEAS

In this chapter, students study segments, lines, planes, and angles. They name and classify triangles by their sides or angles, and they classify quadrilaterals by their angles and sides. Students identify similar and congruent figures, and they find lines of symmetry.

PREREQUISITE SKILLS

The key skills reviewed in the games on these pages are:
- Classifying objects by shape, color, or pattern
- Plotting points in a coordinate plane

Additional practice with prerequisite skills can be found in the Review What You Need to Know exercises on page 420. Additional resources for reviewing prerequisite skills are:
- Skills Review Handbook, pp. 684–707
- Tutor Place
- eTutorial Plus Online

MANAGING THE GAMES

Tips for Success

Students may have difficulty with the Mix and Match game if they try to consider more than one characteristic at a time. Caution them to choose just one characteristic. Then challenge them to make up a game in which two characteristics are chosen.

Reflecting on the Games

In Exercise 1, students focus on strategies that will help them be the last person to cover a shape. Ask them to write other strategies they learned after playing the game a few times.

BEFORE

In previous chapters you've...

- Used ratios and proportions
- Found lengths, perimeters, and areas

Now

In Chapter 9 you'll study...

- Points, lines, and planes
- Angles and angle measures
- Identifying polygons
- Congruent and similar figures
- Line symmetry

WHY?

So you can solve real-world problems about...

- miniature golf, p. 425
- architecture, p. 432
- the Great Pyramid, p. 440
- photography, p. 457

Internet Preview

CLASSZONE.COM
- eEdition Plus Online
- eWorkbook Plus Online
- eTutorial Plus Online
- State Test Practice
- More Examples

Chapter Warm-Up Games

Review skills you need for this chapter in these quick games. Work with a partner.

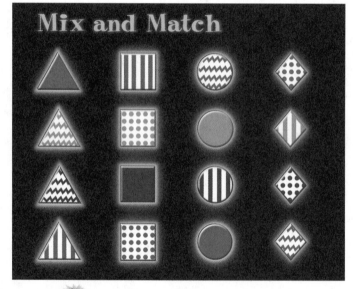

Mix and Match

BRAIN GAME

Key Skill: Classifying objects
Materials: 16 small squares of paper

Computers classify objects by their characteristics. The objects above can be classified based on shape, color, and pattern.

- On your turn, name a characteristic. Use a paper square to cover each object that has that characteristic. For example, you might cover all the green objects, or all the squares, or all the striped objects.

- Take turns, always covering at least one uncovered object. The player who covers the last object wins. Play the game a few times.

Check work.

CHAPTER RESOURCES

These resources are provided to help you prepare for the chapter and to customize review materials:

 Chapter 9 Resource Book
- Tips for New Teachers, pp. 1–2
- Lesson Plan, pp. 5, 13, 23, 32, 41, 50, 60, 68
- Lesson Plan for Block Scheduling, pp. 6, 14, 24, 33, 42, 51, 61, 69

 Technology
- EasyPlanner CD-ROM
- Test and Practice Generator
- Electronic Lesson Presentations CD-ROM
- eTutorial CD-ROM

 Internet
- Classzone
- eEdition Plus Online
- eWorkbook Plus Online
- eTutorial Plus Online
- EasyPlanner Plus Online

ENGLISH LEARNER SUPPORT
- Spanish Study Guide
- Multi-Language Glossary
- Chapter Audio Summaries CDs
- Teacher's Edition, pp. 418E–418F

1. **Purple;** the two uncovered shapes left have no common characteristics, so my partner would only be able to cover one shape on the next turn, leaving me with the last object to cover.

2. *Sample answer:* **(2, 8) and (2, 16); no; any two points with the same x-coordinate and y-coordinates of 8 and 16 will work.**

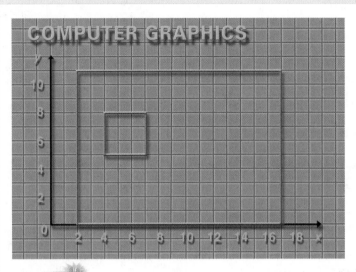

COMPUTER GRAPHICS

 Key Skill:
Plotting points on a coordinate grid

Materials:
graph paper

Computer drawing programs rely on precise instructions. In this game, you'll write instructions for drawing a house on a coordinate grid.

- Follow these instructions to draw a window and the outline of a house:

  Draw a square connecting (4, 5), (4, 8), (7, 8), and (7, 5).

  Draw a rectangle connecting (2, 0), (2, 11), (17, 11), and (17, 0).

  Check work.

- Then write instructions for drawing a door and a roof for the house. Have your partner test your instructions.
  Sample answer: Door: (9, 0), (9, 5), (12, 5), (12, 0); roof: (1, 10), (9.5, 17), (18, 10)

Stop *and* Think

1. **Critical Thinking** Suppose it is your turn in a game of *Mix and Match*. The uncovered shapes are a solid green triangle, a dotted orange square, and a solid purple square. In order to win on your next turn, which characteristic should you name? Explain your thinking. **1–2. See margin.**

2. **Writing** Points (8, 8) and (8, 16) are the corners of a square drawn on a coordinate grid. Name two points that could form the other corners of the square. Are these the only points you could use? Explain your thinking.

Review What You Need to Know
The Review What You Need to Know exercises can help you diagnose whether students have the following skills needed in Chapter 9:

- Identify the first coordinate of an ordered pair (Ex. 1)
- Find the perimeter of a rectangle or square (Exs. 2–5)
- Find the length of a line segment (Exs. 6–9)

 Chapter 9 Resource Book
- Study Guide
  (Lessons 9.1–9.8)

 Tutor Place

NOTETAKING STRATEGIES

A Venn diagram can help students organize concepts and can be used to show how sets of numbers or types of geometric figures are interrelated. In Chapter 11, when students learn about integers, they might find a Venn diagram useful for summarizing what they know about the relationships among different sets of numbers they have studied. Further suggestions for keeping a notebook can be found on page 445.

For more support on notetaking, see:
- Notetaking Guide Workbook
- Notetaking Transparencies

CHAPTER **9**

Getting Ready to Learn

Word Watch

Review Words

perimeter, p. 61
ordered pair, p. 83
coordinates, p. 83

Review What You Need to Know

Using Vocabulary Copy and complete using a review word.

1. The first coordinate in an _?_ tells you how many units to move to the right. **ordered pair**

2. The _?_ of a square can be found using the formula $P = 4s$ where s is the length of each side. **perimeter**

In Exercises 3 and 4, find the perimeter of the rectangle. *(p. 61)*

3. length = 6 in., width = 5 in. **22 in.**   4. length = 10 m, width = 7 m **34 m**

5. Write and solve an equation to find the length of a side of a square that has a perimeter of 48 centimeters. *(p. 61)* **48 = 4s; 12 cm**

Find the length of the line segment to the nearest tenth of a centimeter. *(p. 113)*

6. —————————— 3.2 cm   7. ———————— 1.9 cm

Find the length of the line segment to the nearest eighth of an inch. *(p. 244)*

8. —————————— $1\frac{1}{8}$ in.   9. ——————— $\frac{7}{8}$ in.

You should include material that appears on a notebook like this in your own notes.

Know How to Take Notes

Drawing a Venn Diagram Each oval in a Venn diagram represents a group with something in common. The region or regions where the ovals overlap show what the different groups have in common. The Venn diagram below shows that 2 is both even and prime.

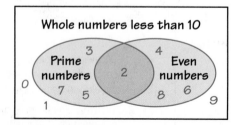

You can use Venn diagrams in your notes for Lesson 9.5 when you learn about different types of quadrilaterals.

Introduction to Geometry

LESSON 9.1

BEFORE	▶ Now	WHY?
You used points and lines to draw diagrams.	You'll identify lines, rays, and segments.	So you can describe maps, as in Exs. 18–21.

Word Watch

point, p. 421
line, p. 421
ray, p. 421
endpoint, p. 421
segment, p. 421
plane, p. 422
intersecting lines, p. 422
parallel lines, p. 422

Geometry In geometry, a **point** is usually labeled with an uppercase letter, such as *A* or *B*. Points are used to name *lines*, *rays*, and *segments*.

Words	Diagram	Symbols
A **line** extends without end in two *opposite* directions.	A ● B ●	$\overleftrightarrow{AB}$ or $\overleftrightarrow{BA}$
A **ray** has one **endpoint** and extends without end in *one* direction.	A ● B ●	$\overrightarrow{AB}$
A **segment** has two endpoints.	A ● B ●	$\overline{AB}$ or $\overline{BA}$

In the chart, notice that there are two ways to name each line or segment but only one way to name the ray. You can name a line using any two points on the line in any order. You must use the endpoints to name a segment, but they can be listed in any order. When you name a ray, you must list the endpoint first.

EXAMPLE 1 **Identifying Lines, Rays, and Segments**

Identify and name the *line*, *ray*, or *segment*.

a. M ● ● N
b. Q ● ● P
c. R ● ● S

Solution

a. The figure is a ray that can be named $\overrightarrow{MN}$.

b. The figure is a segment that can be named $\overline{QP}$ or $\overline{PQ}$.

c. The figure is a line that can be named $\overleftrightarrow{RS}$ or $\overleftrightarrow{SR}$.

Your turn now **Identify and name the *line*, *ray*, or *segment*.**

1. F ● ● G

ray, $\overrightarrow{GF}$

2. H ● ● J

line, $\overleftrightarrow{HJ}$

3. K ● ● L

segment, $\overline{KL}$

---

1 PLAN

SKILL CHECK

1. Draw a segment that is 4 centimeters long.
   Check drawings.

2. Draw a triangle.
   Check drawings.

LESSON OBJECTIVE

Identify lines, rays, and segments.

PACING

Suggested Number of Days
Basic Course: 1 day
Average Course: 1 day
Advanced Course: 1 day
Block: 0.5 block with 9.2

TEACHING RESOURCES

For a complete list of Teaching Resources, see page 418B.

TRANSPARENCY

Warm-Up Exercises for this lesson are available on a transparency.

2 TEACH

MOTIVATING THE LESSON

Ask students to describe *point*, *line*, *ray*, and *segment* in their own words.

TIPS FOR NEW TEACHERS

Be sure students know how to identify points, lines, rays, and segments correctly. See Tips for New Teachers in the *Chapter 9 Resource Book*.

NCTM CURRICULUM STANDARDS
Standard 3: Analyze properties of 2-D shapes
Standard 8: Use the language of math to express ideas
Standard 10: Use representations to communicate ideas

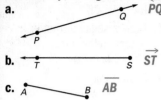
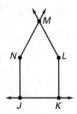
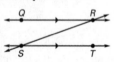

EXAMPLE 2 **Naming Lines, Rays, and Segments**

Use the aerial photo at the right.

a. Name two rays.

b. Name two segments that have *G* as an endpoint.

c. Name a line.

Solution

a. Two rays are $\overrightarrow{JL}$ and $\overrightarrow{JK}$.

b. Two segments that have *G* as an endpoint are $\overline{GJ}$ and $\overline{GH}$.

c. One line is $\overleftrightarrow{GH}$.

Planes and Lines A **plane** is a flat surface that extends without end in all directions. You can represent a plane by a figure that looks like a floor or a wall. In a plane, two different lines will either *intersect* or be *parallel*. **Intersecting lines** meet at a point. **Parallel lines** never meet.

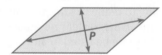 

 with **Reading**

Parallel lines are indicated by special arrows on each line.

EXAMPLE 3 **Intersecting and Parallel Lines**

a. Which lines are intersecting?

b. Which lines are parallel?

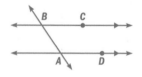

Solution

a. $\overleftrightarrow{AB}$ and $\overleftrightarrow{BC}$ intersect at point *B*.
   $\overleftrightarrow{AD}$ and $\overleftrightarrow{AB}$ intersect at point *A*.

b. $\overleftrightarrow{AD}$ and $\overleftrightarrow{BC}$ are parallel.

Your turn now **Use the diagram at the right.**

4. What is another way to write $\overrightarrow{AD}$? $\overrightarrow{EA}$? $\overrightarrow{AE}$; $\overrightarrow{ED}$

5. Which lines are intersecting? parallel?
   $\overleftrightarrow{AB}$ and $\overleftrightarrow{AE}$, $\overleftrightarrow{DC}$ and $\overleftrightarrow{AE}$; $\overleftrightarrow{AB}$ and $\overleftrightarrow{DC}$

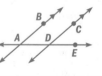

INTERNET
eWorkbook Plus
CLASSZONE.COM

③ APPLY

ASSIGNMENT GUIDE

Basic Course
Day 1: pp. 423–424 Exs. 8–28, 33–39

Average Course
Day 1: pp. 423–424 Exs. 8–19, 22–29, 33–39

Advanced Course
Day 1: pp. 423–424 Exs. 10–22, 25–35*, 39

Block
pp. 423–424 Exs. 8–19, 22–29, 33–39 (with 9.2)

Getting Ready to Practice

Vocabulary **Match the name with the correct figure.**

1. $\overleftrightarrow{XY}$ C

2. $\overrightarrow{XY}$ B

3. $\overline{XY}$ A

A.

B.

C.

Use the diagram at the right. 4–6. Answers may vary.

4. Name a ray. $\overrightarrow{PQ}$

5. Name a segment that has Q as an endpoint. $\overline{LQ}$

6. $\overleftrightarrow{NQ}$ and $\overleftrightarrow{PQ}$, $\overleftrightarrow{NQ}$ and $\overleftrightarrow{ML}$

6. Which lines are intersecting?

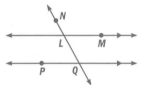

7. Which lines are parallel?
$\overleftrightarrow{ML}$ and $\overleftrightarrow{PQ}$

Practice and Problem Solving

EXTRA PRACTICE

- Student Edition, p. 716
- Chapter 9 Resource Book, pp. 7–9
- Test and Practice Generator

TRANSPARENCY

Even-numbered answers are available on transparencies.

HELP with Homework

Example	Exercises
1	8–10
2	11–15
3	16–17

Online Resources
CLASSZONE.COM
· More Examples
· eTutorial Plus

Identify and name the *line*, *ray*, or *segment*.

8.

ray, $\overrightarrow{HG}$

9.

segment, $\overline{JK}$

10.

line, $\overleftrightarrow{YZ}$

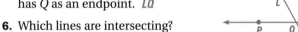

Use the diagram at the right. 11–14. Answers may vary.

11. Name three points. *A, B, C*

12. Name two rays. $\overrightarrow{CB}$, $\overrightarrow{CE}$

13. Name two lines. $\overleftrightarrow{AB}$, $\overleftrightarrow{DE}$

14. Name a segment that has B as an endpoint. $\overline{BC}$

15. Name $\overline{AE}$ in another way. $\overline{EA}$

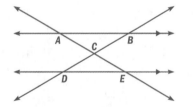

HOMEWORK CHECK

When you review students' homework for this lesson, go over the following exercises to check understanding of key concepts.
Basic: 8, 10, 11, 14, 16
Average: 8, 10, 12, 15, 17
Advanced: 10, 12, 14, 15, 17

TEACHING TIP

In Exercises 12-15, students may confuse rays, lines, and segments. Remind them that the points *A* and *B*, for example, can be used to name a ray, a line, or a segment, depending on the question. Remind them of the definitions on page 421.

Decide whether the lines pictured are *parallel* or *intersecting*.

16. parallel

17. intersecting

16.

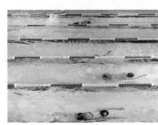

17.

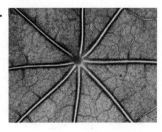

Lesson 9.1 Introduction to Geometry **423**

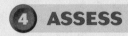

4 ASSESS

ASSESSMENT RESOURCES

For more assessment resources, see:
• Assessment Book
• Test and Practice Generator

MINI-QUIZ

Use the diagram below.

1. Name three points. *A, B,* and *C*

2. Name two rays. $\vec{AB}$, $\vec{AC}$

3. Name a line. $\overleftrightarrow{BC}$

Decide whether the object is best modeled by a *point*, a *ray*, a *segment*, or a *line*.

4. a yard stick **segment**

5. the corner of an envelope **point**

---

5 FOLLOW-UP

RETEACHING/REMEDIATION

• Study Guide in Chapter 9 Resource Book, pp. 10–11
• Tutor Place, Geometry and Measurement Card 1
• eTutorial Plus Online
• Extra Practice, p. 716
• Lesson Practice in Chapter 9 Resource Book, pp. 7–9

CHALLENGE/ENRICHMENT

• Challenge Practice in Chapter 9 Resource Book, p. 12
• Teacher's Edition, p. 418F

ENGLISH LEARNER SUPPORT

• Spanish Study Guide
• Multi-Language Glossary
• Chapter Audio Summaries CDs

25–27, 32. See Additional Answers beginning on page AA1.

---

19. $\vec{SV}$, $\vec{VS}$, $\vec{VO}$, $\vec{OP}$, or $\vec{PO}$

28. False; *A* is the endpoint of $\vec{AB}$, but *B* is the endpoint of $\vec{BA}$.

29. False; $\vec{AB}$ is a ray and $\overleftrightarrow{AB}$ is a line.

30. True; the letters are interchangeable.

31. True; the letters are interchangeable.

INTERNET
State Test Practice
CLASSZONE.COM

Geography Use the map to give an example of the figure.

18. point *S, V, P,* or *O*

19. ray

20. line $\overleftrightarrow{SV}$ or $\overleftrightarrow{PO}$

21. segment $\overline{SV}$, $\overline{VO}$ or $\overline{PO}$

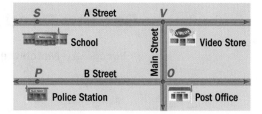

Decide Tell whether the object is best modeled by a *point*, a *ray*, a *segment*, or a *line*.

22. a star in the sky **point**

23. a beam of sunlight **ray**

24. a ruler **segment**

Sketch the figure described. 25–27. See margin.

25. $\overleftrightarrow{WV}$　　　　**26.** $\overleftrightarrow{LK}$　　　　**27.** $\overline{QP}$

Critical Thinking Is the statement *true* or *false*? Explain.

28. $\vec{AB}$ can be written as $\vec{BA}$.

29. $\vec{AB}$ can be written as $\overleftrightarrow{AB}$.

30. $\overline{QP}$ can be written as $\overline{PQ}$.

31. $\vec{PQ}$ can be written as $\vec{QP}$.

32. **Challenge** Draw a diagram in which $\overleftrightarrow{LM}$ is parallel to $\overleftrightarrow{NO}$, $\vec{PQ}$ intersects $\overleftrightarrow{NO}$ at *P* and $\overleftrightarrow{LM}$ at *Q*, and $\vec{QR}$ intersects $\overleftrightarrow{NO}$ at a point *R* between *P* and *O*. **See margin.**

Mixed Review

33. Sketch a line segment that is 65 millimeters long without using a ruler. Then use a ruler to check your estimate. How close was your estimate? *(Lesson 3.2)* **Check drawing; answers may vary.**

34. The regular price of the computer you want is $1100, but the sale price is 25% off the regular price. What is the sale price? *(Lesson 8.7)* **$825**

Basic Skills Copy and complete the statement using <, >, or =.

35. 2.9 ? 3.1 **<**　**36.** 1.8 ? 0.99 **>**　**37.** 12.5 ? 1.25 **>**　**38.** 18.7 ? 18 **>**

Test-Taking Practice

39. Short Response Use the figure at the right to answer the questions. If you drew a line through points *M* and *P*, could $\overleftrightarrow{MP}$ be parallel to $\overleftrightarrow{LM}$? to $\overleftrightarrow{LN}$? Explain.

$\overleftrightarrow{MP}$ cannot be parallel to $\overleftrightarrow{LM}$ because they intersect at point *M*; $\overleftrightarrow{MP}$ could be parallel to $\overleftrightarrow{LN}$ because they do not appear to intersect.

Angles

BEFORE

You named lines, rays, and segments.

▶ **Now**

You'll name, measure, and draw angles.

WHY?

So you can measure angles formed by a kite string as in Exs. 15–17.

In the Real World

 **Word Watch**

angle, p. 425
vertex, p. 425
degrees (°), p. 426

Miniature Golf A miniature golf course has a hole similar to the one shown at the right. You can get a hole-in-one if you hit the ball off of the wall as shown. How can you describe the path of the ball?

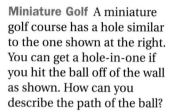

The path of the golf ball forms an *angle*. An **angle** is formed by two rays with the same endpoint. The endpoint is called the **vertex** . The symbol ∠ is used to represent an angle.

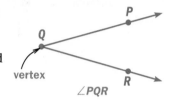

vertex

∠PQR

EXAMPLE 1 Naming Angles

The path of the golf ball above is shown at the right. You can name the angle formed by the path of the golf ball in three ways.

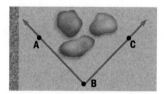

Name the angle by its vertex alone: ∠B.

Name the angle by its vertex and two points, with the vertex as the middle point: ∠ABC.

Name the angle by its vertex and two points, but switch the order of the two points: ∠CBA.

Your turn now Name the angle in three ways.

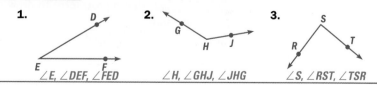

1.

∠E, ∠DEF, ∠FED

2.

∠H, ∠GHJ, ∠JHG

3.

∠S, ∠RST, ∠TSR

NCTM CURRICULUM STANDARDS
Standard 3: Analyze properties of 2-D shapes
Standard 4: Understand the units of measurement; Apply proper tools to find measures

Lesson 9.2   Angles   **425**

TRANSPARENCY

A support transparency is available for Example 2 and Your turn now Exercises 4–7.

TEACHING TIP

To give students more hands-on practice with protractors, have students tear the corner from a piece of paper and measure the right angle with the protractor. Then ask them to cut the angle into two smaller angles and measure them.

 COMMON ERROR

When using a protractor, students may use the wrong scale. Give them examples of which scale to use for angles less than 90° and which to use for angles greater than 90°.

 NOTETAKING

Ask students to make a note in their notebooks that "m∠ABC" means the measure of an angle whose vertex is B and whose sides are $\overrightarrow{BA}$ and $\overrightarrow{BC}$.

4–7. See Additional Answers beginning on page AA1.

Using a Protractor A protractor is a tool you can use to draw and measure angles. Angles are measured in units called **degrees (°)** . To measure an angle, place the center of the protractor on the vertex of the angle and line up one ray with the 0° line. Then read the measure where the other ray crosses the protractor.

 **with Reading**

Some protractors have an inner scale and an outer scale. You read one scale when measuring clockwise and the other scale when measuring counterclockwise. Make sure you use the same scale for each ray of the angle.

The measure of ∠ABC is 122°. You can write this as m∠ABC = 122°.

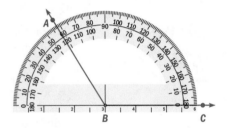

EXAMPLE 2 **Drawing Angles**

Use a protractor to draw an angle that has a measure of 54°.

Solution

① Draw and label a ray.

② Place the center of the protractor at the endpoint of the ray. Line up the ray with the 0° line. Then draw and label a point at the 54° mark on the inner scale.

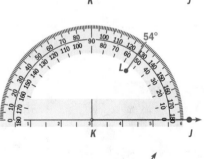

③ Remove the protractor and draw $\overrightarrow{KL}$ to complete the angle.

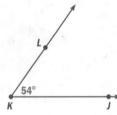

Your turn now Use a protractor to draw an angle that has the given measure. 4–7. See margin.

4. 25°　　　**5.** 85°　　　**6.** 145°　　　**7.** 170°

Estimating Angle Measures You can estimate angle measures by mentally comparing them to 0°, 90°, and 180° on a protractor.

EXAMPLE 3 **Estimating Angle Measures**

Use estimation to name the angle whose measure is closest to the given measure.

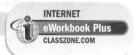

a. 90°   **b.** 15°   **c.** 135°

Solution

Imagine that D is at the center and that $\overrightarrow{DC}$ and $\overrightarrow{DB}$ are on the 0° line.

a. A 90° angle is halfway around a protractor, so $\angle BDA$ and $\angle CDA$ have measures that are equally close to 90°.

b. A 15° angle is close to 0° and less than halfway to 90°, so $\angle CDF$ has the measure that is closest to 15°.

c. A 135° angle is halfway between 90° and 180°, so $\angle CDE$ has the measure that is closest to 135°.

9.2 **Exercises**
More Practice, p. 716

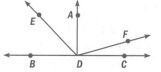
INTERNET
eWorkbook Plus
CLASSZONE.COM

Getting Ready to Practice

1. Vocabulary Name the vertex of $\angle DEF$ and the rays that form the angle.

$E, \overrightarrow{ED}$ and $\overrightarrow{EF}$

Name the angle in three ways.

2.
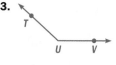
$\angle B, \angle ABC, \angle CBA$

3.

$\angle U, \angle TUV, \angle VUT$

4.

$\angle K, \angle JKL, \angle LKJ$

Use a protractor to draw an angle that has the given measure.

5–8. See margin.

5. 30°   **6.** 45°   **7.** 90°   **8.** 130°

Use estimation to name the angle from Exercises 2–4 above whose measure is closest to the given measure.

9. 100° $\angle JKL$ **10.** 30° $\angle ABC$ **11.** 135° $\angle TUV$

Lesson 9.2   Angles   **427**

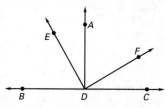

ASSIGNMENT GUIDE

Basic Course
Day 1: pp. 428–429 Exs. 12–19, 29–34
Day 2: pp. 428–429 Exs. 23–27, 35–42

Average Course
Day 1: pp. 428–429 Exs. 12–19, 29–34
Day 2: pp. 428–429 Exs. 22–28, 35–42

Advanced Course
Day 1: pp. 428–429 Exs. 12–17, 29–36
Day 2: pp. 428–429 Exs. 20–28, 39–42, EC: TE p. 418F*

Block
pp. 428–429 Exs. 12–19, 29–34 (with 9.1)
pp. 428–429 Exs. 22–28, 35–42 (with 9.3)

EXTRA PRACTICE
- Student Edition, p. 716
- Chapter 9 Resource Book, pp. 15–17
- Test and Practice Generator

 TRANSPARENCY

Even-numbered answers are available on transparencies. A support transparency is available for Exercises 18–25 and the Brain Game.

HOMEWORK CHECK

When you review students' homework for this lesson, go over the following exercises to check understanding of key concepts.
Basic: 12, 13, 14, 15, 23
Average: 12, 13, 14, 16, 24
Advanced: 12, 13, 14, 17, 25

18–22. See Additional Answers beginning on page AA1.

428

Practice and Problem Solving

 with **Homework**

Example	Exercises
1	12, 14
2	13, 15–22
3	23–25

 **Online Resources**
CLASSZONE.COM
· More Examples
· eTutorial Plus

12. Name the angle shown at the right in three ways. ∠*G*, ∠*LGH*, ∠*HGL*

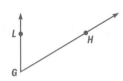

13. Use a protractor to measure the angle in Exercise 12. 60°

14. **Find the Error** Describe and correct the error made in naming the angle.
S is the vertex. The letter *S* should be in the middle, so the angle should be named ∠*QSR*, ∠*RSQ*, or ∠*S*.

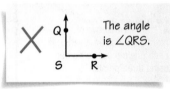
The angle is ∠QRS.

Kites **Trace the red angle that the kite string makes with the ground. Then use a protractor to measure the angle.**

15.   **16.**   **17.**

60°   40°   130°

Use a protractor to draw an angle that has the given measure.
18–22. See margin.

18. 33°   **19.** 72°   **20.** 165°   **21.** 180°

22. Use a protractor to draw and label an angle formed by $\overrightarrow{JK}$ and $\overrightarrow{JL}$ that has a measure of 65°.

Use estimation to match the angle with its measure. Use a protractor to check your answer.

23. 20° C   **24.** 180° A   **25.** 145° B

A.   **B.**   **C.**

Estimation **Tell whether the angle measure is between 0° and 45°, 45° and 90°, 90° and 135°, or 135° and 180°. Then estimate the measure of the angle.** 26–28. Estimates may vary.

26.   **27.**   **28.**

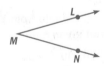   

between 0° and 45°; 35°   between 90° and 135°; 110°   between 45° and 90°; 70°

Mixed Review

Find the sum or difference. *(Lesson 6.2)*

29. $\dfrac{4}{11} + \dfrac{9}{11}$ **30.** $\dfrac{1}{6} + \dfrac{4}{6}$ **31.** $\dfrac{13}{5} - \dfrac{9}{5}$ **32.** $\dfrac{7}{10} - \dfrac{5}{10}$

$\dfrac{13}{11}$ or $1\dfrac{2}{11}$ $\dfrac{5}{6}$ $\dfrac{4}{5}$ $\dfrac{2}{10}$ or $\dfrac{1}{5}$

Solve the proportion. *(Lesson 8.3)*

33. $\dfrac{4}{x} = \dfrac{6}{9}$ 6   **34.** $\dfrac{m}{8} = \dfrac{10}{5}$ 16   **35.** $\dfrac{3}{5} = \dfrac{6}{a}$ 10   **36.** $\dfrac{9}{12} = \dfrac{y}{4}$ 3

Basic Skills   **Write the decimal in words.** 37–40. See margin.

37. 0.0031   **38.** 1.0325   **39.** 52.141   **40.** 496.85

(Margin notes:)

37. thirty-one ten-thousandths

38. one and three hundred twenty-five ten-thousandths

39. fifty-two and one hundred forty-one thousandths

40. four hundred ninety-six and eighty-five hundredths

Test-Taking Practice

INTERNET
State Test Practice
CLASSZONE.COM

41. Multiple Choice The measure of the angle shown at the right is between: **B**

A. 0° and 45°   **B.** 45° and 90°

C. 90° and 135°   **D.** 135° and 180°

42. Multiple Choice Estimate the measure of the angle shown at the right. **H**

F. 35°   **G.** 90°

H. 145°   **I.** 175°

BRAIN GAME

Flag Team Challenge

Trace the blue angles and extend the rays. Then use a protractor to measure the angles. Find the letter that corresponds to each angle measure. The letters will spell the name of the only state whose flag is not rectangular.
OHIO

A = 50°	**U** = 35°	**T** = 150°	**W** = 85°
I = 75°	**O** = 115°	**H** = 105°	

ASSESSMENT RESOURCES

For more assessment resources, see:
- Assessment Book
- Test and Practice Generator

MINI-QUIZ

1. Name the angle in three ways.

∠Q, ∠PQR, ∠RQP

2. Draw an angle with measure 65°. **Check drawings.**

Use estimation to match the angle with its measure.

A.

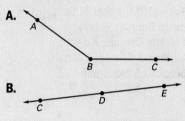

B.

3. 145° **A**   **4.** 180° **B**

RETEACHING/REMEDIATION

- Study Guide in Chapter 9 Resource Book, pp. 18–19
- Tutor Place, Geometry and Measurement Card 2
- eTutorial Plus Online
- Extra Practice, p. 716
- Lesson Practice in Chapter 9 Resource Book, pp. 15–17

CHALLENGE/ENRICHMENT

- Challenge Practice in Chapter 9 Resource Book, p. 21
- Teacher's Edition, p. 418F

ENGLISH LEARNER SUPPORT

- Spanish Study Guide
- Multi-Language Glossary
- Chapter Audio Summaries CDs

LESSON OBJECTIVE

Classify angles and find angle measures.

PACING

Suggested Number of Days
Basic Course: 2 days
Average Course: 2 days
Advanced Course: 2 days
Block: 0.5 block with 9.2
        0.5 block with 9.4

TEACHING RESOURCES

For a complete list of Teaching Resources, see page 418B.

 **TRANSPARENCY**

Warm-Up Exercises for this lesson are available on a transparency.

2 **TEACH**

MOTIVATING THE LESSON

Have students find examples in the classroom of various types of angles.

TIPS FOR NEW TEACHERS

In English, *acute* means "sharp" and *obtuse* means "blunt." Point out that this can help students classify angles. See the Tips for New Teachers in the *Chapter 9 Resource Book.*

Classifying Angles

BEFORE	▶ **Now**	**WHY?**
You named and measured angles.	You'll classify angles and find angle measures.	So you can find the angle measure of the Tower of Pisa, as in Example 4.

📖 **Word Watch**

right angle, p. 430
acute angle, p. 430
obtuse angle, p. 430
straight angle, p. 430
vertical angles, p. 431
complementary angles,
   p. 431
supplementary angles,
   p. 431

Classifying Angles In the photograph at the right, you can see many types of angles. Angles are classified by their measure.

Classifying Angles	
A **right angle** is an angle whose measure is exactly 90°. Indicates a right angle	An **acute angle** is an angle whose measure is less than 90°.
An **obtuse angle** is an angle whose measure is between 90° and 180°.	A **straight angle** is an angle whose measure is exactly 180°.

EXAMPLE 1 **Classifying Angles**

Estimate to classify the angles in the figure as *acute*, *right*, or *obtuse*.

∠A is marked as a right angle.

∠B is an acute angle because m∠B is less than 90°.

∠C is an obtuse angle because m∠C is between 90° and 180°.

∠D is an obtuse angle because m∠D is between 90° and 180°.

Your turn now Classify the angle as *acute*, *right*, *obtuse*, or *straight*.

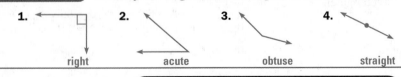

1. right 2. acute 3. obtuse 4. straight

NCTM CURRICULUM STANDARDS
Standard 3: Analyze properties of 2-D shapes
Standard 10: Use representations to communicate mathematical ideas

Vertical Angles When two lines intersect, the angles opposite each other are called **vertical angles.** In the diagram at the right, ∠1 and ∠3 are vertical angles, and ∠2 and ∠4 are vertical angles. Vertical angles have equal measures.

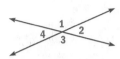

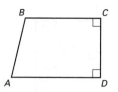
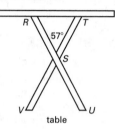
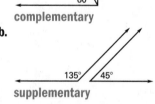
EXAMPLE 2 **Using Vertical Angles**

Find the measure of ∠QRS.

Because ∠QRS and ∠TRU are vertical angles, m∠QRS = m∠TRU = 40°.

ANSWER The measure of ∠QRS is 40°.

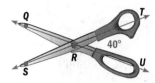

Complementary and Supplementary Angles

Complementary angles Two angles are complementary if the sum of their measures is 90°.

$$m\angle 1 + m\angle 2 = 90°$$

Supplementary angles Two angles are supplementary if the sum of their measures is 180°.

$$m\angle 3 + m\angle 4 = 180°$$

EXAMPLE 3 **Classifying Pairs of Angles**

HELP with Vocabulary

To associate complementary angles with 90° and supplementary angles with 180°, remember that "c" is before "s" in the alphabet and 90 is before 180 on a number line.

Decide whether the angles are *complementary* or *supplementary*.

a.

48° 132°

b.

50°
40°

Solution

a. The angles are supplementary because 48° + 132° = 180°.

b. The angles are complementary because 40° + 50° = 90°.

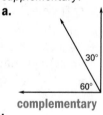

NOTETAKING

Students may have difficulty remembering all the vocabulary in this lesson. Periodically review vocabulary throughout the chapter and have students list vocabulary terms with diagrams in their notebooks.

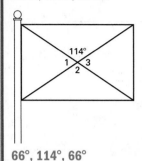
 CONCEPT CHECK

Can complementary angles be obtuse? Why or why not? **No.**
Sample answer: Complementary angles are two angles whose measures have a sum of 90°. Thus, complementary angles must be acute.

 DAILY PUZZLER

Two lines intersect at point *X*. How many angles have vertex *X*? What is the sum of the measures of these angles? **four angles; 360°**

Tower of Pisa
Tuscany, Italy, 1989

EXAMPLE 4 **Solving for an Unknown Measure**

Architecture Before efforts to make the Tower of Pisa more upright began in 1990, the angle between the side of the tower and the ground was about 84.5°. About how many degrees from vertical did the tower lean?

Solution

Start by drawing a diagram. Then find the angle that is complementary to 84.5°.

$$84.5° + x° = 90°$$
$$x = 90 - 84.5$$
$$x = 5.5$$

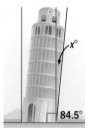

ANSWER The Tower of Pisa leaned about 5.5° from vertical.

9.3 Exercises

More Practice, p. 716

Getting Ready to Practice

Vocabulary **Match the type of angle with an appropriate measure.**

1. acute B   **2.** obtuse D   **3.** right C   **4.** straight A

A. 180°   **B.** 34°   **C.** 90°   **D.** 112°

Use the diagram at the right.

5. Name a pair of vertical angles.

6. Name a pair of complementary angles.

7. Name a pair of supplementary angles.

5. ∠CAB and ∠FAE
6. ∠FAE and ∠EAD
7. Sample answer: ∠DAC and ∠FAD

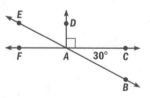

Tell whether the angle measures represent angles that are complementary, supplementary, or neither.

8. 43°, 147° neither   **9.** 22°, 68° complementary   **10.** 34°, 56° complementary   **11.** 64°, 116° supplementary

Use the diagram from Exercises 5–7. Find the angle measure.

12. $m\angle EAF$ 30°   **13.** $m\angle EAD$ 60°   **14.** $m\angle FAB$ 150°

Practice and Problem Solving

with Homework

Example	Exercises
1	15–19
2	20–23
3	24–27
4	28–30

Online Resources
CLASSZONE.COM

· More Examples
· eTutorial Plus

15. right

16. acute

17. obtuse

18. straight

20. ∠HKJ and ∠MKL; ∠JKL and ∠HKM

21. ∠PTN and ∠RTS; ∠PTR and ∠NTS

22. m∠1 = 133°, m∠2 = 47°, m∠3 = 133°

23. m∠1 = 90°, m∠2 = 90°, m∠3 = 90°

Estimate to classify the angle formed by the hands of the clock.

15–18. See margin.

15.
Cairo

16.
Prague

17.
Mexico City

18.
Denver

19. Classify all of the angles in the figure at the right.
∠BAD is obtuse; ∠CAD is right; ∠BAC is acute.

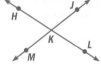

Name the pairs of vertical angles.

20.

21.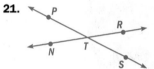

Find the measures of ∠1, ∠2, and ∠3.

22.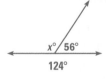

23.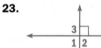

Tell whether the angle measures represent angles that are *complementary*, *supplementary*, or *neither*.

24. 105°, 75°
supplementary

25. 51°, 39°
complementary

26. 15°, 37°
neither

27. 108°, 82°
neither

xy **Algebra Find the value of *x*.**

28.
x° / 56°
124°

29.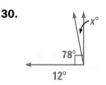
41°
x°
49°

30.
x°
78°
12°

Use a protractor for Exercises 31–34. 31–34. See margin.

31. Draw a right angle.

32. Draw an obtuse angle.

33. Draw an angle complementary to an angle measuring 45°.

34. Draw an angle supplementary to an angle measuring 60°.

Lesson 9.3 Classifying Angles **433**

3 APPLY

ASSIGNMENT GUIDE
Basic Course
Day 1: pp. 433–434 Exs. 15–21, 29–31, 42–46
Day 2: pp. 433–434 Exs. 22–28, 33–37, 47–50

Average Course
Day 1: pp. 433–434 Exs. 15–21, 32–37, 42–45
Day 2: pp. 433–434 Exs. 22–31, 38–40, 46–50

Advanced Course
Day 1: pp. 433–434 Exs. 17–21, 31–37, 42–45
Day 2: pp. 433–434 Exs. 22–30, 38–41*, 48–50

Block
pp. 433–434 Exs. 15–21, 32–37, 42–45 (with 9.2)
pp. 433–434 Exs. 22–31, 38–40, 46–50 (with 9.4)

EXTRA PRACTICE
• Student Edition, p. 716
• Chapter 9 Resource Book, pp. 26–28
• Test and Practice Generator

TRANSPARENCY
Even-numbered answers are available on transparencies. A support transparency is available for Exercises 31–34.

HOMEWORK CHECK
When you review students' homework for this lesson, go over the following exercises to check understanding of key concepts.
Basic: 15, 17, 20, 22, 26
Average: 15, 20, 22, 24, 26
Advanced: 17, 20, 23, 26, 27

31–34. See Additional Answers beginning on page AA1.

433

ASSESS

ASSESSMENT RESOURCES

For more assessment resources, see:
• Assessment Book
• Test and Practice Generator

MINI-QUIZ

1. Classify the angles.

∠*ABC*: right;
∠*CAD*: acute;
∠*BAD*: obtuse

2. Name the pairs of vertical angles.

∠*QPR*, ∠*SPT*; ∠*RPT*, ∠*QPS*

3. Find the value of *x*. **25**

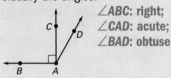

FOLLOW-UP

RETEACHING/REMEDIATION

• Study Guide in Chapter 9 Resource Book, pp. 29–30
• Tutor Place, Geometry and Measurement Cards 3–5
• eTutorial Plus Online
• Extra Practice, p. 716
• Lesson Practice in Chapter 9 Resource Book, pp. 26–28

CHALLENGE/ENRICHMENT

• Challenge Practice in Chapter 9 Resource Book, p. 31
• Teacher's Edition, p. 418F

ENGLISH LEARNER SUPPORT

• Spanish Study Guide
• Multi-Language Glossary
• Chapter Audio Summaries CDs

45. See Additional Answers beginning on page AA1.

434

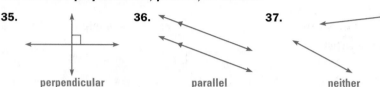

Lines that meet at a 90° angle are called *perpendicular*. Decide if the lines are *perpendicular, parallel,* or *neither.*

35. perpendicular

36. parallel

37. neither

Extended Problem Solving **Use the diagram and information below.**

When you see an object in a mirror, the light from the object bounces off the mirror to reach your eyes. The measure of the angle that is formed by the ray of light and the mirror is the same before and after the light bounces off the mirror.

38. Find the measure of ∠*YBC*. **50°**

39. Find the measure of ∠*ABC*. **80°**

40. **Critical Thinking** What is the measure of ∠*ABC* when you are looking at yourself in the mirror? **0°**

41. **Challenge** Is there a maximum or minimum angle for seeing something reflected in a mirror? Explain. **See margin.**

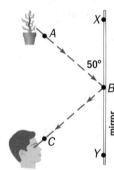

41. Yes. *Sample answer:* The angle must be between 0° and 180° or the image will be in the same plane as the mirror.

Mixed Review

Use the distributive property to evaluate the expression. *(Lesson 4.2)*

42. 5(70 + 6) **380**

43. 7(20 + 4) **168**

44. 4(6 + 0.3) **25.2**

45. Sketch the figures $\overline{AB}$, $\overrightarrow{AB}$, and $\overleftrightarrow{AB}$. *(Lesson 9.1)* **See margin.**

Basic Skills **Find the sum or difference.**

46. 54.2 + 6.12 **60.32**

47. 9.49 + 37.8 **47.29**

48. 18.02 − 0.45 **17.57**

Test-Taking Practice

INTERNET
State Test Practice
CLASSZONE.COM

49. **Multiple Choice** Estimate to classify the angle shown at the right. **A**

A. acute

B. right

C. obtuse

D. straight

50. **Multiple Choice** Which angle measure represents an angle complementary to a 54° angle? **F**

F. 36°

G. 46°

H. 54°

I. 126°

9.4 Hands-on Activity

GOAL
Investigate the sum of the angles of a triangle.

MATERIALS
• ruler
• scissors
• protractor

Investigating Angles of a Triangle

You can use models to find the sum of the angle measures of a triangle.

Explore — Find the sum of the angle measures of a triangle.
Steps 1–2. Check work.

1 Draw a triangle on a piece of paper. Make each side at least 3 inches long.

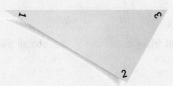

2 Cut out your triangle, and tear off the three corners as shown.

3 Arrange the three corners as shown. What type of angle do they appear to form?
straight angle

4 Repeat Steps 1-3 with a different triangle. What can you conclude about the sum of the angle measures of any triangle?
The sum is 180°.

Your turn now Tell whether the three angle measures could be the angle measures of a triangle. Explain your reasoning. 1–4. See margin.

1. 5°, 80°, 90° **2.** 30°, 70°, 80° **3.** 40°, 54°, 86° **4.** 37°, 42°, 102°

Stop and Think

5. Critical Thinking Choose three angles that you think could form a triangle. Explain how you chose the three angles. Then draw the triangle using a protractor. **A good answer will include three angles whose sum is 180°.**

NCTM CURRICULUM STANDARDS
Standard 3: Analyze properties of 2-D shapes
Standard 7: Make mathematical conjectures
Standard 9: Grasp how mathematical ideas interconnect

Lesson 9.4 Classifying Triangles **435**

1 PLAN

EXPLORE THE CONCEPT
• Find the sum of the angle measures of a triangle.
• This activity helps show the concept presented in the box on page 437.

MATERIALS
Each student or group of students will need a protractor and scissors.

RECOMMENDED TIME
Work activity: 10 min
Discuss results: 5 min

GROUPING
Students can work individually or in pairs. If students work in pairs, ask them to draw different triangles and to compare their results.

2 TEACH

TIPS FOR SUCCESS
To make it easy to identify each vertex, suggest that students mark each one with a dot before tearing.

3 CLOSE

KEY DISCOVERY
The sum of the angle measures of any triangle is 180°.

ASSESSMENT
Tell whether the three angles could be the angle measures of a triangle.
1. 10°, 70°, 80° no
2. 18°, 32°, 130° yes

1–4. See Additional Answers beginning on page AA1.

435

LESSON OBJECTIVE

Classify triangles by their angles and by their sides.

PACING

Suggested Number of Days
Basic Course: 1 day
Average Course: 1 day
Advanced Course: 1 day
Block: 0.5 block with 9.3

TEACHING RESOURCES

For a complete list of Teaching Resources, see page 418B.

TRANSPARENCY

Warm-Up Exercises for this lesson are available on a transparency.

2 TEACH

MOTIVATING THE LESSON

Tell students that triangles can be classified in much the same way that angles are classified.

TIPS FOR NEW TEACHERS

Classifying triangles is usually fairly simple for students, but they may confuse isosceles and equilateral triangles. Point out that all equilateral triangles are also isosceles. See Tips for New Teachers in the *Chapter 9 Resource Book.*

436

Classifying Triangles

BEFORE	▶ Now	WHY?
You classified angles as acute, right, obtuse, or straight.	You'll classify triangles by their angles and by their sides.	So you can classify the triangles of the Great Pyramid, as in Ex. 37.

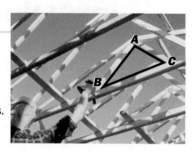

In the Real World

 Word Watch

triangle, p. 436
acute triangle, p. 436
right triangle, p. 436
obtuse triangle, p. 436
equilateral triangle, p. 437
isosceles triangle, p. 437
scalene triangle, p. 437

Carpentry The carpentry work in the photo has many *triangles.* You read △*ABC* as "triangle *ABC.*" A **triangle** is a closed plane figure with three straight sides that connect three points. △*ABC* has sides $\overline{AB}$, $\overline{BC}$, and $\overline{AC}$, and vertices *A*, *B*, and *C*.

Classifying Triangles by Angles		
An **acute triangle** has three acute angles.	A **right triangle** has one right angle.	An **obtuse triangle** has one obtuse angle.

EXAMPLE 1 **Classifying Triangles by Angles**

Classify the triangle by its angles.

a. 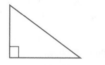   b. 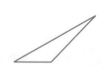   c.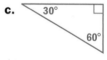

Solution

a. The triangle is obtuse because it has 1 obtuse angle.

b. The triangle is acute because it has 3 acute angles.

c. The triangle is right because it has 1 right angle.

Your turn now **Classify the triangle by its angles.**

1.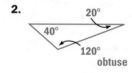
acute

2.
obtuse

3.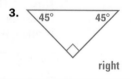
right

NCTM CURRICULUM STANDARDS
Standard 2: Represent situations using algebraic symbols
Standard 3: Analyze properties of 2-D shapes
Standard 9: Grasp how mathematical ideas interconnect

Sides of a Triangle You can use special marks on a drawing to indicate that two sides have the same length as shown at the right.

2 cm
2 cm

Example 1 Classify the triangle by its angles.

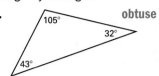

a. obtuse
105° 32° 43°

b. right
56° 34°

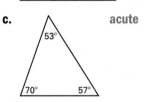

c. acute
53° 70° 57°

Classifying Triangles by Sides

An **equilateral triangle** has three sides of the same length.	An **isosceles triangle** has at least two sides of the same length.	A **scalene triangle** has three sides of different lengths.

EXAMPLE 2 **Classifying Triangles by Sides**

Classify the triangle by its sides.

a.
4 ft 3 ft 2 ft

b.
5 in. 5 in. 5 in.

c.

Solution

  a. The triangle is scalene because all of its sides have different lengths.

  b. The triangle is equilateral because all of its sides have the same length.

  c. The triangle is isosceles because two of its sides have the same length.

Example 2 Classify the triangle by its sides.

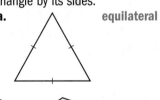

a. equilateral

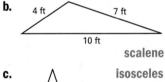

b. 4 ft 7 ft 10 ft
scalene

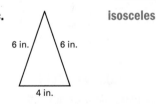

c. isosceles
6 in. 6 in. 4 in.

Angles of a Triangle As you may have noticed in the activity on page 435, the measures of the angles of any triangle add up to 180°.

Sum of Angle Measures of a Triangle

Words The sum of the angle measures of a triangle is 180°.

Algebra $m\angle A + m\angle B + m\angle C = 180°$

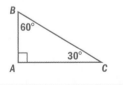
B
60°
30°
A C

MATH REASONING

Ask students why a triangle cannot have more than one right angle or more than one obtuse angle.
With one right angle, the other two angles must have a total measure of 90°, so both must be acute; with one obtuse angle, the other two angles must have a total measure of less than 90°, so both must be acute.

 CONCEPT CHECK

How are triangles classified by their sides? by their angles? **Triangles can be equilateral (3 sides have the same length), isosceles (at least 2 sides have the same length); or scalene (no sides have the same length). Triangles can be equiangular (3 angles have the same measure), acute (3 acute angles), right (1 right angle), or obtuse (1 obtuse angle).**

 DAILY PUZZLER

How many triangles are in the figure below? **10**

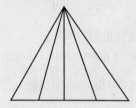

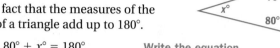

EXAMPLE 3 **Finding Angle Measures of Triangles**

 Algebra **Find the value of *x*.**

Use the fact that the measures of the angles of a triangle add up to 180°.

70°
x°
80°

$70° + 80° + x° = 180°$ Write the equation.

$150 + x = 180$ Simplify.

$x = 180 - 150$ Write a related equation.

$x = 30$

ANSWER The value of *x* is 30.

9.4 **Exercises**
More Practice, p. 716

Getting Ready to Practice

Match the triangle with its description. Use each description once.

1.
25°   80°
75°
A

2.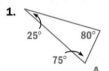
D

3.
100°
30°   50°
B

4.
E

5.
C

6.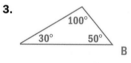
F

A. acute triangle   **B.** obtuse triangle   **C.** right triangle

D. equilateral triangle   **E.** isosceles triangle   **F.** scalene triangle

7. Stamps Classify the stamp shown by its angles and by its sides.
right, isosceles

 Algebra **Find the value of *x*.**

8.
30°
55°
x°
95

9.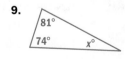
81°
74°   *x*°
25

10.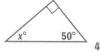
x°   50°
40

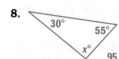

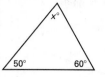

Practice and Problem Solving

HELP with **Homework**

Example	Exercises
1	11-13, 18-19
2	14-17
3	20-22

 **Online Resources**
CLASSZONE.COM
· More Examples
· eTutorial Plus

Classify the triangle by its angles.

11.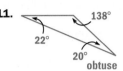
138°
22°
20°
obtuse

12.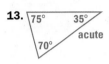
90°   25°
right
65°

13.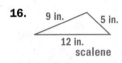
75°   35°
acute
70°

Classify the triangle by its sides.

14.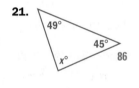
4 ft   4 ft
6 ft
isosceles

15.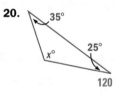
equilateral

16.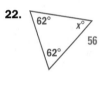
9 in.   5 in.
12 in.
scalene

Flags In Exercises 17–19, use the flag of Guyana, a country in South America.

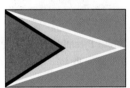

17. Classify the green triangles by their sides.   scalene

18. Classify the red triangle by its angles.   acute

19. Trace the flag. Then draw a line segment on the flag to form two obtuse triangles.   See margin.

xy **Algebra** Find the value of *x*.

20.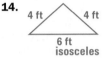
35°
25°
$x°$
120

21.
49°
45°
$x°$ 86

22.
62° $x°$
56
62°

Tell whether the angle measures are those of a triangle. If so, classify the triangle as *acute*, *right*, or *obtuse*.

23. 35°, 35°, 90°
not a triangle

24. 90°, 52°, 38°
is a triangle; right

25. 95°, 25°, 60°
is a triangle; obtuse

26. 56°, 56°, 58°
not a triangle

27. 74°, 55°, 51°
is a triangle; acute

28. 136°, 23°, 32°
not a triangle

Tell whether the statement is *always*, *sometimes*, or *never* true.

29. A right triangle has one right angle.   always

30. In a right triangle, the two acute angles are complementary.   always

31. An obtuse triangle has more than one obtuse angle.   never

Use a protractor to draw the triangle described.   32–35. See margin.

32. acute isosceles

33. obtuse isosceles

34. obtuse scalene

35. right scalene

③ APPLY

ASSIGNMENT GUIDE

Basic Course
Day 1: pp. 439–440 Exs. 11–17, 20–29, 32–36, 40–47

Average Course
Day 1: pp. 439–440 Exs. 11–21, 26–38, 40–42, 45–48

Advanced Course
Day 1: pp. 439–440 Exs. 11–22, 26–31, 34–42*, 47, 48

Block
pp. 439–440 Exs. 11–21, 26–38, 40–42, 45–48 (with 9.3)

EXTRA PRACTICE

• Student Edition, p. 716
• Chapter 9 Resource Book, pp. 35–37
• Test and Practice Generator

TRANSPARENCY

Even-numbered answers are available on transparencies.

HOMEWORK CHECK

When you review students' homework for this lesson, go over the following exercises to check understanding of key concepts.
Basic: 11, 12, 14, 17, 20
Average: 11, 14, 17, 18, 21
Advanced: 11, 15, 17, 18, 22

X COMMON ERROR

For Exercises 32–35, some students may have difficulty drawing a triangle with two characteristics. Encourage them to make a sketch first to predict how the triangle should look. Then they can draw the triangle more precisely with a protractor.

19, 32–35. See Additional Answers beginning on page AA1.

4 ASSESS

ASSESSMENT RESOURCES

For more assessment resources, see:
- Assessment Book
- Test and Practice Generator

MINI-QUIZ

1. Find the value of *x*. **120**

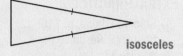

2. Classify the triangle by its angles. **obtuse**

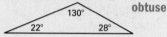

3. Classify the triangle by its sides.

isosceles

5 FOLLOW-UP

RETEACHING/REMEDIATION

- Study Guide in Chapter 9 Resource Book, pp. 38–39
- Tutor Place, Geometry and Measurement Cards 7, 8, 10
- eTutorial Plus Online
- Extra Practice, p. 716
- Lesson Practice in Chapter 9 Resource Book, pp. 35–37

CHALLENGE/ENRICHMENT

- Challenge Practice in Chapter 9 Resource Book, p. 40
- Teacher's Edition, p. 418F

ENGLISH LEARNER SUPPORT

- Spanish Study Guide
- Multi-Language Glossary
- Chapter Audio Summaries CDs

38. See Additional Answers beginning on page AA1.

440

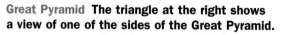

What do you think? **History**

■ **Great Pyramid**

The Great Pyramid is the only one of the Seven Wonders of the World still standing. It is made of over two million stones, most weighing about two and a half tons. About how much does the entire structure weigh?
about 5 million tons

INTERNET
State Test Practice
CLASSZONE.COM

Great Pyramid The triangle at the right shows a view of one of the sides of the Great Pyramid.

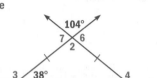

36. What is the value of *x* in the triangle? **77**

37. Classify the triangle by its sides and angles.
acute isosceles triangle

38. **Explain** Use what you know about triangles and angles to find the measures of ∠2, ∠3, ∠4, ∠6, and ∠7. Explain how you found your answers.
See margin.

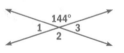

39. **Challenge** In △*JKL*, the measure of ∠*J* is 30°. The measure of ∠*K* is four times the measure of ∠*L*. Find the measure of ∠*K*. What type of triangle is △*JKL*? *m∠K = 120°; obtuse isosceles triangle*

Mixed Review

40. A baseball player pitches $\frac{4}{9}$ of a game. The remaining fraction of the game is evenly divided between two relief pitchers. What fraction of the game did each relief pitcher play? *(Lessons 6.5, 7.4)* $\frac{5}{18}$ **game**

Use the figure shown. *(Lesson 9.3)*

41. Name two pairs of supplementary angles.
Sample answer: ∠1 and ∠2, ∠2 and ∠3

42. Find *m∠*1, *m∠*2, and *m∠*3.
m∠1 = 36°; m∠2 = 144°; m∠3 = 36°

Basic Skills **Write the decimal as a fraction or mixed number.**

43. 0.35 $\frac{7}{20}$ **44.** 0.68 $\frac{17}{25}$ **45.** 6.42 $6\frac{21}{50}$ **46.** 12.37 $12\frac{37}{100}$

Test-Taking Practice

47. **Multiple Choice** What is the measure of ∠*A* in △*ABC*? **C**

A. 115°   **B.** 55°
C. 30°   **D.** 25°

48. **Multiple Choice** Which triangle is obtuse? **F**

F.   **G.**   **H.**   **I.**

9.4 Technology Activity

SPREADSHEET

Angle Measures of Triangles

GOAL Use a spreadsheet to find unknown angle measures of triangles.

> **Example** You can use a spreadsheet to calculate angle measures.

The logo for the Environmental Protection Agency's Research Triangle Park is a triangle that has one 78° angle and one 57° angle. What is the measure of the third angle?

Solution

Create a spreadsheet with the format shown. To calculate the measure of the third angle, you must subtract the sum of the first two angle measures (entered in cells B1 and B2) from 180°. This can be done by entering this formula in cell B3: = 180 − SUM(B1:B2).

	A	B
1	1st angle measure (degrees)	78
2	2nd angle measure (degrees)	57
3	3rd angle measure (degrees)	45

= 180 − SUM(B1:B2) gives the result 180 − (78 + 57), or 45.

ANSWER The measure of the third angle is 45°.

Your turn now Use a spreadsheet to find the value of x.

1.
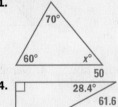
70°
60° x°
50

2.
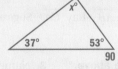
x°
37° 53°
90

3.

34°
34
x° 112°

4.
□ 28.4°
61.6
x°

5.
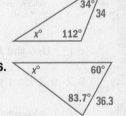
40.3° 32.8°
106.9
x°

6.
x° 60°
83.7° 36.3

7. Art The logo for the National Tsunami Hazard Mitigation Program is a triangle with two 57.5° angles. What is the measure of the third angle? **65°**

8. Science The Nauru99 Triangle is an oceanic and atmospheric research area formed by two research vessels and the island of Nauru. The angle measures at the two research vessels are 80° and 63°. What is the angle measure at the island of Nauru? **37°**

NCTM CURRICULUM STANDARDS
Standard 3: Analyze properties of 2-D shapes
Standard 4: Understand measurable attributes of objects; Apply proper tools to find measures

Lesson 9.4   Classifying Triangles   **441**

 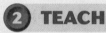

441

Notebook Review

LESSONS 9.1 TO 9.4

Review the vocabulary definitions in your notebook.

Copy the review examples in your notebook. Then complete the exercises.

Check Your Definitions

point, p. 421
line, p. 421
ray, p. 421
endpoint, p. 421
segment, p. 421
plane, p. 422
intersecting lines, p. 422

parallel lines, p. 422
angle, p. 425
vertex, p. 425
degrees (°), p. 426
angles: straight, right, acute, obtuse, p. 430
vertical angles, p. 431

complementary angles, supplementary angles, p. 431
triangles: acute, right, obtuse, equilateral, isosceles, scalene, pp. 436, 437

Use Your Vocabulary

Copy and complete the statement.

1. An ? is formed by two rays with the same endpoint. **angle**

2. Two angles are ? angles if the sum of their measures is 180°. **supplementary**

9.1 Can you identify lines, rays, and segments?

 EXAMPLE Name a line, a ray, and a segment in the figure at the right.

ANSWER Line: $\overleftrightarrow{AB}$ Ray: $\overrightarrow{CA}$ Segment: $\overline{BC}$

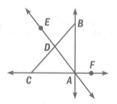

 Use the figure above.   **3.** Name another ray.   **4.** Name another line.

Sample answer $\overrightarrow{EA}$ Sample answer $\overleftrightarrow{FC}$

9.2–9.3 Can you name and classify angles?

 EXAMPLE Name and classify the angle.

a.

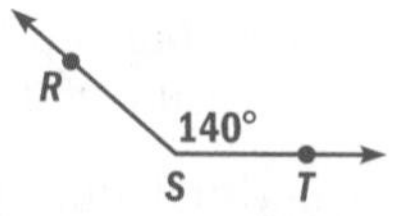

R
140°
S   T

b.

20°
L
M   N

$\angle RST$ is an obtuse angle. $\angle LMN$ is an acute angle.

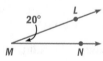 **Classify the angle by its measure.**   **5.** $m\angle A = 100°$ **6.** $m\angle B = 180°$
                                                              obtuse   straight

TRANSPARENCY

A support transparency is available for Review Quiz 1 Exercises 5–7.

9. Subtract the measure from 90°; subtract the measure from 180°.

10. A triangle has 3 angles whose sum is 180°. If there were 2 right angles, then there could only be 2 angles because 90° and 90° add up to 180°.

9.4 Can you classify triangles?

Review

EXAMPLE Find the value of x and classify the triangle by its angles.

$$48° + 32° + x° = 180°$$

$$80 + x = 180$$

$$x = 180 - 80$$

$$x = 100$$

ANSWER The value of x is 100. The triangle is an obtuse triangle.

☑ **Find the value of x. Then classify the triangle by its angles and by its sides.**

7.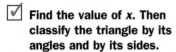

45; right, isosceles

8.

60; acute, equilateral

Stop and Think about Lessons 9.1–9.4 9–10. See margin.

9. **Critical Thinking** Given the measure of an angle, how do you find the measure of a complementary angle? of a supplementary angle?

10. **Writing** Explain why a right triangle cannot have two right angles.

Review Quiz 1

Use the figure to name the following.

1–4. Answers may vary.

1. S

2. $\overrightarrow{PS}$ and $\overrightarrow{QR}$

3. $\overleftrightarrow{PS}$ and $\overleftrightarrow{QR}$

4. $\overline{QR}$

1. a point   2. two rays
3. parallel lines   4. a segment

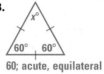

Name the angle in three ways. Then measure it.

5.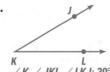

$\angle K, \angle JKL, \angle LKJ$; 30°

6.

$\angle T, \angle STU, \angle UTS$; 120°

7.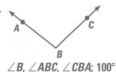

$\angle B, \angle ABC, \angle CBA$; 100°

Tell whether the angle is *acute, obtuse, right,* or *straight.*

8. $m\angle A = 180°$ **9.** $m\angle B = 92°$ **10.** $m\angle C = 18°$ **11.** $m\angle D = 90°$
   straight   obtuse   acute   right

Tell whether the angle measures are those of a triangle.

12. 30°, 60°, 90°   **13.** 45°, 90°, 45°   **14.** 35°, 45°, 110°   **15.** 59°, 43°, 68°
   yes   yes   no   no

Lessons 9.1–9.4   Notebook Review   **443**

EXPLORE THE CONCEPT

- Students investigate relationships among angles of four-sided figures.
- This activity leads into the study of different types of quadrilaterals in Lesson 9.5.

MATERIALS

Each student will need a protractor. See also the Activity master in the *Chapter 9 Resource Book*. A support transparency is available for this Activity.

RECOMMENDED TIME

Work activity: 10 min
Discuss results: 5 min

GROUPING

Students should work individually.

2 TEACH

ALTERNATIVE STRATEGY

To help students generalize, have them visualize the quadrilateral as two triangles that share a common side, a diagonal of the quadrilateral.

3 CLOSE

KEY DISCOVERY

The sum of the angle measures of any quadrilateral is 360°.

ASSESSMENT

Tell whether the four angle measures could be the angle measures of a quadrilateral.

1. 70°, 80°, 100°, 110° yes
2. 18°, 42°, 140° 170° no

444

9.5 Hands-on Activity

GOAL
Investigate relationships among angles of four-sided figures.

MATERIALS
· protractor

Angles of Quadrilaterals

You can use a protractor to investigate angles of four-sided figures.

Explore Investigate the angles of the figures below.

1 Trace the figures below on a piece of paper.

Figure 1   **Figure 2**   **Figure 3**

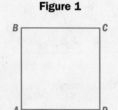   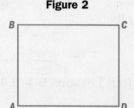   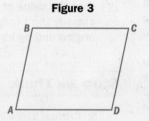

2 Use a protractor to measure the angles. Copy and complete the table.

	m∠A	m∠B	m∠C	m∠D	m∠A + m∠B + m∠C + m∠D
Figure 1	? 90°	? 90°	? 90°	? 90°	? 360°
Figure 2	? 90°	? 90°	? 90°	? 90°	? 360°
Figure 3	? 80°	? 100°	? 80°	? 100°	? 360°

Your turn now

1. Sketch and label a four-sided figure with straight sides. Copy and complete the table in Step 2 for your figure. **A good answer will include any quadrilateral and a completed table that shows the sum of the measures of the angles to be 360°.**

Stop and Think

2. **Writing** Based on the table you completed, write a rule for the sum of the angle measures of a four-sided figure. m∠A + m∠B + m∠C + m∠D = 360°

3. **Critical Thinking** What other angle relationships do you notice in your table? Describe these relationships in words. **Consecutive angles are supplementary and opposite angles have the same measure.**

NCTM CURRICULUM STANDARDS
Standard 3: Analyze properties of 2-D shapes
Standard 4: Understand the processes of measurement
Standard 7: Make mathematical conjectures

Classifying Quadrilaterals

LESSON 9.5

BEFORE | ▶ **Now** | **WHY?**

You classified triangles by their angles and sides. | You'll classify quadrilaterals by their angles and sides. | So you can classify figures in woodwork, as in Exs. 19–21.

Word Watch

quadrilateral, p. 445
parallelogram, p. 445
rectangle, p. 445
rhombus, p. 445
square, p. 445

Quadrilaterals A **quadrilateral** is a plane figure formed by 4 segments called *sides*. Each side intersects exactly 2 other sides, one at each endpoint, and no two sides are part of the same line. The chart below shows some types of quadrilaterals.

Special Quadrilateral	Diagram
A **parallelogram** is a quadrilateral with 2 pairs of parallel sides.	
A **rectangle** is a parallelogram with 4 right angles.	
A **rhombus** is a parallelogram with 4 sides of equal length.	
A **square** is a parallelogram with 4 right angles and 4 sides of equal length.	

with Notetaking

Try making a Venn diagram in your notebook to help you organize the different types of quadrilaterals. For help with Venn diagrams, see p. 703.

EXAMPLE 1 **Classifying Quadrilaterals**

Tell whether the statement is *true* or *false*. Explain your reasoning.

a. All squares are rectangles.

b. Some rhombuses do not have 2 pairs of parallel sides.

Solution

a. True: All squares are parallelograms with 4 right angles, so all squares are rectangles.

b. False: All rhombuses are parallelograms, so all rhombuses have 2 pairs of parallel sides.

NCTM CURRICULUM STANDARDS
Standard 3: Analyze properties of 2-D shapes
Standard 7: Investigate mathematical conjectures
Standard 10: Use representations to communicate ideas

Lesson 9.5 Classifying Quadrilaterals **445**

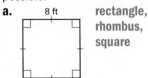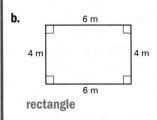

446

Classify Parallelograms You need to look at all the marks and labels on a parallelogram to decide how to classify it. Some parallelograms can be classified in more than one way.

EXAMPLE 2 **Classifying Parallelograms**

Classify the parallelogram in as many ways as possible.

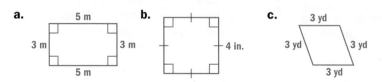

Solution

a. The parallelogram is a rectangle because it has 4 right angles.

b. The parallelogram is a rectangle, a rhombus, and a square because it has 4 right angles and 4 sides of equal length.

c. The parallelogram is a rhombus because it has 4 sides of equal length.

EXAMPLE 3 **Drawing a Quadrilateral**

Draw a quadrilateral that is a rectangle but not a square.

① Draw one side.　② Draw a right angle. Then draw a side with a different length.　③ Draw two more right angles. Then draw the other two sides and angle.

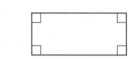

Your turn now Classify the quadrilateral in as many ways as possible.

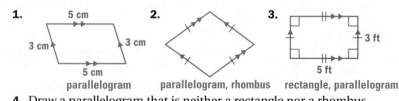

1. **parallelogram**　2. **parallelogram, rhombus**　3. **rectangle, parallelogram**

4. Draw a parallelogram that is neither a rectangle nor a rhombus. See margin.

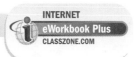

INTERNET
eWorkbook Plus
CLASSZONE.COM

③ **APPLY**

ASSIGNMENT GUIDE

Basic Course
Day 1: pp. 447–448 Exs. 8–14, 27–31
Day 2: pp. 447–448 Exs. 15–22, 32–34

Average Course
Day 1: pp. 447–448 Exs. 8–14, 27–32
Day 2: pp. 447–448 Exs. 15–25, 33–35

Advanced Course
Day 1: pp. 447–448 Exs. 10–14, 22–27*, 34
Day 2: pp. 447–448 Exs. 15–21, 28–31, 35

Block
pp. 447–448 Exs. 8–25, 27–35

Getting Ready to Practice

Vocabulary Copy and complete the statement.

1. A rhombus is a ? with 4 sides of equal length. **parallelogram**

2. A ? is a parallelogram with 4 sides of equal length and 4 right angles. **square**

Tell whether the statement is *true* or *false*. Explain your reasoning.

3–4. See margin.

3. A square is always a rhombus.   **4.** All squares have 4 right angles.

Quilts Classify the quadrilateral in as many ways as possible.

5.    **6.**   **7.**

parallelogram   parallelogram,   parallelogram, rhombus
                       rectangle, rhombus,
                       square

3. True; a rhombus and a square both have 4 sides of equal length.

4. True; a square always has 4 right angles.

Practice and Problem Solving

Copy and complete the statement using *All* or *Some*.

8. ? rectangles are squares. **Some**

9. ? rhombuses are parallelograms. **All**

10. ? squares are rhombuses. **All**

11. ? parallelograms are squares. **Some**

Classify the parallelogram in as many ways as possible.

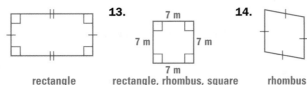

12.   **13.** 7 m   **14.**

         7 m   7 m

          7 m

rectangle   rectangle, rhombus, square   rhombus

15. Draw a rhombus that is not a square. **See margin.**

Critical Thinking Identify all quadrilaterals that always fit the description.

16. 4 equal sides   **17.** 4 right angles   **18.** 2 pairs of parallel sides
rhombus, square   rectangle, square   parallelogram, rectangle,
                                                    rhombus, square

with Homework

Example	Exercises
1	8–11
2	12–14
3	15

Online Resources
CLASSZONE.COM

· More Examples
· eTutorial Plus

EXTRA PRACTICE

• Student Edition, p. 716
• Chapter 9 Resource Book, pp. 44–46
• Test and Practice Generator

④ **TRANSPARENCY**

Even-numbered answers are available on transparencies.

HOMEWORK CHECK

When you review students' homework for this lesson, go over the following exercises to check understanding of key concepts.
Basic: 8, 10, 12, 13, 15
Average: 8, 11, 12, 13, 15,
Advanced: 10, 11, 13, 14, 15

TEACHING TIP

For Exercises 8–11, encourage students to sketch figures to help them decide whether *all* or *some* apply.

15. See Additional Answers beginning on page AA1.

4 ASSESS

ASSESSMENT RESOURCES

For more assessment resources, see:
- Assessment Book
- Test and Practice Generator

MINI-QUIZ

Copy and complete each statement using *All* or *Some*.

1. ? parallelograms are rectangles.
Some

2. ? squares are parallelograms.
All

3. Identify all quadrilaterals that have 4 equal sides and 4 right angles. **squares**

4. Find the value of *x*. **70**

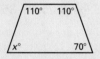

5 FOLLOW-UP

RETEACHING/REMEDIATION

- Study Guide in Chapter 9 Resource Book, pp. 47–48
- Tutor Place, Geometry and Measurement Cards 9, 10
- eTutorial Plus Online
- Extra Practice, p. 716
- Lesson Practice in Chapter 9 Resource Book, pp. 44–46

CHALLENGE/ENRICHMENT

- Challenge Practice in Chapter 9 Resource Book, p. 49
- Teacher's Edition, p. 418F

ENGLISH LEARNER SUPPORT

- Spanish Study Guide
- Multi-Language Glossary
- Chapter Audio Summaries CDs

35. See Additional Answers beginning on page AA1.

448

Woodworking **Use the woodwork shown.**

19. Classify the numbered quadrilaterals.
1 : square; 2 : rectangle; 3 : rhombus

20. What type of quadrilateral is the entire woodwork? **rectangle**

21. How many rhombuses that are not squares are shown on the woodwork?
4

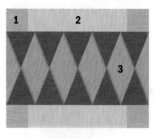

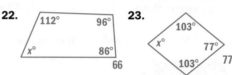 **Algebra** **The sum of the angle measures of a quadrilateral is 360°. Use this information to find the value of *x*.**

22. 112° 96° *x*° 86°

23. 103° *x*° 77° 103° 66 77

24. 62° 106° *x*° 102

25. **Writing** Explain why a rhombus that is also a square is always a rectangle. Squares are always rectangles, so the rhombus must be a rectangle.

26. Yes, the sum of the angles of a quadrilateral is 360°, so with 2 right angles the other two angles just have a sum of 180°; no, with 3 right angles the fourth angle must be 90°, and thus the quadrilateral is a rectangle.

26. **Challenge** Is it possible to draw a quadrilateral that has 2 right angles but is not a rectangle? Is this possible with 3 right angles? Explain.

Mixed Review

27. Order the numbers 42%, 0.45, and $\frac{2}{5}$ from least to greatest. *(Lesson 8.6)*
$\frac{2}{5}$, 42%, 0.45

Tell whether the angle measures are those of a triangle. If so, classify the triangle as *acute*, *right*, or *obtuse*. *(Lesson 9.4)*

28. not a triangle

29. is a triangle; acute

30. is a triangle; obtuse

31. is a triangle; right

28. 28°, 38°, 124° **29.** 20°, 80°, 80° **30.** 23°, 55°, 102° **31.** 45°, 45°, 90°

INTERNET
State Test Practice
CLASSZONE.COM

Basic Skills **Find the total amount spent.**

32. 7 light bulbs for $1.50 each
$10.50

33. 4 bags of pretzels for $2.75 each
$11.00

Test-Taking Practice

34. **Multiple Choice** Which figure is *not* a parallelogram? **B**

A.   B.   C.   D.

35. **Short Response** Explain why a square is a rectangle, a rhombus, a parallelogram, and a quadrilateral. **See margin.**

LESSON 9.6

Polygons

BEFORE
You classified figures by their angles and sides.

▶ **Now**
You'll classify polygons by their sides.

WHY?
So you can classify polygons in street signs, as in Exs. 4–6.

Word Watch

polygon, p. 449
vertex, p. 449
pentagon, p. 449
hexagon, p. 449
octagon, p. 449
regular polygon, p. 450
diagonal, p. 450

In the Real World

Soccer Many soccer balls are made so that the cover shows two different figures. How can you describe these figures?

A **polygon** is a closed plane figure that is formed by three or more segments called sides. Each side intersects exactly two other sides at a **vertex**.

Classifying Polygons				
Triangle	Quadrilateral	Pentagon	Hexagon	Octagon
3 sides	4 sides	5 sides	6 sides	8 sides

HELP with Vocabulary

To help remember how many sides a polygon has, use the following.

"tri" means 3.
"quad" means 4.
"penta" means 5.
"hexa" means 6.
"octa" means 8.

EXAMPLE 1 **Classifying Polygons**

To describe the figures found on the soccer ball shown above, count the number of sides of each figure.

ANSWER The figures are pentagons and hexagons.

Your turn now Classify the polygon.

1.
octagon

2.
quadrilateral

3.
hexagon

SKILL CHECK
1. Which of the following quadrilaterals have all sides equal? square; rectangle, rhombus, parallelogram **square; rhombus**
2. How many sides does a stop sign have? **8**

LESSON OBJECTIVE
Classify polygons by their sides.

PACING
Suggested Number of Days
Basic Course: 1 day
Average Course: 1 day
Advanced Course: 1 day
Block: 0.5 block with 9.7

TEACHING RESOURCES
For a complete list of Teaching Resources, see page 418B.

② TRANSPARENCY
Warm-Up Exercises for this lesson are available on a transparency.

② TEACH

MOTIVATING THE LESSON
Ask students about the shapes they have seen in floor tiles.

TIPS FOR NEW TEACHERS
Make sure students do not confuse arcs with right angle symbols. See Tips for New Teachers in the *Chapter 9 Resource Book.*

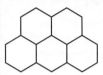
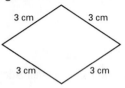
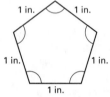

Regular Polygons A **regular polygon** is a polygon with equal side lengths and equal angle measures. A stop sign is an example of a regular octagon.

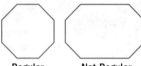

Regular   Not Regular

 EXAMPLE 2 **Classifying Regular Polygons**

Classify the polygon and tell whether it is regular.

a.

10 km
4 km   4 km
10 km

b.

3 in.
3 in.   3 in.
3 in.   3 in.
3 in.

c.

5 m
6 m   6 m
4 m   4 m
7 m

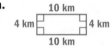 **HELP** **with Reading**

Matching angle marks indicate that the angles have equal measures.

Solution

a. The side lengths of the quadrilateral are not equal, so it is not regular.

b. The side lengths of the hexagon are equal and the angle measures are equal, so it is a regular hexagon.

c. The side lengths of the hexagon are not equal, so it is not regular.

Diagonals A **diagonal** of a polygon is a segment, other than a side, that connects two vertices of the polygon.

EXAMPLE 3 **Diagonals of a Regular Polygon**

How many diagonals can be drawn from one vertex of a regular pentagon? How many triangles do the diagonals form?

Solution

Sketch a regular pentagon and draw all the possible diagonals from one vertex.

ANSWER There are 2 diagonals and 3 triangles.

Your turn now Tell how many triangles are formed by the diagonals from one vertex of the figure.

4. A regular quadrilateral 2   **5.** A regular hexagon 4

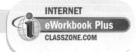
INTERNET
eWorkbook Plus
CLASSZONE.COM

③ APPLY

ASSIGNMENT GUIDE
Basic Course
Day 1: pp. 451–453 Exs. 8–12, 14–21, 27–33
Average Course
Day 1: pp. 451–453 Exs. 8–16, 19–24, 27–29, 32–34
Advanced Course
Day 1: pp. 451–453 Exs. 10–14, 17–29*, 33, 34
Block
pp. 451–453 Exs. 8–16, 19–24, 27–29, 32–34 (with 9.7)

Getting Ready to Practice

Vocabulary **Match the polygon with its correct classification.**

1.
C

2.
A

3.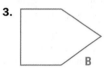
B

A. hexagon   **B.** pentagon   **C.** octagon

Tell whether the figure is a regular polygon.

4.    no   **5.**    yes   **6.** 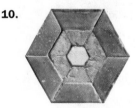   yes

7. **Find the Error** Describe and correct the error in finding the number of diagonals that can be drawn from one vertex of an octagon. *Sample answer:* **There are only 5 diagonals, not 7. Two of the segments drawn from the vertex are sides of the octagon and therefore not diagonals.**

There are 7 diagonals.

Practice and Problem Solving

HELP with **Homework**

Example	Exercises
1	8–10, 16–18
2	8–10, 13
3	11–12

Online Resources
CLASSZONE.COM
· More Examples
· eTutorial Plus

Classify the polygon and tell whether it is regular.

8. 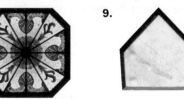   **9.**    **10.**

octagon; not regular   pentagon; not regular   hexagon; regular

11. How many triangles are formed by the diagonals from one vertex of a rectangle? 2

12. Repeat Exercise 11 using a regular octagon. 6

13. **Critical Thinking** What is another name for a regular quadrilateral?
square

EXTRA PRACTICE
- Student Edition, p. 716
- Chapter 9 Resource Book, pp. 54–56
- Test and Practice Generator

TRANSPARENCY
Even-numbered answers are available on transparencies.

HOMEWORK CHECK
When you review students' homework for this lesson, go over the following exercises to check understanding of key concepts.
Basic: 8, 9, 11, 16, 17
Average: 8, 9, 11, 13, 16
Advanced: 10, 11, 12, 13, 18

TEACHING TIP
Encourage students to see the pattern suggested by Exercises 11 and 12. The number of triangles formed by the diagonals from one vertex is two less than the number of sides.

For Exercises 14 and 15, you may need to point out that the angles at the vertex of a polygon are always supplementary. Remind students that the sum of two supplementary angles is 180°.

Advanced Students Ask students to extend the equation in Exercise 23 to find the measure of each angle of a regular polygon with 4 or more sides. Verify that the measure of each angle of a regular pentagon is 108° and the measure of each angle of a regular hexagon is 120°.

16.
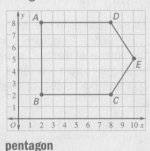
quadrilateral

17.
triangle

18.
pentagon

 with Review

For more help with graphing ordered pairs on a coordinate grid, see page 83.

20. The number of diagonals increases by one as the number of sides increases by one.

(xy) **Algebra** Use supplementary angles to find the value of *x*.

14.

$x°$ 60° 120

15.
$x°$ 108° 72

Geometry **Graph the points on a coordinate grid and connect them to form a polygon. Then classify the polygon.** 16–18. See margin.

16. $A(7, 3)$, $B(3, 3)$, $C(3, 9)$, $D(7, 8)$

17. $A(7, 8)$, $B(7, 3)$, $C(2, 5)$

18. $A(2, 8)$, $B(2, 2)$, $C(8, 2)$, $D(8, 8)$, $E(10, 5)$

Extended Problem Solving **Use the table below for Exercises 19–21.**

19. Copy and complete the table. You may want to draw the polygon described.

Number of sides of regular polygon	4	5	6
Number of diagonals from one vertex	$\frac{?}{1}$	$\frac{?}{2}$	$\frac{?}{3}$

20. **Look for a Pattern** How does the number of diagonals from one vertex change as the number of sides of the polygon increases?

21. **Predict** Use the pattern you found in Exercise 20 to predict the number of diagonals from one vertex of a regular polygon with 9 sides. Then sketch the polygon to check your answer. 6

22. **Critical Thinking** What type of polygon has no diagonals? triangle

23. **Stained Glass Windows** Use the expression below to find the measure of each angle of the regular octagon shown in yellow in the stained glass window at the right. 135°

Number of triangles formed by the diagonals from one vertex	× 180 ÷	Number of sides of the polygon

24. The perimeter of a regular pentagon is 45 inches. What is the length of each side? 9 in.

25. Find the perimeter of a regular octagon that has a side length of 4 meters. 32 m

26. Challenge Draw a regular hexagon. Draw two diagonals from different vertices so that you form two triangles and one quadrilateral. Classify the triangles formed by the diagonals. *See margin for art; isosceles.*

Mixed Review

Draw a quadrilateral that fits the description. *(Lesson 9.5)*
27–28. See margin.

27. at least 3 right angles   **28.** 2 pairs of parallel sides

Choose a Strategy **Use a strategy from the list at the right to solve the following problem. Explain your choice of strategy.**

29. Find the sum of the whole numbers from 1 to 500.

Problem Solving Strategies
- Draw a Diagram
- Solve a Simpler Problem
- Work Backward
- Guess, Check, and Revise

Basic Skills **Use rounding to estimate the sum or difference.**

30. $4.3 + 6.18$ 10   **31.** $2.37 + 3.95$ 6   **32.** $45.15 - 13.8$ 31

Test-Taking Practice

33. Multiple Choice Which figure is a polygon? **D**

A.   **B.**   **C.**   **D.**

34. Short Response Sketch a polygon with ten sides. How many diagonals and triangles can be formed from one vertex of the polygon? **7 diagonals, 8 triangles**

Triangle Teaser

How many triangles are there in the figure?

(Hint: There are more than 16.)
27 triangles

---

29. 125,250. Sample answer: I used Solve a Simpler Problem and found the sum of the first 10 numbers, the second 10 numbers, and when I observed the pattern, used that pattern to find the entire sum.

INTERNET
State Test Practice
CLASSZONE.COM

---

4 ASSESS

ASSESSMENT RESOURCES

For more assessment resources, see:
- Assessment Book
- Test and Practice Generator

MINI-QUIZ

1. Classify the polygon and tell whether it is regular.

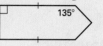

pentagon; not regular

2. How many triangles are formed by the diagonals from one vertex of a pentagon? **3**

3. The perimeter of a regular quadrilateral is 36 inches. What is the length of each side? **9 in.**

4. Find the value of *x*. **80**

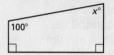

5 FOLLOW-UP

RETEACHING/REMEDIATION
- Study Guide in Chapter 9 Resource Book, pp. 57–58
- Tutor Place, Geometry and Measurement Card 6
- eTutorial Plus Online
- Extra Practice, p. 716
- Lesson Practice in Chapter 9 Resource Book, pp. 54–56

CHALLENGE/ENRICHMENT
- Challenge Practice in Chapter 9 Resource Book, p. 59
- Teacher's Edition, p. 418F

ENGLISH LEARNER SUPPORT
- Spanish Study Guide
- Multi-Language Glossary
- Chapter Audio Summaries CDs

26–28. See Additional Answers beginning on page AA1.

LESSON OBJECTIVE

Identify similar and congruent figures.

PACING

Suggested Number of Days
Basic Course: 2 days
Average Course: 2 days
Advanced Course: 2 days
Block: 0.5 block with 9.6
0.5 block with 9.8

TEACHING RESOURCES

For a complete list of Teaching Resources, see page 418B.

TRANSPARENCY

Warm-Up Exercises for this lesson are available on a transparency.

2 TEACH

MOTIVATING THE LESSON

Give students real-world examples of congruent and similar figures.

ACTIVITY

Goal Use triangles to explore similar and congruent figures.

Key Discovery Congruent figures have the same size and shape. Similar figures have the same shape.

454

Congruent and Similar Figures

LESSON 9.7

BEFORE | **Now** | **WHY?**

You classified polygons by their angles and by their sides. | You'll identify similar and congruent figures. | So you can compare images, such as the photographs in Ex. 13.

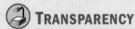 **Word Watch**

congruent, p. 454
similar, p. 454
corresponding parts, p. 455

Activity Use the triangles below to answer the questions.

1–2. See margin.

1 Which triangles are the same size and the same shape? Are their angle measures the same? Are their side lengths the same?

2 Which triangles are the same shape but different sizes? Are their angle measures the same? Are their side lengths the same?

Step 1. first and third triangles; yes; yes

Step 2. first and second triangles, and second and third triangles; yes; no

Comparing Figures Two figures are **congruent** if they have the same size and shape. Two figures are **similar** if they have the same shape but not necessarily the same size.

EXAMPLE 1 **Congruent and Similar Triangles**

Tell whether the triangles are *similar, congruent,* or *neither.*

Solution

$\triangle ABC$, $\triangle FGH$, and $\triangle KLM$ are similar because they have the same shape. $\triangle ABC$ and $\triangle KLM$ are congruent because they have the same size and shape.

Your turn now Tell whether the triangles are *similar, congruent,* or *neither.*

1.
similar

2.
congruent

NCTM CURRICULUM STANDARDS
Standard 3: Analyze properties of 2-D shapes; Use spatial reasoning to solve problems
Standard 8: Use the language of math to express ideas

Corresponding Parts When two figures are similar, their *corresponding angles* have the same measure. When two figures are congruent, their *corresponding parts* have the same measure.
Corresponding parts are the matching sides and angles of two figures.

TIPS FOR NEW TEACHERS
To list corresponding parts, students may need to rotate or flip figures to orient them in the same way. See Tips for New Teachers in the *Chapter 9 Resource Book*.

EXAMPLE 2 Listing Corresponding Parts

△**ABC** and △**DEF** are congruent. List the corresponding parts.

When listing corresponding parts, list corresponding vertices in the same order.

Corresponding angles: ∠A and ∠D, ∠B and ∠E, ∠C and ∠F

Corresponding sides: $\overline{AB}$ and $\overline{DE}$, $\overline{BC}$ and $\overline{EF}$, $\overline{AC}$ and $\overline{DF}$

EXAMPLE 3 Using Corresponding Parts

Bridges In the photograph, △*ABC* and △*DBC* are congruent.

a. If $\overline{AC}$ is about 51 meters long, how long is $\overline{DC}$? Why?

b. If $m\angle A \approx 50°$, what is $m\angle D$? Why?

Solution

a. Corresponding sides of congruent triangles have the same length. So, $\overline{DC}$ has a length of about 51 meters.

b. Corresponding angles of congruent triangles have the same measure. So, $m\angle D \approx 50°$.

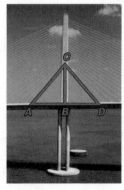

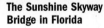
The Sunshine Skyway Bridge in Florida

Your turn now △*GHJ* and △*KML* are similar. List the corresponding parts. Then find $m\angle G$ and $m\angle L$.

3. ∠H and ∠M, ∠J and ∠L, ∠G and ∠K, $\overline{HJ}$ and $\overline{ML}$, $\overline{JG}$ and $\overline{LK}$, $\overline{GH}$ and $\overline{KM}$; $m\angle G = 102°$, $m\angle L = 28°$

3.

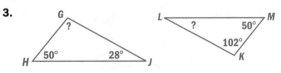

EXTRA EXAMPLES

Example 1 Are the triangles *similar, congruent,* or *neither*?

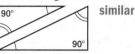
similar

Example 2 △*ABC* and △*RST* are congruent. List the corresponding parts.

∠A and ∠R; ∠B and ∠S; ∠C and ∠T; $\overline{AB}$ and $\overline{RS}$; $\overline{AC}$ and $\overline{RT}$; $\overline{BC}$ and $\overline{ST}$

Example 3 △*ABC* and △*DBC* are congruent.

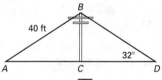

a. How long is $\overline{DB}$? **40 ft**
b. What is $m\angle A$? **32°**

✓ **CONCEPT CHECK**

What is true of congruent triangles? **Corresponding angles have the same measure and corresponding sides have the same length.**

🌎 **DAILY PUZZLER**

A triangle has a perimeter of 24 in. If the length of each side is doubled, what is the new perimeter? **48 in.**

ASSIGNMENT GUIDE

Basic Course
Day 1: pp. 456–457 Exs. 6–10,
18, 22–24
Day 2: pp. 456–457 Exs. 11–15,
25–28

Average Course
Day 1: pp. 456–457 Exs. 6–9,
16–20, 22, 23
Day 2: pp. 456–457 Exs. 11–15,
24–28

Advanced Course
Day 1: pp. 456–457 Exs. 7–9,
14–18, 27
Day 2: pp. 456–457 Exs. 11–13,
19–23*, 28

Block
pp. 456–457 Exs. 6–9, 16–20,
22, 23 (with 9.6)
pp. 456–457 Exs. 11–15, 24–28
(with 9.8)

EXTRA PRACTICE

• Student Edition, p. 716
• Chapter 9 Resource Book,
pp. 62–64
• Test and Practice Generator

 TRANSPARENCY

Even-numbered answers are available on transparencies.

HOMEWORK CHECK

When you review students' homework for this lesson, go over the following exercises to check understanding of key concepts.
Basic: 6, 7, 9, 10, 11
Average: 6, 9, 11, 12, 13
Advanced: 7, 9, 11, 12, 13

 COMMON ERROR

For Exercises 9 and 10, watch for students who mismatch the corresponding angles when one figure of the pair is flipped.

456

9.7 Exercises
More Practice, p. 716

Getting Ready to Practice

Vocabulary Tell whether the statement is *true* or *false*.

1. $\triangle VUW$ is congruent to $\triangle YXZ$ because they have the same size and shape. **false**

2. $\triangle VUW$ is similar to $\triangle YXZ$. **true**

3. In the figures, $\overline{VW}$ corresponds to $\overline{YX}$. **false**

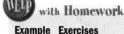 **Algebra** The two figures are congruent. Find the values of *x* and *y*.

4.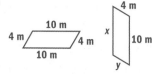

   $x = 10$ m, $y = 4$ m

5.

   $x = 4$ yd, $y = 5$ yd

Practice and Problem Solving

 **with Homework**

Example	Exercises
1	6–8, 13
2	9–10
3	11–12

Online Resources
CLASSZONE.COM
· More Examples
· eTutorial Plus

Tell whether the triangles are *similar*, *congruent*, or *neither*.

6. 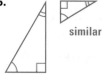 **similar**

7. 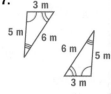 **congruent**

8. 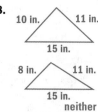 **neither**

List the corresponding parts of the triangles. 9–10. See margin.

9.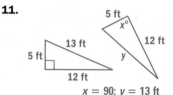

10.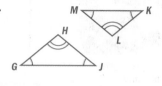

9. $\angle A$ and $\angle D$, $\angle C$ and $\angle F$, $\angle B$ and $\angle E$, $\overline{AC}$ and $\overline{DF}$, $\overline{BC}$ and $\overline{EF}$, $\overline{AB}$ and $\overline{DE}$

10. *Sample answer:* $\angle H$ and $\angle L$, $\angle G$ and $\angle M$, $\angle J$ and $\angle K$, $\overline{GH}$ and $\overline{ML}$, $\overline{HJ}$ and $\overline{LK}$, $\overline{GJ}$ and $\overline{MK}$

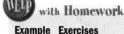 **Algebra** The figures are congruent. Find the values of *x* and *y*.

11.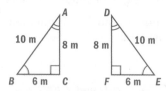

    $x = 90$; $y = 13$ ft

12.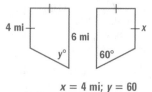

    $x = 4$ mi; $y = 60$

Delicious Fruit Drink!

13. Photography You are viewing photographs on a computer screen at a scale of 2 in. : 1 in. Are the images on the screen and the actual photographs similar? congruent? Explain. Yes; no; they are larger than the actual size.

Decide if the objects are usually *similar*, *congruent*, or *neither*. Explain.
14–17. See margin.

14. buttons on your shirt congruent   **15.** a pair of earrings congruent

16. the drink on the billboard   **17.** a C battery and
and the actual drink similar   a AA battery neither

18. Draw any triangle. Then draw a triangle with the same angle measures but different side lengths. Are the triangles *similar*, *congruent*, or *neither*? Check drawings; similar.

19. △*XYZ* is similar to △*ABC*. List the corresponding parts.
19–21. See margin.

20. Critical Thinking If two figures are congruent, are they also similar? If two figures are similar, are they also congruent? Explain.

21. Challenge Are all squares similar? Are all rectangles similar? Explain.

14–17. Explanations may vary.

14. Congruent; the buttons are the same shape and size.

15. Congruent; the earrings are the same shape and size.

16. Similar; the actual drink and the drink on the billboard are the same shape but not the same size.

17. Neither; the batteries are neither the same shape nor the same size.

19. ∠*Y* and ∠*B*, ∠*X* and ∠*A*, ∠*Z* and ∠*C*, $\overline{YX}$ and $\overline{BA}$, $\overline{YZ}$ and $\overline{BC}$, $\overline{XZ}$ and $\overline{AC}$

20. Yes; no; similar means being alike, but not exactly alike, and congruent means being exactly alike.

Mixed Review

22. Buying CDs A CD that teaches you how to speak Spanish costs $28.75. There is a 6% sales tax and you have $30. Decide whether you can buy the CD. *(Lesson 8.7)* It would cost $30.48 and you only have $30; you do not have enough money.

23. Use a protractor to draw an angle with a measure of 55°. *(Lesson 9.2)* See margin.

Basic Skills **Find the product or quotient.**

24. 3.25×5.6 18.2   **25.** 9.8×0.62 6.076   **26.** $4.85 \div 0.5$ 9.7

21. Yes; yes; all squares are similar, because they all have 4 equal sides and 4 right angles. All rectangles are similar because they all have 4 right angles.

Test-Taking Practice

27. Multiple Choice The triangles shown are congruent. What is the value of *x*? D

A. 2 cm   **B.** 3 cm
C. 5 cm   **D.** 8 cm

28. Multiple Choice The triangles shown are congruent. Find the measure of ∠*G*. I

F. 122°   **G.** 88°
H. 85°   **I.** 65°

Lesson 9.7   Congruent and Similar Figures   **457**

4 **ASSESS**

ASSESSMENT RESOURCES
For more assessment resources, see:
• Assessment Book
• Test and Practice Generator

MINI-QUIZ

1. Tell whether the triangles are *similar*, *congruent*, or *neither*.
similar

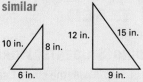

2. The figures are congruent. Find the values of *x* and *y*. 22.6; 12 in.

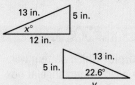

5 **FOLLOW-UP**

RETEACHING/REMEDIATION
• Study Guide in Chapter 9 Resource Book, pp. 65–66
• Tutor Place, Geometry and Measurement Card 17, Ratio, Proportion, and Percent Card 6
• eTutorial Plus Online
• Extra Practice, p. 716
• Lesson Practice in Chapter 9 Resource Book, pp. 62–64

CHALLENGE/ENRICHMENT
• Challenge Practice in Chapter 9 Resource Book, p. 67
• Teacher's Edition, p. 418F

ENGLISH LEARNER SUPPORT
• Spanish Study Guide
• Multi-Language Glossary
• Chapter Audio Summaries CDs

23. See Additional Answers beginning on page AA1.

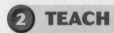

Draw a Diagram
Perform an Experiment
Make a List
Work Backward
Make a Model
Solve a Simpler Problem
Look for a Pattern

1 PLAN

STRATEGY BACKGROUND

The strategy Make a Model is helpful when the real-world objects can be easily created and when it is difficult to visualize the solution. It is useful for real-world problems that involve three-dimensional shapes.

2 TEACH

GUIDING STUDENTS' WORK

Discuss Step 4 with the class. Use a model to show that there will be 2^3 layers and, hence, 8 holes.

EXTRA EXAMPLES

Example Which pattern will form a closed rectangular box when folded? **B**

A.

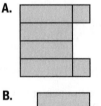

B.

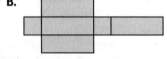

Make a Model

Problem If you fold a rectangular piece of paper in half, and then in half again in the other direction, you will form a similar rectangle. If you punch a hole inside the rectangle through all the layers, how many congruent holes will there be when you unfold the paper?

1 Read and Understand

Read the problem carefully.

You need to fold a rectangular piece of paper in half, then in half again in the other direction, and punch a hole through all the layers.

2 Make a Plan

Decide on a strategy to use.

One way to solve this problem is to make a model. You will need a rectangular piece of paper and a hole punch.

3 Solve the Problem

Reread the problem and make a model.

Begin with a rectangular piece of paper.
Fold the paper in half twice.

Punch a hole inside the rectangle. Unfold the piece of paper and see how many congruent holes you have.

ANSWER There are 4 congruent holes.

4 Look Back

If you make 1 fold, there are 2 layers of paper and 2 holes. If you make 2 folds, there are 4 layers of paper and 4 holes. How many holes would you expect from 3 folds? Try it and see. **8 holes**

NCTM CURRICULUM STANDARDS
Standard 3: Use symmetry to analyze math situations
Standard 6: Solve problems in math and other contexts
Standard 10: Use representations to solve problems

Practice the Strategy

Use the strategy *make a model.*

1. **Paper Cutouts** You fold a rectangular piece of paper in half, then in half again in the other direction. Then you cut out a rectangle through all the layers of paper. What is the maximum number of rectangles you can have when you unfold the paper? the minimum number? **4; 1**

2. **Paper Octagons** Describe how to fold a rectangular piece of paper and make a single cut along a line to form an octagon when the paper is unfolded. **See margin.**

3. **Cubes** Which cube cannot be formed by folding the pattern shown? **C**

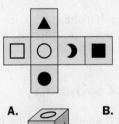

A.   B.

C.   D.

4. **Cube Patterns** Which pattern will form a closed cube when folded? **I**

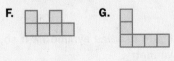

F.   G.

H.   I.

Mixed Problem Solving

Use any strategy to solve the problem.

5. **Furniture** Your bedroom measures 10 feet by 12 feet and your bed measures 6 feet by 3 feet. Could you fit a desk that is 4.5 feet long and 3 feet wide on the same wall as your bed with the long side against the wall? Why or why not? **See margin.**

6. **Random Drawing** Each student in a school with 635 students is assigned a number from 1 to 635 for a random drawing. How many students will be assigned a number with a 2 in it? **208 students**

7. **School Supplies** After purchasing 5 pencils, 5 notebooks, 6 folders, and 3 pens at the prices below, you had $12.35.

Price List	
Notebooks	$4.25 each
Folders	3 for $1
Pens	3 for $4
Pencils	$.25 each

Assume there was no sales tax. How much money did you start with? **$40.85**

8. **Home Improvement** You are building a deck that will be 8 feet by 4 feet. You are using boards that are 8 feet by 4 inches. Will 11 boards be enough? Why or why not? **No.** *Sample answer:* 4 feet is 48 inches, and each board is 4 inches wide, so 48 ÷ 4, or 12 boards are needed.

Lesson 9.8   Line Symmetry   **459**

SKILL CHECK

1. A rectangle is cut along one of its diagonals. Are the resulting triangles congruent? isosceles?
yes; sometimes

LESSON OBJECTIVE

Identify lines of symmetry.

PACING

Suggested Number of Days
Basic Course: 1 day
Average Course: 1 day
Advanced Course: 1 day
Block: 0.5 block with 9.7

TEACHING RESOURCES

For a complete list of Teaching Resources, see page 418B.

TRANSPARENCY

Warm-Up Exercises for this lesson are available on a transparency.

② **TEACH**

MOTIVATING THE LESSON

Ask students to fold a square along one of its sides to make matching halves. Then ask if they can think of another way to fold a square to get two matching halves.

ACTIVITY

Goal Create a figure with symmetry.

Key Discovery Figures have line symmetry if the figure is made up of two congruent parts.

1, 3. See Additional Answers beginning on page AA1.

460

LESSON 9.8

Line Symmetry

BEFORE	Now	WHY?
You learned about congruent and similar figures.	You'll identify lines of symmetry.	So you can find the symmetry of a tennis court, as in Ex. 14.

Activity Create a figure with symmetry.
Steps 1–2. Check work.

① Fold a sheet of paper in half.

② Cut a design out of the folded edge as shown. Unfold the design.

③ Are the figures on the opposite sides of the fold the same size? **yes** the same shape? **yes**

Line Symmetry A figure has **line symmetry** if a line can be drawn that divides the figure into two congruent parts that are mirror images of each other. The line is called the **line of symmetry**.

EXAMPLE 1 **Identifying Lines of Symmetry**

Tell whether the object has line symmetry. If so, draw the line of symmetry.

a.

Yes, this guitar has line symmetry.

b.

No, this guitar does not have line symmetry.

Your turn now Tell whether the figure has line symmetry. If so, copy the figure and draw the line of symmetry.

1.

Yes; see margin for art.

2.

no

3.

Yes; see margin for art.

NCTM CURRICULUM STANDARDS
Standard 3: Analyze properties of 2-D shapes; Use symmetry to analyze math situations
Standard 10: Use representations to communicate ideas

Lines of Symmetry

A figure can have zero, one, or multiple lines of symmetry.

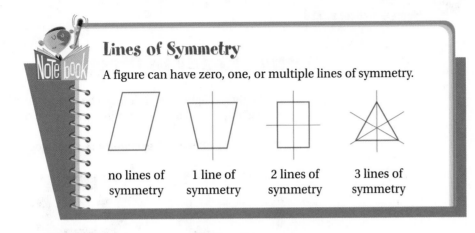

no lines of
symmetry

1 line of
symmetry

2 lines of
symmetry

3 lines of
symmetry

EXAMPLE 2 Multiple Lines of Symmetry

Find the number of lines of symmetry in a square.

Think about how many different ways you can fold a square in half so that the two halves match up perfectly.

vertical fold   **horizontal fold**   **diagonal fold**   **diagonal fold**

ANSWER A square has 4 lines of symmetry.

EXAMPLE 3 Completing Symmetrical Figures

Complete the polygon so that it has the line of symmetry shown.

① Draw the mirror image of each vertex that is not on the line of symmetry.

② Connect the points to complete the mirror image so that the two halves are congruent.

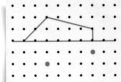

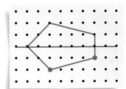

HELP with Solving

To find the mirror image of a point in Example 3, find the distance between the point and the line of symmetry. Place the mirror image point the same distance from the line of symmetry, but on the opposite side.

TIPS FOR NEW TEACHERS

Help students understand line symmetry by doing paper folding. See Tips for New Teachers in the *Chapter 9 Resource Book*.

EXTRA EXAMPLES

Example 1 Tell whether the object has line symmetry. If so, draw the line of symmetry.

Yes; a vertical line of symmetry; check drawings.

Example 2 Find the number of lines of symmetry in an equilateral triangle. **3**

Example 3 Complete the polygon so that it has the line of symmetry shown.

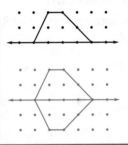

 TRANSPARENCY

A support transparency is available for Example 3.

 CONCEPT CHECK

What is a line of symmetry? **a line that divides a figure into two congruent parts**

 DAILY PUZZLER

How many lines of symmetry does a regular octagon have? **8**

ASSIGNMENT GUIDE

Basic Course
Day 1: pp. 462–463 Exs. 5–11, 14–16, 19–31

Average Course
Day 1: pp. 462–463 Exs. 5–11, 14–17, 19–26, 29–32

Advanced Course
Day 1: pp. 462–463 Exs. 5–8, 12–26*, 30–32

Block
pp. 462–463 Exs. 5–11, 14–17, 19–26, 29–32 (with 9.7)

EXTRA PRACTICE

- Student Edition, p. 716
- Chapter 9 Resource Book, pp. 70–72
- Test and Practice Generator

 TRANSPARENCY

Even-numbered answers are available on transparencies. A support transparency is available for Exercises 11–13.

HOMEWORK CHECK

When you review students' homework for this lesson, go over the following exercises to check understanding of key concepts.
Basic: 5, 7, 8, 9, 11
Average: 5, 7, 8, 10, 11
Advanced: 5, 7, 8, 12, 13

VISUALIZE

After students have copied the figures in Exercises 8–10, suggest that they fold the figures along the line(s) of symmetry so that they can visualize the congruent parts.

8–13. See Additional Answers beginning on page AA1.

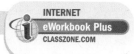

9.8 Exercises
More Practice, p. 716

Getting Ready to Practice

1. **Vocabulary** A figure has ? if it can be divided by a line into two congruent parts that are mirror images of each other. **line symmetry**

Find the number of lines of symmetry in the object.

2.
   2

3.
   0

4.
   1

Practice and Problem Solving

Tell whether the line shown is a line of symmetry.

5.
   no

6.
   yes

7.
   yes

Copy the figure and draw all lines of symmetry. 8–10. See margin.

8.

9.

10.

Copy and complete the figure so that it has the line of symmetry shown. 11–13. See margin.

11.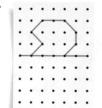

12.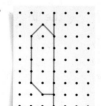

13.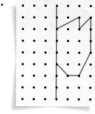

HELP with Homework

Example	Exercises
1	5–10
2	8–10
3	11–13

Online Resources
CLASSZONE.COM
· More Examples
· eTutorial Plus

14. Find the number of lines of symmetry in the tennis court. **2**

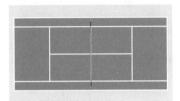

15. Find the number of lines of symmetry in the baseball field. **1**

16. Make a Model Copy the figure at the right. Cut out your copy and use it to find the number of lines of symmetry in the figure. **2**

17. Critical Thinking Is there a type of triangle that has exactly one line of symmetry? If so, identify the type of triangle. **yes; isosceles triangle**

18. Challenge Which quadrilaterals have exactly two lines of symmetry? Sketch the quadrilaterals and show the lines of symmetry.
Rectangles and rhombuses; see margin for art.

Mixed Review

Use mental math to solve the equation. *(Lesson 1.6)*

19. $12 + x = 24$ **12**　**20.** $x - 8 = 22$ **30**　**21.** $3x = 27$ **9**　**22.** $x \div 5 = 4$ **20**

Find the product. *(Lesson 7.2)*

23. $\frac{6}{7} \times \frac{7}{12}$ **$\frac{1}{2}$**　**24.** $\frac{2}{3} \times \frac{1}{2}$ **$\frac{1}{3}$**　**25.** $\frac{3}{2} \times \frac{1}{18}$ **$\frac{1}{12}$**　**26.** $\frac{10}{13} \times \frac{39}{70}$ **$\frac{3}{7}$**

Basic Skills **Estimate the product.** **27–30. Estimates may vary.**

27. 11×24 **240**　**28.** 9×21 **180**　**29.** 32×72 **2100**　**30.** 48×63 **3000**

Test-Taking Practice

31. Multiple Choice Which letter has no lines of symmetry? **B**

A. E　　**B.** F　　**C.** T　　**D.** W

32. Multiple Choice How many lines of symmetry does the letter **H** have?
H

F. none　　**G.** one　　**H.** two　　**I.** four

Lesson 9.8　Line Symmetry　**463**

---

4 ASSESS

ASSESSMENT RESOURCES

For more assessment resources, see:
- Assessment Book
- Test and Practice Generator

MINI-QUIZ

1. Draw all lines of symmetry.

2. Complete the figure so that it has the line of symmetry shown.

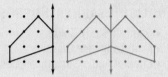

5 FOLLOW-UP

RETEACHING/REMEDIATION
- Study Guide in Chapter 9 Resource Book, pp. 73–74
- Tutor Place, Geometry and Measurement Card 18
- eTutorial Plus Online
- Extra Practice, p. 716
- Lesson Practice in Chapter 9 Resource Book, pp. 70–72

CHALLENGE/ENRICHMENT
- Challenge Practice in Chapter 9 Resource Book, p. 76
- Teacher's Edition, p. 418F

ENGLISH LEARNER SUPPORT
- Spanish Study Guide
- Multi-Language Glossary
- Chapter Audio Summaries CDs

18. See Additional Answers beginning on page AA1.

463

3. rhombus, quadrilateral, parallelogram

4. regular pentagon

5. congruent; $\angle C$ and $\angle F$, $\angle E$ and $\angle H$, $\angle D$ and $\angle G$, $\overline{DE}$ and $\overline{GH}$, $\overline{CE}$ and $\overline{FH}$, $\overline{CD}$ and $\overline{FG}$

Notebook Review

Review the vocabulary definitions in your notebook.

Copy the review examples in your notebook. Then complete the exercises.

Check Your Definitions

quadrilateral, p. 445
parallelogram, p. 445
rectangle, p. 445
rhombus, p. 445
square, p. 445

polygons: pentagon, hexagon, octagon, p. 449
regular polygon, p. 450
diagonal, p. 450

congruent, p. 454
similar, p. 454
corresponding parts, p. 455
line symmetry, p. 460

Use Your Vocabulary

1. Copy and complete: A __?__ is a quadrilateral with two pairs of parallel sides.
   parallelogram

2. Are all rhombuses regular polygons? Why or why not?
   No; all angles do not have to have the same measure.

9.5–9.6 Can you classify quadrilaterals and polygons?

 EXAMPLE Classify the polygon shown.

ANSWER The polygon is a quadrilateral, a parallelogram, a rectangle, a rhombus, and a square.

 Classify the polygon. 3.
3–4. See margin.

4.

9.7 Can you identify similar and congruent figures?

 EXAMPLE The triangles at the right are similar. List the corresponding parts.

ANSWER Corresponding angles: $\angle D$ and $\angle X$, $\angle E$ and $\angle Y$, $\angle F$ and $\angle Z$

Corresponding sides: $\overline{DE}$ and $\overline{XY}$, $\overline{EF}$ and $\overline{YZ}$, $\overline{FD}$ and $\overline{ZX}$

 5. Tell whether the triangles are *similar* or *congruent*. List the corresponding parts.
See margin.

Notebook Review

9. No; a parallelogram is a quadrilateral with 2 pairs of parallel
   sides and a regular hexagon has
   6 sides with 3 pairs of parallel
   sides.

Review Quiz 2

1. quadrilateral, rectangle,
   parallelogram

2. quadrilateral, parallelogram

3. regular octagon

5. ∠J and ∠W, ∠K and ∠X, ∠L
   and ∠Y, ∠M and ∠Z, $\overline{JK}$ and
   $\overline{WX}$, $\overline{KL}$ and $\overline{XY}$, $\overline{LM}$ and $\overline{YZ}$,
   $\overline{JM}$ and $\overline{WZ}$

9.8 Can you find lines of symmetry?

EXAMPLE Tell whether the figure has line
symmetry. If so, draw any lines of symmetry.

ANSWER The figure has one line of symmetry.

☑ **Tell whether the line shown is a line of symmetry.**

6.

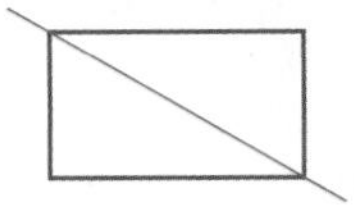

no

7.

no

8.

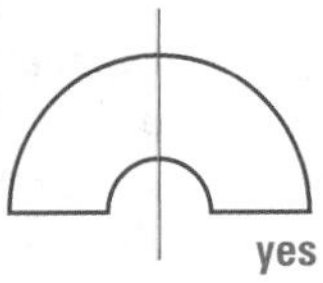

yes

Stop and Think about Lessons 9.5–9.8

9. **Writing** Your friend says that a regular hexagon is a parallelogram.
   Is her statement correct? Explain why or why not. See margin.

Review Quiz 2

Classify the polygon in as many ways as possible. 1–3. See margin.

1.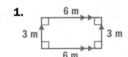

6 m
3 m   3 m
6 m

2.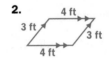

4 ft
3 ft   3 ft
4 ft

3.

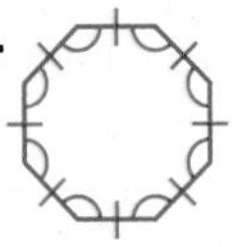

4. A regular pentagon has a perimeter of 15 feet. What is the side length?
   3 ft

Use the congruent quadrilaterals shown.

5. List the corresponding parts. See margin.

6. Find the value of *a*. 12 cm

7. What is *m∠K*? 70°

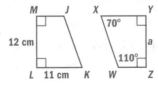

M   J   X   Y
                70°
12 cm   a
                110°
L   11 cm   K   W   Z

Find the number of lines of symmetry in the figure.

8.

2

9.

1

10.

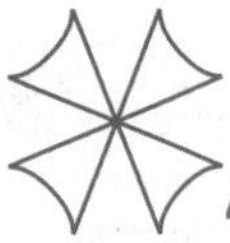

4

1. When two lines intersect, the angles opposite each other are called vertical angles.

Chapter Review

 Vocabulary

ray, p. 421	complementary, p. 431	polygons: pentagon, hexagon, octagon, p. 449
endpoint, p. 421	supplementary, p. 431	
segment, p. 421	triangles: acute, right, obtuse, equilateral, isosceles, scalene, pp. 436, 437	regular polygon, p. 450
intersecting lines, p. 422		
parallel lines, p. 422		diagonal, p. 450
angle, p. 425		congruent and similar figures, p. 454
vertex, p. 425, 449	quadrilateral, p. 445	
degrees(°), p. 426	parallelogram, p. 445	corresponding parts, p. 455
angles: straight, right, acute, obtuse, p. 430	rectangle, p. 445	
	rhombus, p. 445	
vertical angles, p. 431	square, p. 445	line symmetry, p. 460

Vocabulary Review

1. What are vertical angles? **See margin.**

2. Are all rectangles parallelograms? **yes**

3. How many acute angles does an acute triangle have? **3**

4. How many obtuse angles does an obtuse triangle have? **1**

5. What is the relationship between two supplementary angles? **The sum of their measures is 180°.**

Copy and complete the statement.

6. An angle with a measure of 100° is an example of an $\underline{?}$ angle. **obtuse**

7. A straight angle has a measure of $\underline{?}$. **180°**

8. Two figures are $\underline{?}$ if they have the same size and shape. **congruent**

9. A regular polygon has $\underline{?}$ side lengths and $\underline{?}$ angle measures. **equal; equal**

Review Questions

Use the diagram of a gate to name the following. (Lesson 9.1)
10–12. Answers may vary.

10. three points **S, T, V**

11. a horizontal line throught point V $\overleftrightarrow{VW}$

12. a segment that has R as an endpoint $\overline{WR}$

13. a line parallel to the line in Exercise 11 $\overleftrightarrow{ST}$

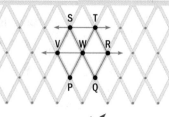

Use the angle at the right. (Lesson 9.2)

14. Name the angle in three ways. What is its vertex? $\angle K, \angle JKL, \angle LKJ; K$

15. Estimate the measure of the angle. Use a protractor to check your estimate. **45°**

Review Questions

Decide whether the angles are *complementary*, *supplementary*, or *neither*.
(Lesson 9.3)

16.

neither

17.

complementary

18.
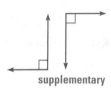
supplementary

19. Draw an obtuse angle. Measure your angle. *(Lesson 9.3)* See margin.

Use the diagram at the right. *(Lesson 9.3)*

20. Are ∠1 and ∠2 vertical angles? Explain why or why not.
No; they are not opposite each other.

21. Find the measures of ∠1, ∠2, and ∠3.
m∠1 = 152°; m∠2 = 28°; m∠3 = 152°

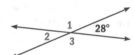

Find the value of *x*. Then classify the triangle by its angles.
(Lesson 9.4)

22.

44; obtuse

23.
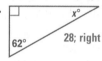
73; acute

24.

28; right

Classify the polygon in as many ways as possible. *(Lessons 9.5, 9.6)*

25.

quadrilateral

26.

See margin.

27.

quadrilateral, parallelogram

28.

pentagon

Tell whether the triangles are *similar* or *congruent*. Then list the corresponding parts. *(Lesson 9.7)* 29–30. See margin.

29.
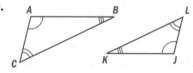

30.

Copy the figure and draw all lines of symmetry. *(Lesson 9.8)* 31–34. See margin.

31.

32.

33.

34.

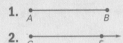
9

Chapter Test

Sketch the figure described. 1–3. See margin.

1. $\overline{AB}$ **2.** $\overrightarrow{GF}$ **3.** $\overleftrightarrow{MN}$

4. Television You are adjusting the volume on the television shown. Are the lines that represent the volume *parallel* or *intersecting*? Explain. **Parallel; the lines do not intersect.**

Use estimation to name the angle in the diagram whose measure is closest to the given measure.

5. 55° ∠VYW   **6.** 10° ∠SYT   **7.** 115° ∠SYV

8. 170° ∠TYW   **9.** 180° ∠SYW   **10.** 80° ∠UYT

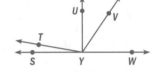

11. Give an example of an acute angle measure and an obtuse angle measure. *Sample answer:* 35°, 160°

12. Find the measure of an angle that is complementary to an angle measuring 25°. **65°**

13. Find the measure of an angle that is supplementary to an angle measuring 80°. **100°**

Find the value of *x*. Then classify the triangle by its angles.

14.
x°
44°
46; right

15.

56°
x°
68; acute

16.
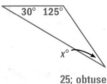
30° 125°
x°
25; obtuse

Classify the quadrilateral in as many ways as possible.

17.

10 in.
rhombus, parallelogram

18.

10 cm
6 cm   6 cm
10 cm
rectangle, parallelogram

19.
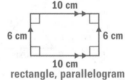
12 m
3 m   3 m
12 m
parallelogram

20. The perimeter of a regular hexagon is 48 centimeters. Find the length of each side. **8 cm**

21. △JKL and △XYZ are congruent. List the corresponding parts. **See margin.**

22. Basketball How many lines of symmetry does the basketball court shown at the right have? **2**

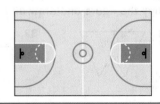

Chapter Standardized Test

Test-Taking Strategy Be careful when choosing an answer. Even though it may seem like the obvious answer, there could be a better choice.

Multiple Choice

1. Which of the following represents a figure that has *M* and *N* as endpoints? **D**

A. $\overleftrightarrow{MN}$ **B.** $\overrightarrow{MN}$ **C.** $\overrightarrow{NM}$ **D.** $\overline{MN}$

2. Which angle has a measure of 102°? **G**

F.   **G.**

H.   **I.**

3. Which statement is true about the figure? **B**

A. It has no acute angles.

B. It has one right angle.

C. It has more than one obtuse angle.

D. All statements are true.

4. Which pair of angle measures represent angles that are complementary? **H**

F. 21°, 59°   **G.** 39°, 61°

H. 24°, 66°   **I.** 85°, 95°

5. What is the value of *x* in the figure? **B**

A. 40   **B.** 50

C. 80   **D.** 90

6. Which angle measures could be those of an acute triangle? **I**

F. 24°, 63°, 73°   **G.** 30°, 60°, 90°

H. 36°, 108°, 36°   **I.** 45°, 85°, 50°

7. Which figure is *not* a polygon? **D**

A.   **B.**

C.   **D.**

Short Response

8. Use the flag of the Bahamas shown below. How many pairs of congruent figures are in the flag? How many lines of symmetry does the flag have? Explain your answers. **See margin.**

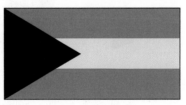

Extended Response

9. Graph the points *A*(2, 4), *B*(4, 4), *C*(4, 8), and *D*(2, 8) and classify the figure they form. Then graph the points *E*(8, 1), *F*(9, 1), *G*(9, 3), and *H*(8, 3) and classify the figure they form. Are the figures *similar*, *congruent*, or *neither*? Explain.
Check graphs; rectangle; rectangle; similar; the rectangles have the same shape but they are not congruent, so they are similar.

8. 1; 1; the two blue sections are congruent. A horizontal line through the center is the only line of symmetry.

9.

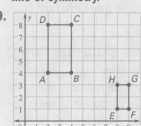

- Students use their knowledge of geometry to classify and describe crystals.
- Classifying triangles was studied in Lesson 9.4. Classifying quadrilaterals and polygons was studied in Lessons 9.5 and 9.6.
- Crystals can be identified by geometric shapes and angle measures.

SCIENCE BACKGROUND

The particles of a mineral are arranged in a structured pattern called a crystal. Scientists may identify a mineral by its crystalline structure. Although a mineral can have multiple crystalline structures, the atomic arrangement of the component elements is the same in all specimens of the mineral.

GROUPING

You may want students to work in groups of four to discuss terminology in the context of polyhedrons.

② **TEACH**

TIPS FOR SUCCESS

Give each group models of prisms and other polyhedrons so they can discuss the way to classify polygons. Introduce informal definitions of *base*, *face*, and *surface*. Have students answer the questions individually and compare their answers.

GUIDING STUDENTS' WORK

The terminology may be confusing for some students, since it may be unfamiliar. Encourage students to make note cards and use them like flash cards to test each other on the types of crystals presented.

470

EXPLORING **MATH** IN **SCIENCE**

The Geometry of Crystals

Classifying Crystals

Crystals occur when the smallest particles of a mineral are arranged in a structured pattern. This pattern determines the outward appearance of a crystal. The different shaped faces you see result from the pattern. Scientists measure the angles between a crystal's faces to help identify the crystal.

A single mineral may have many different crystal forms. For example, the mineral calcite has over 100 different crystal forms. Three of these forms are shown below.

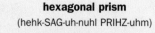

scalenohedron	rhombohedron	hexagonal prism
(skay-LEE-nuh-HEE-druhn)	(RAHM-boh-HEE-druhn)	(hehk-SAG-uh-nuhl PRIHZ-uhm)

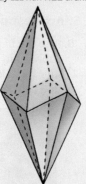 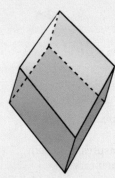 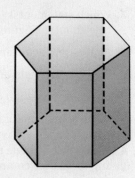

1. The scalenohedron has twelve surfaces, all of which are triangles. Based on the name *scalenohedron*, what kind of triangles do you think the surfaces are? **scalene**

2. Each surface of the rhombohedron is a rhombus. How many surfaces does the rhombohedron have? Based on what you know about rhombuses, what can you say about the lengths of the edges of the rhombohedron? **6; they are all equal.**

3. How many surfaces does the hexagonal prism have? What are the shapes of these surfaces? How many of each type of surface are there? **8; hexagons and rectangles; 2 hexagons and 6 rectangles**

Measuring Angles in Crystals

Crystals in nature tend to be imperfect and distorted. However, scientists can rely on certain geometric properties of a crystal to help identify it. For a particular type of crystal, the angles between certain faces will always be the same. Scientists often measure these angles as part of the process of identifying a crystal.

4. Note the red and blue faces on the crystal forms on page 470. For each crystal form, tell whether the angle between the colored surfaces appears to be a right angle, an acute angle, or an obtuse angle. **scalenohedron: obtuse; rhombohedron: acute; hexagonal prism: obtuse**

5. Table salt is a crystal. Its crystal form is a cube. What kind of angles are there between the surfaces in a salt crystal? **right**

Project IDEAS

- **Experiment** Scientists use a tool called a goniometer to measure the angles between the faces of a crystal. Find out more about goniometers. Then make your own and use it to measure the angles on an everyday object, such as the roof of a birdhouse.
  A good answer will include an accurate goniometer.

- **Report** A diamond is one of three crystal forms of carbon. Find out about the other two crystal forms of carbon. Present your findings to the class using a poster or an oral report.
  A good answer will include clearly presented information.

- **Research** Scientists can also use x-ray lasers to directly measure the angles in crystals. Find information about the use of x-ray measurements in identifying crystals. **A good answer will include well-documented research and clearly presented information.**

- **Career** A scientist who studies crystals is called a crystallographer. Find out what kinds of work crystallographers do. What kind of education is required to be a crystallographer? Present your findings to the class.
  A good answer will include well-documented research and a clear presentation.

INTERNET
Project Support
CLASSZONE.COM

③ APPLY

REFLECTING ON THE ACTIVITY

Common three-dimensional shapes can be used to describe crystals and other solid figures important in science.

PROJECT IDEAS

For additional information on the Project Ideas and for suggestions for more projects, go to classzone.com

④ ASSESS

The rubric below can be used to assess the projects on the pupil page. For more information on rubrics, see the Professional Development Book.

4 The student fully achieves the mathematical and project goals. The crystals are classified correctly. All questions are answered correctly. All work is complete and accurate.

3 The student substantially achieves the mathematical and project goals. The number of surfaces may have been counted incorrectly. There may be some minor misunderstanding of content, errors in computation, or weakness in presentation.

2 The student partially achieves the mathematical and project goals. Some of the questions may not have been answered. Some of the work may be incomplete, misdirected, or unclear.

1 The student makes little progress toward accomplishing the goals of the project because of a lack of understanding or lack of effort. The student did not answer the questions or reflect on the answers to the questions.

REGULAR SCHEDULE

Lesson	Les. Day	BASIC	AVERAGE	ADVANCED
10.1	Day 1	pp. 478–479 Exs. 5–12, 15, 17–27	pp. 478–479 Exs. 5–15, 17–20, 24–27	pp. 478–479 Exs. 7–21*, 25–27
10.2	Day 1	EP p. 714 Exs. 5–8; pp. 482–483 Exs. 7–18, 23–32	pp. 482–483 Exs. 7–13, 16–21, 23–33	pp. 482–483 Exs. 9–13, 16–27*, 31–33
10.3	Day 1	EP p. 711 Exs. 1–4; pp. 488–489 Exs. 14–16, 28–32	pp. 488–489 Exs. 14–16, 25, 28–32	pp. 488–489 Exs. 14–16, 25–29*
	Day 2	pp. 488–489 Exs. 17–23, 33–35	pp. 488–489 Exs. 17–19, 21–24, 33–35	pp. 488–489 Exs. 19–24, 33–35
10.4	Day 1	SRH p. 699 Exs. 1–6; pp. 494–495 Exs. 7–10, 13–16, 24–27	pp. 494–495 Exs. 7–13, 22, 30–34	pp. 494–495 Exs. 9–16, 24–27
	Day 2	pp. 494–495 Exs. 17–21, 28–34	pp. 494–495 Exs. 15–21, 24–29	pp. 494–495 Exs. 17–23*, 28–31, 34
10.5	Day 1	pp. 502–503 Exs. 7–13, 15–19, 24–34	pp. 502–503 Exs. 9–15, 18–22, 24–29, 33–35	pp. 502–503 Exs. 9–13, 16–28*, 33–35
10.6	Day 1	pp. 508–509 Exs. 6–8, 16, 19–23	pp. 508–509 Exs. 6–8, 15–17, 25–28	pp. 508–509 Exs. 6–8, 15–18*, 26–28
	Day 2	pp. 508–509 Exs. 10–14, 24–27	pp. 508–509 Exs. 9–14, 19–22	pp. 508–509 Exs. 9–14, 19–22
10.7	Day 1	pp. 512–513 Exs. 6–15, 20–27	pp. 512–513 Exs. 8–18, 20–27	pp. 512–513 Exs. 8–21*, 24–27
Review	Day 1	pp. 518–519 Exs. 1–30	pp. 518–519 Exs. 1–30	pp. 518–519 Exs. 1–30
Assess	Day 1	Chapter 10 Test	Chapter 10 Test	Chapter 10 Test

YEARLY PACING   Chapter 10 Total – **12 days**   Chapters 1–10 Total – **120 days**   Remaining – **40 days**

*Challenge Exercises   EP = Extra Practice   SRH = Skills Review Handbook   EC = Extra Challenge

BLOCK SCHEDULE

DAY 1	DAY 2	DAY 3	DAY 4	DAY 5	DAY 6
10.1 pp. 478–479 Exs. 5–15, 17–20, 24–27 **10.2** pp. 482–483 Exs. 7–13, 16–21, 23–33	**10.3** pp. 488–489 Exs. 14–19, 21–25, 28–35	**10.4** pp. 494–495 Exs. 7–13, 15–22, 24–34	**10.5** pp. 502–503 Exs. 9–15, 18–22, 24–29, 33–35 **10.6** pp. 508–509 Exs. 6–8, 15–17, 25–28	**10.6 cont.** pp. 508–509 Exs. 9–14, 19–22 **10.7** pp. 512–513 Exs. 8–18, 20–27	**Review** pp. 518–519 Exs. 1–30 **Assess** Chapter 10 Test

YEARLY PACING   Chapter 10 Total – **6 days**   Chapters 1–10 Total – **60 days**   Remaining – **20 days**

Support Materials

📖 CHAPTER RESOURCE BOOK

CHAPTER SUPPORT

Tips for New Teachers	p. 1	Parents as Partners	p. 3

LESSON SUPPORT

	10.1	10.2	10.3	10.4	10.5	10.6	10.7
Lesson Plans (regular and block)	p. 5	p. 13	p. 21	p. 31	p. 43	p. 51	p. 59
Technology Activities & Keystrokes			p. 23	p. 33			
Activity Support Masters							
Activity Masters				p. 34			p. 61
Practice (3 levels)	p. 7	p. 15	p. 24	p. 36	p. 45	p. 53	p. 62
Study Guide	p. 10	p. 18	p. 27	p. 39	p. 48	p. 56	p. 65
Real-World Problem Solving				p. 41			p. 67
Challenge Practice	p. 12	p. 20	p. 29	p. 42	p. 50	p. 58	p. 68

REVIEW

Games Support Masters	p. 30	Cooperative Project with Rubric	p. 72
Chapter Review Games and Activities	p. 69	Extra Credit Project with Rubric	p. 74
Real-Life Project with Rubric	p. 70	Cumulative Practice	p. 76
		Resource Book Answers	A1

📖 ASSESSMENT

Quizzes	p. 118	Alternative Assessments with Rubrics	p. 127
Chapter Tests (3 levels)	p. 120	Unit Test	p. 129
Standardized Test	p. 126	Cumulative Test	p. 131

📑 TRANSPARENCIES

	10.1	10.2	10.3	10.4	10.5	10.6	10.7
Warm-Up / Daily Homework Quiz	✔	✔	✔	✔	✔	✔	✔
Notetaking Guide	✔	✔	✔	✔	✔	✔	✔
Teacher Support				✔			
English/Spanish Problem Solving		✔		✔			✔
Answer Transparencies	✔	✔	✔	✔	✔	✔	✔

💻 TECHNOLOGY

- EasyPlanner CD-ROM
- Test and Practice Generator
- Electronic Lesson Presentations
- eTutorial CD-ROM
- Chapter Audio Summaries CDs
- Classzone.com
- eEdition Plus Online
- eWorkbook Plus Online
- eTutorial Plus Online
- EasyPlanner Plus Online

ADDITIONAL RESOURCES

- Worked-Out Solution Key
- Notetaking Guide
- Practice Workbook
- Tutor Place
- Professional Development Book
- Activities Book
- Poster Package
- Spanish Study Guide
- English/Spanish Chapter Reviews
- Multi-Language Glossary

10 Math Background and Teaching Strategies

Lesson 10.1

MATH BACKGROUND

AREA OF A PARALLELOGRAM The formula for the area of a parallelogram can be justified by relating the parallelogram to a rectangle with length l and width w that has the same area. Thus, since $b = l$ and $h = w$, the formula $A = lw$ becomes $A = bh$.

TEACHING STRATEGIES

Build upon what students already know about finding the area of a rectangle. Draw a rectangle on the board and ask how to find the area. Then draw a dotted line from one vertex to a point on the opposite side. Show how the triangle formed can be cut off and moved to the other side to form a parallelogram.

Discuss the fact that the parallelogram has the same area as the rectangle. Introduce the terminology and symbols for *base*, b, and *height*, h.

Lesson 10.2

MATH BACKGROUND

AREA OF A TRIANGLE The area A of a triangle with base of length b and corresponding height h is $A = \frac{1}{2}bh$. When calculating the area of a triangle, any side can serve as a base. The *perpendicular* distance from the opposite vertex to the line containing the base is the height corresponding to this base. Hence each triangle has three bases and three corresponding heights. In the case of an obtuse triangle, the line segment used to find the height may lie outside the triangle.

TEACHING STRATEGIES

This activity uses what students know about finding the areas of rectangles and triangles to find the area of a trapezoid. Each student will need graph paper and scissors.

Have each student draw a trapezoid on graph paper so that each base is a whole number of units. From each endpoint of the smaller base, have students draw the two heights. Ask students to name what types of figures are formed. Have students cut the trapezoid into these figures and find the area of each part. Students should then add these areas together to find the area of the original trapezoid.

Lesson 10.3

MATH BACKGROUND

CIRCLE A **circle** is a set of points in a plane that are the same distance from a point called the **center**. The **radius** is the distance from the center to a point on the circle. The **diameter** is the distance across the circle through the center. The perimeter of a circle is given the special name **circumference**. In every circle, the ratio of the circumference C to the diameter d is a constant, called π. The number π is an irrational number that can be approximated by 3.14 or $\frac{22}{7}$.

TEACHING STRATEGIES

For this activity, students will need string, scissors, safety compass, centimeter ruler, colored construction paper, poster board, and glue. Have the students work in small groups to create a design of colored circles on poster board. Their circles should vary in size. Students can use a compass to draw smaller circles and string tied to a pencil to draw larger circles. For each circle, have students measure the diameter with a ruler and the circumference with string and a ruler. Have them record their measurements in a table. Then have students find the ratio $C : d$ to the nearest hundredth for each circle. Have all groups display their designs and compare the values they got for $C : d$.

Lesson 10.4

MATH BACKGROUND

AREA OF A CIRCLE The area of a circle is found by using the formula $A = \pi r^2$. As with the area of polygons and other plane figures, the area of a circle is expressed in square units.

CIRCLE GRAPHS A **sector** of a circle is formed by an angle with vertex at the center of the circle. The fact that the sum of the measures of all angles with vertex at a circle's center is 360° is used in making a circle graph.

TEACHING STRATEGIES

The following activity can be used to introduce the formula for the area of a circle. Have students work in pairs; each pair will need circle patterns, scissors, tape, and a ruler. Give each pair two circles, the first with 10 sectors drawn on it and the second with 6 sectors. Have each partner take one circle and cut it apart into the sectors. The sectors should be taped next to each other in an alternating fashion, the points facing down, then up. The figure that is formed should resemble a parallelogram. Have students help each other find an approximation for the area of their parallelogram, by measuring the base (half the circumference) and the height (radius).

Lesson 10.5

MATH BACKGROUND

SOLIDS Just as a two-dimensional figure encloses part of a plane, a three-dimensional figure, called a **solid**, encloses part of space. Geometric solids include **prisms**, **cylinders**, **pyramids**, **cones**, and **spheres**. Pyramids and prisms have polygonal **faces**, **edges**, and **vertices**.

TEACHING STRATEGIES

Use this activity to introduce solids and some of the terminology associated with them. Students will need prisms and pyramids, construction paper, and tape. Have the students work in small groups. Distribute construction paper, tape, a prism, and a pyramid to each group.

Have group members identify the figures as prisms and pyramids and then count the number of edges, faces, and vertices. Each student then creates his or her own solid using construction paper and tape. Have students share their solids with the group, describing them in terms of edges, faces, and vertices. Have each group share their definitions for these terms with the class.

Lesson 10.6

MATH BACKGROUND

SURFACE AREA The **surface area** of a solid is the sum of the areas of its faces. For a prism, this means adding the areas of 6 faces, or adding twice the areas of 3 pairs of congruent faces. If the dimensions of the prism are l, w, and h, then the surface area is given by the formula $S = 2lw + 2lh + 2hw$.

TEACHING STRATEGIES

In order to find the surface area of a prism, students need to be able to visualize, count, and find the areas of the faces of the prism. To help them visualize the faces, ask students to make a net of a prism with specific dimensions, like this.

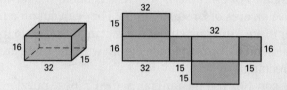

Then ask students to determine how many faces are 16×32 rectangles, how many are 15×32 rectangles, and how many are 15×16 rectangles. Ask how they might use this information to find the surface area of the prism.

Lesson 10.7

MATH BACKGROUND

VOLUME The **volume of a prism** is the amount of space inside it. To find the volume of a rectangular prism, multiply the length by the width by the height of the prism. The formula for the volume of a rectangular prism is $V = lwh$.

TEACHING STRATEGIES

For this activity, students will need a selection of centimeter and inch unit cubes and assorted boxes shaped like rectangular prisms. Have students work in pairs. Give each pair of students either a centimeter cube or an inch cube. Have the groups guess how many of their unit cubes would fit inside each box. Then give them the dimensions of the boxes, in centimeters and in inches. Have students try to find a way to determine how many cubes would fit in one layer of each container and how many layers there would be.

10 Differentiating Instruction

Strategies for Underachievers

PROVIDE TOOLS FOR CONCRETE LEARNING

Many students learn better if they are able to see, touch, and manipulate objects that represent the concept being taught. Chapter 10 provides many opportunities for you to reach these learners.

In Lesson 10.1, to build a concrete understanding of area, have students draw some rectangles on grid paper and count the square units. You may want to have them draw a few rectangles with the same area but different dimensions. For example, 4×6, 12×2, and 8×3 rectangles have an area of 24 square units. They can cut off a triangular piece from one end of the rectangle and slide it to the other end to form a parallelogram with the same area as the rectangle.

In Lesson 10.2 use the tangrams, the Chinese puzzle shapes, introduced on page 479. Use these tangram pieces to reinforce the concept of area. Start with the two small triangle shapes. Arrange them so that they form a square, then a parallelogram, and then a triangle, as illustrated.

Emphasize to students that the area of each of these shapes is the same. Next look at the bases and heights. The parallelogram and the square have the same base and height while the base of the triangle is twice as long as the base of the square. Discuss the formulas and why the formula for area of a triangle would include the factor $\frac{1}{2}$.

In Lesson 10.3, you may want to have students investigate the relationship between the circumference and diameter of a circle. Have students bring in cans, flying discs, or other circular objects. Use string or a tape measure to have students measure the distance around the object (the circumference) and the diameter of the object. Have students divide the circumference by the diameter and put their results on the board or overhead. After all the classroom data has been gathered, do some averaging to see how

close the class results are to π. Check to see if students make the connection that the ratio of the circumference to the diameter is always the same.

GEOMETRIC SOLIDS Students at this age do not have much experience classifying solids. In Lesson 10.5 it is helpful to have geometric solids available in the classroom. You may wish to suggest some items for students to bring from home, such as cereal boxes, cans, tissue boxes, cheese wedges, and so on, that are examples of geometric solids. Alternately, you may wish to have students create these solids out of modeling clay. Students can work in groups to decide which characteristics are the same in all prisms or pyramids and which are different.

In Lesson 10.6, you may wish to bring in some precut rectangular pieces of cardboard so that students can assemble them to form a variety of prisms. In small groups, have students create the prisms and then find their surface areas. The following are suggested sizes in centimeters for the precut rectangles:

3×3 4×4 3×4 4×5 3×5 5×5

Strategies for English Learners

VOCABULARY DEVELOPMENT

ROOTS Many mathematical terms share a Greek or Latin root. Recognizing the root can help students understand the meaning of new words. For example:

Greek or Latin Root	Mathematical Terms
congruere (Latin, *to agree*)	*congru*ent, *congru*ence
polys (Greek, *many*)	*poly*gon, *poly*hedron, *poly*hedral
circum (Latin, *around*)	*circum*ference
circulus (Latin, *circle* or *ring*)	*circ*le, *circul*ar
ferre (Latin, *bear, carry*)	circum*fere*nce

Students will be amazed when you ask them to look in a dictionary to see how many mathematical, scientific, and other words start with *poly*. Encourage students to look for the similarities in words and to watch for prefixes, suffixes, or roots that may give them clues to their meaning.

Strategies for Advanced Learners

INCREASE DEPTH AND COMPLEXITY

To those students who have quickly mastered the concepts in **Lesson 10.2**, have them do the following actvity using a set of all seven tangram pieces.

- **Challenge** Find the area relationships amongst each of the tangram pieces. Assume that the area of the small triangle is 1 square unit. Express the areas of each of the other pieces in terms of the area of the small triangle. Then find the total area of all seven pieces. Finally, determine the fractional part of the whole puzzle that each of the pieces represents. The large triangles are each $\frac{1}{2}$ of the whole. The parallelogram, square, and medium triangle are each $\frac{1}{8}$ of the whole. The two small triangles are each $\frac{1}{16}$ of the whole puzzle.

USE CROSS-CURRICULAR CONNECTIONS

After completing Lesson 10.1, you may wish to have students work with their Social Studies teacher to investigate the origin of the tangram puzzle, and also to research other ancient games and puzzles that involve mathematical concepts.

In conjunction with Exercises 12–14 of Lesson 10.4, you may wish to have students work with their Physical Education teacher to find the areas of your school basketball court, the center circle, the key, and the semicircle at the top of the key. The Physical Education teacher may have some other suggestions for irregular shapes to measure.

In Lesson 10.6, you may wish to have students work with their Art teacher to design a scale model of the ceiling, walls, and floor of their bedroom. Students can find the area of each of these surfaces and research the cost of painting the ceiling, wallpapering the walls, and carpeting the floor.

Differentiating Instruction: Teaching Resources

Differentiating Alternate Assessment

McDougal Littell *Middle School Mathematics* offers teachers a wide variety of alternative assessment for all levels of students. Pictured here are facsimiles of the alternative assessment pages from the *Assessment Book*, and the various types of chapter projects available in the *Chapter 10 Resource Book*.

ASSESSMENT BOOK

The *Assessment Book* contains two pages of alternative assessment for each chapter in the textbook.

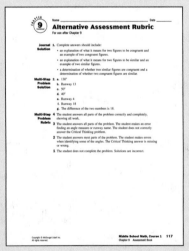

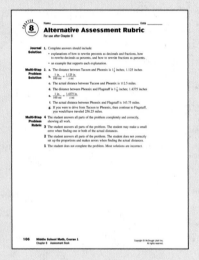

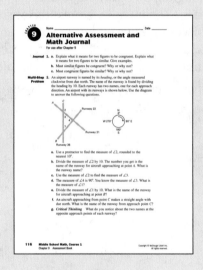

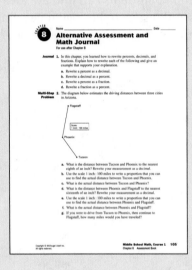

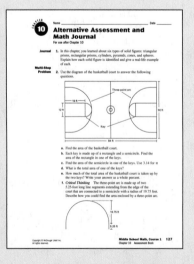

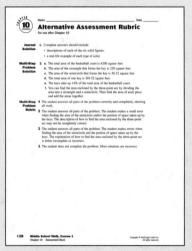

RESOURCE BOOK

The *Chapter Resource Books* contain three different projects for each chapter: Real Life, Cooperative, and Independent Extra Credit. Each project is accompanied by a scoring rubric. Shown below are the three projects for Chapter 10 with their rubrics. A complete discussion of rubrics is available in the *Professional Development Book*.

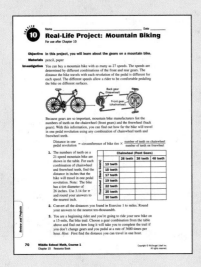

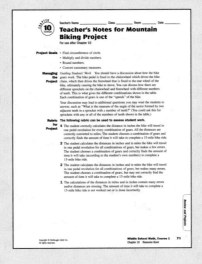

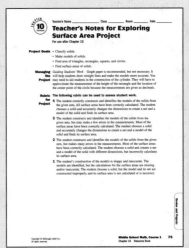

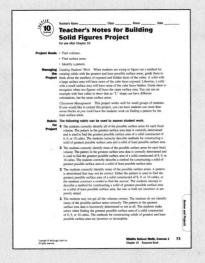

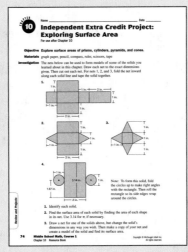

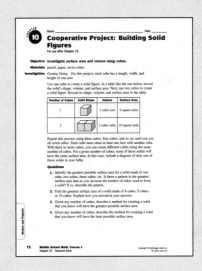

MAIN IDEAS

In this chapter, students find the area of parallelograms, triangles, and circles. They also find the circumference of circles. Students classify solids and find the volume and surface area of rectangular prisms.

PREREQUISITE SKILLS

The key skills reviewed in the game on these pages are:
- Identifying polygons
- Classifying quadrilaterals

Additional practice with prerequisite skills can be found in the Review What You Need to Know exercises on page 474. Additional resources for reviewing prerequisite skills are:
- Skills Review Handbook, pp. 684–707
- Tutor Place
- eTutorial Plus Online

MANAGING THE GAME

Tips for Success

Suggest to students that they copy the kite on a sheet of paper and check off each interior polygon as they count it. Remind them to count the larger polygons that enclose the smaller ones.

Reflecting on the Game

For Exercise 2, you may want to review triangles in more detail by asking students to classify the triangles in the design by their angles and sides.

CHAPTER 10

Geometry and Measurement

BEFORE

In previous chapters you've...

- Solved measurement problems
- Identified and classified polygons

Now

In Chapter 10 you'll study...

- Area of parallelograms and triangles
- Circumference and area of circles
- Solid figures
- Surface area and volume of rectangular prisms

WHY?

So you can solve real-world problems about...

- geography, p. 477
- hang gliders, p. 483
- basketball, p. 492
- skateboarding, p. 503
- aquariums, p. 511

Internet Preview
CLASSZONE.COM

- eEdition Plus Online
- eWorkbook Plus Online
- eTutorial Plus Online
- State Test Practice
- More Examples

Chapter Warm-Up Game

Review skills you need for this chapter in this game. Work with a partner.

Key Skill:
Identifying and classifying polygons

POLYGON COUNT

HOW TO PLAY

In this game, you'll hunt for polygons in the kite design shown on page 473. In the design, angles that appear to be right angles are right angles. Line segments that appear to be parallel are parallel.

1 **MAKE** a polygon tally sheet like the one shown. Use a separate piece of paper.

2 **COUNT** how many of each type of polygon you find in the kite design. You may count each polygon only once. For example, if you count a polygon as a rectangle, you may not count it as a parallelogram. **Check work.**

Polygon Tally Sheet

Triangle	?
Quadrilateral	?
Parallelogram	?
Rectangle	?
Pentagon	?
Hexagon	?

3 **COMPARE** your count with your partner's. Be prepared to justify your thinking.

CHAPTER RESOURCES

These resources are provided to help you prepare for the chapter and to customize review materials:

Chapter 10 Resource Book
- Tips for New Teachers, pp. 1–2
- Lesson Plan, pp. 5, 13, 21, 31, 43, 51, 59
- Lesson Plan for Block Scheduling, pp. 6, 14, 22, 32, 44, 52, 60

Technology
- EasyPlanner CD-ROM
- Test and Practice Generator
- Electronic Lesson Presentations CD-ROM
- eTutorial CD-ROM

Internet
- Classzone
- eEdition Plus Online
- eWorkbook Plus Online
- eTutorial Plus Online
- EasyPlanner Plus Online

ENGLISH LEARNER SUPPORT

- Spanish Study Guide
- Multi-Language Glossary
- Chapter Audio Summaries CDs
- Teacher's Edition, pp. 472E–472F

Stop and Think

1. **Writing** Suppose that the words *rectangle* and *parallelogram* were removed from the tally sheet. How would your polygon count change? Explain your thinking. **All of the rectangles and parallelograms would be counted as quadrilaterals.**

2. **Critical Thinking** In the game *Polygon Count*, some of the polygons you found in the kite design are part of other, larger polygons. Describe some examples. ***Sample answer:*** **The rectangle in the center of the kite is made up of four triangles and one quadrilateral.**

473

Getting Ready to Learn

Review What You Need to Know

Using Vocabulary Copy and complete using a review word.

1. A ? is a quadrilateral with two pairs of parallel sides. **parallelogram**

2. A ? is a triangle that has one right angle. **right triangle**

Evaluate the expression when $x = 10$ and $y = 4$. *(p. 29)*

3. x^2 100   **4.** y^2 16   **5.** $3x^2$ 300   **6.** $2x^2 - y^2$ 184

Find the area of a rectangle with the given dimensions. *(p. 61)*

7. length = 8 ft, width = 4 ft
  32 ft²

8. length = 12 in., width = 6 in.
  72 in.²

The circle graph at the right shows the ages of the first 42 presidents at the time they took office. *(p. 88)*

9. How many presidents were 61 years old or older? **9 presidents**

10. How many presidents were 51 years old or older? **33 presidents**

Ages of U.S. Presidents

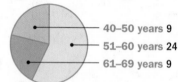

40–50 years 9
51–60 years 24
61–69 years 9

Word Watch

Review Words

area, p. 62
circle graph, p. 88
right triangle, p. 436
parallelogram, p. 445

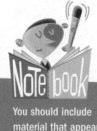

You should include material that appears on a notebook like this in your own notes.

Know How to Take Notes

Learning to Use Formulas You may want to create a special section in your notebook to write formulas. Be sure to write down the complete formula. Tell what each variable represents, and include an example. You learned the formula for the area of a rectangle in Lesson 2.2.

Area of a Rectangle

A is the area, l is the length, and w is the width.

$A = lw$

$\quad = 18 \cdot 9$

$\quad = 162$ square yards

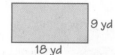

9 yd

18 yd

You will write more formulas in your notebook in Chapter 10.

Hands-on Activity

GOAL

Compare the area of a parallelogram and the area of a rectangle.

MATERIALS

· graph paper
· scissors

Investigating Area

In this activity, you will find the area of a parallelogram.

Explore **You can find the area of a parallelogram by finding the area of a rectangle.**

1 Draw a parallelogram like the one shown below on graph paper. Cut out the parallelogram.

2 Draw a line to make a right triangle as shown.

3 Cut out the triangle. Move the triangle to the other side of the parallelogram to form a rectangle.

  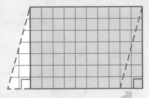

4 You can use the grid squares and the formula $A = lw$ to find the area of the rectangle: $A = 10 \times 7 = 70$. The area of the parallelogram is 70 square units.

Your turn now Follow the steps above to find the area of the parallelogram.

1.

72 square units

2.

20 square units

Stop and Think

3. Writing Explain how the area of a rectangle compares to the area of a parallelogram with the same length and height. They are the same.

NCTM CURRICULUM STANDARDS
Standard 3: Analyze properties of 2-D shapes
Standard 4: Understand measurable attributes of objects; Apply proper techniques to find measures

Lesson 10.1   Area of a Parallelogram   **475**

EXPLORE THE CONCEPT

· Compare the area of a parallelogram and a rectangle.
· The area formula for a parallelogram is given in Lesson 10.1.

MATERIALS

Each student will need graph paper and scissors.

RECOMMENDED TIME

Work activity: 10 min
Discuss results: 5 min

GROUPING

Students should work individually.

2 **TEACH**

DISCUSSION

As students work through Step 4, ask them to explain how the replacements for l and w can be obtained from the diagram in Step 3. **There are l rows of w squares in a rectangle with dimensions l and w.**

3 **CLOSE**

 KEY DISCOVERY

The area of a parallelogram is equal to the area of a rectangle with the same dimensions.

ASSESSMENT

1. A rectangle has height 8 feet and width 6 feet. Find the area of a parallelogram with the same dimensions. **48 ft²**

SKILL CHECK

1. Evaluate xy if $x = 3$ and $y = 4.5$. **13.5**
2. Find the value of x if $8 = 32 \div x$. **4**
3. Solve $\frac{6}{21} = \frac{2}{x}$. $x = 7$

LESSON OBJECTIVE

Find the area of a parallelogram.

PACING

Suggested Number of Days
Basic Course: 1 day
Average Course: 1 day
Advanced Course: 1 day
Block: 0.5 block with 10.2

TEACHING RESOURCES

For a complete list of Teaching Resources, see page 472B.

 TRANSPARENCY

Warm-Up Exercises for this lesson are available on a transparency.

2 **TEACH**

MOTIVATING THE LESSON

Cut an index card along a diagonal to form two triangles. Ask students how you can use the two triangles to form a parallelogram.

TIPS FOR NEW TEACHERS

Be sure students understand that the height h of a parallelogram is the shortest distance from the side chosen as the base b to the side opposite this base. See Tips for New Teachers in the *Chapter 10 Resource Book.*

Area of a Parallelogram

BEFORE	Now	WHY?
You found the area of a rectangle.	You'll find the area of a parallelogram.	So you can estimate the area of Lake Erie, as in Example 3.

 Word Watch

base of a parallelogram, p. 476
height of a parallelogram, p. 476
perpendicular, p. 476

Finding Areas The **base of a parallelogram** is the length of any of its sides. The **height of a parallelogram** is the *perpendicular distance* between the side whose length is the base and the opposite side. Two lines are **perpendicular** if they meet at a right angle.

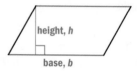

The area of a parallelogram is the product of the base and the height.

Area of a Parallelogram

Words Area = base · height

Algebra $A = bh$

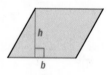

 **with Notetaking**

Include the formula for the area of a parallelogram in your notebook. Include an example like the one shown in Example 1.

EXAMPLE 1 **Finding the Area of a Parallelogram**

Find the area of the parallelogram shown at the right.

2 m
5 m

Solution

$A = bh$ Write the formula for the area of a parallelogram.

$= 5 \cdot 2$ Substitute 5 for b and 2 for h.

$= 10$ Simplify.

ANSWER The area of the parallelogram is 10 square meters.

Your turn now Find the area of the parallelogram described.

1. base = 6 in., height = 10 in. **60 in.²**
2. base = 7 cm, height = 4 cm **28 cm²**

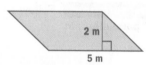

NCTM CURRICULUM STANDARDS
Standard 2: Represent situations using algebraic symbols
Standard 4: Apply proper techniques to find measures
Standard 6: Solve problems in math and other contexts

EXTRA EXAMPLES

Example 1 Find the area of the parallelogram shown below.

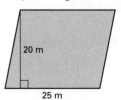

500 m²

20 m

25 m

Example 2 The area of a parallelogram is 84 square feet and the height is 12 feet. What is the base? **7 ft**

Example 3 On a map, the state of Oregon is roughly shaped like a parallelogram, with $b = 3$ inches and $h = 2.5$ inches. If the scale is 1 inch = 115 miles, estimate the area of Oregon. **about 100,000 mi²**

EXAMPLE 2 **Finding an Unknown Dimension**

The area of a parallelogram is 45 square centimeters and the height is 9 centimeters. What is the base?

$A = bh$	Write the formula for the area of a parallelogram.
$45 = b \cdot 9$	Substitute 45 for A and 9 for h.
$b = 45 \div 9$	Write a related division equation.
$b = 5$	Simplify.

ANSWER The base is 5 centimeters.

What do you think?
Geography

EXAMPLE 3 **Estimating Area**

Geography A parallelogram can be used to approximate the shape of Lake Erie. Use the map and the scale to estimate the area of Lake Erie.

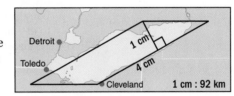

Detroit
Toledo
1 cm
4 cm
Cleveland
1 cm : 92 km

Solution

① Use the scale to find the base, b, and the height, h, in kilometers.

Base	Height
$\dfrac{1\text{ cm}}{92\text{ km}} = \dfrac{4\text{ cm}}{b\text{ km}}$	$\dfrac{1\text{ cm}}{92\text{ km}} = \dfrac{1\text{ cm}}{h\text{ km}}$
$1 \cdot b = 92 \cdot 4$	$1 \cdot h = 92 \cdot 1$
$b = 368$	$h = 92$

② Estimate the area of Lake Erie.

$A = bh$	Write the formula for the area of a parallelogram.
$= 368 \cdot 92$	Substitute 368 for b and 92 for h.
$= 33,856$	Simplify.

ANSWER The area of Lake Erie is about 33,856 square kilometers.

■ **Lake Erie**

The area of Lake Superior is about 82,100 square kilometers. About how many times as great as the area of Lake Erie is the area of Lake Superior?
about 2.4 times

Your turn now Find the unknown length.

3. Area of parallelogram = 72 in.², base = 12 in., height = _?_ **6 in.**

4. Area of parallelogram = 125 mm², height = 5 mm, base = _?_ **25 mm**

MATH REASONING

Students should be able to reason that it is possible to draw different parallelograms with the same area. For example, if the area is fixed at 42 square feet, they could draw one with dimensions 6 feet by 7 feet or one with dimensions 2 feet by 21 feet.

 CONCEPT CHECK

The base of a parallelogram is 6.5 inches and its area is 27.3 square inches. What is the height of the parallelogram? **4.2 in.**

 DAILY PUZZLER

What are the possible bases and heights of three parallelograms whose areas are 12 square feet if the dimensions are whole numbers? Which parallelogram has the greatest perimeter? **12 × 1, 2 × 6, 3 × 4; 12 × 1**

EXTRA PRACTICE

- Student Edition, p. 717
- Chapter 10 Resource Book, pp. 7–9
- Test and Practice Generator

 TRANSPARENCY

Even-numbered answers are available on transparencies.

HOMEWORK CHECK

When you review students' homework for this lesson, go over the following exercises to check understanding of key concepts.
Basic: 5, 7, 10, 11, 15
Average: 5, 8, 10, 11, 15
Advanced: 7, 9, 10, 11, 15

 COMMON ERROR

In Exercises 10 and 11, watch for students who automatically multiply the two numbers given instead of writing the related division equation that will answer the question.

10.1 Exercises

More Practice, p. 717

Getting Ready to Practice

1. Vocabulary To find the area of a parallelogram, you multiply the ? by the ?. **base, height**

Find the area of the parallelogram.

2.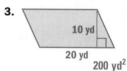
3 ft
15 ft
45 ft²

3.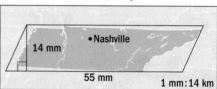
10 yd
20 yd
200 yd²

4. Tennessee A parallelogram can be used to approximate the shape of Tennessee. Use the scale on the map to estimate the area of Tennessee. **150,920 km²**

14 mm · Nashville
55 mm
1 mm : 14 km

Practice and Problem Solving

 **with Homework**

Example	Exercises
1	5–9, 12
2	10, 11
3	15

Online Resources
CLASSZONE.COM
· More Examples
· eTutorial Plus

Find the area of the parallelogram.

A 5.
7 m
12 m
84 m²

6.
10 ft
7 ft
70 ft²

7.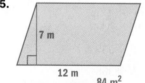
5 in.
6 in.
Rug design (detail) **30 in.²**

8.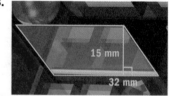
15 mm
32 mm
Digital art (detail) **480 mm²**

9. The height of a parallelogram is 9 meters and the base is 7 meters. What is the area of the parallelogram? **63 m²**

10. The area of a parallelogram is 54 square inches and the height is 9 inches. What is the base of the parallelogram? **6 in.**

11. The area of a parallelogram is 120 square yards and the base is 12 yards. What is the height of the parallelogram? **10 yd**

Tangrams

The tangram pieces in the photo can be arranged to form two congruent squares that fit into the box. Estimate the fraction of the total area of the tangram pieces that is covered by one large triangle.

about $\frac{1}{4}$

13. Check drawings.
Sample answers:
1 centimeter by
12 centimeters,
2 centimeters by
6 centimeters, or
3 centimeters by
4 centimeters

15. 14,400 km^2; high estimate; the parallelogram covers more than just the island of Puerto Rico.

INTERNET
State Test Practice
CLASSZONE.COM

12. **Tangrams** Tangrams are Chinese puzzle shapes that can be arranged into pictures, like the one shown at the right. Find the area of the parallelogram piece. **1290.32 mm^2**

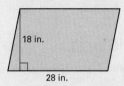

B 13. Draw 2 different parallelograms that each have an area of 12 square centimeters. **See margin.**

14. **Quilts** The base of one parallelogram in a quilt is 6 inches and the height is 3 inches. About how many of these parallelograms do you need to cover an area of 7500 square inches? **about 417 parallelograms**

15. **Estimation** Estimate the area of Puerto Rico. Then tell if your estimate is a *high estimate* or a *low estimate*. Explain your reasoning. **See margin.**

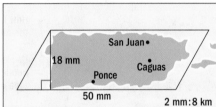

C 16. **Challenge** The base of a parallelogram is 3 inches longer than its height. The height is 7 inches. What is the area of the parallelogram? **70 in.^{2}**

Mixed Review

Solve the equation using mental math. *(Lesson 1.6)*

17. $x + 5 = 12$ 18. $x - 12 = 30$ 19. $4x = 32$ 20. $6x = 72$
     7   42   8   12

21. Sketch 2 different figures that have one line of symmetry. *(Lesson 9.8)*
See margin.

Basic Skills   **Find the product.**

22. $\frac{1}{2} \cdot 4$ 2   23. $\frac{1}{2} \cdot 12$ 6   24. $\frac{1}{2} \cdot 5 \cdot 6$ 15   25. $\frac{1}{2} \cdot 12 \cdot 8$ 48

Test-Taking Practice

26. **Multiple Choice** The height of a parallelogram is 36 meters and the base is 6 meters. What is the area of the parallelogram? **D**

   A. 6 m^2 **B.** 30 m^2 **C.** 42 m^2 **D.** 216 m^2

27. **Multiple Choice** A parallelogram has an area of 300 square feet and a base of 20 feet. What is the height of the parallelogram? **F**

   F. 15 ft   **G.** 15 ft^2 **H.** 6000 ft   **I.** 6000 ft^2

4 ASSESS

ASSESSMENT RESOURCES

For more assessment resources, see:
- Assessment Book
- Test and Practice Generator

MINI-QUIZ

1. Find the area of the parallelogram. **504 in.^{2}**

18 in.
28 in.

2. The height of a parallelogram is 12 meters and the base length is 15 meters. What is the area of the parallelogram? **180 m^2**

3. The area of a parallelogram is 180 square feet and the height is 24 feet. What is the length of the base? **7.5 ft**

5 FOLLOW-UP

RETEACHING/REMEDIATION
- Study Guide in Chapter 10 Resource Book, pp. 10–11
- eTutorial Plus Online
- Extra Practice, p. 717
- Lesson Practice in Chapter 10 Resource Book, pp. 7–9

CHALLENGE/ENRICHMENT
- Challenge Practice in Chapter 10 Resource Book, p. 12
- Teacher's Edition, p. 472F

ENGLISH LEARNER SUPPORT
- Spanish Study Guide
- Multi-Language Glossary
- Chapter Audio Summaries CDs

21. See Additional Answers beginning on page AA1.

LESSON OBJECTIVE

Find the area of a triangle.

PACING

Suggested Number of Days
Basic Course: 1 day
Average Course: 1 day
Advanced Course: 1 day
Block: 0.5 block with 10.1

TEACHING RESOURCES

For a complete list of Teaching Resources, see page 472B.

TRANSPARENCY

Warm-Up Exercises for this lesson are available on a transparency.

2 TEACH

MOTIVATING THE LESSON

Extend the activity by having students show that the area of a triangle is one half the area of a variety of quadrilaterals, including rectangles, squares, and rhombuses.

ACTIVITY

Goal Use a parallelogram to find the area of a triangle.

Key Discovery The area of a triangle is half the area of a parallelogram with the same height and base.

Area of a Triangle

BEFORE
You found the area of a parallelogram.

Now
You'll find the area of a triangle.

WHY?
So you can find the area of a sail, as in Example 2.

Word Watch

base of a triangle, p. 480
height of a triangle, p. 480

Activity You can use a parallelogram to find the area of a triangle.

1. Draw the parallelogram shown at the right on graph paper and cut it out. Find its area.
   60 square units

2. Draw a diagonal like the one shown below. Then cut along the diagonal to form two congruent triangles.

3. How is the area of one triangle related to the area of the parallelogram?

4. Use the formula for the area of a parallelogram to write a rule for the area of a triangle. $A = \frac{1}{2}bh$

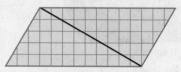

Step 3: It is $\frac{1}{2}$ the area of the parallelogram.

The **base of a triangle** is the length of any of its sides. The **height of a triangle** is the perpendicular distance between the side whose length is the base and the vertex opposite that side.

Area of a Triangle

Words Area of a triangle $= \frac{1}{2} \cdot$ base $\cdot$ height

Algebra $A = \frac{1}{2}bh$

with Solving

As you see in Example 1, the height of an obtuse triangle can be drawn outside the figure.

EXAMPLE 1 Finding the Area of a Triangle

Find the area of the triangle shown.

$A = \frac{1}{2}bh$ — Write the formula for the area of a triangle.

$= \frac{1}{2} \cdot 4 \cdot 11$ — Substitute 4 for b and 11 for h.

$= 22$ — Simplify.

ANSWER The area of the triangle is 22 square feet.

11 ft
4 ft

NCTM CURRICULUM STANDARDS
Standard 2: Represent situations using algebraic symbols
Standard 3: Analyze properties of 2-D shapes
Standard 10: Use representations to solve problems

Your turn now Find the area of the triangle described.

1. base = 12 kilometers, height = 5 kilometers   **30 km²**

2. base = 6 inches, height = 4 inches   **12 in.²**

EXAMPLE 2 **Finding the Area of Combined Figures**

Tall Ships A pattern of a sail for a tall ship is shown. How much material, in square feet, is needed to make the sail?

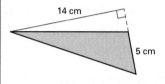

3 ft

6 ft

4 ft

Solution

1 Find the area of each shape.

Area of the triangle: Area of the rectangle:

$A = \frac{1}{2} \cdot 4 \cdot 3$ $A = 4 \cdot 6$

$= 6$ $= 24$

2 Add the areas together to find the total area.
   $6 + 24 = 30$

ANSWER You will need 30 square feet of material to make the sail.

■ Tall Ships

The scale on a model of a tall ship is about 2 in. : 12 ft. The length of the model is 46 inches. What is the approximate length of the actual tall ship?
   276 ft

EXAMPLE 3 **Finding the Height of a Triangle**

The area of a triangle is 36 square inches and the base is 8 inches. What is the height of the triangle?

$A = \frac{1}{2}bh$ Write the formula for the area of a triangle.

$36 = \frac{1}{2} \cdot 8 \cdot h$ Substitute 36 for A and 8 for b.

$36 = 4 \cdot h$ Simplify.

$h = 36 \div 4$ Write a related division equation.

$h = 9$ Simplify.

ANSWER The height of the triangle is 9 inches.

Your turn now Solve the problems below.

3. Find the area of the figure at the right. **55 m²**

4. The area of a triangle is 45 square feet and the base is 10 feet. Find the height. **9 ft**

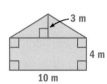

3 m

4 m

10 m

EXTRA EXAMPLES

Example 1 Find the area of the triangle shown. **35 cm²**

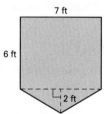

14 cm

5 cm

Example 2 How much material is needed to make the banner shown? **49 ft²**

7 ft

6 ft

2 ft

Example 3 The area of a triangle is 24 cm² and the length of the base is 6 cm. What is the height? **8 cm**

✓ **CONCEPT CHECK**

How do you find the area of a triangle? **Multiply one half the base by the height.**

DAILY PUZZLER

Suppose the total area of the triangle below is 36 cm². What is the area of the shaded region? **12 cm²**

3 APPLY

ASSIGNMENT GUIDE

Basic Course

Day 1: EP p. 714 Exs. 5-8; pp. 482-483 Exs. 7-18, 23-32

Average Course

Day 1: pp. 482-483 Exs. 7-13, 16-21, 23-33

Advanced Course

Day 1: pp. 482-483 Exs. 9-13, 16-27*, 31-33

Block

pp. 482-483 Exs. 7-13, 16-21, 23-33 (with 10.1)

EXTRA PRACTICE

- Student Edition, p. 717
- Chapter 10 Resource Book, pp. 15-17
- Test and Practice Generator

TRANSPARENCY

Even-numbered answers are available on transparencies.

HOMEWORK CHECK

When you review students' homework for this lesson, go over the following exercises to check understanding of key concepts.

Basic: 7, 9, 10, 11, 13

Average: 8, 9, 10, 12, 13

Advanced: 9, 10, 12, 13, 16

COMMON ERROR

In Exercises 3-10, watch for students whose answers are exactly one half the correct answer. This is a common error that occurs when students try to find the area of a triangle mentally by multiplying one half the base and one half the height.

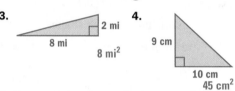

10.2 Exercises

More Practice, p. 717

INTERNET eWorkbook Plus CLASSZONE.COM

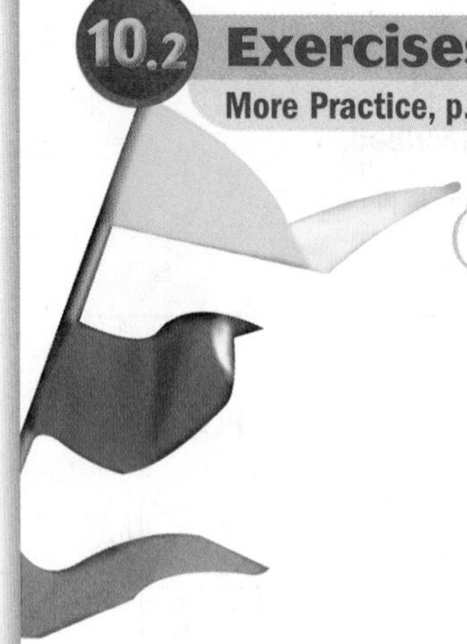

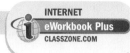

Getting Ready to Practice

Vocabulary **Use the triangle at the right.**

5 yd
6 yd

1. The _?_ of the triangle is 5 yards and the _?_ of the triangle is 6 yards. **height, base**
2. The _?_ of the triangle is 15 square yards. **area**

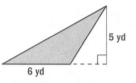

Find the area of the triangle.

3.

2 mi
8 mi

8 mi^2

4.

9 cm
10 cm

45 cm^2

5.

6 ft
2 ft

6 ft^2

6. **Pennant** A pennant is shown at the right. How much blue material, in square inches, was needed to make the pennant? 108 in.^2

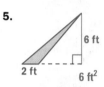

12 in.
18 in.

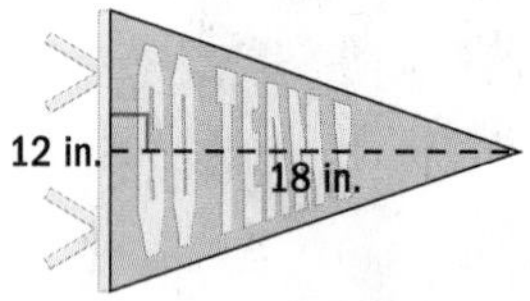

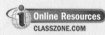

Practice and Problem Solving

HELP with Homework

Example	Exercises
1	7-12
2	10-12
3	13-16

Online Resources CLASSZONE.COM
- More Examples
- eTutorial Plus

Find the area of the triangle.

A 7.

4 ft
10 ft

20 ft^2

8.

12 m
5 m

30 m^2

9.

6 cm
8 cm

24 cm^2

Find the area of the figure indicated.

10.

4 in.
4 in.

8 in.^2

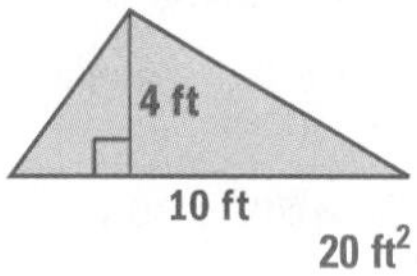

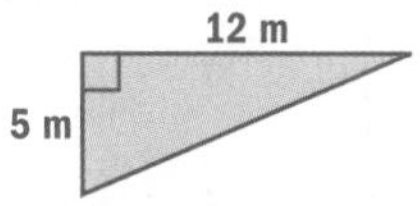

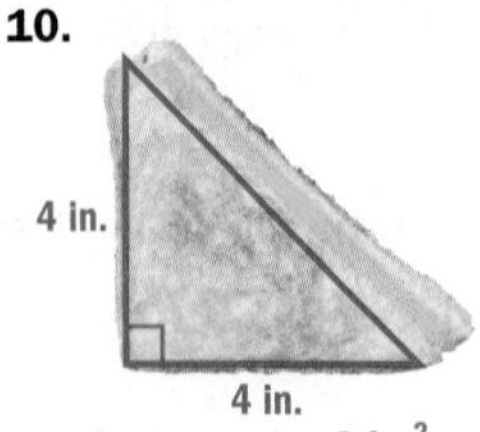

11.

15 in.
15 in.
30 in.

675 in.^2

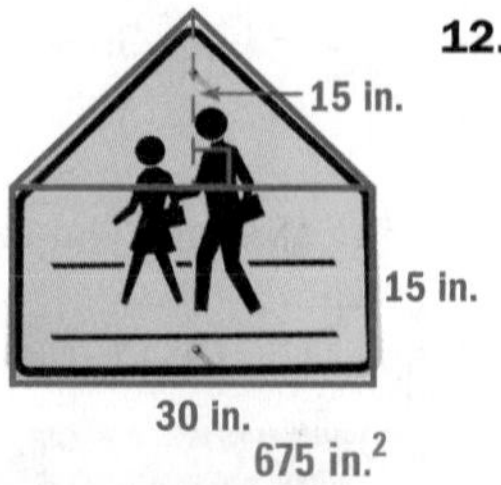

12.

10 cm
23 cm
19 cm

532 cm^2

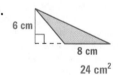

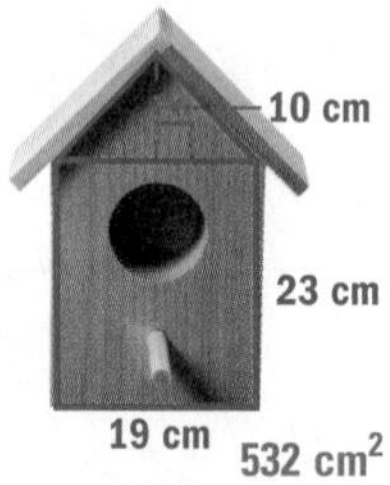

Find the missing dimension of the triangle described.

13. Area: 20 in.^2 base: 8 in. **5 in.**
14. Area: 32 ft^2 height: 4 ft **16 ft**
15. Area: 30 cm^2 height: 6 cm **10 cm**

Hang Gliders

At one time, the world record for a Class 0-1 straight distance glide was 700.6 km. This was 205.6 km longer than the previous record. What was the previous record? **495 km**

19. The area of the triangle with the longer base is twice as great as the area of the other triangle.

20. The height of the triangle is twice as long as the height of the rectangle.

21. about 20% or about $\frac{1}{5}$

22. Divide the hexagon into six congruent triangles and find the area of one triangle. Multiply by 6 to find the area of the hexagon. See margin for art.

INTERNET
State Test Practice
CLASSZONE.COM

---

16. **Hang Gliders** Some hang glider wings are in the shape of a triangle. The base of a wing is 208 inches and the area of the wing is 16,848 square inches. Find the height of the wing. **162 in.**

Algebra **Find the area of the figure when the given lengths, in meters, are $a = 3$, $b = 2$, and $c = 7$.**

B **17.**

13 m²

18.

16.5 m²

19. **Writing** Two triangles have the same height. The base of one triangle is twice as long as the other. How do the two areas compare?
19–22. See margin.

20. **Critical Thinking** A triangle and a rectangle have the same area and the same base. What can you say about their heights?

C **21.** **Puerto Rico** Use the flag of Puerto Rico at the right. How much of the area of the flag does the triangle cover?

22. **Challenge** How can you use triangles to find the area of a regular hexagon? Describe your method and include a drawing.

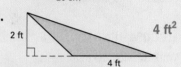
14 in.
9 in.
21 in.

Mixed Review ↻

Tell whether the measure is a *mass*, *capacity*, or *length*.
(Lessons 3.2, 4.7)

23. 4 kg **mass**   24. 917 cm **length**   25. 14 L **capacity**   26. 14.2 g **mass**

27. The area of a parallelogram is 135 square centimeters and the height is 15 centimeters. What is the base? *(Lesson 10.1)* **9 cm**

Basic Skills **Find the product.**

28. (5)(4.5) **22.5**   29. (3.25)(5) **16.25**   30. (7.05)(6) **42.3**   31. (3)(8.21)(4) **98.52**

Test-Taking Practice

32. **Multiple Choice** What is the area of the figure shown? **C**

   A. 12 in.²   **B.** 48 in.²
   C. 60 in.²   **D.** 72 in.²

6 in.
8 in.   4 in.

33. **Short Response** The area of a triangle is 160 square millimeters. The height is 40 millimeters. Explain how to find the base. **See margin.**

---

④ **ASSESS**

ASSESSMENT RESOURCES

For more assessment resources, see:
• Assessment Book
• Test and Practice Generator

MINI-QUIZ

Find the area of the triangle.

1.
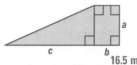
10 cm
20 cm
100 cm²

2.
2 ft
4 ft
4 ft²

Find the missing dimension of the triangle described.

3. Area: 100 cm²
   base: 25 cm **8 cm**

4. Area: 48 m²
   height: 6 m **16 m**

⑤ **FOLLOW-UP**

RETEACHING/REMEDIATION

• Study Guide in Chapter 10 Resource Book, pp. 18–19
• Tutor Place, Geometry and Measurement Card 13
• eTutorial Plus Online
• Extra Practice, p. 717
• Lesson Practice in Chapter 10 Resource Book, pp. 15–17

CHALLENGE/ENRICHMENT

• Challenge Practice in Chapter 10 Resource Book, p. 20
• Teacher's Edition, p. 472F

ENGLISH LEARNER SUPPORT

• Spanish Study Guide
• Multi-Language Glossary
• Chapter Audio Summaries CDs

22, 33. See Additional Answers beginning on page AA1.

483

① PLAN

EXPLORE THE CONCEPT

- Investigate the circumference of a circle.
- This activity leads into the meaning of π and finding the circumference of a circle, which are the topics of lesson 10.3.

MATERIALS

Each student or group of students will need a metric ruler, a compass, scissors, and string.

RECOMMENDED TIME

Work activity: 10 min
Discuss results: 5 min

GROUPING

Students can work individually or in groups of three students. If they work in groups, ask each student to do one of the three steps in the activity.

② TEACH

ALTERNATIVE STRATEGY

You may want students to measure the circumference of different size cans with string and then compare the circumference to the diameter.

③ CLOSE

KEY DISCOVERY

The ratio of the circumference of a circle to its diameter is about 3.14.

ASSESSMENT

1. The circumference of a circle is 12.6 centimeters, and the diameter is about 4 centimeters. Find the ratio of the circumference to the diameter. **about 3.15**

484

10.3 Hands-on Activity

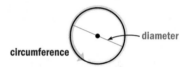

GOAL
Investigate the circumference of a circle.

MATERIALS
- metric ruler   • scissors
- compass
- string

Investigating Circumference

In this activity, you will investigate the relationship between the *diameter* of a circle and the *circumference*, the distance around the circle.

circumference   diameter

Explore   **Find the ratio of the circumference of a circle to the diameter of the circle.**

1 Use a compass to draw a circle with a diameter of 8 centimeters. You will need to set the opening of your compass to 4 centimeters.

2 Cut a piece of string so that the length equals the circumference of the circle. Then measure the string to the nearest tenth of a centimeter.

3 Find the ratio of the circumference to the diameter by dividing the circumference in Step 2 by the diameter given in Step 1. Round your answer to the nearest hundredth.

$$\frac{\text{Circumference in Step 2}}{\text{Diameter in Step 1}} \approx \frac{25.1}{8} \approx 3.14$$

Your turn now   Repeat Steps 1–3 above to find the ratio of the circumference to the diameter for a circle with the given diameter.

1. 2 centimeters
$\frac{6.3}{2} \approx 3.15$

2. 2.5 centimeters
$\frac{7.9}{2.5} \approx 3.16$

3. 3 centimeters
$\frac{9.4}{3} \approx 3.13$

Stop and Think

4. Critical Thinking Is it possible for a circle to have a circumference of 20 centimeters and a diameter of 5 centimeters? Explain.

---

4. No; the ratio of the circumference to the diameter of every circle is about 3.14, and the ratio 20 to 5 is 4.

NCTM CURRICULUM STANDARDS
Standard 4: Understand measurable attributes of objects; Understand the processes of measurement
Standard 10: Use representations to solve problems

Circumference of a Circle

BEFORE | ▶ **Now** | **WHY?**

You found the perimeter of a rectangle. | You'll find the circumference of a circle. | So you can estimate a crater's circumference, as in Example 4.

Finding Circumference A **circle** is the set of all points in a plane that are the same distance from a point called the **center** . The **radius** , *r*, is the distance from the center to any point on the circle. The distance across the circle through its center is the **diameter** , *d*.

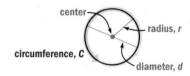

center
radius, *r*
circumference, *C*
diameter, *d*

The distance around a circle is called the **circumference** , *C*.

The ratio of any circle's circumference to its diameter is always the same. This ratio is 3.14159 . . . . It is represented by the Greek letter π, or **pi** . You can use 3.14 or $\frac{22}{7}$ to approximate π.

Circumference of a Circle

Words | **Algebra**

Circumference = pi · **diameter** | $C = \pi d$

Circumference = 2 · pi · **radius** | $C = 2\pi r$

EXAMPLE 1 **Finding the Circumference of a Circle**

Gym Wheel The diameter of a gym wheel is 8 feet. About how far will the wheel go in one rotation? Round your answer to the nearest foot.

Solution

The distance that the gym wheel goes in one rotation is equal to the circumference of the wheel.

$C = \pi d$ | Write the formula for the circumference of a circle.

$\approx (3.14)(8)$ | Substitute 3.14 for π and 8 for *d*.

$= 25.12$ | Simplify.

ANSWER The gym wheel will go about 25 feet in one rotation.

Lesson 10.3 Circumference of a Circle **485**

Example 1 The diameter of a bicycle tire is 26 inches. How far will the tire go in one rotation? **about 82 in.**

Example 2 Find the circumference of the circle shown.

about 43.96 in.

Example 3 Find the circumference of a circle with a diameter of 21 meters. **about 66 m**

📓 **NOTETAKING**

Students should list π and its approximations 3.14 and $\frac{22}{7}$ in their notebooks for future reference.

TEACHING TIP

Students may be confused about when to use 3.14 or when to use $\frac{22}{7}$ as an approximation for π to find the circumference of a circle. Point out that $\frac{22}{7}$ is convenient when the diameter is a multiple of 7.

ⓧ **COMMON ERROR**

Throughout the lesson, watch for students whose answers are exactly twice what they should be. They are calculating the circumference using the formula $C = 2\pi r$ by substituting the length of the diameter for the radius.

 HELP with **Solving**

When the diameter or the radius of a circle is a multiple of 7, use $\frac{22}{7}$ for pi.

4. 31.4 ft; 3.14 because 10 is not a multiple of 7.

5. 110 km; $\frac{22}{7}$ because 35 is a multiple of 7.

6. 264 cm; $\frac{22}{7}$ because 42 is a multiple of 7.

EXAMPLE 2 **Using Radius to Find Circumference**

Find the circumference of the circle shown.

The diameter of a circle is twice the radius. Use $C = 2\pi r$ to find the circumference when you know the radius of a circle.

$C = 2\pi r$ Write the formula for the circumference of a circle.

$\approx (2)(3.14)(6)$ Substitute 3.14 for π and 6 for r.

$= 37.68$ Simplify.

ANSWER The circumference is about 37.68 millimeters.

Your turn now Find the circumference of the circle.

1.

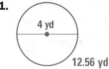

12.56 yd

2.

18.84 m

3.

62.8 cm

EXAMPLE 3 **Choosing an Approximation of Pi**

Find the circumference of a circle with a diameter of 14 centimeters.

Because the diameter is a multiple of 7, use $\frac{22}{7}$ for π.

$C = \pi d$ Use the formula for the circumference of a circle.

$\approx \frac{22}{7} \cdot 14$ Substitute $\frac{22}{7}$ for π and 14 for d.

$= \frac{22 \cdot \overset{2}{\cancel{14}}}{\cancel{7}_1}$ Multiply. Divide out the common factor.

$= 44$ Simplify.

ANSWER The circumference of the circle is about 44 centimeters.

Your turn now Find the circumference of the circle described. Tell what value you used for π. Explain your choice.

4. $d = 10$ ft   **5.** $d = 35$ km   **6.** $r = 42$ cm

EXAMPLE 4 Applying Circumference

Geology The Barringer Meteor Crater has a diameter of about 1186 meters. Find the circumference to the nearest meter.

Solution

$$C = \pi d \qquad \text{Write the formula for the circumference of a circle.}$$

$$\approx (3.14)(1186) \qquad \text{Substitute 3.14 for } \pi \text{ and 1186 for } d.$$

$$= 3724.04 \qquad \text{Simplify.}$$

ANSWER The circumference of the crater is about 3724 meters.

10.3 Exercises

More Practice, p. 717

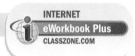
INTERNET
eWorkbook Plus
CLASSZONE.COM

Getting Ready to Practice

Vocabulary Copy and complete the statement.

1. The distance across a circle through its center is the _?_. **diameter**

2. The distance around a circle is the _?_. **circumference**

3. The distance from the center to any point on the circle is the _?_. **radius**

4. The ratio of the circumference of a circle to its diameter is _?_. **pi**

Find the circumference of the circle.

5.

7 cm
22 cm

6.

9 ft
28.26 ft

7.

4 in.
25.12 in.

8.

8 m
50.24 m

9. The radius is given, so the formula $C = 2\pi r$ should be used. The circumference is $2(3.14)(3) = 18.84$ mm.

10. 88 m; $\frac{22}{7}$ because 28 is a multiple of 7.

11. 37.68 yd; 3.14 because 12 is not a multiple of 7.

12. 12.56 in.; 3.14 because 2 is not a multiple of 7.

13. 132 km; $\frac{22}{7}$ because 21 is a multiple of 7.

9. Find the Error Your friend is finding the circumference of a circle with a radius of 3 millimeters. Describe and correct the error.

> $C = \pi d$
> $\approx (3.14)(3)$
> $= 9.42$ mm

Find the circumference of the circle described. Tell what value you used for π. Explain your choice.

10. $d = 28$ m   **11.** $d = 12$ yd   **12.** $r = 2$ in.   **13.** $r = 21$ km

488

③ APPLY

ASSIGNMENT GUIDE

Basic Course
Day 1: EP p. 711 Exs. 1–4;
pp. 488–489 Exs. 14–16,
28–32
Day 2: pp. 488–489 Exs. 17–23,
33–35

Average Course
Day 1: pp. 488–489 Exs. 14–16,
25, 28–32
Day 2: pp. 488–489 Exs. 17–19,
21–24, 33–35

Advanced Course
Day 1: pp. 488–489 Exs. 14–16,
25–29*
Day 2: pp. 488–489 Exs. 19–24,
33–35

Block
pp. 488–489 Exs. 14–19,
21–25, 28–35

EXTRA PRACTICE

- Student Edition, p. 717
- Chapter 10 Resource Book,
  pp. 24–26
- Test and Practice Generator

 TRANSPARENCY

Even-numbered answers are available on transparencies.

HOMEWORK CHECK

When you review students' homework for this lesson, go over the following exercises to check understanding of key concepts.
Basic: 14, 15, 17, 20, 21
Average: 14, 16, 18, 19, 22
Advanced: 14, 16, 19, 21, 24

 COMMON ERROR

Students may use the wrong circumference formula in Exercises 5–8 and 10–13.

17–20. See Additional Answers beginning on page AA1.

488

with **Homework**

Example	Exercises
1	14, 21
2	15, 16, 22–24
3	17–20
4	21–24

Online Resources
CLASSZONE.COM
· More Examples
· eTutorial Plus

What do you think?
Sports

■ **Horse Training**

A *round pen* is a circular pen used for training horses. A round pen with a diameter of 50 feet has a circumference of about 157 feet. Compare this to the perimeter of your classroom.
Answers may vary.

Practice and Problem Solving

Find the circumference of the circular object. Round your answer to the nearest whole number.

A 14. 72 ft

15. 19 in.   3 in.

16. 25 m  4 m

Find the circumference of the circle described. Tell what value you used for π. Explain your choice. 17–20. See margin.

17. $r = 17$ mm   **18.** $d = 70$ yd   **19.** $d = 49$ mi   **20.** $r = 6$ in.

21. Hockey The diameter of a hockey puck is 3 inches. What is the circumference of a hockey puck? **about 9.42 in.**

22. Ribbon You want to wrap a ribbon around a circular candle that has a radius of 4.5 centimeters. You have 30 centimeters of ribbon. Do you have enough ribbon to fit around the candle at least one time? **yes**

B 23. Horse Training A horse trainer stands in the center of a circular track. A horse walks around the track. The trainer is 14 feet from the horse at all times. About how many times must the horse walk around the track in order to travel 440 feet? **about 5 times**

24. Astronomy The radius of the outer edge of the outermost ring of Saturn is about 480,000 kilometers. Find the circumference of the outer edge of the outermost ring to the nearest hundred thousand kilometers. **3,000,000 km**

25. Critical Thinking Which is a better estimate for pi: 3.14 or $\frac{22}{7}$? Explain. **$\frac{22}{7}$; its value is closer to the actual value of pi.**

C 26. Explain The circumference of Earth at the equator is about 24,900 miles. Find the diameter of Earth to the nearest mile. Explain how you found the answer. **7930 mi; divide 24,900 by pi.**

27. Challenge Find the perimeter of the figure at the right. **37.71 ft**

4 ft
3 ft
5 ft
12 ft

Mixed Review

28. Make a frequency table and a line plot of the data. *(Lesson 2.4)*

2, 5, 6, 3, 2, 1, 1, 0, 5, 1, 7, 6, 6, 4, 5, 3, 2, 1, 1, 6 **See margin.**

Choose a Strategy **Use a strategy from the list to solve the following problem. Explain your choice of strategy.**

> **Problem Solving Strategies**
> - Draw a Diagram
> - Make a List
> - Solve a Simpler Problem
> - Make a Model

29. Suppose you fold a piece of paper in half. Then you fold it in half again in the other direction and draw a figure at the folded corner like the one shown. Describe the shape that will be cut out when you unfold the paper.

Basic Skills **Evaluate the expression.**

30. $6(4)^2$
96

31. $(2.5)(5)^2$
62.5

32. $(2.4)(3.1)^2$
23.064

33. $(4 \cdot 3)^2$
144

Test-Taking Practice

34. Multiple Choice The diameter of a bicycle tire is 22 inches. About how far will the tire go in one rotation? **B**

A. 35 in.   **B.** 69 in.   **C.** 139 in.   **D.** 380 in.

35. Multiple Choice What is the approximate circumference of a circle with a radius of 25 centimeters? **G**

F. 78.5 cm   **G.** 157 cm   **H.** 1962.5 cm   **I.** 3925 cm

BRAIN GAME

Tangrams

Tangrams is a puzzle game that was developed in China. The object of the game is to create a design using all seven tangram pieces, also known as *tans*. The tangram pieces may not overlap.

Trace the tangram pieces shown below and cut them out. Then use them to create the design shown at the right. **A sample answer is shown.**

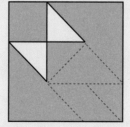

29. The shape will be the letter "X". *Sample answer:* I chose Make a Model so I could see the shape.

---

④ ASSESS

ASSESSMENT RESOURCES

For more assessment resources, see:
- Assessment Book
- Test and Practice Generator

MINI-QUIZ

Find the circumference of the circle.

1.
6 cm

2. 5 in.

about 18.84 cm

about 31.4 in.

3. Find the circumference of a circle with radius 49 feet. **about 308 ft**

4. Find the circumference of a circle with diameter 24 meters. **about 75.36 m**

⑤ FOLLOW-UP

RETEACHING/REMEDIATION
- Study Guide in Chapter 10 Resource Book, pp. 27–28
- Tutor Place, Geometry and Measurement Cards 15, 16
- eTutorial Plus Online
- Extra Practice, p. 717
- Lesson Practice in Chapter 10 Resource Book, pp. 24–26

CHALLENGE/ENRICHMENT
- Challenge Practice in Chapter 10 Resource Book, p. 29
- Teacher's Edition, p. 472F

ENGLISH LEARNER SUPPORT
- Spanish Study Guide
- Multi-Language Glossary
- Chapter Audio Summaries CDs

28. See Additional Answers beginning on page AA1.

1 PLAN

LEARN THE METHOD

- Students will use a calculator to find the circumference of a circle.
- Students can use Method 2 of this activity to complete Exercises 10–13 and 17–20 of Lesson 10.3.

GROUPING

Students can do this activity individually or in pairs. If the students work in pairs, ask one student to use 3.14 as an approximation for π and the other student to use the π key. Then compare answers.

2 TEACH

DISCUSSION

Ask students what value their calculator displays for the number π. After pressing , they should press $=$ to see the value displayed. Remind students that the decimal goes on forever without repeating.

EXTRA EXAMPLES

Example Use a calculator to find the circumference of a circle with diameter 341 feet.
1070.74 ft or 1071.283095 ft

3 CLOSE

ASSESSMENT

Use a calculator to find the circumference of the circle described. Round your answer to the nearest whole number.

1. $d = 18$ ft **57 ft**
2. $r = 24$ in. **151 in.**

490

CALCULATOR

Technology Activity

10.3

Circumference of a Circle

GOAL Use a calculator to find the circumference of a circle.

Example You can find the circumference of a circle using the pi key on a calculator.

The *Place Charles de Gaulle*, a traffic circle which surrounds the Arc de Triomphe in Paris, has a diameter of about 306 meters. What is the circumference of the *Place Charles de Gaulle*?

Solution

Use the formula $C = \pi d$ to find the circumference of a circle. To enter π on a calculator, you can use the approximation 3.14 or you can use the pi key, .

Method 1 Use 3.14 for π.

Keystrokes	Display
3 . 1 4 $\times$ 3 0 6 $=$	960.84

Method 2 Use the π key.

Keystrokes	Display
π $\times$ 3 0 6 $=$	961.327352

ANSWER The circumference of the *Place Charles de Gaulle* is about 961 meters.

HELP with Technology

Although both methods in the Example give approximately the same answer, using the pi key gives a slightly more accurate answer.

Your turn now Use a calculator to find the circumference of the circle described. Round your answer to the nearest whole number.

1. $d = 12$ ft
   38 feet
2. $d = 86$ in.
   270 in.
3. $d = 341$ cm
   1071 cm
4. $d = 7.95$ m
   25 m
5. $r = 15$ km
   94 km
6. $r = 550$ in.
   3456 in.
7. $r = 0.8$ m
   5 m
8. $r = 30.57$ mi
   192 mi
9. **Arctic Circle** The Arctic Circle, located at 66.5° N latitude, has a radius of about 2543 kilometers. What is the circumference of the Arctic Circle to the nearest hundred kilometers?
   about 16,000 km

NCTM CURRICULUM STANDARDS
Standard 2: Represent situations using algebraic symbols
Standard 4: Understand measurable attributes of objects; Apply proper techniques to find measures

Area of a Circle

BEFORE	▶ **Now**	**WHY?**
You found the areas of triangles and parallelograms.	You'll find the area of a circle.	So you can find the area lit by a lighthouse beam, as in Ex. 15.

Word Watch

Review Words
area, p. 62
radius, p. 485
pi, p. 485

(**In the Real World**

Button Designs You are making a design for a circular button. Your design fits on a circle with a radius of 3 centimeters. How much area will be covered by your design?

The area of a circle is the amount of surface covered by the circle.

Area of a Circle

Words Area = (pi)(radius)^2

Algebra $A = \pi r^2$

EXAMPLE 1 **Finding the Area of a Circle**

To answer the question above, find the area of a circle with a radius of 3 centimeters. Round to the nearest square centimeter.

$A = \pi r^2$ Write the formula for the area of a circle.

$\approx (3.14)(3)^2$ Substitute 3.14 for π and 3 for r.

$= 28.26$ Simplify.

ANSWER The area covered by your design is about 28 square centimeters.

Your turn now **Find the area of the circle.**

1. 2 in.

12.56 in.^{2}

2. 4 ft

50.24 ft^2

3. 20 cm

314 cm^2

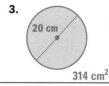

Lesson 10.4   Area of a Circle   **491**

---

① PLAN

SKILL CHECK
1. Find r^2 if $r = 6$. 36
2. $3.14(5)^2 = \underline{?}$ 78.5
3. $\frac{4}{9}(360) = \underline{?}$ 160

LESSON OBJECTIVE
Find the area of a circle.

PACING
Suggested Number of Days
Basic Course: 2 days
Average Course: 2 days
Advanced Course: 2 days
Block: 1 block

TEACHING RESOURCES
For a complete list of Teaching Resources, see page 472B.

⏱ TRANSPARENCY
Warm-Up Exercises for this lesson are available on a transparency.

② TEACH

MOTIVATING THE LESSON
Ask students to design a campaign button showing their own face. Ask how they might determine the size of the photo they could use.

TIPS FOR NEW TEACHERS
Point out that students need only one dimension, the radius, to find the area. Be sure they understand that because the radius is squared, the area is measured in square units. See Tips for New Teachers in the *Chapter 10 Resource Book*.

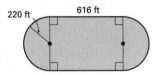
TEACHING TIP

Point out that when a dimension of any figure doubles, its area increases by the square of the doubled dimension, or by a factor of 4.

 COMMON ERROR

Watch for students whose answers are exactly four times the correct answer. This indicates they are using the diameter instead of the radius in the area formula for circles.

Differentiating Instruction

Advanced Students Challenge students to find the area of a circle from its circumference. For example if a circle has circumference 88 feet, they should be able to solve for the radius and find that the area is 617 ft².

 TRANSPARENCY

A support transparency is available for Example 4.

492

EXAMPLE 2 **Finding the Area of Combined Figures**

Basketball Find the area of the free throw area to the nearest square foot.

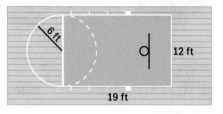

6 ft · 12 ft · 19 ft

Solution

① Find the area of each shape.

Rectangle	Half-circle
$A = lw$	$A = \frac{1}{2}\pi r^2$
$= 19 \cdot 12$	$\approx \frac{1}{2}(3.14)(6)^2$
$= 228$	$= 56.52$

② Add the areas to find the total area: $228 + 56.52 = 284.52$.

ANSWER The area of the free throw area is about 285 square feet.

EXAMPLE 3 **Comparing Areas**

Pizza How many times as great as the area of an 8 inch pizza is the area of a 16 inch pizza?

Solution

① Find the area of each pizza.

8 inch pizza
$A = \pi r^2$
$\approx (3.14)(4)^2$
$= 50.24 \text{ in.}^2$

8 in.

16 inch pizza
$A = \pi r^2$
$\approx (3.14)(8)^2$
$= 200.96 \text{ in.}^2$

16 in.

② Divide the area of the 16 inch pizza by the area of the 8 inch pizza.

$$\frac{200.96}{50.24} = 4$$

ANSWER The area of a 16 inch pizza is 4 times the area of an 8 inch pizza.

Watch Out!

Be sure to read diagrams carefully. The diagrams in Example 3 give the diameters of the pizzas. To find the area of each pizza, you must first find its *radius*.

Your turn now Find the area of the figure to the nearest whole unit.

4.
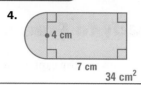
4 cm
7 cm
34 cm²

5.
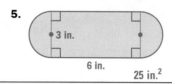
3 in.
6 in.
25 in.²

Making Circle Graphs

A circle graph is made of *sectors* that represent portions of a data set. Each sector is formed by an angle whose vertex is the center of the circle. In a circle graph, the sum of the measures of all these angles is 360°.

EXAMPLE 4 **Making a Circle Graph**

Ski Trails The table shows what fraction of the trails at a ski resort are beginner, intermediate, and expert. Make a circle graph to represent the data.

Types of Ski Trails			
Trail Type	Beginner	Intermediate	Expert
Fraction of Trails	$\frac{3}{10}$	$\frac{1}{2}$	$\frac{1}{5}$

HELP with **Review**
Need help with reading and interpreting circle graphs? See p. 88.

Solution

① Find the angle measure of each sector. Each sector's angle measure is a fraction of 360°. Multiply each fraction in the table by 360° to get the angle measure for each sector.

Beginner

$\frac{3}{10}(360°) = 108°$

Intermediate

$\frac{1}{2}(360°) = 180°$

Expert

$\frac{1}{5}(360°) = 72°$

② Draw the circle graph.

Use a compass to draw a circle.

Use a protractor to draw the angle for each sector.

Label each sector and give your graph a title.

Type of Trail
Beginner
180° 108°
72°
Intermediate
Expert

Lesson 10.4   Area of a Circle   **493**

EXTRA EXAMPLES

Example 4 The table shows what fraction of the students voted for each candidate in a school election. Make a circle graph to represent the data.

Candidate	Jose	Mari	Jeff
Fraction of vote	$\frac{1}{8}$	$\frac{3}{8}$	$\frac{1}{2}$

Number of Votes

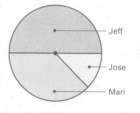
Jeff
Jose
Mari

CROSS-CURRICULUM

Social Studies Students will encounter circle graphs in their social studies texts. Knowing how graphs are made should enhance their understanding of them.

Differentiating Instruction

Less Proficient Students
Students may have difficulty finding the number of degrees in a sector of a circle. Suggest they visualize sectors as pieces of pie. Have them draw pieces of pie and measure their (vertex) angles. Stress that the measures for a whole pie should add up to 360°.

✓ **CONCEPT CHECK**

How do you find the area of a circle if you know its diameter? **Find the radius, which is half the diameter. The area is π multiplied by the square of the radius.**

♞ **DAILY PUZZLER**

A square encloses a circle so that all four sides of the square touch the circle. If the radius of the circle is 8 meters, what is the area of a square? **256 m²**

493

③ APPLY

ASSIGNMENT GUIDE

Basic Course
Day 1: SRH p. 699 Exs. 1–6;
pp. 494–495 Exs. 7–10,
13–16, 24–27
Day 2: pp. 494–495 Exs. 17–21,
28–34

Average Course
Day 1: pp. 494–495 Exs. 7–13,
22, 30–34
Day 2: pp. 494–495 Exs. 15–21,
24–29

Advanced Course
Day 1: pp. 494–495 Exs. 9–16,
24–27
Day 2: pp. 494–495 Exs. 17–23*,
28–31, 34

Block
pp. 494–495 Exs. 7–13, 15–22,
24–34

EXTRA PRACTICE

• Student Edition, p. 717
• Chapter 10 Resource Book,
  pp. 36–38
• Test and Practice Generator

 **TRANSPARENCY**

Even-numbered answers are available on transparencies. A support transparency is available for Exercise 21.

HOMEWORK CHECK

When you review students' homework for this lesson, go over the following exercises to check understanding of key concepts.
Basic: 7, 10, 13, 17, 18
Average: 8, 11, 12, 17, 19
Advanced: 11, 12, 17, 19, 20

6. See Additional Answers beginning on page AA1.

494

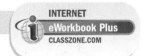

10.4 Exercises

More Practice, p. 717

Getting Ready to Practice

1. **Vocabulary** You can use the expression πr^2 to find the _?_ of a circle.
   area

Find the area of the circle described to the nearest tenth of a unit.

2. $r = 3$ mm
   28.3 mm²

3. $r = 2$ km
   12.6 km²

4. $d = 17$ ft
   226.9 ft²

5. $d = 24$ yd
   452.2 yd²

6. **School Orchestra** Make a circle graph to represent the data in the table. See margin.

Students in the School Orchestra			
Grade	6th	7th	8th
Students	$\frac{7}{20}$	$\frac{2}{5}$	$\frac{1}{4}$

Practice and Problem Solving

HELP with Homework

Example	Exercises
1	7–11, 15–16
2	12–14
3	17
4	18–21

Online Resources
CLASSZONE.COM
· More Examples
· eTutorial Plus

In Exercises 7–11, find the area of the circle to the nearest whole unit.

A 7.
12 ft
452 ft²

8.
30 mi
2826 mi²

9.
18 m
254 m²

10. Find the area of a circle with a radius of 5 feet. 79 ft²

11. Find the area of a circle with a radius of 2.1 centimeters. 14 cm²

Find the area of the figure to the nearest tenth of a unit.

12.
5 ft
4 ft 26.3 ft²

13.
1 m
2.6 m²

14.
13 cm
12 cm
5 cm 96.3 cm²

15. **Lighthouses** A lighthouse beam makes a circle that reaches 18 miles from the lighthouse. Find the area that is lit by the lighthouse beam to the nearest square mile.
   1017 mi²

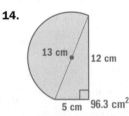
18 mi
lighthouse

B 16. **Lawn Sprinklers** A circular flower garden has an area of about 314 square feet. A sprinkler at the center of the garden covers an area that has a radius of 12 feet. Will the sprinkler water the entire garden?
   yes

17. Eyes In a dark room, the iris of your eye opens until the pupil is about 8 millimeters in diameter. In a lighted room, the pupil has a diameter of about 2 millimeters. How many times as great as the area of the pupil in the lighted room is the area of the pupil in the dark room?

16 times

In Exercises 18–21, use the table of information about animals at an animal shelter.

18. What is the total number of animals available for adoption? **40 animals**

19. Find the fraction of all the animals that are in each category. **19–21. See margin.**

20. Find the angle measures for the sectors of a circle graph.

21. Make a circle graph of the data.

Animals Available for Adoption	
Type of animal	Number available
Dog	10
Cat	15
Rabbit	7
Other	8

19. Dog: $\frac{1}{4}$, Cat: $\frac{3}{8}$, Rabbit: $\frac{7}{40}$, Other: $\frac{1}{5}$

20. Dog: 90°, Cat: 135°, Rabbit: 63°, Other: 72°

C **22. Weather** Weather radar information is displayed on a screen with a scale of 1 in. : 2 mi. The circle on the screen has a radius of 4 inches. About how many square miles does the radar cover? **about 201 mi²**

23. Challenge Use the expression πr^2 to write an expression for the area of a circle when the radius is doubled. **$4\pi r^2$**

Mixed Review

Classify the polygon with the given number of sides. *(Lesson 9.6)*

24. 3 **triangle** **25.** 4 **quadrilateral** **26.** 5 **pentagon** **27.** 6 **hexagon**

Find the circumference of the circle described. *(Lesson 10.3)*

28. $d = 7$ yd **29.** $d = 8$ in. **30.** $r = 3$ m **31.** $r = 6$ ft
22 yd **25.12 in.** **18.84 m** **37.68 ft**

Basic Skills **Find the mean, median, mode(s), and range.**

32. 11, 15, 22, 10, 6, 14, 12, 14
13; 13; 14; 16

33. 120, 85, 61, 101, 88
91; 88; no mode; 59

34. Yes; the area of the surface to be painted, the area of the rectangle minus the area of the circular window, is about 83.44 square feet. Since this is greater than 70 square feet, there is not enough paint.

Test-Taking Practice

INTERNET
State Test Practice
CLASSZONE.COM

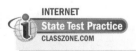

34. Extended Response You are painting a wall that has a circular window. You have enough paint to cover 70 square feet of wall. Do you need to buy more paint? Explain how you got your answer. **See margin.**

4 ft 8 ft 12 ft

---

4 ASSESS

ASSESSMENT RESOURCES

For more assessment resources, see:
• Assessment Book
• Test and Practice Generator

MINI-QUIZ

1. Find the area of the circle to the nearest whole unit. **154 in.²**

7 in.

2. Find the area of a circle with radius 12 meters. **452.16 m²**

3. Find the area of the figure. **89.12 in.²**

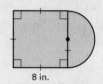
8 in.

5 FOLLOW-UP

RETEACHING/REMEDIATION

• Study Guide in Chapter 10 Resource Book, pp. 39–40
• Tutor Place, Geometry and Measurement Card 16
• eTutorial Plus Online
• Extra Practice, p. 717
• Lesson Practice in Chapter 10 Resource Book, pp. 36–38

CHALLENGE/ENRICHMENT

• Challenge Practice in Chapter 10 Resource Book, p. 42
• Teacher's Edition, p. 472F

ENGLISH LEARNER SUPPORT

• Spanish Study Guide
• Multi-Language Glossary
• Chapter Audio Summaries CDs

21. See Additional Answers beginning on page AA1.

495

1. Name a ray that contains C. **BC⃗**

2. Name a segment that contains A. **AB , AD**

3. Which angle appears to be obtuse? **∠ABC**

LESSON OBJECTIVE

Use a compass and straightedge to construct geometric figures.

2 **TEACH**

Example 1 Draw a vertical segment and copy it. **Check drawings.**

Example 2 Draw an obtuse angle and copy it. **Check drawings.**

 COMMON ERROR

Some students may have difficulty using a compass. Caution them to experiment with the compass and to verify their answers with a ruler and protractor, if they are available.

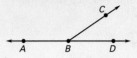
Special Topic

Constructions

GOAL Construct geometric figures.

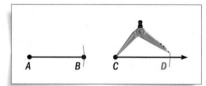

Word Watch

arc, p. 496
perpendicular
  bisector, p. 497
bisector of an angle, p. 497

Copying Figures You can use a compass and a straightedge to construct geometric figures. Use a compass to draw **arcs** , which are parts of circles. Use a straightedge to draw lines, rays, and segments.

EXAMPLE 1 Copying a Segment

Use a compass and a straightedge to copy a segment.

① Draw any $\overline{AB}$. Then draw a ray with endpoint C.

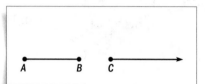

② Draw an arc with center A that passes through B. Using the same compass setting, draw an arc with center C as shown. Label D. $\overline{CD}$ and $\overline{AB}$ have the same length.

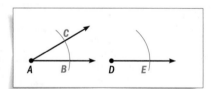

EXAMPLE 2 Copying an Angle

Use a compass and a straightedge to copy an angle.

① Draw any ∠A. Then draw a ray with endpoint D. Draw an arc with center A that intersects the sides of ∠A. Label B and C. Using the same compass setting, draw an arc with center D. Label E.

② Draw an arc with center B that passes through C. Using the same compass setting, draw an arc with center E. Label F. Draw a ray from D through F as shown. ∠D and ∠A have the same measure.

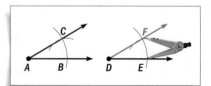

NCTM CURRICULUM STANDARDS
Standard 3: Analyze properties of 2-D shapes; Use symmetry to analyze math situations; Use spatial reasoning to solve problems

Bisecting Figures The **perpendicular bisector** of a segment is the line that divides the segment into two segments of equal length and forms four right angles. The **bisector of an angle** is the ray that divides the angle into two angles with the same measure.

EXAMPLE 3 **Constructing a Perpendicular Bisector**

Construct the perpendicular bisector of a segment.

1. Draw any $\overline{AB}$. Using any compass setting greater than half the length of $\overline{AB}$, draw an arc with center A.

2. Using the same compass setting, draw an arc with center B that intersects the first arc. Label the intersections C and D.

3. Draw $\overleftrightarrow{CD}$, the perpendicular bisector of $\overline{AB}$.

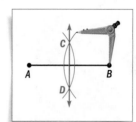

EXAMPLE 4 **Constructing an Angle Bisector**

Construct the bisector of an angle.

1. Draw any $\angle A$. Using any compass setting, draw an arc with center A that intersects the sides of $\angle A$ as shown. Label B and C.

2. Using any compass setting, draw an arc with center B. Using the same compass setting, draw an arc with center C that intersects the first arc as shown. Label the intersection D.

3. Draw $\overrightarrow{AD}$, the bisector of $\angle A$.

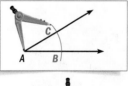

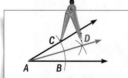

Exercises

In Exercises 1 and 2, use a compass and straightedge.

1. Draw any segment and copy it. Then construct the perpendicular bisector of the segment you constructed. **Check drawing. A good drawing will include all necessary arcs and labels.**

2. Draw any angle and copy it. Then construct the bisector of the angle you constructed. **Check drawing. A good drawing will include all necessary arcs and labels.**

TEACHING TIP

Point out that if a line is known to be a perpendicular bisector of a segment, then on a diagram you can mark a right angle where the line intersects the segment. You can also label the equal halves of the segment.

CONCEPT CHECK

If $\overrightarrow{BD}$ is the bisector of $\angle ABC$, what is true about $\angle ABD$ and $\angle CBD$? **They have the same measure.**

3 APPLY

TRANSPARENCY

Even-numbered answers are available on transparencies.

TEACHING TIP

In Exercises 1 and 2, make sure students also practice the constructions in Examples 1 and 2 by using a straightedge and compass to copy the segment or angle.

1. Check drawing. A good drawing will include all necessary arcs and labels.

2. Check drawing. A good drawing will include all necessary arcs and labels.

LESSONS 10.1 TO 10.4

Notebook Review

Review the vocabulary definitions in your notebook.

Copy the review examples in your notebook. Then complete the exercises.

Check Your Definitions

area, p. 62

base and height of a parallelogram, p. 476

perpendicular, p. 476

base and height of a triangle, p. 480

circle, p. 485

center, p. 485

radius, p. 485

diameter, p. 485

circumference, p. 485

pi (π), p. 485

Use Your Vocabulary

1. Copy and complete: The distance from the center to any point on the circle is called the __?__. **radius**

10.1–10.2 Can you find the area of a parallelogram or triangle?

 EXAMPLE

a. Find the area of the parallelogram.

$A = bh$

$\quad = 15 \cdot 5$

$\quad = 75$

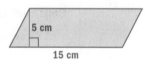

5 cm

15 cm

ANSWER The area of the parallelogram is 75 square centimeters.

b. Find the area of the triangle.

$A = \frac{1}{2}bh$

$\quad = \frac{1}{2} \cdot 22 \cdot 7$

$\quad = 77$

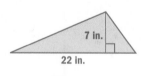

7 in.

22 in.

ANSWER The area of the triangle is 77 square inches.

 Find the area of the parallelogram or the triangle.

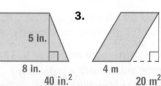

2.

5 in.

8 in.

40 in.²

3.

5 m

4 m

20 m²

4.

3 cm

3 cm

4.5 cm²

10.3–10.4 Can you find circumference and area of a circle?

Review

EXAMPLE Find the circumference and the area of the circle shown at the right.

10 yd

$C = \pi d$ $\qquad$ $A = \pi r^2$

$\approx (3.14)(10)$ $\qquad$ $\approx (3.14)(5)^2$

$= 31.4$ $\qquad$ $= 78.5$

ANSWER The circumference of the circle is about 31.4 yards. The area of the circle is about 78.5 square yards.

✓ **Find the circumference and area of the circle to the nearest whole unit.**

5. $d = 100$ cm
314 cm; 7850 cm^2

6. $d = 42$ mm
132 mm; 1385 mm^2

7. $r = 47$ m
295 m; 6936 m^2

Stop _and_ Think about Lessons 10.1–10.4

8. Writing Compare the formula for the area of a parallelogram to the formula for the area of a triangle. How are they alike? different? **See margin.**

9. Critical Thinking Sketch two different triangles that have an area of 24 square centimeters. **See margin.**

8. They are alike because they both involve a base and a height. They are different in that the formula for the triangle is $\frac{1}{2}$ the formula for the parallelogram.

9. Check drawings. *Sample bases and heights:* 1 centimeter and 48 centimeters, 2 centimeters and 24 centimeters, 3 centimeters and 16 centimeters, 4 centimeters and 12 centimeters, or 6 centimeters and 8 centimeters.

Review Quiz 1

Find the area of the figure to the nearest whole unit.

1.
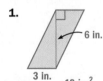
6 in.
3 in.
18 in.^{2}

2.
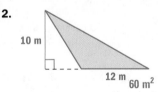
10 m
12 m
60 m^2

3.
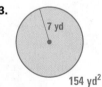
7 yd
154 yd^2

4. A parallelogram has an area of 32 square feet and a height of 4 feet. What is the base? **8 ft**

5. A triangle has a height of 6 meters and an area of 12 square meters. What is the base? **4 m**

6. Find the circumference of a circle with a diameter of 22 feet. **69.08 ft**

7. Communication Cellular telephones send messages within a circular area called a *cell*. Suppose a cell has a radius of about 8 miles. Find the area of the cell to the nearest square mile. **201 mi^2**

Solid Figures

LESSON 10.5

BEFORE	▶ Now	WHY?
You classified polygons by their sides.	You'll classify solids.	So you can name the shape of a skateboard jump, as in Ex. 18.

In the Real World

 Word Watch

solid, p. 500
prism, p. 500
cylinder, p. 500
pyramid, p. 500
cone, p. 500
sphere, p. 500
face, p. 501
edge, p. 501
vertex, p. 501

Candles A **solid** is a three-dimensional figure that encloses a part of space. The candle at the right is an example of a solid. Some solids can be classified by the number and shape of their *bases.* The candle is a *triangular pyramid.*

Classifying Solids

Rectangular prism   Triangular prism
A **prism** is a solid with two parallel bases that are congruent polygons.

A **cylinder** is a solid with two parallel bases that are congruent circles.

A **pyramid** is a solid made up of polygons. The base can be any polygon, and the other polygons are triangles that share a common vertex.

A **cone** is a solid that has one circular base and a vertex that is not in the same plane.

A **sphere** is the set of all points that are the same distance from a point called the center.

EXAMPLE 1   Classifying Solids

Classify the solid.

a.

cone

b.

triangular prism

c.

cylinder

500   Chapter 10   Geometry and Measurement

Faces, Edges, and Vertices Some solids are formed by polygons called **faces**. The segments where the faces meet are **edges**. Each point where the edges meet is called a **vertex**. The plural of vertex is *vertices*.

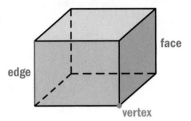

HELP with **Review**

Need help with congruent figures? See p. 454.

EXAMPLE 2 **Counting Faces, Edges, and Vertices**

Count the number of faces, edges, and vertices of the square pyramid shown.

ANSWER There are 4 triangular faces and 1 square base for a total of 5 faces. There are 8 edges. There are 5 vertices.

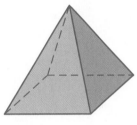

EXAMPLE 3 **Drawing a Solid**

(1 To draw a triangular prism, first draw the congruent bases.

(2 Then connect the corresponding vertices.

(3 Partially erase hidden lines to create dashed lines.

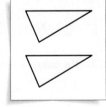

Your turn now Classify the solid. Then count the number of faces, edges, and vertices.

1.

2.

3.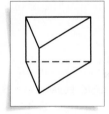

1. triangular pyramid; 4 faces, 6 edges, 4 vertices

2. rectangular prism; 6 faces, 12 edges, 8 vertices

3. triangular prism; 5 faces, 9 edges, 6 vertices

4. A cube is a rectangular prism with square faces. Draw a cube.

See margin.

EXTRA EXAMPLES

Example 1 Classify the roof of the tower.

pyramid

Example 2 Count the number of faces, edges, and vertices of the triangular prism shown.

faces: 5; edges: 9; vertices: 6

Example 3 Draw a pyramid with a square base.
Sample:

NOTETAKING

Stress that students are expected to know the names of the solid figures in this lesson. Encourage students to sketch each of these solids and write notes about them in their notebooks.

CONCEPT CHECK

What is the difference between a rectangular prism and a triangular prism? **The bases of a rectangular prism are rectangles, while those of a triangular prism are triangles.**

DAILY PUZZLER

Can a prism have all faces that are triangles? Explain. **No; if all the faces were triangles, it would be impossible to have two bases.**

4. See Additional Answers beginning on page AA1.

10.5 Exercises

More Practice, p. 717

INTERNET
eWorkbook Plus
CLASSZONE.COM

Getting Ready to Practice

1. Vocabulary Prisms and _?_ have two bases. Pyramids and _?_ have only one base. **cylinders; cones**

Classify the solid.

2.
cylinder

3.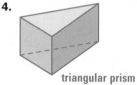
sphere

4.
triangular prism

5. Count the number of faces, edges, and vertices of the solid in Exercise 4.
5 faces, 9 edges, 6 vertices

6. Guided Problem Solving Follow the steps below to make a sketch of a party hat.

① Draw an oval on your paper to represent a circle. Draw a point outside the oval. The point should be directly above the center of the oval. **Steps 1–2. See margin.**

② Draw segments from the right side and the left side of the oval to the point you drew. The segments will look like two sides of a triangle.

③ Classify the solid you drew. **cone**

 with **Homework**

Example	Exercises
1	7–12, 15–17
2	10–12, 18
3	13–14

Online Resources
CLASSZONE.COM
· More Examples
· eTutorial Plus

Practice and Problem Solving

Tell whether the solid has a base. Then classify the solid.

A 7.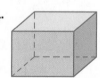
yes; cylinder

8.
no; sphere

9.
yes; cone

Classify the solid. Then count the number of faces, edges, and vertices. **10–12. See margin.**

10.

11.

12.

Draw the solid described. 13–14. See margin.

13. pyramid with a square base   **14.** cylinder

Tell whether the statement is *true* or *false*. If it is false, rewrite the statement to make it true.

15. A cone has two circles as bases.   False. *Sample answer:* A cylinder has two circles as bases.

16. A cylinder can have two triangles as bases. False. *Sample answer:* A prism can have two triangles as bases.

17. A triangular prism has two congruent bases.   true

18. **Skateboarding** A skateboard jump is shown at the right. What type of solid does it resemble? How many faces, edges, and vertices does this solid have? triangular prism; 5 faces, 9 edges, 6 vertices

Copy and complete the statement using *faces*, *edges*, or *vertices*.

B 19. A square pyramid has 8 _?_.   edges   **20.** A hexagonal pyramid has 12 _?_.   edges

21. A hexagonal prism has 8 _?_.   faces   **22.** An octagonal prism has 24 _?_.   edges

C 23. **Challenge** Explain how to find the number of edges of any pyramid whose base is a polygon with *n* sides. Multiply the number of sides, *n*, by 2.

Mixed Review

Estimate the difference. *(Lesson 1.2)* 24–26. Estimates may vary.

24. 502 − 209 300   **25.** 482 − 396 100   **26.** 256 − 89 200

Copy and complete the statement. *(Lesson 4.8)*

27. 5 cm = _?_ mm 50   **28.** 10 kg = _?_ g 10,000   **29.** 35 m = _?_ km 0.035

30. Find the area of a circle with a diameter of 10 centimeters. *(Lesson 10.4)*   78.5 cm²

Basic Skills **Evaluate using the order of operations.**

31. $2(4) + 2(5) + 2(6)$ 30   **32.** $2(4 \times 3) + 2(4 \times 2)$ 40   **33.** $4(6) + 3(4 + 5)$ 51

Test-Taking Practice

34. **Multiple Choice** Which statement about a rectangular prism is false? D

A. It has 8 vertices.   **B.** Its faces are polygons.

C. Its faces are rectangles.   **D.** It has 8 edges.

35. **Short Response** What is the minimum number of edges that a pyramid can have? that a prism can have? Explain your reasoning.
6; 9; a triangle is the polygon with the least number of sides that can be a base.

ASSESSMENT RESOURCES

For more assessment resources, see:
• Assessment Book
• Test and Practice Generator

MINI-QUIZ

Classify the solid. Count the number of edges, vertices, and faces.

1.   **2.**

pyramid; e: 8; v: 5; f: 5   triangular prism; e: 9; v: 6; f: 5

Tell whether the statement is *true* or *false*.

3. A cylinder can have a square base. false

4. A pyramid has at least one side that is a square. false

5 **FOLLOW-UP**

RETEACHING/REMEDIATION

• Study Guide in Chapter 10 Resource Book, pp. 48–49
• Tutor Place, Geometry and Measurement Card 20
• eTutorial Plus Online
• Extra Practice, p. 717
• Lesson Practice in Chapter 10 Resource Book, pp. 45–47

CHALLENGE/ENRICHMENT

• Challenge Practice in Chapter 10 Resource Book, p. 50
• Teacher's Edition, p. 472F

ENGLISH LEARNER SUPPORT

• Spanish Study Guide
• Multi-Language Glossary
• Chapter Audio Summaries CDs

13, 14. See Additional Answers beginning on page AA1.

1 PLAN

STRATEGY BACKGROUND
When you are solving a multi-step problem, you can use the strategy Break into Parts. This strategy enables you to solve simpler problems whose solutions together solve the original problem.

2 TEACH

GUIDING STUDENTS' WORK
For Step 3 you may want to review how to describe the faces of a triangular prism and how to find the area of each face with a formula.

EXTRA EXAMPLES

Example Maria bought 2 pairs of jeans for $22.95 each and 4 T-shirts that cost $10.55 each. The sales tax for her purchases was $5.29. How much did Maria spend in all? **$93.39**

10.6 Problem Solving Strategies

Perform an Experiment
Make a List
Work Backward
Solve a Simpler Problem
Break into Parts
Make a Model
Look for a Pattern

Break into Parts

Problem You want to cover a bookend with fabric. The bookend is a triangular prism with the given dimensions. Find the total area you will be covering.

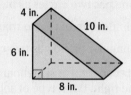

4 in.
10 in.
6 in.
8 in.

1 Read and Understand

Read the problem twice.

You need to find the total area of all the faces of the prism.

2 Make a Plan

Decide on a strategy to use.

One way to solve the problem is to break it into parts and find the area of each face.

3 Solve the Problem

Reread the problem and break it into parts.

First, sketch the 5 faces of the prism: 3 rectangles and 2 triangles. Then find the area of each face.

4 in.	4 in.	4 in.
6 in.	8 in.	10 in.
$A = 6 \cdot 4 = 24$	$A = 8 \cdot 4 = 32$	$A = 10 \cdot 4 = 40$

6 in.   6 in.
8 in.   8 in.

$A = \frac{1}{2}(8)(6) = 24$ $A = \frac{1}{2}(8)(6) = 24$

Add to find the total area: $24 + 32 + 40 + 24 + 24 = 144$

ANSWER The total area you will cover is 144 square inches.

4 Look Back

Check to be sure that your answer has the correct units.

NCTM CURRICULUM STANDARDS
Standard 3: Analyze properties of 3-D shapes
Standard 6: Solve problems in math and other contexts; Apply/adapt strategies to solve problems

Practice the Strategy

Use the strategy *break into parts*.

1. **Neighborhood Party** Use the table below to find the total cost for 100 people to attend a 3 hour neighborhood party. **$2700**

Neighborhood Party Costs	
Tent rental	$250 for 3 hours
Band	$150 per hour
Dinner	$20 per person

2. **Museum Prices** Use the table below to find the total cost for a group of 2 adults, 2 students, 1 senior citizen, and 1 pre-schooler to attend the museum. **$39**

Museum Admission Prices	
Seniors	$7
Adults	$10
Students	$5
Children under 6	$2

3. **Ramps** You want to carpet all sides of the ramp shown except the bottom. The ramp is a triangular prism. How many square feet of carpet do you need? **162 ft²**

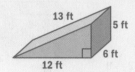

13 ft · 5 ft · 6 ft · 12 ft

4. **Borders** You want to put metal borders on a piece of stained glass in the shape of the figure shown. How much metal will you need? **about 134 in.**

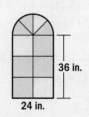

36 in. · 24 in.

Mixed Problem Solving

Use any strategy to solve the problem.

5. **Spinners** You spin the spinner below two times and add the numbers you get. How many different sums are possible? **7 sums**

6. **Money** You spent $25.25 at the bookstore, $19.99 at the home electronics store, $15.75 at a restaurant, and you have $19.01 left. How much money did you start with? **$80**

7. **Find the Pattern** Describe the pattern. Then sketch the next two pictures in the pattern. **See margin.**

8. **Tickets** You go to a concert where the 200 tickets are numbered from 1 to 200. A prize will be given for every ticket whose number includes the digit 7. How many prizes will be given? **38 prizes**

9. **Paper Folding** What is the minimum number of folds you have to make to create nine congruent rectangles from a rectangular piece of paper? **4 folds**

TEACHING TIP

You may want to suggest that students add another column to each table in Exercises 1 and 2 so that they can find the partial cost of each line in the table. This will help them organize the solution for each problem.

☒ COMMON ERROR

For Exercise 4, students may not realize that the curved part of the window is half of a circle with a diameter equal to 24 inches, so the length of this part of the window equals exactly half the circumference of a circle. Point out that the metal border is *around* the window and not part of the interior lattice of the window.

SUGGESTED STRATEGIES

You may wish to suggest the following strategies for the problems in the Mixed Problem Solving:
- Exercise 5: Make a List
- Exercise 6: Work Backward
- Exercise 7: Look for a Pattern
- Exercise 8: Make a List, Solve a Simpler Problem
- Exercise 9: Make a Model

7. Add one dot to each row on the same side of the figure.

Lesson 10.6   Surface Area of a Prism   **505**

LESSON OBJECTIVE

Find the surface area of a prism.

PACING

Suggested Number of Days
Basic Course: 2 days
Average Course: 2 days
Advanced Course: 2 days
Block: 0.5 block with 10.5
0.5 block with 10.7

TEACHING RESOURCES

For a complete list of Teaching Resources, see page 472B.

TRANSPARENCY

Warm-Up Exercises for this lesson are available on a transparency.

TEACH

MOTIVATING THE LESSON

Open up and flatten a cereal box or shoe box. Ask students to describe the 6 rectangular faces in terms of pairs of congruent rectangles.

ACTIVITY

Goal Break a prism into parts to find the surface area.

Key Discovery The surface area of a prism is the sum of six rectangular areas.

Surface Area of a Prism

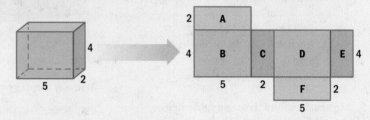

BEFORE	Now	WHY?
You found areas of polygons.	You'll find the surface area of a prism.	So you know how much paper you need for a piñata, as in Ex. 14.

Word Watch

surface area, p. 506

Activity You can break a prism into parts to find the total area.

1. Mentally unfold a box into a *net*, a flat view of the faces of the box.

2. Find the area of each rectangular face of the net. Record your results in a table like the one shown.

Face	A	B	C	D	E	F
Area	?	?	?	?	?	?
	10	20	8	20	8	10

3. Add the areas of the six faces to find the total area.
76 square units

In the activity, you found the *surface area* of a rectangular prism. The **surface area**, S, of a prism is the sum of the areas of its faces.

EXAMPLE 1 **Finding the Surface Area of a Prism**

Find the surface area of the rectangular prism.

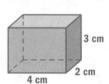

1. Find the area of each face.

   Area of the top or bottom face: $4 \times 2 = 8$
   Area of the front or back face: $4 \times 3 = 12$
   Area of the left or right face: $3 \times 2 = 6$

2. Add the areas of all six faces to find the surface area.

   $$S = 8 + 8 + 12 + 12 + 6 + 6$$
   $$= 52$$

ANSWER The surface area is 52 square centimeters.

EXAMPLE 2 Drawing a Diagram

Find the surface area of a rectangular prism that is 8 inches by 2 inches by 5 inches.

(1) Draw a diagram of the prism and label the dimensions.

(2) Find the area of each face. Then add these areas to find the surface area.

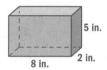

5 in.

2 in.

8 in.

$$S = (8 \times 2) + (8 \times 2) + (8 \times 5) + (8 \times 5) + (5 \times 2) + (5 \times 2)$$

$$= 16 + 16 + 40 + 40 + 10 + 10$$

$$= 132$$

ANSWER The prism has a surface area of 132 square inches.

EXAMPLE 3 Using Surface Area

Painting You want to paint a jewelry box that is 12 inches by 7 inches by 3 inches. The label on the bottle of paint says the paint covers a total area of 300 in.^{2} Do you have enough paint to cover the entire box?

Solution

Find the surface area of the box and compare it to the area the paint will cover.

$$S = 84 + 84 + 36 + 36 + 21 + 21$$

$$= 282$$

ANSWER The surface area of the box is 282 in.^{2} Your bottle of paint covers 300 in.^{2} You do have enough paint to cover the entire box.

Your turn now In Exercises 2 and 3, you may want to draw a diagram.

1. Find the surface area of the rectangular prism shown at the right. **222 mm²**

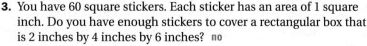

3 mm

5 mm

12 mm

2. A rectangular prism is 3 feet by 4 feet by 6 feet. Find its surface area. **108 ft²**

3. You have 60 square stickers. Each sticker has an area of 1 square inch. Do you have enough stickers to cover a rectangular box that is 2 inches by 4 inches by 6 inches? **no**

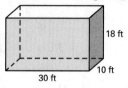

ASSIGNMENT GUIDE

Basic Course
Day 1: pp. 508–509 Exs. 6–8, 16, 19–23
Day 2: pp. 508–509 Exs. 10–14, 24–27

Average Course
Day 1: pp. 508–509 Exs. 6–8, 15–17, 25–28
Day 2: pp. 508–509 Exs. 9–14, 19–22

Advanced Course
Day 1: pp. 508–509 Exs. 6–8, 15–18*, 26–28
Day 2: pp. 508–509 Exs. 9–14, 19–22

Block
pp. 508–509 Exs. 6–8, 15–17, 25–28 (with 10.5)
pp. 508–509 Exs. 9–14, 19–22 (with 10.7)

EXTRA PRACTICE

- Student Edition, p. 717
- Chapter 10 Resource Book, pp. 53–55
- Test and Practice Generator

TRANSPARENCY

Even-numbered answers are available on transparencies.

HOMEWORK CHECK

When you review students' homework for this lesson, go over the following exercises to check understanding of key concepts.
Basic: 6, 7, 10, 11, 14
Average: 6, 8, 10, 12, 14
Advanced: 7, 8, 9, 12, 14

 COMMON ERROR

For Exercises 6–8, students may add the areas of only the faces that are labeled with units. Remind them to add the areas of all six faces.

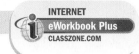
Getting Ready to Practice

1. **Vocabulary** The ? of a prism is the sum of the areas of its faces.   surface area

Find the surface area of the rectangular prism.

2.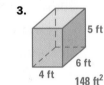
3 m
12 m
4 m   192 m²

3.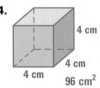
5 ft
6 ft
4 ft   148 ft²

4.
4 cm
4 cm
4 cm   96 cm²

5. **Guided Problem Solving** You make a rectangular cake that is 9 inches wide, 13 inches long, and 2 inches high. You remove it from the pan to frost it. How many square inches of frosting do you need?

   ① Find the area of each of the faces.   top and bottom: 117 in.²; long sides: 26 in.²; short sides: 18 in.²

   ② Tell which face(s) do not need to be frosted.   bottom

   ③ Find the surface area of the part of the cake that needs to be frosted.   205 in.²

Practice and Problem Solving

Find the surface area of the rectangular prism.

A 6.
6 m
18 m
5 m   456 m²

7.
10 yd
10 yd   3 yd
320 yd²

8.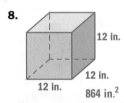
12 in.
12 in.
12 in.   864 in.²

9. **Find the Error** A student finds the surface area of a rectangular prism that is 5 units by 8 units by 6 units. Describe and correct the error.

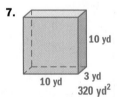

$$\text{Surface area} = (5 \times 8) + (6 \times 8) + (5 \times 6)$$
$$= 40 + 48 + 30$$
$$= 118 \text{ square units}$$

Draw a diagram of the rectangular prism described. Then find the surface area.   10–13. Check drawings.

10. 3 in. by 12 in. by 5 in.   222 in.²
11. 2 m by 6 m by 7 m   136 m²
12. 10 cm by 6 cm by 12 cm   504 cm²
13. 4 ft by 12 ft by 10 ft   416 ft²

9. Each of the areas needs to be multiplied by 2. Surface area = 2(5 × 8) + 2(6 × 8) + 2(5 × 6) = 2(40) + 2(48) + 2(30) = 236 square units.

 with Homework

Example	Exercises
1	6–8
2	9–13
3	14

Online Resources
CLASSZONE.COM
· More Examples
· eTutorial Plus

B 14. Piñata You are making a piñata that is in the shape of a rectangular prism. The prism is 2 feet by 2 feet by 3 feet. You have enough tissue paper to cover 35 square feet of the piñata. Do you have enough tissue paper to cover the entire piñata? **yes**

15. Writing Explain how the surface area changes when all of the dimensions of a rectangular prism are doubled. **The surface area of the larger prism is 4 times the surface area of the smaller prism.**

Each solid is made up of two rectangular prisms. Find the surface area of the solid.

C 16. 156 ft²

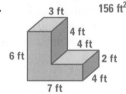
3 ft
4 ft
4 ft
6 ft
2 ft
4 ft
7 ft

17. 490 ft²

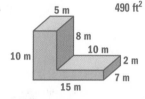
5 m
8 m
10 m
10 m
2 m
7 m
15 m

18. Challenge You need to cover the outside of a 1 foot by 1 foot by 1 foot box with paper. The paper comes in 8 inch by 11 inch sheets. How many sheets of paper will you need to cover the box? Explain.
about 10 sheets

Mixed Review

19. Find the least common multiple of 4 and 6. *(Lesson 5.4)* **12**

Classify the solid. *(Lesson 10.5)*

20. cylinder **21.** 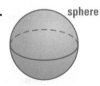 sphere **22.**

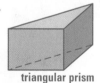
triangular prism

Basic Skills **Solve the equation using mental math.**

23. $15x = 45$ **3**   **24.** $60x = 180$ **3**   **25.** $25x = 250$ **10**   **26.** $120x = 600$ **5**

Test-Taking Practice

28. 3 cans; the surface area of the surface to be painted is 880 square inches. Since 880 ÷ 300 ≈ 3, 3 cans should be bought.

27. Multiple Choice What is the surface area of a rectangular prism that is 4 feet by 6 feet by 8 feet? **B**

A. 384 ft²   **B.** 208 ft²   **C.** 192 ft²   **D.** 104 ft²

28. Short Response A can of paint covers 300 square inches. You want to paint a rectangular box that is 20 inches by 10 inches by 8 inches. How many cans of paint should you buy? Explain your answer.

ASSESSMENT RESOURCES

For more assessment resources, see:
- Assessment Book
- Test and Practice Generator

MINI-QUIZ

Find the surface area of the prism.

1. 2250 m²

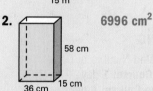
15 m
30 m
15 m

2. 6996 cm²

58 cm
36 cm   15 cm

3. Find the surface area of rectangular prism that is 7 feet by 8 feet by 3 feet. **202 ft²**

RETEACHING/REMEDIATION

- Study Guide in Chapter 10 Resource Book, pp. 56–57
- Tutor Place, Geometry and Measurement Card 21
- eTutorial Plus Online
- Extra Practice, p. 717
- Lesson Practice in Chapter 10 Resource Book, pp. 53–55

CHALLENGE/ENRICHMENT

- Challenge Practice in Chapter 10 Resource Book, p. 58
- Teacher's Edition, p. 472F

ENGLISH LEARNER SUPPORT

- Spanish Study Guide
- Multi-Language Glossary
- Chapter Audio Summaries CDs

28. See Additional Answers beginning on page AA1.

1 PLAN

LESSON OBJECTIVE

Find the volume of a rectangular prism.

PACING

Suggested Number of Days
Basic Course: 1 day
Average Course: 1 day
Advanced Course: 1 day
Block: 0.5 block with 10.6

TEACHING RESOURCES

For a complete list of Teaching Resources, see page 472B.

 TRANSPARENCY

Warm-Up Exercises for this lesson are available on a transparency.

2 TEACH

MOTIVATING THE LESSON

Ask students to put small cubes, such as sugar cubes, in a box, layer by layer. Ask how the number of cubes in a layer can be found.
Multiply the number per row by the number of rows. Then ask how the total number of cubes can be found. **Multiply the number per layer by the number of layers.**

Volume of a Prism

LESSON 10.7

BEFORE	▶ Now	WHY?
You found the surface area of a rectangular prism.	You'll find the volume of a rectangular prism.	So you can find the length of a pool at an aquarium, as in Example 3.

In the Real World

 **Word Watch**

volume, p. 510

Block Puzzles A manufacturer puts puzzles into cube-shaped boxes. Groups of the boxes are stacked, as shown in Example 1, and then put into a rectangular carton for shipping. How many puzzle boxes will fit in one carton?

EXAMPLE 1 Counting Cubes in a Stack

To find the total number of puzzle boxes that will fit in one carton, multiply the number of boxes in one layer by the number of layers. The boxes are stacked in 2 layers. Each layer is a rectangle that is 4 boxes long and 3 boxes wide.

Boxes in one layer × Number of layers = **Number of boxes**

$$3 \times 4 \times 2 = \mathbf{24}$$

ANSWER The manufacturer can fit 24 puzzle boxes in one carton.

The **volume** of a solid, such as the box in Example 1, is the amount of space the solid occupies. Volume is measured in cubic units. One way to find the volume of a rectangular prism is to use the formula below.

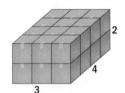 **Volume of a Rectangular Prism**

Words Volume = length · width · height

Algebra $V = lwh$

EXAMPLE 2   **Finding the Volume of a Prism**

Find the volume of the rectangular prism.

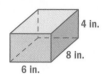

$V = lwh$	Write the volume formula.
$= 8 \cdot 6 \cdot 4$	Substitute for *l*, *w*, and *h*.
$= 192$	Simplify.

ANSWER The volume is 192 cubic inches.

Your turn now   **Find the volume of the rectangular prism.**

1.
4 m
2 m
5 m
40 m³

2.
12 ft
6 ft
6 ft
432 ft³

3.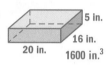
5 in.
16 in.
20 in.
1600 in.³

EXAMPLE 3   **Using the Formula for Volume**

Aquariums A pool at an aquarium is a rectangular prism that is 30 meters wide and 12 meters deep. The volume of the pool is 21,600 cubic meters. How long is the pool?

Solution

$V = lwh$	Write the volume formula.
$21{,}600 = l \cdot 30 \cdot 12$	Substitute for *V*, *w*, and *h*.
$21{,}600 = l \cdot 360$	Simplify.
$l = 21{,}600 \div 360$	Write a related division equation.
$l = 60$	Simplify.

ANSWER The length of the pool is 60 meters.

Sea Lion at Magic Mountain

Your turn now   **In Exercises 4 and 5, the solids are rectangular prisms.**

4. The volume of a swimming pool is 3750 cubic meters. The pool is 25 meters wide and 3 meters deep. How long is the pool? **50 m**

5. The volume of a bathtub is 16 cubic feet. The bathtub is 4 feet long and 2 feet wide. How deep is the bathtub? **2 ft**

ASSIGNMENT GUIDE

Basic Course
Day 1: pp. 512–513 Exs. 6–15, 20–27

Average Course
Day 1: pp. 512–513 Exs. 8–18, 20–27

Advanced Course
Day 1: pp. 512–513 Exs. 8–21*, 24–27

Block
pp. 512–513 Exs. 8–18, 20–27 (with 10.6)

EXTRA PRACTICE

• Student Edition, p. 717
• Chapter 10 Resource Book, pp. 62–64
• Test and Practice Generator

 TRANSPARENCY

Even-numbered answers are available on transparencies.

HOMEWORK CHECK

When you review students' homework for this lesson, go over the following exercises to check understanding of key concepts.
Basic: 6, 7, 9, 10, 11
Average: 8, 9, 10, 12, 13
Advanced: 8, 9, 10, 12, 13

TEACHING TIP

Exercise 17 points out another way to find the volume of a prism, namely to multiply the area of the base by the height. Ask students to imagine a prism as a deck of cards. One card is the area of the base. The stack of cards has the same height as the height of the prism.

10.7 Exercises
More Practice, p. 717

Getting Ready to Practice

1. Vocabulary To find the ? of a rectangular prism, you find the product of the length, the width, and the height. **volume**

Find the volume of the rectangular prism.

2.
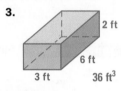
3 cm
7 cm
5 cm
105 cm³

3.
2 ft
6 ft
3 ft
36 ft³

4.
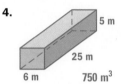
5 m
25 m
6 m
750 m³

5. Guided Problem Solving Use the pasta box shown to find the volume of the part of the pasta box that is not filled with pasta.

MACARONI
Pasta
16 cm
7 cm
13 cm
5 cm

   ① Find the volume of the pasta box shown. **1040 cm³**

   ② Find the volume of the pasta in the pasta box. **455 cm³**

   ③ Subtract the volume of the pasta from the volume of the pasta box. **585 cm³**

Practice and Problem Solving

 **with Homework**

Example	Exercises
1	6–10
2	6–10
3	11–13

Online Resources
CLASSZONE.COM
· More Examples
· eTutorial Plus

Find the volume of the rectangular prism.

A 6.
12 in.
8 in.
3 in.
288 in.³

7.

20 cm
20 cm
20 cm
8000 cm³

8.
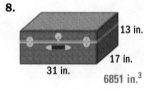
13 in.
17 in.
31 in.
6851 in.³

9. Find the volume of a rectangular prism that is 12 feet by 5 feet by 7 feet. **420 ft³**

10. Planters A planter in the shape of a rectangular prism is 24 inches by 4 inches by 5 inches. How much dirt is needed to fill the planter? **480 in.³**

Find the missing dimension of the rectangular prism described.

11. Volume: 60 ft³
length: 10 ft
width: 2 ft **3 ft**

12. Volume: 96 cm³
length: 16 cm
height: 3 cm **2 cm**

13. Volume: 2500 m³
width: 25 m
height: 5 m **20 m**

Sports

Landing Pits

Some landing pits have a trampoline bed placed about halfway down the pit in order to reduce the number of foam cubes needed. Use the information for Exercise 15 to estimate how many foam cubes are needed if a trampoline bed is placed so that the depth of the landing pit is 4 feet.

about 2560 cubes

Extended Problem Solving In Exercises 14–16, use this information.
A gymnastics center wants to buy foam cubes for a landing pit. The landing pit is a rectangular prism that is 120 inches long by 96 inches wide. The volume is 829,440 cubic inches.

B 14. Find the depth of the landing pit. **72 in.**

15. Estimate Each foam cube has a side length of 6 inches. About how many foam cubes will fit in the landing pit? **about 3840 cubes**

16. A company recommends buying only enough cubes to fill 70% of the landing pit. About how many cubes should the center order?
about 2688 cubes

17. Critical Thinking You find the volume of a rectangular prism using the formula $V = lwh$. Your friend finds the volume of the same prism by multiplying the area of the base by the height. Are the methods the same or are they different? Explain. **Same; the *lw* part of the volume formula is the area of the base.**

18. Writing Explain why the formula $V = s^3$ can be used to find the volume of a cube with a side length of s. **Each edge of a cube has the same length, so the volume is $s \cdot s \cdot s$, or s^3.**

19. Challenge Find all the different whole number lengths, widths, and heights a rectangular prism can have if its volume is 375 cubic centimeters. **3 cm, 5 cm, 25 cm; 15 cm, 5 cm, 5 cm; 1 cm, 1 cm, 375 cm; 1 cm, 15 cm, 25 cm; 1 cm, 3 cm, 125 cm; 1 cm, 75 cm, 5 cm**

Mixed Review

20. Your time in a road race is 40 minutes and 32 seconds. Your friend finishes 3 minutes and 43 seconds later. What is your friend's time? *(Lesson 6.6)* **44 min 15 sec**

21. Find the surface area of a rectangular prism that is 22 centimeters by 4 centimeters by 15 centimeters. *(Lesson 10.6)* **956 cm²**

Basic Skills Copy and complete the statement with <, >, or =.

22. $\frac{7}{10} \underline{?} \frac{3}{10}$ **>**   **23.** $\frac{1}{8} \underline{?} \frac{7}{8}$ **<**   **24.** $\frac{5}{12} \underline{?} \frac{4}{9}$ **<**   **25.** $\frac{2}{3} \underline{?} \frac{10}{15}$ **=**

Test-Taking Practice

26. Multiple Choice What is the volume of a rectangular prism that is 18 meters by 15 meters by 12 meters? **D**

A. 45 m^3 **B.** 90 m^3 **C.** 1332 m^3 **D.** 3240 m^3

27. Multiple Choice The volume of a fish tank is 864 cubic inches. The fish tank is a rectangular prism. The length of the fish tank is 12 inches and the height is 9 inches. What is the width of the fish tank? **G**

F. 4 inches   **G.** 8 inches   **H.** 648 inches   **I.** 843 inches

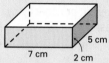

4 ASSESS

ASSESSMENT RESOURCES

For more assessment resources, see:
• Assessment Book
• Test and Practice Generator

MINI-QUIZ

1. Find the volume of the rectangular prism. **70 cm³**

7 cm   2 cm   5 cm

2. Find the missing dimension of a rectangular prism with volume 80 cubic feet, length 10 feet, and width 2 feet. **4 ft**

3. Blocks are popular children's toys that are cubes. How many fit into a carton that measures 3 blocks by 6 blocks by 12 blocks? **216 cubes**

5 FOLLOW-UP

RETEACHING/REMEDIATION

• Study Guide in Chapter 10 Resource Book, pp. 65–66
• Tutor Place, Geometry and Measurement Card 21
• eTutorial Plus Online
• Extra Practice, p. 717
• Lesson Practice in Chapter 10 Resource Book, pp. 62–64

CHALLENGE/ENRICHMENT

• Challenge Practice in Chapter 10 Resource Book, p. 68
• Teacher's Edition, p. 472F

ENGLISH LEARNER SUPPORT

• Spanish Study Guide
• Multi-Language Glossary
• Chapter Audio Summaries CDs

SKILL CHECK

1. $10 + 3(4) = \underline{\ ?\ }$ 22
2. $100 + 3(40) = \underline{\ ?\ }$ 220
3. Simplify $\dfrac{10}{16}$. $\dfrac{5}{8}$

LESSON OBJECTIVE

Find mass, weight, or capacity by reading scales.

2 TEACH

EXTRA EXAMPLES

Example 1 What is the mass of the rock? **2.3 kg or 2300 g**

Example 2 Find the amount of liquid in the beaker. **450 mL**

TEACHING TIP

If possible, ask students to simulate the examples on this page by using actual measuring instruments available to mathematics or science students. If a spring balance is available, ask student to measure the mass of known objects and compare them to their given mass.

514

CHAPTER 10 Special Topic

Mass, Weight, and Capacity

GOAL Determine mass, weight, and capacity by reading scales.

Word Watch

Review Words
mass, p. 187
capacity, p. 188
metric units,
    pp. 187, 188
customary units,
    pp. 344, 355

Metric Measuring Metric units of mass include grams (g), milligrams (mg), and kilograms (kg). Metric units of capacity include liters (L), milliliters (mL), and kiloliters (kL).

EXAMPLE 1 **Measuring Mass in Metric Units**

Use the spring balance to find the mass of the meteorite.

Recall that 1 kg equals 1000 g. Each 1000 g on the scale is divided into 10 equal parts,

so each mark represents $\dfrac{1000}{10}$, or 100 g.

The pointer on the scale is at the sixth mark.

$$\text{Mass} = 6(100)$$
$$= 600$$

ANSWER The mass of the meteorite is 600 g.

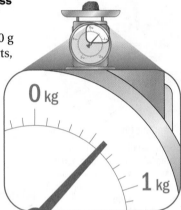

EXAMPLE 2 **Measuring Capacity in Metric Units**

Find the amount of liquid in the measuring cup.

Each 100 mL on the measuring cup is divided into 4 intervals, so each interval

represents $\dfrac{100}{4}$, or 25 mL. The liquid is

3 intervals past 200 mL.

$$\text{Capacity} = 200 + 3(25)$$
$$= 275$$

ANSWER There are 275 mL of liquid in the measuring cup.

Customary Measuring Customary units of weight include ounces (oz), pounds (lb), and tons (T). Customary units of capacity include fluid ounces (fl oz), cups (c), pints (pt), quarts (qt), and gallons (gal).

NCTM CURRICULUM STANDARDS
Standard 4: Understand measurable attributes of
        objects; Understand the units of measurement;
        Understand the systems of measurement

Example 3 Find the weight of the bag of fruit. $3\frac{1}{4}$ lb

Example 4 Find the amount of juice in the measuring cup.

$1\frac{3}{4}$ c

EXAMPLE 3 **Measuring Weight in Customary Units**

Use the spring balance to find the weight of the watermelon.

Each pound on the scale is divided into 16 equal parts, so each mark represents $\frac{1}{16}$ lb. The pointer on the scale is 8 marks past 7 lb.

ANSWER The weight of the watermelon is $7\frac{8}{16}$ lb, or $7\frac{1}{2}$ lb.

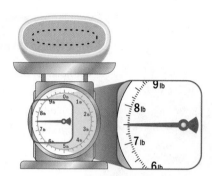

EXAMPLE 4 **Measuring Customary Capacity**

Find the amount of liquid in the measuring cup.

Each cup on the measuring cup is divided into 4 intervals, so each interval represents $\frac{1}{4}$ c. The liquid is 2 intervals past 1 c.

ANSWER The amount of liquid is $1\frac{2}{4}$ c, or $1\frac{1}{2}$ c.

Exercises

1. Find the mass of the oranges.
2.1 kg

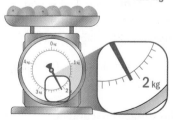

2. Find the amount of liquid in the measuring cup. $2\frac{3}{4}$ c

3. Estimate the total weight in pounds of the books you carried home from school today. Then use a bathroom scale to find the actual weight. Compare your estimate to the actual weight. A good answer will include an estimate and an actual weight.

CONCEPT CHECK

How do you find the weight of an object on a scale? **You determine the weight of one major interval on the scale. Then determine how many times each interval is divided so that you can find the fraction of an interval. Then read the number of major intervals and the fraction of an interval indicated by the pointer.**

3 **APPLY**

TRANSPARENCY

Even-numbered answers are available on transparencies.

TEACHING TIP

In Exercise 3, students will do an experiment to estimate weight. Encourage them to use a bathroom scale to check the weight of several other objects they have estimated.

Notebook Review

LESSONS **10.5** TO **10.7**

Review the vocabulary definitions in your notebook.

Copy the review examples in your notebook. Then complete the exercises.

Check Your Definitions

solid, p. 500	cone, p. 500	vertex, p. 501
prism, p. 500	sphere, p. 500	surface area, p. 506
cylinder, p. 500	face, p. 501	volume, p. 510
pyramid, p. 500	edge, p. 501	

Use Your Vocabulary

1. Copy and complete: A _?_ has one circular base. **cone**

10.5 Can you classify solid figures?

Review **EXAMPLE** Identify the bases of the solid shown at the right. Then classify the solid.

ANSWER The two bases of the solid are circles. The solid is a cylinder.

 2. Classify the solid. Then count the number of faces, edges, and vertices. **triangular prism; 5 faces, 9 edges, 6 vertices**

10.6–10.7 Can you find surface area and volume of a prism?

Review **EXAMPLE** A box measures 14 inches by 18 inches by 4 inches. What is the surface area and the volume of the box?

Surface Area

Area of the top or bottom: $14 \cdot 18 = 252$

Area of the front or back: $4 \cdot 14 = 56$

Area of the left or right: $4 \cdot 18 = 72$

Surface area: $2(252) + 2(56) + 2(72) = 760$

Volume

$V = lwh$

$= 14 \cdot 18 \cdot 4$

$= 1008$

ANSWER The surface area is 760 square inches, and the volume is 1008 cubic inches.

 3. Find the surface area and the volume of the rectangular prism shown at the right. **136 yd², 96 yd³**

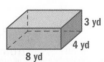

8 yd, 4 yd, 3 yd

Stop *and* Think   about Lessons 10.5–10.7

4. The surface area of a rectangular prism is the sum of the areas of its faces, while the volume is the amount of space the prism occupies.

5. A prism has two bases, while a pyramid has only one.

4. **Writing** Explain the difference between the surface area and the volume of a rectangular prism.

5. **Critical Thinking** Explain how you can tell the difference between a prism and a pyramid.

Review Quiz 2

Classify the solid.

1.

sphere

2.

rectangular prism

3.
rectangular pyramid

4. Count the number of faces, edges, and vertices of the solid in Exercise 2.
6 faces, 12 edges, 8 vertices

5. **Sofa** You are covering a sofa cushion that is a rectangular prism. It measures 18 inches by 21 inches by 4 inches. About how many square inches of fabric do you need? 1068 in.^{2}

6. Find the surface area and the volume of the rectangular prism shown at the right.
504 m^2, 648 m^3

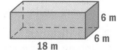
6 m
6 m
18 m

7. A rectangular prism has a width of 5 meters, a height of 3 meters, and a volume of 105 cubic meters. Find the length.
7 m

BrAIN GAME

Counting Blocks

Two views of a tower of blocks are shown. Each block is a cube that measures 1 inch by 1 inch by 1 inch. Find the volume of the tower. Then find the area of the outer surface, including the base. 10 in.^{3}; 36 in.^{2}

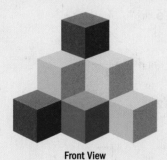
Front View

Back View

ADDITIONAL RESOURCES

The following resources are available to help review the materials in this chapter.

Chapter 10 Resource Book
- Chapter Review Games and Activities, p. 69
- Cumulative Practice, Chs. 1-10

English/Spanish Chapter Reviews and Tests

Chapter Audio Summaries CDs

eTutorial CD-ROM

eWorkbook Plus Online

eTutorial Plus Online

CHAPTER 10

Chapter Review

Vocabulary

base of a parallelogram, p. 476
height of a parallelogram, p. 476
perpendicular, p. 476
base of a triangle, p. 480
height of a triangle, p. 480
circle, p. 485
center, p. 485
radius, p. 485
diameter, p. 485
circumference, p. 485
pi (π), p. 485
solid, p. 500
prism, p. 500
cylinder, p. 500
pyramid, p. 500
cone, p. 500
sphere, p. 500
face, p. 501
edge, p. 501
vertex, p. 501
surface area, p. 506
volume, p. 510

Vocabulary Review

Tell whether the statement is *true* or *false*.

1. The circumference of a circle is measured in square units. **false**
2. The surface area of a prism is measured in square units. **true**
3. The distance from the center of a circle to any point on the circle is called the diameter. **false**

Copy and complete the statement.

4. Two intersecting lines that meet at a right angle are _?_. **perpendicular**
5. The base of a cone is a _?_. **circle**
6. The _?_ of a prism is the sum of the areas of its faces. **surface area**
7. The _?_ of a prism is the amount of space that it occupies. **volume**

Review Questions

Find the area of the figure. *(Lessons 10.1, 10.2, 10.4)*

8.
28 mm
30 mm
840 mm^2

9.
10 mi
10 mi
50 mi^2

10.
16 m
30 m
240 m^2

11.
8 in.
6 in.
48 $in.^2$

12.
3 cm
28.26 cm^2

13.
10 yd
78.5 yd^2

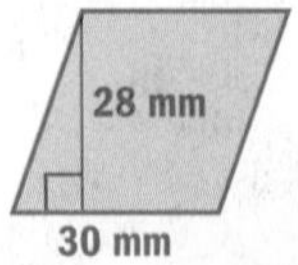

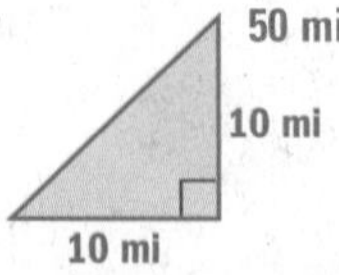

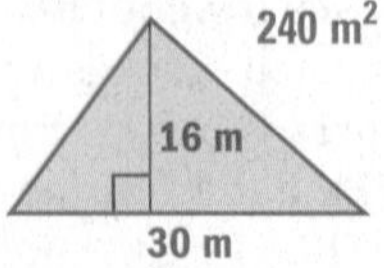

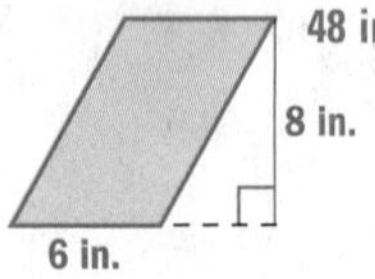

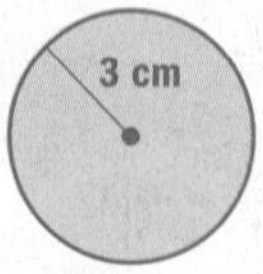

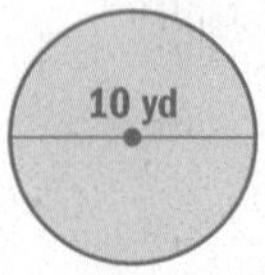

23.
Number of Karate Students

Blue belt
Green belt — Red belt
— Black belt
Orange belt — White belt

Review Questions

14. The area of a parallelogram is 68 square meters and the base is 4 meters. Find the height of the parallelogram. *(Lesson 10.1)* **17 m**

15. The area of a triangle is 100 square inches and the height is 20 inches. What is the base? *(Lesson 10.2)* **10 in.**

Find the circumference of the circle described. *(Lesson 10.3)*

16. diameter = 5 m **15.7 m** **17.** diameter = 35 in. **109.9 in.** **18.** radius = 3 yd **18.84 yd**

19. The trunk of a tree has a circumference of about 75 inches. Find the diameter of the tree to the nearest inch. *(Lesson 10.3)* **24 in.**

Find the area of the figure to the nearest tenth of a unit. *(Lesson 10.4)*

20. 420.5 cm²

20 cm

16 cm

21. 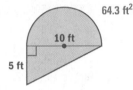 64.3 ft²

10 ft

5 ft

22. 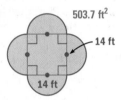 503.7 ft²

14 ft

14 ft

23. Make a circle graph to represent the karate data shown below. *(Lesson 10.4)* **See margin.**

Number of Karate Students at Each Level					
Black Belt	Red Belt	Blue Belt	Green Belt	Orange Belt	White Belt
3	6	15	22	13	8

Classify the solid. *(Lesson 10.5)*

24. cylinder **25.** triangular prism **26.** sphere

27. Count the number of faces, edges, and vertices of the solid in Exercise 25. *(Lesson 10.5)* **5 faces, 9 edges, 6 vertices**

Find the surface area and the volume of the rectangular prism.
(Lessons 10.6, 10.7)

28. 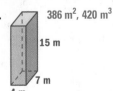 386 m², 420 m³

15 m

7 m
4 m

29. 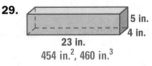

5 in.
4 in.
23 in.
454 in.², 460 in.³

30. 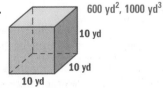 600 yd², 1000 yd³

10 yd
10 yd
10 yd

9. *Sample:*

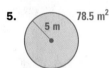

16. Types of Plants Sold

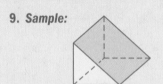

Chapter Test

1. The base of a parallelogram is 6 inches and the height is 4 inches. Find the area of the parallelogram. **24 in.²**

2. The base of a triangle is 10 centimeters and the height is 18 centimeters. Find the area of the triangle. **90 cm²**

3. A parallelogram has an area of 60 square feet and a height of 5 feet. Find the base. **12 ft**

4. Craters Tycho is a crater located on the moon. Tycho has a radius of about 43.5 kilometers. Find the circumference of Tycho to the nearest kilometer. **273 km**

Find the area of the figure.

5. 5 m   **78.5 m²**

6. 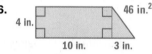 4 in.   10 in.   3 in.   **46 in.²**

7. 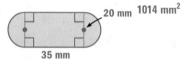 35 mm   20 mm   **1014 mm²**

8. Classify the solid shown at the right. **cone**

9. Draw a triangular prism. **See margin.**

Find the surface area and the volume of the rectangular prism.

10. 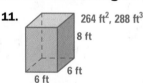 30 in.   5 in.   5 in.
650 in.², 750 in.³

11. 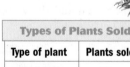 **264 ft², 288 ft³**   8 ft   6 ft   6 ft

12. 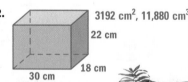 **3192 cm², 11,880 cm³**   22 cm   30 cm   18 cm

13. Count the faces, edges, and vertices of the solid in Exercise 12. **6 faces, 12 edges, 8 vertices**

14. Painting You are painting a rectangular box that is 5 feet by 4 feet by 2 feet. The paint can says that the paint will cover 100 square feet. Do you have enough paint to cover the entire box? **yes**

15. Tissue Box A tissue box measures 9 inches by 5 inches by 3 inches. Find the volume of the tissue box. **135 in.³**

16. Plant Sale The number of plants sold at a plant sale is shown. Make a circle graph to represent the data. **See margin.**

Types of Plants Sold	
Type of plant	**Plants sold**
potted palm	70
geranium	30
African violet	50

Chapter Standardized Test

Test-Taking Strategy Concentrate on the question that you are working on rather than the time that is remaining for the test.

Multiple Choice

1. A parallelogram has an area of 35 square meters. The height of the parallelogram is 7 meters. What is the length of the base? **A**

A. 5 m   **B.** 28 m   **C.** 42 m   **D.** 245 m

2. What is the area of the triangle? **G**

7 cm
10 cm

F. 17 cm^2 **G.** 35 cm^2
H. 70 cm^2 **I.** 140 cm^2

3. What is the approximate circumference of a circle that has a diameter of 6 inches? **B**

A. 9.42 in.   **B.** 18.84 in.
C. 28.26 in.   **D.** 56.52 in.

4. What is the approximate area of a circle that has a radius of 8 feet? **H**

F. 25.12 ft^2 **G.** 50.24 ft^2
H. 200.96 ft^2 **I.** 803.84 ft^2

5. What is the approximate area of the figure? **B**

6 cm

A. 54.84 cm^2 **B.** 64.26 cm^2
C. 73.68 cm^2 **D.** 92.52 cm^2

6. Classify the solid. **H**

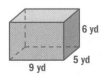

F. Cone
G. Sphere
H. Triangular pyramid
I. Triangular prism

7. Which of the following is *true* about the solid in Exercise 6? **D**

A. There are 12 faces.
B. There are 8 edges.
C. There are 8 vertices.
D. There are 6 edges.

8. What is the surface area of the prism shown? **H**

F. 20 yd^2 **G.** 129 yd^2
H. 258 yd^2 **I.** 270 yd^2

6 yd
9 yd   5 yd

9. What is the volume of the prism shown in Exercise 8? **D**

A. 23 yd^3 **B.** 135 yd^3
C. 225 yd^3 **D.** 270 yd^3

Short Response

10. Can you use this expression to find the area of a half-circle: $\frac{1}{2}\pi r^2$? Explain. See margin.

Extended Response

11. You want to estimate the diameter of a large tree trunk. Your only tools are a large piece of rope and a ruler. Describe the steps you would follow to get a reasonable estimate of the tree's diameter. See margin.

10. Yes; πr^2 is the formula for the area of a circle, and $\frac{1}{2}$ the area is the area of a half circle.

11. *Sample answer:* Wrap the rope once around the tree to find the circumference of the tree. Divide this number by 3.14 to find a reasonable estimate of the diameter.

UNIT 3
Chapters 8–10

BUILDING **Test-Taking Skills**

Strategies for Answering
Context-Based Multiple Choice Questions

Some of the information you need to solve a context-based multiple choice question may appear in a table, a diagram, or a graph.

Problem 1

A magazine ad for a car includes a scale drawing of the car. The actual width of the car is 200 centimeters. What is the actual length of the car?

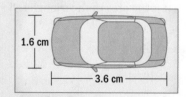

A. 125 cm   B. 203.6 cm   C. 450 cm   D. 720 cm

Solution

Read the problem carefully. Decide what information you are given and how you can use it to solve the problem.

1) From the problem and diagram, you know:

   width on drawing = 1.6 centimeters   actual width = 200 centimeters

   length on drawing = 3.6 centimeters   actual length = ?

You can use the width on the drawing and the actual width to find the scale of the drawing. Then use the scale to find the actual length.

Find the scale.

2) The scale of the drawing is $\frac{1.6 \text{ cm}}{200 \text{ cm}}$ or $\frac{1 \text{ cm}}{125 \text{ cm}}$.

Write and solve a proportion to find the actual length of the car. Use cross products.

3) $\frac{1 \text{ cm}}{125 \text{ cm}} = \frac{\text{Length on drawing}}{\text{Actual length}}$ Write a proportion.

   $\frac{1 \text{ cm}}{125 \text{ cm}} = \frac{3.6 \text{ cm}}{x \text{ cm}}$ Substitute values.

   $1 \cdot x = (125)(3.6)$ The cross products are equal.

   $x = 450$ Multiply.

The actual length is 450 centimeters. The correct answer is C.

Use one of the strategies on pages 202–203.

4) Check to see that your answer is reasonable. For example, because $125 \times 3.6 \approx 100 \times 4 = 400$, the most reasonable answer is C.

Problem 2

A storage chest in the shape of a rectangular prism has the dimensions shown. What is the surface area of the chest?

Surface	Length	Width
front and back	3 ft	2 ft
top and bottom	3 ft	1.5 ft
left and right	2 ft	1.5 ft

F. 13 ft²   **G.** 13.5 ft²   **H.** 27 ft²   **I.** 67.5 ft²

Solution

Read the problem carefully. Recall that the surface area of a prism is the sum of the areas of its faces.

1) Use the table to make a sketch. Find the area of each face of the chest. Then add to find the surface area S.

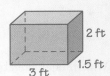

Find the surface area.

2) $S = (3 \times 2) + (3 \times 2) + (3 \times 1.5) +$
   $(3 \times 1.5) + (2 \times 1.5) + (2 \times 1.5)$

   $= 6 + 6 + 4.5 + 4.5 + 3 + 3$

   $= 27$

The surface area is 27 square feet. The correct answer is H.

Watch Out!

It is important to be sure that you know what question you are trying to answer. Some of the choices given may be correct answers to slightly different questions.

Your turn now

1. What is the volume of the storage chest in Problem 2? **B**

  A. 6.5 ft³   **B.** 9 ft³   **C.** 18 ft³   **D.** 27 ft³

2. How many degrees greater than the measure of $\angle A$ is the measure of $\angle B$? **G**

  F. 23°   **G.** 41°

  H. 64°   **I.** 95°

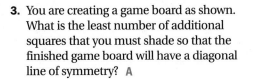

3. You are creating a game board as shown. What is the least number of additional squares that you must shade so that the finished game board will have a diagonal line of symmetry? **A**

  A. 1   **B.** 2   **C.** 3   **D.** 4

Multiple Choice

1. Students voted for their favorite fruit. The results are shown in the circle graph below. What percent of the 250 students who voted chose apples? **A**

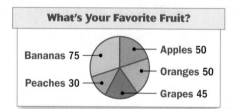

What's Your Favorite Fruit?

Bananas 75
Apples 50
Oranges 50
Peaches 30
Grapes 45

A. 20% **B.** 25% **C.** 50% **D.** 100%

2. Which statement about the figure is *false*? **H**

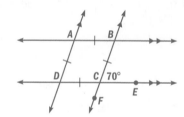

F. $\overleftrightarrow{AB}$ is parallel to $\overleftrightarrow{DC}$.

G. $\overrightarrow{AB}$ has endpoint A.

H. $\angle ECF$ is acute.

I. Quadrilateral $ABCD$ is a rhombus.

3. The table shows the total number of diagonals that can be drawn in a regular polygon with the given number of sides. How many diagonals can be drawn in a regular octagon? **C**

Number of sides	3	4	5	6	7
Number of diagonals	0	2	5	9	14

A. 16 **B.** 18 **C.** 20 **D.** 28

In Exercises 4 and 5, use the scale drawing below. It shows the actual measures of a street sign.

4. About how much metal is needed to make the sign? **G**

F. 97 square inches

G. 453 square inches

H. 471 square inches

I. 510 square inches

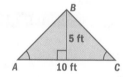

33 in.

12 in.

(1 in.: 18 in.)

5. The actual width of the sign is 12 inches. What is the width of the sign on the scale drawing? **B**

A. 0.6 inch

B. $0.\overline{6}$ inch

C. 0.7 inch

D. 1 inch

In the triangle below, $m\angle ABC = 90°$. Use the diagram in Exercises 6 and 7.

B
5 ft
A   10 ft   C

6. What is the measure of $\angle BAC$? **G**

F. 10° **G.** 45° **H.** 90° **I.** 180°

7. What is the total area of the triangle shown? **A**

A. 25 square feet **B.** 30 square feet

C. 35 square feet **D.** 50 square feet

Short Response

8. Eighteen students in a class of 25 students plan to go on a hiking trip. What percent of the students plan to go on the trip? What percent do not plan to go? Explain how you found your answers.

72%; 28%; $\frac{18}{25} = 0.72 = 72\%$ and $100 - 72 = 28\%$.

9. Engineers tested two cars to find their fuel efficiency. Car A traveled 225 miles and used 14 gallons of gas. Car B traveled 312 miles and used 15 gallons of gas. Which car has better fuel efficiency? Explain. **See margin.**

10. The sales tax rate in Arbordale is 7.5%. Find the amount of sales tax on the purchase of a $19,276 car. Show your work.

$1445.70; 19,276 × 0.075 = 1445.70

11. The Vaughn family wants to spend no more than 24% of their income for their mortgage. Their annual income is $84,000. What is the greatest amount of money they can spend each month on their mortgage if they stay within their budget? Show your steps.

$1680; (84,000 × 0.24) ÷ 12 = 1680

12. Nine apes at a zoo eat a total of 12 pounds of oranges per day. How many pounds of oranges would be needed for 12 apes? How many apes could be fed with 20 pounds of oranges? Explain how you found your answers.

16 lb; 15 apes; $\frac{9 \text{ apes}}{12 \text{ pounds}} = \frac{12 \text{ apes}}{x \text{ pounds}}$, so $x = 16$; $\frac{9 \text{ apes}}{12 \text{ pounds}} = \frac{x \text{ apes}}{20 \text{ pounds}}$, so $x = 15$.

Extended Response

13. A circular rug is shown. How many square feet of floor are covered by this rug? Binding ribbon is sold by the foot. How much binding ribbon is needed to bind off the blue outer edge of the rug? Explain how you found your answers.

4 ft

1 ft

13. 28.26 ft²; 18.84 ft; the radius is 3 feet, so the area is about 3.14 × 9 = 28.26; the diameter is 6 feet, so the circumference is about 3.14 × 6 = 18.84.

14. A popcorn box is shaped like a rectangular prism. It has length 10 cm, width 4.5 cm, and height 16 cm. Sketch the popcorn box. How much cardboard would be needed to make the box, assuming all faces are closed and there are no overlaps? How much popcorn could the box hold? Show how you found your answers.

14. Check drawings; 554 cm²; 720 cm³; S = 2(10 × 4.5) + 2(4.5 × 16) + 2(10 × 16) = 554; V = 10 × 4.5 × 16 = 720.

15. Create a new parallelogram by multiplying the sides and height of the parallelogram shown by 3. Keep the angle measures the same. Is the new parallelogram similar to the old one? Is it congruent to the old one? Explain why or why not. Then find the perimeters and the areas of the old and the new parallelograms. Is the ratio of the areas the same as the ratio of the perimeters? Explain.

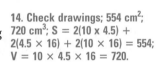

50 mm

13 mm, 12 mm, 13 mm

50 mm

15. Yes; no; the dimensions are proportional but not the same and the angle measures are the same, so they are similar but not congruent; 126 mm and 378 mm; 600 mm² and 5400 mm²; no; the ratio of the areas is 3 times the ratio of the perimeters.

16. The design for a pillow cover is shown. Ignoring color, tell how many lines of symmetry the design has. The measure of ∠1 is 30°. Explain how you can use the symmetry of the design to find the measures of the rest of the numbered angles.

1, 2, 4, 3

2; the triangles containing the numbered angles are all congruent, so the measures of all of the angles are the same.

Cumulative Practice for Chapters 8–10

Chapter 8

Multiple Choice In Exercises 1–10, choose the letter of the correct answer.

1. Mr. and Mrs. Chin have 4 nephews and 2 nieces. What is the ratio of nieces to nephews? *(Lesson 8.1)* **B**

   A. 1 : 3   **B.** 1 : 2   **C.** 2 : 1   **D.** 3 : 1

2. A car travels 3 miles in 4 minutes. At this rate, how far does the car travel in one minute? *(Lesson 8.2)* **F**

   F. 0.75 miles   **G.** 1.33 miles

   H. 12 miles   **I.** 45 miles

3. What is the solution of the proportion $\frac{9}{36} = \frac{y}{16}$? *(Lesson 8.3)* **A**

   A. 4   **B.** $4\frac{1}{2}$ **C.** 108   **D.** 144

4. Henry bought 3 yards of fabric for a costume. He paid $12.60. How much would 5 yards of the fabric cost? *(Lesson 8.3)* **I**

   F. $4.20   **G.** $7.56   **H.** $8.40   **I.** $21

5. A scale drawing of a fountain has a scale of 1 in. : 2 ft. The actual diameter of the circular fountain is 8 feet. What is the diameter on the scale drawing? *(Lesson 8.4)* **B**

   A. 2 in.   **B.** 4 in.   **C.** 8 in.   **D.** 16 in.

6. The distance on a map between Franklin and Lincoln is about 6 inches. Use the scale 1 in. : 10 mi to estimate the actual distance between the towns. *(Lesson 8.4)* **H**

   F. 30 mi   **G.** 40 mi   **H.** 60 mi   **I.** 180 mi

7. How can you write 0.07 as a percent? *(Lesson 8.5)* **B**

   A. 0.07%   **B.** 7%   **C.** 70%   **D.** 700%

8. Which number is *not* equivalent to the other numbers? *(Lesson 8.6)* **F**

   F. $\frac{73}{200}$ **G.** $\frac{3}{8}$ **H.** 0.375   **I.** 37.5%

9. What is 5% of 200? *(Lesson 8.6)* **B**

   A. 5   **B.** 10   **C.** 40   **D.** 82.05

10. You deposit $250 into an account with an annual interest rate of 4%. How much simple interest will you earn on that money in 3 years? *(Lesson 8.7)* **I**

    F. $10   **G.** $20   **H.** $25   **I.** $30

11. **Short Response** Your restaurant bill is $31.96. You want to leave a tip of about 20%. Estimate the amount of the tip. Then estimate your share of the total cost if you divide it into three equal parts. Explain how you found your answers. *(Lesson 8.7)*
    See margin.

12. **Extended Response** A gym bag that costs $35 is on sale for 30% off. You need to pay 6% sales tax on your purchase. *(Lesson 8.7)*

    a. Find the cost of the gym bag. Show your work.

    b. If you pay with two $20 bills, how much change will you receive? Explain.

    a. $25.97; 35 − 35(0.30) = 24.50, 24.50 + 24.50(0.06) = 25.97

    b. $14.03; 40 − 25.97 = 14.03

21. Sample:

$\overline{AB}$ and $\overline{DE}$, $\overline{BC}$ and $\overline{EF}$, $\overline{CA}$ and $\overline{FD}$, $\angle A$ and $\angle D$, $\angle B$ and $\angle E$, $\angle C$ and $\angle F$; they are corresponding parts of congruent triangles.

Test-Taking Skills

Chapter 9

Multiple Choice In Exercises 13–20, choose the letter of the correct answer.

13. Which two symbols *cannot* represent the same figure? *(Lesson 9.1)* **C**

  A. $\overline{AB}$ and $\overline{BA}$ **B.** $\overleftrightarrow{CD}$ and $\overleftrightarrow{DC}$

  C. $\overrightarrow{PQ}$ and $\overrightarrow{QP}$ **D.** $\overrightarrow{RS}$ and $\overrightarrow{RT}$

14. What is the closest approximation to the measure of $\angle P$? *(Lesson 9.2)* **I**

  F. 30°   **G.** 60°

  H. 90°   **I.** 110°

15. Classify an angle with measure 64°. *(Lesson 9.3)* **A**

  A. acute   **B.** straight

  C. obtuse   **D.** right

16. Which angle measure represents an angle that is supplementary to a 37° angle? *(Lesson 9.3)* **I**

  F. 37°   **G.** 53°   **H.** 127°   **I.** 143°

17. The measures of two angles of a triangle are 46° and 42°. Classify the triangle. *(Lesson 9.4)* **B**

  A. acute   **B.** obtuse

  C. equilateral   **D.** right

18. Which statement is true? *(Lesson 9.5)* **H**

  F. Every parallelogram is a rhombus.

  G. Every rhombus is a square.

  H. Every rectangle is a parallelogram.

  I. Every quadrilateral is a rhombus.

19. Which name does *not* apply to the figure shown? *(Lessons 9.4, 9.6)* **B**

  A. equilateral triangle

  B. scalene triangle

  C. regular triangle

  D. polygon

20. How many lines of symmetry does the figure shown have? *(Lesson 9.8)* **G**

  F. 0

  G. 1

  H. 2

  I. 3

21. **Short Response** Draw two congruent right triangles, $\triangle ABC$ and $\triangle DEF$. List the corresponding parts. Explain why $\angle A$ and $\angle D$ have the same measure. *(Lessons 9.4, 9.7)* **See margin.**

22. **Extended Response** In the figure, $m\angle 2 = 50°$. *(Lesson 9.3)*

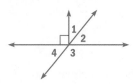

  a. Name two complementary angles. $\angle 1$ and $\angle 2$

  b. Name two vertical angles. $\angle 2$ and $\angle 4$

  c. Name two supplementary angles.

  d. Find the measures of $\angle 1$, $\angle 3$, and $\angle 4$. Explain how you found your answers.

  c. $\angle 3$ and $\angle 4$

  d. $m\angle 1 = 40°$, $m\angle 3 = 130°$, $m\angle 4 = 50°$; $\angle 1$ and $\angle 2$ are complementary, so $m\angle 1 = 90° - 50° = 40°$. $\angle 2$ and $\angle 3$ are supplementary, so $m\angle 3 = 180° - 50° = 130°$. $\angle 4$ and $\angle 2$ are vertical angles, so $m\angle 4 = m\angle 2 = 50°$.

33. Team's Record in One Season

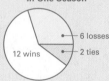

6 losses
2 ties
12 wins

$\frac{12}{20} = 60\%$ wins,

$0.60 \times 360 = 216°$; $\frac{6}{20} =$

30% losses, $0.30 \times 360 =$

$108°$; $\frac{2}{20} = 10\%$ ties,

$0.10 \times 360 = 36°$; draw a circle with sectors having these angles and label each sector.

Chapter 10

Multiple Choice In Exercises 23–32, choose the letter of the correct answer.

23. What is the area of a parallelogram with a base of 14 centimeters and a height of 8 centimeters? *(Lesson 10.1)* **D**

   A. 44 cm   **B.** 112 cm

   C. 44 cm^2 **D.** 112 cm^2

24. The area of a parallelogram is 110 square inches. The height is 10 inches. What is the base? *(Lesson 10.1)* **F**

   F. 11 in.   **G.** 22 in.   **H.** 100 in.   **I.** 110 in.

25. A pennant in the shape of a triangle has an area of 50 square inches. The base is 10 inches. What is the height? *(Lesson 10.2)* **B**

   A. 5 in.   **B.** 10 in.   **C.** 25 in.   **D.** 500 in.

26. What is the area of the figure? *(Lesson 10.2)* **G**

   F. 8 m^2

   G. 10 m^2

   H. 12 m^2

   I. 16 m^2

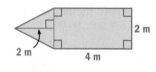

2 m
2 m
4 m

27. What is the approximate circumference of a CD with a radius of 4.5 centimeters? *(Lesson 10.3)* **B**

   A. 14.13 cm   **B.** 28.26 cm

   C. 29.88 cm   **D.** 63.59 cm

28. What is the approximate area of a circle with a diameter of 10 feet? *(Lesson 10.4)* **H**

   F. 15.7 ft^2 **G.** 31.4 ft^2

   H. 78.5 ft^2 **I.** 314 ft^2

29. Which solid has 4 faces? *(Lesson 10.5)* **B**

   A. triangular prism

   B. triangular pyramid

   C. rectangular prism

   D. rectangular pyramid

30. How many edges does a triangular prism have? *(Lesson 10.5)* **H**

   F. 6   **G.** 8   **H.** 9   **I.** 12

31. A box in the shape of a rectangular prism is 9 centimeters by 7 centimeters by 3 centimeters. What is the surface area of the box? *(Lesson 10.6)* **D**

   A. 19 ft^2 **B.** 66 ft^2

   C. 189 ft^2 **D.** 222 ft^2

32. A wading pool is 6 feet by 4 feet by 2 feet. What is its volume? *(Lesson 10.7)* **I**

   F. 12 ft^2 **G.** 12 ft^3 **H.** 48 ft^2 **I.** 48 ft^3

33. **Short Response** A baseball team had 12 wins, 6 losses, and 2 ties during one season. Make a circle graph of the data. Explain your steps. *(Lesson 10.4)* **See margin.**

34. **Extended Response** Kim wants to make a cushion shaped like a rectangular prism for her couch. The cushion will be 16 inches by 18 inches by 4 inches. *(Lessons 10.6, 10.7)*

   a. To find how much fabric she needs to cover the cushion, should Kim find the *surface area* or the *volume?* How much fabric does she need? **surface area; 848 square inches**

   b. To find how much filling Kim needs for the cushion, should she find the *surface area* or the *volume?* How much filling does she need? **volume; 1152 cubic inches**

Integers, Algebra, and Probability

Chapter 11 Integers

- Add, subtract, multiply, and divide integers.
- Identify and graph points in a coordinate plane.
- Identify and perform transformations and tessellations.

Chapter 12 Equations and Functions

- Write and solve equations that model real-life situations.
- Write and evaluate functions and expressions.
- Interpret and create multiple representations of a linear function.

Chapter 13 Probability and Statistics

- Find probabilities and determine the outcomes of events.
- Recognize misleading statistics and graphs.
- Create, analyze, and interpret data displays.

From Chapter 12, p. 605
How much bamboo does a giant panda eat?

529

UNIT RESOURCES

These resources are provided to help you prepare for the unit and to customize review materials:

 Chapter Resource Books
- Chapter 11
- Chapter 12
- Chapter 13

Assessment Book
- Chapters 11–13, pp. 135–174

 Technology
- EasyPlanner CD-ROM
- Test and Practice Generator
- Electronic Lesson Presentations CD-ROM
- eTutorial CD-ROM

 Internet
- Classzone
- eEdition Plus Online
- eWorkbook Plus Online
- eTutorial Plus Online
- EasyPlanner Plus Online

ENGLISH LEARNER SUPPORT

- Spanish Study Guide
- Multi-Language Glossary
- Chapter Audio Summaries CDs
- Teacher's Edition
Chapter 11, pp. 530E–530F
Chapter 12, pp. 580E–580F
Chapter 13, pp. 626E–626F

Chapter 11 Pacing and Assignment Guide

REGULAR SCHEDULE

Lesson	Les. Day	BASIC	AVERAGE	ADVANCED
11.1	Day 1	pp. 535–536 Exs. 11–16, 20–31, 35–37, 40–49	pp. 535–536 Exs. 15–25, 30–38, 40–50	pp. 535–536 Exs. 15–23, 28–39*, 42–45, 48–50
11.2	Day 1	SRH p. 688 Exs. 13–16; pp. 540–541 Exs. 10–13, 35–43, 49–56	pp. 540–541 Exs. 10–13, 34–41, 49–56	pp. 540–541 Exs. 10–13, 35–43, 51–54
	Day 2	pp. 540–541 Exs. 14–29, 44, 57–61	pp. 540–541 Exs. 22–33, 42–47, 59–62	pp. 540–541 Exs. 24–34, 44–48*, 61, 62
11.3	Day 1	SRH p. 688 Exs. 5–8; pp. 546–547 Exs. 11–18, 38–41, 51–57	pp. 546–547 Exs. 15–19, 38–42, 51–61	pp. 546–547 Exs. 15–23, 38–42, 51–54, 63
	Day 2	pp. 546–547 Exs. 22–31, 36, 43–45, 58–63	pp. 546–547 Exs. 24–37, 43–46, 62–64	pp. 546–547 Exs. 32–37, 43–50*, 55–58, 64
11.4	Day 1	pp. 552–553 Exs. 8–19, 24–26, 37–39, 57–59	pp. 552–553 Exs. 12–26, 37–42, 58–60	pp. 552–553 Exs. 12–25, 37–40, 46–48
	Day 2	pp. 552–553 Exs. 28–36, 41, 46–56	pp. 552–553 Exs. 27–36, 46–57	pp. 552–553 Exs. 26–36, 41–45*, 51–54, 60
11.5	Day 1	pp. 556–558 Exs. 12–23, 30–34, 36–43, 48–52	pp. 556–558 Exs. 12–17, 24–39, 44–46, 48–53	pp. 556–558 Exs. 15–17, 24–35, 38–49*, 52, 53
11.6	Day 1	EP p. 709 Exs. 14–18; pp. 564–566 Exs. 9–12, 17–22, 27–30	pp. 564–566 Exs. 9–12, 19–23, 33–36, 47–50	pp. 564–566 Exs. 11–14, 21–23, 29–36, 49
	Day 2	pp. 564–566 Exs. 13–16, 24, 31–34, 39–50	pp. 564–566 Exs. 13–16, 24–28, 38–46	pp. 564–566 Exs. 15–18, 24–26, 37–44*, 50
11.7	Day 1	EP p. 716 Exs. 21–24; pp. 569–571 Exs. 5–8, 15–19, 26–29	pp. 569–571 Exs. 5–8, 15–21, 26–31	pp. 569–571 Exs. 5–8, 15–19, 28–33, 39
	Day 2	pp. 569–571 Exs. 9–14, 21–23, 30–39	pp. 569–571 Exs. 9–14, 22–24, 32–39	pp. 569–571 Exs. 9–14, 22–27*, 34–36
Review	Day 1	pp. 576–577 Exs. 1–62	pp. 576–577 Exs. 1–62	pp. 576–577 Exs. 1–62
Assess	Day 1	Chapter 11 Test	Chapter 11 Test	Chapter 11 Test

YEARLY PACING　　Chapter 11 Total – **14 days**　　Chapters 1–11 Total – **134 days**　　Remaining – **26 days**

*Challenge Exercises　　EP = Extra Practice　　SRH = Skills Review Handbook　　EC = Extra Challenge

BLOCK SCHEDULE

DAY 1	DAY 2	DAY 3	DAY 4	DAY 5	DAY 6	DAY 7
11.1 pp. 535–536 Exs. 15–25, 30–38, 40–50	**11.2 cont.** pp. 540–541 Exs. 22–33, 42–47, 59–62	**11.3 cont.** pp. 546–547 Exs. 24–37, 43–46, 62–64	**11.4 cont.** pp. 552–553 Exs. 27–36, 46–57	**11.6** pp. 564–566 Exs. 9–16, 19–28, 33–36, 38–50	**11.7** pp. 569–571 Exs. 5–24, 26–39	**Review** pp. 576–577 Exs. 1–62
11.2 pp. 540–541 Exs. 10–13, 34–41, 49–56	**11.3** pp. 546–547 Exs. 15–19, 38–42, 51–61	**11.4** pp. 552–553 Exs. 12–26, 37–42, 58–60	**11.5** pp. 556–558 Exs. 12–17, 24–39, 44–46, 48–53			**Assess** Chapter 11 Test

YEARLY PACING　　Chapter 11 Total – **7 days**　　Chapters 1–11 Total – **67 days**　　Remaining – **13 days**

Support Materials

📖 CHAPTER RESOURCE BOOK

CHAPTER SUPPORT

Tips for New Teachers	p. 1	Parents as Partners	p. 3

LESSON SUPPORT

	11.1	11.2	11.3	11.4	11.5	11.6	11.7
Lesson Plans (regular and block)	p. 6	p. 14	p. 23	p. 31	p. 42	p. 52	p. 61
Technology Activities & Keystrokes				p. 33	p. 44		
Activity Support Masters							
Activity Masters						p. 54	
Practice (3 levels)	p. 8	p. 16	p. 25	p. 35	p. 46	p. 55	p. 63
Study Guide	p. 11	p. 19	p. 28	p. 38	p. 49	p. 58	p. 66
Real-World Problem Solving		p. 21		p. 40			
Challenge Practice	p. 13	p. 22	p. 30	p. 41	p. 51	p. 60	p. 68

REVIEW

Games Support Masters	p. 5	Cooperative Project with Rubric	p. 72
Chapter Review Games and Activities	p. 69	Extra Credit Project with Rubric	p. 74
Real-Life Project with Rubric	p. 70	Cumulative Practice	p. 76
		Resource Book Answers	A1

📖 ASSESSMENT

Quizzes	p. 135	Alternative Assessments with Rubrics	p. 144
Chapter Tests (3 levels)	p. 137	Unit Test	p. 168
Standardized Test	p. 143	Cumulative Test	p. 170

📑 TRANSPARENCIES

	11.1	11.2	11.3	11.4	11.5	11.6	11.7
Warm-Up / Daily Homework Quiz	✔	✔	✔	✔	✔	✔	✔
Notetaking Guide	✔	✔	✔	✔	✔	✔	✔
Teacher Support	✔	✔	✔			✔	✔
English/Spanish Problem Solving			✔				
Answer Transparencies	✔	✔	✔	✔	✔	✔	✔

💻 TECHNOLOGY

- EasyPlanner CD-ROM
- Test and Practice Generator
- Electronic Lesson Presentations
- eTutorial CD-ROM
- Chapter Audio Summaries CDs
- Classzone.com
- eEdition Plus Online
- eWorkbook Plus Online
- eTutorial Plus Online
- EasyPlanner Plus Online

ADDITIONAL RESOURCES

- Worked-Out Solution Key
- Notetaking Guide
- Practice Workbook
- Tutor Place
- Professional Development Book
- Activities Book
- Poster Package
- Spanish Study Guide
- English/Spanish Chapter Reviews
- Multi-Language Glossary

530B

Math Background and Teaching Strategies

Lesson 11.1

MATH BACKGROUND

INTEGERS Numbers less than 0 are known as **negative integers**. **Positive integers** are greater than 0. On a number line, negative integers are to the left of 0. Every integer has an **opposite**. Since the number -4 is the number 4 units to the left of 0 on a number line, the opposite of -4 can be found by counting 4 units to the right of 0. Therefore, the opposite of -4 is $+4$. Likewise, the opposite of $+4$ is -4. Positive integers are usually written without the positive sign. Zero is its own opposite and is written without a sign. The set of integers is infinite.

TEACHING STRATEGIES

The ordering of integers is best shown on a number line. To compare two integers, have students first locate each number on the number line. The number to the left is always less than any number to its right.

Lesson 11.2

MATH BACKGROUND

ADDING INTEGERS The **absolute value** of a number is its distance from 0 on a number line. The idea of absolute value is central to the process of **adding integers**. If two integers have the same sign, *add* their absolutes values and give their sum this sign. If two integers have different signs, *subtract* the number with the lesser absolute value from the one with the greater absolute value. Give the result the sign of the number with the greater absolute value.

TEACHING STRATEGIES

A number line is one of the most useful models for understanding addition of integers. To add two integers on a number line, start at the first addend and then go the number of units in the direction indicated by the second addend.

Use this method with several examples so students see that when adding two positive numbers the sum is positive, and when adding two negative numbers the sum is negative. When adding a positive and a negative number, they can tell whether the sum is positive or negative by using the number line to visualize which number is farther from 0. For example, $5 + (-8)$ has a negative sum, since -8 is farther from zero than 5.

Next introduce the idea of absolute value informally as the value of a number if you ignore the sign. Finally, introduce the rules for adding integers.

Lesson 11.3

MATH BACKGROUND

SUBTRACTING INTEGERS The concept of opposite is used to define subtraction of integers. Once the number being subtracted has been changed to its opposite, the subtraction problem becomes an addition problem.

TEACHING STRATEGIES

Give students examples like the ones below. Then ask, them for a rule for subtracting integers.

$$+2 - (-4) = +6 \leftrightarrow +2 + (+4) = +6$$
$$+5 - (+7) = -2 \leftrightarrow +5 + (-7) = -2$$
$$-3 - (-6) = +3 \leftrightarrow -3 + (+6) = +3$$
$$-8 - (+6) = -14 \leftrightarrow -8 + (-6) = -14$$

Lessons 11.4 and 11.5

MATH BACKGROUND

MULTIPLYING INTEGERS The following rules for multiplying integers can be justified by thinking of multiplication as repeated addition, using the commutative property of multiplication, and observing patterns.

- The product of two positive integers or two negative integers is positive.

- The product of two integers with different signs is negative.

DIVIDING INTEGERS The rules for dividing integers can be justified by using the relationship between multiplication and division.

- The quotient of two positive integers or two negative integers is positive.
- The quotient of two integers with different signs is negative.

TEACHING STRATEGIES

Use the idea that multiplication can be thought of a repeated addition and remind students that 3×4 means $4 + 4 + 4 = 12$. Then extend this to the idea that $3 \times (-4)$ means $-4 + (-4) + (-4) = -12$. Again, remind students that multiplication is commutative, so $-4 \times 3 = 3 \times (-4) = -12$. Finally, use a pattern like the following to show that the product of two negative numbers is positive:

$$3 \times (-2) = -6; 2 \times (-2) = -4; 1 \times (-2) = -2; 0 \times (-2) = 0.$$

Notice that the products increase by 2 each time the first factor decreases by 1; therefore, $-1 \times (-2) = 2$, $-2 \times (-2) = 4$, and so on.

For division, write the family of products and quotients for several examples to see why the rules make sense.

$-3 \times 5 = -15$	$-4 \times (-6) = 24$
$5 \times (-3) = -15$	$-6 \times (-4) = 24$
$-15 \div 5 = -3$	$24 \div (-4) = -6$
$-15 \div (-3) = 5$	$24 \div (-6) = -4$

Lesson 11.6

MATH BACKGROUND

COORDINATE PLANE A coordinate grid is used to locate points in a plane. To create a coordinate grid, draw a horizontal number line (the x-axis) and a vertical number line (the y-axis). These lines intersect at a point called the **origin**. These axes divide the coordinate plane into four regions called **quadrants**. You can name any point in a plane with two numbers, called **coordinates**. The first number is the distance from the origin along the x-axis, the x-coordinate. The second is the distance along the y-axis, the y-coordinate. The pair is always named in the order x and then y, so it is called an **ordered pair**.

TRANSLATIONS A **translation** is also called a *slide*. In a translation, every point in the figure slides the same distance in the same direction. You can use a slide arrow to show the direction and distance of the movement.

TEACHING STRATEGIES

For this activity, students will need graph paper, number cubes labeled 0–5, and a coin. Have the students work in pairs. On a coordinate grid, have pairs locate $\triangle ABC$ with vertices $A(0, 0)$, $B(1, 2)$, and $C(1, 0)$. Pairs next create and record a path to show how far their triangle will slide left or right and down or up. They flip the coin, with heads meaning left/down and tails meaning right/up, and toss the cube to determine how far. Using this slide, pairs draw a translation image of $\triangle ABC$. Have them repeat the procedure to locate the vertices of three more translation images.

Lesson 11.7

MATH BACKGROUND

REFLECTIONS In geometry, a **reflection** is a transformation in which a figure is flipped over a line. Each point on a reflection image is the same distance from the **line of reflection** as the corresponding point in the original figure.

In geometry, **rotating** a figure means turning the figure around a point. The point, called the **center of rotation**, can be on the figure or it can be some other point. When you rotate a figure, you describe the rotation by giving the direction, clockwise or counterclockwise, and the **angle of rotation**.

TEACHING STRATEGIES

For this activity students will need paper and tracing paper. Have the students work in pairs. Have each pair of students draw either a triangle or quadrilateral on a sheet of paper. Have them mark a point on the paper outside the figure and label it point P. The tracing paper should then be placed over the other sheet and the figure copied. While one student holds the bottom paper in place, the other student should put a pencil point at P and rotate the tracing. Ask students what type of path the tracing paper is following around the original figure. Now have students choose several other locations for P, including ones outside, on, and inside the figure. Have them rotate the figure around these points and discuss the differences and similarities in the paths.

Differentiating Instruction

Strategies for Underachievers

PROVIDE TOOLS FOR CONCRETE LEARNING

To help reinforce student understanding of positive and negative integers on the number line, you may wish to provide visual reminders to them. Such reminders could include a large number line that wraps around the walls of your classroom or individual number lines that adhere to the tops of student desks.

Continuing from the Hands-on Activity 11.2 into Lesson 11.2 and beyond, you might consider allowing any student who so desires to have access to a set of integer chips for as long as they feel the need to use them. Students will naturally stop using manipulatives when they are ready, and in this case they should be allowed to continue using them as long as they desire. In addition to or instead of using integer chips, some students may also want to continue using a number line for adding and subtracting integers. These students should also be allowed to continue using a number line for as long as necessary.

In Lesson 11.7, you may wish to provide students with patty paper or tissue paper on which they can trace the sample figures in the book. They can then fold the paper along the lines of reflection to see that the original figures align with the reflected figures. Additionally, students can draw an original figure and a line of reflection on a piece of patty paper. They can then fold the paper along the line of reflection and then trace the original figure to draw the reflected figure. This activity could also be conducted using a reflecting tool.

USE SCAFFOLDING

Beginning with the Notebook feature on page 539, you may wish to have underachieving students keep color-coded note cards with the rules for each of the integer operations written on them. Students should have access to these cards for practice assignments and assessments.

Strategies for English Learners

VOCABULARY DEVELOPMENT

Students will need to be very familiar with words we use in measurement. Ask students to brainstorm all the words they can think of that are related to time, such as *morning, evening, afternoon; yesterday, today, tomorrow; second, minute, hour, day, week, weekly, month, monthly, year, annual, annually; lunch time, nighttime, midnight;* days of the week, months of the year; *clock,* and *calendar.* Another good topic to review is measures of length: *inch, centimeter, foot, meter, yard, mile,* and *unit.* Have students write new words in their math journal, draw a picture, or write the word in their primary language to help them remember.

OPPOSITES If students need more practice with opposites, this chapter provides numerous examples, including:

> profit : loss; least : greatest; left : right; right : wrong; product : quotient; off : on; start : end; both : neither; inside : outside.

ANALOGIES If students seem comfortable with opposites and synonyms, introduce the idea of analogies. Put this simple analogy on the board and ask students to think of others, using terms used in mathematics:

> *Addition* is to *sum* as *subtraction* is to _____.

Other possible examples:

> *Left* is to *negative* as *right* is to *positive.*
> *Profit* is to *positive* as *loss* is to *negative.*
> *Numerator* is to *denominator* as *dividend* is to *divisor.*

Strategies for Advanced Learners

In **Lesson 11.4**, some advanced students can be challenged with using exponents and negative bases.

- **Challenge** Compare the values of these expressions:
  $$(-3)^2 \qquad (-3)^3 \qquad (-3)^4 \qquad (-3)^5$$
  What patterns do you see? $(-3)^2 = 9, (-3)^3 = -27$, $(-3)^4 = 81, (-3)^5 = -243$; so, $(-3)^4 > (-3)^2 > (-3)^3 > (-3)^5$; odd powers of negative numbers are negative and even powers are always positive.

- **Challenge** Compare the values of -4^2 and $(-4)^2$.
  $-4^2 = -(4)(4) = -16$ and $(-4)^2 = (-4)(-4) = 16$, so $(-4)^2 > -4^2$.

After completing Lesson 11.5, you may wish to have some students review the commutative and associative properties and how each relates to the four integer operations. Have them use both positive and negative integers to show that both addition and multiplication are commutative and associative, but that subtraction and division are not.

A challenging exercise for **Lesson 11.5** is to show that division by 0 is undefined.

- **Challenge** Show that if a is a nonzero integer, then $a \div 0$ cannot be defined. If $a \div 0$ is defined, then there is a number b such that $a \div 0 = b$. This means there is a related multiplication problem $b \cdot 0 = a$, which means $a = 0$. But a is not 0, so $a \div 0$ cannot be defined.

In conjunction with the Chapter 11 Special Topic on pages 572–573, you may wish to work with an Art teacher and a Language Arts teacher to develop a tessellation project. Students can begin the project by investigating the types of regular polygons or non-regular polygons that will tessellate the plane. Their investigation should include Escher-type tessellations.

Students should choose a fundamental region that will tessellate. Cutting a piece from one side of this fundamental region and pasting it on another side in the same position will create another tessellating region. The resulting tessellation may be done by a translation or by a rotation. Students can experiment with cutting and pasting and then drawing details on their fundamental region in order to create an identifiable object. They can trace their tessellation onto a piece of construction paper, oak tag, or poster board. They can then color their poster and write a creative story about their tessellation creation. Have students be conscious of the size of their fundamental region versus the size of their poster. The region should not be unreasonably large or small compared to the poster.

Consult with the Art teacher about the best media for students to use. The creative writing part of this project can be done in the Language Arts classroom. Tessellation creation projects make excellent displays for open house nights and curriculum fairs.

Differentiating Instruction: Teaching Resources

Differentiating Review, Reteaching, and Remediation

McDougal Littell *Middle School Mathematics* offers teachers a wide variety of reteaching and remediation resources. Pictured here are facsimiles of various pages from the *Notetaking Guide*, the Study Guide pages from the *Chapter 11 Resource Book*, and remediation cards from *Tutor Place*.

NOTETAKING GUIDE

The *Notetaking Guide* easily allows students to take notes on and review each lesson in the textbook by using guided examples and Your Turn Now exercises. The *Notetaking Guide* is available on transparencies also.

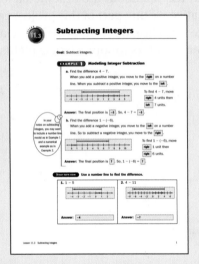

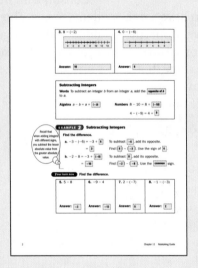

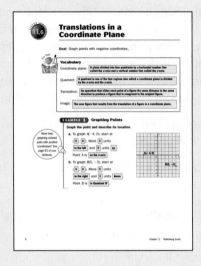

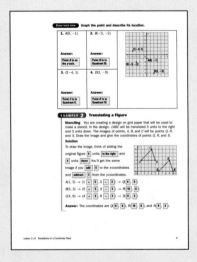

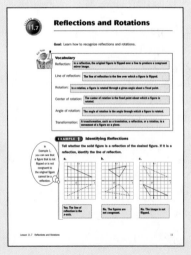

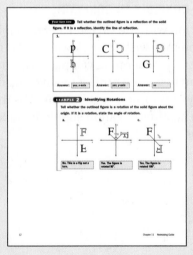

RESOURCE BOOK

The *Chapter Resource Books* contain Study Guide pages with reteaching examples and exercises for each lesson in the textbook. Pictured below are Study Guide pages from the *Chapter 11 Resource Book*. (The Study Guide pages are also available in Spanish in the *Spanish Study Guide*.)

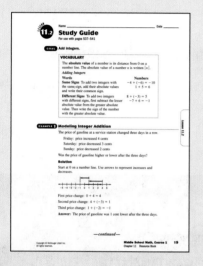

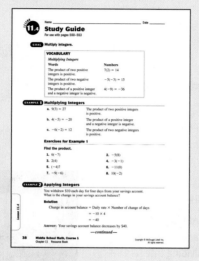

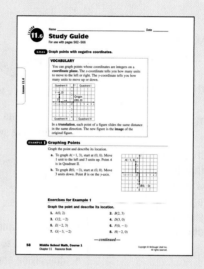

TUTOR PLACE

Tutor Place helps students practice and master essential topics. Instruction is provided by 104 cards containing examples and two sets of practice exercises. Answers are provided in a handy answer key.

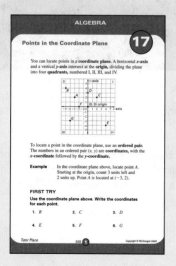

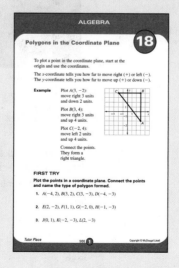

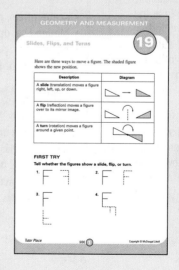

CHAPTER 11

Integers

MAIN IDEAS

In this chapter, students compare and order integers. Next they add, subtract, multiply, and divide integers. Finally, students use their knowledge of integers to plot points in the coordinate plane and do translations, reflections, and rotations in the plane.

PREREQUISITE SKILLS

The key skills reviewed in the games on these pages are:
- Plotting points in the coordinate plane
- Reflecting points in a line of symmetry

Additional practice with prerequisite skills can be found in the Review What You Need to Know exercises on page 532. Additional resources for reviewing prerequisite skills are:
- Skills Review Handbook, pp. 684–707
- Tutor Place
- eTutorial Plus Online

MANAGING THE GAMES

Tips for Success

Stress that connecting the points in order is important in Constellation Mapping, since it is easy to lose the pattern otherwise. In Unidentified Symmetrical Object, remind students that the distance from a point to the line of symmetry is the same on both sides of the line.

Reflecting on the Games

You may want students to discuss the procedure they wrote for Exercise 2. Ask pairs of students to follow the instructions of their partner to see if they get the same result.

Brain Game
See Additional Answers beginning on page AA1.

BEFORE

In previous chapters you've...
- Plotted points
- Studied line symmetry

Now

In Chapter 11 you'll study...
- Comparing and ordering integers
- Adding and subtracting integers
- Multiplying and dividing integers
- Transformations in a coordinate plane

WHY?

So you can solve real-world problems about...
- scuba divers, p. 535
- Mauna Loa, pp. 544–545
- black bears, p. 552
- animation, p. 567

Internet Preview
CLASSZONE.COM
- eEdition Plus Online
- eWorkbook Plus Online
- eTutorial Plus Online
- State Test Practice
- More Examples

Chapter Warm-Up Games

Review skills you need for this chapter in these quick games.

CONSTELLATION MAPPING

- (2, 19), (2, 15), (4, 11), (6, 6), (5, 1)
- (4, 19), (3, 16), (2, 15)
- (4, 11), (7, 13), (9, 11), (8, 7), (10, 2)
- (13, 13), (14, 11), (14, 10), (13, 8), (12, 7)
- (9, 11), (14, 11)
- (6, 6), (7, 6.5), (8, 7)

BRAIN GAME

Key Skill:
Plotting points

Materials:
graph paper

Plot each group of points in the same coordinate plane. Then connect the points in each group in the order they are given. The resulting diagram will be a map of a famous constellation. **See margin.**

UNIDENTIFIED Symmetrical Object

BrAin GAME

Key Skill:
Line symmetry

Materials:
graph paper

- Some of the data beamed to Earth from a distant spaceship's computer have been lost in transmission. Your goal is to reconstruct a picture sent by the ship.

- The picture sent by the ship has line symmetry. Copy the drawing and the line of symmetry shown above onto graph paper. Then reconstruct the picture. **See margin.**

1. A good answer will include clear directions and a clear completed graph.

Stop *and* Think

1. **Extension** The constellation you plotted on page 530 is Orion. Draw a picture of another star grouping, such as the Big Dipper. Then write directions for graphing the star grouping in a coordinate plane.

2. **Writing** Describe the procedure you used to reconstruct the *Unidentified Symmetrical Object*.
   Sample answer: I shaded in the squares on each side of the line of symmetry to match those on the other side of the line.

531

Algebra Evaluate the expression when $a = -2$, $b = -5$, $c = 3$, and $d = 4$.

B 38. $b - a + c$ 0   **39.** $d - b + a$ 7   **40.** $c - a - d$ 1   **41.** $a - b - c$ 0

42. Sunken Ships A diver marks the position of the bow of a sunken ship relative to the water's surface as -44 feet. The position of the stern is -53 feet. Use these integers to write a subtraction problem. What information about the ship can you find by solving the problem?
Sample answer: $-44 - (-53)$; how many feet deeper the stern is.

Evaluate the expression.

43. $5 + (-6) - 14 + 1(9)$ -6

44. $-6 + 5(4) - (-7) + 3^2$ 30

45. $7^2 - 10 + (-3) + 2(8)$ 52

46. $9(3) + (-4) - 6 + 8^2$ 81

Challenge Tell whether the statement is *always*, *sometimes*, or *never* true.

C 47. A negative integer minus a negative integer is negative. sometimes

48. A positive integer minus a positive integer is positive. sometimes

49. A positive integer minus a negative integer is positive. always

50. A negative integer minus a positive integer is negative. always

Mixed Review

Find the product. *(Lesson 7.3)*

51. $2\frac{3}{5} \cdot 3\frac{8}{9}$ $10\frac{1}{9}$ **52.** $1\frac{1}{3} \cdot 4\frac{5}{6}$ $6\frac{4}{9}$ **53.** $3\frac{1}{8} \cdot \frac{7}{5}$ $4\frac{3}{8}$ **54.** $5\frac{1}{7} \cdot 3\frac{2}{9}$ $16\frac{4}{7}$

Find the sum. *(Lesson 11.2)*

55. $6 + (-6)$ 0   **56.** $4 + (-7)$ -3 **57.** $-1 + 5$ 4   **58.** $-8 + (-6)$ -14

Basic Skills **Find the product.**

59. 2.4×3 7.2   **60.** 1.8×1.1 1.98   **61.** 0.63×0.2 0.126   **62.** 0.32×0.09 0.0288

Test-Taking Practice

63. Multiple Choice What is the value of the expression $4 - (-17)$? D

A. -21 **B.** -13 **C.** 13   **D.** 21

64. Short Response At noon the temperature was $8°F$. By 6 P.M. the temperature had dropped $12°$. What was the temperature at 6 P.M.? Show how to solve the problem using a number line and then using the rules for subtracting integers. $-4°F$; see margin for art; $8 - 12 = -4$.

 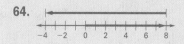

Notebook Review

LESSONS 11.1 TO 11.3

Review the vocabulary definitions in your notebook.

Copy the review examples in your notebook. Then complete the exercises.

Check Your Definitions

integer, p. 533   negative integer, p. 533   absolute value, p. 539

positive integer, p. 533   opposites, p. 534

Use Your Vocabulary

1. Copy and complete: The numbers 12 and -12 are called _?_. **opposites**

2. Copy and complete: The _?_ of -5 is written $|-5|$ and it equals 5. **absolute value**

11.1 Can you compare integers?

Review **EXAMPLE** Compare -7 and -3.

ANSWER Because -7 is to the left of -3 on a number line, $-7 < -3$.

☑ **Copy and complete the statement using < or >.**

3. $5 \underline{\ ?\ } -5$ **>**   4. $-3 \underline{\ ?\ } -2$ **<**   5. $1 \underline{\ ?\ } -4$ **>**   6. $0 \underline{\ ?\ } -1$ **>**

11.2–11.3 Can you add and subtract integers?

Review **EXAMPLE**

a. $-6 + (-7) = -13$ Find $|-6| + |-7|$. Use the common sign.

b. $-8 - (-6) = -8 + 6$ To subtract -6, add its opposite.

$\quad\quad\quad\quad = -2$ Find $|-8| - |6|$. Use the sign of -8.

☑ **Find the sum or difference.**

7. $-9 + 9$ **0**   8. $-2 + (-2)$ **−4** 9. $-13 + 8$ **−5** 10. $11 + (-10)$ **1**

11. $10 - 15$ **−5** 12. $-9 - 8$ **−17** 13. $5 - (-9)$ **14** 14. $-4 - (-7)$ **3**

Stop and Think about Lessons 11.1–11.3

15. Writing Explain the thinking process involved in evaluating $-1 - (-2)$.
Sample answer: Add the opposite of -2. Then find $|-2| - |-1| = 1$.

16. Critical Thinking Use examples to show what is meant by the opposite of the opposite of an integer. *Sample answer:*
$-(-(3)) = (-(-3)) = 3; -(-(-2)) = -(2) = -2.$

Review Quiz 1

Find the opposite and the absolute value of the number.

1. 6 $-6; 6$

2. -4 $4; 4$

3. -10 $10; 10$

4. 0 $0; 0$

Order the integers from least to greatest.

5. $-1, 8, 0, -4, 1$ $-4, -1, 0, 1, 8$

6. $-5, 3, -7, -3, 5$ $-7, -5, -3, 3, 5$

7. $12, -9, 3, -4, 8$ $-9, -4, 3, 8, 12$

8. $-2, 1, 10, -11, -14$
$-14, -11, -2, 1, 10$

Find the sum or difference.

9. $-3 + 6$ 3

10. $6 + (-7)$ -1

11. $11 + (-11)$ 0

12. $-5 + (-15)$ -20

13. $2 - 10$ -8

14. $-14 - 4$ -18

15. $-8 - (-10)$ 2

16. $4 - (-12)$ 16

17. Temperatures The coldest recorded average temperature for Cape Hatteras, North Carolina, during the month of January was about 35°F. The average temperature in Minneapolis-St. Paul, Minnesota, during January of the same year was 2°F below zero. Find the difference between these average temperatures. 37°F

Magic Square

In the magic square at the right, the sum of each row, column, and diagonal is the same. Copy and complete the magic square.

Multiplying Integers

11.4

BEFORE	▶ Now	WHY?
You multiplied whole numbers, fractions, and decimals.	You'll multiply integers.	So you can find changes in water levels, as in Example 2.

Activity   **You can use addition to understand integer multiplication.**

① Copy and complete the table below.

Product	Repeated Addition	Result	
$4 \cdot 2$	$= 2 + 2 + 2 + 2$	$= ?$	8
$4 \cdot 1$	$= 1 + 1 + 1 + 1$	$= ?$	4
$4 \cdot 0$	$= 0 + 0 + 0 + 0$	$= ?$	0
$4 \cdot (-1)$	$= (-1) + (-1) + (-1) + (-1)$	$= ?$	−4
$4 \cdot (-2)$	$= (-2) + (-2) + (-2) + (-2)$	$= ?$	−8

② Describe the pattern of the results. Use the pattern to find $4 \cdot (-3)$.
Each answer is 4 less than the previous answer; **−12**.

③ Copy the table at the right. Then look for a pattern to complete it.

④ What do you observe about the product of two integers with the same sign? with different signs?
The product is positive; the product is negative.

Product	Result	
$2 \cdot (-4)$	$= ?$	−8
$1 \cdot (-4)$	$= ?$	−4
$0 \cdot (-4)$	$= ?$	0
$(-1) \cdot (-4)$	$= ?$	4
$(-2) \cdot (-4)$	$= ?$	8

In the activity, you may have observed the following rules about multiplying integers.

Multiplying Integers

Words	Numbers
The product of two positive integers is positive.	$3(5) = 15$
The product of two negative integers is positive.	$-4(-6) = 24$
The product of a positive integer and a negative integer is negative.	$2(-8) = -16$

EXAMPLE 1 Multiplying Integers

a. $-7(-4) = 28$ The product of two negative integers is positive.

b. $8(-6) = -48$ The product of a positive integer and a negative integer is negative.

c. $-3(10) = -30$ The product of a positive integer and a negative integer is negative.

Your turn now Find the product.

1. $9(8)$ 72   **2.** $-2(-11)$ 22   **3.** $7(-7)$ −49   **4.** $-8(4)$ −32

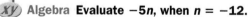

EXAMPLE 2 Applying Integers

Bay of Fundy In the Bay of Fundy, there are about 6 hours between each high and low tide. Suppose that the water level decreases at a rate of about 4 feet per hour during this time. What is the change in the water level?

Bay of Fundy at high tide

Solution

$$\text{Change in water level} = \begin{array}{c}\text{Rate}\\\text{of change}\end{array} \times \begin{array}{c}\text{Number}\\\text{of hours}\end{array}$$

$$= \quad -4 \quad \times \quad 6$$

$$= \quad -24$$

ANSWER The water level decreases by about 24 feet between tides.

EXAMPLE 3 Evaluating Expressions

 Algebra Evaluate $-5n$, when $n = -12$.

$-5n = -5(-12)$ Substitute −12 for n.

$= 60$ The product of two negative integers is positive.

Your turn now Evaluate the expression when $x = 3$ and $y = -2$.

5. $-2x$ −6   **6.** $6y$ −12   **7.** $-5y$ 10   **8.** xy −6

Lesson 11.4   Multiplying Integers   **551**

ASSIGNMENT GUIDE

Basic Course
Day 1: pp. 552–553 Exs. 8–19, 24–26, 37–39, 57–59
Day 2: pp. 552–553 Exs. 28–36, 41, 46–56

Average Course
Day 1: pp. 552–553 Exs. 12–26, 37–42, 58–60
Day 2: pp. 552–553 Exs. 27–36, 46–57

Advanced Course
Day 1: pp. 552–553 Exs. 12–25, 37–40, 46–48
Day 2: pp. 552–553 Exs. 26–36, 41–45*, 51–54, 60

Block
pp. 552–553 Exs. 12–26, 37–42, 58–60 (with 11.3)
pp. 552–553 Exs. 27–36, 46–57 (with 11.5)

EXTRA PRACTICE

- Student Edition, p. 718
- Chapter 11 Resource Book, pp. 35–37
- Test and Practice Generator

⟳ TRANSPARENCY

Even-numbered answers are available on transparencies.

HOMEWORK CHECK

When you review students' homework for this lesson, go over the following exercises to check understanding of key concepts.
Basic: 8, 10, 12, 28, 29
Average: 12, 14, 21, 27, 29
Advanced: 13, 21, 22, 28, 34

11.4 Exercises

More Practice, p. 718

INTERNET
eWorkbook Plus
CLASSZONE.COM

Getting Ready to Practice

Vocabulary Copy and complete the statement.

1. The product of two negative integers is a ? integer. positive

2. The product of a negative integer and a positive integer is a ? integer.
positive

Find the product.

3. 7(3) 21   **4.** −5(2) −10   **5.** 9(−4) −36   **6.** −8(−1) 8

7. Find the Error Describe and correct the error in the solution.

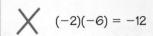
$(-2)(-6) = -12$

The product of two negative integers is positive. The correct solution is $(-2)(-6) = 12$.

Practice and Problem Solving

HELP with Homework

Example	Exercises
1	8–26
2	27, 28
3	29–36

Online Resources
CLASSZONE.COM
· More Examples
· eTutorial Plus

Find the product.

A **8.** 6(4) 24   **9.** 3(8) 24   **10.** 5(−7) −35   **11.** 2(−9) −18

12. −8(3) −24   **13.** −7(6) −42   **14.** −2(−9) 18   **15.** −10(−1) 10

16. 15(−3) −45   **17.** 1(13) 13   **18.** −12(−8) 96   **19.** −7(0) 0

20. 20(11) 220   **21.** 18(−10) −180   **22.** −30(30) −900   **23.** −12(−50) 600

24. Find the product of negative 3 and negative 9.
27

25. Find the product of positive 7 and negative 8.
−56

26. Find the product of negative 10 and positive 5.
−50

27. Diving Think of the surface of the ocean as zero on a number line. A sea otter can dive to −30 meters. A dolphin can dive to a point 10 times as deep. What is the dolphin's position relative to sea level? −300 m

28. Bears A female Asiatic black bear loses about 7 pounds per month during her 6 months of hibernation. What is her change in weight during hibernation? If the bear weighs 210 pounds before hibernation, what does she weigh after hibernation? about −42 lb; about 168 lb

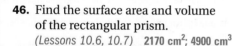 **Algebra** Evaluate the expression when $n = -6$, $p = 5$, and $t = -10$.

B **29.** $7n$ -42 **30.** $-8p$ -40 **31.** $-6n$ 36 **32.** np -30

33. pt -50 **34.** nt 60 **35.** $-2nt$ -120 **36.** $-4pt$ 200

Number Sense Tell whether the statement is *always*, *sometimes*, or *never* true.

37. A negative integer times a negative integer is positive. always

38. A negative integer times a positive integer is negative. always

39. A positive integer times a negative integer is positive. never

40. **Critical Thinking** Evaluate $3(-5)$ and $(-5)3$. What do you notice about the results? What property holds for multiplication of integers?
-15; -15; the results are the same; commutative.

Find the missing numbers in the pattern.

41. $-5, -10, \underline{?}, -40, -80, \underline{?}$ **42.** $-12, \underline{?}, -36, -48, \underline{?}, -72$
$\quad$ -20; -160 $\qquad$ -24; -60

43. $3, \underline{?}, 3, -3, \underline{?}, -3$ **44.** $-4, \underline{?}, -16, 32, \underline{?}, \underline{?}$
$\quad$ -3; 3 $\qquad$ 8; -64; 128

C **45.** **Challenge** Find the missing numbers: $\frac{3}{2}, -\frac{3}{4}, \underline{?}, -\frac{3}{16}, \underline{?}, \underline{?}$.
$\frac{3}{8}, \frac{3}{32}, -\frac{3}{64}$

Mixed Review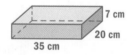

46. Find the surface area and volume of the rectangular prism. *(Lessons 10.6, 10.7)* 2170 cm^2; 4900 cm^3

7 cm
20 cm
35 cm

Find the sum or difference. *(Lessons 11.2, 11.3)*

47. $-4 + 12$ 8 **48.** $5 + (-8)$ -3 **49.** $-7 + (-7)$ -14 **50.** $-11 + 11$ 0

51. $16 - 20$ -4 **52.** $-31 - 9$ -40 **53.** $-36 - (-11)$ -25 **54.** $18 - (-25)$ 43

Basic Skills Find the quotient.

55. $10.9 \div 0.5$ 21.8 **56.** $21 \div 1.2$ 17.5 **57.** $8.52 \div 0.16$ 53.25 **58.** $28.4 \div 0.04$ 710

Test-Taking Practice

59. **Multiple Choice** What is the value of the expression $-5(-9)$? D

A. -45 **B.** -14 **C.** 14 **D.** 45

60. **Multiple Choice** Which statement is true? F

F. $3(-6) = -18$ **G.** $-2(-9) = -18$

H. $4(-7) = 28$ **I.** $-4(-8) = -32$

4 ASSESS

ASSESSMENT RESOURCES
For more assessment resources, see:
• Assessment Book
• Test and Practice Generator

MINI-QUIZ
Find the product.
1. $-4(-3) = \underline{?}$ 12
2. $6(-2) = \underline{?}$ -12
3. $-10(8) = \underline{?}$ -80
4. $12(3) = \underline{?}$ 36
5. Find the missing number in the pattern $-3, -6, \underline{?}, -12, -15.$ -9
6. Evaluate $6a$ when $a = -4$. -24

5 FOLLOW-UP

RETEACHING/REMEDIATION
• Study Guide in Chapter 11 Resource Book, pp. 38–39
• eTutorial Plus Online
• Extra Practice, p. 718
• Lesson Practice in Chapter 11 Resource Book, pp. 35–37

CHALLENGE/ENRICHMENT
• Challenge Practice in Chapter 11 Resource Book, p. 41
• Teacher's Edition, p. 530F

ENGLISH LEARNER SUPPORT
• Spanish Study Guide
• Multi-Language Glossary
• Chapter Audio Summaries CDs

SKILL CHECK

1. $(-6)(3) = \underline{}$ -18
2. $(-5)(-8) = \underline{}$ 40
3. $4(-7) = \underline{}$ -28

LESSON OBJECTIVE

Divide integers.

PACING

Suggested Number of Days
Basic Course: 1 day
Average Course: 1 day
Advanced Course: 1 day
Block: 0.5 block with 11.4

TEACHING RESOURCES

For a complete list of Teaching Resources, see page 530B.

TRANSPARENCY

Warm-Up Exercises for this lesson are available on a transparency.

2 TEACH

MOTIVATING THE LESSON

Describe a sequence of football plays in which a certain number of 5 yard penalties results in a total loss of 30 yards. Discuss how this situation can be represented by $-30 \div (-5) = 6$.

ACTIVITY

Goal Use multiplication to understand integer division.

Key Discovery The quotient of two integers with the same sign is positive. The quotient of two integers with different signs is negative.

Dividing Integers

LESSON 11.5

BEFORE	▶ Now	WHY?
You divided whole numbers, fractions, and decimals.	You'll divide integers.	So you can find average temperatures, as in Example 3.

Word Watch

Review Words
mean, p. 93

Activity **You can use multiplication to understand integer division.**

One way to find the quotient of two integers, such as $-32 \div 4$, is to rewrite the division problem as a multiplication problem.

(1 Rewrite the problem using multiplication.

$-32 \div 4 = \underline{}$ ⟶ $\underline{} \times 4 = -32$

(2 Use mental math to solve the multiplication problem.

$\underline{} \times 4 = -32$ ⟶ $-8 \times 4 = -32$

In Exercises 1–3, rewrite the problem using multiplication to find the quotient. Then use your results in Exercises 4–6.

1. $40 \div (-8) = \underline{}$ -5 2. $-45 \div (-9) = \underline{}$ 5 3. $-20 \div 5 = \underline{}$ -4

4. Is a positive integer divided by a positive integer *positive* or *negative*? positive

5. Is a negative integer divided by a negative integer *positive* or *negative*? positive

6. Is a positive integer divided by a negative integer *positive* or *negative*? negative

7. Is a negative integer divided by a positive integer *positive* or *negative*? negative

---

EXAMPLE 1 **Dividing Integers Using Mental Math**

Divide by solving a related multiplication equation.

   a. $-36 \div (-6) = 6$ Ask, "what number times -6 equals -36?"

   b. $27 \div (-9) = -3$ Ask, "what number times -9 equals 27?"

   c. $-42 \div 7 = -6$ Ask, "what number times 7 equals -42?"

Your turn now Divide by solving a related multiplication equation.

   1. $-30 \div 5$ -6 2. $18 \div (-2)$ -9 3. $-27 \div (-9)$ 3 4. $0 \div (-5)$ 0

NCTM CURRICULUM STANDARDS
Standard 1: Understand meanings of operations;
     Understand how operations are related
Standard 5: Use proper statistical methods to analyze data

Science

Dividing Integers

Words	Numbers
The quotient of two positive integers is positive.	$15 \div 3 = 5$
The quotient of two negative integers is positive.	$-14 \div (-7) = 2$
The quotient of a positive integer and a negative integer is negative.	$12 \div (-4) = -3$
The quotient of a negative integer and a positive integer is negative.	$-10 \div 2 = -5$

EXAMPLE 2 Dividing Integers

a. $-54 \div (-6) = 9$ — The quotient of two negative integers is positive.

b. $14 \div (-2) = -7$ — The quotient of a positive integer and a negative integer is negative.

c. $-24 \div 3 = -8$ — The quotient of a negative integer and a positive integer is negative.

EXAMPLE 3 Finding the Mean of Integers

Antarctica A scientist in Antarctica records the maximum temperature 3 days in a row. Find the mean of the temperatures shown on the thermometers.

$$\text{Mean} = \frac{-6 + (-4) + (-2)}{3}$$

$$= \frac{-12}{3}$$

$$= -4$$

ANSWER The mean of the temperatures is $-4°C$.

■ **Antarctica**

The U.S. has 3 stations in Antarctica: Palmer Station, South Pole Station, and McMurdo Station. The summer population of the stations are about 40, 130, and 1100 respectively. What fraction of the summer population is at McMurdo Station? $\frac{110}{127}$

Your turn now Find the quotient.

5. $-63 \div 7$ -9 **6.** $40 \div (-5)$ -8 **7.** $5 \div (-5)$ -1 **8.** $-22 \div (-2)$ 11

TIPS FOR NEW TEACHERS

Compare the rules for dividing integers with the rules for multiplying integers. See Tips for New Teachers in the *Chapter 11 Resource Book*.

EXTRA EXAMPLES

Example 1
a. $-48 \div (-8) = \underline{?}$ 6
b. $24 \div (-4) = \underline{?}$ -6

Example 2
a. $-32 \div (-8) = \underline{?}$ 4
b. $16 \div (-2) = \underline{?}$ -8
c. $-25 \div 5 = \underline{?}$ -5

Example 3 A submarine cruises below sea level at depths of -100 feet, -120 feet, and -200 feet. Find the mean depth. -140 ft

TEACHING TIP

Summarize the similarities in multiplication and division with the statement, "The product or quotient of two integers is positive if the integers have the same sign and negative if they have different signs."

 CONCEPT CHECK

How do you divide two integers? **Divide the integers. If the integers have the same sign, the quotient is positive. If the integers have different signs, the quotient is negative.**

 DAILY PUZZLER

If $a \div b < 0$ and $b > 0$, what must be true of a? $a < 0$

ASSIGNMENT GUIDE

Basic Course
Day 1: pp. 556–558 Exs. 12–23, 30–34, 36–43, 48–52

Average Course
Day 1: pp. 556–558 Exs. 12–17, 24–39, 44–46, 48–53

Advanced Course
Day 1: pp. 556–558 Exs. 15–17, 24–35, 38–49*, 52, 53

Block
pp. 556–558 Exs. 12–17, 24–39, 44–46, 48–53 (with 11.4)

EXTRA PRACTICE

- Student Edition, p. 718
- Chapter 11 Resource Book, pp. 46–48
- Test and Practice Generator

 TRANSPARENCY

Even-numbered answers are available on transparencies.

HOMEWORK CHECK

When you review students' homework for this lesson, go over the following exercises to check understanding of key concepts.
Basic: 12, 14, 18, 21, 30
Average: 12, 15, 24, 28, 31
Advanced: 15, 17, 25, 30, 33

TEACHING TIP

For Exercises 18–29, suggest that students first divide as if they are dividing whole numbers. They should then use the rules on page 555 to determine the sign of the quotient.

 COMMON ERROR

In Exercises 30–32, students may ignore the signs of the numbers when they find the mean.

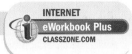

Getting Ready to Practice

1. Vocabulary To find the mean of a group of integers, you add the integers and _?_ by the number of integers. **divide**

Divide by solving a related multiplication equation.

2. $-4 \div 2$ **−2**   **3.** $6 \div (-3)$ **−2**   **4.** $0 \div (-12)$ **0**   **5.** $-2 \div (-2)$ **1**

Find the quotient.

6. $9 \div (-3)$ **−3**   **7.** $15 \div (-3)$ **−5**   **8.** $-10 \div 5$ **−2**   **9.** $-12 \div (-6)$ **2**

10. Find the mean of -8, -3, 2, and -7. **−4**

11. Find the Error Describe and correct the error in the solution.

$$\times \quad -18 \div (-3) = -6$$

A negative integer divided by a negative integer is positive. The solution should be $-18 \div (-3) = 6$.

Practice and Problem Solving

 **with Homework**

Example	Exercises
1	12–17
2	18–29
3	30–34

Online Resources
CLASSZONE.COM
· More Examples
· eTutorial Plus

Divide by solving a related multiplication equation.

A 12. $6 \div (-2)$ **−3**   **13.** $4 \div (-1)$ **−4**   **14.** $-21 \div (-3)$ **7**

15. $-45 \div (-5)$ **9**   **16.** $-30 \div 6$ **−5**   **17.** $-14 \div 7$ **−2**

Find the quotient.

18. $-12 \div (-3)$ **4**   **19.** $-18 \div (-6)$ **3**   **20.** $-24 \div 8$ **−3**

21. $28 \div (-7)$ **−4**   **22.** $39 \div (-13)$ **−3**   **23.** $-30 \div 2$ **−15**

24. $-500 \div 250$ **−2**   **25.** $-90 \div 15$ **−6**   **26.** $110 \div (-11)$ **−10**

27. $750 \div (-50)$ **−15**   **28.** $-128 \div (-32)$ **4**   **29.** $-195 \div (-15)$ **13**

30. Find the mean of -11, -15, 12, and -6. **−5**

31. Find the mean of -9, -2, -8, and 19. **0**

32. Golf Five talented golfers play a game of golf. Their scores are shown below. Find the mean of the scores. **0**

Golfer	Sara	Lauren	Matt	Audrey	Isaias
Score	4	5	−2	−4	−3

Global Temperatures The table shows the highest and lowest recorded temperatures for each continent.

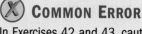

Global Temperatures							
Continent	Africa	Antarctica	Asia	Australia	Europe	North America	South America
High Temperature (°F)	136	59	129	128	122	134	120
Low Temperature (°F)	−11	−129	−90	−9	−67	−81	−27

B 33. Find the mean of the low temperatures. about −59°F

34. Find the mean of the high temperatures. about 118°F

35. **Compare** Find the range of the high temperatures and the range of the low temperatures. Which set of data has the greater range?
77°F; 120°F; the low temperatures

 Algebra **Recall that you can use a fraction bar to express division. Evaluate the expression when $a = -9$, $b = 6$, and $c = -1$.**

36. $\dfrac{36}{a}$ −4 **37.** $\dfrac{b}{-6}$ −1 **38.** $\dfrac{a}{3}$ −3 **39.** $\dfrac{-54}{a}$ 6

40. $\dfrac{-81}{a}$ 9 **41.** $\dfrac{84}{c}$ −84 **42.** $\dfrac{66}{-b}$ −11 **43.** $\dfrac{-72}{-c}$ −72

Extended Problem Solving **The table shows how much money a student earned or spent each day for one week.**

44. Copy the first two columns of the table. Use positive and negative integers to show which amounts represent earnings and which amounts represent money spent.
See margin.

45. Find the mean of the data. 0

46. **Interpret** What can you tell about the student's earning and spending habits from the mean?
The student spent as much as he or she earned.

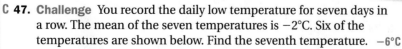

Day	Amount	Activity
Sunday	$20	Earned money weeding gardens
Monday	$5	Earned money running errands
Tuesday	$3	Bought ice cream
Wednesday	$9	Earned money mowing the lawn
Thursday	$0	No activity
Friday	$21	Bought new jeans
Saturday	$10	Went to a movie

C 47. **Challenge** You record the daily low temperature for seven days in a row. The mean of the seven temperatures is −2°C. Six of the temperatures are shown below. Find the seventh temperature. −6°C

−4°C   0°C   −2°C   −3°C   −1°C   2°C

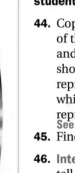

In Exercises 42 and 43, caution students that the negative sign means the opposite of the variable.

TEACHING TIP

Encourage students to solve a simpler problem to help them solve Exercise 47. For example, if the mean of −6, −2 and a third number is −2, then the third number is the number whose sum with −6 and −2 is 3 • (−2), or −6. The third number is therefore 2. Likewise, if the mean of 7 numbers is −2, their sum must be 7 • −2, or −14. Tell them that they need to find the number whose sum with the given numbers is −14.

44.

Day	Amount
Sunday	20
Monday	5
Tuesday	−3
Wednesday	9
Thursday	0
Friday	−21
Saturday	−10

MINI-QUIZ

Find the quotient.

1. $-14 \div (-2) = $? 7
2. $6 \div (-2) = $? -3
3. $-10 \div 5 = $? -2
4. Find the mean of $-3, -6, 9,$ $-12, 27.$ 3
5. Evaluate $\dfrac{24}{a}$ when $a = -12.$ -2

FOLLOW-UP 5

RETEACHING/REMEDIATION

- Study Guide in Chapter 11 Resource Book, pp. 49–50
- eTutorial Plus Online
- Extra Practice, p. 718
- Lesson Practice in Chapter 11 Resource Book, pp. 46–48

CHALLENGE/ENRICHMENT

- Challenge Practice in Chapter 11 Resource Book, p. 51
- Teacher's Edition, p. 530F

ENGLISH LEARNER SUPPORT

- Spanish Study Guide
- Multi-Language Glossary
- Chapter Audio Summaries CDs

48.
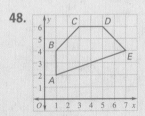

Mixed Review

48. Graph the points $A(1, 2)$, $B(1, 4)$, $C(3, 6)$, $D(5, 6)$, and $E(7, 4)$ on a coordinate grid. Connect the points to form a polygon. Then classify the polygon. *(Lessons 2.6, 9.6)* See margin for art; pentagon

Choose a Strategy Use a strategy from the list to solve the following problem. Explain your choice of strategy.

> **Problem Solving Strategies**
> - Guess, Check, and Revise
> - Perform an Experiment
> - Solve a Simpler Problem
> - Break into Parts

49. How many square inches of carpet are needed to cover the platform shown?

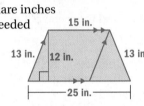

240 in.²; I used Break into Parts because I could find the area of the parallelogram and the area of the triangle and then add to find the area of the platform.

Basic Skills Copy and complete the statement.

50. 9 and 3 hundredths centimeters = ? centimeters 9.03

51. 3 and 1 tenth meters = ? meters 3.1

Test-Taking Practice

52. Multiple Choice Which expression has a value of -8? **B**

  A. $-96 \div (-12)$ **B.** $56 \div (-7)$ **C.** $-32 \div (-4)$ **D.** $56 \div (-8)$

53. Multiple Choice What is the mean of the integers below? **H**

$$-16, -13, -9, -4, 4, 8$$

  F. -8 **G.** -6 **H.** -5 **I.** 5

Mystery Dog

Copy and complete the equations using the numbers listed at the right. Then use the corresponding letters to spell out a type of dog. VIZSLA

Numbers	Letters
48	V
36	Z
−5	L
−6	I
−12	S
−15	A

1. ? $\div (-8) = -6$ 48   **2.** $24 \div $? $= -4$ -6

3. ? $\div (-4) = -9$ 36   **4.** ? $\div (-4) = 3$ -12

5. $35 \div (-7) = $? -5 **6.** $-30 \div $? $= 2$ -15

11.5

CALCULATOR

Technology Activity

Integer Operations

GOAL Use a calculator to perform operations with integers.

Example You can use the ⊡ key to enter negative temperatures.

The average monthly temperatures during the months of December through March in Caribou, Maine, are listed below, to the nearest degree. Find the mean of the temperatures.

$$-10°C \qquad -13°C \qquad -11°C \qquad -4°C$$

Solution

To find the mean of the temperatures, first find the sum of the temperatures. To enter a negative number, use the negation key, ⊡, not the subtraction key, ⊟.

Keystrokes   **Display**

 ⊡ 10 ⊞ ⊡ 13 ⊞ ⊡ 11 ⊞ ⊡ 4 ⊜   **−38**

Then divide the sum by the number of temperatures.

Keystrokes   **Display**

⊡ 38 ÷ 4 ⊜   **−9.5**

ANSWER The mean of the temperatures is −9.5°C.

Your turn now Use a calculator to evaluate the expression.

1. $28 - (-937)$ **965**   2. $402 \times (-59)$ **−23,718** 3. $-45 + 63 - (-30)$ **48**

4. $-33 \times (-74)$ **2442**   5. $810 \div (-45)$ **−18**   6. $-72 \div (-6) + (-93)$ **−81**

7. **Volcanoes** New Zealand has three submarine volcanoes whose elevations are −700 meters, −450 meters, and −140 meters. Find the mean of the elevations. **−430 m**

8. **Money** You have a savings account. During the week you withdraw $75, withdraw $115, deposit $100, and withdraw $55. At the end of the week, do you have more or less money in the account than you had at the beginning of the week? Describe the change in the amount of money. **Less; there is $145 less in the account.**

NCTM CURRICULUM STANDARDS
Standard 1: Understand numbers; Understand meanings of operations
Standard 5: Use proper statistical methods to analyze data

Lesson 11.5   Dividing Integers   **559**

LEARN THE METHOD
- Students will use a calculator to perform operations with integers.
- Students can use a calculator to complete Exercises 30–35 of Lesson 11.5.

2 TEACH

TIPS FOR SUCCESS

While some calculators do not require parentheses to separate a subtraction keystroke from a negative keystroke ($3 - -6$ is allowed), they do not allow you to use the subtraction key to enter a negative number. Caution students that if they always use parentheses around negative numbers and the negation key when appropriate, they will not have difficulty with integer operations.

EXTRA EXAMPLE

Use a calculator to find
$-48 \div 6 + (-7)$. **−15**

3 CLOSE

ASSESSMENT

Use a calculator to evaluate the expression.

1. $-72 \div (-9)$ **8**
2. $-84 \div (-7) + 32$ **44**

STRATEGY BACKGROUND

Encourage students to use the strategy Draw a Graph when a visual representation can help solve a problem. A useful graph may be a map grid, a bar graph, a circle graph, or a line graph.

2 TEACH

GUIDING STUDENTS' WORK

Students may want to draw one straight line from the hotel to the restaurant. Point out that this will not work because they cannot walk through city blocks in a straight line, since there are probably buildings in the way.

EXTRA EXAMPLES

Example Your parents planted a one-foot tree when you were born. When you were 2 years old, the tree was 7 feet tall. When you were 4, the tree was 13 feet tall. Assume the tree grows at a constant rate. What will be the height of the tree when you are 8 years old? **25 ft**

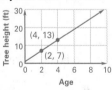

11.6 Problem Solving Strategies

- Make a List
- Work Backward
- Solve a Simpler Problem
- Make a Model
- Draw a Graph
- Break into Parts
- Look for a Pattern

Draw a Graph

Problem You are visiting a city with streets arranged in a grid. You leave your hotel and walk 8 blocks east and 3 blocks north to get to a museum. Then you walk 2 blocks north and 5 blocks west to get to a restaurant. What is the least number of blocks you have to walk to return to your hotel?

1 Read and Understand

Read the problem carefully.

You want to find the least number of blocks from the restaurant to the hotel.

2 Make a Plan

Decide on a strategy to use.

One way to solve this problem is by drawing a graph of your route.

3 Solve the Problem

Reread the problem and draw a graph.

Draw a grid on which each square represents 1 city block. Trace your route and mark key points. Then look for possible routes from the restaurant back to the hotel.

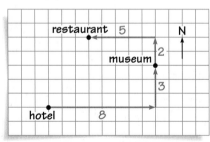

ANSWER There are many possible routes, but the shortest routes are all 8 blocks long.

4 Look Back

The hotel is 5 blocks south and 3 blocks west of the restaurant. So, you must walk 8 blocks total whether you walk south then west, west then south, or some combination of the two.

NCTM CURRICULUM STANDARDS
Standard 3: Use spatial reasoning to solve problems
Standard 6: Solve problems in math and other contexts
Standard 10: Use representations to solve problems

Practice the Strategy

Use the strategy _draw a graph_.

1. **Walking** In a city you walk 2 blocks west, 5 blocks north, then 2 blocks east. Will you reach the same location if you instead walk 5 blocks north? **yes**

2. **Driving** You want to drive from your house to a restaurant as shown on the map below. Write driving directions for a route that makes the least number of turns possible. You may not drive through the parks. **Sample answer: 4 blocks east, 6 blocks south, 4 blocks east**

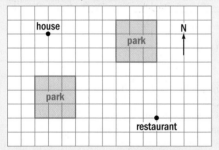

3. **Animation** You are animating Figure _ABCD_ with coordinates _A_(3, 0), _B_(3, 2), _C_(0, 2), and _D_(0, 0). As part of the animation, you double each coordinate to create a new Figure _WXYZ_. Is the new figure similar to the original? Explain. **See margin.**

4. **Page Layout** You are placing digital photos on a page in a yearbook and you want them to be congruent. Will a photo with vertices _A_(0, 10), _B_(0, 7), _C_(2, 7), and _D_(2, 10) be congruent to a photo with vertices _W_(6, 3), _X_(6, 0), _Y_(8, 0), and _Z_(8, 6)? Why or why not? **No; one photo is a rectangle and the other is a different shape.**

5. **Symmetry** A figure is formed by connecting the points (0, 9), (5, 5), (2, 0), (5, −5), (0, −9), (−5, −5), (−2, 0), and (−5, 5) in order. Identify the lines of symmetry. **x-axis and y-axis**

Mixed Problem Solving

Use any strategy to solve the problem.

6. **Mystery Digit** If you evaluate the power 9^{20}, what will the ones' digit be? **1**

7. **Oranges** You take an orange and cut it into two pieces. Then you cut each of those pieces in half. You continue this process 3 more times. How many pieces of the orange do you have? **32 pieces**

8. **Mystery Number** Your friend is thinking of a number. If you double the number, subtract 5, divide by 3, and add 8, you get 11. What is your friend's number? **7**

9. **Bowling** At an amusement park, you roll three balls up a ramp toward the target. Each ball lands in one of three regions on the target. How many different point totals are possible? **9 different totals**

10. **Chess** At the end of each game in a chess tournament, the losing player is required to drop out. If you win the tournament after playing in four games, how many players were there at the beginning of the tournament? **16 players**

TEACHING TIP

For Exercise 2, you may want to label each square as a unit of one block on a side. Encourage students to use colored pencils, if necessary, to label different routes from the house to the restaurant. Exercises 3 and 4 are a good review of coordinates and transformations in the first quadrant. Extend Exercise 3 by asking students to find the area of the original figure and the area of the image. The image has 4 times the area.

(X) COMMON ERROR

Students may draw a figure with no symmetry lines in Exercise 5 if they do not connect the points in the order they are given. Caution them to plot the points carefully and to connect them in order.

SUGGESTED STRATEGIES

You may wish to suggest the following strategies for the problems in the Mixed Problem Solving:
- Exercise 6: Solve a Simpler Problem, Look for a Pattern
- Exercise 7: Make a Model, Look for a Pattern
- Exercise 8: Work Backward
- Exercise 9: Make a List
- Exercise 10: Work Backward

3. Yes; _WXYZ_ is the same shape as _ABCD_ but its sides are twice as long.

Translations in a Coordinate Plane

LESSON 11.6

BEFORE	▶ Now	WHY?
You graphed points with positive coordinates.	You'll graph points with negative coordinates.	So you can describe the path of a tornado, as in Ex. 26.

📖 **Word Watch**

coordinate plane, p. 562
quadrant, p. 562
translation, p. 563
image, p. 563

The Coordinate Plane In Chapter 2 you graphed points whose coordinates were positive or zero on a coordinate grid. Now you'll graph points whose coordinates are integers on a **coordinate plane** as shown below.

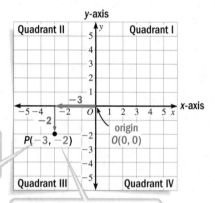

The *x*-coordinate tells you how many units to move to the left or right.

The *y*-coordinate tells you how many units to move up or down.

 **with Review**

Need help graphing ordered pairs with positive coordinates? See p. 83.

EXAMPLE 1 **Graphing Points**

Graph the point and describe its location.

a. To graph $A(-2, 0)$, start at $(0, 0)$. Move 2 units to the left and 0 units up. Point *A* is on the *x*-axis.

b. To graph $B(4, -2)$, start at $(0, 0)$. Move 4 units to the right and 2 units down. Point *B* is in Quadrant IV.

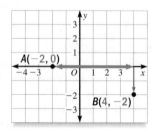

1. Point *A* is on the *y*-axis.

2. Point *B* is in Quadrant III.

3. Point *C* is in Quadrant II.

4. Point *D* is in Quadrant IV.

Your turn now **Graph the point and describe its location.**
1–4. See margin for art.

1. $A(0, -3)$ **2.** $B(-2, -1)$ **3.** $C(-1, 2)$ **4.** $D(1, -4)$

Translations In a **translation**, each point of a figure slides the same distance in the same direction. The new figure is the **image** of the original figure.

For example, each point on △*DEF* has moved 6 units to the right and 3 units up from each point on △*ABC*. △*DEF* is the image of △*ABC*. Notice that in a translation, the image is congruent to the original figure.

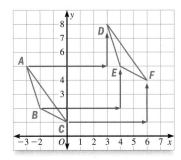

EXAMPLE 2 **Translating a Figure**

Animation In an animation, a kite will be translated 4 units to the right and 5 units down. The images of points *A*, *B*, *C*, and *D* will be points *P*, *Q*, *R*, and *S*. Draw the image and give the coordinates of points *P*, *Q*, *R*, and *S*.

Solution

To draw the image think of sliding the original figure 4 units to the right and 5 units down. You'll get the same image if you add 4 to the *x*-coordinates and subtract 5 from the *y*-coordinates.

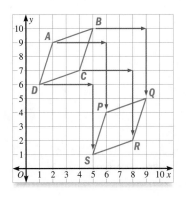

$A(2, 9) \Rightarrow (2 + 4, 9 - 5) \Rightarrow P(6, 4)$

$B(5, 10) \Rightarrow (5 + 4, 10 - 5) \Rightarrow Q(9, 5)$

$C(4, 7) \Rightarrow (4 + 4, 7 - 5) \Rightarrow R(8, 2)$

$D(1, 6) \Rightarrow (1 + 4, 6 - 5) \Rightarrow S(5, 1)$

ANSWER The coordinates are *P*(6, 4), *Q*(9, 5), *R*(8, 2), and *S*(5, 1).

Your turn now Graph the points and connect them to form △*ABC*. Then translate the triangle 3 units to the left and 2 units down to form △*DEF*. Give the coordinates of the vertices of △*DEF*.

5–6. See margin for art.

5. *A*(−4, 1), *B*(−1, −1), *C*(2, 1)
D(−7, −1), *E*(−4, −3), *F*(−1, −1)

6. *A*(2, −1), *B*(−4, 2), *C*(0, −2)
D(−1, −3), *E*(−7, 0), *F*(−3, −4)

TIPS FOR NEW TEACHERS
Explain how to use two integer number lines that are perpendicular to each other as axes in the coordinate plane. See Tips for New Teachers in the *Chapter 11 Resource Book*.

EXTRA EXAMPLES

Example 1 Graph the point.
a. *A*(−4, 0) **b.** *B*(3, −2)

Example 2 Graph the points *A*(−3, 1), *B*(0, 5), and *C*(2, −1) to form △*ABC*. Then translate the triangle 2 units to the right and 3 units down to form △*DEF*.

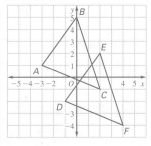

CONCEPT CHECK

How do you translate a figure in the coordinate plane 2 units to the right and 3 units down? **For each point, add 2 to the *x*-coordinate and subtract 3 from the *y*-coordinate.**

DAILY PUZZLER

If you translate a triangle 3 units to the left and 1 unit down the image is △*DEF*, where *D*(−2, −1), *E*(0, −3), and *F*(2, −3). Give the coordinates of the original △*ABC*.
A(1, 0), *B*(3, −2), *C*(5, −2)

5, 6. See Additional Answers beginning on page AA1.

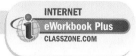

Getting Ready to Practice

Vocabulary Tell whether the statement is *true* or *false*.

1. The y-axis is the horizontal axis on a coordinate plane. **false**

2. A quadrant is one of three sections that make up the coordinate plane.
false

Graph the point and describe its location. 3–6. See margin.

3. $A(5, -1)$ **4.** $B(0, 3)$ **5.** $C(-4, -3)$ **6.** $D(-3, 3)$

7. Graph the points $P(-5, 4)$ and $Q(-2, -2)$. Connect the points to form a segment. Then translate the segment 1 unit to the left and 2 units down to form $\overline{RS}$. Give the coordinates of the endpoints of $\overline{RS}$. See margin.

8. Guided Problem Solving In the diagram, the red boat is the image of the blue boat after a translation. How would you describe the translation to a friend?

   (**1** Find the x-coordinate change. **−5**

   (**2** Find the y-coordinate change. **4**

   (**3** Describe the translation in words.
   Slide the original figure 5 units to the left and 4 units up.

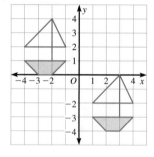

Practice and Problem Solving

Graph the point and describe its location. 9–16. See margin.

A **9.** $A(5, 0)$ **10.** $B(3, 4)$ **11.** $C(-1, 3)$ **12.** $D(0, -7)$

13. $E(-4, -4)$ **14.** $F(-7, -5)$ **15.** $G(3, -2)$ **16.** $H(-5, 2)$

In Exercises 17–22, use the map shown to give the coordinates of the location.

17. school $(-3, 2)$ **18.** library $(0, 3)$

19. statue $(4, -4)$ **20.** post office $(2, 0)$

21. city hall $(3, 4)$ **22.** store $(-2, -2)$

23. Writing Describe in words how to graph a point on a coordinate plane. *Sample answer:* Start at $(0, 0)$. Move to the right or left the number of units given by the x-coordinate. Then move up or down the number of units given by the y-coordinate.

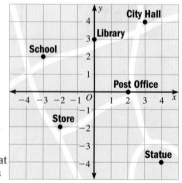

Draw the figure on a coordinate plane. Then translate the figure as described. Give the coordinates of the vertices of the image.

24–25. See margin for art.

24. △QRS: Q(−4, −2), R(6, 3), S(3, −3)
T(−2, −7), U(8, −2), V(5, −8)
Translation: 2 units to the right and 5 units down to form △TUV

25. Rectangle JKLM: J(3, 4), K(4, 3), L(−1, −2), M(−2, −1)
E(−4, 0), F(−3, −1), G(−8, −6), H(−9, −5)
Translation: 7 units to the left and 4 units down to form rectangle EFGH

26. Tornados The graph shows the approximate points where a tornado touched down in South Dakota. Describe the translation between point A and point B, point B and point C, and point A and point C.
See margin.

Critical Thinking Identify the quadrant that contains an ordered pair that fits the given description.

B **27.** (positive, positive) I

28. (negative, negative) III

29. (negative, positive) II

30. (positive, negative) IV

Decide Tell whether the red figure is the image of the blue figure after a translation. If it is, describe the translation. If it is not, explain why not.

31.
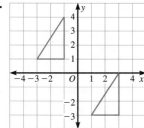

32.
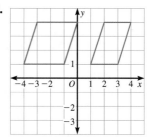

33.
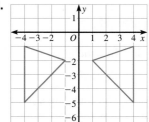

34.
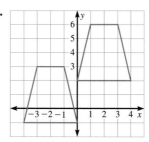

26. A to B: 3 units to the right and 1 unit down; B to C: 5 units to the right and 1 unit down; A to C: 8 units to the right and 2 units down.

31. Yes; slide the figure 4 units to the right and 4 units down.

32. No; each point did not slide the same distance.

33. No; each point did not slide the same distance.

34. Yes, slide the figure 4 units to the right and 3 units up.

⊗ COMMON ERROR

For Exercises 9–16, students may graph the points and describe their locations incorrectly because they confuse the x- and y-coordinates. Emphasize that the x-coordinate is always the first coordinate of the point, and the y-coordinate is always the second coordinate.

📓 NOTETAKING

Encourage students to draw a coordinate grid for Exercises 27–30 in their notebook. Ask them to label the quadrants and write a description in each quadrant about the signs of the x- and y-coordinates.

⊗ COMMON ERROR

For Exercise 33, a common error is to think that the images are translated because they are congruent. While these triangles represent a transformation (a reflection), this is not a translation because each point did not move an equal distance.

24.

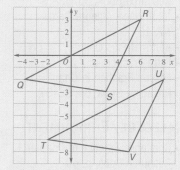

25. See Additional Answers beginning on page AA1.

4 **ASSESS**

ASSESSMENT RESOURCES

For more assessment resources, see:
• Assessment Book
• Test and Practice Generator

MINI-QUIZ

1. Graph the point $C(5, -2)$.

2. Draw the figure with vertices $R(-1, 3)$, $S(2, 4)$, $T(3, 0)$, and $U(2, -1)$. Then translate the figure 4 units left and 1 unit down and label the image *ABCD*.

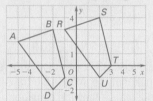

5 **FOLLOW-UP**

RETEACHING/REMEDIATION

• Study Guide in Chapter 11 Resource Book, pp. 58–59
• Tutor Place, Algebra Cards 17, 18
• eTutorial Plus Online
• Extra Practice, p. 718
• Lesson Practice in Chapter 11 Resource Book, pp. 55–57

CHALLENGE/ENRICHMENT

• Challenge Practice in Chapter 11 Resource Book, p. 60
• Teacher's Edition, p. 530F

ENGLISH LEARNER SUPPORT

• Spanish Study Guide
• Multi-Language Glossary
• Chapter Audio Summaries CDs

35, 37, 43. See Additional Answers beginning on page AA1.

566

What do you think? **Art**

■ **Animation**

When animating music, an animator must find the number of frames needed for an entire song. If the length of a song is 3 minutes and the song uses 24 frames per second, how many frames are needed? **4320 frames**

36. Check work. A good answer will include a figure or combination of figures that have been correctly translated.

39. thirty-five hundredths; 35%
40. two hundredths; 2%
41. fifteen hundredths; 15%
42. nine point four hundredths; 9.4%

INTERNET
State Test Practice
CLASSZONE.COM

35. Animation Translations are often used by animators to show movement. Copy the coordinate plane shown. Complete the next two translations of the musical note to continue the pattern. Then shade the notes to make it look like they are fading away into the background. **See margin.**

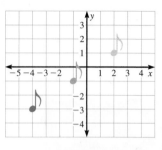

36. Create your own wallpaper border by translating a simple design. Describe your translation in words. **See margin.**

C **37. Challenge** Translate the figure shown by subtracting 2.5 from the *x*-coordinate and adding 0.75 to the *y*-coordinate of each vertex. Graph the image and give the coordinates of its vertices. **See margin.**

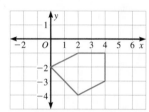

38. Algebra Write the coordinates of the image of the point (x, y) after a translation of *a* units to the right and *b* units down. $(x + a, y - b)$

Mixed Review

Write the number in words and as a percent. *(Lesson 8.5)* 39–42. See margin.

39. 0.35   **40.** 0.02   **41.** $\frac{15}{100}$ **42.** $\frac{9.4}{100}$

43. Draw an obtuse scalene triangle. *(Lesson 9.4)* **See margin.**

44. Find the opposite of 6. *(Lesson 11.1)* -6

Basic Skills **Find the quotient.**

45. $8.4 \div 1.2$ 7   **46.** $49 \div 0.07$ 700 **47.** $1.64 \div 0.8$ 2.05 **48.** $1.65 \div 0.55$ 3

Test-Taking Practice

49. Multiple Choice In which quadrant is the point $(-9, 4)$? B

  A. I   **B.** II   **C.** III   **D.** IV

50. Multiple Choice You translate a point 6 units to the left of the origin, and then 5 units down. Which ordered pair describes the point's new location? F

  F. $(-6, -5)$ **G.** $(0, 5)$ **H.** $(-5, -6)$ **I.** $(5, -6)$

LESSON 11.7

Reflections and Rotations

BEFORE | **Now** | **WHY?**

You learned how to recognize translations.

You'll learn how to recognize reflections and rotations.

So you can identify transformations, as in Exs. 12–14.

Word Watch

reflection, p. 567
line of reflection, p. 567
rotation, p. 568
center of rotation, p. 568
angle of rotation, p. 568
transformation, p. 568

Photography The photograph appears to show eight pelicans. In fact, there are four pelicans reflected in the line to produce a congruent image. In a **reflection**, the original figure is flipped over a line to produce a congruent mirror image. The line is called the **line of reflection**.

line of reflection

EXAMPLE 1 Identifying Reflections

Tell whether the red figure is a reflection of the blue figure. If it is a reflection, identify the line of reflection.

a.

b.

c.

HELP with Solving

In Example 1, you can see that a figure that is not flipped or is not congruent to the original figure cannot be a reflection.

a. Yes. The line of reflection is the *x*-axis.

b. No. The figures are not congruent.

c. No. The image is not flipped.

Your turn now Tell whether the red figure is a reflection of the blue figure. If it is a reflection, identify the line of reflection.

1. yes; *x*-axis

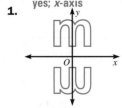

2. yes; *y*-axis

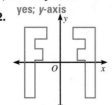

3. no

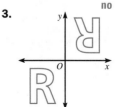

Lesson 11.7   Reflections and Rotations   **567**

1 PLAN

SKILL CHECK
1. $A(3, -4)$ is translated 2 units to the left and 1 unit down. Find the image point. $(1, -5)$
2. How many symmetry lines does a square have? **4**

LESSON OBJECTIVE
Recognize reflections and rotations.

PACING
Suggested Number of Days
Basic Course: 2 days
Average Course: 2 days
Advanced Course: 2 days
Block: 1 block

TEACHING RESOURCES
For a complete list of Teaching Resources, see page 530B.

TRANSPARENCY
Warm-Up Exercises for this lesson are available on a transparency.

2 TEACH

MOTIVATING THE LESSON
Have different pairs of congruent shapes pre-cut so that you can demonstrate reflections and rotations on an overhead screen with a transparent coordinate grid.

TIPS FOR NEW TEACHERS
Be sure students understand how reflections and rotations differ from translations. See Tips for New Teachers in the *Chapter 11 Resource Book.*

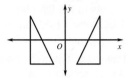
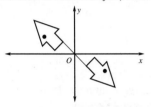
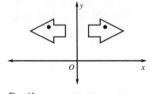
 CONCEPT CHECK

How are reflections and rotations similar? How are they different? **In both transformations, the images are congruent to the original figures. A reflection flips the image over a reflection line, while a rotation turns the image about a point.**

 DAILY PUZZLER

Can you rotate a figure so that you can also find the image by reflecting the figure? **Yes, you can reflect a figure twice over intersecting lines to get a rotation.**

A traditional windmill in Portugal

HELP with **Solving**

You can use tracing paper to help you identify transformations. Trace the original figure, then try to slide, flip, or turn it to produce the image.

Rotations The blue figure below was turned 90° clockwise about the origin to produce the congruent red image. The diagram illustrates a rotation. In a **rotation**, a figure is rotated through a given angle about a fixed point called the **center of rotation**. The angle is called the **angle of rotation**. In this book, you'll be looking at clockwise rotations.

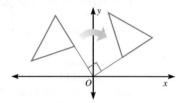

EXAMPLE 2 **Identifying Rotations**

Tell whether the red figure is a rotation of the blue figure about the origin. If it is a rotation, state the angle of rotation.

a.

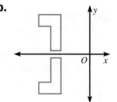

b.

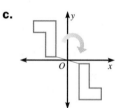

c.

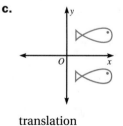

Yes. The figure is rotated 90°.

No. This is a flip, not a turn.

Yes. The figure is rotated 180°.

Transformations A **transformation**, such as a translation, reflection, or rotation, is a movement of a figure on a plane.

EXAMPLE 3 **Identifying Transformations**

Tell whether the transformation is a *translation*, a *reflection*, or a *rotation*.

a.

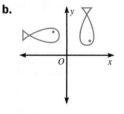

b.

c.

reflection

rotation

translation

INTERNET
eWorkbook Plus
CLASSZONE.COM

Getting Ready to Practice

1. In a reflection, the original figure is flipped over a line to produce a congruent mirror image. In a rotation, the original figure is rotated through a given angle about a fixed point.

1. Vocabulary What is the difference between a reflection and a rotation?

Tell whether the transformation is a *translation*, a *reflection*, or a *rotation*.

2.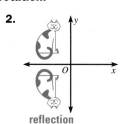
reflection

3.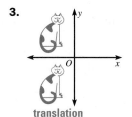
translation

4.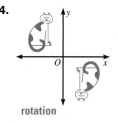
rotation

Practice and Problem Solving

with Homework

Example	Exercises
1	5–7, 9
2	8–10
3	10–13

Online Resources
CLASSZONE.COM
· More Examples
· eTutorial Plus

5. No; the image is not flipped.

6. No; the image is not flipped.

7. Yes, the line of reflection is the y-axis.

9. A appears to be a rotation; B appears to be a reflection.

Tell whether the red figure is a reflection of the blue figure. If it is, identify the line of reflection. If it is not, explain why not. 5–7. See margin.

A 5.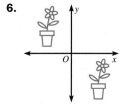

6.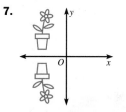

7.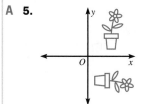

8. Use the figures in Exercises 5–7. Tell whether the red figure is a rotation of the blue figure about the origin. If it is a rotation, state the angle of rotation. yes, 90° rotation; no; no.

Jewelry In Exercise 9, use photographs *A* and *B*.

9. Analyze At a glance, which piece of jewelry has a design that appears to be based on a reflection? Which design appears to be based on a series of rotations about its center?

A.
rotation

B.
reflection

10. Create your own jewelry design based on a series of rotations. Answers will vary.

CROSS-CURRICULUM

Art For Exercises 18–21, point out that transformations are the basis for many patterns used in art, as well as home decorating, jewelry design, and so on. Tiling a floor often uses translations and rotations to generate the pattern.

14.
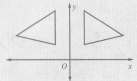

15.

16.
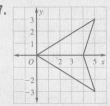

17.
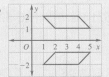

Page 571

22.
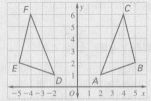

23.
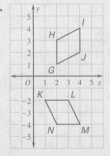

25, 39. See Additional Answers beginning on page AA1.

570

18–21. Descriptions may vary.

18. Can be formed by a reflection; cannot be formed by translations or rotations; the design can be formed by a reflection over a vertical line placed at the middle of the design.

19. Cannot be formed by a reflection; can be formed by a series of translations and by a rotation; the design can be formed by translating the columns or rows of beads up and to the right.

20. Cannot be formed by a reflection; can be formed by a series of translations, but not by a rotation; the design can be formed by translating the leaves up and to the right.

21. Can be formed by a reflection; cannot be formed by a translation, but can be formed by a rotation; the design can be formed by rotating a portion of the design about its center.

Tell whether the transformation is a *translation*, a *reflection*, or a *rotation*.

11.
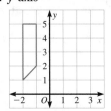
translation

12.
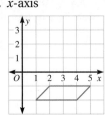
reflection

13.
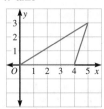
rotation

14. Find the Error The red figure at the right is supposed to be a reflection in the *y*-axis of the blue figure. Find and correct the error. The image is not flipped. See margin for art.

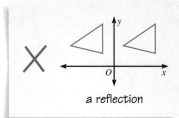
a reflection

Copy and reflect the figure in the indicated axis. 15–17. See margin.

B 15. *y*-axis
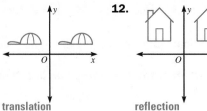

16. *x*-axis
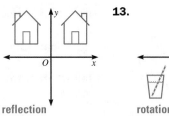

17. *x*-axis
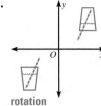

Weaving Ignoring color, tell whether the design can be formed by a reflection. Then tell whether it can be formed by a series of translations or rotations. Describe any transformations that apply. 18–21. See margin.

18.

19.

20.

21.

Chapter 11 Integers

For each figure, graph the points and connect them to form a polygon. Then tell whether the transformation from Figure 1 to Figure 2 is a *translation*, a *reflection*, or a *rotation*. 22–23. See margin for art.

22. Figure 1: *A*(2, 1), *B*(5, 2), *C*(4, 6)
Figure 2: *D*(−2, 1), *E*(−5, 2), *F*(−4, 6)
reflection

23. Figure 1: *G*(2, 1), *H*(2, 3), *I*(4, 4), *J*(4, 2)
Figure 2: *K*(1, −2), *L*(3, −2), *M*(4, −4), *N*(2, −4)
rotation

C 24. Critical Thinking The statement $(x, y) \rightarrow (x, -y)$ is a rule for a reflection. For example, the reflection of point (3, 2) is (3, −2). Use the rule to plot several points and their images. What axis is the line of reflection? Write and test a rule for reflecting points in the other axis.
Check work; *x*-axis; $(x, y) \rightarrow (-x, y)$.

25. Challenge Draw a transformation on a coordinate plane that is a translation, a reflection, and a rotation. See margin.

Mixed Review

Divide. Round to the nearest tenth if necessary. *(Lesson 4.6)*

26. $49 \div 0.8$ **61.25** **27.** $45.6 \div 1.5$ **30.4** **28.** $21.3 \div 0.03$ **710** **29.** $70.56 \div 2.3$ **30.7**

Find the product or quotient. *(Lessons 11.4, 11.5)*

30. $4(-8)$ **−32** **31.** $-6(-9)$ **54** **32.** $-15 \div (-3)$ **5** **33.** $-16 \div 2$ **−8**

Choose a Strategy **Use a strategy from the list to solve the following problem. Explain your choice of strategy.**

34. Your friend treated you to lunch and left a tip of $5. How much was the bill if this was a 20% tip?

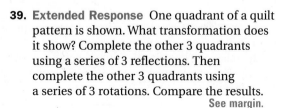
Problem Solving Strategies
▪ Guess, Check, and Revise
▪ Draw a Diagram
▪ Work Backward
▪ Break into Parts

34. $25. *Sample answer:* I used Guess, Check, and Revise because I guessed the amount, checked to see what 20% was, and then revised until I found the correct answer.

Basic Skills **Write the decimal as a fraction or mixed number in simplest form.**

35. 0.6 $\frac{3}{5}$ **36.** 0.75 $\frac{3}{4}$ **37.** 3.08 $3\frac{2}{25}$ **38.** 0.204 $\frac{51}{250}$

39. Translation; see margin for art. The resulting figures are identical.

Test-Taking Practice

39. Extended Response One quadrant of a quilt pattern is shown. What transformation does it show? Complete the other 3 quadrants using a series of 3 reflections. Then complete the other 3 quadrants using a series of 3 rotations. Compare the results.
See margin.

Lesson 11.7 Reflections and Rotations **571**

4 ASSESS

ASSESSMENT RESOURCES

For more assessment resources, see:
• Assessment Book
• Test and Practice Generator

MINI-QUIZ

Tell whether the transformation is a *translation*, a *reflection*, a *rotation*, or *none of these*. If it is a reflection, give the reflecting line. If it is a rotation, give the angle of rotation.

1.

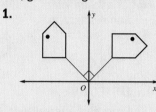

rotation, 90°

2.

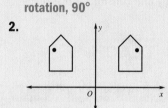

reflection; *y*-axis

5 FOLLOW-UP

RETEACHING/REMEDIATION
• Study Guide in Chapter 11 Resource Book, pp. 66–67
• Tutor Place, Geometry and Measurement Card 19
• eTutorial Plus Online
• Extra Practice, p. 718
• Lesson Practice in Chapter 11 Resource Book, pp. 63–65

CHALLENGE/ENRICHMENT
• Challenge Practice in Chapter 11 Resource Book, p. 68
• Teacher's Edition, p. 530F

ENGLISH LEARNER SUPPORT
• Spanish Study Guide
• Multi-Language Glossary
• Chapter Audio Summaries CDs

571

1. Describe the properties of a *regular* polygon. **All of its angles have equal measures and all of its sides have equal lengths.**

2. Name the geometric figure with 6 sides. **hexagon**

3. Describe a translation. **In a translation, every point of a figure slides the same distance in the same direction.**

LESSON OBJECTIVE

Identify and construct a tessellation.

2 TEACH

Example 1 Tell whether the polygon can form a regular tessellation.
a. square **yes**
b. regular octagon **no**

 COMMON ERROR

Students may think that any regular polygon can tessellate the plane. Point out that only equilateral triangles, squares, and regular hexagons can form regular tessellations.

 **Special Topic**

Tessellations

GOAL Identify and construct tessellations.

 **Word Watch**

tessellation, p. 572
regular tessellation, p. 572

A **tessellation** is a repeating pattern of figures that fill a plane with no gaps or overlaps. A **regular tessellation** is made from only one type of regular polygon. For example, the kitchen floor tiles below suggest a regular tessellation.

Not all regular polygons can form regular tessellations.

EXAMPLE 1 **Forming Regular Tessellations**

Tell whether the polygon can form a regular tessellation.

  a. regular pentagon   **b.** regular hexagon

Solution

a. Start with a regular pentagon. Make 2 copies and fit the pentagons together as shown. The gap around their common vertex cannot be filled by a fourth regular pentagon. So, regular pentagons cannot form a regular tessellation.

b. Start with a regular hexagon. Make 6 copies and fit the hexagons together as shown. The resulting pattern will fill a plane with no gaps or overlaps. So, regular hexagons can form a regular tessellation.

Other Tessellations The only regular polygons that form regular tessellations are equilateral triangles, squares, and regular hexagons. Tessellations can also be formed using more than one regular polygon, or one or more nonregular polygons. The polygons may be translated, reflected, or rotated to fill the plane.

NCTM CURRICULUM STANDARDS
Standard 3: Analyze properties of 2-D shapes; Use spatial reasoning to solve problems
Standard 10: Use representations to solve problems

Example 2 Draw a tessellation of the quadrilateral shown.

EXAMPLE 2 Forming Tessellations

Draw a tessellation of the scalene triangle shown.

Solution

① Locate and mark a point at the middle of one side of the triangle. Rotate the triangle 180° about the point to form a parallelogram.

② Translate the parallelogram as shown so that the pattern fills the plane with no gaps or overlaps.

Exercises

1. See margin for art.
Sample answer: Rotate the triangle 180° about the point at the middle of one side of the triangle to form a parallelogram. Then translate the parallelogram to fill the plane.

1. Draw a regular tessellation of equilateral triangles. Describe any transformations you use.

In Exercises 2–4, use the given triangle and the method in Example 2 to draw a tessellation. 2–4. See margin.

2.

3.

4.

5. You can use any quadrilateral to create a tessellation.

First, locate and mark a point in the middle of one side.

Then, rotate the quadrilateral 180° about the point to form a hexagon.

Finally, translate the hexagons to draw a tessellation.

Draw any quadrilateral and use this method to create a tessellation.
Check drawing.

TEACHING TIP

Encourage students to create tessellations by experimenting with combinations of shapes.

CONCEPT CHECK

Which shapes can form a regular tessellation of the plane?
equilateral triangle, square, and regular hexagon

③ **APPLY**

TRANSPARENCY

Even-numbered answers are available on transparencies.

COMMON ERROR

Exercise 1 may be difficult if students cannot identify the transformation used to make the tessellation. Remind them that this tessellation consists of translations and rotations of equilateral triangles.

TEACHING TIP

After doing Exercise 5, students should be able to conclude that any quadrilateral will tessellate. Ask them to verify that the sum of the angles at a vertex of the tessellation is 360°.

1.
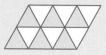

2–4. See Additional Answers beginning on page AA1.

8.
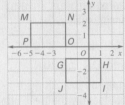

Notebook Review

Review the vocabulary definitions in your notebook.

Copy the review examples in your notebook. Then complete the exercises.

Check Your Definitions

coordinate plane, p. 562	reflection, p. 567	center of rotation, p. 568
quadrant, p. 562	line of reflection, p. 567	angle of rotation, p. 568
translation, p. 563	rotation, p. 568	transformation, p. 568
image, p. 563		

Use Your Vocabulary

1. Copy and complete: In a ?, a figure is turned about a fixed point called the ?. **rotation; point of rotation**

11.4–11.5 Can you multiply and divide integers?

 EXAMPLE $-4(-8) = 32$ The product of two negative integers is positive.

$72 \div (-8) = -9$ The quotient of a positive integer and a negative integer is negative.

 Find the product.   **2.** $6(-6)$ **−36**   **3.** $-7(8)$ **−56**   **4.** $-5(-9)$ **45**

Find the quotient.   **5.** $42 \div (-7)$ **−6**   **6.** $-18 \div 3$ **−6**   **7.** $-20 \div (-5)$ **4**

11.6 Can you translate in a coordinate plane?

EXAMPLE Translate $\triangle ABC$ 3 units to the left and 4 units up to form $\triangle XYZ$. Give the coordinates of points X, Y, and Z.

ANSWER

$A(-1, -1) \implies X(-4, 3)$

$B(3, 0) \implies Y(0, 4)$

$C(2, -3) \implies Z(-1, 1)$

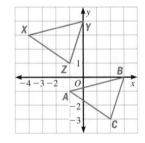

 8. The vertices of rectangle $GHIJ$ are $G(-2, -1)$, $H(1, -1)$, $I(1, -3)$, and $J(-2, -3)$. Draw rectangle $GHIJ$ in a coordinate plane. Then translate it 3 units to the left and 3 units up to form rectangle $QRST$. Give the coordinates of points Q, R, S, and T.
See margin for art; $Q(-5, 2)$, $R(-2, 2)$, $S(-2, 0)$, $T(-5, 0)$.

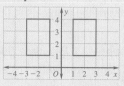
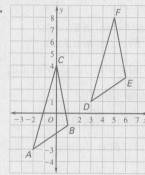
11.7 Can you identify transformations?

 EXAMPLE Tell whether the transformation is a *translation*, a *reflection*, or a *rotation*.

ANSWER The transformation is a reflection in the *y*-axis.

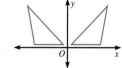

☑ **Tell whether the transformation is a *translation*, a *reflection*, or a *rotation*.**

9.

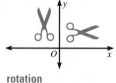

rotation

10.

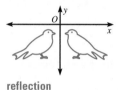

reflection

Stop *and* Think about Lessons 11.4–11.7

11. Writing Explain how to tell if one figure is a translation of another.
Each point of one figure is slid the same distance in the same direction.

12. Critical Thinking Draw a transformation in a coordinate plane that is both a translation and a reflection. Answers may vary.

Review Quiz 2

Find the product or quotient.

1. 7(−7) −49   **2.** −3(9) −27   **3.** −5(−8) 40   **4.** −6(0) 0

5. −140 ÷ 7 −20   **6.** −30 ÷ (−6) 5   **7.** −25 ÷ (−5) 5   **8.** 32 ÷ (−4) −8

9. The vertices of △*ABC* are *A*(−2, −3), *B*(1, −1), and *C*(0, 4). Draw △*ABC* in a coordinate plane. Then translate it 5 units to the right and 4 units up to form △*DEF*. Give the coordinates of points *D*, *E*, and *F.*
See margin for art; *D*(3, 1), *E*(6, 3), *F*(5, 8).

Tell whether the transformation is a *translation*, a *reflection*, or a *rotation*.

10.

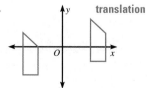

translation

11.

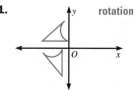

rotation

Chapter Review

Vocabulary

integer, p. 533	quadrant, p. 562	center of rotation, p. 568
positive integer, p. 533	translation, p. 563	angle of rotation, p. 568
negative integer, p. 533	image, p. 563	
opposites, p. 534	reflection, p. 567	transformation, p. 568
absolute value, p. 539	line of reflection, p. 567	
coordinate plane, 562	rotation, p. 568	

Vocabulary Review

Copy and complete the statement.

1. _?_ are integers that are less than zero.
  Negative integers

2. The _?_ is divided into four quadrants.
  coordinate plane

3. The _?_ of 10 is −10.
  opposite

4. In a _?_, each point of a figure slides the same distance in the same direction.
  translation

5. In a rotation, the _?_ is congruent to the original figure. **image**

6. In a reflection, the original figure is flipped over the _?_ to form a congruent mirror image.
  line of reflection

Review Questions

Write the integer that represents the situation. *(Lesson 11.1)*

7. a profit of $25 **$25**

8. 15 degrees below zero
  −15 degrees

9. a decrease of 3 centimeters **−3 cm**

Find the opposite of the integer. *(Lesson 11.1)*

10. 7 **−7**

11. −30 **30**

12. 0 **0**

13. 2 **−2**

Order the integers from least to greatest. *(Lesson 11.1)*

14. 3, −4, 10, 2, −9
  −9, −4, 2, 3, 10

15. −8, 0, −13, 6, −6
  −13, −8, −6, 0, 6

16. 5, −15, 7, −5, −7
  −15, −7, −5, 5, 7

17. −1, 10, −100, 1000, 1
  −100, −1, 1, 10, 1000

Find the absolute value of the number. *(Lesson 11.2)*

18. −21 **21**

19. 8 **8**

20. 100 **100**

21. −10 **10**

Find the sum. *(Lesson 11.2)*

22. 2 + (−3) **−1**

23. 7 + (−4) **3**

24. −1 + 1 **0**

25. −12 + 2 **−10**

26. −9 + 17 **8**

27. −8 + (−9) **−17**

28. −6 + (−11) **−17**

29. −10 + (−20) **−30**

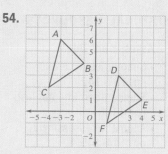

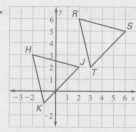

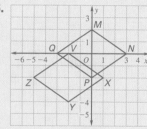

Review Questions

Find the difference. *(Lesson 11.3)*

30. $2 - 6$ −4

31. $5 - 10$ −5

32. $-8 - 3$ −11

33. $-14 - 4$ −18

34. $15 - (-9)$ 24

35. $18 - (-6)$ 24

36. $-13 - (-7)$ −6

37. $-5 - (-25)$ 20

Find the product. *(Lesson 11.4)*

38. $2(-2)$ −4

39. $5(-6)$ −30

40. $3(-11)$ −33

41. $-9(7)$ −63

42. $-10(4)$ −40

43. $-3(-90)$ 270

44. $-7(-8)$ 56

45. $-2(-12)$ 24

Find the quotient. *(Lesson 11.5)*

46. $-20 \div 2$ −10

47. $-35 \div 5$ −7

48. $150 \div (-3)$ −50

49. $24 \div (-6)$ −4

50. $81 \div (-9)$ −9

51. $-12 \div (-4)$ 3

52. $-48 \div (-8)$ 6

53. $-50 \div (-10)$ 5

Draw the figure in a coordinate plane. Then translate the figure as described. Give the coordinates of the vertices of the image. *(Lesson 11.6)* 54–56. See margin for art.

54. $\triangle ABC$: $A(-3, 6)$, $B(-1, 4)$, $C(-4, 2)$ *D*(2, 3), *E*(4, 1), *F*(1, −1)

Translation: 5 units to the right and 3 units down to form $\triangle DEF$

55. $\triangle HJK$: $H(-2, 3)$, $J(2, 2)$, $K(-1, -1)$ *R*(2, 6), *S*(6, 5), *T*(3, 2)

Translation: 4 units to the right and 3 units up to form $\triangle RST$

56. Rhombus $MNPQ$: $M(0, 2)$, $N(3, 0)$, $P(0, -2)$, $Q(-3, 0)$ *V*(−2, 0), *X*(1, −2), *Y*(−2, −4), *Z*(−5, −2)

Translation: 2 units to the left and 2 units down to form rhombus $VXYZ$

Tell whether the transformation is a *translation*, a *reflection*, or a *rotation*. If it is a reflection, identify the line of reflection. If it is a rotation, state the angle of rotation. *(Lesson 11.7)*

57. rotation; 90°

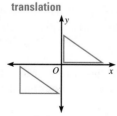

58. translation

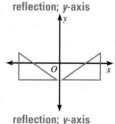

59. reflection; *y*-axis

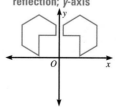

60.

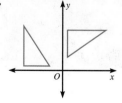

rotation; 180°

61. translation

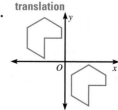

62. reflection; *y*-axis

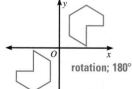

33.

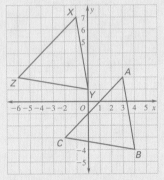

Chapter Test

Write the integer that represents the situation.

1. an increase of $20
$20

2. a profit of $5
$5

3. a loss of 10 meters
−10 m

4. 15 degrees below 0
−15 degrees

Order the integers from least to greatest.

5. −1, 9, −6, 3, 0
−6, −1, 0, 3, 9

6. 21, −22, 13, −14, 4
−22, −14, 4, 13, 21

7. −1, 10, −11, −111, 110
−111, −11, −1, 10, 110

Find the sum.

8. 3 + (−4) −1

9. 9 + (−9) 0

10. 15 + (−5) 10

11. −7 + 2 −5

12. −6 + 11 5

13. −1 + (−1) −2

14. −8 + (−10) −18

15. −12 + (−12) −24

Find the difference.

16. 8 − 9 −1

17. 2 − 12 −10

18. −6 − 10 −16

19. −15 − 15 −30

20. 8 − (−18) 26

21. 5 − (−13) 18

22. −14 − (−7) −7

23. −10 − (−20) 10

Find the product or quotient.

24. 5(−5) −25

25. 8(−9) −72

26. −7(4) −28

27. −3(6) −18

28. 44 ÷ (−2) −22

29. −54 ÷ 9 −6

30. −42 ÷ (−6) 7

31. −10 ÷ (−10) 1

32. Temperature On Monday at noon, the temperature was 23°F. By 9 P.M., the temperature was −4°F. On Tuesday at noon, the temperature was 18°F. By 9 P.M. the temperature was −11°F. On which day did the greater change in temperature occur? Tuesday

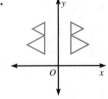

33. Graph the points $A(3, 2)$, $B(4, −4)$, and $C(−2, −3)$. Then translate $\triangle ABC$ 4 units to the left and 5 units up to form $\triangle XYZ$. Give the coordinates of points X, Y, and Z. See margin for art; $X(−1, 7)$, $Y(0, 1)$, $Z(−6, 2)$.

Tell whether the transformation is a *translation*, a *reflection*, or a *rotation*. If it is a reflection, identify the line of reflection. If it is a rotation, state the angle of rotation.

34. rotation; 90°

35. translation

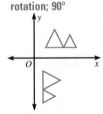

36. reflection; *y*-axis

Chapter Standardized Test

Test-Taking Strategy Don't rush through easy questions. You want to avoid making careless errors.

Multiple Choice

1. What number would you use to represent a decrease of 9 in.? **B**

A. -12 B. -9

C. 3   D. 9

2. Which expression has a value of -3? **G**

F. $9 + (-6)$ G. $-9 + 6$

H. $6 + 9$ I. $-6 + (-9)$

3. What is the value of $-5 - 9$? **A**

A. -14 B. -4 C. 4   D. 14

4. Which expression has a value that is the opposite of 1? **H**

F. $-20 - 19$ G. $-14 + 15$

H. $3 + (-4)$ I. $-9 + 10$

5. What is the value of $-16(-4)$? **D**

A. -64 B. -20 C. 20   D. 64

6. The table shows the temperatures of three of Saturn's moons. Find the mean of the temperatures. **H**

Mimas	$-328°F$
Enceladus	$-330°F$
Tethys	$-305°F$

F. $-330°F$ G. $-328°F$

H. $-321°F$ I. $25°F$

7. Which of the following is true? **B**

A. $-19 > 24$ B. $-5 < -4$

C. $45 < -45$ D. $-12 > -11$

8. Use the figure shown. If you add 2 to each x-coordinate and subtract 3 from each y-coordinate, what will be the coordinates of the vertices of the image? **G**

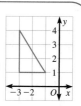

F. $(-5, 4), (-5, 1), (-3, 1)$

G. $(-1, 1), (-1, -2), (1, -2)$

H. $(-1, 1), (-1, -4), (1, -4)$

I. $(-6, 6), (-6, 3), (-4, 3)$

9. Which transformation shows a rotation? **D**

Short Response

10. The base of a 15 foot wall is at an elevation of -7 feet relative to sea level. Write and evaluate an addition expression to represent the elevation of the top of the wall.

$15 + (-7)$; 8 ft

Extended Response

11. Graph the points $A(-2, 4)$, $B(-3, 1)$, and $C(-1, 1)$ and connect them. Translate $\triangle ABC$ 4 units to the right to form $\triangle XYZ$. Give the coordinates of each vertex. Describe a different transformation of $\triangle ABC$ to $\triangle XYZ$.

See margin.

ADDITIONAL RESOURCES

 Assessment Book
• Standardized Chapter Test, p. 143

 Test and Practice Generator

11.

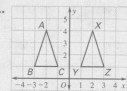

$X(2, 4), Y(1, 1), Z(3, 1)$; reflection over the y-axis

REGULAR SCHEDULE

Lesson	Les. Day	BASIC	AVERAGE	ADVANCED
12.1	Day 1	pp. 585–586 Exs. 11–20, 44–49	pp. 585–586 Exs. 11–21, 30–33, 44–49	pp. 585–586 Exs. 15–21, 30–33, 44, 49
	Day 2	pp. 585–586 Exs. 22–29, 34–38, 50	pp. 585–586 Exs. 22–29, 34–39, 50	pp. 585–586 Exs. 24–29, 34–43*, 50
12.2	Day 1	EP p. 710 Exs. 32, 33, 36, 37; pp. 590–591 Exs. 9–16, 27–34, 49–52	pp. 590–591 Exs. 9–14, 25–34, 49–51	pp. 590–591 Exs. 11–16, 27–31, 45–50*
	Day 2	pp. 590–591 Exs. 17–25, 35–42, 53–55	pp. 590–591 Exs. 17–22, 38–44, 52–56	pp. 590–591 Exs. 19–26, 38–44, 55, 56
12.3	Day 1	EP p. 710 Exs. 34, 35, 38, 39; pp. 594–595 Exs. 9–17, 26–28, 42–47	pp. 594–595 Exs. 9–17, 26–29, 42–47	pp. 594–595 Exs. 12–17, 26–29, 42–47
	Day 2	pp. 594–595 Exs. 18–24, 30–36, 48–52	pp. 594–595 Exs. 21–25, 30–38, 48–52	pp. 594–595 Exs. 21–25, 33–41*, 51, 52
12.4	Day 1	pp. 600–601 Exs. 9, 10, 12–19, 36–39, 43–47	pp. 600–601 Exs. 10, 12–19, 35–41, 52	pp. 600–601 Exs. 10, 14–19, 35–38, 43–48
	Day 2	pp. 600–601 Exs. 11, 20–31, 48–53	pp. 600–601 Exs. 11, 24–34, 45–48, 53	pp. 600–601 Exs. 11, 24–34, 39–42*, 52, 53
12.5	Day 1	pp. 607–609 Exs. 7–10, 15–17, 26–28, 31–35	pp. 607–609 Exs. 7–10, 17–19, 25–29, 31–35	pp. 607–609 Exs. 8–10, 16–19, 27–30*, 39–41
	Day 2	pp. 607–609 Exs. 11–14, 20–24, 36–41	pp. 607–609 Exs. 11–15, 20–24, 36–41	pp. 607–609 Exs. 12–15, 20–26, 31–33, 36
12.6	Day 1	EP p. 718 Exs. 42–46; pp. 615–616 Exs. 7–12, 17–19, 33–38	pp. 615–616 Exs. 7–12, 17–19, 29–31, 33–38	pp. 615–616 Exs. 9–16, 28–30, 35–38, 45
	Day 2	pp. 615–616 Exs. 13–16, 20–22, 24–28, 39–45	pp. 615–616 Exs. 14–16, 20–27, 39–46	pp. 615–616 Exs. 19–27, 31–34*, 39–41, 46
Review	Day 1	pp. 620–621 Exs. 1–62	pp. 620–621 Exs. 1–62	pp. 620–621 Exs. 1–62
Assess	Day 1	Chapter 12 Test	Chapter 12 Test	Chapter 12 Test

YEARLY PACING   Chapter 12 Total – **14 days**   Chapters 1–12 Total – **148 days**   Remaining – **12 days**

*Challenge Exercises   EP = Extra Practice   SRH = Skills Review Handbook   EC = Extra Challenge

BLOCK SCHEDULE

DAY 1	DAY 2	DAY 3	DAY 4	DAY 5	DAY 6	DAY 7
12.1 pp. 585–586 Exs. 11–39, 44–50	**12.2** pp. 590–591 Exs. 9–14, 17–22, 25–34, 38–44, 49–56	**12.3** pp. 594–595 Exs. 9–17, 21–38, 42–52	**12.4** pp. 600–601 Exs. 10–19, 24–41, 45–48, 52, 53	**12.5** pp. 607–609 Exs. 7–15, 17–29, 31–41	**12.6** pp. 615–616 Exs. 7–12, 14–27, 29–31, 33–46	**Review** pp. 620–621 Exs. 1–62 **Assess** Chapter 12 Test

YEARLY PACING   Chapter 12 Total – **7 days**   Chapters 1–12 Total – **74 days**   Remaining – **6 days**

Support Materials

📖 CHAPTER RESOURCE BOOK

CHAPTER SUPPORT

Tips for New Teachers	p. 1	Parents as Partners	p. 3

LESSON SUPPORT

	12.1	12.2	12.3	12.4	12.5	12.6
Lesson Plans (regular and block)	p. 7	p. 16	p. 24	p. 33	p. 41	p. 52
Technology Activities & Keystrokes				p. 43		
Activity Support Masters						
Activity Masters			p. 26			
Practice (3 levels)	p. 9	p. 18	p. 27	p. 35	p. 46	p. 54
Study Guide	p. 12	p. 21	p. 30	p. 38	p. 49	p. 57
Real-World Problem Solving	p. 14					p. 59
Challenge Practice	p. 15	p. 23	p. 32	p. 40	p. 51	p. 60

REVIEW

Games Support Masters	p. 5	Cooperative Project with Rubric	p. 64
Chapter Review Games and Activities	p. 61	Extra Credit Project with Rubric	p. 66
Real-Life Project with Rubric	p. 62	Cumulative Practice	p. 68
		Resource Book Answers	A1

📖 ASSESSMENT

Quizzes	p. 146	Alternative Assessments with Rubrics	p. 155
Chapter Tests (3 levels)	p. 148	Unit Test	p. 168
Standardized Test	p. 154	Cumulative Test	p. 170

🖨 TRANSPARENCIES

	12.1	12.2	12.3	12.4	12.5	12.6
Warm-Up / Daily Homework Quiz	✔	✔	✔	✔	✔	✔
Notetaking Guide	✔	✔	✔	✔	✔	✔
Teacher Support		✔		✔	✔	✔
English/Spanish Problem Solving			✔	✔		
Answer Transparencies	✔	✔	✔	✔	✔	✔

💻 TECHNOLOGY

- EasyPlanner CD-ROM
- Test and Practice Generator
- Electronic Lesson Presentations
- eTutorial CD-ROM
- Chapter Audio Summaries CDs
- Classzone.com
- eEdition Plus Online
- eWorkbook Plus Online
- eTutorial Plus Online
- EasyPlanner Plus Online

ADDITIONAL RESOURCES

- Worked-Out Solution Key
- Notetaking Guide
- Practice Workbook
- Tutor Place
- Professional Development Book
- Activities Book
- Poster Package
- Spanish Study Guide
- English/Spanish Chapter Reviews
- Multi-Language Glossary

Lesson 12.1

MATH BACKGROUND

WRITING EXPRESSIONS AND EQUATIONS In earlier chapters students evaluated expressions and solved equations by replacing a variable with numerical values. Here, they write algebraic expressions for English phrases and algebraic equations for sentences. To write a phrase as an expression, students need to be familiar with key words or groups of words that indicate the operations of arithmetic. To write an equation, they need to first write an expression and then equate that expression with a number or another expression.

TEACHING STRATEGIES

Write a word phrase on the board. Have students discuss what each word means. Then have students discuss how a phrase relates to an algebraic expression. Ask for volunteers to give examples of phrases that can be changed into algebraic expressions.

Help students break down the words, word phrases, and sentences into individual parts as they write expressions and equations. Students tend to focus on the first numbers presented and often subtract or add them without regard to the words used in the text. By underlining and identifying terms such as *combined*, *more than*, and *decreased by*, students will pinpoint the operations required.

Careful reading is also necessary to identify relationships among numbers. Contrast phrases such as "eight less than some number" and "some number less than eight" to emphasize the difference between the expressions $x - 8$ and $8 - x$.

Lesson 12.2

MATH BACKGROUND

SOLVING EQUATIONS When solving an equation, there are three important ideas to keep in mind. The first is to get the variable on one side of the equation by itself. To do this, employ the second idea, which is to use the inverse operation to undo what was done to the variable. The third idea is that an equation must be kept in balance by doing the same thing to both sides. Specifically, to solve an addition equation, use the inverse operation of subtraction. Subtracting the same number from both sides of the equation keeps the equation in balance and results in the variable being isolated on one side of the equation.

TEACHING STRATEGIES

At the concrete level, use markers or algebra tiles to show how to solve addition equations like $x + 4 = 8$. Show how to match the 4 markers on the left side with 4 markers on the right side. Then remove both groups of four, leaving 4 markers on the right. Discuss several examples with small numbers before moving to the more abstract level, where inverse operations can be used to solve equations.

Addition and subtraction are *inverse operations*. Remind students that the number being subtracted from one side of an addition equation must also be subtracted from the other side of the equation to produce a resulting equation that is "balanced," or equal.

Suggest that students write out the steps of their solutions and use colored pencils to help them show what is happening. Students can check their answers by substituting their result back into the original equation.

Lesson 12.3

MATH BACKGROUND

Just as subtraction is used to solve an addition equation, addition is used to solve a subtraction equation. Again, the equation must be kept in balance, so the same number must be *added* to both sides of the subtraction equation.

TEACHING STRATEGIES

Write an equation such as $x - 4 = 16$ on the board. Ask students what operation undoes subtraction and ask how they think the equation might be solved. Remind students to check the solution by substituting the value for x into the equation.

Lesson 12.4

MATH BACKGROUND

The idea of using inverse operations to solve addition and subtraction equations from the previous lessons can be applied to multiplication and division equations. Thus, to solve $3x = 12$, you isolate the variable by dividing both sides by 3 and to solve $\frac{x}{3} = 12$, you isolate the variable by multiplying both sides by 3.

TEACHING STRATEGIES

Write several equations such as $5x = 20$ and $\frac{a}{9} = 3$ on the board. Ask students what they could do to get the variable alone in each equation. Then ask them what they do to the side of the equation that does not contain the variable. Have students explain why this is necessary.

Lesson 12.5

MATH BACKGROUND

FUNCTIONS When students explore patterns and generalize relationships among numbers they are developing an informal understanding of functions. A **function** is a rule or correspondence from one set of numbers (the *domain*) to another set (the *range*). Like a relation, it is a set of ordered pairs. However, in a function, each input value may be paired with one and only one output value. Functions can be given as a *function rule*, which is an equation that relates two variables, or as an *input-output table*.

TEACHING STRATEGIES

Use tables like the ones below to show how function rules can be derived from input-output tables.

Square side length, s	Perimeter, P
1	4
2	8
3	12
4	16
5	20

From this table, develop the function rule $P = 4s$.

Circle diameter length, d	Circumference, C
1	3.14
2	6.28
3	9.42
4	12.56
5	15.70

From this table, develop the function rule $C = 3.14d$.

Lesson 12.6

MATH BACKGROUND

GRAPHS OF FUNCTIONS Functions can be represented by input-output tables, by function rules or equations, by sets of ordered pairs, or by graphs. A graph of a function is useful when you want to predict output values for input values not listed in a table or set of ordered pairs. **Linear functions** are functions whose graphs are straight non-vertical lines that have equations such as $y = 4x - 2$ or $y = 3.6$.

TEACHING STRATEGIES

Remind students of the first-quadrant graphing they learned in Chapter 2 and of the four-quadrant graphing they did in Chapter 11. Then work through an example like the following one to introduce graphing a linear function.

Example

Make an input-output table for the equation $y = 2x + 3$.

x	−2	0	2	4
y	−1	3	7	11

Use the ordered pairs (x, y) from the table to graph the function. Draw a straight line through the graphed points.

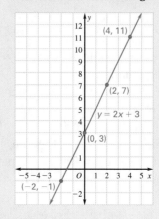

12 Differentiating Instruction

Strategies for Underachievers

ANTICIPATE PROBLEMS WITH VOCABULARY

Strong vocabulary development is an important element for success in translating between English phrases and sentences and algebraic expressions and equations, respectively. In Lesson 12.1, students should write all the entries in the table on page 583, along with any additional phrases, in a personal glossary.

You might suggest that students create a graphic organizer or note cards for organizing and learning this material. If using note cards, you may want to have students color code note cards related to the same operation. For example, one color group might contain all the phrases related to the operation of addition, another color for subtraction, and so on.

PROVIDE TOOLS FOR CONCRETE LEARNING

MANIPULATIVES In Lesson 12.2, the concept of an equation is presented as a balance. This is helpful for some students who will be able to visualize such a balance. Other students, however, may not be as proficient in doing so. These students should be exposed to equations in manipulative form. Each student should be given a set of algebra tiles to manipulate on their own as you present the Examples in Lesson 12.2. Translucent algebra tiles for the overhead projector are a good presentation tool for the teacher. Students who so desire should also be permitted to have these tiles available when completing their assignments and assessment.

USE SCAFFOLDING

In Lesson 12.2, some students may stumble or hesitate when first faced with an equation of the form $7 + x = 8$, rather than in the equivalent form $x + 7 = 8$. If you anticipate such difficulties for some of your students, you may wish to first review with them the concepts of the Commutative Property of Addition. Be sure that they are comfortable with the fact that $4 + 9$ and $9 + 4$, for example, yield the same sum. Encourage these students to use the Commutative Property whenever necessary. They can rewrite any equation such as $3 + x = 9$ as $x + 3 = 9$, if they are more comfortable with the latter form. You can again remind them in Lesson 12.4 of the Commutative Property of Multiplication. Be sure to caution students, however, that there is no commutative property of subtraction or division. Stress that the equation $y - 13 = 9$ is different than the equation $13 - y = 9$.

In Lessons 12.2 through 12.4, you may find that some students will need help with neatly organizing their work and showing the necessary steps. One simple solution is to have students draw a vertical line through the equal sign of each equation they solve, as in the example below.

$$\begin{array}{r} n + 17 = \ \ 41 \\ -17 \ \ \big| -17 \\ \hline n \ \ \big| = \ \ 24 \end{array}$$

Others students, even some who conceptually understand the idea of solving equations, may have difficulty showing the entire procedure required to solve an equation. You may wish to provide these students with a reference sheet showing the correct procedure for solving an equation for each of the four operations. Students should be allowed to model their work after this sheet until they are comfortable doing so on their own.

Strategies for English Learners

FOCUS ON KEY WORDS AND CONCEPTS

OPPOSITES In math class, you might review with students the concept of opposite, which is a key mathematical concept and a good way for English learners to learn and remember vocabulary. Start with some simple opposites such as *tall* and *short*, *in* and *out*, to make sure students have the concept. Then review with the following opposites, which are common and critical to the understanding of mathematics. Give students one word from each pair and ask them to supply the opposite.

odd : even; add : subtract; multiply : divide; sum : difference; plus : minus; positive : negative; true : false

When key words are introduced in each chapter, consider whether each one has an opposite, and, if so, teach it at the same time. Have students keep their lists of opposites in their math journal, and encourage students to draw a picture or write an explanation in their primary language to aid in recall.

Strategies for Advanced Learners

INCREASE DEPTH AND COMPLEXITY

In Lesson 12.4, students who have a well-developed number sense and who are proficient with fractions may be ready to use reciprocals to solve multiplication and division equations. The advantage to using a reciprocal to solve these two types of equations is that multiplying both sides of the equation by the reciprocal of the number by which the variable is multiplied, solves *both* types of equations. Take sufficient time to review multiplication and division of fractions. Be sure that students understand that dividing by 5 is the same as multiplying by $\frac{1}{5}$. Students can then solve the equation $5x = 20$ in the following way.

$$\frac{1}{5} \cdot \frac{5x}{1} = \frac{20}{1} \cdot \frac{1}{5}$$

Equations such as $12 = \frac{d}{8}$ given as Your turn now Exercise 8 on page 599 can be rewritten as $12 = \frac{1}{8}d$. This equation can then be solved by multiplying both sides by 8, which is the reciprocal of $\frac{1}{8}$.

As a challenging activity for **Lesson 12.4**, have students solve the following equations.

- **Challenge** Solve.

  a. $\frac{2}{3}x = 8$ **b.** $\frac{3}{4}x = 15$ **c.** $\frac{4}{5}x = 20$ **d.** $\frac{3}{5}x = 9$

         12   20   25   15

In **Hands-on Activity 12.5**, some students could be challenged with more complex expressions that involve more than one operation.

- **Challenge** Find an expression for each input-output table.

a. $2x + 3$

x	y
0	3
2	7
4	11
6	15

b. $3x - 5$

x	y
2	1
3	4
5	10
6	13

In Problem Solving Strategies 12.6, students can look for patterns that are created by these more complex expressions.

12 Differentiating Instruction: Teaching Resources

Differentiating Technology

McDougal Littell *Middle School Mathematics* offers teachers a wide variety of technology, ranging from calculator activities in the *Chapter Resource Books* to the *Test and Practice Generator CD-ROM* to interactive, online resources and products accessed at Classzone.com.

CLASSZONE.COM

Classzone.com provides helpful online resources for students and teachers, including More Examples, Vocabulary Support, and State Test Practice. Classzone.com is also the access point for the following online products: *eEdition Plus Online*, an interactive, online version of the textbook; *eWorkbook Plus Online*, an interactive practice workbook correlated to the textbook; *eTutorial Plus Online*, an Internet tutorial that makes it easier than ever to help students master skills and concepts; and *EasyPlanner Plus Online*, an online resource with teacher tools and a lesson planner.

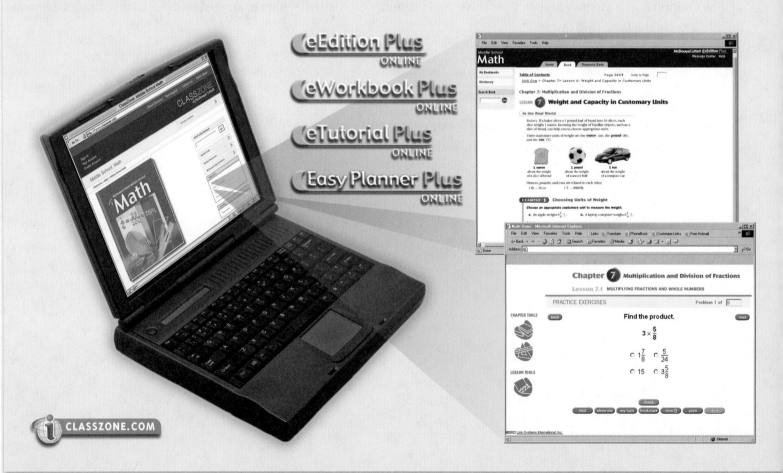

TEST AND PRACTICE GENERATOR CD-ROM

The *Test and Practice Generator* can be used to create numerous practice sheets and quizzes for each lesson and tests for each chapter using both static and algorithmic exercises. Information about creating and editing questions is provided.

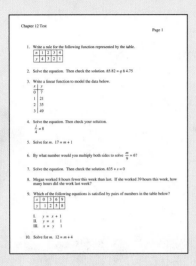

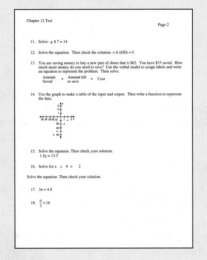

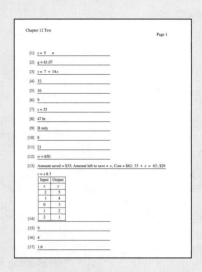

RESOURCE BOOK

The *Chapter Resource Books* contain technology activities that are different from the activities given in the textbook. Also included, where appropriate, are calculator keystrokes that can be used to do the technology activities and exercises that appear in the textbook and in the *Chapter Resource Books*.

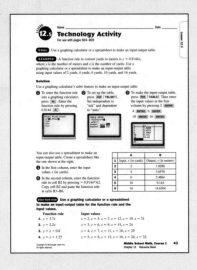

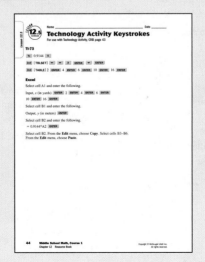

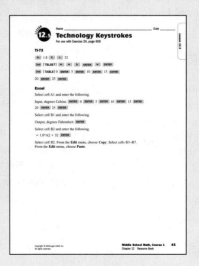

580

OVERVIEW

MAIN IDEAS

In this chapter, students first write variable expressions and equations. They then solve one-step equations by undoing operations in order to isolate the variable. Also, students are introduced to the concept of a function, and they explore that idea using input-output tables as well as ordered pairs, function rules, and graphs.

PREREQUISITE SKILLS

The key skills reviewed in the game on these pages are:
- Evaluating algebraic expressions
- Rounding mixed numbers to the nearest whole number

Additional practice with prerequisite skills can be found in the Review What You Need to Know exercises on page 582. Additional resources for reviewing prerequisite skills are:
- Skills Review Handbook, pp. 684–707
- Tutor Place
- eTutorial Plus

MANAGING THE GAME

Tips for Success

Be sure students can apply the order of operations so they know, for example, that $\frac{1}{2}(4) + 1 = 2 + 1 = 3$ and not $\frac{1}{2}(5) = 2\frac{1}{2}$.

Reflecting on the Game

Ask students to decide which player will win if all players are skillful at evaluating expressions. Lead them to see that the luck of the roll is a factor in winning.

CHAPTER 12
Equations and Functions

BEFORE

In previous chapters you've...
- Used geometry formulas
- Evaluated expressions

Now

In Chapter 12 you'll study...
- Writing expressions and equations
- Solving equations
- Representing functions using tables, equations, and graphs

WHY?

So you can solve real-world problems about...
- the Grand Canyon, p. 586
- shopping, p. 589
- cheerleading, p. 599
- hurricanes, p. 601
- giant pandas, p. 605

Internet Preview
CLASSZONE.COM
- eEdition Plus Online
- eWorkbook Plus Online
- eTutorial Plus Online
- State Test Practice
- More Examples

Chapter Warm-Up Game

Review skills you need for this chapter in this game. Work with a partner.

Key Skill:
Evaluating expressions

EXPRESSION RACE

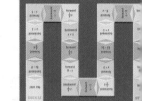

MATERIALS
- *Expression Race* game board
- 1 number cube
- 1 place marker for each player

PREPARE Each player puts a place marker on the START space. Take turns. On your turn, follow the steps on page 581.

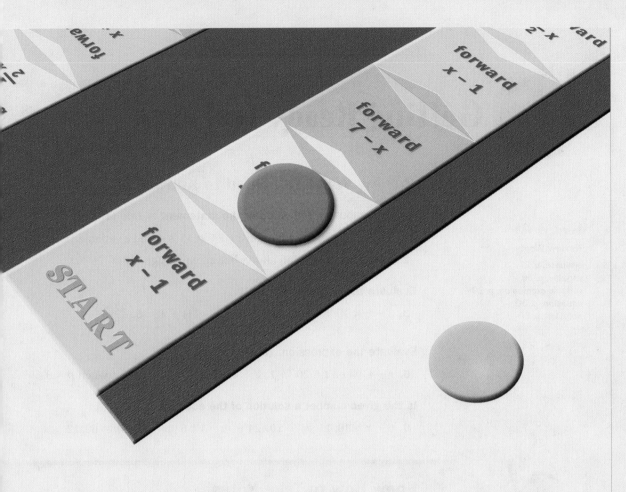

forward
x − 1

forward
7 − x

forward
x − 1

START

 Chapter 12 Resource Book
- Tips for New Teachers, pp. 1–2
- Lesson Plan, pp. 7, 16, 24, 33, 41, 52
- Lesson Plan for Block Scheduling, pp. 8, 17, 25, 34, 42, 53

 Technology
- EasyPlanner CD-ROM
- Test and Practice Generator
- Electronic Lesson Presentations CD-ROM
- eTutorial CD-ROM

 Internet
- Classzone
- eEdition Plus Online
- eWorkbook Plus Online
- eTutorial Plus Online
- EasyPlanner Plus Online

ENGLISH LEARNER SUPPORT

- Spanish Study Guide
- Multi-Language Glossary
- Chapter Audio Summaries CDs
- Teacher's Edition, pp. 580E–580F

 ROLL the number cube. The number you roll is the *x*-value for the expression on the space your marker is on.

 EVALUATE the expression on your space for the *x*-value you rolled. If the result is a fraction, round to the nearest whole number. **Check work.**

MOVE your marker forward or backward the same number of spaces as your result from Step 2.

HOW TO WIN

Be the first player to land on the FINISH space, or be closest to the FINISH space after a set period of time.

Stop *and* Think   1. 1; the value of the expression will be the greatest.

1. **Writing** If you are on the space labeled "Forward 13 − 2x," what is the best number to roll? Explain your thinking.

2. **Critical Thinking** If you rolled a 2 on every turn, would you ever get to the FINISH space? Explain why or why not. What if you rolled a 3 on every turn?
No; you would get stuck going back and forth between the "forward $x − 1$" and "backward $\frac{1}{2}x$" squares; yes.

581

Review What You Need to Know

The Review What You Need to Know exercises can help you diagnose whether students have the following skills needed in Chapter 12:

- Use vocabulary (Exs. 1–2)
- Use the order of operations (Exs. 3–5)
- Evaluate variable expressions (Exs. 6–8)
- Solve equations (Exs. 9–11)

 Chapter 12 Resource Book
- Study Guide (Lessons 12.1–12.6)

 Tutor Place

NOTETAKING STRATEGIES

Students can use flow charts to show the steps of a variety of processes. In Lesson 12.2, for example, they can make a flow chart showing how to solve addition equations. Their steps should include: 1) write the original equation; 2) subtract the number that is added to the variable from both sides of the equation; 3) simplify the expression on each side of the equation; 4) check the solution in the original equation. Further suggestions for keeping a notebook can be found on page 613.

For more support on notetaking, see:
- Notetaking Guide Workbook
- Notetaking Transparencies

Getting Ready to Learn

Word Watch

Review Words

evaluate, p. 21
variable, p. 29
variable expression, p. 29
equation, p. 36
solution, p. 36

Review What You Need to Know

Using Vocabulary **Tell whether the statement is *true* or *false*.**

1. The letter a in the equation $2a + 5 = 15$ is called a variable. **true**

2. A variable expression always has an equal sign. **false**

Evaluate the expression. *(p. 21)*

3. $3 + 9 \times 10$ **93**
4. $15 \div (14 - 11) + 42$ **47**
5. $\dfrac{12 \times 5}{30 \div 3}$ **6**

Evaluate the expression. *(p. 29)*

6. $t + 4$, when $t = 20$ **24**
7. $z \div 4$, when $z = 16$ **4**
8. $7p$, when $p = 8$ **56**

Is the given number a solution of the equation? *(p. 36)*

9. $6 + x = 19; 11$ **no**
10. $24 - m = 17; 6$ **no**
11. $5n = 60; 12$ **yes**

You should include material that appears on a notebook like this in your own notes.

Know How to Take Notes

Making a Flow Chart You can show a mathematical process in your notes using a flow chart like the one below for the order of operations.

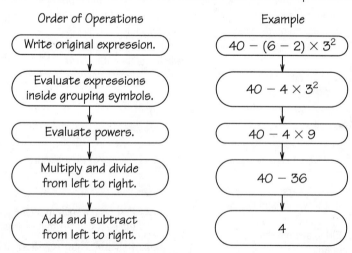

Order of Operations | Example

- Write original expression. → $40 - (6 - 2) \times 3^2$
- Evaluate expressions inside grouping symbols. → $40 - 4 \times 3^2$
- Evaluate powers. → $40 - 4 \times 9$
- Multiply and divide from left to right. → $40 - 36$
- Add and subtract from left to right. → 4

In Lesson 12.6, you can use a flow chart to remember the steps for identifying linear equations.

LESSON 12.1

Writing Expressions and Equations

BEFORE You evaluated numerical and variable expressions.

Now You'll write variable expressions and equations.

WHY? So you can find the time left on a videotape, as in Ex. 38.

Word Watch

Review Words
variable expression, p. 29
equation, p. 36

In the Real World

Art Show Your school's art show has *x* pieces in it. You expect to add 3 pieces. What will be the total number of pieces in the show? You will see a way to express the total in Example 1.

To write phrases and sentences as variable expressions or equations, look for key words that indicate addition, subtraction, multiplication, or division.

Addition	Subtraction	Multiplication	Division
plus	minus	times	divided by
the sum of	the difference of	the product of	the quotient of
increased by	decreased by	multiplied by	
total	fewer than	of	
more than	less than		
added to	subtracted from		

EXAMPLE 1 Expressions: Adding and Subtracting

Write the phrase as an expression. Let *x* represent the number.

Phrase	Expression
3 pieces added to *x* pieces in the show	$x + 3$
The sum of 4 and a number	$4 + x$
The difference of 12 and a number	$12 - x$
9 less than the number of boys	$x - 9$

 **Your turn now** Write the phrase as a variable expression.

1. 16 decreased by a number *d*
$16 - d$
2. The total of 10 and a number *n*
$10 + n$
3. A number *h* increased by 15
$h + 15$
4. 10 subtracted from a number *m*
$m - 10$
5. Four fewer than a number *g*
$g - 4$
6. Seven more than a number *k*
$k + 7$

Lesson 12.1   Writing Expressions and Equations   **583**

① PLAN

SKILL CHECK
Evaluate when $x = 2$.
1. $16x$ — 32
2. $x + (-3)$ — -1
3. $27 \div x$ — 13.5
4. $x - 4.5$ — -2.5

LESSON OBJECTIVE
Write variable expressions and equations.

PACING
Suggested Number of Days
Basic Course: 2 days
Average Course: 2 days
Advanced Course: 2 days
Block: 1 block

TEACHING RESOURCES
For a complete list of Teaching Resources, see page 580B.

 **TRANSPARENCY**
Warm-Up Exercises for this lesson are available on a transparency.

② TEACH

MOTIVATING THE LESSON
Ask students how they could use mathematical expressions to describe aspects of their daily lives.

TIPS FOR NEW TEACHERS
Be sure students can recognize and write the symbol for each of the four arithmetic operations. See the Tips for New Teachers in the *Chapter 12 Resource Book*.

CONCEPT CHECK

What are some of the key words that indicate addition, subtraction, multiplication, and division? *Plus*, *total*, and *more than* for addition; *minus*, *difference*, and *less than* for subtraction; *times* and *product* for multiplication; *divided by* and *quotient of* for division.

 DAILY PUZZLER

The sum of a number y and itself is equal to the quotient of the same number and itself. Write an equation to model that situation. Then find the value of y. $y + y = \frac{y}{y}$ or $2y = 1$;
The value of y is 0.5.

Watch Out!
Order is important with subtraction and division. "The quotient of a number and 6" means $\frac{y}{6}$, not $\frac{6}{y}$.

EXAMPLE 2 **Expressions: Multiplying and Dividing**

Write the phrase as an expression. Let y represent the number.

Phrase	Expression
The **product of** 5 and the number of girls	$5 \cdot y$, or $5y$
8 **multiplied by** a number	$y \cdot 8$, or $8y$
The **quotient of** a number and 6	$\frac{y}{6}$
24 **divided by** the number of hours	$\frac{24}{y}$

Writing Equations To translate a sentence into an equation, look for key words like *is* or *equals* to find the place for the equal sign.

EXAMPLE 3 **Writing Simple Equations**

Write the sentence as an equation.

Sentence	Equation
A number x minus 5 **is** 12.	$x - 5 = 12$
15 times a number y **is** 75.	$15y = 75$

EXAMPLE 4 **Modeling a Situation**

Restaurant Three friends share the cost of a dinner equally. The cost of the dinner is $27. Write a multiplication equation that you could use to find the amount a that each friend pays.

Solution

Number of friends $\cdot$ Amount each pays $=$ Total cost

$$3a = 27$$

Your turn now In Exercises 7–10, write the sentence as an equation.

7. A number n added to 4 is 11.

8. The quotient of x and 96 is 8.

9. A number p times 3 is 36.

10. Twelve minus a number q is 2.

11. Today's high temperature of 59°F is 3°F less than yesterday's high temperature t. Write a subtraction equation you could use to find t.

7. $n + 4 = 11$
8. $\frac{x}{96} = 8$
9. $3p = 36$
10. $12 - q = 2$
11. $t - 3 = 59$

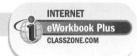

Getting Ready to Practice

1. Vocabulary The phrase *decreased by* represents the operation of ? .

subtraction

Write the phrase as an expression. Let x represent the number.

2. 13 more than a number $x + 13$

3. A number times 7 $7x$

4. A number divided by 16 $\frac{x}{16}$

5. 21 minus a number $21 - x$

In Exercises 6–9, write the sentence as an equation.

7. $\frac{h}{6} = 2$

6. A number y added to 4 is 7.
$4 + y = 7$

7. A number h divided by 6 is 2.

8. 6 times a number t is 42.
$6t = 42$

9. The difference of s and 32 is 6.
$s - 32 = 6$

10. Test Scores You have 29 correct answers on a test, which is four more correct answers than Sara has. Write an equation you could use to find s, the number of correct answers Sara has. *Sample answer: $s + 4 = 29$*

Practice and Problem Solving

25. $\frac{32}{r} = 2$

30–33. Sample answers are given.

30. a number n plus 4

31. 7 less than a number y

32. the product of 8 and a number r

33. a number d divided by 3

Write the phrase as an expression. Let x represent the number.

A 11. A number divided by 9 $\frac{x}{9}$

12. A number decreased by 4 $x - 4$

13. 16 subtracted from a number
$x - 16$

14. The total of 17 and a number
$17 + x$

15. 20 multiplied by a number $20x$

16. The quotient of a number and 2 $\frac{x}{2}$

17. A number increased by 18 $x + 18$

18. 10 minus a number $10 - x$

19. 27 less than a number $x - 27$

20. The product of 6 and a number $6x$

21. Writing Explain how the phrases representing the expressions $y - 2$ and $2 - y$ are different. *Sample answer: $y - 2$ means 2 less than y, while $2 - y$ means y less than 2.*

Write the sentence as an equation.

22. 11 fewer than a number k is 3.
$k - 11 = 3$

23. A number n plus 6 is 30.
$n + 6 = 30$

24. A number c times 15 is 90.
$15c = 90$

25. 32 divided by a number r is 2.
See margin.

26. The sum of 9 and q is 15.
$9 + q = 15$

27. The product of x and 3 is 123.
$3x = 123$

28. The quotient of 50 and w is 10.
$\frac{50}{w} = 10$

29. A number t decreased by 4 is 26.
$t - 4 = 26$

Write a phrase for the variable expression. 30–33. See margin.

B 30. $n + 4$

31. $y - 7$

32. $8r$

33. $\frac{d}{3}$

with Homework

Example	Exercises
1	11–21
2	11–20
3	22–29
4	34–38

Online Resources
CLASSZONE.COM

· More Examples
· eTutorial Plus

③ **APPLY**

ASSIGNMENT GUIDE

Basic Course
Day 1: pp. 585–586 Exs. 11–20, 44–49
Day 2: pp. 585–586 Exs. 22–29, 34–38, 50

Average Course
Day 1: pp. 585–586 Exs. 11–21, 30–33, 44–49
Day 2: pp. 585–586 Exs. 22–29, 34–39, 50

Advanced Course
Day 1: pp. 585–586 Exs. 15–21, 30–33, 44, 49
Day 2: pp. 585–586 Exs. 24–29, 34–43*, 50

Block
pp. 585–586 Exs. 11–39, 44–50

EXTRA PRACTICE

• Student Edition, p. 719
• Chapter 12 Resource Book, pp. 9–11
• Test and Practice Generator

TRANSPARENCY

Even-numbered answers are available on transparencies.

HOMEWORK CHECK

When you review students' homework for this lesson, go over the following exercises to check understanding of key concepts.
Basic: 11, 13, 17, 22, 34
Average: 15, 17, 18, 23, 35
Advanced: 17, 20, 24, 36, 38

TEACHING TIP

For Exercises 22–29, ask students to start by separating each sentence into three parts: the word "is"; the phrase (or number) on one side of "is"; and the number on the other side of "is."

4 ASSESS

ASSESSMENT RESOURCES

For more assessment resources, see:
- Assessment Book
- Test and Practice Generator

MINI-QUIZ

1. Write each phrase as an expression. Let t represent the number.
   a. 5 fewer than a number $t - 5$
   b. the product of a number and 6 $6t$

2. Write the sentence as an equation.
   a. A number z more than 3 is 5. $3 + z = 5$
   b. 18 divided by a number w is 4.5. $\frac{18}{w} = 4.5$

3. You have read 195 pages of a book, which is 23 pages fewer than the total number t of pages in the book. Write an equation to find t. $t - 23 = 195$

5 FOLLOW-UP

RETEACHING/REMEDIATION

- Study Guide in Chapter 12 Resource Book, pp. 12–13
- Tutor Place, Algebra Cards 1, 7
- eTutorial Plus Online
- Extra Practice, p. 719
- Lesson Practice in Chapter 12 Resource Book, pp. 9–11

CHALLENGE/ENRICHMENT

- Challenge Practice in Chapter 12 Resource Book, p. 15
- Teacher's Edition, p. 580F

ENGLISH LEARNER SUPPORT

- Spanish Study Guide
- Multi-Language Glossary
- Chapter Audio Summaries CDs

40–44. See Additional Answers beginning on page AA1.

586

What do you think?
Recreation

■ **Grand Canyon**

In the Grand Canyon, the temperature increases as you go down. When it is 75°F at the top of the canyon, it might be 110°F at the bottom. What is the change in the temperature? 35°F

INTERNET
State Test Practice
CLASSZONE.COM

Interpret In Exercises 34–37, match the situation with the equation that describes it.

A. $x - 8 = 24$ B. $8x = 24$ C. $8 + x = 24$ D. $\frac{x}{8} = 24$

34. You have $8. How much more do you need to make a $24 purchase? C

35. You pay $24 for shoes after an $8 discount. What was the original price? A

36. The total cost of tickets for a concert is split equally among 8 friends, with each paying $24. What is the total cost of the tickets? D

37. You earn $24 for eight hours of work. How much do you earn per hour? B

38. **Videotape** You record 95 minutes of material on a videotape. The tape can fit 120 minutes of material. Write an addition equation you could use to find m, the number of minutes left on the tape. $95 + m = 120$

39. **Grand Canyon** In Grand Canyon National Park, the elevation of the North Kaibab trailhead is 8241 feet. The elevation of Bright Angel Camp is 2400 feet. Write two equations you could use to find c, the difference in elevation between the trailhead and Bright Angel Camp.
$2400 + c = 8241; \ 8241 - c = 2400$

Challenge Write a sentence about a real-world situation that could be represented by the equation. 40–43. See margin.

C 40. $6 + y = 20$ 41. $k - 25 = 60$ 42. $4m = 32$ 43. $\frac{r}{5} = 25$

Mixed Review

44. Graph each figure. Then tell whether Figure 2 is a reflection of Figure 1. If it is a reflection, identify the line of reflection. *(Lesson 11.7)*
   See margin.
   Figure 1: $A(-1, 1), B(-3, 0), C(-3, 4)$ **Figure 2:** $P(1, 1), Q(3, 0), R(3, 4)$

Basic Skills Solve the equation using mental math.

45. $d + 6 = 15$ 9   46. $45 - f = 10$ 35   47. $8g = 88$ 11   48. $48 \div x = 6$ 8

Test-Taking Practice

49. **Multiple Choice** Which of the following can represent "twelve more than seventeen bicycles"? B

   A. $17 - 12$ B. $17 + 12$ C. $12 > 17$ D. $17 \div 12$

50. **Multiple Choice** Nathan has 12 video games. He receives more for his birthday. He now has 28 video games. Which equation could you use to find v, the number of video games he receives for his birthday? F

   F. $12 + v = 28$ G. $12 - v = 28$ H. $12v = 28$ I. $\frac{28}{v} = 12$

12.2 Hands-on Activity

GOAL
Use algebra tiles to solve addition equations.

MATERIALS
· algebra tiles

Algebra Tiles

You can solve some simple equations using these two types of algebra tiles.

x-tile

Represents the variable x.

1-tile

Represents positive 1.

Explore   Use algebra tiles to solve the equation $x + 3 = 7$.

① Represent the equation using an x-tile and ten 1-tiles.

② To solve the equation, you must get the x-tile by itself on one side. You can take away three 1-tiles from each side. By taking away the same amount on each side, you keep the two sides equal.

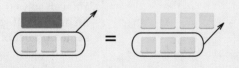

③ Notice that one x-tile remains on the left side and four 1-tiles remain on the right side. So, $x = 4$.

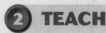

Your turn now   Use algebra tiles to solve the equation.

1. $x + 2 = 3$ **1** **2.** $x + 3 = 6$ **3** **3.** $x + 1 = 4$ **3** **4.** $x + 4 = 8$ **4**

5. $1 + x = 7$ **6** **6.** $4 + x = 7$ **3** **7.** $2 + x = 9$ **7** **8.** $3 + x = 5$ **2**

Stop and Think

 9. **Writing** Describe how you could solve equations like those in Exercises 1–8 without using algebra tiles.
Subtract the number that is with the x from both sides of the equation.

NCTM CURRICULUM STANDARDS
Standard 1: Understand meanings of operations
Standard 2: Use models to understand relationships; Use models to represent relationships

Lesson 12.2   Solving Addition Equations   **587**

① **PLAN**

EXPLORE THE CONCEPT
• Students use algebra tiles to solve addition equations.
• This Activity is used again in Example 1 of Lesson 12.2.

MATERIALS
Each student or group of students will need a set of algebra tiles. A support transparency is available for this Activity.

RECOMMENDED TIME
Work activity: 15 min
Discuss results: 5 min

GROUPING
Students can work individually or in groups of two. If students work in pairs, they can take turns choosing the tiles for the equation and removing the tiles to solve the equation.

② **TEACH**

TIPS FOR SUCCESS
Have students describe each of steps 1, 2, and 3 algebraically. That will prepare them for the series of solution steps in Example 2 of Lesson 12.2.

③ **CLOSE**

KEY DISCOVERY
To solve addition equations, you remove the same number of tiles from both sides.

ASSESSMENT
Solve the equation.
1. $5 + x = 10$ **5**
2. $8 = 7 + x$ **1**

587

SKILL CHECK

1. $25 - \underline{\ ?\ } = 0$ 25
2. $13.2 - \underline{\ ?\ } = 0$ 13.2
3. $4\frac{1}{3} - \underline{\ ?\ } = 0$ $4\frac{1}{3}$

LESSON OBJECTIVE

Solve one-step addition equations.

PACING

Suggested Number of Days
Basic Course: 2 days
Average Course: 2 days
Advanced Course: 2 days
Block: 1 block

TEACHING RESOURCES

For a complete list of Teaching Resources, see page 580B.

 TRANSPARENCY

Warm-Up Exercises for this lesson are available on a transparency.

2 TEACH

MOTIVATING THE LESSON

For real-life actions such as buttoning a coat, ask students to describe the reverse action. Then have them discuss what mathematical action will reverse adding a number to a variable.

TIPS FOR NEW TEACHERS

Be sure students understand that when an equation is written "$x = $," then the other side of the equation is the solution. See the Tips for New Teachers in the *Chapter 12 Resource Book.*

Solving Addition Equations

LESSON 12.2

BEFORE	▶ Now	WHY?
You solved equations using mental math.	You'll solve one-step addition equations.	So you can find the cost of time on a parking meter, as in Ex. 25.

 **Word Watch**

Review Words
variable, p. 29
solution, p. 36
solve, p. 37

Algebra Tiles One way to solve addition equations is to use algebra tiles.

An *x*-tile represents the variable *x*.   **A 1-tile represents positive 1.**

You can model an equation by imagining that tiles are placed on a balance scale, as shown below.

$$x + 2 \ = \ 4$$

You can solve the equation by removing tiles until the *x*-tile is by itself on one side. If you remove tiles from one side, you must remove the same number of tiles from the other side to keep the scale balanced.

EXAMPLE 1   **Solving Equations Using Algebra Tiles**

Use algebra tiles to solve $x + 2 = 4$.

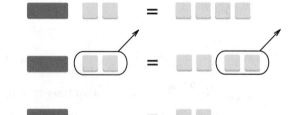

(1 Represent the equation using algebra tiles.

(2 Take away two 1-tiles from each side.

(3 The remaining tiles show that the value of *x* is 2.

ANSWER The solution is 2.

Your turn now   Use algebra tiles to solve the equation.

1. $x + 1 = 5$ 4   **2.** $x + 3 = 9$ 6   **3.** $4 + x = 4$ 0   **4.** $7 + x = 8$ 1

NCTM CURRICULUM STANDARDS
Standard 2: Represent situations using algebraic symbols; Analyze situations using algebraic symbols; Use models to represent relationships

The idea behind the algebra tile method can be used to solve equations with numbers that are hard to model with tiles.

Solving Addition Equations

To solve an addition equation, subtract the same number from each side so that the variable is by itself on one side.

EXAMPLE 2 Solving an Addition Equation

Solve the equation $y + 25 = 140$.

$$
\begin{aligned}
y + 25 &= 140 && \text{Write the original equation.} \\
\underline{-25} \quad &\underline{-25} && \text{Subtract 25 from each side.} \\
y &= 115 && \text{Simplify.}
\end{aligned}
$$

✓ **Check** $y + 25 = 140$ Write the original equation.

$115 + 25 \overset{?}{=} 140$ Substitute 115 for y.

$140 = 140$ ✓   Solution checks.

with Solving

After solving an equation, you should always check your solution.

EXAMPLE 3 Using an Addition Equation

Shopping You buy some clothing that costs $17.45. What is the amount of change c that the clerk should give you if you pay with a $20 bill?

Solution

$\text{Cost} + \text{Change} = \text{Amount paid}$ Write a verbal model.

$$
\begin{aligned}
17.45 + c &= 20.00 && \text{Write an equation.} \\
\underline{-17.45} \quad &\underline{-17.45} && \text{Subtract 17.45 from each side.} \\
c &= 2.55 && \text{Simplify.}
\end{aligned}
$$

ANSWER The clerk should give you $2.55 in change.

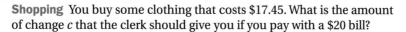 **Solve the equation. Then check the solution.**

5. $p + 24 = 88$ 64   **6.** $15 + q = 105$ 90   **7.** $r + 39 = 76$ 37

8. $s + 2.5 = 10.7$ 8.2   **9.** $8.35 + t = 10.55$ 2.2   **10.** $u + 1.85 = 50$ 48.15

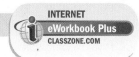
INTERNET
eWorkbook Plus
CLASSZONE.COM

Getting Ready to Practice

Vocabulary Tell whether the given number is a solution of the equation.

1. $x + 3 = 8; 5$ yes   **2.** $x + 1.1 = 3.7; 2.6$ yes **3.** $3.5 + x = 3.5; 3.5$ no

Solve the equation. Then check the solution.

4. $x + 5 = 7$ 2   **5.** $m + 9 = 15$ 6 **6.** $6 + y = 6$ 0   **7.** $15 + p = 50$ 35

8. Guided Problem Solving A video game has 16 levels. You have reached level 5. Write and solve an addition equation to find the number of levels you have left.

  ① What is the unknown value? Choose a variable to represent it.

  ② Write an equation using the information in the problem.

  ③ Solve the equation. Check your solution.

8. **Step 1:** The number of levels you have left.
Sample answer: n

Step 2: $5 + n = 16$

Step 3: 11

Practice and Problem Solving

Solve the equation.

A **9.** $x + 1 = 8$ 7   **10.** $x + 5 = 11$ 6   **11.** $x + 2 = 2$ 0   **12.** $4 + x = 9$ 5

13. $10 + x = 15$ 5 **14.** $6 + x = 13$ 7   **15.** $4 + x = 20$ 16 **16.** $x + 3 = 18$ 15

17. $a + 13 = 26$ 13 **18.** $b + 22 = 40$ 18 **19.** $d + 27 = 34$ 7 **20.** $c + 35 = 35$ 0

21. $42 + g = 70$ 28 **22.** $17 + h = 66$ 49 **23.** $j + 68 = 100$ 32 **24.** $k + 8 = 73$ 65

25. Parking Meter You have 10 minutes left at a parking meter. After you put in a quarter, you have 25 minutes left. Write and solve an addition equation to find q, the number of minutes a quarter is worth.

$10 + q = 25; 15$ min

26. Find the Error Describe and correct the error in the solution of the equation $b + 6 = 18$.
6 should be subtracted from each side.
The solution should be: $b + 6 = 18$
$\underline{\quad -6 = -6}$
$b \quad = 12$

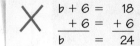

$$\begin{aligned} b + 6 &= \quad 18 \\ + 6 &= +6 \\ \hline b \quad &= \quad 24 \end{aligned}$$

The solution is 24.

Estimation Estimate the solution of the equation. 27–28. Estimates may vary.

B **27.** $x + 3\frac{6}{7} = 27\frac{24}{25}$ 24   **28.** $y + 10\frac{1}{12} = 24\frac{13}{15}$ 15

With **Homework**

Example   Exercises
1   9–16
2   9–24, 26
3   25

Online Resources
CLASSZONE.COM
· More Examples
· eTutorial Plus

Choose a Method Solve the equation. Tell whether you used *algebra tiles*, *mental math*, or *paper and pencil*. **29–40. Methods may vary.**

29. $x + 3 = 9$ **6**

30. $y + 25 = 80$ **55**

31. $z + 5.6 = 8.3$ **2.7**

32. $q + 8 = 12$ **4**

33. $20 + p = 37$ **17**

34. $0.08 + r = 1.28$ **1.2**

35. $m + 3.7 = 9.9$ **6.2**

36. $n + 0.8 = 1.5$ **0.7**

37. $9.5 + d = 14.3$ **4.8**

38. $1.4 + a = 2.2$ **0.8**

39. $0.3 + b = 2$ **1.7**

40. $4 + c = 4$ **0**

41. Geometry The perimeter of the triangle shown is 11.1 kilometers. Write and solve an addition equation to find the length of the third side. $3.6 + 2.55 + x = 11.1$; 4.95 km

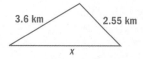
3.6 km   2.55 km   x

Extended Problem Solving **Lois is training for a marathon. Her goal is to travel 28 miles for the week.**

42. Mental Math Lois travels 6 miles on Monday, 8 miles on Wednesday, and 6 miles on Thursday. How many miles has she traveled so far? **20 mi**

43. Use Exercise 42 to write an addition equation you could use to find the number of miles Lois has left to travel to meet her goal. $20 + m = 28$

44. Explain Solve the equation you wrote in Exercise 43. Explain how to check your solution. **8 mi; add 20 and 8, if the sum is 28, the solution is correct.**

Challenge Solve the equation.

C 45. $x + 5 = 4$ **−1**

46. $10 + x = -4$ **−14**

47. $3 + x = -7$ **−10**

48. $-3 + x = 9$ **12**

Mixed Review

49. Prime; its only factors are 1 and itself.

49. Tell whether 97 is *prime* or *composite*. Explain. *(Lesson 5.1)*

50. Write the sentence as an equation: The difference of 26 and a number c is 19. *(Lesson 12.1)* $26 - c = 19$

**Basic Skills** Find the sum.

51. $12.4 + 5.6$ **18**

52. $4.7 + 9.9$ **14.6**

53. $0.25 + 2.09$ **2.34**

54. $2.4 + 23.05$ **25.45**

Test-Taking Practice

55. Multiple Choice What is the solution of $12 + x = 21$? **B**

A. 6   **B.** 9   **C.** 11   **D.** 33

56. Short Response Write and solve an equation for the sentence: A number x added to 33 is 50. Explain how you found your solution.
$33 + x = 50$; 17; subtract 33 from each side.

Lesson 12.2   Solving Addition Equations   **591**

4 ASSESS

ASSESSMENT RESOURCES

For more assessment resources, see:
- Assessment Book
- Test and Practice Generator

MINI-QUIZ

1. Solve the equation $x + 2 = 12$ using algebra tiles. **10**

2. Solve $p + 28 = 55$. **27**

3. This month you have talked 153 minutes on a cell phone. You can use 250 minutes before you have to pay extra fees. Write and solve an addition equation to find the number m of minutes before you have to pay extra fees. $153 + m = 250$; 97 min

5 FOLLOW-UP

RETEACHING/REMEDIATION

- Study Guide in Chapter 12 Resource Book, pp. 21–22
- Tutor Place, Algebra Cards 9, 12
- eTutorial Plus Online
- Extra Practice, p. 719
- Lesson Practice in Chapter 12 Resource Book, pp. 18–20

CHALLENGE/ENRICHMENT

- Challenge Practice in Chapter 12 Resource Book, p. 23
- Teacher's Edition, p. 580F

ENGLISH LEARNER SUPPORT

- Spanish Study Guide
- Multi-Language Glossary
- Chapter Audio Summaries CDs

LESSON 12.3

Solving Subtraction Equations

BEFORE	▶ **Now**	**WHY?**
You solved one-step addition equations.	You'll solve one-step subtraction equations.	So you can find the number of berries in a carton, as in Ex. 24.

(**In the Real World**

 **Word Watch**

Review Words
variable, p. 29
solution, p. 36
solve, p. 37

Collecting You gave away 2 scallop shells from your collection and now you have 5 scallop shells left. How many scallop shells did you have at the start?

An equation that represents this situation is $x - 2 = 5$, where x is the number of scallop shells you had in your collection at the start.

EXAMPLE 1   **Working Backward**

One way to solve the equation above to find the number of scallop shells you had in your collection at the start is to work backward.

After giving away 2 scallop shells, you have 5 scallop shells. $x - 2 = 5$

To find the value x you had before subtracting 2, you can add 2 to *undo* the subtraction. $5 + 2 = x$

ANSWER You had 7 scallop shells in your collection at the start.

✓ **Check** $x - 2 = 5$ **Write the original equation.**

          $7 - 2 \stackrel{?}{=} 5$ **Substitute 7 for x.**

             $5 = 5$ ✓   **Solution checks.**

Isolating the Variable You can also solve the equation in Example 1 by getting the variable by itself as you did in Lesson 12.2. You would write the following steps.

$$\begin{aligned} x - 2 &= 5 \\ \underline{+ 2} \quad &\underline{+ 2} \\ x &= 7 \end{aligned}$$

By adding 2 to each side of the equation, you undo the subtraction while keeping the two sides of the equation equal to each other.

NCTM CURRICULUM STANDARDS
Standard 1: Understand how operations are related
Standard 2: Represent situations using algebraic symbols; Analyze situations using algebraic symbols

Solving Subtraction Equations

To solve a subtraction equation, add the same number to each side so that the variable is by itself on one side.

EXAMPLE 2 Solving Subtraction Equations

Solve the equation.

a. $14 = n - 6$ **b.** $m - 3.1 = 11.95$

Solution

a. In this equation, the variable is on the right side of the equation.

$$\begin{aligned} 14 &= n - 6 \qquad &&\text{Write the original equation.}\\ +6 \quad &\ +6 \qquad &&\text{Add 6 to each side.}\\ \overline{20} &= n \qquad &&\text{Simplify.} \end{aligned}$$

b.

$$\begin{aligned} m - 3.1 &= 11.95 \qquad &&\text{Write the original equation.}\\ +3.1 \quad &\ +3.1 \qquad &&\text{Add 3.1 to each side.}\\ \overline{m} &= 15.05 \qquad &&\text{Simplify.} \end{aligned}$$

Watch Out!

 Line up decimal points correctly before adding decimals.

WRONG	RIGHT
11.95	11.95
+ 3.1	+ 3.1
12.26	15.05

EXAMPLE 3 Using a Subtraction Equation

Elevator You are riding an elevator. You go down 14 floors and exit on the 23rd floor. On what floor did you enter the elevator?

Solution

Let f represent the number of the floor on which you entered the elevator.

$$\begin{aligned} f - 14 &= 23 \qquad &&\text{Write an equation.}\\ +14 \quad &\ +14 \qquad &&\text{Add 14 to each side.}\\ \overline{f} &= 37 \qquad &&\text{Simplify.} \end{aligned}$$

ANSWER You entered the elevator on the 37th floor.

 CONCEPT CHECK

For a subtraction equation such as $y - 15 = 37$, what can you do to solve the equation? **Add the number 15 to each side of the equation.**

DAILY PUZZLER

The solution to an equation is 13.71, and you can find the solution by adding 5.28 to each side of the equation. What is the equation? $x - 5.28 = 8.43$

Your turn now Solve the equation. Then check the solution.

1. $q - 7 = 2$ **9**   **2.** $25 = s - 17$ **42**   **3.** $3.2 = r - 2.1$ **5.3**

ASSIGNMENT GUIDE

Basic Course
Day 1: EP p. 710 Exs. 34, 35,
   38, 39; pp. 594–595
   Exs. 9–17, 26–28, 42–47
Day 2: pp. 594–595 Exs. 18–24,
   30–36, 48–52

Average Course
Day 1: pp. 594–595 Exs. 9–17,
   26–29, 42–47
Day 2: pp. 594–595 Exs. 21–25,
   30–38, 48–52

Advanced Course
Day 1: pp. 594–595 Exs. 12–17,
   26–29, 42–47
Day 2: pp. 594–595 Exs. 21–25,
   33–41*, 51, 52

Block
pp. 594–595 Exs. 9–17, 21–38,
   42–52

EXTRA PRACTICE

- Student Edition, p. 719
- Chapter 12 Resource Book,
  pp. 27–29
- Test and Practice Generator

 **TRANSPARENCY**

Even-numbered answers are available on transparencies.

HOMEWORK CHECK

When you review students' homework for this lesson, go over the following exercises to check understanding of key concepts.
Basic: 9, 15, 22, 24, 30
Average: 9, 16, 23, 24, 31
Advanced: 12, 16, 23, 24, 33

TEACHING TIP

In Exercises 9–23, point out to students that each variable must be greater than or equal to the number on the other side of the equation. Students can use that fact as a rough check of their answers.

Getting Ready to Practice

1. **Vocabulary** When solving an addition or a subtraction equation, you should get the __?__ by itself on one side of the equation. **variable**

Tell whether the given number is a solution of the equation.

2. $x - 3 = 9$; 6 no   3. $x - 8 = 8$; 0 no   4. $x - 7.1 = 10.4$; 17.5 yes

Solve the equation. Then check the solution.

5. $p - 2 = 7$ 9   6. $z - 1 = 4$ 5   7. $16 = m - 6$ 22

8. **Guided Problem Solving** Your class is planting trees in parks. After planting 17 trees, the class has 14 trees left to plant. Write and solve a subtraction equation to find the number of trees the class started with.

   ① What is the unknown value? Choose a variable to represent it.
   The number of trees the class started with. *Sample answer: t*

   ② Write a subtraction equation using the information in the problem.
   $t - 17 = 14$

   ③ Solve the equation. Check your solution. **31 trees**

Practice and Problem Solving

25. You do the same thing to both sides to solve either an addition equation or a subtraction equation; to solve an addition equation, you subtract; to solve a subtraction equation, you add.

 with **Homework**

Example	Exercises
1	9–17
2	9–23, 25, 30–35
3	24

 **Online Resources**
CLASSZONE.COM
· More Examples
· eTutorial Plus

Solve the equation.

A 9. $w - 7 = 6$ 13   10. $y - 8 = 5$ 13   11. $z - 2 = 1$ 3

12. $p - 3 = 0$ 3   13. $q - 5 = 10$ 15   14. $r - 9 = 7$ 16

15. $b - 4 = 19$ 23   16. $d - 6 = 12$ 18   17. $c - 0 = 11$ 11

18. $3 = m - 15$ 18   19. $7 = n - 8$ 15   20. $22 = p - 12$ 34

21. $20 = g - 13$ 33   22. $25 = h - 19$ 44   23. $39 = j - 14$ 53

24. **Berries** You eat 9 strawberries from a carton. There are 12 strawberries remaining in the carton. How many strawberries were in the full carton? Write and solve a subtraction equation for the situation.
   21 strawberries; $x - 9 = 12$

25. **Writing** Compare solving a subtraction equation to solving an addition equation. How are the steps alike? How are they different? See margin.

Number Sense Without solving the equations, tell which equation has a greater solution. Explain.

B 26. $x - 50 = 3271$ or $x - 500 = 3271$
   $x - 500 = 3271$; the sum of 500 and 3271 is greater than the sum of 50 and 3271.

27. $x - 368 = 532$ or $x - 368 = 475$
   $x - 368 = 532$; the sum of 368 and 532 is greater than the sum of 368 and 475.

Compare In Exercises 28 and 29, write and solve two different subtraction equations for the situation. Compare the solutions.

28. Paper Route You are delivering newspapers on your paper route. You have to deliver to 8 more houses. You have already delivered to 21 houses. How many houses are on your route?
$x - 21 = 8; x - 8 = 21;$ 29 houses; the solutions are the same.

29. Sports You have lost track of how many softball games your team played this season. You know your team won 12 games. Your friend reminds you that your team lost 9 games. How many games did your team play? $x - 12 = 9; x - 9 = 12;$ 21 games; the solutions are the same.

Solve the equation.

30. $x - 4.2 = 7.1$ 11.3   **31.** $x - 2.8 = 6.5$ 9.3   **32.** $13.4 = x - 1.8$ 15.2

33. $x - 17.06 = 13$ 30.06 **34.** $x - 5.97 = 3.86$ 9.83 **35.** $6.02 = x - 9.3$ 15.32

C 36. $a - 1\frac{1}{3} = 2\frac{1}{6}$ $3\frac{1}{2}$ **37.** $b - \frac{5}{8} = 3\frac{1}{4}$ $3\frac{7}{8}$ **38.** $c - 2\frac{2}{3} = 3\frac{3}{4}$ $6\frac{5}{12}$

Challenge Solve the equation.

39. $x - 15 = -2$ 13   **40.** $x - 10 = -20$ −10   **41.** $x - (-9) = -17$ −26

Mixed Review

Plot the point. Name the quadrant that contains the point.
(Lesson 11.6) 42–44. See margin.

42. $A(4, -5)$ **43.** $B(-3, 2)$ **44.** $C(-6, -1)$

Solve the equation. *(Lesson 12.2)*

45. $x + 4 = 6$ 2   **46.** $b + 5 = 8$ 3   **47.** $9 + p = 17$ 8

Basic Skills Find the quotient.

48. $456 \div 57$ 8   **49.** $252 \div 28$ 9   **50.** $64.6 \div 9.5$ 6.8

Test-Taking Practice

51. Multiple Choice What is the solution of the equation $p - 16 = 24$? D

   A. 8   **B.** 12   **C.** 32   **D.** 40

52. Multiple Choice Which equation does *not* have 8 as a solution? H

   F. $t - 1 = 7$ **G.** $t - 5 = 3$ **H.** $t - 6 = 14$ **I.** $0 = t - 8$

ASSESSMENT RESOURCES
For more assessment resources, see:
• Assessment Book
• Test and Practice Generator

MINI-QUIZ

1. You used 6 gallons of gas from a full tank of x gallons. Now the tank has 11 gallons. Work backward to find how many gallons are in a full tank. **17 gal**

Solve each equation.

2. $a - 2\frac{1}{2} = 4\frac{3}{4}$ $7\frac{1}{4}$

3. $17.1 = b - 4.3$ **21.4**

4. After you wrote a check for $12.50, the balance in your checking account was $112.40. Write an equation that you can use to find the balance B before you wrote the check. Find that balance.
$B - 12.50 = 112.40;$ **$124.90**

RETEACHING/REMEDIATION
• Study Guide in Chapter 12 Resource Book, pp. 30–31
• Tutor Place, Algebra Cards 8, 12
• eTutorial Plus Online
• Extra Practice, p. 719
• Lesson Practice in Chapter 12 Resource Book, pp. 27–29

CHALLENGE/ENRICHMENT
• Challenge Practice in Chapter 12 Resource Book, p. 32
• Teacher's Edition, p. 580F

ENGLISH LEARNER SUPPORT
• Spanish Study Guide
• Multi-Language Glossary
• Chapter Audio Summaries CDs

42–44. See Additional Answers beginning on page AA1.

LESSONS 12.1 TO 12.3

Notebook Review

Review the vocabulary definitions in your notebook.

Copy the review examples in your notebook. Then complete the exercises.

Check Your Definitions

variable expression, p. 29

equation, p. 36

solution, p. 36

solve, p. 37

Use Your Vocabulary

1. Explain the difference between a variable expression and an equation.
   A variable expression contains variables and numbers, but no equal sign. An equation contains variables, numbers, and an equal sign.

12.1 Can you write variable expressions and equations?

 EXAMPLE

Words	Algebra
A number y increased by 8	$y + 8$
The difference of 2 and a number y	$2 - y$
The product of 10 and a number y is 30.	$10y = 30$

✓ **Write the phrase as an expression. Let x represent the number.**

2. A number divided by 7 $\frac{x}{7}$ 3. A number times 6 $6x$

4. 80 less than a number $x - 80$ 5. 25 plus a number $25 + x$

6. Write the sentence as an equation: Forty more than a number p is 62.
   $40 + p = 62$

12.2–12.3 Can you solve addition and subtraction equations?

 EXAMPLE

a. $\begin{aligned} 13 &= f + 8 \\ \underline{-8} &\quad \underline{-8} \\ 5 &= f \end{aligned}$

b. $\begin{aligned} g - 4 &= 11 \\ \underline{+4} &\quad \underline{+4} \\ g &= 15 \end{aligned}$

✓ **Solve the equation.**

7. $x + 8 = 15$ 7   8. $10 + y = 30$ 20   9. $32 = a + 17$ 15

10. $b + 0.7 = 1.9$ 1.2   11. $23.2 + c = 40$ 16.8   12. $15 = q - 5$ 20

13. $r - 10 = 11$ 21   14. $s - 25 = 18$ 43   15. $5.7 = t - 24$ 29.7

about Lessons 12.1–12.3

16. Writing Explain how writing an equation to model a situation is similar to translating one language into another language. *Sample answer:* Each word is translated into a special symbol.

17. Critical Thinking Write two different addition or subtraction equations that have the same solution.
Sample answer: $3 + x = 4$; $5 + x = 6$

Review Quiz 1

Write the phrase as an expression. Let *x* represent the number.

1. A number decreased by 5 $x - 5$

2. The total of 14 and a number $14 + x$

3. A number multiplied by 9 $9x$

4. The quotient of a number and 10 $\dfrac{x}{10}$

Write the sentence as an equation. Let *y* represent the number.

5. 8 more than a number is 35. $8 + y = 35$

6. 48 divided by a number is 6. $\dfrac{48}{y} = 6$

7. 3 times a number is 0. $3y = 0$

8. 10 less than a number is 10. $y - 10 = 10$

Solve the equation.

9. $x + 15 = 29$ 14

10. $3 + y = 14$ 11

11. $24 = f + 17$ 7

12. $d - 5 = 9$ 14

13. $z - 14 = 2$ 16

14. $12 = a - 12$ 24

15. Lizards A Komodo dragon can grow to be 120 inches long. Suppose one of these lizards is 92 inches long. Write and solve an addition equation to find *x*, the number of inches it still needs to grow to be 120 inches long. $92 + x = 120$; 28 in.

BRAIN GAME

Symbologic

Use the first two symbol equations to complete the third equation.

□ + ● + ● = △ + ●

□ + △ + □ = ● + ●

□ + □ + □ = __?__ a circle

SKILL CHECK

1. $12 \div \underline{?} = 1$ 12
2. $\frac{1}{5} \times \underline{?} = 1$ 5
3. $2.7 \div \underline{?} = 1$ 2.7
4. $1 = \frac{1}{9} \times \underline{?}$ 9

LESSON OBJECTIVE

Solve multiplication and division equations.

PACING

Suggested Number of Days
Basic Course: 2 days
Average Course: 2 days
Advanced Course: 2 days
Block: 1 block

TEACHING RESOURCES

For a complete list of Teaching Resources, see page 580B.

 **TRANSPARENCY**

Warm-Up Exercises for this lesson are available on a transparency. A support transparency is available for this Activity.

2 TEACH

MOTIVATING THE LESSON

Extend the Activity by having students solve other multiplication equations using algebra tiles.

ACTIVITY

Goal Students use algebra tiles to solve a multiplication equation.

Key Discovery You can solve a multiplication equation by dividing both sides of the equation by the number that the variable is multiplied by.

LESSON 12.4

Solving Multiplication and Division Equations

BEFORE   ▶ **Now**   **WHY?**

You solved one-step addition and subtraction equations. | You'll solve multiplication and division equations. | So you can make predictions about a hurricane's travel time, as in Ex. 33.

 **Word Watch**

Review Words
variable, p. 29
solution, p. 36
solve, p. 37

Activity You can use algebra tiles to solve a multiplication equation.

① Use algebra tiles to represent the equation $2x = 6$.

② Divide the x-tiles into two equal groups. Divide the 1-tiles into the same number of equal groups.

③ Match a group on the left with a group on the right. Explain how this tells you the solution of the equation.
One x-tile equals three 1-tiles, so the solution is 3.

Use algebra tiles to solve the equation.

1. $2x = 8$ 4   2. $3x = 9$ 3   3. $4x = 12$ 3

The activity shows how you can solve a multiplication equation using algebra tiles. You can also use division to solve a multiplication equation.

EXAMPLE 1   **Solving a Multiplication Equation**

Solve the equation $5x = 20$.

$5x = 20$ Write the original equation.

$\dfrac{5x}{5} = \dfrac{20}{5}$ Divide each side by 5.

$x = 4$ Simplify.

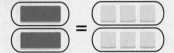 **with Review**

As you saw on page 253, the fraction bar is a way to express division. You will write division using a fraction bar when you solve multiplication and division equations.

Your turn now   Solve the equation. Then check the solution.

1. $4n = 20$ 5   2. $3m = 15$ 5   3. $24 = 2p$ 12   4. $65 = 5q$ 13

NCTM CURRICULUM STANDARDS
Standard 2: Represent situations using algebraic symbols; Analyze situations using algebraic symbols; Use models to represent relationships

Solving Multiplication and Division Equations

You can use multiplication and division to undo each other when trying to get the variable by itself on one side of an equation.

Multiplication Equations To solve a multiplication equation, *divide* each side by the number the variable is multiplied by.

Division Equations To solve a division equation, *multiply* each side by the divisor.

EXAMPLE 2 Solving a Division Equation

Solve the equation $\frac{x}{7} = 3$.

$\frac{x}{7} = 3$	Write the original equation.
$7 \cdot \frac{x}{7} = 7 \cdot 3$	Multiply each side by 7.
$x = 21$	Simplify.

EXAMPLE 3 Using an Equation

Cheerleading In cheerleader tryouts, 27 students are placed in groups of 3 to make human pyramids. Write and solve a multiplication equation to find n, the number of pyramids the 27 students form.

Solution

$27 = 3n$	Write an equation.
$\frac{27}{3} = \frac{3n}{3}$	Divide each side by 3.
$9 = n$	Simplify.

ANSWER The 27 students will form 9 pyramids.

Your turn now Solve the equation. Then check the solution.

5. $\frac{a}{2} = 7$ 14 **6.** $\frac{b}{5} = 6$ 30 **7.** $45 = \frac{c}{3}$ 135 **8.** $12 = \frac{d}{8}$ 96

ASSIGNMENT GUIDE

Basic Course
Day 1: pp. 600–601 Exs. 9, 10, 12–19, 36–39, 43–47
Day 2: pp. 600–601 Exs. 11, 20–31, 48–53

Average Course
Day 1: pp. 600–601 Exs. 10, 12–19, 35–41, 52
Day 2: pp. 600–601 Exs. 11, 24–34, 45–48, 53

Advanced Course
Day 1: pp. 600–601 Exs. 10, 14–19, 35–38, 43–48
Day 2: pp. 600–601 Exs. 11, 24–34, 39–42*, 52, 53

Block
pp. 600–601 Exs. 10–19, 24–41, 45–48, 52, 53

EXTRA PRACTICE
- Student Edition, p. 719
- Chapter 12 Resource Book, pp. 35–37
- Test and Practice Generator

TRANSPARENCY

Even-numbered answers are available on transparencies.

HOMEWORK CHECK

When you review students' homework for this lesson, go over the following exercises to check understanding of key concepts.
Basic: 9, 10, 11, 20, 28
Average: 10, 11, 12, 24, 29
Advanced: 10, 11, 24, 29, 32

TEACHING TIP

For Exercises 12–27 and 36–41, ask students to begin by asking "What operation was done to the variable?"

600

INTERNET
eWorkbook Plus
CLASSZONE.COM

Getting Ready to Practice

1. Vocabulary You can solve a multiplication equation by _?_. You can solve a division equation by _?_. division; multiplication

Solve the equation. Then check the solution.

2. $5x = 35$ 7   **3.** $14 = 7y$ 2   **4.** $14 = \dfrac{a}{2}$ 28   **5.** $\dfrac{c}{6} = 2$ 12

In Exercises 6 and 7, write the sentence as an equation. Then solve the equation.

6. Five times a number x is 105.   **7.** 24 is a number c divided by 2.
$5x = 105$; 21 $24 = \dfrac{c}{2}$; 48

8. Pretzels You purchase 8 soft pretzels for your friends. You pay $14. Write a multiplication equation you can use to find the cost of a soft pretzel. Then solve the equation. $8p = 14$; $1.75

Practice and Problem Solving

Copy and complete the solution.

A **9.** $5x = 10$ 5; 5; 2   **10.** $27 = 9x$ 9; 9; 3   **11.** $\dfrac{x}{9} = 4$ 9; 9; 36

$\dfrac{5x}{?} = \dfrac{10}{?}$ $\dfrac{27}{?} = \dfrac{9x}{?}$ $\underline{?} \cdot \dfrac{x}{9} = \underline{?} \cdot 4$

$x = \underline{?}$ $\underline{?} = x$ $x = \underline{?}$

Solve the equation.

12. $4m = 32$ 8   **13.** $3n = 60$ 20   **14.** $5p = 0$ 0   **15.** $7q = 63$ 9

16. $35 = 7g$ 5   **17.** $42 = 3h$ 14   **18.** $72 = 6j$ 12   **19.** $51 = 17k$ 3

20. $\dfrac{t}{10} = 12$ 120   **21.** $\dfrac{u}{5} = 10$ 50   **22.** $\dfrac{w}{6} = 15$ 90   **23.** $\dfrac{x}{21} = 4$ 84

24. $5 = \dfrac{a}{4}$ 20   **25.** $12 = \dfrac{b}{7}$ 84   **26.** $9 = \dfrac{c}{30}$ 270   **27.** $7 = \dfrac{d}{14}$ 98

In Exercises 28–31, write the sentence as an equation. Then solve the equation.

28. 112 is 8 times a number y.   **29.** Eleven times a number b is 44.
$112 = 8y$; 14 $11b = 44$; 4
30. A number f divided by 6 is 9.   **31.** 27 is a number n divided by 3.
30–31. See margin.

32. Pens Four friends share a box of pens. Each receives 3 pens. Write and solve a division equation to find the number of pens in the box.

$\dfrac{x}{4} = 3$; 12 pens

---

30. $\dfrac{f}{6} = 9$; 54

31. $27 = \dfrac{n}{3}$; 81

with Homework

Example	Exercises
1	9, 10, 12–19
2	11, 20–27
3	28–34

Online Resources
CLASSZONE.COM
· More Examples
· eTutorial Plus

Hurricanes

The product of a hurricane's speed (in miles per hour) and its rainfall (in inches) is about 100. What rainfall can you expect from a storm traveling 5 miles per hour?

20 in.

INTERNET
State Test Practice
CLASSZONE.COM

B 33. Hurricanes A hurricane is traveling at an average speed of 24 miles per hour. Write and solve a multiplication equation to predict how many hours it will take to travel 1728 miles if it continues at this speed.
24h = 1728; 72 h

34. Sports A team won 45% of its games this year. The team won 9 games. Write and solve a multiplication equation to find the number of games the team played. 0.45x = 9; 20 games

35. Critical Thinking Explain why you can multiply each side of the equation $\frac{1}{4}x = 20$ by the reciprocal of $\frac{1}{4}$ to solve the equation.
Multiplying by 4, the reciprocal of $\frac{1}{4}$, is the same as dividing by $\frac{1}{4}$.

Solve the equation.

36. $5m = 28$ 5.6   **37.** $40 = 9p$ $4\frac{4}{9}$ **38.** $\frac{x}{4} = 2.7$ 10.8

C 39. $8q = -56$ -7 **40.** $-450 = -10s$ 45   **41.** $\frac{w}{5} = -4$ -20

42. Challenge An *acre* covers 43,560 square feet. The unit is based on early farmers' fields that were 10 times as long as they were wide. Find $10x$ and x, the length and width, in feet, of such a field. 10x = 660 ft, x = 66 ft

A = 43,560 ft²

10x

x

Mixed Review

Evaluate the expression when $x = 3$. *(Lesson 1.5)*

43. $5x + 4$ 19   **44.** $8 + 7x$ 29   **45.** $30 - 3x$ 21

Solve the equation. *(Lesson 12.3)*

46. $b - 8 = 17$ 25   **47.** $x - 12 = 5$ 17   **48.** $41 = m - 19$ 60

Basic Skills Copy and complete the statement using <, >, or =.

49. $\frac{3}{8}$? $\frac{3}{4}$ <   **50.** $\frac{7}{9}$? $\frac{2}{3}$ >   **51.** $\frac{1}{2}$? $\frac{8}{16}$ =

Test-Taking Practice

52. Multiple Choice Solve the equation $12x = 120$. A

   A. 10   **B.** 108   **C.** 132   **D.** 1440

53. Multiple Choice Solve the equation $\frac{z}{8} = 7$. I

   F. $\frac{7}{8}$ **G.** 8   **H.** 15   **I.** 56

Lesson 12.4   Solving Multiplication and Division Equations   **601**

4 ASSESS

ASSESSMENT RESOURCES

For more assessment resources, see:
• Assessment Book
• Test and Practice Generator

MINI-QUIZ

Solve each equation.

1. $\frac{x}{10} = 3$ 30

2. $6y = 66$ 11

3. $54 = 9z$ 6

4. $32 = \frac{w}{4}$ 128

5. The 32 members of a tennis team are placed in groups of 4 to practice playing doubles. Write and solve a multiplication equation to find t, the number of groups the 32 players form. 4t = 32; 8

5 FOLLOW-UP

RETEACHING/REMEDIATION

• Study Guide in Chapter 12 Resource Book, pp. 38–39
• Tutor Place, Algebra Cards 10–12
• eTutorial Plus Online
• Extra Practice, p. 719
• Lesson Practice in Chapter 12 Resource Book, pp. 35–37

CHALLENGE/ENRICHMENT

• Challenge Practice in Chapter 12 Resource Book, p. 40
• Teacher's Edition, p. 580F

ENGLISH LEARNER SUPPORT

• Spanish Study Guide
• Multi-Language Glossary
• Chapter Audio Summaries CDs

601

Solve each equation.

1. $x + 5 = 11$ 6

2. $2x = 16$ 8

3. $x - 4 = 0$ 4

4. $\frac{x}{3} = 0$ 0

LESSON OBJECTIVE

Solve one-step inequalities.

2 TEACH

TEACHING TIP

As you begin this Special Topic, ask students what number satisfies $x = 5$. Then introduce the inequalities $x < 5$ and $x > 5$ and ask what numbers might satisfy them.

EXTRA EXAMPLES

Example 1 Write each sentence as an inequality. Let x represent the number.
a. 16 is greater than a number. **$16 > x$**
b. Twice a number is less than or equal to 15. **$2x \leq 15$**
c. 5 less than a number is greater than or equal to 1. **$x - 5 \geq 1$**

Example 2 A plane holds 185 passengers. After the 28 members of Alicia's class join those already on board, the plane is still not full. Write an inequality to find the number n of people already on the plane. **$n + 28 < 185$**

CHAPTER 12 Special Topic

Solving Inequalities

GOAL Solve one-step inequalities.

Word Watch

inequality, p. 602
solve an inequality, p. 602
solution of an inequality, p. 602
graph of an inequality, p. 603

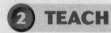

HELP with Review

Need help writing expressions? See pages 583–584.

An **inequality** is a statement formed by placing an inequality symbol between two expressions. To translate sentences into inequalities, look for the following phrases.

Phrase	Symbol
is less than	$<$
is less than or equal to	$\leq$
is greater than	$>$
is greater than or equal to	$\geq$

EXAMPLE 1   Writing Simple Inequalities

Write the sentence as an inequality. Let x represent the number.

Sentence	Inequality
A number is less than 5.	$x < 5$
Twice a number is greater than or equal to 8.	$2x \geq 8$
A number minus 7 is less than or equal to 5.	$x - 7 \leq 5$

EXAMPLE 2   Modeling a Situation

Restaurant A restaurant can seat 54 people. If a party of 12 joins the number of people already seated, the restaurant will still not be full. Write an inequality you could use to find the number of people n that are already seated in the restaurant.

Solution

$$\underset{\text{seated}}{\text{Number already}} + \underset{\text{join}}{\text{Number who}} < \underset{\text{can seat}}{\text{Number restaurant}}$$

$$n + 12 < 54$$

Solving Inequalities You **solve** an inequality by finding the *solution*. The **solution** of an inequality is the set of all values of the variable that make the inequality true. Solving an inequality is similar to solving an equation. You perform the same operation on each side of the inequality in order to get the variable by itself.

NCTM CURRICULUM STANDARDS
Standard 2: Represent situations using algebraic symbols; Use models to understand relationships; Use models to represent relationships

EXAMPLE 3 Solving an Inequality

Solve the inequality $x + 2 \geq 3$.

$x + 2 \geq 3$	Write the original inequality.
$x + 2 - 2 \geq 3 - 2$	Subtract 2 from each side.
$x \geq 1$	Simplify.

Graphing Solutions The **graph** of an inequality is all the points on a number line that represent the solution of the inequality. An open dot on a graph indicates a number that is not part of the solution.

EXAMPLE 4 Graphing Solutions of an Inequality

Solve the inequality $3x < 21$. Then graph the solution.

$3x < 21$	Write the original inequality.
$\dfrac{3x}{3} < \dfrac{21}{3}$	Divide each side by 3.
$x < 7$	Simplify.

7 is not part of the solution, so use an open dot at 7 on the graph.

Exercises

1. **Saving** A bicycle costs $275. If you double the amount you've saved, you will have more than enough to buy the bicycle. Write an inequality you could use to find how much you have saved. $2x > 275$

Solve the inequality. Then graph the solution. 2–9. See margin.

2. $x + 1 > 3$
3. $x + 2 \leq 2$
4. $x - 4 < 0$
5. $x - 2 \geq 5$

6. $3x \leq 9$
7. $2x > 12$
8. $\dfrac{x}{2} \geq 1$
9. $\dfrac{x}{3} < 4$

10. **Modeling Inequalities** Label 11 cards with the integers -5 through 5. Arrange the cards face up in order from least to greatest. If the integer on a card is a solution of the inequality $3x \leq 6$, leave the card face up. If not, turn the card over. Use your results to solve the inequality $3x \leq 6$. $x \leq 2$

EXPLORE THE CONCEPT

- Students find an expression for an input-output table.
- This Activity leads to writing function rules for input-output tables in Lesson 12.5.

MATERIALS

Each student or group of students will need paper and pencil.

GROUPING

Students can work individually or in groups of two. If students work in pairs, they can take turns suggesting and checking expressions.

TEACH

TIPS FOR SUCCESS

As students work through Steps 1–3, be sure they understand that the expression $2x$ is a first guess, or conjecture, for the input-output relationship. Since that expression does not work for all of the input-output pairs, a new guess is needed. The expression $x + 2$ is the second conjecture.

CLOSE

🔍 **KEY DISCOVERY**

In an expression like $x + 4$ or $3x$, if x is replaced by an input value, then a single output value results.

ASSESSMENT

1. Find an expression for the input-output table. $\frac{x}{2}$

Input	2	4	6	8	10
Output	1	2	3	4	5

604

12.5 **Hands-on Activity**

GOAL
Find an expression for an input-output table.

MATERIALS
- paper
- pencil

Input-Output Tables

Imagine a machine that evaluates expressions. The value of the variable is the *input* and the value of the expression is the *output*.

$9 \rightarrow \boxed{x - 6} \rightarrow 3$

Explore — Find an expression for an input-output table.

1 Look for a relationship between the first input and the first output. Write an expression that gives the value of the output when the input is x. The first output is twice the first input, so try $2x$.

Input	Output
2	4
3	5
4	6
5	7

$2 \rightarrow \boxed{2x} \rightarrow 4$

2 Check whether the expression works for the next input-output pair.

$3 \rightarrow \boxed{2x} \rightarrow 6$ — The output should be 5.

3 If the expression doesn't work, try another expression using a different operation. The first output is 2 more than the first input, so try $x + 2$.

$2 \rightarrow \boxed{x + 2} \rightarrow 4$ $3 \rightarrow \boxed{x + 2} \rightarrow 5$ $4 \rightarrow \boxed{x + 2} \rightarrow 6$ $5 \rightarrow \boxed{x + 2} \rightarrow 7$

Your turn now — Find an expression for the input-output table.

1.

Input	12	11	10	9
Output	10	9	8	7

$x - 2$

2.

Input	3	7	10	12
Output	9	21	30	36

$3x$

Stop and Think

3. Critical Thinking A machine performs one of the four basic operations. Can a given input value produce more than one output value? **no**

NCTM CURRICULUM STANDARDS
Standard 2: Understand patterns; Understand functions; Represent situations using algebraic symbols

LESSON 12.5

Functions

BEFORE	Now	WHY?
You evaluated variable expressions.	You'll evaluate functions and write function rules.	So you can find miles driven on a road trip, as in Ex. 29.

Word Watch

function, p. 605
input, p. 605
output, p. 605

In the Real World

Giant Pandas Giant pandas eat about 30 pounds of bamboo every day. About how many pounds of bamboo will a giant panda eat in 2 days? in 3 days? in 4 days?

The *function rule* below relates the pounds of bamboo a panda eats to the number of days.

$$\text{Pounds of bamboo} = 30 \times \text{Number of days}$$

A **function** is a pairing of each number in one set with a number in a second set. Starting with a number in the first set, called an **input**, the function pairs it with exactly one number in the second set, called an **output**.

EXAMPLE 1 Evaluating a Function

To solve the problem above about giant pandas, you can make an *input-output table*. Use the function rule $p = 30d$, where d is the number of days (input) and p is the pounds of bamboo eaten (output).

Input Days, d	Substitute in the function $p = 30d$	Output Pounds eaten, p
1	$p = 30(1)$	30
2	$p = 30(2)$	60
3	$p = 30(3)$	90
4	$p = 30(4)$	120

ANSWER A giant panda will eat about 60 pounds of bamboo in 2 days, about 90 pounds in 3 days, and about 120 pounds in 4 days.

Your turn now Make an input-output table using the function rule and the input values $x = 5, 6, 7, 8,$ and 9. 1–4. See margin.

1. $y = x - 1$ **2.** $y = 10 - x$ **3.** $y = 5x$ **4.** $y = 2x + 3$

SKILL CHECK
Evaluate each expression for $n = 5$.
1. $7n$ **35** **2.** $2n + 3$ **13**
3. $\dfrac{n}{10}$ $\dfrac{1}{2}$ **4.** $5 - 3n$ **−10**

LESSON OBJECTIVE
Evaluate and write functions.

PACING
Suggested Number of Days
Basic Course: 2 days
Average Course: 2 days
Advanced Course: 2 days
Block: 1 block

TEACHING RESOURCES
For a complete list of Teaching Resources, see page 580B.

TRANSPARENCY
Warm-Up Exercises for this lesson are available on a transparency.

2 TEACH

MOTIVATING THE LESSON
Show students other real-life examples of functions.

TIPS FOR NEW TEACHERS
In Example 1, be sure students understand d represents an input value and p represents a corresponding output value. See Tips for New Teachers in *Chapter 12 Resource Book*.

1–4. See Additional Answers beginning on page AA1.

605

HELP with **Reading**

A function rule is written so that it tells you what to do to the input to get the output. In Example 2, the rule $y = x - 4$ tells you to subtract 4 from the input to get the output.

HELP with **Solving**

It can be helpful to choose letters that remind you of what the variables stand for. Example 3 uses s and t, the first letters of the words *squares* and *triangles*.

EXAMPLE 2   Using a Table to Write a Rule

Write a function rule for the input-output table.

a.

Input, x	Output, y
10	6
11	7
12	8
13	9

b.

Input, m	Output, n
0	0
3	1
6	2
9	3

Solution

a. Each output y is 4 less than the input x. A function rule is $y = x - 4$.

b. Each output n is the input m divided by 3. A function rule is $n = \frac{m}{3}$.

EXAMPLE 3   Making a Table to Write a Rule

Pattern Make an input-output table using the number of squares s as the input and the number of triangles t as the output. Then write a function rule that relates s and t.

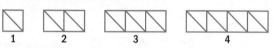

1   2   3   4

Solution

Each output value is 2 times the input value. There are 2 triangles for every square.

ANSWER A function rule for this pattern is $t = 2s$.

Squares, s	Triangles, t
1	2
2	4
3	6
4	8

Your turn now   **Write a function rule for the relationship.**

5. First make an input-output table. Use the number of dots in the bottom row n as the input and the total number of dots t as the output. **See margin.**

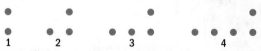

1   2   3   4

6. Use the input-output table at the right. $y = \frac{x}{9}$

Input, x	9	18	27	36
Output, y	1	2	3	4

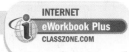
INTERNET
eWorkbook Plus
CLASSZONE.COM

Getting Ready to Practice

1. Vocabulary In a function, each _?_ has exactly one _?_ . **input; output**

Make an input-output table using the function rule and the input values $x = 2, 4, 6, 8,$ and 10. 2–5. See margin.

2. $y = x + 8$ **3.** $y = 2x$ **4.** $y = \dfrac{x}{2}$ **5.** $y = 3x - 2$

6. School Dance The table shows the amount c your class charges for t tickets to the school dance. Write a function rule that relates the input t and the output c. **$c = 6t$**

Tickets, t	Cost, c
2	$12
3	$18
4	$24
5	$30

Practice and Problem Solving

Make an input-output table using the function rule and the input values $x = 3, 6, 9, 12,$ and 15. 7–14. See margin.

A **7.** $y = 6x$ **8.** $y = x + 10$ **9.** $y = 15 - x$ **10.** $y = \dfrac{x}{3}$

11. $y = 4x + 1$ **12.** $y = 8x - 5$ **13.** $y = 2x - 4$ **14.** $y = 20 - x$

15. Measurement A function rule to convert inches to centimeters is $c = 2.54i$, where c is the number of centimeters and i is the number of inches. Make an input-output table using the input values of 3 inches, 6 inches, 9 inches, 12 inches, and 36 inches. Round to the nearest tenth of a centimeter. **See margin.**

Write a function rule for the input-output table.

16.

Original price, p	Sale price, s
$50	$45
$60	$55
$70	$65
$80	$75

$s = p - 5$

17.

Age now, n	Age in 15 years, t
10	25
11	26
12	27
13	28

$t = n + 15$

18.

Boxes, b	1	2	3	4
Muffins, m	12	24	36	48

$m = 12b$

19.

Invited guests, g	80	100	120	140
Banquet tables, t	8	10	12	14

$t = \dfrac{g}{10}$

 **with Homework**

Example	Exercises
1	7–15
2	16–19
3	20–24

Online Resources
CLASSZONE.COM
· More Examples
· eTutorial Plus

Lesson 12.5   Functions   **607**

③ APPLY

ASSIGNMENT GUIDE

Basic Course
Day 1: pp. 607–609 Exs. 7–10, 15–17, 26–28, 31–35
Day 2: pp. 607–609 Exs. 11–14, 20–24, 36–41

Average Course
Day 1: pp. 607–609 Exs. 7–10, 17–19, 25–29, 31–35
Day 2: pp. 607–609 Exs. 11–15, 20–24, 36–41

Advanced Course
Day 1: pp. 607–609 Exs. 8–10, 16–19, 27–30*, 39–41
Day 2: pp. 607–609 Exs. 12–15, 20–26, 31–33, 36

Block
pp. 607–609 Exs. 7–15, 17–29, 31–41

EXTRA PRACTICE
• Student Edition, p. 719
• Chapter 12 Resource Book, pp. 46–48
• Test and Practice Generator

TRANSPARENCY
Even-numbered answers are available on transparencies.

HOMEWORK CHECK
When you review students' homework for this lesson, go over the following exercises to check understanding of key concepts.
Basic: 7, 9, 16, 17, 20
Average: 8, 10, 17, 18, 21
Advanced: 10, 17, 18, 21, 23

2–5, 7–15. See Additional Answers beginning on page AA1.

Make an input-output table. Then write a function rule for the relationship. 20–22. See margin.

20. input: cats
output: paws

21. input: hours
output: minutes

22. input: feet
output: yards

Geometry Make an input-output table. Then write a function rule that relates the input *n* and the output *p*. 23–24. See margin.

23. Each figure is made up of equilateral triangles. Let *n* represent the number of triangles and let *p* represent the perimeter of the figure.

1   2   3   4   5

24. Each figure is made up of 5-pointed stars. Let *n* represent the number of stars and let *p* represent the number of points.

1   2   3   4

25. Writing Create your own visual pattern that can be represented with a function rule, as in Exercises 23 and 24. Make an input-output table and write the function rule. A good answer will include an obvious pattern and a clear input-output table and rule.

26. Temperature To convert degrees Celsius *C* to degrees Fahrenheit *F*, you can use the function rule $F = 1.8C + 32$. Make an input-output table using the input values of 0°C, 5°C, 10°C, 15°C, 20°C, and 25°C.
See margin.

Copy and complete the table using the function rule given.

27. $k = j + 25$

j	0	3	8	?	?
k	?	?	?	40	100

Row 1: 15, 75; Row 2: 25, 28, 33

28. $q = 1.6p$

p	10	15	?	?	?
q	?	?	32	40	56

Row 1: 20, 25, 35; Row 2: 16, 24

C 29. Road Trip While on a road trip, you record the following times and miles driven. Assume you travel at a constant rate. Copy and complete the table. Then write a function rule that relates the input *t* and the output *d*. Row 1: 6:00; Row 2: 300, 540; Row 3: 250; $d = \dfrac{5}{6}t$

Time	9:00	10:30	11:00	1:00	2:00	?
Time elapsed, t	0	90	120	240	?	?
Miles driven, d	0	75	100	200	?	450

30. Challenge Make an input-output table using $x = y^2$ and the values $y = -4, -2, 0, 2,$ and 4. Does the equation represent a function if *x* is considered the input and *y* is considered the output? See margin.

Mixed Review

31. Find the time that has elapsed from 11:59 A.M. to 4:43 P.M. *(Lesson 6.6)*
4 h 44 min

Solve the equation. *(Lesson 12.4)*

32. $9t = 81$ **9** **33.** $2x = 26$ **13** **34.** $\frac{n}{6} = 7$ **42** **35.** $\frac{f}{4} = 12$ **48**

Choose a Strategy **Use a strategy from the list to solve the following problem. Explain your choice of strategy.**

> **Problem Solving Strategies**
> - Perform an Experiment
> - Make a List or Table
> - Solve a Simpler Problem
> - Draw a Graph

36. In a city, you walk 3 blocks north, 5 blocks east, 2 blocks north, 6 blocks west, and 6 blocks south. Describe the shortest walking route to get back to your starting point. **Walk 1 block east and 1 block north; I used Draw a Graph so I could see the path taken.**

Basic Skills **Graph the points on the same coordinate grid.**
37–40. See margin.

37. $(0, 5)$ **38.** $(2, 0)$ **39.** $(1, 3)$ **40.** $(4, 2)$

Test-Taking Practice

41. **Extended Response** Make input-output tables for converting from dollars to quarters and from quarters to nickels. Write function rules for the conversions. Then use your results to write a function rule for converting from dollars directly to nickels. **See margin.**

Function Assembly Line

Each machine takes input and gives output as shown. What is the final output if the machines are used in the given order? The starting input is ⟨O⟩ and the output of each machine becomes the input of the next machine.

1–3. See margin.

1. Machine 1, Machine 3

2. Machine 4, Machine 2

3. Machine 2, Machine 3, Machine 1

ASSESSMENT RESOURCES

For more assessment resources, see:
- Assessment Book
- Test and Practice Generator

MINI-QUIZ

1. Use the rule $y = 2.5x$ to find the values of y for the input values $x = 0, 2, 4,$ and 6. **0, 5, 10, 15**

2. Write a function rule for the input-output table.

Input, x	0	1	2	3
Output, y	-7	-6	-5	-4

$y = x - 7$

3. Make an input-output table using the number of large triangles L as the input and the number of small triangles s as the output. Then write a function rule that relates L and s.

1   2   3

Check tables; $s = 3L$.

RETEACHING/REMEDIATION
- Study Guide in Chapter 12 Resource Book, pp. 49–50
- eTutorial Plus Online
- Extra Practice, p. 719
- Lesson Practice in Chapter 12 Resource Book, pp. 46–48

CHALLENGE/ENRICHMENT
- Challenge Practice in Chapter 12 Resource Book, p. 51
- Teacher's Edition, p. 580F

ENGLISH LEARNER SUPPORT
- Spanish Study Guide
- Multi-Language Glossary
- Chapter Audio Summaries CDs

37–41, Brain Game. See Additional Answers beginning on page AA1.

The strategy Look for a Pattern involves three steps: (1) Identify data in the problem that may be useful; (2) Find what the data have in common; and (3) Use the common element as a pattern to continue that pattern beyond the given data. Students often find the third step to be the easiest because after identifying useful data and finding a pattern, they understand how to continue the pattern.

2 TEACH

GUIDING STUDENTS' WORK

Some students may need help in the "clock arithmetic" for finding the length of each period. Encourage them to use clock faces or other techniques to subtract or add clock times.

EXTRA EXAMPLES

Example A movie is being shown all day. The first three starting times are 11:30 A.M., 1:05 P.M., and 2:40 P.M., and that pattern continues. If you get to the movie theater at 8:50 P.M., how long will you wait until the next showing? **The rest of the starting times for the afternoon and evening shows are 4:15, 5:50, 7:25, 9:00, and 10:35. If you get there at 8:50, you have 10 minutes until the 9:00 showing.**

12.6 Problem Solving Strategies

- Draw a Diagram
- Work Backward
- Solve a Simpler Problem
- Make a Model
- Look for a Pattern
- Break into Parts
- Draw a Graph

Look for a Pattern

Problem You need to leave school at 1:15 P.M. for a short appointment and you expect to return a half hour later. You know that the first three class periods start at 8:15 A.M., 9:04 A.M., and 9:53 A.M. and that all eight periods are the same length. Will you return in time for your 8th period class?

① Read and Understand

Read the problem carefully.

You want to find when 8th period begins and the time you'll return.

② Make a Plan

Decide on a strategy to use.

One way to solve the problem is to look for a pattern in the class starting times.

③ Solve the Problem

Reread the problem and look for a pattern.

First, figure out how you get from one starting time to the next. Do you add, subtract, multiply, or divide?

8:15   9:04   9:53
$+49$ $+49$

You *add* 49 minutes to find the starting time for the next period.

Continue the pattern by adding 49 minutes to each starting time until you reach 8th period.

Period	1st	2nd	3rd	4th	5th	6th	7th	8th
Starting time	8:15	9:04	9:53	10:42	11:31	12:20	1:09	1:58

$+49$ $+49$ $+49$ $+49$ $+49$ $+49$ $+49$

You'll return 30 minutes after 1:15 P.M., which is at 1:45 P.M.

ANSWER You will return in time for your 8th period class that begins at 1:58 P.M., because your return time of 1:45 P.M. is earlier than 1:58 P.M.

④ Look Back

Because 49 minutes is 11 minutes less than an hour, you can instead think of adding 1 hour and subtracting 11 minutes to get the next time.

NCTM CURRICULUM STANDARDS
Standard 2: Understand patterns
Standard 6: Solve problems in math and other contexts; Apply/adapt strategies to solve problems

Practice the Strategy

Use the strategy _look for a pattern_.

1. **Bus Travel** A bus left at 4:55 P.M., 5:07 P.M., 5:19 P.M., and 5:31 P.M. Assume the bus schedule continues to follow a pattern. Describe the pattern and predict when the next bus will leave if it is now 6:20 P.M. **add 12 min; 6:31 P.M.**

2. **Train Travel** A train schedule lists departures at 8:03 A.M., 8:34 A.M., 9:05 A.M., and 9:36 A.M. Assume the departure times continue to follow a pattern. Predict the departure times for the next three trains. **10:07 A.M., 10:38 A.M., 11:09 A.M.**

3. **Number Patterns** Describe the pattern. Then find the next three numbers. **subtract 5; −7, −12, −17**
   13, 8, 3, −2, _?_ , _?_ , _?_

4. **Letter Patterns** Describe the pattern. Then find the next two letters. **skip 3 letters in the alphabet; Q, U**
   A, E, I, M, _?_ , _?_

5. **Necklace** A friend asks you to finish stringing beads on a necklace. Describe the pattern the friend used and find the next five beads to continue the pattern. **See margin.**

6. **Auto Repair** You buy a set of socket wrenches that come in $\frac{15}{16}$, 1, $1\frac{1}{16}$, and $1\frac{1}{8}$ inch sizes. Predict the next two sizes. $1\frac{3}{16}$ **in.,** $1\frac{1}{4}$ **in.**

7. **Secret Code** A number from 1–26 was assigned to each letter of the alphabet. Decode the secret message.

   6   3–12–15–4–12–17

   10–22   9–18–11–26–5. **See margin.**

Mixed Problem Solving

Use any strategy to solve the problem.

8. **Coordinate Graphing** Begin at (3, 4). Move up 6 units. Then move to the right 2 units and then down 12 units. What are the coordinates of your new position? **(5, −2)**

9. **Money** You spend $4.25 on lunch, lend a friend $2.50, find a quarter, buy a snack for $1.35, and then have $2.35 left. How much money did you have before lunch? **$10.20**

10. **Street Numbers** You paint house numbers on curbs for homeowners. You have number stencils, but you are missing the number 3. How many numbers between 1 and 200 are you unable to paint? **38**

11. **Playhouse** You are building a playhouse. Calculate the surface area of the exterior surfaces. Do not include the door or the floor. **100 ft²**

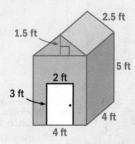

COMMON ERROR

In Exercise 1, students may calculate the pattern that a bus leaves every 12 minutes, and conclude that the bus after 6:20 would be at 6:32. Ask them if a bus actually leaves at exactly 6:20.

TEACHING TIP

For Exercise 2, ask students to write the times in two columns:
   8:03   8:34
   9:05   9:36
Then they can see that in each column, the time between trains is 1 hour 2 minutes. They can easily write the times in each column, and then list the times chronologically.

SUGGESTED STRATEGIES

You may wish to suggest the following strategies for the problems in the Mixed Problem Solving:
- Exercise 8: Draw a Graph
- Exercise 9: Work Backward
- Exercise 10: Solve a Simpler Problem, Break into Parts
- Exercise 11: Break into Parts

5. The bead pattern is: large blue bead, small yellow bead, two small green beads, small yellow bead. This pattern of five beads repeats. So the next five beads are: small yellow bead, two small green beads, small yellow bead, large blue bead.

7. Message: I forgot my lunch. Note that the pattern used is: I = 6, J = 7, K = 8, ..., Y = 22, Z = 23, A = 24, B = 25, C = 26, D = 1, E = 2, F = 3, G = 4, H = 5.

Name the coordinates of each point.

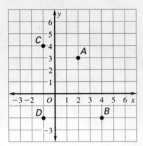

1. A (2, 3) **2.** B (4, −2)
3. C (−1, 4) **4.** D (−1, −2)

LESSON OBJECTIVE

Graph linear functions.

PACING

Suggested Number of Days
Basic Course: 2 days
Average Course: 2 days
Advanced Course: 2 days
Block: 1 block

TEACHING RESOURCES

For a complete list of Teaching Resources, see page 580B.

 TRANSPARENCY

Warm-Up Exercises for this lesson are available on a transparency.

MOTIVATING THE LESSON

Use a coordinate grid on the overhead projector to graph ordered pairs from an input-output table for $y = 2x - 1$. Ask students what seems to be true about the points.

 **LESSON 12.6**

Graphing Functions

BEFORE	Now	WHY?
You graphed ordered pairs in a coordinate plane.	You'll graph linear functions in a coordinate plane.	So you can predict time spent making signs, as in Ex. 28.

 **Word Watch**

linear function, p. 613

In the Real World

Walking You are training for a long distance walking race. In your practice walks, you maintain a steady rate of about 15 minutes per mile. How can you use a graph to represent this relationship?

The number of miles you walk x and the number of minutes it takes y are related by the rule $y = 15x$. So, the distances and times for practice walks are represented by points on the graph of the function $y = 15x$.

EXAMPLE 1 **Graphing a Function**

To graph the function $y = 15x$ mentioned above, follow the steps below.

(1 Make an input-output table for the function $y = 15x$.

Input, x	Output, y
0	0
1	15
2	30
3	45

(2 Write the input and output values as ordered pairs: (input, output).

(0, 0), (1, 15), (2, 30), (3, 45)

(3 Graph the ordered pairs. Notice that the points all lie along a straight line. If you chose other input values for your table, the points you would graph would also lie along that same line.

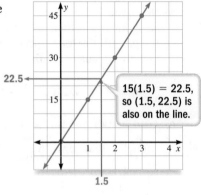

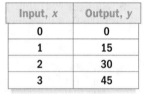
15(1.5) = 22.5, so (1.5, 22.5) is also on the line.

(4 Draw a line through the points. That line represents the complete graph of the function $y = 15x$.

Your turn now Copy the table and graph from Example 1. Then evaluate the function for the given input. Graph the ordered pair to check whether the point is on the line. 1–3. The graphed points are on the line.

1. $x = 6$ 90 **2.** $x = 2.5$ 37.5 **3.** $x = \frac{1}{2}$ $7\frac{1}{2}$

NCTM CURRICULUM STANDARDS
Standard 2: Understand functions
Standard 9: Use connections among mathematical ideas
Standard 10: Use representations to solve problems

Representing Functions

There are many ways to represent the same function.

Words A number is the sum of another number and one.

Algebra $y = x + 1$

Ordered Pairs $(-2, -1)$, $(-1, 0)$, $(0, 1)$, $(1, 2)$, $(2, 3)$

Input-Output Table

Input, x	Output, y
-2	-1
-1	0
0	1
1	2
2	3

Graph

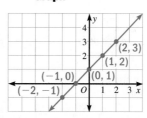

Types of Functions A **linear function** is a function whose graph is a straight line. Not all functions are linear functions.

EXAMPLE 2 **Identifying Linear Functions**

with Notetaking

It may be helpful to include a flow chart in your notes on identifying linear functions. Your flow chart should include steps for graphing ordered pairs, as in Example 1, and a step for deciding whether you can draw a line through the points.

Tell whether the function is *linear* or *not linear*. Explain.

a.

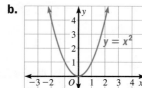

The function is linear, because the graph is a straight line.

b.

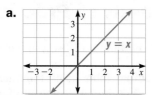

The function is not linear, because the graph is not a straight line.

Your turn now Graph the function using the input values $x = 1, 2, 3, 4,$ and 5. Tell whether the function is *linear* or *not linear*. Explain.

4–6. See margin.

4. $y = x - 1$ **5.** $y = 3 - x$ **6.** $y = 2x + 1$

7. Can a graph in the shape of a V represent a linear function? Explain.

No; the graph is not a straight line.

Lesson 12.6   Graphing Functions   **613**

TIPS FOR NEW TEACHERS

Be sure students understand that first coordinates are input values and that second coordinates are output values. See Tips for New Teachers in the *Chapter 12 Resource Book*.

EXTRA EXAMPLES

Example 1

a. Graph the function $y = -2x$. and use the graph to find the value of y for an x value of -1.5. **3**

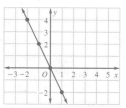

Example 2 Tell whether the function is *linear* or *not linear*. Explain.

a.

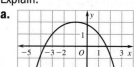

The function is not linear because the graph is not a straight line.

b.

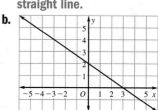

The function is linear because the graph is a straight line.

 TRANSPARENCY

A support transparency is available for Examples 1 and 3.

4–6. See Additional Answers beginning on page AA1.

613

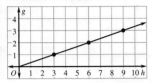

You can use the graph of a linear function to help make predictions.

EXAMPLE 3 **Looking for a Pattern**

Pools The graph shows the time it takes to fill a wading pool to various depths. Predict how long it takes to fill the pool to a depth of 15 inches.

Solution

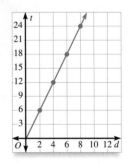

① Write some ordered pairs from the graph.

$(2, 6)$, $(4, 12)$, $(6, 18)$, $(8, 24)$

② Write a function rule.

$t = 3d$, where *d* is depth in inches and *t* is time in minutes

③ Evaluate the function when $d = 15$.

$t = 3(15) = 45$

ANSWER The water will be 15 inches deep in about 45 minutes.

 with Solving

In many situations, including those in Examples 1 and 3, it does not make sense to have values less than 0. In Example 3, it also does not make sense for *d*-values to be greater than the height of the pool.

12.6 Exercises

More Practice, p. 719

INTERNET
eWorkbook Plus
CLASSZONE.COM

Getting Ready to Practice

1. **Vocabulary** A function whose graph is a straight line is a ? function.
   linear

Make an input-output table using the function rule and the input values *x* = 0, 1, 2, 3, and 4. Graph the function. 2–3. See margin.

2. $y = 5 + x$
3. $y = 2x - 3$

Lunch The table shows the cost of a salad with a cup of soup for lunch.

Ounces of salad, *s*	Total cost of lunch, *t*
2	$2.50
4	$3.00
6	$3.50
8	$4.00

4. Write the values in the table as ordered pairs (ounces, total cost).
   (2, 2.50), (4, 3.00), (6, 3.50), (8, 4.00)

5. Use the ordered pairs from Exercise 4 to graph the function. Is the function linear? **See margin for art; yes.**

6. Use the graph to find the cost of a 7 ounce salad with a cup of soup.
   $3.75

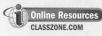
20. Linear; the graph is a straight line.

21. Linear; the graph is a straight line.

22. Not linear; the graph is not a straight line.

23. Extend the line so it passes through the point with *x*-coordinate 8.5 and determine the *y*-coordinate to find the number of skiers; use the function rule and substitute 8.5 for *x*.

Practice and Problem Solving

Graph the ordered pairs. Draw a line through the points. 7–10. See margin.

A **7.** $(-3, -1)$, $(0, 0)$, $(3, 1)$, $(6, 2)$ **8.** $(-1, 2)$, $(1, 2)$, $(3, 2)$, $(5, 2)$

9. $(0, -1)$, $(2, 2)$, $(4, 5)$, $(6, 8)$ **10.** $(0, 6)$, $(1.5, 4.5)$, $(3, 3)$ $(4.5, 1.5)$

Make an input-output table using the function rule and the input values $x = 0, 1, 2, 3,$ and 4. Graph the function. 11–19. See margin.

11. $y = x + 4$ **12.** $y = 3x$ **13.** $y = 7 - x$

14. $y = 5x + 1$ **15.** $y = x + 2.5$ **16.** $y = \frac{1}{2}x$

17. $y = \frac{1}{2}x + 2$ **18.** $y = x - 3$ **19.** $y = 10 - 3x$

Decide Tell whether the function is *linear* or *not linear*. Explain.
20–22. See margin.

20. $y = 2x - 3$ **21.** $y = 5 - x$ **22.** $y = x^2 - 1$

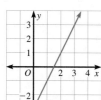 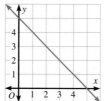

23. Writing The number of skiers a ski lift carries is estimated by the function rule $y = 2x$, where x is the number of hours and y is the number of skiers in thousands. How can you use a graph of the function to find the number of skiers carried in 8.5 hours? How can you find the number of skiers carried in 8.5 hours without making a graph?
See margin.

Look for a Pattern Graph the ordered pairs and draw a line through the points. Write a function rule for the ordered pairs. 24–27. See margin.

B **24.** $(0, 1)$, $(1, 2)$, $(2, 3)$, $(3, 4)$, $(4, 5)$ **25.** $(-1, 3)$, $(0, 4)$, $(1, 5)$, $(2, 6)$, $(3, 7)$

26. $(0, 0)$, $\left(\frac{1}{2}, 1\right)$, $(1, 2)$, $\left(1\frac{1}{2}, 3\right)$, $(2, 4)$ **27.** $(0, 5)$, $(1, 4)$, $(2, 3)$, $(3, 2)$, $(4, 1)$

28. Signs You are making signs for your school's art festival. The table shows the amount of time it takes you to make signs. Use ordered pairs from the table to graph the function. Then predict how many signs you can make in 5 hours (300 minutes). **See margin for art; 15 signs.**

Number of signs	Time (min)
2	40
4	80
6	120
8	160

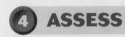
ASSESSMENT RESOURCES

For more assessment resources, see:
- Assessment Book
- Test and Practice Generator

MINI-QUIZ

1. Graph the function $y = 3x$.

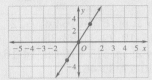

2. The graph shows the number of reams of paper R used at a copy shop in h hours. Predict how many reams of paper will be used in 24 hours. **48 reams**

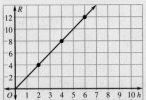

5 **FOLLOW-UP**

RETEACHING/REMEDIATION
- Study Guide in Chapter 12 Resource Book, pp. 57–58
- eTutorial Plus Online
- Extra Practice, p. 719
- Lesson Practice in Chapter 12 Resource Book, pp. 54–56

CHALLENGE/ENRICHMENT
- Challenge Practice in Chapter 12 Resource Book, p. 60
- Teacher's Edition, p. 580F

ENGLISH LEARNER SUPPORT
- Spanish Study Guide
- Multi-Language Glossary
- Chapter Audio Summaries CDs

29, 30, 32, 46. See Additional Answers beginning on page AA1.

HELP with **Solving**

You don't always use x and y to label the axes of your graphs. In Ex. 30, the horizontal axis should be labeled s and the vertical axis should be labeled V.

Extended Problem Solving In Exercises 29–31, use the function $V = s^3$ to find the volume of a cube, where s is the side length of the cube.

C **29. Evaluate** Make an input-output table using the input values 1, 2, 4, 8, and 16.
29–30. See margin.

30. Graph Graph the ordered pairs from the table. Is the function linear?

31. Compare How does the volume of a cube change when its side length doubles? **8 times as large**

32. Challenge The function for finding the area of a circle is $A = \pi r^2$, where r is the radius of the circle. Make an input-output table for the function. Graph the function. How does the area change if the input value is doubled? tripled? quadrupled? **See margin.**

Mixed Review

Write the fraction or mixed number as a decimal. Use bar notation to show a repeating decimal. *(Lesson 5.8)*

33. $\dfrac{3}{10}$ 0.3   **34.** $\dfrac{11}{6}$ $1.8\overline{3}$ **35.** $1\dfrac{4}{11}$ $1.\overline{36}$ **36.** $6\dfrac{3}{8}$ 6.375

Copy and complete the statement. *(Lesson 8.1)*

37. $\dfrac{2}{3} = \dfrac{8}{?}$ 12   **38.** $\dfrac{20}{?} = \dfrac{4}{5}$ 25   **39.** $\dfrac{?}{11} = \dfrac{18}{22}$ 9   **40.** $\dfrac{40}{100} = \dfrac{?}{25}$ 10

41. Write a function rule for the input-output table. *(Lesson 12.5)*
$y = x + 8$

Input, x	7	8	9	10
Output, y	15	16	17	18

Basic Skills **You have \$21. Determine how many packs of trading cards you can buy for the given price.**

42. \$3 per pack
7 packs

43. \$1.50 per pack
14 packs

44. \$1.75 per pack
12 packs

Test-Taking Practice

45. Multiple Choice What ordered pairs are part of the graph of the function $y = 5x + 7$? **D**

A. (5, 7), (10, 14), (15, 21)   **B.** (0, 7), (1, 2), (2, −3)

C. (0, 5), (1, 12), (2, 19)   **D.** (1, 12), (2, 17), (4, 27)

46. Short Response On the same coordinate plane, graph the functions $y = 3x + 4$, $y = 3x$, and $y = 3x - 4$. Use the input values $x = 0, 1, 2, 3,$ and 4. What do you notice about the graphs? **See margin.**

INTERNET
State Test Practice
CLASSZONE.COM

12.6

CALCULATOR

Technology *Activity*

Graphing Linear Functions

GOAL Use a graphing calculator to graph linear functions.

 Example You can graph linear functions using a graphing calculator.

At a local bank, a money order costs the amount of the money order plus a $1 fee. A function rule for the money order is $y = x + 1$, where x is the amount of the money order and y is the total cost. Graph this function.

Solution

1 To enter the function rule into a graphing calculator, press Y= . With the cursor next to $Y_1=$, enter the function rule by pressing x + 1.

2 To display the graph, press GRAPH . If you use the standard viewing window, the graph shows values from -10 through 10 along the x- and y-axes.

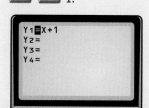

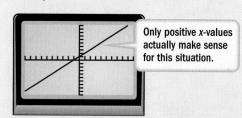

Only positive x-values actually make sense for this situation.

Your turn now Use a graphing calculator to graph the function. In Exercises 11 and 12, also tell what x-values make sense. 1–10. See margin

1. $y = x + 2$
2. $y = x - 4$
3. $y = 3x$
4. $y = \frac{x}{3}$
5. $y = \frac{1}{5}x$

6. $y = 3 - x$
7. $y = 3x - 5$
8. $y = 2x + 1$
9. $y = 1 - 4x$
10. $y = -x$

11. **Geometry** The function rule $y = 3.14x$ can be used to estimate the circumference of a circle, where x is the diameter of the circle.
See margin for art. Only positive numbers make sense since you cannot have a negative diameter.

12. **Snow** Under certain weather conditions, the function rule $y = 0.1x$ can be used to estimate the number of inches of water y contained in x inches of snow. See margin for art. Only positive numbers make sense since you cannot have negative inches of snow.

Lesson 12.6   Graphing Functions   **617**

1 **PLAN**

LEARN THE METHOD
• Students will use a graphing calculator to graph linear functions.
• Students can use a graphing calculator to complete Exercises 11–19 of Lesson 12.6.

2 **TEACH**

TIPS FOR SUCCESS
Be sure students know how to correct keyboarding errors and how to clear prior functions and their graphs.

EXTRA EXAMPLES

Example Use a graphing calculator to graph $y = x + 1.5$.

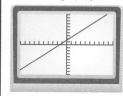

3 **CLOSE**

ASSESSMENT

1. The formula $y = 1.414x$ can be used to estimate the length of the diagonal of a square where x is the side of the square. Graph this function.

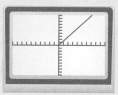

1–12. See Additional Answers beginning on page AA1.

Notebook Review (page 619)

7.

Input, x	Output, y
0	5
1	6
2	7
3	8
4	9

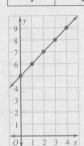

8–10. See Additional Answers beginning on page AA1.

 LESSONS 12.4 TO 12.6

Notebook Review

 NoTebook

Review the vocabulary definitions in your notebook.

Copy the review examples in your notebook. Then complete the exercises.

Check Your Definitions

function, p. 605   input, output, p. 605   linear function, p. 613

Use Your Vocabulary

1. Copy and complete: You can use a table of ? and ? values to graph a function. **input; output**

2. How can you tell from its graph whether a function is linear?
   The graph is a straight line.

12.4 Can you solve multiplication and division equations?

 EXAMPLE

a. $2x = 10$

$\dfrac{2x}{2} = \dfrac{10}{2}$

$x = 5$

b. $7 = \dfrac{z}{3}$

$3 \cdot 7 = 3 \cdot \dfrac{z}{3}$

$21 = z$

 Solve the equation.

3. $6p = 18$ 3   **4.** $68 = 4q$ 17   **5.** $15 = \dfrac{w}{8}$ 120   **6.** $\dfrac{x}{2} = 10$ 20

12.5–12.6 Can you evaluate and graph functions?

 EXAMPLE Graph the function $y = x - 2$.

	Table		Ordered Pairs	Graph
Input, x	$y = x - 2$	Output, y		
0	$y = 0 - 2$	-2	$(0, -2)$	
1	$y = 1 - 2$	-1	$(1, -1)$	
2	$y = 2 - 2$	0	$(2, 0)$	
3	$y = 3 - 2$	1	$(3, 1)$	

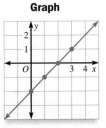

☑ **Make an input-output table using the function rule and the input values x = 0, 1, 2, 3, and 4. Graph the function.** 7–10. See margin.

7. $y = x + 5$ **8.** $y = 17 - x$ **9.** $y = 4x - 5$ **10.** $y = \frac{1}{2}x + 4$

11. Write a function rule for the input-output table.

$w = \frac{d}{7}$

Days, d	7	14	21	28
Weeks, w	1	2	3	4

Stop and Think about Lessons 12.4–12.6

12. Explain The formula for the area of a rectangle is $A = lw$, where w is the width and l is the length. Explain how to solve for the length of a rectangle if you are given the area and the width.
Substitute the given values for *A* and *w* and solve the equation for *l*.

Review Quiz 2

Solve the equation.

1. $10w = 20$ 2

2. $13x = 78$ 6

3. $72 = 2z$ 36

4. $77 = 7y$ 11

5. $\frac{a}{5} = 8$ 40

6. $\frac{b}{13} = 4$ 52

7. $24 = \frac{c}{2}$ 48

8. $6 = \frac{d}{30}$ 180

Write the sentence as an equation. Then solve the equation.

9. Five times a number r is 75.
$5r = 75; 15$

10. A number d divided by 7 is 8.

10. $\frac{d}{7} = 8$; 56

11. Wages You earn $5 per hour raking. Write and solve a multiplication equation to find t, the number of hours you must work to earn $35.
$5t = 35; 7$ h

Write a function rule for the input-output table.

12.

Tickets, t	Cost, c
2	$8
4	$16
6	$24
8	$32

$c = 4t$

13.

Sale price, s	Original price, p
$70	$80
$63	$73
$85	$95
$56	$66

$p = s + 10$

Make an input-output table using the function rule and the input values x = 3, 6, 9, and 12. Graph the function. 14–17. See margin.

14. $y = x$

15. $y = 5x - 10$

16. $y = 14 - x$

17. $y = \frac{1}{3}x + 3$

Review Quiz 2

14.

Input, x	Output, y
3	3
6	6
9	9
12	12

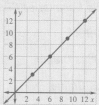

15.

Input, x	Output, y
3	5
6	20
9	35
12	50

16.

Input, x	Output, y
3	11
6	8
9	5
12	2

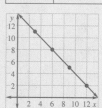

17. See Additional Answers beginning on page AA1.

619

ADDITIONAL RESOURCES
The following resources are available to help review the materials in this chapter.

Chapter 12 Resource Book
- Chapter Review Games and Activities, p. 61
- Cumulative Practice, Chs. 1–12

English/Spanish Chapter Reviews and Tests

Chapter Audio Summaries CDs

eTutorial CD-ROM

eWorkbook Plus Online

eTutorial Plus Online

3. Sample:

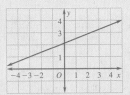

4. Sample:

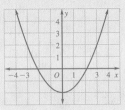

Page 621

48.

Input, x	Output, y
0	0
5	50
10	100
15	150
20	200

49.

Input, x	Output, y
0	15
5	25
10	35
15	45
20	55

---

12 Chapter Review

Vocabulary

function, p. 605　　　input, output, p. 605　　　linear function, p. 613

Vocabulary Review

1. In the function $y = 3x + 1$, what variable represents the input? the output? x; y

2. In a function, what is special about the relationship of inputs and outputs?
Each input has exactly one output.

3. Sketch an example of a linear function.
3–4. See margin.

4. Sketch an example of a function that is not linear.

Review Questions

Write the phrase as an expression. Let x represent the number.
(Lesson 12.1)

5. The difference of 7 and a number　$7 - x$

6. A number times 16　$16x$

7. 15 more than a number　$15 + x$

8. The quotient of a number and 2　$\frac{x}{2}$

Write the sentence as an equation. *(Lesson 12.1)*

9. A number n divided by 3 is 15.　$\frac{n}{3} = 15$

10. Five less than a number p is 7.　$p - 5 = 7$

11. The product of 2 and a number q is 10.　$2q = 10$

12. 100 is 40 increased by a number r.　$100 = 40 + r$

Solve the equation. *(Lessons 12.2, 12.3)*

13. $a + 8 = 12$　4
14. $3 + b = 21$　18
15. $32 = 12 + c$　20
16. $22 = d + 18$　4

17. $69 = f + 17$　52
18. $32 + e = 51$　19
19. $g + 2.7 = 4.6$　1.9
20. $12.5 = 1.9 + h$　10.6

21. $x - 7 = 9$　16
22. $p - 8 = 21$　29
23. $q - 31 = 13$　44
24. $2 = r - 29$　31

25. $19 = s - 19$　38
26. $57 = t - 24$　81
27. $18 = w - 3.8$　21.8
28. $z - 4.02 = 1.86$　5.88

29. **Sports** Your friend hits a golf ball 250 yards. Your ball lands 35 yards short of it. Write and solve an addition equation to find the distance your ball traveled. *(Lesson 12.2)*　$x + 35 = 250$; 215 yd

30. **Employees** Eleven employees of a company are out of the office. There are 98 employees currently in the office. Write and solve a subtraction equation to find the total number of employees. *(Lesson 12.3)* **Sample answer:** $x - 11 = 98$; 109 employees

Review Questions

Solve the equation. *(Lesson 12.4)*

31. $4p = 36$ 9   **32.** $5q = 105$ 21   **33.** $58 = 2r$ 29   **34.** $140 = 7s$ 20

35. $3t = 132$ 44   **36.** $10u = 1000$ 100   **37.** $135 = 9w$ 15   **38.** $0 = 12x$ 0

39. $\frac{a}{5} = 4$ 20   **40.** $\frac{b}{2} = 25$ 50   **41.** $10 = \frac{c}{3}$ 30   **42.** $12 = \frac{d}{10}$ 120

43. $\frac{h}{7} = 5$ 35   **44.** $\frac{k}{6} = 12$ 72   **45.** $\frac{m}{20} = 4$ 80   **46.** $\frac{n}{11} = 15$ 165

47. Geometry A rectangle has a width of 3 feet and an area of 57 square feet. Write and solve a multiplication equation to find the length of the rectangle. *(Lesson 12.4)* $3l = 57$; 19 ft

Make an input-output table using the function rule and the input values $x = 0, 5, 10, 15,$ and 20. *(Lesson 12.5)*   48–51. See margin.

48. $y = 10x$ **49.** $y = 2x + 15$ **50.** $y = 100 - x$ **51.** $y = \frac{x}{5}$

Write a function rule for the input-output table. *(Lesson 12.5)*

52.

Words, w	Pages, p
250	1
500	2
750	3
1000	4

$p = \frac{w}{250}$

53.

Sale, s	Regular, r
$5.00	$7.50
$10.00	$12.50
$15.00	$17.50
$20.00	$22.50

$r = s + 2.50$

54.

Gallons, g	Cups, c
1	16
2	32
3	48
4	64

$c = 16g$

Make an input-output table. Then write a function rule for the relationship. *(Lesson 12.5)*   55–56. See margin.

55. input: months; output: years   **56.** input: age now; output: age in 20 years

Make an input-output table using the function rule and the input values $x = 0, 2, 4, 6,$ and 8. Graph the function. *(Lesson 12.6)*

57–59. See margin.

57. $y = 12 - x$ **58.** $y = 3x - 4$ **59.** $y = \frac{1}{2}x + 3$

Graph the ordered pairs. Write a function rule for the ordered pairs. *(Lesson 12.6)*   60–61. See margin.

60. $(0, 0), (2, 1), (4, 2), (6, 3), (8, 4)$

61. $(1, 8), (2, 7), (3, 6), (4, 5), (5, 4)$

62. Tell whether the function at the right is *linear* or *not linear*. Explain. *(Lesson 12.6)*

Linear; the graph is a straight line.

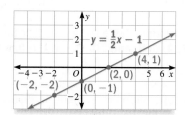

50.

Input, x	Output, y
0	100
5	95
10	90
15	85
20	80

51.

Input, x	Output, y
0	0
5	1
10	2
15	3
20	4

55.

Months, m	Years, y
12	1
24	2
36	3
48	4

$y = \frac{m}{12}$

56.

Input, x	Output, y
5	25
10	30
15	35
20	40

$y = x + 20$

57.

Input, x	Output, y
0	12
2	10
4	8
6	6
8	4

58–61. See Additional Answers beginning on page AA1.

23.

Input, x	Output, y
0	0
3	15
6	30
9	45
12	60

24.

Input, x	Output, y
0	6
3	18
6	30
9	42
12	54

25.

Input, x	Output, y
0	60
3	54
6	48
9	42
12	36

26.

Input, x	Output, y
0	0
3	1
6	2
9	3
12	4

27.

Kilometers, k	Meters, m
1	1000
2	2000
3	3000
4	4000

$m = 1000k$

28–33. See Additional Answers beginning on page AA1.

12 Chapter Test

Write the sentence as an equation.

1. Five times a number b is 30. $5b = 30$

2. 15 is a number c divided by 3. $15 = \frac{c}{3}$

3. A number d decreased by 5 is 22. $d - 5 = 22$

4. The sum of e and 25 is 100. $e + 25 = 100$

Solve the equation.

5. $x + 4 = 15$ 11

6. $7 + y = 13$ 6

7. $z + 9 = 18$ 9

8. $25 = w + 3$ 22

9. $a - 8 = 24$ 32

10. $b - 17 = 15$ 32

11. $44 = c - 12$ 56

12. $d - 52 = 9$ 61

13. Pottery A pottery class has 26 students. Seventeen of the students are girls. Write and solve an addition equation to find the number of boys in the class. $17 + x = 26$; 9 boys

Solve the equation.

14. $15p = 60$ 4

15. $9q = 99$ 11

16. $198 = 6r$ 33

17. $52 = 2s$ 26

18. $\frac{m}{7} = 7$ 49

19. $\frac{n}{13} = 4$ 52

20. $9 = \frac{w}{20}$ 180

21. $16 = \frac{x}{3}$ 48

22. Music Jorge practiced his trumpet three times as long as Randy did. Jorge practiced for 105 minutes. Write and solve a multiplication equation to find how long Randy practiced.

$3x = 105$; 35 min

Make an input-output table using the function rule and the input values x = 0, 3, 6, 9, and 12. 23–26. See margin.

23. $y = 5x$

24. $y = 4x + 6$

25. $y = 60 - 2x$

26. $y = \frac{x}{3}$

Make an input-output table. Then write a function rule for the relationship. 27–29. See margin.

27. input: kilometers
output: meters

28. input: age as freshman
output: age as senior

29. input: side length of square
output: area of square

Make an input-output table using the function rule and the input values x = 2, 4, 6, 8, and 10. Graph the function. 30–32. See margin.

30. $y = 12 - x$

31. $y = 3x - 4$

32. $y = \frac{1}{2}x + 1$

33. Graph the ordered pairs (7, 3), (8, 4), (9, 5), (10, 6), and (11, 7). Write a function rule for the ordered pairs. See margin.

Chapter Standardized Test

Test-Taking Strategy If you find yourself becoming tense and worried, stop and take some deep breaths. This can help you to feel calmer and more relaxed.

ADDITIONAL RESOURCES

 Assessment Book
• Standardized Chapter Test, p. 154

 Test and Practice Generator

Multiple Choice

1. What equation represents "25 less than a number k is 17"? **A**

  A. $k - 25 = 17$ **B.** $25 - k = 17$

  C. $17 - k = 25$ **D.** $25 + k = 17$

2. Your friend has done one fourth the number of math puzzles you have done. If z is the number of puzzles you have done, what is an expression for the number your friend has done? **H**

  F. $z - \frac{1}{4}$ **G.** $z + \frac{1}{4}$ **H.** $\frac{z}{4}$ **I.** $4z$

3. What is the solution of the equation $x + 12 = 24$? **B**

  A. 2   **B.** 12   **C.** 18   **D.** 40

4. What is the solution of the equation $11 = n - 5$? **H**

  F. -6 **G.** 6   **H.** 16   **I.** 55

5. Which whole number is closest to the solution of the equation $t - 15.2 = 23.9$? **D**

  A. 8   **B.** 9   **C.** 38   **D.** 39

6. You buy a pair of soccer shin guards for d dollars. If you give the clerk $20 and receive $2.05 in change, which equation can you use to find d? **I**

  F. $d + 20 = 2.05$ **G.** $2.05d = 20$

  H. $d - 2.05 = 20$ **I.** $20 = d + 2.05$

7. What is the solution of the equation $9p = 108$? **B**

  A. 2   **B.** 12   **C.** 99   **D.** 972

8. What is the solution of the equation $\frac{b}{5} = 18$? **H**

  F. $\frac{18}{5}$ **G.** 13   **H.** 90   **I.** 95

9. What is the solution of the equation $20 = \frac{d}{20}$? **D**

  A. $\frac{1}{20}$ **B.** 1   **C.** 40   **D.** 400

10. What is the output y of the function $y = 3x - 5$ when the input x is 5? **I**

  F. 0   **G.** 3   **H.** 5   **I.** 10

11. Which function rule has the following graph? **D**

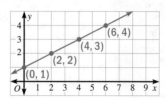

  A. $y = 2x + 1$ **B.** $y = x + 2$

  C. $x = 2y + 1$ **D.** $y = \frac{1}{2}x + 1$

Short Response

12. Graph the function $y = 5 - x$. Use the input values $x = 0, 1, 2, 3$, and 4. Show your steps.
See margin.

Extended Response

13. A triangle has a base of 10 centimeters. Choose various heights h as inputs. For each input, find the area A of the triangle as the output. Record your results in an input-output table. Graph the ordered pairs (h, A). Write a function rule relating h and A.
See margin.

12. See Additional Answers beginning on page AA1.

13. *Sample answer:*

Height, h	Area, A
2	10
4	20
6	30
8	40
10	50

$A = 5h$

- Students explore the relationship between the circumference of an elephant's footprint and its shoulder height.
- Circumference was studied in Lesson 10.3. Graphing functions was studied in Lessons 12.5 and 12.6.
- Scientists can use the circumference of an elephant's footprint to help them estimate the height of the elephant.

SCIENCE BACKGROUND

Gathering data about the size of wild animals is just one of the many aspects of learning about them. The animals' habitats, longevity, and breeding habits are also useful to biologists working to protect endangered species.

2 TEACH

TIPS FOR SUCCESS

After students complete Exercises 1 and 2, ask them to compare their graphs and conclusions with those of other students. Then have them work individually on Exercises 3-5. Use Exercise 6 for class discussion.

GUIDING STUDENTS' WORK

In Exercises 4 and 5, be sure students plot the points and include their line on the graph they made for Exercise 1. Suggest that they use a second color for the new points and the line.

1, 4. See Additional Answers beginning on page AA1.

EXPLORING **MATH** IN **SCIENCE**

Investigating
Elephant
TRACKS

Measuring Elephants

Scientists who study elephants often need to know the sizes of the animals they observe. However, it can be very difficult to get a wild elephant to stand still while a human measures it.

Instead, scientists have found a method of estimating the shoulder height of an elephant by using the circumference of the elephant's forefoot. Scientists can find the circumference of the forefoot easily by measuring the tracks left by an elephant passing through the mud.

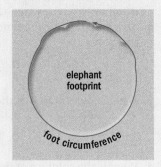

elephant footprint

foot circumference

The table below contains measurements of 16 elephants from Africa.

Elephant Measurements								
Forefoot circumference (cm)	110	112	145	130	120	120	107	117
Shoulder height (cm)	252	204	309	284	272	267	239	237
Forefoot circumference (cm)	105	115	117	140	117	110	120	110
Shoulder height (cm)	229	239	252	304	249	244	224	249

1. Use the data in the table to make a graph. Put foot circumference on the x-axis, numbering from 100 to 150 and using increments of 5. Put shoulder height on the y-axis, numbering from 200 to 310 and using increments of 10. **See margin.**

2. **Critical Thinking** What patterns do you notice in your graph? In general, what happens to an elephant's shoulder height as the foot circumference increases? **The points seem to rise from left to right; it increases.**

Testing a Formula

Scientists in the field use a rule of thumb to estimate elephant heights. According to this rule of thumb, an elephant's shoulder height is about twice the circumference of the elephant's forefoot.

3. Express the scientists' rule of thumb as a formula. Let x be the forefoot circumference. Let y be the shoulder height. $y = 2x$

4. Use your formula from Exercise 3. Copy and complete the input-output table. Then plot the information from the table on your graph from Exercise 1. Draw a line through the new points. This line represents the scientists' prediction of an elephant's height, based on its foot circumference. **See margin for art.**

Input, x	Output, y
110	220 ?
120	240 ?
140	280 ?

5. Compare the data points you plotted in Exercise 1 with the line you drew in Exercise 4. Do most of the data points fall above or below the line? Do any of the points fall on the line? **above; no**

6. Critical Thinking Do you think that the scientists' rule of thumb is a good one? If you use the rule of thumb, are you likely to overestimate or underestimate the height of an elephant? Explain your thinking. *Sample answer*: Yes; underestimate; most of the points on the graph I made were above the line for $y = 2x$.

Project IDEAS

- **Experiment** Measure the foot length and the height of each student in your class. Make a graph of the data. What patterns do you notice in your graph? **A good answer will include accurate data and graphs.**

- **Report** Find out about the sizes, weights, and life spans of a particular type of elephant. Use a poster to present your information. **A good answer will include accurate data and a neat, accurate poster.**

- **Research** Scientists who study animals in the wild use a variety of methods to observe and understand their subjects. Learn more about the methods scientists use to study a particular animal and present your findings to the class.
A good answer will include well-documented research and a clear presentation.

- **Career** People who study data and look for patterns are called statisticians. Learn more about the different kinds of work statisticians do. Present your findings to the class.
A good answer will include well-documented research and a clear presentation.

INTERNET
Project Support
CLASSZONE.COM

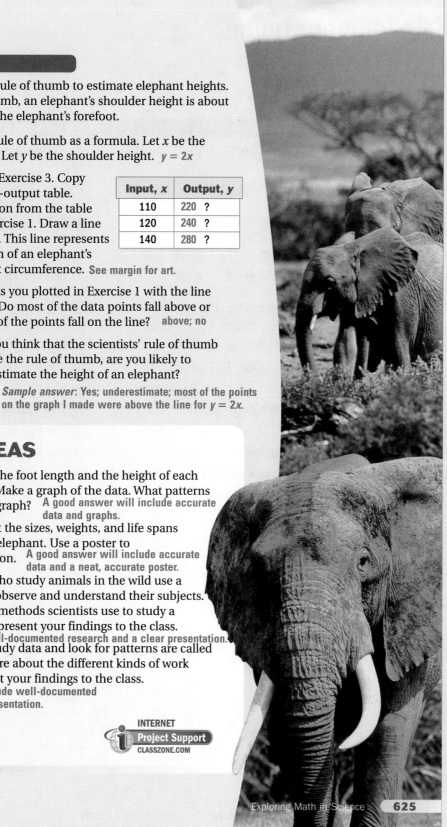

Exploring Math in Science   **625**

REFLECTING ON THE ACTIVITY

Useful information about wild animals can be obtained indirectly through scientific observation.

PROJECT IDEAS

For additional information on the Project Ideas and for suggestions for more projects, go to classzone.com

④ ASSESS

The rubric below can be used to assess the projects on the pupil page. For more information on rubrics, see the Professional Development Book.

4 The student fully achieves the mathematical and project goals. The graph is drawn correctly, and the formula expressing the relationship between the circumference of the elephant's footprint and its shoulder height is correct. All questions are answered correctly. All work is complete and accurate.

3 The student substantially achieves the mathematical and project goals. The graph or the input-output table may have small errors. There may be some minor misunderstanding of content, errors in computation, or weakness in presentation.

2 The student partially achieves the mathematical and project goals. Some of the questions may not have been answered. Some of the work may be incomplete, misdirected, or unclear.

1 The student makes little progress toward accomplishing the goals of the project because of a lack of understanding or lack of effort. The student did not answer the questions or notice any patterns in the graph.

Pacing and Assignment Guide

REGULAR SCHEDULE

Lesson	Les. Day	BASIC	AVERAGE	ADVANCED
13.1	Day 1	pp. 633–634 Exs. 7–12, 20, 25–27, 33–35	pp. 633–634 Exs. 7–12, 19–21, 28–31, 38–40	pp. 633–634 Exs. 9–12, 25–29, 33–36, 39
	Day 2	pp. 633–634 Exs. 13–18, 22–24, 36–39	pp. 633–634 Exs. 13–18, 23–27, 33–37	pp. 633–634 Exs. 15–24, 30–32*, 40
13.2	Day 1	SRH p. 703 Exs. 1–5; pp. 638–639 Exs. 4–10, 12–14, 17–25	pp. 638–639 Exs. 6–15, 17–20, 23–26	pp. 638–639 Exs. 6–20*, 24–26
13.3	Day 1	pp. 644–645 Exs. 6–20, 24, 27–35	pp. 644–645 Exs. 7–14, 18–25, 27–36	pp. 644–645 Exs. 7–9, 12–27*, 31–36
13.4	Day 1	SRH p. 704 Exs. 5–7, p. 705 Exs. 5–8; pp. 650–652 Exs. 5–16, 20–24	pp. 650–652 Exs. 5–17, 20–25	pp. 650–652 Exs. 5–21*, 24, 25
13.5	Day 1	SRH p. 709 Exs. 11, 12, 22, 23; pp. 655–656 Exs. 5–7, 12–14, 25, 26	pp. 655–656 Exs. 5–8, 17–22	pp. 655–656 Exs. 5–8, 16–21*
	Day 2	pp. 655–656 Exs. 9–11, 17–24	pp. 655–656 Exs. 9–15, 23–26	pp. 655–656 Exs. 9–15, 24–26
13.6	Day 1	pp. 659–661 Exs. 4–10, 20–23	pp. 659–661 Exs. 4–11, 20–23	pp. 659–661 Exs. 4–11, 19–21*
	Day 2	pp. 659–661 Exs. 11–13, 15–17, 24–26	pp. 659–661 Exs. 12–18, 24–26	pp. 659–661 Exs. 12–18, 24–26
13.7	Day 1	pp. 664–665 Exs. 7–9, 11–13, 15–20	pp. 664–665 Exs. 7–13, 15–20	pp. 664–665 Exs. 7–16*, 20
Review	Day 1	pp. 668–669 Exs. 1–30	pp. 668–669 Exs. 1–30	pp. 668–669 Exs. 1–30
Assess	Day 1	Chapter 13 Test	Chapter 13 Test	Chapter 13 Test

YEARLY PACING   Chapter 13 Total – **12 days**   Chapters 1–13 Total – **160 days**   Remaining – **0 days**

*Challenge Exercises   EP = Extra Practice   SRH = Skills Review Handbook   EC = Extra Challenge

BLOCK SCHEDULE

DAY 1	DAY 2	DAY 3	DAY 4	DAY 5	DAY 6
13.1 pp. 633–634 Exs. 7–21, 23–31, 33–39	**13.2** pp. 638–639 Exs. 6–15, 17–20, 23–26 **13.3** pp. 644–645 Exs. 7–14, 18–25, 27–36	**13.4** pp. 650–652 Exs. 5–17, 20–25 **13.5** pp. 655–656 Exs. 5–8, 17–22	**13.5 cont.** pp. 655–656 Exs. 9–15, 23–26 **13.6** pp. 659–661 Exs. 4–11, 20–23	**13.6 cont.** pp. 659–661 Exs. 12–18, 24–26 **13.7** pp. 664–665 Exs. 7–13, 15–20	**Review** pp. 668–669 Exs. 1–30 **Assess** Chapter 13 Test

YEARLY PACING   Chapter 13 Total – **6 days**   Chapters 1–13 Total – **80 days**   Remaining – **0 days**

Support Materials

📖 CHAPTER RESOURCE BOOK

CHAPTER SUPPORT

Tips for New Teachers	p. 1	Parents as Partners	p. 3

LESSON SUPPORT

	13.1	13.2	13.3	13.4	13.5	13.6	13.7
Lesson Plans (regular and block)	p. 6	p. 15	p. 25	p. 34	p. 42	p. 50	p. 58
Technology Activities & Keystrokes	p. 8						p. 60
Activity Support Masters							
Activity Masters		p. 17					
Practice (3 levels)	p. 9	p. 18	p. 27	p. 36	p. 44	p. 52	p. 62
Study Guide	p. 12	p. 21	p. 30	p. 39	p. 47	p. 55	p. 65
Real-World Problem Solving		p. 23					p. 67
Challenge Practice	p. 14	p. 24	p. 32	p. 41	p. 49	p. 57	p. 68

REVIEW

Games Support Masters	pp. 5, 33	Cooperative Project with Rubric	p. 72
Chapter Review Games and Activities	p. 69	Extra Credit Project with Rubric	p. 74
Real-Life Project with Rubric	p. 70	Cumulative Practice	p. 76
		Resource Book Answers	A1

📖 ASSESSMENT

Quizzes	p. 157	Alternative Assessments with Rubrics	p. 166
Chapter Tests (3 levels)	p. 159	Unit Test	p. 168
Standardized Test	p. 165	Cumulative Test	p. 170

📝 TRANSPARENCIES

	13.1	13.2	13.3	13.4	13.5	13.6	13.7
Warm-Up / Daily Homework Quiz	✔	✔	✔	✔	✔	✔	✔
Notetaking Guide	✔	✔	✔	✔	✔	✔	✔
Teacher Support							
English/Spanish Problem Solving	✔	✔	✔		✔		
Answer Transparencies	✔	✔	✔	✔	✔	✔	✔

💻 TECHNOLOGY

- EasyPlanner CD-ROM
- Test and Practice Generator
- Electronic Lesson Presentations
- eTutorial CD-ROM
- Chapter Audio Summaries CDs
- Classzone.com
- eEdition Plus Online
- eWorkbook Plus Online
- eTutorial Plus Online
- EasyPlanner Plus Online

ADDITIONAL RESOURCES

- Worked-Out Solution Key
- Notetaking Guide
- Practice Workbook
- Tutor Place
- Professional Development Book
- Activities Book
- Poster Package
- Spanish Study Guide
- English/Spanish Chapter Reviews
- Multi-Language Glossary

13 Math Background and Teaching Strategies

Lesson 13.1

MATH BACKGROUND

In an experiment, the **probability** that an **event** will occur is a ratio that gives the frequency of **favorable outcomes** to the total number of outcomes. Probabilities are numbers between 0 and 1 and can be expressed as ratios, fractions, decimals, or percents. An impossible event has 0 probability; a certain event has a probability of 1. The sum of the probabilities of an event and its **complement** is 1.

TEACHING STRATEGIES

Discuss with students what it means to say that something happens by chance. Ask students to describe situations when an outcome is determined by chance, such as flipping a coin, rolling a number cube, or drawing a name from a hat. Then ask them what it means to say that an event is impossible.

Lesson 13.2

MATH BACKGROUND

LISTING OUTCOMES A **tree diagram** is one devise for finding and listing all possible outcomes for an event. The outermost branches of the completed tree are the possible outcomes. A table can also be used to systematically account for all possible outcomes.

COMBINATIONS AND PERMUTATIONS A **combination** is a grouping of objects in which the order of listing the objects does not make a difference. A **permutation** is a grouping in which order *does* make a difference.

TEACHING STRATEGIES

For this activity students will need poster board and markers. Have the students work in small groups. Tell each group that they will introduce three new flavors of ice cream: Razzle-Dazzle Raspberry (R), Macadamia Magic (M), and Crunchy Coffee (C). As part of the promotion, each customer who comes into the store is offered a free sample of a "Mystery Flavor" labeled R, M, or C. Assuming that the chance of a customer choosing each flavor is equally likely,

have groups draw a tree diagram to show the possible choices of the first three customers. Discuss the 27 possible outcomes if order makes a difference as contrasted to the 10 possible outcomes if order does not make a difference.

Lesson 13.3

MATH BACKGROUND

A **compound event** consists of the outcomes of two or more events. Two events are said to be **independent events** if the outcome of one has no effect on the outcome of the other. One way to find the probability of two or more independent events is to list all possible outcomes and then count the favorable outcomes.

TEACHING STRATEGIES

Discuss examples of independent events like the following:

- Tossing a coin and landing on heads, and rolling a number cube and getting a 5

- Choosing a card from a deck of cards and getting a three, replacing it, and choosing a second card and getting an ace

- Rolling a die and getting a 4, and then rolling a second die and getting a 1

Then ask students how you might find the probability of both events occurring.

Lesson 13.4

MATH BACKGROUND

GRAPHS Because statistics are often used to prove a point, they can easily be twisted in favor of that point and can be misleading. One way graphs of statistical data can be misleading is by using distorted or inappropriate scales. If, for example, the increments on the vertical scale are very small, then the change over time will appear to be exaggerated.

AVERAGES Averages can also be misleading if an inappropriate average is represented as being "typical" of the data.

TEACHING STRATEGIES

Make an overhead transparency of the two graphs below.

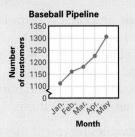
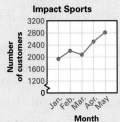

Have students give a visual impression of the data. Then ask them to analyze the data and explain why the visual impression is misleading.

Lesson 13.5

MATH BACKGROUND

In a **stem-and-leaf plot**, the numbers on the left side of the vertical line are the *stems* and the numbers on the right side are the *leaves*. To make an *ordered* stem-and-leaf plot, arrange the leaves from least to greatest, starting from the left.

TEACHING STRATEGIES

Draw this stem-and-leaf plot on the board. It represents the ages of people at an afternoon movie.

Stem	Leaf
0	3 5 6 8
1	2 3 5 7 9
2	0 2 4 6 7
3	0 1 4

Tell students the stem digits represent the number of tens and the leaf digits represent the number of ones in the ages. Ask how many people are represented in the plot. Ask students for the least and greatest ages. Discuss with students why they think this diagram is named a stem-and-leaf plot.

Lesson 13.6

MATH BACKGROUND

A **box-and-whisker plot** can be useful for analyzing and visualizing large sets of data. A box-and-whisker plot shows the **median**, the **upper** and **lower quartiles**, and the **lower** and **upper extremes** in the distribution. A **double box-and-whisker plot** can be used to compare two sets of data.

TEACHING STRATEGIES

Using the following data, construct a box-and-whisker plot with the students.

18 27 34 52 54 59 61 68 78 82 85 87 91 93 100

First find the median. The numbers are already ordered from least to greatest, so 68 is the median.

Next, consider only the values to the left of the median: 18, 27, 34, 52, 54, 59, 61. Their median is 52, the lower quartile.

Now consider only the values to the right of the median: 78, 82, 85, 87, 91, 93, 100. Their median is 87, the upper quartile.

Note that the lower extreme is 18 and the upper extreme is 100. Use these values to draw the plot on the board.

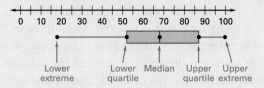

Lesson 13.7

MATH BACKGROUND

DATA DISPLAYS Tables and graphs are visual means for organizing and displaying data. Line graphs show trends, while circle graphs provide quick comparisons. Other displays, like stem-and-leaf plots and box-and-whisker plots, describe the distribution of data. Choosing the best type of graph for specific data and a specific purpose is a useful skill.

TEACHING STRATEGIES

Write the following data on the board.

A Typical School Day for Judith

7 A.M. to 8 A.M.	Prepare for school
8 A.M. to 2 P.M.	In school
2 P.M. to 6 P.M.	After-school job
6 P.M. to 7 P.M.	Dinner
7 P.M. to 9 P.M.	Homework and Study
9 P.M. to 11 P.M.	Read
11 P.M. to 7 A.M.	Sleep

Have students work in small groups to discuss the kinds of graphs that would be appropriate for displaying the data. Have them discuss which type of graphs, if any, would be inappropriate.

CHAPTER 13 Differentiating Instruction

Strategies for Underachievers

ANTICIPATE PROBLEMS WITH VOCABULARY

In this chapter your students will encounter many new vocabulary terms. They will also encounter some important review terms as well. Beginning with Lesson 13.1, students should write all new vocabulary terms in a personal glossary. With each new lesson in Chapter 13, they should add to this glossary. Students should also draw diagrams or pictures for each entry, as appropriate.

You might suggest that students create a graphic organizer or note cards for organizing and learning this vocabulary. If using note cards, you may want to have students color code cards related to the same topic. For example, one color group might contain all the vocabulary terms related to average, such as *mean, median, mode,* and so on.

PROVIDE TOOLS FOR CONCRETE LEARNING

CALCULATORS Students should have access to calculators for the duration of this chapter so that they can focus upon the concepts of probability being introduced.

MODIFY DEPTH AND COMPLEXITY

In Lesson 13.6, students may have difficulty constructing a box-and-whisker plot. If this is the case, do not pursue construction any further. Instead, focus on the interpretation of a box-and-whisker plot. Do not avoid box-and-whisker plots entirely, as interpretation of a box-and-whisker plot is a popular item on standardized tests.

Strategies for English Learners

DISSECT WORD PROBLEMS

It is sometimes difficult for teachers to gauge how much English some English learners understand. English learners who are quiet may be struggling to comprehend, or they may comprehend well and be shy about speaking. To get a sense of which students are having the most difficulty, ask students to take several word problems and highlight the words or sentences they need to learn, and circle the words or sentences they know already. Read at least one word problem together each day and talk about it.

Some word problems are open-ended, that is, they require students to provide an explanation, not just a short answer. Here is an example of an open-ended question:

MUSIC Use the data set below. The values represent the lengths (in seconds) of the songs on a CD.

227, 248, 228, 233, 241, 266, 231, 81, 279,
261, 305, 254, 305, 206, 302, 263, 282

Find the mean, median, and mode(s) of the data set. Which of these measures do you think are good representations of the length of a typical song on the CD? Explain.

Another type of open-ended question might ask students to describe a procedure in their own words.

WRITING Describe in words how to graph the ordered pair in a coordinate plane.

a. (3, 4)   **b.** (2, 26)   **c.** (24, 0)

These kinds of problems present three challenges for English learners: (1) They have to understand what is being asked; (2) They have to do the mathematics; and (3) They need to find the English words to describe their thinking. Practice some simple organizational techniques students can use to explain their answers. Encourage students to attempt these problems even if they are unsure about their English writing skills. Reassure them that a good explanation that uses mathematical terms and symbols will usually be accepted, even when the problem asks students to describe in words. Using basic phrases such as *first step, second step, third step,* and *final step,* or *if, then,* coupled with mathematical expressions or drawings may be enough for an explanation. Have students look through this chapter and find word problems that require more than a numerical answer. They should find phrases such as *describe the pattern, explain your thinking, explain your reasoning, tell why,* and *justify your predictions.*

Strategies for Advanced Learners

INCREASE DEPTH AND COMPLEXITY

In Hands-on Activity 13.1, advanced students may be intrigued to investigate the results of rolling solids with different numbers of faces. Encourage them to repeat this activity using a number tetrahedron (4 sides), a number octahedron (8 sides), a number dodecahedron (12 sides), and a number icosahedron (20 sides).

In the Example in Technology Activity 13.1, you may wish to have some students complete the event 10 times, 100 times, and 1000 times. They should then check their answers to see how close they come to $\frac{1}{2}$. Ask them which of the following is closest to $\frac{1}{2}$: $\frac{6}{10}$, $\frac{51}{100}$, or $\frac{501}{1000}$. Have students consider polls which pose a question to 10 people, 100 people, or 1000 people. Then ask them which poll should have the most reliable results. Have students check newspapers and other media for polls to see how many people are being surveyed.

Those students who are interested in computers may wish to investigate how random number generators work. Random number generators vary in quality. Ask students to consider what makes a superior or an inferior random number generator.

The following can be used as a culminating challenge activity for **Chapter 13**.

- **Challenge** Have students work in groups of 10. Have students accurately measure the heights of all the students in the group and the height of the teacher. Students should choose whether to use inches or centimeters for their measurements. Half of the group can create a poster-size stem-and-leaf plot for the data, and the other half can create a poster-size box-and-whisker plot. Returning to the whole group, students can determine the mean and the median of the data and discuss the importance of any outliers and whether the mean or the median would be the most representative average for the data. Check work.

USE CROSS-CURRICULAR CONNECTIONS

In Lesson 13.1, the cube along with the tetrahedron, octahedron, dodecahedron, and icosahedron represent the entire set of what are called the "Platonic Solids." You might wish to work with a Language Arts teacher and have some students investigate and report on these Platonic Solids. Also, you might wish to work with a Technology Specialist and have some students develop a presentation of the Platonic Solids using computer graphics or have them work with their Social Studies and Language Arts teachers to investigate and report on Plato and other Greek mathematicians.

While discussing misleading statistics in Lesson 13.4, you may wish to work with the School Psychologist or Guidance Counselor to discuss how some people try to mislead others, and to provide your students strategies to keep them from being misled.

Differentiating Instruction: Teaching Resources

Differentiating Enrichment and Activities

McDougal Littell *Middle School Mathematics* offers teachers enrichment for all levels of students. Pictured on these pages are facsimiles of the Real-World Problem Solving pages, Chapter Review Games, and Chapter Projects from the *Chapter 13 Resource Book* and a number of activities from the *Special Activities Book*. Also available is the *Poster Package* containing large, full-color posters, one for each unit.

RESOURCE BOOK

The *Chapter Resource Books* contain Real-World Problem Solving activities for various lessons in the textbook, Chapter Review Games for a motivating review of each chapter, and Chapter Projects with rubrics that apply the mathematics of the chapter.

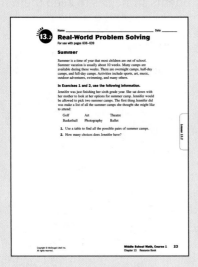

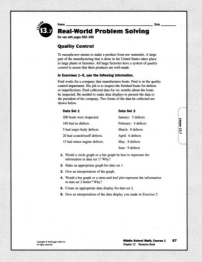

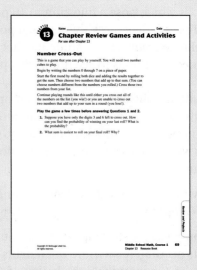

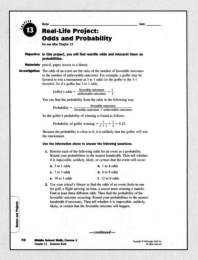

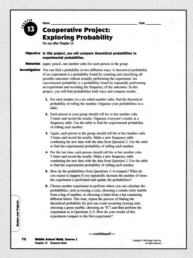

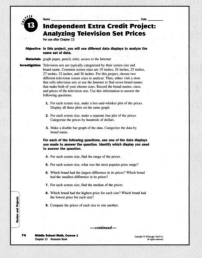

SPECIAL ACTIVITIES BOOK

The *Special Activities Book* contains numerous activities including activities for the start of school, activities for substitute teachers, activities for use before holiday breaks, and short change-of-pace activities.

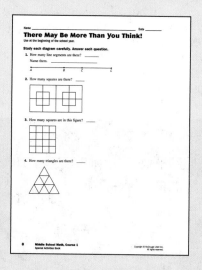

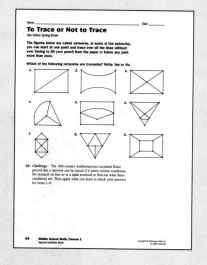

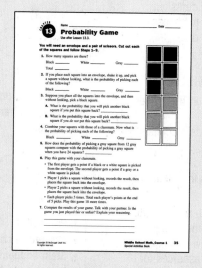

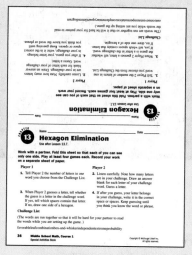

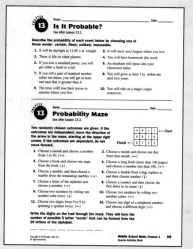

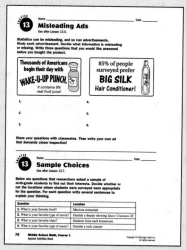

MAIN IDEAS

In this chapter, students find the probability of an event, and the complement of an event. They also use tree diagrams and tables to list outcomes. They use their knowledge of outcomes to find the probability of independent events. Students look at misleading statistics, and they learn to make stem-and-leaf plots and box-and-whisker plots. Finally, students use their knowledge of data to choose appropriate displays for data.

PREREQUISITE SKILLS

The key skills reviewed in the games on these pages are:
- Comparing fractions, decimals, and percents
- Solving proportions
- Ordering numbers from least to greatest

Additional practice with prerequisite skills can be found in the Review What You Need to Know exercises on page 628. Additional resources for reviewing prerequisite skills are:
- Skills Review Handbook, pp. 684–707
- Tutor Place
- eTutorial Plus Online

MANAGING THE GAMES

Tips for Success

One way to compare the numbers in the games is to express all the numbers as decimals. Suggest that students who struggle do this.

Reflecting on the Games

Remind students that if the numerators of two fractions are the same, the larger fraction is the one with the smaller denominator. Use this relationship to help answer Exercise 1.

13

Probability and Statistics

BEFORE

In previous chapters you've...
- Solved proportions
- Compared percents, decimals, and fractions

Now

In Chapter 13 you'll study...
- Probability
- Misleading statistics
- Stem-and-leaf plots
- Box-and-whisker plots
- Choosing a data display

WHY?

So you can solve real-world problems about...
- football, p. 630
- pottery, p. 636
- storms, p. 651
- communication, p. 665

Internet Preview
CLASSZONE.COM
- eEdition Plus Online
- eWorkbook Plus Online
- eTutorial Plus Online
- State Test Practice
- More Examples

Chapter Warm-Up Games

Review skills you need for this chapter in these quick games.

Spider Web Maze

BrAIN GAME

Key Skill:
Comparing percents, decimals, and fractions

- Copy the spider web maze. Start at 1% near the center of the web. Your goal is to escape to 100% at the top of the web.

- Move along the threads of the web. You may only move to a number that is greater than the number you are on. You may not pass through the spider at the center of the web. **Check work.**

Chapter 13 Resource Book
- Tips for New Teachers, pp. 1–2
- Lesson Plan, pp. 6, 15, 25, 34, 42, 50, 58
- Lesson Plan for Block Scheduling, pp. 7, 16, 26, 35, 43, 51, 59

Technology
- EasyPlanner CD-ROM
- Test and Practice Generator
- Electronic Lesson Presentations CD-ROM
- eTutorial CD-ROM

Internet
- Classzone
- eEdition Plus Online
- eWorkbook Plus Online
- eTutorial Plus Online
- EasyPlanner Plus Online

ENGLISH LEARNER SUPPORT

- Spanish Study Guide
- Multi-Language Glossary
- Chapter Audio Summaries CDs
- Teacher's Edition, pp. 626E–626F

Butterfly Challenge

Texan-Crescent
$$\frac{3}{10} = \frac{?}{40}$$

Indian
$$\frac{2}{5} = \frac{?}{20}$$

Nymph
$$\frac{4}{7} = \frac{?}{35}$$

Buckeye
$$\frac{2}{9} = \frac{?}{18}$$

Empress
$$\frac{7}{8} = \frac{?}{24}$$

Silverspot
$$\frac{2}{3} = \frac{?}{15}$$

Red-Rim
$$\frac{3}{7} = \frac{?}{14}$$

Morpho
$$\frac{3}{8} = \frac{?}{24}$$

Orion
$$\frac{1}{6} = \frac{?}{108}$$

BrAIN GAME

Key Skill:
Solving proportions

- Copy and solve the proportions. Order your answers from least to greatest. Write the butterfly names associated with your answers in the same order. **Row 1: 12, 8, 20; Row 2: 4, 21, 10; Row 3: 6, 9, 18; 4, 6, 8, 9, 10, 12, 18, 20, 21**
- The first letters of the names will spell out the name of a butterfly whose name is also a word that means "sulfur." **Buckeye, Red-Rim, Indian, Morpho, Silverspot, Texan-Crescent, Orion, Nymph, Empress**

BRIMSTONE

1. *Sample answer:*
$\frac{6}{10}$ and $\frac{6}{15}$; $\frac{2}{6}$ and $\frac{35}{100}$

2. Row 1: 120, 40, 140; Row 2: 36, 168, 30; Row 3: 42, 72, 108; 30, 36, 40, 42, 72, 108, 120, 140, 168; Silverspot, Buckeye, Indian, Red-Rim, Morpho, Orion, Texan-Crescent, Nymph, Empress

TEN MONTHS

Stop *and* Think

1. **Critical Thinking** Give an example from *Spider Web Maze* in which simplifying helped you compare two fractions. Give an example in which you changed a fraction to a decimal in order to compare two numbers.

2. **Extension** For each proportion in *Butterfly Challenge*, find one of the cross products. Order these products from least to greatest. Write the butterfly names associated with the products in the same order. The last letters of the names will spell out the lifespan of the butterfly whose name you spelled in the puzzle.

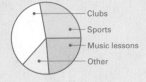

Getting Ready to Learn

Review What You Need to Know ↻

Using Vocabulary **Copy and complete using a review word.**

1. If a value occurs the most often in a data set, then it is called the ? . **mode**

2. The ? is the sum of the data values divided by the number of values. **mean**

Find the mean, median, mode(s), and range of the data. *(p. 93)*

3. 13, 2, 23, 12, 2, 3, 8   **9; 8; 2; 21**
4. 8, 9, 3, 4, 8, 6, 9, 8, 9, 6   **7; 8; 8 and 9; 6**

Write the fraction as a decimal and as a percent. *(p. 399)*

5. $\frac{1}{4}$ **0.25; 25%**   6. $\frac{5}{5}$ **1; 100%**   7. $\frac{2}{3}$ **0.$\overline{6}$; 66.$\overline{6}$%**   8. $\frac{1}{8}$ **0.125; 12.5%**

The table shows the results of a survey asking 100 students their favorite after-school activity. *(p. 491)*

Activity	Students
sports	28
music lessons	24
clubs	35
other	13

9. Make a circle graph of the data. **See margin.**

10. Which activity is preferred by slightly less than one fourth of the students? **music lessons**

Word Watch

Review Words

circle graph, p. 88
mean, p. 93
median, p. 93
mode, p. 93
range, p. 94
decimal, p. 108
fraction, p. 228
percent, p. 395

You should include material that appears on a notebook like this in your own notes.

Know How to Take Notes

Summarizing Material At the end of the year, write a summary of key ideas from different lessons that are related to each other. Include definitions and examples of the key ideas.

Simplifying Fractions

$$\frac{10}{80} = \frac{1 \times 10}{8 \times 10}$$

$$= \frac{1 \times \cancel{10}^{1}}{8 \times \cancel{10}_{1}}$$

$$= \frac{1}{8}$$

Fractions to Decimals

$$\frac{1}{8} \rightarrow 8\overline{)1.000}$$
.125
8
20
16
40
40
0

Decimals to Percents

$$0.125 = \frac{125}{1000}$$

$$= \frac{12.5}{100}$$

$$= 12.5\%$$

You can use this tool to connect Chapter 13 with other chapters.

13.1 Hands-on *Activity*

GOAL
Use an experiment to test predictions.

MATERIALS
· number cube

Conducting an Experiment

You can predict the results of rolling a number cube and use an experiment to test your predictions.

Explore Make and test predictions about rolling a number cube.

1 Predict whether a number *less than 2*, *equal to 2*, or *greater than 2* will occur most often when you roll a number cube 30 times. Explain your answer.
Greater than 2; there are more possible outcomes.

2 Make a frequency table like the one at the right. Then roll a number cube 30 times and record your results in the frequency table.
See margin.

Number on cube	Tally	Frequency
1	?	?
2	?	?
3	?	?
4	?	?
5	?	?
6	?	?

3 What fraction of the results is less than 2? equal to 2? greater than 2? Do your results match your predictions?
Sample answer: $\frac{1}{6}, \frac{1}{6}, \frac{2}{3}$; answers may vary.

Your turn now

1. Predict whether a number *less than 4, equal to 4,* or *greater than 4* will occur most often when you roll a number cube 30 times. Then repeat the experiment above to test your prediction.
Less than 4; good answers should include a frequency table that looks similar to the table from Step 2 in Explore.

Stop *and* Think

Sample answer: $\frac{1}{2}, \frac{1}{6}, \frac{1}{3}$

2. Critical Thinking When you roll a number cube, do you think that any one of the numbers is more likely to occur than each of the other numbers? Use the data in the two frequency tables you made above to support your answer. **No.** *Sample answer:* Each number on a fair number cube is equally likely to occur when it is rolled.

NCTM CURRICULUM STANDARDS
Standard 5: Collect, organize, and display data; Develop inferences that are based on data; Evaluate predictions that are based on data

Lesson 13.1   Introduction to Probability   **629**

---

① PLAN

EXPLORE THE CONCEPT
• Students will roll a number cube to test predictions.
• This Activity leads into the idea of experimental probability, the topic of Lesson 13.1.

MATERIALS
Each student or group of students will need a number cube.

RECOMMENDED TIME
Work activity: 10 min
Discuss results: 5 min

GROUPING
Students can work individually or in groups of 3. If they work in groups, ask one student to roll the cube, one to tally the outcomes, and one to complete the frequency table.

② TEACH

TIPS FOR SUCCESS
As students work through Step 3, point out that they need to add the results for rolling a 3, 4, 5, or 6 in order to find the frequency of rolling a number greater than 2.

③ CLOSE

 KEY DISCOVERY
Rolling any of the 6 numbers on a number cube is equally likely.

ASSESSMENT
1. Out of 60 rolls of a number cube, predict the fraction of results greater than 3. $\frac{1}{2}$

Step 2. See Additional Answers beginning on page AA1.

629

LESSON OBJECTIVE

Write probabilities.

PACING

Suggested Number of Days
Basic Course: 2 days
Average Course: 2 days
Advanced Course: 2 days
Block: 1 block

TEACHING RESOURCES

For a complete list of Teaching Resources, see page 626B.

 TRANSPARENCY

Warm-Up Exercises for this lesson are available on a transparency.

2 **TEACH**

MOTIVATING THE LESSON

Ask students to predict how many times heads will be the outcome if they toss a coin 50 times.

TIPS FOR NEW TEACHERS

Point out that the probability of an outcome is never higher than one, and that the probability of the complementary event is always 1—(the probability of the event). See Tips for New Teachers in the *Chapter 13 Resource Book*.

630

LESSON **13.1**

Introduction to Probability

BEFORE	Now	WHY?
You wrote ratios.	You'll write probabilities.	So you can find the likelihood of winning a raffle, as in Ex. 27.

In the Real World

 Word Watch

outcome, p. 630
event, p. 630
favorable outcomes, p. 630
probability, p. 630
complementary events,
   p. 632

Football A coin toss determines starting plays in a football game. A team captain calls "heads." How likely is it that the captain's team will win the toss?

Tossing a coin is an example of an *experiment*. An **outcome**, such as "heads," is a possible result of an experiment. An **event** is a collection of outcomes. Once you specify an event, the outcomes for that event are called **favorable outcomes**. You can find *probabilities* by counting favorable outcomes.

Finding Probabilities

The **probability** that an event will occur when all outcomes of an experiment are equally likely is as follows.

$$\text{Probability of event} = \frac{\text{Number of favorable outcomes}}{\text{Number of possible outcomes}}$$

EXAMPLE 1 **Finding a Probability**

In the coin toss problem above, there is 1 favorable outcome, which is "heads." The 2 possible outcomes are "heads" and "tails."

$$\text{Probability of winning the toss} = \frac{\text{Number of favorable outcomes}}{\text{Number of possible outcomes}} = \frac{1}{2}$$

ANSWER The captain's team is as likely to win the toss as to lose it.

NCTM CURRICULUM STANDARDS
Standard 5: Understand basic concepts of probability;
     Apply basic concepts of probability
Standard 6: Solve problems in math and other contexts

Probabilities As shown in Example 1, an event that has a probability of $\frac{1}{2}$ is likely to occur half the time. The probability P of an event is a measure of the likelihood that the event will occur. You can write probabilities as fractions, decimals, and percents.

$P = 0$	$P = 0.25$	$P = 0.50$	$P = 0.75$	$P = 1$
Impossible	Unlikely	Likely to occur half the time	Likely	Certain

EXAMPLE 2 **Describing Probabilities**

HELP with **Solving**

When you flip a coin, roll a number cube, or randomly choose objects from a bag, you are assuming that all the outcomes are equally likely to occur.

You roll a number cube. Find and describe the probability of the event.

a. You roll an odd number.

Because there are 3 odd outcomes,

$P = \frac{3}{6} = 0.5 = 50\%.$

ANSWER You are likely to roll an odd number half the time.

b. You roll a whole number.

Because all 6 outcomes are whole numbers, $P = \frac{6}{6} = 1 = 100\%.$

ANSWER You are certain to roll a whole number.

c. You roll a 7.

Because 7 is not one of the outcomes, $P = \frac{0}{6} = 0 = 0\%.$

ANSWER It is impossible to roll a 7.

d. You roll a number less than 3.

Because there are 2 outcomes less than 3, $P = \frac{2}{6} = 0.\overline{3} = 33\frac{1}{3}\%.$

ANSWER You are unlikely to roll a number less than 3.

Your turn now **Find the probability of the event.**

1. You roll a number greater than 3 on a number cube. $\frac{1}{2}$

2. You randomly choose a red marble from a bag of 4 green, 2 blue, and 7 red marbles. $\frac{7}{13}$

TEACHING TIP

Point out that in real-life, probabilities are described with phrases like, "the chance of rain is 30%", "the probability that the baby will have blue eyes is one-fourth", and so on. Do a group activity that asks students to write examples of probability phrases from real life.

✗ COMMON ERROR

Watch for students who have the incorrect probabilities because they did not consider all of the possible outcomes. Encourage them to make an organized list of outcomes before finding the probability.

Example 3 The outcomes on the spinner are equally likely. Find each probability.

a. You spin an even number. $\frac{1}{2}$

b. You spin a number less than 4. $\frac{3}{8}$

 NOTETAKING

Ask students to write the definitions of new vocabulary words in their notebooks. They should include *experiment*, *outcome*, *favorable outcome*, *event*, *equally likely*, *probability*, and *complementary probability*.

MULTIPLE REPRESENTATIONS

Ask students to represent all of the outcomes of an event as fractions of a rectangle. This will help them make the connections to fractions as probabilities as well as help them include all of the outcomes.

 CONCEPT CHECK

How do you find the probability of an event? **Divide the number of favorable outcomes by the number of possible outcomes.**

 DAILY PUZZLER

Suppose you roll a number cube. What is the probability you will toss either an odd number or an even number? Explain. **1; all outcomes are either odd or even.**

Complementary Events Two events are **complementary events**, or *complements* of each other, if they have no outcomes in common and if together they contain all the outcomes of the experiment.

EXAMPLE 3 **Complementary Events**

The outcomes on the spinner are equally likely. You spin the spinner.

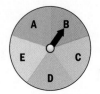

a. Find the probability of spinning a vowel.

b. Describe the complement of the event in part (a) and find its probability.

Solution

a. Because 2 of the 5 letters are vowels, $P = \frac{2}{5}$.

b. The complement of spinning a vowel is spinning a consonant. Because 3 of the 5 letters are consonants, $P = \frac{3}{5}$.

13.1 **Exercises**
More Practice, p. 720

INTERNET
eWorkbook Plus
CLASSZONE.COM

Getting Ready to Practice

Vocabulary **List all the favorable outcomes for the given event.**

1. Spinning a vowel on the spinner
   spinning an A, E, or O

2. Rolling an integer on a number cube
   rolling a 1, 2, 3, 4, 5, or 6

3. Randomly choosing a red marble
   choosing marble 1, 2, 3, or 6

4. **Socks** A drawer contains 6 blue and 4 red socks. You randomly choose one sock. Find the probability that you choose a red sock. $\frac{2}{5}$

A hat holds 10 tiles labeled A, C, R, U, 1, 4, 5, 7, 8, and 9.

5. You randomly choose one tile. Find the probability that it is a letter. $\frac{2}{5}$

6. Describe the complement of the event in Exercise 5 and find its probability. **choosing a number;** $\frac{3}{5}$

Practice and Problem Solving

You roll a number cube. Find the probability of the event.

A **7.** You roll a 1. $\frac{1}{6}$ **8.** You roll a prime number. $\frac{1}{2}$

9. You roll an 8. 0   **10.** You roll a multiple of 3. $\frac{1}{3}$

Tell whether the event is *impossible, unlikely, likely,* **or** *certain.*

11. A student randomly chosen from a class is right-handed. **likely**

12. It will be Monday in one of the next 10 days. **certain**

13. June will have 31 days this year. **impossible**

14. A person bowls a perfect score. **unlikely**

You spin the spinner, which is divided into equal parts. Find the probability of the event. Then tell whether the event is *impossible, unlikely, likely,* **or** *certain.*

15. You spin a 5. $\frac{1}{8}$; unlikely   **16.** You spin an integer. 1; certain

17. You spin an 8. $\frac{1}{8}$; unlikely   **18.** You spin a factor of 12. $\frac{5}{8}$; likely

19. Find the Error Describe and correct the error in finding the probability of rolling a 5 on a number cube. **See margin.**

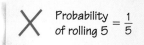
✗ Probability of rolling 5 $= \frac{1}{5}$

20. Video Games You randomly choose a level from 12 different levels in a video game. You don't know which 4 levels have secret warp zones. Find the probability that you choose a level that has a secret warp zone. $\frac{1}{3}$

21. Alphabet A bag holds 26 letter tiles. Each tile has a different letter of the alphabet. You randomly choose one tile. Find the probability that it is a consonant. $\frac{21}{26}$

Describe the complement of the event. Then find its probability.

22. You roll an odd number on a number cube. **rolling an even number;** $\frac{1}{2}$

23. You randomly choose a consonant from the letters in MATH. **choosing a vowel;** $\frac{1}{4}$

24. You randomly choose a red tile from a box of 4 red and 8 blue tiles. **choosing a blue tile;** $\frac{2}{3}$

B 25. Groundhogs The groundhog Punxsutawney Phil is said to predict six more weeks of winter if he sees his shadow on February 2. From 1901 to 2000, Phil saw his shadow 87 of the 100 recorded years. You randomly choose one year from 1901 to 2000. Find the probability that you select a year in which Phil saw his shadow. $\frac{87}{100}$

MINI-QUIZ

You roll a number cube. Find the probability of the event.

1. You roll a number that is not prime. $\frac{1}{2}$

2. You roll a multiple of 4. $\frac{1}{6}$

3. For the spinner below, find the probability of spinning a number less than 2. Then find the complement of that event.

$\frac{1}{6}$; $\frac{5}{6}$

5 **FOLLOW-UP**

RETEACHING/REMEDIATION
- Study Guide in Chapter 13 Resource Book, pp. 12–13
- Tutor Place, Fractions Card 19; Ratios, Proportions, and Percents Card 16
- eTutorial Plus Online
- Extra Practice, p. 720
- Lesson Practice in Chapter 13 Resource Book, pp. 9–11

CHALLENGE/ENRICHMENT
- Challenge Practice in Chapter 13 Resource Book, p. 14
- Teacher's Edition, p. 626F

ENGLISH LEARNER SUPPORT
- Spanish Study Guide
- Multi-Language Glossary
- Chapter Audio Summaries CDs

34–36. See Additional Answers beginning on page AA1.

634

26. **Piano Keys** A piano has 52 white keys and 36 black keys. Eight keys produce a C note. You randomly play one key. Find the probability that it produces a C note. $\frac{1}{11}$

27. **Raffles** The probability of losing a raffle is 98%. Describe the complement of losing a raffle and find its probability. **winning a raffle; 2%**

28. **CD Changer** A CD changer holds 3 CDs. Each CD has 12 songs. You let the CD changer randomly select which song to play first. Find the probability that your favorite song is played first. $\frac{1}{36}$

29. **Critical Thinking** Can the probability of an event be greater than 1? Can the probability of an event be less than 0? Explain. **See margin.**

29. No; no; there cannot be more than the number of possible outcomes, nor can there be fewer than 0 outcomes.

31. $\frac{1}{5}$; there is one favorable outcome and there are 5 unfavorable outcomes.

Odds The *odds in favor* of an event is the ratio of favorable outcomes to unfavorable outcomes. You want to roll a 6 on a number cube.

C 30. List all the favorable outcomes. Then list all the unfavorable outcomes. **rolling a 6; rolling a 1, 2, 3, 4, or 5**

31. Find the odds in favor of rolling a 6. Explain your answer. **See margin.**

32. **Challenge** An experiment is *fair* if each event is equally likely to occur. You roll a number cube to find out which of two players goes first in a game. Describe two ways that you can fairly decide who goes first. *Sample answer:* The person who rolls a 1, 2, or 3 goes first, or the person who rolls a 4, 5, or 6 goes first.

Mixed Review

33. Find the volume of a rectangular prism that is 12 inches by 3 inches by 6 inches. *(Lesson 10.7)* **216 in.³**

Graph the function using the input values $x = 0, 3, 6,$ and 9. *(Lesson 12.6)*
34–36. See margin.

34. $y = x + 7$
35. $y = x - 4$
36. $y = 2x$

Basic Skills Order the numbers from least to greatest.

37. 6.23, 62.3, 623, 0.623, 6230
    0.623, 6.23, 62.3, 623, 6230

38. 1441, 1.441, 144.1, 0.1441, 14.41
    0.1441, 1.441, 14.41, 144.1, 1441

Test-Taking Practice

39. **Multiple Choice** The outcomes on the spinner are equally likely. You spin the spinner. Find the probability of spinning a multiple of 4. **B**

A. $\frac{1}{2}$ B. $\frac{3}{4}$ C. $\frac{7}{8}$ D. 1

40. **Multiple Choice** A bag holds 6 red, 8 yellow, and 6 green marbles. You randomly choose one marble. Find the probability that it is red. **G**

F. $\frac{3}{20}$ G. $\frac{3}{10}$ H. $\frac{1}{3}$ I. $\frac{3}{5}$

13.1

Technology Activity

Testing Probabilities

GOAL Use a calculator to generate a random set of data so you can test probabilities.

HELP with Technology

The display **RANDI(1, 6)** tells you that the integers 1 through 6 are the only possible outcomes of the simulation.

Example You can use the random integer feature **RANDI** to generate a random set of integers.

Generate a random set of data to show the results of 10 rolls on a number cube. Then compare your results with the probability of rolling an odd number.

Solution

To simulate rolling a number cube, use the random integer feature **RANDI**.

Keystrokes

PRB ◀ = 1 2nd [,] 6)

Display

RANDI(1, 6)

Press = 10 times to generate the results of rolling a number cube 10 times. Record your results as you generate them. Suppose you generate the following numbers:

2, 4, 5, 6, 3, 1, 3, 4, 3, and 5.

In the simulation, 6 of the 10 results are odd numbers.

ANSWER You generated an odd number $\frac{6}{10}$, or $\frac{3}{5}$, of the time. This is slightly greater than the probability of rolling an odd number, $\frac{1}{2}$.

Your turn now Use a calculator to solve the problems below.

1. Let 1 represent heads and 2 represent tails. Generate a random set of data to show the results of 15 coin tosses. Then compare your results with the probability of getting heads.
   A good answer should be close to $\frac{1}{2}$.

2. A spinner is divided into three equal sections. Let 1 and 2 represent red and 3 represent green. Generate a random set of data to show the results of 24 spins. Then compare your results with the probability of spinning green.
   A good answer should be close to $\frac{1}{3}$.

NCTM CURRICULUM STANDARDS
Standard 5: Devise questions that can be addressed with data; Collect, organize, and display data; Understand basic concepts of probability

Lesson 13.1   Introduction to Probability   **635**

---

1 PLAN

LEARN THE METHOD
- Students will use a calculator to randomly generate a set of data so that they can test probabilities.
- Students can use randomly generated numbers to determine experimental probabilities for Exercises 7–9 on page 633.

GROUPING

Students can do this activity individually or in pairs. If the students work in pairs, ask one student to tally the results from the calculator in a frequency chart.

2 TEACH

DISCUSSION

You may want to ask students to repeat the number cube simulation more than once and then compare results. If students work in groups, find a class average of the probability of rolling an odd number.

Example What calculator instruction would you use to simulate spinning a spinner with 8 equally likely events?
RANDI(1, 8)

3 CLOSE

ASSESSMENT

Let 1 represent heads and 2 represent tails. Generate a random set of data and show the results for 10 tosses. Use the data to find the probability of tossing a head.

Sample answer: $\frac{1}{2}$

635

LESSON OBJECTIVE

Use diagrams, tables, and lists to find the outcomes of an event.

PACING

Suggested Number of Days
Basic Course: 1 day
Average Course: 1 day
Advanced Course: 1 day
Block: 0.5 block with 13.3

TEACHING RESOURCES

For a complete list of Teaching Resources, see page 626B.

 **TRANSPARENCY**

Warm-Up Exercises for this lesson are available on a transparency.

2 TEACH

MOTIVATING THE LESSON

Describe how a single cell splits into two cells, each then splitting into two more cells, and so on. Ask students to make a diagram to show this.

TIPS FOR NEW TEACHERS

Suggest students use a whole sheet of paper for a tree diagram, leaving lots of space between the main branches. See Tips for New Teachers in the *Chapter 13 Resource Book*.

1–2. See Additional Answers beginning on page AA1.

Finding Outcomes

BEFORE	▶ Now	WHY?
You identified outcomes.	You'll use diagrams, tables, and lists to find outcomes.	So you can arrange a movie schedule, as in Ex. 11.

 **Word Watch**

tree diagram, p. 636
combination, p. 637
permutation, p. 637

In the Real World

Pottery Your art class is painting pottery for an art fair. You can choose a small or a large size, and you can paint a vase, a jar, or a plate. What are the different kinds of pottery you can paint?

A **tree diagram** can help you organize a list of possible outcomes by placing different choices on different branches of the "tree."

EXAMPLE 1 **Using Tree Diagrams**

To find all possible outcomes in the problem above, use a tree diagram.

① List the sizes.   **② For each size list the items.**   **③ Find the outcomes.**

small	vase	small vase
	jar	small jar
	plate	small plate
large	vase	large vase
	jar	large jar
	plate	large plate

Your turn now **Use a tree diagram to find all the possible outcomes.**
1–2. See margin.

1. You can order a tuna, ham, roast beef, or egg sandwich. You can choose rye, white, wheat, or oatmeal bread. Find all the possible sandwiches.

2. A roller hockey team is choosing jerseys. The body can be red, white, purple, green, or blue. The sleeves can be black, red, or blue. Find all the possible jerseys that the team can choose from.

NCTM CURRICULUM STANDARDS
Standard 5: Collect, organize, and display data
Standard 6: Build knowledge through problem solving
Standard 10: Use representations to communicate ideas

Combinations and Permutations To choose outcomes, you need to decide whether the order of the objects matters. A **combination** is a grouping of objects in which order is not important. A **permutation** is an arrangement of objects in which order is important.

EXAMPLE 2 Finding Combinations

Sundaes You can choose 2 toppings for a sundae from nuts, sprinkles, caramel, and marshmallows. Find all the possible pairs of toppings.

Solution

Each outcome is a combination because it doesn't matter which topping you choose first. Use a table to show all the possible pairs of toppings.

Nuts	Sprinkles	Caramel	Marshmallows	Outcomes
X	X			nuts, sprinkles
X		X		nuts, caramel
X			X	nuts, marshmallows
	X	X		sprinkles, caramel
	X		X	sprinkles, marshmallows
		X	X	caramel, marshmallows

EXAMPLE 3 Finding Permutations

Find all the two-digit numbers that can be formed using two different digits from 1, 4, 7, and 9.

Solution

Each outcome is a permutation because the order of the digits matters. You can use an organized list to arrange all the possible outcomes.

Starts with 1:	Starts with 4:	Starts with 7:	Starts with 9:
14 17 19	41 47 49	71 74 79	91 94 97

Your turn now Find all the possible outcomes.

3. You can choose two toppings for a pizza from pepperoni, olives, mushrooms, and onions. Find all the possible pairs of toppings.

4. You are placing a math book, a novel, and a dictionary on a shelf. Find all the possible ways you can order the books on the shelf.

3. pepperoni and olives, pepperoni and mushrooms, pepperoni and onions, olives and mushrooms, olives and onions, mushrooms and onions

4. math book, novel, dictionary; math book, dictionary, novel; dictionary, math book, novel; dictionary, novel, math book; novel, dictionary, math book; novel, math book, dictionary

EXTRA EXAMPLES

Example 1 At the ice cream shop, you can choose a sugar or waffle cone, and vanilla, chocolate, or strawberry ice cream. Make a tree diagram to list all the possible outcomes. **Check diagrams; outcomes: sugar cone, vanilla; sugar cone, chocolate; sugar cone, strawberry; waffle cone, vanilla; waffle cone, chocolate; waffle cone, strawberry**

Example 2 When you order a pizza, you can choose two pizza toppings from sausage, pepperoni, cheese, or peppers. Find all possible pairs of toppings. **sausage, pepperoni; sausage, cheese; sausage, peppers; pepperoni, cheese; pepperoni, peppers; cheese, peppers**

Example 3 List all the two-letter pairings that can be formed from the letters in CAT. **CA, CT, AC, AT, TC, TA**

 NOTETAKING

Encourage students to write the description of a combination versus a permutation in their notebooks, along with examples.

CONCEPT CHECK

How would you find all two-digit combinations of the numbers 6, 7, 8? **Pair 6 with 7 and with 8 to get 67, 68. Then pair 7 with 6 and 8 to get 76 and 78. Lastly, pair 8 with 6 and 7 to get 86 and 87.**

 DAILY PUZZLER

At a restaurant, you have 3 entrée choices, 2 salad choices, and 3 dessert choices. If you can choose one of each, how many choices are there? **18**

ASSIGNMENT GUIDE

Basic Course
Day 1: SRH p. 703 Exs. 1–5;
pp. 638–639 Exs. 4–10,
12–14, 17–25

Average Course
Day 1: pp. 638–639 Exs. 6–15,
17–20, 23–26

Advanced Course
Day 1: pp. 638–639 Exs. 6–20*,
24–26

Block
pp. 638–639 Exs. 6–15, 17–20,
23–26 (with 13.3)

EXTRA PRACTICE

- Student Edition, p. 720
- Chapter 13 Resource Book, pp. 18–20
- Test and Practice Generator

Ⓐ **TRANSPARENCY**

Even-numbered answers are available on transparencies.

HOMEWORK CHECK

When you review students' homework for this lesson, go over the following exercises to check understanding of key concepts.
Basic: 4, 5, 6, 8, 10
Average: 6, 7, 8, 9, 10
Advanced: 6, 7, 8, 9, 10

Ⓧ **COMMON ERROR**

If students have trouble creating the diagrams for Exercises 4–7, give them help with diagrams similar to the one shown for Exercise 3.

3–9. See Additional Answers beginning on page AA1.

Getting Ready to Practice

1. **Vocabulary** Choosing any 2 DVDs from 5 DVDs describes a ?. Arranging 4 letters to make a word describes a ?.
   combination; permutation

2. **Outfits** You pack a solid shirt, a striped shirt, a plaid shirt, tan shorts, and jeans for a weekend trip. Find all the different outfits you can wear.

   2. solid shirt and tan shorts, solid shirt and jeans, striped shirt and tan shorts, striped shirt and jeans, plaid shirt and tan shorts, plaid shirt and jeans

3. **Car Ride** You are taking a car ride with your aunt and uncle. Only your aunt and uncle can drive. Copy and complete the tree diagram at the right. Then find all the possible ways that two people can sit in front.
   See margin.

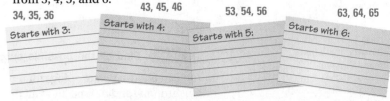

Practice and Problem Solving

 with Homework

Example	Exercises
1	4–7
2	8–10
3	8–10

ⓘ **Online Resources**
CLASSZONE.COM
· More Examples
· eTutorial Plus

In Exercises 4–7, use a tree diagram to find all the possible outcomes.
4–7. See margin.

A 4. Wrapping paper: gold, silver
   Bow: red, blue, white, green

5. Room: kitchen, bathroom
   Paint color: white, beige, gray

6. Pet: dog, cat, horse, gerbil, bird
   Gender: male, female

7. City: Dallas, New York, Miami
   Month of travel: June, July, August

8. **Phones** A phone company offers 5 phone plan options: call waiting, call forwarding, voice mail, three-way calling, and caller ID. You can choose 3 options. Use a table to find all the possible sets of 3 options.
   See margin.

9. **Sculptures** You have 5 different colors of clay: blue, green, yellow, red, and purple. Each clay sculpture you can make uses exactly 2 different colors. Use a table to find all the different sculptures you can make.
   See margin.

10. **Numbers** Copy and complete the cards below to list all the two-digit numbers that can be formed using two different digits from 3, 4, 5, and 6.

    34, 35, 36   43, 45, 46   53, 54, 56   63, 64, 65

    Starts with 3:   Starts with 4:   Starts with 5:   Starts with 6:

11. comedy and drama, comedy and science fiction, comedy and adventure, drama and comedy, drama and science fiction, drama and adventure, science fiction and comedy, science fiction and drama, science fiction and adventure, adventure and comedy, adventure and drama, adventure and science fiction

B 11. **Movies** You rent 4 movies for a party: a comedy, a drama, a science fiction movie, and an adventure movie. Find all the possible orders in which to show two of the movies. See margin.

12. Writing Write a problem that can be solved using the tree diagram at the right. **See margin.**

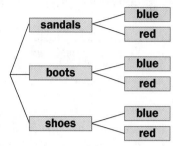

13. Eating Out For the first course, you can order soup or salad. For the main course, you can order pasta, seafood, or beef. For dessert, you can order pie, cake, or ice cream. Find all the possible meals. **See margin.**

14. Ice Skating Jenna, Karen, Angela, and Terry draw numbers from a hat to determine the order in an ice skating competition. Find all the ways that the skaters can be arranged if Jenna skates first. **See margin.**

15. Critical Thinking The sixth-grade class is electing 4 class officers:
C president, vice-president, secretary, and treasurer. The class is also choosing a 5-person fundraising committee. Tell which situation is a combination and which is a permutation. Explain your reasoning. **See margin.**

16. Challenge The rides at a fair are a Ferris wheel, a carousel, a log ride, and bumper cars. Find all the different ways you can go on the rides. **See margin.**

12. *Sample answer:* You are buying new footwear. You can choose from sandals, boots, and shoes, each come in either blue or red. Find all possibilities of footwear you can buy.

14. Jenna, Karen, Angela, and Terry; Jenna, Karen, Terry, and Angela; Jenna, Angela, Karen, and Terry; Jenna, Angela, Terry, and Karen; Jenna, Terry, Karen, and Angela; Jenna, Terry, Angela, and Karen

Mixed Review

17. A circular garden has a radius of 6 meters. Find its area. *(Lesson 10.4)*
113.04 m²

A bag has 6 tiles labeled A, B, E, L, R, and U. You randomly choose one tile. Find the probability of the event. *(Lesson 13.1)*

18. You choose an R. $\frac{1}{6}$ **19.** You choose a vowel. **20.** You choose an S. 0
$\frac{1}{2}$

Basic Skills **Write the fraction in simplest form.**

21. $\frac{4}{10}$ $\frac{2}{5}$ **22.** $\frac{6}{9}$ $\frac{2}{3}$ **23.** $\frac{10}{12}$ $\frac{5}{6}$ **24.** $\frac{12}{20}$ $\frac{3}{5}$

Test-Taking Practice

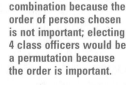
15. Choosing a 5-person committee would be a combination because the order of persons chosen is not important; electing 4 class officers would be a permutation because the order is important.

25. Multiple Choice Tom, Gerald, and John are competing as a team in a speedskating relay race. In how many different ways can they arrange themselves for the race? **B**

A. 3 **B.** 6 **C.** 9 **D.** 12

26. Short Response Juggling balls come in blue, green, red, orange, and purple. A juggler wants to choose exactly 3 of these colors at once. How many different groups of colors can the juggler choose from? Explain how you got your answer. **10; make a list of all possible combinations.**

13, 16. See Additional Answers beginning on page AA1.

MINI-QUIZ

1. Use a tree diagram to find all of the possible outcomes. The choice of color for a uniform is red or blue and the choice of fabric is cotton, rayon, or polyester. **Check diagrams; outcomes: red, cotton; red, rayon, red, polyester; blue, cotton, blue, rayon; blue, polyester**

2. You have four different entertainment options on vacation: ride a bicycle (B), go to a movie (M), rent a canoe (C), or go shopping (S). Find all possible orders in which to do two options. **BM, BC, BS, MB, MC, MS, CB, CM, CS, SB, SM, SC**

The strategy Act It Out helps students visualize the problem they need to solve. When it is appropriate, this strategy allows students to simulate the conditions of the problem so that they can understand it better.

TEACH 2

GUIDING STUDENTS' WORK

Students should notice that while all four students are in each arrangement, Anne must be first or second. It is important that students list each arrangement as they form it so that no order is repeated.

EXTRA EXAMPLES

Example John, Juan, and Sean are to arrange themselves in a line so that a student whose name begins with the letter J must be last. How many arrangements can they make?
4 arrangements

13.3 **Problem Solving Strategies**

- Guess, Check, and Revise
- Solve a Simpler Problem
- Make a Model
- Break into Parts
- Act it Out
- Draw a Graph
- Look for a Pattern

Act It Out

Problem Holly, Paul, Anne, and Jim are rehearsing a dance routine. How many different ways can you arrange the four dancers in a line if Anne must be first or second?

1 Read and Understand

Read the problem carefully.

You need to place four people in a line. Anne must be either first or second in line.

2 Make a Plan

Decide on a strategy to use.

You can solve the problem by acting it out. You need four people to act out the roles of Holly, Paul, Anne, and Jim.

3 Solve the Problem

Reread the problem and act it out.

Work in a group of four students playing the roles of Holly, Paul, Anne, and Jim. Arrange yourselves in as many ways as possible. List the arrangements.

If Anne is first, then the possible arrangements are as follows.

Anne, Holly, Paul, Jim	Anne, Holly, Jim, Paul
Anne, Paul, Holly, Jim	Anne, Paul, Jim, Holly
Anne, Jim, Paul, Holly	Anne, Jim, Holly, Paul

If Anne is second, then the possible arrangements are as follows.

Holly, Anne, Paul, Jim	Holly, Anne, Jim, Paul
Paul, Anne, Holly, Jim	Paul, Anne, Jim, Holly
Jim, Anne, Paul, Holly	Jim, Anne, Holly, Paul

ANSWER There are 12 ways to arrange the dancers in a line if Anne is the first or second person in line.

4 Look Back

You can solve the problem a different way. Use a tree diagram to find all the possible ways to arrange the four dancers. Then count all the outcomes in which Anne is either first or second.

NCTM CURRICULUM STANDARDS
Standard 6: Solve problems in math and other contexts; Apply/adapt strategies to solve problems
Standard 10: Use representations to communicate ideas

Practice the Strategy

Use the strategy *act it out*.

1. **Tug-of-War** Lauren, Luis, Carol, and Nia are a team playing tug-of-war. How many different ways can you arrange them if Luis cannot be the person in front? **18 ways**

2. **Trading Cards** You have $4. You sell a trading card for $1 and then buy 2 more trading cards for $2 each. Then you sell both of those cards for $3 each. How much money do you have now? **$7**

3. **Socks** A bag has 4 socks of different colors: blue, red, white, and black. How many different ways can you choose two socks? **6 ways**

4. **Seating** Betty, Louis, Carl, Mary, Phil, and Kate are sitting in seats 1 through 6 shown below. Phil is sitting in seat 3. Betty is sitting across from Phil. Carl is sitting between Betty and Kate. Mary is sitting across from Carl. In which seat is Louis sitting? **seat 1**

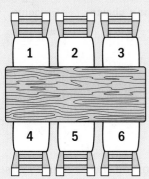

5. **Games** A game starts with 6 tokens on a table. Two players take turns removing 1, 2, or 3 tokens. The player who removes the last token on his or her turn wins. If you go first, how many tokens should you remove to guarantee that you win the game?
2 tokens

Mixed Problem Solving

Use any strategy to solve the problem.

6. **Graphing** Starting at $(-2, -4)$, go up 4 units, then to the left 2 units, then down 3 units, and then to the right 7 units. What are the coordinates of your new position?
(3, −3)

7. **Talent Show** You sold 35 tickets to a community talent show. Tickets cost $3 per adult and $2 per child. You raised $84 for the show. How many adult tickets did you sell? **14 adult tickets**

8. **Counting Off** There are 20 people seated in a room. They count off by 2's starting with the number 2. All the people with numbers that are divisible by 4 stand up. Then the people with numbers that are divisible by 8 sit down. How many people are now seated? **15 people**

9. **Cubes** The rectangular prism below is made up of cubes. The cubes in the top and bottom rows are blue. The cubes in the middle two rows are red. How many more blue faces than red faces are showing on the six sides of the prism?
30 more blue faces

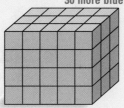

TRANSPARENCY
Even-numbered answers are available on transparencies.

TEACHING TIP

For Exercise 2, you may want to provide play money and trading cards so that students can act out the question. Have students work in pairs, and give each student $4 and 5 trading cards. Exercise 3 can be simulated with colored marbles or colored chips. Encourage students to write down each solution and compare their solutions with a partner.

SUGGESTED STRATEGIES

You may wish to suggest the following strategies for the problems in the Mixed Problem Solving:

- Exercise 6: Draw a Graph
- Exercise 7: Guess, Check, and Revise
- Exercise 8: Act It Out
- Exercise 9: Make a Model

SKILL CHECK

1. At a fair, you can choose between candy or popcorn and between a soft drink or orange juice. What are the different outcomes? **candy, soft drink; candy, orange juice; popcorn, soft drink; popcorn, orange juice**

2. At an ice cream shop, you can choose one of the flavors chocolate, vanilla, butter pecan, or pistachio. Find the probability of choosing pistachio ice cream. $\frac{1}{4}$

PACING

Suggested Number of Days
Basic Course: 1 day
Average Course: 1 day
Advanced Course: 1 day
Block: 0.5 block with 13.2

 TRANSPARENCY

Warm-Up Exercises for this lesson are available on a transparency.

MOTIVATING THE LESSON

Have students list the activities they might choose to do on a Saturday.

LESSON 13.3

Probability of Independent Events

BEFORE	Now	WHY?
You found the probability of a single event.	You'll find the probability of two independent events.	So you can analyze a game, as in Example 3.

Word Watch

independent events, p. 642

(**In the Real World**

Recreation You and your friend each randomly choose to go swimming or play basketball on Saturday. What is the probability that both of you choose basketball?

Two events are **independent** if the occurrence of one event does not affect the likelihood that the other event will occur.

EXAMPLE 1 Two Independent Events

To answer the question above, make a tree diagram of the possible outcomes. Note that your choice does not affect your friend's choice.

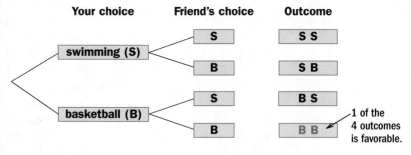

ANSWER The probability that both of you choose basketball is $\frac{1}{4}$.

Your turn now Use the situation in Example 1.

1. Find the probability that both of you choose the same activity. $\frac{1}{2}$

2. Find the probability that at least one of you chooses swimming. $\frac{3}{4}$

NCTM CURRICULUM STANDARDS
Standard 5: Apply basic concepts of probability
Standard 6: Solve problems in math and other contexts
Standard 10: Use representations to solve problems

EXAMPLE 2 Probability of a Sum

The spinners at the right are each divided into equal parts. You spin the spinners. Find the probability that the sum is at least 4.

You can use a table of sums to list all the possible outcomes.

	1	2	3	4	5	6
1	2	3	4	5	6	7
2	3	4	5	6	7	8

← 9 of the 12 sums are at least 4.

ANSWER The probability that the sum is at least 4 is $\frac{9}{12} = \frac{3}{4}$.

EXAMPLE 3 Three Independent Events

Games You are playing a game in which 3 canes are tossed. One side of each cane is flat, and the other side is round. Find the probability that all 3 canes land the same side up.

Solution

You can use a tree diagram to find all the possible outcomes.

First cane	Second cane	Third cane	Outcome
round (R)	R	R	R R R
		F	R R F
	F	R	R F R
		F	R F F
flat (F)	R	R	F R R
		F	F R F
	F	R	F F R
		F	F F F

ANSWER The probability that all 3 canes land the same side up is $\frac{2}{8} = \frac{1}{4}$.

**2 canes round side up
1 cane flat side up**

Your turn now Find the probability of the event.

3. The sum in Example 2 is at most 4. $\frac{5}{12}$

4. Exactly 1 cane in Example 3 lands flat side up. $\frac{3}{8}$

TIPS FOR NEW TEACHERS
Using a tree diagram or table may be necessary to determine all of the outcomes of independent events. Make sure you review how to find outcomes. See Tips for New Teachers in the *Chapter 13 Resource Book*.

EXTRA EXAMPLES

Example 1 You and your friend can each randomly choose between a folk concert and a rock concert. What is the probability that both of you will choose the folk concert? $\frac{1}{4}$

Example 2 The spinners below are divided into equal parts. You spin the spinners. Find the probability that the sum of the outcomes is at least 6. $\frac{1}{4}$

Example 3 Three coins are tossed. Find the probability that all three coins land with heads up. $\frac{1}{8}$

✓ CONCEPT CHECK

How do you find the probability of two independent events occurring?
List all possible outcomes. Then compare the favorable outcomes with the total number of outcomes.

🌐 DAILY PUZZLER

One spinner gives 4 possible equally likely outcomes, and another spinner gives 6. Without using a table or diagram, how many possible outcomes are there? **24**

ASSIGNMENT GUIDE

Basic Course
Day 1: pp. 644–645 Exs. 6–20, 24, 27–35

Average Course
Day 1: pp. 644–645 Exs. 7–14, 18–25, 27–36

Advanced Course
Day 1: pp. 644–645 Exs. 7–9, 12–27*, 31–36

Block
pp. 644–645 Exs. 7–14, 18–25, 27–36 (with 13.2)

EXTRA PRACTICE

- Student Edition, p. 720
- Chapter 13 Resource Book, pp. 27–29
- Test and Practice Generator

 TRANSPARENCY

Even-numbered answers are available on transparencies.

HOMEWORK CHECK

When you review students' homework for this lesson, go over the following exercises to check understanding of key concepts.
Basic: 6, 12, 14, 18, 19
Average: 7, 13, 14, 18, 20
Advanced: 7, 14, 16, 18, 21

COMMON ERROR

In Exercises 8–11, students sometimes do not know the correct probability because they do not treat the problem as two independent events. For example, in Exercise 8, since the probability of getting heads is $\frac{1}{2}$ on each coin, they think the answer should be $\frac{1}{2}$. Suggest they make a tree diagram so they will understand how many outcomes there are.

13.3 Exercises
More Practice, p. 720

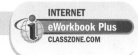

Getting Ready to Practice

Vocabulary **You randomly choose two marbles from a bag of 6 red and 4 blue marbles. Tell whether the two events are independent. Explain.**

1. You choose a red marble and put it back in the bag. Then you choose a blue marble. **Independent; the first event does not affect the second event because you put the first marble back in the bag.**

2. You choose a blue marble but don't put it back in the bag. Then you choose a red marble. **Not independent; the first event affects the second event because you do not put the marble back in the bag.**

Each spinner is divided into equal parts. You spin the spinners. Find the probability of the event.

3. You spin green on both spinners. $\frac{1}{6}$

4. You spin red on at least 1 spinner. $\frac{5}{6}$

5. **Carnival** You and a friend each randomly choose among the dunk tank, face painting, and the balloon throw for your first carnival activity. Find the probability that you both choose the same activity. $\frac{1}{3}$

Practice and Problem Solving

 **with Homework**

Example	Exercises
1	6–11, 18
2	12–17
3	19–22

Online Resources
CLASSZONE.COM
· More Examples
· eTutorial Plus

The spinner is divided into equal parts. You spin it twice. Find the probability of the event.

A 6. You spin two odd numbers. $\frac{1}{4}$

7. You spin at least one even number. $\frac{3}{4}$

You toss a coin twice. Find the probability of the event.

8. You get heads both times. $\frac{1}{4}$ 9. You get heads 0 times. $\frac{1}{4}$

10. You get tails at least 1 time. $\frac{3}{4}$ 11. You get tails exactly 1 time. $\frac{1}{2}$

A bag contains three tiles numbered 1, 2, and 3. Another bag contains four tiles numbered 1, 3, 5, and 7. You randomly draw one tile from each bag. Find the probability of the event.

12. The sum is 8. $\frac{1}{6}$ 13. The sum is 9. $\frac{1}{12}$ 14. The sum is odd. $\frac{1}{3}$

15. The sum is prime. $\frac{1}{3}$ 16. The sum is 11. 0   17. The sum is even. $\frac{2}{3}$

18. **Hidden Coin** You are guessing which of 2 hands is holding a coin. Find all the possible results of playing the game twice. Then find the probability that you guess correctly both times.
right and right, right and left, left and right, left and left; $\frac{1}{4}$

You toss a coin three times. Find the probability of the event.

B **19.** You get heads 3 times. $\frac{1}{8}$　**20.** You get tails exactly 1 time. $\frac{3}{8}$

21. You get tails at least 2 times. $\frac{1}{2}$　**22.** You get heads at most 2 times. $\frac{7}{8}$

23. Order the events in Exercises 19–22 from least likely to occur to most likely to occur. **heads 3 times, tails exactly 1 time, tails at least 2 times, heads at most 2 times**

24. Acting It Out You have 3 shirts: solid, striped, and floral. You have 2 pairs of shorts: khaki and plaid. You have 3 sweaters: orange, green, and blue. You randomly choose one of each type of clothing. Find the probability that you choose a floral shirt, plaid shorts, and a green sweater. $\frac{1}{18}$

C **25. Critical Thinking** A bag contains only blue and red tiles. You draw a blue tile but do not put it back in the bag. Does this *increase*, *decrease*, or *not change* the probability that the next tile chosen is red? Explain. **Increase; there are now fewer total tiles but the same number of red tiles.**

26. Challenge You forgot the last 2 digits of your user ID for a games website. You know that both digits are odd. Find the probability that you type the correct last digits by randomly typing 2 odd numbers. $\frac{1}{25}$

Mixed Review

Find the mean, median, and mode(s) of the data. *(Lesson 2.8)*

27. 14, 16, 12, 11, 14, 15, 13, 20
14.375; 14; 14

28. 15, 28, 21, 17, 28, 20, 21
about 21.4; 21; 21 and 28

Solve the proportion. *(Lesson 8.3)*

29. $\frac{4}{3} = \frac{x}{12}$ **16**　**30.** $\frac{5}{25} = \frac{s}{15}$ **3**　**31.** $\frac{10}{30} = \frac{6}{c}$ **18**　**32.** $\frac{24}{9} = \frac{8}{n}$ **3**

Basic Skills **Find the total amount spent.**

33. 6 bottles of water for $.95 each **$5.70**　**34.** 2 boxes of cereal for $3.45 each **$6.90**

Test-Taking Practice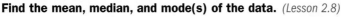

35. Multiple Choice You are guessing on 2 multiple-choice questions. Each question has answer choices A, B, and C. Find the probability that you answer both questions correctly. **A**

　A. $\frac{1}{9}$　　**B.** $\frac{1}{6}$　　**C.** $\frac{1}{2}$　　**D.** $\frac{2}{3}$

36. Multiple Choice A token is red on one side and yellow on the other side. You toss it twice. Find the probability that you get red both times. **G**

　F. $\frac{1}{8}$　　**G.** $\frac{1}{4}$　　**H.** $\frac{1}{2}$　　**I.** $\frac{2}{3}$

ASSESSMENT RESOURCES

For more assessment resources, see:
- Assessment Book
- Test and Practice Generator

MINI-QUIZ

1. The spinner is divided into four equal parts. You spin it twice. Find the probability of spinning two even numbers. $\frac{1}{4}$

2. You toss a coin twice. Find the probability of getting two tails. $\frac{1}{4}$

3. You toss a coin three times. Find the probability of getting two tails and one head. $\frac{3}{8}$

4. You toss a coin three times. Find the probability of getting at least two tails. $\frac{1}{2}$

5 **FOLLOW-UP**

RETEACHING/REMEDIATION

- Study Guide in Chapter 13 Resource Book, pp. 30–31
- eTutorial Plus Online
- Extra Practice, p. 720
- Lesson Practice in Chapter 13 Resource Book, pp. 27–29

CHALLENGE/ENRICHMENT

- Challenge Practice in Chapter 13 Resource Book, p. 32
- Teacher's Edition, p. 626F

ENGLISH LEARNER SUPPORT

- Spanish Study Guide
- Multi-Language Glossary
- Chapter Audio Summaries CDs

ADDITIONAL RESOURCES

The following resources are available to help review the materials in Lessons 13.1–13.3.

 Chapter 13 Resource Book
- Lesson Practice
- Study Guide

 Assessment Book
- Chapter 13 Quiz 1

 Technology
- Test and Practice Generator
- eTutorial CD-ROM

 Internet
- Classzone
- eWorkbook Plus Online
- eTutorial Plus Online

ENGLISH LEARNER SUPPORT

- Spanish Study Guide
- Multi-Language Glossary
- Chapter Audio Summaries CDs

2. A combination is a grouping of objects in which order is not important. A permutation is an arrangement of objects in which order is important.

LESSONS 13.1 TO 13.3

Notebook Review

Review the vocabulary definitions in your notebook.

Copy the review examples in your notebook. Then complete the exercises.

Check Your Definitions

outcome, p. 630
event, p. 630
favorable outcomes, p. 630

probability, p. 630
complementary events, p. 632
tree diagram, p. 636

combination, p. 637
permutation, p. 637
independent events, p. 642

Use Your Vocabulary

1. Describe the complement of rolling an even number on a number cube.
   rolling an odd number

2. **Writing** Explain how a combination and a permutation are different.
   See margin.

13.1 Can you find probabilities of single events?

Review

EXAMPLE The probability of rolling an even number on a number cube is as follows.

$$\frac{\text{Number of favorable outcomes}}{\text{Number of possible outcomes}} = \frac{3}{6} = \frac{1}{2}$$

 You roll a number cube. Find the probability of the event.

3. You roll a 5. $\frac{1}{6}$ 4. You roll an 8. 0 5. You roll a factor of 24. $\frac{5}{6}$

13.2–13.3 Can you find outcomes and probabilities?

Review

EXAMPLE You toss a coin twice. Find the probability that you get tails both times.

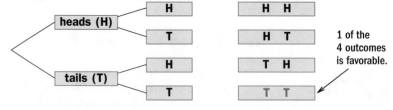

1 of the 4 outcomes is favorable.

ANSWER The probability that you get tails both times is $\frac{1}{4}$.

 6. Find all the different ways you can arrange the letters of the word ACT. Then find the probability that you randomly choose an arrangement in which the letter C is not the first letter.
ACT, ATC, CAT, CTA, TAC, TCA; $\frac{2}{3}$

Stop and Think about Lessons 13.1–13.3

7. Writing Explain whether a percent greater than 100% can represent a probability.

8. Critical Thinking How are the probabilities of two complementary events related? Explain your answer.

Review Quiz 1

A bag contains twelve tiles numbered 1 through 12. You randomly choose one tile from the bag. Find the probability of the event.

1. You choose a 7. $\frac{1}{12}$

2. You choose an even number. $\frac{1}{2}$

3. You choose a multiple of 3. $\frac{1}{3}$

4. You choose a 15. 0

5. Posters A poster comes in 3 sizes: 1 foot by 2 feet, 2 feet by 4 feet, and 3 feet by 6 feet. You can choose a black-and-white or a colored poster. List all the different kinds of posters you can choose from.

6. Find all the two-digit numbers that can be formed using two different digits from 1, 2, 4, and 6. 12, 14, 16, 21, 24, 26, 41, 42, 46, 61, 62, 64

7. Phone Numbers You forgot the first two digits of your friend's phone number. You know that each of the digits is 7 or 8. Find the probability that you get the correct first two digits by randomly choosing 7 or 8. $\frac{1}{4}$

Create a Spinner

Create a spinner that has 6 equal parts. Use the clues below to find out which numbers to put on the spinner.

- The probability of spinning a 4 is $\frac{1}{3}$.

- The probability of spinning a 2 is $\frac{1}{6}$.

- The probability of spinning a factor of 15 is $\frac{1}{2}$.

- The sum of the odd numbers on the spinner is 13.
  one 2, one 3, two 4s, two 5s

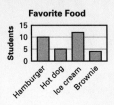

Favorite Food

1. Which food received the most votes? **Ice cream**

2. Which food received twice as many votes as hot dogs? **Hamburgers**

LESSON OBJECTIVE

Recognize how statistics can be misleading.

PACING

Suggested Number of Days
Basic Course: 1 day
Average Course: 1 day
Advanced Course: 1 day
Block: 0.5 block with 13.5

TEACHING RESOURCES

For a complete list of Teaching Resources, see page 626B.

 TRANSPARENCY

Warm-Up Exercises for this lesson are available on a transparency.

2 TEACH

MOTIVATING THE LESSON

Ask students to recall surveys they or their parents have participated in.

ACTIVITY

Goal Use graphs to influence the way people interpret data.

Key Discovery The scale of a graph influences the way people interpret the data.

Steps 1–2. See Additional Answers beginning on page AA1.

648

LESSON 13.4

Misleading Statistics

BEFORE	Now	WHY?
You made conclusions based on graphs of data.	You'll recognize how statistics can be misleading.	So you can interpret a graph of storms, as in Exs. 7–9.

Word Watch

Review Words

scale, p. 68
bar graph, p. 79
line graph, p. 84
mean, p. 93
median, p. 93
mode, p. 93

Step 3. The graph in Step 1; the bar for soda looks much longer than the other bars.

Activity You can use graphs to influence the way people interpret data.

The table at the right shows the results of a survey asking 100 students their favorite drink.
Steps 1–2. See margin.

Drink	Students
Milk	25
Juice	21
Soda	31
Water	23

1 Draw a bar graph of the data with a scale from 0 to 35 in increments of 5.

2 Draw a bar graph of the data with a scale from 0 to 50 in increments of 10.

3 Which graph is more likely to persuade someone that students drink too much soda? Explain your choice.

Misleading Graphs How someone draws a graph can affect how the information is interpreted. Bar and line graphs could be misleading if the scale appears to distort the data in some way.

EXAMPLE 1 Potentially Misleading Graphs

Movies The bar graph shows the number of admissions to movie theaters in the United States in 3 different years. Without using the scale, compare admissions in 1990 and 2000. Then compare the admissions using the scale.

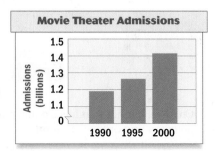

Movie Theater Admissions

Solution

Admissions in 1990 appear to have been about half the number in 2000, because the 1990 bar is half as high as the 2000 bar.

Admissions in 1990 were actually about 85% of admissions in 2000, because $1.2 \div 1.4 \approx 85\%$. The break in the scale distorts the relative heights of the bars.

NCTM CURRICULUM STANDARDS
Standard 5: Develop inferences that are based on data
Standard 8: Communicate thinking clearly to others; Analyze the thinking/strategies of others

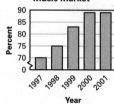

TIPS FOR NEW TEACHERS
Demonstrate the importance of the scale in a bar graph by showing two graphs of students' heights. The scale on one graph should start at 0. The scale on the other graph should start just below the shortest height in the class. See Tips for New Teachers in the *Chapter 13 Resource Book*.

Your turn now Solve the problem below.

1. Tell which line graph makes the average price of a movie ticket in the United States appear to increase more dramatically. Explain.
   The graph on the right; the line appears to be steeper.

Misleading Averages An *average* can be represented by the mean, the median, or the mode. You may get a misleading impression of a data set if the average that is used does not represent the data well.

with Review

Need help with finding the mean, median, and mode? See p. 93.

EXAMPLE 2 **Misleading Averages**

Cameras A store owner says that the average price of a digital camera at the store is $65. The prices of the 10 digital cameras sold at the store are:

$65, $65, $80, $90, $95, $100, $112, $120, $168, and $215.

Does $65 describe the prices well? Why might a store owner use this number?

3. Sample answer: To convince people that the average donation contains a lot of books.

Solution

The mode, $65, does not describe the data well because it is less than most of the prices. A store owner might use $65 as the average price to convince people that the store sells very inexpensive digital cameras.

with Solving

If one data value is very small or very large compared to the other data, then the mean could be distorted.

Your turn now The numbers of monthly book donations to a library are listed below. Use these data in Exercises 2 and 3.

23, 28, 36, 45, 25, 31, 39, 47, 28, 32, 40, 226

2. Does 50 describe the numbers of donations well? Why or why not?
   No; it is greater than most of the donations.
3. Why might a library use 50 as the average number of donated books?
   See margin.

EXTRA EXAMPLES

Example 1 Without using the scale in the bar graph below, compare the percents of CDs sold in 1998 and 2001. Then compare the percents using the scale.

CD Sales as Percent of Music Market

The 1998 percent looks to be about half the 2001 percent because the bar is half as tall. Using the scale, there is actually only a difference of 14%.

Example 2 A store owner says the average price of a CD is $18. The prices for 10 randomly selected CDs are $12, $22, $18, $15, $18, $18, $19, $11, $13, $12. Does $18 describe the prices well? *No, $18 is higher than many of the prices.*

✓ **CONCEPT CHECK**

Describe how graphs can be misleading. *They can misrepresent the data by using a scale that makes comparisons inaccurate.*

 DAILY PUZZLER

Find the average price of the CDs in Extra Example 2. *$15.80*

ASSIGNMENT GUIDE

Basic Course
Day 1: SRH p. 704 Exs. 5–7,
p. 705 Exs. 5–8; pp. 650–652
Exs. 5–16, 20–24

Average Course
Day 1: pp. 650–652 Exs. 5–17,
20–25

Advanced Course
Day 1: pp. 650–652 Exs. 5–21*,
24, 25

Block
pp. 650–652 Exs. 5–17, 20–25
(with 13.5)

EXTRA PRACTICE

- Student Edition, p. 720
- Chapter 13 Resource Book, pp. 36–38
- Test and Practice Generator

TRANSPARENCY

Even-numbered answers are available on transparencies.

HOMEWORK CHECK

When you review students' homework for this lesson, go over the following exercises to check understanding of key concepts.
Basic: 5, 6, 7, 8, 10
Average: 5, 6, 7, 9, 10
Advanced: 5, 6, 8, 10, 11

TEACHING TIP

For Exercise 4, you may need to remind students about how to find the mean, median, and mode for a set of data. Tell them that the mean is the average, the median is the middle value, and the mode is the value that appears most often. Refer them to Chapter 2.

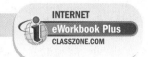

13.4 Exercises
More Practice, p. 720

INTERNET
eWorkbook Plus
CLASSZONE.COM

Getting Ready to Practice

1. **Vocabulary** Describe how the scale affects a graph's appearance.
   It can distort the data.

Jumping **The bar graph shows various long jump records.**

2. Without looking at the scale, about how many times greater does the record for kangaroos appear to be than the record for humans? for frogs? **3 times; 2 times**

3. Using the scale, is the record for kangaroos *less than* or *greater than* two times the record for humans? for frogs? **less than; less than**

Long Jump Records

Human
Frog
Kangaroo

0 28 32 36 40 44
Distance (ft)

4. **Guided Problem Solving** Jill says that her average score on a game is 500. Do the scores below support this? Why would Jill say this?

   350, 305, 300, 200, 500, 325, 375, 225, 275, 500

   (1 Find the mean, median, and mode(s) of the scores. **335.5; 315; 500**

   (2 Does 500 describe Jill's scores well? Why or why not?
      No; it is greater than all of the other scores.

   (3 Why would Jill use 500 as her average score? **To make her scores look higher than they actually are.**

Practice and Problem Solving

A 5. **Dogs** Which line graph would a dog walker use to persuade you to get your dog walked for 60 minutes? Explain. **B; the line in graph B is not as steep as the line in graph A.**

A. **Cost of Walking Dogs**

Cost (dollars)
25
20
15
10
5
0
0 10 20 30 40 50 60 70
Minutes

B. **Cost of Walking Dogs**

Cost (dollars)
50
40
30
20
10
0
0 10 20 30 40 50 60 70
Minutes

HELP with Homework

Example	Exercises
1	5, 7–9
2	6, 10–11

Online Resources
CLASSZONE.COM
· More Examples
· eTutorial Plus

6. **Skateboarding** A reporter says that the average age of the athletes in a skateboarding competition is 18 years. All the ages are listed below. Why do you think this average was used? Is there a better one?

   15, 17, 29, 17, 15, 16, 15, 20   To make the athletes appear to be older; yes, the median is better.

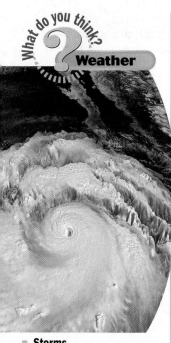
Storms The bar graph shows how many hurricanes and tropical storms started in various months from 1995 to 2001 in the Eastern Pacific.

7. Without looking at the scale or the data values, about how many times more storms appeared to start from July to September than from April to June? **2 times more**

8. Using the data values, about how many times more storms actually started from July to September than from April to June? **about 4 times more**

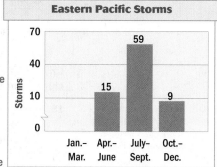

Eastern Pacific Storms

9. Would a travel agent use *the data values* or *the bars on the graph* to convince someone not to travel to the Eastern Pacific in the summer? **the data values**

Baseball The numbers of games won by a baseball team in 10 seasons are listed below.

82, 94, 97, 88, 88, 71, 69, 55, 59, 72

10. A sports report states that the average number of wins by the team is 88. Does 88 describe the numbers of wins well? Why or why not?
No, it is greater than more than half of the number of wins.

11. Why might a report use 88 as the average number of wins?
To make it appear that the team usually wins a lot of games.

Electives The circle graph shows the results of a survey asking students their favorite elective. **12–13. See margin.**

B 12. Without looking at the percents, which elective appears to have the most responses? Explain.

13. Draw a circle graph that more accurately shows the actual percent for each elective.

Favorite Electives

Music 35%　Languages 20%
Other 10%　Art 35%

Houses The list below shows the prices of several houses in a region.

$115,000, $115,000, $130,000, $140,000, $145,000, $150,000, $152,000, $190,000, $198,000, $215,000

14. A real estate agent says that the average cost of a home in the region is $115,000. Does $115,000 describe the prices well? Why or why not?

15. Why might a real estate agent use $115,000 as the average price?

16. Which average provides you with the information you would most want to know when buying a house? Why?

14. No; it is lowest when compared to the rest of the prices shown.

15. *Sample answer:* To show that the houses in the region are not that expensive.

16. *Sample answer:* The one that represents the data well. In this example, the median, which is $147,500, may best represent the data.

Lesson 13.4　Misleading Statistics　**651**

Differentiating Instruction

Advanced Students In Exercise 5, ask students to generalize about how a change in a vertical scale affects a line graph. **A greater interval between the numbers flattens out the graph.**

Ⓧ **COMMON ERROR**

Exercises 10–11 illustrate a common error made when reporting data. The error is to assume the middle value of a set of data is the average. Remind students that they need to put the data values in order before they determine what the middle value is.

12. Art; it appears to have the largest section of the graph.

13.　**Favorite Electives**

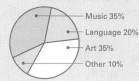

Music 35%
Language 20%
Art 35%
Other 10%

MINI-QUIZ

1. The graph shows the annual food costs in the U.S. for four different years. Without using the scale, compare the costs for 1994 and 1998. Then compare these costs using the scale.

Annual Food Costs in the U.S.

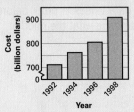

The 1998 costs appear to be twice those in 1994 because the 1998 bar is twice as tall as the 1994 bar. The 1998 costs were really about 19% greater than the 1994 costs.

5 FOLLOW-UP

RETEACHING/REMEDIATION

- Study Guide in Chapter 13 Resource Book, pp. 39–40
- eTutorial Plus Online
- Extra Practice, p. 720
- Lesson Practice in Chapter 13 Resource Book, pp. 36–38

CHALLENGE/ENRICHMENT

- Challenge Practice in Chapter 13 Resource Book, p. 41
- Teacher's Edition, p. 626F

ENGLISH LEARNER SUPPORT

- Spanish Study Guide
- Multi-Language Glossary
- Chapter Audio Summaries CDs

17. See Additional Answers beginning on page AA1.

652

C 17. Bears The table shows the number of grizzly bears that were born in Yellowstone from 1992 to 1998. Draw a bar graph that makes the number of newborns in 1998 appear to be twice the number in 1992.

See margin.

Year	1992	1993	1994	1995	1996	1997	1998
Newborns	60	41	47	37	72	62	70

Challenge **The graph below shows the numbers, in millions, of CD shipments in the United States in 1998 and 1999.**

18. About 4 times greater. *Sample answer:* The pictures make it appear that 4 times as many CDs were shipped in 1999 than were shipped in 1998, when there were actually about $1\frac{1}{8}$ times as many shipped.

18. About how many times greater in area is the picture for 1999 than the picture for 1998? Explain how this may distort the data.

19. Was the actual number of shipments in 1999 *less than* or *greater than* twice the number of shipments in 1998? less than

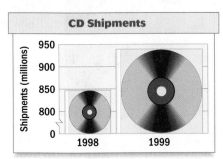

Mixed Review

20. Write *6 more than a number* as a variable expression. *(Lesson 12.1)*
$n + 6$

21. You toss a coin twice. Find the probability that you get heads at least one time. *(Lesson 13.3)* $\frac{3}{4}$

Basic Skills **Find the range of the data.**

22. 14, 16, 11, 10, 13, 15, 21, 18 **11**   **23.** 532, 416, 501, 543, 580, 499 **164**

Test-Taking Practice

INTERNET
State Test Practice
CLASSZONE.COM

24. Twice as tall; no; the scale shows that Building B is only about 75 meters taller than Building A, which is about 175 meters tall.

24. Short Response The bar graph shows the heights of two buildings. Without looking at the scale, tell how many times taller Building B appears than Building A. Does your answer represent the actual relationship? Explain.

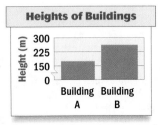

25. Multiple Choice The list below shows the number of cars at a car wash each day last week. You want it to seem as successful as possible. Which value would you use as the average number of cars washed per day? **A**

73, 80, 106, 73, 73, 85, 98

A. mean   **B.** median   **C.** mode   **D.** range

Stem-and-Leaf Plots

BEFORE ▶ **Now** **WHY?**

You organized data using line plots and frequency tables.

You'll organize data using stem-and-leaf plots.

So you can organize scores in bowling games, as in Ex. 12.

Word Watch

stem-and-leaf plot, p. 653
leaf, p. 653
stem, p. 653

In the Real World

Internet The table lists how long, in minutes, you were online each day for the past 21 days. How can you display the data so you can see them grouped in an orderly way?

You can use a *stem-and-leaf plot* to organize a large set of data. In a **stem-and-leaf plot**, each data value has two parts, a *stem* and a *leaf*. The **leaf** is the last digit on the right. The **stem** is the remaining digits. For example, the leaf of the data value 37 is 7. The stem is 3.

Daily Internet Use (minutes)			
SUNDAY	22	27	42
MONDAY	41	23	19
TUESDAY	15	35	29
WEDNESDAY	28	54	53
THURSDAY	50	70	31
FRIDAY	19	40	31
SATURDAY	44	37	35

EXAMPLE 1 Making a Stem-and-Leaf Plot

To organize the minutes online in the table above, you can make a stem-and-leaf plot. The numbers range from 15 to 70. So, the least stem is 1 and the greatest stem is 7.

① Order the stems from least to greatest.

```
1 |
2 |
3 |
4 |
5 |
6 |
7 |
```

② Write the leaves next to their stems.

```
1 | 9 5 9
2 | 2 7 3 9 8
3 | 5 1 1 7 5
4 | 2 1 0 4
5 | 4 3 0
6 |
7 | 0  ← This stands for 53.
```

③ Order the leaves from least to greatest.

```
1 | 5 9 9
2 | 2 3 7 8 9
3 | 1 1 5 5 7
4 | 0 1 2 4
5 | 0 3 4
6 |
7 | 0   Key: 5 | 3 = 53
```

Watch Out!

Be sure to include all of the stems between the least and the greatest. In Example 1, 6 is a stem even though none of the data values have a 6 in the tens' place.

1.

```
1 | 4 5 6
2 | 1 2 2 4 8
3 | 0 1 3 9
4 |
5 | 1   Key: 3 | 1 = 31
```

Your turn now Make a stem-and-leaf plot of the data.

1. 31, 14, 22, 51, 33, 16, 21, 24, 22, 15, 30, 28, 39

NCTM CURRICULUM STANDARDS
Standard 5: Collect, organize, and display data; Use proper statistical methods to analyze data
Standard 8: Use the language of math to express ideas

---

① PLAN

SKILL CHECK
Use the set of numbers 14, 18, 13, 19, and 15.
1. Find the median.   15
2. Find the mean.   15.8
3. Find the mode.   none
4. Find the range.   6

LESSON OBJECTIVE

Organize data with a stem-and-leaf plot.

PACING

Suggested Number of Days
Basic Course: 2 days
Average Course: 2 days
Advanced Course: 2 days
Block: 0.5 block with 13.4
         0.5 block with 13.6

TEACHING RESOURCES

For a complete list of Teaching Resources, see page 626B.

TRANSPARENCY

Warm-Up Exercises for this lesson are available on a transparency.

② TEACH

MOTIVATING THE LESSON

Make a list of students' heights and create a stem-and-leaf plot. Students should see that a stem-and-leaf plot is a good way to condense data.

TIPS FOR NEW TEACHERS

Point out that some plots include stems with no leaves. See Tips for New Teachers in the *Chapter 13 Resource Book*.

653

NOTETAKING

Ask students to write the steps for making a stem-and-leaf plot in their notebooks.

 CONCEPT CHECK

How do you make a stem-and-leaf plot? **Identify the leaf as the last digit of each number and the stem as the remaining digit(s). List the stems in order and then add the leaves from least to greatest.**

 DAILY PUZZLER

The patients in a hospital range in age from 2 years to 102 years. What stems would you need in a stem-and-leaf plot for their ages? **0, 10, 20, 30, 40, 50, 60, 70, 80, 90, 100**

EXAMPLE 2 **Interpreting Stem-and-Leaf Plots**

Diners The stem-and-leaf plot shows the ages of people at a diner.

a. What is the range of the ages?

b. Describe the age group with the most people.

```
0 | 4 6 7 9
1 | 0 1 1 2 2 2 2 4 9
2 | 2 5 8
3 | 0 1 4      Key: 3 | 1 = 31
```

Solution

a. The youngest person at the diner is 4 years old, because the least data value is 0 | 4. The oldest person is 34 years old, because the greatest data value is 3 | 4. The range is 30 years, because $34 - 4 = 30$.

b. Most of the people at the diner are between 10 and 19 years old, because most of the data values have a stem of 1.

EXAMPLE 3 **Finding the Mean, Median, and Mode**

Use the stem-and-leaf plot.

a. Find the mean.

b. Find the median.

c. Find the mode.

```
5 | 7 7
6 | 1 2 7
7 | 0 4      Key: 5 | 7 = 5.7
```

Solution

Make an ordered list of the 7 values in the stem-and-leaf plot.

5.7, 5.7, 6.1, 6.2, 6.7, 7.0, 7.4

a. Mean $= \dfrac{5.7 + 5.7 + 6.1 + 6.2 + 6.7 + 7.0 + 7.4}{7} = \dfrac{44.8}{7} = 6.4$

b. The median is 6.2, because the middle value is 6.2.

c. The mode is 5.7, because it occurs the most times.

Your turn now Use the stem-and-leaf plot in Example 2.

2. Describe the ages of the people at the diner who are not in the most common age group. **people between the ages of 0 to 9 and 20 to 39**

3. Find the mean, median, and mode(s) of the data. **16.5; 12; 12**

INTERNET
eWorkbook Plus
CLASSZONE.COM

Getting Ready to Practice

1. Vocabulary Identify the stems and the leaves in the stem-and-leaf plot. **stems: 1, 2, 3; leaves: 2, 4, 7, 1, 9, 5, 6, 8, 9**

```
1 | 2 4 7
2 | 1 9
3 | 5 6 8 9    Key: 1|4 = 14
```

Pets The list below shows the weights, in pounds, of pets owned by students.

25, 7, 8, 10, 13, 22, 10, 15, 12, 13, 9, 40, 15, 21, 14

2. Find the least stem and the greatest stem for the data. **0,4**

3. Make a stem-and-leaf plot of the data. **See margin.**

4. Which stem has the most leaves? Explain what this means.
1; most of the weights are in the 10-19 pound range.

Practice and Problem Solving

Make a stem-and-leaf plot of the data. **5–7. See margin.**

A 5. 15, 18, 24, 32, 28, 18, 21, 16, 32, 41, 25, 31, 18, 25

6. 67, 55, 61, 69, 50, 51, 67, 62, 39, 50, 35, 62, 58, 60

7. 15, 38, 9, 33, 16, 7, 5, 35, 30, 35, 55, 49, 41, 52, 51

8. Find the Error Describe and correct the error in making the stem-and-leaf plot.
See margin.

```
1 | 5 9
2 | 0 2
4 | 3 3 7   Key: 4|3 = 43
```

Tennis The stem-and-leaf plot shows the lengths, in minutes, of mixed doubles finals matches in Wimbledon tennis for a period of years.

9. Find the mean, median, mode(s), and range. **about 80.7; 73; 73; 62**

10. Which stem has the most leaves? Explain what this means. **7; most of the tennis matches lasted from 70 to 79 minutes.**

11. Describe the relationship between the shortest and longest matches in two different ways. *Sample answer:* The longest match lasted 62 minutes longer than the shortest match; the shortest match lasted more than an hour less than the longest match.

```
 5 | 9
 6 | 6 9
 7 | 1 1 3 3 3 5
 8 | 5 5
 9 | 3 7
10 | 0
11 |
12 | 1    Key: 12|1 = 121
```

3.
```
0 | 7 8 9
1 | 0 0 2 3 3 4 5 5
2 | 1 2 5
3 |
4 | 0   Key: 2|1 = 21
```

 **with Homework**

Example	Exercises
1	5–8
2	9–11
3	9–11

 **Online Resources**
CLASSZONE.COM
· More Examples
· eTutorial Plus

3 APPLY

ASSIGNMENT GUIDE
Basic Course
Day 1: SRH p. 709 Exs. 11, 12, 22, 23; pp. 655–656 Exs. 5–7, 12–14, 25, 26
Day 2: pp. 655–656 Exs. 9–11, 17–24
Average Course
Day 1: pp. 655–656 Exs. 5–8, 17–22
Day 2: pp. 655–656 Exs. 9–15, 23–26
Advanced Course
Day 1: pp. 655–656 Exs. 5–8, 16–21*
Day 2: pp. 655–656 Exs. 9–15, 24–26
Block
pp. 655–656 Exs. 5–8, 17–22 (with 13.4)
pp. 655–656 Exs. 9–15, 23–26 (with 13.6)

EXTRA PRACTICE
• Student Edition, p. 720
• Chapter 13 Resource Book, pp. 44–46
• Test and Practice Generator

TRANSPARENCY
Even-numbered answers are available on transparencies.

HOMEWORK CHECK
When you review students' homework for this lesson, go over the following exercises to check understanding of key concepts.
Basic: 5, 6, 7, 9, 10
Average: 5, 7, 9, 10, 11
Advanced: 6, 7, 9, 10, 11

5–8. See Additional Answers beginning on page AA1.

655

For more assessment resources, see:
- Assessment Book
- Test and Practice Generator

MINI-QUIZ

1. Make a stem-and-leaf plot of these data: 12, 10, 19, 21, 32, 33, 30, 20, 19, 15, 16.

```
1 | 0 2 5 6 9 9
2 | 0 1
3 | 0 2 3
```

2. Use the stem-and-leaf plot.

```
1 | 0 1 1 2
2 | 1 3 4 4 5 6 8
3 |
4 | 0 4 4 4 8
```

a. Find the mean. **27.2**
b. Find the median. **24.5**
c. Find the mode. **44**
d. What is the range? **38**
e. Describe the group with the most data values. **the group with values from 20 to 29**

---

5 **FOLLOW-UP**

RETEACHING/REMEDIATION

- Study Guide in Chapter 13 Resource Book, pp. 47–48
- eTutorial Plus Online
- Extra Practice, p. 720
- Lesson Practice in Chapter 13 Resource Book, pp. 44–46

CHALLENGE/ENRICHMENT

- Challenge Practice in Chapter 13 Resource Book, p. 49
- Teacher's Edition, p. 626F

ENGLISH LEARNER SUPPORT

- Spanish Study Guide
- Multi-Language Glossary
- Chapter Audio Summaries CDs

17–20. See Additional Answers beginning on page AA1.

12.
```
18 | 1
19 | 0 5 6 9
20 | 2 4
21 | 0 5 7
22 | 2 2
23 | 0 5
24 |
25 | 1    Key: 19 | 6 = 196
```

15. *Sample answer:* Mode; a lighter phone would be preferable over a heavier phone.

INTERNET
State Test Practice
CLASSZONE.COM

26.
```
7 | 8 9
8 | 3 6 6 8
9 | 3 4 6 6 9
Key: 7 | 9 = 79
```
90s; the most leaves are after the 9.

Bowling **The table shows your bowling scores in several games.**

B 12. Make a stem-and-leaf plot of the scores. Use the key 19 | 6 = 196.
See margin.
13. Suppose your goal was to score at least 230 in 10 of the games. By how many games did you miss your goal?
7 games

Bowling Scores				
181	222	196	210	217
195	199	204	215	190
202	251	222	230	235

Cell Phones **In Exercises 14 and 15, use the stem-and-leaf plot.**
It shows the weights, in ounces, of 15 cell phones at a store.

14. Find the mean, median, and mode(s).
6.1; 6.0; 4.8
15. **Writing** Which number would you use as the average weight? Explain.
See margin.
C 16. **Challenge** The least value of a data set is 12.3. The greatest value is 90.7. Is it appropriate to make a stem-and-leaf plot of the data? Explain.
Sample answer: No; the values are too wide spread for a stem-and-leaf plot.

```
4 | 0 3 8 8
5 | 0 4 9
6 | 0 1 2
7 | 1 2 9
8 | 2 6    Key: 8 | 6 = 8.6
```

Mixed Review

Graph the integer on a number line. *(Lesson 11.1)* 17–20. See margin.

17. −6   **18.** 5   **19.** 0   **20.** −2

21. Your score on a cooking contest is 7. All the scores of the 10 contestants are listed below. What average can you use so you can say that your score is above average? Explain. *(Lesson 13.4)* Mode; the mode is 5, so you could say your score of 7 is above average.

7, 10, 10, 6, 9, 5, 8, 7, 5, 5

Basic Skills **Copy and complete the statement with <, >, or =.**

22. 35.89 ? 35.889 **>**   **23.** 2.162 ? 2.1005 **>**   **24.** 6.017 ? 6.01700 **=**

Test-Taking Practice

25. **Multiple Choice** Use the stem-and-leaf plot to find the median of the data. **B**

```
0 | 9 9
1 | 5 5 6 7 9
2 | 0 0 0 1 2    Key: 2 | 0 = 20
```

A. 8   **B.** 18   **C.** 20   **D.** 22

26. **Short Response** Make a stem-and-leaf plot of Gary's test scores below. Did Gary get mostly 90s, 80s, or 70s? Explain.

78, 96, 96, 83, 94, 88, 93, 79, 99, 86, 86

Box-and-Whisker Plots

LESSON 13.6

BEFORE ▶ **Now** **WHY?**

You represented data using stem-and-leaf plots.

You'll represent data using box-and-whisker plots.

So you can compare durations of solar eclipses, as in Ex. 11.

In the Real World

Ticket Prices The notebook shows the ticket prices for different concerts that you attended. How can you display the data so you can see how spread out they are?

Ticket Prices
$14 $36 $9 $12
$24 $27 $22 $42
$25 $19 $18

A **box-and-whisker plot** divides a data set into four parts, two below the median and two above it. The **lower quartile** is the median of the lower half of the data. The **upper quartile** is the median of the upper half. The **lower extreme** is the least data value. The **upper extreme** is the greatest data value.

EXAMPLE 1 **Making a Box-and-Whisker Plot**

To display the ticket prices above, make a box-and-whisker plot.

(1) Order the data to find the median, the quartiles, and the extremes.

Lower half   Upper half

9   12   14   18   19   22   24   25   27   36   42

Lower extreme   Lower quartile   Median   Upper quartile   Upper extreme

(2) Plot the five values below a number line.

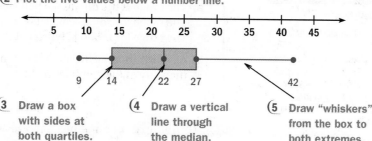

9   14   22   27   42

(3) Draw a box with sides at both quartiles.

(4) Draw a vertical line through the median.

(5) Draw "whiskers" from the box to both extremes.

Your turn now **Make a box-and-whisker plot of the data.** 1–2. See margin.

1. 5, 9, 16, 8, 6, 15, 14, 5, 15, 12   **2.** 35, 19, 63, 48, 67, 50, 44, 58, 53

---

1 PLAN

SKILL CHECK
Use the set of numbers 22, 25, 28, 19, 16, 22, and 24.
1. Find the median.   22
2. Find the range.   12

LESSON OBJECTIVE
Represent data with box-and-whisker plots.

PACING
Suggested Number of Days
Basic Course: 2 days
Average Course: 2 days
Advanced Course: 2 days
Block: 0.5 block with 13.5
       0.5 block with 13.7

TEACHING RESOURCES
For a complete list of Teaching Resources, see page 626B.

TRANSPARENCY
Warm-Up Exercises for this lesson are available on a transparency.

2 TEACH

MOTIVATING THE LESSON
Ask students to name the various ways they already know for displaying data. Then explain that this lesson will give them another way.

TIPS FOR NEW TEACHERS
Be sure students understand that just as the median divides the data into halves, the quartiles divide the data into quarters. See Tips for New Teachers in the *Chapter 13 Resource Book.*

1–2. See Additional Answers beginning on page AA1.

657

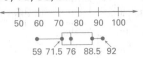
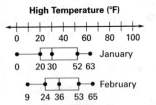

658

What do you think?
Science

■ **Jellyfish**

A moon jellyfish is shown in the photo above. The largest jellyfish can grow up to 90 inches in body width. How does this width compare to the body widths of the moon jellyfish samples in Example 3? **The largest jellyfish has a greater body width than the moon jellyfish samples in Example 3.**

EXAMPLE 2 **Reading a Box-and-Whisker Plot**

Identify the median, the lower and upper quartiles, and the lower and upper extremes in the box-and-whisker plot below.

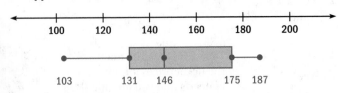

ANSWER The median is 146. The lower quartile is 131. The upper quartile is 175. The lower extreme is 103. The upper extreme is 187.

EXAMPLE 3 **Interpreting Box-and-Whisker Plots**

Jellyfish The box-and-whisker plots below represent the body widths, in inches, of a sample of jellyfish from two different species.

a. Find the range of the body widths.

b. Compare the body widths in the two samples.

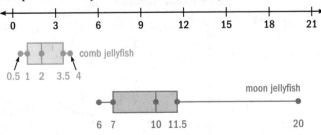

Solution

a. The range is the difference between the extremes. The range for comb jellyfish is 3.5 inches, because $4 - 0.5 = 3.5$. The range for moon jellyfish is 14 inches, because $20 - 6 = 14$.

b. All of the moon jellyfish in the sample have a greater body width than any of the comb jellyfish.

Your turn now Use the box-and-whisker plots above.

3. Find the range of the data in Example 2. **84**

4. Identify the median, the lower and upper quartiles, and the lower and upper extremes for the body widths of the moon jellyfish in Example 3. **median = 10, lower quartile = 7, upper quartile = 11.5, lower extreme = 6, upper extreme = 20**

INTERNET
eWorkbook Plus
CLASSZONE.COM

Getting Ready to Practice

1. Vocabulary Identify the median, the lower quartile, the upper quartile, the lower extreme, and the upper extreme in the box-and-whisker plot.

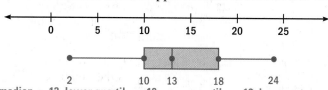

median = 13, lower quartile = 10, upper quartile = 18, lower extreme = 2, upper extreme = 24

2. Find the Error Describe and correct the error in finding the upper quartile.

The upper quartile is the average of 20 and 21, or 20.5.

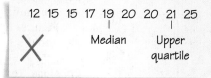

3. Recycling The list below shows the numbers of recyclable cans collected by ten classes. Make a box-and-whisker plot of the data.   *See margin.*

36, 42, 12, 39, 34, 71, 33, 32, 40, 32

Practice and Problem Solving

DVD Players The box-and-whisker plot below shows the prices, in dollars, of various DVD players offered at a store. Identify the value.

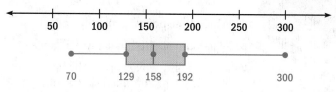

A **4.** lower extreme 70   **5.** upper quartile 192   **6.** median 158

Make a box-and-whisker plot of the data. *7–10. See margin.*

7. 9, 11, 15, 8, 6, 18, 13, 14, 10   **8.** 22, 7, 4, 29, 15, 30, 8, 9, 11

9. 37, 14, 30, 24, 32, 16, 20, 13   **10.** 17, 3, 42, 39, 10, 12, 33, 25

11. Solar Eclipses In a total solar eclipse, the moon is between Earth and the Sun. The list below shows the lengths, in seconds, of 13 total solar eclipses from 1981 to 2000. Make a box-and-whisker plot of the data.

122, 311, 120, 119, 226, 153, 413, 321, 263, 129, 170, 249, 143

See margin.

with Homework

Example	Exercises
1	7–12
2	4–6, 13
3	14–17

Online Resources
CLASSZONE.COM
· More Examples
· eTutorial Plus

Assignment Guide
Basic Course
Day 1: pp. 659–661 Exs. 4–10, 20–23
Day 2: pp. 659–661 Exs. 11–13, 15–17, 24–26
Average Course
Day 1: pp. 659–661 Exs. 4–11, 20–23
Day 2: pp. 659–661 Exs. 12–18, 24–26
Advanced Course
Day 1: pp. 659–661 Exs. 4–11, 19–21*
Day 2: pp. 659–661 Exs. 12–18, 24–26
Block
pp. 659–661 Exs. 4–11, 20–23 (with 13.5)
pp. 659–661 Exs. 12–18, 24–26 (with 13.7)

Extra Practice
• Student Edition, p. 720
• Chapter 13 Resource Book, pp. 52–54
• Test and Practice Generator

Transparency
Even-numbered answers are available on transparencies.

Homework Check
When you review students' homework for this lesson, go over the following exercises to check understanding of key concepts.
Basic: 4, 5, 7, 9, 15
Average: 5, 7, 10, 13, 14
Advanced: 6, 8, 11, 13, 14

3, 7–11. See Additional Answers beginning on page AA1.

TEACHING TIP

For Exercise 19, ask students to describe the strategy they used to find the data set. Have them explain the strategy to a partner so that they can compare strategies and data sets.

12.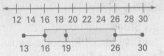

Page 661

26. Order the data, then find the median, and upper and lower quartiles. Draw the number line and plot the points for the upper and lower extremes, upper and lower quartiles, and median. Draw the vertical bars and the box and shade the box. Draw the whiskers to complete.

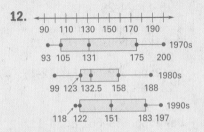

Extended Problem Solving **Use the table shown for Exercises 12–14.** The table shows the running times, in minutes, of the movies that won the award for Best Picture from 1970 to 1999.

12. **Graph** Make a box-and-whisker plot of each set of data using the same number line. See margin.

13. **Interpret** Identify the median and the range of the running times for each decade.

14. **Compare** Compare and contrast the running times of the Best Pictures in the 1970s, the 1980s, and the 1990s.
The median of the running times increased each decade, while the range decreased.

13. 1970s: median = 131, range = 107; 1980s: median = 132.5, range = 89; 1990s: median = 151, range = 79

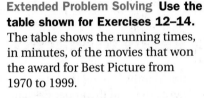

Running Times of Best Pictures (minutes)		
1970s	**1980s**	**1990s**
170	124	183
104	123	118
175	188	131
129	132	197
200	158	142
133	150	177
119	120	160
93	160	194
183	133	122
105	99	121

Bobsleds **The box-and-whisker plots show the differences, in seconds, between the gold and silver medalists' times in men's Olympic bobsled events from 1928 to 2002.**

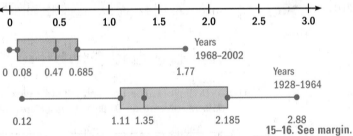

15. 1968-2002; the median and upper and lower quartiles for 1968-2002 are all less than the median and upper and lower quartiles for 1928-1964.

16. 1928-1964; the range for 1928-1964 is 2.76, while the range for 1968-2002 is 1.77.

15. Which time period generally had a lesser time difference? Explain.

16. Which time period had a wider range of time differences? Explain.

17. In a box-and-whisker plot, the box represents about 50% of the data. The whiskers each represent about 25% of the data. About what percent of the time differences from 1928 to 1964 were between 1.11 seconds and 2.88 seconds? 75%; 25%

C 18. **Critical Thinking** Explain why the medians of the lower half and the upper half of a set of data are called quartiles. They divide the data set into fourths.

19. **Challenge** Make a data set of 10 values that meets these conditions:
median = 123
lower quartile = 92
upper extreme = 170
range = 87

Sample answer: 83, 90, 92, 110, 121, 125, 130, 160, 165, 170

15–16. See margin.

Mixed Review

Choose a Strategy Use a strategy from the list to solve the following problem. Explain your choice of strategy.

Problem Solving Strategies
- Guess, Check, and Revise
- Draw a Diagram
- Make a Table
- Look for a Pattern

20. A ferry arrives at 11:07 A.M., 11:21 A.M., 11:35 A.M., and 11:49 A.M. Predict when the next two ferries will arrive.

20. 12:03 P.M., 12:17 P.M.
Sample answer: I used Look for a Pattern to find that a ferry arrives every 14 minutes.

Basic Skills Find the sum or difference.

21. $10.3 + 1.7$ **12** **22.** $2.6 + 94.8$ **97.4** **23.** $3.07 - 0.589$ **2.481** **24.** $21.9 - 6.7$ **15.2**

Test-Taking Practice

25. Multiple Choice Find the range in the box-and-whisker plot. **B**

18   30   46 52 58

A. 22 **B.** 40 **C.** 46 **D.** 52

26. Short Response Make a box-and-whisker plot of the data. Explain your steps. **See margin.**

13, 14, 22, 25, 30, 29, 27, 18, 19, 14, 18, 19

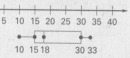

BRAIN GAME

Solve the Riddle

Who earns a living by driving customers away?   A TAXI DRIVER

Each data value has a letter underneath it.

16	19	18	15	20	10	27	14	30	8	13	12	8	7	23
(A)	(S)	(F)	(V)	(X)	(E)	(U)	(O)	(D)	(I)	(L)	(B)	(I)	(T)	(R)

Replace each **?** with the letter of the correct data value.

?	?	?	?	?	?	?	?	?	?	?
mean	lower extreme	mean	upper quartile	mode	upper extreme	range	mode	median	lower quartile	range

---

4 ASSESS

ASSESSMENT RESOURCES

For more assessment resources, see:
- Assessment Book
- Test and Practice Generator

MINI-QUIZ

1. Make a box-and-whisker plot of the data 12, 10, 16, 23, 32, 33, 30, 20, 18, 15, and 16.

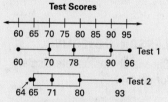

5 10 15 20 25 30 35 40

10 15 18   30 33

2. Use the box-and-whisker plot.

Test Scores

60 65 70 75 80 85 90 95

60   70   78   90 96   Test 1

64 65 71   80   93   Test 2

a. Find the median score for each test. **Test 1: 78; Test 2: 71**

b. Find the lower and upper quartile of Test 2. **65; 80**

c. Find the range of Test 1. **36**

d. In general, which test had lower scores? **Test 2**

5 FOLLOW-UP

RETEACHING/REMEDIATION

- Study Guide in Chapter 13 Resource Book, pp. 55–56
- eTutorial Plus Online
- Extra Practice, p. 720
- Lesson Practice in Chapter 13 Resource Book, pp. 52–54

CHALLENGE/ENRICHMENT

- Challenge Practice in Chapter 13 Resource Book, p. 57
- Teacher's Edition, p. 626F

ENGLISH LEARNER SUPPORT

- Spanish Study Guide
- Multi-Language Glossary
- Chapter Audio Summaries CDs

SKILL CHECK

For Exercises 1–3, use data values 10, 18, 15, 19, 21, 20.

1. Make a stem-and-leaf plot of the data.

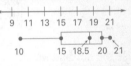

```
1 | 0 5 8 9
2 | 0 1
```

2. Make a box-and-whisker plot of the data.

```
9  11  13  15  17  19  21
   10      15  18.5  20  21
```

LESSON OBJECTIVE

Choose an appropriate display for data.

PACING

Suggested Number of Days
Basic Course: 1 day
Average Course: 1 day
Advanced Course: 1 day
Block: 0.5 block with 13.6

TEACHING RESOURCES

For a complete list of Teaching Resources, see page 626B.

TRANSPARENCY

Warm-Up Exercises for this lesson are available on a transparency.

2 TEACH

MOTIVATING THE LESSON

Ask students to cut out graphs from the newspaper and name the type of display used. Ask them to discuss why the display is appropriate.

LESSON 13.7

Choosing an Appropriate Data Display

BEFORE
You created different data displays.

Now
You'll choose appropriate data displays.

WHY?
So you can graph the results of a competition, as in Ex. 10.

Word Watch

Review Words
line plot, p. 73
bar graph, p. 79
line graph, p. 84
circle graph, p. 88
stem-and-leaf plot, p. 653
box-and-whisker plot, p. 657

Data Displays Below is a summary of the different ways you can display data and how each display is often used.

Appropriate Data Displays	
A **line plot** shows how often each number occurs.	
A **bar graph** shows how different categories of data compare.	
A **line graph** represents data that change over time.	
A **circle graph** represents data as parts of a whole.	
A **stem-and-leaf plot** displays all the data values and orders the data from least to greatest.	1 | 0 1 2 2 2 | 4 8 8 3 | 9
A **box-and-whisker plot** shows the spread of data using the median, the quartiles, and the extremes.	

EXAMPLE 1 Choosing Between Two Displays

Stamps Which graph makes it easier to compare the number of people who prefer sports stamps to the total number of people?

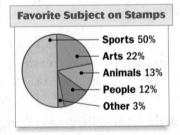

Favorite Subject on Stamps
Sports 50%
Arts 22%
Animals 13%
People 12%
Other 3%

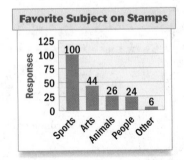

Favorite Subject on Stamps
Sports 100, Arts 44, Animals 26, People 24, Other 6

ANSWER The circle graph shows the whole, so it makes it easier to see that 50% of the people chose sports as their favorite stamp subject.

EXAMPLE 2 Making an Appropriate Display

Sunglasses You ask 20 people at a beach how many pairs of sunglasses they own. The list below shows their responses. Make a data display that shows the spread of data.

0, 1, 1, 1, 2, 2, 2, 2, 2, 3, 3, 3, 3, 3, 4, 4, 4, 6, 6, 10

Solution

You can use a box-and-whisker plot to show the spread of data. The box tells you that about half of the people own 2 to 4 pairs of sunglasses.

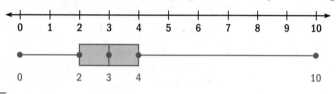

EXAMPLE 3 Choosing the Appropriate Display

Weather The data displays organize the daily high temperatures, in degrees Fahrenheit, during a recent month in Boston, Massachusetts. Which display is appropriate for finding the median high temperature?

```
3 | 6
4 | 0 1 4 5 7 8 9 9 9
5 | 3 3 3 4 6 6 6 8 8
6 | 0 0 2 3 5 5 7
7 | 2 3
8 | 4 5
```

Key: 3 | 6 = 36°F

Daily High Temperatures (°F)

- 30°– 49° 10 days
- 50°– 69° 16 days
- 70°– 89° 4 days

Solution

The stem-and-leaf plot is appropriate for finding the median high temperature, 56°F, because it displays the data in order. The circle graph is not appropriate because it does not display the temperatures.

 **with Notetaking**

For each type of data display you studied in this book, you may want to include an example in your notebook along with a summary of the information that you can read from the display.

Your turn now Choose an appropriate display for the given situation.

1. You record the temperature, in degrees Fahrenheit, at noon for seven days in a row. The data are listed below. Which data display would you use to show how the temperature changed during that time?   *line graph*

| 50°F | 42°F | 30°F | 32°F | 45°F | 55°F | 50°F |

TIPS FOR NEW TEACHERS
Discuss specific examples of each type of display shown in the chart on this page. See Tips for New Teachers in the *Chapter 13 Resource Book*.

EXTRA EXAMPLES

Example 1 In Example 1, which graph makes it clearer that more people prefer stamps with animals than stamps with people? **The bar graph is better because the exact numbers are given.**

Example 2 Which two types of display are best when data categories rather than data values are given? **bar graphs and circle graphs**

Example 3 The data displays show quiz scores for a class. Which display is better for finding the median quiz score?

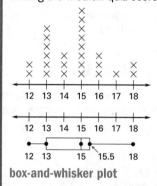

box-and-whisker plot

✓ CONCEPT CHECK

How do you choose the best display for data? **Study the data and decide what information you want people to get from it.**

DAILY PUZZLER

The data value 10 in Example 2 is called an *outlier*. What do you think the term means? *Sample answer:* A number that is much greater or much less than other data values.

664

ASSIGNMENT GUIDE

Basic Course
Day 1: pp. 664–665 Exs. 7–9, 11–13, 15–20

Average Course
Day 1: pp. 664–665 Exs. 7–13, 15–20

Advanced Course
Day 1: pp. 664–665 Exs. 7–16*, 20

Block
pp. 664–665 Exs. 7–13, 15–20 (with 13.6)

EXTRA PRACTICE

- Student Edition, p. 720
- Chapter 13 Resource Book, pp. 62–64
- Test and Practice Generator

 TRANSPARENCY

Even-numbered answers are available on transparencies.

HOMEWORK CHECK

When you review students' homework for this lesson, go over the following exercises to check understanding of key concepts.
Basic: 7, 8, 9, 11, 12
Average: 7, 8, 9, 11, 12
Advanced: 7, 9, 10, 11, 12

TEACHING TIP

Ask students to compare their answers for Exercises 8–10 in groups. If the answers do not agree, ask them to justify their choice to others in the group.

8, 10–12, 16, 20. See Additional Answers beginning on page AA1.

13.7 Exercises

More Practice, p. 720

9.

```
1 | 9
2 |
3 | 1 4 8 9
4 | 1 2 5 9
5 | 8
6 | 0
7 | 0    Key: 3 | 4 = 34
median = 41.5
```

 **with Homework**

Example	Exercises
1	7
2	8–10
3	11, 12

Online Resources
CLASSZONE.COM
· More Examples
· eTutorial Plus

Getting Ready to Practice

Vocabulary **Match the data display with its description.**

1. line plot **C**

2. circle graph **E**

3. line graph **B**

4. stem-and-leaf plot **A**

5. bar graph **D**

A. shows all values and orders data

B. displays data changing over time

C. uses X's to show how often a number occurs

D. shows how data in various categories compare

E. represents data as parts of a whole

6. **Soccer** Which data displays make it possible to compare the number of soccer players in each age group in the table? *line plot, line graph, bar graph, stem-and-leaf plot*

Age	11	12	13
Players	1	9	3

Practice and Problem Solving

A 7. Tell which data display makes it easier to see the number of students who read 5 books last month. *line plot*

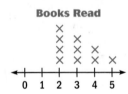

Books Read

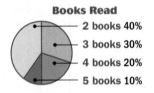

Books Read
- 2 books 40%
- 3 books 30%
- 4 books 20%
- 5 books 10%

8. **Stocks** The closing prices of a company stock on Monday through Friday are listed in order below. Make a data display that shows the change in price over the week. *See margin.*

$26.20, $25.50, $25.00, $24.80, $24.65

9. **Concerts** The list below shows the ages of the first twelve people who enter a concert hall. Make a data display that orders the ages from least to greatest. Then use the display to find the median of the ages.
See margin.

34, 19, 60, 45, 42, 38, 49, 58, 70, 41, 39, 31

10. **Bicycle Stunts** The list shows the scores of 10 athletes at a bicycle stunt competition. Make a data display that shows the median and the spread of the scores. *See margin.*

Bicycle Stunt Scores				
91.4	91.0	90.3	90.0	89.7
89.4	87.5	86.7	84.3	84.1

Communication In Exercises 11 and 12, use the table below. It shows the results of a survey asking 100 students their favorite way to get in touch with friends.

B **11.** Tell whether a *line graph* or a *bar graph* is appropriate for displaying the data. Then use your choice to make a display of the results of the survey.
Bar graph; see margin for art.

12. Make a data display that is appropriate for comparing the results for each category to the overall results of the survey.
See margin.

Form of communication	Responses
instant messaging	33
e-mail	20
telephone	28
letter writing	11
other	8

13. Line plot and stem-and-leaf plot; a line plot shows the number of each piece of data and a stem-and-leaf plot shows each piece of data.

13. Critical Thinking Name two data displays that you can use to find the mode of a set of data. Explain your reasoning.

C **14. Challenge** Describe how you might use the following data displays to show where most of the data belong: bar graph, line plot, circle graph, and stem-and-leaf plot.

14. *Sample answer:* Bar graph: look for the longest bar; line plot: look for the most Xs; circle graph: look for the largest area; stem-and-leaf plot: look for the stem with the most leaves.

15.

```
0 | 8 9
1 | 0 2 2 2 4 5 6 8
2 |
3 | 2 2 4 5 6 7
4 | 1      Key: 3 | 2 = 32
```

Mixed Review

15. Make a stem-and-leaf plot of the data. *(Lesson 13.5)*

32, 34, 14, 8, 18, 32, 36, 35, 9, 15, 12, 41, 37, 12, 16, 12, 10

16. Make a box-and-whisker plot of the data. *(Lesson 13.6)* **See margin.**

23, 62, 32, 32, 10, 24, 35, 27, 22, 21, 19, 16

Basic Skills Evaluate the expression.

17. $24 - 3^3 \div 9$ **21**   **18.** $61 - 5 \times 2^3$ **21**   **19.** $7 \times 6 + 68 \div 4$ **59**

Test-Taking Practice

20. Extended Response The table shows the cost to mail a post card in the United States in different years. Tell which data display you would use to show the changing cost to mail a post card over the years. Explain your choice. Then make the data display.
I would use a line graph because it shows how the cost changed over time. See margin for art.

Year	Cost of post card
1960	$.03
1970	$.05
1980	$.10
1990	$.15
2000	$.20

ASSESSMENT RESOURCES

For more assessment resources, see:
• Assessment Book
• Test and Practice Generator

MINI-QUIZ

1. Tell which display makes it easier to see the number of movies seen by students last month.

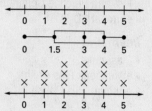

The line plot allows you to count the number of movies.

2. The number of miles walked during a walkathon are given below. Make a data display that orders the miles from least to greatest. Use the display to find the median.
1, 4, 2, 5, 2, 10, 6, 4, 3, 3, 4, 1, 4, 3, 4, 4, 5, 4, 2, 6, 2, 6, 10 **4 mi**

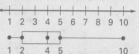

RETEACHING/REMEDIATION

• Study Guide in Chapter 13 Resource Book, pp. 65–66
• eTutorial Plus Online
• Extra Practice, p. 720
• Lesson Practice in Chapter 13 Resource Book, pp. 62–64

CHALLENGE/ENRICHMENT

• Challenge Practice in Chapter 13 Resource Book, p. 68
• Teacher's Edition, p. 626F

ENGLISH LEARNER SUPPORT

• Spanish Study Guide
• Multi-Language Glossary
• Chapter Audio Summaries CDs

665

4.
```
0 | 5 7 8
1 | 0 2 5 9
2 | 4 8
3 | 1 6
4 |
5 | 0
```
Key: 3 | 1 = 31

LESSONS 13.4 TO 13.7

Notebook Review

 **Note book**

Review the vocabulary definitions in your notebook.

Copy the review examples in your notebook. Then complete the exercises.

Check Your Definitions

stem-and-leaf plot, p. 653	box-and-whisker plot, p. 657	upper quartile, p. 657
leaf, p. 653		lower extreme, p. 657
stem, p. 653	lower quartile, p. 657	upper extreme, p. 657

Use Your Vocabulary

1. Identify the stem and the leaf in the number 36. stem: 3, leaf: 6

2. Identify the lower quartile in the set of data:
15, 17, 17, 18, 20, 21, 22, 26, 29. 17

13.4 Can you recognize misleading statistics?

 Review

EXAMPLE Explain why the bar graph could be misleading.

Value A appears to be one fourth of Value B. However, using the scale, Value A is about 63% of Value B, because $100 \div 160 \approx 63\%$.

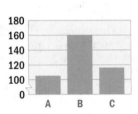

3. Use the graph in the Example above. What fraction of Value B does Value C appear to be without using the scale? using the scale?
about $\frac{1}{2}$; about 72%

13.5 Can you make stem-and-leaf plots?

 Review

EXAMPLE Make a stem-and-leaf plot of the data.

15, 11, 9, 7, 32, 21, 16, 9, 13, 17, 15, 8, 30, 20, 23

(1 Order the stems from least to greatest.
```
0 |
1 |
2 |
3 |
```

(2 Write the leaves next to their stems.
```
0 | 9 7 9 8
1 | 5 1 6 3 7 5
2 | 1 0 3
3 | 2 0
```

(3 Order the leaves from least to greatest.
```
0 | 7 8 9 9
1 | 1 3 5 5 6 7
2 | 0 1 3
3 | 0 2
```
Key: 2 | 3 = 23

4. Make a stem-and-leaf plot of the data.
5, 10, 12, 31, 28, 50, 8, 7, 15, 19, 24, 36 See margin.

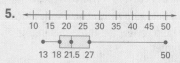
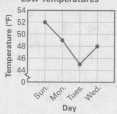
Review Quiz 2

1. The graph on the left; the line is steeper and makes the prices appear to have increased quickly.

2.
```
0 | 4 8
1 | 6
2 | 1 4 6
3 | 3 6 9
4 |
5 | 0
```
Key: 3 | 3 = 33

3.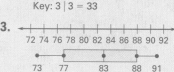

4.

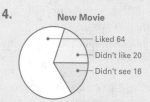

13.6–13.7 Can you make appropriate data displays?

 EXAMPLE Make a box-and-whisker plot to show the spread of data.

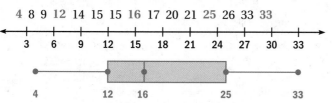

4 8 9 12 14 15 15 16 17 20 21 25 26 33 33

5. Make a box-and-whisker plot of the data.

13, 16, 21, 31, 50, 18, 24, 19, 27, 22 5–6. See margin.

6. The low temperature in a city was 52°F on Sunday, 49°F on Monday, 45°F on Tuesday, and 48°F on Wednesday. Make a data display that shows the change in temperature over the four days.

Stop *and* **Think** about Lessons 13.4–13.7

7. Writing Describe how the scale can affect your impression of the data in a line graph and in a bar graph. The scale can appear to distort the data.

Review Quiz 2

1. Which line graph might a travel agent use to convince people that train travel is becoming too expensive? Explain your choice. 1–4. See margin.

2. Make a stem-and-leaf plot of the data: 36, 33, 21, 8, 39, 24, 26, 50, 4, 16.

3. Make a box-and-whisker plot of the data: 80, 81, 90, 83, 74, 73, 91, 84, 86.

4. Survey In a survey of 100 people, 64 people liked a new movie, 20 people didn't like the movie, and the rest have not seen it. Make a data display that compares the results for each response to all the responses.

12. taco with mild sauce, taco with hot sauce, taco with extra hot sauce, burrito with mild sauce, burrito with hot sauce, burrito with extra hot sauce, enchilada with mild sauce, enchilada with hot sauce, enchilada with extra hot sauce

13. Pittsburgh hat, Pittsburgh T-shirt, Pittsburgh poster, Dallas hat, Dallas T-shirt, Dallas poster, Miami hat, Miami T-shirt, Miami poster, Los Angeles hat, Los Angeles T-shirt, Los Angeles poster

14. printer and camera, printer and scanner, camera and scanner

Chapter Review

Vocabulary

outcome, p. 630	combination, p. 637	stem, p. 653
event, p. 630	permutation, p. 637	box-and-whisker plot, p. 657
favorable outcomes, p. 630	independent events, p. 642	lower quartile, p. 657
probability, p. 630	stem-and-leaf plot, p. 653	upper quartile, p. 657
complementary events, p. 632	leaf, p. 653	lower extreme, p. 657
tree diagram, p. 636		upper extreme, p. 657

Vocabulary Review

Copy and complete the statement.

1. Two events are ? if they have no outcomes in common and if together they contain all the outcomes of the experiment. **complementary**

2. Two events are ? if the occurrence of one event does not affect the likelihood that the other event will occur. **independent**

3. An arrangement of objects in which order is important is called a ? . **permutation**

4. In a stem-and-leaf plot, the ? is the last digit on the right, and the ? is the remaining digits. **leaf, stem**

5. In a box-and-whisker plot, the ? is the least data value, and the ? is the greatest data value. **lower extreme, upper extreme**

6. Outcomes for which an event occurs are called ? outcomes. **favorable**

Review Questions

You roll a number cube. Find the probability of the event. *(Lesson 13.1)*

7. You roll a number less than 4. $\frac{1}{2}$

8. You roll a number greater than 6. 0

9. You roll a factor of 60. 1

10. You don't roll a multiple of 3. $\frac{2}{3}$

11. **Birthdays** You randomly choose a birthday in July. Find the probability that it is not an even date. *(Lesson 13.1)* $\frac{16}{31}$

Use a tree diagram to find all the possible outcomes. *(Lesson 13.2)* 12–14. See margin.

12. Dish: taco, burrito, enchilada
    Sauce: mild, hot, extra hot

13. City: Pittsburgh, Dallas, Miami, Los Angeles
    Souvenir: hat, T-shirt, poster

14. **Computers** You can choose 2 free accessories from among a printer, a camera, and a scanner when you buy a computer. Find all the possible pairs of accessories you can choose from. *(Lesson 13.2)*

15. Leah and Sarah, Leah and
Jenny, Leah and Michelle,
Sarah and Leah, Sarah and
Jenny, Sarah and Michelle,
Jenny and Leah, Jenny and
Sarah, Jenny and Michelle,
Michelle and Leah, Michelle
and Sarah, Michelle and Jenny

Review Questions

15. Diving Leah, Sarah, Jenny, and Michelle are competing in a diving competition. Find all the possible top two placements. *(Lesson 13.2)* See margin.

The spinners at the right are each divided into equal parts. You spin the spinners. Find the probability of the event. *(Lesson 13.3)*

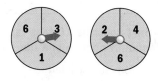
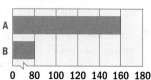

16. You spin a sum of 5. $\frac{2}{9}$ **17.** You spin two sixes. $\frac{1}{9}$

18. You spin an odd sum. $\frac{2}{3}$ **19.** You spin two prime numbers. $\frac{1}{9}$

20. Your friend is thinking of a two-digit number. You know that the first digit is 6 or 7, and the second digit is 1 or 2. Find the probability that you randomly choose the correct number. *(Lesson 13.3)* $\frac{1}{4}$

21. What fraction of Value A does Value B appear to be without using the scale? If you use the scale, what fraction of Value A is Value B? *(Lesson 13.4)* $\frac{1}{5}; \frac{1}{2}$

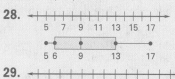
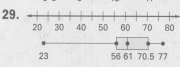

A
B
0   80 100 120 140 160 180

Basketball The list below shows the total points earned by a basketball team during each finals match. *(Lesson 13.4)*

98, 78, 100, 98, 82, 79, 88

22. A local sports reporter states that the average points per game is 98. Does 98 describe the total points well? Why or why not?   No; most of the totals are less than 98.

Make a stem-and-leaf plot of the data. *(Lesson 13.5)*

23. 45, 52, 59, 32, 48, 55, 41, 60   23–24. See margin.

24. 18, 24, 27, 14, 33, 28, 45, 72, 49, 12, 25

Use the stem-and-leaf plot below to find the quantity. *(Lesson 13.5)*

25. mean 48

26. median 50

27. mode 50

```
3 | 4 6 7 7
4 |
5 | 0 0 0 1 6
6 | 2 5        Key: 3 | 7 = 37
```

Make a box-and-whisker plot of the data. *(Lesson 13.6)*

28. 13, 5, 10, 6, 17, 8, 5, 7, 13, 9, 11   28–29. See margin.

29. 65, 70, 76, 59, 41, 23, 77, 58, 71, 63, 59, 54

30. Music After playing 3 new songs, a disc jockey records that 186 callers prefer the first song, 79 callers prefer the second song, and 310 callers prefer the third song. Which data display would you use to compare the responses for the first song to all the responses? *(Lesson 13.7)* circle graph

23.
```
3 | 2
4 | 1 5 8
5 | 2 5 9
6 | 0
    Key: 4 | 8 = 48
```

24.
```
1 | 2 4 8
2 | 4 5 7 8
3 | 3
4 | 5 9
5 |
6 |
7 | 2
    Key: 3 | 3 = 33
```

28.
5 7 9 11 13 15 17
5 6   9   13   17

29.
20 30 40 50 60 70 80
23   56 61 70.5 77

5. solid shirt with overalls, solid shirt with jeans, striped shirt with overalls, striped shirt with jeans, checkered shirt with overalls, checkered shirt with jeans, plaid shirt with overalls, plaid shirt with jeans

6. museum and aquarium, museum and circus, museum and amusement park, aquarium and circus, aquarium and amusement park, circus and amusement park

7. brother, sister, cousin; brother, cousin, sister; cousin, brother, sister; cousin, sister, brother; sister, cousin, brother; sister, brother, cousin

14.
```
3 | 9
4 |
5 | 4 9
6 | 3 8
7 |
8 | 1 8
9 | 0 3 5 7
```
Key: 5 | 4 = 54

15.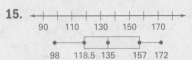

```
   90  110  130  150  170
```
98   118.5 135   157   172

Chapter Test

A bag contains 10 tiles labeled 1, 4, 7, 8, L, T, M, O, U, and Z. You randomly choose one tile. Find the probability of the event.

1. You choose a letter. $\frac{3}{5}$ **2.** You choose an odd number. $\frac{1}{5}$

3. You choose a factor of 16. $\frac{3}{10}$ **4.** You don't choose a consonant. $\frac{3}{5}$

5. Clothing You have 4 shirts: solid, striped, checkered, and plaid. You have 2 pairs of pants: overalls and jeans. Use a tree diagram to find all the possible outfits you can wear. See margin.

6. Vacation You want to go to a museum, an aquarium, a circus, and an amusement park during your vacation. You have time for only 2 places. Find all the combinations of 2 places that you can choose from. See margin.

7. Photos You are arranging your brother, sister, and cousin for a photo. Find all the possible ways you can arrange them in a row. See margin.

Each spinner is divided into equal parts. You spin the spinners. Find the probability of the event.

8. You spin green on both spinners. $\frac{1}{12}$ **9.** You spin blue on at least 1 spinner. $\frac{1}{2}$

10. You spin yellow on exactly 1 spinner. 0   **11.** You don't spin red on either spinner. $\frac{1}{2}$

12. Fuel Prices Which line graph would someone use to convince people that the price per gallon of gasoline in a state was stable over seven months? Explain. The graph on the left; the line appears to decrease very little.

13. In-line Skates An advertiser says that the average price of inline skates at a store is $130. The list below shows the prices of inline skates offered at the store. Why do you think this average was used? To make the price appear to be low.

$150, $250, $200, $190, $150, $100, $130, $130, $130, $190

14. Make a stem-and-leaf plot of the data.
90, 81, 93, 95, 68, 63, 97, 88, 59, 39, 54
14–15. See margin.

15. Make a box-and-whisker plot of the data.
98, 117, 129, 154, 160, 145, 120, 135, 172

16. License Plates You record the states of the first 200 license plates of vehicles you see enter a highway. You find 134 Oklahoma plates, 35 Texas plates, and 31 Louisiana plates. Which data display would you use to compare the number of Texas plates to total plates? circle graph

Chapter Standardized Test

Test-Taking Strategy Work at your own pace. Do not think about how fast other students complete the test.

Multiple Choice

1. A bag holds 9 red and 3 blue marbles. If you randomly choose one marble from the bag, find the probability that it is blue. **A**

A. $\frac{1}{4}$ **B.** $\frac{1}{3}$ **C.** $\frac{5}{12}$ **D.** $\frac{7}{12}$

2. Find the mode in the stem-and-leaf plot below. **H**

```
4 | 3 5 8
5 | 2 5 5 9
6 | 0 0 0 6
7 | 2            Key: 5|9 = 59
```

F. 55   **G.** 57   **H.** 60   **I.** 72

3. You toss a coin twice. Find the probability of getting heads at least one time. **C**

A. $\frac{1}{4}$ **B.** $\frac{1}{2}$ **C.** $\frac{3}{4}$ **D.** 1

4. You can choose 2 kinds of flowers for a garden from lilies, daisies, roses, carnations, and irises. Find all the possible pairs of flowers. **H**

F. 3   **G.** 7   **H.** 10   **I.** 14

5. You roll a number cube. Which event is most likely to occur? **B**

A. You roll a 9.   **B.** You roll an integer.

C. You roll a 5.   **D.** Your roll is even.

6. How many different ways can you arrange two letters from the word MATH? **I**

F. 4   **G.** 6   **H.** 8   **I.** 12

7. Find the range in the box-and-whisker plot below. **C**

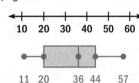

A. 22   **B.** 36   **C.** 46   **D.** 57

8. You are guessing on 1 true-and-false question and 1 multiple-choice question with answer choices A, B, C, and D. Find the probability that you answer both questions correctly. **F**

F. $\frac{1}{8}$ **G.** $\frac{1}{6}$ **H.** $\frac{1}{4}$ **I.** $\frac{1}{3}$

9. Which data display would you use to show the value of a baseball card over 50 years? **D**

A. bar graph   **B.** stem-and-leaf plot

C. line plot   **D.** line graph

Short Response

10. Bob's scores in a board game are 430, 290, 330, 330, 610, and 380. Bob says that his average score is 395. Explain whether 395 describes the scores well. Then tell why Bob would use 395 as his average score.
See margin.

Extended Response

11. In a survey of 425 students, 254 liked a science museum, 102 didn't like the museum, and the rest did not have an opinion. Draw a bar graph that makes it appear that one third as many students didn't like the museum as students who did.
See margin.

10. No, because most scores are less than 395; to make his average appear to be better than it really is.

11. Museum Preference

Strategies for Answering
Extended Response Questions

Scoring Rubric

Full credit
- answer is correct, *and*
- work or reasoning is included

Partial credit
- answer is correct, but reasoning is incorrect, *or*
- answer is incorrect, but reasoning is correct

No credit
- no answer is given, *or*
- answer makes no sense

Problem

Salad ingredients cost $.25 per ounce at a salad bar. You plan to buy a salad and a $1.00 bottle of juice. Make a function table to show the total cost of the juice and salad for 0, 1, 2, 3, 4, 5, and 6 ounces of salad. Graph the function. Find the cost of juice and a 10 ounce salad, and explain how you found your answer.

Full credit solution

The function table is correct and reflects an understanding of the relationship between the number of ounces of salad and the total cost of the juice and the salad.

Let x represent the number of ounces of salad. Let y represent the cost in dollars of the juice and salad.

Ounces of salad, x	0	1	2	3	4	5	6
Total cost, y	$1.00	$1.25	$1.50	$1.75	$2.00	$2.25	$2.50

The graph correctly represents the data in the table.

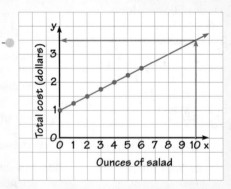

The answer is correct. The explanation is clear and reflects correct mathematical thinking.

The total cost of juice and a 10 ounce salad is $3.50.

To find my answer, I drew a line through the plotted points. I found 10 ounces on the x-axis. Then I drew lines up to the graph and across to the y-axis, meeting the y-axis at $3.50.

Partial credit solution

The function table is correct and reflects an understanding of the relationship between the number of ounces of salad and the total cost of the juice and the salad.

Ounces of salad, x	Total cost, y
0	$1.00
1	$1.25
2	$1.50
3	$1.75
4	$2.00
5	$2.25
6	$2.50

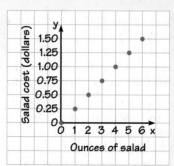

The graph correctly represents the data in the table.

The answer is incorrect. — The total cost is $4.50.

The explanation does not reflect correct mathematical reasoning. — To find my answer, I used the table. Five ounces cost $2.25, so 10 ounces cost twice that, or $4.50.

Watch Out!

Scoring is often based on how clearly you explain your reasoning.

1. Partial credit; answers are correct, but reasoning is incorrect; change the table and graph so they are identical to those on page 672.

Your turn now

1. One student's answer to the problem on page 672 is given below. Score the solution as *full credit, partial credit,* or *no credit.* Explain your choice. If you choose *partial credit* or *no credit,* explain how you would change the answer to earn a score of *full credit.*

Ounces of salad, x	Total cost, y
0	$0
1	$.25
2	$.50
3	$.75
4	$1.00
5	$1.25
6	$1.50

The total cost of juice and a 10 ounce salad is $3.50.

To find my answer, I multiplied the salad cost per ounce by the number of ounces and added the juice cost. Salad costs $.25 per ounce, so 10 ounces cost $2.50. So, the total cost is $2.50 + $1.00, or $3.50.

1.

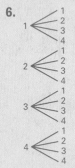

4°; graph 17 and −7 on the number line. Divide the segment between 17 and −7 into 6 equal parts, which is 4.

2. D and F, E and I, H and J; B, C, E, and I, and D, F, H, and J; for the reflections, look for the dots that can be placed side by side and a line of symmetry drawn; for the rotations, look for the dots that are turned about a point.

3. mean = $(−5 + 2 + 1 + 2 + (−4) + (−3) + 2) \div 7 = −1$, median (fourth value) = 0, mode = 2, range = $2 − (−5) = 7$; mode, because it is the greatest value.

5. $65 + 40n$

Input, n	Output
1	105
2	145
3	185

6.

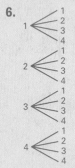

There are 4 possible sums of 5 out of 16 outcomes, so the probability is $\frac{4}{16} = \frac{1}{4}$.

7. See Additional Answers beginning on page AA1.

Extended Response

1. The temperature was 17°F at 4:00 P.M. By 10:00 P.M. the temperature had dropped to −7°F. The temperature decreased by the same amount each hour. Use a number line to show how many degrees the temperature decreased each hour. Explain your work. **See margin.**

2. The first ten letters of the Braille alphabet are shown below. These ten letters are formed by arranging 1 to 4 dots in a 2 by 2 grid as shown. Which of these Braille letters are reflections of each other? Which are rotations of each other? Explain how you found your answers. **See margin.**

For example:

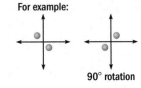

90° rotation

A   B   C   D   E   F   G   H   I   J

3. The lowest daily temperatures for one week are listed below. Find the mean, median, mode, and range of the data. Show your work. Which average does not represent the data well? Why? **See margin.**

   −5°F   0°F   1°F   2°F   −4°F   −3°F   2°F

4. Brad has $10 to spend. He will buy a sticker book. How much money will he have left after he buys the sticker book? With the money that Brad has left, what is the greatest number of stickers n he can buy? Write and solve a multiplication equation to answer this question. Show your work.
$4.00; 10; $0.40n = 4.00$, $n = 10$

Item	Price
sticker book	$6.00
stamp book	$4.95
stamps	$.35
stickers	$.40

5. A CD player costs $185. Nathan has already saved $65. Nathan will save $40 a week from a baby-sitting job. Write a function rule to represent the amount of money Nathan will have after n weeks. Then use an input-output table to find how many weeks Nathan needs to baby-sit to have enough money to buy the CD player. **See margin.**

6. The spinner at the right is divided into four equal sections. Make a tree diagram to show all the possible outcomes when you spin the spinner two times. Use the tree diagram to find the probability that the sum of the numbers from two spins is 5. Show your work. **See margin.**

7. The data below show the sizes of classes at North Junior High School. Make a stem-and-leaf plot of the data. Then make a box-and-whisker plot of the data. Compare the information you can get from each data display. **See margin.**

   15, 23, 38, 12, 24, 26, 14, 23, 34, 34, 23, 17, 30, 23, 24, 28,
   32, 26, 28, 17, 21, 29, 31, 26, 21

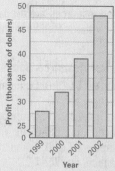

Company Profits

Multiple Choice

8. A test has 20 questions that are each worth 5 points. The teacher marked −2 next to four of the questions on Maura's test. What was Maura's score on the test? **D**

A. −8   **B.** 8   **C.** 90   **D.** 92

9. Suppose s represents the number of cups of sugar in a recipe. The amount of flour is twice the amount of sugar. Which expression represents the number of cups of flour? **H**

F. $s - 2$ **G.** $s + 2$ **H.** $2s$ **I.** $\frac{s}{2}$

10. After Julie gave Cara $7, Cara had a total of $40. Which equation could you use to find the amount of money m that Cara originally had? **B**

A. $m - 7 = 40$ **B.** $m + 7 = 40$

C. $7m = 40$ **D.** $\frac{m}{7} = 40$

Short Response

13. Tim is a contestant in a game show. He has a score of −$250. He correctly answers a question worth $500, but then misses a question worth $150 to end the game. If the other player has a final score of $25, does Tim win? Explain.

Yes; −250 + 500 − 150 = 100 > 25.

14. Make a bar graph of the company profit data shown that makes it appear that the profits have increased much more steeply than they actually have. Explain why your graph gives this impression. **See margin.**

Year	1999	2000	2001	2002
Profits	$28,000	$32,000	$39,000	$48,000

11. Carl has $3. How many different lunches of one sandwich and one drink can he order? **G**

F. 3
G. 4
H. 6
I. 9

Item	Cost
tuna	$2.50
hot dog	$1.75
chicken	$2.95
milk	$.60
juice	$.50
lemonade	$1.00

12. A survey asks students to name their favorite type of music. Which type of graph would be the best for displaying the data? **B**

A. line graph

B. bar graph

C. stem-and-leaf plot

D. box-and-whisker plot

15. Find all the possible orders in which a salesperson can visit Boston, Chicago, and New York. If the order is chosen randomly, what is the probability that the salesperson will visit Chicago first? Explain. **See margin.**

16. The graph shows the relationship between time traveled, t, and distance, D, for a car driven at a constant rate. Write a rule for the function. Use the rule to predict the number of hours it takes to drive 240 miles at this rate. Explain.

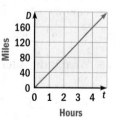

$D = 40t$; 6 h; substitute 240 into the equation for D and solve; 240 = 40t, t = 6.

It appears that the profits have increased by about 4 times from 1999 to 2002 when they have not even doubled. The graph gives this impression because of the break in the vertical axis.

15. Boston, Chicago, New York; Boston, New York, Chicago; Chicago, Boston, New York; Chicago, New York, Boston; New York, Chicago, Boston; New York, Boston, Chicago; $\frac{1}{3}$; Chicago is first $\frac{2}{6}$ or $\frac{1}{3}$ of the time.

Test-Taking Skills

675

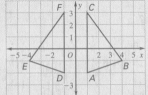
Cumulative Practice for Chapters 11–13

Chapter 11

Multiple Choice In Exercises 1–10, choose the letter of the correct answer.

1. The peak of a mountain is 10,016 feet above sea level. Which number would you use to represent the height of the peak? *(Lesson 11.1)* **D**

   A. −10,016 feet   **B.** −5008 feet

   C. 5008 feet   **D.** 10,016 feet

2. Which list of integers is in order from greatest to least? *(Lesson 11.1)* **H**

   F. 0, 2, −27, −28   **G.** 2, 0, −28, −27

   H. 2, 0, −27, −28   **I.** −28, −27, 0, 2

3. Which expression does not have the same value as the other three expressions? *(Lessons 11.1, 11.2)* **C**

   A. the absolute value of 7

   B. the absolute value of −7

   C. the opposite of 7

   D. the opposite of −7

4. Find the sum −12 + 6. *(Lesson 11.2)* **G**

   F. −18   **G.** −6   **H.** 6   **I.** 18

5. What is the value of the expression −6 − (−9)? *(Lesson 11.3)* **C**

   A. −15   **B.** −3   **C.** 3   **D.** 15

6. A record high temperature is 134°F. A record low is −80°F. What is the difference in these temperatures? *(Lesson 11.3)* **H**

   F. −54°F   **G.** 54°F   **H.** 214°F   **I.** 224°F

7. Which statement is true? *(Lesson 11.4)* **D**

   A. 4(−4) = 16   **B.** −8(4) = 32

   C. 4(3) = −12   **D.** −9(−9) = 81

8. Find the quotient −54 ÷ (−9). *(Lesson 11.5)* **H**

   F. −7   **G.** −6   **H.** 6   **I.** 7

9. The yards gained and lost during a football game were −3, 2, 4, −2, −7, and 0. Find the mean of the data. *(Lesson 11.5)* **B**

   A. −1.2   **B.** −1   **C.** 1   **D.** 1.2

10. Use the figure shown. You translate the figure 1 unit to the right and 2 units down. Which point is not a vertex of the translated figure? *(Lesson 11.6)* **I**

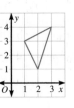

   F. (2, 1)   **G.** (3, −1) **H.** (4, 2)   **I.** (5, 3)

11. Short Response Graph the point (−2, −3). Then graph the image when the point is translated 2 units to the left and 5 units up. State the quadrants in which the point and its image are located. Explain how you found your answers. *(Lesson 11.6)*
See margin.

12. Extended Response *(Lesson 11.7)*

   a. Graph △ABC with vertices A(1, −2), B(4, −1), and C(1, 3). Graph △DEF with vertices D(−1, −2), E(−4, −1), and F(−1, 3). See margin.

   b. Tell whether the transformation from △ABC to △DEF is a *translation*, a *reflection*, or a *rotation*. Then describe the transformation.
   reflection; over the y-axis

23. $2a = 20$; 10 angelfish; divided both sides of the equation $2a = 20$ by 2.

24. a.

Input, t	Output, d
1	50
2	100
3	150
4	200

b. $d = 50t$

c.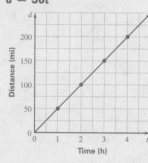

Chapter 12

Multiple Choice In Exercises 13–22, choose the letter of the correct answer.

13. Write the phrase as an expression: 16 decreased by f. *(Lesson 12.1)* **D**

A. $f - 16$ **B.** $16 \div f$

C. $16 \cdot f$ **D.** $16 - f$

14. Karen had 32 CDs. She was given c more CDs. She now has 41 CDs. Which equation can you use to find c? *(Lesson 12.1)* **F**

F. $32 + c = 41$ **G.** $32 - c = 41$

H. $32c = 41$ **I.** $32 \div c = 41$

15. What would you do to both sides of the equation $24 + x = 39$ to solve it? *(Lesson 12.2)* **C**

A. add 24   **B.** add 39

C. subtract 24   **D.** subtract 39

16. What is the solution of the equation $x + 13 = 20$? *(Lesson 12.2)* **G**

F. -7 **G.** 7   **H.** 17   **I.** 33

17. Which equation does *not* have 12 as a solution? *(Lesson 12.3)* **D**

A. $t - 4 = 8$ **B.** $t - 6 = 6$

C. $t - 7 = 5$ **D.** $t - 1 = 13$

18. What is the solution of the equation $9p = 81$? *(Lesson 12.4)* **G**

F. -9 **G.** 9   **H.** 72   **I.** 729

19. What is the solution of the equation $\frac{x}{3} = 27$? *(Lesson 12.4)* **D**

A. 9   **B.** 24   **C.** 30   **D.** 81

20. When the input x is 8, what is the output of the function $y = 4x - 10$? *(Lesson 12.5)* **G**

F. 4.5   **G.** 22   **H.** 32   **I.** 38

21. Which equation is a function rule for the input-output table shown? *(Lesson 12.5)* **D**

Input, x	0	2	4	6	8
Output, y	3	5	7	9	11

A. $y = \dfrac{x}{3}$ **B.** $y = 3x$

C. $y = x - 3$ **D.** $y = x + 3$

22. Which function rule has the graph shown? *(Lesson 12.6)* **G**

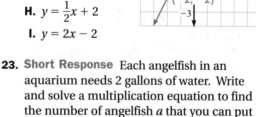

F. $y = x + 2$

G. $y = 2x + 2$

H. $y = \frac{1}{2}x + 2$

I. $y = 2x - 2$

23. **Short Response** Each angelfish in an aquarium needs 2 gallons of water. Write and solve a multiplication equation to find the number of angelfish a that you can put in a 20 gallon tank. Explain how you found your answer. *(Lesson 12.2)* **See margin.**

24. **Extended Response** Your brother is planning a car trip. He expects to drive at an average speed of 50 miles per hour. *(Lessons 12.5, 12.6)* **See margin.**

  a. Make an input-output table that represents the relationship between the time t and the distance d he drives. Use the input values $t = 1, 2, 3,$ and 4.

  b. Write a function rule that relates t and d.

  c. Graph the function.

33. See Additional Answers beginning on page AA1.

34. a.

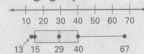

```
1 | 3 4 5 5 5
2 | 7 8 9 9
3 | 6 7
4 | 0
5 | 3 9
6 | 7
```
Key: 3 | 6 = 36

the age group 10–19

b.

c. No; 15 is near the youngest age, there are many more people older than 15 in the club.

Chapter 13

Multiple Choice In Exercises 25–32, choose the letter of the correct answer.

25. There are nine cards in a bag, numbered 1 through 9. You randomly choose one card. What is the probability that it is an even number? *(Lesson 13.1)* **A**

A. $\frac{4}{9}$ **B.** $\frac{1}{2}$ **C.** $\frac{5}{9}$ **D.** 1

26. Find the probability of the complement of rolling a 4 on a number cube. *(Lesson 13.1)* **I**

F. 0   **G.** $\frac{1}{6}$ **H.** $\frac{1}{4}$ **I.** $\frac{5}{6}$

27. Alberto, Chris, Edgar, and Manny are running in a relay race. How many ways can you order the first two runners? *(Lesson 13.2)* **D**

A. 2   **B.** 6   **C.** 8   **D.** 12

28. The spinner is divided into equal parts. You spin the spinner twice. Find the probability that you get an even number at least one time. *(Lesson 13.3)* **I**

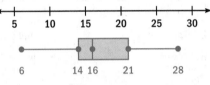

F. 0   **G.** $\frac{1}{4}$ **H.** $\frac{1}{2}$ **I.** $\frac{3}{4}$

29. Which is least likely to affect how the information in a bar graph is interpreted? *(Lesson 13.4)* **B**

A. Using very small increments in the scale

B. Drawing the bars horizontally

C. Putting a vertical break in the scale

D. Using very large increments in the scale

30. What is the median of the data shown in the stem-and-leaf plot? *(Lesson 13.5)* **H**

```
1 | 3 7 8
2 | 1 1 6 8
3 | 0
4 | 0 8 9      Key: 3 | 0 = 30
```

F. 13   **G.** 21   **H.** 26   **I.** 49

31. Use the box-and-whisker plot shown to find the difference between the upper quartile and the lower quartile. *(Lesson 13.6)* **A**

A. 7   **B.** 14   **C.** 21   **D.** 22

32. Which display would best show increases in parking fees over time? *(Lesson 13.7)* **H**

F. stem-and-leaf plot   **G.** line plot

H. line graph   **I.** circle graph

33. Short Response Choices at Casa Burrito are: vegetarian, chicken, or beef; regular-size or large; with mild salsa or hot salsa. Use a tree diagram to find all the different burrito orders possible. *(Lesson 13.2)*
See margin.

34. Extended Response A model train club says that the average age of its members is 15. The ages of all the members are listed below. *(Lessons 13.4, 13.5, 13.6)* **See margin.**

27, 40, 14, 59, 28, 29, 15, 13, 29, 37, 53, 15, 67, 36, 15

a. Make a stem-and-leaf plot of the ages. Which age group has the most people?

b. Make a box-and-whisker plot of the data.

c. Does 15 describe the ages well? Explain.

End-of-Course Test

Number Sense, Measurement, and Decimals

Find the sum, difference, product, or quotient.

1. $839 + 296$ 1135   **2.** $156 - 39$ 117   **3.** 18×36 648   **4.** $424 \div 8$ 53

5. $6.468 + 4.22$ 10.688   **6.** $5.174 - 2.01$ 3.164   **7.** $8 - 3.21$ 4.79   **8.** 0.826×3 2.478

9. 3.4×5.06 17.204   **10.** 3.4×0.001 0.0034   **11.** $128 \div 0.4$ 320   **12.** $9.186 \div 1000$ 0.009186

13. Write your answers to Exercises 8 and 9 in words. two and four hundred seventy-eight thousandths; seventeen and two hundred four thousandths

Estimate the sum, difference, product, or quotient using the given method.

14. 49×89 (rounding) 4500   **15.** $537 - 22$ (rounding) 520

16. $353 \div 39$ (compatible numbers) 9   **17.** $3.13 + 4.45 + 2.92$ (front-end estimation) 10.5

18. The data show the ages of students enrolled in a diving class. Make a frequency table and a bar graph of the data. Then find the mean, median, mode(s), and range of the data. Choose the best average(s) to represent the data. Explain your choice. **See margin.**

    12, 13, 16, 12, 15, 12, 11, 15, 12, 12

Evaluate the expression.

19. $30 - 4 \times 6$ 6   **20.** $6 \times (8 - 2) \div 4$ 9   **21.** 2×5^2 50

22. $\frac{x}{7}$, when $x = 84$ 12   **23.** $6 + 3n$, when $n = 5$ 21   **24.** y^3, when $y = 2$ 8

Order the numbers from least to greatest.

25. 18.14, 18.04, 18.41, 18.4, 18.401   **26.** 5.6, 5.59, 5.505, 5.575, 5.063
    18.04, 18.14, 18.4, 18.401, 18.41   5.063, 5.505, 5.575, 5.59, 5.6

Choose an appropriate unit in the given system(s) to measure the item.

27. height of a tree (metric, customary)   **28.** length of a highway (metric, customary)
       meters, feet or yards   kilometers, miles
29. capacity of a fish tank (metric)   **30.** mass of a pencil (metric)
       liters   milligrams or grams

Solve.

31. Jill bought a pen for $2.39 and a pad of graph paper for $3.98. How much change should she get from a $20 bill? $13.63

32. Find the area and perimeter of a square with side length 4.7 meters. $A = 22.09 \text{ m}^2$; $P = 18.8 \text{ m}$

18.

Age of student	Tally	Frequency
11	I	1
12	IIII	5
13	I	1
14		0
15	II	2
16	I	1

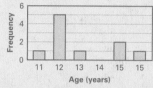

Ages of Students in Diving Class

13, 12, 12, 5; the mean is the best average because there are about as many ages above it as below it.

Fraction Concepts and Operations

Write the prime factorization of the number.

33. 40 $2^3 \times 5$ **34.** 72 $2^3 \times 3^2$ **35.** 56 $2^3 \times 7$ **36.** 120 $2^3 \times 3 \times 5$

Find the GCF and LCM of the numbers.

37. 16, 24 8, 48 **38.** 12, 40 4, 120 **39.** 7, 18 1, 126

Order the fractions from least to greatest.

40. $\frac{1}{3}, \frac{1}{9}, \frac{1}{12}, \frac{1}{4}$ $\frac{1}{12}, \frac{1}{9}, \frac{1}{4}, \frac{1}{3}$ **41.** $\frac{3}{8}, \frac{2}{5}, \frac{1}{2}, \frac{7}{20}$ $\frac{7}{20}, \frac{3}{8}, \frac{2}{5}, \frac{1}{2}$ **42.** $\frac{2}{3}, \frac{9}{10}, \frac{3}{4}, \frac{4}{5}$ $\frac{2}{3}, \frac{3}{4}, \frac{4}{5}, \frac{9}{10}$

Write the decimals as fractions or mixed numbers in simplest form and write the fractions or mixed numbers as decimals.

43. 0.26 $\frac{13}{50}$ **44.** 5.6 $5\frac{3}{5}$ **45.** 3.06 $3\frac{3}{50}$ **46.** 0.175 $\frac{7}{40}$

47. $\frac{19}{25}$ 0.76 **48.** $2\frac{3}{8}$ 2.375 **49.** $\frac{1}{6}$ $0.1\overline{6}$ **50.** $\frac{17}{1000}$ 0.017

Estimate and then find the sum, difference, product, or quotient. 51–58. Estimates may vary.

51. $\frac{5}{8} + \frac{7}{8}$ $1\frac{1}{2}; 1\frac{1}{2}$ **52.** $7\frac{1}{5} + 3\frac{2}{3}$ $11; 10\frac{13}{15}$ **53.** $6 - 2\frac{3}{7}$ $3\frac{1}{2}; 3\frac{4}{7}$ **54.** $9\frac{1}{2} - 4\frac{5}{6}$ $4\frac{1}{2}; 4\frac{2}{3}$

55. $\frac{3}{5} \times \frac{2}{3}$ $\frac{1}{2}; \frac{2}{5}$ **56.** $3\frac{1}{4} \times 6\frac{2}{3}$ $21; 21\frac{2}{3}$ **57.** $\frac{4}{9} \div 3$ $\frac{1}{6}; \frac{4}{27}$ **58.** $2\frac{5}{6} \div 1\frac{3}{5}$ $2; 1\frac{37}{48}$

Add or subtract.

59. 7 h 41 min 45 sec
      + 8 h 34 min 18 sec
      ── 16 h 16 min 3 sec

60. 8 h 12 min
      − 3 h 58 min
      ── 4 h 14 min

61. 2 yd 2 ft
      + 3 yd 2 ft
      ── 6 yd 1 ft

In Exercises 62–64, choose an appropriate customary unit of measure.

62. weight of an orange ounces **63.** capacity of a bathtub gallons **64.** capacity of a teaspoon fluid ounces

65. Atiba was $53\frac{7}{8}$ inches tall last year. This year, he is $56\frac{1}{4}$ inches tall. How many inches did he grow over the past year? $2\frac{3}{8}$ in.

66. Nick jogged $4\frac{1}{10}$ miles on Sunday and $2\frac{2}{5}$ miles on Tuesday. How many more miles did he jog on Sunday than on Tuesday? $1\frac{7}{10}$ mi

83.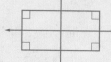

89. *Sample:*

Proportions, Percent, and Geometry

Solve the proportion.

67. $\frac{12}{x} = \frac{4}{7}$ 21 **68.** $\frac{9}{12} = \frac{x}{48}$ 36 **69.** $\frac{4}{18} = \frac{6}{x}$ 27 **70.** $\frac{x}{42} = \frac{5}{6}$ 35

Write the number as a fraction, a decimal, and a percent.

71. $\frac{2}{5}$ **72.** $\frac{3}{8}$ **73.** 54% **74.** 6% **75.** 0.125

$\frac{2}{5}$; 0.4; 40% $\frac{3}{8}$; 0.375; 37.5% $\frac{27}{50}$; 0.54; 54% $\frac{3}{50}$; 0.06; 6% $\frac{1}{8}$; 0.125; 12.5%

Find the percent of the number.

76. 7% of 83 5.81 **77.** 85% of 500 425 **78.** $66\frac{2}{3}$% of 90 60 **79.** 14.5% of 8 1.16

In Exercises 80–83, use the diagram shown.

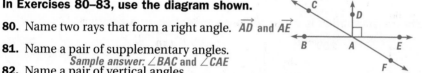

80. Name two rays that form a right angle. $\overrightarrow{AD}$ and $\overrightarrow{AE}$

81. Name a pair of supplementary angles.
Sample answer: ∠BAC and ∠CAE

82. Name a pair of vertical angles.
Sample answer: ∠BAC and ∠FAE

83. Use a protractor to draw an angle that has the same measure as ∠CAE. See margin.

Classify the figure in as many ways as possible. Then find the area.

84.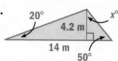

85.

86.

scalene, obtuse triangle; 29.4 m² parallelogram; 50.4 ft² circle; 314 cm²

87. In Exercise 84, find the value of x. 40 **88.** In Exercise 86, find the circumference. 62.8 cm

89. Draw a rectangle and show its lines of symmetry. See margin.

In Exercises 90–92, name the solid that matches the description.

90. Its one base is a circle. **91.** Its two bases are circles. **92.** Its one base can be a triangle.
cone cylinder pyramid

93. A jewelry box is 3 in. by 4 in. by 5 in. Find its surface area and volume. S = 94 in.², V = 60 in.³

94. The regular price of a sweatshirt is $22.50. Find the cost after a discount of 20%. $18

95. Two cities are 60 miles apart. How many centimeters apart are the cities on a map with a scale of 1 cm : 80 mi? 0.75 cm

106.

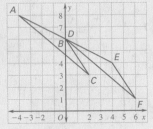

107.

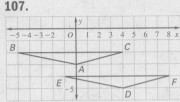

119.

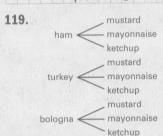

ham — mustard, mayonnaise, ketchup

turkey — mustard, mayonnaise, ketchup

bologna — mustard, mayonnaise, ketchup

20.

```
5 | 0
6 | 0 5
7 | 0 5 5
8 | 5 7 8
9 | 0 2 5 8
```

Key: 7 | 0 = 70

```
+--+--+--+--+--+--+--
  50  60  70  80  90  100
  •------|------•----•--•
  50    67.5   85 91 98
```

Sample answer: The stem-and-leaf plot shows the data grouped by the first digit in each number. It shows the data in order from least to greatest, so it is easy to find the median, range, and mode using this plot. The box-and-whisker plot shows the least and greatest values, as well as the lower quartile, median, and upper quartile. It is easy to find the median and range using this plot.

Integers, Algebra, and Probability

Order the integers from least to greatest.

96. $6, -16, 0, -6, 8$ $-16, -6, 0, 6, 8$

97. $0, -8, 5, -10, -5, 8$ $-10, -8, -5, 0, 5, 8$

Find the sum, difference, product, or quotient.

98. $16 + (-10)$ 6

99. $-5 + (-7)$ -12

100. $-9 - 2$ -11

101. $-4 - (-7)$ 3

102. $-8 \div (-2)$ 4

103. $-6(5)$ -30

104. $(-7)(-4)$ 28

105. $30 \div (-6)$ -5

Graph the points and connect them to form $\triangle ABC$. **Then translate** $\triangle ABC$ **4 units to the right and 2 units down to form** $\triangle DEF$. **Give the coordinates of the vertices of** $\triangle DEF$. 106–107. See margin for graphs.

106. $A(-4, 8), B(0, 6), C(2, 3)$
$D(0, 6), E(4, 4), F(6, 1)$

107. $A(0, -3), B(-5, -2), C(4, -2)$
$D(4, -5), E(-1, -4), F(8, -4)$

Tell whether the transformation is a *translation*, **a** *reflection*, **or a** *rotation*.

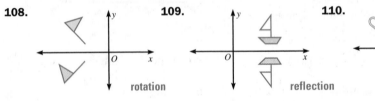

108. rotation

109. reflection

110. translation

Write the equation.

111. 16 more than a number is 28.
$16 + n = 28$

112. 6 less than a number is 8.
$n - 6 = 8$

Solve the equation.

113. $89 = x + 18$ 71

114. $m - 24 = 56$ 80

115. $6q = -42$ -7

116. $\frac{w}{12} = 6$ 72

You roll a number cube. Find the probability of the event.

117. You roll a number less than 7. 1

118. You roll a factor of 40. $\frac{2}{3}$

119. Use a tree diagram to find all the possible sandwiches you can make using either ham, turkey, or bologna and either mustard, mayonnaise, or ketchup. See margin.

120. The data show Pam's Spanish test grades. Make a stem-and-leaf plot and a box-and-whisker plot of the data. Then write a paragraph explaining each plot. See margin.

87, 75, 90, 65, 98, 75, 85, 70, 60, 88, 92, 50, 95

Contents of Student Resources

684

1. (5 × 1000) + (8 × 100) + (9 × 10); five thousand eight hundred ninety

2. (5 × 10,000) + (2 × 100) + (8 × 1); fifty thousand, two hundred eight

3. (9 × 100,000) + (6 × 1000) + (2 × 100) + (1 × 1); nine hundred six thousand, two hundred one

4. (1 × 1,000,000) + (3 × 100,000) + (5 × 10,000) + (6 × 100) + (1 × 1); one million, three hundred fifty thousand, six hundred one

Skills Review

Skills Review Handbook

Whole Number Place Value

The **whole numbers** are the numbers 0, 1, 2, 3, ... A **digit** is any of the numbers 0, 1, 2, 3, 4, 5, 6, 7, 8, or 9. The value of each digit in a whole number depends on its position within the number. For example, in the whole number 127,891, the 8 has a value of 800 because it is in the hundreds' place and 8 × 100 = 800.

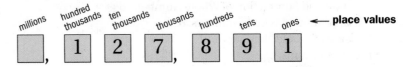

millions, hundred thousands, ten thousands, thousands, hundreds, tens, ones ← place values

| | , | 1 | 2 | 7 | , | 8 | 9 | 1 |

EXAMPLE Write the number 4062 in expanded form and in words.

Expanded form: 4062 = 4000 + 60 + 2   The zero in the hundreds' place is a placeholder.

= (4 × 1000) + (6 × 10) + (2 × 1)

Words: four thousand, sixty-two

EXAMPLE Write the number in standard form.

a. (6 × 100,000) + (4 × 1000) + (2 × 100) + (3 × 1) = 600,000 + 4000 + 200 + 3

= 604,203

b. seventy-three thousand, five hundred six

Write 7 in the ten thousands' place, 3 in the thousands' place, 5 in the hundreds' place, and 6 in the ones' place. Write a zero as a placeholder in the tens' place. The answer is 73,506.

● Practice

Identify the place value of the red digit. Then write the number in expanded form and in words.   1–4. See margin.

1. 5890   **2.** 50,208   **3.** 906,201   **4.** 1,350,601

Write the number in standard form.

5. (1 × 100,000) + (5 × 1000) + (3 × 100)   105,300

6. (7 × 10,000) + (9 × 10) + (3 × 1)   70,093

7. forty-two thousand, six hundred   42,600

8. six hundred fifty-one thousand, forty-one   651,041

Ordering Whole Numbers

A **number line** is a line whose points are associated with numbers. The numbers from left to right are in order from least to greatest. You can graph whole numbers on a number line to compare and order them. You can also compare the digits in each place from left to right.
The symbol < means *is less than* and the symbol > means *is greater than*.

Skills Review

EXAMPLE Use a number line to order 18, 9, 21, and 12.

Graph all the numbers on the same number line.

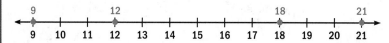

ANSWER From the number line, you can see that the order from least to greatest is 9, 12, 18, 21 and from greatest to least is 21, 18, 12, 9.

EXAMPLE Compare the numbers.

a. 3496 and 3469

Compare each place from left to right.

3496   The thousands' and hundreds'
        digits are the same.
3469   The tens' digits are different.
        9 is greater than 6.

ANSWER 3496 is greater than 3469.
            Write 3496 > 3469.

b. 9801 and 10,981

Compare each place from left to right.

9,801   No ten-thousands' digit means
         0 ten-thousands.
10,981   The ten-thousands' digit is 1.
         1 is greater than 0.

ANSWER 9801 is less than 10,981.
            Write 9801 < 10,981.

● Practice

Use a number line to order the numbers from least to greatest.

1. 11, 0, 8, 3, 10   0, 3, 8, 10, 11

2. 21, 17, 7, 11, 20
       7, 11, 17, 20, 21

3. 87, 78, 90, 85, 79
       78, 79, 85, 87, 90

4. 101, 110, 107, 97, 111
       97, 101, 107, 110, 111

5. 521, 518, 508, 512, 510
       508, 510, 512, 518, 521

6. 1010, 998, 1001, 1011
       998, 1001, 1010, 1011

Compare the numbers.

7. 207 and 148   207 > 148

8. 2095 and 2905   2095 < 2905

9. 3465 and 3492   3465 < 3492

10. 873 and 1073   873 < 1073

11. 21,539 and 9847
        21,539 > 9847

12. 103,264 and 13,264
        103,264 > 13,264

Rounding Whole Numbers

To **round** a whole number means to approximate the number to a given place value. For example, 84 rounded to the nearest ten is 80, because 84 is closer to 80 than to 90. When rounding to a specified place value, look at the digit to the right of that place value.

If the digit to the right is less than 5 (0, 1, 2, 3, or 4), round down.

If the digit to the right is 5 or greater (5, 6, 7, 8, or 9), round up.

EXAMPLE **Round the number to the place value of the red digit.**

    a. 479   **b.** 35,174

Solution

  a. Because the 4 is in the hundreds' place, round 479 to the nearest hundred. Notice that 479 is between 400 and 500, so it will round to one of these two numbers.

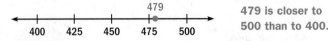

                                             479 is closer to 500 than to 400.

     The digit to the right of the 4 is a 7. Because 7 is greater than 5, you round up.

     ANSWER 479 rounded to the nearest hundred is 500.

  b. Because the 5 is in the thousands' place, round 35,174 to the nearest thousand. Notice that 35,174 is between 35,000 and 36,000, so it will round to one of these two numbers.

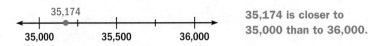

                                             35,174 is closer to 35,000 than to 36,000.

     The digit to the right of the 5 is a 1. Because 1 is less than 5, you round down.

     ANSWER 35,174 rounded to the nearest thousand is 35,000.

● Practice

Round the number to the place value of the red digit.

1. 86   90   **2.** 21   20   **3.** 247   200   **4.** 558   560   **5.** 4283 4280

6. 9561   10,000   **7.** 10,954   11,000   **8.** 36,982   36,980   **9.** 143,543   **10.** 593,121

                                                                                         144,000   600,000

Number Fact Families

Inverse operations are operations that "undo" each other, such as addition and subtraction or multiplication and division. A **number fact family** consists of three numbers related by inverse operations. For example, the facts $6 \times 2 = 12$, $2 \times 6 = 12$, $12 \div 6 = 2$, and $12 \div 2 = 6$ are in the same fact family.

EXAMPLE Copy and complete the number fact family.

$$4 + 2 = 6 \qquad 2 + \underline{\;?\;} = 6 \qquad 6 - \underline{\;?\;} = 2 \qquad 6 - \underline{\;?\;} = 4$$

Solution

The numbers in this fact family are 4, 2, and 6. Identify which of the three numbers is missing in each of the last three equations.

The 4 is missing in $2 + \underline{\;?\;} = 6$ and in $6 - \underline{\;?\;} = 2$.
The 2 is missing in $6 - \underline{\;?\;} = 4$.

ANSWER The complete number fact family is:
$4 + 2 = 6$; $2 + 4 = 6$; $6 - 4 = 2$; $6 - 2 = 4$.

EXAMPLE Write a related division equation for $4 \times 7 = 28$.

Think of the number fact family that contains the multiplication fact $4 \times 7 = 28$. The three numbers in this fact family are 4, 7, and 28, so the two related division equations are $28 \div 4 = 7$ and $28 \div 7 = 4$.

You can also think about "undoing" the multiplication. You multiply 4 and 7 to get 28, so divide 28 by 4 to get 7 or divide 28 by 7 to get 4.

Practice

In Exercises 1–4, copy and complete the number fact family.

1. $14 - 9 = 5 \qquad 14 - \underline{\;?\;} = 9 \qquad \underline{\;?\;} + 9 = 14 \qquad 9 + \underline{\;?\;} = \underline{\;?\;}$ 5; 5; 5; 14

2. $2 \times 8 = 16 \qquad 8 \times \underline{\;?\;} = 16 \qquad 16 \div \underline{\;?\;} = 8 \qquad \underline{\;?\;} \div \underline{\;?\;} = 2$ 2; 2; 16; 8

3. $32 \div \underline{\;?\;} = 4 \qquad 32 \div \underline{\;?\;} = 8 \qquad 8 \times \underline{\;?\;} = 32 \qquad \underline{\;?\;} \times \underline{\;?\;} = 32$ 8; 4; 4; 4; 8

4. $\underline{\;?\;} + 5 = 11 \qquad \underline{\;?\;} + 6 = 11 \qquad 11 - \underline{\;?\;} = 5 \qquad \underline{\;?\;} - \underline{\;?\;} = 6$ 6; 5; 6; 11; 5

5. Write a related subtraction equation for $7 + 8 = 15$. $15 - 8 = 7$ or $15 - 7 = 8$

6. Write a related multiplication equation for $54 \div 6 = 9$. $6 \times 9 = 54$ or $9 \times 6 = 54$

Addition and Subtraction on a Number Line

To **add** two whole numbers on a number line:

(1 Start at 0. Move to the *right* as far as the first number.

(2 To add the second number, continue from the location of the first number and move to the *right* the number of units indicated by the second number. The final location is the answer.

EXAMPLE Use a number line to add 4 + 5.

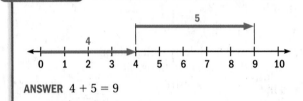

Start at 0.
Move 4 units to the *right*.
Then move 5 more units to the *right*.

ANSWER 4 + 5 = 9

To **subtract** two whole numbers on a number line:

(1 Start at 0. Move to the *right* as far as the first number.

(2 To subtract the second number, continue from the location of the first number and move to the *left* the number of units indicated by the second number. The final location is the answer.

EXAMPLE Use a number line to subtract 11 − 7.

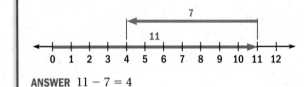

Start at 0.
Move 11 units to the *right*.
Then move 7 units to the *left*.

ANSWER 11 − 7 = 4

● Practice

Use a number line to add or subtract the numbers.

1. 8 + 5 13

2. 7 + 8 15

3. 4 + 7 11

4. 3 + 9 12

5. 10 + 3 13

6. 12 + 12 24

7. 8 + 12 20

8. 15 + 8 23

9. 10 − 4 6

10. 12 − 6 6

11. 14 − 6 8

12. 15 − 7 8

13. 17 − 9 8

14. 22 − 8 14

15. 19 − 3 16

16. 18 − 5 13

Addition and Subtraction of Whole Numbers

A **sum** is the result when you add two or more numbers. A **difference** is the result when you subtract two numbers. To add and subtract whole numbers, write the numbers in columns by place value. Start computing with the digits in the ones' place. Moving to the left, add or subtract the digits one place value at a time, regrouping as needed.

Skills Review

EXAMPLE Find the sum 287 + 36.

1 Add the ones. Then regroup the 13 ones as **1** ten and **3** ones.

$$
\begin{array}{r}
1 \\
287 \\
+\ 36 \\
\hline
3
\end{array}
$$

2 Add the tens. Then regroup the 12 tens as **1** hundred and **2** tens.

$$
\begin{array}{r}
1\ 1 \\
287 \\
+\ 36 \\
\hline
23
\end{array}
$$

3 Add the hundreds.

$$
\begin{array}{r}
1\ 1 \\
287 \\
+\ 36 \\
\hline
323
\end{array}
$$

EXAMPLE Find the difference 305 − 86.

1 Start with the ones. There are not enough ones in 305 to subtract 6. You will need to regroup. There are no tens, so go to the hundreds' place.

$$
\begin{array}{r}
305 \\
-\ 86
\end{array}
$$

2 Regroup the 3 hundreds as 2 hundreds and 10 tens. Then regroup the 10 tens as **9** tens and **10** ones. Now subtract one place value at a time.

$$
\begin{array}{r}
9 \\
2\ \cancel{10}\ 15 \\
\cancel{3}\ \cancel{0}\ \cancel{5} \\
-\ \ \ 8\ 6 \\
\hline
2\ 1\ 9
\end{array}
$$

5 ones plus **10** ones from regrouping makes **15** ones.

✓**Check** Because addition and subtraction are *inverse operations*, you can check your answer by adding: 219 + 86 = 305.

Practice

Find the sum or difference.

1. 43 + 28   71

2. 81 + 59   140

3. 192 + 48   240

4. 85 + 357   442

5. 235 + 165   400

6. 586 + 287   873

7. 283 + 1129   1412

8. 3547 + 385   3932

9. 75 − 58   17

10. 62 − 17   45

11. 245 − 26   219

12. 574 − 67   507

13. 326 − 177   149

14. 402 − 258   144

15. 1461 − 282   1179

16. 4340 − 173   4167

Multiplication of Whole Numbers

A **product** is the result when you multiply two or more numbers. To **multiply** two whole numbers, multiply the entire top number by the digit in each place value of the bottom number to obtain partial products. Then add the partial products.

EXAMPLE Find the product 263 × 54.

(1 Multiply 263 by the ones' digit in 54.

$$
\begin{array}{r}
2\,1 \\
263 \\
\times\ 54 \\
\hline
1052 \\
\end{array}
$$

(2 Multiply by the tens' digit. Start the partial product in the tens' place.

$$
\begin{array}{r}
3\,1 \\
263 \\
\times\ 54 \\
\hline
1052 \\
1315 \\
\end{array}
$$

(3 Add the partial products.

$$
\begin{array}{r}
263 \\
\times\ 54 \\
\hline
1052 \\
1315 \\
\hline
14{,}202 \\
\end{array}
$$

To multiply a whole number by a *power of 10*, such as 10, 100 or 1000, write the number followed by the number of zeros in the power. Because multiplying by such powers of 10 shifts each digit of the number to a higher place value, the zeros are needed as placeholders.

EXAMPLE Find the product.

a. 74×100

b. 234×1000

Solution

a. 100 is a power of 10 with 2 zeros, so write 2 zeros after 74.

ANSWER $74 \times 100 = 7400$

b. 1000 is a power of 10 with 3 zeros, so write 3 zeros after 234.

— Place commas as necessary.

ANSWER $234 \times 1000 = 234{,}000$

● Practice

Find the product.

1. 41×80 3280
2. 73×34 2482
3. 26×37 962
4. 68×42 2856

5. 217×28 6076
6. 483×53 25,599
7. 975×62 60,450
8. 371×88 32,648

9. 1987×74 147,038
10. 6581×25 164,525
11. 4657×10 46,570
12. 9876×100 987,600

13. 123×100 12,300
14. 2568×1000 2,568,000
15. $2319 \times 10{,}000$ 23,190,000
16. $7923 \times 100{,}000$ 792,300,000

Division of Whole Numbers

In a division problem, the number being divided is called the **dividend** and the number it is being divided by is called the **divisor**. The result of the division is called the **quotient**. To **divide** two whole numbers, you use the following pattern: divide, multiply, subtract, bring down. Continue this pattern until there are no more digits to bring down. If the divisor does not divide the dividend evenly, then there is a **remainder**.

EXAMPLE Find the quotient 236 ÷ 4.

(1) Decide where to write the first digit of the quotient. Because 4 is between 2 and 23, place the first digit above the 3.

(2) Because 23 ÷ 4 is between 5 and 6, multiply 4 by **5**. Then subtract **20** from 23. Be sure the difference is less than the divisor.

(3) Bring down the next digit, **6**. Divide 36 by 4. Because 36 ÷ 4 = **9**, multiply 4 by **9**. Subtract 36. The remainder is 0.

$$
\begin{array}{r} \square \leftarrow \text{first digit of quotient} \\ \text{divisor} \rightarrow 4)\overline{236} \\ \text{dividend} \end{array}
$$

$$
\begin{array}{r} 5 \\ 4)\overline{236} \\ \underline{20} \\ 3 \end{array}
$$

$$
\begin{array}{r} 59 \\ 4)\overline{236} \\ \underline{20} \\ 36 \\ \underline{36} \\ 0 \end{array}
$$

EXAMPLE Find the quotient 7346 ÷ 24.

(1)
$$
\begin{array}{r} \square \leftarrow \text{first digit of quotient} \\ 24)\overline{7346} \end{array}
$$

(2)
$$
\begin{array}{r} 30 \leftarrow \text{Bring down} \\ 24)\overline{7346} \\ \underline{72} \\ 14 \end{array}
$$
the **4**. But 24 < 14, so write a **0**.

(3)
$$
\begin{array}{r} 306 \text{ R2} \leftarrow \text{remainder} \\ 24)\overline{7346} \\ \underline{72} \\ 146 \\ \underline{144} \\ 2 \end{array}
$$
Then bring down the **6** to continue dividing.

✓ **Check** (24 × 306) + 2 = 7346, so the answer 306 R2 is correct.

Practice

Find the quotient.

1. 6)852   142

2. 5)650   130

3. 7)378   54

4. 7)126   18

5. 3645 ÷ 9   405

6. 2388 ÷ 4   597

7. 580 ÷ 10   58

8. 783 ÷ 12   65 R3

9. 436 ÷ 33   13 R7

10. 2100 ÷ 100   21

11. 1617 ÷ 65   24 R57

12. 1488 ÷ 72   20 R48

Estimating Sums

To **estimate** the solution of a problem means to find an approximate answer. One way to estimate a sum when all the numbers have the same number of digits is to use **front-end estimation**. First add the digits in the *greatest* place to get a low estimate. Then use the remaining digits to adjust the sum and get a closer estimate.

EXAMPLE Estimate the sum 465 + 342 + 198.

(1 Add the digits in the greatest place: the hundreds' place.

$$
\begin{array}{r}
465 \\
342 \\
+\ 198 \\
\hline
800
\end{array}
$$

(2 Estimate the sum of the remaining digits. Look for more hundreds.

$$
\begin{array}{r}
465 \searrow \\
342 \rightarrow \text{about } 100 \\
+\ 198 \rightarrow \text{about } 100 \\
\hline
\text{about } 200 \text{ more}
\end{array}
$$

(3 Add the two sums.

$$
\begin{array}{r}
800 \\
+\ 200 \\
\hline
1000
\end{array}
$$

ANSWER The sum 465 + 342 + 198 is *about* 1000.

When numbers being added have about the same value, you can use *clustering* to estimate their sum.

EXAMPLE Estimate the sum 72 + 68 + 65.

The numbers all cluster around the value 70.

$$
\begin{array}{r}
72 \\
68 \\
+\ 65
\end{array}
\quad \longrightarrow \quad
\begin{array}{r}
70 \\
70 \\
+\ 70
\end{array}
\qquad 3 \times 70 = 210
$$

ANSWER The sum 72 + 68 + 65 is *about* 210.

Practice

Estimate the sum.   1–9. Estimates may vary.

1. 290 + 419 + 578 1300

2. 549 + 127 + 328 1000

3. 643 + 294 + 861 1800

4. 328 + 560 + 781 + 533 2200

5. 1289 + 2716 + 5952 10,000

6. 6429 + 5381 + 7232 19,000

7. 42 + 43 + 36 + 37 160

8. 99 + 100 + 95 + 107 400

9. 274 + 292 + 307 + 315 1200

Estimating Differences

One way to estimate a difference is to find a low estimate and a high estimate.

EXAMPLE Find a low and high estimate for the difference 534 − 278.

① For the **low estimate**, round the greater number down and the lesser number up to decrease the difference.

$$\begin{array}{r} 534 \\ -\ 278 \end{array} \longrightarrow \begin{array}{r} 500 \\ -\ 300 \\ \hline 200 \end{array}$$

② For the **high estimate**, round the greater number up and the lesser number down to increase the difference.

$$\begin{array}{r} 534 \\ -\ 278 \end{array} \longrightarrow \begin{array}{r} 600 \\ -\ 200 \\ \hline 400 \end{array}$$

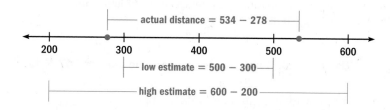

actual distance = 534 − 278

200   300   400   500   600

low estimate = 500 − 300

high estimate = 600 − 200

ANSWER The difference 534 − 278 is between 200 and 400.

● Practice

Find a low and high estimate for the difference.

1.   924   700; 900
      − 105

2.   876   400; 600
      − 328

3.   724   400; 600
      − 286

4.   639   100; 300
      − 427

5.   642   300; 500
      − 268

6.   745   500; 700
      − 197

7.   839   400; 600
      − 381

8.   593   0; 200
      − 402

9.   2768   0; 2000
      − 1319

10.   2913   0; 2000
       − 1245

11.   7943   3000; 5000
       − 3872

12.   5639   2000; 4000
       − 2088

13.   6543   4000; 6000
       − 1739

14.   7561   4000; 6000
       − 2972

15.   8421   1000; 3000
       − 6384

16.   5129   2000; 4000
       − 2876

Estimating Products

One way to estimate a product is to find a low estimate and a high estimate.

EXAMPLE Find a low and high estimate for the product 253 × 15.

For the low estimate, round both factors *down*.

$$\begin{array}{r} 200 \\ \times\ 10 \\ \hline 2000 \end{array}$$

For the high estimate, round both factors *up*.

$$\begin{array}{r} 300 \\ \times\ 20 \\ \hline 6000 \end{array}$$

ANSWER The product 253 × 15 is between 2000 and 6000.

Another way is to use compatible numbers. **Compatible numbers** are numbers that are easy to use in computations.

EXAMPLE Use compatible numbers to estimate the product 147 × 12.

Replace 147 and 12 with two numbers that are easy to multiply.

$$\begin{array}{r} 147 \\ \times\ 12 \end{array} \longrightarrow \begin{array}{r} 150 \\ \times\ 10 \\ \hline 1500 \end{array}$$

ANSWER The product 147 × 12 is *about* 1500.

● Practice

Find a low and high estimate for the product.

1. 42 × 21 800; 1500 **2.** 63 × 59 3000; 4200 **3.** 74 × 38 2100; 3200 **4.** 92 × 29 1800; 3000

5. 129 × 34 3000; 8000 **6.** 563 × 48 20,000; 30,000 **7.** 67 × 215 12,000; 21,000 **8.** 26 × 749 14,000; 24,000

9. 4786 × 73 280,000; 400,000 **10.** 1793 × 41 40,000; 100,000 **11.** 13 × 6721 60,000; 140,000 **12.** 64 × 8516 480,000; 630,000

Use compatible numbers to estimate the product. 13–28. Estimates may vary.

13. 213 × 53 10,500 **14.** 395 × 43 16,000 **15.** 528 × 98 52,800 **16.** 821 × 78 64,000

17. 22 × 742 14,000 **18.** 14 × 683 10,500 **19.** 52 × 932 45,000 **20.** 62 × 287 18,000

21. 865 × 712 630,000 **22.** 912 × 233 180,000 **23.** 268 × 543 150,000 **24.** 387 × 603 240,000

25. 2751 × 32 90,000 **26.** 8613 × 44 360,000 **27.** 98 × 7361 736,100 **28.** 67 × 1322 70,000

Estimating Quotients

One way to estimate a quotient is to find a low estimate and a high estimate by using numbers that divide with no remainder.

EXAMPLE Find a low and high estimate for the quotient 2692 ÷ 8.

Replace 2692 with numbers that are easily divisible by 8.

For the **low estimate**, use a number less than 2692.

$$\overset{300}{8\overline{)2400}}$$

For the **high estimate**, use a number greater than 2692.

$$\overset{400}{8\overline{)3200}}$$

ANSWER The quotient 2692 ÷ 8 is between 300 and 400.

Another way to estimate a quotient is to use compatible numbers.

EXAMPLE Use compatible numbers to estimate the quotient 99 ÷ 23.

Look for numbers close to 99 and 23 that divide evenly.

$$23\overline{)99} \quad \Longrightarrow \quad \overset{4}{25\overline{)100}}$$

ANSWER The quotient 99 ÷ 23 is *about* 4.

● Practice

Find a low and high estimate for the quotient.

1. 211 ÷ 4   50; 60   **2.** 423 ÷ 5   80; 90   **3.** 394 ÷ 6   60; 70   **4.** 449 ÷ 8   50; 60

5. 198 ÷ 6   30; 40   **6.** 347 ÷ 9   30; 40   **7.** 1946 ÷ 7   200; 300   **8.** 2124 ÷ 4   500; 600

9. 2198 ÷ 6   300; 400   **10.** 2476 ÷ 9   200; 300 **11.** 3601 ÷ 8   400; 500   **12.** 1396 ÷ 3   400; 500

13. 5989 ÷ 5   1100; 1200 **14.** 7431 ÷ 4   1800; 1900 **15.** 6172 ÷ 7   800; 900 **16.** 4382 ÷ 9   400; 500

Use compatible numbers to estimate the quotient.   17–28. Estimates may vary.

17. 125 ÷ 62   2   **18.** 239 ÷ 38   6   **19.** 489 ÷ 48   10   **20.** 342 ÷ 81   4

21. 973 ÷ 87   10   **22.** 391 ÷ 42   10   **23.** 632 ÷ 87   7   **24.** 439 ÷ 58   7

25. 4201 ÷ 43   100   **26.** 2702 ÷ 73   40   **27.** 7378 ÷ 92   80   **28.** 1024 ÷ 28   30

Solving Problems Using Addition and Subtraction

You can use the following guidelines to tell whether to use addition or subtraction to solve a word problem.

Use *addition* when you need to combine, add on, or find a total.

Use *subtraction* when you need to compare, take away, find how many are left, or find how many more you need.

EXAMPLE You paid $15 for a T-shirt and $35 for a pair of jeans. How much did you pay in all?

You need to find a total, so you need to add.

$15 + $35 = $50

ANSWER You paid $50 in all.

EXAMPLE You need to make 40 muffins for a bake sale. You already made 24 muffins. How many more do you need to make?

You need to find how many more you need, so you need to subtract.

$40 - 24 = 16$

ANSWER You need to make 16 more muffins.

Practice

1. You have $13 to spend. You buy a poster for $4. How much money do you have left? $9

2. You spend $19 for a movie on DVD and $8 for a movie on video tape. How much more did you spend for the DVD movie? $11

3. You buy 18 pencils and 8 pens. How many items did you buy in all?   26 items

4. You have 27 stamps in your stamp collection. Your friend gives you 8 stamps. How many stamps do you have in your collection now?   35 stamps

5. You need $25 for school supplies. You have $18. How much more money do you need for school supplies? $7

6. You have to sell 31 tickets for the dance. You have already sold 14 of them. How many more do you have to sell?   17 tickets

Solving Problems Using Multiplication and Division

You can use the following guidelines to tell whether to use multiplication or division to solve a word problem.

Use *multiplication* when you need to combine or join together the total number of objects in groups of equal size.

Use *division* when you need to find the number of equal groups or find the number in each equal group.

EXAMPLE **You buy 4 packages of markers. Each package contains 8 markers. How many markers did you buy?**

You need to combine groups of equal size, so you need to multiply.

$4 \times 8 = 32$

ANSWER You bought 32 markers.

EXAMPLE **You have 20 beads. You put an equal number of beads on 5 bracelets. How many beads do you put on each bracelet?**

You need to find the number in each equal group, so you need to divide.

$20 \div 5 = 4$

ANSWER You put 4 beads on each bracelet.

Practice

1. You order 6 packages of folders for the school store. Each package contains 10 folders. How many folders do you get?   60 folders

2. You have 30 plants. You split the plants evenly among 5 pots. How many plants do you put in each pot?   6 plants

3. You buy 32 bottles of water in boxes of 8. How many boxes did you buy?   4 boxes

4. You have 4 boxes of straws. Each box contains 12 straws. How many straws do you have?   48 straws

5. You buy 5 CDs at a yard sale for $4 each. How much did you spend? $20

6. You need to make 96 cookies. One batch of cookies makes 24. How many batches do you need to make?   4 batches

Operations with Money

You can use the following guidelines to tell whether to use subtraction or addition to solve a money problem.

Use *addition* when finding the total cost of several items.

Use *subtraction* when finding how much change you should receive.

EXAMPLE You buy a book for $4.89. You give the clerk $10.00. How much change do you receive?

You are finding the amount of change, so you need to subtract.

Subtract as you would with whole numbers.

$$
\begin{array}{r}
9 \\
9\ \cancel{10}\ 10 \\
\cancel{10}\ .\ \cancel{0}\ \cancel{0} \\
-\ \ 4\ .\ 8\ 9 \\
\hline
5\ .\ 1\ 1
\end{array}
$$

> Place the decimal point in the answer so that it lines up with the other decimal points.

ANSWER Your change is $5.11.

EXAMPLE You buy shoes for $28.99, a backpack for $32.50, and jeans for $29.95. How much do you spend in all?

You are finding the total cost of several items, so you need to add.

Add as you would with whole numbers.

$$
\begin{array}{r}
2\ 2\ 1 \\
28.99 \\
32.50 \\
+\ 29.95 \\
\hline
91.44
\end{array}
$$

> Place the decimal point in the answer so that it lines up with the other decimal points.

ANSWER You spent $91.44 in all.

● Practice

1. You buy a carton of juice for $2.98. You give the clerk $5. How much change do you receive? $2.02

2. You buy a calendar for $12.48. You give the clerk $13.03. How much change do you receive? $.55

3. You buy a package of CDs for $18.98, a printer cartridge for $21.35, and a box of printer paper for $17.75. How much do you spend in all? $58.08

Adding and Subtracting Decimals

Skills Review

You add and subtract decimals one place value at a time from right to left in the same way you add and subtract whole numbers. Line up the decimal points in your calculation and place a decimal point in your answer.

EXAMPLE Find the sum 16.8 + 29.5.

(1 Line up the decimal points. Add the tenths. Regroup the 13 tenths as **1** one and **3** tenths.

$$
\begin{array}{r}
1 \\
1\ 6\ .\ 8 \\
+\ 2\ 9\ .\ 5 \\
\hline
3
\end{array}
$$

(2 Add the ones. Regroup the 16 ones as **1** ten and **6** ones. Then add the tens. Write the decimal point.

$$
\begin{array}{r}
1\ \ 1 \\
1\ 6\ .\ 8 \\
+\ 2\ 9\ .\ 5 \\
\hline
4\ 6\ .\ 3
\end{array}
$$

Line up the decimal point in the sum with the other decimal points.

EXAMPLE Find the difference 18.25 − 6.79.

(1 Line up the decimal points. Regroup to be able to subtract the hundredths. The 2 tenths become **1** tenth and **10** hundredths. Then subtract the hundredths.

$$
\begin{array}{r}
1\,15 \\
1\ 8\ .\ 2\cancel{5} \\
-\ \ \ 6\ .\ 7\ 9 \\
\hline
6
\end{array}
$$

← 5 hundredths plus **10** hundredths from regrouping makes **15** hundredths.

(2 Regroup to be able to subtract the tenths. The 8 ones become **7** ones and **10** tenths. Now subtract the tenths. Then subtract the ones and the tens. Write the decimal point.

$$
\begin{array}{r}
11 \\
7\ \ \cancel{1}\,15 \\
1\cancel{8}\ .\ \cancel{2}\cancel{5} \\
-\ \ \ 6\ .\ 7\ 9 \\
\hline
1\ 1\ .\ 4\ 6
\end{array}
$$

Line up the decimal point in the difference with the other decimal points.

● Practice

Find the sum or difference.

1. 17.9 + 23.5   41.4

2. 25.8 + 17.3   43.1

3. 56.3 + 86.7   143

4. 2.76 + 8.54   11.3

5. 6.91 + 4.38   11.29

6. 7.35 + 8.96   16.31

7. 10.65 + 9.48   20.13

8. 24.76 + 8.08   32.84

9. 48.55 + 8.67   57.22

10. 18.2 − 10.8   7.4

11. 36.4 − 19.9   16.5

12. 64.3 − 25.6   38.7

13. 9.75 − 2.87   6.88

14. 7.14 − 2.94   4.2

15. 8.75 − 2.99   5.76

16. 45.78 − 6.89   38.89

17. 28.93 − 9.06   19.87

18. 72.17 − 8.28   63.89

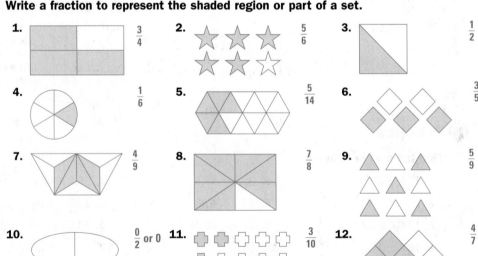

Modeling Fractions

A **fraction** is used to describe one or more parts of a whole or a set. The top part of a fraction is called the **numerator**. It tells how many parts of the whole or how many objects from the set to consider. The bottom part of a fraction is called the **denominator**. It tells how many equal sized parts make up the whole or how many objects make up the set.

EXAMPLE Write a fraction to represent the shaded region or part of a set.

a.

b.

Solution

a. The region is divided into 3 equal parts and 2 of the parts are shaded. The fraction that represents the shaded part of the set is $\frac{2}{3}$.

b. There are 8 objects in this set and five of the objects are shaded. The fraction that represents the shaded part of the set is $\frac{5}{8}$.

● Practice

Write a fraction to represent the shaded region or part of a set.

1. $\frac{3}{4}$
2. $\frac{5}{6}$
3. $\frac{1}{2}$
4. $\frac{1}{6}$
5. $\frac{5}{14}$
6. $\frac{3}{5}$
7. $\frac{4}{9}$
8. $\frac{7}{8}$
9. $\frac{5}{9}$
10. $\frac{0}{2}$ or 0
11. $\frac{3}{10}$
12. $\frac{4}{7}$

Units of Time

Use the equivalent units of time
given at the right to change one unit
of time to another.

Divide to change from a smaller unit to a larger unit.
Multiply to change from a larger unit to a smaller unit.

Skills Review

> **1 week = 7 days**
> **1 day = 24 hours**
> **1 hour = 60 minutes**
> **1 minute = 60 seconds**

EXAMPLE **Copy and complete.**

a. 28 days = $\underline{?}$ weeks

b. 3 hours 15 minutes = $\underline{?}$ minutes

c. 67 seconds = $\underline{?}$ minutes $\underline{?}$ seconds

Solution

a. You are changing days to weeks,
a smaller unit to a larger unit. There
are 7 days in one week, so divide by 7.

$$28 \text{ days} = (28 \div 7) \text{ weeks}$$
$$= 4 \text{ weeks}$$

b. You are changing hours to minutes,
a larger unit to a smaller unit. There
are 60 minutes in one hour, so multiply
by 60. Then add the extra minutes.

$$3 \text{ hours 15 minutes} = [(3 \times 60) + 15] \text{ minutes}$$
$$= (180 + 15) \text{ minutes}$$
$$= 195 \text{ minutes}$$

c. You are changing seconds to minutes,
a smaller unit to a larger unit. There are
60 seconds in one minute, so divide by 60.
If there is a remainder, write it as seconds.

$$\begin{array}{r} 1 \leftarrow \text{minutes} \\ 60\overline{)67} \\ \underline{60} \\ 7 \leftarrow \text{extra seconds} \end{array}$$

1 minute 7 seconds

Practice

Copy and complete.

1. 4 hours = $\underline{?}$ minutes   240

2. 3 weeks = $\underline{?}$ days   21

3. 96 hours = $\underline{?}$ days   4

4. 420 seconds = $\underline{?}$ minutes   7

5. 1 week 5 days = $\underline{?}$ days   12

6. 2 hours 25 minutes = $\underline{?}$ minutes   145

7. 2 days 4 hours = $\underline{?}$ hours   52

8. 3 minutes 10 seconds = $\underline{?}$ seconds   190

9. 16 days = $\underline{?}$ weeks $\underline{?}$ days   2; 2

10. 90 minutes = $\underline{?}$ hours $\underline{?}$ minutes   1; 30

11. 40 hours = $\underline{?}$ days $\underline{?}$ hours   1; 16

12. 200 seconds = $\underline{?}$ minutes $\underline{?}$ seconds   3; 20

Perimeter and Area

Perimeter is the distance around a figure measured in linear units.

Area is the amount of surface covered by a figure measured in square units.

EXAMPLE Find the perimeter of the rectangle below.

To find the perimeter, add the side lengths.
3 in. + 6 in. + 3 in. + 6 in. = 18 in.

ANSWER The perimeter is 18 inches.

```
      6 in.
3 in.        3 in.
      6 in.
```

EXAMPLE Find the area.

a.

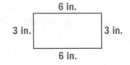

Find the area by counting the number of squares inside the figure. There are 21 squares. So the area is 21 square units.

b.

Count the **whole squares**. Estimate how many more whole squares can be made by the **partial squares**. The total area is about 12 + 8 = 20 square units.

Practice

Find the perimeter.

1.
```
    3 in.   10 in.
2 in.      2 in.
    3 in.
```

2.
```
     8 ft   24 ft
4 ft       4 ft
     8 ft
```

3.
```
         15 cm
  6 cm   4 cm
    5 cm
```

Find the area.

4. 24 square units

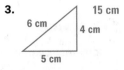

5. 21 square units

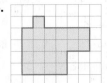

6. 16 square units

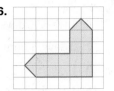

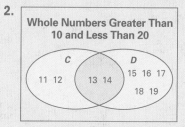

Venn Diagrams and Logical Reasoning

A **Venn diagram** uses shapes to show how sets are related.

EXAMPLE Draw and use a Venn diagram.

a. Draw a Venn diagram of the whole numbers between 0 and 10 where set A consists of even whole numbers and set B consists of multiples of 3.

b. If an even whole number is between 0 and 10, then is it *always, sometimes,* or *never* a multiple of 3?

c. If a number is in set B, then is it *always, sometimes,* or *never* in set A?

Solution

a.

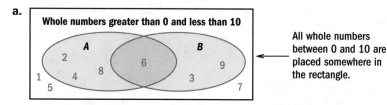

Whole numbers greater than 0 and less than 10

A   2   6   B   9
1   4   8   3
5   7

All whole numbers between 0 and 10 are placed somewhere in the rectangle.

b. This statement is *sometimes* true because 6 is an even whole number that is a multiple of 3, but 2, 4, and 8, the other even whole numbers between 0 and 10, are not multiples of 3.

c. This statement is *sometimes* true because 3 and 9 are in set B only, but 6 is in sets B and A.

Practice

Draw a Venn diagram of the sets described.   1–2. See margin.

1. Use the set of whole numbers less than 15. Set A consists of multiples of 3 and set B consists of multiples of 4.

2. Use the set of whole numbers between 10 and 20. Set C consists of numbers less than 15 and set D consists of numbers greater than 12.

Use the Venn diagrams from Exercises 1 and 2 to tell whether the statement is *always, sometimes,* or *never* true. Explain your reasoning.
                                                    3–5. Explanations may vary.
3. If a number is in set A, then it is in set B.
    Sometimes; 12 is in both set A and set B, but 6, for example, is only in set A.
4. If a number is between 12 and 15, then it is in both set C and set D.
    Always; 13 and 14 are less than 15 and greater than 12, so they are in both sets.
5. If a number is greater than 15, then it is in set C. Never; set C consists of numbers less than 15.

Reading Bar Graphs

Data are numbers or facts. One way to display data is in **bar graphs**, which use bars to show how quantities compare.

EXAMPLE A group of students collected data on the number of students in each sixth grade math period at their school. The bar graph below displays the data they collected.

  a. Which class has the most students?

  b. Which class has 15 students?

Solution

  a. The longest bar in the bar graph represents period 3, which shows a class with 25 students. So period 3 has the most students.

  b. Look at the vertical scale and locate 15. Then find the bar that ends at 15. The bar that shows 15 students represents period 5.

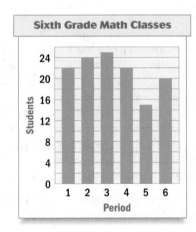

Sixth Grade Math Classes

Practice

Use the bar graph above.

1. How many students are in period 6?   **20 students**

2. Which two periods have the same number of students?   **periods 1 and 4**

3. Which period has 24 students?   **period 2**

4. Which period has the fewest students?   **period 5**

5. How many more students are in period 1 than in period 5?   **7 more students**

6. Which period has two more students than period 4?   **period 2**

7. Which two periods have a difference of 1 in the number of students they have?   **periods 2 and 3**

Reading Line Graphs

You can use a line graph to display data. A **line graph** uses line segments to show how quantities change over time.

EXAMPLE The line graph below shows the data you collected on the depth of a creek behind your house each day for one week.

a. Did the depth of the creek *increase* or *decrease* from Monday to Tuesday?

b. On which day was the creek 6 inches deep when you measured it?

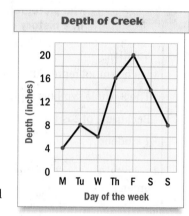

Depth of Creek

Solution

a. If the line rises from left to right, the data increase. If the line falls from left to right, the data decrease. Because the line from Monday to Tuesday rises, the depth of the creek increased.

b. Look at the vertical scale and locate 6. Then find the bullet on the horizontal line with the value of 6. The creek was 6 inches deep when you measured it on Wednesday.

● Practice

Use the line graph above.

1. On which day was the creek 16 inches deep when you measured it?   Thursday

2. Between which two days did the depth of the creek decrease by 2 inches?   Tuesday and Wednesday

3. How deep was the creek on Sunday?   8 in.

4. On which day was the creek the deepest?   Friday

5. Did the depth of the creek *increase* or *decrease* from Friday to Saturday?   decrease

6. On which two days was the depth of the creek the same when you measured it?   Tuesday and Sunday

7. On which day was the creek the shallowest?   Monday

8. Between which two days did the depth of the creek increase the most? How much was the increase?   Wednesday and Thursday; 10 in.

Reading a Pictograph

A **pictograph** is a way to display data using pictures. To read a pictograph, find the key and read the amount that each symbol represents. Multiply that amount by the number of whole symbols shown for the category. Then find and add on the value of any partial symbols.

EXAMPLE The pictograph shows data on the eye colors of students in a history class. How many students have green eyes?

Solution

Each symbol represents 2 students.

The 3 whole symbols represent $3 \times 2 = 6$ students.

Because $\frac{1}{2}$ of 2 is 1, the half symbol represents 1 student.

ANSWER $6 + 1 = 7$, so there are 7 students with green eyes.

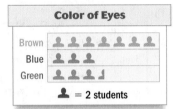

Color of Eyes	
Brown	👤👤👤👤👤👤👤
Blue	👤👤👤
Green	👤👤👤⌐

👤 = 2 students

Practice

Use the pictograph above.

1. Which eye color do most students have? How many students have this eye color? brown; 14 students

2. Which eye color do the fewest students have? How many students have this eye color? blue; 6 students

Use the pictograph at the right.

3. How many pictures were taken on Tuesday?
   8 pictures
4. On which day were the most pictures taken? How many pictures were taken?
   Friday; 16 pictures
5. About how many fewer pictures were taken on Thursday than on Monday?
   about 4 pictures
6. How many pictures were taken on Wednesday? 12 pictures

7. On which day was the number of pictures taken twice the number taken on Tuesday? Friday

Number of Pictures Taken	
Monday	📷 📷 📷 📷
Tuesday	📷 📷
Wednesday	📷 📷 📷
Thursday	📷 📷 📷
Friday	📷 📷 📷 📷

📷 = 4 pictures

1.

CDs Sold in One Day

2. Pets Owned by Students

Making a Pictograph

To make a pictograph, first choose a symbol and find an appropriate amount for that symbol to represent. Then draw the graph.

EXAMPLE

You collected data on the types of bagels sold in one hour at a bagel shop. Make a pictograph of the data.

Bagels Sold in One Hour	
Type of bagel	Number sold
plain	12
sesame	7
rye	4
cinnamon raisin	10
egg	11

Solution

Choose a symbol to represent 2 bagels. Half of a symbol represents 1 bagel. Write the types of bagels along the left hand side of the graph. Then draw symbols to represent the number of bagels of each type sold that hour.

Bagels Sold in One Hour

Plain ⊙⊙⊙⊙⊙⊙
Sesame ⊙⊙⊙(
Rye ⊙⊙
Cinn. Raisin ⊙⊙⊙⊙⊙
Egg ⊙⊙⊙⊙⊙(

⊙ = 2 bagels

● Practice

Make a pictograph of the data. 1–2. See margin.

1.

CDs Sold in One Day	
Type of CD	Number sold
country	15
rock	25
pop	35

2.

Pets Owned by Students	
Pet	Number of students
dog	24
cat	18
turtle	6
rabbit	3
hamster	21

9. add 4 to the previous number; 21, 25

10. subtract 7 from the previous number; 22, 15

11. divide the previous number by 2; 100, 50

Extra Practice

Chapter 1

1.1 **Find the sum, difference, product, or quotient.**

1. $262 - 59$ 203
2. $47 + 158$ 205
3. $306 \div 6$ 51
4. 34×21 714

5. 34×5 170
6. $348 - 72$ 276
7. $156 \div 4$ 39
8. $13 + 19$ 32

1.1 **Describe the pattern. Then find the next two numbers.** 9–11. See margin.

9. 5, 9, 13, 17, $\underline{?}$, $\underline{?}$
10. 50, 43, 36, 29, $\underline{?}$, $\underline{?}$
11. 1600, 800, 400, 200, $\underline{?}$, $\underline{?}$

1.2 **Estimate the sum, difference, product, or quotient.**
12–19. Estimates may vary.

12. $257 + 91$ 350
13. $435 - 69$ 370
14. 173×29 5100
15. $381 \div 52$ 8

16. $680 + 134$ 810
17. $805 - 37$ 760
18. $583 \div 61$ 10
19. 48×32 1500

1.2 **20.** You are buying spring water for use by runners at a road race. The water comes in cases of 36 bottles each. You buy 12 cases. Estimate the number of bottles you buy. **about 400 bottles**

1.3 **Find the value of the power.**

21. 7^3 343
22. 6^4 1296
23. 2 cubed 8
24. 12 squared 144

1.4 **Evaluate the expression.**

25. $27 - 17 + 4$ 14
26. $5 \times 12 \div 20$ 3
27. $18 + 9 \div 3$ 21
28. $4 + 3^3$ 31

29. $9 \times (2 + 6) \div 12$ 6
30. $100 \div 5^2 + 5$ 9
31. $10 - 2 \times 3 + 7$ 11
32. $\dfrac{8^2}{9 - 5}$ 16

1.5 **Evaluate the expression when $x = 9$ and $y = 4$.**

33. $3x$ 27
34. $4x + y$ 40
35. $92 - x^2$ 11
36. $2x \div 3 + 5$ 11

37. $y + x + 1$ 14
38. $6 - y$ 2
39. $x - y \div 2$ 7
40. $x + y^2$ 25

1.5 **41.** Let a represent your age in years. Your cousin is 9 years older. You can use the expression $a + 9$ to represent your cousin's age. Use the expression to find how old your cousin is if you are 13 years old. **22 years old**

1.6 **Solve the equation using mental math.**

42. $2b = 8$ 4
43. $8 + z = 11$ 3
44. $x - 2 = 21$ 23
45. $18 \div x = 9$ 2

46. $1 + x = 4$ 3
47. $13 - q = 9$ 4
48. $70 \div t = 10$ 7
49. $4 \cdot c = 0$ 0

1.7 **50.** The product of two whole numbers is 56. Their difference is 10. Find the two numbers. Begin by making a list of all the pairs of numbers whose product is 56. **14, 4**

Extra Practice

Chapter 2

2.1 **1.** Find the length of the line segment to the nearest centimeter. **6 cm**

_____

2.1 **Choose an appropriate customary unit and metric unit for the length.**

2. your height
inches, centimeters

3. distance between towns
miles, kilometers

4. thickness of a ruler
inches, millimeters

2.2 **Find the perimeter and the area of the rectangle or square.**

5. a rectangle that is 6 in. by 3 in.
18 in.; 18 in.²

6. a square that is 12 mi by 12 mi
48 mi; 144 mi²

2.3 **The scale on a map is 1 cm : 120 km. Find the actual distance, in kilometers, for the given length on the map.**

7. 2 cm 240 km   **8.** 5 cm 600 km   **9.** 7 cm 840 km   **10.** 18 cm 2160 km

2.4 **The following data show the heights, in inches, of flowers in a flower box.**

4, 6, 5, 5, 5, 6, 8, 4, 6, 5, 5, 6, 5 11–12. See margin.

11. Make a frequency table of the data.   **12.** Make a line plot of the data.

2.5 **13.** Make a bar graph of the fish swimming speed data at the right.
See margin.

Fish	Carp	Cod	Mackerel	Pike
Speed (km/h)	6	8	11	6

2.6 **Graph the points on the same coordinate grid.** 14–18. See margin.

14. (0, 0)   **15.** (7, 1)   **16.** (2, 3)   **17.** (5, 4)   **18.** (1, 0)

2.6 **19.** Make a line graph of the running data at the right.
See margin.

Time spent running (seconds)	0	10	20	30	40
Distance from start (meters)	0	25	40	45	45

2.7 **The circle graph shows the number of bagels sold at a bakery in one day.**

20. What type of bagel was most popular?
sesame bagel

21. Suppose 300 bagels were sold at the bakery. Predict how many sesame bagels would be sold.
120 sesame bagels

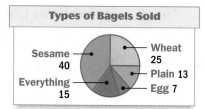

Types of Bagels Sold

Sesame 40
Wheat 25
Plain 13
Egg 7
Everything 15

2.8 **Find the mean, median, mode(s), and range. Then choose the best average(s) to represent a typical data value. Explain your choice.**

22. Number of telephones in students' homes: 3, 2, 3, 4, 1, 2, 4, 2, 3, 2 See margin.

23. Temperatures at 6 A.M. (°F): 22, 25, 30, 31, 34, 40, 49
33, 31, no mode, 27; mean; it is in the middle of all the data.

11.

Heights	Tally	Frequency
4	II	2
5	IIII I	6
6	IIII	4
7		0
8	I	1

12.

× × × × × × ×
4 5 6 7 8
Flower Heights (in.)

13.

Fish Swimming Speed
Speed (km/h)
Carp Cod Mackerel Pike
Fish

14–18.

17
16
15
14 18

19.

Distance From Start
Distance (m)
10 20 30 40
Time (sec)

22. 2.6, 2.5, 2, 3; median; it is in the middle of all of the data.

3. eight thousandths

4. two and nine hundredths

5. one and eleven hundredths

6. twelve and seven hundred
   twenty-one thousandths

7. seven and two hundred
   seventy-five ten-thousandths

Chapter 3

3.1 **Write the number as a decimal.**

1. fifty and forty-two hundredths 50.42   **2.** seventy-two thousandths 0.072

3.1 **Write the decimal in words.** 3–7. See margin.

3. 0.008   **4.** 2.09   **5.** 1.11   **6.** 12.721   **7.** 7.0275

3.2 **8.** Find the length of the word *mathematics* to the nearest tenth
   of a centimeter. 2.2 cm

3.2 **9.** A pencil is 15 centimeters long. Write the length of the pencil to the
   nearest hundredth of a meter. 0.15 meter

3.3 **Copy and complete the statement with <, >, or =.**

10. 5.7 ? 7.5 <   **11.** 13.76 ? 13.81 <   **12.** 6.05 ? 6.50 <

13. 17.98 ? 17.89 >   **14.** 0.03 ? 0.003 >   **15.** 0.84 ? 0.840 =

3.3 **Order the numbers from least to greatest.**

16. 0.90, 0.09, 0.99   **17.** 2.3, 2.12, 2.01   **18.** 4.5, 4.05, 4.55
   0.09, 0.90, 0.99   2.01, 2.12, 2.3   4.05, 4.5, 4.55

3.4 **Round the decimal as specified.**

19. 13.2709 (nearest tenth) 13.3   **20.** 0.090909 (nearest hundredth) 0.09

3.4 **Round the decimal to the place value of the leading digit.**

21. 0.7004 0.7   **22.** 0.06111 0.06   **23.** 0.0089 0.009   **24.** 0.000192 0.0002

3.5 **Use rounding to estimate the sum or difference.**

25. 3.9 − 2.1 2   **26.** 4.7 + 5.2 10   **27.** 6.7 + 12.4 19   **28.** 19.73 − 5.82 14

3.5 **Use front-end estimation to estimate the sum.**

29. 13.89 + 8.72 + 9.45 32   **30.** 6.25 + 8.33 + 9.40 24   **31.** 7.30 + 2.50 + 3.80 14

3.6 **Find the sum or difference.**

32. 3.8 + 9.2 13   **33.** 2.11 + 8.7 10.81   **34.** 13.2 − 4.7 8.5   **35.** 8.24 − 6.1 2.14

3.6 **Evaluate the expression when $x = 0.35$ and $y = 2.19$.**

36. $x + 0.062$ 0.412   **37.** $2.1 + x$ 2.45   **38.** $8.5 − y$ 6.31   **39.** $y − x$ 1.84

3.6 **40.** Tell which property is being illustrated: $1.8 + 6.3 = 6.3 + 1.8$.
   commutative property of addition

Chapter 4

4.1 **Find the product. Use estimation to check your answer.**

1. 4×8.13 32.52   **2.** 27.5×6 165   **3.** 22×5.69 125.18   **4.** 3.897×14 54.558

4.2 **Use the distributive property to find the product.**

5. $6(8.2 + 3)$ 67.2   **6.** $6(20 - 3)$ 102   **7.** $7(29)$ 203   **8.** $8(4.8)$ 38.4

4.3 **Multiply. Use estimation to check that the product is reasonable.**

9. 0.8×2.6 2.08   **10.** 9.2×0.36 3.312   **11.** 4.09×1.23 5.0307   **12.** 0.005×2.1 0.0105

4.4 **Copy the answer and place the decimal point in the correct location.**

13. $35.2 \div 11 = \mathbf{32}$ 3.2   **14.** $492.17 \div 7 = \mathbf{7031}$ 70.31   **15.** $29 \div 8 = \mathbf{3625}$ 3.625

4.4 **Divide. Round to the nearest tenth if necessary.**

16. $9.9 \div 11$ 0.9   **17.** $13.5 \div 9$ 1.5   **18.** $21 \div 8$ 2.6   **19.** $4.2 \div 4$ 1.1

4.5 **Find the product or quotient using mental math.**

20. 16.9×1000 16900   **21.** 2.05×100 205   **22.** 40×0.01 0.4   **23.** 17.98×0.1 1.798
24. $0.008 \div 10$ 0.0008   **25.** $935 \div 1000$ 0.935   **26.** $8.3 \div 0.01$ 830   **27.** $9.38 \div 0.1$ 93.8

4.6 **Divide. Round to the nearest tenth if necessary.**

28. $0.9 \div 0.3$ 3   **29.** $4.2 \div 3.5$ 1.2   **30.** $50 \div 1.5$ 33.3   **31.** $39 \div 7.8$ 5
32. $9.25 \div 0.4$ 23.1   **33.** $9.9 \div 0.03$ 330   **34.** $8.3 \div 0.41$ 20.2   **35.** $6.32 \div 7.4$ 0.9

4.7 **Choose an appropriate metric unit to measure the item.**

36. mass of a marble   milligrams   **37.** mass of a cat   kilograms

38. capacity of a soup spoon   milliliters   **39.** capacity of a water tank   kiloliters

40. mass of a facial tissue   milligrams   **41.** capacity of a large can of paint   liters

4.8 **Copy and complete the statement.**

42. $188 \text{ mg} = \underline{\ ?\ } \text{ g}$ 0.188   **43.** $480 \text{ L} = \underline{\ ?\ } \text{ mL}$ 480,000   **44.** $3.8 \text{ km} = \underline{\ ?\ } \text{ m}$ 3800
45. $67.4 \text{ kg} = \underline{\ ?\ } \text{ g}$ 67,400   **46.** $25 \text{ mL} = \underline{\ ?\ } \text{ L}$ 0.025   **47.** $100 \text{ cm} = \underline{\ ?\ } \text{ mm}$ 1000

4.8 **Copy and complete the statement with <, >, or =.**

48. $212 \text{ m} \underline{\ ?\ } 0.1 \text{ km}$ >   **49.** $4.9 \text{ mm} \underline{\ ?\ } 5 \text{ cm}$ <   **50.** $0.025 \text{ L} \underline{\ ?\ } 249 \text{ mL}$ <
51. $1.6 \text{ kL} \underline{\ ?\ } 160,000 \text{ mL}$ >   **52.** $980 \text{ g} \underline{\ ?\ } 0.98 \text{ kg}$ =   **53.** $3800 \text{ mg} \underline{\ ?\ } 4.9 \text{ g}$ <

1. 406 is divisible by 2, but not by 3, 4, 6, 9, or 10.

2. 721 is not divisible by 2, 3, 5, 6, 9, or 10.

3. 534 is divisible by 2, 3, and 6, but not by 5, 9, or 10.

4. 1557 is divisible by 3 and 9, but not by 2, 5, 6, or 10.

5. 510 is divisible by 2, 3, 5, 6, and 10, but not by 9.

Extra Practice

Chapter 5

5.1 **Test the number for divisibility by 2, 3, 5, 6, 9, and 10.** 1–5. See margin.

1. 406   **2.** 721   **3.** 534   **4.** 1557   **5.** 510

5.1 **Tell whether the number is *prime*, *composite*, or *neither*.**

6. 13 prime   **7.** 8 composite   **8.** 25 composite   **9.** 1 neither   **10.** 71 prime

5.1 **Write the prime factorization of the number.**

11. 95 5×19 **12.** 330   **13.** 76 $2^2 \times 19$ **14.** 400 $2^4 \times 5^2$ **15.** 175 $5^2 \times 7$

$2 \times 3 \times 5 \times 11$

5.2 **Find the GCF of the numbers.**

16. 15, 21 3   **17.** 8, 20 4   **18.** 16, 24 8   **19.** 25, 50, 70 5

5.3 **Write two fractions that are equivalent to the given fraction.** 20–24. Sample answers are given.

20. $\frac{1}{4}$ $\frac{2}{8}, \frac{3}{12}$ **21.** $\frac{2}{5}$ $\frac{4}{10}, \frac{6}{15}$ **22.** $\frac{5}{6}$ $\frac{10}{12}, \frac{15}{18}$ **23.** $\frac{3}{10}$ $\frac{6}{20}, \frac{9}{30}$ **24.** $\frac{4}{7}$ $\frac{8}{14}, \frac{12}{21}$

5.3 **Tell whether the fraction is in simplest form. If not, simplify it.**

25. $\frac{5}{9}$ yes   **26.** $\frac{18}{27}$ no; $\frac{2}{3}$ **27.** $\frac{3}{42}$ no; $\frac{1}{14}$ **28.** $\frac{17}{20}$ yes   **29.** $\frac{12}{15}$ no; $\frac{4}{5}$

5.4 **Find the LCM of the numbers.**

30. 3, 9 9   **31.** 8, 12 24   **32.** 20, 30 60   **33.** 4, 8, 10 40

5.5 **Order the fractions from least to greatest.** $\frac{5}{9}, \frac{7}{12}, \frac{11}{18}, \frac{2}{3}$ $\frac{3}{20}, \frac{2}{9}, \frac{4}{15}, \frac{2}{5}$

34. $\frac{1}{2}, \frac{2}{5}, \frac{3}{8}$ $\frac{3}{8}, \frac{2}{5}, \frac{1}{2}$ **35.** $\frac{13}{15}, \frac{9}{10}, \frac{4}{5}$ $\frac{4}{5}, \frac{13}{15}, \frac{9}{10}$ **36.** $\frac{7}{12}, \frac{2}{3}, \frac{5}{9}, \frac{11}{18}$ **37.** $\frac{2}{5}, \frac{4}{15}, \frac{3}{20}, \frac{2}{9}$

5.6 **Rewrite the number as an improper fraction or mixed number.**

38. $1\frac{3}{4}$ $\frac{7}{4}$ **39.** $3\frac{8}{9}$ $\frac{35}{9}$ **40.** $5\frac{3}{10}$ $\frac{53}{10}$ **41.** $2\frac{3}{7}$ $\frac{17}{7}$ **42.** $1\frac{6}{11}$ $\frac{17}{11}$

43. $\frac{13}{6}$ $2\frac{1}{6}$ **44.** $\frac{21}{4}$ $5\frac{1}{4}$ **45.** $\frac{17}{5}$ $3\frac{2}{5}$ **46.** $\frac{20}{3}$ $6\frac{2}{3}$ **47.** $\frac{19}{12}$ $1\frac{7}{12}$

5.6 **Order the numbers from least to greatest.** $\frac{17}{8}, 2\frac{1}{4}, \frac{55}{24}, 2\frac{1}{3}$

48. $2\frac{1}{2}, \frac{19}{16}, \frac{35}{12}$ $\frac{19}{16}, 2\frac{1}{2}, \frac{35}{12}$ **49.** $2\frac{1}{4}, \frac{17}{8}, 2\frac{1}{3}, \frac{55}{24}$ **50.** $\frac{13}{8}, 1\frac{2}{5}, \frac{7}{4}, 2$ $1\frac{2}{5}, \frac{13}{8}, \frac{7}{4}, 2$

5.7 **Write the decimal as a fraction or mixed number in simplest form.**

51. 0.95 $\frac{19}{20}$ **52.** 3.8 $3\frac{4}{5}$ **53.** 2.08 $2\frac{2}{25}$ **54.** 6.09 $6\frac{9}{100}$ **55.** 0.645 $\frac{129}{200}$

5.8 **Write the fraction or mixed number as a decimal.**

56. $\frac{5}{8}$ 0.625   **57.** $\frac{7}{4}$ 1.75   **58.** $\frac{8}{15}$ $0.5\overline{3}$ **59.** $5\frac{1}{6}$ $5.1\overline{6}$ **60.** $\frac{57}{40}$ 1.425

Chapter 6

6.1 **Estimate the sum or difference.**

1. $\dfrac{15}{16} - \dfrac{5}{8}$ $\dfrac{1}{2}$

2. $\dfrac{1}{8} + \dfrac{5}{6}$ 1

3. $\dfrac{7}{12} - \dfrac{8}{15}$ 0

4. $\dfrac{5}{12} + \dfrac{3}{5}$ 1

5. $7\dfrac{1}{8} - 2\dfrac{5}{6}$ 4

6. $1\dfrac{2}{3} + 2\dfrac{7}{9}$ 5

7. $5\dfrac{8}{15} + 3\dfrac{5}{12}$ 9

8. $6\dfrac{2}{9} - 1\dfrac{6}{7}$ 4

Find the sum or difference.

6.2

9. $\dfrac{5}{8} + \dfrac{1}{8}$ $\dfrac{3}{4}$

10. $\dfrac{7}{12} + \dfrac{5}{12}$ 1

11. $\dfrac{8}{15} - \dfrac{4}{15}$ $\dfrac{4}{15}$

12. $\dfrac{5}{9} - \dfrac{4}{9}$ $\dfrac{1}{9}$

13. $\dfrac{17}{20} - \dfrac{9}{20}$ $\dfrac{2}{5}$

14. $\dfrac{2}{11} + \dfrac{7}{11}$ $\dfrac{9}{11}$

15. $\dfrac{7}{10} - \dfrac{3}{10}$ $\dfrac{2}{5}$

16. $\dfrac{5}{14} + \dfrac{3}{14}$ $\dfrac{4}{7}$

6.3

17. $\dfrac{5}{9} - \dfrac{1}{6}$ $\dfrac{7}{18}$

18. $\dfrac{2}{3} - \dfrac{1}{2}$ $\dfrac{1}{6}$

19. $\dfrac{11}{16} + \dfrac{1}{4}$ $\dfrac{15}{16}$

20. $\dfrac{2}{7} + \dfrac{2}{3}$ $\dfrac{20}{21}$

21. $\dfrac{11}{15} - \dfrac{1}{10}$ $\dfrac{19}{30}$

22. $\dfrac{6}{13} + \dfrac{1}{3}$ $\dfrac{31}{39}$

23. $\dfrac{7}{20} + \dfrac{3}{5}$ $\dfrac{19}{20}$

24. $\dfrac{9}{16} - \dfrac{1}{8}$ $\dfrac{7}{16}$

6.4

25. $6\dfrac{5}{6} - 4\dfrac{1}{6}$ $2\dfrac{2}{3}$

26. $2\dfrac{5}{12} + 4\dfrac{2}{3}$ $7\dfrac{1}{12}$

27. $3\dfrac{1}{2} + 12\dfrac{3}{4}$ $16\dfrac{1}{4}$

28. $9\dfrac{2}{3} - 1\dfrac{3}{8}$ $8\dfrac{7}{24}$

29. $1\dfrac{5}{14} + 6\dfrac{3}{14}$ $7\dfrac{4}{7}$

30. $12\dfrac{1}{2} - 3\dfrac{1}{5}$ $9\dfrac{3}{10}$

31. $3\dfrac{7}{8} - 3\dfrac{3}{4}$ $\dfrac{1}{8}$

32. $2\dfrac{5}{9} + 4\dfrac{1}{6}$ $6\dfrac{13}{18}$

6.5

33. $3\dfrac{2}{13} - 1\dfrac{9}{13}$ $1\dfrac{6}{13}$

34. $8\dfrac{3}{4} - 6\dfrac{4}{5}$ $1\dfrac{19}{20}$

35. $2\dfrac{3}{8} - \dfrac{5}{8}$ $1\dfrac{3}{4}$

36. $4 - 2\dfrac{3}{4}$ $1\dfrac{1}{4}$

37. $4\dfrac{1}{10} - 3\dfrac{1}{2}$ $\dfrac{3}{5}$

38. $4\dfrac{1}{6} - 1\dfrac{2}{3}$ $2\dfrac{1}{2}$

39. $9 - 6\dfrac{4}{5}$ $2\dfrac{1}{5}$

40. $5\dfrac{2}{3} - 4\dfrac{3}{4}$ $\dfrac{11}{12}$

6.6 **Add or subtract the measures of time.**

41.
```
  6 h 15 min
− 2 h 40 min
  3 h 35 min
```

42.
```
      45 min
+ 4 h 25 min
  5 h 10 min
```

43.
```
1 h 24 min 38 sec
+    56 min 12 sec
2 h 20 min 50 sec
```

44.
```
  4 h 17 min
−      38 min
  3 h 39 min
```

45.
```
  5 h 28 min
+ 1 h 47 min
  7 h 15 min
```

46.
```
  3 h  4 min 12 sec
+ 2 h 17 min 35 sec
  5 h 21 min 47 sec
```

6.6 **Find the elapsed time.**

47. 6:00 A.M. to 8:30 A.M.
2 h 30 min

48. 9:00 A.M. to 3:15 P.M.
6 h 15 min

49. 6:30 P.M. to 12:15 A.M.
5 h 45 min

50. 7:30 A.M. to 9:10 P.M.
13 h 40 min

51. 3:40 P.M. to 5:15 P.M.
1 h 35 min

52. 11:40 P.M. to 2:30 A.M.
2 h 50 min

6.6

53. You went on a hike with a group of friends from 8:15 A.M. to 4:30 P.M. How long were you hiking?   8 h 15 min

Chapter 7

7.1 **Use compatible numbers to estimate the product.**

1. $25 \times \frac{3}{8}$ 9

2. $10 \times \frac{1}{3}$ 3

3. $\frac{9}{10} \times 32$ 27

4. $\frac{5}{7} \times 34$ 25

Find the product.

7.1 **5.** $8 \times \frac{3}{4}$ 6

6. $6 \times \frac{5}{8}$ $3\frac{3}{4}$

7. $\frac{4}{7} \times 28$ 16

8. $\frac{2}{3} \times 7$ $4\frac{2}{3}$

7.2 **9.** $\frac{5}{3} \times \frac{3}{4}$ $1\frac{1}{4}$

10. $\frac{7}{12} \times \frac{8}{9}$ $\frac{14}{27}$

11. $\frac{1}{3} \times \frac{2}{9}$ $\frac{2}{27}$

12. $\frac{4}{9} \times \frac{3}{8} \times \frac{2}{3}$ $\frac{1}{9}$

7.3 **13.** $4 \times 1\frac{5}{6}$ $7\frac{1}{3}$

14. $\frac{2}{5} \times 3\frac{2}{5}$ $1\frac{9}{25}$

15. $1\frac{3}{4} \times \frac{2}{3}$ $1\frac{1}{6}$

16. $2\frac{1}{4} \times 1\frac{1}{3}$ 3

Find the quotient.

7.4 **17.** $\frac{5}{6} \div 4$ $\frac{5}{24}$

18. $1 \div \frac{5}{12}$ $2\frac{2}{5}$

19. $\frac{1}{5} \div \frac{5}{4}$ $\frac{4}{25}$

20. $\frac{2}{3} \div \frac{1}{9}$ 6

7.5 **21.** $2\frac{1}{4} \div \frac{3}{4}$ 3

22. $\frac{7}{8} \div 1\frac{1}{2}$ $\frac{7}{12}$

23. $1\frac{4}{5} \div 4$ $\frac{9}{20}$

24. $12 \div 1\frac{1}{2}$ 8

25. $3\frac{1}{2} \div 1\frac{1}{5}$ $2\frac{11}{12}$

26. $5\frac{2}{5} \div 1\frac{1}{8}$ $4\frac{4}{5}$

27. $6 \div 2\frac{2}{5}$ $2\frac{1}{2}$

28. $3\frac{3}{4} \div 6\frac{1}{2}$ $\frac{15}{26}$

7.5 **Solve the problem. Explain why you chose the operation you used.**

29. You buy 10 yards of fabric to make some costumes. If each costume needs $3\frac{5}{8}$ yards of fabric, do you have enough fabric to make 3 costumes?
No. *Sample answer:* Use multiplication to find the total amount of fabric needed.

30. Amy is $1\frac{1}{3}$ feet taller than Frank. Frank is $4\frac{1}{4}$ feet tall. How tall is Amy?
$5\frac{7}{12}$ ft. *Sample answer:* Use addition to find her height.

7.6 **Copy and complete the statement using an appropriate customary unit.**

31. weight of a horse = 850 __?__
pounds

32. capacity of a washing machine = 19 __?__
gallons

33. weight of a jar of jam = 10 __?__
ounces

34. capacity of a can of soup = 12 __?__
fluid ounces

7.7 **Copy and complete the statement.**

35. 3 gal 2 qt = __?__ qt 14

36. 2 yd 6 in. = __?__ in. 78

37. 25 oz = __?__ lb __?__ oz, or __?__ lb
1; 9; $1\frac{9}{16}$

7.7 **Change the measurement to the specified unit.**

38. $3\frac{1}{4}$ cups to fluid ounces
26 fl oz

39. $1\frac{1}{8}$ tons to pounds
2250 lb

40. 9 pints to gallons
$1\frac{1}{8}$ gal

7.7 **Find the sum or difference.**

41. 3 lb 6 oz + 2 lb 10 oz
6 lb

42. 3 ft 5 in. − 1 ft 9 in.
1 ft 8 in.

43. 1 yd 2 ft + 2 yd 2 ft
4 yd 1 ft

Chapter 8

8.1 **Write the ratio in simplest form.**

1. $12 : 18$ $2 : 3$ **2.** 6 to 3 2 to 1 **3.** $2 : 10$ $1 : 5$ **4.** 5 to 20 1 to 4 **5.** $16 : 12$ $4 : 3$

Copy and complete the statement.

8.1 **6.** $\frac{3}{8} = \frac{9}{?}$ 24 **7.** $\frac{10}{?} = \frac{1}{2}$ 20 **8.** $\frac{?}{12} = \frac{7}{6}$ 14 **9.** $\frac{3}{5} = \frac{?}{15}$ 9

8.2 **10.** $\frac{\$5}{2 \text{ items}} = \frac{?}{12 \text{ items}}$ \$30 **11.** $\frac{38 \text{ cm}}{30 \text{ min}} = \frac{?}{15 \text{ min}}$ 19 cm **12.** $\frac{?}{3 \text{ classes}} = \frac{25 \text{ students}}{1 \text{ class}}$ 75 students

8.2 **Write the unit rate.**

13. $\frac{2750 \text{ visitors}}{10 \text{ hours}}$ $\frac{275 \text{ visitors}}{1 \text{ hour}}$ **14.** $\frac{90 \text{ meters}}{18 \text{ seconds}}$ $\frac{5 \text{ meters}}{1 \text{ second}}$ **15.** $\frac{5000 \text{ words}}{25 \text{ pages}}$ $\frac{200 \text{ words}}{1 \text{ page}}$ **16.** $\frac{40,000 \text{ bits}}{5 \text{ minutes}}$ $\frac{8000 \text{ bits}}{1 \text{ minute}}$

8.3 **Solve the proportion.**

17. $\frac{81}{6} = \frac{27}{r}$ 2 **18.** $\frac{16}{x} = \frac{40}{25}$ 10 **19.** $\frac{8}{20} = \frac{b}{28}$ 28 **20.** $\frac{a}{51} = \frac{10}{15}$ 34

8.4 **A scale drawing of a room has a scale of 1 in. : 8 ft. In the drawing, the floor of the room is 2.5 inches long by 2 inches wide.**

21. What are the actual dimensions of the floor of the room? 20 ft by 16 ft

22. What is the ratio of the floor area of the room in the drawing to the floor area of the actual room? 1 : 64

8.5 **Write the percent as a decimal and a fraction.**

23. 18% 0.18, $\frac{9}{50}$ **24.** 69% 0.69, $\frac{69}{100}$ **25.** 2.5% 0.025, $\frac{1}{40}$ **26.** 45% 0.45, $\frac{9}{20}$

8.6 **Write the fraction or decimal as a percent.**

27. $\frac{17}{20}$ 85% **28.** $\frac{3}{8}$ 37.5% **29.** 0.83 83% **30.** 0.9 90% **31.** 0.005 0.5%

8.6 **Order the numbers from least to greatest.**

32. $0.24, \frac{7}{25}, \frac{1}{4}, 23\%$ **33.** $67\%, \frac{5}{6}, 0.76, \frac{2}{3}$ **34.** $0.2, \frac{3}{20}, 14\%, 0.018$
23%, 0.24, $\frac{1}{4}$, $\frac{7}{25}$ $\frac{2}{3}$, 67%, 0.76, $\frac{5}{6}$ 0.018, 14%, $\frac{3}{20}$, 0.2

8.7 **Find the percent of the number.**

35. 20% of 90 18 **36.** 8% of 4 0.32 **37.** 16% of 350 56 **38.** $33\frac{1}{3}\%$ of 150 50

8.7 **39.** A bank account pays 4% annual interest. How much simple interest will \$2000 earn in 6 years? \$480

8.7 **40.** You want to buy a sweater that costs \$18.50. The sales tax is 5%. You realize that you have only \$20 with you. Can you buy the sweater? yes

1. Sample answer: $\vec{BC}$ and $\vec{BF}$; $\overline{BD}$ and $\overline{BA}$

6.

19. $\overline{XY}$ and $\overline{DE}$, $\overline{YZ}$ and $\overline{EF}$, $\overline{ZX}$ and $\overline{FD}$; $\angle X$ and $\angle D$, $\angle Y$ and $\angle E$, $\angle Z$ and $\angle F$

21.

23.

24.

Chapter 9

Use the diagram at the right.

9.1   **1.** Name two rays and two segments with endpoint B. **See margin.**

2. Name two parallel lines. $\overleftrightarrow{EA}$ and $\overleftrightarrow{DB}$

3. Name two lines that intersect at D. $\overleftrightarrow{ED}$ and $\overleftrightarrow{DF}$

9.2   **4.** Name three angles with vertex B. **Sample answer:** $\angle DBC$, $\angle FBA$, $\angle FBC$

5. Name an angle in the diagram whose measure is 50°. $\angle AED$

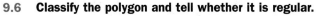

9.2   **6.** Use a protractor to draw an angle that has a measure of 108°. **See margin.**

Use the diagram at the right.

9.3   **7.** Classify each angle as *acute, right, obtuse,* or *straight:* $\angle RQS$, $\angle QSU$, $\angle QSR$, $\angle QST$. **right; obtuse; acute; straight**

8. Find the measures of $\angle TSU$, $\angle VQS$, and $\angle RST$. **30°; 70°; 150°**

9.4   **9.** Find the measures of $\angle QRS$, $\angle QVR$, and $\angle QVS$. **60°; 100°; 80°**

10. Classify each triangle by its angles as *acute, right,* or *obtuse:* $\triangle STU$, $\triangle SVQ$, $\triangle QRV$, $\triangle QRS$. **obtuse; acute; obtuse; right**

9.5   **Copy and complete the statement using *All, Some,* or *No.***

11. ? squares are parallelograms. **All**

12. ? rhombuses are squares. **Some**

13. ? rectangles are rhombuses. **No**

14. ? quadrilaterals have four right angles. **Some**

9.6   **Classify the polygon and tell whether it is regular.**

15.
triangle; no

16.
pentagon; yes

17.
hexagon; no

18.
rhombus; no

9.7   **$\triangle XYZ$ and $\triangle DEF$ are congruent.**

19. List the corresponding parts. **See margin.**

20. How long is $\overline{EF}$? Explain. **28 ft; it is the same length as $\overline{YZ}$.**

9.8   **Tell whether the figure has line symmetry. If so, copy the figure and draw all lines of symmetry.**

21.
Yes; see margin.

22.
no

23.
Yes; see margin.

24.
Yes; see margin.

Chapter 10

10.1 Find the unknown measure of the parallelogram described.

1. base = 12 ft, height = 30 ft, Area = ?
360 ft²

2. base = 5 m, Area = 20 m², height = ?
4 m

10.2 Find the area of the triangle.

3. 13.5 mm² 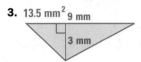 9 mm
3 mm

4. 12 m²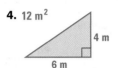
4 m
6 m

5. 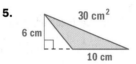 30 cm²
6 cm
10 cm

10.3 Find the circumference of the circle described. Tell what value you used for π. Explain your choice. 6–9. See margin.

6. r = 80 m **7.** d = 35 cm **8.** d = 9 mm **9.** r = 7 in.

10.4 Find the area of the circle described. Round to the nearest tenth of a unit.

10. r = 42 m
5539.0 m²

11. d = 8 cm
50.2 cm²

12. d = 200 mm
31,400 mm²

13. r = 15 ft
706.5 ft²

10.4 Find the area of the figure to the nearest whole unit.

14. 6 mi
8 mi
38 mi²

15. 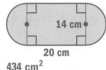 14 cm
20 cm
434 cm²

16.
4 ft
4 ft
29 ft²

10.4 17. The table shows how many of the 40 volunteers will be assigned to each of the three types of jobs. Make a circle graph of the data.
See margin.

Spring Fundraiser Volunteers			
Job	tickets	snacks	booths
Number of volunteers	8	6	26

10.5 Draw the solid described. 18–19. See margin.

18. cone

19. pyramid with a rectangular base

10.5 20. Count the number of faces, edges, and vertices of the solid you drew in Exercise 19. 5 faces, 8 edges, 5 vertices

10.6 Draw a diagram of the rectangular prism described. Then find the surface area. 21–22. See margin for art.

21. 5 cm by 5 cm by 3 cm 110 cm²

22. 6 in. by 4 in. by 10 in. 248 in.²

10.7 23. Find the volumes of the prisms described in Exercises 21 and 22. 75 cm³; 240 in.³

6. 502.4 m; 3.14; 80 is not a multiple of 7.

7. 110 cm; $\frac{22}{7}$; 35 is a multiple of 7.

8. 28.26 mm; 3.14; 9 is not a multiple of 7.

9. 44 in.; $\frac{22}{7}$; 7 is a multiple of 7.

17. Spring Fundraiser Volunteers

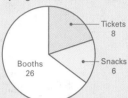
Tickets 8
Snacks 6
Booths 26

18.

19.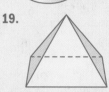

21.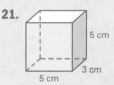
5 cm
3 cm
5 cm

22.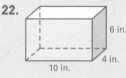
6 in.
4 in.
10 in.

42.

43.

44.

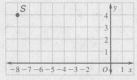

45.

46.

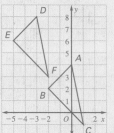

47.

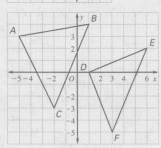

48.

Chapter 11

11.1   **1.** Find the opposites of the integers 4, −18, and 0.   −4, 18, 0

11.1   **Copy and complete the statement using < or >.**

    2. −4 _?_ 0   <   **3.** 2 _?_ −5   >   **4.** −10 _?_ −11   >   **5.** −8 _?_ 13   <

11.1   **Order the integers from least to greatest.**

    6. 3, −4, 7, 2, −1   **7.** 0, 2, −3, 5, 3   **8.** −5, 6, −1, −4, −3   **9.** −7, 9, −9, 8, −6
      −4, −1, 2, 3, 7   −3, 0, 2, 3, 5   −5, −4, −3, −1, 6   −9, −7, −6, 8, 9

Find the sum or difference.

11.2   **10.** 8 + (−22)   −14   **11.** −6 + 10   4   **12.** 6 + (−12)   −6   **13.** −5 + (−5)   −10

    14. 2 + (−15)   −13   **15.** −14 + 14   0   **16.** −20 + 16   −4   **17.** −9 + (−5)   −14

11.3   **18.** 2 − 7   −5   **19.** 13 − (−3)   16   **20.** −7 − 9   −16   **21.** −24 − (−7)   −17

    22. 16 − (−17)   33   **23.** −10 − 18   −28   **24.** −9 − (−11)   2   **25.** 8 − 17   −9

Find the product or quotient.

11.4   **26.** 13(4)   52   **27.** −8(5)   −40   **28.** −6(10)   −60   **29.** −7(−20)   140

    30. 0(−12)   0   **31.** −4(−8)   32   **32.** 14(−5)   −70   **33.** −11(−9)   99

11.5   **34.** −9 ÷ (−1)   9   **35.** −200 ÷ 25   −8   **36.** 42 ÷ (−6)   −7   **37.** −70 ÷ (−14)   5

    38. 110 ÷ (−5)   −22   **39.** −45 ÷ 15   −3   **40.** −51 ÷ (−17)   3   **41.** 300 ÷ (−12)   −25

11.6   **Graph the point and describe its location.**   42–46. See margin for art.

    42. $P(3, -7)$ **43.** $Q(4, 4)$ **44.** $R(-2, -6)$ **45.** $S(-8, 4)$ **46.** $T(-5, 0)$
        Quadrant IV   Quadrant I   Quadrant III   Quadrant II   x-axis

11.6   **Draw the figure on a coordinate plane. Then translate the figure as described. Give the coordinates of the vertices of the image.**   47–48. See margin for art.

    47. $\triangle ABC$: $A(0, 4)$, $B(-2, 2)$, $C(1, -1)$ **48.** $\triangle ABC$: $A(-5, 3)$, $B(1, 4)$, $C(-2, -3)$

        Translation: 3 units to the left and   Translation: 5 units to the right and
        4 units up to form $\triangle DEF$ 2 units down to form $\triangle DEF$
        $D(-3, 8)$, $E(-5, 6)$, $F(-2, 3)$ $D(0, 1)$, $E(6, 2)$, $F(3, -5)$

11.7   **Tell whether the transformation is a _translation_, a _reflection_, or a _rotation_.**

    49. reflection   **50.** rotation   **51.** translation   **52.** reflection

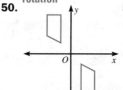
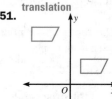
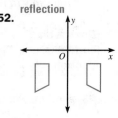

Chapter 12

12.1 **Write the phrase as an expression. Let *n* represent the number.**

1. A number increased by 7 $n + 7$

2. 30 multiplied by a number $30n$

3. A number subtracted from 20 $20 - n$

4. The quotient of a number and 50 $\frac{n}{50}$

12.1 **Write the sentence as an equation.**

5. The product of 8 and a number *n* is 32. $8n = 32$

6. The sum of 7 and a number *x* is 19. $7 + x = 19$

7. A number *y* divided by 6 is 5. $\frac{y}{6} = 5$

8. 15 less than a number *k* is 6. $k - 15 = 6$

Solve the equation.

12.2 **9.** $9 + p = 38$ 29

10. $x + 17 = 50$ 33

11. $16 + z = 30$ 14

12. $q + 2.8 = 4.7$ 1.9

12.3 **13.** $8 = z - 8$ 16

14. $x - 31 = 41$ 72

15. $1 = n - 24$ 25

16. $w - 4.8 = 2.5$ 7.3

12.4 **17.** $30 = 3n$ 10

18. $20c = 100$ 5

19. $8n = 72$ 9

20. $68 = 4x$ 17

21. $\frac{x}{12} = 5$ 60

22. $10 = \frac{b}{8}$ 80

23. $\frac{x}{7} = 3$ 21

24. $\frac{n}{5} = 13$ 65

12.5 **Make an input-output table using the function rule and the input values *x* = 4, 8, 12, 16, and 20.** 25–28. See margin.

25. $y = x - 3$

26. $y = 5x$

27. $y = 2x + 5$

28. $y = \frac{x}{4}$

12.5 **29.** Write a function rule for the input-output table. $c = 6p$

Price of each item, *p*	$10	$20	$30	$40	$50
Total cost of items, *c*	$60	$120	$180	$240	$300

12.5 **Make an input-output table. Then write a function rule for the relationship.** 30–31. See margin.

30. input: dollars
output: cents

31. input: quarts
output: gallons

12.6 **Make an input-output table using the function rule and the input values *x* = 0, 1, 2, 3, and 4. Graph the function.** 32–35. See margin.

32. $y = 10 - x$

33. $y = x - 2$

34. $y = 2x + 1$

35. $y = \frac{1}{2}x + 3$

12.6 **Graph the ordered pairs and draw a line through the points. Write a function rule for the ordered pairs.** 36–37. See margin.

36. $(-2, 1), (-1, 2), (0, 3), (1, 4), (2, 5)$

37. $(-6, -2), (-3, -1), (0, 0), (3, 1), (6, 2)$

Extra Practice

25.

Input, *x*	Output, *y*
4	1
8	5
12	9
16	13
20	17

26.

Input, *x*	Output, *y*
4	20
8	40
12	60
16	80
20	100

27.

Input, *x*	Output, *y*
4	13
8	21
12	29
16	37
20	45

28.

Input, *x*	Output, *y*
4	1
8	2
12	3
16	4
20	5

30. *Sample answer:* $c = 100d$

Dollars, *d*	Cents, *c*
1	100
2	200
3	300
4	400
5	500

31. *Sample answer:* $g = \frac{q}{4}$

Quarts, *q*	Gallons, *g*
2	$\frac{1}{2}$
4	1
6	$1\frac{1}{2}$
8	2

32–37. See Additional Answers beginning on page AA1.

720

6. white cover with black printing, white cover with blue printing, red cover with black printing, red cover with blue printing, gold cover with black printing, gold cover with blue printing

11.
```
0 | 4 6 7 7 8 8 8 9
1 | 1 2 5 6 8 9
2 | 0 0 1 4 4 9
```
   Key: 1 | 5 = 15

12. 14.3, 13.5, 8

13. 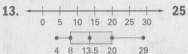 25

Chapter 13

13.1 **A box contains seven tiles numbered 1 through 7. You randomly choose a tile. Find the probability of the event.**

1. You choose an odd number. $\frac{4}{7}$ 2. You choose a multiple of 3. $\frac{2}{7}$

3. You choose a number less than 10. 1   4. You choose the number 18. 0

13.1 5. Describe the complement of the event in Exercise 2. Then find its probability. **You do not choose a multiple of 3;** $\frac{5}{7}$.

13.2 6. The cover of a yearbook can be white, red, or gold. The printing on the cover can be black or blue. Use a tree diagram to find all the possible covers. **See margin.**

13.2 7. An electronic lock has four buttons, labeled 1, 2, 3, and 4. List all possible two-digit numbers that can be formed using these four buttons. Include repeated digits, such as 11. **11, 12, 13, 14, 21, 22, 23, 24, 31, 32, 33, 34, 41, 42, 43, 44**

13.3 **You toss a coin and then you roll a number cube. Find the probability of the event.**

8. You get tails and then roll a 2. $\frac{1}{12}$ 9. You get heads and then roll an even number. $\frac{1}{4}$

13.4 10. A family, using the data below, claims that the average water bill on their street is $147. Does $147 describe the average water bill well? Why or why not? **No; all but one of the bills is less than $147.**

$98, $105, $105, $106, $110, $118, $125, $125, $130, $448

In Exercises 11–13, use the list of data below. The data show the number of students using the library's study room each day. 11–13. See margin.

9, 4, 8, 11, 24, 8, 20, 15, 29, 7, 6, 7, 8, 16, 20, 19, 24, 21, 12, 18

13.5 11. Make a stem-and-leaf plot of the data.   12. Find the mean, median, and mode(s).

13.6 13. Make a box-and-whisker plot of the data. Find the range.

13.7 **Choose an appropriate data display for the given situation. Explain your choice.**

14. Each student in a math class gives the number of pets in his or her family. You want to find the most common number of pets. **Bar graph; it shows how different categories compare.**

15. You have data on the average rainfall in your town each year for the past 50 years and want to see how the average has changed over time. **Line graph; it shows change over time.**

16. You want to compare the number of votes each candidate for class president received to the total number of votes cast. **Circle graph; it shows data as part of a whole.**

Table of Symbols

Symbol	Meaning	Page
+	plus	5
=	equals, is equal to	5, 36
−	minus	6
×	times	6
÷	divided by	6
R	remainder	6
≈	is about equal to	13
4^3	4 to the 3rd power	17
( )	parentheses—a grouping symbol	21
$\frac{14}{2}$	14 divided by 2	22
$3 \cdot x$ $3(x)$ $3x$	3 times x	30
$\stackrel{?}{=}$	is equal to?	36
≠	is not equal to	36
(4, 3)	ordered pair of numbers	83
28.6	decimal point	108
<	is less than	118, 602
>	is greater than	118, 602
...	continues on	235
$1.1\overline{6}$	repeating decimal 1.16666...	254
$a : b, \frac{a}{b}$	ratio of a to b	374

Symbol	Meaning	Page
%	percent	395
$\overleftrightarrow{AB}$	line AB	421
$\overrightarrow{AB}$	ray AB	421
$\overline{AB}$	segment AB	421
⇉	parallel lines	422
$\angle PQR$	angle PQR	425
°	degree(s)	426
$m\angle B$	measure of angle B	426
⌐	right angle	430
$\triangle ABC$	triangle with vertices A, B, and C	436
π	pi—a number approximately equal to 3.14	485
−3	negative 3	533
−3	the opposite of 3	534
$|a|$	the absolute value of a number a	539
≤	is less than or equal to	602
≥	is greater than or equal to	602

Table of Measures

Time

60 seconds (sec) = 1 minute (min)
60 minutes = 1 hour (h)
24 hours = 1 day
7 days = 1 week
4 weeks (approx.) = 1 month

$\left.\begin{array}{c}\text{365 days} \\ \text{52 weeks (approx.)} \\ \text{12 months}\end{array}\right\}$ = 1 year

10 years = 1 decade
100 years = 1 century

METRIC

Length

10 millimeters (mm) = 1 centimeter (cm)
$\left.\begin{array}{c}\text{100 cm} \\ \text{1000 mm}\end{array}\right\}$ = 1 meter (m)
1000 m = 1 kilometer (km)

Area

100 square millimeters = 1 square centimeter
(mm^2) $\qquad$ (cm^2)
10,000 cm^2 = 1 square meter (m^2)
10,000 m^2 = 1 hectare (ha)

Volume

1000 cubic millimeters = 1 cubic centimeter
(mm^3) $\qquad$ (cm^3)
1,000,000 cm^3 = 1 cubic meter (m^3)

Liquid Capacity

$\left.\begin{array}{l}\text{1000 milliliters (mL)} \\ \text{1000 cubic centimeters (cm}^3)\end{array}\right\}$ = 1 liter (L)
1000 L = 1 kiloliter (kL)

Mass

1000 milligrams (mg) = 1 gram (g)
1000 g = 1 kilogram (kg)
1000 kg = 1 metric ton (t)

Temperature   Degrees Celsius (°C)

0°C = freezing point of water
37°C = normal body temperature
100°C = boiling point of water

UNITED STATES CUSTOMARY

Length

12 inches (in.) = 1 foot (ft)
$\left.\begin{array}{c}\text{36 in.} \\ \text{3 ft}\end{array}\right\}$ = 1 yard (yd)
$\left.\begin{array}{c}\text{5280 ft} \\ \text{1760 yd}\end{array}\right\}$ = 1 mile (mi)

Area

144 square inches $(in.^2)$ = 1 square foot (ft^2)
9 ft^2 = 1 square yard (yd^2)
$\left.\begin{array}{c}\text{43,560 ft}^2 \\ \text{4840 yd}^2\end{array}\right\}$ = 1 acre (A)

Volume

1728 cubic inches $(in.^3)$ = 1 cubic foot (ft^3)
27 ft^3 = 1 cubic yard (yd^3)

Liquid Capacity

8 fluid ounces (fl oz) = 1 cup (c)
2 c = 1 pint (pt)
2 pt = 1 quart (qt)
4 qt = 1 gallon (gal)

Weight

16 ounces (oz) = 1 pound (lb)
2000 lb = 1 ton

Temperature   Degrees Fahrenheit (°F)

32°F = freezing point of water
98.6°F = normal body temperature
212°F = boiling point of water

Table of Measures

Table of Formulas

Geometric Formulas

Rectangle

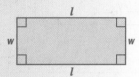

Area (p. 62)
A = length · width
$A = lw$

Perimeter (p. 61)
$P = 2$ · length + 2 · width
$P = 2l + 2w$

Square

Area (p. 62)
A = (side length)^2
$A = s^2$

Perimeter (p. 62)
$P = 4$ · side length
$P = 4s$

Parallelogram

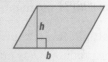

Area (p. 476)
A = base · height
$A = bh$

Triangle

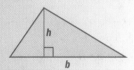

Area (p. 480)

$A = \frac{1}{2}$ · base · height

$A = \frac{1}{2}bh$

Circle

Area (p. 491)
A = (pi)(radius)^2 = πr^2

Circumference (p. 485)
C = pi · diameter = πd
$C = 2$ · pi · radius = $2\pi r$

Rectangular Prism

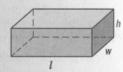

Surface Area (p. 506)
S = sum of areas of faces

Volume (p. 510)
V = length · width · height
$V = lwh$

Other Formulas

Distance traveled	(p. 154)	$d = rt$ where d = distance, r = rate, and t = time
Simple interest	(p. 408)	$I = Prt$ where I = simple interest, P = principal, r = annual interest rate, and t = time in years
Temperature	(p. 317)	$F = \frac{9}{5}C + 32$ and $C = \frac{5}{9}(F - 32)$ where F = degrees Fahrenheit and C = degrees Celsius

Table of Properties

Number Properties

Addition Property of 0 (p. 37)

The sum of any number and 0 is that number.

Numbers $7 + 0 = 7$

Algebra $a + 0 = a$

Multiplication Property of 0 (p. 37)

The product of any number and 0 is 0.

Numbers $4 \times 0 = 0$

Algebra $a \times 0 = 0$

Multiplication Property of 1 (p. 37)

The product of any number and 1 is that number.

Numbers $3 \times 1 = 3$

Algebra $a \times 1 = a$

Commutative Property of Addition (p. 137)

You can add numbers in any order.

Numbers $2 + 5 = 5 + 2$

Algebra $a + b = b + a$

Associative Property of Addition (p. 137)

The value of a sum does not depend on how the numbers are grouped.

Numbers $(2 + 4) + 6 = 2 + (4 + 6)$

Algebra $(a + b) + c = a + (b + c)$

Commutative Property of Multiplication (p. 155)

You can multiply numbers in any order.

Numbers $2 \times 6.5 = 6.5 \times 2$

Algebra $a \cdot b = b \cdot a$

Associative Property of Multiplication (p. 155)

The value of a product does not depend on how the numbers are grouped.

Numbers $(6 \times 2.5) \times 4 = 6 \times (2.5 \times 4)$

Algebra $(a \cdot b) \cdot c = a \cdot (b \cdot c)$

Distributive Property (p. 159)

You can multiply a number and a sum by multiplying the number by each part of the sum and then adding these products. The same property applies with subtraction.

Numbers $3(4 + 6) = 3(4) + 3(6)$
$2(8 - 5) = 2(8) - 2(5)$

Algebra $a(b + c) = ab + ac$
$a(b - c) = ab - ac$

Cross Products Property (p. 383)

In a proportion, the cross products are equal.

Numbers If $\frac{3}{4} = \frac{6}{8}$, then $3 \cdot 8 = 4 \cdot 6$.

Algebra If $\frac{a}{b} = \frac{c}{d}$ and b and d do not equal 0, then $ad = bc$.

Glossary

	Example
a	
absolute value (p. 539) The absolute value of a number is its distance from 0 on a number line. The absolute value of *a* is written $\lvert a \rvert$.	$\lvert 2 \rvert = \lvert -2 \rvert = 2$ 2 units 2 units −2 −1 0 1 2
acute angle (p. 430) An angle whose measure is less than 90°.	
acute triangle (p. 436) A triangle with three acute angles.	
angle (p. 425) A figure formed by two rays with the same endpoint.	D E F ∠DEF, or ∠E, or ∠FED
angle of rotation (p. 568) *See* rotation.	
annual interest rate (p. 408) The percent of the principal you earn or pay per year.	If you deposit $100 in a bank account that pays 4% per year, then 4% is the *annual interest rate*.
area (pp. 62, 702) The amount of surface covered by a figure. Area is measured in square units such as square feet (ft^2) or square meters (m^2).	3 units 4 units *Area* = 12 square units
associative property of addition (p. 137) The value of a sum does not depend on how the numbers are grouped.	$(a + b) + c = a + (b + c)$ $(2 + 5) + 4 = 2 + (5 + 4)$
associative property of multiplication (p. 155) The value of a product does not depend on how the numbers are grouped.	$(a \cdot b) \cdot c = a \cdot (b \cdot c)$ $(2 \times 6.5) \times 4 = 2 \times (6.5 \times 4)$
average (p. 649) A single number used to describe what is typical of a set of data. *See* mean, median, *and* mode.	

	Example
axes (pp. 83, 562) A horizontal number line, the *horizontal axis*, and a vertical number line, the *vertical axis*, that meet at (0, 0).	*See* coordinate plane.

b

bar graph (pp. 79, 704) A graph in which the lengths of bars are used to represent and compare data.	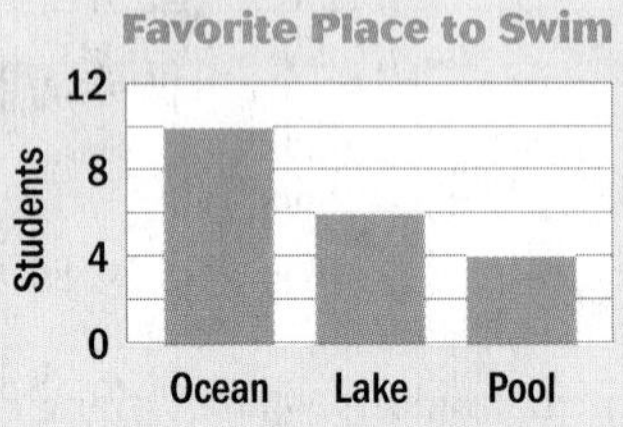 **Favorite Place to Swim**
base of a parallelogram (p. 476) The base of a parallelogram is the length of any of its sides.	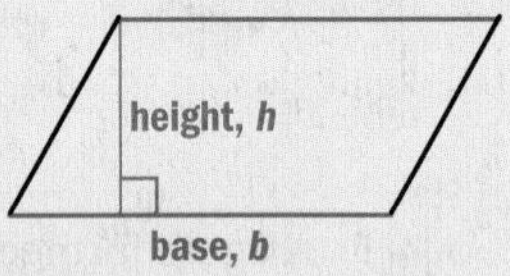
base of a power (p. 16) The base of a power is the repeated factor.	The *base* of the power 2^3 is 2.
base of a solid (p. 500) *See* prism, cylinder, pyramid, *and* cone.	
base of a triangle (p. 480) The length of any of its sides.	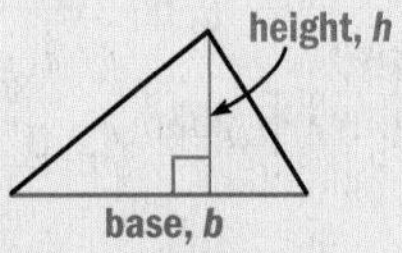
benchmark (p. 57) A familiar object that can be used to approximate the size of a unit.	The length of a small paper clip is about one inch.
box-and-whisker plot (p. 657) A display that divides a data set into four parts, two below the median and two above it.	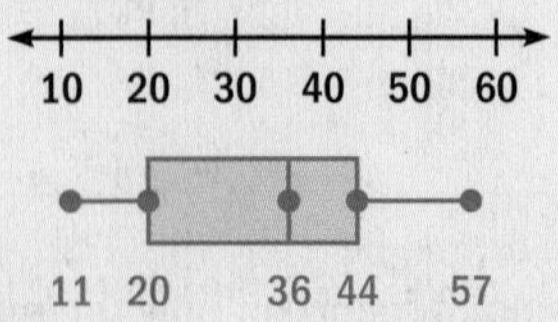

c

capacity (p. 188) Capacity measures the amount that a container can hold.	

	Example
center of a circle (p. 485) The point inside a circle that is the same distance from all points on the circle.	*See* circle.
center of rotation (p. 568) *See* rotation.	
circle (p. 485) The set of all points in a plane that are the same distance from a point called the *center*.	
circle graph (p. 88) A graph that represents data as parts of a circle. The entire circle represents all of the data.	**Opinions of Roller Coasters**
circumference (p. 485) The distance around a circle.	
clustering (p. 692) A method of estimating a sum when numbers being added have about the same value.	You can estimate the sum 72 + 69 + 65 as 3(70) = 210.
combination (p. 637) A grouping of objects in which order is not important.	Counting the ways to choose two essays to write from eight possibilities involves a *combination*.
common factor (p. 222) A whole number that is a factor of two or more nonzero whole numbers.	The *common factors* of 64 and 120 are 1, 2, 4, and 8.
common multiple (p. 235) A whole number that is a multiple of two or more nonzero whole numbers.	The *common multiples* of 6 and 8 are 24, 48, 72, 96, ...
commutative property of addition (p. 137) In a sum, you can add numbers in any order.	$a + b = b + a$ $2 + 5 = 5 + 2$

	Example
commutative property of multiplication (p. 155) In a product, you can multiply numbers in any order.	$a \cdot b = b \cdot a$ $2 \times 6.5 = 6.5 \times 2$
compatible numbers (pp. 13, 694) Numbers that are easy to use in computations.	You can estimate the quotient $2605 \div 7$ by using the *compatible numbers* 2800 and 7. Because $2800 \div 7 = 400$, $2605 \div 7 \approx 400$.
complementary angles (p. 431) Two angles whose measures have a sum of 90°.	
complementary events (p. 632) Events that have no outcomes in common and that together contain all the outcomes of the experiment.	Rolling an odd number on a number cube and rolling an even number on a number cube are *complementary events*, or *complements*.
composite number (p. 215) A whole number greater than 1 that has factors other than itself and 1.	6 is a *composite number* because its factors are 1, 2, 3, and 6.
cone (p. 500) A solid that has one circular base and a vertex that is not in the same plane.	
congruent figures (p. 454) Figures with the same size and shape.	
coordinate grid (p. 83) *See* coordinate plane.	
coordinate plane (p. 562) A plane divided into four *quadrants* by a horizontal number line called the *x*-axis and a vertical number line called the *y*-axis.	

	Example
coordinates (pp. 83, 562) The numbers in an ordered pair that locate a point on a coordinate grid. *See also* x-coordinate *and* y-coordinate.	The numbers 4 and 3 in the *ordered pair* (4, 3) are the *coordinates* of the graph of (4, 3), which is located 4 units to the right and 3 units up from (0, 0).
corresponding parts (p. 455) The matching sides and angles of two figures.	 Corresponding parts: $\angle U$ and $\angle X$, $\angle V$ and $\angle Y$, $\angle W$ and $\angle Z$, $\overline{UV}$ and $\overline{XY}$, $\overline{VW}$ and $\overline{YZ}$, $\overline{UW}$ and $\overline{XZ}$.
cross products (p. 383) For the proportion $\frac{a}{b} = \frac{c}{d}$, where $b \neq 0$ and $d \neq 0$, the cross products are *ad* and *bc*.	In the proportion $\frac{2}{3} = \frac{8}{12}$, the *cross products* are 2 • 12 and 3 • 8.
cube (pp. 459, 501) A rectangular prism with 6 congruent square faces.	*See* solid.
cubed (p. 17) A number cubed is the third power of the number.	4 *cubed* indicates 4^3, or 64.
cylinder (p. 500) A solid with two parallel bases that are congruent circles.	bases

d

data (pp. 72, 704) Information, often given in the form of numbers or facts.	
decimal (p. 108) A number that is written using the base-ten place value system. Each place value is ten times the place value to the right.	The *decimal* 3.12 represents 3 ones plus 1 tenth plus 2 hundredths, or three and twelve hundredths.
degree (°) (p. 426) A unit used to measure angles. There are 180° on a *protractor*, a semicircular tool used to measure degrees.	**The measure of the angle is 90°.**

	Example
denominator (pp. 228, 700) The number below the fraction bar in a fraction. It represents the number of equal parts into which the whole is divided or the number of objects that make up the set.	In the fraction $\frac{3}{4}$, the *denominator* is 4.
diagonal (p. 450) A segment, other than a side, that connects two vertices of a polygon.	diagonals
diameter of a circle (p. 485) The distance across the circle through its center.	*See* circumference.
difference (pp. 6, 689) The result when two numbers are subtracted.	The *difference* of 7 and 3 is $7 - 3$, or 4.
digit (p. 684) Any of the numbers 0, 1, 2, 3, 4, 5, 6, 7, 8, or 9.	In the whole number 127,891, the *digit* 8 has a value of 800, or 8×100, because it is in the hundreds' place.
discount (p. 407) An amount subtracted from the regular price of an item to get the sale price.	When $40 sneakers are on sale at 25% off, the *discount* is 25% of $40, or $10.
distributive property (p. 159) You can multiply a number and a sum by multiplying the number by each part of the sum and then adding these products. The same property applies with subtraction.	$a(b + c) = ab + ac$ $3(4 + 6) = 3(4) + 3(6)$ $a(b - c) = ab - ac$ $2(8 - 5) = 2(8) - 2(5)$
dividend (pp. 6, 691) A number that is divided by another number.	In $18 \div 6 = 3$, the *dividend* is 18.
divisible (p. 214) A number is divisible by another number if that other number is a factor of the first.	Because $3 \times 4 = 12$, 12 is *divisible* by 3 and by 4.
divisor (pp. 6, 691) The number by which another number is divided.	In $18 \div 6 = 3$, the *divisor* is 6.

Glossary

	Example
double bar graph (p. 80) A bar graph that shows two sets of data on the same graph.	**Favorite Zoo Animal** (graph with y-axis Students labeled 0, 10, 20, 30; x-axis Lion, Monkey, Elephant, Other) ■ Sixth grade ■ Seventh grade

e

edges of a solid (p. 501) The segments where the faces meet.	*See* vertex of a solid.
elapsed time (p. 299) The amount of time between a start time and an end time.	The *elapsed time* from 7:15 A.M. to 12 P.M. is 4 hours and 45 minutes.
endpoint (p. 421) *See* segment *and* ray.	
equation (p. 36) A mathematical sentence formed by placing an equal sign (=) between two expressions.	$3y = 21$ and $x - 3 = 7$ are *equations*.
equilateral triangle (p. 437) A triangle with three sides of the same length.	(triangle figure)
equivalent fractions (p. 228) Fractions that represent the same number.	$\frac{5}{15}$ and $\frac{20}{60}$ are *equivalent fractions* that both represent $\frac{1}{3}$.
equivalent ratios (p. 375) Ratios that can be written as equivalent fractions.	*See* equivalent fractions.
estimate (p. 692) To find an approximate solution to a problem.	You can *estimate* the sum $88 + 51$ as $90 + 50$, or 140.
evaluate (pp. 21, 29) To find the value of an expression.	To *evaluate* $2t - 1$ when $t = 3$, substitute 3 for t and find the value of $2 \times 3 - 1$. So, $2t - 1 = 5$ when $t = 3$.
event (p. 630) A collection of outcomes of an experiment.	The *event* "getting an odd number" on a number cube consists of the outcomes 1, 3, and 5.

	Example
exponent (p. 16) The exponent of a power is the number of times the factor is repeated.	The *exponent* of the power 2^3 is 3.

f

	Example
faces of a solid (p. 501) The polygons that form the solid figure.	*See* vertex of a solid.
factor (p. 16) When whole numbers other than zero are multiplied together, each number is a factor of the product.	Because $2 \times 3 \times 7 = 42$, 2, 3, and 7 are *factors* of 42.
factor tree (p. 216) A diagram that can be used to write the prime factorization of a number.	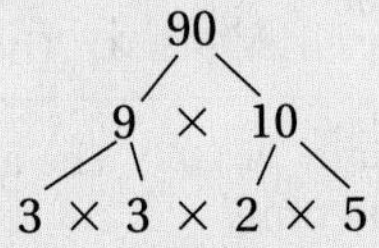 90 9 $\times$ 10 3 $\times$ 3 $\times$ 2 $\times$ 5
favorable outcomes (p. 630) Once you specify an event, the outcomes for that event are *favorable outcomes*.	If you toss a number cube, the *favorable outcomes* for getting an odd number are 1, 3, and 5.
fraction (p. 228, 700) A number of the form $\frac{a}{b}$ ($b \neq 0$) used to describe parts of a whole or a set.	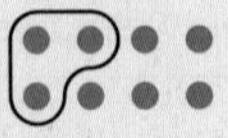 $\frac{3}{8}$
frequency table (p. 72) A table that displays the number of times each item or category occurs in a data set.	Art Project | Tally | Frequency painting | ⊪ ॥ | 6 sculpture | ॥॥॥ | 4 drawing | ॥ | 2
front-end estimation (p. 131, 692) A method of estimating a sum by adding the front-end digits and using the remaining digits to adjust the sum.	To estimate the sum $3.75 + 1.28 + 6.93$, first add the ones: $3 + 1 + 6 = 10$. Then estimate the sum of the remaining digits: $0.75 + 0.28 + 0.93 \approx 2$. The sum is about $10 + 2$, or 12.
function (p. 605) A pairing of two values, called an *input* and an *output*. In a function, each input has exactly one output.	

Input, x	Output, y
-2	-1
-1	0
0	1
1	2
2	3

Glossary

	Example
g	
graph of an inequality (p. 603) All the points on a number line that represent the solution of the inequality.	The number line shows the solution of $x < 2$. The open dot at 2 shows that 2 is not part of the solution.
greatest common factor (GCF) (p. 222) The largest of the common factors of two or more nonzero whole numbers.	The *greatest common factor* of 64 and 120 is the greatest of the common factors 1, 2, 4, and 8, which is 8.
grouping symbols (p. 21) Symbols such as parentheses, brackets, or fraction bars that group parts of an expression.	The parentheses in $12 \div (4 - 1)$ are *grouping symbols* that indicate that the subtraction is done first.
h	
height of a parallelogram (p. 476) The perpendicular distance between the side whose length is the base and the opposite side.	
height of a triangle (p. 480) The perpendicular distance between the side whose length is the base and the vertex opposite that side.	
hexagon (p. 449) A polygon with six sides.	

	Example
i	
image (pp. 562, 567, 568) The new figure that results from the translation, reflection, or rotation of a figure in a coordinate plane.	*See* translation, rotation, *and* reflection.
improper fraction (p. 244) Any fraction in which the numerator is greater than or equal to the denominator.	$\frac{21}{8}$ and $\frac{6}{6}$ are *improper fractions*.
independent events (p. 642) Events for which the occurrence of one event does not affect the likelihood that the other event will occur.	Rolling a number cube and then flipping a coin are *independent events*.
inequality (p. 602) A statement formed by placing an inequality symbol such as < (is less than) or > (is greater than) between two expressions.	$2 > x$, $n + 12 < 54$, and $x - 7 \leq 5$ are *inequalities*.
input (p. 605) *See* function.	
input-output table (p. 605) A table used to represent a function by listing the *output* for each of several different *inputs*.	*See* function.
integers (p. 533) The numbers . . . , −5, −4, −3, −2, −1, 0, 1, 2, 3, 4, 5, ...	*See* number line.
interest (p. 408) An amount of money paid for the use of money.	*See* simple interest.
intersecting lines (p. 422) Lines in a plane that meet at a point.	
inverse operations (p. 687) Operations that "undo" each other, such as addition and subtraction or multiplication and division.	
isosceles triangle (p. 437) A triangle with at least two sides of the same length.	
l	
leading digit (p. 13) The leading digit of a whole number is the first digit at the left.	The *leading digit* of 59 is 5.
leaf (p. 653) The last digit on the right of a number displayed in a stem-and-leaf plot.	*See* stem-and-leaf plot.

	Example
least common denominator (LCD) (p. 239) The least common multiple of the denominators of two or more fractions.	The *least common denominator* of $\frac{5}{6}$ and $\frac{7}{9}$ is the least common multiple of 6 and 9, or 18.
least common multiple (LCM) (p. 236) The smallest of the common multiples of two or more nonzero whole numbers.	The *least common multiple* of 9 and 12 is the smallest of the common multiples 36, 72, 108, . . . , or 36.
line (p. 421) A set of points that extends without end in two opposite directions.	$\overleftrightarrow{RS}$ or $\overleftrightarrow{SR}$
line graph (pp. 84, 705) A graph that represents data using points connected by line segments to show how quantities change over time.	
line of reflection (p. 527) *See* reflection.	
line of symmetry (p. 460) *See* line symmetry.	
line plot (p. 73) A number line diagram that uses X marks to show the frequencies of items or categories being tallied.	
line symmetry (p. 460) A figure has line symmetry if a line can be drawn that divides the figure into two congruent parts that are mirror images of each other. The line is the *line of symmetry*.	lines of symmetry

	Example

linear function (p. 613) A function whose graph is a straight line.

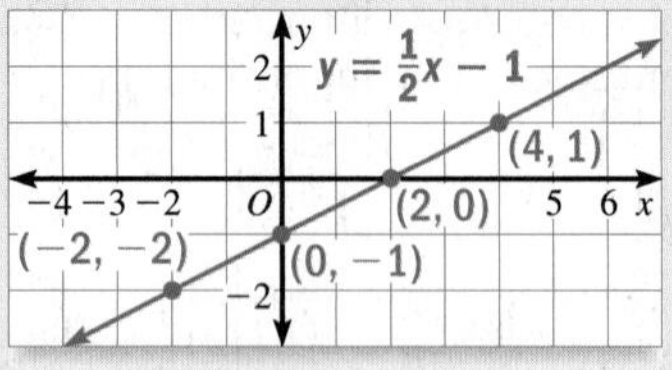

$y = \frac{1}{2}x - 1$

(4, 1)
(2, 0)
(-2, -2)
(0, -1)

---

lower extreme (p. 657) The least value of a data set.

See box-and-whisker plot.

---

lower quartile (p. 657) The median of the lower half of a data set.

See box-and-whisker plot.

---

m

mean (p. 93) The sum of the data values divided by the number of values.

The *mean* of the values 7, 10, 9, and 6 is

$$\frac{7 + 10 + 9 + 6}{4} = \frac{32}{4} = 8.$$

---

median (p. 93) The middle data value when the values are written in numerical order. If a data set has an even number of values, the median is the mean of the two middle values.

The *median* of the ages

36, 36, 37, 37, 39, 40, 41

is 37, because 37 is the middle number.

---

mixed number (p. 244) The sum of a whole number and a fraction less than 1.

$2\frac{5}{8}$ is a *mixed number*.

---

mode (p. 93) The data value that occurs most often. A data set can have one mode, more than one mode, or no mode.

In the data set

36, 36, 37, 37, 39, 40, 41,

both 36 and 37 occur twice, so there are two *modes*, 36 and 37.

---

multiple (p. 235) A multiple of a whole number is the product of the number and any nonzero whole number.

The *multiples* of 2 are 2, 4, 6, 8, 10, ...

---

n

negative integers (p. 533) Integers that are less than 0.

The *negative integers* are −1, −2, −3, −4, ...

	Example
net (p. 506) A two-dimensional figure that can be folded to form a solid.	 **Net** **Solid**
number fact family (p. 687) Four number facts consisting of three numbers related by inverse operations.	The facts $8 + 2 = 10$, $10 - 2 = 8$, $2 + 8 = 10$, and $10 - 8 = 2$ are in the same *number fact family*.
number line (pp. 118, 685) A line whose points are associated with numbers. You can use a number line to compare and order numbers. The numbers on a number line increase from left to right.	
numerator (pp. 228, 700) The number above the fraction bar in a fraction. It represents the number of equal parts out of the whole or the number of objects from the set that are being considered.	In the fraction $\frac{3}{4}$, the *numerator* is 3.
numerical expression (p. 21) An expression, consisting of numbers and operations to be performed, that represents a particular value.	The *numerical expression* $2 \times 3 - 1$ represents 5.

O

obtuse angle (p. 430) An angle whose measure is between 90° and 180°.	
obtuse triangle (p. 436) A triangle with one obtuse angle.	

	Example
octagon (p. 449) A polygon with eight sides.	
opposites (p. 534) Numbers that are the same distance from 0 on a number line, but are on opposite sides of 0.	3 and -3 are *opposites*.
order of operations (p. 21) The order in which to perform operations when evaluating expressions with more than one operation.	$1 + 3^2(5 - 1) = 1 + 3^2(4) = 1 + 9(4) = 1 + 36 = 37$
ordered pair (pp. 83, 562) *See* coordinates.	*See* coordinate plane.
origin (pp. 83, 562) The point (0, 0) on a coordinate plane.	*See* coordinate plane.
outcome (p. 630) A possible result of an experiment.	When you toss a coin, the *outcomes* are heads and tails.
output (p. 605) *See* function.	

P

	Example
parallel lines (p. 422) Lines in the same plane that never meet.	
parallelogram (p. 445) A quadrilateral with two pairs of parallel sides.	
pentagon (p. 449) A polygon with five sides.	
percent (p. 395) A ratio that compares a number to 100. *Percent* means "per hundred."	$43\% = \frac{43}{100} = 0.43$
perimeter (pp. 61, 702) The distance around a figure, measured in linear units such as feet, inches, or meters.	 *Perimeter* $= 5 + 7 + 8$, or 20 cm

	Example
permutation (p. 637) An arrangement of objects in which order is important.	Counting the ways to list the members of the student council in a program involves a *permutation*.
perpendicular lines (p. 476) Two lines are perpendicular if they meet at a right angle.	
pi (π) (p. 485) The ratio of the circumference of a circle to its diameter.	You can use 3.14 or $\frac{22}{7}$ to approximate π.
pictograph (p. 706) A graph that uses pictures or symbols to display data.	**Color of Eyes** = 2 students
place value (pp. 108, 684) The place value of each digit in a number depends on its position within the number.	In 723, the 2 is in the tens' place and it has a value of 20.
plane (p. 422) A flat surface that extends without end in all directions.	
point (p. 421) A position in space represented with a dot.	$\bullet P$
polygon (p. 449) A closed plane figure that is formed by three or more segments called sides. Each side intersects exactly two other sides at a *vertex*.	 vertex
positive integers (p. 533) Integers that are greater than 0.	The *positive integers* are 1, 2, 3, 4, ...
power (p. 16) An expression, such as 2^3, that represents a product with a repeated factor.	The third *power* of 2 is $2^3 = 2 \times 2 \times 2$, which represents the product of three factors of 2.

	Example
prime factorization (p. 216) A whole number written as the product of prime factors.	The *prime factorization* of 20 is $2^2 \times 5$.
prime number (p. 215) A whole number greater than 1 whose only factors are 1 and itself.	59 is a *prime number*, because its only factors are 1 and itself.
principal (p. 408) An amount of money that is saved or borrowed.	If you deposit $100 in a bank account that pays 4% annual interest, then the *principal* is $100.
prism (p. 500) A solid with two parallel bases that are congruent polygons.	 bases **Rectangular Prism**　**Triangular Prism**
probability of an event (p. 630) A measure of the likelihood that the event will occur, computed as $\dfrac{\text{number of favorable outcomes}}{\text{number of possible outcomes}}$ when all the outcomes are equally likely.	If you toss a number cube, the *probability* that you roll an odd number is $\frac{3}{6} = 0.5 = 50\%$.
product (pp. 6, 690) The result when two or more numbers are multiplied.	The *product* of 3 and 4 is 3×4, or 12.
proper fraction (p. 245) A fraction in which the numerator is less than the denominator.	$\frac{2}{3}$ is a *proper fraction*.
proportion (p. 383) An equation you write to show that two ratios are equivalent.	The equation $\frac{2}{3} = \frac{8}{12}$ is a *proportion*.
pyramid (p. 500) A solid made up of polygons. The base can be any polygon, and the other polygons are triangles that share a common vertex.	 base

q

quadrants (p. 562) The four regions into which a coordinate plane is divided by the *x*-axis and the *y*-axis. *See also* coordinate plane.	*See* coordinate plane.
quadrilateral (p. 445) A plane figure formed by four segments called sides. Each side intersects exactly two other sides, one at each endpoint, and no two sides are part of the same line.	

	Example
quotient (pp. 6, 691) The result of a division.	The *quotient* of 18 and 6 is 18 ÷ 6, or 3.
r	
radius of a circle (p. 485) The distance from the center to any point on the circle. The plural of radius is *radii*.	*See* circumference.
range (p. 94) The difference between the greatest data value and the least data value.	In the data set 36, 36, 37, 37, 39, 40, 41, the *range* is 41 − 36 = 5.
rate (p. 379) A ratio of two measures that have different units.	The International Space Station orbits Earth at an average *rate* of 15 miles every 3 seconds, or 5 miles per second.
ratio (p. 374) The ratio of a number a to a nonzero number b is the quotient when a is divided by b.	The *ratio* of a to b can be written as $\frac{a}{b}$, as $a : b$, or as "a to b."
ray (p. 421) A part of a line that has one *endpoint* and extends without end in one direction.	 $\overrightarrow{AB}$ **with endpoint A.**
reciprocals (p. 334) Two numbers whose product is 1.	Because $\frac{3}{5} \times \frac{5}{3} = 1$, $\frac{3}{5}$ and $\frac{5}{3}$ are *reciprocals*.
rectangle (p. 445) A parallelogram with four right angles.	
rectangular prism (p. 500) A prism with rectangular bases.	*See* prism.
reflection (p. 567) An operation that flips a figure over a line called the *line of reflection* to produce a congruent mirror image.	 The *x*-axis is the *line of reflection*.

	Example
regular polygon (p. 450) A polygon with equal side lengths and equal angle measures.	 **Regular** **Not Regular**
remainder (pp. 6, 691) If a divisor does not divide a dividend evenly, the remainder is the whole number left over after the division.	$\begin{array}{r} 8\ \text{R4} \\ 7\overline{)60} \\ 56 \\ \hline 4 \end{array}$ ← *remainder*
repeating decimal (p. 254) A decimal that has one or more digits that repeat forever.	0.3333... and $2.\overline{01}$ are *repeating decimals*.
rhombus (p. 445) A parallelogram with four sides of equal length.	
right angle (p. 430) An angle whose measure is exactly 90°.	
right triangle (p. 436) A triangle with one right angle.	
rotation (p. 568) An operation that rotates a figure through a given *angle of rotation* about a fixed point, the *center of rotation*, to produce a congruent image.	 The origin is the center of rotation and the angle of rotation is 90°.

	Example
round (pp. 124, 686) To approximate a number to a given place value.	518 *rounded* to the nearest ten is 520, and 518 *rounded* to the nearest hundred is 500.
S	
scale (p. 68) In a scale drawing, a key that tells how the drawing's dimensions and the actual dimensions are related.	If the scale on a scale drawing is 1 in. : 10 ft, then each inch on the drawing represents 10 feet on the scale drawing.
scale drawing (p. 68) A drawing of an object with the same shape as the original object, but not the same size.	
scalene triangle (p. 437) A triangle with three sides of different lengths.	
segment (p. 421) A part of a line that consists of two *endpoints* and all the points between them.	 $\overline{AB}$ or $\overline{BA}$ with *endpoints A and B.*
similar figures (p. 454) Figures with the same shape but not necessarily the same size.	
simple interest (p. 408) Interest paid only on the principal.	If you deposit $100 in a bank account that pays 4% annual interest, you will earn $100(0.04), or $4, *simple interest* in one year.
simplest form of a fraction (p. 229) A fraction is in simplest form if its numerator and denominator have a greatest common factor of 1.	The *simplest form* of the fraction $\frac{4}{12}$ is $\frac{1}{3}$.
solid (p. 500) A three-dimensional figure that encloses a part of space.	

	Example
solution of an equation (p. 36) A number that, when substituted for a variable, makes the equation true.	10 is the *solution of the equation* $x - 3 = 7$.
solution of an inequality (p. 602) The group of all values of the variable that make the inequality true.	The *solution of the inequality* $x + 2 \geq 3$ is $x \geq 1$, or all numbers that are greater than or equal to 1.
solve an equation (p. 37) To find all the solutions of an equation by finding all the values of the variable that make the equation true.	To *solve the equation* $n \div 4 = 7$, find the number that can be divided by 4 to equal 7; $28 \div 4 = 7$, so the solution is 28.
solve an inequality (p. 602) Find all values of the variable that make the inequality true.	To *solve* $x + 2 \geq 3$, subtract 2 from each side to get $x \geq 1$.
sphere (p. 500) The set of points in space that are a given distance from a given point.	
square (p. 445) A parallelogram with four right angles and four sides of equal length.	
squared (p. 17) A number squared is the second power of the number.	3 *squared* indicates 3^2, or 9.
stem (p. 653) All the digits except the last digit on the right of a number displayed in a stem-and-leaf plot.	*See* stem-and-leaf plot.
stem-and-leaf plot (p. 653) A data display that can be used to organize a large set of data.	0 | 7 8 9 9 1 | 1 3 5 5 6 7 2 | 0 1 3 3 | 0 2 Key: $2\|3 = 23$ stem / \ leaf
straight angle (p. 430) An angle whose measure is exactly 180°.	
sum (pp. 5, 689) The result when two or more numbers are added.	The *sum* of 2 and 5 is $2 + 5$, or 7.

	Example
supplementary angles (p. 431) Two angles whose measures have a sum of 180°.	48° 132°
surface area of a prism (p. 506) The sum of the areas of the faces of the prism. Surface area is measured in square units.	4 in. 8 in. 6 in. *Surface Area* = 2(8 × 6) + 2(8 × 4) + 2(6 × 4) = 208 square inches

t

terminating decimal (p. 254) A decimal that has a final digit.	0.084 and 0.6 are *terminating decimals*.
transformation (p. 568) A movement of a figure in a coordinate plane. Three types of transformations are *translations*, *reflections*, and *rotations*.	*See* translation, rotation, *and* reflection.
translation (p. 562) An operation that slides each point of a figure the same distance in the same direction to produce a figure that is congruent to the original figure.	
tree diagram (p. 636) A diagram that shows all the possible outcomes as choices on different branches of the "tree."	H — H HH, T HT; T — H TH, T TT
triangle (p. 436) A closed plane figure with three straight sides that connect three points.	

	Example
triangular prism (p. 500) A prism with triangular bases.	*See* prism.

unit rate (p. 379) A rate with a denominator of 1.	55 miles per hour and $.25 per ounce are *unit rates*.
upper extreme (p. 657) The greatest value of a data set.	*See* box-and-whisker plot.
upper quartile (p. 657) The median of the upper half of a data set.	*See* box-and-whisker plot.

variable (p. 29) A symbol, usually a letter, that represents one or more numbers.	x is a *variable* in $4x - 3$ and in $x + 3 = 5$.
variable expression (p. 29) An expression consisting of one or more numbers, variables, and operations to be performed.	$4x - 3$ and $2t^2$ are *variable expressions*.
Venn diagram (p. 703) A diagram that uses shapes to show how sets are related.	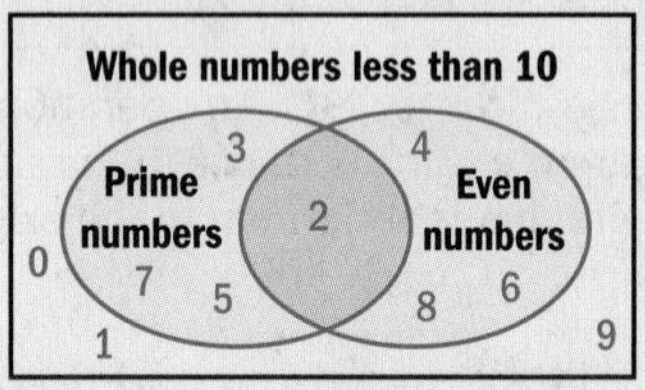
verbal model (p. 41) Words that describe how real-life values are related. Verbal models can be expressed using math symbols.	You pay $50 for a gym membership and $3 per visit. Find your total cost for 20 visits. *Verbal model:* $$\text{Total cost} = \text{Membership cost} + \text{Visits cost}$$
vertex of a polygon (p. 449) A point at which two sides of a polygon meet. The plural of vertex is *vertices*.	*See* polygon.
vertex of a solid (p. 501) A point where the edges meet. The plural of vertex is *vertices*.	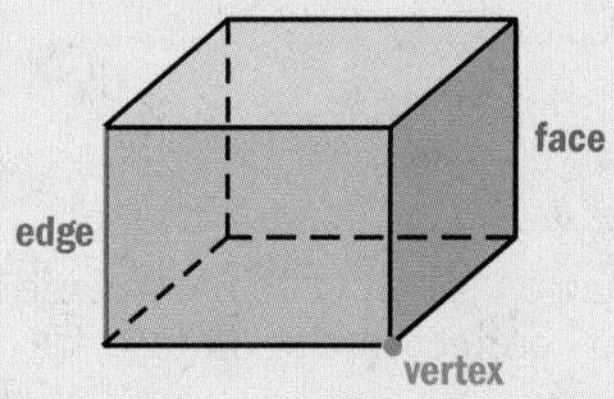

Glossary

	Example
vertex of an angle (p. 425) The endpoint of the rays that form the angle.	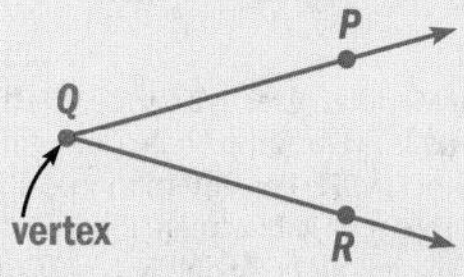
vertical angles (p. 431) When two lines intersect, the angles opposite each other are vertical angles.	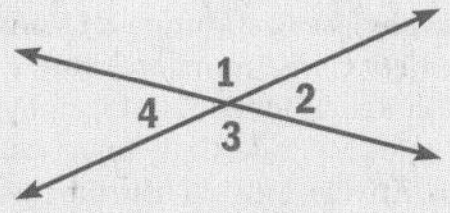 $\angle 1$ and $\angle 3$ are vertical angles; $\angle 2$ and $\angle 4$ are also vertical angles.
volume of a solid (p. 510) The amount of space that the solid occupies. Volume is measured in cubic units.	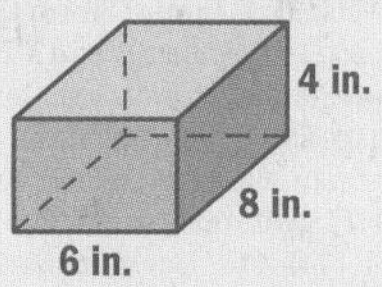 $Volume = lwh = 6 \cdot 8 \cdot 4 =$ 192 cubic inches

W

whole numbers (p. 684) The numbers 0, 1, 2, 3	

X

x-axis (p. 562) The horizontal axis in a coordinate plane. *See also* coordinate plane.	*See* coordinate plane.
x-coordinate (p. 562) The first coordinate in an ordered pair, which tells you how many units to move to the left or right.	In the ordered pair $(-3, -2)$, the *x*-coordinate, -3, tells you to move 3 units to the left. *See also* coordinate plane.

Y

y-axis (p. 562) The vertical axis in a coordinate plane. *See also* coordinate plane.	*See* coordinate plane.
y-coordinate (p. 562) The second coordinate in an ordered pair, which tells you how many units to move up or down.	In the ordered pair $(-3, -2)$, the *y*-coordinate, -2, tells you to move 2 units down. *See also* coordinate plane.

Credits

CR1

Squared Studios/PhotoDisc: Market Fresh/Object Series CD#49; **351** *bl* Nik Wheeler/Corbis; **352** *tl* Courtesy of Marklin, Inc. Train Model: Marklin German Federal Railroad class 18.4 Steam Locomotive. Length: 40-1/8", Gauge: 1, Scale: 1:32.; **353** *bl* DanFornari©WHOI, *cr* James Marshall/Corbis; **354** *tl* Bettmann/Corbis; **359** *tr* John Warden/Index Stock Imagery/Picturequest; **360** *cr* LightWave, *br* Artville: Musical Instruments; **369** *bl* PhotoDisc: Supporting Cast: Teens/Objects Series CD#39; **370, 371** *tr* Ken O'Donoghue; **374** *bl* PhotoDisc: Supporting Cast: Teens/Objects Series CD#39; **375** *cl* PhotoDisc; **376** *bc* EyeWire: CD/Instrumental Objects; **377** *tl* Medford Taylor/National Geographic Image Collection; **381** *tl* Charles W. Melton, *cr* Jeremy Barker; **382** *tl* Buddy Mays/Words & Pictures/Picturequest; **384** *cl* Stephen Studd/Getty Images; **387** *tl* Tim Flach/Getty Images; **388** *cl* Seitzinger/Derbymania; **389** *bl* Ralf-Finn Hestoft/Index Stock Imagery/Picturequest; **390** *cr* CSA Plastock/Photonica; **395** *tr* Lawrence Manning/Corbis; **396** *cl* Comstock: CD Pets & Vets; **398** *cl* PhotoDisc: Backgrounds & Objects CD #8, PhotoDisc: Tools of the Trade CD #48, *tl* PhotoSpin/PowerPhotos: Africa Vol 16, PhotoDisc: Tools of the Trade CD #48; **399** *bl* David Young-Wolff/PhotoEdit; **400** *bl* Burgess Blevins/Getty Images; **401** *bl* PhotoDisc; **402** *cl* James J. Bissell/SuperStock; **404** *cr* Frank Siteman; **405** *tr* Ryan McVay/Getty Images; **407** *cl* Kevin Horan/Getty; **409** *cl* Frank Siteman; **410** *tl* PhotoDisc; **415** *br* Bruce Burkhardt/Corbis; **416** *br* PhotoDisc; **419** *c* PhotoDisc: InfoMedia 2/Objects CD#26; **422** *tr* USGS; **423** *bc* LightWave, *br* Geoff du Feu/Getty Images; **425** *bl* Chuck Savage/Corbis; **428** *cl* Jeff Hunter/Getty Images; **430** *tr* Bob Krist/Corbis/Stock Market; **432** *tl* Hideo Kurihara/Getty; **434** *tl* Jim Karageorg/Masterfile; **436** *tr* Pete Saloutos/Corbis; **438** *br* U.S. Postal Service; **440** *tl* Barnabas Bosshart/Corbis; **447** *tl* Cathy Melloan/PhotoEdit; **449** *tr* Gary Holscher/Getty Images; **451** *cl, c, cr* Masterfile, *bl* Cathy Melloan/PhotoEdit, *bc* Christine Osborne/Corbis; **452** *br* Tuthill, David W., *bl* Tony Freeman/Photoedit/Picturequest; **455** *cr* Michael Cerone/SuperStock, *cl* Raymond Gehman/Corbis; **458** *br* Frank Siteman; **459** *tr* Corbis Images/PictureQuest; **460** *cl* The Fusions Collection/Stockbyte: Music (cd 36), *cr* The Fusions Collection/Stockbyte: Music (cd 36); **462** *tl* Comstock: Whimsical Pop-Ins, *tr* Photospin-PowerPhotos: Frames Vol. 14, *tc* haitianartwork.com, *cr* PhotoDisc: Sports Goods CD25, *cl* Corbis: Sports Objects (vol. 174), *c* Artville: Bugs and Insects; **463** *tl* Peter Grumann/Getty Images; **470** *l* Jose Manuel Sanchis Calvete/Corbis; **471** *right* Photo Disk/Objects of Nature CD #38, *c* Eduardo Fuss; **472, 473** Jay Syverson/Corbis; **477** *cl* Roger Ressmeyer/Corbis; **478** *bc* Michael Freeman/Corbis, *br* Digital Art/Corbis; **479** *tl* Arthur Bickerstaffe, *tr* Ken O'Donoghue; **481** *cl* PhotoDisc; **482** *tl* Mike Zens/Corbis, *bl* Corbis Images/Picturequest, *bc* PhotoDisc: Government and Social Issues CD#25, *br* Lawrence Manning/Corbis; **483** *tl* Kevin Fleming/Corbis, *cr* Stockbyte: Flags-The Americas (cd 68); **485** *bl* Michael Lamarra; **487** *tl* PhotoDisc; **488** *tl* Dave Bartruff/Corbis, *tc* C Squared Studios/Artville: Musical Instruments, *tr* William Sallaz/Duomo/Corbis, *cl* LightWave; **491** *tr* © Rubberball Productions/Rubberball Production/Picturequest ; **492** *tl* Bob Daemmrich/Stock Market/Picturequest ; **493** *cr* Jack Affleck/Index Stock Imagery/Picturequest; **494** *bl* John Lund/Getty Images; **497** *cl* Stockbyte CD 29 HouseholdObjects (cd 29); **500** *tr, bl* Ken O'Donoghue; **502** *cr* Ken O'Donoghue, *c* PhotoDisc: Sports Goods CD#25, *cl* EyeWire: Instrumental Objects; **503** *tl* Jacob Taposchaner/Getty Images; **504** *cr* Frank Siteman; **505** *tr* Frank Wartenberg/Corbis; **507** *cl* Ken O' Donoghue; **509** *tl* Richard Cummins/Corbis; **510** *tr, cl, bl* Ken O'Donoghue, toy cube courtesy of Regan Universal Press/Andrews McMeel Publishing, **511** *cl* Joseph Sohm/Corbis; **513** *tl* Marvin Sharp/Sharp's Images Photography; **515** *tl* PhotoSpin PowerPhotos: Food Basics Vol. 2; **519** *cr* Stockbyte: Busy Kids 1 (cd 55); **520** *br* PhotoDisc, Inc.; **529** *bl* Keren Su/Corbis; **530** *cr* Copyright © 2002 SPACE.com, Inc. All rights reserved; **531** *tr* Rick Fischer/Masterfile; **533** *bl* Corbis: Space and Spaceflight (vol. 56), *tr* EAC Images/NASA/Aurora & Quanta Productions; **534** *bl* Chris Trotman/Corbis; **535** *tl* PhotoDisc; **538** *bl* Comstock: Sportsview 1; **541** *tl* Bettmann/Corbis; **545** *bl* Oregon State University/University of Hawaii School of Ocean and Earth Science and Technology/USGS; **546** *bl* Stockbyte: Food Cutouts 3 (cd 61); **547** *tl* Stephen Frink/Getty Images; **551** *cr* Francois Gohier/Photo Researchers, Inc., *cl* Francois Gohier/Photo Researchers, Inc.; **552** *br* Alexis

Nees/Animals Animals; **555** *bl* Jose Azel/Aurora & Quanta Productions; **557** *tr* NASA/USGS/Stockli, Nelson, Hasler/Laboratory for Atmospheres/Goddard Space Flight Center, *bl* Bob Daemmrich/Stock, Boston Inc./Picturequest ; **560** *br* Frank Siteman; **561** *tr* Mantha Granger/Edge productions, Cognoscenti Map Guides; **565** *tl* Corbis: Storm Chaser (vol. 107); **566** *tl* Michael Newman/PhotoEdit/Picturequest; **567** *tr* Steve Bloom/Getty Images; **568** *tl* George Hunter/Getty Images; **569** *br* Mary Louise Brimberg/National Geographic Image Collection, *bl* Bridgeman Art Library; **570** *bl* Coco McCoy/Rainbow/PictureQuest, *c* Bill Gillette/Stock Boston Inc./Picturequest, *cr* Neil Beer/Photodisk, *bc* The Design Library/photostogo.com/Index Stock Photography, Inc, *br* © Danny Lehman/Corbis; **572** *tc; bl* Philadelphia Museum of Art/Corbis; **573** *tl* Priscilla Connell/Photostogo/Index Stock Photography, Inc.; **576** *cr* George D. Lepp/Corbis; **578** *br* Sergei Ilnitsky/Corbis; **583** *bl, tr* Ken O'Donoghue; **584** *bl* Tom Stewart/Corbis Stock Market; **586** *tl* Tom Bean/Corbis; **589** *bl* Ryan McVay/PhotoDisc: Shopping Spree VL 05; **591** *cl* Jim Cummins/Getty; **592** *tr, bl* Ken O'Donoghue; **594** *tl* Stephen McBrady/PhotoEdit/Picturequest; **595** *tl* Rubberball Prod: CD Silhouettes of Occupations; **599** *bl* Tony Anderson/Getty; **601** *tl* AFP Photo/RobertSullivan/Corbis; **603** *bl* Dana White/PhotoEdit; **605** *tr* Keren Su/Corbis, *bl* John Giustina/Getty; **607** *tl* Brad Hitz/Getty; **608** *bl* Mark E. Gibson; **610** *br* Frank Siteman; **611** *tr* Tim Macpherson/Getty; **612** *bl* Maxime Laurent/Digitalvision: Urban Leisure; **615** *bl* Charles Gupton/Corbis Stock Market; **620** *br* C-Squared Studios/PhotoDisc/Getty Images; **622** *cr* EyeWire: Instrumental Objects; **624** *l* Ian Murphy/Getty Images, *tc* Stan Osolinski/Getty Images; **625** *r* Stan Osolinski/Getty Images, *br* Nicholas Parfitt/Getty Images; **627** *cr, tl* PhotoDisc: Nature, Wildlife, Environment CD#44; **630** *bl* Ron Avery/SuperStock, *tr* Steve Skjold/Skjold Stock Photography; **631** *bl* Ken O'Donoghue; **633** *cl* Jason Cohn/Corbis; **636** *tr, cl* Steve Skjold/Skjold Stock Photography; **637** *cl* Comstock: Food Icons; **639** *tl* Chris Trotman/Corbis; **640** *r* Frank Siteman; **641** *tr* David Young-Wolff/PhotoEdit; **643** *cl* Ken O'Donoghue, *tr* Anne-Marie Weber/Getty Images; **651** *tl* NASA; **654** *tl* Richard Cummins/Corbis, *cr* PhotoDisc; **655** *tl* Chris Whitehead/Getty Images; **656** *tl* Alistair Berg/Getty; **658** *cl* Atlantech,Inc: SeaLifeStyles; **659** *tl* David Young-Wolff/Getty; **660** *cl* Wally McNamee/Corbis; **663** *tl* Stephanie Rausser/Getty Images; **664** *bl* Rubberball Prod.: Silhouettes of Sports 2; **669** *br* Michelle D. Bridwell/PhotoEdit.

Illustration

Rob Dunlavey
52, 150, 151, 264, 265, 370, 371, 473, 580, 581

Laurie O'Keefe
116, 118, 267, 291

School Division, Houghton Mifflin Co.
347, 422

Sam Ward
xxv, 17, 24, 25, 45, 47, 62, 73, 97, 120, 123, 131, 156, 167, 173, 182, 190, 195, 219, 238, 248, 255, 274, 275, 303, 330, 332, 343, 378, 385, 397, 403, 438, 453, 457, 495, 508, 536, 590, 600, 609, 634, 645, 661

CR2

Chapter 1

1.1 Getting Ready to Practice (p. 7) **5.** 81
7. 432 **9.** 783 **11.** 55 R2 **13.** subtract 10; 20, 10
15. $156

1.1 Practice and Problem Solving (pp. 8–9)
17. 16 **19.** 19 R1 **21.** 236 **23.** 600 **25.** 687
27. 57 R7 **29.** 613 **31.** 7719 **33.** subtract 2; 22, 20
35. add 8; 36, 44 **37.** 13 **39.** 14 days **41.** false;
product **43.** true **45.** 1 **47.** 6 **49.** 47 litters
51. Add 67 five times. **57.** 90 **59.** 300 **61.** 1000
63. 5000 **65.** 4 **67.** 11 **69.** 27 **71.** 5

1.2 Getting Ready to Practice (p. 14) **1.** yes
3. no; 7200 **5.** 600, 100; 500 **7.** 4000, 6000; 10,000

1.2 Practice and Problem Solving
(pp. 14–15) **9–31.** Estimates may vary. **9.** 100
11. 100 **13.** 400 **15.** 300 **17.** 500 **19.** 1500
21. 80 **23.** 10 **25.** 100 **27.** 900 **29.** 4800 **31.** 20
33. about 200 students **35.** yes **37.** no **39.** no
41. *Sample answer:* about 130 mi **43.** Low. *Sample
answer:* You want to be sure you have enough
paint. **47.** 2064 **49.** 714 **51.** 64 **53.** 121

1.3 Getting Ready to Practice (p. 18)
1. base; 27 **3.** exponent; 1

1.3 Practice and Problem Solving (pp. 18–19)
7. 8^2 **9.** 9^4 **11.** 7^4 **13.** *Sample answer:* 4^3 means
$4 \times 4 \times 4$, not 4×3; $4 \times 4 \times 4 = 64$. **15.** 144
17. 10,000 **19.** 32 **21.** 1 **23.** 64 **25.** 1000
27. 1,000,000 **29.** 1, 1, 1; the value is 1. **31.** 4^3
33. 10^3 **35.** 5^3 **37.** 25^5 **39.** 64 tiles **41.** 84 people
43. 8, 5 **45.** 200 **47.** 350 **49.** tens **51.** hundreds

1.3 Technology Activity (p. 20) **1.** 390,625
3. 1,048,576 **5.** 2,825,761 **7.** 191,102,976
9. 42,144,192 **11.** 442,050,625 **13.** 19,683
15. 2,476,099 **17.** 1,048,576

1.4 Getting Ready to Practice (p. 23)
1. grouping symbols **3.** 8 **5.** 8 **7.** 2

1.4 Practice and Problem Solving
(pp. 23–25) **9.** 3 **11.** 6 **13.** 1 **15.** 24 **17.** 2 **19.** 3
21. 13 **23.** 4 **25.** 8 **27.** $18; multiply $4 by 3.

Subtract the product from $30. **29.** *Sample
answer:* in order from left to right; The same rule
applies: multiply and divide in order from left to
right. **31.** false; 13 **33.** true **35.** true **41.** 177
43. 14 **45.** 114 **47.** 188 seats **55.** $7 **57.** $4 \times 4 \times
4 \times 4 = 256$ **59.** $1 \times 1 \times 1 \times 1 \times 1 = 1$ **61.** 4, 41,
404, 414

1.1–1.4 Notebook Review (pp. 26–27)
1. divide; subtract **2.** base: 9; exponent: 5
3. 1135 **4.** 454 **5.** 1495 **6.** 64 R3
7–10. Estimates may vary. **7.** 190 **8.** 470 **9.** 900
10. 68 **11.** 25 **12.** 64 **13.** 19 **14.** 8 **15.** High;
low; if both numbers are rounded up, the estimate
will be greater than the actual sum. If both
numbers are rounded down, the estimate will be
less than the actual sum.

1.5 Getting Ready to Practice (p. 31) **1.** *a*
3. *Sample answer:* 3(2) means to multiply 3 and 2.
$3t = 3(2) = 6$ **5.** 63 **7.** 11 **9.** 12 **11.** 15

1.5 Practice and Problem Solving
(pp. 31–33) **13.** 16 **15.** 6 **17.** 5 **19.** 45 **21.** 7 **23.** 7
25. 3 **27.** 4 mi **29.** 12 ft **31.** 14 ft **33.** 9 **35.** 2
37. 21 **39.** 15 **41.** 36 **43.** 4 **45.** 18 mi. *Sample
answer:* The rate, *r*, is 6 miles per hour and the
time, *t*, is 3 hours. Substitute these values into the
expression *r* • *t* and multiply. **47.** my friend; me
49. 9 **51.** 20 **53.** 33 **55.** 28 **59.** 26 **61.** 3 **63.** ×;
+; ×. *Sample answer:* Guess, Check, and Revise;
it is the best choice of the strategies listed.
65. true **67.** true **69.** false; 6 **71.** true

1.6 Problem Solving Strategies (p. 35)
1. 7 pots of tulips and 5 pots of daffodils
3. 8 questions worth 5 points and 5 questions worth
12 points **5.** 18 ft **7.** 3 months **9.** $A - 6 = B$

1.6 Getting Ready to Practice (p. 38)
1. solution **3.** 5 is a solution. **5.** 5 is a solution.
7. 3 **9.** 10 **11.** 13 **13.** 9

1.6 Practice and Problem Solving
(pp. 39–40) **15.** 3 is a solution. **17.** 2 is not a
solution. **19.** 9 is not a solution. **21.** 7 is not a
solution. **23.** 8 is a solution. **29.** 14 **31.** 8 **33.** 3

35. 9 **37.** 13 **39.** 11 **41.** 0 **43.** The 0 in the second line should be 1. $5x = 5$; $5(1) = 5$; So, 1 is the solution. **45-53.** Methods will vary. **45.** 12 is not a solution. **47.** 8 is not a solution. **49.** 18 is not a solution. **51.** 7 is a solution. **53.** 26 is not a solution. **55.** 60 h **61.** about 1200 people **63.** 24 **65.** 6 **67.** $20 \div 2$

1.7 Getting Ready to Practice (p. 44)

1. Step 1: Read and Understand: Read the problem carefully. Identify the question and any important information. Step 2: Make a Plan: Decide on a problem solving strategy. Step 3: Solve the Problem: Use the problem solving strategy to answer the question. Step 4: Look Back: Check that your answer is reasonable.

1.7 Practice and Problem Solving

(pp. 44–45) **3.** 7 posts **5.** $277 **7.** 6 and 4 **9.** *Sample answer:* Have 6 people represent adults. Give each of these people $12. Have 4 people represent children. Give each of these people $7. Put all of the money together and count it to find the total cost. **11.** 6 tickets **13.** 8 people; 10 people **15.** 17^2 **17.** 8^4 **19.** 8 **21.** 10 **23.** 20,000 **25.** 900,000

1.5–1.7 Notebook Review (pp. 46–47)

1. variable **2.** Yes; because $3 \cdot 5 = 15$. **3.** 25 **4.** 2 **5.** 6 **6.** 6 **7.** 1 **8.** 8 **9.** $140 **10.** No; any number times 0 is always 0. **11.** *Sample answer:* It helps you to make sure your answer is reasonable.

Chapter Review (pp. 48–49)
1. order of operations **3.** base **5.** equation **7.** 1113 **9.** 525 **11.** 78 R3 **13.** 413 **15.** add 9; 45, 54 **17.** subtract 10; 27, 17 **19-25.** Estimates may vary. **19.** 400 **21.** 20 **23.** 1800 **25.** 400 **27.** 343 **29.** 625 **31.** 169 **33.** 2500 **35.** 5 **37.** 6 **39.** 80,000 **41.** 3 **43.** 3 **45.** 4 **47.** 10 **49.** 9 **51.** 7 **53.** 15 **55.** 25 **57.** 66 in. **59.** 5 **61.** 0 **63.** 60 **65.** 4 **67.** $3.20

Chapter 2

2.1 Getting Ready to Practice (p. 58) **1.** ft
3. cm **5.** Answers may vary. **7.** miles; kilometers

2.1 Practice and Problem Solving

(pp. 58–60) **9.** 2 in. **11.** 38 mm; 4 cm **17.** miles; kilometers **19.** feet; meters **21.** inches; centimeters **23.** feet; meters **25-29.** Sample answers are given. **25.** 3 elbow to knuckle units; 3 ft **27.** 26 paper clips; 26 in. **29.** 45 little fingers; 45 cm **31.** *Sample answer:* The left end of the eraser is not lined up at the mark for 0. The length of the eraser is about 2 inches. **33.** reasonable **35.** not reasonable; millimeters **41.** *Sample answer:* It will depend on how close the width of the table and the width of the doorway are to each other. If they are very close, then an actual measurement is needed. If they are not close, then an estimate is sufficient. **43.** A good answer should mention a benchmark that is familiar to students and about 1 mile long. *Sample answer:* Imagine how long the distance is in the chosen benchmark. **45.** 16 **47.** 14 **49.** 12 in., 12 in., and 8 in. *Sample answer:* I used Guess, Check, and Revise because I thought guessing the lengths of the sides and then checking to see if they worked was the easiest strategy to use.

2.2 Getting Ready to Practice (p. 63)

1. perimeter; area **3.** $P = 18$ ft; $A = 14$ ft^2 **5.** Step 1: perimeter; Step 2: $64 = 4s$; Step 3: 16 ft

2.2 Practice and Problem Solving

(pp. 64–65) **7.** area **9.** $P = 20$ in; $A = 21$ in.^{2} **11.** $P = 32$ yd; $A = 64$ yd^2 **13.** $P = 72$ ft; $A = 323$ ft^2 **15.** area **17.** perimeter **19.** 1600 ft^2 **21.** $42 = l \cdot 3$; 14 in. **23.** $100 = 4s$; 25 ft **25.** The square has an area of 64 square inches and the rectangle has an area of 128 square inches. The area of the rectangle is twice the area of the square. **27.** No; a low estimate for the area of the lawn is $30 \cdot 50 = 1500$ square feet, which is exactly the area the fertilizer will cover. **29.** *Sample answer:* One rectangle has sides of length 3 and 5, while the second rectangle has sides of length 2 and 6. **31.** 48 ft^2 **33.** 64 **35.** 1000 **37.** 3 cm **39.** *Sample answer:* 1490

2.3 Problem Solving Strategies (p. 67)

1. 7 yd by 1 yd, 6 yd by 2 yd, 5 yd by 3 yd, 4 yd by 4 yd   **3.** *Sample answer:* Place the 5 centimeter rod end to end with the 7 centimeter rod to make a 12 centimeter rod. Use the difference between this combination and the 13 centimeter rod to measure 1 centimeter.   **5.** 1 mi   **7.** 6   **9.** any animal name that has three letters in it, such as "cat"

2.3 Getting Ready to Practice (p. 70)

1. Each inch on the scale drawing represents 40 miles on the actual object.   **3.** 3 cm   **5.** 10 cm

2.3 Practice and Problem Solving
(pp. 70–71)   **7.** 300 mi   **9.** 750 mi   **11.** 6 cm
13. 2 in.   **15.** 7 in.   **17.** *Sample answer:* The actual length of 20 feet corresponds to 5 feet in the scale. So you should multiply 2 inches by 4, and the length of the model is 8 inches.

The length of the model is 8 inches.
19. 5 cm   **21.** 4500 m   **23.** 20; 120 times taller
25. reasonable   **27.** 0, 1, 3, 4, 8, 16   **29.** 11, 14, 22, 23, 25

2.4 Getting Ready to Practice (p. 74)

1. frequency   **3.**

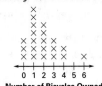

Number of Bicycles Owned

2.4 Practice and Problem Solving
(pp. 74–75)

5.

Type of call	Tally	Frequency
building fires	JHT I	6
other fires	JHT JHT II	12
hazardous materials	JHT II	7
rescues	III	3
false alarms	JHT II	7
mutual aid	IIII	4

7. 39 calls

9.

Point values of shots	Tally	Frequency
1	JHT II	7
2	JHT JHT I	11
3	III	3

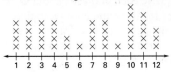

2 occurs most often and 3 occurs least often.

Number of Shots with Given Value

11. *Sample answer:* The frequency table is easier to use to find the number of occurrences. The line plot is easier to use to see the items that occurred most or least often.   **13.** 4 days   **15.** No. *Sample answer:* The items being tallied are not numbers, so a line plot cannot be used to display the data.
17. Check line plots of birth months of classmates.

Birth Months of United States Presidents

19. 2 more students   **21.** 0, 7, 14, 21, 28, 35
23. 0, 20, 40, 60, 80, 100

2.1–2.4 Notebook Review (pp. 76–77)
1. The area of a figure is the amount of surface the figure covers. The perimeter of a figure is the distance around the figure.   **2.** $P = 28$ in.; $A = 49$ in.^{2}
3. 4 in.; 4 in.   **4.** 64 m   **5.** 96 m   **6.** 64 m   **7.** 192 m

8.

Number	Tally	Frequency
10	II	2
11	III	3
12	III	3
13	III	3
14	I	1
15	III	3

9. A good situation for an estimate will be one in which an exact measurement is not needed, such as the distance between a city in California and a city in New York. **10.** Frequency tables and line plots are similar in that they both tell how frequent a number occurs. They are different in that the frequency table makes it easier to see the number of occurrences, whereas the line plot makes it easier to see which item occurred most or least often.

2.5 Getting Ready to Practice (p. 81)

1. *Sample answer:* Start the scale at 0 and end at a value greater than the greatest data value. Use equal increments along the scale.

3.
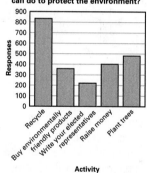
What is the most important thing kids can do to protect the environment?

2.5 Practice and Problem Solving
(pp. 81–82) **5.**
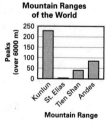
Mountain Ranges of the World

7.
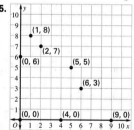
Cost of Food

9. ice cream   **11.** *Sample answer:* If the greatest data value in the scale is much greater than the actual greatest data value and the increments are too large, the differences in the bars will seem to be less than they really are.   **15.** 4   **17.** 8
19. \$4.75   **21.** \$2.25

2.6 Getting Ready to Practice (p. 85) **1.** *C*
3. *E*   **5.** 160; 200   **7.** No. *Sample answer:* They watched less television from 1992 to 1996, and then more television from 1996 to 2000.

2.6 Practice and Problem Solving
(pp. 85–86) **8–15.**
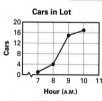

17.

Cars in Lot

19.
Number of Students

21.

Countries Connected to Internet   about 125 countries

SA4

23. 127 beats per minute   **25.** 2 inches on the map represents 15 miles on the ground.   **27.** 18   **29.** 75

2.6 Technology Activity (p. 87)

1.

■ Male population
□ Female population

2.7 Getting Ready to Practice (p. 89)

5. Look at the sections for ages from 0 to 34. They make up about half of the circle, which means they make up about half of the population.

2.7 Practice and Problem Solving

(pp. 90–91) **7.** A   **9.** Arctic Ocean   **11.** 335 million km^2 **13.** 148 doubles   **15.** 108 home runs
17. $160,000   **19.** about $1900   **21.** fall; bar graph
23. 276 people   **27.** 6   **29.**

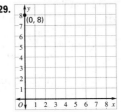

31. 156   **33.** 225

2.8 Getting Ready to Practice (p. 95)

1. range; median   **3.** mean = 8, median = 8, mode = 8, range = 5   **5.** Step 1: mean = 26, median = 23, mode = 21; Step 2: The mean is a little higher than the typical age; the median represents the data well; the mode is a little lower than the typical age. Step 3: median

2.8 Practice and Problem Solving

(pp. 95–97) **7.** mean = 11, median = 9, mode = 5, range = 20   **9.** mean = 31, median = 33, modes = 25 and 37, range = 24   **11.** mean = 40, median = 30, mode = 30, range = 70   **13.** mean = 155, median = 175, mode = 180; *Sample answer:* The median or the mode is the best average to represent a typical score because either is closer to the middle of the set.   **15.** mean = 73, median = 73, mode = 77, range = 10   **17.** green   **19.** No;

no; the data sets are not numerical.   **21.** 832
23. No; 8; the mean given is too close to the least data value.   **25.** No; 16; the mean given is too close to the greatest data value.   **27.** true
29. false   **31.** A good answer should include these two points for each of the three averages. • The data set listed should actually have the average given. • The context should make it very clear that the given average is most descriptive of the data set.   **35.** 25 people   **37.** thirty-five   **39.** six hundred seven

2.5–2.8 Notebook Review (pp. 98–99)

1. ordered pair   **2.** Add the values and divide by the number of values.   **3.** *Sample answer:* Start the scale at 0 and end the scale at 16, using equal increments of 2.

4.

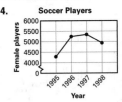

5.

6. Lake Ontario   **7.** mean = 50, median = 45, modes = 39 and 45, range = 43   **8.** *Sample answer:* Start the scale at 0 and end the scale at a value greater than the greatest data value, using equal increments along the scale.   **9.** *Sample answer:* Data values that are much less or much greater than most of the other data values can make the mean less or greater than the average that best represents the data.

Chapter Review (pp. 100–101)

1. The answer should include any three of the following: inch, foot, yard, mile.   **3.** false   **5.** coordinate
7. median; median; average   **9.** feet; meters
11. miles; kilometers   **13.** paper clip; 3 in.
15. *Sample answer:* 3 little fingers; 35 mm; 4 cm
17. $P = 36$ yd; $A = 81$ yd^2 **19.** 256 in.

21.

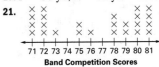

23-26.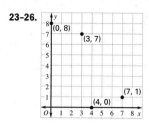

27.

29. 20 more wins **31.** mean = 120, median = 100, mode = 100, range = 130 **33.** Median. *Sample answer:* It is the closest to most of the data.

Chapter 3

3.1 Getting Ready to Practice (p. 109)
1. hundredths **3.** hundred-thousandths
5. *Sample answer:* There is no *and* after "hundred," so the number should have a zero to the left of the decimal point. The answer should be 0.412. **7.** 6.009 **9.** eight and fourteen ten-thousandths **11.** twenty-four and six thousandths

3.1 Practice and Problem Solving
(pp. 109–111) **13.** 7 **15.** 15; 150 **21.** 30.15
23. 0.705 **25.** 86.0143 **27.** four and sixteen hundredths **29.** seventeen and twenty-two thousandths **31.** ten and two hundred fifty-five ten-thousandths **33.** 1.99 km **35.** $.20
37. $.70 **39.** 0.09; 0.002 **41.** 0.007; 0.0002
43. one and five hundredths carats
45. 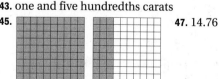 **47.** 14.76

49. 85.30 **51.** Russia **55.** 5. *Sample answer:* I chose Draw a Diagram because it was easy to draw and label booths and spaces until the length is about 50 feet. **57.** four million, twenty-seven thousand

3.2 Getting Ready to Practice (p. 115)
1. 0.01 **3.** 100 **5.** Step 1: 4 mm; Step 2: 0.4; Step 3: 2.4 cm

3.2 Practice and Problem Solving
(pp. 115–117) **7.** 5.02 **9.** 12.004 **11.** 0.88 m
13. *A*; 1.3 cm; *B*; 3.9 cm; *C*; 4.5 cm; *D*; 7.4 cm; *E*; 9.0 cm **15.** 3.4 cm **17.** 0.96 cm **19.** 1.14 m
21. Answers may vary. **23.** Answers may vary.
25. 1.372 m **27.** 2 cm **29.** greater than
31. equal to

3.3 Getting Ready to Practice (p. 120)
1. 7.55 **3.** 7.38 **5.** $2.79, $3.07, $3.29, $3.70, $3.79, $3.92

3.3 Practice and Problem Solving
(pp. 120–121) **7.** > **9.** > **11.** > **13.** = **15.** Yes; since 27.36 < 27.4, the book will stand upright.
17. 9.06, 9.07, 9.1 **19.** 0.1, 0.9, 1.1, 1.5 **21.** 0.98, 1.05, 1.15, 1.2 **23.** 0.055, 0.065, 0.55, 0.555, 0.56
25. Mauna Kea, Haleakala, West Maui, West Molokai **27.** *Sample answer:* 8.7 **29.** *Sample answer:* 3.65 **33.** 28.0016 **35.** 107,000

3.1–3.3 Notebook Review (pp. 122–123)
1. hundredths **2.** *Sample answer:* It separates the whole number part from the decimal part.
3. eleven and two tenths centimeters; 11.2 cm
4. twenty-six hundredths meter; 0.26 m **5.** > **6.** <
7. = **8.** 0.082, 0.09, 0.75, 0.91, 0.94 **9.** *Sample answer:* Five hundred ten-thousandths means the last digit in the decimal is in the ten-thousandths place. Five hundred ten thousandths means the last digit in the decimal is in the thousandths place. **10.** *Sample answer:* The last 0 in 0.50 represents 0 hundredths. Since 50 hundredths and 5 tenths represent the same part of one whole, they are equal.

3.4 Getting Ready to Practice (p. 126)
1. 2; 0.02 **3.** 1; 0.001 **5.** 8.2 **7.** 10.629
9. 8,400,000; 8.4 million

3.4 Practice and Problem Solving
(pp. 127–128) **11.** 10 **13.** 1.4 **15.** 3 **17.** 9.0
19. 3.90 **21.** 7.296 **23.** 0.03 **25.** 0.009 **27.** 0.0002
29. 0.00010 **31.** *Sample answer:* because many of
the scores would round to 81 **33.** 15,900,000;
15.9 million **35.** 10,000,000; 10.0 million
37. 1.29 **39.** 1.71 **41.** California: 76,700,000,
76.7 million; Illinois: 41,900,000, 41.9 million;
New York: 62,000,000, 62.0 million; Ohio:
60,200,000, 60.2 million; Washington: 48,100,000,
48.1 million **43.** *Sample answer:* 3.9, 4.2, 4.45
45. *Sample answer:* 3.35, 3.42, 3.44 **49.** *Sample answer:* 800 **51.** *Sample answer:* 310 **53.** =
55. 1926 **57.** 115

3.5 Getting Ready to Practice (p. 132)
1. 1 and 5 **3.** 18 **5.** Step 1: Check drawings. Step
2: 150 cm; Step 3: 150 centimeters is less than
157.16 centimeters, so they will fit beneath the
shelf.

3.5 Practice and Problem Solving
(pp. 132–133) **7.** 12 **9.** 2 **11.** 3 **13.** 8 **15.** 25
17. 0 **19.** $4.00; high; $1.15 was rounded down.
21. 15 **23.** 12 **25.** 11 **27.** Mount Kosciusko: 1.38,
Vinson Massif: 3.04, Mount Elbrus: 3.5, Mount
Kilimanjaro: 3.7, Mount McKinley: 3.85, Mount
Aconcagua: 4.33, Mount Everest: 5.50; 3.7 mi
29. *Sample answer:* The median; it is closer to
more of the heights than the mean is. **31.** 16
33. 5 **35.** 17.802 **37.** $12.00 **39.** $1.50

3.6 Problem Solving Strategies (p. 135)
1. 7 medals **3.** 3 buses **5.** no **7.** 652, 265, 256,
526, 562 **9.** $30

3.6 Getting Ready to Practice (p. 138)
1. commutative **3.** 18.64 **5.** 3.75 **7.** associative
property

3.6 Practice and Problem Solving
(pp. 139–140) **9.** 9.26 **11.** 24.54 **13.** 9.961 **15.** 3.26
17. 4.47 **19.** 2.76 **21.** 6.92 **23.** 5.74 **25.** 11.15
27. associative property; 19.5 **29.** commutative
property; 6.74 **31.** $4.76 **33.** 28.25 **35.** 21 cm
37. 12.3 m **39.** whistle

41.

Number	Tally	Frequency
0	I	1
1	IIII	4
2	II	2
3	IIII	4
4	III	3
5	IIII I	5
6	II	2
7	I	1
8	I	1
9	II	2

43. 168 **45.** 864

3.6 Technology Activity (p. 141) **1.** 7.385
3. 8.653 **5.** 4.852 **7.** 20.1 in. **9.** 7.514 mi

3.4–3.6 Notebook Review (pp. 142–143)
1. low **2.** commutative property **3.** 5.6
4. 3.047 **5.** 11 **6.** 7 **7.** 17 **8.** 16.298 **9.** 8.288
10. It increases the estimate and makes it more
accurate. **11.** *Sample answer:* With the decimal
points lined up, you add digits with the same
place value.

Chapter Review (pp. 144–145) **1.** fifteen
and three hundred sixty-eight thousandths
3. commutative property **5.** 12.2 **7.** 6.011 **9.** 4.4
11. 3.5 cm **13.** 17.02, 17.12, 17.20, 17.21 **15.** >
17. < **19.** = **21.** < **23.** 0.007 **25.** 1.61 **27.** 12
29. 4 **31.** 12 **33.** 9 **35.** 27 **37.** 18 **39.** 0.2 mi
41. $.68, $1.13, $1.49, $1.50, $1.62, $1.85; Paris;
London **43.** 5.98 **45.** 7.27 **47.** 8.143 **49.** 4.805
51. 5.63 **53.** 7.36 **55.** 12.657 **57.** 1.656

Chapter 4

4.1 Getting Ready to Practice (p. 155)
1. associative property of multiplication **3.** 15.60
5. 0.6; 3 times 2 tenths is 6 tenths. **7.** 15.82; 3 and
164 thousandths times 5 is 15 and 82 hundredths.

4.1 Practice and Problem Solving
(pp. 156–157) **9.** 0.8; 4 times 2 tenths is 8 tenths.
11. 0.06; 2 times 3 hundredths is 6 hundredths.
13. 7.857 **15.** *Sample answer:* There should be
four decimal places in the answer and there are

only three. Add a zero before the 112 and place the decimal point correctly. The correct product is 0.0112. **17.** 19.53 **19.** 95.58 **21.** 17.6 **23.** 24.576 **25.** 31.875 **27.** 0.09 **29.** 83; associative **31.** $338.45 **33.** $41.69 **35.** *Sample answer:* 24 × 1 is 24, which is less than the actual product. **37.** *Sample answer:* It does not change the answer in any way or have any effect on the value of the number; if there is a digit in the tenths place, there must be a digit in the hundredths place for money. **39.** 15 **43.** 60 **45.** *Sample answer:* 14 **47.** *Sample answer:* 11 **49.** hundred **51.** ten thousand

4.1 Technology Activity (p. 158) **1.** $1474.48; $76,672.96 **3.** $1408.40; $73,236.80

4.2 Getting Ready to Practice (p. 161) **1.** 2(3.1) + 2(7.4) **3.** 50, 7 **5.** 3.2, 8

4.2 Practice and Problem Solving (pp. 161–162) **7.** 332 **9.** 58 **11.** 67.2 **13.** 75 **15.** 271.8 **17.** 90.86 **19.** The 2 was distributed to the 32 and not to the 6. The solution should be 2(32 + 6) = 2(32) + 2(6) = 64 + 12 = 76. **21.** 7, 7 **23.** 60 **25.** 686 **27.** 369 **29.** 46 **31.** 48.3 **33.** $14.75 **35.** 5¢ **37.** 66 in. **39.** $5x + 26$ **45.** 7.06, 7.6, 7.61, 7.63 **47.** 5.93 **49.** 2.528 **51.** 30,000

4.3 Getting Ready to Practice (p. 166) **1.** sum **3.** 0.8 **5.** 15.708 **7.** 17.325 ft^2

4.3 Practice and Problem Solving (pp. 167–168) **9.** 0.27 **11.** *Sample answer:* The original problem has two decimal places, so the answer should also have two decimal places. The solution should be

```
      7.5
   ×  3.8
    6 00
   22 5
   28.50
```

13. 60.532 **15.** 0.18 **17.** 2.976 **19.** 14.3444 **21.** 14.95 **23.** 0.09008 **25.** 84.4262 **27.** 2.89 ft^2 **29.** 2.25 in. **31.** > **33.** < **35.** no; 3.78 **37.** yes **39.** ham: $4.12; cheese: $2.40; turkey: $5.31; total: $11.83 **41.** *Sample answer:* Use zero as a placeholder when the number of decimal places needed is greater than the number of digits in the product. For example, 0.2 × 0.036 = 0.0072, where the two zeros before the 7 were added to create four decimal places. **43.** Less than. *Sample answer:* A model can be used to show that the number of squares shaded for the product is less than the number of squares shaded for either of the two numbers.

45–48.

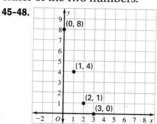

49. fifteen and two hundredths miles **51.** 335 **53.** 15

4.4 Getting Ready to Practice (p. 171) **1.** quotient **3.** divisor **5.** 4.4 **7.** 1.2

4.4 Practice and Problem Solving (pp. 171–173) **9.** 8.25 **11.** 1.75 **13.** 7.4 **15.** 0.7 **17.** 3.5 **19.** 4.8 **21.** 4.0 **23.** 6.7 **25.** 9.5 **27.** 1.9 **29.** 3.7 min **31.** $9.80 **33.** $11.50 **35.** 0.308 **37.** 0.310 **39.** 0.4 **41.** 3.6 **43.** = **45.** 8 tram cars **47.** 11.25 mL. *Sample answer:* An estimate can be used because the amount is so small. **49.** 10 **51.** 0.01 **53.** 9 **55.** 2 **57.** 34.146 **59.** 8.3889 **61.** *Sample answer:* 790 **63.** *Sample answer:* 1000

4.1–4.4 Notebook Review (pp. 174–175) **1.** distributive property **2.** 5.226 **3.** 0.6 **4.** 12.48 **5.** 290 **6.** 184 **7.** 417 **8.** 153 **9.** 0.42 **10.** 40.392 **11.** 0.0852 **12.** 7.3 **13.** 6.5 **14.** 3.3 **15.** 0.2 **16.** *Sample answer:* Write 5.1 as 5 + 0.1 and use the distributive property. So, 7(5 + 0.1) = 35 + 0.7 = 35.7. **17.** Add the number of decimal places in each of the two factors to find the number of decimal places in the product. Because 2 + 1 = 3, the product has 3 decimal places.

4.5 Getting Ready to Practice (p. 178) **1.** 10, 100 **3.** 75.8 **5.** 0.1635 **7.** 1.34 **9.** 521 **11.** 5670 in.^{2}

4.5 Practice and Problem Solving

(pp. 178–179) **17.** 743.4 **19.** 5020 **21.** 10
23. 0.03457 **25.** 1257 **27.** 317.25
29. 87,200 microns **31.** 375 **33.** 634 **35.** 9.1
37. 81,000 **39.** > **43.** 20.89 **45.** 1.27 **47.** 0.0896
49. 48.3042 **51.** $.09 **53.** $8.68

4.6 Getting Ready to Practice (p. 182)

1. dividend: 8.49, divisor: 0.3 **3.** 28$\overline{)476}$ **5.** 21$\overline{)0.4}$
7. 500 **9.** 2.05

4.6 Practice and Problem Solving

(pp. 182–184) **11.** 91 ÷ 43 **13.** 700 ÷ 38
15. 132 ÷ 55 **17.** 1390 ÷ 32 **19.** 80 **21.** 8.6
23. 3.1 **25.** 1.5 **27.** 75.7 **29.** 2.3 **31.** 365.76 cm.
Sample answer: Multiplication will show how long
the pictures are. **33.** 4.6 cm. *Sample answer:*
Division will give the width of the rectangle.
35. $1.11 **37.** $2.59 **39.** 0.03 **41.** 800 **43.** 108
45. 304.3 **47.** 32.5 mi/gal **49.** *Sample answer:*
1.8 + 1.7 = 3.5, 7.1 − 3.6 = 3.5, 1.75 × 2 = 3.5,
10.5 ÷ 3 = 3.5 **51.** 1.65 **53.** 13.18 **55.** 5.0 times
greater **57.** = **59.** < **63.** 6 **65.** 28 **67.** 3
69. 32.148 **71.** banana; 30 students
73. 95 students

4.7 Problem Solving Strategies (p. 186)

1. *Sample answer:* Jump rope 10 times.
3. 5 toothpicks **5.** 1 ft by 100 ft, 2 ft by 50 ft, 4 ft
by 25 ft, 5 ft by 20 ft, 10 ft by 10 ft **7.** 23 and 25

4.7 Getting Ready to Practice (p. 189)

1. capacity **3.** length **5.** kilogram **7.** capacity

4.7 Practice and Problem Solving

(pp. 189–190) **9.** mass **11.** capacity **13.** length
15. length **17.** nickel **19.** Grams. *Sample answer:*
It is closest to the mass of a paper clip. **21.** liter
23. kilogram **25.** milliliter **27.** Liters. *Sample
answer:* The amounts used would be closest
to the capacity of a large bottle of water.
29. 2886.8 L; 2.8868 kL **31.** 1000 **33.** 6000
35. 0.004 **39.** 0.093 **41.** 0.057 **43.** 0.374
45. *Sample answer:* 5 **47.** *Sample answer:* 100

4.8 Getting Ready to Practice (p. 193)

1. meter, gram, liter **3.** 0.52 **5.** 800

4.8 Practice and Problem Solving

(pp. 193–195) **7.** divide **9.** multiply **11.** 10
13. 1000 **15.** 0.8 **17.** 0.255 **19.** 4000 **21.** 800
23. 8100 **25.** 0.75 L **27.** 0.64 m **29.** < **31.** <
33. > **35.** arm span **37.** 7.26 kg; 5.98 kg; 2.72 kg;
6.79 kg **39.** mean = 4.998 kg, median = 5.25 kg,
mode = 2.72 kg. *Sample answer:* Mean; it is closer
to the middle of all the data. **41.** 1.44 km²
43. The answer in square meters will be 1,000,000
times the answer in square kilometers. **45.** yes
49. 64 **51.** 64 **53.** 2.4 **55.** 32.618 **57.** 4.587
59. 3160 **61.** 101, 105, 110, 150

4.5–4.8 Notebook Review (pp. 196–197)

1. mass, capacity **2.** *Sample answer:* Multiply
both the divisor and the dividend by a power of 10
that will make the divisor a whole number.
3. 380.6 **4.** 4.591 **5.** 62.137 **6.** 97,800 **7.** 1069.0
8. 43.7 **9.** 23.8 **10.** 606.4 **11.** gram **12.** milliliter
13. 0.0245 **14.** 21,200 **15.** 2 **16.** divide; multiply

Chapter Review (pp. 198–199)

1. distributive
property **3.** milliliter, liter, kiloliter **5.** multiply
7. 20.9 **9.** 144.532 **11.** 102 **13.** 1304.96
15. $130.50 **17.** 231 **19.** 16 **21.** 44.5 **23.** 235
25. 2.96 **27.** 0.5202 **29.** 0.0427 **31.** 2.6256
33. 12.645 **35.** 3.9483 **37.** 2.4 **39.** 6.9 **41.** 9.7
43. 4.1 **45.** 19.8 **47.** 1.6 **49.** 90 **51.** 12.5
53. $1.35 **55.** 24 **57.** 0.6569 **59.** 0.08147
61. 3.2 mm **63.** milligram **65.** milliliter
67. gram **69.** 0.729 **71.** 54,900 **73.** 17
75. 30,000 **77.** 2.7 mg, 0.027 kg, 270 g
79. 8 cm, 0.8 m, 8000 mm

Chapter 5

5.1 Getting Ready to Practice (p. 216)

1. *Sample answer:* All even numbers are divisible
by 2. **3.** *Sample answer:* A number is divisible by
5 if it ends in a 5 or a 0. **5.** composite **7.** prime
9. **11.**

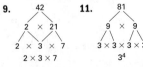

5.1 Practice and Problem Solving

(pp. 217–219) **13.** 1, 2, 7, 14 **15.** 1, 19 **17.** 1, 2, 4, 5,
10, 20, 25, 50, 100 **19.** 1, 11, 121 **21.** 140 is

divisible by 2, 5, and 10, but not by 3, 6, or 9. **23.** 282 is divisible by 2, 3, and 6, but not by 5, 9, or 10. **25.** 1578 is divisible by 2, 3, and 6, but not by 5, 9, or 10. **27.** 8745 is divisible by 3 and 5, but not by 2, 6, 9, or 10. **29.** prime **31.** composite **33.** prime **35.** composite **37.** Yes. *Sample answer:* 117 is divisible by 3. **39.** 3×13 **41.** $3^2 \times 7$ **43.** 2×3^3 **45.** $2 \times 3 \times 5^2$ **49.** true **51.** false **53.** 2, 3, 4, or 6; 24, 16, 12, or 8 **55.** *Sample answer:* 6; if there are 6 students per team, there will be 8 teams, or 4 pairs of teams. In the first round of races, 4 teams will win and 4 will lose. So there will be 4 teams left for the runoff. **57.** 30 **59.** 90 **61.** 53×67 **65.** 296 **67.** 216 **69.** 32.1 **71.** 3.0 **73.** 103 stickers

5.2 Problem Solving Strategies (p. 221)
1. 4 possibilities **3.** 5 ways **5.** 6 code words **7.** 12 tacks **9.** No; the cars will only hold 20 people and they need to hold 21 people.

5.2 Getting Ready to Practice (p. 224)
1. 2 **3.** 15

5.2 Practice and Problem Solving
(pp. 224–225) **5.** The factor of 14 is not included in the factors of 28. So the GCF is 14. **7.** 12 **9.** 11 **11.** 8 **13.** 18 **15.** 4 **17.** 1 **19.** 8 **21.** 13 **23.** 16 people **25.** sometimes **27.** always **33.** 0.0005 **35.** 900 **37.** $\frac{3}{8}$

5.3 Getting Ready to Practice (p. 230) **1.** yes
3. no; $\frac{1}{3}$ **9.** blue: $\frac{5}{18}$; orange: $\frac{1}{2}$; green: $\frac{2}{9}$

5.3 Practice and Problem Solving
(pp. 231–232) **11–17.** Answers may vary.
11. $\frac{2}{20}$, $\frac{3}{30}$ **13.** $\frac{6}{10}$, $\frac{9}{15}$ **15.** $\frac{18}{40}$, $\frac{27}{60}$ **17.** $\frac{6}{200}$, $\frac{9}{300}$
19. 45 **21.** 4 **23.** 54 **25.** 7 **27.** no; $\frac{1}{3}$ **29.** yes
31. no; $\frac{8}{9}$ **33.** no; $\frac{2}{7}$ **35.** $\frac{1}{2}$ **37.** 5 **39.** 54
41. $\frac{1}{16}$ **43.** sometimes **49.** 2 **51.** 4 **53.** $\frac{4}{12}$.
Sample answer: I used Make a Table to solve the problem so I could keep track of the numerators and denominators and their relationships.
55. 1200 **57.** 120,000

5.1–5.3 Notebook Review (pp. 233–234)
1. prime number **2.** 3, 9, composite number **3.** 49 is not divisible by 2, 3, 5, 6, 9, or 10. **4.** 252 is divisible by 2, 3, 6, and 9, but not by 5 or 10. **5.** 396 is divisible by 2, 3, 6, and 9, but not by 5 or 10. **6.** 1402 is divisible by 2, but not by 3, 5, 6, 9, or 10. **7.** 12 **8.** 27 **9.** $\frac{1}{7}$ **10.** $\frac{2}{3}$ **11.** $\frac{5}{16}$ **12.** $\frac{4}{9}$
13. *Sample answer:* You can use the rules to quickly determine a factor of a number.
14. *Sample answer:* 8 and 16; multiplied 8 by two different numbers.

5.4 Getting Ready to Practice (p. 237)
1. 7, 14, 21 **3.** 11, 22, 33 **5.** 96 **7.** Step 1: 6, 12, 18, 24, 30, 36, . . .; 3, 6, 9, 12, 15, 18, 21, . . .; Step 2: 6, 12, 18; Step 3: game 6; 3 times

5.4 Practice and Problem Solving
(pp. 237–238) **9.** 40 **11.** 60 **13.** 16 **15.** 72 **17.** 84 **19.** 396 **21.** 135 **23.** 360 **25.** 300th customer; find the LCM of 20 and 75. **27.** 3 and 17 **29.** 4 and 16 **31.** 2.056 **33.** 54.5 **35.** 0.25 **37.** *Sample answer:* $\frac{6}{20}$, $\frac{9}{30}$ **39.** *Sample answer:* $\frac{24}{34}$, $\frac{36}{51}$ **41.** > **43.** <

5.5 Getting Ready to Practice (p. 241)
1. the least common multiple of the denominators **3.** 6; > **5.** 20; <

5.5 Practice and Problem Solving
(pp. 241–242) **7.** > **9.** > **11.** > **13.** < **15.** = **17.** > **19.** $\frac{7}{8}$ in. album **21.** $\frac{5}{8}$, $\frac{2}{3}$, $\frac{3}{4}$ **23.** $\frac{4}{5}$, $\frac{17}{20}$, $\frac{9}{10}$ **25.** $\frac{5}{9}$, $\frac{7}{12}$, $\frac{3}{4}$ **27.** $\frac{3}{8}$, $\frac{4}{9}$, $\frac{11}{24}$ **29.** The bracelet containing $\frac{2}{3}$ gold. **31.** Africa **33.** South America **37.** 12,000 **39.** $\frac{1}{4}$ **41.** $\frac{2}{5}$ **43.** 137 **45.** 1402

5.6 Getting Ready to Practice (p. 246)
1. A fraction is improper if its numerator is greater than or equal to its denominator. **3.** 13 **5.** 3 **7.** = **9.** <

5.6 Practice and Problem Solving
(pp. 247–248) **11.** $2\frac{1}{8}$ in.; $\frac{17}{8}$ in. **13.** $\frac{9}{2}$ **15.** $\frac{17}{5}$ **17.** $\frac{23}{3}$ **19.** $\frac{21}{2}$ **21.** $2\frac{2}{3}$ **23.** $3\frac{3}{5}$ **25.** $6\frac{1}{2}$ **27.** $1\frac{5}{7}$

29. $2\frac{3}{4}, 3, \frac{7}{2}$ **31.** $5, \frac{41}{8}, 5\frac{1}{6}, \frac{17}{3}$ **33.** $\frac{6}{6}$ **35.** $\frac{14}{14}$

37. *Sample answer:* $1\frac{4}{5}$ **39.** *Sample answer:* $3\frac{1}{4}$

43. 19 **45.** 18 **47.** twenty-three and five tenths
49. seventy-eight and fifteen hundredths
51. 10,000 **53.** 4390

5.7 Getting Ready to Practice (p. 251)

1. When the GCF of the numerator and
denominator is 1. **3.** 27 **5.** 2 **7.** Write a mixed
number with the whole number being 128 and
the fraction $\frac{4}{10}$ which simplifies to $\frac{2}{5}$.

5.7 Practice and Problem Solving

(pp. 251–252) **9.** $0.53; \frac{53}{100}$ **11.** $3.11; 3\frac{11}{100}$ **13.** $\frac{18}{25}$

15. $9\frac{3}{10}$ **17.** $3\frac{1}{100}$ **19.** $\frac{403}{500}$ **21.** $\frac{1}{40}$ **23.** $9\frac{401}{1000}$

25. clothing, food, gifts, electronics, furniture
27. $\frac{1177}{2500}$ in. **33.** 0.7 **35.** 0.6 **37.** $\frac{11}{36}, \frac{1}{2}, \frac{13}{18}, \frac{5}{6}$

39. 300

5.8 Getting Ready to Practice (p. 255)

1. terminating **3.** repeating **5.** $0.\overline{1}$ **7.** $8.0\overline{4}$
9. 0.4 **11.** 2.75 **13.** 0.67 lb

5.8 Practice and Problem Solving

(pp. 255–256) **15.** 0.388888 . . . **17.** 0.49159159 . . .
19. 0.8 **21.** 2.84 **23.** 3.75 **25.** $0.2\overline{7}$ **27.** $5.\overline{8}$

29. $0.58\overline{3}$ **31.** $1\frac{3}{4}; 1.75$ **33.** 0.92; 0.08 **35.** true
37. $0.0\overline{9}, 0.1\overline{8}, 0.2\overline{7}; 0.\overline{36}, 0.\overline{45}$ **39.** 0.5 **41.** 2.000
43. grams **45.** milligrams **47.** $2^2 \times 17$
49. $2^3 \times 3^2 \times 7$ **51.** *Sample answer:* 10,000

5.8 Technology Activity (p. 257) **1.** 0.83

3. 0.31 **5.** 5.38 **7.** 13.39 **9.** 29.19 **11.** 50.82
13. $13.38

5.4–5.8 Notebook Review (pp. 258–259)

1. Multiples of 6: 6, 12, 18, 24, 30, 36, 42, 48, 54,
60, 66, 72, 78, 84, 90, 96; multiples of 8: 8, 16, 24,
32, 40, 48, 56, 64, 72, 80, 88, 96; no; the LCM
of 6 and 8 is 24, not 48. **2.** repeating decimal
3. $\frac{7}{25}, \frac{3}{10}, \frac{2}{5}, \frac{7}{10}$ **4.** $1\frac{1}{4} < \frac{5}{3}$ **5.** $\frac{7}{2} > 3\frac{1}{8}$ **6.** $\frac{13}{20}$
7. 2.65 **8.** Find the smallest of all of the common
multiples; use the prime factorization and

multiply together the prime factors, using each
the greatest number of times it is a factor of any of
the numbers. *Sample answer:* Use prime
factorization if the numbers are large and list
multiples if the numbers are small. **9.** Yes.
Sample answer: It is hard to compare them in
different forms.

Chapter Review (pp. 260–261) **1.** a multiple
shared by two or more numbers **3.** *Sample
answer:* 2, 3, 5; their only factors are 1 and itself.
5. equivalent **7.** proper fraction **9.** 150 is
divisible by 2, 3, 5, 6, and 10, but not by 9. **11.** 430
is divisible by 2, 5, and 10, but not by 3, 6, or 9.
13. 1464 is divisible by 2, 3, and 6, but not by 5, 9,
or 10. **15.** 2970 is divisible by 2, 3, 5, 6, 9, and 10.
17. $2^4 \times 5$ **19.** $2^2 \times 3^3$ **21.** $3^2 \times 23$ **23.** $3^2 \times 7^2$

25. 4 **27.** 5 **29.** 9 **31.** 13 **33.** no; $\frac{3}{8}$ **35.** no; $\frac{11}{31}$

37. 20 **39.** 76 **41.** 104 **43.** 40 **45.** 60 min **47.** >

49. < **51.** $\frac{5}{28}, \frac{3}{14}, \frac{1}{4}$ **53.** $\frac{1}{72}, \frac{1}{24}, \frac{1}{18}, \frac{1}{12}$ **55.** $\frac{21}{5}$

57. $2\frac{5}{9}$ **59.** $4\frac{4}{5}$ **61.** $\frac{121}{200}$ **63.** 3.4 **65.** 2.125

Chapter 6

6.1 Getting Ready to Practice (p. 269)

1. Fractions; whole number **3.** 0 **5.** 4

7. *Sample answer:* 7 **9.** *Sample answer:* $\frac{1}{2}$

6.1 Practice and Problem Solving

(pp. 269–270) **11.** 1 **13.** 4 **15–25.** Estimates may
vary. **15.** 0 **17.** 0 **19.** 1 **21.** 5 **23.** 5 **25.** 3
27. 5 c **29.** high estimate; so that you will not run
out of paint **31.** high **33.** low **37.** 5 **39.** 6
41. $\frac{8}{3}$ **43.** $\frac{33}{4}$ **45.** 1012 **47.** 577

6.2 Getting Ready to Practice (p. 273)

1. numerators; common denominator **3.** $1\frac{1}{5}$

5. $\frac{3}{4}$

6.2 Practice and Problem Solving

(pp. 273–275) **7.** $\frac{2}{3}$ **9.** $\frac{7}{9}$ **11.** $\frac{1}{2}$ **13.** $\frac{1}{2}$ **15.** $1\frac{1}{7}$

17. $\frac{5}{8}$ **19.** $1\frac{4}{7}$ **21.** $\frac{4}{5}$ **23.** $\frac{1}{2}$ of the drawing

25. $1\frac{1}{2}$ ft **27.** 1 mi **29.** $\frac{1}{4}$ **31.** $\frac{1}{2}$ **33.** 1 **35.** $\frac{21}{25}$

37. $\frac{3}{100}$ **41.** 10 **43.** 36 **45.** 195 **47.** 2430

6.3 Getting Ready to Practice (p. 279)

1. LCD **3.** $1\frac{1}{18}$ **5.** $\frac{1}{2}$

6.3 Practice and Problem Solving

(pp. 279–281) **7.** $\frac{5}{9}$ **9.** $\frac{11}{30}$ **11.** $1\frac{5}{14}$ **13.** $\frac{5}{12}$ **15.** $\frac{11}{12}$

17. $\frac{23}{40}$ **19.** $\frac{2}{3}$ **21.** $\frac{13}{28}$ **23.** $\frac{1}{5}$ in. **25.** $\frac{5}{6}$ **27.** $\frac{1}{6}$ **29.** $\frac{1}{9}$

31. $1\frac{1}{12}$ **33.** $1\frac{7}{8}$ in. **35.** $1\frac{3}{14}$ yd **37.** $\frac{1}{12}$ **39.** $\frac{8}{15}$

41. central and southern regions **43.** *Sample answer:* Yes, as long as he or she adds the fractions $\frac{6}{8}$ and $\frac{4}{8}$ and then simplifies the answer of $\frac{10}{8}$ to $1\frac{1}{4}$.

45. $1\frac{5}{12}$ **51.** $1\frac{1}{5}$ **53.** $1\frac{1}{2}$ **55.** 450, 455, 504, 540, 545

6.1–6.3 Notebook Review (pp. 282–283)

1. *Sample answer:* Since $\frac{1}{2}$ is halfway between 3 and 4, round up to 4. **2.** 24 **3–6.** Estimates may vary. **3.** 1 **4.** $\frac{1}{2}$ **5.** 1 **6.** 6 **7.** $\frac{2}{3}$ **8.** $1\frac{1}{2}$

9. $\frac{2}{5}$ **10.** $\frac{1}{4}$ **11.** $\frac{9}{10}$ **12.** $1\frac{1}{8}$ **13.** $\frac{13}{28}$ **14.** $\frac{1}{18}$

15. *Sample answer:* It depends on whether the fraction itself is closer to 1 or $\frac{1}{2}$. If the fraction is closer to 1, then the estimate is closer if you round the mixed number to the nearest whole number. If the fraction is closer to $\frac{1}{2}$, then the estimate is closer if you round the mixed number to the nearest half. **16.** Yes. *Sample answer:* The denominators must be the same before you can add or subtract fractions.

6.4 Getting Ready to Practice (p. 286) 1. $2\frac{3}{4}$

3. $4\frac{3}{4}$ **5.** $3\frac{5}{7}$ **7.** $6\frac{1}{4}$ **9.** $1\frac{2}{5}$ **11.** $3\frac{3}{4}$ **13.** $1\frac{5}{12}$ ft

6.4 Practice and Problem Solving

(pp. 287–288) **15.** $10\frac{1}{3}$ **17.** $7\frac{9}{10}$ **19.** $10\frac{5}{12}$

21. $16\frac{1}{9}$ **23.** $3\frac{7}{12}$ **25.** $2\frac{7}{12}$ **27.** $1\frac{5}{8}$ in.

29. $11\frac{14}{15}$; pencil and paper **31.** $9\frac{5}{6}$; mental math

33. 8; mental math **35.** 4; mental math **37.** $7\frac{1}{3}$

39. $\frac{1}{2}$ **41.** $3\frac{1}{2}$ **43.** $1\frac{1}{4}$ **45.** $37\frac{1}{2}$ cents **47.** $6\frac{1}{12}$; answers may vary. **49.** $10\frac{1}{2}$ ft **51.** < **53.** < **55.** $\frac{1}{2}$

57. $\frac{1}{24}$ **59.** 190,000 **61.** 8,900,000

6.5 Getting Ready to Practice (p. 292)

1. 7 **3.** 4 **5.** $1\frac{1}{3}$ **7.** $1\frac{3}{4}$ **9.** $9\frac{3}{4}$ mi

6.5 Practice and Problem Solving

(pp. 292–294) **11.** $2\frac{1}{2}$ **13.** $4\frac{5}{7}$ **15.** $2\frac{1}{8}$ **17.** $9\frac{7}{15}$

19. $1\frac{9}{14}$ **21.** $\frac{3}{4}$ **23.** $1\frac{3}{4}$ mi **25.** *Sample answer:* $4\frac{2}{5}$ should be renamed as $3\frac{7}{5}$; the solution should be $4\frac{2}{5} - 1\frac{4}{5} = 3\frac{7}{5} - 1\frac{4}{5} = 2\frac{3}{5}$. **27.** Yes; you cannot subtract $\frac{5}{6}$ from $\frac{1}{2}$. **29.** Yes; you cannot subtract $\frac{5}{7}$ from $\frac{4}{7}$. **31.** No; you can subtract 0 from $\frac{2}{5}$.

33. Yes; you cannot subtract $\frac{3}{4}$ from $\frac{2}{3}$. **35.** $\frac{1}{4}$

37. $\frac{1}{8}$ **39.** $\frac{1}{3}$ ft **41.** $1\frac{1}{3}$ **43.** $1\frac{19}{20}$ **45.** $4\frac{1}{6}$ **47.** $\frac{3}{4}$

49. $21\frac{3}{4}$ in. **51.** $19\frac{1}{2}$ in. **55.** $5\frac{1}{9}$ **57.** $3\frac{3}{4}$ **59.** 3.3 m. *Sample answer:* I used Draw a Diagram because the picture helped me see what I needed to find. **61.** 4; 50 **63.** 660

6.5 Technology Activity (p. 295) 1. The A4 size is $2\frac{3}{8}$ inches wider and $3\frac{5}{12}$ inches longer.

3. The two sizes are the same width, and the U.S. legal size is 3 inches longer.

6.6 Problem Solving Strategies (p. 297)

1. 79 points **3.** 60 **5.** Wednesday **7.** Row 1: remove 8; Row 2: remove 3; Row 3: remove 6 **9.** 32 yd^2

6.6 Getting Ready to Practice (p. 300)

1. 2 **3.** 5 **5.** 1 h 36 min **7.** 6 h 31 min 22 sec **9.** 5 h 15 min

6.6 Practice and Problem Solving

(pp. 300–301) **11.** 3 h 25 min **13.** 5 h 33 min 35 sec
15. 2 h 15 min **17.** 2 h **19.** 4 h 35 min
21. 7 h 50 min **23.** 6 h 20 min **25.** 1 h 35 min
27. yes **29.** 10:05 P.M. **31.** yes **33.** no **35.** $\frac{3}{4}$
37. $1\frac{11}{18}$ **39.** 320 **41.** 1800

6.4–6.6 Notebook Review (pp. 302–303)

1. *Sample answer:* 3 can be rewritten as $2\frac{3}{3}$, so $3\frac{1}{3}$
is equal to $2\frac{4}{3}$. **2.** elapsed time **3.** $8\frac{5}{7}$ **4.** $9\frac{7}{24}$
5. $5\frac{5}{14}$ **6.** $5\frac{2}{3}$ **7.** $2\frac{7}{12}$ **8.** $2\frac{13}{15}$ **9.** $1\frac{3}{8}$ **10.** $1\frac{2}{5}$
11. 6 h 15 min **12.** 8 h 15 min **13.** *Sample
answer:* Sometimes you have to rename.

Chapter Review (pp. 304–305) **1.** half, mixed

numbers **3.** elapsed time **5–13.** Estimates may
vary. **5.** $1\frac{1}{2}$ **7.** 1 **9.** 12 **11.** 3 **13.** 5 h **15.** $1\frac{2}{3}$
17. $\frac{3}{5}$ **19.** $\frac{3}{5}$ **21.** $\frac{1}{10}$ **23.** $\frac{1}{12}$ in. **25.** $8\frac{1}{7}$ **27.** $3\frac{17}{21}$
29. $11\frac{1}{2}$ **31.** $4\frac{13}{30}$ **33.** $2\frac{8}{9}$ **35.** $5\frac{7}{10}$ **37.** $1\frac{5}{16}$ lb
39. 4 h 40 min 7 sec **41.** 2 h **43.** 6 h 15 min
45. 6 h 4 min

Chapter 7

7.1 Getting Ready to Practice (p. 315) **1.** yes
3. $3\frac{1}{2}$ **5.** 15 **7.** 4 **9.** 6

7.1 Practice and Problem Solving

(pp. 316–317) **11.** $2\frac{4}{7}$ **13.** $7\frac{1}{2}$ **15.** $\frac{5}{6}$ **17.** $2\frac{1}{2}$ **19.** 6
21. 40 **23.** 40 min **25.** $2\frac{1}{2}$ mi **27.** 20; 5 **29.** 30; 12
31. 48; 42 **33.** 33; 22 **35.** Parks: 48 million acres;
Preserves: 21 million acres; Recreation areas:
3 million acres; Monuments and other: 3 million
acres **37.** High; yes. *Sample answer:* If the rack is
too large, it will still hold all of the CDs; however,
if it is too small, it will not hold all of them.
39. 100 **41.** 44 **43.** 95°F **49.** 1.3413 **51.** 0.04366
53. $\frac{1}{2}$ **55.** 0 **57.** $\frac{2}{3}$

7.2 Getting Ready to Practice (p. 323) **1.** if
the GCF of the numerator and denominator is 1

3. $\frac{3}{10}$ **5.** $\frac{7}{10}$ **7.** $\frac{2}{3}$ **9.** The GCF of 3 and 9 is 3, and
9 divided by 3 is 3, not 2. The solution is $\frac{5}{12}$.

7.2 Practice and Problem Solving

(pp. 323–325) **11.** $\frac{4}{21}$ **13.** $\frac{3}{16}$ **15.** $\frac{3}{20}$ **17.** $\frac{4}{45}$ **19.** $\frac{1}{35}$
21. $\frac{6}{55}$ **23.** $\frac{2}{15}$ **25.** $\frac{1}{4}$ **27.** $\frac{1}{2}$ **29.** $\frac{3}{5}$ **31.** $\frac{5}{16}$ **33.** $\frac{1}{7}$
35. $\frac{3}{8}$ mi **37.** < **39.** = **41.** < **43.** $\frac{11}{12}$ **45.** $\frac{9}{50}$
47. $\frac{4}{13}$ **49.** $\frac{5}{28}$ **53.** 3 **55.** 4 **57.** 10 **59.** 18
61. *Sample answer:* 1000

7.3 Getting Ready to Practice (p. 328)

1. *Sample answer:* $2\frac{1}{2}$; $\frac{5}{4}$ **3.** no **5.** Yes; divide 9
into 18 and 9, and divide 5 into 25 and 10. **7.** 34
9. $2\frac{11}{12}$

7.3 Practice and Problem Solving

(pp. 328–330) **11.** $\frac{11}{12}$ **13.** $11\frac{1}{3}$ **15.** $2\frac{11}{12}$ **17.** $3\frac{4}{15}$
19. $9\frac{1}{3}$ **21.** 2 **23.** $1\frac{1}{8}$ **25.** $22\frac{1}{2}$ **27.** 15 **29.** 16
31. $1\frac{1}{32}$ yd^2 **33.** 70 min **35.** $5\frac{3}{4}$ must be changed
to an improper fraction and then multiplied by 3.
The solution should be $3 \times \frac{23}{4} = \frac{69}{4} = 17\frac{1}{4}$.
37. $9\frac{1}{24}$ **39.** $14\frac{7}{12}$ **41.** 5 × 3. *Sample answer:*
With 5 × 3, one factor is rounded up and one is
rounded down, so the estimate will be better.
43. $5\frac{8}{25}$ in.^{2} **45.** 24 ft **49.** 6 h 27 min
51. the number of groups

7.1–7.3 Notebook Review (pp. 331–332)

1. improper fractions **2.** 3; $3\frac{1}{6}$ **3.** 9; $8\frac{1}{4}$
4. 6; $5\frac{5}{8}$ **5.** 8; $8\frac{4}{7}$ **6.** $\frac{2}{7}$ **7.** $4\frac{2}{3}$ **8.** $5\frac{1}{4}$ **9.** $22\frac{1}{2}$
10. The product will be less than the whole
number if the fraction is less than 1, and greater
than the whole number if the fraction is greater
then 1 (an improper fraction).

7.4 Getting Ready to Practice (p. 336)

1. no **3.** yes **5.** $\frac{9}{2} \times \frac{4}{3} = 6$ **7.** $\frac{2}{3} \times \frac{1}{4} = \frac{1}{6}$

9. Step 1: $12 \div \frac{5}{8}$; Step 2: $19\frac{1}{5}$; Step 3: *Sample answer:* You can only make 19 magnets because you cannot make $\frac{1}{5}$ of a magnet.

7.4 Practice and Problem Solving

(pp. 336–338) **11.** $\frac{7}{3}$ **13.** $\frac{3}{1}$ or 3 **15.** $\frac{1}{10}$ **17.** $\frac{2}{7}$ **19.** $\frac{5}{8}$ **21.** 1 **23.** 5, 30 **25.** The dividend must be multiplied by the reciprocal of the divisor. The solution should be $\frac{3}{4} \div \frac{1}{8} = \frac{3}{4} \times \frac{8}{1} = 6$. **27.** $1\frac{11}{24}$ **29.** 14 **31.** $\frac{2}{5}$ **33.** $\frac{5}{9}$ **35.** $\frac{1}{20}$ **37.** $2\frac{7}{10}$ **39.** 45 mi/h **41.** 8 teacups; 5 mugs **43.** More teacups; it takes less clay to make a teacup. **45.** <; you are dividing $\frac{3}{5}$ into smaller parts. **47.** <; you are dividing 6 by a fraction greater than 1. **49.** $1\frac{2}{3}$ **51.** $1\frac{4}{5}$ **53.** \$12 per hour **55.** 12 lots; cut in half **59.** *Sample answer:* 8 **61.** *Sample answer:* 5 **63.** 3 **65.** $4\frac{8}{9}$ **67.** \$5.22 **69.** \$7.61

7.5 Getting Ready to Practice (p. 341)

1. $\frac{8}{19}$ **3.** $\frac{7}{30}$; $\frac{7}{36}$ **5.** $\frac{3}{8}$; $5\frac{1}{4}$

7.5 Practice and Problem Solving

(pp. 341–343) **7.** $3\frac{3}{4} \div \frac{3}{4}$; 5 **9.** No. *Sample answer:* Mixed numbers must be converted to improper fractions before the reciprocal can be found. **11.** 39 **13.** $\frac{7}{10}$ **15.** $\frac{2}{15}$ **17.** $1\frac{3}{5}$ **19.** 7 **21.** $\frac{17}{31}$ **23.** 9 books **25.** *Sample answer:* 6 **27.** *Sample answer:* 5 **29.** $1\frac{3}{16}$ lb. *Sample answer:* Use subtraction to find the difference in weights. **31.** $5\frac{7}{8}$ ft. *Sample answer:* Use multiplication by one half to find half *of* the total length. **33.** divide by 2; $\frac{1}{32}$, $\frac{1}{64}$ **35.** greater than 1; 8 **37.** less than 1; $\frac{9}{10}$ **39.** $5\frac{1}{2}$ yd **41.** $2\frac{7}{40}$ **43.** $3\frac{3}{4} \div 31$ **45.** about 8 min **47.** $5\frac{7}{10}$ **51.** $9\frac{2}{7}$ **53.** $3\frac{5}{9}$ **55.** 38

7.6 Getting Ready to Practice (p. 346)

1. fluid ounces, cups, pints, quart, gallons **3.** pounds **5.** cups

7.6 Practice and Problem Solving

(pp. 346–347) **11.** gallons **13.** cups **15.** gallons **17.** pints **19.** weight **21.** capacity **23.** capacity **25.** More than. *Sample answer:* A bathroom sink is larger than a quart of milk. **27.** Less than. *Sample answer:* An ice cube tray holds only about half a quart of water. **29.** *Sample answer:* 1 ounce: 5 quarters; 1 pound: loaf of bread; 1 ton: ten 200 lb men; 1 fluid ounce: 2 tablespoons; 1 cup: small glass; 1 pint: tall glass; 1 quart: large mayonnaise jar; 1 gallon: 2 rectangular cartons of ice cream **31.** 760 **33.** 0.175 **35.** 0.075 **37.** $0.\overline{2}$ **39.** no

7.7 Problem Solving Strategies

(p. 349) **1.** *Sample answer:* You can use a proportion to solve the problem; 50 hot dogs. **3.** **5.** 8 vocabulary questions and 3 short answer questions **7.** 20 **9.** $9\frac{1}{2}$ in. by 12 in.

7.7 Getting Ready to Practice (p. 352) **1.** 1

3. 16 **5.** 720 **7.** 4300 **9.** 51 ft **11.** 11 lb 2 oz; 1 lb 4 oz

7.7 Practice and Problem Solving

(pp. 353–354) **13.** 13 **15.** 5, 4 **17.** $7\frac{1}{2}$ **19.** 12,000 lb **21.** 5 qt **23.** $3\frac{3}{4}$ ft **25.** 10 oz **27.** $4\frac{1}{4}$ pt **29.** 7 c **31.** $1\frac{1}{2}$ qt **33.** 12 ft 3 in. **35.** 7 gal **37.** 6 T 1919 lb **39.** $17\frac{3}{5}$ T **41.** about 50 mi **43.** <. *Sample answer:* I chose paper and pencil because it is hard to find $\frac{7}{8}$ times 5280 mentally. **45.** =. *Sample answer:* I chose paper and pencil because it is hard to multiply $1\frac{2}{3}$ by 8 mentally. **47.** >. *Sample answer:* I chose paper and pencil because it is hard to divide 280 by 16 mentally. **51.** 9, 3 **53.** $\frac{28}{45}$ **55.** $\frac{1}{76}$ **57.** 6 **59.** 9

7.7 Technology Activity (p. 355) **1.** 79; 55; 862 **3.** 26; 110; 35

7.4–7.7 Notebook Review (pp. 356–357)

1. reciprocal **2.** $1\frac{4}{21}$ **3.** $\frac{4}{35}$ **4.** $\frac{5}{32}$ **5.** $3\frac{6}{7}$ **6.** 750 **7.** $\frac{7}{16}$ **8.** 58 **9.** 8 yd; 2 yd 2 ft **10.** pounds **11.** *Sample answer:* To use division, divide 30 by 4 and simplify. To multiply by a form of 1, multiply 30 quarts by $\frac{1 \text{ gallon}}{4 \text{ quarts}}$ and simplify. The methods are similar in that you end up dividing by 4 in both.

Chapter Review (pp. 358–359) **1.** true **3.** false **5.** false **7.** true **9.** true **11.** 7 **13.** 35 **15.** $5\frac{1}{4}$ h **17.** $\frac{1}{5}$ **19.** $\frac{9}{23}$ **21.** $\frac{1}{18}$ **23.** $\frac{7}{30}$ **25.** $1\frac{1}{5}$ **27.** $15\frac{1}{3}$ **29.** 8 **31.** 6 **33.** $\frac{1}{3}$ **35.** 16 **37.** $1\frac{1}{10}$ **39.** $\frac{9}{25}$ **41.** 13; yes; 60 divided by $4\frac{1}{2}$ is $13\frac{1}{3}$, so there is $\frac{1}{3}$ of a sandwich left over. **43.** pounds **45.** ounces **47.** 44 **49.** $1\frac{1}{2}$ **51.** 3750 lb **53.** 12 qt **55.** 4 lb 11 oz

Chapter 8

8.1 Getting Ready to Practice (p. 376)

1. 5 : 12, 5 to 12 **3.** $\frac{2}{5}$ **5.** 4 **7.** 8 **9.** 18

8.1 Practice and Problem Solving

(pp. 376–378) **11.** $\frac{13}{20}$, 13 : 20 **13.** 9 **15.** 3 **17.** $\frac{31}{76}$, 31 : 76, 31 to 76 **19.** $\frac{1}{2}$ **21.** $\frac{2}{3}$ **23.** Joel **25.** John **27.** 34. *Sample answer:* Subtract the number of altos, basses, and tenors from the total number of singers. **29.** $\frac{1}{8}$ **31.** Rewrite both fractions with the least common denominator. The fraction with the greater numerator is the larger fraction. **35.** 16,000 **37.**

Explanations may vary.
39. 50 **41.** 0.07

8.2 Getting Ready to Practice (p. 381)
1. unit rate **3.** equivalent **5.** 180,000 L

8.2 Practice and Problem Solving

(pp. 381–382) **7.** 12 oz **9.** 18 mi **11.** $\frac{3 \text{ m}}{1 \text{ sec}}$ **13.** not equivalent **15.** $\frac{20 \text{ words}}{5 \text{ min}}$; $\frac{4 \text{ words}}{1 \text{ min}}$ **17.** $\frac{160 \text{ mi}}{4 \text{ h}}$; $\frac{40 \text{ mi}}{1 \text{ h}}$ **19.** 21,000,000 gal **21.** $\frac{2.21 \text{ lb}}{1 \text{ kg}}$ **23.** $\frac{2.54 \text{ cm}}{1 \text{ in.}}$ **25.** 18 oz box; the unit price for the 18 ounce box is about $.22 and the unit price for the 12 ounce box is $.25. **27.** No; the unit rate for both rates is $\frac{5 \text{ mi}}{1 \text{ sec}}$. **29.** 6 m **31.** 8 **33.** 18

8.3 Getting Ready to Practice

(p. 385) **1.** $3x$, 72 **3.** yes **5.** no **7.** 30 **9.** 8 **11.** 72 in.

8.3 Practice and Problem Solving

(pp. 386–387) **13.** yes **15.** no **17.** 1 **19.** 3 **21.** 10 **23.** 100 **25.** 30 **27.** 10 **29.** 350 gal **31.** 9 questions **33.** *Sample answer:* mental math; 6 **35.** *Sample answer:* related equation; 33 **37.** 12; 20 **39.** yes **41.** *Sample answer:* Since multiplying 12 by $1\frac{1}{2}$ gives 18, multiply 30 by $1\frac{1}{2}$ to find the unknown value, 45. **43.** *Sample answer:* 3.52 lb **45.** 34 cm; 42 cm^2

8.4 Getting Ready to Practice (p. 390)
1. 1 in. to 5 ft; $\frac{1 \text{ in.}}{5 \text{ ft}}$ **3.** about 300 ft

8.4 Practice and Problem Solving

(pp. 390–391) **5.** 10 cm **7.** 400 mi **9.** 225 mi **11.** A good answer should include the use of the ratio $\frac{1}{2}$ in proportions to find the width and length of the enlarged rectangle. For Rectangle 1, the enlarged rectangle will be 8 cm × 4 cm. For Rectangle 2, the enlarged rectangle will be 6 cm × 10 cm. For Rectangle 3, the enlarged rectangle will be 12 cm × 12 cm. **13.** For all rectangles, the ratio of the perimeters is $\frac{1 \text{ cm}}{2 \text{ cm}}$ and the ratio of the areas is $\frac{1 \text{ cm}^2}{4 \text{ cm}^2}$. The ratio of the perimeters is the same as the scale, and the ratio of the areas is the square of the scale. **15.** $\frac{1 \text{ cm}}{5 \text{ m}}$ **17.** No; no. *Sample answer:* Since 12 inches = 1 foot, the number 12 should be squared to find the number of square inches in 1 square foot. Similarly, since 3 feet = 1 yard, the number 3 should be squared to find the number of square feet in 1 square yard. **19.** pounds **21.** 33 **23.** 16 **25.** 7.1 **27.** 0.68

8.1–8.4 Notebook Review (pp. 392–393)
1. rate **2.** ratios, equivalent **3.** 12 and $4x$
4. 45 sec **5.** <; $0.\overline{6} < 0.\overline{7}$ **6.** $2.50 **7.** 12 **8.** 125 ft
9. *Sample answer:* They both are ratios of measures that have different units. A rate can have a denominator other than 1, but a unit rate must have a denominator of 1.

8.5 Getting Ready to Practice (p. 397) **1.** 100
3. eighty-one hundredths, 81% **5.** sixty-three hundredths, 63% **7.** 20% of the students

8.5 Practice and Problem Solving
(pp. 397–398) **9.** 68%, 0.68, $\frac{68}{100} = \frac{17}{25}$ **11.** forty-two hundredths, 42% **13.** fifty-seven hundredths, 57%
15. twenty-eight hundredths, 28%
17. two-hundred hundredths, 200% **23.** 36%, 0.36, $\frac{36}{100} = \frac{9}{25}$ **25.** 43%; add 22% for 4 or 5 days to 21% for 6 or 7 days to get 43%. **27.** 1 day or less: 0.19, $\frac{19}{100}$; 2 or 3 days: 0.38, $\frac{38}{100} = \frac{19}{50}$; 4 or 5 days: 0.22, $\frac{22}{100} = \frac{11}{50}$; 6 or 7 days: 0.21, $\frac{21}{100}$ **29.** >
35. 2 h 15 min **37.** 1.57, 3.8, 4.1 **39.** 9, 9.2, 9.4

8.6 Getting Ready to Practice (p. 401)
1. 60% **7.** 64% do not sew

8.6 Practice and Problem Solving
(pp. 402–403) **9.** 65% **11.** 28% **13.** 20% **15.** 8.4%
17. 58.7% **19.** 1.5% **21.** 90% **23.** 15%, 0.16, $\frac{1}{4}$
25. 50%, $\frac{2}{3}$, $\frac{7}{10}$, 0.77 **27.** 0.3, 33%, $\frac{1}{3}$, 34%
29. 27.5% **31.** 56% **33.** *Sample answer:* mental math; 36% **35.** *Sample answer:* calculator; 44%
37. 350% **39.** 0.4% **41.** John; Vince **43.** 29
45. $\frac{3000 \text{ ants}}{1 \text{ h}}$ **47.** 0.37, $\frac{37}{100}$ **49.** 0.96, $\frac{24}{25}$ **51.** 150
53. 1.875

8.7 Problem Solving Strategies (p. 405)
1. 14; 33 **3.** 10,000 **5.** 6 **7.** 2 packages of pencils and 6 packages of pens, or 7 packages of pencils and 3 packages of pens **9.** 18 different meals

8.7 Getting Ready to Practice (p. 408)
1. I = simple interest; P = principal; r = annual interest rate; t = time in years **3.** 9 **5.** 60

8.7 Practice and Problem Solving
(pp. 409–410) **7.** 42 **9.** 10 **11.** 54 **13.** 8.1 **15.** 37.2
17. 21 **19.** 1% is $\frac{1}{100}$. The answer should be $\frac{1}{100} \times 400 = \frac{400}{100} = 4$. **21.** $52.50 **23.** $55
25. $5.04 **27.** $3.20 **29.** $12.80 **31–35.** Estimates may vary. **31.** 600 **33.** 40 **35.** 72 **37.** double the answer; triple the answer **39.** $244; $258.64
41. buying the package **43.** 10; 8; 10; 22
45. 700 m **47.** 9.25 **49.** 12.7

8.7 Technology Activity (p. 411) **1.** 7.2
3. 7.809 **5.** 24.057 **7.** $19.50 **9.** $32.18

8.5–8.7 Notebook Review (pp. 412–413)
1. principal **2.** 0.16, $\frac{16}{100} = \frac{4}{25}$ **3.** 70% **4.** 24%
5. 24% **6.** 87.5% **7.** 100 **8.** 63 **9.** 2.4 **10.** 110.5
11. $9 **12.** *Sample answer:* Change the percent to either a fraction or a decimal and multiply. Consider if it is easier to change the percent to a fraction or to a decimal, and whether the number is easy to divide by the denominator of the fraction.

Chapter Review (pp. 414–415) **1.** false **3.** true
5. cross products **7.** 9 **9.** 4 **11.** $\frac{1}{2}$ **13.** $\frac{1}{4}$
15. $\frac{60 \text{ mi}}{1 \text{ h}}$ **17.** 9 **19.** 30 **21.** 175 ft $\times$ 75 ft
23. thirty-four hundredths, 34%
25. five hundredths, 5% **27.** 0.64, $\frac{64}{100} = \frac{16}{25}$
29. 0.90, $\frac{90}{100} = \frac{9}{10}$ **31.** 40% **33.** 62.5%
35. 0.2, 25%, $\frac{1}{3}$, 0.35, 40%, $\frac{3}{5}$ **37.** 12 **39.** 400
41. $17.25

Chapter 9

9.1 Getting Ready to Practice (p. 423)

5. *Sample answer:* $\overleftrightarrow{LQ}$ **7.** $\overleftrightarrow{ML}$ and $\overleftrightarrow{PQ}$

9.1 Practice and Problem Solving

(pp. 423–424) **9.** segment, $\overline{JK}$ **11.** *Sample answer:*
A, B, C **13.** *Sample answer:* $\overleftrightarrow{AB}$, $\overleftrightarrow{DE}$ **15.** $\overline{EA}$
17. intersecting   **19.** $\overrightarrow{SV}$, $\overrightarrow{VS}$, $\overrightarrow{VO}$, $\overrightarrow{OP}$, or $\overrightarrow{PO}$
21. $\overrightarrow{SV}$, $\overrightarrow{VO}$, or $\overrightarrow{PO}$ **23.** ray   **25.**

27. 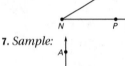   **29.** False; $\overrightarrow{AB}$ is a ray and $\overleftrightarrow{AB}$
is a line.   **31.** True; the letters are interchangeable.
33. Answers may vary.   **35.** <   **37.** >

9.2 Getting Ready to Practice (p. 427)

1. E; $\overrightarrow{ED}$ and $\overrightarrow{EF}$ **3.** $\angle U$, $\angle TUV$, $\angle VUT$

5. *Sample:*

7. *Sample:*   **9.** $\angle JKL$ **11.** $\angle TUV$

9.2 Practice and Problem Solving

(pp. 428–429) **13.** 60°   **15.** 60°   **17.** 130°
19. *Sample:*

21. *Sample:*
27. *Sample answer:* Between 90° and 135°; 110°
29. $\frac{13}{11}$ or $1\frac{2}{11}$ **31.** $\frac{4}{5}$ **33.** 6   **35.** 10   **37.** thirty-one
ten-thousandths   **39.** fifty-two and one hundred
forty-one thousandths

9.3 Getting Ready to Practice (p. 432)

5. $\angle CAB$ and $\angle FAE$ **7.** *Sample answer:* $\angle DAC$ and
$\angle FAD$ **9.** complementary   **11.** supplementary
13. 60°

9.3 Practice and Problem Solving

(pp. 433–434) **15.** right   **17.** obtuse   **19.** $\angle BAD$ is
obtuse; $\angle CAD$ is right; $\angle BAC$ is acute.   **21.** $\angle PTN$
and $\angle RTS$; $\angle PTR$ and $\angle NTS$ **23.** $m\angle 1 = 90°$,
$m\angle 2 = 90°$, $m\angle 3 = 90°$ **25.** complementary
27. neither   **29.** 49°   **31.** *Sample:*

33. *Sample:*   **35.** perpendicular

37. neither   **39.** 80°   **43.** 168   **45.**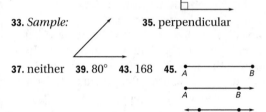

47. 47.29

9.4 Getting Ready to Practice (p. 438)

7. right, isosceles   **9.** 25

9.4 Practice and Problem Solving

(pp. 439–440) **11.** obtuse   **13.** acute   **15.** equilateral
17. scalene   **19.**    **21.** 86

23. not a triangle   **25.** is a triangle; obtuse
27. is a triangle; acute   **29.** always   **31.** never
33. *Sample:*

35. *Sample:*

37. acute isosceles triangle   **41.** *Sample answer:*
$\angle 1$ and $\angle 2$, $\angle 2$ and $\angle 3$ **43.** $\frac{7}{20}$ **45.** $6\frac{21}{50}$

9.4 Technology Activity (p. 441) **1.** 50   **3.** 34
5. 106.9   **7.** 65°

9.1–9.4 Notebook Review (pp. 442–443)

1. angle   **2.** supplementary   **3.** *Sample answer:*
$\overrightarrow{EA}$ **4.** *Sample answer:* $\overleftrightarrow{FC}$ **5.** obtuse   **6.** straight
7. 45; right, isosceles   **8.** 60; acute, equilateral

9. Subtract the measure from 90°; subtract the measure from 180°. **10.** A triangle has 3 angles whose sum is 180°. If there were 2 right angles, then there could only be 2 angles because 90° and 90° add up to 180°.

9.5 Getting Ready to Practice (p. 447)
1. parallelogram **3.** True; a rhombus and a square both have 4 sides of equal length. **5.** parallelogram **7.** parallelogram, rhombus

9.5 Practice and Problem Solving
(pp. 447–448) **9.** All **11.** Some **13.** rectangle, rhombus, square **15.**

17. rectangle, square **19.** 1: square; 2: rectangle; 3: rhombus **21.** 4 **23.** 77 **25.** Squares are always rectangles, so the rhombus must be a rectangle.

27. $\frac{2}{5}$, 42%, 0.45 **29.** is a triangle; acute

31. is a triangle; right **33.** $11.00

9.6 Getting Ready to Practice (p. 451) **5.** yes
7. *Sample answer:* There are only 5 diagonals, not 7. Two of the segments drawn from the vertex are sides of the octagon and therefore not diagonals.

9.6 Practice and Problem Solving
(pp. 451–453) **9.** pentagon; not regular **11.** 2
13. square **15.** 72 **17.** 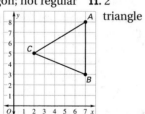 triangle

19.

Number of sides in polygon	4	5	6
Number of diagonals from one vertex	1	2	3

21. 6 **23.** 135° **25.** 32 m **27.** *Sample:*

29. 125,250; I used Solve a Simpler Problem and found the sum of the first 10 numbers, the second 10 numbers, and when I observed the pattern, used that pattern to find the entire sum. **31.** 6

9.7 Getting Ready to Practice (p. 456)
1. false **3.** false **5.** $x = 4$ yd, $y = 5$ yd

9.7 Practice and Problem Solving
(pp. 456–457) **7.** congruent **9.** $\angle A$ and $\angle D$, $\angle C$ and $\angle F$, $\angle B$ and $\angle E$, $\overline{AC}$ and $\overline{DF}$, $\overline{BC}$ and $\overline{EF}$, $\overline{AB}$ and $\overline{DE}$ **11.** $x = 90$; $y = 13$ ft **13.** Yes; no; they are larger than the actual size. **15.** Congruent. *Sample answer:* The earrings are the same shape and size. **17.** Neither. *Sample answer:* The batteries are neither the same shape nor the same size. **19.** $\angle Y$ and $\angle B$, $\angle X$ and $\angle A$, $\angle Z$ and $\angle C$; $\overline{YX}$ and $\overline{BA}$, $\overline{YZ}$ and $\overline{BC}$, $\overline{XZ}$ and $\overline{AC}$

23.  **25.** 6.076

9.8 Problem Solving Strategies (p. 459)
1. 4; 1 **5.** Yes. *Sample answer:* If the long side of the bed is placed against the 12 foot wall, then 6 feet of space along that wall remains for the desk. **7.** $40.85

9.8 Getting Ready to Practice (p. 462)
1. line symmetry **3.** 0

9.8 Practice and Problem Solving
(pp. 462–463) **5.** no **7.** yes **9.**

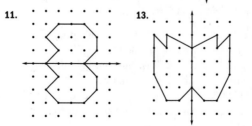

11. **13.**

15. 1   **17.** yes; isosceles triangle   **19.** 12   **21.** 9
23. $\frac{1}{2}$ **25.** $\frac{1}{12}$ **27.** *Sample answer:* 240
29. *Sample answer:* 2100

9.5–9.8 Notebook Review (pp. 464–465)
1. parallelogram   **2.** No; all angles do not have to
have the same measure.   **3.** rhombus,
quadrilateral, parallelogram   **4.** regular pentagon
5. congruent; $\angle C$ and $\angle F$, $\angle E$ and $\angle H$, $\angle D$ and
$\angle G$, $\overline{DE}$ and $\overline{GH}$, $\overline{CE}$ and $\overline{FH}$, $\overline{CD}$ and $\overline{FG}$ **6.** no
7. no   **8.** yes   **9.** No; a parallelogram is a
quadrilateral with 2 pairs of parallel sides and a
regular hexagon has 6 sides with 3 pairs of parallel
sides.

Chapter Review (pp. 466–467)   **1.** When two
lines intersect, the angles opposite each other are
called vertical angles.   **3.** 3   **5.** The sum of their
measures is 180°.   **7.** 180°   **9.** equal; equal
11. $\overleftrightarrow{VW}$ **13.** $\overleftrightarrow{ST}$ **15.** 45°   **17.** complementary
19. *Sample:*

21. $m\angle 1 = 152°$; $m\angle 2 = 28°$; $m\angle 3 = 152°$
23. 73; acute   **25.** quadrilateral   **27.** quadrilateral,
parallelogram   **29.** similar; $\angle A$ and $\angle J$, $\angle B$ and $\angle K$,
$\angle C$ and $\angle L$; $\overline{AB}$ and $\overline{JK}$; $\overline{BC}$ and $\overline{KL}$; $\overline{AC}$ and $\overline{JL}$
31.   **33.**

Chapter 10

10.1 Getting Ready to Practice (p. 478)
1. base, height   **3.** 200 yd²

10.1 Practice and Problem Solving
(pp. 478–479)   **5.** 84 m²   **7.** 30 in.²   **9.** 63 m²
11. 10 yd   **13.** Check drawings. *Sample answer:*
1 cm by 12 cm, 2 cm by 6 cm, or 3 cm by 4 cm
15. 14,400 km²; high estimate; the parallelogram
covers more than just the island of Puerto Rico.

17. 7   **19.** 8   **21.** *Sample:*
23. 6   **25.** 48

10.2 Getting Ready to Practice (p. 482)
1. height, base   **3.** 8 mi²   **5.** 6 ft²

10.2 Practice and Problem Solving
(pp. 482–483)   **7.** 20 ft²   **9.** 24 cm²   **11.** 675 in.²
13. 5 in.   **15.** 10 cm   **17.** 13 m²   **19.** The area of the
triangle with the longer base is twice as great as
the area of the other triangle.   **21.** about 20% or
about $\frac{1}{5}$ **23.** mass   **25.** capacity   **27.** 9 cm
29. 16.25   **31.** 98.52

10.3 Getting Ready to Practice (p. 487)
1. diameter   **3.** radius   **5.** 22 cm   **7.** 25.12 in.
9. The radius is given, so the formula $C = 2\pi r$
should be used. The circumference is $2(3.14)(3) =$
18.84 mm.   **11.** 37.68 yd; 3.14 because 12 is not a
multiple of 7.   **13.** 132 km; $\frac{22}{7}$ because 21 is a
multiple of 7.

10.3 Practice and Problem Solving
(pp. 488–489)   **15.** 19 in.   **17.** 106.76 mm; 3.14
because 17 is not a multiple of 7.   **19.** 154 mi; $\frac{22}{7}$
because 49 is a multiple of 7.   **21.** about 9.42 in.
23. about 5 times   **25.** $\frac{22}{7}$; its value is closer to the
actual value of pi.   **29.** The shape will be the letter
"X". *Sample answer:* I chose Make a Model so I
could see the shape.   **31.** 62.5   **33.** 144

10.3 Technology Activity (p. 490)   **1.** 38 feet
3. 1071 cm   **5.** 94 km   **7.** 5 m   **9.** about 16,000 km

10.4 Getting Ready to Practice (p. 494)
1. area   **3.** 12.6 km²   **5.** 452.2 yd²

10.4 Practice and Problem Solving
(pp. 494–495)   **7.** 452 ft²   **9.** 254 m²   **11.** 14 cm²
13. 2.6 m²   **15.** 1017 mi²   **17.** 16 times
19. Dog: $\frac{1}{4}$, Cat: $\frac{3}{8}$, Rabbit: $\frac{7}{40}$, Other: $\frac{1}{5}$

5 unfavorable outcomes.   **33.** 216 in.^{3}

35. 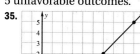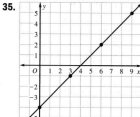   **37.** 0.623, 6.23, 62.3, 623, 6230

seafood, and ice cream; soup, beef, and ice cream; salad, pasta, and ice cream; salad, seafood, and ice cream; salad, beef, and ice cream
15. Choosing a 5-person fundraising committee would be a combination because the order of the persons being chosen is not important; electing 4 class officers would be a permutation because the order is important.   **17.** 113.04 m^2
19. $\frac{1}{2}$ **21.** $\frac{2}{5}$ **23.** $\frac{5}{6}$

13.1 Technology Activity (p. 635)   **1.** A good answer should be close to $\frac{1}{2}$.

13.2 Getting Ready to Practice (p. 638)
1. combination; permutation

3.

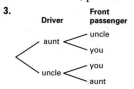

aunt and uncle, aunt and you, uncle and you, uncle and aunt

13.2 Practice and Problem Solving
(pp. 638–639)   **5.** white paint in kitchen, white paint in bathroom, beige paint in kitchen, beige paint in bathroom, gray paint in kitchen, gray paint in bathroom   **7.** Dallas in June, Dallas in July, Dallas in August, New York in June, New York in July, New York in August, Miami in June, Miami in July, Miami in August   **9.** blue and green, blue and yellow, blue and red, blue and purple, green and yellow, green and red, green and purple, yellow and red, yellow and purple, red and purple
11. comedy and drama, comedy and science fiction, comedy and adventure, drama and comedy, drama and science fiction, drama and adventure, science fiction and comedy, science fiction and drama, science fiction and adventure, adventure and comedy, adventure and drama, adventure and science fiction   **13.** soup, pasta, and pie; soup, seafood, and pie; soup, beef, and pie; salad, pasta, and pie; salad, seafood, and pie; salad, beef, and pie; soup, pasta, and cake; soup, seafood, and cake; soup, beef, and cake; salad, pasta, and cake; salad, seafood, and cake; salad, beef, and cake; soup, pasta, and ice cream; soup,

13.3 Problem Solving Strategies (p. 641)
1. 18 ways   **3.** 6 ways   **5.** 2 tokens   **7.** 14 adult tickets   **9.** 30 more blue faces

13.3 Getting Ready to Practice (p. 644)
1. Independent; the first event does not affect the second event because you put the first marble back in the bag.   **3.** $\frac{1}{6}$ **5.** $\frac{1}{3}$

13.3 Practice and Problem Solving
(pp. 644–645)   **7.** $\frac{3}{4}$ **9.** $\frac{1}{4}$ **11.** $\frac{1}{2}$ **13.** $\frac{1}{12}$ **15.** $\frac{1}{3}$ **17.** $\frac{2}{3}$
19. $\frac{1}{8}$ **21.** $\frac{1}{2}$ **23.** heads 3 times, tails exactly 1 time, tails at least 2 times, heads at most 2 times
25. Increase; there are now fewer total tiles but the same number of red tiles.   **27.** 14.375; 14; 14
29. 16   **31.** 18   **33.** $5.70

13.1–13.3 Notebook Review (pp. 646–647)
1. rolling an odd number   **2.** A combination is a grouping of objects in which order is not important. A permutation is an arrangement of objects in which order is important.   **3.** $\frac{1}{6}$ **4.** 0
5. $\frac{5}{6}$ **6.** ACT, ATC, CAT, CTA, TAC, TCA; $\frac{2}{3}$ **7.** No, a percent greater than 100% is always greater than 1 and probabilities cannot be greater than 1.
8. The sum of their probabilities is 1. *Sample answer:* They have no outcomes in common and contain all the outcomes of the experiment.

13.4 Getting Ready to Practice (p. 650)
1. It can distort the data.   **3.** less than; less than

13.4 Practice and Problem Solving
(pp. 650–652)   **5.** B; the line in graph B is not as steep as than the line in graph A.   **7.** 2 times more

9. the data values   **11.** To make it appear that the team usually wins a lot of games.

13.

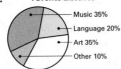

Favorite Electives

- Music 35%
- Language 20%
- Art 35%
- Other 10%

15. *Sample answer:* To show that the houses in the region are not that expensive.

17. *Sample:*

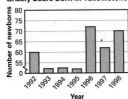

Grizzly Bears Born in Yellowstone

21. $\frac{3}{4}$ **23.** 164

13.5 Getting Ready to Practice (p. 655)

1. stems: 1, 2, 3; leaves: 2, 4, 7, 1, 9, 5, 6, 8, 9

3.
```
0 | 7 8 9
1 | 0 0 2 3 3 4 5 5
2 | 1 2 5
3 |
4 | 0
```
Key: 2 | 1 = 21

13.5 Practice and Problem Solving (pp. 655–656)

5.
```
1 | 5 6 8 8 8
2 | 1 4 5 5 8
3 | 1 2 2
4 | 1
```
Key: 3 | 2 = 32

7.
```
0 | 5 7 9
1 | 5 6
2 |
3 | 0 3 5 5 8
4 | 1 9
5 | 1 2 5
```
Key: 3 | 5 = 35

9. about 80.7; 73; 73; 62   **11.** *Sample answer:* The longest match lasted 62 minutes longer than the shortest match; the shortest match lasted more than an hour less than the longest match.

13. 7 games   **15.** *Sample answer:* Mode; a lighter phone would be preferable over a heavier phone.

17–20.

21. Mode; the mode is 5, so you could say your score of 7 is above average.   **23.** >

13.6 Getting Ready to Practice (p. 659)

1. median = 13, lower quartile = 10, upper quartile = 18, lower extreme = 2, upper extreme = 24   **3.**

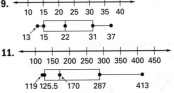

13.6 Practice and Problem Solving (pp. 659–661) **5.** 192   **7.**

9.

11.

13. 1970s: median = 131, range = 107; 1980s: median = 132.5, range = 89; 1990s: median = 151, range = 79   **15.** 1968–2002; the median and upper and lower quartiles for 1968–2002 are all less than the median and upper and lower quartiles for 1928–1964.   **17.** 75%   **21.** 12   **23.** 2.481

13.7 Practice and Problem Solving (pp. 664–665) **7.** line plot

9.
```
1 | 9
2 |
3 | 1 4 8 9
4 | 1 2 5 9
5 | 8
6 | 0
7 | 0
```
Key: 3 | 4 = 34   median = 41.5

11. bar graph

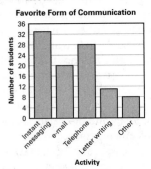

Favorite Form of Communication

13. Line plot and stem-and-leaf plot; a line plot shows the number of each piece of data and a stem-and-leaf plot shows each piece of data.

15.

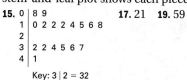

```
0 | 8 9
1 | 0 2 2 2 4 5 6 8
2 |
3 | 2 2 4 5 6 7
4 | 1
Key: 3 | 2 = 32
```

17. 21   **19.** 59

13.4–13.7 Notebook Review (pp. 666–667)

1. stem: 3, leaf: 6   **2.** 17   **3.** about $\frac{1}{2}$; about 72%

4.

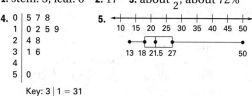

```
0 | 5 7 8
1 | 0 2 5 9
2 | 4 8
3 | 1 6
4 |
5 | 0
Key: 3 | 1 = 31
```

5.

(line plot from 10 to 50: 13 18 21.5 27, 50)

6.

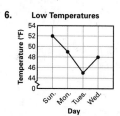

Low Temperatures

7. The scale can appear to distort the data.

Chapter Review (pp. 668–669)

1. complementary   **3.** permutation   **5.** lower extreme, upper extreme   **7.** $\frac{1}{2}$ **9.** 1   **11.** $\frac{16}{31}$

13. Pittsburgh hat, Pittsburgh T-shirt, Pittsburgh poster, Dallas hat, Dallas T-shirt, Dallas poster, Miami hat, Miami T-shirt, Miami poster, Los Angeles hat, Los Angeles T-shirt, Los Angeles poster   **15.** Leah and Sarah, Leah and Jenny, Leah and Michelle, Sarah and Leah, Sarah and Jenny, Sarah and Michelle, Jenny and Leah, Jenny and Sarah, Jenny and Michelle, Michelle and Leah, Michelle and Sarah, Michelle and Jenny

17. $\frac{1}{9}$ **19.** $\frac{1}{9}$ **21.** $\frac{1}{5}$; $\frac{1}{2}$ **23.**

```
3 | 2
4 | 1 5 8
5 | 2 5 9
6 | 0
Key: 4 | 8 = 48
```

25. 48   **27.** 50   **29.**

(line plot from 20 to 80: 23, 56 61 70.5 77)

Skills Review Handbook

Whole Number Place Value (p. 684)
1. $(5 \times 1000) + (8 \times 100) + (9 \times 10)$; five thousand eight hundred ninety   **3.** $(9 \times 100,000) + (6 \times 1000) + (2 \times 100) + (1 \times 1)$; nine hundred six thousand, two hundred one   **5.** 105,300
7. 42,600

Comparing and Ordering Whole Numbers (p. 685)   **1.** 0, 3, 8, 10, 11   **3.** 78, 79, 85, 87, 90
5. 508, 510, 512, 518, 521   **7.** 207 > 148
9. 3465 < 3492   **11.** 21,539 > 9847

Rounding Whole Numbers (p. 686)   **1.** tens' place; 90   **3.** ones' place; 200   **5.** 4280   **7.** 11,000
9. 144,000

Fact Families (p. 687)   **1.** 5; 5; 5; 14   **3.** 8; 4; 4; 4; 8
5. $15 - 8 = 7$ or $15 - 7 = 8$

Addition and Subtraction on a Number Line (p. 688)   **1.** 13   **3.** 11   **5.** 13   **7.** 20   **9.** 6
11. 8   **13.** 8   **15.** 16

Addition and Subtraction of Whole Numbers (p. 689)   **1.** 71   **3.** 240   **5.** 400   **7.** 1412
9. 17   **11.** 219   **13.** 149   **15.** 1179

Multiplication of Whole Numbers (p. 690)
1. 3280   **3.** 962   **5.** 6076   **7.** 60,450   **9.** 147,038
11. 46,570   **13.** 12,300   **15.** 23,190,000

Division of Whole Numbers (p. 691)   **1.** 142
3. 54   **5.** 405   **7.** 58   **9.** 13 R7   **11.** 24 R57

Estimating Sums (p. 692)   **1-9.** Estimates may vary.   **1.** 1300   **3.** 1800   **5.** 10,000   **7.** 160   **9.** 1200

Estimating Differences (p. 693)   **1.** 700; 900
3. 400; 600   **5.** 300; 500   **7.** 400; 600   **9.** 0; 2000
11. 3000; 5000   **13.** 4000; 6000   **15.** 1000; 3000

Estimating Products (p. 694)   **1.** 800; 1500
3. 2100; 3200   **5.** 3000; 8000   **7.** 12,000; 21,000
9. 280,000; 400,000   **11.** 60,000; 140,000
13-27. Estimates may vary.   **13.** 10,500   **15.** 52,800
17. 14,000   **19.** 45,000   **21.** 630,000   **23.** 150,000
25. 90,000   **27.** 736,100

Estimating Quotients (p. 695) **1.** 50; 60
3. 60; 70 **5.** 30; 40 **7.** 200; 300 **9.** 300; 400
11. 400; 500 **13.** 1100; 1200 **15.** 800; 900
17-27. Estimates may vary. **17.** 2 **19.** 10 **21.** 10
23. 7 **25.** 100 **27.** 80

**Solving Problems Using Addition and
Subtraction** (p. 696) **1.** $9 **3.** 26 items **5.** $7

**Solving Problems Using Multiplication
and Division** (p. 697) **1.** 60 folders **3.** 4 boxes
5. $20

Operations with Money (p. 698) **1.** $2.02
3. $58.08

Adding and Subtracting Decimals (p. 699)
1. 41.4 **3.** 143 **5.** 11.29 **7.** 20.13 **9.** 57.22
11. 16.5 **13.** 6.88 **15.** 5.76 **17.** 19.87

Modeling Fractions (p. 700) **1.** $\frac{3}{4}$ **3.** $\frac{1}{2}$ **5.** $\frac{5}{14}$
7. $\frac{4}{9}$ **9.** $\frac{5}{9}$ **11.** $\frac{3}{10}$

Units of Time (p. 701) **1.** 240 **3.** 4 **5.** 12 **7.** 52
9. 2; 2 **11.** 1; 16

Perimeter and Area (p. 702) **1.** 10 in. **3.** 15 cm
5. 21 square units

Venn Diagrams and Logical Reasoning
(p. 703) **1.**

Whole Numbers Less Than 15

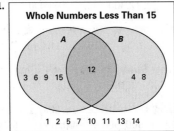

A: 3 6 9 15 | 12 | B: 4 8
1 2 5 7 10 11 13 14

3. Sometimes. *Sample answer:* 12 is in both set *A*
and set *B*, but 6, for example, is only in set *A*.
5. Never. *Sample answer:* Set *C* consists of
numbers less than 15.

Reading Bar Graphs (p. 704) **1.** 20 students
3. period 2 **5.** 7 more students **7.** periods 2 and 3

Reading Line Graphs (p. 705) **1.** Thursday
3. 8 in. **5.** decrease **7.** Monday

Reading a Pictograph (p. 706) **1.** brown;
14 students **3.** 8 pictures **5.** about 4 pictures
7. Friday

Making a Pictograph (p. 707)
1. *Sample:*

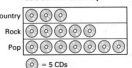

CDs Sold in One Day
Country
Rock
Pop
= 5 CDs

Extra Practice

Chapter 1 (p. 708) **1.** 203 **3.** 51 **5.** 170 **7.** 39
9. add 4 to the previous number; 21, 25
11. divide the previous number by 2; 100, 50
13-19. Estimates may vary. **13.** 370 **15.** 8 **17.** 760
19. 1500 **21.** 343 **23.** 8 **25.** 14 **27.** 21 **29.** 6
31. 11 **33.** 27 **35.** 11 **37.** 14 **39.** 7 **41.** 22 years
old **43.** 3 **45.** 2 **47.** 4 **49.** 0

Chapter 2 (p. 709) **1.** 6 cm **3.** miles, kilometers
5. 18 in.; 18 in.^{2} **7.** 240 km **9.** 840 km
11.

Heights	Tally	Frequency
4	II	2
5	IIII I	6
6	IIII	4
7		0
8	I	1

13.

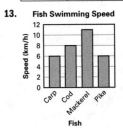

Fish Swimming Speed

14-18.

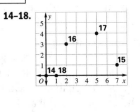

19.

Distance From Start

21. 120 sesame bagels

23. 33, 31, no mode, 27; mean; it is in the middle
of all the data.

Chapter 3 (p. 710) **1.** 50.42 **3.** eight thousandths
5. one and eleven hundredths **7.** seven and two
hundred seventy-five ten-thousandths **9.** 0.15 m
11. < **13.** > **15.** = **17.** 2.01, 2.12, 2.3 **19.** 13.3
21. 0.7 **23.** 0.009 **25.** 2 **27.** 19 **29.** 32 **31.** 14
33. 10.81 **35.** 2.14 **37.** 2.45 **39.** 1.84

Chapter 4 (p. 711) **1.** 32.52 **3.** 125.18 **5.** 67.2
7. 203 **9.** 2.08 **11.** 5.0307 **13.** 3.2 **15.** 3.625
17. 1.5 **19.** 1.1 **21.** 205 **23.** 1.798 **25.** 0.935
27. 93.8 **29.** 1.2 **31.** 5 **33.** 330 **35.** 0.9
37. kilograms **39.** kiloliters **41.** liters **43.** 480,000
45. 67,400 **47.** 1000 **49.** < **51.** > **53.** <

Chapter 5 (p. 712) **1.** 406 is divisible by 2, but
not by 3, 4, 6, 9 or 10. **3.** 534 is divisible by 2, 3,
and 6, but not by 5, 9, or 10. **5.** 510 is divisible by
2, 3, 5, 6, and 10, but not by 9. **7.** composite
9. neither **11.** 5×19 **13.** $2^2 \times 19$ **15.** $5^2 \times 7$
17. 4 **19.** 5 **21.** Sample answer: $\frac{4}{10}, \frac{6}{15}$
23. Sample answer: $\frac{6}{20}, \frac{9}{30}$ **25.** yes **27.** no; $\frac{1}{14}$
29. no; $\frac{4}{5}$ **31.** 24 **33.** 40 **35.** $\frac{4}{5}, \frac{13}{15}, \frac{9}{10}$ **37.** $\frac{3}{20}, \frac{2}{9}$,
$\frac{4}{15}, \frac{2}{5}$ **39.** $\frac{35}{9}$ **41.** $\frac{17}{7}$ **43.** $2\frac{1}{6}$ **45.** $3\frac{2}{5}$ **47.** $1\frac{7}{12}$
49. $\frac{17}{8}, 2\frac{1}{4}, \frac{55}{24}, 2\frac{1}{3}$ **51.** $\frac{19}{20}$ **53.** $2\frac{2}{25}$ **55.** $\frac{129}{200}$
57. 1.75 **59.** $5.1\overline{6}$

Chapter 6 (p. 713) **1.** $\frac{1}{2}$ **3.** 0 **5.** 4 **7.** 9 **9.** $\frac{3}{4}$
11. $\frac{4}{15}$ **13.** $\frac{2}{5}$ **15.** $\frac{2}{5}$ **17.** $\frac{7}{18}$ **19.** $\frac{15}{16}$ **21.** $\frac{19}{30}$ **23.** $\frac{19}{20}$
25. $2\frac{2}{3}$ **27.** $16\frac{1}{4}$ **29.** $7\frac{4}{7}$ **31.** $\frac{1}{8}$ **33.** $1\frac{6}{13}$ **35.** $1\frac{3}{4}$
37. $\frac{3}{5}$ **39.** $2\frac{1}{5}$ **41.** 3 h 35 min **43.** 2 h 20 min 50 sec
45. 7 h 15 min **47.** 2 h 30 min **49.** 5 h 45 min
51. 1 h 35 min **53.** 8 h 15 min

Chapter 7 (p. 714) **1.** 9 **3.** 27 **5.** 6 **7.** 16 **9.** $1\frac{1}{4}$
11. $\frac{2}{27}$ **13.** $7\frac{1}{3}$ **15.** $1\frac{1}{6}$ **17.** $\frac{5}{24}$ **19.** $\frac{4}{25}$ **21.** 3
23. $\frac{9}{20}$ **25.** $2\frac{11}{12}$ **27.** $2\frac{1}{2}$ **29.** No. Sample answer:
Use multiplication to find the total amount of
fabric needed. **31.** pounds **33.** ounces **35.** 14
37. 1; 9; $1\frac{9}{16}$ **39.** 2250 lb **41.** 6 lb **43.** 4 yd 1 ft

Chapter 8 (p. 715) **1.** 2 : 3 **3.** 1 : 5 **5.** 4 : 3 **7.** 20
9. 9 **11.** 19 cm **13.** $\frac{275 \text{ visitors}}{1 \text{ hour}}$ **15.** $\frac{200 \text{ words}}{1 \text{ page}}$
17. 2 **19.** 28 **21.** 20 ft by 16 ft **23.** 0.18, $\frac{9}{50}$
25. 0.025, $\frac{1}{40}$ **27.** 85% **29.** 83% **31.** 0.5%
33. $\frac{2}{3}$, 67%, 0.76, $\frac{5}{6}$ **35.** 18 **37.** 56 **39.** $480

Chapter 9 (p. 716) **1.** Sample answer: $\overrightarrow{BC}$ and
$\overrightarrow{BF}$; $\overline{BD}$ and $\overline{BA}$ **3.** $\overleftrightarrow{ED}$ and $\overrightarrow{DF}$ **5.** $\angle AED$
7. right; obtuse; acute; straight **9.** 60°; 100°; 80°
11. All **13.** No **15.** triangle; no **17.** hexagon; no
19. $\overline{XY}$ and $\overline{DE}$, $\overline{YZ}$ and $\overline{EF}$, $\overline{ZX}$ and $\overline{FD}$; $\angle X$ and
$\angle D$, $\angle Y$ and $\angle E$, $\angle Z$ and $\angle F$
21. yes **23.** yes

Chapter 10 (p. 717) **1.** 360 ft² **3.** 13.5 mm²
5. 30 cm² **7.** 110 cm; $\frac{22}{7}$; 35 is a multiple of 7.
9. 44 in.; $\frac{22}{7}$; 7 is a multiple of 7. **11.** 50.2 cm²
13. 706.5 ft² **15.** 434 cm²

17.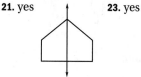

Spring Fundraiser Volunteers

Tickets 8

Booths 26

Snacks 6

19.

21.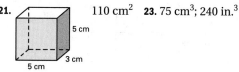

110 cm² **23.** 75 cm³; 240 in.³

5 cm

5 cm   3 cm

Chapter 11 (p. 718) **1.** −4, 18, 0 **3.** > **5.** <
7. −3, 0, 2, 3, 5 **9.** −9, −7, −6, 8, 9 **11.** 4
13. −10 **15.** 0 **17.** −14 **19.** 16 **21.** −17
23. −28 **25.** −9 **27.** −40 **29.** 140 **31.** 32
33. 99 **35.** −8 **37.** 5 **39.** −3 **41.** −25

43. Quadrant I

45. 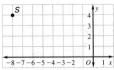 Quadrant II

47. 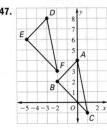 $D(-3, 8)$, $E(-5, 6)$, $F(-2, 3)$

49. reflection **51.** translation

Chapter 12 (p. 719) **1.** $n + 7$ **3.** $20 - n$
5. $8n = 32$ **7.** $\dfrac{y}{6} = 5$ **9.** 29 **11.** 14 **13.** 16
15. 25 **17.** 10 **19.** 9 **21.** 60 **23.** 21

25.

Input, x	Output, y
4	1
8	5
12	9
16	13
20	17

27.

Input, x	Output, y
4	13
8	21
12	29
16	37
20	45

29. $c = 6p$

31. *Sample answer:*

Quarts, q	Gallons, g
2	$\frac{1}{2}$
4	1
6	$1\frac{1}{2}$
8	2

$g = \dfrac{q}{4}$

33.

Input, x	Output, y
0	-2
1	-1
2	0
3	1
4	2

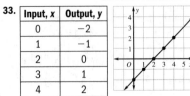

35.

Input, x	Output, y
0	3
1	$3\frac{1}{2}$
2	4
3	$4\frac{1}{2}$
4	5

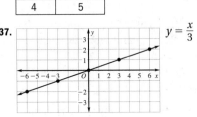

37. $y = \dfrac{x}{3}$

Chapter 13 (p. 720) **1.** $\dfrac{4}{7}$ **3.** 1 **5.** You do not choose a multiple of 3; $\dfrac{5}{7}$. **7.** 11, 12, 13, 14, 21, 22, 23, 24, 31, 32, 33, 34, 41, 42, 43, 44 **9.** $\dfrac{1}{4}$

11.
```
0 | 4 6 7 7 8 8 8 9
1 | 1 2 5 6 8 9
2 | 0 0 1 4 4 9
```
Key: 1 | 5 = 15

13. 25

15. Line graph; it shows change over time.

Teacher's Edition Index

Pupil's Edition in black
Teacher's Edition in blue

b

c

Additional Answers

Chapter 1

1.7 Getting Ready to Practice (p. 44) **1.** 1. Read and Understand: Read the problem carefully. Identify the question and any important information. 2. Make a Plan: Decide on a problem solving strategy. 3. Solve the Problem: Use the problem solving strategy to answer the question. 4. Look Back: Check that your answer is reasonable. **2.** Step 1: All the ways to make 40 cents in change using only dimes and nickels; Step 2: It helps you look at different ways to make 40 cents in an organized way; Step 3: 5 ways; Step 4: *Sample answer:* If you use 5 dimes, the total value would be 50 cents, which is too much. You cannot have any fewer than 0 dimes, so the answer is reasonable.

Chapter 2

2.3 Your turn now (p. 72) **1.** *Sample answer:* Fill in the first column and write in the headings for the last two columns. Make a tally mark each time a project is chosen. After all of the tally marks are recorded, write the total in the Frequency column. This way of recording the data is more organized and takes less time.

2.

Letter	Tally	Frequency
M	I	1
I	IIII	4
S	IIII	4
P	II	2

2.3 Your turn now (p. 73)

3.

Number of letters	Tally	Frequency
3	IIII	4
4	JHT I	6
5	III	3
6	II	2
7	I	1
8	II	2
9	II	2

4.

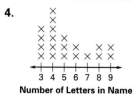

Number of Letters in Name

2.4 Getting Ready to Practice (p. 74)

2.

Number of bicycles	Tally	Frequency
0	III	3
1	JHT II	7
2	JHT	5
3	III	3
4	II	2
5		0
6	I	1

3.

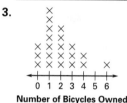

Number of Bicycles Owned

2.5 Practice and Problem Solving (pp. 74–75)

5.

Type of call	Tally	Frequency
building fires	JHT I	6
other fires	JHT JHT II	12
hazardous materials	JHT II	7
rescues	III	3
false alarms	JHT II	7
mutual aid	IIII	4

8.

Section	Tally	Frequency
woodwinds	JHT IIII	9
percussion	II	2
brass	JHT JHT I	11
strings	JHT JHT JHT JHT IIII	24

The string section is the largest.

9.

Point values of shots	Tally	Frequency
1	JHT II	7
2	JHT JHT I	11
3	III	3

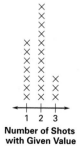

Number of Shots with Given Value

AA1

10.

Number of weeks	Tally	Frequency
0	II	2
1	I	1
2	II	2
3		0
4	IIII IIII I	11
5	I	1
6	IIII	4
7		0
8	IIII	5

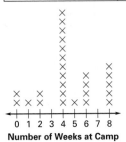

0 1 2 3 4 5 6 7 8
Number of Weeks at Camp

12.

Weather	Tally	Frequency
sunny	IIII IIII	10
partly cloudy	IIII I	6
cloudy	IIII III	8
rainy	IIII I	6

14. 24 days; add the number of sunny, partly cloudy, and cloudy days, or subtract the rainy days from the total number of days in the month.

17.

1 2 3 4 5 6 7 8 9 10 11 12
Birth Months of United States Presidents

2.4 Test-Taking Practice (p. 75)

24.

Number of students	Tally	Frequency
23	I	1
24	III	3
25	II	2
26	IIII	4
27	I	1
28	I	1

23 24 25 26 27 28
Number of Students

2.5 Hands-on Activity (p. 78)

2.

Last digit	Tally	Frequency
0	II	2
1	II	2
2	II	2
3	III	3
4	III	3
5	I	1
6	III	3
7	II	2
8	III	3
9	IIII	4

3. *Sample answer:* Compare the lengths of the bars created by shading boxes. The longest bar corresponds to the greatest frequency and the shortest bar corresponds to the lowest frequency.

2.5 Your turn now (p. 80)

1.

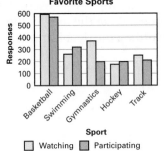

Favorite Sports

Responses
600 500 400 300 200 100 0

Basketball Swimming Gymnastics Hockey Track

Sport

☐ Watching ■ Participating

2.5 Getting Ready to Practice (p. 81)

3. What is the most important thing kids can do to protect the environment?

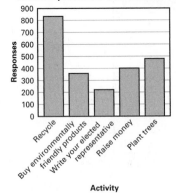

Responses
900 800 700 600 500 400 300 200 100 0

Recycle / Buy environmentally friendly products / Write your elected representative / Raise money / Plant trees

Activity

2.5 Practice and Problem Solving (pp. 81–82)

5.

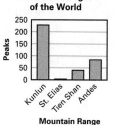
Mountain Ranges of the World

6.

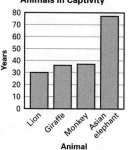
Maximum Life Span of Animals in Captivity

7.

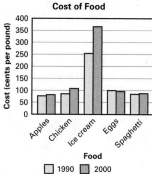
Cost of Food

8.

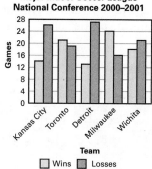
Major Indoor Soccer League National Conference 2000–2001

13.

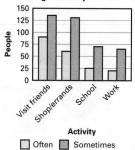
Skating as Transportation

2.5 Mixed Review (p. 82)

18.

Scores	Tally	Frequency
6	II	2
7	IIII	5
8	III	3
9	IIII	5
10	I	1

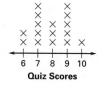
Quiz Scores

2.6 Your turn now (p. 83)

1–4.

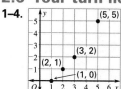

2.6 Your turn now (p. 84)

7.

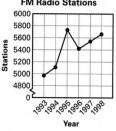
FM Radio Stations

2.6 Getting Ready to Practice (p. 85)

6.

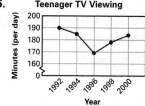
Teenager TV Viewing

2.6 Practice and Problem Solving (pp. 85–86)

8–15.

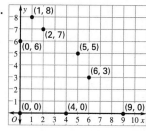

16.

Endangered or Threatened Bird Species in the U.S.

17.

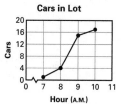
Cars in Lot

18.

Tickets Sold

19.

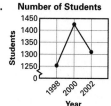
Number of Students

20.

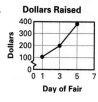
Dollars Raised

AA3

21. **Countries Connected to Internet**

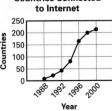

22. **Recommended Heart Rate**

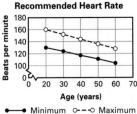

— ● — Minimum   ○--○ Maximum

2.6 Mixed Review (p. 86)

26. **Postcards Sent Each Day**

2.6 Technology Activity (p. 87)

1. **United States Population**

■ Male population
□ Female population

2. **United States Population**

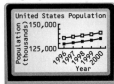

□─□ Male population
■─■ Female population

2.7 Practice and Problem Solving (pp. 90–91)

20. **Favorite Season**

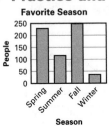

2.7 Mixed Review (p. 91)

29.

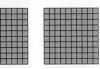

2.8 Hands-on Activity (p. 92) **1.** Step 1: 2, 5, 5, 5, 7, 9, 9; Step 2: height of middle stack: 5; typical height: 5; Step 3: typical height: 6   **2.** Step 1: 2, 2, 6, 7, 8; Step 2: height of middle stack: 6; typical height: 2; Step 3: typical height: 5   **3.** Exercise 1: Yes. *Sample answer:* Both numbers are very close together; Exercise 2: No. *Sample answer:* 2 is much smaller than 5 and 6, so 2 would not really be considered "typical" for this data set.

2.8 Practice and Problem Solving (pp. 95–97)
13. Mean = 155, median = 175, mode = 180. *Sample answer:* The median or the mode is the best average to represent a typical score because either is closer to the middle of the set.
14. mean = 80, median = 71, mode = 71; the mean is the best average to represent a typical score because it is the closest to the middle of the set.

Chapter 3

3.1 Practice and Problem Solving (pp. 109–111)

45.

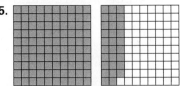

53.

10; 100; 1000

54. **Checking e-mail**

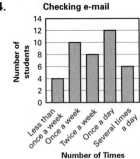

3.2 Hands-on Activity (p. 112)

2. *Sample answer:* To find the length in centimeters, divide by 10 to get 11 R2. The quotient is the number of centimeters and the remainder is the number of millimeters. So the length is 11 centimeters 2 millimeters.

3. *Sample answer:* Divide by 100 and write the quotient as the number of meters and the remainder as the number of centimeters.

3.4 Practice and Problem Solving (pp. 127–128)

41. California: 76,700,000, 76.7 million; Illinois: 41,900,000, 41.9 million; New York: 62,000,000, 62.0 million; Ohio: 60,200,000, 60.2 million; Washington: 48,100,000, 48.1 million

42.

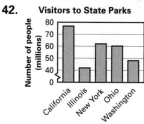

Visitors to State Parks

43–46. Sample answers are given.

43. 3.9, 4.2, 4.45

44. 14.75, 14.9, 15.3

45. 3.35, 3.42, 3.44

46. 8.66, 8.68, 8.72

3.5 Practice and Problem Solving (pp. 132–133)

30. A good answer should include these points:
- In a sum, an overestimate can occur when one or both numbers are rounded up.
- In a sum, an underestimate can occur when one or both numbers are rounded down.
- In a difference, an overestimate can occur when the number being subtracted from is rounded up and/or the number being subtracted is rounded down.
- In a difference, an underestimate can occur when the number being subtracted from is rounded down and/or the number being subtracted is rounded up.

3.6 Practice and Problem Solving (pp. 139–140)

41.

Number	Tally	Frequency
0	I	1
1	IIII	4
2	II	2
3	IIII	4
4	III	3
5	IIII	5
6	II	2
7	I	1
8	I	1
9	II	2

Exploring Math in Science (pp. 148–149)

1.

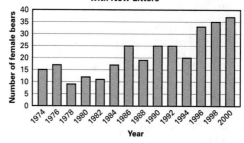

Female Grizzly Bears in Yellowstone National Park with New Litters

2.

Grizzly Bear Cubs in Yellowstone National Park

5.

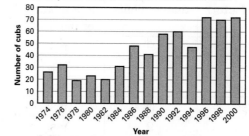

Average Litter Sizes of Grizzly Bears

Sample answer: The litter sizes increased slightly, then decreased, then increased a little more, and then decreased again; yes.

Chapter 4

4.3 Mixed Review (p. 168)

45–48.

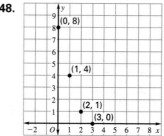

Unit 1 Practicing Test-Taking Skills (p. 207)

16b.

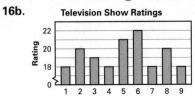

Television Show Ratings

Chapter 5

5.1 Hands-on Activity (p. 213)

2.

Number	Is 9 a factor?	Sum of digits	Is 9 a factor of the sum?
18	Yes	9	Yes
60	No	6	No
80	No	8	No
99	Yes	18	Yes
315	Yes	9	Yes
329	No	14	No

3. If the sum of the digits of a number is divisible by 3, then the number is divisible by 3; if the sum of the digits of a number is divisible by 9, then the number is divisible by 9.

5.1 Practice and Problem Solving (pp. 217–219)

21. 140 is divisible by 2, 5, and 10, but not by 3, 6, or 9.   **22.** 144 is divisible by 2, 3, 6, and 9, but not by 5 or 10.   **23.** 282 is divisible by 2, 3, and 6, but not by 5, 9, or 10.   **24.** 315 is divisible by 3, 5, and 9, but not by 2, 6, or 10.   **25.** 1578 is divisible by 2, 3, and 6, but not by 5, 9, or 10.   **26.** 4860 is divisible by 2, 3, 5, 6, 9, and 10.
27. 8745 is divisible by 3 and 5, but not by 2, 6, 9, or 10.
28. 9990 is divisible by 2, 3, 5, 6, 9, and 10.

5.2 Problem Solving Strategies (p. 221)

2.

Pennies	Nickels	Dimes	Quarters
10	1	1	0
10	3	0	0
5	0	2	0
5	2	1	0
5	4	0	0
0	1	2	0
0	3	1	0
0	5	0	0
0	0	0	1

Chapter 6

6.1 Practice and Problem Solving (pp. 269–270)

34. *Sample answer:* $\frac{3}{4}$ is halfway between $\frac{1}{2}$ and 1, so it can be rounded to either number.   **35.** *Sample answer:* You and a friend are putting apples in boxes. At lunch time, you have $13\frac{1}{2}$ boxes of apples and your friend has $14\frac{3}{4}$ boxes of apples. Not counting partial boxes, how many full boxes of apples do you and your friend have all together at lunch time?

Exploring Math in Science (pp. 308–309)

1.

	Jan.	Feb.	Mar.	Apr.
Elapsed Time	10 h 48 min	11 h 27 min	12 h 9 min	12 h 54 min
	May	**June**	**July**	**Aug.**
Elapsed Time	13 h 30 min	14 h 45 min	13 h 31 min	12 h 54 min
	Sep.	**Oct.**	**Nov.**	**Dec.**
Elapsed Time	12 h 9 min	11 h 25 min	10 h 47 min	10 h 32 min

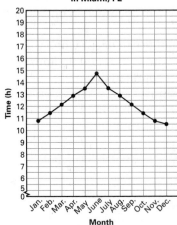

Elapsed Time from Sunrise to Sunset in Miami, FL

5.

	Jan.	Feb.	Mar.	Apr.
Elapsed Time	6 h 52 min	9 h 39 min	12 h 20 min	15 h 18 min
	May	**June**	**July**	**Aug.**
Elapsed Time	17 h 58 min	19 h 22 min	18 h 0 min	15 h 16 min
	Sep.	**Oct.**	**Nov.**	**Dec.**
Elapsed Time	12 h 21 min	9 h 31 min	6 h 47 min	5 h 27 min

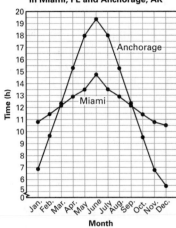

Elapsed Time from Sunrise to Sunset in Miami, FL and Anchorage, AK

Chapter 7

7.3 Brain Game (p. 330) **1.** A good answer may be the name of the person chosen. **2.** Length and width may vary. *Sample answer:* estimated the fractional parts **3.** A good answer will include the unit of measure squared. **4.** The differences occurred because the size of the units used varied.

7.7 Problem Solving Strategies (p. 349)
2. *Sample answer:* One dot is added to both ends of the horizontal and vertical "segment".   **3.**

Chapter 8

8.1 Mixed Review (p. 378)
37.

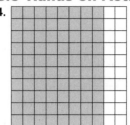

Sample answer: I used the strategy Solve a Related Problem to continue the number pattern.

8.5 Hands-on Activity (p. 394)
4.

8.6 Practice and Problem Solving (pp. 402–403)
22. $0.64, \frac{67}{100}, 68\%$ **23.** $15\%, 0.16, \frac{1}{4}$ **24.** $82\%, \frac{17}{20}, 0.88$
25. $50\%, \frac{2}{3}, \frac{7}{10}, 0.77$ **26.** $0.72, \frac{3}{4}, 79\%, \frac{4}{5}$ **27.** $0.3, 33\%, \frac{1}{3}, 34\%$

Chapter 9

9.1 Practice and Problem Solving (pp. 423–424)
25. W V **26.** L K
27. Q P **32.**

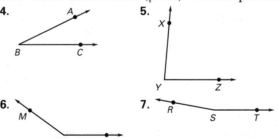

9.2 Your turn now (p. 426) **4–7.** Sample answers are given.
4.   **5.**
6.   **7.**

9.2 Getting Ready to Practice (p. 427)
5–8. Sample answers are given.
5.   **6.**

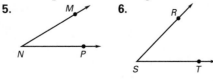

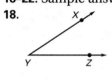

7.

8.

9.2 Practice and Problem Solving (pp. 428–429)

18–22. Sample answers are given.

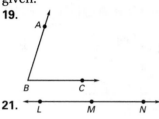

18.

19.

20.

21.

22.

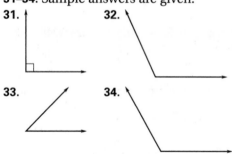

9.3 Practice and Problem Solving (pp. 433–434)

31–34. Sample answers are given.

31.

32.

33.

34.

9.3 Mixed Review (p. 434)

45.

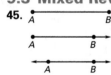

9.4 Hands-on Activity (p. 435)
1. No; the sum of the measures of the angles is 175°, which is less than 180°. **2.** Yes; the sum of the measures of the angles is 180°. **3.** Yes; the sum of the measures of the angles is 180°. **4.** No; the sum of the measures of the angles is 181°, which is more than 180°.

9.4 Practice and Problem Solving (pp. 439–440)

19.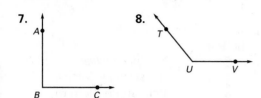

32–35. Sample answers are given.

32.

33.

34.

35.

38. $m\angle 2 = 104°$ because it is a vertical angle with the 104° angle. $m\angle 6 = m\angle 7 = 76°$ because $\angle 6$ is supplementary with the 104° angle and $\angle 6$ and $\angle 7$ are vertical angles. $m\angle 3 = 142°$ because it is supplementary with the 38° angle. $m\angle 4 = 142°$ because it is supplementary with a 38° angle.

9.5 Your turn now (p. 446)
4. *Sample:*

9.5 Practice and Problem Solving (pp. 447–448)
15.

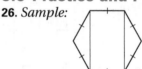

9.5 Test-Taking Practice (p. 448) **35.** A square is a rectangle because they both have 4 right angles. A square is a rhombus because they both have 4 sides of equal length. A square is a parallelogram because they both have 2 pairs of parallel sides. A square is a quadrilateral because it is formed by 4 segments called sides.

9.6 Practice and Problem Solving (pp. 451–453)
26. *Sample:*

9.6 Mixed Review (p. 453)
27–28. Sample answers are given.

27. **28.**

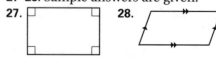

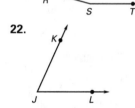

AA8

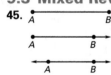

Additional Answers

9.7 Mixed Review (p. 457)

23.

9.8 Your turn now (p. 460)

1.   **3.**

9.8 Practice and Problem Solving (pp. 462–463)

8. 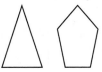   **9.** 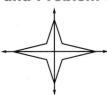   **10.**

11.

12.

13.

18.

Chapter 10

10.1 Mixed Review (p. 479)

21. *Sample:*

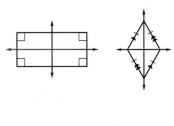

10.2 Practice and Problem Solving (pp. 482–483)

22.

10.2 Test-Taking Practice (p. 483)

33. Substitute 160 for A and 40 for h in the formula $A = \frac{1}{2}bh$ to get $160 = \frac{1}{2}b(40)$. Simplify to $160 = 20b$. Then write a related division equation, $b = 160 \div 20$, and simplify to find that the length of the base is 8 millimeters.

10.3 Practice and Problem Solving (p. 488)

17. 106.76 mm; 3.14 because 17 is not a multiple of 7.

18. 220 yd; $\frac{22}{7}$ because 70 is a multiple of 7.   **19.** 154 mi;

$\frac{22}{7}$ because 49 is a multiple of 7.   **20.** 37.68 in.; 3.14 because 6 is not a multiple of 7.

10.3 Mixed Review (p. 489)

28.

Number	Tally	Frequency
0	I	1
1	IIIII	5
2	III	3
3	II	2
4	I	1
5	III	3
6	IIII	4
7	I	1

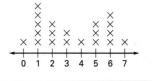

10.4 Getting Ready to Practice (p. 494)

6.

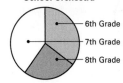

Students in the School Orchestra
- 6th Grade
- 7th Grade
- 8th Grade

10.4 Practice and Problem Solving (pp. 494–495)

21.

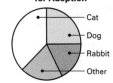

Animals Available for Adoption
- Cat
- Dog
- Rabbit
- Other

10.5 Your turn now (p. 501)

4.

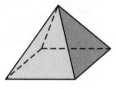

10.5 Getting Ready to Practice (p. 502)

6. Step 1:   •   Step 2:

10.5 Practice and Problem Solving (pp. 502–503)

13.

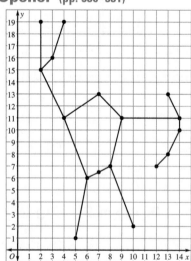

14.

10.6 Test-Taking Practice (p. 509) **28.** 3 cans; the area of the surface to be painted is 880 square inches. Since 880 ÷ 300 ≈ 3, 3 cans should be bought.

Chapter 11

Chapter Opener (pp. 530–531)

Brain Game

Brain Game

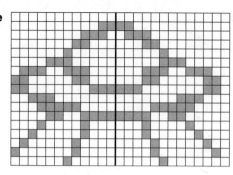

Getting Ready to Learn (p. 532)

11. triangle

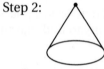

12. rectangle

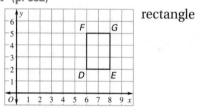

11.1 Getting Ready to Practice (p. 535)

7. $-9, -3, 0, 2, 7$

8. $-8, -5, -2, 6, 10$

9. $-9, -5, -3, -2, 0$

11.6 Your turn now (p. 562)

1–4.

11.6 Your turn now (p. 563)

5.

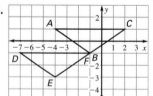

6.

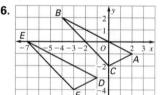

11.6 Getting Ready to Practice (p. 564)

3.

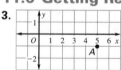

Point *A* is in Quadrant IV.

4.

Point *B* is on the *y*-axis.

5. 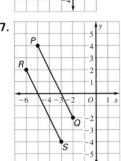 Point C is in Quadrant III.

6. Point D is in Quadrant II.

7. 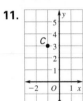 $R(-6, 2)$, $S(-3, -4)$

25.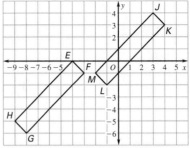

35.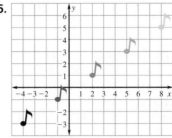

11.6 Practice and Problem Solving (pp. 564–566)

9.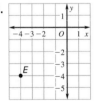

Point A is on the x-axis.

10. 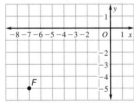 Point B is in Quadrant I.

11. 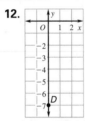 Point C is in Quadrant II.

12. Point D is on the y-axis.

37.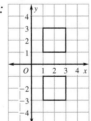
$(-0.5, -0.25)$, $(1.5, -0.25)$, $(1.5, -2.25)$, $(-0.5, -3.25)$, $(-2.5, -1.25)$

11.6 Mixed Review (p. 566)

43. *Sample:*

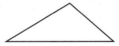

11.7 Practice and Problem Solving (pp. 569–571)

25. *Sample:*

13.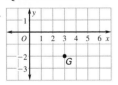

14.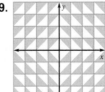

Point E is in Quadrant III.

Point F is in Quadrant III.

15.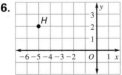

16.

Point G is in Quadrant IV.

Point H is in Quadrant II.

11.7 Test-Taking Practice (p. 571)

39.

AA11

Special Topic Exercises (p. 573)

2. **3.**

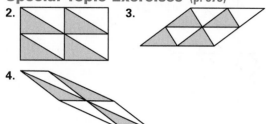

4.

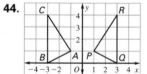

Chapter 12

12.1 Practice and Problem Solving (pp. 585–586)

40–43. Sample answers are given.   **40.** You have $6. How much more do you need to make a $20 purchase?   **41.** You pay $60 for a coat after a $25 discount. What was the original price? **42.** You bought 4 books of equal value for $32. What was the cost of each book?   **43.** The cost of a dinner was split equally among 5 friends with each paying $25. What was the total cost of the dinner?

12.1 Mixed Review (p. 586)

44. 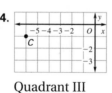 reflection; y-axis

12.3 Mixed Review (p. 595)

42.

Quadrant IV

43.

Quadrant II

44.

Quadrant III

Special Topic Exercises (p. 603)

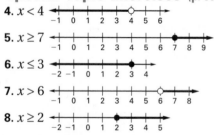

4. $x < 4$

5. $x \geq 7$

6. $x \leq 3$

7. $x > 6$

8. $x \geq 2$

9. $x < 12$

12.5 Your turn now (p. 605)

1.

Input, x	$y = x - 1$	Output, y
5	$y = 5 - 1$	4
6	$y = 6 - 1$	5
7	$y = 7 - 1$	6
8	$y = 8 - 1$	7
9	$y = 9 - 1$	8

2.

Input, x	$y = 10 - x$	Output, y
5	$y = 10 - 5$	5
6	$y = 10 - 6$	4
7	$y = 10 - 7$	3
8	$y = 10 - 8$	2
9	$y = 10 - 9$	1

3.

Input, x	$y = 5x$	Output, y
5	$y = 5(5)$	25
6	$y = 5(6)$	30
7	$y = 5(7)$	35
8	$y = 5(8)$	40
9	$y = 5(9)$	45

4.

Input, x	$y = 2x + 3$	Output, y
5	$y = 2(5) + 3$	13
6	$y = 2(6) + 3$	15
7	$y = 2(7) + 3$	17
8	$y = 2(8) + 3$	19
9	$y = 2(9) + 3$	21

12.5 Your turn now (p. 606)

5. $t = n + 1$

Input, n	Output, t
1	2
2	3
3	4
4	5

12.5 Getting Ready to Practice (p. 607)

2.

Input, x	$y = x + 8$	Output, y
2	$y = 2 + 8$	10
4	$y = 4 + 8$	12
6	$y = 6 + 8$	14
8	$y = 8 + 8$	16
10	$y = 10 + 8$	18

3.

Input, x	$y = 2x$	Output, y
2	$y = 2(2)$	4
4	$y = 2(4)$	8
6	$y = 2(6)$	12
8	$y = 2(8)$	16
10	$y = 2(10)$	20

4.

Input, x	$y = \dfrac{x}{2}$	Output, y
2	$y = \dfrac{2}{2}$	1
4	$y = \dfrac{4}{2}$	2
6	$y = \dfrac{6}{2}$	3
8	$y = \dfrac{8}{2}$	4
10	$y = \dfrac{10}{2}$	5

5.

Input, x	$y = 3x - 2$	Output, y
2	$y = 3(2) - 2$	4
4	$y = 3(4) - 2$	10
6	$y = 3(6) - 2$	16
8	$y = 3(8) - 2$	22
10	$y = 3(10) - 2$	28

12.5 Practice and Problem Solving (pp. 607–608)

7.

Input, x	$y = 6x$	Output, y
3	$y = 6(3)$	18
6	$y = 6(6)$	36
9	$y = 6(9)$	54
12	$y = 6(12)$	72
15	$y = 6(15)$	90

8.

Input, x	$y = x + 10$	Output, y
3	$y = 3 + 10$	13
6	$y = 6 + 10$	16
9	$y = 9 + 10$	19
12	$y = 12 + 10$	22
15	$y = 15 + 10$	25

9.

Input, x	$y = 15 - x$	Output, y
3	$y = 15 - 3$	12
6	$y = 15 - 6$	9
9	$y = 15 - 9$	6
12	$y = 15 - 12$	3
15	$y = 15 - 15$	0

10.

Input, x	$y = \dfrac{x}{3}$	Output, y
3	$y = \dfrac{3}{3}$	1
6	$y = \dfrac{6}{3}$	2
9	$y = \dfrac{9}{3}$	3
12	$y = \dfrac{12}{3}$	4
15	$y = \dfrac{15}{3}$	5

11.

Input, x	$y = 4x + 1$	Output, y
3	$y = 4(3) + 1$	13
6	$y = 4(6) + 1$	25
9	$y = 4(9) + 1$	37
12	$y = 4(12) + 1$	49
15	$y = 4(15) + 1$	61

12.

Input, x	$y = 8x - 5$	Output, y
3	$y = 8(3) - 5$	19
6	$y = 8(6) - 5$	43
9	$y = 8(9) - 5$	67
12	$y = 8(12) - 5$	91
15	$y = 8(15) - 5$	115

13.

Input, x	$y = 2x - 4$	Output, y
3	$y = 2(3) - 4$	2
6	$y = 2(6) - 4$	8
9	$y = 2(9) - 4$	14
12	$y = 2(12) - 4$	20
15	$y = 2(15) - 4$	26

14.

Input, x	$y = 20 - x$	Output, y
3	$y = 20 - 3$	17
6	$y = 20 - 6$	14
9	$y = 20 - 9$	11
12	$y = 20 - 12$	8
15	$y = 20 - 15$	5

15.

Inches, i	$c = 2.54i$	Centimeters, c
3	$c = 2.54(3)$	7.6
6	$c = 2.54(6)$	15.2
9	$c = 2.54(9)$	22.9
12	$c = 2.54(12)$	30.5
36	$c = 2.54(36)$	91.4

24. $p = 5n$

Stars, n	Points, p
1	5
2	10
3	15
4	20

26.

Celsius, C	$F = 1.8C + 32$	Fahrenheit, F
0	$F = 1.8(0) + 32$	32
5	$F = 1.8(5) + 32$	41
10	$F = 1.8(10) + 32$	50
15	$F = 1.8(15) + 32$	59
20	$F = 1.8(20) + 32$	68
25	$F = 1.8(25) + 32$	77

30. no

Input, y	$x = y^2$	Output, x
−4	$x = (-4)^2$	16
−2	$x = (-2)^2$	4
0	$x = (0)^2$	0
2	$x = (2)^2$	4
4	$x = (4)^2$	16

12.5 Mixed Review (p. 609)

37–40.

41.

Dollars, d	Quarters, q
1	4
2	8
3	12
4	16
5	20

$q = 4d$

Quarters, q	Nickels, n
1	5
2	10
3	15
4	20
5	25

$n = 5q$; $n = 20d$

12.5 Brain Game (p. 609)

1. 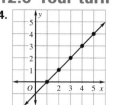   2. 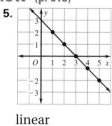   3.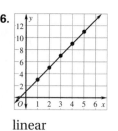

12.6 Your turn now (p. 613)

4.

linear

5.

linear

6.

linear

12.6 Getting Ready to Practice (p. 614)

2.

Input, x	Output, y
1	5
2	6
3	7
4	8
5	9

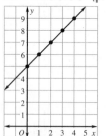

3.

Input, x	Output, y
0	−3
1	−1
2	1
3	3
4	5

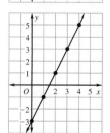

5.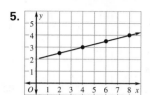

12.6 Practice and Problem Solving (pp. 615–616)

7.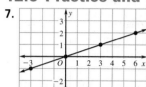

8.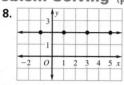

9.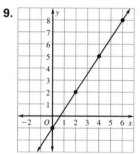

10.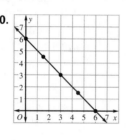

11.

Input, x	Output, y
0	4
1	5
2	6
3	7
4	8

12.

Input, x	Output, y
0	0
1	3
2	6
3	9
4	12

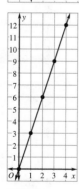

13.

Input, x	Output, y
0	7
1	6
2	5
3	4
4	3

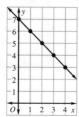

14.

Input, x	Output, y
0	1
1	6
2	11
3	16
4	21

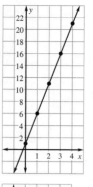

15.

Input, x	Output, y
0	2.5
1	3.5
2	4.5
3	5.5
4	6.5

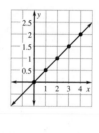

16.

Input, x	Output, y
0	0
1	$\frac{1}{2}$
2	1
3	$1\frac{1}{2}$
4	2

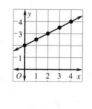

17.

Input, x	Output, y
0	2
1	$2\frac{1}{2}$
2	3
3	$3\frac{1}{2}$
4	4

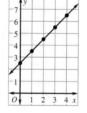

18.

Input, x	Output, y
0	−3
1	−2
2	−1
3	0
4	1

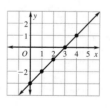

19.

Input, *x*	Output, *y*
0	10
1	7
2	4
3	1
4	−2

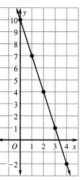

24. 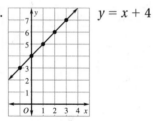 $y = x + 1$ **25.** 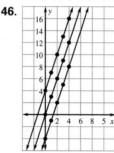 $y = x + 4$

26. 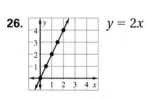 $y = 2x$ **27.** 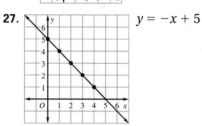 $y = -x + 5$

28. 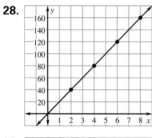   **29.**

Sides, *s*	Volume, *V*
1	1
2	8
4	64
8	512
16	4096

30. 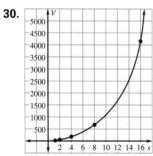 no

32. *Sample answer:*

Radius, *r*	Area, *A*
1	3.14
2	12.56
3	28.26
4	50.24
5	78.5

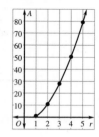

The area is 4 times greater;
9 times greater; 16 times greater.

12.6 Test–Taking Practice (p. 616)

46. The lines are parallel, with the graph of $y = 3x + 4$ lying 4 units above the graph of $y = 3x$ and the graph of $y = 3x - 4$ lying 4 units below the graph of $y = 3x$.

12.6 Technology Activity (p. 617)

1. 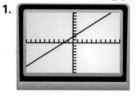   **2.**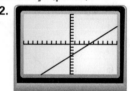

3. 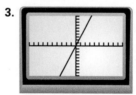   **4.**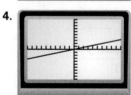

5. 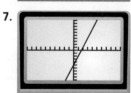   **6.**

7. 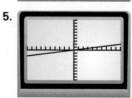   **8.**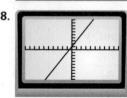

9.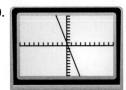

10.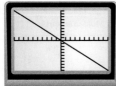

11.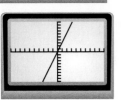

12.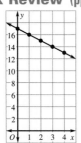

12.4–12.6 Notebook Review (pp. 618–619)

8.

Input, x	Output, y
0	17
1	16
2	15
3	14
4	13

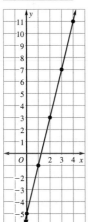

9.

Input, x	Output, y
0	−5
1	−1
2	3
3	7
4	11

10.

Input, x	Output, y
0	4
1	$4\frac{1}{2}$
2	5
3	$5\frac{1}{2}$
4	6

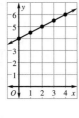

Review Quiz 2 (p. 619)

17.

Input, x	Output, y
3	4
6	5
9	6
12	7

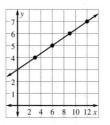

Chapter Review (pp. 620–621)

58.

Input, x	Output, y
0	−4
2	2
4	8
6	14
8	20

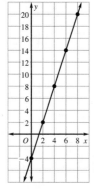

59.

Input, x	Output, y
0	3
2	4
4	5
6	6
8	7

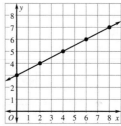

60. 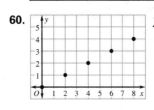 $y = \dfrac{x}{2}$

61. 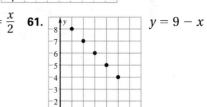 $y = 9 - x$

Chapter Test (p. 622)

28.

Age as freshman, f	Age as senior, s
14	17
15	18
16	19

$s = f + 3$

29.

Sides, s	Area, A
1	1
2	4
3	9
4	16

$A = s^2$

30.

Input, x	Output, y
2	10
4	8
6	6
8	4
10	2

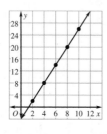

31.

Input, x	Output, y
2	2
4	8
6	14
8	20
10	26

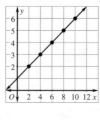

32.

Input, x	Output, y
2	2
4	3
6	4
8	5
10	6

33.

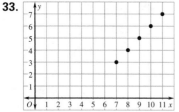

$y = x - 4$

Chapter Standardized Test (p. 623)

12.

Input, x	$y = 5 - x$	Output, y
0	$y = 5 - 0$	5
1	$y = 5 - 1$	4
2	$y = 5 - 2$	3
3	$y = 5 - 3$	2
4	$y = 5 - 4$	1

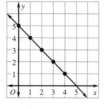

Exploring Math in Science (pp. 624–625)

1.

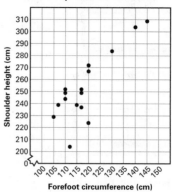

African Elephant Measurements

4.

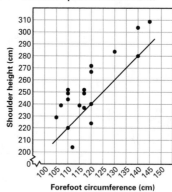

African Elephant Measurements

Chapter 13

13.1 Hands–on Activity (p. 629) **Step 2**. Good answers should include a completed table with a frequency close to 5 for each number on the cube.

13.1 Practice and Problem Solving (pp. 633–634)

34.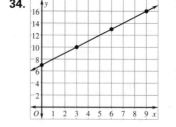

35.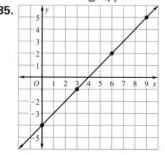

36.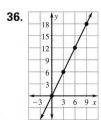

13.2 Your turn now (p. 636) **1.** tuna on rye, tuna on white, tuna on wheat, tuna on oatmeal, ham on rye, ham on white, ham on wheat, ham on oatmeal, roast beef on rye, roast beef on white, roast beef on wheat, roast beef on oatmeal, egg on rye, egg on white, egg on wheat, egg on oatmeal **2.** red with black sleeves, red with red sleeves, red with blue sleeves, white with black sleeves, white with red sleeves, white with blue sleeves, purple with black sleeves, purple with red sleeves, purple with blue sleeves, green with black sleeves, green with red sleeves, green with blue sleeves, blue with black sleeves, blue with red sleeves, blue with blue sleeves

13.2 Getting Ready to Practice (p. 638)

3. aunt and uncle, aunt and you, uncle and you, uncle and aunt

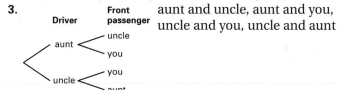

13.2 Practice and Problem Solving (pp. 638–639)
4. gold paper and red bow, gold paper and blue bow, gold paper and white bow, gold paper and green bow, silver paper and red bow, silver paper and blue bow, silver paper and white bow, silver paper and green bow **5.** white paint in kitchen, white paint in bathroom, beige paint in kitchen, beige paint in bathroom, gray paint in kitchen, gray paint in bathroom **6.** male dog, male cat, male horse, male gerbil, male bird, female dog, female cat, female horse, female gerbil, female bird **7.** Dallas in June, Dallas in July, Dallas in August, New York in June, New York in July, New York in August, Miami in June, Miami in July, Miami in August **8.** call waiting, call forwarding, voice mail; call waiting, call forwarding, three-way calling; call waiting, call forwarding, caller ID; call waiting, voice mail, three-way calling; call waiting, voice mail, caller ID; call waiting, three-way calling, caller ID; call forwarding, voice mail, three-way calling; call forwarding, voice mail, caller ID; call forwarding, three-way calling, caller ID; voice mail, three-way calling, caller ID **9.** blue and green, blue and yellow, blue and red, blue and purple, green and yellow, green and red, green and purple, yellow and red, yellow and purple, red and purple

13. soup, pasta, and pie; soup, seafood, and pie; soup, beef, and pie; salad, pasta, and pie; salad, seafood, and pie; salad, beef, and pie; soup, pasta, and cake; soup, seafood, and cake; soup, beef, and cake; salad, pasta, and cake; salad, seafood, and cake; salad, beef, and cake; soup, pasta, and ice cream; soup, seafood, and ice cream; soup, beef, and ice cream; salad, pasta, and ice cream; salad, seafood, and ice cream; salad, beef, and ice cream **16.** Ferris wheel, carousel, log ride, and bumper cars; Ferris wheel, carousel, bumper cars, and log ride; Ferris wheel, log ride, carousel, and bumper cars; Ferris wheel, log ride, bumper cars, and carousel; Ferris wheel, bumper cars, carousel, and log ride; Ferris wheel, bumper cars, log ride, and carousel; carousel, Ferris wheel, log ride, and bumper cars; carousel, Ferris wheel, bumper cars, and log ride; carousel, log ride, Ferris wheel, and bumper cars; carousel, log ride, bumper cars, and Ferris wheel; carousel, bumper cars, Ferris wheel, and log ride; carousel, bumper cars, log ride, and Ferris wheel; log ride, Ferris wheel, carousel, and bumper cars; log ride, Ferris wheel, bumper cars, and carousel; log ride, carousel, Ferris wheel, and bumper cars; log ride, carousel, bumper cars, and Ferris wheel; log ride, bumper cars, Ferris wheel, and carousel; log ride, bumper cars, carousel, and Ferris wheel; bumper cars, Ferris wheel, log ride, and carousel; bumper cars, Ferris wheel, carousel, and log ride; bumper cars, log ride, Ferris wheel, and carousel; bumper cars, log ride, carousel, and Ferris wheel; bumper cars, carousel, Ferris wheel, and log ride; bumper cars, carousel, log ride, and Ferris wheel

13.4 In-lesson Activity (p. 648)

Step 1.

Step 2.

13.4 Practice and Problem Solving (pp. 651–652)
17. *Sample:*

13.5 Practice and Problem Solving (pp. 655–656)

5.
1	5 6 8 8 8
2	1 4 5 5 8
3	1 2 2
4	1

Key: 2 | 1 = 21

6.
3	5 9
4	
5	0 0 1 5 8
6	0 1 2 2 7 7 9

Key: 5 | 1 = 51

7.
0	5 7 9
1	5 6
2	
3	0 3 5 5 8
4	1 9
5	1 2 5

Key: 3 | 5 = 35

8. The stem of 3 is missing.

1	5 9
2	0 2
3	
4	3 3 7

Key: 4 | 3 = 43

13.5 Mixed Review (p. 656)

17–20.

13.6 Your turn now (p. 657)

1.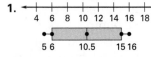

2.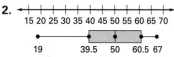

13.6 Getting Ready to Practice (p. 659)

3.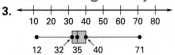

13.6 Practice and Problem Solving (pp. 659–661)

7.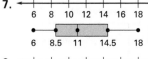

8.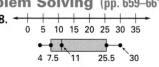

9.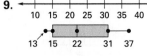

10.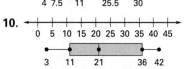

11.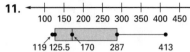

13.7 Practice and Problem Solving (pp. 664–665)

8.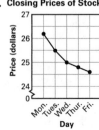
Closing Prices of Stock

10.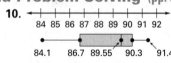

11.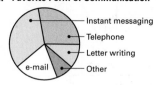
Favorite Form of Communication

12. Favorite Form of Communication
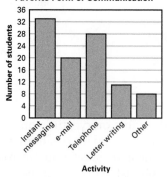
- Instant messaging
- Telephone
- Letter writing
- e-mail
- Other

13.7 Mixed Review (p. 665)

16.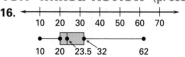

13.7 Test–Taking Practice (p. 665)

20.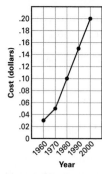
Mailing Cost of a Postcard in the U.S.

Unit 4 Practicing Test–Taking Skills (p. 674)

7.
1	2 4 5 7 7
2	1 1 3 3 3 3 4 4 6 6 6 8 8 9
3	0 1 2 4 4 8

Key: 2 | 1 = 21

The stem-and-leaf plot shows which stem has the most data and makes it easy to find the median, mode, and range. The box-and-whisker plot makes it easy to find the median and the range.

33.

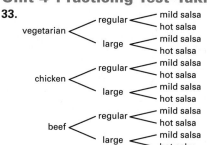

35.

Input, x	Output, y
0	3
1	$3\frac{1}{2}$
2	4
3	$4\frac{1}{2}$
4	5

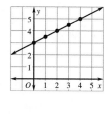

36.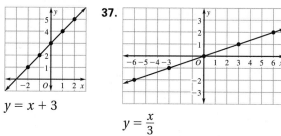

$y = x + 3$

37.

$y = \dfrac{x}{3}$

Extra Practice

Chapter 12 (p. 719)

32.

Input, x	Output, y
0	10
1	9
2	8
3	7
4	6

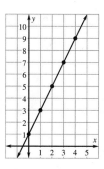

33.

Input, x	Output, y
0	−2
1	−1
2	0
3	1
4	2

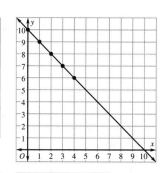

34.

Input, x	Output, y
0	1
1	3
2	5
3	7
4	9

McDougal Littell Middle School Math, Course 1

This middle school math program provides the math your students need to know in a way they can understand. Fully integrated problem solving, notetaking, and assessment strategies help your students succeed.

Features	Benefits
Chapter Warm-Up Games See pp. 2–3, 264–265, 370–371.	These quick, easy-to-play games review skills needed for the upcoming chapter. The *Stop and Think* questions lead students to reflect on key mathematical ideas, as well as providing writing opportunities and ways to develop critical thinking skills.
Before, Now, Why? See pp. 310–311, 313.	At the start of each chapter and lesson, this feature makes a connection to prior knowledge and answers the question, "Why should I learn this?"
Word Watch, Vocabulary Questions See pp. 372, 374, 376, 392, 414.	*Word Watch* alerts students to the key review words and new words they should know. Questions that help students understand and review vocabulary occur throughout each chapter.
Notetaking Strand See pp. 312, 313, 321, 331.	*Know How to Take Notes* strategies appear at the beginning of each chapter. Additional help with notetaking is integrated throughout the chapter to show students how to take good notes and to remind them to write important concepts in their notebooks. *Notebook Reviews* reinforce the importance of vocabulary and help students prepare for tests.
Stepped-Out Examples See pp. 30, 160, 278, 384, 491, 589.	Clear, step-by-step examples help make the math clear and accessible to students. Each step of the example includes an explanation, and color coding is used to help students understand mathematical relationships.
Hands-On Activities See pp. 10–11, 163, 318–319, 444, 537.	These optional activities help students develop conceptual understanding through exploration, reflection, and critical thinking.
Problem Solving Strategies See pp. 66, 134, 220, 458, 610.	These strategies are taught and practiced in each chapter so that students are continually extending and reinforcing their skills.
Building Test-Taking Skills See pp. 202, 362, 522, 672.	This unique feature helps students learn how to analyze and respond to multiple choice, short response, and extended response questions.
Exploring Math in Science See pp. 148, 308, 470, 624.	These cross-curricular extensions offer opportunities for projects and cooperative learning.